*A*ndrew Lloyd-Webber (left) who composed the score for *Phantom of the Opera* which set a Broadway record for advance sales of $19 000 000 in 1987.

*N*orris McWhirter (right with stopwatch) timing Roger Bannister's four-minute mile. With his twin brother Ross he founded *The Guinness Book of Records* in 1954, since when worldwide sales of all editions have surpassed 62·8 million copies

*P*er Lindstrand who piloted the first hot-air balloon to cross the Atlantic in July 1987. In June 1988 he also set a new altitude record for a hot-air balloon of 19 811 m *64 996 ft* over Laredo, Texas.

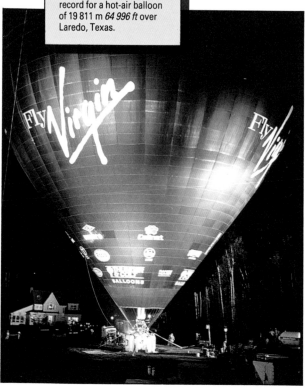

*I*an Botham who became the first Test cricketer to score 3000 runs and take 300 wickets. He is also the only Test player to have scored a hundred and take eight wickets in a Test match innings.

Eleanor Campbell

Eleanor Campbell

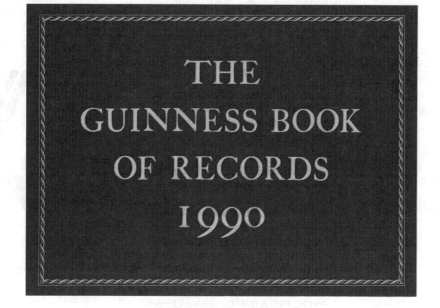

THE
GUINNESS BOOK
OF RECORDS
1990

EDITOR
Donald McFarlan

EDITORIAL ADVISOR
Norris D. McWhirter

Acknowledgements

The Editor of the *Guinness Book of Records* wishes to thank:

DEPUTY EDITORS
Sheila Goldsmith
Nicholas Heath-Brown
Stewart Newport
Sheelagh Thomas

SPORTS EDITOR
Peter J Matthews

ART EDITOR
David L Roberts

PICTURE EDITOR
Alex P Goldberg

INFORMATION SYSTEMS MANAGER
Alex E Reid

ADMINISTRATION ASSISTANT
Ann Collins

PRODUCTION MANAGER
Chris Lingard

EDITORIAL ASSISTANT
Muriel Ling

SECRETARIAL SUPPORT
Anne Belsham
Julie O'Leary
Tina Rozasty

PRESS OFFICER
Anna Nicholas

CONTRIBUTORS: Robin Adams; Andrew Adams; C V Appleton; John W Arblaster AIM; Moira Banks; Howard Bass; Michael Benton; David Boddington; Richard Boehmer; Robert Brooke; Henry G Button; A C Carder; Nobby Clarke; Colin Dyson; Keith Escott; Clive Everton,; Frank L Forster; Andrew Frankel; Bill Frindall; Tim Furniss; Steven Goldberg; Ian Goold; Valerie Govig; Stan Greenberg; Liz Hawley; Albert Herbert; Ron Hildebrandt; Sir Peter Johnson; Alan Jones; Gene Jones; John Lawson; Peter Lunn; John Marshall; Andy Milroy; Alan Mitchell BA, BAgr (For); David Mondey; John Moody; Ian Morrison; Susann Palmer; Colin Pelton; Tessa Pocock; John Randall; Chris Rhys; Patrick Robertson; Jack Rollin; Adrian Room; Irvin Saxton; Robert Shopland; Colin C Smith; Graham Snowdon; William Stephens; Ron Stewart; Lance Tingay; Juhani Virola; Dr A C Waltham; David Wells; Rick Wilson; Gerald L Wood FZS; Tony Wood.

Grateful acknowledgement is made to the governing bodies and organisations who have helped in our researches.

COVER DESIGN: The Partners: Photography by Ian McKinnell.

ARTWORK, MAPS AND DIAGRAMS: Ad Vantage Studios - Ron Harding and Jon Lucas; Rhoda and Robert Burns; Chris Forsey; Peter Harper; Matthew Hillier and Carol Wright.

PROOFREADING: Helen Dore.

British Library Cataloguing in Publication Data
Guinness book of records.-36th edition
1. Records of achievement-Collections-Serials
031'.02

ISBN 0-85112-341-4

Standard Book Number IBSN: 0-85112-341-4
Standard Book Number IBSN: 0-85112-927-7 (*Limp Edition*)

'Guinness' is a registered trade mark of Guinness Publishing Ltd.
Printed and bound in Spain by Printer Industria Gráfica S.A., Barcelona

Introduction

The story of the Guinness Book

On Saturday 10 Nov 1951, Sir Hugh Beaver (1890–1967) was out shooting on The North Slob, by the river Slaney in County Wexford in the south–east of Ireland. Some golden plover were missed by the party. That evening at Castlebridge House it was realised that it was not possible to confirm in reference books whether or not the golden plover was Europe's fastest game bird.

At last we stick our necks out (see p 34) and confirm that the Red grouse *Lagopus lagopus scoticus* is Britain's fastest game bird.

In August 1954 argument arose as to whether grouse were even faster. Sir Hugh, managing director of Guinness thought that there must be numerous other questions debated nightly in the 81 400 pubs in Britain and in Ireland, but there was no book with which to settle arguments about records.

On 12 September 1954, Sir Hugh invited Norris and Ross McWhirter to see if their fact and figure agency in London could help. An office was set up at 107 Fleet Street and intense work began on the first slim 198 page edition. The printers bound the first copy on 27 August 1955. Well before Christmas the Guinness Book was No. 1 on the bestsellers list. It has occupied this position every year since, except 1957 and 1959 when it was not republished.

The first US edition appeared in New York in 1956 followed by editions in French (1962) and German (1963). In 1967 there were first editions in Japanese, Spanish, Danish and Norwegian, while the following year editions were published in Swedish, Finnish and Italian. In the 'seventies there followed Dutch (1971); Portuguese (1974); Czechoslovak (1976); Hebrew, Serbo-Croat and Icelandic (all in 1977) and Slovenian (1978). In the 1980s translations into Greek, Indonesian, Chinese, Turkish,

The Editor with Dr Who (Sylvester McCoy) at the culmination of Wolverhampton's 'Let's get leadless' campaign. It is not known if Dr Who's normal mode of transport is as environmentally sound.

Hindi, Malay, Arabic, Thai, Tamil, Telugu, Malayalam, Kannada and Hungarian brought the total to 262 editions in 35 languages. In 1989 arrangements were concluded for the publication of the first Russian edition.

In November 1974 the Guinness Book earned its own place in the Guinness Book. It had become the top selling copyright book in publishing history with sales of 23·9 million. In October 1988 the global sales surpassed 60 million which is equivalent to 168 stacks each as high as Mount Everest.

Iveagh

THE RT HON EARL OF IVEAGH: PRESIDENT
GUINNESS PLC OCTOBER 1989

Editorial policy

Our main concern is to publish those records which improve upon previous records or which are newly significant in having become the subject of widespread and preferably international interest. However, in no circumstances will we *undertake* to publish any record *and reserve the right to determine in our sole discretion the records to be published*.

It should be stressed that unique occurrences, interesting peculiarites or 'firsts' are not necessarily records. Records in our sense have to be both measurable and comparable. Records which are *qualified* in some way simply cannot be accommodated in the space available.

If you wish to claim a record, please send *written* corroboration in the form of press coverage and signed authenti-

cation by independent adult witnesses of standing in their community. Signed log books should show there has been unremitting surveillance where appropriate. Colour action photographs or transparencies should also be supplied and may be considered for publication. *Please do not send video tapes unless requested to do so.*

We do not publish gratuitously dangerous categories such as the lowest height for a handcuffed free-fall parachutist or the thinnest burning rope suspending a man in a strait-jacket from a helicopter. Also, it has been decided that this is the last edition which will carry 'sport endurance events' (which are listed at the end of Sports, Games and Pastimes for the final time).

If an activity is one controlled by a recognised world or national governing body, that body should be consulted and involved in ratifying it. Guidance regarding the breaking of records is available from this office upon *postal* application and receipt of pre-paid postage and should be sought at *least* one month before completing plans for a record attempt. In addition, a last-minute check should also be made in case the published record has recently been broken.

EDITOR: DONALD McFARLAN
OCTOBER 1989 GUINNESS PUBLISHING LTD
33 LONDON ROAD, ENFIELD,
MIDDLESEX EN2 6DJ, ENGLAND

Contents

CHAPTER 1

THE HUMAN BEING

Origins 6
Dimensions 6
Reproductivity 11
Longevity 13
Physiology and Anatomy 15

CHAPTER 2

THE LIVING WORLD

General Records 22
Mammals 22
Pets 32
Birds 33
Reptiles 35
Amphibians 37
Fishes 38
Starfishes 39
Crustaceans 39
Arachnids 40
Insects 40
Centipedes 42
Millipedes 42
Segmented Worms 43
Molluscs 43
Ribbon Worms 44
Jellyfishes and Corals 44
Sponges 44
Extinct Animals 44
Plant Kingdom 47
Kingdom Protista 52
Kingdom Fungi 52
Kingdom Procaryota 52
Parks, Zoos, Oceanaria, Aquaria 52

CHAPTER 3

THE NATURAL WORLD AND SPACE

Earth: Structure and Dimensions 54
Natural Phenomena 60
Weather 61
Gems and Jewels 65
The Solar System 65
Stars 68
The Universe 69
Telescopes 69

CHAPTER 4

SCIENCE AND TECHNOLOGY

Elements 72
Numbers 73
Physical Extremes 73
Borings and Mines 75
Power 77
Engineering 78
Clocks and Computers 81
Telecommunications 82
Rocketry and Missiles 82
Space Flight 82

CHAPTER 5

BUILDINGS AND STRUCTURES

Buildings for Working 86
Buildings for Living 88
Buildings for Entertainment 92
Towers and Masts 94
Bridges 95
Canals 96
Dams 97
Tunnels 97
Specialised Structures 98

CHAPTER 6

TRANSPORT

Ships 104
Road Vehicles 109
Railways 118
Aircraft 120
Roads 127

CHAPTER 7

THE BUSINESS WORLD

Commerce 130
Economics 133
Agriculture 138

CHAPTER 8

THE ARTS AND ENTERTAINMENT

Painting 144
Sculpture 145
Antiques 145
Language and Literature 146
Music 155
Theatre 159
Recorded Sound 160
Photography 164
Cinema 164
Radio 166
Television 167

CHAPTER 9

HUMAN ACHIEVEMENTS

Endurance and Endeavour 170
Miscellaneous Endeavours 173
Food and Drink 178
Manufactured Articles 187

CHAPTER 10

THE HUMAN WORLD

Political and Social 194
Royalty and Heads of State 197
Legislatures 199
Honours, Decorations and Awards 202
Miltary and Defence 204
Judicial 209
Education 215
Religion 216

CHAPTER 11

SPORTS

Records for 92 Sports, Games and Pastimes, from Aerobatics to Yachting commence on page 220

COMMONWEALTH GAMES 308
ENDURANCE MARATHONS 310
STOP PRESS 311
INDEX 313

Oldest triplets in the UK
Faith Alice, Hope Fanny and Charity Sarah Stockdale of Cracoe, near Skipton, North Yorkshire born 28-9 Dec 1857 were the longest lived on record. Charity was the first to die on 30 July 1944 aged 86 years 213 days.
(Photo: Ronald Chapman for Guinness Publishing).

Origins

EARLIEST MAN

SCALE OF TIME

If the age of the Earth-Moon system (latest estimate 4450 million years) is likened to a single year, Hominids appeared on the scene at about 4.15 p.m. on 31 December, Britain's earliest known inhabitants arrived at about 11.10 p.m., the Christian era began about 14 seconds before midnight and the life span of a 120-year-old person (pp 13 & 14) would be about three-quarters of a second. Present calculations indicate that the Sun's increased heat, as it becomes a 'red giant', will make life insupportable on Earth in about 5500 million years. Meanwhile there may well be colder epicycles. The period of 1000 million years is sometimes referred to as an aeon.

Man (Homo sapiens) is a species in the sub-family Homininae of the family Hominidae of the super-family Hominoidea of the sub-order Simiae (or Anthropoidea) of the order Primates of the infra-class Eutheria of the sub-class Theria of the class Mammalia of the sub-phylum Vertebrata (Craniata) of the phylum Chordata of the sub-kingdom Metazoa of the animal kingdom.

Earliest Primate ■ These appeared in the Palaeocene epoch about 69 million years ago. The earliest members of the sub-order Anthropoidea are known from both Africa and South America in the early Oligocene, 34–30 million years ago, when the two infra-orders, Platyrrhini and Catarrhini, from the New and Old Worlds respectively, were already distinct.

Earliest Hominid ■ Characteristics typical of the Hominidae such as the large brain and bipedal locomotion do not appear until much later. The earliest undoubted hominid relic found is an Australopithecine jaw bone with two molars 2 in *5 cm* in length found by Kiptalam Chepboi near Lake Baringo, Kenya in February 1984 and dated to 4 million years by associated fossils and to 5·6–5·4 million years through rock correlation by potassium-argón dating.

The most complete of the earliest hominid skeletons is that of 'Lucy' (40 per cent complete) found by Dr Donald C. Johanson and T. Gray at Locality 162 by the Awash River, Hadar, in the Afar region of Ethiopia on 30 Nov 1974. She was estimated to be *c.* 40 years old when she died 3 million years ago, and she was 106 cm *3 ½ ft* tall.

Parallel tracks of hominid footprints extending over 24 m *80 ft* were discovered at Laetoli, Tanzania in 1978, first by Paul Abell, in volcanic ash dating to 3·5 million years ago. The height of the smallest of the seemingly three individuals was estimated to be 120 cm *3 ft 11 in.*

Earliest genus–Homo ■ The earliest species of this genus is *Homo habilis* or 'Handy Man' so named by Professor Raymond Arthur Dart (b. Brisbane 4 Feb 1893) in 1964. The greatest age attributed to fossils of this genus is 1·9 million years for the skull KNM-ER (Kenya National Museum-East Rudolf) 1470 discovered in 1972 by Bernard Ngeneo at Koobi Fora by Lake Turkana, northern Kenya. It was reconstructed by Dr Maeve Leakey (*née* Epps).

The earliest stone tools are abraded core-choppers dating from *c.* 2·5 million years. They were found at Hadar, Ethiopia in November–December 1976 by Hélène Roche (France). Finger–(as opposed to fist–) held quartz slicers found by Roche and Dr John Wall (NZ) close to the Hadar site by the Gona River are also dated to *c.* 2.5 million years.

Earliest Homo erectus ■ This species (upright man), directly ancestral to *Homo sapiens*, was discovered by Kamoya Kimeu on the surface at the site of Nariokotome III to the west of Lake Turkana, Kenya in August 1985. The skeleton of this 1·64 m *5 ft 5 in* 12-year-old-boy is the most complete of this species ever found; only a few small pieces are missing. It is dated to 1·6 million years.

Europe ■ A *Homo erectus* skull from a site at Bilzingsleben, East Germany, has been dated by uranium dating techniques and electron-spin resonance (ESR) to not less than 350 000 and possible more than 400 000 years.

Great Britain ■ A Lower Palaeolithic hand-axe factory and occupation site at Boxgrove, Sussex is thought to be possibly more than 450 000 years old. The oldest actual human remains ever found in Britain are pieces of a brain case from a specimen of *Homo sapiens*, recovered in June 1935 and March 1936 by Dr Alvan T. Marston from the Boyn Hill terrace in the Barnfield Pit, near Swanscombe, Kent. The remains were associated with a middle Acheulian tool culture and probably date to the Holsteinian interglacial (*c.* 230 000 BC).

Three hominid teeth, mandible fragments and a vertebra were found in Pontnewydd Cave, Lower Elwy Valley, North Wales, from October 1980. They were dated by the Thorium/Uranium disequilibrium method to a little over 200 000 years.

In 1988 a jaw bone of *Home Sapiens Sapiens* (ie completely modern man) from a cave near Torquay, Devon was dated to 31 000 years old by radio-carbon dating; this is 13 000 years older than a previously dated skeleton of this species.

Dimensions

GIANTS

The true height of human giants is frequently obscured by exaggeration and commercial dishonesty. The only admissible evidence on the actual height of giants is that collected since 1870 under impartial medical supervision. Unfortunately medical authors themselves are not always blameless in including fanciful, as opposed to measured, heights.

The assertion that Goliath of Gath (*c.* 1060 BC) stood 6 cubits and a span 290 cm *(9 ft 6 ½ in)* suggests a confusion of units or some over-zealous exaggeration by the Hebrew chroniclers. The Jewish historian Flavius Josephus (born AD 37/38, died *c.* AD 100) and some of the manuscripts of the Septuagint (the earliest Greek translation of the Old Testament) attribute to Goliath the wholly credible height of 4 Greek cubits and a span 208 cm *(6 ft 10 in)*).

Giants exhibited in circuses and exhibitions are, as a matter of routine, under contract not to be anthropometrically assessed and are, almost traditionally, billed by their promoters at heights up to 45 cm *18 in* in excess of their true heights. The most recent example of this practice was Muhammed Aalam Channa (b. 1956) of Pakistan who allegedly measured 250·8 cm *8 ft 2 ¾ in*. On 21 Aug 1987 he

---

ROBERT WADLOW

Weighing 3·85 kg *8½lb* at birth, the abnormal growth of Robert Wadlow started at the age of 2 following a double hernia operation. His height progressed as follows:

AGE	HEIGHT		WEIGHT	
	cm	ft in	kg	lb
5	163	5 4	48	105
8	183	6 0	77	169
9	189	6 2¼	82	180
10	196	6 5	95	210
11	200	6 7	–	–
12	210	6 10½	–	–
13	218	7 1¾	116	255
14	226	7 5	137	301
15	234	7 8	161	355
16	240	7 10¼	170	374
17	245	8 0½	143[1]	315
18	253	8 3½	–	–
19	258	8 5½	218	480
20	261	8 6¼	–	–
21	265	8 8¼	223	491
22·4[2]	272	8 11¹/₁₀	199	439

[1] *Following severe influenza and infection of the foot.*

[2] *Still growing during his terminal illness.*

GIANTS

The only other men for whom heights of 245 cm *8 ft* or more have been reliably reported are the nine listed below. In seven cases, gigantism was followed by acromegaly, a disorder which causes an enlargement of the nose, lips, tongue, lower jaw, hands and feet, due to renewed activity and increase in growth hormone by an already swollen pituitary gland, which is located at the base of the brain.

John William Rogan (1871–1905), of Gallatin, Tennessee, USA [1] 264 cm *8 ft 8 in.*

John F. Carroll (1932–69) of Buffalo, New York State, USA [2] 263·5 cm *8 ft 7¾ in.*

Välnö Myllyrinne (1909–63) of Helsinki, Finland [3] 251·4 cm *8 ft 3 in.*

Don Koehler (1925–81) of Denton, Montana, USA [4] 248·9 cm *8 ft 2 in,* latterly lived in Chicago.

Bernard Coyne (1897–1921) of Anthon, Iowa, USA [5] 248·9 cm *8 ft 2 in.*

Patrick Cotter (O'Brien) (1760–1806) of Kinsale, County Cork, Republic of Ireland [6] 246 cm *8 ft 1 in.*

'Constantine' (1872–1902) of Reutlingen, West Germany [7] 245·8 cm *8 ft 0·8 in.*

Gabriel Estavao Monjane (b. 1944–fl. 1989) of Monjacaze, Mozambique [8] *c.* 245·7 cm *8 ft ¾ in.*

Sulaimān 'Ali Nashnush (b. 1943–fl. 1968) of Tripoli, Libya [9] 245 cm *8 ft 0·4 in.*

[1] *Measured in a sitting position. Unable to stand owing to ankylosis (stiffening of the joints through the formation of adhesions) of the knees and hips. Weighed only 79 kg 175 lb.*

[2] *Severe kyphoscoliosis (two-dimensional spinal curvature). The figure represents his height with assumed normal spinal curvature, calculated from a standing height of 245 cm 8 ft measured on 14 Oct 1959. His standing height was 234 cm 7 ft 8¼ in shortly before his death.*

[3] *Stood 222 cm 7 ft 3½ in at the age of 21 years. Experienced a second phase of growth in his late thirties and measured 246·8 cm 8 ft 1·2 in at the time of his death. In 1931 he reportedly weighed 196·8 kg 31 st.*

[4] *Abnormal growth started at the age of 10. He had a twin sister who is 175 cm 5 ft 9 in tall. His father was 187 cm 6 ft 2 in and his mother 177 cm 5 ft 10 in.*

[5] *Eunuchoidal giant (Daddy long-legs syndrome). Rejected by Army in 1918 when 236 cm 7 ft 9 in. Still growing at time of death.*

[6] *Revised height based on skeletal remeasurement after bones exhumed on 19 Dec 1972.*

[7] *Eunuchoidal. Height estimated, as both legs were amputated after they turned gangrenous. He claimed a height of 259 cm 8 ft 6 in.*

[8] *Latest measurement taken in May 1987. Recently had a successful hip operation in South Africa.*

[9] *Operation to correct abnormal growth successfully carried out in Rome in 1960.*

Note: *fl* is the abbreviation for *floruit*, Latin for living at the relevant date.

was anthropometrically assessed in New York, N.Y., USA and found to measure 233·6 cm *7 ft 8 in.*

TALLEST MEN

Modern opinion is that the tallest man in medical history of whom there is irrefutable evidence was the pre-acromegalic giant Robert Pershing Wadlow, born at 6.30 a.m. on 22 Feb 1918 in Alton, Illinois, USA. On 27 Jun 1940 Dr C.M. Charles, Associate Professor of Anatomy at Washington University's School of Medicine in St Louis, Missouri, and Dr Cyril Mac-Bryde measured Robert Wadlow at 272 cm *8 ft 11·1 in* (arm-span 288 cm *9 ft 5 ¾ in*) in St Louis. Wadlow died 18 days later at 1.30 a.m. on 15 Jul 1940 weighing 199 kg *31 st 5 lb* in an hotel in Manistee, Michigan, as a result of a septic blister on his right ankle, caused by a poorly fitting brace. Because of his rapid growth he had limited feeling in his legs below the knees. Wadlow was still growing during his terminal illness and would probably have ultimately reached or just exceeded 274 cm *9 ft* in height if he had survived for another year. His greatest recorded weight was 222·7 kg *(35 st 1 lb)* on his 21st birthday, and scaled 199 kg *(31 st 5 lb)* at the time of his death. His shoes were size 37AA (47 cm *18 ½ in*) and his hands measured 32·4 cm *12 ¾ in* from the wrist to the tip of the middle finger (cf. the depth of this page at 28·5 cm *11 ¾ in*).

He was buried in Oakwood Cemetery, Alton, Illinois, in a coffin measuring 328 cm *10 ft 9 in* in length, 81 cm *32 in* wide and 76 cm *30 in* deep.

Engand ■ William Bradley (1787–1820), born in Market Weighton, now Humberside, stood 236 cm *7 ft 9 in.* John Middleton (1578–1623), the famous Childe of Hale, from near Liverpool, was credited with a height of 282 cm *9 ft 3 in* but a life-size impression of his right hand (length 29·2 cm *11 ½ in,* cf. Wadlow's 32·4 cm *12 ¾ in*) painted on a panel in Brasenose College, Oxford indicates his true stature was nearer 236 cm *7 ft 9 in.* In 1634 the death was reported in Leeds, Yorkshire, of a 16-year-old boy known as 'Big George' who stood 228·6 cm *7 ft 6 in.* Albert Brough (1871–1919), a Nottingham publican, reached a height of 232 cm *7 ft 7 ½ in.* Frederick Kempster (1889–1918) of Avebury, Wiltshire, was reported to have measured 255 cm *8 ft 4 ½ in* at the time of his death, but photographic evidence suggests that his height was 235 cm *7 ft 8 ½ in.* He measured 234 cm *7 ft 8·1 in* in 1913. Henry Daglish, who stood 231 cm *7 ft 7 in* died in Upper Stratton, Wiltshire, on 15 Mar 1951, aged 25. He started growing abnormally at the age of 17 years. The much-publicised Edward (Ted) Evans (1924–58) of Englefield Green, Surrey, was reputed to be 282 cm *9 ft 3 in* but actually stood 235 cm *7 ft 8 ½ in.*

Scotland ■ The tallest recorded 'true' (non-pathological) giant, was Angus Macaskill (1823–63), born on the island of Berneray, in the Sound of Harris, Western Isles. He stood 236 cm *7 ft 9 in* and died in St Ann's, on Cape Breton Island, Nova Scotia, Canada.

Wales ■ William Evans (1599–1634) of Monmouthshire, now Gwent, who was porter to King James I, stood 228·6 cm *7 ft 6 in.*

Ireland ■ Patrick Cotter (O'Brien) (1760–1806), born in Kinsale, County Cork was 246 cm *8 ft 1 in* tall . He died at Hotwells, Bristol (see table p. 6).

Isle of Man ■ The tallest Manxman on record was Arthur Caley of Sulby. He was variously credited with heights of 249 cm *8 ft 2 in* and 254 cm *8 ft 4 in,* but actually stood 228·6 cm *7 ft 6 in.* He died at Clyde, New Jersey, USA on 12 Feb 1889 aged 60.

Living ■ The acromegalic giant, Gabriel Estavao Monjane (b. 1944) of Monjacaze, Mozambique, East Africa, stands today at 245·7 cm *8 ft ¾ in,* and he weighs 181 kg *28 st.* He measured 226 cm *7 ft 5 in* at the age of 16 and was anthropometrically assessed by Dr Manuel Alberto in Lourenco Marques, Portugal in December 1965, when his standing height was found to be 238·5 cm *7 ft 10 in.* Soon afterwards he joined a Portuguese circus which billed him at 265 cm *8 ft 8 ⅓ in.*

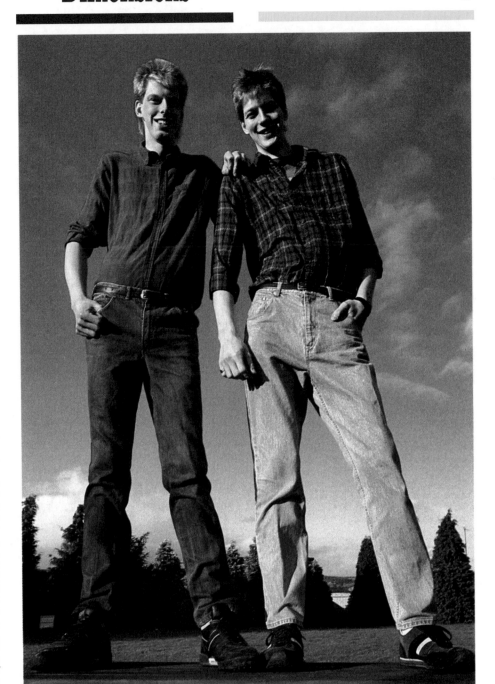

Britain's tallest twins ● 20-year old twins Andrew and Timothy Hull are the current record holders. (Photo: John D. James for Guinness Publishing).

The tallest man now living in Great Britain is Christopher Paul Greener (b. New Brighton, Merseyside, 21 Nov 1943) of Hayes, Kent, who measures 229 cm *7 ft 6 ¼ in* (weight 165 kg *26 st*).

The tallest Scotsman now living is George Gracie (b. 1938) of Forth, Strathclyde. He stands 221 cm *7 ft 3 in* and weighs 203 kg *32 st.* His brother Hugh (b. 1941) is 215 cm *7 ft 0 ½ in.*

TALLEST WOMEN

Giantesses are rarer than giants but their heights are still spectacular. The tallest woman in history was the acromegalic giantess Zeng Jinlian (pronounced San Chunglin) (b. 26 Jun 1964) of Yujiang village in the Bright Moon Commune, Hunan Province, central China who was 247 cm *8 ft 1 ¾ in* when she died on 13 Feb 1982. This figure, however, represented her height with assumed normal spinal curvature because she suffered from severe scoliosis and could not stand up straight. She began to grow

abnormally from the age of 4 months and stood 156 cm *5 ft 1 ½ in* before her 4th birthday (cf. 163 cm *5 ft 4 in* for Robert Wadlow at the age of 5) and 217 cm *7 ft 1 ½ in* when she was 13. Her hands measured 25·5 cm *10 in* and her feet 35·5 cm *14 in* in length. Both her parents and her brother are normal in size. The eunuchoidal giantess Ella Ewing (1875-1913) of Gorin, Missouri, USA was billed at 249 cm *8 ft 2 in* , but this height was exaggerated. She measured 224 cm *7 ft 4 ½ in* at the age of 23 years, and may have attained 228·6 cm *7 ft 6 in* by the time of her death.

United Kingdom ■ The tallest ever recorded in medical history was Jane ('Ginny') Bunford, born on 26 Jul 1895 at Bartley Green, Northfield, Birmingham. Her skeleton, now preserved in the Anatomical Museum in the Medical School at Birmingham University, has a mounted height of 223·3 cm *7 ft 4 in.* Her abnormal growth started at the age of 11 following a head injury, and on her 13th birthday she measured 198 cm *6 ft 6 in.* Shortly before her death on 1 Apr 1922 she stood 231 cm *7 ft 7 in* tall, but she had severe kyphoscoliosis and would have measured at least 241 cm *7 ft 11 in* if she had been able to stand fully erect.

Living ■ The world's tallest woman is Sandy Allen

EXAGGERATED HEIGHTS

The following lists a number of well-known giants whose heights have been exaggerated.

NAME	DATES	COUNTRY	HEIGHT CLAIMED			HEIGHT ACTUAL		
			cm	ft	in	cm	ft	in
Edouard Beaupre	1881–1904	Canada	251·4	8	3	236·2	7	9
Muhammad Aalam Channa[1]	1956–fl. 1989	Pakistan	250·8	8	2¾	233·6	7	8
Fernard (Atlas) Bacheland	1923–76	Belgium	279·4	9	2	234·3	7	8¼
Joachim Eleizegue	1822–fl. 1845	Spain	238·7	7	10	233·6	7	8
Chang Wu-Gow	1846–93	China	279·4	9	2	233·6	7	8
Johann Petrussen	1914–fl. 1986	Iceland	264·1	8	8	231·1	7	7
Max Palmer	1928–fl. 1986	USA	245·1	8	0½	231·1	7	7
Rigardus Riynhout	1922–fl. 1955	Netherlands	278·1	9	1½	229·8	7	6½
Baptiste Hugo	1879–1916	France	269·2	8	10	229·8	7	6½
Bernardo Gigli	1736–62	Italy	243·8	8	0	229·8	7	6½
James Toller	1795–1819	England	259·0	8	6	228·6	7	6
Eddie Carmel[2]	1938–72	Israel	275·5	9	0½	228·6	7	6
Daniel Cajanus	1724–49	Finland	283·2	9	3½	222·2	7	3½
Patrick Murphy	1834–62	Ireland	269·2	8	10	222·2	7	3½
Jakop Loli (The Pomeranian Giant)	1783–1839	USSR	255·2	8	4½	220·9	7	3
Paul Henoch	1852–76	Germany	251·4	8	3	218·4	7	2

[1] Channa was medically assessed in New York on 21 Aug 1987 and found to measure 233·6 cm 7 ft 8 in (238·7 cm 7 ft 10 in in his shoes)

[2] The height of Eddie Carmel was estimated from photographs and that of Cajanus from evidence by bones. Each of the other actual heights was obtained from independent medical authority.

The embalmed body of Beaupre in the anatomical museum of the University of Montreal measures 217 cm 7 ft 1 ⅜ in in length.

born in Chicago, Illinois, USA on 18 Jun 1955 and now working as a secretary in Indianapolis, Indiana. A 2·95 kg 6 ½ lb baby, her abnormal growth began soon after birth. At 10 years of age she stood 190·5 cm 6 ft 3 in and measured 216 cm 7 ft 1 in when she was 16. On 14 Jul 1977 this acromegalic giantess underwent a pituitary gland operation which inhibited further growth at 231·7 cm 7 ft 7 ¼ in. She now weighs 209·5 kg 33 st and takes a size 16 EEE American shoe (14 ½ UK or 50 PP C).

In April 1986 a eunuchoidal giantess known only as Mulia (b. 1956) from an unnamed village in Borneo was flown to a hospital in Surabaja, Java, for an operation to check her exceptional growth. She measured 155 cm 5 ft 1 in (weight 41·2 kg 6 ½ st) at the age of 13 years and began growing abnormally 2 years later. Since 1977 she had been unable to stand erect due to her medical condition, and thus had to be measured in a prone position at the hospital. She recorded a length of 233 cm 7 ft 7 ¾ in which, allowing for some elongation, indicated a standing height of c.228·6 cm 7 ft 6 in. Her weight was 77 kg 12 st 14 lb. Since then there has been no further news about this giantess and it is therefore not known if the operation was a success.

Twins *Male* ■ The world's tallest identical twins are Michael and James Lanier (b. 27 Nov 1969) from Troy, Michigan, USA. They measured 216 cm 7 ft 1 in at the age of 14 years and both now stand 223·3 cm 7 ft 4 in. Their sister Jennifer is 157·4 cm 5 ft 2 in tall.

The tallest ever in Britain were the Knipe brothers (b. 1761) of Magherfelt, near Londonderry, Northern Ireland who both measured 218·4 cm 7 ft 2 in.

Britain's tallest living twins are Andrew (b. 23 Oct 1968) and Timothy (b. 24 Oct 1968) Hull of Redditch, Worcs, who are 206·5 cm 6 ft 9·3 in and 209 cm 6 ft 10·3 in respectively.

Female ■ Identical twins Pamela and Patricia Terry (b. 27 Jul 1951) from Ohio, USA both measure 182·88 cm 6 ft.

Married couple ■ Anna Hanen Swan (1846–88) of Nova Scotia, Canada, was billed at 246 cm 8 ft 1 in but actually measured 227 cm 7 ft 5½ in. At St Martin's-in-the-Fields, London on 17 Jun 1871 she married Martin van Buren Bates (1845–1919) of Whitesburg, Letcher County, Kentucky, USA, who stood 219 cm 7 ft 2½ in, making them the tallest married couple on record.

DWARFS

The strictures which apply to giants apply equally to dwarfs, except that exaggeration gives way to understatement. In the same way as 274 cm 9 ft may be regarded as the limit towards which the tallest giants tend, so 58 cm 23 inches must be regarded as the limit towards which the shortest adult ateliotic dwarfs or midgets tend (cf. the average length of new-born babies is 46–50 cm 18–20 in). In ateliosis or hypophyseal infantilism the skeleton remains in its infantile state. In the case of child dwarfs their *ages* are often enhanced by their agents or managers.

Shortest female ■ The shortest mature human of whom there is independent evidence was the ateliotic dwarf Pauline Musters ('Princess Pauline'), a Dutch midget. She was born at Ossendrecht, on 26 Feb 1876 and measured 30 cm 11·8 in at birth. At 9 years of age she was 55 cm 21·65 in tall and weighed only 1·5 kg 3 lb 5 oz. She died on 1 Mar 1895 in New York City, at the age of 19, of pneumonia, with meningitis, her heart weakened from alcoholic excesses. Although she was billed at 48 cm 19 in, she had earlier been medically assessed and found to be 59 cm 23·2 in tall. A *post mortem* examination showed her to be exactly 61 cm 24 in (there was some elongation after death). Her mature weight varied from 3·4–4 kg 7½–9 lb and her 'vital statistics' were 47–48–43 cm 18½–19–17 in, which suggests she was overweight.

In 1979 a height of 50 cm 19·68 in and a weight of 1·98 kg 4 lb 6 oz were reported for a 9-year-old Greek girl named Stamatoula (b. Sep 1969), length 15 cm 5·9 in). When she died on 22 Aug 1985 at the Lyrion Convent, Athens, Greece she measured 67 cm 26·4 in and weighed 5 kg 11 lb. The child, believed to be the survivor of twins, suffered from Seckel's syndrome, also known as 'bird-headed dwarfism', because victims have prominent eyes and noses.

United Kingdom ■ The shortest mature human ever recorded in Britain was Joyce Carpenter (b. 21 Dec 1929), of Charford, now Hereford and Worcester, who stood 74 cm 29 in tall and weighed 13·6 kg 30 lb. She suffered from Morquio's disease which causes deformities of the spine and shortening of the neck and trunk. She died on 7 Aug 1973 aged 43.

Shortest male ■ The shortest recorded adult male dwarf was Calvin Phillips, born on 14 Jan 1791 in Bridgewater, Massachusetts, USA. He weighed 907 g 2 lb at birth and stopped growing at the age of

5. When he was 19 he measured 67 cm 26½ in tall and weighed 5·4 kg 12 lb with his clothes on. He died 2 years later, in April 1812, from progeria, a rare disorder characterised by dwarfism and premature senility.

In 1938 a height of 48 cm 19 in was attributed to Paul Del Rio (b. Madrid, 1920) by *Life Magazine* when he visited Hollywood, but the fact that his presence created no great impression among other dwarfs in the film capital and that he weighed as much as 5·4 kg 12 lb suggests that he was closer to 66 cm 26 in tall.

William E. Jackson, *alias* 'Major Mite', born 2 Oct 1864 in Dunedin, New Zealand, measured 23 cm 9 in long and weighed 340 g 12 oz at birth. In November 1880 he stood 53 cm 21 in and weighed 4 kg 9 lb. He died in New York City on 9 Dec 1900, when he measured 69 cm 27 in.

In 1983 a height of 65 cm 25·6 in was reported for Dimitris Morokos (b. 1963) of Poros, Greece, but this height has not yet been confirmed. He died 2 years later in 1985 aged 22 years.

The most famous midget in history was Charles Sherwood Stratton, *alias* 'General Tom Thumb', born on 4 Jan 1838. When he joined up with Phineas T. Barnum, the famous American showman, his birth date was changed to 4 Jan 1832 so that when billed at 77 cm 30½ in at the age of 18 he was in fact 12. He died in his birthplace of Bridgeport, Connecticut, USA of apoplexy on 15 Jul 1883 aged 45 (not 51) and was 102 cm 3 ft 4 in (31·7 kg 70 lb).

Hopkins Hopkins (1737–54) of Llantrisant, Mid-Glamorgan, who suffered from progeria (a rare childhood disorder characterised by dwarfism and premature senility), was 79 cm 31 in tall. He weighed 8·62 kg 19 lb at the age of 7 and 6 kg 13 lb at the time of his death. There are an estimated 3000 people of severely restricted growth (i.e. under 142 cm 4 ft 8 in) living in Britain today.

Living ■ The world's shortest known mobile living adult human is believed to be Nelson de la Rosa Aquino (b. June 1968), of Santo Domingo, Dominican Republic, who suffers from Seckel's Syndrome. On 2 Apr 1987 he was examined by the Head of the Dominican Republic Medical Association who revealed that this tiny prodigy measured 72 cm 28·3 in in height and weighed only 6·81 kg 15 lb. (Compare 3·4 kg 7½ lb for an average baby at birth.) Other statistics include a 44·4 cm 17½ in chest and 40·6 cm 16 in waist. The doctor also reported that Nelson had stopped growing. The rest of his family are all of normal size. Madge Bester (b. 26 Apr 1963) of Johannesburg, South Africa, is only 65 cm 25·5 in tall, but she suffers from *Osteogeneses imperfecta* and is confined to a wheelchair. In this disease there is an inherited abnormality of collagen which, with calcium salts, provide the rigid structure of bones. It is characterised by brittle bones and other deformities of the skeleton. Her mother Winnie is not much taller, measuring 70 cm 27·5 in and she too is confined to a wheelchair.

In January 1989 an unconfirmed height of 54·6 cm 21·5 in and a weight of 4·9 kg 11 lb were reported for another dwarf suffering from Seckel's syndrome. Sallih Djail of Barika, Algeria, who is allegedly 23 years old, says that he was 22·8 cm 9 in long at birth and stopped growing at the age of 8 months. If his height and age are correct then Sallih is the shortest human being ever recorded in medical history, but this case has yet to be fully authenticated.

The Portuguese dwarf Antonio Ferreiro, a former holder of the 'shortest human' title 75 cm 29 ½ in died in Lisbon on 11 Feb 1989 aged 44. He was a drummer in a pop group.

The shortest adult living in Britain is Michael Henbury-Ballan (b. 26 Nov 1958) of Bassett, Southampton, who is 94 cm 37 in tall and weighs 35 kg 5½ st. A 2·66 kg 5 lb 14 oz baby, he stopped growing at 13 years. His fraternal twin brother Malcolm is 175 cm 5 ft 9 in tall weighs only 73 kg 11 st

7 lb. In 1981 a height of 96·5 cm *38 in* was reported for an unnamed woman (b. 1963) living in Brighton, Sussex.

Patrick Scanlan (b.1966) of Maida Vale, London stands 91·4 cm *36 in* tall and weighs only 19 kg *42 lb*, but he suffers from MPS (Mucopolysaccharide), an enzyme disease that causes severe bone abnormalities, including curvature of the spine, and cannot stand erect. He stopped growing at the age of 4 years. He is able to joke that when he grows up 'I'd like to be a lumberjack on a mushroom farm'.

Twins ■ The shortest ever recorded were the primordial dwarfs Matjus and Bela Matina (b. 1903–*fl.* 1935) of Budapest, Hungary who later became naturalised Americans. They both measured 76 cm *30 in*.

The world's shortest living twins are John and Greg Rice (b. 3 Dec 1951) of West Palm Beach, Florida, USA who both measure 86·3 cm *34 in*. The shortest identical twin sisters are Dorene Williams of Oakdale and Darlene McGregor of Almeda, California, USA (b. 1948) who both stand 124·4 cm *4 ft 1 in* .

Oldest ■ There are only two centenarian dwarfs on record. The older was Hungarian-born Miss Susanna Bokoyni ('Princess Susanna') of Newton, New Jersey, USA who died aged 105 years on 24 Aug 1984. She was 101 cm *3 ft 4 in* tall and weighed 16·78 kg *37 lb*. The other was Miss Anne Clowes of Matlock, Derbyshire, who died on 5 Aug 1784 aged 103 years. She was 114 cm *3 ft 9 in* tall and weighed 21·7 kg *48 lb*.

Most variable stature ■ Adam Rainer, born in Graz, Austria, in 1899, measured 118 cm *3 ft 10·45 in* at the age of 21. He then suddenly started growing at a rapid rate, and by 1931 he had reached 218 cm *7 ft 1 ¾ in*. He became so weak as a result that he was bed-ridden for the rest of his life. At the time of his death on 4 Mar 1950 aged 51 he measured 234 cm *7 ft 8 in* and was the only person in medical history to have been both a dwarf and a giant.

Most dissimilar couple ■ On 30 Jun 1984 (200·6 cm *6 ft 7 in*) Nigel Wilks (b. 1963) of Kingston upon Hull, Humberside married (119·3 cm *3 ft 11 in*) Beverly Russell (b. 1963) who suffers from achondroplasia. Their son Daniel, 4·22 kg *9 lb 5 oz*, was born by Caesarian section on 22 Mar 1986.

TRIBES

Tallest ■ The tallest major tribes in the world are the slender Tutsi (also known as the Watussi) of Rwanda and Burundi, Central Africa, and the Dinka of the Sudan. In the case of the Tutsi average adult males and females stand 195·5 cm *6 ft 5 in* and 177·8 cm *5 ft 10 in* respectively.

The Tehuelches of Patagonia, long regarded as of gigantic stature (*i.e.* 213–244 cm *7–8 ft*), have in fact an average height (males) of 177 cm *5 ft 10 in* and apparently do not exceed 198 cm *6 ft 6 in*. In 1912 the average height of men living in Balmaclellan, in the Kircudbright district of Dumfries and Galloway, was reported to be 179 cm *5 ft 10·4 in.*

Shortest ■ The smallest pygmies are the Mbuti of the Ituri Forest, Zaïre, Central Africa with an average height of 137 cm *4 ft 6 in* for men and 135 cm *4 ft 5 in* for women, with some groups averaging only 132 cm *4 ft 4 in* for men and 124 cm *4 ft 1 in* for women. According to recent medical research pygmy children are not significantly shorter than the children of other tribes. But they do not grow in adolescence because they cannot produce enough of a hormone called Insulin–like Growth Factor (IGF).

WEIGHT

Heaviest men ■ The heaviest in medical history was Jon Brower Minnoch (b. 29 Sep 1941) of Bainbridge Island, Washington State, USA, who had suffered from obesity since childhood. The 185 cm *6 ft 1 in* former taxi-driver was 181 kg *28 st* in 1963, 317 kg *50 st* in 1966 and 442 kg *69 st 9 lb* in Septem-

ber 1976. Eighteen months later, in March 1978, Minnoch was rushed to University Hospital, Seattle, saturated with fluid and suffering from heart and respiratory failure. It took a dozen firemen and an improvised stretcher to move him from his home to a ferry-boat. When he arrived at the hospital he was put in two beds lashed together. It took 13 people just to roll him over. By extrapolating his intake and elimination rates, consultant endocrinologist Dr Robert Schwartz calculated that Minnoch must have weighed more than 635 kg *99 st 1 lb* when he was admitted, a great deal of which was water accumulation due to his congestive heart failure. After nearly 2 years on a 1200-calories-a-day diet the choking fluid had gone, and he was discharged at 216 kg *34 st*. But the weight crept back again, and in October 1981 he had to be readmitted, after putting on 91 kg *over 14 st 1 lb*. When he died on 10 Sep 1983 he weighed more than 363 kg *just over 57 st*.

Living ■ The heaviest living man is T. J. Albert Jackson (b. Kent Nicholson), also known as 'Fat Albert' of Canton, Mississippi, USA (see table). He recently tipped the scales at 404 kg *63 st 9 lb*. He has a 305 cm *120 in* chest, a 294 cm *116 in* waist, 178 cm *70 in* thighs and a 75 cm *29 ½ in* neck. Albert Pernitsch of Grafkorn, Austria also claims to be the world's heaviest man, but the greatest weight recorded for him so far is 399 kg *62 st 1 lb*.

When an attempt was made to weigh Walter Hudson (b. November 1944) of New York, NY, USA on an industrial scale which registered up to 454 kg *71 st 1 lb* the machine broke down, but the 178 cm *5 ft 10 in* tall super heavyweight was later found to weigh 545 kg *85 st*. He measured 269·2 cm *106 in* around the chest and 279·4 cm *110 in* around the waist. On 14 Sep 1987 he made the headlines when he became wedged in his bedroom doorway and had to be rescued by firemen. It took nine men to carry him back to the reinforced bed in which he had been virtually a prisoner for 27 years. Hudson, a

---

SUPER HEAVYWEIGHTS

Jon Brower Minnoch (1941–83) USA 185 cm *(6 ft 1 in)* **635 kg** *100 st*

Walter Hudson (b. 1944) USA 178 cm *(5 ft 10 in)* **544 kg** *85 st 7 lb*

Michael Walker *né* Francis Lang (b. 1934) USA 188 cm *(6 ft 2 in)*[1] **538 kg** *84 st 11 lb*

Robert Earl Hughes (1926–58) USA 184 cm *(6 ft 0 ½ in)* **485 kg** *76 st 5 lb*

Mike Parteleno (b. 1958) USA 183 cm *(6 ft)* **463 kg** *73 st*

Mills Darden (1798–1857) USA 229 cm *(7 ft 6 in)* **462 kg** *72 st 12 lb*

Michael Edelman (b. 1964) USA **457 kg** *72 st*

John Finnerty (b. 1952) USA **453 kg** *71 st 6 lb*

'Big Tex' (1902–*fl* 1956) USA 186 cm *(6 ft 1½ in)* **419 kg** *66 st*

Mickey Mounds (b. 1953) USA **413 kg** *65 st*[2]

John Hanson Craig (1856–94) USA 195 cm *(6 ft 5 in)*[3] **411 kg** *64 st 11 lb*

Michael Hebranko (b. 1954) Brooklyn, New York, USA 183 cm *6 ft* **410·5 kg** *64 st 9 lb*

Arthur Knorr (1914–60) USA 185 cm *(6 ft 1 in)*[4] **408 kg** *64 st 4 lb*

T. J. Albert Jackson (b. 1941) Canton, Mississippi, USA 193 cm *(6 ft 4 in)* **404 kg** *63 st 9 lb*

[1] *Peak weight attained in 1971 as a result of drug-induced bulimia. Reduced to 167 kg 26 st 1 lb by February 1980.*

[2] *Reduced to 165 kg 26 st by February 1989.*

[3] *Won $1000 in a 'Bonny Baby' contest in New York City in 1858.*

[4] *Gained 136 kg 21 st 1 lb in his last 6 months.*

---

foodaholic since his early childhood, is now on a special weight–loss programme and by June 1988 had lost 286 kg *45 st*.

Great Britain ■ Peter Yarnall of East Ham, London, weighed 374 kg *58 st* and was 177·8 cm *5 ft 10 in* tall. The former docker began putting on weight at a very rapid rate in 1978 and for the last 2 years of his life he was completely bed-ridden. He died on 30 Mar 1984 aged 34 years and it took 10 firemen 5 hours to demolish the wall of his bedroom and winch his body down to street level. His coffin measured 233 cm *7 ft 4 in* in length, 122 cm *4 ft* across and had a depth of 83·8 cm *2 ft 9 in*.

Only three other British men had a recorded weight of more than 317·5 kg *49 st*. The most celebrated one was Daniel Lambert (1770–1809) of Leicester, Leicestershire. He stood 180 cm *5 ft 11 in* tall and weighed 335 kg *52 st* shortly before his death and had a girth of more than 233 cm *92 in*. Another was William Campbell (b. Glasgow 1856) who died on 16 Jun 1878 when a publican at High Bridge, Newcastle upon Tyne, Tyne and Wear. He was 190 cm *6 ft 3 in* tall and weighed 340 kg *53 st 8 lb* with a 216 cm *85 in* waist and a 244 cm *96 in* chest. The third was the Welshman Melvin (or Melvyn) Jones (b. 1934) who died in Liverpool on 25 Jul 1988 and was buried in Bangor, Gwynedd. He stood 170 cm *5 ft 7 in* tall and weighed 329 kg *51 st*.

In 1928 an unnamed boy was excluded from a Leicester school on account of his abnormal size. He died at the age of 13 when he was over 190·5 kg *29 st*.

Living *Great Britain* ■ The 210·8 cm *6 ft 11 in* professional wrestler Martin Ruane alias Luke McMasters ('Giant Haystacks') who was born in Camberwell, London in 1946 and once claimed to have tipped the scales at 317 kg *50 st*. His weight now fluctuates between 286 kg *45 st* and 292 kg *26 st*. Arthur Armitage (b. 28 Jun 1929) of Knottingley, West Yorkshire, weighed 305 kg *48 st* (height 175 cm *5 ft 9 in*) in October 1986. Since then, however, he has gone on another crash diet and by March 1989 had stabilised at 190 kg *30 st* . Norman Smith (b. 10 May 1957) of Slough, Berks reached a peak weight of 303 kg *47 st 11 lb* (height 184 cm *6 ft ½ in*) on 10 Mar 1988, but since then he has also gone on a crash diet and was last reported down to 265 kg *41 st 10 lb* .

Wales ■ Melvin Jones (see above).

Ireland ■ The heaviest is reputed to have been Roger Byrne, who was buried in Rosenallis, County Laoighis (Leix), on 14 Mar 1804. He died in his 54th year and his coffin and its contents weighed 330 kg *52 st*. Roly McIntyre (b. 1952) of Kesh, Fermanagh, Northern Ireland scaled a peak 262 kg *41 st 4 lb* in April 1983.

Slimming *Men* ■ By July 1979 Jon Brower Minnoch (1941–83) (see above) had reduced to 216 kg *34 st*, thus indicating a weight loss of at least 419 kg *66 st* in 2 years, or an average of 4 kg *8·8 lb* per week. The greatest slimming feat with published information is that of Michael Hebranko (b.1954), of Brooklyn, New York, USA, who in July 1987 weighed 410·5 kg *64 st 9 lb*. Within 15 months he lost over 226·8 kg *35 st 10 lb* and by June 1989 weighed 98·4 kg *15 ½ st 7 lb* having lost a total of 312 kg *49 st 2 lb* within a period of less than 24 months. His waist measurement was 292·1 cm *115 in* but is now 91-96 cm *36-38 in*, a reduction of 200·6 cm *79 in*.

Paul M. Kimelman (b. 1943) of Pittsburgh, Pennsylvania, USA reduced from 216 kg *34 st 11 lb* to 59 kg *9 st 4 lb* between 1 Jan 1967 and 3 Aug 1967, a loss of 162 kg *25 st* in 215 days. Roly McIntyre (b. 1952) of Kesh, Fermanagh, N. Ireland (see heaviest men) reduced from 262 kg *41 st 4 lb* to 84·8 kg *13 st 5 lb* during the 22-month period Apr 1983–Feb 1985.

On 14 Mar 1982 surgeons at a hospital in New York City, NY, USA removed 67 kg *10 st* of adipose tissue from the abdominal wall of a 362 kg *57 st* man. They had to use a hoist to lift the layers of fat as they were removed. Ron Allen (b. 1947) sweated off 9·7 kg

$21\,^1\!/_2$ lb of his 113·4 kg *17 st 1 lb* in Nashville, Tennessee, USA in 24 hours in August 1984.

Women ■ The US circus fat lady Mrs Celesta Geyer (b. 1901), *alias* Dolly Dimples, reduced from 251 kg *39 st* to 69 kg *10 st 1 lb* in 1950–1, a loss of 182 kg *28 st* in 14 months. Her vital statistics diminished *pari passu* from 200–213–213 cm *79–84–84 in* to a svelte 86–71–91 cm *34–28–36 in*. Her book *'How I Lost 28 st'* was not a best-seller because of the difficulty of would-be readers identifying themselves with the dress-making and other problems of losing more than 178 kg *28 st* when 150 cm *4 ft 11 in* tall. In December 1967 she was reportedly down to 50 kg *7 st 12 lb*. In February 1951 Mrs Gertrude Levandowski (b. 1893) of Burnips, Michigan, successfully underwent a protracted operation for the removal of a ovarian cyst which subsequently reduced her weight from 280 kg *44 st* to 140 kg *22 st* (see also p.20).

The feminine champion in Britain was Mrs Dolly Wager (b. 1933) of Charlton, London, who, between September 1971 and 22 May 1973 reduced from 200 kg *31 st 7 lb* to 69·8 kg *11 st* so losing 130 kg *20 st 7 lb* with Weight Watchers.

Weight gaining ■ Jon Minnoch (see p. 9) in October 1981 when readmitted to University of Washington Hospital, Seattle, Washington State, USA had regained 91 kg *14 st* in 7 days. Arthur Knorr (see table p. 9) gained 136 kg *21 st* in the last 6 months of his life. Miss Doris James of San Francisco, California, USA is alleged to have gained 147 kg *23 st 3 lb* in the 12 months before her death in August 1965, aged 38, at a weight of 306 kg *48 st 3 lb*. She was only 157 cm *5 ft 2 in* tall.

Greatest differential ■ The greatest recorded for a married couple is *c.* 589 kg *92 st 12 lb* in the case of Jon Brower Minnoch (see p. 9) and his 50 kg *7 st 12 lb* wife Jeannette in Mar 1978. She bore him two sons.

The UK record is held by the wrestler Martin Ruane, *alias* Giant Haystacks (see p.9) and his 47·6 kg *7 ½ st* wife Rita, where their weight differential at one time may have been 270 kg *42 ½ st*. They have three sons.

Heaviest women ■ In 1888 a weight of 385·5 kg *60 st 10 lb* was also reported for an unnamed negress living in Boston, Massachusetts, USA, but further details are lacking. When Mrs Percy Pearl Washington, who suffered from polydipsia, died in hospital in Milwaukee, USA on 9 Oct 1972 the scales registered only up to 362·8 kg *57 st 2 lb*, but she was credited with an unconfirmed weight of 399·1 kg *62 st 12 lb*. She was 183 cm *6 ft* tall and wore a US size 62 dress. Ida Maitland (1898–1932) of Springfield, Mississippi, USA reportedly weighed 413 kg *65 st 1 lb*, but this claim has never been substantiated.

Great Britain and Ireland ■ The heaviest woman ever recorded in Britain was Mrs Muriel Hopkins (b. 1931) of Tipton, West Midlands, who weighed 278 kg *43 st 11 lb* (height 180 cm *5 ft 11 in*) in 1978. Shortly before her death on 22 Apr 1979 she reportedly scaled 330 kg *52 st*, but this was only an estimate, and her actual weight was found to be 301 kg *47 st 7 lb*. Her coffin measured 190 cm *6 ft 3 in* in length, 137 cm *4 ft 5 in* wide and was 114 cm *3 ft 9 in* deep.

Living ■ The heaviest woman ever recorded was probably Rosie Carnemolla (b. 1944) of Poughkeepsie, North Dakota, USA, who recorded a peak weight of 385·5 kg *60 st 10 lb* on 13 Mar 1988. A week later she was put on a carefully controlled diet which reduced her weight by 113 kg *17 st 12 lb* in 6 months, and then underwent a gastric exclusion operation to reduce the size of her stomach. By September 1988 the former food addict was down to 158·7 kg *25 st* during which time her waistline had declined from 249 cm *98 in* to 117 cm *46 in* and her US size 70 dress to 46. She is hoping to reach her target weight of 68 kg *10 st 10 lb* by the end of 1989.

Heaviest twins ■ Billy Leon (1946–79) and Benny Loyd (b. 7 Dec 1946) McCrary *alias* McGuire of Hendersonville, North Carolina, USA were normal in size until the age of 6 when they both contracted German measles. In November 1978 they were weighed at 337 kg *53 st 1 lb* (Billy) and 328 kg *51 st 9 lb* (Benny) and had 213 cm *84 in* waists. As professional tag wrestling performers they were *billed* at weights up to 349 kg *55 st*. Billy died at Niagara Falls, Ontario, Canada on 13 Jul 1979 after a mini-motorcycle accident.

People suffering from the Prader–Willi syndrome, a rare brain disorder which makes them constantly crave for food, have been known to get so fat that they die from asphyxiation.

Lightest ■ The lightest adult was Lucia Zarate (b. San Carlos, Mexico 2 Jan 1863, d. Oct 1889), an emaciated Mexican ateleiotic dwarf of 67 cm *26 ½ in*, who weighed 2125 kg *4·7 lb* at the age of 17. She 'fattened up' to 5·9 kg *13 lb* by her 20th birthday. At birth she weighed 1·1 kg *2 ½ lb*.

The thinnest recorded adults of normal height are those suffering from Simmonds' Disease (Hypophyseal cachexia). Losses up to 65 per cent of the original body-weight have been recorded in females, with a 'low' of 20 kg *3 st 3 lb* in the case of Emma Shaller (b. St Louis, Missouri 8 Jul 1868, d. 4 Oct 1890), who stood 157 cm *5 ft 2 in*. Edward C. Hagner (1892–1962), *alias* Eddie Masher (USA) is alleged to have weighed only 22 kg *3 st 6 lb* at a height of 170 cm *5 ft 7 in*. He was also known as ' Skeleton Dude'. In August 1825 the biceps measurement of Claude-Ambroise Seurat (b. 10 Apr 1797, d. 6 Apr 1826) of Troyes, France was 10 cm *4 in* and the distance between his back and his chest was less than 7·6 cm *3 in*. According to one report he stood

171 cm *5 ft 7¹/₂ in* and weighed 35 kg *5 st 8 lb*, but in another account he was described as 163 cm *5 ft 4 in* and only 16 kg *2 st 8 lb*. It was recorded that the American exhibitionist Rosa Lee Plemons (b. 1873) weighed 12 kg *27 lb* at the age of 18.

Great Britain ■ The lightest adult was Hopkins Hopkins (Dwarfs, see p. 8). Robert Thorn (b. 1842) of March, Cambridgeshire weighed 22 kg *49 lb* at the age of 32. He was 137 cm *4 ft 6 in* tall and had a 68 cm *27 in* chest (expanded) 11·4 cm *4¹/₂ in* biceps, and a 7·6 cm *3 in* wrist. A doctor who examined him said he had practically no muscular development, 'although he could run along the road'.

In July 1977 the death was reported of an 83-year-old woman in Mexborough, South Yorkshire who scaled only 15 kg *2 st 5 lb* (height not recorded).

Reproductivity

MOTHERHOOD

Most children ■ The greatest officially recorded number is 69 by the first of the two wives of Feodor Vassilyev (b.1707–*fl.* 1782), a peasant from Shuya, 241 km *150 miles* east of Moscow,USSR. In 27 confinements she gave birth to 16 pairs of twins, 7 sets of triplets and 4 sets of quadruplets. The case was reported by the Monastery of Nikolskiy on 27 Feb 1782 to Moscow. At least 67 survived infancy. Empress Ekaterina II (The Great) (1762–96) was said to have expressed interest. The children, of whom almost all survived to their majority, were born in the period *c.* 1725–65.

The world's most prolific mother is currently Leontina Albina (*née* Espinosa) (b. 1925) of San Antonio, Chile, who in 1981 produced her 55th and last child. Her husband Gerardo Secunda Albina (variously Alvina) (b. 1921) states that they were married in Argentina in 1943 and had 5 sets of triplets (all boys) before coming to Chile. Only 40 (24 boys and 16 girls) survive. Eleven children died at birth or were lost in an earthquake.

On 31 Jan 1989 farmer's wife Mrs. Maria Olivera (b. 1939) of San Juan, Argentina, gave birth to her 32nd child. They are all still alive.

Great Britain ■ Elizabeth, wife of John Mott and married in 1676, of Monks Kirby, Warwickshire, produced 42 live-born children. She died in 1720, 44 years later. According to an inscription on a gravestone in Conway Church cemetery, Gwynedd, North Wales, Nicholas Hookes (d. 27 Mar 1637) was the 41st child of his mother Alice Hookes, but further details are lacking. It has not been possible to corroborate or refute this report. Mrs Elizabeth Greenhille (d. 1681) of Abbots Langley, Hertfordshire is alleged to have produced 39 children (32 daughters, 7 sons) in a record 38 confinements. Her son Thomas was author of *Art of Embalming* (1705). Mrs Rebecca Town (1805–51) of Keighley, Yorkshire, had 30 children, but only one survived to the age of 3. Mrs Ada Watson (b. 23 June 1886) of Cambridge gave birth to 25 children in 22 confinements, including 3 sets of twins, all of whom attained their majority, during the period 1904–31. She died in Roehampton, London, on 5 Feb 1974.

Great Britain's champion mothers of today are believed to be Mrs Margaret McNaught (b. 1923), of Balsall Heath, Birmingham (12 boys and 10 girls, all single births – 2 boys died in infancy) and Mrs Mabel Constable (b. 1920), of Long Itchington, Warwickshire who also has had 22 children including a set of triplets and two sets of twins. In December 1949 it was reported that Mrs Mabel Murphy (b.1898) of Lisnaskea, Co. Fermanagh, N. Ireland had produced 28 children (12 still-born) in 32 years of marriage, but this claim has not yet been fully substantiated. Ireland's champion is Mrs Kathleen Scott (b. 4 July 1914) of Dublin, who gave birth to her 24th child on 9 Aug 1958. Twenty of her children are still alive. Mrs Jessie Campbell (b. 1946) of Straun, Isle of Skye, Scotland gave birth to her 20th child in 1988.

Oldest mother ■ Medical literature contains

extreme but unauthenticated cases of septuagenarian mothers, such as Mrs Ellen Ellis, aged 72, of Four Crosses, Clwyd, who allegedly produced a stillborn 13th child on 15 May 1776 in her 46th year of marriage. Many very late maternities will be cover-ups for illegitimate grandchildren. The oldest recorded mother for whom the evidence satisfied medical verification was Mrs Ruth Alice Kistler (*née* Taylor), formerly Mrs Shepard (1899–1982), of Portland, Oregon, USA. A birth certificate indicates that she gave birth to a daughter, Suzan, at Glendale, near Los Angeles, California, on 18 Oct 1956, when her age was 57 years 129 days. In the *Gazette Médicale de Liège* (1 Oct 1891) Dr E. Derasse reported the case of one of his patients who gave birth to a healthy baby when aged 59 years 5 months. He had managed to obtain her birth certificate. The woman already had a married daughter aged 40 years.

Great Britain ■ Mrs Kathleen Campbell (b.23 Apr 1932) of Ilkeston, Derbyshire, gave birth to a 2·92 kg *6 lb 7 oz* baby boy at Nottingham City Hospital on 9 Sep 1987 aged 55 years 141 days. She already had 6 children aged 22 to 16 years. Mrs Elizabeth Pearce gave birth to a son when aged 54 years 40 days. According to a report in the *Lancet* (1867) a woman reputedly 62 gave birth to triplets. She had previously had 10 children.

According to figures published by the Office of Population Censuses and Surveys in 1986 a woman that year gave birth to a boy when aged 56 years, but at the moment further information is lacking.

Ireland ■ Mrs Mary Higgins of Cork, Co. Cork (b. 7 Jan 1876) gave birth to a daughter, Patricia, on 17 Mar 1931 when aged 55 years 69 days.

Longest and shortest pregnancy ■ Claims up to 413 days have been widely reported but accurate data are bedevilled by the increasing use of oral contraceptive pills which is a cause of amenorrhoea. *The US Medical Investigator* of 27 Dec 1884 reported a case of 15 months 20 days and the *Histoire de l'Académie* of 1751 the most extreme case of 36 months. In the pre-pill era English law has accepted pregnancies with extremes of 174 days (*Clark* v. *Clark*, 1939) and 349 days (*Hadlum* v. *Hadlum*, 1949). In May 1961 a Burmese woman aged 54 gave birth by caesarean section in Rangoon to a 1·3 kg *3 lb* calcified baby after 25 years' gestation. She had gone into labour in 1936, but no child was born.

Premature – Living ■ James Elgin Gill was born to his parents, Brenda and James, on 20 May 1987 in Ottawa, Ontario, Canada 128 days premature and weighing 624 g *1 lb 6 oz*.

Joanne and Mark Holding (non-identical twins) were born on 28 Feb 1988 in Portsmouth, Hants 105 days premature, Joanne weighed 0·880 kg *1 lb 15 oz* and Mark was 0·825 kg *1 lb 8 oz*.

Andy and Tina Piper of St Leonards-on-Sea, East Sussex, were delivered of quadruplets on 10 April 1988 at exactly 26 weeks term. Oliver,1·16 kg *2 lb 9 oz*, Francesca 0·96 kg *2 lb 2 oz*, Charlotte 1·03 kg *2 lb 4¹/₂ oz* and Georgina 1·05 kg *2 lb 5 oz* were all born at The Royal Sussex County Hospital, Brighton, Sussex.

BABIES

Heaviest ■ Big babies (i.e. over 4·5 kg *10 lb*) are usually born to mothers who are large, overweight or have some medical problem.

The heaviest of normal parentage were boys of 10·2 kg *22 lb 8 oz* born to Sig Carmelina Fedele of Aversa, Italy in September 1955 and by caesarian section to Mrs Christina Samane at Sipetu Hospital, Transkei, South Africa on 24 May 1982. The latter boy named Sithandawe who suffers from Weaver's syndrome (excessive growth in children because of abnormalities in the parents' genes) weighed 70 kg *11 st* and stood 165 cm *5 ft 5 in* on his 6th birthday. Mrs Anna Bates *née* Swan (1846–88), the 227 cm *7 ft 5¹/₂ in* Canadian giantess (see also p.8), gave birth

Reproductivity

to a boy weighing 10·77 kg *23 lb 12 oz* (length 76 cm *30 in*) at her home in Seville, Ohio, USA on 19 Jan 1879, but the baby died 11 hours later. Her first child, an 8·16 kg *18 lb* girl (length 61 cm *24 in*) was still-born in 1872. On 9 Jan 1891 Mrs Florentin Ortega of Buenos Aires, Argentina produced a still-born boy weighing 11·3 kg *25 lb*. In May 1939 a deformed baby weighing 13·26 kg *29 lb 4 oz* was born in a hospital at Effingham, Illinois, USA, but died 2 hours later.

United Kingdom ■ It was reported in a letter to the *British Medical Journal* (1 Feb 1879) from a doctor in Torpoint, Cornwall that a child born on Christmas Day 1852 weighed 9·53 kg *21 lb*. The only other reported birth weight in excess of 9·07 kg *20 lb* is 9·13 kg *20 lb 2 oz* for a boy with a 36·8 cm *14¹⁄₂ in* chest born to a 33-year-old schoolmistress in Crewe, Cheshire, on 12 Nov 1884. On 15 Oct 1785 the 'Irish Fairy', Mrs Catherine Kelly, who stood 86·3 cm *34 in* and weighed 9·97 kg *22 lb*, died in Norwich, Norfolk, after giving birth to a 3·17 kg *7 lb* baby which lived only 2 hours.

Most bouncing baby ■ Thomas Hills Everitt (1779–1880) of Enfield, Middlesex weighed 57 kg *126 lb* at the age of 9 ¹⁄₂ months. He stood 99 cm *3 ft 3 in* tall and had a girth of 94 cm *37 in*. T. J. Albert Jackson, the world's heaviest living man (see p. 9), weighed 47·6 kg *105 lb* and stood 124 cm *4 ft 1 in* tall at the age of 12 months. Therese Parentean, who died in Rouyn, Quebec, Canada on 11 May 1936 aged 9 years, weighed 154 kg *24 st 4 lb* (cf. 171 kg *27 st* for Robert Earl Hughes at the age of 10 [see table, and Largest chest measurements, p.16).

Lightest ■ The lowest birth weight recorded for a surviving infant, of which there is definite evidence, is 283 g *10 oz* in the case of Mrs Marian Taggart *née* Chapman (b. 5 June 1938, d. 31 May 1983) who was born six weeks premature in South Shields, Tyne and Wear. She was born unattended (length 31 cm) and was nursed by Dr D. A. Shearer, who fed her hourly for the first 30 hours with brandy, glucose and water through a fountain-pen filler. At 3 weeks she weighed 821 g *1 lb 13 oz* and by her first birthday 6·29 kg *13 lb 14 oz*. Her weight on her 21st birthday was 48·08 kg *7 st 8 lb*.

A weight of 227 g *8 oz* was reported on 20 Mar 1938 for a baby born prematurely to Mrs John Womack, after she had been knocked down by a lorry in East St Louis, Illinois, USA. The baby was taken alive to St Mary's Hospital, but died a few hours later. On 23 Feb 1952 it was reported that a 170 g *6 oz* baby only 17 cm *6¹⁄₂ in* long lived for 12 hours in a hospital in Indianapolis, Indiana, USA. A twin was still-born.

Coincident birthdates ■ The only verified example of a family producing 5 single children with coincident birthdays is that of Catherine (1952), Carol (1953), Charles (1956), Claudia (1961) and Cecilia (1966), born to Ralph and Carolyn Cummins of Clintwood, Virginia, USA all on 20 February. The random odds against five single siblings sharing a birthdate would be one in 17 797 577 730—more than 3¹⁄₂ times the world's population.

The three children of the Henriksen family of Andenes, Norway, Heidi (b. 1960) Olav (b. 1964) and Lief-Martin (b. 1968) all celebrate their birthday infrequently, because these all fall on Leap Day – February 29. Ralph Bertram Williams was born on 4 July 1982 in Wilmington, North Carolina, USA. His father, grandfather and, in 1876, his great-grandfather were also born on 4 July.

Most southerly birth ■ Emilio Marcos Palma (Argentina), born 7 Jan 1978 at the Sargento Cabral Base, Antarctica, is the only person alive who can claim to be the first born on any continent. The mother was flown from Argentina at governmental expense.

Test-tube baby *Earliest* ■ Lesley Brown, 31, was delivered by caesarian section of Louise Brown (2·6 kg *5 lb 12 oz*) in Oldham General Hospital, Lancashire, at 11.47 p.m. on 25 Jul 1978. Louise was externally conceived on 10 Nov 1977.

MULTIPLE BIRTHS

HIGHEST NUMBER REPORTED AT SINGLE BIRTH *World*
10 (decaplets) (2 male, 8 female) Bacacay, Brazil, 22 Apr 1946 (also report from Spain, 1924 and China, 12 May 1936)

HIGHEST NUMBER MEDICALLY RECORDED[1]
World
9 (nonuplets) (5 male, 4 female) to Mrs Geraldine Brodrick at Royal Hospital, Sydney, Australia on 13 June 1971. 2 males stillborn. Richard (12 oz *340 g*) survived 6 days
9 (all died) to patient at University of Pennsylvania, Philadelphia, USA 29 May 1972
9 (all died) reported from Bagerhat, Bangladesh, c. 11 May 1977 to 30-year-old mother

United Kingdom
7 (septuplets) (4 boys and 3 girls) to Mrs Susan Halton (b. 1960) at Liverpool Maternity Hospital on 15 Aug 1987. The last survivor Kane 680 g *1 lb 8 oz* died on 31 Aug 1987. 6 (sextuplets) (all female) to Mrs Janet Walton (b. 1952) at Liverpool Maternity Hospital on 18 Nov 1983. All survive. (4 male, 2 female) to Mrs Jane Underhill (b. 1957) at Rosie Maternity Hospital, Cambridge, on 2 May 1985. After 9 months only 3 survived. (3 male, 3 female) to Mrs Susan Coleman at Homerton, East London on 12 Nov 1986. All survive. (2 male, 4 female) to Mrs Sheila Ann Thorns (*née* Manning) at New Birmingham Maternity Hospital on 2 Oct 1968. Three survive.(1 male, 5 female) to Mrs Rosemary Letts (*née* Egerton) at University College Hospital, London, on 15 Dec 1969. One boy and 4 girls survive

HIGHEST NUMBER SURVIVING[2] *World*
6 out of 6 (3 males, 3 females) to Mrs Susan Jane Rosenkowitz (*née* Scoones) (b. Colombo, Sri Lanka, 28 Oct 1947) at Mowbray, Cape Town, South Africa on 11 Jan 1974. In order of birth they were: David, Nicolette, Jason, Emma, Grant and Elizabeth. They totalled 10·915 kg *24 lb 1 oz*
6 out of 6 (4 males, 2 females) to Mrs Rosanna Giannini (b. 1952) at Careggi Hospital, Florence, Italy on 11 Jan 1980. They are Francesco, Fabrizio, Giorgio Roberto, Letizia and Linda

United Kingdom
6 out of 6 (see above): Mrs Janet Walton and Mrs Susan Coleman

QUINTUPLETS *World Heaviest*
11·35 kg *25 lb* Mrs Lui Saulien, Chekiang, China, 7 Jun 1953
11·35 kg *25 lb* Mrs Kamalammal, Pondicherry, India, 30 Dec 1956

World Most Sets
No recorded case of more than a single set

QUADRUPLETS *World Heaviest*
10·35 kg *22 lb 13 oz* Mrs Ayako Takeda, Tsuchihashi Maternity Hospital, Kagoshima, Japan, 4 Oct 1978 (4 girls)

World Most Sets
4 Mde Feodor Vassilyev, Shuya, Russia (d. *ante* 1770)

TRIPLETS[3] *World Heaviest*
26 lb 6 oz (unconfirmed) Iranian case (2 male, 1 female) 18 Mar 1968

UK Heaviest
10·886 kg *24 lb* Mrs Mary McDermott, of Bearpark, Co. Durham, 18 Nov 1914

World Most Sets
15 Maddalena Granata, Italy (1839–*fl.* 1886)

TWINS *World Heaviest*
12·590 kg *27 lb 12 oz* (surviving) Mrs J. P. Haskin, Fort Smith, Arkansas, USA, 20 Feb 1924

UK Heaviest
The 16·1 kg *35 lb 8 oz* reported in the *Lancet* from Derbyshire, on 6 Dec 1884 for the Warren Case (2

males liveborn) is believed to have been a misprint for 11·6 kg *25 lb 8 oz*
World Most Sets
16 Mde Vassilyev (see above). *Note also* Mrs Barbara Zulu of Barbeton, South Africa bore 3 sets of girls and 3 mixed sets in 7 years (1967–73)
UK Most Sets
15 Mrs Mary Jonas of Chester (d. 4 Dec 1899)–all sets were boy and girl

---

[1] Mrs Edith Bonham (d. 1469) of Wishford Magna, Wiltshire reportedly had septuplets.
[2] The South African press were unable to verify the birth of 5 babies to Mrs Charmaine Craig (*née* Peterson) in Cape Town on 16 Oct 1980 and a 6 th on 8 Nov. The reported names were Frank, Salome, John, Andrew, William and belatedly Deborah.
[3] Mrs Anna Steynvaait of Johannesburg, South Africa produced 2 sets within 10 months in 1960.

MULTIPLE BIRTHS

Lightest twins ■ Mary, 453 g *16 oz*, and Margaret, 538 g *19 oz*, were born on 16 Aug 1931 to Mrs Florence Stimson, Queens Road, Old Fletton, Peterborough, England.

'Siamese' twins ■ Conjoined twins derived the name 'Siamese' from the celebrated Chang and Eng Bunker ('Left' and 'Right' in Thai) born at Meklong on 11 May 1811 of Chinese parents. They were joined by a cartilaginous band at the chest and married in April 1843 the Misses Sarah and Adelaide Yates of Wilkes County, North Carolina, USA and fathered ten and twelve children respectively. They died within three hours of each other on 17 Jan 1874, aged 62. The only known British example to reach maturity were the pygopagus twins Daisy and Violet Hilton born in Brighton, now East Sussex, on 5 Feb 1908 (joined at the buttocks). They died in Charlotte, North Carolina, USA on 5 Jan 1969, aged 60, from Hong Kong flu. The earliest successful separation of Siamese twins was performed on xiphopagus (joined at the sternum) girls at Mt Sinai Hospital, Cleveland, Ohio, USA by Dr Jac S. Geller on 14 Dec 1952.

The rarest form of conjoined twins is Dicephales tetrabrachius dipus (two heads, four arms and two legs). The only known examples are the pair Masha and Dasha born in the USSR on 4 Jan 1950, Nadir and Juraci Climerio de Oliverra of Santo Amaro de Purifcacao, Bahia, Brazil, born on 2 Jun 1957, an unnamed pair separated in a 10-hour operation in Washington, DC, on 23 Jun 1977, Fonda Michelle and Shannon Elaine Beaver of Forest City, North Carolina, USA born on 9 Feb 1980 and successfully separated in February 1981. Hassan and Hussein (b. Sep 1986) of Sudan were successfully separated at Great Ormond Street Hospital, London on 29 Apr 1987, and another successful separation was carried out on Viet and Duc (b. 1981) at a hospital in Ho Chi Minh City (formerly Saigon) Vietnam on 4 Oct 1988.

Britain's only known pair were the 'Scottish brothers', who were born near Glasgow in 1490. They were brought to the Court of King James IV of Scotland in 1491, and lived under the king's patronage for the rest of his reign. They died in 1518 aged 28 years, one brother succumbing five days before the other, who 'moaned piteously as he crept about the castle gardens, carrying with him the dead body of the brother from whom only death could separate him and to whom death would again join him'.

The oldest surviving unseparated twins are the craniopagus pair Yvonne and Yvette McCarther (b. 1949) of Los Angeles, California, USA (heads are fused at the crown). They have rejected an operation to separate them.

Most twins *Geographically* ■ In Chungchon, South Korea it was reported in September 1981 that there were unaccountably 38 pairs in only 275 families-the highest ever recorded ratio. The highest ratio of twins in Britain is to be found on the island of North Uist in the Outer Hebrides, Scotland. In June 1985 there were 36 sets aged from 82 to 2 years, a ratio of 1 to 40.(Cf. the national average of 1 to 100.)

Reproductivity

Longest separated twins ■ Philip and Barbara McAuley of Preston, Lancashire (b. 27 May 1916) became separated when over a year old on 30 Jun 1917. Officers of the Salvation Army reunited them for the first time after almost exactly 70 years in London on 29 Jun 1987.

Longest separation ■ Through the agency of the Salvation Army William James Pring of Clacton-on-Sea (b. 4 Apr 1904) was reunited with his sister Elsie May of Southampton, Hampshire (now Mrs Ashford, b. 7 Nov 1897) on 20 Nov 1988 after exactly 81 years' separation. The Army's investigations took just over 2 weeks.

Fastest triplet birth ■ This was 2 minutes in the case of Bradley, Christopher and Carmon born naturally to Mrs James E. Duck of Memphis, Tennessee, USA on 21 Mar 1977.

First test-tube quintuplets ■ Alan, Brett, Connor, Douglas and Edward, were born to Linda and Bruce Jacobssen at University College Hospital, London on 26 Apr 1985.

Quindecaplets ■ It was announced by Dr Gennaro Montanino of Rome that he had removed by hysterotomy at 4 months of the pregnancy the foetuses of 10 girls and 5 boys from the womb of a 35-year-old housewife on 22 Jul 1971. A fertility drug was responsible for this unique and unsurpassed instance of quindecaplets.

Longest interval between twins ■ Mrs Danny Berg (b. 1953) of Rome, Italy who had been on hormone treatment after suffering two miscarriages, gave birth normally to a baby girl, Diana, on 23 Dec 1987, but she was not delivered of the other twin, Monica, by caesarian until 30 Jan 1988. Mrs. Mary Wright, 38, gave birth to Amy and Elizabeth 18 months apart from eggs fertilised by her husband in March 1984. Elizabeth was born at Stoke-on-Trent, Staffordshire, on 22 Apr 1987 from an egg which had been in frozen storage for 29 months.

DESCENDANTS

In polygamous countries, the number of a person's descendants can become incalculable. The last Sharifian Emperor of Morocco, Moulay Ismail (1672–1727), known as 'The Bloodthirsty', was reputed to have fathered a total of 525 sons and 342 daughters by 1703 and a 700th son in 1721.

In April 1984 the death was reported of Adam Borntrager, aged 96, of Medford, Wisconsin, USA who had had 707 direct descendants of whom all but 32 were living. The total comprised 11 children, 115 grand-529 great-grand and 20 great-great-grandchildren. Mrs Peter L. Schwartz (1902–88) had 14 children, 13 of whom are still living,175 grandchildren, 477 great-grandchildren and 20 great-great-grandchildren. Both families are of the Amish Mennonite sect who eschew cars, telephones, electric light and higher education.

Mrs Sarah Crawshaw (d. 25 Dec 1844) left 397 descendants according to her gravestone in Stones Church, Ripponden, Halifax, West Yorkshire.

Seven-generation family ■ Augusta Bunge (née Pagel) (b.13 Oct 1879) of Wisconsin, USA, learned that her great-great-great-great-granddaughter had become a grandmother by receiving the news of the birth of her great-great–great-great-great-grandson Christopher John Bollig (b. 21 Jan 1989).

Great grandmother ■ Harriet Holmes of Newfoundland, Canada (b. 17 Jan 1899) became the youngest 3 greats-grandmother known when aged 88 years 50 days.

Most living ascendants ■ Megan Sue Austin (b. 16 May 1982) of Bar Harbor, Maine, USA had a full set of grandparents and great-grandparents and five great-great-grandparents, making 19 direct ascendants.

Longevity

No single subject is more obscured by vanity, deceit, falsehood and deliberate fraud than the extremes of human longevity. Extreme claims are generally made on behalf of the very aged rather than *by* them.

Many hundreds of claims throughout history have been made for persons living well into their second century and some, insulting to the intelligence, for people living even into their third. Centenarians surviving beyond their 113th year are in fact of the extremest rarity and the present absolute proven limit of human longevity does not yet admit of anyone living to celebrate any birthday after their 120th.

The largest group of people in the world with reliable long pedigrees is the British peerage. After ten centuries this has produced only three centenarian peers, of whom only two reached their 101st birthdays. This poor record is possibly not unconnected with the extreme draughtiness of many of their residences and the amount of lead in their game.

Several celebrated super-centenarians (over 110 years) are believed to have been double lives (father and son, relations with the same names or successive bearers of a title). The most famous example was Christian Jakobsen Drackenberg allegedly born in Stavanger, Norway on 18 Nov 1626 and died in Aarhus, Denmark aged seemingly 145 years 326 days on 9 Oct 1772. A number of instances have been commercially sponsored, while a fourth category of recent claims are those made for political ends, such as the 100 citizens of the Russian Soviet–Federative Socialist Republic (population 117 494 000 at mid-1960) claimed in March 1960 to be between 120 and 156. From data on documented centenarians, actuaries have shown that only one 115-year life can be expected in 2100 million lives (cf. world population was estimated to be *c.* 5000 million by mid-1987).

The height of credulity was reached on 5 May 1933, when a news agency gullibly filed a story from China with a Peking date-line that Li Chung-yun, the 'oldest man on Earth', born in 1680, had just died aged 256 years (*sic*).

The most extreme case of longevity recently claimed in the USSR has been 168 years for Shirali 'Baba' Muslinov of Barzavu, Azerbaijan, who died on 2 Sep 1973 and was reputedly born on 26 Mar 1805.

> **Longest search** ● Mrs Elsie May Ashford (née Pring) meeting her brother William James Pring for the first time in 81 years on 20 Nov 1988. They were reunited by Major Colin Fairclough of The Salvation Army.

No interview with this man was ever permitted to any Western journalist or scientist. He was even said to have celebrated, in 1966, the 100th birthday of his third wife Hartun and that of one of his grandchildren in August 1973. It was reported in 1979 that 241 centenarians had been found in the Abkhazian Republic of Georgia, (pop 520 000) USSR, where aged citizens are invested with an almost saint-like status. 2·58 per cent of the population were aged over 90–24 times the proportion in the USA.

Dr Zhores Aleksandrovich Medvedev (b. Tbilisi, 14 Nov 1925), the Russian gerontologist who was refused a visa to return to the USSR in 1973, referring to USSR claims in Washington, DC, on 30 Apr 1974 stated, 'The whole phenomenon looks like a falsification' adding, 'He [Stalin] liked the idea that [other] Georgians lived to be 100 or more. Local officials tried hard to find more and more cases for Stalin.' He points out (a) the *average* life-span in the regions claiming the highest incidence of centenarians is lower than the USSR average and (b) in contradistinction to the rest of the world, the incidence of centenarians claimed in the Caucasus had declined rapidly from 8000 in 1950 to 4500 in 1970.

It was announced in February 1984 that the 1982 census in China revealed only 3765 centenarians, of whom two-thirds were women. According to a 1985 census carried out in the Chinese Province of Xinjiang Urgur there were 850 centenarians in the area, four aged between 125 and 103 years. In the USA the mid-1983 figure was 32 000. Birth and death registration, however, became complete only in 1933 and was only 30·9 per cent by 1915.

According to research carried out by scientists at the Scripps Institution of Oceanography at La Jolla, California, USA, in 1979, it is now possible to work out a person's age within a 10 per cent margin of error by examining the amino-acids in teeth and eyes.

Oldest authentic centenarian *World* ■ The greatest *authenticated* age to which any human has ever lived is a unique 120 years 237 days in the case of Shigechiyo Izumi of Asan on Tokunoshima, an island 1320 km *820 miles* south west of Tokyo, Japan. He was born at Asan on 29 Jun 1865 and recorded as a 6-year-old in Japan's first census of 1871. He died in his double-glazed bungalow at 12.15 GMT on 21 Feb 1986 after developing pneumonia.

Oldest living *World* ■ The oldest living person in the world whose date of birth can be reliably authenticated is Carrie C. White (neé Joyner) who was born in Gadsden, Florida, USA on 18 Nov 1874. She now lives in a nursing home in Palatka, Florida.

United Kingdom ■ With an estimated population of some 4000 centenarians only 22 per cent are male. While husbands have a better chance than bachelors, it appears that spinsters have a better chance than wives of reaching 100 years!

The only UK citizens with birth and death certificates more than 112 years apart have been Mrs Anna Williams (1873–1987) (114 years 208 days), Miss Alice Stevenson (1861–1973) (112 years 39 days) and Miss Janetta Jane Thomas (1869–1982) (112 years 35 days).

Britain's oldest proven man is John Evans (b. 19 Aug 1877) who on 26 May 1989 reached the age of 111 years 282 days and who, thereby, overtook the previous holder John Mosley Turner (b. 15 Jun 1856), who died on 22 Mar 1968 aged 111 years 281 days.

Oldest living *United Kingdom* ■ Miss Charlotte Hughes (neé Milburn) (b. 1 Aug 1877) of Marske-on-Sea, Cleveland is Britain's oldest lady.

John Evans, of Llewitha, Swansea, West Glamorgan, is the oldest living man; he was born on 19 Aug 1877. Formerly a miner having first gone down the mines in 1889 he had a heart pacemaker fitted when he was 108 years old, on 19 Mar 1986, and celebrated his 110th birthday with his first ever visit to London.

Family centenarians ■ The first recorded case in the UK of four siblings being centenarians occurred on 2 Apr 1984 when Mrs Lily Beatrice Parsons (*née* Andrews) reached her 100th birthday. Her three sisters were Mrs Florence Eliza White (1874–1979), Mrs Maud Annie Spencer (1876–1978), Mrs Eleanor Newton Webber (1880–1983). The family came from Teignmouth, Devon.

Oldest quadruplets ■ The Ottman quads of Munich, West Germany–Adolf, Anne-Marie, Emma and Elisabeth celebrated their 77th birthday on 5 May 1989.

Oldest triplets ■ Faith, Hope and Charity Caughlin were born at Marlboro, Massachusetts, USA on 27 Mar 1868. The first to die was Mrs (Ellen) Hope Daniels aged 93 on 2 Mar 1962.

The longest-lived triplets recorded in Great Britain have been Faith Alice, Hope Fanny and Charity Sarah Stockdale of Cracoe, near Skipton, North Yorkshire, born on 28–9 Dec 1857. Charity was the first to die on 30 Jul 1944 aged 86 years 213 days.

Oldest twins ■ Eli Shadrack and John Meshak Phipps were born on 14 Feb 1803 at Affinghton, Virginia, USA. Eli died at Hennessey, Oklahoma, USA on 23 Feb 1911 aged 108 years 9 days on which day John was still living in Shenandoah, Iowa, USA. On 17 Jun 1984, identical twin sisters, Mildred Widman Philippi and Mary Widman Franzini of St Louis, Missouri, USA celebrated their 104th birthday. Mildred died on 4 May 1985, 44 days short of the twins' would-be 105th birthday. The chances of identical twins both reaching 100 are now probably about one in 50 million.

Living ■ The identical twin spinsters, Alice Maria and Emily Edith Weller were both born within 15 min of each other on 20 Apr 1888 in Epsom, Surrey. They now live in a nursing home in Brighton, East Sussex and attribute their long life to 'hard work, good food and caring parents'.

The oldest twins on record in Great Britain were the twins May and Marjorie Chavasse of Oxford, who were born on 29 Aug 1886. Their brother, Captain Noel Chavasse (also a twin), was one of only three ever to have been awarded a bar to the Victoria Cross, won posthumously in the First World War. Marjorie died on 27 Jul 1987 aged 100 years 332 days, and May on 26 Feb 1989 103 years 213 days.

Most reigns ■ The greatest number of reigns during which any English subject could have lived is ten. A person born on the day (11 April) that Henry VI was deposed in 1471 had to live to only the comparatively modest age of 87 years 7 months and 6 days to see the accession of Elizabeth I on 17 Nov 1558. Such a person could have been Thomas Carn of London, reputedly born in 1471 and died 28 Jan 1578 in his 107th year.

Long spans ■ The last Briton with 18th-century paternity was Miss Alice J. Grigg of Belvedere, Kent (d. 28 Apr 1970) whose father William was born on 26 Oct 1799. The father of Baroness Elliot of Harwood (b. 15 Jan 1903), Sir Charles Tennant Bt, was born in Glasgow in the reign of George IV on 4 Nov 1823.

Oldest mummy ■ Mummification (from the Persian word *mūm*, wax) dates from 2600 BC or the 4th dynasty of the Egyptian pharaohs. The oldest known mummy is that of a high-ranking young woman who was buried *c.* 2600BC on a plateau near the Great Pyramid of Cheops at Gaza, Egypt. Her remains, which appear to represent the first attempts at mummification, were discovered in a 1·83 m *6 ft* deep excavation on 17 Mar 1989, but only her skull was intact. She is believed to have lived in the lost kingdom of Ankh Ptah, about which very little is known. The oldest surviving mummy is of *Wati*, a court musician of *c.* 2400 BC from the tomb of Nefer in Saqqâra, Egypt, found in 1944.

Authentic National Longevity Records

	Years	Days		Born		Died	
Japan	120	237	Shigechiyo Izumi	29 Jun	1865	21 Feb	1986
United Kingdom[1]	114	208	Anna Eliza Williams (Mrs) (*née* Davies)	2 Jun	1873	27 Dec	1987
United States[2]	114		Carrie White (Mrs) (*née* Joyner)	18 Nov	1874	*fl.* Mar	1989
France	114		Jeanne Louise Calment	21 Feb	1875	*fl.* Mar	1989
Canada[3]	113	124	Pierre Joubert	15 Jul	1701	16 Nov	1814
Australia	112	330	Caroline Maud Mockridge	11 Dec	1874	6 Nov	1987
Spain[4]	112	228	Josefa Salas Mateo	14 Jul	1860	27 Feb	1973
Norway	112	61	Maren Bolette Torp	21 Dec	1876	20 Feb	1989
Morocco	>112		El Hadj Mohammed el Mokri (Grand Vizier)		1844	16 Sep	1957
Poland	112	+	Roswlia Mielczarak (Mrs)		1868	7 Jan	1981
Ireland[5]	111	327	The Hon. Katherine Plunket	22 Nov	1820	14 Oct	1932
Scotland[5]	111	238	Kate Begbie (Mrs)	9 Jan	1877	5 Sep	1988
South Africa[6]	111	151	Johanna Booyson	17 Jan	1857	16 Jun	1968
Czechoslovakia	111	+	Marie Bernatkova	22 Oct	1857	*fl.* Oct	1968
Netherlands[7]	111		Christina van Druten-Hoogakker	20 Jan	1876	8 Dec	1987
Channel Islands (Guernsey)	110	321	Margaret Ann Neve (*née* Harvey)	18 May	1792	4 Apr	1903
Northern Ireland	110	234	Elizabeth Watkins (Mrs)	10 Mar	1863	31 Oct	1973
Sweden[8]	110	200+	Wilhelmine Sande (Mrs)	24 Oct	1874	21 Jan	1986
Yugoslavia	110	150+	Demitrius Philipovitch	9 Mar	1818	*fl.* Aug	1928
Greece[9]	110	+	Lambrini Tsiatoura (Mrs)		1870	19 Feb	1981
USSR[10]	110	+	Khasako Dzugayev	7 Aug	1860	*fl.* Aug	1970
Italy	110	+	Damiana Sette (Sig)		1884	25 Feb	1985
Finland	109	182	Andrei Akaki Kuznetsoff	17 Oct	1873		1984
Tasmania (State of)	109	179	Mary Ann Crow (Mrs)	2 Feb	1836	31 Jul	1945
Belgium	108	327	Mathilda Vertommen-Hellemans	12 Aug	1868	4 Jul	1977
Germany[11]	108	128	Luise Schwarz	27 Sep	1849	2 Feb	1958
Iceland	108	45	Halldóra Bjarndóttir	14 Oct	1873	28 Nov	1981
Portugal[12]	108	+	Maria Luisa Jorge	7 Jun	1859	*fl.* Jul	1967
Malaysia	106	+	Hassan Bin Yusoff	14 Aug	1865	*fl.* Jan	1972
Luxembourg	105	228	Nicolas Wiscourt	31 Dec	1872	17 Aug	1978

[1] *London-born Miss Isabella Shepheard was allegedly 115 years old when she died at St Asaph, Clwyd, North Wales, on 20 Nov 1948, but her actual age was believed to have been 109 years 90 days. Charles Alfred Nunez Arnold died in Liverpool on 15 Nov 1941 reputedly aged 112 years 66 days based on a baptismal claim (London, 10 Sep 1829). Mrs Elizabeth Cornish (née Veale) who was buried at Stratton, Cornwall on 10 Mar 1691 or 2 was reputedly baptised on 16 Oct 1578, 113 years 4 months earlier.*

[2] *Ex-slave Mrs Martha Graham died at Fayetteville, North Carolina on 25 Jun 1959 reputedly aged 117 or 118. Census researches by Eckler show that she was seemingly born in Dec 1844 and hence aged 114 years 6 months. Mrs Rena Glover Brailsford died in Summerton, South Carolina, USA on 6 Dec 1977 reputedly aged 118 years. Mrs Rosario Reina Vasquez who died in California on 2 Sep 1980 was reputedly born in Sonora, Mexico on 3 Jun 1866, which would have made her 114 years 93 days. The 1900 US Federal Census for Crawfish Springs Militia District of Walker County, Georgia, records an age of 77 for a Mark Thrash. If the Mark Thrash (reputedly born in Georgia in December 1822) who died near Chattanooga, Tennessee on 17 Dec 1943 was he, and the age attributed was accurate, then he would have survived for 121 years.*

[3] *Mrs Ellen Carroll died in North River, Newfoundland, Canada on 8 Dec 1943, reputedly aged 115 years 49 days.*

[4] *Senor Benita Medrana of Avila died on 28 Jan 1979 allegedly aged 114 years 335 days.*

[5] *Lachlen McDonald, who died 7 Jun 1858 in Harris, Outer Hebrides, was recorded as being '110 years' on his death certificate.*

[6] *Mrs Susan Johanna Deporter of Port Elizabeth, South Africa, was reputedly 114 years old when she died on 4 Aug 1954. Mrs Sarah Lawrence, Cape Town, South Africa was reputedly 112 on 3 Jun 1968.*

[7] *Thomas Peters was recorded to have been born on 6 Apr 1745 in Leeuwarden and died aged 111 years 354 days on 26 Mar 1857 in Arnhem*

[8] *Mrs W. Sande was born in present-day Norway.*

[9] *The claim that Liakon Efdokia died 17 Jan 1982 aged 118 years 13 days is not substantiated by the censuses of 1971 or 1981. Birth registration before 1920 was fragmentary.*

[10] *There are allegedly 21 700 centenarians in the USSR (cf. 7000 in the USA). Of these 21 000 are ascribed to the Georgian SSR, i.e. one in every 232. In July 1962 it was reported that 128, mostly male, were in the one village of Medini.*

[11] *West Germany: an unnamed female died in 1979 aged 112 years and an unnamed male died, aged also 112 years, in 1969. The Austrian record is 108 years (female d. 1975) and the Swiss record is also 108 years (female d. 1967).*

[12] *Senhora Jesuina da Conceicao of Lisbon was reputedly 113 years old when she died on 10 Jun 1965.*

Note: *fl.* is the abbreviation for *floruit*, Latin for he (or she) was living at the relevant date.

Physiology and Anatomy

Hydrogen (63 per cent) and oxygen (25·5 per cent) constitute the commonest of the 24 elements in the human body. In 1972 four more trace elements were added—fluorine, silicon, tin and vanadium. The 'essentiality' of nickel remains a matter of controversy.

HANDS, FEET AND HAIR

Touch ■ The extreme sensitivity of the fingers is such that a vibration with a movement of 0·02 of a micron can be detected.

Longest finger nails ■ The aggregate measurement of those of Shridhar Chillal (b. 1937) of Pune, India, on 17 Mar 1989, was 426·72 cm *168 in* for the 5 nails on his left hand (thumb 99·06 cm *39 in,* first finger 74.99 cm *29 ½ in,* second finger and third fingers 83·82 cm *33 in,* and the fourth 85 cm *33 ½ in*). He last cut his nails in 1952. Finger nails grow about 0·05 cm *0·02 in* a week–four times faster than toe nails.

Least toes ■ The two-toed syndrome exhibited by some members of the Wadomo tribe of the Zambezi Valley, Zimbabwe, and the Kalanga tribe of the eastern Kalahari Desert, Botswana, is hereditary via a single mutated gene. These 'ostrich people', as they are known, are not handicapped by their deformity, and can walk great distances without discomfort.

Largest feet ■ If cases of elephantiasis are excluded, then the biggest feet known are those of Muhammad Aalam Channa of Pakistan who wears a size 22 sandal. The owner of Britain's largest feet is John Thrupp (b.1964) of Stratford–upon–Avon, Warks,who wears a size 21 shoe. He is 2·11 m *6 ft 11 in* tall. Chris Greener, Britain's tallest man (see p. 7) takes size 17.

Longest hair ■ In 1780 a head of hair measuring 3·65 m *12 ft* in length and dressed in a style known as the Plica Polonica (hair closely matted together) was sent to Dresden after adorning the head of a Polish peasant woman for 52 years. The plait of hair was 30·4 cm *11·9 in* in circumference. Swami Pandarasannadhi, the head of the Tirudaduturai monastery, Tanjore district, Madras, India, was reported in 1949 to have hair 7·92 m *26 ft* in length but no photographic or scientific evidence has ever been supplied in order to support this extreme measurement. In March 1989 a length of 6·4 m *21 ft* was claimed for the hair of 74-year-old Mata Jagdamba, a Yogni living in Ujjain, North India. The length of hair of Miss Skuldfrid Sjorgren (b. Stockholm) was reported from Toronto, Canada in 1927 to have reached twice her height at 3·20 m *10 ft 6 in.* The hair of Diane Witt of Worcester, USA measured 315 cm *10 ft 9 in* in May 1989. She last cut her hair 7 years ago. Human hair grows at the rate of about 1·27 cm *0·5 in* in a month. If left uncut it will usually grow to a maximum of 61–91 cm *2–3 ft.*

Longest beard ■ That of Hans N. Langseth (b. 1846 near Eidsroll, Norway) measured 5·33 m *17½ ft* at the time of his burial at Kensett, Iowa in 1927 after 15 years' residence in the United States. It was presented to the Smithsonian Institution, Washington, DC in 1967. Richard Latter (b. Pembury, Kent, 1831) of Tunbridge Wells, Kent, who died in 1914 aged 83, reputedly had a beard 4·87 m *16 ft* long but contemporary independent corroboration is lacking and photographic evidence indicates this figure was exaggarated. The beard of the bearded lady Janice Deveree (b. Bracken Co., Kentucky, 1842) was measured at 36 cm *14 in* in 1884. The beard of Mlle Hélène Antonia of Liège, Belgium, a 17th-century exhibitionist, was said to have reached to her hips.

Longest moustache ■ That of Birger Pellas (b. 21 Sep 1934) of Malmö, Sweden, grown since 1973 reached 286 cm *9 ft 4½ in* on 3 Feb 1989.

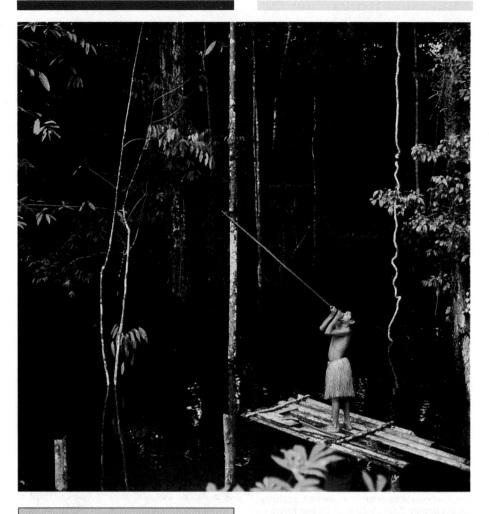

Colour blindness ● The Brazilian Indians along with the Fijians possess the lowest rate of red-green colour blindness in the world. (Photo: Daily Telegraph)

Karna Ram Bheel (1928–87) was granted permission by a New Delhi prison governor in February 1979 to keep his 238 cm *7 ft 10 in* moustache which he had grown since 1949 during his life sentence. He used mustard, oil, butter and cream to keep it in trim.

The longest moustache in Great Britain has been that of John Roy (1910–88), of Weeley, near Clacton, Essex. It attained a peak span of 189 cm *6 ft 2 ½in* between 1939 and 2 Apr 1976. He accidentally sat on it in the bath in 1984 and lost 42 cm *16½ in.* He then took off the same amount from the other side to even the moustache. The current UK champion is Mike Solomons of Long Ditton, Surrey with 81·3 cm *32 in* as of March 1989.

DENTITION

Earliest ■ The first deciduous or milk teeth normally appear in infants at 5–8 months, these being the mandibular and maxillary first incisors. There are many records of children born with teeth, the most distinguished example being Prince Louis Dieudonné, later Louis XIV of France, who was born with two teeth on 5 Sep 1638. Molars usually appear at 24 months, but in Pindborg's case published in Denmark in 1970, a 6-week premature baby was documented with 8 natal teeth of which 4 were in the molar region.

Most ■ Cases of the growth in late life of a third set of teeth have been recorded several times. A reference to a case in France of a fourth dentition, known as Lison's case, was published in 1896. A triple row of teeth was noted in 1680 by Albertus Hellwigius.

Most dedicated dentist ■ Brother Giovanni Battista Orsenigo of the Ospedale Fatebenefratelli, Rome, a religious dentist, conserved all the teeth he extracted in three enormous cases during the time he exercised his profession from 1868 to 1904. In 1903 the number was counted and found to be 2 000 744 teeth, indicating an average of 185 teeth or nearly 6 total extractions a day.

Strongest bite ■ In August 1986, Richard Hofmann (b. 1949) of Lake City, Florida, USA, achieved a bite strength of 442 kg *975 lb* for approx. 2 seconds in a research test using a gnathodymometer at the College of Dentistry, University of Florida, USA. This figure is over 6 times normal biting strength.

Most valuable tooth ■ In 1816 a tooth belonging to Sir Isaac Newton (1643–1727) was sold in London for £730. It was purchased by a nobleman who had it set in a ring which he wore constantly.

Earliest false teeth ■ From discoveries made in Etruscan tombs, partial dentures of bridge-work type were being worn in what is now Tuscany, Italy, as early as 700 BC. Some were permanently attached to existing teeth and others were removable.

OPTICS

Highest visual acuity ■ The human eye is capable of judging relative position with remarkable accuracy, reaching limits of between 3 and 5 sec of arc.

In April 1984 Dr Dennis M. Levi of the College of Optometry, University of Houston, Texas, USA, repeatedly identified the position of a thin white line within 0·85 sec of arc. This is equivalent to a displacement of some 6 mm *¼ in* at a distance of 1·6 km *1 mile.*

Colour sensitivity ■ The unaided human eye, under the best possible viewing conditions, comparing large areas of colour, in good illumination, using both eyes, can distinguish 10 000 000 different colour surfaces. The most accurate photoelectric spectrophotometers possess a precision probably only 40 per cent as good as this. About 7·5 per cent of men and 0·1 per cent of women are colour blind. The most extreme form, monochromatic vision, is very rare. The highest rate of red–green colour blindness is in Czechoslovakia and the lowest rate among Fijians and Brazilian Indians. ·

DRUGS

Most powerful drugs ■ The most powerful commonly available drug is d-Lysergic Acid Diethylamide tartrate (LSD-25, $C_{20}H_{25}N_3O$) first produced in 1938 for common cold research and as a hallucinogen by Dr Albert Hoffman (Swiss) on 16–19 Apr 1943. The most potent analgesic drug is the morphine-like R33799 confirmed in 1978 to have almost 12 000 times the potency of morphine. Interferon was reported available for $10 per millionth of a microgramme.

BONES

Longest ■ Excluding a variable number of sesamoids (small rounded bones) there are 206 bones in the adult human body, compared with 300 for children (as they grow some bones fuse together to make one). The thigh bone or *femur* is the longest. It constitutes usually 27 $^1/_2$ per cent of a person's stature, and may be expected to be 50 cm *19 $^3/_4$ in* long in a 183 cm *6 ft* tall man. The longest recorded bone was the femur of the German giant Constantine, who died in Mons, Belgium, on 30 Mar 1902, aged 30 (see p. 6). It measured 76 cm *29.9 in*. The femur of Robert Wadlow, the tallest man ever recorded, measured an estimated 75 cm *29.5 in.*

Smallest ■ The *stapes* or stirrup bone, one of the three auditory ossicles in the middle ear, measures from 2·6 to 3·4 mm *0·10 to 0.17 in* in length and weighs from 2·0 to 4·3 mg *0.03 – 0·065 grains.*

MUSCLES

Largest ■ Muscles normally account for 40 per cent of the body weight and the bulkiest of the 639 named muscles in the human body is the *gluteus maximus* or buttock muscle, which extends the thigh.

Smallest ■ The *stapedius*, which controls the *stapes* (see above), an auditory ossicle in the middle ear, is less than 0·127 cm *1/20 th of an inch* long.

Largest chest measurements ■ The largest are among endomorphs (those with a tendency towards globularity). In the extreme case of Hughes (see table p. 9) this was 315 cm *124 in*, and T. J. Albert

Most prescribed drug ● A cluster of crystals of ranitidine, the active ingredient in anti-ulcer Zantac, the top selling prescribed drug, photographed here under polarised light. (Photo: Glaxo Holdings plc)

Jackson, currently the heaviest living man (see p. 9) has a chest measurement of 304·8 cm *120 in*. The largest chest ever recorded in Britain was that of William Campbell (see p. 9) which measured 244 cm *96 in*. Among muscular subjects (mesomorphs) of normal height *expanded* chest measurements above 142 cm *56 in* are extremely rare.

Arnold Schwarzenegger (b.1948) of Graz, Austria, 185 cm *6 ft 1 in* former Mr Universe and 'the most perfectly developed man in the history of the world', had a chest measurement of 145 cm *57 in* (bicep 55·8 cm *22 in*) at his best bodyweight of 107 kg *235 lb*. This was exceeded by Jamie Reeves (b. 1962) of Sheffield, Yorks, who has a chest measurement of 152·4 cm *60 in* at a height of 193 cm *6 ft 4 in* , he weighs 146 kg *23 st*. Vasiliy Alekseyev (b. 1942), the 186 cm *6 ft 1 $^1/_4$ in* Russian super-heavyweight weight-lifting champion, had a 153·6 cm *60 $^1/_2$ in* chest at his top weight of 158·7 kg *350 lb*. Power-lifter Rick Brown (b. 4 Apr 1960) of Los Angeles, California, USA, known to his friends as 'Grizzly', has a chest measurement of 167·6 cm *66 in* at a bodyweight of 166 kg *26 st 1 lb*, but the largest muscular chest measurement recorded so far is that of another American power-lifter named Isaac 'Dr Size' Nesser (b. 21 Apr 1962) of Greensburg, Pennsylvania, USA who measures 172·87 cm *68·06 in*. He stands 177·8·8 cm *5 ft 10 in* and weighs 164·2 kg *25 st 1 lb*.

Largest and smallest biceps ■ Isaac 'Dr Size' Nesser has biceps of 66·35 cm *26 $^1/_8$ in* cold (not pumped).The biceps of Robert Thorn (see p. 11) measured 11·4 cm *4 $^1/_4$ in* when 'pumped up'.

Largest and smallest waists ■ The largest waist ever recorded was that of Walter Hudson (see table p.9) which measured 302 cm *119 in* at his peak weight of 545 kg *85 st 7 lb*. Queen Catherine di Medici (1519–89) decreed a waist measurement of 35 cm *13.77 in* for ladies of the French Court, but this was at a time when females were more diminutive.

The smallest recorded waist among women of normal stature in the 20th century is a reputed 33 cm *13 in* in the cases of the French actress Mlle Polaire (real name Emile Marie Bouchand)(1881–1939) and Mrs Ethel Granger (1905–82) of Peterborough, Cambridge, who reduced from a natural 56 cm *22 in* over the period 1929–39.

Longest necks ■ The maximum measured exten-

sion of the neck by the successive fitting of copper coils, as practised by the women of the Padaung or Kareni tribe of Burma, is 40 cm *15 $^3/_4$ in*. When the rings are removed the muscles developed to support the head and neck shrink to their normal length.

BRAINS

Heaviest ■ The brain of an average adult male (*i.e.* 20–55 years) weighs 1424 g *3 lb 2·2 oz*, decreasing gradually to 1395 g *3 lb 1·1 oz* with advancing age. The heaviest brain ever recorded was that of a 50-year-old male which weighed 2049 g *4 lb 8·29 oz* reported by Dr Thomas F. Hegert, chief medical examiner for District 9, State of Florida, USA, on 23 Oct 1975. The brain of Ivan Sergeyvich Turgenev (1818–83), the Russian author, weighed 2012 g *4 lb 6·9 oz*. In January 1891 the *Edinburgh Medical Journal* reported the case of a 75-year-old man in the Royal Edinburgh Asylum whose brain weighed 1829 g *4 lb 0·5 oz*. The largest female brain weighed 1565 g *3 lb 7·3 oz* and belonged to a murderess.

Human brains are getting heavier. Examination of *post-mortem* records shows that the average male brain weight has increased from 1372 g *3 lb 0·4 oz* in 1860 to 1424 g *3 lb 2·2 oz* today. Women's brains have also put on weight, from 1242 g *2 lb 11·8 oz* to 1265 g *2 lb 12·6 oz* and in recent years have been growing almost as fast as men's.

Professor Marian Diamond of the University of California at Berkeley announced on 13 Feb 1985 that the neuron to glial cell ratio in Section 39 of the brain of Albert Einstein (1879–1955) was 1·12 as opposed to the standard 1·936 – a difference of 72·8 per cent.

Lightest ■ The lightest 'normal' or non-atrophied brain on record was one weighing 1096 g *2 lb 6·7 oz* reported by Dr P. Davis and Professor E. Wright of King's College Hospital, London in 1977. It belonged to a 31-year-old woman.

Human computer ■ The fastest extraction of a 13th root from a 100-digit number is in 1 min 28·8 sec by the Dutchman Willem Klein (1912–86) on 7 Apr 1981 at the National Laboratory for High Energy Physics (KEK), Tsukuba, Japan. Mrs Shakuntala Devi of India demonstrated the multiplication of two 13-digit numbers which were randomly selected 7 686 369 774 870 × 2 465 099 745 779 by the Computer Department of Imperial College, London on 18 Jun 1980, in 28 seconds. Her answer which was correct was 18 947 668 177 995 426 462 773 730. Some experts on calculating prodigies refuse to give credence to Mrs Devi on the grounds that it is so vastly superior to the calculating feats of any other invigilated prodigy that the invigilation must have been defective.

Memory ■ Bhandanta Vicitsara recited 16 000 pages of Buddhist canonical texts in Rangoon, Burma in May 1974. Gon Yang-ling, 26, has memorised more than 15 000 telephone numbers in Harbin, China according to the Xinhua News Agency. Rare instances of eidetic memory–the ability to re-project and hence 'visually' recall material–are known to science.

Dominic O'Brien of Wonersh, Guildford, Surrey memorised a random sequence of twenty-five separate packs of cards (1300) which had been all shuffled together on a single sighting with four errors at the University of Surrey, Guildford on 11 Jun 1989.

Between 9 Apr–11 Jun 1989 the record for memorising playing cards was broken six times by three contenders, namely Tony Power, Allan Griffith and Dominic O'Brien. Each briefly held the record no less than twice.

Barbara 'Squeek' Moore performed on the piano from memory 1852 songs at the Philadelphia Bourse Building, Pennsylvania, USA from 25 Oct to 13 Nov 1988.

The greatest number of places of π ■ Hideaki Tomoyori (b. 30 Sep 1932), of Yokohama, Japan, recited 'pi' from memory to 40 000 places in 17 hr

21 min including 4 hr 15 min breaks on 9–10 Mar 1987 at the Tsukuba University Club House. On a Japanese TV programme, Mr Tomoyori also demonstrated his ability to recite correctly the 20 consecutive digits following a randomly selected series of numbers.

The British record is 20 013 by Creighton Herbert James Carvello (b. 19 Nov 1944) on 27 Jun 1980 in 9 hr 10 min at Saltscar Comprehensive School, Redcar, Cleveland. *Note:* It is only the *approximation* of π at $^{22}/_7$ which recurs after its sixth decimal place and can, of course, be recited *ad nauseam*. The true value is a string of random numbers fiendishly difficult to memorise. The average ability for memorising random numbers is barely more than 8, as proved by the common inability to memorise 9 or 10 digit telephone numbers.

VOICE

Highest and lowest ■ Before this century the extremes were a staccato E in *alt altissimo* (e[iv]) by Ellen Beach Yaw (USA) (1869–1947) in Carnegie Hall, New York, USA on 19 Jan 1896, and an A₁ (55 Hz (cycles per sec)) by Kasper Foster (1617–73). Madeleine Marie Robin (1918–60), the French operatic coloratura, could produce and sustain the B above high C in the Lucia mad scene in Donizetti's *Lucia di Lammermoor*. Since 1950 singers have achieved high and low notes far beyond the hitherto accepted extremes. However, notes at the bass and treble extremities of the register tend to lack harmonics and are of little musical value. Frl Marita Gunther, trained by Alfred Wolfsohn, has covered the range of the piano from the lowest note, A₁₁ to c[v]. Of this range of 7¼ octaves, 6 octaves were considered to be of musical value. Roy Hart, also trained by Wolfsohn, has reached notes below the range of the piano. Barry Girard of Canton, Ohio, USA in May 1975 reached the E (4340 Hz) above the piano's top note. The highest note put into song is G[iv] first occurring in Mozart's *Popoli di Tessaglia*. The lowest vocal note in the classical repertoire is in Mozart's *Il Seraglio* in Osmin's aria which calls for a low D (73.4 Hz). Dan Britton reached the 4th E below middle C at 20·6 Hz at Anoka County Fair, Minnesota, USA on 31 Jul 1984. Stefan Zucker sang A in *alt altissimo* for 3·8 sec in the tenor role of Salvini in the première of Bellini's *Adelson e Salvini* in New York on 12 Sep 1972.

Greatest range ■ The normal intelligible outdoor range of the male human voice in still air is 180 m *200 yd*. The *silbo*, the whistled language of the Spanish-speaking Canary Island of La Gomera, is intelligible across the valleys, under ideal conditions, at 8 km *5 miles*. There is a recorded case, under freak acoustic conditions, of the human voice being detectable at a distance of 17 km *10½ miles* across still water at night. It was said that Mills Darden (see table p. 9) could be heard 9 km *6 miles* away when he bellowed at the top of his voice.

Because of their greater optimum frequency, female screams tend to record higher readings on decibel meters than male bellows. The highest scientifically measured emission has been one of 128 dBA by the screaming of Simon Robinson of McLaren Vale, South Australia at 'The Guinness Challenge' at the Australian Grand Prix, Adelaide, on 11 Nov 1988.

Shouting ■ Donald H. Burns of St George's, Bermuda, USA won the Loudest Cry trophy in the Seventh International Town Criers' Championship in Halifax, Nova Scotia, Canada on 15 Sep 1984 with a shout recorded at 113 decibels.

The greatest number of wins in the national Town Criers' Contest is 11 (between 1939–73) by Ben Johnson of Fowey, Cornwall. The first national feminine champion has been Mrs Henrietta Sargent, towncrier, of The Three Horse Shoes, Cricklade, Wilts in 1980. On being told she had beaten the other 31 contestants she said, 'I'm speechless'.

Lowest detectable sound ■ The intensity of noise or sound is measured in terms of pressure. The pressure of the quietest sound that can be detected by a person of normal hearing at the most sensitive frequency of *c.* 2750 Hz is 2×10^{-5} pascal. One tenth of the logarithm to this standard provides a unit termed a decibel (dBA). A noise of 30 decibels is negligible.

Highest noise levels ■ Prolonged noise above 150 decibels will cause permanent deafness while above 192 dBA a lethal over-pressure shock wave can be formed. Equivalent continuous sound levels (LEQ) above 90 dBA are impermissible in factories, but this compares with 125 emitted by racing cars, 130 by amplified music and 170 by some toy guns.

Highest detectable pitch ■ The upper limit is reckoned to be 20 000 Hz (cycles per sec), although it has been alleged that children with asthma can detect sounds of 30 000 Hz. Bats emit pulses at up to 90 000 Hz. It was announced in February 1964 that experiments in the USSR had conclusively proved that oscillations as high as 200 000 Hz can be detected if the oscillator is pressed against the skull.

Fastest talker ■ Few people are able to speak *articulately* at a sustained speed above 300 words per minute. The fastest broadcaster has been regarded as Gerry Wilmot (b. Victoria, BC, Canada, 6 Oct 1914), the ice hockey commentator in the late forties. Raymond Glendenning (1907–74), the BBC commentator, once spoke 176 words in 30 sec while commentating on a greyhound race. In public life the highest speed recorded is a 327 words per min burst in a speech made in December 1961 by John Fitzgerald Kennedy (1917–63), then President of the United States. John Moschitta (USA) recited 545 words in 55·8 sec or 586 words per minute on 24 May 1988 in Los Angeles, California, USA. John Helm of Yorkshire TV can recite the 92 Football League clubs in 26 sec.

Backwards Talking ■ Steve Briers recited the entire lyrics of Queen's album A Night at the Opera on the Radio 1 Roadshow at Tenby, Dyfed on 26 Jul 1988. He achieved 2343 words in 15 min 7 sec.

BLOOD

Groups ■ The preponderance of one blood group varies greatly from one locality to another. On a world basis Group O is the most common (46 per cent), but in some areas, for example Norway, Group A predominates.

The full description of the commonest sub-group in Britain is O MsNs, P+, Rr, Lu(a−), K−, Le(a−b+),

> **Backwards talking** ● Steve Briers who recited the entire lyrics of Queen's album *A Night at the Opera* on the Radio 1 Roadshow at Tenby, Dyfed on 26 July 1988. (Photo: Gareth Davies)

Fy(a+b+), Jk(a+b+), which occurs in one in every 270 people.

The rarest blood group on the ABO system, one of 14 systems, is AB, which occurs in less than 3 per cent of persons in the British Isles. The rarest type in the world is a type of Bombay blood (sub-type h-h) found so far only in a Czechoslovak nurse in 1961 and in a brother (Rh positive) and sister (Rh negative) named Jalbert in Massachusetts, reported in February 1968.

Richest natural resources ■ Joe Thomas of Detroit, Michigan, USA was reported in August 1970 to have the highest known count of Anti-Lewis B, the rare blood antibody. A US biological supply firm pays him $1500 per US quart *1·13 litres*. The Internal Revenue regard this income as a taxable liquid asset.

Donor and recipient ■ Since September 1966, Allen Doster, a self-employed beautician, has, to February 1989, made a total of 1037 platelet donations by both manual and machine plasmapheresis at Roswell Park Memorial Institute, New York, USA. The current limit in the USA on machine platelet pheresis donations is 24 per year.

Tammy Hill (b.1978) of Accrington, Lancs, has 7094 litres *12 480 pt* of blood pumped through her body once every fortnight. She suffers from a rare disease that creates massive amounts of fat in her blood and without this treatment, at Alder Hay Hospital, Liverpool, she could suffer a heart attack.

A 50-year-old haemophiliac Warren C. Jyrich required 2400 donor units *1080 litres* of blood when undergoing open heart surgery at the Michael Reese Hospital, Chicago, USA in December 1970.

Largest vein ■ The largest is the *inferior vena cava*, which returns the blood from most of the body below the level of the heart.

Most alcoholic subject ■ California University Medical School, Los Angeles, USA reported in December 1982 the case of a confused but conscious 24-year-old female, who was shown to have a blood alcohol level of 1510 mg per 100 ml — nearly 19 times the UK driving limit (80 mg of alcohol per 100 ml of blood) and triple the normally lethal limit. After two days she discharged herself. The late Samuel Riley (b. 1922) of Sefton Park, Merseyside, was found by a disbelieving pathologist to have a level of 1220 mg on 28 Mar 1979.

William Pitt the Younger (1759–1806) the British Prime Minister, once allegedly drank 574 bottles of claret, 854 bottles of Madeira and 2410 bottles of Port in one year!

Tommy Johns of Brisbane, Queensland, Australia, died in April 1988 from a brain tumour aged 66 years after having been arrested nearly 3000 times for being drunk and disorderly in a public place. (See Chapter 10, Most Appearances).

BODY TEMPERATURE

Highest ■ Willie Jones, a 52-year-old black man, was admitted to Grady Memorial Hospital, Atlanta, Georgia, USA on 10 Jul 1980 with heat stroke on a day when the temperature reached 32·2° C *90° F* with 44 per cent humidity. His temperature was found to be 46·5° C *115·7° F*. After 24 days he was discharged 'at prior baseline status'.

Lowest ■ There are three recorded cases of patients surviving body temperatures as low as 16° C *60·8° F*. Dorothy Mae Stevens (1929–74) who was found in an alley in Chicago, Illinois, USA on 1 Feb 1951 and whose pulse dropped to 12 beats per min; Vickie Mary Davis aged 2 years 1 month in an unheated house in Marshalltown, Iowa, USA on 21 Jan 1956 and 2-year-old Michael Troke in the snow near his home in Milwaukee, Wisconsin, USA on 19 Jan 1985, all with this temperature. People may die of hypothermia with body temperatures of 35·0° C *95° F*.

ILLNESS AND DISEASE

Commonest ■ The commonest non-contagious disease is periodontal disease, such as gingivitis (inflammation of the gums) which subclinically afflicts some 80 per cent of the US population. In Great Britain 13 per cent of people have lost all their teeth before they are 21 years old. During their lifetime few completely escape its effects. Infestation with pinworm (*Enterobius vermicularis*) approaches 100 per cent in some tropical areas of the world.

The commonest contagious disease in the world is coryza (acute nasopharyngitis) or the common cold. The greatest reported loss of working time in Britain is from neurotic disorders, which accounted for 31 488 800 or 8·25 per cent, of the total of 381 151 800 days lost from mid-1987 to mid-1988.

The most resistant recorded case to being infected at the Medical Research Council Common Cold Unit, Salisbury, Wilts is J. Brophy, who has had one mild reaction in 24 visits.

Rarest ■ Medical literature periodically records hitherto undescribed diseases. A disease as yet undiagnosed but predicted by a Norwegian doctor is podocytoma of the kidney–tumour of the epithelial cells lining the glomerulus of the kidney.

The last case of endemic smallpox was recorded in Ali Maow Maalin in Merka, Somalia on 26 Oct 1977. Paul Braddon of Rusper, West Sussex was reported on 2 Aug 1983 to be the first person to contract malaria in Britain for more than 35 years.

Kuru, or laughing sickness, afflicts only the Fore tribe of eastern New Guinea and is 100 per cent fatal. This was formerly attributed to the cannibalistic practice of eating human brains.

The rarest fatal diseases in England and Wales have been those from which the last deaths (all males) were all recorded more than 40 years ago–yellow fever (1930), cholera nostras (1928) and bubonic plague (1926).

Most infectious ■ The pneumonic form of plague, as evidenced by the Black Death of 1347–51,had a mortality rate of about 99·99 per cent.

Highest mortality rate ■ The virus AIDS (acquired immune-deficiency syndrome), first recognised in 1978, was first identified in January 1983 at the Pasteur Institute, Paris by Luc Montagnier, Françoise Barré-Sinoussi and Jean-Claude Chermann as a Human T-lymphotrophic Type III (HTLV III) virus.

The World Health Organisation reported 108 176 cases to July 1988. The US death toll from AIDS has been predicted to reach 179 000 by 1991, with care costs possibly reaching $16 000 million. Uncertainty on the percentage of sero-positive HIV carriers and the duration of incubation only make it possible to

assert that the toll will be of the order 100 000 to 300 000 by this date.

Rabies in humans has been regarded as uniformly fatal when associated with the hydrophobia symptom. A 25-year-old woman, Candida de Sousa Barbosa of Rio de Janeiro, Brazil, following surgery by Dr Max Karpin, was believed to be the first ever survivor of the disease in November 1968. Some sources prefer the case of an unnamed 7-year-old boy living near Tampa Florida, USA, who, on 23 Jun 1953, was bitten on the chest by a rabid Common vampire bat (*Desmodus rotundus*). The boy was put on a course of prophylactic immunization and eventually made a full recovery.

Leading cause of death ■ In industrialised countries arteriosclerosis (thickening of the arterial wall) underlies much coronary and cerebrovascular disease. Deaths from diseases of the circulatory system totalled 278 849 in England and Wales in 1984.

Most notorious carrier ■ The most publicised of all typhoid carriers has been Mary Mallon (real name Maria Anna Caduff), known as Typhoid Mary, who was born in Graubunden, Switzerland, in 1855 and arrived as an immigrant in New York City, NY, USA, on 11 Jan 1868. In her job as a cook she was the source of 53 outbreaks, including the 1903 epidemic of 1400 cases in Ithaca, and 3 deaths. She was placed under permanent detention at Riverside Hospital on North Brother Island, East River, from 1915 until her death from broncho-pneumonia on 11 Nov 1938.

Parkinson's disease ■ Named after 'An Essay on the Shaking Palsy' of 1817 by Dr James Parkinson (1755–1824) and for which the earliest treatments were not published until 1946, the most protracted case was 62 years in the case of Frederick G. Humphries (d. 23 Feb 1985) of Croydon, London. His symptoms were detected in 1923.

MEDICAL EXTREMES

Heart stoppage ■ The longest is 4 hr in the case of a Norwegian fisherman, Jan Egil Refsdahl (b. 1936), who fell overboard in the icy waters off Bergen on 7 Dec 1987. He was rushed to nearby Haukeland Hospital after his body temperature fell to 24° C *77° F* and his heart stopped beating, but he made a full recovery after he was connected to a heart–lung machine normally used for heart surgery.

***Post mortem* birth** ■ The longest gestation interval in a *post mortem* birth was one of 84 days in the case of a baby girl born on 5 Jul 1983 from a clinically dead woman in Roanoke, Virginia, USA who had been kept on life support since April.

Pulse rates ■ A normal adult rate is 70–72 beats per min at rest for males and 78–82 for females. Rates increase to 200 or more during violent exercise. When Charles Thompson of Cwmbran, Gwent was admitted to hospital for a hip joint replacement operation on 16 Aug 1987 he was found to have a resting pulse rate of 28 beats per min.

Longest coma ■ Elaine Esposito (b. 3 Dec 1934) of Tarpon Springs, Florida, USA, never stirred after an appendicectomy on 6 Aug 1941, when she was 6, in Chicago, Illinois, USA and died on 25 Nov 1978 aged 43 years 357 days, having been in a coma for 37 years 111 days.

Longest dream ■ Dreaming sleep is characterised by rapid eye movements known as REM described in 1953 by William Dement of the University of Chicago, USA. The longest recorded period of REM is one of 2 hr 23 min on 15 Feb 1967 at the Department of Psychology, University of Illinois, Chicago on Bill Carskadon, who had had his previous sleep interrupted. In July 1984 the Sleep Research Centre, Haifa, Israel recorded nil REM in a 33-year-old male who had a shrapnel brain injury.

Largest stone ■ The largest reported in medical literature was one of 6·29 kg *13 lb 14 oz* removed from an 80-year-old woman by Dr Humphrey Arthure at Charing Cross Hospital, London, on 29

Dec 1952. In August 1987 it was reported that 23 530 gallstones had been removed from an 85–year old woman, by Mr K. Whittle Martin at Worthing Hospital, West Sussex, after she complained of severe abdominal pain.

Longest in 'iron lung' ■ Mrs Laurel Nisbet (1912–85) of La Crescenta, California, USA, was in an 'iron lung' for 37 years 58 days continuously since 25 Jun 1948. The longest survival in an 'iron lung' in Britain was 30 years (1949–79) by Denis Atkin in Lodge Moor Hospital, Sheffield, South Yorks. John Prestwich (b. 24 Nov 1938) of Kings Langley, Herts has been dependent on a negative pressure respirator since 24 Nov 1955. Paul Bates (1935–89) of Horsham, West Sussex, was harnessed to a mechanical positive pressure respirator on 13 Aug 1954. He had received an estimated 252 141 743 respirations via his trachea up to early 1989.

Longest on haemodialysis ■ Raymond Jones (b. 14 Apr 1929) of Slough, Berks, who has suffered from kidney failure from the age of 34, has received continuous haemodialysis since 13 Oct 1963 averaging three visits per week to the Royal Free Hospital, Hampstead, London. In this time he seen his children grow up, marry and themselves have children.

Fastest nerve impulses ■ The results of experiments published in 1966 have shown that the fastest messages transmitted by the human nervous system travel as fast as 288 km/h *180 mph*. With advancing age impulses are carried 15 per cent more slowly.

Fastest reactions ■ The fastest recorded apparent reaction times for sprinters at the 1980 Olympic Games were 0·12 sec for Romy Müller (GDR) in the women's 200 m semi-final and 0·124 sec for Wilbert Greaves (GB) in the 110 m hurdles heats. Both may have been anticipatory. These compare with 0·011 sec for the cockroach *Periplaneta americana*.

Hiccoughing ■ The longest recorded attack is that afflicting Charles Osborne (b. 1894) of Anthon, Iowa, USA, for the past 67 years from 1922. He contracted it when slaughtering a hog and has been unable to find a cure, but leads a reasonably normal life in which he has had two wives and fathered eight children. He has admitted, however, that he cannot keep in his false teeth. In July 1986 he was reported to be hiccoughing at 20–25 per minute from his earlier high of 40.

Sneezing ■ The most chronic fit ever recorded is that of Donna Griffiths (b. 1969) of Pershore, Hereford and Worcester. She started sneezing on 13 Jan 1981 and surpassed the previous duration record of 194 days on 27 Jul 1981. She sneezed an estimated million times in the first 365 days. She achieved her first sneeze-free day on 16 Sep 1983–the 978th day. The highest speed at which expelled particles have ever been measured to travel is 167 km/h *103·6 mph*.

Snoring ■ The highest measured sound level recorded by any chronic snorer are peaks of 90 decibels measured at the Department of Medicine, the University of British Columbia, Vancouver, Canada, during the evening of 3 Nov 1987. The meter was placed 60 cm *2 ft* above the head of Mark Thompson Hebbard (b.28 Feb 1947) of Richmond, British Columbia, Canada who maintained an overall level of 90 decibels. As a Vancouver city traffic bylaw for tolerable loudness is set at 80 decibels he wonders if he is legally entitled to sleep there.

Yawning ■ In Lee's case, reported in 1888, a 15-year-old female patient yawned continuously for a period of 5 weeks.

Sleeplessness ■ Researches indicate that on the Circadian cycle for the majority peak efficiency is attained between 8 and 9 p.m. and the low point comes at 4 a.m. The longest recorded period for which a person has voluntarily gone without sleep is 453 hr 40 min by Robert McDonald of California, USA in a rocking chair on 14 Mar–2 Apr 1986 (see Chapter 9 p. 184). Victims of the very rare condition chronic colestites (total insomnia) have been known

Aids virus ● The virus AIDS (acquired immune-deficiency syndrome) was first recognised in 1978 and identified in January 1983 at the Pasteur Institute, Paris by Luc Montagnier, Françoise Barré-Sinoussi and Jean-Claude Chermann as a Human T-lymphotrophic Type III (HTLV III) virus. (Photo: Science Photo Library)

to go without definable sleep for many years. Jesus de Frutos (b. 1925) of Segovia, Spain asserts that he has only dozed since 1954.

Sleepwalking ■ On 6 Apr 1987 Michael Dixon (b. 1976) was found wandering barefoot, dazed and in his pyjamas along a railway track in Peru, Indiana, USA. He had sleepwalked out of his home in Danville, Illinois, USA 160 km *100 miles* away after travelling on a freight train.

Motionlessness ■ Antonio Gomes dos Santos (b. 1963) of Nazaré, Portugal, continuously stood motionless for 15 hr 2 min 55 sec on 30 Jul 1988 at the Amoreiras Shopping Centre, Lisbon, Portugal. The longest recorded case of involuntarily being made to stand to attention was when Corporal Everett D. Reamer of the 60th Coast Artillery Regiment AA Battery F, USA FFE was so punished in Camp No 1, Osaka, Japan for 132 consecutive hours from 8.00 a.m. 15 Aug until 8.00 p.m. 20 Aug 1944.

Fire breathers and extinguishers ■ Reg Morris blew a flame from his mouth to a distance of 9·4 m *31 ft* at the Miner's Rest, Chasetown, Staffordshire on 29 Oct 1986. On 25 June 1988 Reg Morris also extinguished 22 888 torches of flame in his mouth in 2 hr at Yew Tree School, Walsall, West Midlands. On 26 Jul 1986 at Port Lonsdale, Victoria, Australia, Sipra Ellen Lloyd set a female record of 8357.

Human salamanders ■ The highest dry-air temperature endured by naked men in the US Air Force experiments in 1960 was 204·4°C *400° F* and for heavily clothed men 260° C *500° F.* Steaks require only 162·8° C *325° F.* Temperatures of 140° C *284° F* have been found quite bearable in sauna baths.

A group of 11 people led by Steven Neil Bisyak of Redmond, Washington, USA, participated in a firewalk with an average temperature of 841° C *1546° F* on 19 Dec 1987 at Redmond. There is an annual firewalk during the feast of St Constantine each May in Aghia Eleni, northern Greece.

Swallowing ■ The worst reported case of compulsive swallowing was an insane female Mrs H. aged 42, who complained of a 'slight abdominal pain'. She had 2533 objects, including 947 bent pins, in her stomach. These were removed by Drs

Chalk and Foucar in June 1927 at the Ontario Hospital, Canada. In a more recent case 212 objects were removed from the stomach of a man admitted to Groote Schuur Hospital, Cape Town, South Africa in May 1985. They included 53 toothbrushes, 2 telescopic aerials, 2 razors and 150 handles of disposable razors. Another compulsive swallower in the USA, a 24-year-old psychoneurotic woman, gulped down a 12·7 cm *5 in* long iron hinge bolt from a hospital door which amazingly passed through the curve of the duodenum and the intestinal tract and broke the bed-pan when the patient successfully passed the object. The heaviest object extracted from a human stomach has been a 2·53 kg *5 lb 3 oz* ball of hair in Swain's case from a 20-year-old female compulsive swallower in the South Devon and East Cornwall Hospital, England on 30 Mar 1895.

Sword ■ Edward Benjamin 'Count Desmond' (b. 1941 of Binghamton, NY, USA) swallowed thirteen 58·4 cm *23 in* long blades to below his xiphisternum and injured himself in the process.
No further claims will be published.

Heaviest smoker ■ King Zog I of Albania (1895–1961) reportedly smoked 300 cigarettes in a day.

Hunger strike ■ Doctors estimate a well-nourished individual can survive without medical consequences on a diet of sugar and water for 30 days or more. The longest period for which anyone has gone without solid food is 382 days by Angus Barbieri (b. 1940) of Tayport, Fife, who lived on tea, coffee, water, soda water and vitamins in Maryfield Hospital, Dundee, Angus, from June 1965 to July 1966. His weight declined from 214·1 kg *33 st 10 lb* to 80·74 kg *12 st 10 lb.*
Records claimed, unless there is unremitting medical surveillance, are inadmissible.

The longest recorded hunger strike was 385 days from 28 Jun 1972 to 18 Jul 1973 by Denis Galer Goodwin in Wakefield Prison, West Yorkshire, protesting his innocence of a rape charge. He was fed by tube orally.

The longest recorded case of survival without food *and* water is 18 days by Andreas Mihavecz, then 18, of Bregenz, Austria who was put into a holding cell on 1 Apr 1979 in a local government building in Höchst, Austria but was totally forgotten by the police. On 18 Apr 1979 he was discovered close to death having had neither food nor water. He had been a passenger in a crashed car.

Underwater ■ The world record for voluntarily staying underwater is 13 min 42·5 sec by Robert Foster, then aged 32, an electronics technician of

Richmond, California, USA who stayed under 3·05 m *10 ft* of water in the swimming pool of the Bermuda Palms Motel at San Rafael, California, USA on 15 Mar 1959. He hyperventilated with oxygen for 30 min before his descent.

In 1986 2-year-old Michelle Funk of Salt Lake City, Utah, USA, made a full recovery after spending 66 minutes underwater. The toddler fell into a swollen creek near her home while playing. When she was eventually discovered rescue workers found she had no pulse or heart beat. Her life was saved by the first successful bypass machine to warm her blood, which had dropped to 66° F. Doctors at the hospital described the time she had spent under water as the 'longest documented submergence with an intact neurological outcome'.

g forces ■ The acceleration g, due to gravity, is 32 ft 1·05 in per sec per sec *978·02 cm/sec²* at sea level at the Equator. A *sustained* acceleration of 20 g, with a peak of 25 g, was withstood in a dry capsule during astronautic research by Dr Carter Collins of California, USA. The highest g value endured on a water-braked rocket sled is 82·6 g for 0·04 of a sec by Eli L. Beeding Jr at Holloman Air Force Base, New Mexico, on 16 May 1958. He was put in hospital for 3 days.

Fire walking ● One of a group of 11 people led by Steven Neil Bisyak of Redmond, Washington, USA participating in a firewalk with an average temperature of 841° F *1546° F* on 19 Dec 1987 at Redmond.

A land diver of Pentecost Island, Vanuatu formerly the New Hebrides dived from a platform 24·76 m *81 ft 3 in* high with liana vines attached to his ankles on 15 May 1982. The body speed was 15·24 m *50 ft* per sec 54 km/h *34 mph*. The jerk transmitted a momentary g force in excess of 110.

Longest stay in hospital ■ Miss Martha Nelson was admitted to the Columbus State Institute for the Feeble-Minded in Ohio, USA in 1875. She died in January 1975 aged 103 years 6 months in the Orient State Institution, Ohio after spending more than 99 years in institutions.

Pill-taking ■ The highest recorded total of pills swallowed by a patient is 565 939 between 9 Jun 1967 and 19 Jun 1988 by C. H. A. Kilner (1926–88) of Bindura, Zimbabwe.

Most injections ■ A diabetic, Mrs Evelyn Ruth Winder (b. 1921) of Invercargill, New Zealand gave an estimated 60 028 insulin injections to herself over 58 years to May 1989.

Most tattoos ■ The seeming ultimate in being tattooed is represented by Wilfred Hardy of Huthwaite, Notts, England. Not content with a perilous approach to within 96 per cent of totality, he has been tattooed on the inside of his cheek, his tongue, gums and eyebrows. Walter Stiglitz of North Plainfield, New Jersey, USA in April 1989 claimed 5488 separate tattoos by different artists. The world's most decorated woman is strip artiste Krystyne Kolorful (b. 5 Dec 1952, Alberta, Canada). Her 95 per cent body suit took 10 years to complete and cost $15 000. Britain's most decorated woman is Rusty Field (b. 1944) of Norfolk, who after 12 years under the needle of Bill Skuse has come to 85 per cent of totality. Both the 1980 and 1981 World's Most Beautiful Tattooed Lady Contest in the USA were won by Britain's Susan James (b.1959).

OPERATIONS

Longest ■ The most protracted reported operation, for surgical as opposed to medical control purposes, has been one of 96 hr performed on Mrs Gertrude Levandowski (see also p.10) during the period 4–8 Feb 1951 in Chicago, Illinois, USA. The patient suffered from a weak heart and surgeons had to exercise the utmost caution during the operation. The 'most delayed' operation on record is one of 22 years for Miss Christine Madden (b.1959) of Ward End, Birmingham. She had her tonsils out on 20 Feb 1989 after awaiting a call from the hopsital since the age of 7 years. In February 1989 it was reported that Joan Brown of Birmingham went on a waiting list for the removal of her tonsils in 1939 and again in 1958 - she is still waiting.

Most ■ Padmabhushan Dr M. C. Modi, a pioneer of mass eye surgery in India since 1943, has performed as many as 833 cataract operations in one day, visited 45 000 villages and 100 000 patients making a total of 564 834 operations to January 1989.

Dr Robert B. McClure (b. 1901) of Toronto, Canada performed a career total of 20 423 major operations in 1924–78.

Joseph Ascough (1935–87) of Nottingham, underwent his 341st operation (for the removal of papillomas from his wind pipe) in September 1987. These wart-like growths which impede breathing first formed when he was 18 months old.

On 2 Mar 1977 Mr Jens Kjaer Jension (b. 1914) of Hoven, Denmark, was discharged from a local hospital after having had 32 131 thorns removed from his body over a period of six years and 248 visits. In 1967 he had tripped and fallen into a pile of spiky berberry cuttings in his garden and was rushed unconscious to hospital. Even today he is still troubled by thorns working their way out through the skin of his legs.

Oldest subject ■ The greatest recorded age at which anyone has undergone an operation is 111 years 105 days in the case of James Henry Brett, Jr (1849–1961) of Houston, Texas, USA. He underwent a

hip operation on 7 Nov 1960. The oldest age established in Britain was the case of Miss Mary Wright (b. 28 Feb 1862) who died during a thigh operation at Boston, Lincs on 22 Apr 1971 aged 109 years 53 days.

Transplants *Heart* ■ The first operation was performed on Louis Washkansky, aged 55, at the Groote Schuur Hospital, Cape Town, South Africa, between 1.00 a.m. and 6 a.m., on 3 Dec 1967, by a team of 30 headed by Professor Christiaan Neethling Barnard (b. Beaufort West, South Africa 8 Oct 1922). The donor was Miss Denise Ann Darvall, aged 25. Washkansky lived for 18 days. Britain's first transplant operation took place at the National Heart Hospital, London on 3 May 1968. The patient, Frederick West, survived for 46 days.

Longest surviving ■ Emmanuel Vitria, of Marseilles, France (b. 24 Jan 1920) who received the heart of Pierre Ponson, 20, at the Salvator Hospital, Marseilles on 27 Nov 1968, and died after 18 years 162 days on 9 May 1987. The surgeon, Edmund Henry, died of a heart attack in 1972 aged 61.

Britain's longest-surviving heart transplant patient was Nigel Olney (b.1944) who underwent surgery at Papworth Hospital, Cambridge, Cambs on 29 Jan 1980. In June 1988 he was involved in a car accident, shortly after he received a second transplant but died on 21 Dec 1988. The current holder is Derrick H Morris (b. 24 Mar 1930) who underwent surgery at Harefield Hospital, Middx on 23 Feb 1980.

The first transplantee to give birth was Betsy Sneith, 23, with a baby girl Sierra (3·45 kg *7 lb 10 oz*) at Stanford University, California, USA on 17 Sep 1984. She had received a donor heart in February 1980. Paul Holt of Vancouver, British Columbia, Canada underwent a heart transplant at Loma Linda Hospital,in California, USA on 16 Oct 1987 aged 2 hrs 34 min. He was born 6 weeks premature at 2·9 kg *6 lb 6 oz*. The youngest transplant patient in the UK was Hollie Roffey who received a new heart when aged only 10 days at the National Heart Hospital in London on 29 July 1984, but she survived only 10 days.

Heart—lung—liver ■ The first triple transplant took place on 17 Dec 1986 at Papworth Hospital, Cambridge, Cambs when Mrs Davina Thompson (b. 28 Feb 1951) of Rawmarsh, South Yorks, underwent surgery for 7 hours by a team of 15 headed by chest surgeon Mr John Wallwork and Professor Sir Roy Calne. Mark Dolby (b. 19 Feb 1961) is the second person to receive a triple transplant operation, heart–lung–liver. The operation was the first performed at Harefield Hospital, Middx on 21 Aug 1987.

Kidney ■ R. H. Lawler (b. 1895) (USA) performed the first transplant of the kidney in the human in 1950. The longest survival, being between identical twins, has been 20 years. Mr. William Nicholas of Norfolk survived for 22 years, he died on 19 November 1988.

Five-organ transplant ■ Tabatha Foster (1984–1988) of Madisonville, Kentucky, USA, when aged 3 years 143 days, received a transplanted liver, pancreas, small intestine, portions of stomach and large intestine in a 15-hour operation at the Children's Hospital, Pittsburgh, USA on 31 Oct 1987. She had never eaten solid food before the operation.

Artificial heart ■ On 1–2 Dec 1982 at the Utah Medical Center, Salt Lake City, USA Dr Barney B. Clark, 61, of Des Moines, Washington, USA was the first recipient of an artificial heart. The surgeon was Dr William C. DeVries. The heart was a Jarvik 7 designed by Dr Robert K. Jarvik (b Midland, Michigan 11 May 1946). Dr Clark died on 23 Mar 1983, 112 days later. William J. Schroeder survived 620 days in Louisville, Kentucky from 25 Nov 1984 to 7 Aug 1986. Britain's first artificial heart patient was Raymond Cook of Hucknall, Notts who temporarily received a Jarvik 7 on 2 Nov 1986 at Papworth Hospital, Cambridge, Cambs.

Earliest appendicectomy ■ The earliest recorded successful appendix operation was performed in 1736 by Claudius Amyand (1680–1740). He

was Serjeant Surgeon to King George II (reigned 1727–60).

Earliest anaesthesia ■ The earliest recorded operation under general anaesthesia was for the removal of a cyst from the neck of James Venable by Dr Crawford Williamson Long (1815–78), using diethyl ether ($C_2H_5)_2O$, in Jefferson, Georgia, on 30 Mar 1842. The earliest amputation under an anaesthetic in Great Britain was by Dr William Scott and Dr James McLauchlan at the Dumfries and Galloway Infirmary, Scotland on 19 Dec 1846.

Most durable cancer patient ■ The most extreme recorded case of survival from diagnosed cancer is that of Mrs Winona Mildred Melick (*née* Douglass) (b. 22 Oct 1876) of Long Beach, California, USA. She had four cancer operations in 1918, 1933, 1966 and 1968 but died from pneumonia on 28 Dec 1981, 67 days after her 105th birthday.

Tracheostomy ■ Mrs Winifred Campbell (b. 6 Jul 1902) of Wanstead, London has spoken through a silver tube in her throat for 82 years.

Munchausen's syndrome ■ The most extreme recorded case of this rare and incurable condition (a continual desire to have medical treatment) was William McIlroy (b. 1906), who cost the National Health Service an estimated £2·5 million during his 50-year career as a hospital patient. During that time he had 400 major and minor operations, and stayed at 100 different hospitals using 22 aliases. The longest period he was ever out of hospital was for six months. In 1979 the Irishman hung up his bedpan for the last time, saying he was sick of hospitals, and retired to an old people's home, where he died in 1983.

Largest tumour ■ The largest tumour ever recorded was Spohn's case of an ovarian cyst weighing 148·7 kg *23 st 6 lb* taken from a woman in Texas, USA in 1905. She made a full recovery.

Surgical instruments ■ The largest are robot retractors used in abdominal surgery, introduced by Abbey Surgical Instruments of Chingford, Essex in 1968 and weighing 5 kg *11 lb*. Some bronchoscopic forceps measure 60 cm *23 ¹⁄₂ in* in length. The smallest are Elliot's eye trephine, which has a blade 0·2 cm *0·078 in* in diameter and 'straight' stapes picks with a needle-type tip or blade of 0·3 mm *0·013 in* long.

PSYCHIC FORCES

Extra-sensory perception ■ The two most extreme published examples of ESP in scientific literature have been those of the Reiss case of a 26-year-old female at Hunter College, New York State, USA in 1936 and of Pavel Stepánek (Czechoslovakia) in 1967–68. Any importance which might be attached to their cases was diminished by subsequent developments. The Reiss subject refused to undergo any further tests under stricter conditions. When Stepánek was retested at Edinburgh University with plastic cards he 'failed to display any clairvoyant ability'. Much smaller departures from the laws of probability have however been displayed in less extreme cases carried out under strict conditions.

Most durable ghost ■ Ghosts are not immortal and would seem to deteriorate after 400 years. The most outstanding exception to their normal 'half-life' recorded in the British Isles would seem to be the late Bronze Age (*c.* 700 BC) horseman who frequents the B3081 near Sixpenny Handley, Dorset.

Pluckley in Kent is generally thought to be the most haunted village in England boasting at least 12 spiritous inhabitants. These include both a White and a Red Lady at St Nicholas Church, a Highwayman at Fright Corner, a Screaming Man at the brickworks and a spectral Coach and Horses at various locations. Both pubs in the village seem to cater for more than one kind of spirit and dancing round the Devil's Bush three times is supposed to guarantee the personal appearance of its namesake – provided the dancer is naked of course.

CHAPTER 2

Largest carnivore
Weights in excess of 907 kg 2000lb have been reported for the polar bear (Ursus maritimus), but the average adult male weighs 386 - 408 kg 850 - 900lb and measures 2·4m 7¾ft nose-to-tail. In 1960 a polar bear allegedly weighing 1002kg 2210lb before skinning was shot at the polar entrance to Kotzebue Sound, north-west Alaska, by Arthur Dubs of Medford, Oregon, USA. In April 1962 the 3.38m 11ft 1¼in tall mounted specimen was put on display at the Seattle World Fair, but further details are lacking.
(Photo: Bruce Coleman)

Animal Kingdom General Records

Noisiest ■ The noisiest land animals in the world are the Howling monkeys (*Alouatta*) of Central and South America. The males have an enlarged bony structure at the top of the windpipe which enables the sound to reverberate, and their fearsome screams have been described as a cross between the bark of a dog and the bray of an ass increased 1000-fold. Once they are in full voice they can clearly be heard for distances up to 16 km *10 miles* away.

Most fertile ■ It has been calculated that a single Cabbage aphid (*Brevicoryne brassica*) can give rise in a year to a mass of descendants weighing 822 000 000 tonnes, more than three times the total weight of the world's human population. Fortunately the mortality rate is tremendous!

Strongest ■ In proportion to their size the strongest animals are the larger beetles of the Scarabaeidae, which are found mainly in the tropics. In tests carried out on a Rhinoceros beetle (*Dynastinae*) it was found that it could support 850 times its own weight on its back (cf. 25 per cent of its bodyweight for an adult elephant). A Dor beetle (*Geotrupes stercorosus*) shifted a load weighing 80 g *2·82 oz* or 400 times its own bodyweight from one point to another and also managed to lift 100 g *3½ oz.*

Strongest bite ■ Experiments carried out with a Snodgrass gnathodynamometer (shark bite-meter) at the Lerner Marine Laboratory in Bimini, Bahamas, revealed that a 2 m *6 ft 6¾ in* long Dusky shark (*Carcharhinus obscurus*) could exert a force of 60 kg *132 lb* between its jaws. This is equivalent to a pressure of 3 tonnes per cm² or *19·6 tons per in²* at the tips of the teeth. The crushing power of a 6 m *19 ft 8 in* long Great white shark (*Carcharodon carcharias*) has not yet been established.

Suspended animation ■ In 1846 two specimens of the desert snail *Eremina desertorum* were presented to the British Museum (Natural History) as dead exhibits. They were glued to a small tablet and placed on display. Four years later, in March 1850, the Museum staff, suspecting that one of the snails was still alive, removed it from the tablet and placed it in tepid water. The snail moved and later began to feed. This hardy little creature lived for a further two years before it fell into a torpor and died.

Regeneration ■ The sponge (*Porifera*) has the most remarkable powers of regeneration of lost parts of any animal, and it can regrow its entire body from a tiny fragment of itself. If a sponge is squeezed through a fine-meshed silk gauze each piece of separated tissue will live as an individual.

Most dangerous ■ The world's most dangerous animals (excluding Man) are the malarial mosquitoes of the genus *Plasmodium* which, if we exclude wars and accidents, have probably been responsible directly or indirectly for 50 per cent of all human deaths since the Stone Age. Even today, despite major campaigns to eradicate it, at least 200 million people are affected by the disease each year, and more than one million babies and children die annually from malaria in Africa alone.

Largest colonies ■ The Black-tailed prairie dog (*Cynomys ludovicianus*) of the western USA and northern Mexico builds the largest colonies. One single 'town' discovered in 1901 was estimated to cover an area measuring 384 × 160 km *240 × 100 miles.* It contained about 400 000 000 individuals.

Greatest concentration ■ The greatest concentration of animals ever recorded was an unbelievably huge swarm of Rocky Mountain locusts (*Melanoplus spretus*) which passed over Nebraska, USA on 15-25 Aug 1875. According to one local scientist, who watched their movements for five days, these locusts covered an area of 514 374 km² *198 600 miles²* as they flew over the American State. If he over-estimated the size of the swarm by 50 per cent (most locusts do not fly at night) it still covered an area of 257 187 km² *99 300 miles²*, which is approximately the area of Colorado or Oregon. It has been calculated that this swarm of Rocky Mountain locusts contained at least 12 500 000 000 000 insects weighing 25 000 000 tonnes. For reasons unexplained this pest mysteriously disappeared in 1902 and has not been seen since.

Most prodigious eater ■ The larva of the Polyphemus moth (*Antheraea polyphemus*) of North America consumes an amount equal to 86 000 times its own birth weight in the first 48 hours of its life. In human terms, this would be equivalent to a 3·17 kg *7 lb* baby taking in 273 tonnes *269 tons* of nourishment!

Champion slimmer ■ During the seven-month lactation period a 120 tonne female Blue whale (*Balaenoptera musculus*) can lose up to 25 per cent of her bodyweight nursing her calf.

Most valuable ■ The most valuable animals in cash terms are thoroughbred racehorses. The most paid for a yearling is $13·1 million on 23 Jul 1985 at Keeneland, Kentucky, USA by Robert Sangster and partners for *Seattle Dancer* (see Chapter 11, Horseracing).

Mammals *Mammalia*

Largest and heaviest ■ The longest and heaviest mammal in the world, and the largest animal ever recorded, is the Blue or Sulphur-bottom whale (*Balaenoptera musculus*), also called Sibbald's rorqual. The longest specimen ever recorded was a female landed at the Compania Argentina de Pesca, Grytviken, South Georgia, in 1909 which measured 33·58 m *110 ft 2½ in* in length. Another female measuring 27·6 m *90 ft 6 in* caught in the Southern Ocean by the Soviet Slava whaling fleet on 20 Mar 1947 weighed 190 tonnes *187 tons*. Its tongue and heart weighed 4·29 tonnes *4·22 tons* and 698·5 kg *1540 lb* respectively.

British Isles ■ A 26·8 m *88 ft* Blue whale was killed near the Bunaveneader station in Harris in the Western Isles, Scotland in 1904. In December 1851 the carcass of a Blue whale measuring 28·87 m *94 ft 9 in* in length (girth 13·7 m *42 ft*) was brought into Bantry harbour, Co. Cork, after it had been found floating dead in the sea. A specimen stranded on the west coast of Lewis, Western Isles, *c.* 1870 was credited with a length of 32 m *105 ft* but the carcass was cut up by the local people before this measurement could be verified. The length was probably exaggerated or taken along the curve of the body instead of in a straight line from the tip of the snout to the notch in the flukes.

Blue whales inhabit the colder seas and migrate to warmer waters in the winter for breeding. Observations made in the Antarctic in 1947–8 showed that a Blue whale can maintain a speed of 20 knots (*37 km/h*) for ten minutes when frightened. It has been calculated that a 27 m *90 ft* Blue whale travelling at 20 knots *37 km/h* would develop 527 cv *520 hp*. Newborn calves measure between 6·5–8·6 m *21 ft 3½ in–28 ft 6 in* in length and weigh up to 3000 kg *2·95 tons*.

The barely visible ovum of the Blue whale calf weighing a fraction of a milligram grows to a weight of *c.* 26 tonnes in 22 ¾ months made up of 10 ¾ months gestation and the first 12 months of life. This is an equivalent to an increase of 30 000 million-fold.

The low frequency pulses made by Blue whales when communicating with each other have been measured up to 188 decibels, making them the loudest sounds emitted by any living source. They have been detected 850 km *530 miles* away.

It has been estimated that there are only about 10–12 000 Blue whales roaming the world's oceans today as a result of over-hunting. This compares with a peak estimate of *c.* 220 000 at the turn of the century. The species has been protected *de jure* since 1967, although non-member countries of the International Whaling Commission, e.g. Panama, Taiwan, South Korea and the Philippines, are not bound by this agreement. An indefinite world-wide ban on commercial whaling came into force at the start of the 1985/86 season, but Japan, Norway and Iceland are still slaughtering Minke, Fin and Sei whales (*Balaenoptera acutorostrata*, *B. physalus* and *B. borealis*) under the guise of 'research whaling'. In 1988 Iceland caught 68 Fin whales and ten Sei whales and 300 Minke whales were captured by Japanese whalers in the southern ocean. The ban on commercial whaling will be re-assessed in 1990.

Deepest dive ■ On 14 Oct 1955 a 14·32 m *47 ft* bull Sperm whale (*Physeter catodon* = *macrocephalus*) was found at a depth of 620 fathoms (*1134 m*), its jaw entangled with a submarine cable running between Santa Elena, Ecuador and Chorillos, Peru. At this depth the whale withstood a pressure of 11 583 kPa *1680 lb/in²* of body surface. In 1970 American scientists, by triangulating the location clicks of Sperm whales, calculated that the *maximum* depth reached by this species was 2500 m *8202 ft*. However on 25 Aug 1969 another bull Sperm whale was killed 160 km *100 miles* south of Durban after it had surfaced from a dive lasting 1 hr 52 min, and inside its stomach were found two small sharks which had been swallowed about an hour earlier. These were later identified as *Scymnodon* sp., a type of dogfish found only on the sea floor. At this point from land the depth of water is in excess of 1646 fathoms (*3193 m*) for a radius of 48–64 km *30–40 miles*, which suggests that the Sperm whale sometimes descends to a depth of over 1640 fathoms *3000 m* when seeking

Largest colonies ● The Black-tailed prairie dog (*Cynomys ludovicianus*) of the western USA and northern Mexico builds the largest colonies. One single 'town' discovered in 1901 was estimated to cover an area measuring 384 × 160 km *240 × 100 miles.* It contained about 400 000 000 individuals. (Photo: Jacana)

food and is limited by pressure of time rather than by pressure of pressure.

Largest on land ■ The largest living land animal is the African bush elephant (*Loxodonta africana*). The average adult bull stands 3·2 m *10 ft 6 in* at the shoulder and weighs 5·7 tonnes *5·6 tons*. The largest specimen ever recorded was a bull shot 40 km *25 miles* north–northeast of Mucusso, southern Angola on 7 Nov 1974. Lying on its side this elephant measured 4·16 m *13 ft 8 in* in a projected line from the highest point of the shoulder to the base of the forefoot, indicating that its standing height must have been about 3·96 m *13 ft*. Other measurements included an overall length of 10·67 m *35 ft* (tip of extended trunk to tip of extended tail) and a forefoot circumference of 1·8 m *5 ft 11 in*. The weight was computed to be 12·24 tonnes (*12·5 tons*).

The tallest elephant ever recorded was a bull shot by J. M. A. Oosterveen (Holland) south of Sesfontein in Damaraland, Namibia, south-west Africa on 4 Apr 1978 after it had allegedly killed eleven people and caused widespread crop damage. Lying on its side this mountain of flesh measured 4·42 m *14 ft 6 in* in a projected line from the shoulder to the base of the forefoot, indicating that its standing height must have been about 4·21 m *13 ft 10 in*. Other measurements included an overall length of 10·38 m *34 ft 1 in*, and a forefoot circumference of 1·57 m *5 ft 2 in*. The endangered desert elephants of Damaraland (reduced to 84 individuals in August 1981) is the tallest race in the world because it has proportionately longer legs than other elephants, and this particular animal weighed an estimated 8 tonnes.

British Isles ■ A full-grown Red deer (*Cervus elaphus*) stag stands 1·11 m *3 ft 8 in* at the shoulder and weighs 104–113 kg *230–250 lb*. The heaviest ever recorded was a stag killed at Glenfiddich, Banff, Scotland in 1831, which weighed 238 kg *525 lb*. The heaviest park Red deer on record was a stag weighing 215 kg *476 lb* (height at shoulder 1·37 m *4 ft 6 in*) killed at Woburn, Bedfordshire in 1836. The so-called Wild pony (*Equus caballus*) may weigh up to 320 kg *700 lb* but there are no truly feral populations living today.

Largest marine ■ The largest toothed mammal ever recorded is the Sperm whale (*Physeter macrocephalus*), also called the Cachalot. In the summer of 1950 a record-sized bull measuring 20·7 m *67 ft 11 in* was captured off the Kurile Islands, north-west Pacific, by a USSR whaling fleet. Bulls of much larger size were reported in the early days of whaling. The 5 m *16 ft 4³⁄₄ in* long lower jaw of a Sperm whale exhibited in the British Museum (Natural History) belonged to a bull measuring nearly 25·6 m *84 ft*, and similar lengths have been reported for other outsized individuals killed.

British Isles ■ Thirteen cachalots have been stranded on British coasts since 1913. The largest, a bull measuring 19 m *61 ft 5 in*, was washed ashore at Birchington, Kent on 18 Oct 1914. Another huge bull was stranded at Derryloughan, Co. Galway, Ireland on 2 Jan 1952 and reportedly measured 19·8 m *65 ft*, but the carcass was so badly decomposed that there must have been some length extension.

Tallest land ■ The Giraffe (*Giraffa camelopardalis*), which is now found only in the dry savannah and semi-desert areas of Africa south of the Sahara, is the tallest living animal. The tallest ever recorded was a Masai bull (*G. camelopardalis tippelskirchi*) named 'George', received at Chester Zoo, on 8 Jan 1959 from Kenya. His 'horns' *almost* grazed the roof of the 6·09 m *20 ft* high Giraffe House when he was nine years old. George died on 22 Jul 1969. Less credible heights of up to 7 m *23 ft* (between pegs) have been claimed for bulls shot in the field.

Smallest land mammal ■ The endangered Kitti's hog-nosed bat (*Craseonycteristhonglongyai*), also called the Bumblebee bat, is confined to about 21 limestone caves (population more than 2000) on the Kwae Noi River, Kanchanaburi, Thailand, and mature specimens (both sexes) have a wing span of c. 160 mm *6·29 in* and weigh 1·75–2 g *0·062–0·071 oz*.

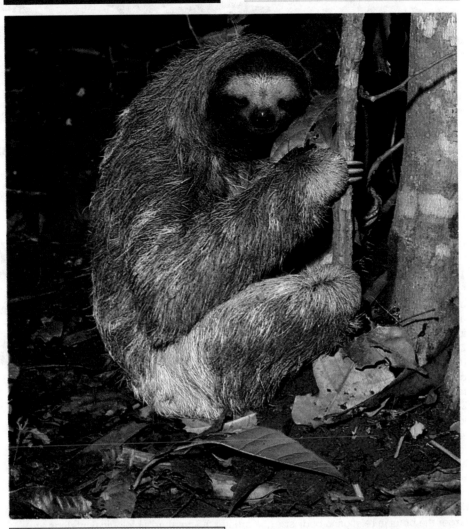

Insectivore ■ Mature specimens of Savi's white-toothed pygmy shrew (*Suncus etruscus*), also called the Etruscan shrew, which is found along the coast of the Mediterranean and southwards to Cape Province, South Africa have a head and body length of 36–52 mm *1·32–2·04 in*, a tail length of 24–29 mm *0·94–1·14 in* and weigh between 1·5 and 2·5 g *0·052 and 0·09 oz*.

Great Britain ■ Mature specimens of the European pygmy shrew (*Sorex minutus*) have a head and body length of 43–64 mm *1·69–2·5 in*, a tail length of 31–46 mm *1·22–1·81 in* and weigh between 2·4 and 6·1 g *0·084–0·213 oz*.

Smallest marine ■ In terms of weight, the smallest totally marine mammal is probably Commerson's dolphin (*Cephalorhynchus commersonii*), also known as Le Jacobite, which is found in the waters off the southern tip of South America. In one series of six adult specimens the weights ranged from 23 kg *50·7 lb* to 35 kg *77·1 lb*. The Sea otter (*Enhydra lutris*) of the north Pacific is of comparable size (25–38·5 kg *55–81·4 lb*), but this species sometimes comes ashore during storms.

Rarest land ■ A number of mammals are known only from a single or type specimen. One of these is the Small-toothed fruit bat (*Neopteryx frosti*), collected from Tamalanti, West Celebes, in 1938. The Thylacine or Tasmanian tiger (*Thylacinus cynocephalus*), feared extinct since the last captive specimen died in Beaumaris Zoo, Hobart, Tasmania on 7

Sep 1936, was positively identified in July 1982 when a wildlife ranger saw one of these predatory marsupials in the spotlight of his parked car. Since then, however, there have been no more positive sightings. The Red wolf (*Canis rufus*) of south-east USA became extinct in the wild in the early 1970s, but there are now over 50 individuals (not all of them genetically pure) held by the US Fish and Wildlife Service. In June 1988 it was announced that two pairs released in North Carolina by the captive breeding programme had produced cubs. The Black-footed ferret (*Mustela nigripes*) of the northern USA is also extinct in the wild, but in 1988 the captive population (25), housed in a special centre in Cheyenne, Wyoming, USA more than doubled when the second breeding season produced 38 pups. The ferret will be reintroduced in Wyoming in the early 1990s.

Rarest marine ■ Longman's beaked whale (*Indopacetus pacificus*) is known only from two skulls. The type specimen was discovered on a beach near MacKay, Queensland, Australia in 1922, and the second near Muqdisho, Somalia, east Africa in 1955. The Vaquita or Gulf porpoise (*Phocoena sinus*) has not been sighted since 1980, and may now be extinct. Many hundreds of thousands have been accidentally killed by gillnet fishing in the last 45 years.

Fastest land ■ Over a short distance (i.e. up to 549 m *600 yd*) the Cheetah or Hunting leopard (*Acinonyx jubatus*) of the open plains of east Africa, Iran, Turkmenia and Afghanistan has a probable maximum speed of 96–101 km/h *60–63 mph* on suitably level ground. Speeds of 114, 135 and even 145 km/h, *71, 84 and 90 mph* have been claimed for this animal, but these figures must be considered exaggerated. Tests in London in 1937 showed that on an oval greyhound track over 316 m *345 yd* a female Cheetah's average speed over three runs was 69·8 km/h *43·4 mph* (cf. 72·27 km/h *44·91 mph* for the fastest racehorse, see Chapter 11), but this specimen

1.COMMON DOLPHIN (*Delphinus delphis*)

1.COMMON DOLPHIN
(*Delphinus delphis*) - this
dolphin can hear frequencies
as high as 280kHz (cf. 20 kHz
for the adult human limit).
2.COMMERSON'S DOLPHIN
(*Cephalorhynchus
commersonii*) - probably the smallest totally marine
mammal in terms of weight. In one series of six adult specimens the weights ranged from
23 kg *50·7 lb* to 35 kg *77·1 lb*. **3.FRANCISCANA** (*Pontoporia blainvillei*) - this dolphin has the
longest beak in proportion to its body length of any small cetacean. This species is found in the
shallow coastal waters of South America from Valdés Peninsula and La Plata delta, Argentina
to São Paulo, Brazil. **4.VAQUITA** (*Phocoena sinus*) - one of the rarest marine mammals. It
has not been sighted since 1980, and may now be extinct. Hundreds of thousands have
been accidentally caught in gill nets, in the last 45 years. **5.BOTTLENOSE DOLPHIN** (*Tursiops
truncatus*) - this species is probably the most familiar to visitors of oceanariums and
dolphinariums and is arguably the most intelligent cetacean if the theory of encephaliation (the
larger the brain in relation to body size, the greater the creature's biological intelligence)
is considered. **6.KILLER WHALE** (*Orcinus orca*) - the fastest marine mammal. On 12 Oct
1958 a bull Killer whale measuring an estimated 6·10-7·62 m *20-25 ft* in length was
timed at 30 knots (*55·5 km/h*) in the east Pacific. The Killer whale is also the
most widely distributed of all cetaceans and is the largest of the
dolphins, males reaching a length of 9·5 m *31·16 ft*. **7.DALL'S
PORPOISE** (*Phocoenoides dalli*) - speeds of up to
30 knots (*55.5 km/h*) in short bursts have also
been reported for Dall's porpoise in
the North Pacific. It is also
claimed that this species
never sleeps at all.

6.KILLER WHALE (*Orcinus orca*)

7.DALL'S PORPOISE (*Phocoenoides dalli*)

DOLPHINS & PORPOISES

3.FRANCISCANA (*Pontoporia blainvillei*)

4.VAQUITA (*Phocoena sinus*)

2.COMMERSON'S DOLPHIN
(*Cephalorhynchus commersonii*)

5.BOTTLENOSE DOLPHIN (*Tursiops truncatus*)

(Artwork: Matthew Hillier/Guinness Publishing)

was not running flat out and had great difficulty negotiating the bends. The fastest land animal over a sustained distance (i.e. 914 m *1000 yd* or more) is the Pronghorn antelope (*Antilocapra americana*) of the western United States. Specimens have been observed to travel at 56 km/h *35 mph* for 6 km *4 miles*, at 67 km/h *42 mph* for 1·6 km *1 mile* and 88·5 km/h *55 mph* for 0·8 km *half a mile*.

British ■ Over a sustained distance the Roe deer (*Capreolus capreolus*), can cruise at 40–48 km/h *25–30 mph* for more than 32 km *20 miles*, with occasional bursts of up to 64 km/h *40 mph*. On 19 Oct 1970 a frightened runaway Red deer registered a speed of 67·5 km/h *42 mph* on a police radar trap as it charged through a street in Stalybridge, Manchester.

Fastest marine ■ On 12 Oct 1958 a bull Killer whale (*Orcinus orca*) measuring an estimated 6·1–7·62 m *20–25 ft* in length was timed at 30 knots (*55·5 km/h*) in the east Pacific. Speeds of up to 30 knots in short bursts have also been reported for Dall's porpoise (*Phocoenoides dalli*).

Slowest ■ The Ai or Three-toed sloth (*Bradypus tridactylus*) of tropical America has an average ground speed of 1·83–2·44 m *6–8 ft* a minute (0·109–0·158 km/h *0·068–0·098 mph*), but in the trees it can 'accelerate' to 4·57 m *15 ft* a minute (0·272 km/h *0·17 mph*) (cf. these figures with the 0·05 km/h *0·03 mph* of the common garden snail and the 0·27 km/h *0·17 mph* of the giant tortoise).

Sleepiest ■ Some armadillos (*Dasypodidae*), opossums (*Didelphidae*) and sloths (*Bradypodidae*) spend up to 80 per cent of their lives sleeping or dozing, while it is claimed that Dall's porpoise (*Phocoenoides dalli*) never sleeps at all.

Longest hibernation ■ The Barrow ground squirrel (*Spermophilus parryi barrowensis*) of Point Barrow, Alaska, USA, hibernates for nine months of the year. During the remaining three months it feeds, breeds and collects food for storage in its burrow.

Oldest ■ No other mammal can match the extreme proven 120 years attained by Man (*Homo sapiens*) (see Chapter 1). It is probable that the closest

---

Longest gestation period ● The longest of all mammalian gestation periods is that of the Asiatic elephant (*Elephas maximus*), with an average of 609 days or just over 20 months and a maximum of 760 days—more than two and a half times that of a human. By 1981 only *c.* 35 000 survived. (Photo: Keystone Collection)

---

approach is made by the Asiatic elephant (*Elephas maximus*). The greatest age that has been verified with absolute certainty is 78 years in the case of a cow named 'Modoc', who died at Santa Clara, California, USA, on 17 Jul 1975. She was imported into the USA from Germany in 1898 at the age of two years. Nepal's royal elephant 'Prem Prasad' was reportedly 81 when he died at Kasra, Chitwan, on 27 Feb 1985, but his actual age was believed to have been 65–70 years. Sri Lanka's famous bull elephant 'Rajah', who had led the annual Perahera procession through Kandi carrying the Sacred Tooth of the Buddha since 1931, died on 16 Jul 1988 allegedly aged 81 years.

Highest living ■ The Yak (*Bos grunniens*), of Tibet and the Szechwanese Alps, China, occasionally climbs to an altitude of 6100 m *20 000 ft* when foraging.

Largest herds ■ The largest herds on record were those of the Springbok (*Antidorcas marsupialis*) during migration across the plains of the western parts of southern Africa in the 19th century. In 1849 John (later Sir John) Fraser observed a *trekbokken* that took three days to pass through the settlement of Beaufort West, Cape Province. Another herd seen moving near Nels Poortje, Cape Province in 1888 was estimated to contain 100 million head, although 10 million is probably a more realistic figure. A herd estimated to be 24 km *15 miles* wide and more than 160 km *100 miles* long was reported from Karree Kloof, Orange River, South Africa in July 1896.

Longest mammalian gestation period ■ The Asiatic elephant (*Elephas maximus*), has an average gestation period of 609 days or just over 20 months and a maximum of 760 days—more than two and a half times that of a human. By 1981 only *c.* 35 000 survived.

Shortest mammalian gestation period ■ The gestation periods of the American opossum (*Didelphis marsupialis*), also called the Virginian opossum, the rare Water opossum or Yapok (*Chironectes minimus*) of central and northern South America, and the Eastern native cat (*Dasyurus viverrinus*) of Australia are all normally 12–13 days but they can be as short as eight days.

Largest litter ■ The greatest number of young born to a *wild* mammal at a single birth is 31 (30 of which survived) in the case of the Tailless tenrec (*Tenrec ecaudatus*) found in Madagascar and the Comoro Islands. The normal litter size is 12–15, although females can suckle up to 24.

Youngest breeder ■ The Streaked tenrec (*Hemicentetes semispinosus*) of Madagascar is weaned after only five days, and females can breed 3–4 weeks after birth.

CARNIVORES

Largest living terrestrial carnivore ■ The average adult male Kodiak bear (*Ursus arctos middendorffi*), which is found on Kodiak Island and the adjacent Afognak and Shuyak islands in the Gulf of Alaska, USA, has a nose-to-tail length of 2·4 m *8 ft* (tail about 10 cm *4 in*). It stands 1·32 m *52 in* at the shoulder and weighs between 476 kg and 533 kg *1050 lb–1175 lb*. In 1894 a weight of 751 kg *1656 lb* was recorded for a male shot at English Bay, Kodiak Island, whose *stretched* skin measured 4·11 m *13 ft 6 in* from the tip of the nose to the root of the tail. This weight was exceeded by a 'cage-fat male' in the Cheyenne Mountain Zoological Park, Colorado Springs, Colorado, USA which scaled 757 kg *1670 lb* at the time of its death on 22 Sep 1955. In 1981 an unconfirmed weight of over 907 kg *2000 lb* was reported for a Peninsula giant bear (*Ursus a. gyas*) from Alaska on exhibition at the Space Farms Zoological Park at Beemerville, New Jersey, USA. Weights in excess of 907 kg *2000 lb* have been reported for the Polar bear (*Ursus maritimus*), but the average adult male weighs 386–408 kg *850–900 lb* and measures 2·4 m *7¾ ft* nose-to-tail. In 1960 a Polar bear allegedly weighing 1002 kg *2210 lb* before skinning was shot at the polar entrance to Kotzebue Sound, north-west Alaska, by Arthur Dubs of Medford, Oregon, USA. In April 1962 the 3·38 m *11 ft 1¼ in* tall mounted specimen was put on display at the Seattle World Fair, but further details are lacking.

Britain ■ The largest land carnivore found in Britain is the Badger (*Meles meles*). The average adult boar (sows are slightly smaller) measures 90 cm *3 ft* in length – including a 10 cm *4 in* tail – and weighs 12·3 kg *27 lb* in the early spring and 14·5 kg *32 lb* at the end of the summer when it is in 'grease'. In December 1952 a boar weighing 27·2 kg *60 lb* was killed near Rotherham, South Yorks.

Smallest ■ The smallest living member of the order Carnivora is the Least weasel (*Mustela rixosa*), also called the Dwarf weasel, which is circumpolar in distribution. Four races are recognised, the smallest of which is *M. r. pygmaea* of Siberia. Mature specimens have an overall length of 177–207 mm *6·96–8·14 in* and weigh between 35 and 70 g *1¼–2½ oz*.

Largest feline ■ The largest member of the cat family (Felidae) is the protected long-furred Siberian tiger (*Panthera tigris altaica*), also called the Amur or Manchurian tiger. Adult males average 3·15 m *10 ft 4 in* in length (nose to tip of extended tail), stand 99–107 cm *39–42 in* at the shoulder and weigh about 265 kg *585 lb*. In 1950 a male weighing 384 kg *846·5 lb* was shot in the Sikhote Alin Mts, Maritime Territory, USSR. In November 1967 David Hasinger of Philadelphia, Pennsylvania, USA shot an outsized Indian tiger (*Panthera tigris tigris*) in northern Uttar Pradesh which measured 3·22 m *10 ft 7 in* between pegs (3·37 m *11 ft 1 in* over the curves) and weighed 389 kg *857 lb* (cf. 2·82 m *9 ft 3 in* and 190 kg *420 lb* for an average adult male). It is now on display in the US Museum of Natural History, Smithsonian Institution, Washington, DC, USA.

The largest tiger ever held in captivity, and the heaviest 'big cat' on record, is a nine-year-old Siberian male named 'Jaipur', owned by animal trainer Joan Byron-Marasek of Clarksburg, New

Largest primate ● The Mountain gorilla (*Gorilla g. beringei*) of the volcanic mountain ranges of western Rwanda, south-western Uganda and eastern Zaïre (see above) is not as big as the Eastern lowland gorilla (*Gorilla g. graueri*), i.e. 172·5 cm *5 ft 8 in* and 155 kg *343 lb*, although most of the exceptionally large gorillas taken in the field have been of this race. The greatest height (top of crest to heel) recorded for a gorilla in the wild is 1·88 m *6 ft 2 in* for a bull of the mountain race shot by T. Alexander Barns in the Eastern Congo (Zaïre) *c.* 1920. (Photo: Paysan Archive)

Jersey, USA. This specimen measures 3·32 m *10 ft 11 in* in total length and tipped the scales at 423 kg *932 lb* in October 1986.

The average adult African lion (*Panthera leo*) measures 2·7 m *9 ft* overall, stands 91–97 cm *36–38 in* at the shoulder and weighs 181–185 kg *400–410 lb*. The heaviest wild specimen on record was one weighing 313 kg *690 lb* shot by Lennox Anderson just outside Hectorspruit in the eastern Transvaal, South Africa in 1936. In July 1970 a weight of 375 kg *826 lb* was reported for a black-maned lion named 'Simba' (b. Dublin Zoo, 1959) at Colchester Zoo, Essex. He died on 16 Jan 1973 at the now defunct Knaresborough Zoo, North Yorks, where his stuffed body had been on display. An adult male Litigon (an Indian lion/Tigon cross) named 'Cubanacan' at Alipore Zoological Gardens, Calcutta, India, is also believed to weigh at least 363 kg *800 lb*. This animal stands 1·32 m *52 in* at the shoulder (cf. 1·11 m *44 in* for the lion 'Simba') and measures a record 3·5 m *11 ft 6 in* in total length.

Smallest feline ■ The smallest member of the cat family is the Rusty-spotted cat (*Felis rubiginosa*) of southern India and Sri Lanka. The average adult male has an overall length of 64–71 cm *25–28 in* (tail 23–25 cm *9–10 in*) and weighs about 1·35 kg *3 lb*.

PRIMATES

Largest living ■ The average adult male Eastern lowland gorilla (*Gorilla g. graueri*) of the lowland

forests of eastern Zaïre and south-western Uganda, stands 175 cm *5 ft 9 in* tall and weighs 165 kg *360 lb*. The Mountain gorilla (*Gorilla g. beringei*) of the volcanic mountain ranges of western Rwanda, south-western Uganda and eastern Zaïre is also of comparable size i.e. 172·5 cm *5 ft 8 in* and 155 kg *343 lb*, and most of the exceptionally large gorillas taken in the field have been of this race. The greatest height (top of crest to heel) recorded for a gorilla in the wild is 1·88 m *6 ft 2 in* for a bull of the mountain race shot by T. Alexander Barns in the Eastern Congo (Zaïre) *c.* 1920. The tallest gorilla ever kept in captivity is reportedly an Eastern lowland male named 'Colossus' (b. 1966) who is currently on display at a zoo in Gulf Breeze, Florida, USA. He allegedly stands 1·88 m *6 ft 2 in* tall and weighs 260·8 kg *575 lb* but these figures have not yet been confirmed. A Western lowland gorilla called 'Baltimore Jack', who was received at Baltimore Zoo, Maryland, USA in 1956 and later sold to Phoenix Zoo, Arizona, USA, had exceptionally long legs for a gorilla. He reportedly stood 1·91 m *6 ft 3 in* tall, but his actual height was somewhere between 1·7 m *5 ft 7 in* and 1·75 m *5 ft 9 in* (weight 126 kg *300 lb*). He died in 1972.

The heaviest gorilla ever kept in captivity was a male of the mountain race named 'N'gagi', who died in San Diego Zoo, California, USA on 12 Jan 1944 aged 18 years. He scaled 310 kg *683 lb* at his heaviest in 1943, and weighed 288 kg *636 lb* at the time of his death. He was 1·72 m *5 ft 7¾ in* tall and boasted a record chest measurement of 198 cm *78 in*.

Britain's largest captive gorilla is probably 'Djoum' (b. 1969) of Howletts Zoo, Kent, whose weight is stable at 213 kg *470 lb*. Another male example of the Western lowland gorilla (*Gorilla g. gorilla*) named 'Bukhama' (b. 1960) at Dudley Zoo, West Midlands, was reportedly 227 kg *500 lb* in 1969, but this primate has not been weighed since.

Smallest ■ Adult specimens of the rare Pen-tailed shrew (*Ptilocercus lowii*) of Malaysia, have a total length of 230–330 mm *9–13 in* (head and body 100–140 mm *3·93–5·51 in*, tail 130–190 mm *5·1–7·5 in*) and weigh 35–50 g *1·23–1·76 oz*. The Pygmy marmoset (*Cebuella pygmaea*) of the Upper Amazon

Smallest primate ● The Lesser mouse-lemur (*Microcebus murinus*) of Madagascar is comparable in length to the Pen-tailed shrew (*Ptilocercus lowii*) but it is heavier, adults weighing 45–80 g *1·58–2·82 oz*. (Photo: Jacana)

Basin and the Lesser mouse-lemur (*Microcebus murinus*) of Madagascar are also of comparable length but heavier, adults weighing 50–75 g *1·76–2·64 oz* and 45–80 g *1·58–2·82 oz* respectively.

Rarest ■ The Greater bamboo Broad-nosed gentle lemur (*Hapalemur simus*) of Madagascar reportedly became extinct in the early 1970s, but in 1986 a group consisting of 60–80 individuals was discovered living in a remote rain forest near Ranomafana in the south-eastern part of the island by an expedition from Duke University, Durham, North Carolina, USA. The Golden-rumped tamarin (*Leontopithecus chrysopygus*), which is now restricted to two areas of forest in the state of Sao Paulo, south-east Brazil, is also on the verge of extinction, with only 75–100 surviving in 1986.

Oldest ■ The greatest irrefutable age reported for a non-human primate is *c.* 59 years in the case of a male Orang-utan (*Pongo pygmaeus*) named 'Guas', who died in Philadelphia Zoological Garden, Pennsylvania, USA on 9 Feb 1977. When he was received on 1 May 1931 he was at least 13 years of age. The oldest Chimpanzee (*Pan troglodytes*) on record was a male named 'Jimmy' at Seneca Zoo, Rochester, NY, USA who died on 17 Sep 1985 aged 55 years 6 months. The famous Western lowland gorilla 'Massa' (b. July 1931) died on 30 Dec 1984 aged 53 years 5 months.

The oldest female gorilla on record was 'Carolyn' (b. 1939) of New York Zoological Park (Bronx Zoo), USA who died on 27 Sep 1986 aged 47 years.

Strongest ■ In 1924 'Boma', a 74·8 kg *165 lb* male chimpanzee at Bronx Zoo, New York, USA recorded a right-handed pull (feet braced) of 384 kg *847 lb* on a dynamometer (cf. 95 kg *210 lb* for a man of the same weight). On another occasion an adult female chimpanzee named 'Suzette' (estimated weight 61 kg *135 lb*) at the same zoo registered a right-handed pull of 572 kg *1260 lb* while in a rage. A record from the USA of a 45 kg *100 lb* chimpanzee achieving a two-handed dead lift of 272 kg *600 lb*

with ease suggests that a male gorilla could with training raise 907 kg *2000 lb*.

MONKEYS

Largest ■ The only species of monkey reliably credited with weights of more than 45 kg *100 lb* is the Mandrill (*Mandrillus sphinx*) of equatorial west Africa. The greatest reliable weight recorded is 54 kg *119 lb* for a captive male but an unconfirmed weight of 59 kg *130 lb* has been reported. (Adult females are about half the size of males.)

Smallest ■ The smallest known monkey is the Pygmy marmoset (*Cebuella pygmaea*) of the Upper Amazon Basin. (See Primates, Smallest.)

Rarest ■ (see Primates, Rarest)

Oldest ■ The world's oldest monkey, a male White-throated capuchin (*Cebus capucinus*) called 'Bobo', died on 10 Jul 1988 aged 53 years following complications related to a stroke. He was originally imported from South America and donated to the Mesker Park Zoo in Evansville, Indiana, USA on 1 Jan 1935. When the zoo disbanded its monkey colony he was given to Dr Raymond T. Bartus, founder of the Geriatric Research Programme at Lederle Laboratories, American Cyanamid Co., Pearl River, NY, USA, and lived in the geriatric monkey colony from 31 Oct 1981 until his death.

PINNIPEDS Seals, Sea-lions, Walruses

Largest ■ The largest of the 34 known species of pinniped is the Southern elephant seal (*Mirounga leonina*), which inhabits the sub-Antarctic islands. Adult bulls average 5 m *16½ ft* in length (tip of inflated snout to the extremities of the outstretched tail flippers), 3·7 m *12 ft* in maximum bodily girth and weigh about 2268 kg (*5000 lb*). The largest accurately measured specimen on record was a bull killed in Possession Bay, South Georgia, USA on 28 Feb 1913 which measured 6·5 m *21 ft 4 in* after flensing (original length about 6·85 m *22½ ft*) and probably weighed at least 4 tonnes. There are old records of bulls measuring 7·62–9·14 m *25–30 ft* and even 10·66 m *35 ft* but these figures must be considered exaggerated. Adult cows are much smaller, averaging 3 m *10 ft* in length and weighing about 680 kg *1500 lb*.

Britain ■ The largest pinniped among British fauna is the Grey seal (*Halichoerus grypus*), also called the Atlantic seal. In one sample taken during the breeding season at the Farne Islands, Northumberland the heaviest (a male) weighed 310 kg *683½ lb* (length from nose to tip of flippers 2·45 m *8 ft ½ in*).

Smallest ■ The smallest pinnipeds are the Ringed seal (*Phoca hispida*) of the Arctic and the closely-related Baikal seal (*P. sibirica*) of Lake Baikal and the Caspian seal (*P. caspica*) of the Caspian Sea, USSR. Adult specimens (males) measure up to 1·67 m *5 ft 6 in* in length and reach a maximum weight of 127 kg *280 lb*. Females are about two-thirds this size.

Britain ■ The average adult male Common seal (*Phoca vitulina*) measures 1·5–1·98 m *4 ft 11 in–6 ft 6 in* in length and weighs up to 149·6 kg *330 lb*. Females are four-fifths this size. During the period July–September 1988, 2000 seals died as a result of a virus, and up to 80 per cent of the population (30 000) of the Common seal may have succumbed.

Most abundant ■ In 1978 the total population of the Crabeater seal (*Lobodon carcinophagus*) of Antarctica was believed to be nearly 15 000 000.

Rarest ■ The last reliable sighting of the Caribbean or West Indian monk seal (*Monachus tropicalis*) was on Serranilla Bank off the coast of Mexico's Yucatan peninsula in 1952. In 1974 two seals were seen near Cay Verde and Cay Burro, south-east Bahamas, but a search in 1979 found nothing. It has been suggested that these sightings (and others) may have been Californian sea-lions (*Zalophus californianus*) which had escaped from captivity and

have been recorded in the Gulf of Mexico on several occasions.

Fastest ■ The highest swimming speed recorded for a pinniped is a 40 km/h *25 mph* short spurt by a Californian sea-lion. The fastest-moving pinniped on land is the Crabeater seal which has been timed at speeds up to 19 km/h *11·8 mph*.

Deepest dive ■ In *c.* May 1988 a team of scientists from the University of California at Santa Cruz, USA tested out the diving abilities of the Northern elephant seal (*Mirounga anguistirostris*) off Ano Nuevo Point, California. One female reached a record depth of 1257 m *4135 ft*, and another one remained under water for 48 minutes. Similar experiments carried out by Australian scientists on Southern elephant seals in the Southern Ocean recorded a dive of 1134 m *3720 ft*, and other dives lasting nearly two hours were observed. It was also discovered that the seals regularly swam down to about 820 m *2500 ft* and when they surfaced again apparently had no 'oxygen debt'.

Oldest ■ A female Grey seal shot at Shunni Wick in the Shetland Islands on 23 Apr 1969 was believed to be 'at least 46 years old' based on a count of dentine rings. The captive record is an estimated 41 years for a bull Grey seal 'Jacob' held in Skansen Zoo (1901–42).

RODENTS

Largest ■ The Capybara (*Hydrochoerus hydrochaeris*), also called the Carpincho or Water hog, of tropical South America, has a head and body length of 0·99–1·4 m *3¼–4½ ft* and can weigh up to 113 kg *250 lb* (cage-fat specimen). Britain's largest rodent is the Coypu (*Myocastor coypus*), also known as the Nutria, which was introduced from Argentina by East Anglian fur-breeders in 1929. Three years later, the first escapes were recorded and by 1960 at least 200 000 Coypus were living in East Anglia. About 80 per cent were killed by the severe winter of 1963/4, and since then the Ministry of Agriculture has carried out a campaign of extermination against this species. During the period 1981–7 trappers shot 34 000 coypus and the last known colony at St Neot's on the Great Ouse, Huntingdonshire, was eliminated in 1987. Since then only two isolated coypus have been found plus the corpse of an old male killed on a road at Barton Bendish, Norfolk, on 18 Jul 1988. The trapping campaign will continue until the end of 1989. Adult males measure 76–91 cm *30–36 in* in length (including short tail) and weigh up to 13 kg *28 lb* in the wild state (18 kg *40 lb* in captivity).

Smallest ■ The Northern pygmy mouse (*Baiomys taylori*) of central Mexico and southern Arizona and Texas, measures up to 109 mm *4·3 in* in total length and weighs 7–8 g *0·24–0·28 oz*.

Britain ■ The Old World harvest mouse (*Micromys minutus*), measures up to 135 mm *5·3 in* in total length and weighs 7–10 g *0·24–0·35 oz*.

Rarest ■ The rarest rodents in the world are Garrido's hutia (*Capromys garridoi*) of the Canarreos Archipelago, Cuba and the Little earth hutia (*C. sanfelipensis*) of Juan Garcia Cay, an islet off southern Cuba. The latter species has not been recorded since its discovery in 1970.

Oldest ■ The greatest reliable age reported for a rodent is 27 years 3 months for a Sumatran crested porcupine (*Hystrix brachyura*) which died in National Zoological Park, Washington, DC, USA on 12 Jan 1965.

Fastest breeder ■ The female Meadow vole (*Microtus agrestis*), found in Britain, can reproduce from the age of 25 days and have up to 17 litters of 6–8 young in a year.

INSECTIVORES

Largest ■ The Moon rat (*Echinosorex gymnurus*), also known as Raffles' gymnure, which is found in Burma, Thailand, Malaysia, Sumatra and Borneo has a head and body length of 265–445 mm *10·43–*

17·52 in, a tail measuring 200–210 mm *7·87–8·26 in* and weighs up to 1400 g *3·08 lb*. The European hedgehog (*Erinaceus europaeus*) is much shorter in overall length (196–298 mm *7·71–11·73 in*), but well-fed examples have been known to scale as much as 1900 g *4·19 lb*. Although the much larger anteaters (families Tachyglossidae and Myrmecophagidae) feed on termites and other soft-bodied insects, they are not insectivores but belong to the orders Monotremata and Edentata ('without teeth').

Smallest ■ The smallest insectivore is Savi's white-toothed pygmy shrew (*Suncus etruscus*). (See Mammals, Smallest.)

Oldest ■ The greatest reliable age recorded for an insectivore is 16 + years for a Lesser hedgehog-tenrec (*Echinops telfairi*), which was born in Amsterdam Zoo, Netherlands in 1966 and was later sent to Jersey Zoo. It died on 27 Nov 1982.

BATS

Largest ■ The only flying mammals are bats (order Chiroptera), of which there are about 950 living species. That with the greatest wing span is the Bismarck flying fox (*Pteropus neohibernicus*) of the Bismarck Archipelago and New Guinea. One specimen preserved in the American Museum of Natural History has a wing spread of 165 cm *5 ft 5 in*, but some unmeasured bats probably reach 183 cm *6 ft*.

Britain ■ Mature specimens of the very rare large Mouse-eared bat (*Myotis myotis*) have a wing span of 355–450 mm *13·97–17·71 in* and weigh up to 45 g *1·58 oz* in the case of females.

Smallest ■ The smallest bat in the world is Kitti's hog-nosed bat. See page 23.

British ■ The smallest native British bat is the Pipistrelle (*Pipistrellus pipistrellus*). Mature specimens have a wing span of 190–250 mm *7·48–9·84 in* and weigh between 3 and 8 g *0·1–0·28 oz*.

Rarest ■ At least three species of bat are known only from the type specimen. They are: the Small-toothed fruit bat (*Neopteryx frosti*) from Tamalanti, West Celebes (1938/39); *Paracoelops megalotis* from Vinh, Vietnam (1945); and *Latidens salimalii* from the High Wavy Mountains, southern India (1948).

Britain ■ The rarest bat on the British list (15 species) is now the large Mouse-eared bat of southern England, the population of which is down from 48 to a single male which has lived in Sussex for 15 years forlornly waiting for a mate. (The last known surviving female was killed by the felling of a tree in Sussex in 1977).

In 1987 a vagrant Northern bat (*Eptesicus nilssoni*) was found hibernating in Surrey by two journalists. A native of Europe and Russia, it was the first recorded example of this species in Britain.

Fastest ■ Because of the great practical difficulties few data on bat speeds have been published. The greatest velocity attributed to a bat is 51 km/h *32 mph* in the case of a Mexican free-tailed bat, but this may have been wind-assisted. In one American experiment using an artificial mine tunnel and 17 different kinds of bat, only four of them managed to exceed 20·8 km/h *13 mph* in level flight.

Oldest ■ The greatest age reliably reported for a bat is 32 years for a banded female Little brown bat (*Myotis lucifugus*) in the USA in 1987.

Highest detectable pitch ■ Because of their ultrasonic echolocation bats have the most acute hearing of any terrestrial animal. Vampire bats (*Desmodontidae*) and fruit bats (*Pteropodidae*) can hear frequencies as high as 120–210 kHz (cf. 20 kHz for the adult human limit but 280 kHz for the Common dolphin (*Delphinus delphis*).

Largest colonies ■ The largest concentration of bats found living anywhere in the world today is that of the Mexican free-tailed bat (*Tadarida brasiliensis*) in Bracken Cave, San Antonio, Texas, USA where up to 20 million animals assemble after migration.

Largest insectivore ● Although the European hedgehog (*Erinaceus europaeus*) is much shorter at 196–298 mm *7·71–11·73 in* than the Moon rat (*Echinosorex gymnurus*) in overall length, well-fed examples have been known to scale as much as 1900 g *4·19 lb*. (Photo: Bruce Coleman)

Britain ■ A bat colony in Greywell Canal Tunnel, Hampshire contains about 2000 individuals made up of six different species.

Deepest ■ A Little brown bat has been recorded at a depth of 1160 m *3805 ft* in a zinc mine in New York State, USA. The mine serves as winter quarters for 1000 members of this species, which normally roost at a depth of 200 m *656 ft*.

ANTELOPES

Largest ■ The rare Giant eland (*Tragelaphus derbianus*), of western and central Africa may surpass 907 kg *2000 lb*. The Common eland (*T. oryx*) of eastern and southern Africa has the same shoulder height of up to 1·78 m *5 ft 10 in* but is not quite so massive, although there is one record of a 1·65 m *5 ft 5 in* bull shot in Malawi *c.* 1937 which weighed 943 kg *2078 lb*.

Smallest ■ Mature specimens of the Royal antelope (*Neotragus pygmaeus*) of western Africa measure 25–31 cm *10–12 in* at the shoulder and weigh only 3–3·6 kg *7–8 lb*, which is the size of a large Brown hare (*Lepus europaeus*). Salt's dik-dik (*Madoqua saltina*) of north-eastern Ethiopia and Somalia weighs only 2·2–2·7 kg *5–6 lb* when adult, but this species stands about 35·5 cm *14 in* at the withers.

Rarest ■ Until recently, the Arabian oryx (*Oryx leucoryx*) had not been reported in the wild since 1972 when three were killed and four others captured on the Jiddat-al-Harasis plateau, South Oman. Between March 1980 and August 1983 a total of 17 antelopes from the World Herd at San Diego Zoo, California, USA were released into the open desert in South Oman under the protection of a nomadic tribe. Since then there have been at least 43 live births and at the beginning of 1989, the wild herd totalled 60. The Arabian oryx has also been successfully reintroduced into the Shaumari Reserve in Jordan, where there are now 90 of these animals.

Oldest ■ The greatest reliable age recorded for an antelope is 25 years 4 months for an Addax (*Addax nasomaculatus*) which died in Brookfield Zoo, Chicago, Illinois, USA on 15 Oct 1960.

DEER

Largest ■ The largest deer is the Alaskan moose (*Alces alces gigas*). Adult bulls average 1·83 m *6 ft* at the shoulder and weigh *c.* 500 kg *1100 lb*. A bull standing 2·34 m *7 ft 8 in* between pegs and weighing an estimated 816 kg *1800 lb* was shot on the Yukon River in the Yukon Territory, Canada in September 1897. Unconfirmed measurements of up to 2·59 m *8 ft 6 in* at the shoulder and estimated weights of up to 1180 kg *2600 lb* have been claimed. The record antler spread or 'rack' is 199 cm *78¹/₂ in* (skull and antlers 41 kg *91 lb*). They were taken from a moose killed near the headwaters of the Stewart River in the Yukon, Canada in October 1897 and are now on display in the Field Museum, Chicago, Illinois, USA.

Britain ■ The largest deer is the Red deer (See page 23).

Smallest ■ The smallest true deer (family Cervidae) is the Northern pudu (*Pudu mephistopheles*) of Ecuador and Colombia. Mature specimens measure 33–35 cm *13–14 in* at the shoulder and weigh 7·2–8·1 kg *16–18 lb*. The smallest ruminant is the Lesser Malay chevrotain (*Tragulus javanicus*) of south-east Asia, Sumatra and Borneo. Adult specimens measure 20–25 cm *8–10 in* at the shoulder and weigh 2·7–3·2 kg *6–7 lb*.

Rarest ■ Until recently, Fea's muntjac (*Muntiacus feae*) was known only from two specimens collected on the borders of southern Burma and western Thailand. In December 1977 a female was received at Dusit Zoo, Bangkok, followed by two females in

1981 and three males and three females from Xizang, Tibet from February 1982–April 1983.

Oldest ■ The greatest reliable age recorded for a deer is 26 years 8 months for a Red deer (*Cervus elaphus scoticus*) which died in Milwaukee Zoo, Wisconsin, USA on 28 Jun 1954.

MARSUPIALS

Largest ■ The adult male Red kangaroo (*Macropus rufus*) of central, southern and eastern Australia stand up to 213 cm *7 ft* tall, measure up to 245 cm *8 ft ¹/₂ in* in total length and weigh up to 85 kg *187 lb*.

Smallest ■ The smallest known marsupial is the rare Long-tailed planigale (*Planigale ingrami*), a flat-skulled mouse, of north-eastern and north-western Australia. Adult males have a head and body length of 55–63 mm *2·16–2·48 in*, a tail length of 57–60 mm *2·24–2·36 in* and weigh 3·9–4·5 g *0·13–0·19 oz*.

Oldest ■ The greatest reliable age recorded for a marsupial is 26 years 22 days for a Common wombat (*Vombatus ursinus*) which died in London Zoo on 20 Apr 1906.

Fastest speed ■ The highest speed recorded for a marsupial is 64 km/h *40 mph* for a mature female Eastern grey kangaroo. One large male Red Kangaroo was paced for 1·6 km *1 mile* at 56 km/h *35mph*, and dropped dead from his exertions and was obviously too heavy for sustained flight at that speed.

Highest jump ■ A captive Eastern grey once cleared a 2·44 m *8 ft* fence when a car backfired and there is also a record of a hunted Red kangaroo clearing a stack of timber 3·1 m *10 ft* high.

Longest jump ■ During the course of a chase in New South Wales in January 1951 a female Red kangaroo made a series of bounds which included one of 12·80 m *42 ft*. There is also an unconfirmed report of an Eastern grey kangaroo jumping nearly 13·5 m *44 ft 8¹/₂ in* on the flat.

TUSKS

Longest ■ The longest recorded elephant tusks (excluding prehistoric examples) are a pair from Zaïre preserved in the National Collection of Heads and Horns kept by the New York Zoological Society in Bronx Park, New York City, USA. The right tusk measures 3·49 m *11 ft 5¹/₂ in* along the outside curve and the left 3·35 m *11 ft*. Their combined weight is 133 kg *293 lb*. A single tusk of 3·5 m *11 ft 6 in* has been reported. Ivory rose from $2·30 to $34/lb in the period 1970–80.

Heaviest ■ A pair of tusks in the British Museum (Natural History) which were collected from an aged bull shot by an Arab with a muzzle-loading gun at the foot of Mt Kilimanjaro, Kenya in 1897, originally weighed 109 kg *240 lb* (length 3·11 m *10 ft 2¹/₂ in*) and 102 kg *225 lb* (length 3·18 m *10 ft 5¹/₂ in*) respectively, giving a total weight of 211 kg *465 lb*, but their combined weight today is 200 kg *440¹/₂ lb*. A single elephant tusk collected in Benin, west Africa and exhibited at the Paris Exposition in 1900 weighed 117 kg *258 lb*.

HORNS

Longest ■ The longest horns grown by any living animal are those of the Water buffalo (*Bubalus arnee =B. bubalis*) of India. One huge bull shot in 1955 had horns measuring 4·24 m *13 ft 11 in* from tip to tip along the outside curve across the forehead. The longest single horn on record was one measuring 206 cm *81¹/₄ in* on the outside curve found on a specimen of domestic Ankole cattle (*Bos taurus*) near Lake Ngami, Botswana. The largest spread recorded for a Texas longhorn steer is 3·2 m *10 ft 6 in*. They are currently on exhibition at the Hermitage Museum, Big Springs, Texas, USA.

HORSES AND PONIES

The world's equine population is estimated to

be 75 000 000. For record horse prices see Agriculture Chap 7.

Earliest domestication ■ The first domestication of the horse reportedly occurred in what is now the Ukraine, USSR *c.* 6500 years ago when paleolithic hunters tamed some for their flesh and milk.

Largest ■ A 19.2 hand (*1·98 m*) pure-bred red roan Belgian (Brabant) stallion named 'Brooklyn Supreme' (1928–48) owned by C. G. Good of Ogden, Iowa, USA weighed 1451 kg *3200 lb* at its heaviest in 1938 and had a chest girth of 259 cm *102 in*. Each of his 3·4 kg *7¹/₂ lb* shoes measured 35·5 cm *14 in* across and required 76·2 cm *30 in* of iron (cf. 55·8 cm *22 in* for 'Wandle Goliath' - see below).

In April 1973 a weight of 1459 kg *3218 lb* was reported for an 18.2 hand (*1·88 m*) Belgian (Brabant) mare named 'Wilma du Bos' (foaled 15 Jul 1966) shortly before she was shipped from Antwerp to her new owner, Mrs Virgie Arden of Reno, Nevada, USA, but at the time she was heavily in foal (maximum girth 3·65 m *12 ft*). When this horse arrived in New York she scaled 1399 kg *3086 lb*, but after foaling her weight returned to her normal 1088–1134 kg *2400–2500 lb*.

Britain ■ The 17.2 hand (*1·78 m*) Shire stallion 'Honest Tom 5123' (foaled in 1884) owned by James Forshaw of Littleport, Cambs, scaled 1325 kg *2912 lb* in 1891. The heaviest horse living in Britain today is the 19.1 ¹/₂ hand (*1·97 m*) Shire gelding 'Extra Stout' (foaled 1980) owned by Samuel Smith's Old Brewery, Tadcaster, Yorkshire. He recorded a weight of 1180 kg *2602 lb* on 9 Mar 1989. The 17.2 hand (*1·78 m*) champion Percheron stallion 'Pinchbeck Union Crest' (1964-88), owned by George Sneath of Pinchbeck, Spalding, Lincs fluctuated between 1143 kg *2520 lb* and 1194 kg *2632 lb*. His famous father 'Saltmarsh Silver Crest' (1955-78) scaled 1257 kg *2772 lb* at his heaviest.

Tallest ■ The tallest documented horse on record was the Shire gelding 'Sampson' (later renamed 'Mammoth') bred by Thomas Cleaver of Toddington Mills, Beds. This horse (foaled in 1846) measured 21.2 ¹/₂ hands (*2·19 m*) in 1850 and was later said to have weighed 1524 kg *30 cwt*.

The Shire geldings 'Wandle Goliath' (foaled 1977) owned by Young & Company's Brewery, Wandsworth, London, and 'Extra Stout' (see above), both measure 19.1 ¹/₂ hands (*1·97 m*).

Smallest ■ The Falabella of Argentina was developed over a period of 70 years by inbreeding and crossing a small group of undersized horses originally discovered in the southern part of the country. Most adult specimens stand less than 76 cm *30 in* and average 36–45 kg *80–100 lb*. The smallest mature horse bred by Julio Falabella of Recco de Roca before he died in 1981 was a mare which stood 38 cm *15 in* and weighed 11·9 kg *26¹/₄ lb*. On 30 Nov 1975 Dr T. H. Hamison of the Circle Veterinary Center, Spartanburg, South Carolina, USA certified that the stallion 'Little Pumpkin' (foaled 15 Apr 1973) owned by J. C. Williams Jr of Della Terra Mini Horse Farm, Inman, South Carolina, USA, stood 35·5 cm *14 in* and weighed 9·07 kg *20 lb*.

Oldest ■ The greatest reliable age recorded for a horse is 62 years in the case of 'Old Billy' (foaled 1760), believed to be a cross between a Cleveland and Eastern blood, who was bred by Mr Edward Robinson of Wild Grave Farm in Woolston, Lancs. In 1762 or 1763 he was sold to the Mersey and Irwell Navigation Company and remained with them in a working capacity (i.e. marshalling and towing barges) until 1819 when he was retired to a farm at Latchford, near Warrington, where he died on 27 Nov 1822. The skull of this horse is preserved in the Manchester Museum, and his stuffed head (fitted with false teeth) is now on display in Bedford Museum.

The greatest reliable age recorded for a pony is 54 years for a stallion owned by a farmer in central France (*fl.* 1919). A roan pony named 'Bonnie Lass', owned by twin sisters Sylvia Moore and Mrs

Marion Atkinson of Old Harlow, Essex, died on 2 May 1987 aged 42 years. Exactly a year to the day later a moorland pony called 'Joey' belonging to June and Rosie Osborne of the Glebe Equestrian Centre, Wickham Bishop, Essex died aged 44 years. The greatest age recorded for a thoroughbred racehorse is 42 years in the case of the chestnut gelding 'Tango Duke' (foaled 1935), owned by Mrs Carmen J. Koper of Barongarook, Victoria, Australia. The horse died on 25 Jan 1978.

Strongest ■ The greatest load ever hauled by a pair of draught-horses was allegedly one weighing 130·9 tonnes (*144 short tons*) which two Shires with a combined weight of 1587 kg *3500 lb* pulled on a sledge litter for a distance of 402 m *440 yd* along a frozen road at the Nester Estate near Ewen, Michigan, USA on 26 Feb 1893, but this tonnage was exaggerated. The load, which comprised 50 logs of white pine scaling 36 055 board feet, actually weighed in the region of 42·3 tonnes *42·3 short tons*. On 23 Apr 1924 a Shire gelding named 'Vulcan', owned by Liverpool Corporation, registered a pull equal to a starting load of 29·47 tonnes *29 tons* on a dynamometer at the British Empire Exhibition at Wembley, and a pair of Shires *easily* pulled a starting load of 51 tonnes *50 tons*, the maximum registered on the dynamometer.

Largest mules ■ 'Apollo' (b. Tennessee 1977) and 'Anak' (b. Kentucky 1976) owned by Herbert L. Mueller of Columbia, Illinois, USA are the largest mules on record. 'Apollo' measures 19.1 hands (*1·995 m*) and weighs 998 kg *2200 lb* and 'Anak' is 18.3 hands (*1·905 m*) and 952·2 kg *2100 lb*, giving a combined weight of 1960·5 kg *4300 lb*. Both are the hybrid offspring of Belgian mares and Mammoth jacks.

DOGS

UK canine population 6 600 000 (1989 estimate), compared with 52 000 000 for the USA and 400 000 000 for the world.

Heaviest ■ The heaviest breeds of domestic dog (*Canis familiaris*) are the Old English mastiff and the St Bernard, both of which (males) regularly weigh 77–91 kg *170–200 lb* at maturity. The heaviest (and longest) dog ever recorded is 'Alcama Zorba de La-Susa' (whelped 26 Sep 1981), an Old English mastiff owned by Chris Eraclides of London. In September 1987 this canine super-heavyweight tipped the scales at 144·66 kg *319 lb* (shoulder height 88·7 cm *35 in*). Despite his enormous size, however, he does not carry any surplus weight because his diet is strictly controlled. Unfortunately, in March 1989, 'Zorba' was left in the charge of a relative who overfed him and he ballooned to 153·5 kg *338 lb* but he is now back to his ideal weight. Other statistics include a chest girth of 144·7 cm *57 in*, an 87·7 cm *36¹/₂ in* neck, and a nose to tail length of 254·4 cm *8 ft 3 in*. One of his sons 'Chandor' (whelped 6 Aug 1987) weighed 120·6 kg *266 lb* at the age of 18 months (cf. 108 kg *238 lb* for 'Zorba' at two years).

The heaviest St Bernard on record is 'Benedictine Jr. Schwarzwald Hof' (whelped 1982) owned by breeders Thomas and Anne Irwin of Grand Rapids, Michigan, USA. His last recorded weight was 140·6 kg *310 lb* (height at shoulder 99 cm *39 in*).

Tallest ■ The Great Dane and the Irish wolfhound both can exceed 99 cm *39 in* at the shoulder. In the case of the Great Dane the extreme recorded example was 'Shamgret Danzas' (whelped in 1975), owned by Mr and Mrs Peter Comley of Milton Keynes, Bucks. He stood 105·4 cm *41¹/₂ in* or 106·6 cm *42 in* when his hackles went up and weighed up to 108 kg *17 st*. He died on 16 Oct 1984. The Irish wolfhound 'Broadbridge Michael' (1920–9), owned by Mrs Mary Beynon of Sutton-at-Hone, Kent, stood 100·3 cm *39¹/₂ in* at the age of two years.

Smallest ■ *Miniature* versions of the Yorkshire terrier, the Chihuahua and the Toy poodle have been known to weigh less than 453 g *16 oz* when adult.

The smallest mature dog on record was a matchbox-sized Yorkshire terrier owned by Mr Arthur F. Marples of Blackburn, Lancs, a former editor of *Our Dogs*. This tiny atom, which died in 1945 aged nearly two years, stood 6·3 cm *2½ in* at the shoulder and measured 9·5 cm *3¾ in* from the tip of its nose to the root of its tail. Its weight was an incredible 113 g *4 oz*.

The smallest living adult dog is a miniature Chihuahua named 'Peanuts' (whelped 23 Sep 1986) owned by Floyd and Grace Parker of Wilson's Mills, North Carolina, USA. She measures 25 cm *9·84 in* head to tail, 14 cm *5·5 in* at the shoulder and tipped the scales at 630 g *18 oz* on 25 Oct 1988.

Oldest ■ Most dogs live between 8 and 15 years, and authentic records of dogs living over 20 years are rare. They are generally the smaller breeds. The greatest reliable age recorded for a dog is 29 years 5 months for an Australian cattle-dog named 'Bluey', owned by Mr Les Hall of Rochester, Victoria, Australia. The dog was obtained as a puppy in 1910 and worked among cattle and sheep for nearly 20 years. He was put to sleep on 14 Nov 1939.

British ■ A Welsh collie named 'Taffy' owned by Mrs Evelyn Brown of Forge Farm, West Bromwich, West Midlands lived for 27 years and 313 days. He was whelped on 2 Apr 1952 and died on 9 Feb 1980.

Strength ■ The greatest load ever shifted by a dog was 2905 kg *6400½ lb* of railroad steel pulled by a 80 kg *176 lb* St Bernard named 'Ryettes Brandy Bear' at Bothell, Washington State, USA on 21 Jul 1978. The four-year-old dog, owned by Douglas Alexander of Monroe, Washington, pulled the weight on a four-wheeled carrier across a concrete surface for a distance of 4·57 m *15 ft* in less than 90 sec. Ten days earlier the same dog had moved 2993 kg *6600 lb*, but was 12·7 cm *5 in* short of the 4·5 m *15 ft* minimum distance when the 90 seconds were up.

At the American Dog Breeders' Association Inc. Annual Weight-Pull 'National' held at Oklahoma City, Oklahoma, USA on 15–16 Oct 1988 an American pit bull terrier named 'Kissy Bear', owned by Robert Gaines of San Antonio, Texas, USA pulled 2678·5 kg *5905 lb* in 20·05 sec. At the same meeting 'Cutty Sark', a 15·4 kg *34 lb* American pit bull terrier, pulled 1404 kg *3096 lb* (91·1 kg per kg *90·8 lb per lb* of body weight) in 19·64 sec. He is owned by Billy Hayes of Palquemine, Louisiana, USA.

Longest trail ■ The 1688 km *1049 mile* Iditarod Trail from Anchorage to Nome, Alaska, USA has been in being since 1910 at the course of an annual race from 1967. The only four-time winner has been Rick Swenson (1977-79-81-82) who lost by 1 sec in 1978. The record was set by Susan Butcher (winner in 1986-87-88) in 1987 with 11 days 2 hours 5 mins 13 sec.

On 8 Feb 1988 the Rev Donald Ewen McEwen, owner-musher of Nekanesu Kennels, Eldorado, Ontario, Canada drove a 76-dog sled for 3·2 km *2 miles* single-handedly on the ice and about the shore of Lingham Lake. The team, consisting of 25 Siberian huskies and 51 Alaskan huskies, was assembled for the filming of an English TV commercial.

Rarest ■ At the last count (18 March 1988) there were only 70 living examples of the American hairless terrier, 68 of them owned by Willie and Edwin Scott of Trout, Louisiana, USA.

Guide dog ■ The longest period of *active service* reported for a guide dog is 14 years 8 months (August 1972-March 1987) in the case of a Labrador-Retriever bitch named 'Cindy–Cleo' (whelped 20 Jan 1971), owned by Mr Aron Barr of Tel Aviv, Israel. The dog died on 10 Apr 1987.

Largest litter ■ 'Lena', an American foxhound bitch owned by Commander W. N. Ely of Ambler, Pennsylvania, USA produced a litter of 23 on 19 Jun 1944. All the puppies survived. On 6–7 Feb 1975 'Careless Ann', a St Bernard owned by Robert and Alice Rodden of Lebanon, Missouri, USA, also produced a litter of 23, 14 of which survived, and the same number (16 survived) was thrown by 'Shalimar

Bootsie', a Great Dane owned by Mrs Marjorie Harris of Little Hall, nr. Colchester, Essex in June 1987.

Most prolific ■ The greatest sire of all time was the champion greyhound 'Low Pressure', nicknamed 'Timmy', whelped in September 1957 and owned by Mrs Bruna Amhurst of Regent's Park, London. From December 1961 until his death on 27 Nov 1969 he fathered 2414 registered puppies, with at least 600 others unregistered.

Most valuable ■ In 1907 Mrs Clarice Ashton Cross of Ascot, Berks turned down an offer of £32 000 from the American financier and industrialist J. Pierpont Morgan for her famous Pekingese 'Ch. Ch'êrh of Alderbourne' (1904–*fl.* 1914). Mr Morgan then came back with an 'open' cheque, but again she turned him down. The largest legacy devoted to a dog was by Miss Ella Wendel of New York who 'left' her standard poodle 'Toby' £15 million in 1931.

Smallest living adult dog ● 'Peanuts' the miniature Chihuahua, measures a mere 25 cm *9·84 in* head to tail and weighs only 630 g *18 oz*. She is owned by Floyd and Grace Parker of Wilson's Mills, North Carolina, USA.

Highest jump ■ The canine 'high jump' record for a leap and a scramble over a smooth wooden wall (without any ribs or other aids) is held by a German shepherd dog named 'Max of Pangoula', who scaled an 3·48 m *11 ft 5⅛ in* wall, at Chikurubi prison's dog training·school near Harare, Zimbabwe on 18 Mar 1980. His trainer was Chief Prison Officer Alec Mann. 'Duke', a three-year-old German shepherd dog, handled by Cpl Graham Urry of RAF Newton, Notts, scaled a ribbed wall with regulation shallow slats to a height of 3·58 m *11 ft 9 in* on the BBC *Record Breakers* TV programme on 11 Nov 1986.

Longest jump ■ A greyhound named 'Bang'

jumped 9·14 m *30 ft* while coursing a hare at Brecon Lodge, Glos in 1849. He cleared a 1·4 m *4 ft 6 in* gate and landed on a hard road, but despite a damaged pastern bone he still managed to kill the hare.

Ratting ■ During the five-year period 1820–4 a 11·8 kg *26 lb* 'bull and terrier' dog named 'Billy' despatched 4000 rats in 17 hr, a remarkable feat considering that he was blind in one eye. His most notable feat was the killing of 100 rats in 5 min 30 sec at the cockpit in Tufton Street, Westminster, London on 23 Apr 1825. He died on 23 Feb 1829 aged 13 yrs. James Searle's famous 'bull and terrier' bitch 'Jenny Lind' was another outstanding ratter. On 12 Jul 1853 she was backed to kill 500 rats in under 3 hr at The Beehive in Old Crosshall Street, Liverpool, and completed the job in 1 hr 36 min.

Tracking ■ In 1925 a Dobermann pinscher named 'Sauer', trained by Detective-Sergeant Herbert Kruger, tracked a stock-thief 160 km *100 miles* across the Great Karroo, South Africa by scent alone. In 1923 a collie dog named 'Bobbie', lost by his owners while they were on holiday in Wolcott, Indiana, USA, turned up at the family home in Silverton, Oregon, USA six months later, after covering a distance of some 3200 km *2000 miles*. The dog, later identified by householders who had looked after him along the route, had apparently travelled back through the states of Illinois, Iowa, Nebraska and Colorado, before crossing the Rocky Mountains in the depths of winter.

Top show dogs ■ The greatest number of Challenge Certificates won by a dog is the 78 compiled by the famous Chow chow 'Ch. U'Kwong King Solomon' (whelped 21 Jun 1968). Owned and bred by Mrs Joan Egerton of Bramhall, Cheshire, 'Solly' won his first CC at the Cheshire Agricultural Society Championship Show on 4 Jun 1969, and his 78th CC was awarded at the City of Birmingham Championship Show on 4 Sep 1976. He died on 3 Apr 1978. The greatest number of 'Best-in-Show' awards won by any dog in all-breed shows is the career total of 203 compiled by the Scottish terrier bitch 'Ch. Braeburn's Close Encounter' (whelped 22 Oct 1978) up to 10 Mar 1985. She is owned by Sonnie Novick of Plantation Acres, Florida, USA. 'Ch. Clayfield's Mon Ami', a German Shepherd bitch whelped in 1973, won a unique ten Dog Show championships on 4 continents from 1975 to 1987. She is owned by Neal, Sharon, Buffy and Holly Leas of West Des Moines, Iowa, USA.

Largest show ■ At the Ladies' Kennel Association Show (LKA) held at the Birmingham National Exhibition Centre on 14–15 Dec 1984 there were 21 212 entries and a total of 14 611 dogs exhibited.

Top trainer ■ The most successful dog trainer in the world was Mrs Barbara Woodhouse (1910–88) of Rickmansworth, Herts, who trained 19 000 dogs to obey the basic commands during the period 1951 to her retirement in 1985 following a stroke. The fastest

LARGEST PET LITTERS

Animal/Breed	No.	Owner	Date	
CAT *Burmese/Siamese*	15[1]	Mrs Valerie Gane, Church Westcote, Kingham, Oxon	7 Aug	1970
DOG *American foxhound*	23[2]	Cdr W. N. Ely, Ambler, Pennsylvania, USA	19 Jun	1944
DOG *St Bernard*	23[3]	R. and A. Rodden, Lebanon, Missouri, USA	6/7 Feb	1975
DOG *Great Dane*	23[4]	Mrs Marjorie Harris, Little Hall, Essex	June	1987
RABBIT *New Zealand white*	24	Joseph Filek, Sydney, Cape Breton, Nova Scotia, Canada		1978
GUINEA PIG (CAVY)	12	Laboratory specimen		1972
HAMSTER *Golden*	26[5]	L. and S. Miller, Baton Rouge, Louisiana, USA	28 Feb	1974
MOUSE *House*	34[6]	Marion Ogilvie, Blackpool, Lancs	12 Feb	1982
GERBIL *Mongolian*	14[7]	Sharon Kirkman, Bulwell, Notts	May	1983
DOMESTIC FERRET	15	John Cliff, Denstone, Uttoxeter, Staffs		1981

[1] 4 still born [2] all survived [3] 14 survived [4] 16 survived [5] 18 killed by mother [6] 33 survived [7] Litter of 15 recorded 1960s by George Meares, geneticist-owner of gerbil breeding farm, St Petersburg, Florida, USA. Used special food formula.

CAGED PET LONGEVITY

Animal/Species	Name, Owner, etc.	Years	Months
HAMSTER *Golden*	Reported 1984, Cambridge	19	–
RABBIT	*Flopsy* caught 6 Aug 1964 d. 29 Jun 1983 (owner Mrs L. B. Walker) Longford, Tasmania	18	10 ¾
GUINEA PIG	*Snowball* d. 14 Feb 1979 (owner, M. A. Wall) Bingham, Notts.	14	10 ½
GERBIL *Mongolian*	*Sahara* May 1973–4 Oct 1981 (owner Aaron Milstone) Lathrup Village, Michigan, USA	8	4 ½
MOUSE *House*	*Fritzy* 11 Sep 1977–24 April 1985 (owner Mrs Bridget Beard) West House School, Edgbaston, Birmingham	7	7
RAT *Common*	Died: *c.* 1924 Philadelphia, Pennsylvania, USA.	5	8

19 years reported for a laboratory specimen in Cambridge.

trainer is Mr Armand Rabuttinio of Aston, Pennsylvania, USA. His highest total for a single day (9 a.m.–6 p.m.) is 132 dogs at a training marathon held at Upland, Pennsylvania, USA on 12 Jun 1982.

Drug sniffing ■ The greatest drug-sniffing dogs on record are a pair of Malinoises called 'Rocky' and 'Barco'. These Belgian sheepdogs (whelped 1984) are members of an American stop-and-search team which patrols the Rio Grande Valley ('Cocaine Alley') along the southern Texas border. In 1988 alone they were involved in 969 seizures of drugs worth $182 million, and they are so proficient at their job that Mexican drug smugglers have put a $30 000 price on their heads. 'Rocky' and 'Barco' were recently awarded honorary titles of Sergeant Major and always wear their stripes when they are on duty. The only drug-sniffing dog with a 100 per cent arrest record was a German shepherd of the US Army called 'General'. During the period April 1974 to March 1976 this canine detective and his handler, SP4 Michael R. Harris of the 591st Military Police Company in Fort Bliss, Texas, USA, carried out 220 searches for narcotics, arrested 220 people for possession and uncovered 330 caches of drugs. The German shepherd 'Blue' of the Los Angeles Police Department was reported in January 1986 to have

assisted in apprehending 253 suspected felons. In October 1988 another German shepherd owned by the Essex Police sniffed out 2 tonnes of cannabis worth £6 million when it was sent into a remote cottage on the outskirts of Harlow, Essex.

CATS

UK feline population 6 500 000 (1988 estimate), compared with 54 600 000 for the USA.

Largest ■ The largest of the 330 breeds of cat is the Ragdoll with males weighing 6·8–9·07 kg *15–20 lb*. In the majority of domestic cats (*Felis catus*), the average weight of the male (tom) at maturity is 3·9 kg *8·6 lb*, compared with 3·2 kg *7·2 lb* for the adult female or queen. Neuters and spays average out somewhat heavier. The heaviest domestic cat on record was a neutered male tabby named 'Himmy', owned by Thomas Vyse of Redlynch, Cairns, Queensland, Australia. At the time of his death (from respiratory failure) on 12 Mar 1986 aged 10 years 4 months he weighed 21·3 kg *46 lb 15¼ oz* (neck 38·1 cm *15 in*, waist 83·8 cm *33 in*, length 96·5 cm *38 in*). In Feb 1988 an unconfirmed weight of 21·7 kg *48 lb* was reported for a cat named 'Edward Bear', owned by Miss Jackie Fleming of Sydney, NSW, Australia.

Britain ■ An 11-year-old male tabby called 'Poppa', owned by Miss Gwladys Cooper of Newport, Gwent, South Wales, scaled 20·19 kg *44½ lb* in November 1984 and died on 25 Jun 1985.

Smallest ■ The smallest breed of domestic cat is the Singapura or 'Drain Cat' of Singapore. Adult

males average 2·72 kg *6 lb* in weight and adult females 1·81 kg *4 lb*. A male Siamese cross named 'Ebony-Eb-Honey Cat' owned by Miss Angelina Johnston of Boise, Idaho, USA tipped the scales at only 0·79 kg *1 lb 12 oz* in February 1984 when aged 23 months.

Oldest ■ Cats are generally longer-lived than dogs. The average life expectancy of entire well-fed males raised under household conditions, and receiving good medical attention, is 13–15 years (15–17 years for intact females), but neutered males and females live on the average one to two years longer. The oldest cat ever recorded was probably the tabby 'Puss', owned by Mrs T. Holway of Clayhidon, Devon, who celebrated his 36th birthday on 28 Nov 1939 and died the next day. A more recent and better-documented case was that of the female tabby 'Ma', owned by Mrs Alice St George Moore of Drewsteignton, Devon. This cat was put to sleep on 5 Nov 1957 aged 34. The oldest cat living in Britain today is believed to be a female black moggy named 'Kitty', owned by Mr George Johnston of Croxton, Staffs. She was discovered as a stray (with four kittens) in November 1957, and celebrated her 31st birthday in 1988.

Oldest twins ■ The oldest twin cats on record were 'Beau' and 'Bubbles' (b. 17 Oct 1963) owned by Diane Phelps of Dearborn, Michigan, USA. 'Bubbles' died on 29 Apr 1985 aged 21 years 6 months and 'Beau' was put to sleep on 28 Dec 1985 aged 22 years 2 months. They were longhair and part Persian.

Largest kindle ■ A litter of 19 kittens (four stillborn) was delivered by caesarean section to 'Tarawood Antigone', a four-year-old brown Burmese, on 7 Aug 1970. Her owner, Mrs Valerie Gane of Church Westcote, Kingham, Oxon, said it was the result of a mis-mating with a half-Siamese. Of the 15 survivors, 14 were males and one female.

Smallest rabbit ● The Netherland dwarf has a weight range of 0·9–1·13 kg *2–2⅓ lb* when fully grown. This tiny bundle is a Red-eyed White Netherland Dwarf buck. (Photo: Bruce Coleman)

Longest ears ● The longest ears are found in the Lop family (four strains), and in particular the English Lop. The ears of a typical example measure about 61 cm *24 in* from tip to tip (taken across the skull), and 14 cm *5·51 in* in width. In 1901 Captain Youden exhibited a specimen in England which had 77·4 cm *30·5 in* ears; it is not known, however, if this was a natural attainment or weights had been used to stretch the ears and left the veins inside badly varicosed. (Photo: Bruce Coleman)

The largest live litter (all of which survived) was one of 14 kittens born in December 1974 to a Persian cat named 'Bluebell', owned by Mrs Elenore Dawson of Wellington, Cape Province, South Africa.

Most prolific ■ A tabby named 'Dusty' (b. 1935) living in Bonham, Texas, USA produced 420 kittens during her breeding life. She gave birth to her last kindle (a single kitten) on 12 Jun 1952. In May 1987 'Kitty' (see page 32) produced two kittens at the age of 30 years (breeding total to date 212 kittens), making her the oldest feline mother on record.

Most valuable ■ In 1988 Mr Carl Mayes, a breeder in Atlanta, Georgia, USA turned down an offer of $10 000 for his male Singapura 'Bull', the best-known example of its breed in the USA.

Best climber ■ On 6 Sep 1950 a four-month-old kitten belonging to Josephine Aufdenblatten of Geneva, Switzerland followed a group of climbers up to the top of the 4478 m *14 691 ft* Matterhorn in the Alps.

Mousing champion ■ A female tortoiseshell named 'Towser' (b. 21 Apr 1963) owned by Glenturret Distillery Ltd near Crieff, Tayside, Scotland notched up an estimated lifetime score of 28 899. She averaged three mice per day until her death on 20 Mar 1987.

RABBITS AND HARES

Largest ■ The largest breed of domestic rabbit (*Oryctolagus cuniculus*) is the Flemish giant. Adults weigh 7–8·5 kg *15·4–18·7 lb* (average toe-to-toe length when fully stretched 91 cm *36 in*), but weights up to 11·3 kg *25 lb* have been reliably reported for this breed. In April 1980 a five-month-old French Lop doe weighing 12 kg *26·45 lb* was exhibited at the Reus Fair, north-east Spain. The heaviest recorded wild rabbit (av. weight 1·58 kg *3½ lb*) was one of 3·74 kg *8 lb 4 oz*, killed by Norman Wilkie of Markinch, Fife, Scotland while ferreting on 20 Nov 1982.

Smallest ■ The Netherland dwarf and the Polish both have a weight range of 0·9–1·13 kg *2–2½ lb* when fully grown. In 1975 Jacques Bouloc of Coulommière, France announced a new cross of the above breeds which weighed 396 g *14 oz*.

Most prolific ■ The most prolific domestic breeds are the New Zealand white and the Californian. Does produce 5–6 litters a year, each containing 8–12 kittens during their breeding life (cf. five litters and three to seven young for the wild rabbit).

Longest ears ■ The longest ears are found in the Lop family (four strains), and in particular the English Lop. The ears of a typical example measure about 61 cm *24 in* from tip to tip (taken across the skull), and 14 cm *5·51 in* in width. In 1901 Captain Youden exhibited a specimen in England which had 77·4 cm *30·5 in* ears; it is not known, however, if this was a natural attainment or if weights had been used to stretch the ears and left the veins inside badly varicosed.

Largest hare ■ In November 1956 a Brown hare weighing 6·83 kg *15 lb 1 oz* was shot near Welford, Northamptonshire. The average adult weight is 3·62 kg *8 lb*.

Birds *Aves*

Largest ratite ■ The largest living bird is the North African ostrich (*Struthio c. camelus*), which is found in reduced numbers south of the Atlas Mountains from Upper Senegal and Niger across to the Sudan and central Ethiopia. Male examples (adult hens are smaller) of this flightless or ratite subspecies have been recorded up to 2·74 m *9 ft* in height and 156·5 kg *345 lb* in weight.

Largest carinate ■ The world's heaviest flying birds are the Kori bustard or Paauw (*Ardeotis kori*) of eastern South Africa and the Great bustard (*Otis tarda*) of Europe and Asia. Weights up to 18·14 kg *40 lb* have been reported for the former shot in South

Africa, and there is an isolated record of 21 kg *46·2 lb* for a cock bird shot in Manchuria which was too heavy to fly. The heaviest Great bustard on record weighed 15·8 kg *35 lb*. The Mute swan (*Cygnus olor*), which is resident in Britain, can reach 18·14 kg *40 lb* on very rare occasions, and there is a record from Poland of a cob weighing 22·5 kg *49·6 lb* which had temporarily lost the power of flight.

Bird of prey ■ The heaviest bird of prey is the Andean condor (*Vultur gryphus*), adult males averaging 9·09–11·3 kg *20–25 lb*. A weight of 14·1 kg *31 lb* has been claimed for an outsized male Californian condor (*Gymnogyps californianus*) now preserved in the California Academy of Sciences, Los Angeles, USA. This species is appreciably smaller than the Andean condor and rarely exceeds 10·4 kg *23 lb*.

Largest wingspan ■ The Wandering albatross (*Diomedea exulans*) of the southern oceans has the largest wingspan of any living bird, adult males averaging 3·15 m *10 ft 4 in* with wings tightly stretched. The largest recorded specimen was a very old male 3·63 m *11 ft 11 in* caught by members of the Antarctic research ship USNS *Eltanin* in the Tasman Sea on 18 Sep 1965. Unconfirmed measurements up to 4·22 m *13 ft 10 in* have been claimed for this species. The only other bird reliably credited with a wingspan in excess of 3·35 m *11 ft* is the vulture-like Marabou stork (*Leptoptilus crumeniferus*) of tropical Africa. In 1934 an extreme measurement of 4·06 m *13 ft 4 in* was reported for a male shot in central Africa by naturalist Richard Meinertzhagen (1879–1967), but this species rarely exceeds 2·74 m *9 ft*.

Smallest ■ The smallest bird in the world is the Bee hummingbird (*Mellisuga helenae*) of Cuba and the Isle of Pines. Adult males (females are slightly larger) measure 57 mm *2·24 in* in total length, half of which is taken up by the bill and tail. It weighs 1·6 g *0·056 oz*, which means it is lighter than a Privet hawk-moth (*Sphinx ligustri*) (2·4 g *0·084 oz*) (see Nest, smallest).

The smallest bird of prey is the 35 g *1·23 oz* White-fronted falconet (*Microhierax latifrons*) of north-western Borneo, which is sparrow-sized. The smallest seabird is the Least storm petrel (*Halocyptena microsoma*), which breeds on many of the small islands in the Gulf of California, north-western Mexico. Adult specimens average 140 mm *5½ in* in total length and weigh *c.* 28 g *1 oz*.

The smallest regularly breeding British bird is the Goldcrest (*Regulus regulus*) also known as the Golden crested wren. Adult specimens measure 90 mm *3·5 in* in length and weigh between 3·8 and 4·5 g *0·108* and *0·127 oz*, which means it is half the weight of the Common wren (*Troglodytes troglodytes*).

Most abundant *Wild bird* ■ The Red-billed quelea (*Quelea quelea*), a seed-eating weaver of the drier parts of Africa south of the Sahara, has an estimated adult breeding population of 1 500 000 000 and at least 1 000 000 000 of these 'feathered locusts' are slaughtered annually without having any impact on the population. One huge roost in the Sudan contained 32 000 000 birds.

Sea bird ■ The most abundant is probably the very small Wilson's storm petrel (*Oceanites oceanicus*) which breeds on the Antarctic continent and adjacent sub-Antarctic islands. No population estimates have been published, but the numbers must run into hundreds of millions.

Domesticated bird ■ The most abundant species is the Chicken, the tame version of the wild Red jungle fowl (*Gallus gallus*) of south-east Asia. According to the FAO (Food and Agriculture Organisation of the United Nations), the world's chicken population stood at 8 295 760 000 in 1985, which means there are 1·6 chickens for every member of the human race.

Nesting bird ■ Of the estimated 126–150 wild bird species found in Britain the commonest is now the

Blackbird (*Turdus merula*), with a breeding population of 5 million pairs. It is followed by the Robin (*Erithicius rubecula*) and the Blue tit (*Parus caeruleus*) with 4 million pairs each, the House sparrow (*Passer domesticus*) with 3 million pairs and the Song thrush (*Turdus philamelos*) with 2½ million pairs. Between 1964–74 the population of the Wren (*Troglodytes troglodytes*) increased tenfold, after a series of mild winters, and at the end of this period there were an estimated 10 million pairs. This species, however, is severely affected by cold weather, and the harsh winter of 1978/9 alone reduced the Wren population by 40 per cent.

Rarest ■ The number of threatened bird species worldwide has risen in the past ten years from 290 to 1029 as a result of human activity, according to a survey published in October 1988. Because of the practical difficulties in assessing bird populations in the wild, it is virtually impossible to establish the identity of the world's rarest living bird.

The strongest contender, up until very recently, was the Dusky seaside sparrow (*Ammospiza nigrescens*), formerly of Titusville Marshes, Florida, USA, but the last known example (a male) died at Discovery Island, Disney World, Orlando, Florida, USA on 16 May 1987. Some of its tissues has been frozen in the hope that future technology might allow a pure strain of Dusky seaside sparrow to be resurrected through genetic cloning.

The Guam flycatcher (*Myiagra freycineti*) and the Rufous fantail (*Rhipidura rufifrons*), also of Guam, were last seen in 1984 and may now also be extinct, and the Guam rail (*Rallus owstons*) has only been sighted three times since 1985. The Oa (*Moho braccatus*) of Kauai in the Hawaiian Islands, reportedly extinct, was rediscovered in 1960 in the mountain rain forests of the Alahari swamp. Its nest was found in 1979 and it was seen again in 1981. It is now protected and there may be one or two pairs left. The Crested shellduck (*Tadorna cristata*) is known from only three specimens. The last sighting was in 1971 but it may still survive in the remoter Japanese coastal regions or in adjacent waters. The Imperial woodpecker (*Campephilus imperiali*) of Mexico has not been sighted since 1958 on the Sonora-Chihuahua border, but there were unconfirmed reports from south-west Chihuahua in 1977. The Socorro dove (*Zenaida graysoni*) of Socorro Island off the west coast of Mexico is now extinct in the wild and survives only in captivity. The Itombwe owl is known only from the type specimen collected in 1951 while sleeping in long grass high in the Itombwe mountains, eastern Zaïre, and the Kibale ground-thrush (*Turdus kibalensis*) of western Uganda is known only from two males collected in 1966. The Sea cliff swallow (*Hirunda perdita*) is known only from a dead specimen picked up on an islet off Port Sudan in 1984, and has not been recorded since.

In 1979 the Chatham Island black robin (*Petroica traversi*) was another bird on the verge of extinction with only five surviving. By cross-fostering the chicks of this wild song bird with local tom tits, however, (the first of its kind), members of the New Zealand Wildlife Service managed to increase the population to 38 by 1984. Today there are over 100 of these robins spread amongst several islands. Another remarkable fact is that every living example of this species is descended from the female known as 'Old Blue'. She lived for *c.* 14 years (over twice the normal lifespan) and remained fertile right up to the end. The death of this amazing little bird was officially announced in New Zealand Parliament and her body has now been preserved in a museum.

Spix's macaw (*Cyanopsitta spixii*) of Brazil, the world's most endangered parrot, became extinct in the wild *c.* 1988. There are only ten left in captivity, eight of them in Brazil.

The last wild California condor (*Gymnogyps californianus*) was captured on 19 Apr 1987 in Kern County, California, USA to join 26 others held for captive breeding in San Diego Wildlife Park and Los Angeles Zoo. On 29 Apr 1988 the first California condor ever born in captivity was successfully hatched out at San Diego Wildlife Park and the chick was successfully fed for six months with condor hand puppets.

The world's rarest, most restricted and most highly threatened bird is now probably the Aldabra brush warbler (*Nesillas aldabrabus*). Not discovered until 1967, five individuals (three males and two females) were ringed between July 1974 and February 1977. One of the males was re-sighted in 1978 and again in September 1983, but that was the last confirmed record. This species is restricted to a coastal strip 2 km *1·24 miles* long and 50 m *54 yds* wide on the northern tip of Aldabra Atoll in the Indian Ocean.

British Isles ■ According to the British Ornithologists' Union there are over 50 species of birds which have been recorded only once in the British Isles - most of them since the end of the Second World War in 1945.

That which has not recurred for the longest period is the Black-capped petrel (*Pterodroma hasitata*), of the West Indies. A specimen was caught alive on a heath at Southacre, near Swaffham, Norfolk in March or April 1850. On 28–29 May 1979 an Aleutian tern (*Sterna aleutica*) was sighted on the Farne Islands, Northumberland. This bird breeds on the coasts of Alaska and eastern Siberia, and until then had never been recorded outside the North Pacific.

On 3 Aug 1988 a Tristram's storm-petrel (*Oceanodroma tristrami*) was sighted off Sennen, near Land's End, Cornwall, more than 12 874 km *8000 miles* from its natural haunts in Japanese waters. It had never been recorded in the Atlantic before.

The most tenuously established British bird is the Snowy owl (*Nyctea scandiaca*). During the period 1967–75 one pair bred regularly on Fetlar, Shetland Isles and reared a total of 21 young, but soon afterwards the old male took off for an unknown destination, having driven off all the young males, and left the females without a mate. From 19–22 Apr 1979 an adult male was seen on Fair Isle some 129 km *80 miles* further south, but it did not find its way to Fetlar. In 1984 four females were seen on Fetlar, but once again no males were in evidence. A total of 91 females have now been observed during the period 1958–86.

In 1916 an English vicar stole the eggs of the last White-tailed sea eagle (*Haliaeetus albicilla*) on Skye in the Inner Hebrides, Scotland. During the period 1975–7 an attempt to reintroduce this bird on the island of Rum was made, and 13 eaglets from Norway were released. In the summer of 1985 the first chick raised in the wild in Britain for more than 70 years took to the air. The parents of the chick successfully raised two more the following year and another two in 1987 and 1988 respectively. In November 1988 a White-tailed sea eagle was spotted near a bird reserve at Elmley, Isle of Sheppey, Kent.

Britain's rarest breeding bird is the Red-backed shrike (*Lanius collurio*) of southern and eastern England. In 1952 there were over 300 breeding pairs, but only 1-3 pairs in 1988. The Shore lark (*Eremophila alpestris*) of the east coast and the Ruff (*Philomachus pugnax*) of East Anglia are both now down to three breeding pairs.

Britain's rarest breeding sea bird is the Mediterranean black-headed gull (*Larus melanocephalus*) which first bred at Needs Oar Point Nature Reserve, Hants, in 1968. Its range has been slowly extending in recent years.

Fastest flying ■ The fastest living creature is the Peregrine falcon (*Falco peregrinus*) when stooping from great heights during territorial displays. In one series of experiments carried out in Germany the highest speed recorded for peregrines at a 30-degree angle of stoop was 270 km/h *168 mph*, and at 45 degrees the maximum velocity was 350 km/h *217 mph*.

The White-throated spinetail swift (*Hirundapus caudacutus*) of Asia and the Alpine swift (*Apus melba*) are also extremely fast during courtship display flights, and the former has been timed at speeds up to 170 km/h *105·6 mph* in tests carried out in the USSR.

The fastest fliers in level flight are found among the ducks and geese (*Anatidae*), and some powerful species such as the Red-breasted merganser (*Mergus serrator*), the Eider (*Somateria mollissima*), the Canvasback (*Aythya valisineria*) and the Spur-winged goose (*Plectropterus gambiensis*) can probably exceed an air speed of 104 km/h *65 mph*.

Britain's fastest game bird is the Red grouse (*Lagopus l. scoticus*) which, in still air, has recorded burst speeds up to 92·8–100·8 km/h *58–63 mph* over very short distances.

> **Longest bill** ● The longest bill in relation to overall body length is that of the Sword-billed hummingbird (*Ensifera ensifera*) of the Andes from Venezuela to Bolivia. It measures 10·2 cm *4 in* in length and is longer than the bird's actual body if the tail is excluded. (Artwork: Matthew Hillier)

Air speeds up to 112 km/h *70 mph* have been claimed for the Golden plover (*Pluvialis apricaria*) when flushed, but it is extremely doubtful whether this rapid-flying bird can exceed 80–88 km/h *50–55 mph* - even in an emergency.

Slowest flying ■ Probably at least 50 per cent of the world's flying birds cannot exceed an air speed of 64 km/h *40 mph* in level flight. The slowest flying bird is the American woodcock (*Scolopax minor*), which has been timed at 8 km/h *5 mph* without sinking during courtship flights.

Fastest wing beat ■ The wing beat of the Horned sungem (*Heliactin cornuta*) of tropical South America has a rate of 90 beats per sec.

Longest lived ■ The greatest irrefutable age reported for any bird is 80 + years for a male Sulphur-crested cockatoo (*Cacatua galerita*) named 'Cocky', who died at London Zoo in 1982. He was presented to the Zoo in 1925, and had been with his previous owner since 1902 when he was already fully mature. In 1987 an unconfirmed age of *c*. 82 years was reported for a male Siberian white crane (*Crus leucogeranus*) named 'Wolfe' at the International Crane Foundation, Baraboo, Wisconsin, USA. The bird was said to have hatched out in a zoo in Switzerland *c*. 1905. He died in late 1988 after breaking his bill while repelling a visitor near his pen.

In 1964 the death was reported of a male Andean condor called 'Kuzya' at Moscow Zoo, USSR, aged 72 + years. As this bird was already fully grown when it was received in 1892, it must have been at least 77.

The oldest ringed sea bird on record is a female Royal albatross (*Diomedea epomophora*) named

'Grandma' ('Blue White'), who laid another egg at Taiaroa Head, near Dunedin, South Island, New Zealand in November 1988, aged 60 years. She was banded for the first time in 1937 when she was a breeding adult, and such birds do not start breeding until they are nine years old. Since then she has raised ten chicks of her own and fostered three others. Her mate 'Green White Green' is 47.

Longest flights ■ The greatest distance covered by a ringed bird is 22 530 km *14 000 miles* by an Arctic tern (*Sterna paradisea*), which was banded as a nestling on 5 Jul 1955 in the Kandalaksha Sanctuary on the White Sea coast and was captured alive by a fisherman 13 km *8 miles* south of Fremantle, Western Australia on 16 May 1956. The bird had flown south via the Atlantic Ocean and then circled Africa before crossing the Indian Ocean. It did not survive to make the return journey. There is also another report of an Arctic tern flying from Greenland to Australasia, but further details are lacking.

Highest flying ■ Most migrating birds fly at relatively low altitudes (i.e. below 91 m *300 ft*) and it is only a few dozen species that fly higher than 914 m *3000 ft*.

The highest acceptable altitude recorded for a bird is 11 277 m *37 000 ft* for a Ruppell's vulture (*Gyps rueppellii*) which collided with a commercial aircraft over Abidjan, Ivory Coast, western Africa, on 29 Nov 1973. The impact damaged one of the aircraft's engines, causing it to shut down, but the plane landed safely without further incident. Sufficient feather remains of the bird were recovered to allow the US Museum of Natural History to make a positive identification, but this was a freakish altitude even for this high-level soarer, which is rarely seen above 6096 m *20 000 ft*.

On 15 Nov 1988 a Pan American 747 jet carrying 269 passengers from New York to London was forced to make an emergency landing at Gander, Newfoundland, Canada for repairs after something crashed into its nose cone damaging vital radar equipment at a height of 10 058 m *33 000 ft*. According to one report the damage was caused by a Greater snow goose (*Anser c. coerulescens*) but no bloodstains or feathers were found sticking to the nose cone when it was inspected. A more acceptable explanation is that the dent was caused by metal fatigue (there was a great deal of turbulence) or the airliner had been struck by space debris.

Britain ■ On 9 Dec 1967 about 30 Whooper swans (*Cygnus cygnus*) were recorded at an altitude of just over 8230 m *27 000 ft* flying in from Iceland to winter at Loch Foyle, Northern Ireland. They were spotted by an airline pilot over the Outer Hebrides, and the height was also confirmed on radar by air traffic control in Northern Ireland.

Most airborne ■ The most aerial of all birds is the Sooty tern (*Sterna fuscata*) which, after leaving the nesting grounds, remains continuously aloft from three to ten years as a sub-adult, before returning to land to breed. The most aerial land bird is the Common swift (*Apus apus*) which remains airborne for two to three years, during which time it sleeps, drinks, eats and even mates on the wing.

Fastest swimmer ■ The Gentoo penguin (*Pygoscelis papua*) has a maximum burst speed of c. 27·4 km/h *17 mph*.

Deepest dive ■ In 1969 a depth of 265 m *870 ft* was recorded for a small group of ten Emperor penguins (*Aptenodytes forsteri*) at Cape Crozier, Antarctica by a team of American scientists. One bird remained submerged for 18 minutes.

Vision ■ Birds of prey (Falconiformes) have the keenest eyesight in the avian world, and large species with eyes similar in size to those of man have visual acuity at least two times stronger than human vision. It has also been calculated that a large eagle can detect a point object at a distance 3–8 times greater than that achieved by man. Thus the Golden eagle (*Aquila chrysaetos*) can detect an 46 cm *18 in* long hare at a range of 3·2 km *2 miles* in good light and against a contrasting background, and a Peregrine falcon can spot a pigeon at a range of over 8 km *5 miles*. In experiments carried out on the Tawny owl (*Strix aluco*) at the University of Birmingham, England in 1977, it was revealed that the bird's eye on average was only 2½ times more sensitive than the human eye. It was also discovered that the Tawny owl sees perfectly adequately in daylight and that its visual acuity is only slightly inferior to that of the human.

g force ■ American scientific experiments have revealed that the beak of the Red-headed woodpecker (*Melanerpes erythrocephalus*) hits the bark of a tree with an impact velocity of 20·9 km/h *13 mph*. This means that when the head snaps back the brain is subject to a deceleration of about 10 g *0·35 oz*.

Longest feathers ■ The longest feathers grown by any bird are those of the Phoenix fowl or Onagadori (a strain of Red junglefowl *Gallus gallus*) which has been bred in south-western Japan since the mid-17th century. In 1972 a tail covert measuring 10·6 m *34 ft 9½ in* was reported for a rooster owned by Masasha Kubota of Kochi, Shikoku. Among flying birds the tail feathers of the male Crested pheasant (*Rheinhartia ocellata*) of south-east Asia regularly reach 173 cm *5 ft 8 in* in length and 13 cm *5 in* wide, and the central tail feathers of the Reeves' pheasant

(*Syrmaticus reevesi*) of central and northern China have exceptionally reached 2·43 m *8 ft*.

Most and least feathers ■ In a series of 'feather counts' on various species of bird a Whistling swan (*Cygnus columbianus*) was found to have 25 216 feathers, 20 177 of which were on the head and neck. The Ruby-throated hummingbird (*Archilochus colubris*) has only 940.

Largest egg ■ The average Ostrich (*Struthio camelus*) egg measures 15–20 cm *6–8 in* in length, 10–15 cm *4–6 in* in diameter and weighs 1·65–1·78 kg *3·63–3·88 lb* (around two dozen hens' eggs in volume). It requires about 40 min for boiling. The shell, though 1·5 mm *0·059 in* thick, can support the weight of a 127 kg *20 st* man. On 28 Jun 1988 a two year old cross between a Northern and a Southern ostrich (*Struthio c. camelus*) × (*Struthio c. australis*) laid an egg weighing a record 2·3 kg *5·07 lb* at the Kibbutz Ha'on collective farm, Israel.
The largest egg laid by any bird on the British list is that of the Mute swan (*Cygnus olor*), which measures 109–124 mm *4·3–4·9 in* in length, 71–78·5 mm *2·8–3·1 in* in diameter, and weighs 340–368 g *12–13 oz*.

Smallest egg ■ The smallest egg laid by any bird is that of the Vervain hummingbird (*Mellisuga minima*) of Jamaica. Two specimens measuring less than 10 mm *0·39 in* in length weighed 0·365 g *0·0128 oz* and 0·375 g *0·0132 oz* respectively. The smallest egg laid by a bird on the British list is that of the Goldcrest, which measures 12·2–14·5 mm *0·48–0·57 in* in length and between 9·4 and 9·9 mm *0·37–0·39 in* in diameter with a weight of 0·6 g *0·021 oz*. Eggs emitted from the oviduct before maturity, known as 'sports', are not reckoned to be of significance.

Longest incubation ■ The longest normal incubation period is that of the Wandering albatross, with a normal range of 75–82 days. There is an isolated case of an egg of the Mallee fowl (*Leipoa ocellata*) of Australia taking 90 days to hatch against its normal incubation of 62 days.

Shortest incubation ■ The shortest incubation period is the ten days of the Great spotted woodpecker (*Dendrocopus major*) and the Blackbilled cuckoo (*Coccyzus erythropthalmus*). The idlest of cock birds include hummingbirds (family Trochilidae), Eider duck (*Somateria mollissima*) and Golden pheasant (*Chrysolophus pictus*) among whom the hen bird does 100 per cent of the incubation, whereas the female Common kiwi (*Apteryx australis*) leaves this to the male for 75–80 days.

Longest bills ■ The bill of the Australian pelican (*Pelicanus conspicillatus*) measures 34–47 cm *13·3–18·5 in* long. The longest bill in relation to overall body length is that of the Sword-billed hummingbird (*Ensifera ensifera*) of the Andes from Venezuela to Bolivia. It measures 10·2 cm *4 in* in length and is longer than the bird's actual body if the tail is excluded.

Shortest bills ■ The shortest bills in relation to body length are found among the smaller swifts (*Apodidae*) and in particular that of the Glossy swiftlet (*Collocalia esculenta*) which is almost non-existent.

Cuckoos ■ It is unlikely that the Cuckoo (*Culculus canorus*) has ever been *heard and seen* in Britain earlier than 2 Mar, on which date one was observed under acceptable conditions by Mr William A. Haynes of Trinder Road, Wantage, Oxon in 1972. The two latest dates are 16 Dec 1912 at Anstey's Cove, Torquay, Devon and 26 Dec 1897 or 1898 in Cheshire.

Bird-spotter ■ The world's leading bird-spotter or 'twitcher' is Norman Chesterfield (b. 8 Mar 1913) of Wheatley, Ontario, Canada, who did not buy his first pair of binoculars until 1955. By February 1989 he had logged 6437 of the 9016 known species. The British life list record is 462 by Ron Johns (b. 1941) of Slough, Bucks who started spotting in 1952. The British year

list record is 340 by Lee Evans (b. 1960) of Luton, Beds established in 1985. In an average year he travels 96 000 km *60 000 miles*. The greatest number of species spotted in a 24-hour period is 342 by Kenyans Terry Stevenson, John Fanshawe and Andy Roberts on day two of the Birdwatch Kenya '86 event held on 29–30 Nov. The 48-hour record is held by Don Turner and David Pearson of Kenya who spotted 494 species at the same event.

Peter G. Kaestner of Washington, DC, USA was the first person to see at least one species of each of the world's 159 bird families. He saw his final family on 1 Oct 1986. Since then Dr Ira J. Abramson of North Miami, Florida, USA and Dr Martin H. Edwards have also succeeded in this achievement.

Largest nest ■ A nest measuring 2·9 m *9½ ft* wide, 6 m *20 ft* deep was built by a pair of Bald eagles (*Haliaeetus leucocephalus*) and possibly their successors near St Petersburg, Florida, USA. It was examined in 1963 and was estimated to weigh more than 2 tonnes. The Golden eagle (*Aquila chrysaetos*) also constructs huge nests, and one 4·57 m *15 ft* deep was reported from Scotland in 1954. It had been used for 45 years. The incubation mounds built by the Mallee fowl (*Leipoa ocellata*) of Australia are much larger, having been measured up to 4·57 m *15 ft* in height and 10·6 m *35 ft* across, and it has been calculated that the nest site may involve the mounding of 289 m³ *300 yd³* of matter weighing 300 tonnes *295 tons*.

Smallest nest ■ The smallest nests are built by hummingbirds (*Trochilidae*). That of the Vervain hummingbird (*Mellisuga minima*) is about half the size of a walnut, while the deeper one of the Bee hummingbird is thimble-sized. The smallest British nest is that of the Goldcrest, which measures about 8–9 cm *3·14–3·54 in* in diameter.

DOMESTICATED BIRDS

Earliest domesticated ■ The earliest domesticated bird was the Greylag goose (*Anser*) of the Neolithic period (20 000 years ago) of south-eastern Europe and Asia Minor.

Oldest ■ The longest-lived domesticated bird (excluding the Ostrich which has lived up to 68 years) is the Domestic Goose (*Anser anser domesticus*) which normally lives about 25 years. On 16 Dec 1976 a gander named 'George', owned by Mrs Florence Hull of Thornton, Lancs, died aged 49 years 8 months. He was hatched out in April 1927. The longest-lived small cagebird is the Canary (*Serinus canaria*). The oldest example on record was a 34-year-old cock bird named 'Joey', owned by Mrs K. Ross of Hull. The bird was purchased in Calabar, Nigeria in 1941 and died on 8 Apr 1975. The oldest budgerigar (*Melopsittacus undulatus*) was a hen bird named 'Charlie', owned by Miss J. Dinsey of Stonebridge, London, which died on 20 Jun 1977 aged 29 years 2 months.

Most talkative ■ A number of birds are renowned for their talking ability (i.e. the reproduction of words) but the African grey parrot (*Psittacus erythacus*) reigns supreme in this department. A female specimen named 'Prudle', formerly owned by Mrs Lyn Logue (died January 1988) and now in the care of Mrs Iris Frost of Seaford, East Sussex, won the 'Best talking parrot-like bird' title at the National Cage and Aviary Bird Show in London each December for 12 consecutive years (1965–76). Prudle, who has a vocabulary of nearly 800 words, was taken from a nest at Jinja, Uganda in 1958. She retired undefeated.

Reptiles *Reptilia*

(Crocodiles, snakes, turtles, tortoises, lizards)

CROCODILIANS

Largest ■ The largest reptile in the world is the Estuarine or Saltwater crocodile (*Crocodylus porosus*) of south-east Asia, the Malay Archipelago,

Indonesia, northern Australia, Papua New Guinea, Vietnam and the Philippines. Adult males average 4·2–4·8 m *14–16 ft* in length and scale about 408–520 kg *900–1150 lb*. In July 1957 an unconfirmed – but probably authentic – length of 8·63 m *28 ft 4 in* was reported for an Estuarine crocodile shot by Mrs Kris Pawlowski of Mt Isa on MacArthur Bank in the Norman River, Queensland, Australia. Her husband Ron, a leading authority on this species, and a very reliable observer, was present when the crocodile was shot, and a photographic record existed until 1968. The 'official' Australian record is 6·15 m *20 ft 2 in* for a male harpooned in the MacArthur River near Barroloola, Northern Territories by Keith Adams, a film maker. At the present time there are four protected Estuarine crocodiles at the Bhitarkanika Wildlife Sanctuary, Orissa State, eastern India which measure more than 6 m *19 ft 8 in* in length. The largest individual is over 7 m *23 ft* long.

Captive ■ The largest crocodile ever held in captivity is an Estuarine/Siamese hybrid name 'Yai' (b. 10 Jun 1972) at the famous Samutprakarn Crocodile Farm and Zoo, Thailand. He measures 6 m *19 ft 8 in* in length and weighs 1114·27 kg *2465 lb*.

Smallest ■ Osborn's dwarf crocodile (*Osteolaemus osborni*), found in the upper region of the Congo River, west Africa rarely exceeds 1·2 m *3 ft 11 in* in length.

Oldest ■ The greatest age authenticated for a crocodilian is 66 years for a female American alligator (*Alligator mississipiensis*) which arrived at Adelaide Zoo, South Australia, on 5 Jun 1914 as a two-year-old, and died there on 26 Sep 1978 aged 66 years. Another female of this species named 'Smiley' at the Maritime Museum Aquarium, Gothenburg, Sweden, died on 10 Feb 1987 aged 65 years after the electricity heating its pool was accidentally turned down.

Rarest ■ The total population of the protected Chinese alligator (*Alligator sinensis*) of the lower Chang Jiang (Yangtse Kiang) River of Anhui, Zhejiang and Jiangsu Provinces, is currently estimated at 700–1000 individuals.

LIZARDS

Largest ■ See illustration below.

The longest lizard in the world is the slender Salvadori monitor (*Varanus salvadori*) of New Guinea which has been reliably measured up to 4·75 m *15 ft 7 in*. Nearly 70 per cent of the total length, however, is taken up by the tail.

Smallest ■ *Sphaerodactylus parthenopion*, a tiny gecko indigenous to the island of Virgin Gorda, one of the British Virgin Islands, is believed to be the world's smallest lizard. It is known only from 15 specimens, including some gravid females found between 10 and 16 Aug 1964. The three largest females measured 18 mm *0·67 in* from snout to vent, with a tail of approximately the same length. It is possible that another gecko, *S. elasmorhynchus*, may be even smaller. The only known specimen was an apparently mature female with a snout-vent length of 17 mm *0·67 in* and a tail of the same measurement. It was found on 15 Mar 1966 among the roots of a tree in the western part of the Massif de la Hotte in Haiti.

Oldest ■ The greatest age recorded for a lizard is more than 54 years for a male Slow worm (*Anguis fragilis*) kept in the Zoological Museum in Copenhagen, Denmark from 1892 until 1946.

Fastest ■ The highest speed measured for any reptile on land is 29 km/h *18 mph* for a Six-lined race runner (*Chemidophorus sexlineatus*) near McCormick, South Carolina, USA, in 1941.

CHELONIANS

Largest ■ The largest living chelonian is the Leatherback turtle (*Dermochelys coriacea*), which is circumglobal in distribution. The average adult measures 1·83–2·13 m *6–7 ft* from the tip of the beak to the end of the tail (carapace 1·52–1·67 m *5–5 ½ ft*), about 2·13 m *7 ft* across the front flippers and weighs anything up to 453 kg *1000 lb*. The greatest weight reliably recorded is 865 kg *1908 lb* for a male captured off Monterey, California, USA on 29 Aug 1961 which measured 2·54 m *8 ft 4 in* overall.

British ■ The largest Leatherback turtle ever recorded in British waters was a male found dead on the beach at Harlech, Gwynedd, Wales on 26 Sep 1988. It measured 2·44 m *8 ft* in total length and 2·44 m *8 ft* across the front flippers. It tipped the scales at an astonishing 961·1 kg *2120 lb*. It is now in the possession of the National Museum of Wales, Cardiff, where it will eventually be put on public display. Most museums refuse to exhibit large turtles because they can drip oil for up to 50 years.

Tortoise ■ The largest living tortoise is the Aldabra giant tortoise *Geochelone gigantea* of the Indian Ocean islands of Aldabra, Mauritius, and the Seychelles (introduced 1874). A male named 'Esmerelda', a long-time resident on Bird Island in the Seychelles, recorded a weight of 298 kg *657 lb* on 26 Feb 1989.

Smallest ■ The smallest marine turtle in the world is the Atlantic ridley (*Lepidochelys kempii*), which has a shell length of 50–70 cm *19·7–27·6 in* and does not exceed 36 kg *80 lb*.

Longest lived ■ The greatest authentic age recorded for a tortoise is over 152 years for a male Marion's tortoise (*Testudo sumeirii*), brought from the Seychelles to Mauritius in 1766 by the Chevalier de Fresne, who presented it to the Port Louis army garrison. This specimen (it went blind in 1908) was accidentally killed in 1918. The greatest proven age of a continuously observed tortoise is more than 116 years for a Mediterranean spur-thighed tortoise (*Testudo graeca*). The oldest turtle on record was an Alligator snapping turtle (*Macrochelys temminckii*) at Philadelphia Zoo, Pennsylvania, USA. When it was accidentally killed on 7 Feb 1949 it was 58 years 9 months 1 day.

Fastest ■ The highest speed claimed for any reptile in water is 35 km/h *22 mph* by a frightened Pacific leatherback turtle. The National Tortoise Championship record is 5·48 m *18 ft* up a 1:12 gradient in 43·7 sec (0·45 km/h *0·28 mph*) by 'Charlie' at Tickhill, South Yorks on 2 Jul 1977.

Slowest ■ In a recent 'speed' test carried out in the Seychelles a male giant tortoise (*Geochelone gigan-*

tea) could cover only 4·57 m *5 yd* in 43·5 sec (0·37 km/h *0·23 mph*) despite the enticement of a female.

Deepest dive ■ In May 1987 it was reported by Dr Scott Eckert that a Leatherback turtle (*Dermochelys coriacea*) fitted with a pressure-sensitive recording device had dived to a depth of 1200 m *3973 ft* off the Virgin Islands in the West Indies.

Rarest ■ The world's rarest chelonian is the protected Short-necked swamp tortoise (*Pseudemydura umbrina*), which is confined to Ellen Brook and Twin reserves near Perth, Western Australia. The total wild population is now only 20–25, with another 22 held at Perth Zoo.

SNAKES

Longest ■ The Reticulated python (*Python reticulatus*) of south-east Asia, Indonesia and the Philippines, regularly exceeds 6·24 m *20 ft 6 in*. In 1912 a specimen measuring 10 m *32 ft 9 ½ in* was shot near a mining camp on the north coast of Celebes in the Malay Archipelago.

Britain ■ The longest snake found in Britian is the Grass snake (*Natrix natrix*), which is found throughout southern England, parts of Wales and in Dumfries and Galloway, Scotland. The longest accurately measured specimen was probably a female killed in South Wales in 1887 which measured 1·775 m *5 ft 10 in*. In September 1816 a 2·13 m *7 ft* female was allegedly killed by a labourer at Trebun, Anglesey, North Wales and 'left for public curiosity at Llangefni', but further details are lacking.

In captivity ■ The longest (and heaviest) snake ever held in captivity was a female reticulated python named 'Colossus' who died in Highland Park Zoo, Pennsylvania, USA on 15 Apr 1963. She measured 8·68 m *28 ft 6 in* in length, and scaled 145 kg *320 lb* at her heaviest.

Shortest ■ The shortest snake in the world is the very rare thread snake *Leptotyphlops bilineata* which is known only from the islands of Martinique, Barbados and St Lucia in the West Indies. In one series of eight specimens the two longest both measured 108 mm *4·25 in*.

Heaviest ■ The Anaconda (*Eunectes murinus*) of tropical South America and Trinidad is nearly twice as heavy as a reticulated python (*Python reticulatus*) of the same length. A female shot in Brazil *c.* 1960 was not weighed, but as it measured 8·45 m *27 ft 9 in* in length with a girth of 111 cm *44 in* it must have scaled nearly 227 kg *500 lb*. The average adult length is 5·48–6·09 m *18–20 ft*.

The heaviest venomous snake is probably the Eastern diamondback rattlesnake (*Crotalus adamanteus*) of the south-eastern United States. One specimen measuring 2·36 m *7 ft 9 in* in length weighed 15 kg *34 lb*. Adult examples average 1·52–1·83 m *5–6 ft* in length and scale 5·5–6·8 kg *12–15 lb*. One huge individual measured 2·36 m *7 ft 9 in* in length and weighed 15·4 kg *34 lb*. The Western diamondback rattlesnake (*C. atrox*) of the southwestern United States is second to the Eastern diamondback in terms of size and a 2·26 m *7 ft 5 in*

example weighed 10·88 kg *24 lb*. The West African Gaboon viper (*Bitis gabonica*) of the tropical rain forests is probably even bulkier than these two rattlesnakes, but this species's average length of 1·22–1·52 m *4–5 ft* does not exceed 2·06 m *6 ft 9 in*. A 1·83 m *6 ft* long female weighed 11·34 kg *25 lb* and another female measuring 1·74 m *5 ft 8½ in* scaled 8·2 kg *18 lb* with an empty stomach. In February 1973 a posthumous weight of 12·75 kg *28 lb* was reported for a 4·39 m *14 ft 5 in* long King cobra (*Ophiophagus hannah*) at New York Zoological Park (Bronx Zoo). It had been ill for some time.

Oldest ■ The greatest irrefutable age recorded for a snake is 40 years 3 months and 14 days for a male Common boa (*Boa constrictor constrictor*) named 'Popeye' who died at Philadelphia Zoo, Pennsylvania, USA on 15 Apr 1977.

Fastest ■ The fastest-moving land snake is probably the slender Black mamba (*Dendroaspis polylepis*) of the eastern part of tropical Africa. A speed of 16–19 km/h *10–12 mph* may be possible for short bursts over level ground. The British grass snake has a maximum speed of 6·8 km/h *4·2 mph*.

Most venomous ■ The Sea snake (*Hydrophis belcheri*) has a myotoxic venom a hundred times as toxic as that of the Australian taipan (*Oxyuranus scutellatus*). The snake abounds round Ashmore Reef in the Timor Sea, off the coast of north-west Australia. The most venomous land snake is the 2 m *6 ft 6¾ in* long Smooth-scaled snake (*Parademansia microlepidotus*) of the Diamantina River and Cooper's Creek drainage basins in Channel County, Queensland and western NSW which has a venom nine times as toxic as that of the Tiger snake (*Notechis scutatus*) of South Australia and Tasmania. One specimen yielded 110 mg *0·00385 oz* of venom after milking, a quantity sufficient to kill 125 000 mice, but so far no human fatalities have been reported. More people die of snakebite in Sri Lanka than any comparable area in the world. An average of 800 people are killed annually on the island by snakes, and 95 per cent of the fatalities are caused by the Common krait (*Bungarus caeruleus*), the Sri Lankan cobra (*Naja naja naja*) and Russell's viper (*Vipera russelli pulchella*).

Britain ■ The only venomous snake in Britain is the adder (*Vipera berus*). Since 1890 ten people have died after being bitten by this snake, including six children. The most recent recorded death was on 1 Jul 1975 when a five-year-old was bitten at Callander, Perthshire and died 44 hours later. The longest recorded specimen was a female measuring 110·5 cm *43½ in* which was killed by Graham Per-

kins of Paradise Farm, Pontrilas, Hereford & Worcester in August 1977.

Longest venomous ■ The longest venomous snake in the world is the King cobra (*Ophiophagus hannah*), also called the Hamadryad, of south-east Asia and the Philippines, which has an average adult length of 3·65–4·57 m *12–15 ft*. A 5·54 m *18 ft 2 in* specimen, captured alive near Fort Dickson in the state of Negri Sembilan, Malaya in April 1937, later grew to 5·71 m *18 ft 9 in* in London Zoo. It was destroyed at the outbreak of war in 1939.

Shortest venomous ■ The Namaqua dwarf adder (*Bitis schneider*) of Namibia, south-west Africa has an average adult length of 200 mm *7·87 in*.

Longest fangs ■ The longest fangs of any snake are those of the highly venomous Gaboon viper (*Bitis gabonica*) of tropical Africa. In a 1·83 m *6 ft* long specimen they measured 50 mm *1·96 in*. On 12 Feb 1963 a Gaboon viper under severe stress sank its fangs into its own back at Philadelphia Zoo, Pennsylvania, USA and died as a result from traumatic injury to a vital organ. It did not, as has been widely reported, succumb to its own venom.

Rarest ■ The rarest snake is probably the Keelscaled boa (*Casarea dussumieri*) of Round Island, western Indian Ocean. In 1983 only 58 specimens were collected, marked and released and at least another nine specimens are held at Jersey Zoo, Channel Islands. The Round Island boa (*Bolyeria multicarinata*) is only known from two specimens collected in the past 40 years and probably became extinct in 1980.

Britain ■ The rarest snake of Britain's three indigenous species is the Smooth snake (*Coronella austriaca*) of southern England with a total wild population of *c.* 2000.

Amphibians *Amphibia*

Largest ■ The largest species of amphibian is the Chinese giant salamander (*Andrias davidianus*), which lives in north-eastern, central and southern China. The average adult measures 114 cm *3 ft 9 in* in length and weighs 25–30 kg *55–66 lb*. One specimen collected in Hunan Province measured 1·8 m *5 ft 11 in* in length and scaled 65 kg *143 lb*.

Britain ■ The largest British amphibian is the Common toad (*Bufo bufo*) which is found throughout England, Scotland and Wales. A huge female collected from Marlpit Pond, Boxley, Kent, measured 99 mm *3·89 in* snout to vent and weighed 118 g *4·16 oz*.

Smallest ■ The smallest known amphibian is the Short-headed toad *Psyllophryne didactyla* (family Brachycephalidae) of south-eastern Brazil, adult specimens having an average snout-vent length of 9·8 mm *0·38 in*.

Britain ■ The smallest found in Britain is the Palmate newt (*Triturus helveticus*). Adult specimens measure 7·5–9·2 cm *2·95–3·62 in* in length and weigh up to 2·39 g *0·083 oz*. The Natterjack or Running toad (*Bufo calamita*) has a maximum snout-vent length of only 80 mm *3·14 in* (female) but it is a bulkier animal.

Oldest ■ The greatest authentic age recorded for an amphibian is 55 years for a Japanese giant salamander which died in Amsterdam Zoo, Netherlands in 1881.

Longest gestation ■ The viviparous Alpine black salamander (*Salamandra atra*) has a gestation period of up to 38 months at altitudes above 1400 m *4600 ft* in the Swiss Alps, but this drops to 24–26 months at lower altitudes.

Rarest ■ Only five specimens of the Israel painted frog (*Discoglossus nigriventer*) of Lake Huleh have been reported since 1940.

Britain ■ The *introduced* Green tree frog (*Hyla arborea*) is now confined to a single site on the outskirts of London.

Highest and lowest ■ The greatest altitude at which an amphibian has been found is 8000 m *26 246 ft* for a Common toad collected in the Himalayas. This species has also been found at a depth of 340 m *1115 ft* in a coal mine.

Most poisonous ■ The most active known poison is the batrachotoxin derived from the skin secretions of the Golden poison-dart frog (*Phyllobates terribilis*) of western Colombia, South America which was not discovered until 1973. Its skin secretions are at least 20 times more toxic than those of any other known dart-poison frog (human handlers have to wear thick gloves), and an average adult specimen contains enough poison (1900 micrograms) to kill nearly 1500 people. Rather surprisingly, this species is preyed upon by the frog-eating snake *Leimadophis epinephelus*, which is thought to be immune to its poison.

Largest frog ■
The largest known frog is the rare Goliath frog (*Conraua goliath*) of Cameroun and Equatorial Guinea. A female weighing 3306 g *7 lb 4·5 oz* was caught in the River Mbia, Equatorial Guinea on 23 Aug 1960. It had a snout-vent length of 34 cm *13·38 in* and measured 81·5 cm *32·08 in* overall with legs extended. A slightly longer female (35·6 cm *14 in*) collected in the same river in December 1966 weighed 3100 g *6 lb 13¼ oz.*

Britain ■ The largest frog found in Britain is the *introduced* Marsh frog (*Rana r. ridibunda*). Adult males have been measured up to 96 mm *3·77 in* snout-vent, and adult females up to 133 mm *5·25 in*, the weight ranging from 60 to 95 g *1·7–3 oz.*

The largest captive frog living in Britain today is a male African bull frog (*Pyxicephalus adspersus*) named 'Colossus' (b. 1978), owned by Mr Steve Crabtree of Southsea, Hants. It has a snout-vent length of 22·2 cm *8¾ in*, a girth of 45·7 cm *18 in* and weighs 1·89 kg *4 lb 3 oz.*

Smallest frog ■
The smallest frog in the world, and the second smallest anuran, is *Sminthillus limbatus*, of Cuba. Adult specimens have a snout-vent length of 8·5–12·4 mm *0·44–0·48 in.*

Longest jump ■
(*Competition frog jumps are invariably the aggregate of three consecutive leaps*). The greatest distance covered by a frog in a triple jump is 10·3 m *33 ft 5½ in* by a South African sharp-nosed frog (*Ptychadena oxyrhynchus*) named 'Santjie' at a frog Derby held at Lurula Natal Spa, Paulpietersburg, Natal on 21 May 1977. At the famous annual Calaveras Jumping Jubilee held at Angels Camp, California, USA on 18 May 1986 an American bull frog (*Rana catesbeiana*) called 'Rosie the Ribeter', owned and trained by Lee Giudicci of Santa Clara, California, USA leapt 6·55 m *21 ft 5¾ in*. 'Santjie' would have been ineligible for this contest because entrants must measure at least 10·16 cm *4 in* 'stem to stern'.

Largest toad ■
The largest known toad is the Marine toad (*Bufo marinus*) of tropical South America and Queensland, Australia (introduced). An average adult specimen weighs 453 g *1 lb*. The largest toad ever recorded was a female Marine toad (*Bufo marinus*) nick-named 'Totally Awesome' (Toad A) owned by Blank Park Zoo, Des Moines, Iowa, USA. She was purchased from an animal dealer in Miami, Florida on 11 May 1983, when she weighed about 0·9 kg *2 lb*, and attained a peak 2·31 kg *5 lb 1½ oz* (snout-vent length 24·13 cm *9½ in*) on 19 Nov 1987. She died on 8 Apr 1988, most probably from old age.

Britain ■ The largest toad and heaviest amphibian found in Britain is the Common toad. (See Largest British amphibian.)

Smallest toad ■
The smallest toad in the world is the Short-headed toad. (See Smallest amphibian.)

Fishes

Agnatha, Gnathostomata

Largest marine ■
The largest fish in the world is the rare plankton-feeding Whale shark (*Rhincodon typus*), which is found in the warmer areas of the Atlantic, Pacific and Indian Oceans. The longest scientifically-measured one on record was a 12·65 m *41½ ft* specimen captured off Baba Island near Karachi, Pakistan on 11 Nov 1949. It measured 7 m *23 ft* round the thickest part of the body and weighed an estimated 15 tonnes.

British Isles ■ An 11·12 m *36 ft 6 in* Basking shark (*Cetorhinus maximus*) was washed ashore at Brighton, East Sussex in 1806. It weighed an estimated 8 tonnes.

Carnivorous ■ The largest carnivorous fish (excluding plankton-eaters) is the comparatively rare Great white shark (*Carcharodon carcharias*), also called the 'Man-eater'. Adult specimens (females are larger than males) average 4·3–4·6 m

14–15 ft in length and generally scale between 522–771 kg *1150–1700 lb*, but larger individuals have been recorded. The length and weight record is held by a 6·4 m *21 ft* female caught off Castillo de Cojimar, Cuba, in May 1945. It weighed 3313 kg *7302 lb* and yielded a 455·8 kg *1005 lb* liver. On 17 Apr 1987 a female Great white shark with a 'straight-line' measurement of 7·13 m *23 ft 5 in* and an estimated weight of 3000 kg *6613 lb* was caught off Malta by Alfred Cutajar. Unfortunately the preserved jaws do not confirm this extreme measurement. A formula based on the size of the shark's teeth and the perimeter measurement of its upper jaw indicate a more acceptable measurement of 5·33–5·48 m *17½–18 ft.*

Bony ■ The longest of the bony or 'true' fishes (Pisces) is the Oarfish (*Regalecus glesne*), also called the 'King of the Herrings', which has a worldwide distribution. In *c.* 1885 a 7·6 m *25 ft* long example weighing 272 kg *600 lb* was caught by fishermen off Pemaquid Point, Maine, USA. Another Oarfish, seen swimming off Asbury Park, New Jersey, USA by a team of scientists from the Sandy Hook Marine Laboratory on 18 Jul 1963, was estimated to measure 15·2 m *50 ft* in length. The heaviest bony fish in the world is the Ocean sunfish (*Mola mola*), which is found in all tropical, sub-tropical and temperate waters. On 18 Sep 1908 a specimen was accidentally struck by the SS *Fiona* off Bird Island about 65 km *40 miles* from Sydney, New South Wales, Australia and towed to Port Jackson. It measured 4·26 m *14 ft* between the anal and dorsal fins and weighed 2235 kg *4927 lb.*

The largest bony fish found in British waters is the Ocean sunfish. A specimen weighing 363 kg *800 lb* stranded near Montrose, Angus on 14 Dec 1960 was sent to the Marine Research Institute in Aberdeen.

Largest freshwater ■
The largest fish which spends its whole life in fresh or brackish water is the rare Pa beuk or Pla buk (*Pangasianodon gigas*). This *was* exceeded by the European catfish or Wels (*Silurus glanis*) in earlier times (in the 19th century lengths up to 4·57 m *15 ft* and weights up to 336·3 kg *720 lb* were reported for Russian specimens), but today anything over 1·83 m *6 ft* and 91 kg *200 lb* is considered large. The Arapaima (*Arapaima glanis*), also called the Pirarucu, found in the Amazon and other South American rivers and often claimed to be the largest freshwater fish, averages 2 m *6½ ft* and 68 kg *150 lb*. The largest 'authentically recorded' measured 2·48 m *8 ft 1½ in* in length and weighed 147 kg *325 lb*. It was caught in the Rio Negro, Brazil in 1836. In September 1978, a Nile perch (*Lates niloticus*) weighing 188·6 kg *416 lb* was netted in the eastern part of Lake Victoria, Kenya.

British ■ The largest fish ever caught in a British river was a Common sturgeon (*Acipenser sturio*) weighing 230 kg *507½ lb* and measuring 2·74 m *9 ft*, which was accidentally netted in the Severn at Lydney, Glos on 1 Jun 1937. Larger specimens have been taken at sea – notably one weighing 317 kg *700 lb* and 3·18 m *10 ft 5 in* long netted by the trawler *Ben Urie* off Orkney and landed on 18 Oct 1956.

Smallest marine ■
The shortest recorded marine fish – and the shortest known vertebrate – is the dwarf goby *Trimmatom nanus* of the Chagos Archipelago, central Indian Ocean. In one series of 92 specimens collected by the 1978–9 Joint Services Chagos Research Expedition of the British Armed Forces the adult males averaged 8·6 mm *0·338 in* in length and the adult females 8·9 mm *0·35 in*. The lightest of all vertebrates and the smallest catch possible for any fisherman is the dwarf goby *Schindleria praematurus* from Samoa which measures 12–19 mm *0·47–0·74 in*. Mature specimens have been known to weigh only 2 mg, which is equivalent to *14·175 to the oz.*

British ■ Guillet's goby (*Lebutus guilleti*) does not exceed 24 mm *0·94 in*. It has been recorded from the English Channel, the west coast of Ireland and the Irish Sea.

Shark ■ The Spined pygmy shark (*Squaliolus*

laticaudus) of the western Pacific matures at 150 mm *5·9 in* in length.

Smallest freshwater ■
The shortest and lightest freshwater fish is the Dwarf pygmy goby *Pandaka pygmaea*, a colourless and nearly transparent species found in the streams and lakes of Luzon in the Philippines. Adult males measure only 7·5–9·9 mm *0·28–0·38 in* in length and weigh 4–5 mg *0·00014–0·00018 oz*. The world's smallest commercial fish is the now endangered Sinarapan (*Mistichthys luzonensis*), a goby found only in Lake Buhi, Luzon, Philippines. Adult males measure 10–13 mm *0·39–0·51 in* in length, and a dried 454 g *1 lb* fish cake contains about 70 000 of them!

Fastest ■
The maximum swimming speed of a fish is dependent on its length and temperature. The Cosmopolitan sailfish (*Istiophorus platypterus*) is considered to be the fastest species of fish over short distances, although the practical difficulties of measuring make data extremely difficult to secure. In a series of speed trials carried out at the Long Key Fishing Camp, Florida, USA, one sailfish took out 91 m *100 yd* of line in 3 sec which is equivalent to a velocity of 109 km/h *68 mph* (compare 96 km/h *60 mph* for the cheetah).

Some American fishermen believe that the Bluefin tuna (*Thunnus thynnus*) is the fastest fish in the sea, and burst speeds up to 56 knots (*104km/h*) have been claimed for this species, but the highest speed recorded so far is 70 km/h *43·4 mph* in a 20-second dash. The yellowfin tuna (*Thunnus albacares*) and the wahoo (*Acanthocybium solandri*) are also extremely fast, having been timed at 74·59 km/h *46·35 mph* and 77·05 km/h *47·88 mph* resepectively during 10–20 second sprints.

Oldest ■
Aquaria are of too recent origin to be able to establish with certainty which species of fish can be regarded as being the longest lived. Early indications are, however, that it may be the Lake sturgeon (*Acipenser fulvescens*) of North America. In one study of the growth rings (annuli) of 966 specimens caught in the Lake Winnebago region, Wisconsin, USA between 1951 and 1954 the oldest sturgeon was found to be a male 2·01 m *6 ft 7 in*), which gave a reading of 82 years and was still growing. The perch-like marine fish *Notothenia neglecta* of the Antarctic Ocean, whose blood contains a natural anti-freeze, is reported to live up to 150 years, but this claim has not yet been verified. In July 1974 a growth ring count of 228 years (sic) was reported for a female Koi fish, a form of fancy carp, named 'Hanako' living in a pond in Higashi Shirakawa, Gifu Prefecture, Japan, but the greatest authoritatively accepted age for this species is 'more than 50 years'. In 1948 the death was reported of an 88-year-old female European eel (*Anguilla anguilla*) named 'Putte' in the aquarium at Halsingborg Museum, southern Sweden. She was allegedly born in the Sargasso Sea, in the North Atlantic, in 1860, and was caught in a river as a three-year-old elver.

Oldest goldfish ■
Goldfish (*Carassius auratus*) have been reported to live for over 50 years in China.

British ■ A specimen named 'Fred', owned by Mr A. R. Wilson of Worthing, West Sussex, died on 1 Aug 1980, aged 41 years.

Shortest-lived ■
The shortest-lived fishes are probably certain species of the sub-order Cyprinodontei (Killifish), found in Africa and South America, which normally live about eight months.

Most abundant ■
The most abundant species is probably the 76 mm *3 in* long deep-sea Bristlemouth *Cyclothone elongata* which has a world-wide distribution. It would take about 500 of them to weigh 0·45 kg *1 lb*.

Deepest ■
The greatest depth from which a fish has been recovered is 8300 m *27 230 ft* in the Puerto Rico Trench (8366 m *27 488 ft*) in the Atlantic by Dr Gilbert L. Voss of the US research vessel *John Elliott* who took a 16·5 cm *6½ in* long *Bassogigas profundissimus* in April 1970. It was only the fifth such

brotulid ever caught. Dr Jacques Piccard and Lieutenant Don Walsh, US Navy, reported they saw a sole-like fish about 33 cm *1 ft* long (tentatively identified as *Chascanopsetta lugubris*) from the bathyscaphe *Trieste* at a depth of 35 820 ft *10 917 m* in the Challenger Deep (Marianas Trench) in the western Pacific on 24 Jan 1960. This sighting, however, has been questioned by some authorities, who still regard the brotulids of the genus *Bassogigas* as the deepest-living vertebrates.

Most eggs ■ The Ocean sunfish (*Mola mola*) produces up to 30 000 000 eggs, each of them measuring about 1·3 mm *0·05 in* in diameter, at a single spawning.

Least eggs ■ The mouth-brooding cichlid *Tropheus moorii* of Lake Tanganyika, east Africa, produces seven eggs or less during normal reproduction.

Most valuable ■ The world's most valuable fish is the Russian sturgeon (*Huso huso*). One 1227 kg *2706 lb* female caught in the Tikhaya Sosna River in 1924 yielded 245 kg *541 lb* of best-quality caviar which would be worth £189 350 on today's market.

The 76 cm *30 in* long Ginrin Showa koi which won supreme championship in nationwide Japanese koi shows in 1976, 1977, 1979 and 1980 was sold two years later for 17 000 000 yen. In March 1986 this ornamental carp was acquired by Mr Derry Evans, owner of the Kent Koi Centre near Sevenoaks, Kent for an undisclosed sum, but the 15-year-old fish died five months later. It has since been stuffed and mounted to preserve its beauty.

Most venomous ■ See below.

Most ferocious ■ The razor-toothed piranhas of the genera *Serrasalmus, Pygocentrus* and *Pygopristis* are the most ferocious freshwater fish in the world. They live in the sluggish waters of the large rivers of South America, and will attack any creature, regardless of size, if it is injured or making a commotion in the water. On 19 Sep 1981 more than 300 people were reportedly killed and eaten when an over-loaded passenger-cargo boat capsized and sank as it was docking at the Brazilian port of Obidos. According to one official only 178 of the estimated people aboard the boat survived.

Most electric ■ The most powerful electric fish is the Electric eel (*Electrophorus electricus*), which is found in the rivers of Brazil, Colombia, Venezuela and Peru. An average-sized specimen can discharge 400 volts at 1 ampere, but measurements up to 650 volts have been recorded.

Starfishes *Asteroidea*

Largest ■ The largest of the 1600 known species of starfish in terms of total arm span is the very fragile brisingid *Midgardia xandaros*. A specimen collected by the Texas A & M University research vessel *Alaminos* in the southern part of the Gulf of Mexico in the late summer of 1968 measured 1380 mm *54·33 in* tip to tip, but the diameter of its disc was only 26 mm *1·02 in*. Its dry weight was 70 g *2·46 oz*. The heaviest species of starfish is the five-armed *Thromidia catalai* of the western Pacific. One specimen collected off Ilot Amedee, New Caledonia on 14 Sep 1969 and later deposited in Noumea Aquarium weighed an estimated 6 kg *13·2 lb* (total arm span 630 mm *24·8 in*).

British ■ The largest starfish found in British waters is the Spiny starfish (*Marthasterias glacialis*). In January 1979 Jonathon MacNeil from Isle of Barra, Western Isles, found a specimen on the beach which originally spanned 76·2 cm *30 in*.

Smallest ■ The smallest known starfish is the asterinid sea star *Patiriella parvivipara* discovered by Wolfgang Zeidler on the west coast of the Eyre peninsula, South Australia in 1975. It has a maximum radius of only 4·7 mm *0·18 in* and a diameter of less than 9 mm *0·35 in*.

Most destructive ■ The Crown of Thorns (*Acanthaster planci*) of the Indo-Pacific region and the Red Sea can destroy 300–400 cm² *46·5–62 in²* of coral a day.

Deepest ■ The greatest depth from which a starfish has been recovered is 7584 m *24 881 ft* for a

> **Most venomous fish ●** The most venomous fish in the world are the Stonefish (Synanceidae) of the tropical waters of the Indo-Pacific, and in particular *Synanceja horrida* which has the largest venom glands of any known fish. Direct contact with the spines of its fins, which contain a strong neurotoxic poison, often proves fatal. (Photo: Paysan Archive)

specimen of *Porcellanaster ivanovi* collected by the USSR research ship *Vityaz* in the Marianas Trench, in the west Pacific, *c.* 1962.

Crustaceans *Crustacea*

(Crabs, lobsters, shrimps, prawns, crayfish, barnacles, water fleas, fish lice, woodlice, sandhoppers, krill, etc.)

Largest marine ■ The largest of all crustaceans (although not the heaviest) is the Taka-ashi-gani or Giant spider crab (*Macrocheira kaempferi*), also called the Stilt crab, which is found in deep waters off the south-eastern coast of Japan. Mature specimens usually have a body measuring 254 × 305 mm *10 × 12 in* and a claw span of 2·43–2·74 m *8–9 ft*, but unconfirmed measurements up to 5·79 m *19 ft* have been reported. A specimen with a claw span of 3·69 m *12 ft 1 ½ in* weighed 18·6 kg *41 lb*.

The largest species of lobster, and the heaviest of all crustaceans, is the American or North Atlantic lobster (*Homarus americanus*). On 11 Feb 1977 a specimen weighing 20·14 kg *44 lb 6 oz* and measuring 1·06 m *3 ft 6 in* from the end of the tail-fan to the tip of the largest claw was caught off Nova Scotia, Canada, and later sold to a New York restaurant owner.

Europe ■ The largest crustacean found in British waters is the Common or European lobster (*Homarus vulgaris*), which averages 900–1360 g *2–3 lb*. In June 1931 an outsized specimen weighing 5·80 kg *20 ½ lb* and measuring 1·26 m *4 ft 1 ½ in* in total length was caught in a caisson during the construction of No 3 jetty at Fowey, Cornwall. Its crushing claw weighed 1188 g *2 lb 10 oz* after the meat had been removed. Another European lobster weighing a record 10 kg *22 lb* was caught off the west coast of Floroe, Norway, by an amateur fisherman in March 1988, but died before it reached Bergen in October 1988. The largest crab found in British waters is the Edible or Great crab (*Cancer pagurus*). In 1895 a crab measuring 279 mm *11 in* across the shell and weighing 6·35 kg *14 lb* was caught off the coast of Cornwall.

Smallest ■ Water fleas of the genus *Alonella* may measure less than 0·25 mm *0·0098 in* in length. They are found in British waters. The smallest known lobster is the Cape lobster (*Homarus capensis*) of South Africa, which measures 10–12 cm *3·9–4·7 in* in total length.

Oldest ■ Very large specimens of the American lobster (*Homarus americanus*) may be as much as 50 years old.

Deepest ■ The greatest depth from which a crustacean has been recovered is 10 500 m *34 450 ft* for *live* amphipods from the Challenger Deep, Marianas Trench, West Pacific by the US research vessel *Thomas Washington* in November 1980. Amphipods and isopods have also been collected in the Ecuadorean Andes at a height of 4053 m *13 300 ft.*

Largest concentration ■ The largest single concentration of crustaceans ever recorded was an enormous swarm of krill (*Euphausia superba*) estimated to weigh 10 million tonnes and tracked by US scientists off Antarctica in March 1981.

Arachnids *Arachnida*
SPIDERS (order Araneae)

Largest ■ The world's largest known spider is the Goliath bird-eating spider (*Theraphosa leblondi*) of the coastal rainforests of Surinam, Guyana (formerly British Guyana) and French Guiana, north-eastern South America; isolated specimens have also been reported from Venezuela and Brazil. In February 1985 Charles J Seiderman of New York City, NY, USA, captured a huge female just north of Paramarido, Surinam. This spider had a maximum leg span of 266·7 mm *10¹/₂ in* (total body length 102 mm *4 in*), 25 mm *1 in* long fangs and weighed a peak 122·2 g *4·3 oz* before its death from moulting problems in Jan 1986. An outsized male example collected by members of the Pablo San Martin Expedition at Rio Cavro, Venezuela in April 1965 had a leg span of 280 mm *11·02 in*, but the female is built on much heavier lines.

British ■ Of the 617 known species of British spider covering an estimated population of over 500 000 000 000 the Cardinal spider (*Tegenaria gigantea*) of southern England has the greatest leg span. In October 1985 Mrs Lyndsay Jarrett of Marston Meysey, Wilts collected an outsized female in her home with a span of 139 mm *5·5 in.*

The well-known 'Daddy Longlegs' spider (*Pholcus phalangioides*) rarely exceeds 114 mm *4¹/₂ in* in leg span, but one outsized specimen collected in England measured 15·2 cm *6 in* across. The heaviest spider found in Britain is the orb weaver *Araneus quadratus.* On 10 Sep 1979 a female weighing 2·25 g *0·079 oz* was collected at Lavington, West Sussex by J. R. Parker.

Smallest ■ The smallest known spider is *Patu marplesi* (family Symphytognathidae) of Western Samoa in the Pacific. The type specimen (male) found in moss at *c.* 600 m *2000 ft* in Madolelei, Upolu, Western Samoa in Jan 1965 measured 0·43 mm *0·017 in* overall, which means that it was about the size of a full-stop on this page.

Britain ■ The extremely rare money spider *Glyphesis cottonae* is found only in a swamp near Beaulieu Road Station, Hampshire and on Thursley Common, Surrey. Adult specimens of both sexes have a body length of 1 mm *0·039 in.*

Most common ■ The Crab spiders (family Thomisidae) have a world-wide distribution.

Britain ■ The orb weaver *Araneus diadematus* has been recorded from all but four counties in Great Britain and Ireland.

Rarest ■ The most elusive of all spiders are the rare Trapdoor spiders of the genus *Liphistius*, which are found in south-east Asia.

Britain ■ The most elusive spiders in Britain are the four species which are known only from the type specimen. These are the jumping spiders *Salticus mutabilis* (one male Bloxworth, Dorset, 1860) and *Heliophanus melinus* (one female Bloxworth, 1870);

the Crab spider *Philodromus buxi* (one female Bloxworth, pre-1879); and the Cobweb spider *Robertus insignis* (one male Norwich, 1906).

Oldest ■ The longest-lived of all spiders are the primitive *Mygalomorphae* (tarantulas and allied species). One female therasophid collected in Mexico in 1935 lived for an estimated 26–28 years. The longest-lived British spider is probably the Purse web spider (*Atypus affinis*). One specimen was kept in a greenhouse for nine years.

Fastest ■ The fastest-moving arachnids are the long-legged Sun-spiders of the genus *Solpuga*, which live in the arid semi-desert regions of Africa and the Middle East. They feed on geckos and other lizards and can reach speeds of over 16 km/h *10 mph.*

Largest webs ■ Aerial webs spun by the tropical orb weavers of the genus *Nephila* have been measured up to 573 cm *18 ft 9³/₄ in* in circumference.

Smallest webs ■ The smallest webs are spun by spiders such as *Glyphesis cottonae* (see Britain's smallest) which cover about 480 mm *0·75 in².*

Most venomous ■ The world's most venomous spiders are the Brazilian wandering spiders of the genus *Phoneutria*, and particularly *P. fera*, which has the most active neurotoxic venom of any living spider. These large and highly aggressive creatures frequently enter human dwellings and hide in clothing or shoes. When disturbed they bite furiously several times, and hundreds of accidents involving these species are reported annually. Fortunately an effective antivenin is available, and when deaths do occur they are usually children under the age of seven.

SCORPIONS (Scorpiones)

Largest ■ The largest living scorpion (750 species) is *Heterometrus swammerdami* of southern India, males averaging 180 mm *7·1 in* from the tips of the pincers to the end of the sting. A specimen collected in Madras Province on 14 Sep 1869, and now in the possession of the Bombay Natural History Society, measures 247 mm *9·7 in* (tip of head to point of sting 187 mm *7·4 in*, length of body 82 mm *3·2 in*). Another one found under a rock in the village of Krishnarajapuram, West Bengal during the Second World War and taken to the local military hospital for examination was even larger, measuring 292 mm *11·5 in.*

Smallest ■ The smallest scorpion in the world is *Microbothus pusillus* from the Red Sea coast, which measures about 13 mm *0·5 in* in total length.

Most venomous ■ The most venomous scorpion in the world is the Palestine yellow scorpion (*Leiurus quinquestriatus*), which ranges from the eastern part of North Africa through the Middle East to the shores of the Red Sea. Happily the amount of venom it delivers is very small (0·255 mg *0·000 009 oz*) and adult lives are seldom endangered, but it has been responsible for a number of fatalities among young children under the age of five.

Insects *Insecta*

Heaviest ■ The heaviest living insects are the Goliath beetles (family Scarabaeidae) of Equatorial Africa. The largest members of the group are *Goliathus regius, G. goliathus* (=*G. giganteus*) and *G. druryi*, and in one series of fully-grown males (females are smaller) the lengths from the tips of the small frontal horns to the end of the abdomen measured up to 110 mm *4·33 in* and the weights ranged from 70 to 100 g *2·5–3·5 oz.* The Elephant beetles (*Megasoma*) of central America and the West Indies attain the greatest dimensions in terms of volume, but they lack the massive build-up of heavy chiton forming the thorax and anterior sternum of the Goliaths, and this gives them a distinct weight advantage.

Britain ■ The heaviest insect found in Britain is the Stag beetle (*Lucanus cervus*) which is widely distributed over southern England. The largest specimen on record was a male collected at Sheerness, Kent in 1871 and now preserved in the British Museum (Natural History), which measures 87·4 mm *3·04 in* in length (body plus mandibles) and probably weighed over 6 g *0·21 oz* when alive.

Largest cockroach ■ The world's largest cockroach is *Megaloblatta longipennis* of Colombia, South America. A preserved female in the collection of Akira Yokokura of Yamagata, Japan measures 97 mm *3·81 in* in length and 45 mm *1·77 in* across.

Longest ■ The longest insect in the world is the Giant stick-insect *Pharnacia serratipes* of Indonesia, females of which have been measured up to 330 mm *13 in.* The longest known beetle (excluding antennae) is the Hercules beetle (*Dynastes hercules*) of Central and South America, which has been measured up to 190 mm *7·48 in.* More than half the length however, is taken up by the prothoracic horn.

Smallest ■ The smallest insects recorded so far are the 'Feather-winged' beetles of the family Ptiliidae (=Trichopterygidae) and the 'Battledore-wing fairy flies' (parasitic wasps) of the family Mymaridae. They are smaller than some of the protozoa (single-celled animals). The male Bloodsucking banded louse *Enderleinellus zonatus*, ungorged, and the parasitic wasp *Caraphractus cinctus* may each weigh as little as 0·005 mg, or *5 670 000 to an oz.* Eggs of the latter each weigh 0·0002 mg or *141 750 000 to an oz.*

Rarest ■ It has recently been estimated that there may be as many as 30 million species of insect – more than all other phylums and classes put together – but thousands are known only from a single or type specimen.

Fastest flying ■ Experiments have proved that the widely publicised claim by an American scientist in 1926 that the deer bot-fly (*Cephenemyia pratti*) could attain a speed of 1316 km/h *818 mph* (*sic*) at an altitude of 3657 m *12 000 ft* was wildly exaggerated. If true, the fly would have had to develop the equivalent of 1·1 kW *1·5 hp* and consume 1¹/₂ times its own weight in food per second to acquire the energy that would be needed, and even if this were possible it would still be crushed by the air pressure and incinerated by the friction. Acceptable modern experiments have now established that the highest maintainable air speed of any insect including the Deer bot-fly, hawk moths (*Sphingidae*), horse flies (*Tabanus bovinus*) and some tropical butterflies (*Hesperiidae*) is 39 km/h *24 mph*, rising to a maximum of 58 km/h *36 mph* for the Australian dragon fly *Austrophlebia costalis*, for short bursts.

Fastest moving ■ The fastest moving insects are large tropical cockroaches (*Dictyoptera*), and specimens measuring about 30 mm *1·18 in* in length have been timed at 120–130 cm/sec *4·28–4·64km/h 2·68–2·90 mph* or 40–43 body lengths per second.

Highest g force ■ The Click beetle (*Athous haemorrhoidalis*) (a common British species) averages 400 g when 'jack-knifing' into the air to escape predators. One example measuring 12 mm *0·47 in* in length and weighing 40 mg *0·00014 oz* which jumped to a height of 30 cm *11 ¾ in* was calculated to have 'endured' a peak brain deceleration of 2300 g by the end of the movement.

Oldest ■ The longest-lived insects are the Splendour beetles (Buprestidae). On 27 May 1983 a *Buprestis aurulenta* appeared from the staircase timber in the home of Mr W. Euston of Prittlewell, Southend-on-Sea, Essex after 47 years as a larva.

Loudest ■ The loudest of all insects is the male cicada (family Cicadidae). At 7400 pulses/min its tymbal organs produce a noise (officially described by the US Department of Agriculture as 'Tsh-ee-EEEE-e-ou') detectable more than a quarter of a mile *400 m* distant.

British ■ The only British species is the very rare Mountain cicada (*Cicadetta montana*), which is confined to the New Forest area in Hampshire.

Fastest wing beat ■ The fastest wing beat of any insect under natural conditions is 62 760 per min by a tiny midge of the genus *Forcipomyia*. In experiments with truncated wings at a temperature of 37° C *98·6° F* the rate increased to 133 080 beats/min. The muscular contraction–expansion cycle in 0·00045 or 1/2218th of a sec further represents the fastest muscle movement ever measured.

Slowest wing beat ■ The slowest wing beat of any insect is 300 per min by the Swallowtail butterfly (*Papilio machaon*). The average is 460–636 per min.

Largest termite mound ■ In 1968 W. Page photographed a specimen south of Horgesia, Somalia estimated to be 8·7 m *28·5 ft* tall.

DRAGONFLIES
Largest ■ *Megaloprepus caeruleata* of Central and South America has been measured up to 120 mm *4·72 in* across the wings and 191 mm *7·52 in* in body length.

Britain ■ *Anax imperator* has a wing span measurement of up to 106 mm *4·17 in.*

Smallest ■ The smallest dragonfly in the world is *Agriocnemis naia* of Burma. A specimen in the British Museum (Natural History) had a wing expanse of 17·6 mm *0·69 in* and a body length of 18 mm *0·71 in.*

Britain ■ The smallest is *Lestes dryas*, which has a body length of 20–25 mm *0·78–0·98 in.*

FLEAS
Largest ■ Siphonapterologists recognise 1830 varieties, of which the largest known is *Hystrichopsylla schefferi*, which was described from a single specimen taken from the nest of a Mountain beaver (*Aplodontia rufa*) at Puyallup, Washington State, USA in 1913. Females measure up to 8 mm *0·31 in* in length, which is the diameter of a pencil.

Britain ■ The largest flea (61 species) found in Britain is the Mole and vole flea (*H. talpae*)–females have been measured up to 6 mm *0·23 in.*

Longest jump ■ The champion jumper among fleas is the Common flea (*Pulex irritans*). In one American experiment carried out in 1910 a specimen allowed to leap at will performed a long jump of 330 mm *13 in* and a high jump of 197 mm *7 ¾ in.* In jumping 130 times its own height a flea subjects itself to a force of 200 g.

BUTTERFLIES AND MOTHS (order Lepidoptera)

Largest ■ The largest known butterfly is the protected Queen Alexandra's birdwing (*Ornithop-*

tera alexandrae) which is restricted to the Popondetta Plain in Papua New Guinea. Females may have a wing span exceeding 280 mm *11·02 in* and weigh over 25 g *0·88 oz.* The largest moth in the world (although not the heaviest) is the Hercules moth (*Cosdinoscera hercules*) of tropical Australia and New Guinea. A wing area of up to 263·2 cm² *40·8 in²* and a wing span of 280 mm *11 in* have been recorded. In 1948 an unconfirmed measurement of 360 mm *14·17 in* was reported for a female captured near the post office at the coastal town of Innisfail, Queensland, Australia, now in the Oberthur collection. The rare Owlet moth (*Thysania agrippina*) of Brazil has been measured up to 308 mm *12·16 in* wing span in the case of a female taken in 1934 and now in the collection of John G. Powers in Ontario, Canada.

Britain ■ The largest butterfly found in Britain is the Monarch butterfly (*Danaus plexippus*), also called the Milkweed or Black-veined brown butterfly, a rare vagrant which breeds in the southern United States and Central America. It has a wing span of up to 127 mm *5 in* and weighs about 1 g *0·04 oz.* The largest *native* butterfly is the Swallowtail (*Papilio*

machaon britannicus), females of which have a wing span up to 100 mm *3·93 in.* This species is now confined to fens in Suffolk, Cambs and the Norfolk Broads.

The largest (but not the heaviest) of the 21 000 species of insect found in Britain is the very rare Death's head hawkmoth (*Acherontia atropos*). One female found dead in a garden at Tiverton, Devon in 1931 had a wing span of 145 mm *5·75 in* and weighed nearly 3 g *0·10 oz.* On 9 Jun 1988 a giant moth with a wingspan of 15·2 cm *6 in* was found by workmen at a plant hire firm in Wolleston, Northants. It was later identified as a Great peacock silk moth (*Saturnia*

Heaviest insects ● The heaviest living insects are the Goliath beetles (family Scarabaeidae) of Equatorial Africa. The largest members of the group are *Goliathus regius*, *G. goliathus* (=*G. giganteus*), and *G. druryi*. In one series of fully-grown males (females are smaller) the weight ranged from 70 to 100 g *2·5–3·5 oz.* (Photo: Paysan Archive)

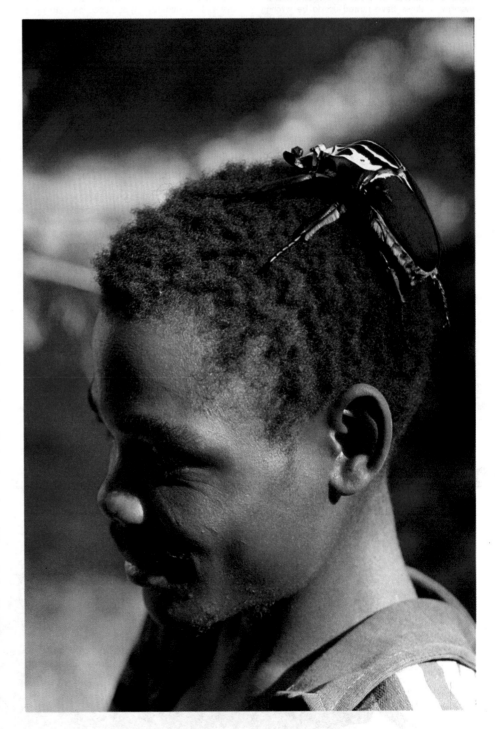

pyri) which had probably escaped from a butterfly house.

Smallest ■ The recently discovered *Micropsyche ariana* has a wing span of 7 mm *0·275 in*. The type specimen was collected on Mt Khwajaghar in the Koh-i-Baba range, Afghanistan. The smallest of the 140 000 known species of Lepidoptera are the moths *Johanssonia acetosea* found in Britain, and *Stigmella ridiculosa* from the Canary Islands, which have a wing span of *c.* 2 mm *0·08 in* with a similar body length.

Britain ■ The Small blue (*Cupido minimus*) has a wing span of 19–25 mm *0·75–1·0 in.*

Rarest ■ The birdwing butterfly *Ornithopteria* (=*Troides*) *allottei* of Bougainville, Solomon Islands is known from less than a dozen specimens. A male from the collection of C. Rousseau Decelle was auctioned for £750 in Paris on 24 Oct 1966.

Britain ■ Britain's rarest butterfly (59 species) is the Large tortoiseshell (*Nymphalis polychloros*) which has not been seen in its last stronghold, Dorset, for several decades. There have been a number of isolated 'sightings' in southern England but the majority of these have turned out to be wrongly identified commas (*Polygonia C-album*). In May 1987 a large tortoiseshell was positively identified at Radipole Lake Nature Reserve, Weymouth, but this was probably a vagrant from the Continent or an escapee from a private breeder. The Chequered skipper (*Carterocephalus palaemon*) which became extinct in 1975 is now confined to western Inverness-shire and northern Argyll, Scotland. The Large blue (*Maculinea arion*) was officially declared extinct in 1979, but eggs were brought over from the island of Oland, Sweden in 1984 and hatched successfully on a site in the West Country. In 1986 another 220 eggs were obtained from Sweden, and the caterpillars distributed. At least 75 butterflies emerged and flew

the following summer, and it is estimated that 4500 eggs were laid by the butterflies in 1987. The next summer 150 adult Blues were recorded. They have now been introduced to half a dozen other suitable sites.

Most acute sense of smell ■ The most acute sense of smell exhibited in nature is that of the male Emperor moth (*Eudia pavonia*) which, according to German experiments in 1961, can detect the sex attractant of the virgin female at the almost unbelievable range of 11 km *6·8 miles* upwind. This scent has been identified as one of the higher alcohols ($C_{16}H_{29}OH$), of which the female carries less than 0·0001 mg.

Largest butterfly farm ■ The Australian Butterfly Sanctuary at Kuranda, Queensland, Australia is the world's largest butterfly farm in terms of flight space. The main flight 'aviary' consists of huge all-weather aluminium-framed glasshouse with an internal flight capacity of 3660 m³ *129 250 ft³*. The Sanctuary encompasses 2·8 ha *7 acres*, 1·2 ha *3 acres* of which are under cultivation with butterfly-food plants, and the other 1·6 ha *4 acres* natural rain-forest. Since Australian Law forbids the importation of live insect material, all butterfly eggs, pupae and larvae are bred in the Sanctuary.

Europe ■ The Stratford-upon-Avon Butterfly Farm has a flight area of 582 m² *6264 ft²*, and can accommodate 2000 exotic butterflies in authentic rain forest conditions. The total of all flight areas at the butterfly farm, which opened on 15 Jul 1985, is 807 m² *8686 ft².*

Centipedes *Chilopoda*

Longest ■ The longest known species of centipede is a large variant of the widely distributed *Scolopendra morsitans*, found on the Andaman

Islands in the Bay of Bengal. Specimens have been measured up to 330 mm *13 in* in length and 38 mm *1·5in* in breadth.

Britain ■ *Haplophilus subterraneus* has been measured up to 70 mm *2·75 in* in length and 1·4 mm *0·05 in* across the body.

Shortest ■ The shortest recorded centipede is an unidentified species which measures only 5 mm *0·19 in.*

Britain ■ *Lithobius dubosequi* measures up to 9·5 mm *0·374 in* in length.

Most legs ■ *Himantarum gabrielis* found in southern Europe has 171–177 pairs of legs when adult.

Fastest ■ The fastest centipede is probably *Scrutigera coleoptrata* of southern Europe which can travel at 1·8 km/h *1·1 mph.*

Millipedes *Diplopoda*

Longest ■ Both *Graphidostreptus gigas* of Africa and *Scaphistostreptus seychellarum* of the Seychelles in the Indian Ocean have been measured up to 280 mm *11·02 in* in length and 20 mm *0·78 in* in diameter.

Britain ■ *Cylindroiulus londinensis* measures up to 50 mm *1·96 in.*

Shortest ■ The shortest millipede in the world is the British species *Polyxenus lagurus*, which measures 2·1–4·0 mm *0·082–0·15 in.*

Most legs ■ The greatest number of legs reported for a millipede is 375 pairs (750 legs) for *Illacme plenipes* of California, USA.

Largest land gastropod ● A lifesize illustration of the African giant snail (*Achatina* sp.), the largest land gastropod. A specimen named 'Gee Geronimo' owned by Christopher Hudson (1955–79) of Hove, East Sussex, measured 39·3 cm *15½ in* from snout to tail when fully extended (shell length 27·3 cm *10¾ in*) in December 1978 and weighed exactly 900 g *2 lb*. The snail was collected in Sierra Leone in June 1976. (Artwork: Matthew Hillier/Guinness Publishing)

Segmented Worms
Annelida

Longest ■ The longest known species of earthworm is *Microchaetus rappi* (=*M. microchaetus*) of South Africa. In *c.* 1937 a giant measuring 6·7 m *22 ft* in length when naturally extended and 20 mm *0·78 in* in diameter was collected in the Transvaal.

Britain ■ The longest segmented worm found in Britain is the King rag worm (*Nereis virens*). On 19 Oct 1975 a specimen measuring 111·7 cm *44 in* when fully extended was collected by Mr James Sawyer in Hauxley Bay, Northumberland.

The longest earthworm found in Britain is *Lumbricus terrestris*. The normal range is 90–300 mm *3·54–11·81 in* but this species has been reliably measured up to 350 mm *13·78 in* when naturally extended. Measurements up to 508 mm *20 in* have been claimed, but in each case the body was probably macerated first. On 2 Feb 1988 an 'earthworm' reported to measure 1·83 m *6 ft* in length was found on an allotment in Stratton St Margaret, Wilts. The specimen was later sent to the British Museum (Natural History) for identification, where it was found to be the intestine of a hedgehog. In May 1988 a man living in Herne Bay, Kent found a *live* 1·98 m *6 ft 6 in* long earthworm in his garden after a heavy rainstorm and took it to Bramble Wildlife Park near Canterbury for examination. Unfortunately the earthworm fragmented soon afterwards and the parts were discarded before experts could make a positive identification.

Shortest ■ *Chaetogaster annandalei* measures less than 0·5 mm *0·019 in* in length.

Worm charming ■ At the first World Worm Charming Championship held at Willaston near Nantwich, Cheshire, on 5 Jul 1980 a local farmer's son, Tom Shufflebotham (b. 1960), charmed a record 511 worms out of the ground (a 3 m² *3·28 yd²* plot) in the alloted time of 30 minutes. Garden forks or other implements are vibrated in the soil by competitors to coax up the worms, but water is banned.

Molluscs *Mollusca*

(Squids, octopuses, shellfish, snails, etc.)

Largest invertebrate ■ The Atlantic giant squid *Architeuthis dux* is the world's largest known invertebrate. The heaviest ever recorded was a 2 tonne monster which ran aground in Thimble Tickle Bay, Newfoundland, Canada on 2 Nov 1878. There are numerous types of squids ranging in size from 1·5 cm *0·75 in* to the longest ever recorded – a 17·37 m *57 ft* giant *Architeuthis longimanus* which was washed up on Lyall Bay, Cook Strait, New Zealand in October 1887. Its two long slender tentacles each measured 15·01 m *49 ft 3 in*.

British ■ The largest squid ever recorded in British waters was an *Architeuthis monachus* found at the head of Whalefirth Voe, Shetland on 2 Oct 1959 which measured 7·31 m *24 ft* in total length.

Largest octopus ■ The largest octopus known to science is *Octopus apollyon* of the coastal

waters of the North Pacific. One huge individual caught single-handed by skin-diver Donald E. Hagen in Lower Hoods Canal, Puget Sound, Washington State, USA on 18 Feb 1973 had a relaxed radial spread of 7·01 m *23 ft* and weighed 53·8 kg *118 lb 10 oz.*

British ■ The largest octopus found in British waters is the Common octopus (*Octopus vulgaris*). It

may span 2·13 m *7 ft* and weigh more than 4·5 kg *10 lb.*

Largest eye ■ The Atlantic giant squid has the largest eye of any animal – living or extinct. It has been estimated that the one recorded at Thimble Tickle Bay had eyes 400 mm *15·75 in* in diameter – almost the width of this open book!

Oldest mollusc ■ The longest-lived mollusc is the Ocean quahog (*Arctica islandica*), a thick-shelled clam found in mid-Atlantic. A specimen with 220 annual growth rings was collected in 1982.

SHELLS

Largest ■ The largest of all existing bivalve shells is the Marine giant clam *Tridacna gigas*, found on the Indo-Pacific coral reefs. An outsized specimen measuring 115 cm *45·2 in* in length and weighing 333 kg *734 lb* was collected off Ishigaki Island, Okinawa, Japan in 1956 but was not scientifically examined until August 1984. It probably scaled just over 340 kg *750 lb* when alive (the soft parts weigh up to 9·1 kg *20 lb*). Another giant clam collected at Tapanoeli (Tapanula) on the north-west coast of Sumatra before 1817 and now preserved at Arno's Vale, Northern Ireland, measures 137 cm *54 in* in length and weighs 230 kg *507 lb.*

British ■ The largest bivalve shell found in British waters is the Fan mussel (*Pinna fragilis*). One specimen found at Tor Bay, Devon measured 37 cm *14·56 in* in length and 20 cm *7·87 in* in breadth.

Smallest ■ The smallest known shell-bearing species is the gastropod *Ammonicera rota*, which is found in British waters. It measures 0·5 mm *0·02 in* in diameter. The smallest bivalve shell is the Coinshell *Neolepton sykesi*, which is known only from a few examples collected off Guernsey, Channel Islands and western Ireland. It has an average diameter of 1·2 mm *0·047 in.*

Slowest growth ■ The slowest growth in the Animal Kingdom is that of the Deep-sea clam *Tindaria callistisormis* of the North Atlantic which takes *c.* 100 years to reach a length of 8 mm *0·31 in.*

Most expensive ■ The value of a sea-shell does not necessarily depend on its rarity or its prevalence. Some rare shells are inexpensive because there is no demand for them, while certain common shells fetch high prices because they are not readily accessible. In theory the most valuable shells in the world should be some of the unique examples collected in deep-sea trawls, but these shells are always dull and unattractive and hold very little interest for the collector. The most sought-after shell at present is probably *Cypraea fultoni*. In 1987 two live specimens were taken by a Russian trawler off Mozambique in the Indian Ocean. The larger of the two was later sold in New York to collector Dr Massilia Raybaudi of Italy for $24 000. The other was put up for sale at $17 000. A third, *C. fultoni*, went for $6600 in June 1987 to a Carmel, California collector. This collector also purchased a *C. teramachii* for $6500 in a one-week buying spree. Another *C. fultoni* in the American Museum of Natural History, New York was valued at $14 000 a few years ago.

GASTROPODS

Largest ■ The largest known gastropod is the Trumpet or Baler conch (*Syrinx aruanus*) of Australia. One outsized specimen collected off Western Australia in 1979 and now owned by Don Pisor (who bought it from a fisherman in Kaoh-siung, Taiwan in November 1979) of San Diego, California measures 77·2 cm *30·39 in* in length and has a maximum girth of 101 cm *39·76 in*. It weighed nearly 18·14 kg *40 lb* when alive. For largest known land gastropod see left. The largest land snail found in Britain is the

Roman or Edible snail (*Helix pomatia*), which measures up to 10 cm *4 in* in overall length and weighs up to 85 g *3 oz.*

Fastest ■ The fastest-moving species of land snail is probably the Common garden snail (*Helix aspersa*). On 17 Jul 1988 a garden snail named 'Tracker' completed a 33 cm *13 in* course at Cougham, Norfolk in a record 2 min 31 sec. The snail won a silver tankard stuffed with lettuce leaves. The snail-racing equivalent of a four minute mile is 61 cm *24 in* in 3 min or a 5 ¹/₂ day mile. On 9 Jul 1988 another garden snail called 'Hercules' dragged a 241 g *8·5 oz* stone for 47 cm *18¹/₂ in* across a table in 10 min in the Basque town of Val de Trapagua, Spain.

Ribbon Worms

Nemertina

Longest ■ The longest of the 550 recorded species of ribbon worm, also called nemertines (or nemerteans), is the 'Boot-lace' worm (*Lineus longissimus*), which is found in the shallow waters of the North Sea. A specimen washed ashore at St Andrews, Fife, Scotland, in 1864 after a severe storm measured more than 55 m *180 ft* in length.

Immolation ■ Some ribbon worms absorb themselves when food is scarce. One specimen under observation digested 95 per cent of its own body in a few months without apparently suffering any ill-effects. As soon as food became available the lost tissue was restored.

Jellyfishes and Corals *Cnidaria*

Largest jellyfish ■ The largest jellyfish is the Arctic giant jellyfish (*Cyanea capillata arctica*) of the north-western Atlantic. One washed up in Massachusetts Bay had a bell diameter of 2·28 m *7 ft 6 in* and tentacles stretching 36·5 m *120 ft.*

British ■ The largest cnidarian found in British waters is the rare 'Lion's mane' jellyfish (*Cyanea capillata*), also known as the Common sea blubber. One specimen measured at St Andrew's Marine Laboratory, Fife, had a bell diameter of 91 cm *35·8 in* and tentacles stretching over 13·7 m *45 ft.*

Most venomous cnidarian ■ The beautiful but deadly Australian sea wasp (*Chironex fleckeri*) is the most venomous jellyfish in the world. Its cardiotoxic venom has caused the deaths of 66 people off the coast of Queensland since 1880, with victims dying within 1–3 minutes if medical aid is not available. One effective defence is women's panty hose, outsize versions of which are now worn by Queensland lifesavers at surf carnivals.

Coral ■ The world's greatest stony coral structure is the Great Barrier Reef off Queensland, north-east Australia. It stretches 2028 km *1260 miles* and covers 207 000 km² *80 000 miles².*

The world's largest reported known example of discrete coral is a stony colony of *Galaxea fascicularis* found in Sakiyama Bay off Irimote Island, Okinawa on 7 Aug 1982 by Dr Shohei Shirai of the Institute for Development of Pacific Natural Resources. It has a long axis measurement of 7·8 m *23 ft 9 in*, a height of 4 m *13 ft 1¹/₂ in* and a maximum circumference of 19·5 m *59 ft 5 in.*

Sponges *Porifera*

Largest ■ The largest known sponge is the barrel-shaped Loggerhead sponge (*Spheciospongia vesparium*) of the West Indies and the waters off Florida, USA. Individuals measure

up to 105 cm *3 ft 6 in* in height and 91 cm *3 ft* in diameter. Neptune's cup or goblet (*Poterion patera*) of Indonesia grows to 120 cm *4 ft* in height, but it is a less bulky animal. In 1909 a Wool sponge (*Hippospongia canaliculatta*) measuring 183 cm *6 ft* in circumference was collected off the Bahamas. When first taken from the water it weighed between 36 and 41 kg *80–90 lb* but after it had been dried and relieved of all excrescences it scaled 5·44 kg *12 lb* (this sponge is now preserved in the US National Museum, Washington, DC, USA).

Smallest ■ The widely distributed *Leucosolenia blanca* measures 3 mm *0·11 in* in height when fully grown.

Deepest ■ Sponges have been recovered from depths of up to 5637 m *18 500 ft.*

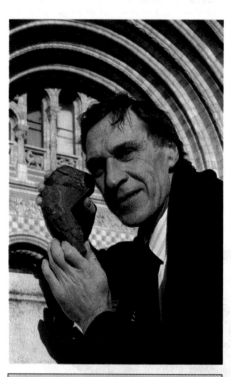

Oldest reptile fossil ● The oldest reptile fossil nicknamed 'Lizzie the Lizard' was found on a site in Scotland by palaeontologist Stan Wood in March 1988. The 20·32 cm *8 in* reptile is estimated to be 340 million years old, 40 million years older than previously discovered reptiles. (Photo: Graham Gauld Public Relations Ltd)

● Below: an artist's impression of Lizzie. (Artwork: Matthew Hillier for Guinness Publishing)

Extinct Animals

The first dinosaur to be scientifically described was *Megalosaurus bucklandi* ('great fossil lizard') in 1824. The remains of this bipedal flesh-eater had been found by workmen before 1818 in a slate quarry near Woodstock, Oxfordshire and were later placed in the University Museum, Oxford. It was not until 1841, however, that the name Dinosauria ('terrible lizards') was given to these newly-discovered giants.

Earliest known ■ The earliest known dinosaur was a yet unnamed prosauropod ('before the lizard feet'), which may have given rise to the mighty sauropods. In 1984 a partial skeleton of this reptile, which measured 2·44 m *8 ft* in length and weighed an estimated 67 kg *147 lb* when alive, was discovered in the Petrified Forest National Park, Arizona, USA by a team from the University of California at Berkeley. It may have been related to the plateosaurids ('fleet lizards') which lived from the early Jurassic.

Largest ■ The largest terrestrial vertebrates of all time were the brachiosaurs ('arm lizards') of the Tendaguru and Morrison Formations of Africa and North America respectively, which lumbered across the landscape 150 million years ago. Estimated weights up to 190 tonnes have been published for the biggest members of this family (*Brachiosauridae*), but such weights are unlikely. Present estimates range from 30 to 80 tonnes for *Brachiosaurus*. Most of the brachiosaurs discovered so far weighed a more acceptable 35–40 tonnes, but they could have been up to 33 per cent heavier in prime fat-bearing condition. The largest (and tallest) species for which the whole skeleton is known was the gracile *Brachiosaurus (Giraffatitan) brancai* from the famous Tendaguru site in Tanzania, which was excavated by a German expedition during the period 1909–11. The bones were later shipped back to the Humboldt Museum für Naturkunde in East Berlin, Germany for preparation and assembly and the specimen (a composite of several partial skeletons of different sizes) was finally put on display in 1937. As it stands today the world's largest mounted dinosaur measures 22·2 m *72 ft 9¹/₂ in* overall length (height at shoulder 6 m *19 ft 8 in*) and has a raised head height of 14 m *46 ft.* It weighed an estimated 31·5 tonnes. The isolated fibula of another *Brachiosaurus* in the same museum is 13 per cent larger than its equivalent in the mounted skeleton and it has been calculated that the bone must have come from a sauropod measuring 25 m *82 ft* in total length (shoulder height 6·79 m *22 ft 3¹/₂ in*) and has an estimated height of 16 m *52¹/₂ ft* to the top of its raised head. It weighed 45 tonnes. *Brachiosaurus (B) altithorax* from western Colorado, USA was also in the same class but heavier-bodied, and probably weighed about 50 tonnes in lean condition.

Three large sauropods have been described from the Uncompahgre Plateau of western Colorado, USA, but they have not been fully described. *Dystylosaurus edwini* ('two beam lizard'), found in 1979, is based on a single giant vertebra, and it is probably a brachiosaurid, like *Ultrasaurus macintoshi* ('extreme lizard'), also found in 1979. The latter is said to have had a body length of 30 m *(98 ft)* and a body weight of 100–130 tonnes. *Supersaurus vivianae* ('super lizard'), found in the same general area in 1972, has shoulder bones and neck vertebrae that suggest a height of 16·5 m *(54 ft)* and a total body length of 25–30 m *(82–98 ft)*. *Supersaurus* is probably a diplodocid.

Trackways are also a good indication of size, and the print named *Breviparopus*, found at Taghbalout, Morocco together with those of the brachiosaur *Pleurocoelus* from the Paluxy River, Texas, USA, suggest that they were also in the very large size class i.e. 50 tonnes.

Titanosaurs ■ A small number of titanosaurs ('giant lizards') have also been described as super-sized, and *Antarctosaurus giganteus* ('Antarctic lizard') of South America, India and Kazakhstan probably rivalled the largest brachiosaurs in terms of weight. There is also an enormous incomplete femur (original length at least 244 cm *8 ft*) in the Museum of La Plata, Argentina that must have come from a titanosaur (*A. giganteus*) massing about 55 tonnes.

Diplodocid ■ In 1985 the remains of a huge diplodocid said to be 'the largest dinosaur ever known' (*sic*) were excavated from a site near Albuquerque, New Mexico, USA. According to a palaeontologist at the New Mexico Museum of Natural History this giant sauropod, informally dubbed *Seismosaurus* ('earthquake lizard'), measured an estimated 30–36 m *100–120 ft* in total length and weighed at least 80 tonnes, but it is doubtful whether this new species was as heavy as *Supersaurus vivianae*.

Size limits ■ The largest known sauropods appear to weigh around the 50–100 tonne mark, but this doesn't necessarily represent the ultimate weight limit for a land vertebrate. Theoretical calculations suggest that some dinosaurs approached the maximum body weight possible for a terrestrial animal, namely 120 tonnes. At weights greater than that, the legs would have to be so massive to support the bulk that the dinosaur could not have moved!

Britain ■ Britain's largest known dinosaur was the diplodocid *Cetiosaurus oxoniensis* ('whale lizard'), from the upper beds of the Great Oolite at Enslow Bridge, near Oxford. Up until recently this sauropod, which roamed across southern England about 170 million years ago, was credited with lengths up to 21 m *69 ft* overall and a maximum weight of 27 tonnes but in the summer of 1981 the proximal end of a *Cetiosaurus* femur over one-third larger than any others previously found was dug up by workmen in the village of Clifton Regnes, Olney, Bucks. The bone is now in the possession of the Hansford family of Ballater, Aberdeenshire and, judging by its size, this sauropod must have measured an estimated 25·6 m *84 ft* in length and weighed c. 45 tonnes. This mass may nearly have been matched by the brachiosaur *Pelorosaurus* ('monstrous lizard') which, on the evidence of a haemal arch (the bone running beneath the vertebrae of the tail) found on the Isle of Wight may have reached 24 m *80 ft*.

Longest ■ Up until very recently the longest dinosaurs on record were believed to be certain attenuated diplodocids. A complete reconstruction of a *Diplodocus carnegii* in the Carnegie Museum of Natural History in Pittsburgh, Pennsylvania, USA measures 26·6 m *87 ft 6 in* in total length – head and body 6·7 m *22 ft*, body 4·5 m *15 ft*, tail 15·4 m *50 ft 6 in* – and has a mounted height of 3·58 m *11 ft 9 in* at the pelvis, the highest point on the body. But this giant was a lightweight relatively speaking and only weighed an estimated 10·7 tonnes. By comparison, *Supersaurus vivianae* (see page 44) measured an estimated 25–30 m *82–98 ft* in total length, while *Breviparopus* (see page 44) attained the astonishing length of 48 m *157 ft* – making it the longest vertebrate on record! Note, however, that this estimate is based on footprints only.

Britain ■ Britain's longest known dinosaurs were *Cetiosaurus oxoniensis* and *Pelorosaurus* (see above).

Largest land predator ■ The largest flesh-eating dinosaur recorded so far is *Tyrannosaurus rex* ('king tyrant lizard'), which stalked across what are now the states of Montana, Wyoming and Texas in the USA, and Alberta and Saskatchewan in Canada 70 million years ago. A composite skeleton of this nightmarish beast in the American Museum of Natural History, New York, USA has a bipedal height of 5·6 m *18 ft 6 in* (total length 10·6 m *34 ft 9 in*), and weighed an estimated 5·7 tonnes (close to 7 tonnes with large fat reserves). This individual, however, may have been a sub-adult, because the upper jaw-bone (maxilla) of another *Tyrannosaurus* in the Museum of Paleontology at the University of California, Berkeley, is 29 per cent longer (90 cm *35·4 in*) than the one in the American Museum of Natural History. This indicated a 14 m *44 ft* theropod weighing anything up to 12 tonnes! Its Mongolian relative *Tarbosaurus bataar* ('alarming lizard'), known from 13 skeletons, had a longer skull than *Tyrannosaurus* but was less heavily

built. It measured 10–14 m *33–46 ft* in total length while *Dynamosaurus imperiosus* ('dynamic lizard') of Shandung Province, China, was also in the same size league measuring up to 14 m *46 ft* overall (bipedal length 6·1 m *20 ft*), but these tyrannosaurids were not so heavily built as their North American relative.

Allosaurs ■ Some of the allosaurs ('other lizards') of North America, Africa, Australia and China also reached exceptional sizes, and one individual excavated near Kenton, Oklahoma, USA in 1934 measured 12·8 m *42 ft* in total length and had a bipedal height of 4·9 m *16 ft*. It was built on even more massive lines than the tyrannosaurids and was named *Saurophagus maximus* 'lizard eater'. Later, however, the bones were re-examined and found to be those of a large allosaur, or an *Acrocanthosaurus* ('very spiky reptile') which measured about 12 m *39 ft* overall. Seven skeletons of this terrifying meat-eater have been found in Oklahoma since 1950. Another allosaur from China, *Yangchuanosaurus magnus*, has been described as the largest non-tyrannosaurid carnosaur so far recorded, with a skull even more massive than that of *T. rex*. It measured over 10·36 m *34 ft* in length overall. *Spinosaurus aegyptiacus* ('thorn lizard') of Niger and Egypt was even longer than the largest-known tyrannosaurid, with a total length of c. 15 m *49 ft*, and combined its tremendous length with 1·6 m *5 ft 3 in* long blade-like spines running down its back, but it was a much more lightly-built theropod than the tyrannosaurids and probably did not exceed 4 tonnes.

Ornithomimosaurs ■ Most of the ornithomimosaurs ('ostrich mimic lizard') were of modest size, but one giant form, *Deinocheirus mirificus* ('terrible hand'), is represented by a pair of arms each 2·6 m (*8 ft*) long, from Mongolia. These suggest a total body size of 7·8 m (*24 ft*) or more.

undescribed plant-eating fabrosaurid from Colorado, USA measured 75 cm *29·5 in* from the snout to the tip of the tail and weighed about 6·8 kg *15 lb*.

Longest neck ■ The sauropod *Mamenchisaurus* ('mamenchi lizard') of the Late Jurassic of Sichuan, south-central China, has the longest neck of any animal that has ever lived. It measures 11 m *36 ft* or half the total length of the dinosaur.

Longest trackway ■ In 1983 a series of four *Apatosaurus* (= *Brontosaurus*) trackways which ran parallel for a distance of over 215 m *705 ft* were recorded from 145-million-year-old Morrison strata in south-east Colorado, USA.

Fastest ■ Trackways can be used to estimate dinosaur speeds, and one from the Late Morrison of Texas discovered in 1981 indicated that a carnivorous dinosaur had been moving at 40 km/h *25 mph*. Some of the ornithomimids (ostrich dinosaurs) were even faster, and the large-brained 100 kg *220 lb* *Dromiceiomimus* ('emu mimic') of the late Cretaceous of southern Alberta, Canada could probably outsprint an ostrich, which has a top speed of 72 km/h *45 mph*.

Largest footprints ■ In 1932 the gigantic footprints of a large bipedal hadrosaurid (duckbill) measuring 1·36 m *53·5 in* in length and 81 cm *31·8 in* wide were discovered at Salt Lake City, Utah, USA and other reports from Colorado and Utah refer to

Largest skull ● The skulls of the long-frilled ceratopsids were the largest of all known land animals and culminated in the long-frilled *Torosaurus sp.*, ('bull lizard'). This herbivore had a 2032 kg *4480 lb* skull measuring up to 3 m *9 ft 10 in* in length (including fringe) compared to the 0·81 m *2 ft 8 in* long skull of the White rhino (*Ceratotherium simum*). (Artwork: Matthew Hillier for Guinness Publishing)

The megalosaurids ('great lizards') also produced some enormities, including *Megalosaurus ingens* from the Tendaguru site in Tanzania, and *Bahariasaurus* from Egypt and Algeria, both of which were nearly as large as *T. rex*.

Smallest ■ The chicken-sized *Compsognathus* ('pretty jaw') of southern West Germany and south-east France, and an

Extinct Animals

footprints 95–100 cm *37·4–39·4 in* wide. Footprints attributed to the largest brachiosaurids also range up to 100 cm *39·3 in* wide for the hind feet.

Most brainless ■ *Stegosaurus* ('plated lizard'), which roamed across the states of Colorado, Oklahoma, Utah and Wyoming, USA about 150 million years ago, measured up to 9 m *30 ft* in total length but had a walnut-sized brain weighing only 70 g *2¹⁄₂ oz*. This represented 0·004 of 1 per cent of its computed body weight of 1 ¾ tonnes (cf. 0·074 of 1 per cent for an elephant and 1·88 per cent for a human).

Largest eggs ■ The largest known dinosaur eggs are those of *Hypselosaurus priscus* ('high ridge lizard'), a 12·19 m *40 ft* long titanosaurid which lived about 80 000 000 years ago. Some examples found in the valley of the Durance near Aix-en-Provence, southern France in October 1961 would have had, uncrushed, a length of 300 mm *12 in* and a diameter of 255 mm *10 in* (capacity 3·3 litres *5·8 pt*).

Largest claws ■ The therizinosaurids ('scythe lizards') from the Late Cretaceous of the Nemegt Basin, southern Mongolia, had the largest claws of any known animal, and in the case of *Therizinosaurus cheloniformis* measured up to 91·4 cm *36 in* round the outer curve (cf. 20·3 cm *8 in* for *T. rex*). It has been suggested that these sickle claws were designed for grasping and tearing apart large victims, but this creature had a feeble skull partially or entirely lacking teeth and probably lived on termites.

In January 1983, amateur fossil collector William Walker found a 30 cm *11·8 in* long claw-bone in a clay pit near Dorking, Surrey. Further excavations by a team from the British Museum (Natural History) revealed that the owner of this claw (believed to be a spinosaur) measured more than 9 m *29 ft 6 in* overall (estimated weight 2 tonnes) and had a bipedal height of 3–4 m *9 ft–13 ft*. It was also distinguished from other therapods by having 128 teeth instead of the usual 64. This enigma, said to be the most important dinosaur fossil found in Europe this century, was subsequently named *Baryonyx walkeri* ('heavy claw').

Largest skull ■ The skulls of the long-frilled ceratopsids were the largest of all known land animals and culminated in the long-frilled *Torosaurus sp.* ('bull lizard'). This herbivore, which measured c. 7·6 m *25 ft* in total length and weighed up to 8 tonnes, had a skull measuring up to 3 m *9 ft 10 in* in length (including fringe) and weighing up to 2 tonnes. It ranged from Montana to Texas, USA.

Disappearance ■ No wholly satisfactory theory has been offered for the dinosaurs' sudden extinction, but one school of thought is that 65 million years ago an asteroid hit the earth, thus triggering volcanic activity and producing lethal doses of acid rain over a period of 10 000 years.

Largest flying creature ■ The largest flying creature was the pterosaur *Quetzalcoatlus northropi* ('feathered serpent') which glided over what is now Texas, Wyoming and New Jersey, USA, Alberta, Canada, Senegal in Africa, and Jordan about 70 million years ago. Partial remains discovered in Big Bend National Park, western Texas, USA in 1971 indicate that this reptile must have had a wing span of 11–12 m *36–39 ft* and weighed about *113 kg* 250 lb.

Britain ■ *Ornithodesmus latidens*, from the Wealden Shales of Atherfield, Isle of Wight about 120 million years ago, had a wing expanse of c. 5 m *16 ft 4¹⁄₄ in*.

Largest marine reptile ■ *Kronosaurus queenslandicus*, a short-necked pliosaur from the Early Cretaceous (135 million years ago) of Australia, had a 3·04 m *10 ft* long skull containing 80 massive teeth and measured up to 15·2 m *50 ft* in length.

Britain ■ Britain's largest marine reptile was *Stretosaurus macromerus*, a short-necked pliosaur from the Kimmeridge Clay of Stretham, Cambs and Oxon. A mandible found at Cumnor, Oxfordshire and now in the University Museum, Oxford has a restored length of over 3 m *9 ft 10 in* and must have belonged

to a reptile measuring at least 14 m *46 ft* in total length.

Largest crocodile ■ The largest known crocodile was the euschian *Deinosuchus riograndensis* ('terrible crocodile'), which lived in the lakes and swamps of what is now the state of Texas, USA about 75 million years ago. Fragmentary remains discovered in Big Bend National Park, western Texas, USA indicate a hypothetical length of 16 m *52 ft 6 in*, compared with the 15·2 m *50 ft* of the huge gharial *Rhamphosuchus* of northern India (2 million years ago) and the 14 m *46 ft* of *Sarcosuchus imperator* of Niger.

Largest chelonians ■ The largest prehistoric chelonian was *Stupendemys geographicus*, a pelomedusid turtle which lived about 5 million years ago. Fossil remains discovered by Harvard University palaeontologists in northern Venezuela in 1972 indicate that this turtle had a carapace (shell) measuring 218–230 cm *7 ft 2 in–7 ft 6¹⁄₂ in* in mid-line length and measured 3 m *9 ft 10 in* in overall length. It had a computed weight of 2041 kg *4500 lb* in life.

Largest tortoise ■ The largest prehistoric tortoise was probably *Geochelone* (= *Colossochelys*) *atlas*, which lived in what is now northern India, Burma, Java, the Celebes and Timor, about 2 million years ago. In 1923 the fossil remains of a specimen with a carapace 180 cm *5 ft 11 in* long (223 cm *7 ft 4 in* over the curve) and 89 cm *2 ft 11 in* high were discovered near Chandigarh in the Siwalik Hills, India. This animal had a total length of 2·44 m *8 ft* and is computed to have weighed 852 kg *2100 lb* when it was alive.

Longest snake ■ The longest prehistoric snake was the python-like *Gigantophis garstini*, which inhabited what is now Egypt about 38 million years ago. Parts of a spinal column and a small piece of jaw discovered at Fayum in the Western Desert indicate a length of c. 11 m *37 ft*. Another huge fossil snake from Middle Eocene in Mali was originally credited with a length of 23 m *75 ft* (sic), but this measurement was over-estimated. It was actually 9 m *30 ft*.

Largest amphibian ■ The largest amphibian ever recorded was the gharial-like *Prionosuchus plummeri* which lived 270 million years ago. In 1972 the fragmented remains of a specimen measuring an estimated 9 m *30 ft* in life were discovered in northern Brazil.

Largest fish ■ No prehistoric fish larger than living species has yet been discovered. The claim that the Great shark (*Carcharodon megalodon*), which abounded in Miocene seas some 15 000 000 years ago, measured 24 m *80 ft* in length, based on ratios from fossil teeth has now been shown to be in error. The modern estimate is that this shark did not exceed 13·1 m *43 ft*.

Largest insect ■ The largest prehistoric insect was the dragonfly *Meganeura monyi*, which lived about 300 million years ago. Fossil remains (i.e. impressions of wings) discovered at Commentry, central France, indicate a wing extending up to 70 cm *27·5 in*.

Britain ■ Britain's largest dragonfly was *Pupus diluculum* (family Meganeuridae), which is known only from a wing impression found on a lump of coal in Bolsover colliery, Derby in July 1978. It had an estimated wing span of 50–60 cm *19·68–23·62 in* and lived about 300 million years ago, making it the oldest flying creature so far recorded.

Largest bird ■ The largest prehistoric bird was the flightless *Dromornis stirtoni*, a huge emu-like creature which lived in central Australia 11 million years ago. Fossil leg bones found near Alice Springs in 1974 indicate that the bird must have stood c. 3 m *10 ft* in height and weighed c. 500 kg *1100 lb*. The giant moa *Dinornis maximus* of New Zealand was even taller, attaining a maximum height of 3·6 m *12 ft*, but it weighed only about 227 kg *500 lb*.

Flying bird ■ The largest known flying bird was the Giant teratorn (*Argentavis magnificens*) which

lived in Argentina about 6 million years ago. Fossil remains discovered at a site 160 km *100 miles* west of Buenos Aires, Argentina in 1979 indicate that this gigantic vulture had a wing span of 7·0–7·6 m *23–25 ft* and weighed about 120 kg *265 lb*.

Sea-bird ■ In 1987 an expedition from the Charleston Museum of South Carolina, USA discovered the fossil remains of a 30 million-year-old giant sea-bird (*Pseudodontornis sp.*), which was related to the pelicans and cormorants. It had a wingspan of c. 5·8 m *19 ft* and weighed about 41 kg *90 lb*.

Largest land mammal ■ The largest land mammal ever recorded was *Paraceratherium* (= *Baluchitherium*), a long-necked hornless rhinocerotid which roamed across western Asia and Europe (Yugoslavia) about 35 million years ago. A restoration in the American Museum of Natural History, New York, USA measures 5·41 m *17 ft 9 in* to the top of the shoulder hump and 11·27 m *37 ft* in total length, and this particular specimen must have weighed about 20 tonnes. The bones of this gigantic browser were first discovered in the Bugti Hills in east Baluchistan, Pakistan in 1907–8.

Largest marine mammal ■ The serpentine *Basilosaurus* (*Zeuglodon*) *cetoides*, which swam in the seas over modern-day Arkansas and Alabama 50 million years ago, measured up to 21·3 m *70 ft* in length.

Largest mammoth ■ The largest prehistoric elephant was the Steppe mammoth *Mammuthus (Parelephas) trogontherii*, which roamed over what is now central Europe a million years ago. A fragmentary skeleton found in Mosbach, West Germany indicates a shoulder height of 4·5 m *14 ft 9 in*.

Largest primate ■ The largest known primate was *Gigantopithecus*, of the Middle Pleistocene of what is now northern Vietnam and southern China. Males would have stood an estimated 2·74 m *9 ft* tall and weighed about 272 kg *600 lb*. It is risky, however, to correlate tooth size and jaw depth of primates with their height and bodyweight, and *Gigantopithecus* may have had a disproportionately large head, jaws and teeth for his body size. The only remains that have been discovered so far are three partial lower jaws and more than 1000 teeth.

Antlers ■ The prehistoric Giant deer (*Megaloceros giganteus*), which lived in northern Europe and northern Asia as recently as 8000 BC, had the longest horns of any known animal. One specimen recovered from an Irish bog had greatly palmated antlers measuring 4·3 m *14 ft* across, which correspond to a shoulder height of 1·83 m *6 ft* and a weight of 499 kg *1100 lb*.

Tusks ■ The longest tusks of any prehistoric animal were those of the Straight-tusked elephant *Palaeoloxodon antiquus germanicus*, which lived in northern Germany about 300 000 years ago. The average length in adult bulls was 5 m *16 ft 5 in*. A single tusk of a Woolly mammoth (*Mammuthus primigenius*) preserved in the Franzens Museum at Brno, Czechoslovakia measures 5·02 m *16 ft 5¹⁄₂ in* along the outside curve. In c. August 1933, a single tusk of an Imperial mammoth (*Mammuthus imperator*) measuring 4·87 + m *16 + ft* (anterior end missing) was unearthed near Post, Gorza County, in Texas, USA. In 1934 this tusk was presented to the American Museum of Natural History in New York City.

The heaviest single fossil tusk on record is one weighing 150 kg *330 lb* with a maximum circumference of 89 cm *35 in* now preserved in the Museo Civico di Storia Naturale in Milan, Italy. The specimen (in two pieces) measures 3·58 m *11 ft 9 in* in length.

The heaviest recorded fossil tusks are a pair belonging to a 4·06 m *13 ft 4 in* tall Columbian mammoth (*Mammuthus columbi*) in the State Museum, Lincoln, Nebraska, USA, which have a combined weight of 226 kg *498 lb* and measure 4·21 m *13 ft 9 in* and 4·14 m *13 ft 7 in* respectively. They were found near Campbell, Nebraska, USA in April 1915.

Plant Kingdom *Plantea*

The medicinal value of plants was known to Neanderthal man in Iraq *c.* 60 000 BC. The earliest evidence for a garden is a relief of proto-dynastic age *c.* 3000 BC in Egypt depicting a specimen palm in a protective enclosure amid irrigation or decorative waterways. Though the Romans had gardens in England from AD 43 the earliest surviving garden is at Romsey Abbey, Hants laid out *c.* 1092.

Oldest ■ 'King Clone', the oldest known clone of the Creosote plant (*Larrea tridentata*), found in south-west California, USA, was estimated in February 1980 by Professor Frank C. Vasek to be 11 700 years old. It is possible that crustose lichens in excess of 500 mm *19·6 in* in diameter may be as old. In 1981 it was estimated that Antarctic lichens of more than 100 mm *3·9 in* in diameter are at least 10 000 years old.

Rarest ■ Plants thought to be extinct are rediscovered each year and there are thus many plants of which specimens are known in but a single locality. Cuttings from a Café marron tree (*Ramosmania heterophylla*), a single specimen growing on Rodriguez Island, Indian Ocean, reported in April 1986 were flown to the Royal Botanic Gardens, Kew, west London in an attempt to propagate it and preserve the species. *Pennantia baylisiana*, a tree found in 1945 on Three Kings Island, off New Zealand, only exists as a female and cannot fruit. In May 1983 it was reported that there was a sole surviving specimen of the Lady's slipper orchid (*Cypripedium calceolus*) in Britain.

Northernmost ■ The Yellow poppy (*Papaver radicatum*) and the Arctic willow (*Salix arctica*) survive, the latter in an extremely stunted form, on the northernmost land (83° N).

Southernmost ■ Lichens resembling *Rhinodina frigida* have been found in Moraine Canyon in 86°09′S 157°30′W in 1971 and in the Horlick Mountain area, Antarctica in 86°09′S 131°14′W in 1965. The southernmost recorded flowering plant is the Antarctic hair grass (*Deschampsia antarctica*) which was found in latitude 68°21′S on Refuge Island, Antarctica on 11 Mar 1981.

Highest ■ The greatest certain altitude at which any flowering plants have been found is 6400 m *21 000 ft* on Kamet (7756 m *25 447 ft*) by N. D. Jayal in 1955. They were *Ermania himalayensis* and *Ranunculus lobatus*.

Roots ■ The greatest reported depth to which roots have penetrated is a calculated 120 m *400 ft* in the case of a wild fig tree at Echo Caves, near Ohrigstad, eastern Transvaal, South Africa. An elm tree root of at least 110 m *360 ft* was reported from Auchencraig, Largs, Ayrshire *c.* 1950. A single Winter rye plant (*Secale cereale*) has been shown to produce 622·8 km *387 miles* of roots in 0·051 m³ *1·83 ft³* of earth.

Worst weeds ■ The most intransigent weed is the mat-forming Water weed *Salvinia auriculata*, found in Africa. It was detected on the filling of Kariba Lake in May 1959 and within 11 months had choked an area of 199 km² *77 miles²* rising by 1963 to 1002 km² *387 miles²*. The world's worst land weeds are regarded as Purple nut sedge, Bermuda grass, Barnyard grass, Jungle-rice, Goose grass, Johnson grass, Guinea grass, Cogon grass and Lantana.

Britain ■ The most damaging and widespread cereal weeds in Britain are the wild oats *Avena fatua* and *A. ludoviciana*. Their seeds can withstand temperatures of 115·6° C *240° F* for 15 min and remain viable. The largest weed in Britain is the Giant hogweed (*Heracleum mantegazzianum*) which established itself from seeds brought from the Caucasus before 1862. It reaches 3·65 m *12 ft*.

Most spreading ■ The greatest area covered by a single clonal growth is that of the wild Box huckleberry (*Gaylussacia brachyera*), a mat-forming evergreen shrub first reported in 1796. A colony

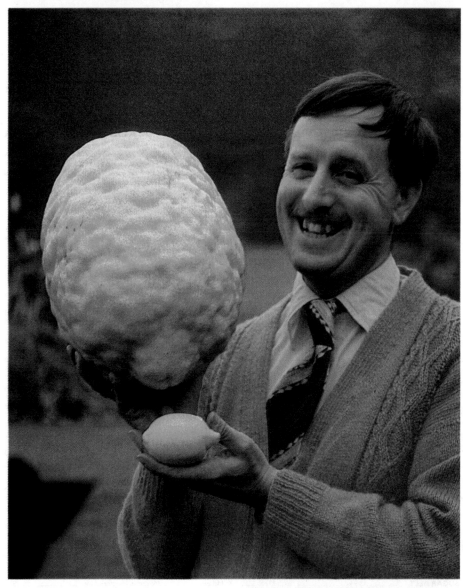

covering about 40 ha *100 acres* was found on 18 Jul 1920 near the Juniata River, Pennsylvania, USA. It has been estimated that this colony began 13 000 years ago.

Smallest flowering and fruiting ■ The floating flowering Aquatic duckweed (*Wolffia angusta*) of Australia, described in 1980, is only 0·6 mm *0·00236 in* in length and 0·33 mm *0·00129 in* in width. It weighs about 0·00015 g *1/190 000 of an oz*, its fruit resembling a tiny fig weighing 0·00007 g or *400 000 to the oz*.

The smallest land plant regularly flowering in Britain is the Chaffweed (*Cetunculus minimus*), a single seed of which weighs 0·00003 of a gramme.

Fastest growing ■ The case of a *Hesperoyucca whipplei* of the family Liliaceae growing 3·65 m *12 ft* in 14 days was reported from Tresco Abbey, Isles of Scilly in July 1978.

Slowest flowering ■ The slowest flowering of all plants is the rare *Puya raimondii*, the largest of all herbs, discovered at 3960 m *13 000 ft* in Bolivia in 1870. The panicle emerges after about 80–150 years of the plant's life. One planted near sea level at the University of California's Botanical Garden, Berkeley, USA in 1958 grew to 7·6 m *25 ft* and bloomed as early as August 1986 after only 28 years. It then dies. (See also Largest blooms.)

Oldest pot plant ■ The succulent *Fockea crispa* was potted by Baron Jacquin (1728–1817) at the Schönbrunn gardens, Vienna, Austria *c.* 1801.

Biggest collection ■ Dr Julian A. Steyermark (d. 15 Oct 1988) of the Missouri Botanical Garden, St Louis, Missouri, USA, had by Oct 1988 made an

unrivalled total of 138 000 collections of which 132 223 were his own continuous number series.

Largest aspidistra ■ The aspidistra (*Aspidistra elatior*) was introduced to Britain as a parlour palm from Japan and China in 1822.

The biggest aspidistra in the world measures 142 cm *56 in* and belongs to Cliff Evans of Kiora, Moruya, NSW, Australia.

Britain ■ The biggest aspidistra known in Britain is one 127 cm *50 in* tall with more than 500 leaves spanning 1·52 m *5 ft*, grown by Gertie James in Staveley, Chesterfield.

Earliest flower ■ The oldest fossil of a flowering plant with palm-like imprints was found in Colorado, USA in 1953 and dated about 65 million years old.

Largest cactus ■ The largest of all cacti is the Saguaro (*Cereus giganteus* or *Carnegiea gigantea*), found in Arizona, south-eastern California and Sonora, Mexico. The green fluted column is surmounted by candelabra-like branches rising to a height of 16 m *52 ft 6 in* in the case of a specimen measured on the boundary of the Saguaro National Monument, Arizona, USA. They have waxy white blooms which are followed by edible crimson fruit.

UNITED KINGDOM
FRUIT, VEGETABLES, FLOWERS

Many data subsequent to 1958 come from the annual *Garden News* and Phostrogen Ltd Giant Vegetable and Fruit Contest and the Super Sunflower Contest.

TYPE	SIZE (Weight/Dimensions)		GROWER	LOCATION	YEAR
APPLE	1·357 kg	3 lb 1 oz	V. Loveridge	Ross-on-Wye, Hereford & Worcs	1965
ARTICHOKE	3·625 kg	8 lb	A. R. Lawson	Tollerton, North Yorks	1964
BEETROOT	13·49 kg	29 lb 12 oz	E. Stone	East Woodyates, Wilts	1988
BROAD BEAN	59·3 cm	23 ³⁄₈ in	T. Currie	Jedburgh, Borders	1963
	59·3 cm	23 ³⁄₈ in	Mrs M. Adrian	Irvine, Strathclyde	1982
BROCCOLI	13·100 kg	28 lb 14 ¼ oz	J. T. Cooke	Funtington, W. Sussex	1964
BRUSSELS SPROUT[1]	7·285 kg	16 lb 1 oz	E. E. Jenkins	Shipston-on-Stour, Warwicks	1974
CABBAGE*	54·88 kg	121 lb	E. Stone	East Woodyates, Wilts	1988
CABBAGE, RED [2]	19·05 kg	42 lb	R. Straw	Staveley, Derby	1925
CARROT[3]	4·649 kg	10 lb 4 oz	E. Stone	East Woodyates, Wilts	1984
CAULIFLOWER	23·900 kg	52 lb 11 ½ oz	J. T. Cooke	Funtington, W. Sussex	1966
CELERY	16·1 kg	35 lb 8 oz	E. Stone	East Woodyates, Wilts	1986
CUCUMBER[4]	7·25 kg (indoor)	15·99 lb	R. Butcher	Stockbridge, Hants	1988
	3·740 kg (outdoor)	8 lb 4 oz	C. Bowcock	Willaston, Merseyside	1973
	110 cm	43 ½ in	A. C. Rayment	Chelmsford, Essex	1984–6
DAHLIA[5]	3·17 m	10 ft 5 in	R. Lond	Diss, Norfolk	1985
DWARF BEAN	43·4 cm	17 ½ in	C. Bowcock	Willaston, Merseyside	1973
GLADIOLUS	2·55 m	8 ft 4 ½ in	A. Breed	Melrose, Roxburgh	1981
GOOSEBERRY	58·5 g	2·06 oz	A. Dingle	Macclesfield, Cheshire	1978
GOURD	88·900 kg	196 lb	J. Leathes	Herringfleet Hall, Suffolk	1846
GRAPEFRUIT*[6]	1·673 kg	3 lb 11 oz	Willington G.C.	Willington, Beds	1986
HOLLYHOCK	7·39 m	24 ft 3 in	W. P. Walshe	Eastbourne, E. Sussex	1961
KALE[7]	3·65 m tall	12 ft	B. T. Newton	Mullion, Cornwall	1950
LEEK, BLANCH	4·235 kg	9 lb 5 ½ oz	C. Bowcock	Willaston, Merseyside	1973
LEEK, POT	5·5 kg	12 lb 2 oz	P. Harrigan	Linton, Northumberland	1987
LEMON[8]	2·13 kg	4 lb 11 oz	Pershore College	Pershore, H & W	1986
LETTUCE	11·335 kg	25 lb	C. Bowcock	Willaston, Merseyside	1974
LUPIN*	1·90 m	6 ft 3 in	K. S. Barnes	Guildford, Surrey	1988
MANGOLD	24·720 kg	54 ½ lb	P. F. Scott	Sutton, Humberside	1971
MARROW	47·85 kg	105 lb 8 oz	D. C. Payne	Tewkesbury, Glos.	1982
MELON[9]	6·42 kg	14 lb 2 ¾ oz	R. D. Sainsbury	Paull, Hull, Humberside	1985
MUSHROOM[10]	1·72 m diam.	68 in	G. Long	Listowel, Co. Kerry	1987
ONION	4·164 kg	9 lb 2 ⅞ oz	K. Foster	Richmond, North Yorks	1988
PARSNIP	3·62 m	142 ¾ in	K. Lloyd	Cydweli, Dyfed	1984
PEAPOD[11]	25·7 cm	10 ⅛ in	T. Currie	Jedburgh, Borders	1964
PEAR[12]	1·200 kg	2 lb 10 ½ oz	Mrs K. Loines	Hythe, Hants	1973
PETUNIA*[13]	2·53 m	8 ft 4 in	G. A. Warner	Dunfermline, Fife	1978
POTATO[14]	3·200 kg	7 lb 1 oz	J. H. East	Spalding, Lincs.	1963
	3·200 kg	7 lb 1 oz	J.P. Busby	Atherstone, Warwicks.	1982
PUMPKIN[15]	201·4 kg	444 lb	R. A. Butcher	Stockbridge, Hants	1984
RADISH[16]	10·26 kg	22·63 lb	B. Lavery	Llanharri, Mid Glamorgan	1988
RHUBARB	2·665 kg	5 lb 14 oz	E. Stone	East Woodyates, Wilts	1985
RUNNER BEAN	100·3 cm	39 ½ in	J. Taylor	Shifnal, Shropshire	1986
SAVOY CABBAGE	17·450 kg	38 lb 8 oz	W. H. Neil	Retford, Notts.	1966
SHALLOT*	2·636 kg (4 bulbs)	5 lb 13 oz	R. Miller	Woodbury, Devon.	1987
STRAWBERRY	231 g	8·17 oz	G. Anderson	Folkestone, Kent	1983
SUGAR BEET[17]	13·9 kg	30 lb 10 oz	K. McLean	Meldreth, Hertfordshire	1984
SUNFLOWER[18]	7·17 m tall	23 ft 6 ½ in	F. Kelland	Exeter, Devon	1976
SWEDE	22·11 kg	48 lb 12 oz	A. Foster	Alnwick, Northumberland	1980
TOMATO[19]	2·537 kg	5 lb 9 ½ oz	R. G. Burrows	Huddersfield, West Yorks	1985
TOMATO PLANT[20]	13·96 m (length)	45 ft 9 ½ in	Chosen Hill School	Gloucester, Glos.	1981
TOMATO TRUSS	9·175 kg	20 lb 4 oz	C. Bowcock	Willaston, Merseyside	1973
TURNIP[21]	16·783 kg	37 lb	G. Farquhar	Tillyfourie, Grampian	1987

[1] A Brussels sprout plant measuring 3·55 m 11 ft 8 in was grown by Ralph G. Sadler of Watchbury Farm, Barford, Warwicks on 6 Jul 1978.
[2] The Swalwell, County Durham red cabbage of 1865 grown by William Collingwood (d. 8 Oct 1867) reputedly weighed 55·7 kg 123 lb and was 6·57 m 259 in in circumference.
[3] A specimen of 7 kg 15 lb 7 oz was grown by Miss I. G. Scott of Nelson, New Zealand in October 1978. A 3·44 m 135 ½ in specimen grown by Bernard Lavery of Llanharri, South Wales was recorded in 1988.
[4] A Vietnamese variety 1·83 m 6 ft long was reported by L. Szabo of Debrecen, Hungary in September 1976.
[5] A 6·3 m 20 ft 8 in dahlia was grown by R. D. Blythe of Nannup, Western Australia in 1988.
[6] A 2·966 kg 6 lb 8 ¹⁄₁₀oz specimen was weighed for Joshua and Allison Sosnow in Tucson, Arizona, USA on 21 Dec 1984.
[7] Gosse Haisma of Bunbury, Western Australia grew a stalk to 5·54 m 18 ft 2 in.
[8] An 3·88 kg 8 lb 8 oz lemon with a 74·9 cm 29 ¹⁄₂in girth was grown by Charlotte and Donald Knutzen of Whittier, California, USA in August 1983.
[9] Jason Bright, 10, of Hope, Arkansas, USA, grew a watermelon reported by Grace's Gardens in September 1985 to weigh 118 kg 260 lb and overtaking the joint record set by his father and grandfather.
[10] This mushroom weighed 10·8 kg 24 lb. A specimen of the edible Termitomyces titanicus found near Kitwe, Zambia on 18 Dec 1978 measured 63 cm 26 in in diameter and weighed 2·5 kg 5 ½lb. A mushroom of 'nearly 100 lb' and 51 cm 20 in thick was reported from Potenza, Italy on 30 Oct 1985.
[11] A 63·5 cm 25 in peapod was grown by Chad McInville in Jul 1986.
[12] A specimen weighing 1·405 kg 3 lb 1 ½ oz was harvested on 10 May 1979 at Messrs K. & R. Yeomans, Arding, Armidale, NSW, Australia. It was reported in the 4 Nov 1831 edition of The Standard that Mrs G. Chambers of Faversham, Kent had grown seven 'extraordinary large pears', the heaviest weighing 2 lb 14 ¹⁄₂oz 1·318 kg.
[13] Bert Lawrence of Windham, New York, USA grew a petunia plant measured on 19 Sep 1985 at 4·16 m 13 ft 8 in.
[14] One weighing 8·275 kg 18 lb 4 oz reported dug up by Thomas Siddal in his garden in Chester on 17 Feb 1795. A yield of 233·5 kg 515 lb was achieved from a 1·1 kg 2 ½lb parent seed by Bowcock planted in April 1977. Six tubers weighing 24·72 kg 54 lb 8 oz by Alan Nunn of Rhodes, Middleton, Lancs were reported on 18 Sep 1949.
[15] A pumpkin (C. maxima) of 304·3 kg 671 lb (3·63 m 143 ¼ in girth) grown by Robert Gancarz of Jacobstown, New Jersey, USA won the World Pumpkin Confederation contest at Collins, New York, on 13 Oct 1986.
[16] A radish of 12·25 kg 27 lb and 69·8 cm 27 ½ in long was grown by Ron Whitford in Wollongong, Australia in November 1985.
[17] One weighing 20·63 kg 45 ½ lb was grown by R. Meyer of Brawley, California, USA in 1974.
[18] A sunflower of 7·76 m 25 ft 5 ½ in was grown by Martien Heijms of Oirschot, Netherlands in 1986. A sunflower with a head measuring 82 cm 32 ¼in in diameter was grown by Mrs Emily Martin of Maple Ridge, British Columbia, Canada in Sep 1983.
[19] Gordon Graham of Edmond, Oklahoma, grew a tomato of 3·51 kg 7 lb 12 oz in 1986.
[20] Gordon Graham of Edmond, Oklahoma, grew a tomato plant of 16·3 m 53 ft 6 in in 1985. Charles H. Wilber grew a cherry tomato plant with a height of 8·71 m 28 ft 7 in recorded in November 1985. It was reported at the Tsukuba Science Expo Centre, Japan on 28 Feb 1988 that a single plant produced 16 897 tomatoes.
[21] A 33·1 kg 73 lb turnip was reported in December 1768 and one of 23·1 kg 51 lb from Alaska in 1981.
* Not in official contest.

The heaviest orange ever reported is one weighing 2·5 kg 5 lb 8 oz exhibited in Nelspruit, South Africa on 19 Jun 1981. It was the size of a human head, and was soon stolen.

An armless cactus 24 m *78 ft* in height was measured in April 1978 by Hube Yates in Cave Creek, Arizona. It was toppled in a windstorm in July 1986 at an estimated age of 150 years.

Mosses ■ The smallest of mosses is the microscopic Pygmy moss (*Ephemerum*) and the longest is the Brook moss (*Fontinalis*), which forms streamers up to 91 cm *3 ft* long in flowing water.

SEAWEED

Longest ■ The longest species of seaweed is the Pacific giant kelp (*Macrocystis pyrifera*), which, although it does not exceed 60 m *196 ft* in length, can grow 45 cm *18 in* in a day.

British ■ The longest of the 700 species of British seaweed is the Brown seaweed *Chorda filum* which grows up to a length of 6·10 m *20 ft*. The Japanese *Sargassum muticum* introduced *c.* 1970 can grow to 9·0 m *30 ft*.

Deepest ■ The greatest depth at which plant life has been found is 269 m *884 ft* by Mark and Diane Littler (USA) off San Salvadore Island, Bahamas in October 1984. These maroon-coloured algae survived though 99·9995 per cent of sunlight was filtered out.

VINES AND VINEYARDS

Largest vine ■ This was planted in 1842 at Carpinteria, California, USA. By 1900 it was yielding more than 9 tonnes of grapes in some years, and averaging 7 tonnes per year. It died in 1920. A single bunch of grapes (Red Thomson seedless) weighing 9400 grammes *20 lb 11 ½ oz* was weighed in Santiago, Chile in May 1984.

Britain ■ Britain's largest vine (1898–1964) was at Kippen, Stirling with a girth, measured in 1956, of 1·52 m *5 ft*. England's largest vine is the Great Vine, planted in 1768 at Hampton Court, London. Its girth is 215·9 cm *85 in* with branches up to 34·7 m *114 ft* long and an average yield of 318·8 kg *703 lb*. In 1988 Leslie Stringer of Dartford, Kent obtained a yield of 1757·7 kg *3875 lb* from a vine in Banstead, Surrey planted in 1962.

Largest vineyard ■ The world's largest vineyard extends over the Mediterranean façade between the Rhône and the Pyrenees in the *départements* Hérault, Gard, Aude and Pyrénées-Orientales in an area of 840 000 ha *2 075 685 acres* of which 52·3 per cent is *monoculture viticole*.

Most northerly vineyard ■ A vineyard at Sabile, Latvia, USSR is just north of Lat. 57° N.

Britain ■ The most northerly commercial vineyard in Britain is that at Renishaw Hall, Nr Chesterfield, Derbyshire with 2600 vines, at Lat. 53° 18′N.

Most southerly vineyard ■ The most southerly commercial vineyards are to be found in central Otago, South Island, New Zealand south of Lat. 45° S.

Renton Burgess Vineyard, south of Alexandra, South Island, New Zealand, is in Lat. 44°36′S.

BLOOMS AND FLOWERS

Largest ■ The largest of all blooms are the parasitic Stinking corpse lily (*Rafflesia arnoldii*). They attach themselves to the cissus vines of the jungle in south-east Asia and measure up to 91 cm *3 ft* across and 1·9 cm *¾ in* thick, and attain a weight of 7 kg *15 lb*. True to name, the plant is extremely offensive in scent.

British ■ The largest bloom of any indigenous British flowering plant is that of the Wild white water lily (*Nymphaea alba*), which measures 15 cm *6 in* across.

Inflorescence ■ The largest known inflorescence as distinct from the largest of all blooms is that of *Puya raimondii*, a rare Bolivian monocarpic member of the Bromeliaceae family with an erect panicle (diameter 2·4 m *8 ft*) which emerges to a height of 10·7 m *35 ft*. Each of these bears up to 8000 white blooms (see also Slowest flowering plant). The flower-spike of an agave was in 1974 measured to be 15·8 m *52 ft* long in Berkeley, California, USA.

Blossoming plant ■ The giant Chinese wisteria (*Wisteria sinensis*) at Sierra Madre, California, USA was planted in 1892 and now has branches 152 m *500 ft* long. It covers nearly an acre, weighs 228 tonnes *225 tons* and has an estimated 1 500 000 blossoms during its blossoming period of five weeks, when up to 30 000 people pay admission to visit it.

Most valuable ■ The Burpee Co $10 000 prize offered in 1954 for the first all-white marigold was won on 12 Aug 1975 by Alice Vonk of Sully, Iowa, USA.

Largest arrangement ■ The largest arrangement of a single variety of flower was made by Johan Weisz, floral designer of Amsterdam, and 15 assistants at the City Hall, Aalsmeer, Netherlands from 23–25 Sep 1986. It consisted of 35 000 'Zurella' roses and measured 21·8 m *71 ft 6 in* in length, 7·68 m *25 ft 2 in* in width and 7·59 m *24 ft 11 in* high.

Largest bouquet ■ Thirty-six people took 335 hr to make an 11·23 m *36 ft 10 in* high bouquet of 9299 flowers at Annecy, France on 19 Sep 1986.

Largest wreath ■ A wreath built by the Clemsonville Christmas Tree Farm of Union Bridge, Maryland, USA in December 1988 measured 34·5 m *113 ft* in diameter and weighed 3683·2 kg *8120 lb*.

Longest daisy chain ■ The longest daisy chain, made in 7 hr, measuring 2·12 km *6980 ft 7 in* was made by villagers of Good Easter, Chelmsford, Essex on 27 May 1985. The team is limited to 16.

Largest rhododendron ■ Examples of the scarlet *Rhododendron arboreum* reach a height of 19·8 m *65 ft* on Mt Japfu, Nagaland, India. The cross-section of the trunk of a *Rhododendron giganteum*, reputedly 27·43 m *90 ft* high from Yunnan, China is preserved at Inverewe Gardens, Highland, Scotland.

UK ■ The largest in the United Kingdom is one 7·60 m *25 ft* tall and 82·9 m *272 ft* in circumference at Government House, Hillsborough, Co. Down, Northern Ireland. A specimen 10·65 m *35 ft* high and 99 cm *3 ft 3 in* in circumference has been measured at Tregothan, Truro.

Largest chrysanthemum ■ François Santini of Laboratoire Algochimie, Château Renault, Indre-et-Loire, France, grew a 2·5 m *8·2 ft* tall chrysanthemum with a total of 4041 blooms.

Longest philodendron ■ A 224·0 m *735 ft* long philodendron grows in the home of Mr M. J. Linhart in Thornton, Leics.

Largest rose tree ■ A 'Lady Banks' rose tree at Tombstone, Arizona, USA has a trunk 101 cm *40 in* thick, stands 2·74 m *9 ft* high and covers an area of 499 m² *5380 ft²* supported by 68 posts and several thousand feet of piping. This enables 150 people to be seated under the arbour. The cutting came from Scotland in 1884.

Smallest sunflower ■ A fully-mature sunflower measuring a mere 5·6 cm *2·2 in* tall was grown by Michael Lenke in Lake Oswego, Oregon, USA in 1985 using a patented 'Bonsai' technique.

ORCHIDS

Tallest ■ The largest of all orchids is *Grammatophyllum speciosum*, native to Malaysia. Specimens have been recorded up to 7·62 m *25 ft* in height.

Largest flower ■ The largest orchid flower is that of *Phragmipedium caudatum*, found in tropical areas of America. Its petals grow up to 46 cm *18 in* long, giving it a maximum outstretched diameter of 91 cm *3 ft*. The flower is, however, much less bulky than that of the Stinking corpse lily (see above). *Galeola foliata* a saprophyte of the Vanilla family, has been recorded at a height of 15 m *49 ft*. It grows in the decaying rain forests of Queensland, Australia but is not free-standing.

Britain ■ The first flowering in Britain of *Grammato-*

Fastest growing ● The above *Hesperoyucca whipplei* of the family Liliaceae growing 3·65 m *12 ft* in 14 days was reported from Tresco Abbey, Isles of Scilly in July 1978.

phyllum wallisii from Mindanao, Philippines at Burnham Nurseries, Kingsteignton, Devon in 1982 produced 557 flowers.

Smallest ■ The smallest orchid is *Platystele jungermannoides*, found in Central America. Its flowers are 1 mm *0·04 in* across.

Most expensive ■ The highest price ever paid for an orchid is 1150 guineas (£1207·50), paid by Baron Schröder to Sanders of St Albans for an *Odontoglossum crispum* (variety *pittianum*) at an auction by Protheroe & Morris of Bow Lane, London on 22 Mar 1906. A Cymbidium orchid called 'Rosanna Pinkie' was sold in the United States for $4500 in 1952.

FRUITS AND VEGETABLES

Most nutritive ■ An analysis of the 38 commonly eaten raw (as opposed to dried) fruits shows that the one with the highest calorific value is avocado (*Persea americana*), with 163 cals per 100 g. Avocados probably originated in Central and South America and also contain vitamins A, C and E and 2·2 per cent protein.

Least nutritive ■ That with the lowest calorific value is cucumber with 73 calories per lb *16 cals per 100 g*.

Asparagus ■ Joaquin Calvo Peligros of Madrid, Spain found a 2 m 18 cm *7·15 ft* long asparagus with a 2 cm *0·78 in* diameter on 'La Maraña' hill, Carveña, Madrid on 1 May 1988.

Chilli ■ A 6·6 m *21 ft 7 in* chilli plant was grown by Shri Kishan Joshi of Almora, India in 1985–6.

Cucumber ■ Mrs Eileen Chappel of Bowen Hills, Queensland, Australia grew a cucumber weighing 30 kg *66 lb* in April 1989.

Peach ■ The largest peach reported in Britain is one of 411 g *14½ oz*, 30·4 cm *12 in* in August 1984 from a 26-year-old Italian tree grown by Mrs Jean Bird of London SW6.

Pineapple ■ A pineapple weighing 7·96 kg *17 lb 8 oz* was harvested by Dole Philippines Inc. at South

Cotabato, Philippines in November 1984. Pineapples up to 13 kg *28·6 lb* were reported in 1978 from Tarauaca, Brazil.

Potato display ■ A record display of 369 varieties of potato (*Solanum tuberosum*) was mounted on BBC *Record Breakers* by Donald MacLean on 16 Sep 1984.

HERBS

Herbs are not botanically defined but consist of plants whose leaves or roots are of culinary or medicinal value.

Most heavily consumed ■ The most heavily consumed is coriander (*Coriandrum sativum*). It is used in curry powder, confectionery, in bread and in gin.

FERNS

Largest ■ The largest of all the more than 6000 species of fern is the Tree fern (*Alsophila excelsa*) of Norfolk Island, in the South Pacific, which attains a height of up to 18·28 m *60 ft*.

Britain ■ The highest in Britain is a bracken *Pteridium aquilinum* measuring over 4·8 m *16 ft* in Ruislip, Middlesex in 1970.

Smallest ■ The world's smallest ferns are *Hecistopteris pumila*, found in Central America, and *Azolla caroliniana*, which is native to the United States and has fronds down to 12 mm *½ in*.

GRASSES

Commonest ■ The world's commonest grass is *Cynodon dactylon* or Bermuda grass. The 'Callie' hybrid, selected in 1966, grows as much as 15·2 cm *6 in* a day and stolons reach 5·5 m *18 ft* in length.

Fastest growing ■ Some species of the 45 genera of bamboo have been measured to grow at up to 91 cm *36 in* per day (0·00003 km/h *0·00002 mph*).

Tallest ■ A Thorney bamboo culm (*Bambusa arundinacea*) felled at Pattazhi, Travancore, India in November 1904 measured 37·0 m *121 ½ ft*. The tallest of the 160 grasses found in Great Britain is the Common reed (*Phragmites communis*), which reaches a height of 2·97 m *9 ft 9 in*.

Shortest ■ The shortest grass native to Great Britain is the very rare sand bent (*Mibora minima*) from Anglesey, which has a maximum growing height of under 15 cm *6 in*.

LEAVES

Largest ■ The largest leaves of any plant belong to the Raffia palm (*Raphia raffia*) of the Mascarene Islands in the Indian Ocean, and the Amazonian bamboo palm (*R. toedigera*) of South America, whose leaf blades may measure up to 19·81 m *65 ft* in length with petioles up to 3·96 m *13 ft*. The largest undivided leaf is that of *Alocasia macrorrhiza*, found in Sabah, East Malaysia. One found in 1966 was 3·02 m *9 ft 11 in* long and 1·92 m *6 ft 3½ in* wide, with a unilateral area of 3·17 m² *34·2 ft²*.

Britain ■ The largest leaves to be found in outdoor plants in Great Britain are those of *Gunnera manicata* from Brazil with leaves 1·82–3·04 m *6–10 ft* across on prickly stems 1·52–2·43 m *5–8 ft* long.

Fourteen-leafed clover ■ A fourteen-leafed white clover (*Trifolium repens*) was found by Randy Farland near Sioux Falls, South Dakota, USA on 16 Jun 1975. A fourteen-leafed red clover (*Trifolium pratense*) was also reported by Paul Haizlip, 12 at Bellevue, Washington State, USA on 22 Jun 1987.

SEEDS

Largest ■ The largest seed in the world is that of the Double coconut or Coco de mer (*Lodoicea seychellarum*), the single-seeded fruit of which may weigh 18 kg *40 lb*. This grows only in the Seychelles, in the Indian Ocean.

Smallest ■ The smallest seeds are those of epiphytic orchids, at 35 000 000 to the oz (cf. grass pollens at up to 6 000 000 000 grains/oz). A single plant of the American ragweed can generate 8 000 000 000 pollen grains in five hours.

Plants

Most viable ■ The most protracted claim for the viability of seeds is that made for the Arctic lupin (*Lupinus arcticus*) found in frozen silt at Miller Creek in the Yukon, Canada in July 1954 by Harold Schmidt. The seeds were germinated in 1966 and were dated by the radiocarbon method of associated material to at least 8000 BC and more probably to 13 000 BC.

Most conquering conker ■ The highest recorded battle honours for an untreated conker (fruit of the Common horse-chestnut or *Aesculus hippocastanum*) is a 'five thousander plus', which won the BBC Conker Conquest in 1954. A professor of botany has however opined that this heroic specimen might well have been a 'ringer', probably an ivory or tagua nut (*Phytelephas macrocarpa*). The Guinness Book of Records *will not publish any category for the largest collection of conkers for fear that trees might suffer wholesale damage.*

HEDGES

Tallest ■ The Meikleour beech hedge in Perthshire was planted in 1746 and has now attained a trimmed height of 26 m *85 ft*. It is 550 m *600 yd* long. Some of its trees now exceed 32 m *105 ft*.

Tallest yew ■ A yew hedge in Earl Bathurst's Park, Cirencester, Glos, was planted in 1720, and runs for 155 m *170 yd*, reaches 11 m *36 ft*, is 4·5 m *15 ft* thick at its base and takes 20 man-days to trim.

Tallest box ■ The tallest box hedge is 10·7 m *35 ft* in height at Birr Castle, Offaly, Ireland dating from the 18th century.

TREES AND WOOD

Most massive ■ The most massive living thing on Earth is the biggest known Giant Sequoia (*Sequoiadendron giganteum*) named the 'General Sherman', standing 83·8 m *274·9 ft* tall, in the Sequoia National Park, California, USA. It has a true girth of 25·1 m *82·3 ft* (1989) (at 1·4 m *4·5 ft* above the ground). The 'General Sherman' has been estimated to contain the equivalent of 600 120 board feet of timber, sufficient to make 5 000 000 000 matches. The foliage is blue-green, and the red-brown tan bark may be up to 61 cm *24 in* thick in parts. Estimates place its weight, including its root system, at 2500 tonnes but the timber is light (288·3 kg/m³ *18 lb/ft³*). This 2500–3000-year-old monster has an annual growth rate of almost a millimetre (*0·039 in*)–the volume contained in a tree 15 m *49·2 ft* tall and 30 cm *1 ft* in diameter. The largest known petrified tree is one of this species with a 89·9 m *295 ft* trunk near Coaldale, Nevada, USA.

The seed of a 'big tree' weighs only 4·7 mg *1/6000th of an oz*. Its growth at maturity may therefore represent an increase in weight of 1 300 000 million-fold.

The tree canopy covering the greatest area is the great Banyan *Ficus benghalensis* in the Indian Botanical Garden, Calcutta with 1775 prop or supporting roots and a circumference of 412 m *1350 ft*. It covers overall some 1·2 ha *3 acres* and dates from *ante* 1787. However, it is reported that a 550-year-old Banyan tree (known as 'Thimmamma Marrimanu') in Gutibayalu village near Kadiri Taluk, Andhra Pradesh, India spreads over 2·1 ha *5·2 acres*.

Greatest girth ■ 'El Arbol del Tule', in the state of Oaxaca, in Mexico is a 41 m *135 ft* tall Montezuma cypress (*Taxodium mucronatum*) with a girth of 35·8 m *117·6 ft* at a height of 1·52 m *5 ft* above the ground in 1982.

A figure of 57·9 m *190 ft* in circumference was recorded for the pollarded European chestnut (*Castanea sativa*) known as the 'Tree of the 100 Horses' (Castagno di Cento Cavalli) on Mount Etna, Sicily, Italy in 1770 and 1780. It is now in three parts widely separated.

Measurements up to 54·5 m *180 ft* in circumference have been attributed to Baobab trees (*Adansonia digitata*).

Britain ■ A sweet ('Spanish') chestnut (*Castanea sativa*) in the grounds of Canford School, near Poole, Dorset, has a bole 13·33 m *43 ft 9 in* in circumference. The largest-girthed living British oak is one at Bowthorpe Farm near Bourne, south Lincs, measured in September 1973 to be 11·91 m *39 ft 1 in*. The largest 'maiden' (i.e. not pollarded) oak is the Majesty Oak at Fredville Park, near Nonington, Kent, with a girth of 11·60 m *38 ft 1 in* (1973). The largest yew with a clear bole at 1·52 m *5 ft* is 10·79 m *35 ft 5 in* at Ulcombe Church, Kent.

Fastest growing ■ Discounting bamboo, which is not botanically classified as a tree but as a woody grass, the fastest rate of growth recorded is 10·74 m *35 ft 3 in* in 13 months by an *Albizzia falcata* planted on 17 Jun 1974 in Sabah, Malaysia. The youngest recorded age for a tree to reach 30·48 m *100 ft* is 64 months for one of the species planted on 24 Feb 1975, also in Sabah.

The world's most productive forest is a plantation of eucalypts (*Eucalyptus grandis*) at Aracruz, Brazil, where the average growth rate is 70 m³ per ha per year (*2472 ft³ per 2·47 acre per year*).

Slowest growing ■ The speed of growth of trees depends largely upon conditions, although some species, such as box and yew, are always slow-growing. The extreme is represented by the *Dioon edule* (Cycadaceae) measured in Mexico in 1981–6 by Dr Charles M. Peters. He found the average annual growth rate to be 0·76 mm *0·03 in* and a 120-year old specimen of 9·9 cm *3·9 in* tall. The growing of miniature trees or *bonsai* is an oriental cult mentioned as early as *c.* 1320.

Tallest ■ According to the researches of Dr A. C. Carder, the tallest tree ever measured was an Australian Eucalyptus (*Eucalyptus regnans*) at Watts

TALLEST TREES IN THE BRITISH ISLES *(By species)*

World's tallest

Species	Location	Height
ALDER (Italian)	Westonbirt, Gloucester	34m 111ft
ALDER (Common)	Ashburnham Park, East Sussex	32m 105ft
ASH	Old Roar Ghyll, St. Leonards, East Sussex	41m 135ft
BEECH	Hallyburton House, Perthshire	46m 150ft
BEECH (Copper)¹	Dalguise House, Perthshire	38m 124ft
BIRCH (Swedish)	Taymouth Castle, Perthshire	34m 111ft
CEDAR (Blue Atlas)	Brockhampton Pk, Hereford & Worcs	38m 125ft
CEDAR (of Lebanon)	Leaton Knolls, Shropshire	42m 140ft
CHESTNUT (Horse)	Ashford Chase, Petersfield, Hampshire	39m 130ft
CHESTNUT (Sweet)	Tyninghame, E.Lothian	36m 118ft
CYPRESS (Lawson)	Strone House, Argyll	40m 133ft
CYPRESS (Leyland)	Bicton, Sidmouth, Devon	36m 118ft
CYPRESS (Monterey)	Moreton House, Devon	40m 131ft
DOUGLAS FIR	The Hermitage, Perthshire	61m 200ft
ELM² (Smooth Leaf)	No large trees left standing	
ELM² (Huntingdon)	Howlett's Park Zoo, Canterbury, Kent	40m 132ft
ELM (Wych)²	Castle Howard, Yorks	41m 134ft
EUCALYPTUS	Glencormack, Co. Wicklow	44m 144ft
GRAND FIR	Strone, Cairndow, Argyll	62m 203ft
GINKGO	Sezincote, Glos.	30m 98ft
HEMLOCK (Western)	Murthly Castle, Dunkeld, Perthshire	52m 170ft
HOLLY	Ashburnham Park, Battle, East Sussex	24m 80ft
HORNBEAM	Wrest Park, Shefford, Bedfordshire	32m 105ft
LARCH (European)	Glenlee, Dumfries & Galloway	46m 150ft
LARCH (Japanese)	Blair Castle, Fife	37m 123ft

River, Victoria, Australia, reported in 1872 by trained forester William Ferguson. It measured 132·58 m *435 ft* and almost certainly measured over 152·4 m *500 ft* originally. A *Eucalyptus regnans* at Mt Baw Baw, Victoria, Australia is believed to have measured 143 m *470 ft* in 1885. The closest measured rivals to these champions have been:

m	ft	
126·5	415	Douglas-Fir *Pseudotsuga menziesii*, Lynn Valley, British Columbia, 1902
119·7	393	The Mineral Douglas-fir *Pseudotsuga menziesii*, Washington State, USA, 1905
115·8	380	Nisqually fir *Pseudotsuga menziesii*, Nisqually River, Washington State, USA, 1899
114·3	375	Cornthwaite Mountain ash *Eucalyptus regnans*, Thorpdale, Victoria, Australia, 1880
112	367·6	Coast redwood *Sequoia sempervirens*, Guerneville, California, USA, 1873. This tree was felled for timber in 1875.

Tallest standing tree in the world. The 'Harry Cole' tree, Humboldt County, California, measured by Ron Hildebrant of Petaluna, California in July 1988 was found to be at least 113 m *371 ft* tall.

Currently the tallest standing broadleaf tree is a Mountain ash (*Eucalyptus regnans*) in the Styx Valley, Tasmania at 95 m *312 ft*.

Great Britain ■ The tallest trees in Great Britain are a Grand fir (*Abies grandis*) at Strone, Cairndow, Argyllshire and Douglas-firs at The Hermitage, Perth, and in Moniac Glen, Inverness. In June 1985 all were 61–62 m *200–203 ft*. Only the Strone Grand fir can be measured from both sides. At 62 m *203 ft* and still making visible annual increase, this is the best claimant. The tallest in England is a Douglas-fir (*Pseudotsuga menziesii*) measured at 53 m *174 ft* at Broadwood, Dunster, Somerset. The tallest measured in Northern Ireland is a Giant Sequoia (*Sequoiadendron giganteum*), measured in 1983 to be 50 m *164 ft* tall at Caledon Castle, Co. Tyrone. The tallest in Wales is a grand fir at Leighton Park, Powys (pl. 1886) measured in 1982 to be 58 m *190 ft*.

Ireland ■ The tallest tree in Ireland is a Sitka spruce (*Picea sitchensis*) 50·59 m *166 ft* tall at Curraghmore, Waterford, measured in March 1974.

Christmas ■ The world's tallest cut Christmas tree was a 67·36 m *221 ft* tall Douglas-fir (*Pseudotsuga menziesii*) erected at Northgate Shopping Center, Seattle, Washington State, USA in December 1950.

Britain ■ An 25·98 m *85 ft 3¼ in* long spruce (*Picea abies*) from Norway erected for the Canterbury Cathedral appeal on the South Bank, London on 20 Nov 1975.

Oldest ■ The oldest recorded tree was a Bristlecone pine (*Pinus longaeva*) designated WPN-114, which grew at 3275 m *10 750 ft* above sea level on the north-east face of Mt Wheeler, eastern Nevada, USA. It was found to be 5100 years old. The oldest known *living* tree is the Bristlecone pine named 'Methuselah' at 3050 m *10 000 ft* in the California side of the White Mountains, confirmed as 4700 years old. In March 1974 it was reported that this tree had produced 48 live seedlings. Dendrochronologists estimate the *potential* life-span of a Bristlecone pine at nearly 5500 years, but that of a California big tree (*Sequoia giganteum*) at perhaps 6000 years. No single cell lives more than 30 years.

British ■ Of all British trees that with the longest life is the Yew (*Taxus baccata*), for which a maximum age well in excess of 1000 years is usually conceded. The oldest known is the Fortingall Yew near Aberfeldy, Perthshire, part of which still grows. In 1777 this tree was over 15·24 m *50 ft* in girth and it cannot be much less than 3500 years old today.

Earliest species ■ The earliest species of tree still surviving is the Maiden-hair tree (*Ginkgo biloba*), of Zhexiang, China, which first appeared about 160 000 000 years ago, during the Jurassic era. It was 'rediscovered' by Kaempfer (Netherlands) in 1690 and reached England c. 1754. It has been grown in Japan since c. 1100 where it was known as *ginkyō* ('silver apricot') and is now known as *icho*.

Most leaves ■ Little work has been done on the laborious task of establishing which species has most leaves. A large oak has perhaps 250 000 but a cypress may have some 45–50 million leaf scales.

Remotest ■ The tree believed to be the remotest from any other is a Norwegian spruce, the only one on Campbell Island, Antarctica. Its nearest companion would be over 145 km *120 miles* away on the Auckland Islands.

Rarest ■ A single specimen of the Café marron bush *Ramosmania heterophylla* survives at the Royal Botanic Gardens, Kew, west London. It is 12·7 cm *5 in* tall and was last seen in Mauritius in 1940.

Most expensive ■ The highest price ever paid for a tree is $51 000 for a single Starkspur Golden Delicious apple tree from near Yakima, Washington State, USA, bought by a nursery in Missouri in 1959.

Largest forest ■ The largest afforested areas in the world are the vast coniferous forests of the northern USSR, lying between latitude 55° N and the Arctic Circle. The total wooded area amounts to 1100 million ha *2 700 000 000 acres* (25 per cent of the world's forests), of which 38 per cent is Siberian larch. The USSR is 34 per cent afforested. The largest are of forest in the tropics remains the Amazon Basin amounting to approximately 330 million ha (*81·5 million acres*).

UK ■ The largest forest in England is the Kielder Forest District (39 380 ha *97 309 acres*), in Northumberland. The largest in Wales is Coed Morgannwg (Forest of Glamorgan) (17 845 ha *44 095 acres*). Scotland's most extensive forest is the Newton Stewart Forest District (35 275 ha *87 165 acres*) in Dumfries &

---

[1] *It was toppled by severe winds on 16th Oct 1987. On the night of 16-17 Oct 1987 an estimated 15 million trees were destroyed by high winds at an estimated cost of £15 million.*
[2] *It was estimated in 1980 that more than 17 million of the 23 million elms in southern England had since 1968 been killed by the fungus that causes Dutch elm disease Ceratocystis ulmi.*

(Artwork: Rhoda & Robert Burns/Drawing Attention)

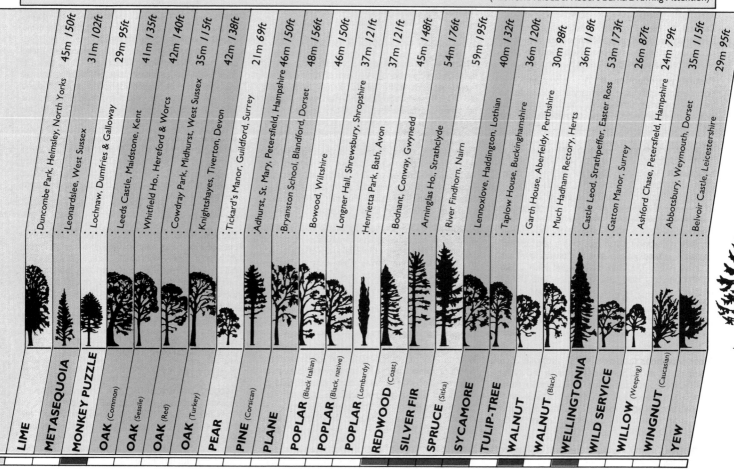

Galloway. The United Kingdom is 7 per cent afforested.

Longest avenue ■ The longest avenue of trees has been the now partly felled private avenue of 1750 beeches in Savernake Forest near Marlborough, Wilts. It measures 5·79 km *3·6 miles*.

Heaviest wood ■ Black ironwood (*Olea laurifolia*), also called South African ironwood, has a specific gravity of up to 1·49, and weighing up to 1490 kg/m³ *93 lb/ft³*.

British ■ The heaviest British wood is boxwood (*Buxus sempervirens*) with an extreme of 1025 kg/m³ *64 lb/ft³*.

Lightest wood ■ The lightest wood is *Aeschynomene hispida*, found in Cuba, which has a specific gravity of 0·044 and a weight of only 44 kg/m³ *2³/₄ lb/ft³*. The wood of the Balsa tree (*Ochroma pyramidale*) is of very variable density – between 40 and 384 kg/m³ *2¹/₂ and 24 lb/ft³*. The density of cork is 240 kg/m³ *15 lb/ft³*.

Kingdom Protista

Protista were first discovered in 1676 by Antonie van Leeuwenhoek of Delft (1632–1723), a Dutch microscopist. Among Protista are characteristics common to both plants and animals. The more plant-like are termed Protophyta (protophytes), including unicellular algae, and the more animal-like are placed in the phylum Protozoa (protozoans), including amoeba and flagellates.

Largest ■ The largest protozoans in terms of volume which are known to have existed were calcareous foraminifera (Foraminiferida) belonging to the genus *Nummulites*, a species of which, in the Middle Eocene rocks of Turkey, attained 22 cm *8·6 in* in diameter. The largest existing protozoan, a species of the fan-shaped *Stannophyllum* (Xenophyophorida), can exceed this in length (25 cm *9·8 in* has been recorded) but not in volume.

Smallest protophytes ■ The marine microflagellate alga *Micromonas pusilla*, has a diameter of less than 2 microns or micrometres (2×10^{-6} m) or *0·00008 in*.

Fastest ■ The protozoan *Monas stigmatica* has been measured to move a distance equivalent to 40 times its own length in a second. No human can cover even seven times his own length in a second.

Fastest reproduction ■ The protozoan *Glaucoma*, which reproduces by binary fission, divides as frequently as every three hours. Thus in the course of a day it could become a '6 greats grandparent' and the progenitor of 510 descendants.

Kingdom Fungi

Largest ■ Marcia Wallgren of Yellow Springs, Ohio, USA, found a Puff ball (*Calvatia gigantea*) 195·58 cm *77 in* in circumference in 1988. A 32·6 kg *72 lb* example of the edible mushroom (*Polyporus frondosus*) was reported by Joseph Opple near Solon, Ohio, USA in September 1976. The largest officially recorded tree fungus was a specimen of *Oxyporus (Fomes) nobilissimus*, measuring 142 cm *56 in* by 94 cm *37 in* and weighing at least 136 kg *300 lb* found by J. Hisey in Washington State, USA in 1946.

UK ■ An Ash fungus (*Fomes fraxineus*) measuring 127 cm by 38 cm *50 in* by *15 in* wide, was found by the forester A. D. C. LeSueur on a tree at Waddesdon, Bucks in 1954.

Most poisonous toadstool ■ The yellowish-olive Death cap (*Amanita phalloides*) is regarded as the world's most poisonous fungus. It is found in England. From 6–15 hours after tasting, the effects are vomiting, delirium, collapse and death. Among its victims was Cardinal Giulio di' Medici, Pope Clement VII (b. 1478) on 25 Sep 1534.

UK ■ In the United Kingdom there were 39 fatalities from fungus poisoning between 1920 and 1950. As the poisonous types are mostly *Amanita* varieties, it is reasonable to assume that the deaths were predominantly due to *Amanita phalloides*. The most recent fatality was probably in 1960.

Aeroflora ■ Fungi were once classified in the subkingdom Protophyta of the kingdom Protista. The highest total fungal spore count was 161 037 per m³ near Cardiff on 21 July 1971. A plane tree pollen count of 2160 per m³ was recorded near London on 9 May 1971. The lowest counts of airborne allergens are nil.

Britain ■ A grass pollen count of 2824 per m³ was recorded at Aberystwyth on 29 Jun 1961.

Procaryota

Earliest ■ The earliest life form reported from Britain is *Kakabekia barghoorniana*, a microorganism similar in form to an orange slice, found near Harlech, Gwynedd, Wales in 1964 and dated to 4000 million years ago in July 1986.

BACTERIA

Antonie van Leeuwenhoek (1632–1723) was the first to observe bacteria, in 1675. The largest of the bacteria is the sulphur bacterium *Beggiatoa mirabilis*, which is from 16 to 45 microns in width and which may form filaments several millimetres long.

The bacteria *Thermoactinomyces vulgaris* have been found alive in cores of mud taken from the bottom of Windermere, Cumbria, England and have been dated to 1500 years before the present.

Smallest free-living entity ■ The smallest of all free-living organisms are pleuro-pneumonia-like organisms (PPLO) of the *Mycoplasma*. One of these, *Mycoplasma laidlawii*, first discovered in sewage in 1936, has a diameter during its early existence of only 100 millimicrons, or *0·000004 in*. Examples of the strain known as H.39 have a maximum diameter of 300 millimicrons and weigh an estimated $1·0 \times 10^{-16}$ gramme. Thus a 190 tonne Blue whale would weigh $1·9 \times 10^{24}$ or 1·9 quadrillion times as much.

Highest ■ In April 1967 the US National Aeronautics and Space Administration (NASA) reported that bacteria had been discovered at an altitude of 41 100 m (41·13 km) *135 000 ft (25·56 miles)*.

Oldest ■ The oldest deposits from which living bacteria are claimed to have been extracted are salt layers near Irkutsk, USSR, dating from about 600 000 000 years ago, but the discovery was not accepted internationally. The US Dry Valley Drilling Project in Antarctica claimed resuscitated rod-shaped bacteria from caves up to a million years old.

Fastest ■ The rod-shaped bacillus *Bdellovibrio bacteriovorus*, by means of a polar flagellum rotating 100 times/sec, can move 50 times its own length of 2 μm per sec. This would be the equivalent of a human sprinter reaching 320 km/h *200 mph* or a swimmer crossing the English Channel in 6 min.

Toughest ■ The bacterium *Micrococcus radiodurans* can withstand atomic radiation of 6·5 million röntgens or 10 000 times that fatal to the average man. In March 1983 John Barras (University of Oregon, USA) reported bacteria from sulphurous sea bed vents thriving at 306°C *583°F* in the East Pacific Rise at Lat. 21°N.

VIRUSES

Largest ■ Dmitriy Ivanovsky (1864–1920) first reported filterable objects in 1892 but Martinus Willem Beijerink (1851–1931) first confirmed the nature of viruses in 1898. These are now defined as aggregates of two or more types of chemical (including either dna or rna) which are infectious and potentially pathogenic. The longest known is the rod-shaped *Citrus tristeza* virus with particles measuring 2000×10 nm (1 nanometre $= 1 \times 10^{-9}$ m).

Smallest ■ The smallest known viruses are the nucleoprotein plant viruses such as the satellite of tobacco *Necrosis virus* with spherical particles 17 nm in diameter. A putative new infectious submicroscopic organism but without nucleic acid, named a 'prion', was announced from the University of California in February 1982. Viroids (rna cores without protein coating) are much smaller than viruses. They were discovered by Theodor O. Diener (USA) in February 1972. Dr Rohwer of Bethesda, Maryland, USA stated in September 1984 that scrapie-specific protein was smaller than the concept of a 'yet to be identified prion'.

Parks, Zoos, Oceanaria, Aquaria

PARKS

Largest ■ The Wood Buffalo National Park in Alberta, Canada (established 1922), has an area of 45 211 197 ha *11 172 000 acres* (45 480 km² *17 560 miles²*). The largest national park in Great Britain is the Lake District National Park which has an area of 2240 km² *866 miles²*. The largest private park in the United Kingdom is Woburn Park (1200 ha *3000 acres*), near Woburn Abbey, the seat of the Dukes of Bedford.

ZOOS

It has been estimated that throughout the world there are some 757 zoos with an estimated annual attendance of 350 000 000.

Largest game reserve ■ The world's largest zoological reserve is the Etosha National Park, Namibia. Established in 1907 its area has grown to 99 525 km² *38 427 miles²*.

Oldest zoo ■ The earliest known collection of animals was that set up by Shulgi, a 3rd-dynasty ruler of Ur from 2097–2094 BC at Puzurish in south-east Iraq. The oldest known zoo is that at Schönbrunn, Vienna, Austria, built in 1752 by the Holy Roman Emperor Franz I for his wife Maria Theresa. The oldest existing public zoological collection in the world is that of the Zoological Society of London, founded in 1826. Its collection, housed partly in Regent's Park, London (14·5 ha *36 acres*) and partly at Whipsnade Park, Beds (219 ha *541 acres*) (opened 23 May 1931), is the most comprehensive in the United Kingdom. The stocktaking on 1 Jan 1989 accounted for a total of 11 108 specimens. These comprised 2628 mammals, 1916 birds, 489 reptiles, 175 amphibians, an estimated total of 2300 fish and an estimated total of 3600 invertebrates excluding some common species. The record annual attendances are 3 031 571 in 1950 for Regent's Park and 756 758 in 1961 for Whipsnade.

Earliest without bars ■ The earliest zoo without bars was that at Stellingen, near Hamburg, West Germany. It was founded in 1907 by Carl Hagenbeck (1844–1913), who made use of deep pits and large pens instead of cages to separate the exhibits from visitors.

OCEANARIA

Earliest ■ The world's first oceanarium is Marineland of Florida, opened in 1938 at a site 29 km *18 miles* south of St Augustine, Florida, USA. Up to 26·3 million litres *5 800 000 gal* of sea-water are pumped daily through two major tanks, one rectangular (30·48 m *100 ft* long by 12·19 m *40 ft* wide by 5·48 m *18 ft* deep) containing 1·7 million litres *375 000 gal*, and one circular (71 m *233 ft* in circumference and 3·65 m *12 ft* deep) containing 1·5 million litres *330 000 gal*. The tanks are seascaped, including coral reefs and even a shipwreck.

AQUARIA

Largest aquarium ■ The Sydney Aquarium, Australia, opened on 13 Jul 1988, holds a total of 3 315 398 litres *875 838 gal* of water. It contains over 5000 fish displayed in a variety of habitats including two massive floating oceanariums, 21 major aquarium tanks, 29 smaller aquarium tanks and four crocodile and turtle pools.

CHAPTER 3

Largest peninsula
Clearly visible in this photograph taken during the
Apollo 11 mission is Arabia, the worlds largest
peninsula, with an area of about 3.250.000 km².
(Photo: NASA/Science Photo Library)

The Natural World and Space

THE EARTH

The Earth is not a true sphere, but flattened at the poles and hence an oblate spheroid. The polar diameter of the Earth, which is 12 713·505 km *7899·806 miles*, is 42·769 km *26·575 miles* less than the equatorial diameter (12 756·274 km *7926·381 miles*). The Earth has a pear-shaped asymmetry with the north polar radius being 45 m *148 ft* longer than the south polar radius. There is also a slight ellipticity of the equator since its long axis (about longitude 37° W) is 159 m *522 ft* greater than the short axis. The greatest departures from the reference ellipsoid are a protuberance of 73 m *240 ft* in the area of Papua New Guinea and a depression of 105 m *344 ft* south of Sri Lanka, in the Indian Ocean.

The greatest circumference of the Earth, at the equator, is 40 075·02 km *24 901·46 miles*, compared with 40 007·86 km *24 859·73 miles* at the meridian. The area of the surface is estimated to be 510 065 600 km^2 *196 937 400 miles^2*. The period of axial rotation, *i.e.* the true sidereal day, is 23 hr 56 min 4·0996 sec, mean time.

The mass of the Earth was first assessed by Dr Nevil Maskelyne (1732–1811) in Perthshire, Scotland in 1774. The modern value is 5·974 × 10^{21} tonnes and its density is 5·515 times that of water. The volume is an estimated 1 083 207 000 000 km^3 *259 875 300 000 miles^3*. The Earth picks up cosmic dust but estimates vary widely with 30 000 tonnes a year being the upper limit. Modern theory is that the Earth has an outer shell or lithosphere 80 km *50 miles* thick, then an outer and inner rock layer or mantle extending 2809 km *1745 miles* deep, beneath which there is an iron-rich core of radius 3482 km *2164 miles*. If the iron-rich core theory is correct, iron would be the most abundant element in the Earth. At the centre of the core the estimated density is 13·09 g/cm^3, the temperature 4500° C and the pressure 364 GPa or 23 600 tons f/in^2.

Structure and Dimensions

OCEANS

The area of the Earth covered by sea is estimated to be 362 033 000 km^2 *139 781 000 miles^2* or 70·98 per cent of the total surface. The mean depth of the hydrosphere was once estimated to be 3795 m *12 450 ft*, but recent surveys suggest a lower estimate, of 3554 m *11 660 ft*. The total weight of the water is estimated to be 1·32 × 10^{18} tonnes, or 0·022 per cent of the Earth's total weight. The volume of the oceans is estimated to be 1 349 900 000 km^3 *323 900 000 miles^3* compared to 35 000 000 km^3 *8 400 000 miles^3* of fresh water.

Largest ■ The largest ocean in the world is the Pacific. Excluding adjacent seas, it represents 45·9 per cent of the world's oceans and covers 166 241 000 km^2 *64 185 600 miles^2* in area. The average depth is 4188 m *13 740 ft*. The shortest navigable trans-Pacific distance from Guayaquil, Ecuador to Bangkok, Thailand is 17 550 km *10 905 miles*.

Deepest ■ The deepest part of the ocean was first pinpointed in 1951 by HM Survey Ship *Challenger* in the Mariana Trench in the Pacific Ocean. The depth was measured by wide-band sounding at 10 863 m *35 639 ft*. Subsequent visits have resulted in slightly deeper measurements. A survey by the Soviet research ship *Vityaz* in 1957 produced a depth which was later refined to 11 034 m *36 200 ft*, and on 23 Jan 1960 the US Navy bathyscaphe *Trieste* descended to the bottom at 10 916 m *35 813 ft*. A more recent visit produced a figure of 10 924 m ± 10 m *35 839 ft ± 33 ft*, from data obtained by the survey vessel *Takuyo* of the Hydrographic Department, Japan Maritime Safety Agency in 1984, using a narrow multi-beam echo sounder.

A metal object, say a kilogram ball of steel, dropped into water above this trench would take nearly 64 min to fall to the sea bed, where hydrostatic pressure is over 1250 bars *18 000 lb/in^2*.

THE WORLD'S WATER

Whilst the volume of the world's oceans is estimated to be 1 349 900 000km^3 323 900 000 miles^3, the volume of fresh water is just 35 000 000km^3 8 400 000 miles^3. The pint of Guinness on the left shows a comparison between each ocean as a percentage of the total volume of the oceans, and the one on the right represents the world's fresh water if the total volume of the oceans is a full pint. (Artwork: Peter Harper)

SEA WATER 1349 900 000km^3

- Other Seas 2%
- Arctic 1%
- Atlantic 24%
- Indian 21%
- Pacific 52%

FRESH WATER 35 000 000km^3

The deepest point in the territorial waters of the United Kingdom is an area 6 cables (*1100 m*) off the island of Raasay, off Skye, in the Inner Sound at Lat. 57° 30′ 33″ N, Long. 5° 57′ 27″ W.

Largest sea ■ The largest of the world's seas is the South China Sea, with an area of 2 974 600 km^2 *1 148 500 miles^2*.

Largest gulf ■ The largest gulf in the world is the Gulf of Mexico, with an area of 1 500 000 km^2 *580 000 miles^2* and a shoreline of 4990 km *3100 miles* from Cape Sable, Florida, USA, to Cabo Catoche, Mexico.

Largest bay ■ The largest bay in the world measured by shoreline length is Hudson Bay, northern Canada, with a shoreline of 12 268 km *7623 miles* and with an area of 822 300 km^2 *317 500 miles^2*. The area of the Bay of Bengal is however 2 172 000 km^2 *839 000 miles^2*.

Great Britain ■ Great Britain's largest bay is Cardigan Bay which has a 225 km *140 mile* long shoreline and measures 116 km *72 miles* across from the Lleyn Peninsula, Gwynedd to St David's Head, Dyfed, Wales.

Longest fjord ■ The world's longest fjord is the Nordvest Fjord arm of the Scoresby Sund in eastern Greenland, which extends inland 313 km *195 miles* from the sea. The longest Norwegian fjord is the Sogne Fjord, which extends 183 km *113·7 miles* inland from Sygnefest to the head of the Lusterfjord arm at Skjolden. It averages barely 4·75 km *3 miles* in width and has a deepest point of 1245 m *4085 ft*. If measured from Huglo along the Bømlafjord to the head of the Sørfjord arm at Odda, Hardangerfjorden can also be said to extend 183 km *113·7 miles*. The longest Danish fjord is Limfjorden (160 km *100 miles*).

Longest sea loch ■ Loch Fyne, Scotland, extends 60·5 km *37·6 miles* inland into Strathclyde.

Highest seamount ■ The highest known submarine mountain, or seamount, is one discovered in 1953 near the Tonga Trench, between Samoa and New Zealand. It rises 8690 m *28 500 ft* from the sea bed, with its summit 365 m *1200 ft* below the surface.

Remotest spot from land ■ The world's most distant point from land is a spot in the South Pacific, approximately 48° 30′ S, 125° 30′ W, which is about 2670 km *1660 miles* from the nearest points of land, namely Pitcairn Island, Ducie Island and Cape Dart, Antarctica. Centred on this spot, therefore, is a circle of water with an area of about 22 421 500 km^2 *8 657 000 miles^2* — about 18 000 km^2 *7000 miles^2* larger than the USSR, the world's largest country.

Most southerly ■ The most southerly part of the oceans is 85° 34′ S, 154° W, at the snout of the Robert Scott Glacier, 490 km *305 miles* from the South Pole.

Temperature ■ The temperature of the water at the surface of the sea varies from −2° C *28·5° F* in the White Sea to 35·6° C *96° F* in the shallow areas of the Persian Gulf in summer. Ice-focused solar rays have been known to heat lake water to nearly 26·8° C *80° F*. The normal Red Sea temperature is 22° C *71·6° F*. The highest temperature recorded in the ocean is 404° C *759° F*, for a spring measured by an American research submarine some 480 km *300 miles* off the American west coast, in an expedition under the direction of Professor Jack Diamond of Oregon State University, USA in 1985. Remote probes measured the temperature of the spring which was kept from vaporising by the weight of water above it.

Clearest ■ The Weddell Sea, 71° S, 15° W off Antarctica, has the clearest water of any sea. A 'Secchi' disc was visible to a depth of 80 m *262 ft* on 13 Oct 1986, as measured by Dutch researchers of the German Alfred-Wegener Institute. Such clarity corresponds to what scientists consider attainable in distilled water.

STRAITS

Longest ■ The longest straits in the world are the Tatarskiy Proliv or Tartar Straits between Sakhalin Island and the USSR mainland running from the Sea of Japan to Sakhalinsky Zaliv — 800 km *497 miles*, thus marginally longer than the Malacca Straits.

Broadest ■ The broadest named straits in the world are the Davis Straits between Greenland and Baffin Island with a minimum width of 338 km

210 miles. The Drake Passage between the Diego Ramirez Islands, Chile and the South Shetland Islands is 1140 km *710 miles* across.

Narrowest ■ The narrowest navigable straits are those between the Aegean island of Euboea and the mainland of Greece. The gap is only 40 m *45 yd* wide at Khalkis. The Seil Sound, Inner Hebrides, Scotland narrows to a point only 6 m *20 ft* wide where the Clachan bridge joins the island of Seil to the mainland, and is said to span the Atlantic.

WAVES

Highest ■ The highest officially-recorded sea wave was calculated at 34 m *112 ft* from trough to crest; it was measured by Lt Frederic Margraff USN from the USS *Ramapo* proceeding from Manila, Philippines, to San Diego, California, USA, on the night of 6–7 Feb 1933, during a 68-knot (*126 km/h*) hurricane. The highest instrumentally measured wave was one 26·2 m *86 ft* high, recorded by the British ship *Weather Reporter*, in the North Atlantic on 30 Dec 1972 in Lat. 59° N, Long. 19° W. It has been calculated on the statistics of the Stationary Random Theory that one wave in more than 300 000 may exceed the average by a factor of 4. On 9 Jul 1958 a landslip caused a 160 km/h *100 mph* wave to wash 524 m *1720 ft* high along the fjord-like Lituya Bay in Alaska, USA.

Highest seismic ■ The highest estimated height of a *tsunami* (often wrongly called a tidal wave) was one of 85 m *278 ft*, which appeared off Ishigaki Island, Ryukyu Chain on 24 Apr 1771. It tossed a 750-tonne block of coral more than 2·5 km *1·3 miles. Tsunami* (a Japanese word meaning *nami*, a wave; *tsu*, overflowing) have been observed to travel at 790 km/h *490 mph.* Evidence for a 300 m *1000 ft* ocean wave having occurred about 100 000 years ago was reported on 4 Dec 1984. This is believed to have broken on the southern shore of Lanai, Hawaiian Islands and was due to a meteorite, a volcanic eruption or a submarine landslide.

CURRENTS

Greatest ■ The greatest current in the oceans is the Antarctic Circumpolar Current or West Wind

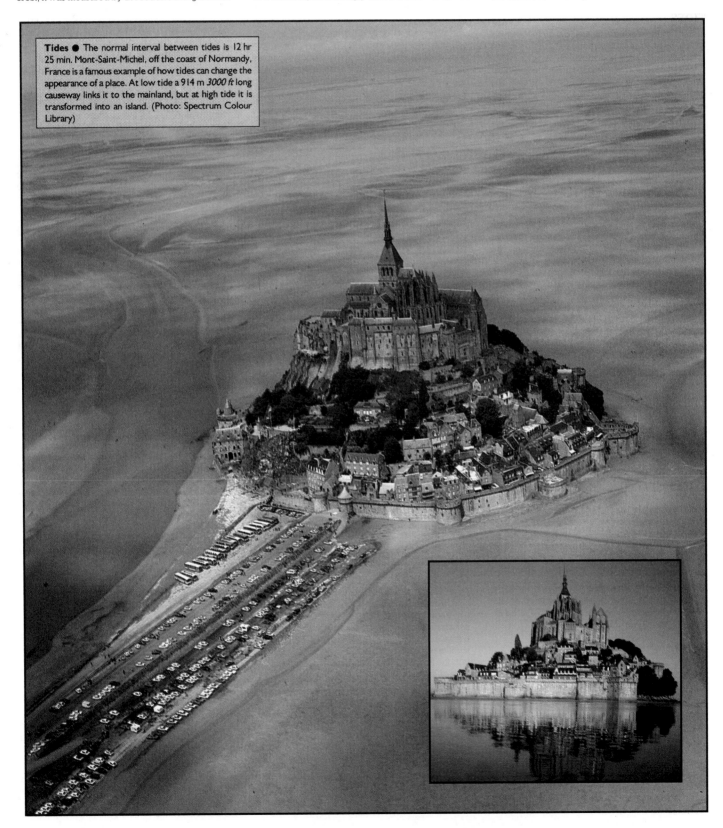

Tides ● The normal interval between tides is 12 hr 25 min. Mont-Saint-Michel, off the coast of Normandy, France is a famous example of how tides can change the appearance of a place. At low tide a 914 m *3000 ft* long causeway links it to the mainland, but at high tide it is transformed into an island. (Photo: Spectrum Colour Library)

Drift Current which was measured in 1969 in the Drake Passage between South America and Antarctica to be flowing at a rate of 270 000 000 m³ *9500 million ft³* per sec — nearly treble that of the Gulf Stream. Its width ranges from 300–2000 km *185–1240 miles* and has a proven surface flow rate of ¹/₁₀ of a knot *0·75 km/h.*

Strongest ■ The world's strongest currents are the Nakwakto Rapids, Slingsby Channel, British Columbia, Canada (Lat. 51° 05′ N, Long. 127° 30′ W) where the flow rate may reach 16 knots *29·6 km/h.*

Great Britain ■ The fastest current in British territorial waters is 10·7 knots *19·8 km/h* in the Pentland Firth between the Orkney Islands and Caithness.

TIDES

Extreme tides are due to lunar and solar gravitational forces affected by their perigee, perihelion and syzygies. Barometric and wind effects can superimpose an added 'surge' element. Coastal and sea-floor configurations can accentuate these forces. The normal interval between tides is 12 hr 25 min.

Greatest ■ The greatest tides occur in the Bay of Fundy, which divides the peninsula of Nova Scotia, Canada, from the United States' north-easternmost state of Maine and the Canadian province of New Brunswick. Burncoat Head in the Minas Basin, Nova Scotia, has the greatest mean spring range with 14,50 m *47·5 ft.* A range of 16·6 m *54¹/₂ ft* was recorded at springs in Leaf Basin in 1953. Tahiti experiences virtually no tide.

Great Britain ■ The place with the greatest mean spring range in Great Britain is Beachley, on the Severn, with a range of 12·40 m *40·7 ft,* compared with the British Isles' average of 4·57 m *15 ft.* Prior to 1933, tides as high as 8·80 m *28·9 ft* above and 6·80 m *22·3 ft* below datum (total range 15·60 m *51·2 ft*) were recorded at Avonmouth though an extreme range of 15·90 m *52·2 ft* for Beachley was officially accepted. In 1883 a freak tide of greater range was reported from Chepstow, Gwent.

ICEBERGS

Largest and tallest ■ The largest iceberg on record was an antarctic tabular 'berg of over 31 000 km² *12 000 miles²* (335 km *208 miles* long and 97 km *60 miles* wide and thus larger than Belgium) sighted 240 km *150 miles* west of Scott Island, in the South Pacific Ocean, by the USS *Glacier* on 12 Nov 1956. The 61 m *200 ft* thick arctic ice island T.1 (360 km² *140 miles²*), discovered in 1946, was tracked for 17 years. The tallest iceberg measured was one of 167 m *550 ft* reported off western Greenland by the US icebreaker *East Wind* in 1958.

Most southerly arctic ■ The most southerly arctic iceberg was sighted in the Atlantic by a USN weather patrol in Lat. 28° 44′ N, Long. 48° 42′ W in April 1935. The southernmost iceberg reported in British home waters was sighted 96 km *60 miles* from Smith's Knoll, on the Dogger Bank, in the North Sea.

Most northerly antarctic ■ The most northerly antarctic iceberg was a remnant sighted in the Atlantic by the ship *Dochra* in Lat. 26° 30′ S, Long. 25° 40′ W, on 30 Apr 1894.

LAND

There is satisfactory evidence that at one time the Earth's land surface comprised a single primeval continent of 2 × 10⁸ km² *80 million miles²,* now termed Pangaea, and that this split about 190 million years ago, during the Jurassic period, into two super-continents, which are termed Laurasia (Eurasia, Greenland and Northern America) and Gondwanaland (Africa, Arabia, India, South America, Oceania and Antarctica), named after Gondwana, India, which itself split 120 million years ago. The South Pole was apparently in the area of the Sahara as recently as the Ordovician period of *c.* 450 million years ago.

ROCKS

The age of the Earth is generally considered to be within the range of 4530 ± 20 million years, by analogy with directly measured ages of meteorites and of the Moon. However, no rocks of this great age have yet been found on the Earth since geological processes have presumably destroyed them.

Oldest ■ The greatest reported age for any scientifically dated rock is 4300 million years in the case of zircon crystals found by Bob Pidgeon and Simon Wilde 700 km *935 miles* in the Jack Hills, north-east of Perth, Western Australia. The find was reported in July 1986.

On 6 Apr 1988 Japanese scientists claimed that 10 small diamonds found in Zaire were 6000 million years old.

The oldest rocks in Great Britain are the original volcanic products from which were formed the gneiss and granulite rocks of the Scourian complex in the north-west Highlands and the Western Isles which were crystallised 2800 million years ago.

Largest ■ The largest isolated monolith in the world is the 377 m *1237 ft* high Mount Augustus (1105 m *3627 ft* above sea level), discovered on 3 Jun 1858, 320 km *200 miles* east of Carnarvon, Western Australia. It is an upfaulted monoclinal gritty conglomerate 8 km *5 miles* long and 3 km *2 miles* across and thus twice the size of the celebrated monolithic arkose Ayer's Rock (335 m *1100 ft*), 400 km *250 miles* south-west of Alice Springs, in Northern Territory, Australia. It was estimated in 1940 that La Gran Piedra, a volcanic plug located in the Sierra Maestra, Cuba weighs 61 355 tonnes.

CONTINENTS

Largest ■ Of the Earth's surface 41·25 per cent, or 210 400 000 km² *81 200 000 miles²* is covered by continental masses of which only about two-thirds or 29·02 per cent of the Earth's surface (148 021 000 km² *57 151 000 miles²*) is land above water, with a mean height of 756 m *2480 ft* above sea level. The Eurasian land mass is the largest, with an area (including islands) of 53 698 000 km² *20 733 000 miles².* The Afro-Eurasian land mass, separated artificially only by the Suez Canal, covers an area of 84 702 000 km² *32 704 000 miles²* or 57·2 per cent of the Earth's land mass.

Smallest ■ The smallest is the Australian mainland, with an area of 7 618 493 km² *2 941 526 miles²,* which, together with Tasmania, New Zealand, New Guinea and the Pacific Islands, is described sometimes as Oceania.

Land remotest from the sea ■ The point of land remotest from the sea is at Lat. 46° 16·8′ N Long. 86° 40·2′ E in the Dzoosotoyn Elisen (desert), northern Xinjiang Uygur Zizhiqu (Sin Kiang), China's most north-westerly province. It was visited by Nicholas Crane and Dr Richard Crane (GB) on 27 Jun 1986 and is at a straight-line distance of 2648 km *1645 miles* from the nearest open sea.

Great Britain ■ The point furthest from the sea in Great Britain is a point near Meriden, West Midlands, England, which is 117 km *72 ¹/₂ miles* equidistant from the Severn Bridge, the Dee and Mersey estuaries and the Welland estuary in the Wash. The equivalent point in Scotland is in the Forest of Atholl, north-west Tayside, 65 km *40 ¹/₂ miles* equidistant from the head of Loch Leven, Inverness Firth and the Firth of Tay.

Peninsula ■ The world's largest peninsula is Arabia, with an area of about 3 250 000 km² *1 250 000 miles².*

ISLANDS

Largest ■ Discounting Australia, which is usually regarded as a continental land mass, the largest island in the world is Greenland (renamed Kalaatdlit Nunaat on 1 May 1979), with an area of about 2 175 000 km² *840 000 miles².* There is evidence that Greenland is in fact several islands overlaid by an

ice cap without which it would have an area of 1 680 000 km² *650 000 miles².* The largest sand island in the world is Fraser Island, Queensland, Australia with a 120 km *75 mile* long sand dune.

Great Britain ■ The mainland of Great Britain is the eighth largest island in the world, with an area of 218 024 km² *84 186 miles².* It stretches 971 km *603 ¹/₂ miles* from Dunnet Head in the north to Lizard Point in the south and 463 km *287 ¹/₂ miles* across from Porthaflod, Dyfed to Lowestoft, Suffolk. The island of Ireland (84 418 km² *32 594 miles²*) is the 20th largest in the world.

Freshwater ■ The largest island surrounded by fresh water is the Ilha de Marajó (48 000 km² *18 500 miles²*), in the mouth of the River Amazon, Brazil. The world's largest inland island (i.e land surrounded by rivers) is Ilha do Bananal, Brazil (18 130 km² *7000 miles²*). The largest island in a lake is Manitoulin Island (2766 km² *1068 miles²*) in the Canadian (Ontario) section of Lake Huron.

Great Britain ■ The largest lake island in Great Britain is Inchmurrin in Loch Lomond, Strathclyde/Central, Scotland with an area of 115 ha *284 acres.*

Remotest ■ The remotest island in the world is Bouvet Øya (formerly Liverpool Island), discovered in the South Atlantic by J. B. C. Bouvet de Lozier on 1 Jan 1739, and first landed on by Capt George Norris on 16 Dec 1825. Its position is 54° 26′ S, 3° 24′ E. This uninhabited Norwegian dependency is about 1700 km *1050 miles* from the nearest land—the uninhabited Queen Maud Land coast of eastern Antarctica.

The remotest inhabited island in the world is Tristan da Cunha, discovered in the South Atlantic by Tristão da Cunha, a Portuguese admiral, in March 1506. It has an area of 98 km² *38 miles²* (habitable area 31 km² *12 miles²*). The first permanent inhabitant was Thomas Currie, who landed in 1810. The island was annexed by the United Kingdom on 14 Aug 1816. After evacuation in 1961 (due to volcanic activity), 198 islanders returned in November 1963. The nearest inhabited land to the group is the island of St Helena, 2120 km *1320 miles* to the north-east. The nearest continent, Africa, is 2735 km *1700 miles* away.

The remotest of the British islets is Rockall. It is officially given as being 307 km *191 miles* west of St Kilda, Western Isles, although in June 1986 it was found by an RAF *Nimrod* to be 1509 m *4950 ft* to the south-east of its official location. This 21 m *70 ft* high rock measuring 25 m *83 ft* across was not formally annexed until 18 Sept 1955. It was 'occupied' by Tom McClean for 38 days 22 hr 52 min from 25 May to 4 Jul 1985. The remotest British island which has ever been inhabited is North Rona which is 70·8 km *44 miles* from the next nearest land at Cape Wrath and the Butt of Lewis. It was evacuated *c.* 1844. Muckle Flugga, off Unst, in the Shetlands, is the northernmost inhabited with a population of 3 (1971) and is in a latitude north of southern Greenland. Just to the north of it is the rock of Out Stack in Lat. 60° 51′ 35·7″ N.

Greatest archipelago ■ The world's greatest archipelago is the 5600 km *3500 mile* long crescent of more than 13 000 islands which forms Indonesia.

Highest rock pinnacle ■ The world's highest rock pinnacle is Ball's Pyramid near Lord Howe Island in the Pacific, which is 561 m *1843 ft* high, but has a base axis of only 200 m *220 yd.* It was first scaled in 1965.

Northernmost land ■ On 26 Jul 1978 Uffe Petersen of the Danish Geodetic Institute observed the islet of Oodaq Ø 30 m *100 ft* across, 1·36 km *1478 yd* north of Kaffeklubben Ø off Pearyland, Greenland in Lat. 83° 40′ 32·5″ N. Long. 30° 40′ 10·1″ W. It is 706·4 km *438·9 miles* from the North Pole.

Southernmost land ■ The South Pole, unlike the North Pole, is on land. The Amundsen–Scott South Polar station was built there at an altitude of 2855 m *9370 ft* in 1957. It is drifting bodily with the ice cap

8–9 m *27–30 ft* per annum in the direction 43° W and was replaced by a new structure in 1975.

Newest ■ The world's newest island is the lava islet of Fukuto Kuokanoba near Iwo Jima in the Pacific reported in January 1986. It measures 650 × 450 m *2132 × 1476 ft* and is 12 m *40 ft* above sea level.

Largest atoll ■ The largest atoll in the world is Kwajalein in the Marshall Islands, in the central Pacific Ocean. Its slender 283 km *176 mile* long coral reef encloses a lagoon of 2850 km² *1100 miles²*. The atoll with the largest land area is Christmas Atoll, in the Line Islands, in the central Pacific Ocean. It has an area of 642 km² *248 miles²* of which 323 km² *125 miles²* is land. Its principal settlement, London, is only 4 km *2¹/₂ miles* distant from another settlement, Paris.

Longest reef ■ The Great Barrier Reef off Queensland, north-eastern Australia, is 2027 km *1260 statute miles* in length. Between 1959 and 1971 a large section between Cooktown and Townsville was destroyed by the Crown of Thorns starfish (*Acanthaster planci*).

DEPRESSIONS

Deepest ■ The deepest depression so far discovered is the bed rock in the Bentley sub-glacial trench, Antarctica at 2538 m *8326 ft* below sea level. The greatest submarine depression is an area of the north-west Pacific floor which has an average depth of 4570 m *15 000 ft*. The deepest exposed depression on land is the shore surrounding the Dead Sea, now 400 m *1312 ft* below sea level. The deepest point on the bed of this saltiest of all lakes is 728 m *2388 ft* below sea level. The rate of fall in the lake surface since 1948 has been 350 mm *13·78 in* per annum. The deepest part of the bed of Lake Baykal in Siberia, USSR is 1485 m *4872 ft* below sea level.

Great Britain ■ The lowest-lying area in Great Britain is in the Holme Fen area of the Great Ouse, in Cambridgeshire, at 2·75 m *9 ft* below sea level. The deepest depression in England is the bed of part of Lake Windermere, 28·65 m *94 ft* below sea level, and in Scotland the bed of Loch Morar, Inverness, 300·8 m *987 ft* below sea level.

Largest ■ The largest exposed depression in the world is the Caspian Sea basin in the Azerbaydzhani, Russian, Kazakh and Turkmen Republics of the USSR and northern Iran (Persia). It is more than 518 000 km² *200 000 miles²*, of which 371 800 km² *143 550 miles²* is lake area. The preponderant land area of the depression is the Prikaspiyskaya Nizmennost, lying around the northern third of the lake and stretching inland for a distance of up to 450 km *280 miles*.

CAVES

Longest ■ The most extensive cave system in the world is that under the Mammoth Cave National Park, Kentucky, USA, first discovered in 1799. On 9 Sept 1972 an exploration group led by Dr John P. Wilcox completed a connection, pioneered by Mrs Patricia Crowther on 30 Aug, between the Flint Ridge Cave system and the Mammoth Cave system, so making a combined system with a total mapped passageway length which is now over 530 km *330 miles*.

Great Britain ■ The longest cave system in Great Britain is the Ease Gill system, West Yorks which now has 52·4 km *32¹/₂ miles* of explored passage.

Largest ■ The world's largest cave chamber is the Sarawak Chamber, Lubang Nasib Bagus, in the Gunung Mulu National Park, Sarawak, discovered and surveyed by the 1980 British–Malaysian Mulu Expedition. Its length is 700 m *2300 ft*, and its average width is 300 m *980 ft*, and it is nowhere less than 70 m *230 ft* high. It would be large enough to garage 7500 buses.

Greatest descent ■ The world depth record was set by the Groupe Vulcain in the Gouffre Jean

Bernard, France at 1535 m *5036 ft* in October 1983. However, this cave, explored via multiple entrances, has never been entirely descended, so the 'sporting' record for the greatest descent into a cave is recognised as 1508 m *4947 ft* in the Shakta Pantjukhina in the Russian Caucasus Mountains by a team of Ukranian cavers in 1988.

Longest stalactite ■ The longest known stalactite in the world is a wall-supported column extending 59 m *195 ft* from roof to floor in the Cueva de Nerja, near Málaga, in Spain. Probably the longest free-hanging stalactite in the world is one of 7 m *23 ft* in the Poll an Ionain cave in County Clare, Ireland.

Tallest stalagmite ■ The tallest known stalagmite in the world is La Grande Stalagmite in the Aven Armand cave, Lozère, France, which has attained a height of 29 m *98 ft* from the cave floor. It was found in September 1897. The tallest cave column is considered to be the 39 m *128 ft* high Flying Dragon Pillar in Nine Dragons Cave (Daji Dong), Guizhou, China.

DEEPEST CAVES
BY COUNTRIES

Depth			
m	ft		
1535	5036	Réseau Jean Bernard	France
1508	4947	Shakta Pantjukhina	USSR
1408	4619	Puerta de Illamina	Spain
1353	4439	Sistema Huautla	Mexico
1219	3999	Schwersystem	Austria
1215	3986	Complesso Fighiera Corchia	Italy
1159	3802	Anou Ifflis	Algeria
1020	3346	Siebenhengste System	Switzerland
897	2943	Jama u Vjetrena brda	Yugoslavia
889	2917	Nettlebed System	New Zealand
783	2569	Jaskinia Sniezna	Poland
751	2464	Ghar Parau, Zagros	Iran
308	1010	Ogof Ffynnon Ddu	Wales
214	702	Giant's Hole System	England
179	587	Reyfad Pot	N. Ireland
140	459	Carrowmore Cavern	Rep. of Ireland
76	249	Cnoc nan Uamh	Scotland

MOUNTAINS

Highest ■ An eastern Himalayan peak of 8848 m *29 028 ft* above sea level on the Tibet–Nepal border (in an area first designated Chu-mu-lang-ma on a

map of 1717) was discovered to be the world's highest mountain in 1852 by the Survey Department of the Government of India, from theodolite readings taken in 1849 and 1850. In 1860 its height was computed to be 8840 m *29 002 ft*. On 25 Jul 1973 the Chinese announced a height of 8848·2 m *29 029 ft 3 in*. It was named Mt Everest after Col. Sir George Everest, CB. (1790–1866), formerly Surveyor-General of India.

Everest's status as the world's highest mountain, maintained for 135 years (1852–1987), was most recently challenged by K2 (formerly Godwin Austen), also known as Chogori, in the disputed Kashmiri Northern Areas of Pakistan, in an announcement on 6 Mar 1987 by the US K2 Expedition. Their satellite transit surveyor yielded altitudes of between 8858 and 8908 m *29 064–29 228 ft* as against the hitherto official 19th-century figure of 8611 m *28 250 ft*, and the 20th-century proposed height of 8760 m *28 740 ft*. However, on 13 Aug 1987 the Chinese reaffirmed their heights of 8848·2 m *29 029 ft 3 in* for Everest and 8611 m *28 250 ft* for K2. The Research Council in Rome announced on 23 Oct 1987 that new satellite measurements restored Everest to primacy, at 8863 m *29 078 ft*, and put K2 down to 8607 m *28 238 ft*. It was on 31 Jul 1954 that K2 was first climbed, by A. Campagnoni and L. Lacedelli of Italy, 14 months after the summit of Everest had been reached. (For details of Everest ascents, see under Mountaineering in Chapter 11.)

The mountain whose summit is farthest from the Earth's centre is the Andean peak of Chimborazo (6267 m *20 561 ft*), 158 km *98 miles* south of the equator in Ecuador, South America. Its summit is 2150 m *7057 ft* further from the Earth's centre than the summit of Mt Everest. The highest mountain on the equator is Volcán Cayambe (5878 m *19 285 ft*), Ecuador, in Long. 77° 58′ W. A mountaineer atop the summit would be moving at 1671 km/h *1038 mph* relative to the Earth's centre due to the Earth's rotation.

The highest insular mountain in the world is Puncak Jayak (formerly Puncak Sukarno, formerly Carstensz Pyramide) in Irian Jaya, Indonesia. A survey by the Australian Universities' Expedition in 1973 yielded a height of 4884 m *16 023 ft*. Ngga Pula, now 4861 m *15 950 ft*, was in 1936 possibly *c.* 4910 m *c. 16 110 ft* before the melting of its snow cap.

The highest mountain in the United Kingdom is Ben Nevis (1343 m *4406 ft* excluding the 3·65 m *12 ft* cairn), 6·85 km *4¹/₄ miles* south-east of Fort William, Argyll, Scotland. It was climbed before 1720 but though acclaimed the highest in 1790 was not confirmed to be higher than Ben Macdhui (1310 m *4300 ft*) until 1847. In 1834 Ben Macdhui and Ben Nevis (Gaelic, *Beinn Nibheis*) (first reference, 1778) were respectively quoted as 1393 m *4570 ft* and 1332 m *4370 ft*. The highest mountain in England is

Scafell Pike (978 m *3210 ft*) in Cumbria; in Wales the highest is Snowdon (*Yr Wyddfa*) (1085 m *3560 ft*) in Gwynedd; and in Ireland it is Carrauntual (1041 m *3414 ft*) in County Kerry.

There is some evidence that, before being ground down by the ice cap, mountains in the Loch Bà area of the Isle of Mull, Strathclyde were 4575 m *15 000 ft* above sea level. There are 577 peaks and tops over 915 m *3000 ft* in the whole British Isles and 165 peaks and 136 tops in Scotland higher than England's highest point, Scafell Pike. The highest mountain off the mainland is Sgùrr Alasdair (1008 m *3309 ft*) on Skye, named after Alexander (Gaelic, *Alasdair*) Nicolson, who made the first ascent in 1873.

Unclimbed ■ The highest unclimbed mountain is Lhotse Middle Peak (8430 m *27 657 ft*) in the Khumbu district of the Nepal Himalaya. It is the 10th highest individually recognised summit in the world.

Tallest ■ The world's tallest mountain measured from its submarine base (3280 fathoms *6000 m*) in the Hawaiian Trough to its peak is Mauna Kea (Mountain White) on the island of Hawaii, with a combined height of 10 203 m *33 476 ft* of which 4205 m *13 796 ft* are above sea level. Another mountain whose dimensions, but not height, exceed those of Mt Everest is the volcanic Hawaiian peak of Mauna Loa (Mountain Long) at 4170 m *13 680 ft*. The axes of its elliptical base, 4975 m *16 322 ft* below sea level, have been estimated at 119 m *74 miles* and 85 km *53 miles*. It should be noted that Cerro Aconcagua (6960 m *22 834 ft*) is more than 11 826 m *38 800 ft* above the 4875 m *16 000 ft* deep Pacific abyssal plain or 13 055 m *42 834 ft* above the Peru–Chile Trench which is 290 km *180 miles* distant in the South Pacific.

Greatest ranges ■ The world's greatest land mountain range is the Himalaya-Karakoram, which contains 96 of the world's 109 peaks of over 7315 m *24 000 ft*. Himalaya derives from the sanskrit *him*, snow; *alaya*, home. The greatest of all mountain ranges is, however, the submarine Indian/East Pacific Oceans Cordillera extending 30 900 km *19 200 miles* from the Gulf of Aden to the Gulf of California by way of the seabed between Australia and Antarctica with an average height of 2430 km *8000 ft* above the base ocean depth.

Longest lines of sight ■ Vatnajökull (2118 m *6952 ft*), Iceland has been seen by refracted light from the Faeroe Islands 550 km *340 miles* distant. In Alaska Mt McKinley (6193 m *20 320 ft*) has been sighted from Mt Sanford (4949 m *16 237 ft*) from a distance of 370 km *230 miles*. McKinley, so named in 1896, was called Denali (Great One) in the Athabascan language of North American Indians and is the highest mountain in the United States.

Greatest plateau ■ The most extensive high plateau in the world is the Tibetan Plateau in Central Asia. The average altitude is 4875 m *16 000 ft* and the area is 200 000 km² *77 000 miles²*.

Sheerest wall ■ Mt Rakaposhi (7772 m *25 498 ft*) rises 5·99 vertical kilometres *3·72 miles* from the Hunza Valley, Pakistan in 10 horizontal kilometres *6·21 miles* with an overall gradient of 31°.

The 975 m *3200 ft* wide north-west face of Half Dome, Yosemite, California, USA is 670 m *2200 ft* high but nowhere departs more than 7 degrees from the vertical. It was first climbed (Class VI) in 1957 by Royal Robbins, Jerry Gallwas and Mike Sherrick.

Highest halites ■ Along the northern shores of the Gulf of Mexico for 1160 km *1725 miles* there exist 330 subterranean 'mountains' of salt, some of which rise more than 18 300 m *60 000 ft* from bed rock and appear as the low salt domes first discovered in 1862.

Lowest hill ■ Official maps of Seria, Brunei show an artificial hillock named Bukit Thompson by the 13th hole on the Panaga Golf Course at 4·5 m *15 ft*.

WATERFALLS

Highest ■ The highest waterfall (as opposed to vaporised 'Bridal Veil') in the world is the Salto Angel

in Venezuela, on a branch of the River Carrao, an upper tributary of the Caroni, with a total drop of 979 m *3212 ft*—the longest single drop is 807 m *2648 ft*. The 'Angel Falls' were named after the United States pilot Jimmy Angel (d. 8 Dec 1956), who recorded them in his log book on 14 Nov 1933. The falls, known by the Indians as Cherun-Meru, were first reported by Ernesto Sanchez La Cruz in 1910.

The tallest waterfall in the United Kingdom is Eas a'Chùal Aluinn, from Glas Bheinn (774 m *2541 ft*), Sutherland, Scotland, with a drop of 200 m *658 ft*. In England there is no clear-cut tallest waterfall. Cautley Spout, in Howgill Falls, Cumbria, with very broken cascades down a deep gully, has a total drop of 180 m *591 ft*. Hardraw Force, in Wensleydale, North Yorks has the longest unbroken drop, of 27 m *90 ft*. The cascade in the Gaping Gill Cave, Ingleborough, North Yorks descends 111 m *365 ft*. The highest Welsh waterfall is the Pistyll-y-Llyn on the Powys–Dyfed border which exceeds 90 m *300 ft* in descent. The highest falls in Ireland are the Powerscourt Falls (106 m *350 ft*), on the River Dargle, County Wicklow.

Greatest ■ On the basis of the average annual flow, the greatest waterfalls in the world are the Boyoma (formerly Stanley) Falls in Zaïre with 17 000 m³/sec *600 000 cusec*. The peak flow of the Guaíra (Salto das Sete Quedas) on the Alto Paraná river between Brazil and Paraguay at times attained a peak flow rate of 50 000 m³/sec *1 750 000 cusec*.

It has been calculated that, when some 5 500 000 years ago the Mediterranean basins began to be

filled from the Atlantic through the Straits of Gibraltar, a waterfall 26 times greater than the Guaíra and perhaps 800 m *2625 ft* high was formed.

Widest ■ The widest waterfalls in the world are the Khône Falls (15–21 m *50–70 ft* high) in Laos, with a width of 10·8 km *6·7 miles* and a flood flow of 42 500 m³/sec *1 500 000 cusec*.

RIVERS

Longest ■ The two longest rivers in the world are the Nile (*Bahr-el-Nil*), flowing into the Mediterranean, and the Amazon (*Amazonas*), flowing into the South Atlantic. Which is the longer is more a matter of definition than simple measurement.

The length of the Nile watercourse, as surveyed by M. Devroey (Belgium) before the loss of a few miles of meanders due to the formation of Lake Nasser, behind the Aswan High Dam, was 6670 km *4145 miles*. This course is unitary from a hydrological standpoint and runs from the source in Burundi of the Luvironza branch of the Kagera feeder of the Victoria Nyanza via the White Nile (*Bahrel-Jebel*) to the delta in the Mediterranean.

The true source of the Amazon was discovered in 1953 to be a stream named Huarco, deriving from the Misuie Glacier (5400 m *17 715 ft*) in the Arequipa Andes of Peru. This stream progressively becomes the Toro then the Santiago then the Apurimac, which in turn is known as the Ene and then the Tambo before its confluence with the Amazon prime tributary the Ucayali. The length of the Amazon from this source to the South Atlantic via the Canal do Norte was measured in 1969 and found to be 6448 km *4007 miles* (usually quoted to the rounded-off figure of 6437 km *4000 miles*).

If, however, a vessel navigating down the river follows the 'arm' (carrying 10 per cent of the river's water) to the south of Ilha de Marajó through the Furo Tajapuru and Furo dos Macacos into the Pará, the total length of the water-course becomes 6750 km 4195 miles. *The Rio Pará is* not however a tributary *of the Amazon, being hydrologically part of the basin of the Tocantins which itself however flows into the Bahía de Marajó and out into the South Atlantic.*

The longest river in Great Britain is the Severn, which empties into the Bristol Channel and is 354 km *220 miles* long. Its basin extends over 11 419 km² *4409 miles²*. It rises in north-western Powys, Wales, and flows through Shropshire, Hereford & Worcester, Gloucestershire and Avon and has a record 17 tributaries. The longest river wholly in England is the Thames, which is 346 km *215 miles* long to The Nore. Its remotest source is at Seven Springs, Glos, whence the River Churn joins the other head waters. The source of the Thames proper is Trewsbury Mead, Coates, Cirencester, Glos. The basin measures 9948 km² *3841 miles²*. The Yorkshire Ouse's 11 tributaries aggregate 1012 km *629 miles*.

The longest river wholly in Wales is the Usk, with a length of 104·5 km *65 miles*. It rises on the border of Dyfed and Powys and flows out via Gwent into the Severn Estuary. The longest river in Scotland is the Tay, with Dundee, Tayside, on the shore of the estuary. It is 188 km *117 miles* long from the source of its remotest head-stream, the River Tummel, Tayside and has the greatest volume of any river in Great Britain, with a flow of up to 1387 m³/sec *49 000 cusec*. Of Scottish rivers the Tweed and the Clyde have most tributaries with 11 each.

The longest river in Ireland is the Shannon, which is longer than any river in Great Britain. It rises 78·6 m *258 ft* above sea level, in County Cavan, and flows through a series of loughs to Limerick. It is 386 km *240 miles* long, including the 90 km *56 mile* long estuary to Loop Head. The basin area is 15 695 km² *6060 miles²*.

Shortest ■ The world's shortest river with a name is the Roe River, near Great Falls, Montana, USA which flows into the Missouri River and has an official length of 61 m *200·13 ft*.

Largest basin ■ The largest river basin in the world is that drained by the Amazon (6448 km *4007 miles*). It covers about 7 045 000 km² *2 720 000 miles²*. It has about 15 000 tributaries and subtributaries, of which four are more than 1609 km *1000 miles* long. These include the Madeira, the longest of all tributaries, with a length of 3380 km *2100 miles*, which is surpassed by only 14 rivers in the whole world.

Longest sub-tributary ■ The longest sub-tributary is the Pilcomayo (1609 km *1000 miles*) in South America. It is a tributary of the Paraguay (2415 km *1500 miles* long), which is itself a tributary of the Paraná (4025 km *2500 miles*).

Longest estuary ■ The world's longest estuary is that of the often frozen Ob', in the northern USSR, at 885 km *550 miles*. It is up to 80 km *50 miles* wide.

Largest delta ■ The world's largest delta is that created by the Ganges (Ganga) and Brahmaputra in Bangladesh and West Bengal, India. It covers an area of 75 000 km² *30 000 miles²*.

Greatest flow ■ The greatest flow of any river in the world is that of the Amazon, which discharges an average of 120 000 m³/sec *4 200 000 cusec* into the Atlantic Ocean, increasing to more than 200 000 m³/sec *7 000 000 cusec* in full flood. The lowest 1450 km *900 miles* of the Amazon average 90 m *300 ft* in depth.

Submarine ■ In 1952 a submarine river 400 km *250 miles* wide, known as the Cromwell current, was discovered flowing eastward 90 m *300 ft* below the surface of the Pacific for 5625 km *3500 miles* along the equator. Its volume is 1000 times that of the Mississippi.

Subterranean ■ In August 1958 a crypto-river was tracked by radio isotopes flowing under the Nile with 6 times its mean annual flow or 500 000 million m³ *20 million million ft³*.

Largest swamp ■ The world's largest tract of swamp is in the basin of the Pripet or Pripyat River—a tributary of the Dnieper in the USSR. These swamps cover an estimated area of 46 950 km² *18 125 miles²*.

RIVER BORES

The bore on the Ch'ient'ang'kian (Hang-chou-fe) in eastern China is the most remarkable of the 60 in the world. At spring tides the wave attains a height of up to 7·5 m *25 ft* and a speed of 13–15 knots *24–27 km/h*. It is heard advancing at a range of 22 km *14 miles*. The annual downstream flood wave on the Mekong sometimes reaches a height of 14 m *46 ft*. The greatest volume of any tidal bore is that of the Canal do Norte (16 km *10 miles* wide) in the mouth of the Amazon.

The most notable of the eight river bores in the United Kingdom is that on the Severn, which attained a height of 2·8 m *9¼ ft* on 15 Oct 1966 downstream of Stonebench, and a speed of 20 km/h *13 mph*. It travels from Framilode towards Gloucester.

LAKES AND INLAND SEAS

Largest ■ The largest inland sea or lake in the world is the Kaspiskoye More (Caspian Sea) in the southern USSR and Iran. It is 1225 km *760 miles* long and its total area is 371 800 km² *143 550 miles²*. Of the total area some 143 200 km² *55 280 miles²* (38·5 per cent) are in Iran, where it is named the Darya-ye-Khazar. Its maximum depth is 1025 m *3360 ft* and its surface is 28·5 m *93 ft* below sea level. Its estimated volume is 89 600 km³ *21 500 miles³* of saline water. Its surface has varied between 32 m *105 ft* (11th century) and 22 m *72 ft* (early 19th century) below sea level.

Deepest ■ The deepest lake in the world is Ozero (Lake) Baykal in central Siberia, USSR. It is 620 km *385 miles* long and between 32–74 km *20–46 miles* wide. In 1957 the lake's Olkhon Crevice was measured to be 1940 m *6365 ft* deep and hence 1485 m *4872 ft* below sea level.

The deepest lake in Great Britain is the 16·57 km *10·30 mile* long Loch Morar, in Inverness. Its surface is 9 m *30 ft* above sea level and its extreme depth 310 m *1017 ft*. England's deepest lake is Wast Water (78 m *258 ft*), in Cumbria. The lake with the greatest mean depth is Loch Ness with 130 m *427 ft*.

Highest ■ The highest navigable lake in the world is Lake Titicaca, partly in Peru and partly in Bolivia, with an area of about 8285 km² *3200 miles²*. It is 209 km *130 miles* long, has a maximum depth of 370 m *1214 ft*, and is situated at 3811 m *12 506 ft* above sea level. There are higher lakes in the Himalayas, but most are glacial and of a temporary nature only. A survey of the area carried out in 1984 showed a lake at a height of 5414 m *17 762 ft* named Panch Pokhri which was 1·6 km *1 mile* long.

The highest lake in the United Kingdom is the 0·76 ha *1·9 acre* Lochan Buidhe at 1097 m *3600 ft* above sea level in the Cairngorm Mountains, Scotland. England's highest is Broad Crag Tarn (837 m *2746 ft* above sea level) on Scafell Pike, Cumbria and the highest named freshwater lake in Wales is The Frogs Pool, a tarn near the summit of Carnedd Llywelyn, Gwynedd at 830 m *2723 ft*.

Freshwater ■ The freshwater lake with the greatest surface area is Lake Superior, one of the Great Lakes of North America. The total area is 82 350 km² *31 800 miles²*, of which 53 600 km² *20 700 miles²* are in Minnesota, Wisconsin and Michigan, USA and 27 750 km² *11 100 miles²* in Ontario, Canada. It is 182 m *1600 ft* above sea level. The freshwater lake with the greatest volume is Lake Baykal in Siberia, USSR with an estimated volume of 23 000 km³ *5520 miles³*.

The largest lake in the United Kingdom is Lough Neagh (14·6 m *48 ft* above sea level) in Northern Ireland. It is 28·9 km *18 miles* long and 17·7 km *11 miles* wide and has an area of 381·73 km² *147·39 miles²*. Its extreme depth is 31 m *102 ft*.

Freshwater loch ■ The largest lake in Great Britain, and the largest inland loch in Scotland, is Loch Lomond (7 m *23 ft* above sea level), which is 36·44 km *22·64 miles* long and has a surface area of 70·04 km² *27·45 miles²*. It is situated in the Strathclyde and Central regions and its greatest depth is 190 m *623 ft*. The lake or loch with the greatest volume is, however, Loch Ness with 7 443 000 000 m³ *262 845 000 000 ft³*. The longest lake or loch is Loch Ness which measures 38·99 km *24·23 miles*, although the three arms of the Y-shaped Loch Awe, Strathclyde aggregate 40·99 km *25·47 miles*. The largest lake in England is Windermere, in Cumbria. It is 17 km *10½ miles* long and has a surface area of 14·74 km² *5·69 miles²*. Its greatest depth is 66·75 m *219 ft* in the northern half. The largest *natural* lake in Wales is Llyn Tegid, with an area of 4·38 km² *1·69 miles²*, although the largest lake in Wales is that formed by the reservoir at Lake Vyrnwy, where the total surface area is 453·25 ha *1120 acres*.

Freshwater loughs ■ The largest lough in the Republic of Ireland is Lough Corrib in Mayo and Galway. It measures 43·5 km *27 miles* in length and is 11·25 km *7 miles* across at its widest point with a total surface area of 168 km² *65 miles²*.

Lake in a lake ■ The largest lake in a lake is Manitou Lake (106·42 km² *41·09 miles²*) on the world's largest lake island Manitoulin Island (2766 km² *1068 miles²*) in the Canadian part of Lake Huron. The lake itself contains a number of islands.

Underground ■ Reputedly the world's largest underground lake is the Lost Sea, 91 m *300 ft* subterranean in the Craighead Caverns, Sweetwater, Tennessee, USA measuring 1·8 ha *4½ acres* and discovered in 1905.

Largest lagoon ■ Lagoa dos Patos in southernmost Brazil is 254 km *158 miles* long and extends over 10 645 km² *4110 miles²*.

OTHER FEATURES

Desert ■ Nearly an eighth of the world's land surface is arid with a rainfall of less than 25 cm *9·8 in* per annum. The Sahara in North Africa is the largest in the world. At its greatest length it is 5150 km *3200 miles* from east to west. From north to south it is between 1275 and 2250 km *800 and 1400 miles*. The area covered by the desert is about 8 400 000 km² *3 250 000 miles²*. The land level varies from 132 m *436 ft* below sea level in the Qattâra Depression, Egypt to the mountain Emi Koussi (3415 m *11 204 ft*) in Chad. The diurnal temperature range in the western Sahara may be more than 45° C or *80° F*.

Sand dunes ■ The world's highest measured sand dunes are those in the Saharan sand sea of Isaouane-N-Tifernine of east central Algeria in Lat. 26° 42' N, Long. 6° 43' E. They have a wave-length of 5 km *3·1 miles* and attain a height of 430 m *1410 ft*.

Largest gorge ■ The largest land gorge in the world is the Grand Canyon on the Colorado River in north-central Arizona, USA. It extends from Marble Gorge to the Grand Wash Cliffs, over a distance of 349 km *217 miles*. It varies in width from 6–20 km *4–13 miles* and is some 1615 m *5300 ft* deep. The submarine Labrador Basin canyon is 3440 km *c. 2150 miles* long.

Deepest canyon ■ The deepest canyon is El Cañon de Colca, Peru, reported in 1929, which is 3223 m *10 574 ft* deep. It was first traversed by the Polish Expedition CANOANDES' 79-kayak team from 12 May–14 Jun 1981. A stretch of the Kali River in central Nepal flows 5485 m *18 000 ft* below its flanking summits of the Dhaulagiri and Annapurna groups. The deepest submarine canyon yet discovered is one 40 km *25 miles* south of Esperance, Western Australia, which is 1800 m *6000 ft* deep and 32 km *20 miles* wide.

Cliffs ■ The highest sea cliffs yet pinpointed anywhere in the world are those on the north coast of east Moloka'i, Hawaii near Umilehi Point, which descend 1005 m *3300 ft* to the sea at an average gradient of >55°.

The highest cliffs in north-west Europe are those on the north coast of Achill Island, in County Mayo, Ireland, which are 668 m *2192 ft* sheer above the sea at Croaghan. The highest cliffs in the United Kingdom are the 396 m *1300 ft* Conachair cliffs on St Kilda, Western Isles (425 m *1397 ft*). The highest sheer sea cliffs on the mainland of Great Britain are at Clo Mor, 4·8 km *3 miles* south-east of Cape Wrath, Sutherland, Scotland which drop 280·7 m *921 ft*. England's highest cliff (gradient >45°) is Great Hangman Hill, near Combe Martin, in north Devon, which descends from 318 m *1043 ft* to the sea in 300 m *984 ft*, the last 213 m *700 ft* of which is sheer.

Natural arches ■ The longest natural arch in the world is the Landscape Arch in the Arches National Park, 40 km *25 miles* north of Moab in Utah, USA. This natural sandstone arch spans 88 m *291 ft* and is set about 30 m *100 ft* above the canyon floor. In one place erosion has narrowed its section to 1·82 m *6 ft*. Larger, however, is the Rainbow Bridge, Utah, USA discovered on 14 Aug 1909, which although only 84·7 m *278 ft* long, is more than 6·7 m *22 ft* wide.

Longest glaciers ■ It is estimated that 15 600 000 km² *6 020 000 miles²*, or 10·5 per cent of the Earth's land surface, is permanently glaciated. The world's longest known glacier is the Lambert Glacier, discovered by an Australian aircraft crew in Australian Antarctic Territory in 1956–7. It is up to 64 km *40 miles* wide and, with its upper section, known as the Mellor Glacier, it measures at least 402 km *250 miles* in length. With the Fisher Glacier limb, the Lambert forms a continuous ice passage about 514 km *320 miles* long. The longest Himalayan glacier is the Siachen (75·6 km *47 miles*) in the Karakoram range, though the Hispar and Biafo combine to form an ice passage 122 km *76 miles* long. The fastest-moving major glacier is the Quarayaq in Greenland flowing 20–24 m *65–80 ft* per day.

Greatest avalanches ■ The greatest natural avalanches, though rarely observed, occur in the Himalayas but no estimates of their volume have been published. It was estimated that 3 500 000 m³

120 000 000 ft³ of snow fell in an avalanche in the Italian Alps in 1885. The 400 km/h *250 mph* avalanche triggered by the Mount St Helens eruption in Washington State, USA on 18 May 1980 was estimated to measure 2800 million m³ *96 000 million ft³* (see Accidents and Disasters, Chapter 10).

Natural Phenomena

EARTHQUAKES ■ (Seismologists record all dates with the year *first*, based not on local time but on Universal Time/Greenwich Mean Time).

Greatest ■ It is estimated that each year there are some 500 000 detectable seismic or micro-seismic disturbances of which 100 000 can be felt and 1000 cause damage. The deepest recorded hypocentres are of 720 km *447 miles* in Indonesia in 1933, 1934 and 1943.

The most commonly used scale to measure the size of earthquakes is Richter's magnitude scale (1954). It is named after Dr Charles Richter (1900–85) and the most commonly used form is M_s, based on amplitudes of surface waves, usually at a period of 20 sec. The largest reported magnitudes on this scale are about 8.9, but the scale does not properly represent the size of the very largest earthquakes, above M_s about 8, for which it is better to use the concept of seismic moment, M_o, devised by K. Aki in 1966. Moment can be used to derive a 'moment magnitude', M_w, first used by Hiroo Kanamori in 1977. The largest recorded earthquake on the M_w scale is the Chilean shock of 1960 May 22, which had $M_w = 9.5$, but only 8.3 on the M_s scale. For the largest events such as the Chilean shock of 1960, the energy released is more than 10^{19} joules.

Worst death toll ■ The greatest chronicled loss of life occurred in the earthquake which rocked every city of the Near East and eastern Mediterranean *c.* July 1201. Contemporary accounts estimate the loss of life at 1 100 000. Less uncertain is the figure of 830 000 fatalities in a prolonged 'quake (*ti chen*) in the Shensi, Shansi and Honan provinces of China, of 1556 Feb 2 (new style) (Jan 23 os). The highest death toll in modern times has been in the Tangshan 'quake (Mag. 7.9) in eastern China on 1976 Jul 27 (local time was 3 a.m. July 28). A first figure published on 4 Jan 1977 revealed 655 237 killed, later adjusted to 750 000. On 22 Nov 1979 the New China News Agency unaccountably reduced the death toll to 242 000. As late as January 1982 the site of the city was still a prohibited area.

Material damage ■ The greatest physical devastation was in the 'quake on the Kwanto plain, Japan, of 1923 Sept 1 (Mag. 8.2, epicentre in Lat. 35° 15′ N, Long. 139° 30′ E); in Sagami Bay the sea bottom in one area sank 400 m *1310 ft*. The official total of persons killed and missing in this *Shinsai* or great 'quake and the resultant fires was 142 807. In Tokyo and Yokohama 575 000 dwellings were destroyed. The cost of the damage was estimated at £1000 million (now £17 000 million).

Great Britain and Ireland ■ The total of the undisputed death toll for Great Britain is two—an apprentice, Thomas Grey, struck by falling masonry from Christ's Hospital Church, near Newgate, London at 6 p.m. on 6 Apr 1580, and another youth, Mabel Everet, who died of injuries 4 days later.

The East Anglian or Colchester earthquake of 1884 Apr 22 (9.18 a.m.) (epicentres Lat. 51° 48′ N, Long. 0° 53′ E, and Lat. 51° 51′ N, Long. 0° 55′ E) caused damage estimated at more than £12 000 to 1250 buildings. Langenhoe Church was wrecked. Windows and doors were rattled over an area of 137 250 km² *53 000 miles²* and the shock was felt in Exeter and Ostend, Belgium. It has been estimated to have been of Magnitude 5.2 on the Richter scale.

The highest instrumentally measured Magnitude is 6.0 for the Dogger Bank event of 1931 Jun 7. The strongest Scottish tremor occurred at Inverness at 10.45 p.m. on 1816 Aug 13, and was felt over an area of 130 000 km² *50 000 miles²*. The strongest Welsh tremor occurred in Swansea at 9.45 a.m. on 1906 June 27 (epicentre Lat. 51° 38′ N, Long. 4° W). It was felt over an area of 97 900 km² *37 800 miles²*.

No earthquake with its epicentre in Ireland has ever been instrumentally measured, though the effects of the North Wales shock of 1984 Jul 19 (Mag. 5 to 5.5) dislocated traffic lights in Dublin. However, there was a shock in August 1734 which damaged 100 dwellings and 5 churches.

VOLCANOES

The total number of known active volcanoes in the world is 850 of which many are submarine. The greatest active concentration is in Indonesia, where 77 of its 167 volcanoes have erupted within historic times. The name volcano derives from the now dormant Vulcano Island (from the god of fire Vulcanus) in the Mediterranean.

> **Highest active volcano** ● The highest volcano regarded as active is Ojos del Salado (which has fumaroles), at a height of 6885 m *22 588 ft*, in the Andes on the border between Chile and Argentina. (Photo: Dr. J.H. Rogers)

Greatest explosion ■ The greatest explosion (possibly since Santoríni in the Aegean Sea, 96 km *60 miles* north of Crete, in 1628 BC) occurred at *c.* 10 a.m. (local time), or 3.00 a.m. GMT, on 27 Aug 1883, with an eruption of Krakatoa, an island (then 47 km² *18 miles²*) in the Sunda Strait, between Sumatra and Java, in Indonesia. 163 villages were wiped out, and 36 380 people killed by the wave it caused. Rocks were thrown 55 km *34 miles* high and dust fell 5330 km *3313 miles* away 10 days later. The explosion was recorded 4 hours later on the island of Rodrigues, 4776 km *2968 miles* away, as 'the roar of heavy guns', and was heard over 1/13th part of the surface of the globe. This explosion, estimated to have had about 26 times the power of the greatest H-bomb test, was still only a fifth part of the Santoríni cataclysm.

Greatest eruption ■ The total volume of matter discharged in the eruption of Tambora, a volcano on the island of Sumbawa, in Indonesia, 5–7 Apr 1815, was 150–180 km³. The energy of this 2245 km/h *1395 mph* eruption, which lowered the height of the island by 1250 m *4100 ft* from 4100 m *13 450 ft* to 2850 m *9350 ft*, was 8.4×10^{19} joules. A crater 11 km *7 miles* in diameter was formed. Some 90 000 were killed or died of famine. This compares with a probable 60–65 km³ ejected by Santoríni and 20 km³ ejected by Krakatoa. The internal pressure at Tambora has been estimated at 3270 kg/cm² or *20.76 tons/in²*.

The ejecta in the Taupo eruption in New Zealand *c.* AD 130 has been estimated at 30 000 million tonnes of pumice moving at one time at 700 km/h *400 mph*. It flattened 16 000 km² *6180 miles²* (over 26 times the devastated area of Mount St Helens). Less than 20 per cent of the 14×10^9 tonnes of pumice ejected in this most violent of all documented volcanic events fell within 200 km *125 miles* of the vent.

Longest lava flow ■ The longest lava flow in historic times is a mixture of pahoehoe ropey lava (twisted cord-like solidifications) and aa blocky lava, resulting from the eruption of Laki in 1783 in southeast Iceland which flowed 65–70 km *40.5–43.5 miles*. The largest known prehistoric flow is the Roza basalt flow in North America *c.* 15 million years ago, which had an unsurpassed length (480 km *300 miles*) and area (40 000 km² *15 400 miles²*).

Largest active ■ Mauna Loa in Hawaii has a dome 120 km *75 miles* long and 103 km *64 miles* wide with a lava flow that occupies more than 5180 km² *2000 miles²* of the island. Its pit crater, Mokuaweoweo, measures 10.4 km² *4 miles²* and is 150–180 m *500–600 ft* deep. It rises 4168 m *13 677 ft* and has averaged one eruption every 3½ years since 1832, most recently in April 1984.

Highest active ■ The highest volcano regarded as active is Ojos del Salado (which has fumaroles), at a height of 6885 m *22 588 ft*, on the frontier between Chile and Argentina.

Highest dormant ■ The highest dormant volcano is Volcán Llullaillaco (6739 m *22 109 ft*), on the frontier between Chile and Argentina.

Highest extinct ■ The highest extinct volcano in the world is Cerro Aconcagua ('stone sentinel') (6960 m *22 834 ft*) on the Argentinian side of the Andes. It was first climbed on 14 Jan 1897 by Mathias Zurbriggen—the highest summit climbed until 12 June 1907.

Northernmost and southernmost ■ The northernmost volcano is Beeren Berg (2276 m *7470 ft*) on the island of Jan Mayen (71° 05′ N) in the Greenland Sea. It erupted on 20 Sept 1970 and the island's 39 inhabitants (all male) had to be evacuated. It was possibly discovered by Henry Hudson the English navigator and explorer (d. 1611) in 1607 or 1608, but was definitely visited by Jan Jacobsz Mayen (Netherlands) in 1614. It was annexed by Norway on 8 May 1929. The Ostenso seamount (1775 m *5825 ft*) 556 km *346 miles* from the North Pole in Lat. 85° 10′ N, Long. 133° W was volcanic. The most

WORLD'S STRONGEST EARTHQUAKES

Progressive list of instrumentally recorded earthquakes

Kanamori Scale Magnitudes M_w	Richter Scale Magnitude M_s	Location		Date
8.8	8.6	Ecuador	1906	31 Jan
9.0	8¼	Kamchatka, USSR	1952	4 Nov
9.1	7¾	Andreanol, Aleutian Is., USA	1957	9 Mar
9.2	8.4	Alaska, USA	1964	28 Mar
9.5	8.3	Chile	1960	22 May

$\log E = 1.5M + 4.8$ *(joules)*

southerly known active volcano is Mt Erebus (3795 m *12 450 ft*) on Ross Island (77° 35′ S), in Antarctica. It was discovered on 28 Jan 1841 by the expedition of Captain (later Rear-Admiral Sir) James Clark Ross, RN (1800–62), and first climbed at 10 a.m. on 10 Mar 1908 by a British party of five, led by Professor (later Lieut-Col Sir) Tannatt William Edgeworth David (1858–1934).

Largest crater ■ The world's largest *caldera* or volcano crater is that of Toba, north-central Sumatra, Indonesia covering 1775 km² *685 miles²*.

GEYSERS

Tallest ■ The Waimangu (Maori 'black water') geyser, in New Zealand, erupted to a height in excess of 457 m *1500 ft* in 1904, but has not been active since it erupted violently at 6.20 a.m. on 1 Apr 1917 and killed 4 people. Currently the world's tallest active geyser is the US National Parks' Service Steamboat Geyser, in Yellowstone National Park, Wyoming, which from 1962 to 1969 erupted with intervals ranging from 5 days to 10 months to a height of 76–115 m *250–380 ft*. The greatest measured water discharge has been 37 850 hl *825 000 gal* by the Giant Geyser, also in Yellowstone National Park, which has been dormant since 1955. The *Geysir* ('gusher') near Mt Hekla in south-central Iceland, from which all others have been named, spurts, on occasions, to 55 m *180 ft*, while the adjacent Strokkur spurts at 10–15 min intervals.

Weather

The meteorological records given below necessarily relate largely to the last 140–160 years, since data before that time are both sparse and often unreliable. Reliable registering thermometers were introduced as recently as *c.* 1820. The longest continuous observations have been maintained at the Radcliffe Observatory, Oxford since 1815 though discontinuous records have enabled the Chinese to assert that 903 BC was a very bad winter.

Palaeo-entomological evidence is that there was a southern European climate in England *c.* 90 000 BC, while in *c.* 6000 BC the mean summer temperature reached 19·4° C *67° F*, or 3·3° C *6° F* higher than the present. It is believed that 1·2 million years ago the world's air temperature averaged 35° C *95° F*. The earliest authentic recording of British weather relates to the period 26 Aug–17 Sep 55 BC. The earliest reliably known hot summer was in AD 664 during our driest-ever century and the earliest known severe winter was that of AD 763–4. In 1683–4 there was frost in London from November to April. Frosts were recorded during August in the period 1668–89.

Most equable temperature ■ The location with the most equable recorded temperature over a short period is Garapan, on Saipan, in the Mariana Islands, Pacific Ocean. During the 9 years from 1927 to 1935, inclusive, the lowest temperature recorded was 19·6° C *67·3° F* on 30 Jan 1934 and the highest was 31·4° C *88·5° F* on 9 Sep 1931, giving an extreme range of 11·8° C *21·2° F*. Between 1911 and 1966 the Brazilian off-shore island of Fernando de Noronha had a minimum temperature of 18·6° C *65·5° F* on 17 Nov 1913 and a maximum of 32·0° C *89·6° F* on 2 Mar 1965, an extreme range of 13·4° C *24·1° F*.

Greatest temperature ranges ■ The greatest recorded temperature ranges in the world are around the Siberian 'cold pole' in the eastern USSR. Temperatures in Verkhoyansk (67° 33′ N, 133° 23′ E) have ranged 106·7° C *192° F* from −70° C *−94° F* (unofficial) to 36·7° C *98° F*. The greatest temperature variation recorded in a day is 55·5° C *100° F* (a fall from 6·7° C *44° F* to −48·8° C *−56° F*) at Browning, Montana, USA on 23–24 Jan 1916. The most freakish rise was 27·2° C *49° F* in 2 min at Spearfish, South Dakota, USA from −20° C *−4° F* at 7.30 a.m. to 7·2° C *45° F* at 7.32 a.m. on 22 Jan 1943. The British record is 29° C *52·2° F* (−7° C *19·4° F* to 22° C *71·6° F*) at Tummel Bridge, Tayside on 9 May 1978.

EXTREME TEMPERATURES
(Progressive recordings)

HIGH

53·0° C	127·4°F	Ouargla, Algeria	27 Aug	1884
54·4° C	130°F	Amos, California, USA	17 Aug	1885
54·4° C	130°F	Mammoth Tank, California, USA	17 Aug	1885
56·7° C	134°F	Death Valley, California, USA	10 Jul	1913
58·0° C	136·4°F	Al'Aziziyah (el-Azizia), Libya*	13 Sep	1922

* *Obtained by the US National Geographical Society but not officially recognised by the Libyan Ministry of Communications.*

A reading of 60° C 140° F at Delta, Mexico, in August 1953 is not now accepted because of over-exposure to roof radiation. The official Mexican record of 58·0° C 136·4° F at San Luis, Sonora on 11 Aug 1933 is not internationally accepted.

A freak heat flash reported from Coimbra, Portugal, in September 1933 said to have caused the temperature to rise to 70°C 158° F for 120 sec is apocryphal.

LOW

−58·3° C	−73°F	Floeberg Bay, Ellesmere I., Canada		[1] 1852
−68° C	−90·4°F	Verkhoyansk, Siberia, USSR	3 Jan	1885
−68° C	−90·4°F	Verkhoyansk, Siberia, USSR	5 & 7 Feb	1892
−68° C	−90·4°F	Oymyakon, Siberia, USSR[2]	6 Feb	1933
−73·5° C	−100·4°F	South Pole, Antarctica	11 May	1957
−74·5° C	−102·1°F	South Pole, Antarctica	17 Sep	1957
−78·3° C	−109·1°F	Sovietskaya, Antarctica	2 May	1958
−80·7° C	−113·3°F	Vostok, Antarctica	15 Jun	1958
−81·2° C	−114·1°F	Sovietskaya, Antarctica	19 Jun	1958
−83·0° C	−117·4°F	Sovietskaya, Antarctica	25 Jun	1958
−85·7° C	−122·4°F	Vostok, Antarctica	7–8 Aug	1958
−86·7° C	−124·1°F	Sovietskaya, Antarctica	9 Aug	1958
−87·4° C	−125·3°F	Vostok, Antarctica	25 Aug	1958
−88·3° C	−126·9°F	Vostok, Antarctica	24 Aug	1960
−89·2° C	−128·6°F	Vostok, Antactica	21 Jul	1983

[1] *The earliest recorded occasion that mercury froze (at −40° C or −40° F) was by M. V. Lomonosov, near Moscow c. 1750.*

[2] *Population in 1986 reported to be 4000—the world's coldest inhabited place.*

Longest freeze ■ The longest recorded unremitting freeze in the British Isles was one of 40 days at the Great Dun Fell radio station, Appleby, Cumbria, from 23 Jan to 3 Mar 1986. Less rigorous early data include a frost from 5 Dec 1607 to 14 Feb 1608 and a 91-day frost on Dartmoor, Devon in 1854–5. No temperature lower than 1° C *34° F* has ever been recorded on Bishop Rock, Isles of Scilly.

Upper atmosphere ■ The lowest temperature ever recorded in the atmosphere was −143° C *−225·4° F* at an altitude of about 80·5–96·5 km *50–60 miles*, during noctilucent cloud research above Kronogård, Sweden from 27 Jul to 7 Aug 1963. A jet stream moving at 656 km/h *408 mph* at 47 000 m *154 200 ft* (46 km *29·2 miles*) was recorded by Skua rocket above South Uist, Outer Hebrides, Scotland on 13 Dec 1967.

Thickest ice ■ The greatest recorded thickness of ice is 4·78 km *2·97 miles* measured by radio echo soundings from a US Antarctic research aircraft at 69° 9′ 38″ S 135° 20′ 25″ E 400 km *250 miles* from the coast in Wilkes Land on 4 Jan 1975.

Deepest permafrost ■ The deepest recorded permafrost is more than 1370 m *4500 ft* reported from the upper reaches of the Viluy River, Siberia, USSR in February 1982.

Most recent white Christmas and Frost Fair ■ London has experienced 8 'white' or snowing Christmas Days since 1900. These have been 1906, 1917 (slight), 1923 (slight), 1927, 1938, 1956 (slight), 1970 and 1981. These were more frequent in the 19th century and even more so before the change of the calendar which by removing 3–13 Sep brought forward all dates subsequent to 2 Sep 1752 by 11 days. The last of the 9 recorded Frost Fairs held on the Thames since 1564/5 was from December 1813 to 26 Jan 1814.

Most intense rainfall ■ Difficulties attend rainfall readings for very short periods but the figure of 38·1 mm *1½ in* in 1 min at Barst, Guadeloupe on 26 Nov 1970, is regarded as the most intense recorded in modern times. The cloudburst of 'near 609 mm *2 ft* in less than a quarter of half an hour' at Oxford on the afternoon of 31 May (old style) 1682 is regarded as unacademically recorded. The most intense rainfall in Britain recorded to modern standards has been 51 mm *2 in* in 12 min at Wisbech, Cambs on 27 Jun 1970.

Falsest St Swithin's Days ■ The legend that the weather on St Swithin's Day, celebrated on 15 Jul (old and new style) since AD 912, determines the rainfall for the next 40 days is one which has long persisted. There was a brilliant 13½ hr sunshine in London on 15 Jul 1924, but 30 of the next 40 days were wet. On 15 Jul 1913 there was a 15-hr downpour, yet it rained on only 9 of the subsequent 40 days in London.

Best and worst British summers ■ According to Professor Gordon Manley's survey over the period 1728–1978 the best (i.e. driest and hottest) British summer was that of 1976 and the worst (*i.e.* wettest and coldest) that of 1879. Temperatures of >32° C *89·8° F* were recorded on 13 consecutive days (25 Jun–7 Jul 1976) within Great Britain including 35·9° C *96·6° F* at Cheltenham on 3 Jul. In 1983 there were 40 days >26·6° C *80° F* in Britain between 3 Jul–31 Aug including 17 consecutively (3–19 Jul). London experienced its hottest month (July) since records began in 1840.

Humidity and discomfort ■ Human comfort or discomfort depends not merely on temperature but on the combination of temperature, humidity, radiation and wind-speed. The United States Weather Bureau uses a Temperature-Humidity Index, which equals two-fifths of the sum of the dry and wet bulb thermometer readings plus 15. A THI of 98·2 has been twice recorded in Death Valley, California—on

Lightning ● Lightning is the discharge of an electric field which has developed within a cloud; the discharge may occur within the cloud, from one cloud to another or between cloud and ground. However, since air is normally non-conductive, discharge can only occur after channels of ionised air have been established. Every few million strokes there is a giant discharge, in which the cloud-to-earth and return strokes flash from and to the top of the thunder clouds. In these 'positive giants' energy of up to 3000 million joules (3×10^{16} ergs) has been recorded. The temperature reaches about 30 000° C, which is more than 5 times greater than that of the surface of the Sun. This photograph shows lightning over the town of Tamworth in New South Wales, Australia. (Photo: Science Photo Library)

Roy C. Sullivan (USA) is the only person to have survived a lightning strike seven times, in 1942, 1969, 1970, 1972, 1973, 1976 and finally in 1977. He is seen here in 1973 following his 5th mishap, which '... set my hat on fire, my hair on fire, went down my left arm and leg, knocked my left shoe off then crossed over to my right leg.'

Weather

27 Jul 1966 (119° F and 31 per cent) and on 12 Aug 1970 (117° F and 37 per cent). A person driving at 72 km/h *45 mph* in a car without a windscreen in a temperature of −42·7° C *−45° F* would, by the chill factor, experience the equivalent of −87· 2° C *−125° F, i.e.* within 2·0° C *3·5° F* of the world record.

Largest mirage ■ The largest mirage on record was that sighted in the Arctic at 83° N 103° W by Donald B. MacMillan in 1913. This type of mirage, known as the Fata Morgana, appeared as the same 'hills, valleys, snow-capped peaks extending through at least 120 degrees of the horizon' that Peary had misidentified as Crocker Land 6 years earlier. On 17 Jul 1939 a mirage of Snaefells Jokull (1437 m *4715 ft*) on Iceland was seen from the sea at a distance of 539–563 km *335–350 miles.*

Longest-lasting rainbow ■ A rainbow lasting over 3 hours was reported from the coastal border of Gwynedd and Clwyd, North Wales on 14 Aug 1979.

Lightning ■ The visible length of lightning strokes varies greatly. In mountainous regions, when clouds are very low, the flash may be less than 91 m *300 ft* long. In flat country with very high clouds, a cloud-to-earth flash may measure 6 km *4 miles* though in the most extreme cases such flashes have been measured at 32 km *20 miles.* The intensely bright central core of the lightning channel is extremely narrow. Some authorities suggest that its diameter is as little as 1·27 cm *½ in.* This core is surrounded by a 'corona envelope' (glow discharge) which may measure 3–6 m *10–20 ft* in diameter.

The speed of a discharge varies from 160–1600 km/sec *100–1000 miles/sec* for the downward leader track, and reaches up to 140 000 km/sec *87 000 miles/sec* (nearly half the speed of light) for the powerful return stroke. In Britain there is an average of 3·7 strikes per km² per annum (6 strikes per mile²), and an average of 4200 per annum over London alone.

Highest waterspout ■ The highest waterspout of which there is a reliable record was one observed on 16 May 1898 off Eden, New South Wales, Australia. A theodolite reading from the shore gave its height as 1528 m *5014 ft.* It was about 3 m *10 ft* in diameter. The Spithead waterspout off Ryde, Isle of Wight on 21 Aug 1878 was measured by sextant to be 1600 m or *'about a mile'* in height. A more realistic estimate of a waterspout was one which developed off Yarmouth, Isle of Wight on 6 Aug 1987. It was some 762 m *2500 ft* in height.

Cloud extremes ● The cloud form with the greatest vertical range is cumulonimbus, which has been observed to reach a height of nearly 20 000 m *68 000 ft* in the tropics. This photograph was taken from the American shuttle STS-6 *Challenger* over Zaïre. (Photo: Science Photo Library)

Cloud extremes ■ The highest standard cloud form is cirrus, averaging 8250 m *27 000 ft* and above, but the rare nacreous or mother-of-pearl formation sometimes reaches nearly 24 000 m *80 000 ft* (see also Noctilucent clouds, p. 66). Cirrus cloud at 8075 m *26 500 ft* contains unfrozen but super-cooled water at −35° C *−31° F.* The lowest is stratus, below 1066 m *3500 ft.* The cloud form with the greatest vertical range is cumulonimbus, which has been observed to reach a height of nearly 20 000 m *68 000 ft* in the tropics.

Tornadoes (see also Accidents and Disasters, Chapter 10) ■ Britain's strongest tornado was at Southsea, Portsmouth on 14 Dec 1810 (Force 8 on the Meaden-TORRO scale). The Newmarket tornado (Force 6) of 3 Jan 1978 caused property damage estimated at up to £1 000 000. On 23 Nov 1981, 58 tornadoes were reported in one day from Anglesey to eastern England.

Highest shade temperature ■ The highest ever recorded shade temperature is 58° C *136·4° F* at al'Azīzīyah, Libya (alt. 111 m *367 ft*) on 13 Sep 1922. The highest in Britain is 36·8° C *98·2° F* at Raunds (Northants), Epsom (Surrey), and Canterbury (Kent) on 9 Aug 1911. The 38·6° C *100·5° F* which was once reported from Tonbridge (Kent) was a non-standard exposure and is estimated to be equivalent to 36–36·7° C *97–98° F.*

Lowest screen temperature ■ A record low of −89·2° C *−128·6° F* was registered at Vostok, Antarctica (alt. 3419 m *11 220 ft*) on 21 Jul 1983. The coldest permanently inhabited place is the Siberian village of Oymyakon (pop. 4000) (63° 16′ N, 143° 15′ E), (700 m *2300 ft*) in the USSR where the temperature reached −67·7° C *−89·9° F* in 1933. Britain's lowest was −27·2° C *−17° F* on 11 Feb 1895 and again on 10 Jan 1982, both times at Braemar, Grampian, Scotland. The −30·5° C *−23° F* at Blackadder, Borders, on 4 Dec 1879, and the −28·9° C *−20° F* at Grantown-on-Spey on 24 Feb 1955, were not standard exposures. The lowest official temperature in England is −26·1° C *−15° F* at Newport, Salop on 10 Jan 1982. The lowest maximum temperature for a day was −19·1° C *−2·3° F* at Braemar, again on 10 Jan 1982.

Greatest rainfall ■ A record 1870 mm *73·62 in* of rain fell in 24 hours in Cilaos (alt. 1200 m *3937 ft*), La Réunion, Indian Ocean on 15 and 16 Mar 1952. This is equal to 7554 tonnes of rain per acre. For a calendar month, the record is 9300 mm *366·14 in,* at Cherra-

Driest place ● It was at the famous seaside resort of Margate, in Kent (shown here) that the lowest rainfall in Britain in a single year was recorded, when there were just 236 mm *9·29 in* of rain in 1921. (Photo: Spectrum)

punji, Meghalaya, India in July 1861, and the 12 month record was also at Cherrapunji with 26 461 mm *1041·78 in* between 1 Aug 1860 and 31 Jul 1861.

In Great Britain, the 24 hour record is 279 mm *11 in* at Martinstown, Dorset, on 18 and 19 Jul 1955. 1436 mm *56·54 in* fell in October 1909 at Llyn Llydau, Snowdon, Gwynedd, and over a 12 month period 6527 mm *257 in* fell at Sprinkling Tarn, Cumbria, in 1954.

Wettest place ■ By average annual rainfall, the wettest place in the world is Tutunendo, in Colombia, with 11 770 mm *463·4 in* per annum. Styhead Tarn (487 m *1600 ft*), in Cumbria, with 4391 mm *172·9 in,* is Britain's wettest place.

Greatest snowfall ■ 31 102 mm *1224 ¹/₂ in* of snow fell over a 12 month period from 19 Feb 1971 to 18 Feb 1972 at Paradise, Mt Rainier, in Washington State, USA. The record for a single snowstorm is 4800 mm *189 in* at Mt Shasta Ski Bowl, California, USA from 13–19 Feb 1959 and for a 24 hr period it is 1930 mm *76 in* at Silver Lake, Colorado, USA on 14–15 Apr 1921. The greatest depth of snow on the ground was 1146 cm *37 ft 7 in* at Tamarack, California, USA in March 1911. Britain's 12 month record is the 1524 mm *60 in* which fell both in Upper Teesdale and also in the Denbighshire Hills, Clwyd, in 1947. London's earliest recorded snow was on 25 Sep 1885, and the latest on 27 May 1821. Less reliable reports suggest snow on 12 Sep 1658 (old style) and on 12 Jun 1791.

Maximum sunshine ■ The annual average at Yuma, Arizona, USA is 90 per cent (over 4000 hours). St Petersburg, Florida, USA, recorded 768 consecutive sunny days from 9 Feb 1967 to 17 Mar 1969. The best in Britain was 78·3 per cent of the maximum possible in one month (382 hours out of 488) at Pendennis Castle, Falmouth, Cornwall in June 1925.

Minimum sunshine ■ At the South Pole there is

nil sunshine for 182 days every year and at the North Pole the figure is nil for 176 days. From 18 Nov to 8 Feb each winter the south-eastern end of the village of Lochranza, Isle of Arran, Strathclyde is in shadow of mountains, and for the whole of December 1890, a figure of nil was registered at Westminster, London.

Barometric pressure ■ The highest barometric pressure ever recorded was 1083·8 mb (*32 in*), at Agata, Siberia, USSR (alt. 262 m *862 ft*) on 31 Dec 1968. The highest in Britain was 1054·7 mb (*31·15 in*), in Aberdeen on 31 Jan 1902.

The lowest was 870 mb (*25·69 in*), 482 km *300 miles* west of Guam, Pacific Ocean, in Lat. 16°44' N, Long. 137° 46' E on 12 Oct 1979. Britain's lowest is 925·5 mb (*27·33 in*), at Ochtertyre, near Crieff, Tayside on 26 Jan 1884.

Highest surface wind-speed ■ A surface wind-speed of 371 km/h *231 mph* was recorded at Mt Washington (1916 m *6288 ft*), New Hampshire, USA on 12 Apr 1934. The highest speed measured to date in a tornado is 450 km/h *280 mph* at Wichita Falls, Texas, USA on 2 Apr 1958. The record high surface wind-speed for Britain is 278 km/h *172 mph* (150 knots), on Cairn Gorm Summit (1245 m *4084 ft*), on 20 Mar 1986. A figure of 285·2 km/h *177·2 mph* at RAF Saxa Vord, Unst, in the Shetlands, Scotland on 16 Feb 1962, was not recorded with standard equipment. British tornadoes may reach 290 km/h *180 mph.*

There were gales of great severity on 15 Jan 1362, 26 Nov 1703 and 16 Oct 1987.

Thunder-days ■ Kampala, Uganda averages 242 days of thunder each year. Between Lat. 35° N and 35° S there are some 3200 thunderstorms each 12 night-time hours, some of which can be heard at a range of 29 km *18 miles.* The record number of thunder-days recorded in a specific place in a calendar year in Britain is 38, twice. The first time was in 1912, at Stonyhurst, in Lancashire, and the second was in 1967, at Huddersfield, in West Yorks.

Hottest place ■ On an annual mean basis, with readings taken over a six year period from 1960 to 1966, the temperature at Dallol, in Ethiopia, was 34·4° C *94° F.* In Death Valley, California, USA, maximum temperatures of over 48·9° C *120° F* were recorded on 43 consecutive days, between 6 Jul and 17 Aug 1917. At Marble Bar, Western Australia (maximum 49·4° C *121° F*), 162 consecutive days with maximum temperatures of over 37·8° C *100° F* were recorded between 30 Oct 1923 and 8 Apr 1924. At Wyndham, also in Western Australia, the temperature reached 32·2° C *90° F* or more on 333 days in 1946. In Britain, annual mean temperatures of 11·5° C *52·7° F* were recorded both at Penzance, in Cornwall, and the Isles of Scilly in the period 1931 to 1960.

Coldest place ■ Polus Nedostupnosti, Pole of Cold (78° S, 96° E), Antarctica is the coldest place in the world, with an extrapolated annual mean of −57·8° C *−72° F.* The coldest measured mean is −56·6° C *−70° F,* at Plateau Station, Antarctica. For Britain it is 6·34° C *43·41° F,* at Braemar, Grampian, Scotland based on readings taken between 1952 and 1981.

Most rainy days ■ Mt Wai-'ale-'ale (1569 m *5148 ft*), Kauai, Hawaii, has up to 350 rainy days per annum. The place in the British Isles which has had the most rainy days in a calendar year is Ballynahinch, in Galway, Ireland with 309 in 1923.

Driest place ■ The annual mean rainfall in the Desierto de Atacama, near Calama, Chile is nil. In Britain, the lowest annual mean rainfall on record is at St Osyth, Lee Wick Farm, Essex, with 513 mm *20·2 in*, based on the period 1964 to 1982. The lowest rainfall recorded in a single year was 236 mm *9·29 in* at one station in Margate, Kent in 1921.

Longest drought ■ Desierto de Atacama, in Chile experienced a drought for some 400 years up to 1971. Britain's longest drought lasted 73 days, from 4 Mar to 15 May 1893, at Mile End, Greater London.

Heaviest hailstones ■ The heaviest hailstones on record, weighing 1·02 kg *2¼ lb*, are reported to have killed 92 people in the Gopalganj district of Bangladesh on 14 Apr 1986. The *Canton Evening News* reported 5 killed and 225 injured by a hailstorm on 14 Apr 1981, with stones weighing up to 13·6 kg *30 lb* (sic). The heaviest hailstones in Britain fell on 5 Sept 1958, at Horsham, West Sussex, and weighed 141 g *5 oz*. Much heavier ones are sometimes reported, but usually these are coalesced rather than single stones. An ice block of 1–2 kg *35–70 oz* was reputed at Withington, Manchester on 2 Apr 1973.

Longest sea level fogs ■ Sea level fogs—with visibility less than 914·4 m *1000 yd*—persist for weeks on the Grand Banks, Newfoundland, Canada, with the average being more than 120 days per year. The duration record for Britain is 4 days 18 hours, twice, in both cases in London. The first time was from 26 Nov to 1 Dec 1948 and the second from 5 to 9 Dec 1952. Lower visibilities occur at higher altitudes. Ben Nevis is reputedly in cloud 300 days per year.

Windiest place ■ The Commonwealth Bay, George V Coast, Antarctica, where gales reach 320 km/h *200 mph* is the world's windiest place. In Britain, an average reading of 33·1 km/h *20·6 mph* was registered at Fair Isle in the period 1974–1978.

Gems, Jewels and Precious Stones

OPAL

Largest. 113·81 troy oz. The 17 700 carat *Olympic Australis* (SiO_2nHO_2O) found in Coober Pedy, South Australia in August 1956, owned by Altmann and Cherny Pty Ltd, is on public display in Melbourne, Australia and valued at $1·8 million (US).

Black Opal A 443·56 carat 2·85 troy oz black opal named *Pacific* measuring 75 x 50 x 16 mm was found in January 1989 by operatives of the Black Opal International Pty Ltd at Lightning Ridge, New South Wales, Australia. This unique black gem opal coloured green/blue in large block pattern will be displayed at gem exhibitions throughout the world during 1989-90.

DIAMOND

Largest. 3106 carats. Found on 25 Jan 1905 in the Premier Mine, Pretoria, South Africa and named *The Cullinan* after the mine's discoverer Sir Thomas Cullinan. Presented to King Edward VII in 1907. Currently the largest uncut stone is of 599 carats, found near Pretoria, South Africa in Jul 1986 and revealed by De Beers on 11 Mar 1988. It is expected to yield a 350 carat cut stone.

Largest cut. 530·2 carats. A 74-facet pear-shaped gem named *The Star of Africa*, cleaved from *The Cullinan* by Jak Asscher and polished by Henri Koe in Amsterdam in 1908. Now in the Royal Sceptre.

Smallest. 0·000 102 2 carat. D. Drukker & Zn NV of Amsterdam, Netherlands have produced a 57-facet brilliant with a diameter of 0·22 mm *0·009 in*.

Large opal ● This 443·56 carat black opal measuring 75 x 50 x 16 mm was certified in March 1989. (Photo: Australian Opal and Gemstone Photo Library).

Rarest colour. Blood red. The largest is a 5·05 carat flawless stone found in Tichtenburg, South Africa in 1927 and now in a private collection in the United States.

Highest priced. $9 130 000. The flawless pear-shaped 85·91 carat, sold to Laurence Graff of London at Sotheby's New York, USA on 19 Apr 1988. The record per carat is £241 457 ($406 450) for a 3·10 carat red (cranberry hue) diamond from the Argyle mine, Western Australia sold to Laurence Graff at Christies', New York on 11 Apr 1989. A record price of £5.8 million ($10 million) was paid for a rough uncut diamond by Chow Tai Fook of Hong Kong on 4 Mar 1989.

JADE

Largest. 143 tonnes. On 17 Sep 1978 a boulder of nephrite jade was reported $Ca_2(Mg,Fe)_5(Sl_4O_{11})_2(OH)_2$ of 603 m³ *21 300 ft³* found in China.

TOPAZ

Largest. 22 892·5 carats. The rectangular, cushion-cut *American Golden Topaz* with 172 facets and 149·2 mm in overall width has been on display at the Smithsonian Institution, Washington, DC, USA since 4 May 1988.

GOLD

Largest nugget. 214·32 kg *7560 oz*. The *Holtermann Nugget* found on 19 Oct 1872 in the Beyers & Holtermann Star of Hope mine, Hill End, New South Wales, Australia, contained some 99·8 kg *220 lb* gold in a 285·7 kg *630 lb* slab of slate.

Largest pure nugget. The *Welcome Stranger* found at Moliagul, Victoria, Australia in 1869 yielded 69·92 kg *2248 troy oz* pure gold from 70·92 kg *2280 ¼ oz*.

EMERALD

Largest cut. 86 136 carats. This natural beryl Gleim [$Be_3Al_2(SiO_3)_6$] was found in Carnaiba, Brazil in August 1974. It was carved by Richard Chan in Hong Kong and valued at £718 000 in 1982.

RUBY

Largest star. 2475 carats. *Rajarathna*, India, displays an animated star of 6 lines and is cut as a cabochon.

Largest double star. 1370 carats. A cabochon cut gem, *Neelanjahi*, owned by G. Vidyaraj, Bangalore, India, displays 12 star lines and measures 7·62 cm *3 in* in height and 5·08 cm *2 in* in diameter.

Largest. 8500 carats. In July 1985 jeweller James Kazanjian of Beverly Hills, California, USA displayed a 14 cm *5½ in* tall red corundum (Al_2O_3) carved into the Liberty Bell.

PEARL

Largest. 6·37 kg *14 lb 1 oz*. The *Pearl of Lao-tze* (also known as the *Pearl of Allah*) was found at Palawan, Philippines on 7 May 1934 in the shell of a giant clam. The property of Wilburn Dowell Cobb until his death, this 24 cm *9½ in* long by 14 cm *5½ in* diameter molluscan concretion was bought at auction on 15 May 1980 in San Francisco, California, USA by Peter Hoffman and Victor Barbish for $200 000. An appraisal by the San Francisco Gem Laboratory in May 1984 suggested a value of $40–42 000 000.

Highest priced. Sfr 1 210 000 (£460 076) *La Régente*, an egg-shaped pearl weighing 15·13 g *302·68 grains* and formerly part of the French Crown Jewels, was sold at Christie's, Geneva, Switzerland, on 12 May 1988.

SAPPHIRE

Largest. 2302 carats. Found at Anakie, Queensland, Australia in *c.* 1935, this corundum (Al_2O_3) was carved into a 1318 carat head of Abraham Lincoln and is now in the custody of the Kazanjian Foundation of Los Angeles, California, USA. A sapphire crystal found by Steve Meyer and Craig Peden near Canton, North Carolina, USA in December 1987 has been provisionally estimated at 3500 carats.

Largest cut. 1444 carats. A bust of General Dwight David Eisenhower that was carved in 1953-5 from a 2097-carat black star stone.

Largest Star. The 1145 carat blue-silver 'Star of the Carolinas', was found in 1988 at the Old Pressley Sapphire Mine in Canton, in Western North Carolina, USA.

Highest priced. £579 300. A step-cut single stone of 66·03 carats from the Rockefeller Collection was sold by auction on 8 May 1980 at Sotheby's, Zurich, Switzerland.

AMBER

Largest. 15·25 kg *33 lb 10 oz*. The 'Burma Amber' is located in the Natural History Museum, London. Amber is a fossil resin derived from extinct coniferous trees, and often contains trapped insects.

The Universe & Space

LIGHT-YEAR—that distance travelled by light (speed 299 792·458 km/s *186 282·397 miles/sec* or 1 079 252 848·8 km/h *670 616 629·2 mph in vacuo*) in one tropical year (365·24219878 mean solar days at January 0·12 hours Ephemeris time in AD 1900) and is equivalent to 9 460 528 405 000 km *5 878 499 814 000 miles*. The unit was first used in March 1888 and fixed at this constant in October 1983.
MAGNITUDE—a measure of stellar brightness such that the light of a star of any magnitude bears a ratio of 2·511 886 to that of a star of the next magnitude. Thus a fifth magnitude star is 2·511 886 times as bright, while one of the first magnitude is exactly 100 (or 2·511 886⁵) times as bright, as a sixth magnitude star. In the case of such exceptionally bright bodies as Sirius, Venus, the Moon (magnitude −12·71) or the Sun (magnitude −26·78), the magnitude is expressed as a minus quantity.
PROPER MOTION—that component of a star's motion in space which, at right angles to the line of sight, constitutes an apparent change of position of the star in the celestial sphere.

METEOROIDS

Meteoroids are of cometary or asteroidal origin. A meteor is the light phenomenon caused by the entry of a meteoroid into the Earth's atmosphere.

Meteor shower ■ The greatest 'shower' on record occurred on the night of 16–17 Nov 1966, when the Leonid meteors (which recur every 33¼ years) were visible between western North America and eastern USSR. It was calculated that meteors passed over Arizona, USA, at a rate of 2300 per min for a period of 20 min from 5 a.m. on 17 Nov 1966.

METEORITES

Meteorites ■ When a *meteoroid* (consisting of broken fragments of cometary or asteroidal origin and ranging in size from fine dust to bodies several kilometres in diameter) penetrates to the Earth's surface, the remnant, which could be either aerolite (stony) or siderite (metallic), is described as a *meteorite*. Such events occur about 150 times per year over the whole land surface of the Earth.

The most anxious time of day for meteorophobes should be 3 p.m. In historic times, the only recorded person injured by a meteorite was Mrs Ann Hodges of Sylacauga, Alabama, USA. On 30 Nov 1954 a 4 kg *9 lb* stone, some 18 cm *7 in* in length, crashed through the roof of her home, hitting Mrs Hodges on the arm and bruising her hip. The physician who examined her, Dr Moody D. Jacobs, declared her fit but she was subsequently hospitalised as a result of the attendant publicity.

Oldest ■ A revision by T. Kirsten in 1981 of the age estimates of meteorites which have remained essentially undisturbed after their formation suggest that the oldest which has been accurately dated is the Krähenberg meteorite at 4600 ± 20 million years which predates the Solar System by about 70 million years. It was reported in August 1978 that dust grains in the Murchison meteorite which fell in Australia in September 1969 may also be older than the Solar System.

Largest ■ There was a mysterious explosion of 12½ megatons in Lat. 60° 55′ N, Long. 101° 57′ E, in the basin of the Podkamennaya Tunguska river, 40 miles north of Vanavar, in Siberia, USSR, at 00 hrs 17 min 11 sec UT on 30 June 1908. The cause was variously attributed to a meteorite (1927), a comet (1930), a nuclear explosion (1961) and to anti-matter (1965). This devastated an area of about 3885 km² *1500 miles²* and the shock was felt as far as 1000 km (more than *600 miles*) away. The theory is now favoured that this was the terminal flare of stony debris from a comet, possibly Encke's comet, at an altitude of only 6 km or less than *20 000 ft*. A similar event may have occurred over the Isle of Axholm, Humberside, England a few thousand years before. A stony meteorite with a diameter of 10 km *6·2 miles* striking the Earth at 55 925 mph *25 km/sec* would generate an explosive energy equivalent to 100 million megatons. Such events should not be expected to recur more than once in 75 million years.

The largest known meteorite was found in 1920 at Hoba West, near Grootfontein in south-west Africa and is a block 2·75 m *9 ft* long by 2·43 m *8 ft* broad, estimated to be 59 tonnes *130 000 lb*. The largest meteorite exhibited by any museum is the 'Tent' meteorite, weighing 30 883 kg *68 085 lb (30·39 tons)* found in 1897 near Cape York, on the west coast of Greenland, by the expedition of Commander (later Rear-Admiral) Robert Edwin Peary (1856–1920). It was known to the Eskimos as the Ahnighito and is now exhibited in the Hayden Planetarium in New York City, USA. The largest piece of stony meteorite recovered is a piece of 1770 kg *3902 lb*, part of a 4 tonne shower which struck Jilin (formerly Kirin), China on 8 Mar 1976.

The heaviest of the 22 meteorites known to have fallen on the British Isles since 1623 was one weighing at least 46·25 kg *102 lb* (largest piece 7·88 kg *17 lb 4 oz*), which fell at 4.12 p.m. on 24 Dec 1965 at Barwell, Leics. Scotland's largest recorded meteorite fell in Strathmore, Tayside on 3 Dec 1917. It weighed 10·09 kg *22¼ lb* and was the largest of four stones totalling 13·324 kg *29 lb 6 oz*. The largest recorded meteorite to fall in Ireland was the Limerick Stone of 29·5 kg *65 lb*, part of a shower weighing more than 48 kg *106 lb* which fell near Adare, Limerick, on 10 Sep 1813. The larger of the two recorded meteorites to land in Wales was one

weighing 794 g *28 oz* of which a piece weighing 723 g *25½ oz* went through the roof of the Prince Llewellyn Hotel in Beddgelert, Gwynedd, shortly before 3.15 a.m. on 21 Sep 1949. Debris from the Bovedy Fall in Northern Ireland in 1969 spread over 80 km *50 miles*.

Craters ■ It has been estimated that some 2000 asteroid-Earth collisions have occurred in the last 600 million years. 102 collision sites or astroblemes have been recognised. A crater 241 km *150 miles* in diameter and 805 m *½ mile* deep was postulated in 1962 in Wilkes Land, Antarctica. It would be caused by a 13 000 million tonnes meteorite striking at 70 811 km/h *44 000 mph*. Soviet scientists reported in December 1970 an astrobleme with a 95 km *60 mile* diameter and a maximum depth of 400 m *1300 ft* in the basin of the River Popigai. There is a crater-like formation or astrobleme 442·5 km *275 miles* in diameter on the eastern shore of the Hudson Bay, Canada, where the Nastapoka Islands are just off the coast.

One of the largest and best preserved craters is the Coon Butte or Barringer crater, discovered in 1891 near Canyon Diablo, Winslow, northern Arizona, USA. It is 1265 m *4150 ft* in diameter and now about 175 m *575 ft* deep, with a parapet rising 40–48 m *130–155 ft* above the surrounding plain. It has been estimated that an iron-nickel mass of some 2 000 000 tonnes and diameter of 61–79 m *200–260 ft* gouged this crater in *c.* 25 000 BC. Evidence was published in 1963 discounting a meteoric origin for the crypto-volcanic Vredefort Ring (diameter 41·8 km *26 miles*), to the south-west of Johannesburg, South Africa, but this has now been re-asserted. The New Quebec (formerly the Chubb) 'Crater', first sighted on 20 June 1943 in northern Ungava, Canada, is 404 m *1325 ft* deep and measures 10·9 km *6·8 miles* round its rim.

Tektites ■ The largest of which details have been published has been of 3·2 kg *7·04 lb* found in 1932 at Muong Nong, Saravane Province, Laos and now in the Louvre Paris Museum. Eight SNC meteorites named after their find sites at Shergotty, India; Nakla, Egypt and Chassigny, France, are believed to have emanated from Mars.

Fireball *Brightest* ■ The brightest ever photographically recorded was by Dr Zdenek Ceplecha over Sumava, Czechoslovakia on 4 Dec 1974 with a momentary magnitude of −22 or 10 000 times brighter than a full Moon.

AURORAE

Most frequent ■ Polar lights, known since 1560 as Aurora Borealis or Northern Lights in the northern hemisphere, and since 1773 as Aurora Australis in the southern, are caused by electrical solar discharges in the upper atmosphere and occur most frequently in high latitudes. Aurorae are visible at some time on *every* clear dark night in the polar areas within 20 degrees of the magnetic poles. The extreme height of aurorae has been measured at 1000 km *620 miles*, while the lowest may descend to 72·5 km *45 miles*. Reliable figures exist only from 1952, since when the record high and low number of nights of auroral displays in Shetland (geomagnetic Lat. 63°) has been 203 (1957) and 58 (1965). The most recent great display in north-west Europe was that of 4–5 Sep 1958.

Lowest latitudes ■ Extreme cases of displays in very low latitudes are Cuzco, Peru (2 Aug 1744); Honolulu, Hawaii (1 Sep 1859) and, questionably, Singapore (25 Sep 1909).

Noctilucent clouds ■ These remain sunlit long after sunset owing to their great altitude and are thought to consist of ice crystals or meteoric dust. Regular observations (at heights of *c.* 85 km *52 miles*) in Western Europe date only from 1964, since when the record high and low number of nights on which these phenomena have been observed have been 43 (1979) and 15 (1970).

THE MOON

The Earth's closest neighbour in space and its only

natural satellite is the Moon which has an average of 3475·1 km *2159·3 miles* and a mass of 7·348 x 10¹⁹ tonnes or 0·0123 Earth masses so the density is 3·344 x that of water. The Moon orbits at a mean distance of 384 399·1 km *238 854.5 miles* centre–to–centre although the centre of mass is displaced from the centre of figure by 1·8 km *1·1 miles* towards the Earth so that the distance surface-to-surface is 376 285 km *233 813 miles*. In the present century the closest approach (smallest perigee) was 356 375 km *221 441 miles* centre-to-centre on 4 Jan 1912 and the farthest distance largest apogee) was 406 711 km *252 718 miles* on 2 Mar 1984. The orbital period (sidereal month) is 27.321661 days giving an average orbital velocity of 3683 km/h *2289 mph*. The currently accepted 'giant impact' theory of the lunar origin suggests that the Moon was formed just outside of the Earth's Roche Limit (about 18 500 km *11 500 miles* from the Earth's centre) from the debris resulting from a glancing collision between the Earth and a Mars-size planetesimal. That this event must have occurred in the early history of the Solar System is indiciated by the fact that the oldest lunar rocks and soils brought back to Earth by the *Apollo* programme crews are of a similar age to the oldest known meteorites (about 4500 million years). The first direct hit on the Moon was achieved at 2 min 24 sec after midnight (Moscow time) on 14 Sep 1959, by the Soviet space probe *Lunar II* near the *Mare Serenitatis*. The first photographic images of the hidden side were collected by the USSR *Lunar III* from 6.30 am on the 7 Oct 1959, from a range of up to 70 400 km *43 750 miles* and transmitted to the Earth from a distance of 470 000 km *292 000 miles*.

Crater *Largest and deepest* ■ Only 59 per cent of the Moon's surface is directly visible from the Earth because it is in 'captured rotation', i.e. the period of rotation is equal to the period of orbit. The largest wholly visible crater is the walled plain Bailly, towards the Moon's South Pole, which is 295 km *183 miles* across, with walls rising to 4250 m *14 000 ft*. The Orientale Basin, partly on the averted side, measures more than 965 km *600 miles* in diameter. The deepest crater is the Newton crater, with a floor estimated to be between 7000 and 8850 m *23 000–29 000 ft* below its rim and 2250 m *14 000 ft* below the level of the plain outside. The brightest directly visible spot on the Moon is *Aristarchus*.

Highest mountains ■ In the absence of a sea level, lunar altitudes are measured relative to an adopted reference sphere of radius 1 738 km *1079·943 miles*. Thus the greatest elevation attained on this basis by any of the 12 US astronauts has been 7830 m *25 688 ft* on the Descartes Highlands by Capt John Watts Young USN and Major Charles M. Duke Jr on 27 Apr 1972.

Temperature extremes ■ When the Sun is overhead the temperature on the lunar equator reaches 117·2° C *243° F* (17·2 ° C *31 ° F* above the boiling point of water). By sunset the temperature is 14·4° C *58° F* but after nightfall it sinks to −162·7° C *−261° F.*

THE SUN

Distance extremes ■ The true distance of the Earth from the Sun is 1·00000102 astronomical units or 149 598 020 km *92 955 900 miles*. The orbit is elliptical and the distance of the Sun varies between a minimum (perihelion) of 147 097 800 km *91 402 300 miles* and a maximum (aphelion) of 152 098 200 km *94 509 400 miles*. Based on an orbital circumference of 939 886 400 km *584 018 400 miles* and an orbital period (sidereal year) of 365·256366 days then the average orbital velocity is 107 210 kmh *66 620 mph*, but this varies between a minimum of 105 450 kmh *65 500 mph* at aphelion and a maximum of 109 030 kmh *67 750 mph* at perihelion.

Temperature and dimensions ■ The Sun has a stellar classification of a *yellow dwarf* type G2 although its mass at 1·9889 x 10²⁷ tonnes *1·9575 x 10²⁷ tons* is 332 946·04 times that of the Earth and represents over 99 per cent of the total mass of the Solar System. The solar diameter at 1392 140 km

865 040 miles leads to a density of 1·408 times that of water. The Sun has a central temperature of about 15 400 000 K and a core pressure of 25·4 PPa *1 650 000 000 tons/in²* and uses up about 4 million tonnes of hydrogen per sec, equal to an energy output of 3·85 x 10²⁶ watts, although it will take 10 000 million years to exhaust its energy supply (about 5 000 million years from the present). The luminous intensity of the Sun is 2·7 x 10²⁷ candela which is equal to a luminance of 4·5 x 10⁸ candela/m² *290 000 candela/in²*.

Sunspots ■ To be visible to the *protected* naked eye, a sunspot must cover about one two-thousandth part of the Sun's disc and thus have an area of about 1300 million km² *500 000 000 miles²*. The largest sunspot ever noted was in the Sun's southern hemisphere on 8 Apr 1947. Its area was about 18 000 million km² *7000 million miles²* with an extreme longitude of 300 000 km *187 000 miles* and an extreme latitude of 145 000 km *90 000 miles*. Sunspots appear darker because they are more than 1500 deg C cooler than the rest of the Sun's surface temperature of 5507° C. In October 1957 a smoothed sunspot count showed 263, the highest recorded index since records started in 1755 (cf. previous record of 239 in May 1778). In 1943 one sunspot lasted for 200 days from June to December.

ECLIPSES

Earliest recorded ■ For the Middle East, lunar eclipses have been extrapolated to 3450 BC and solar ones to 4200 BC. The oldest recorded total solar eclipse is on a clay tablet found in 1948 among the ruins of the ancient city of Ugarit (now in Syria). A re-assessment in 1989 suggests that this records the eclipse of the 5 Mar 1223 BC! No centre of the path of totality for a solar eclipse crossed London for the 575 years from 20 Mar 1140 to 3 May 1715. On 14 Jun 2151 at 18.25 GMT the eclipse will be 99 per cent total in central London but total in Sheffield and Norfolk. The most recent occasion when a line of totality of a solar eclipse crossed Great Britain was on 29 Jun 1927 for 24·5 sec at West Hartlepool, Cleveland and the next instance will clip the coast at St Just, Cornwall at 10.10 a.m. on Wednesday 11 Aug 1999. On 30 Jun 1954 a total eclipse was witnessed from Unst, Shetland Islands but the centre of the path of totality was to its north.

Longest duration ■ The maximum *possible* duration of an eclipse of the Sun is 7 min 31 sec. The longest actually *measured* was on 20 Jun 1955 (7 min 8 sec), seen from the Philippines. One of 7 min 29 sec should occur in mid-Atlantic on 16 Jul 2186, which will then be the longest for 1469 years. The longest possible in the British Isles is 5 min 30 sec. That of 15 Jun 1885 lasted nearly 5 min, as will that of 20 Jul 2381 in the Borders area. Durations can be extended by observers being airborne as on 30 Jun 1973 when an eclipse was 'extended' to 72 min aboard Concorde. An annular eclipse may last for 12 min 24 sec. The longest totality of any lunar eclipse is 104 minutes and has occurred many times.

Most and least frequent ■ The highest number of eclipses possible in a year is seven, as in 1935, when there were five solar and two lunar eclipses; or four solar and three lunar, as occurred in 1982. The lowest possible number in a year is two, both of which must be solar, as in 1944 and 1969.

COMETS

Earliest recorded ■ Records date from the 7th century BC. The speeds of the estimated 2 000 000 comets vary from 1125 km/h *700 mph* in outer space to 2 000 000 km/h *1 250 000 mph* when near the Sun. The successive appearances of Halley's Comet have been traced back to 467 BC. It was first depicted in the Nuremberg Chronicle of AD 684. The first prediction of its return by Edmund Halley (1656–1742) proved true on Christmas Day 1758, 16 years after his death. On 13–14 Mar 1986, the European satellite *Giotto* (launched 2 Jul 1985) penetrated to within 540 km *335 miles* of the nucleus of Halley's Comet. It was established that this was 15 km *9·3 miles* in length and velvet black in colour.

Closest approach ■ On 1 Jul 1770, Lexell's Comet, travelling at a speed of 38·5 km/sec *23·9 miles/sec* (relative to the Sun), came to within 1 200 000 km *745 000 miles* of the Earth. However, the Earth is believed to have passed through the tail of Halley's Comet, most recently on 19 May 1910.

Largest ■ The tail of the brightest of all comets, the Great Comet of 1843, trailed for 330 000 000 km *205 000 000 miles*. The bow shock of Holmes Comet of 1892 once measured 2 400 000 km *1 500 000 miles* in diameter.

Shortest period ■ Of all the recorded periodic comets (these are members of the Solar System), the one which most frequently returns is Encke's Comet, first identified in 1786. Its period of 1206 days (3.3 years) is the shortest established. Not one of its 53 returns (including that of 1983) has been missed by astronomers. Now increasingly faint, it is expected to 'die' by February 1994. The most frequently observed comets are Schwassmann-Wachmann I, Kopff and Oterma which can be observed every year between Mars and Jupiter.

Longest period ■ At the other extreme is Delavan's Comet of 1914, whose path was not accurately determined. It is not expected to return for perhaps 24 million years.

PLANETS

Largest ■ The nine major planets (including the Earth) are bodies within the Solar System and which revolve round the Sun in definite orbits. The search for Planet X continues. Jupiter, with an equatorial diameter of 142 984 km *88 846 miles* and a polar diameter of 133 708 km *83 082 miles* is the largest of the nine major planets, with a mass 317·828 times, and a volume 1323·3 times that of the Earth. It also has the shortest period of rotation resulting in a Jovian day of only 9 hr 50 min 30·003 sec in the equatorial zone.

Smallest, coldest and outermost ■ Pluto was first recorded by Clyde William Tombaugh (b. 4 Feb 1906) at Lowell Observatory, Flagstaff, Arizona, USA on 18 Feb 1930 from photographs he took on 23 and 29 Jan. His find was announced on 13 March. Pluto's companion Charon was announced on 22 Jun 1978 from the US Naval Observatory, Flagstaff, Arizona. Pluto, with a mass of about 1/500th of that of the Earth, has a diameter of 2284 km *1419 miles* and Charon 1192 km *741 miles*. Their surface temperature is an estimated −214°C *−353°F*. Their mean distance from the Sun is 5 913 514 000 km *3 674 488 000 miles* with a period of revolution of 248·54 years. Because of their orbital eccentricity they will have been temporarily closer to the Sun than Neptune in the period from 23 Jan 1979 to 15 Mar 1999.

Fastest ■ Mercury, which orbits the Sun at an average distance of 57 909 200 km *35 983 100 miles*, has a period of revolution of 87·9686 days, so giving the highest average speed in orbit of 172 248 km/h *107 030 mph*.

Hottest ■ For Venus a surface temperature of 462° C *864°F* has been estimated from measurements made from the USSR *Venera* and US Pioneer Cytherean surface probes.

Nearest ■ The fellow planet closest to the Earth is Venus, which is, at times, only 41 360 000 km *25 700 000 miles* inside the Earth's orbit, compared with Mars's closest approach of 55 680 000 km *34 600 000 miles* outside the Earth's orbit. Mars, known since 1965 to be cratered, has temperatures ranging from 29·4° C *85° F* to −123° C *−190° F*.

Surface features ■ By far the highest and most spectacular is Olympus Mons (formerly Nix Olympica) in the Tharsis region of Mars with a diameter of 500–600 km *310–370 miles* and a height of 26 ±3 km *75 450–95 150 ft* above the surrounding plain. Venus has a canyon some 1600 km *1000 miles* south of Venusian equator 6·4 km *21 000 ft* deep and 400 km *250 miles* long. The ice cliff on the Uranian moon Miranda is 5·20 km *65 000 ft* high.

Brightest and faintest ■ Viewed from the Earth,

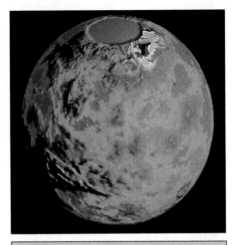

Nearest planet ● A global topographic map of the planet Venus based on radar data received from the Pioneer probe. The northern 'continent' Ishtar can be clearly seen. (Photo: NASA/Science Photo Library).

by far the brightest of the five planets visible to the naked eye is Venus, with a maximum magnitude of −4·4. Uranus, the first to be discovered by telescope when it was sighted by Sir William Herschel from his garden at 19, New King St., Bath on 13 Mar 1781, is only marginally visible with a magnitude 5·5. The faintest is Pluto, with a magnitude of 15·0.

Densest and least dense ■ Earth is the densest planet with an average figure of 5·515 times that of water, whilst Saturn has an average density only about one-eighth of this value or 0·685 times that of water.

Conjunctions ■ The most dramatic recorded conjunction (coming together) of the other seven principal members of the Solar System (Sun, Moon, Mercury, Venus, Mars, Jupiter and Saturn) occurred on 5 Feb 1962, when 16° were seen during an eclipse in the Pacific area. It is possible that the seven-fold conjunction of September 1186 spanned only 12°. The next notable conjunction will take place on 5 May 2000.

Largest scale model ■ The largest scale model of the Solar System was inaugurated by the Futures' Museum, Falun, Sweden on 29 Nov 1986. A model of the Earth of diameter 13 mm *½ in* was placed in the museum. The Sun 1·5 m *5 ft* and the planets which ranged from 3·5 mm *0·13 in* to 140 mm *5·½ in* were positioned in the nearby city of Borlange some 16·2 km *10 miles* away. *Proxima Centauri* was posi-

Newest supernova ● This, the most recently discovered supernova, was sighted by Ian Shelton on the morning of 23 Feb 1987 and lies in the Large Magellanic Cloud. Designated – 69 202 it is some 170 000 light-years distant. (Photo; European Space Agency).

tioned at the Museum of Victoria, Melbourne, Australia.

SATELLITES

Most ■ Of the nine major planets, all but Venus and Mercury have satellites. The planet with the most is Saturn with at least 17 satellites. The Earth and Pluto are the only planets with a single satellite. The distance from their parent planets varies from the 9377 km *5827 miles* of *Phobos* from the centre of Mars to the 23 700 000 km *14 700 000 miles* of Jupiter's outer satellite *Sinope* (Jupiter IX). The Solar System has a total of 54 established satellites.

Largest and smallest ■ The largest and heaviest satellite is *Ganymede* (Jupiter III), which is 2·017 times heavier than our own Moon and has a diameter of 5262 km *3270 miles*. The smallest satellite is *Leda* (Jupiter XIII) with a diameter of less than 15 km *9·3 miles*.

Largest asteroids ■ In the belt which lies between Mars and Jupiter, there are some 45 000 (about 4100 numbered to October 1989) minor planets or asteroids which are, for the most part, too small to yield to diameter measurement. The largest and first discovered (by G. Piazzi at Palermo, Sicily on 1 Jan 1801) of these is *Ceres*, which has a diameter of 936 km *582 miles*. The only one visible to the naked eye is asteroid 4 *Vesta* (diameter 519 km *322 miles*) discovered on 29 Mar 1807 by Dr Heinrich Wilhelm Olbers (1758–1840), a German amateur astronomer. The closest measured approach to the Earth by an asteroid was 780 000 km *485 000 miles* in the case of *Hermes* on 30 Oct 1937 (asteroid now lost). The most distant detected is 2060 *Chiron*, found between Saturn and Uranus on 18–19 Oct 1977, by Charles T. Kowal from the Hale Observatory, California, USA.

STARS

Largest and most massive ■ The variable star

Eta Carinae, which is 9100 light-years distant in the Carina Nebula in our own galaxy, has a mass at least 200 times greater than our own Sun. *Betelgeux* (top left star of Orion) has a diameter of 700 million km *400 million miles* or about 500 times greater than the Sun. In 1978 it was found to be surrounded not only by a dust 'shell' but also an outer tenuous gas halo up to $8·5 \times 10^{11}$ km *$5·3 \times 10^{1}$ miles* in diameter, that is over 1100 times the diameter of the star. The light from *Betelgeux* left in AD 1680.

Smallest and lightest ■ A mass of 0·014 that of the Sun is estimated for the very faint star RG 0058.8-2807 which was discovered by I. Neill Reid and Gerard Gilmore using the UK Schmidt telescope and was announced in April 1983. The white dwarf star L362-81 has an estimated diameter of 5600 km *3500 miles* or only 0·0040 that of the Sun.

Brightest ■ Sirius A (*Alpha Canis Majoris*), also known as the Dog Star, is apparently the brightest star of the 5776 stars of naked eye visibility in the heavens, with an apparent magnitude of −1·46. It is in the constellation *Canis Major* and is visible in the winter months of the northern hemisphere, being due south at midnight on the last day of the year. Sirius is 8·64 light-years distant and has a luminosity 26 times as much as that of the Sun. It has a diameter of 2·33 million km *1·45 million miles* and a mass of $4·26 \times 10^{27}$ tonnes. The faint white dwarf companion Sirius B has a diameter of only 10 000 km *6000 miles* but is 350 000 times heavier than the Earth. The magnitude of Sirius should rise to a maximum of −1·67 by c. AD 61 000.

Farthest ■ The Solar System, with its Sun's nine principal planets, 54 satellites, asteroids and comets, is located in the outer regions of our Milky Way Galaxy orbiting at a mean distance of 29 700 light years and with an orbital eccentricity of 0·07. The present distance from the centre is 27 700 light years and it will reach the minimum distance of 27 600 light years (perigalacticon) in about 15 million years time.

The Galaxy has a diameter of about 70 000 light years so the most distant star will be at 66 700 light years when the Solar System is farthest from the centre (apogalacticon), while at present the most distant stars are at 62 700 light years. The present orbital velocity of the Sun and a large number of nearby stars have been averaged to 792 000 kmh *492 000 mph* (the 'Local Standard of Rest') which would lead to an orbital period of 237 million years. However, the Sun's actual velocity is 97 200 kmh *60 400 mph* faster than this average.

Nearest ■ Excepting the special case of our own Sun (*q.v.* above) the nearest star is the very faint *Proxima Centauri*, discovered in 1915, which is 4·22 light-years ($4·00 \times 10^{13}$ km *24 800 000 000 000 miles*) away. The nearest 'star' visible to the naked eye is the southern hemisphere binary *Alpha Centauri*, or *Rigel Kentaurus* (4·35 light-years distant), with an apparent magnitude of −0·29. It was discovered by Nicolas L. da Lacaille (1713–62) in c. 1752. In AD 29700 this binary will reach a minimum distance of 2·84 light-years and should then be the second brightest 'star' with an apparent magnitude of −1·20.

Most and least luminous ■ If all the stars could be viewed at the same distance the most luminous would be the variable *Eta Carinae* (see Most Massive Star), which now has a total luminosity 6 500 000 times that of the Sun but at its peak brightness in 1843 was at least ten times more luminous than this. The visually brightest star is the hypergiant *Cygnus OB2 No.12*, 5900 light-years distant, which has an absolute visual magnitude of −9·9 and is therefore visually 810 000 times more luminous than the Sun. This brightness may be matched by the supergiant IV b 59 in the nearby galaxy Messier 101 but this would depend on the distance adopted for this galaxy (estimates varying between 15 600 000 and 19 700 000 light-years). The variable *eta Carinae* in 1843 had an absolute brightness 70 million times that of the Sun. The faintest star detected is the recently

THE MOST DISTANT MEASURED HEAVENLY BODIES

The possible existence of galaxies external to our own Milky Way system was mooted in 1789 by Sir William Herschel (1738–1822). These extra-galactic nebulae were first termed 'island universes'. Sir John Herschel (1792–1871) opined as early as 1835 that some might be more than 250 000 000 000 million miles distant. The first direct measurement of any body outside our Solar System was in 1838. Distances in the table below assume that the edge of the observable Universe is at a distance of 14 000 million light years.

Estimated Distance in Light-years[1]	Object	Method	Astronomers	Observatory	Date
about 6 (now 11·08)	61 Cygni	Parallax	F. Bessel	Königsberg, Germany	1838
>20 (now 26)	Vega	Parallax	F. G. W. Struve	Dorpat (now Tartu), Estonia	1840
c. 200	Limit	Parallax			by 1900
900 000 (now 2·15 million)[2]	Galaxy M31	Cepheid variable	E. P. Hubble (1889–1953)	Mt. Wilson, Cal., USA	1924

Millions of Light–Years	Recession Speed % of c	Object	Redshift[3]	Astronomers	Observatory	Date
c.200	1·4	NGC 7619		M. L. Humason	Mt. Wilson, Cal., USA	early 1928
>2100	>15·0	Ursa Major No. 2		Humason & E. P. Hubble	Mt. Wilson, Cal., USA	by 1936[4]
4600	32·6	Cluster 1448	0·403		Palomar, Cal., USA	1956
5100	36·2	3C 295 in Boötes	0·461	R. Minkowski	Palomar, Cal., USA	1956
5700	41·0	QSO 3C 147	0·545	M. Schmidt & T. A. Matthews	Palomar, Cal., USA	June 1960
11 200	80·1	QSO 3C 9	2·01	M. Schmidt	Palomar, Cal., USA	Feb 1964[5]
11 400	81·3	QSO 0106 +01	2·11	E. M. Burbridge *et al.*	Palomar, Cal., USA	Apr 1965
11 400	81·4	QSO 1116 +12	2·12	C. R. Lynds & A. N. Stockton M. Schmidt	Steward, Ariz., USA Palomar, Cal., USA	Mar 1966 Mar 1966
11 500	82·4	QSO Pks 0237 −23	2·22	H. C. Arp *et al.*	Palomar, Cal., USA	Dec 1966
11 700	83·7	QSO 4C 25.05	2·36	E. T. Olsen & M. Schmidt	Palomar, Cal., USA	Dec 1967[6]
12 300	87·5	QSO 4C 05.34	2·88	R. Lynds & D. Wills	Kitt Peak, Arizona, USA	Mar 1970
12 600	90·2	QSO OH 471	3·40	R. F. Carswell & P. A. Strittmatter	Steward, Ariz., USA	Mar 1973
12 700	90·7	QSO OQ 172	3·53	E. J. Wampler *et al.*	Lick, Cal., USA	May 1973
12 800	91·6	QSO Pks 2000 −330	3·78	B. A. Peterson *et al.*	Siding Spring, NSW, Australia	Apr 1982[7]
12 800	91·7	QSO Pks 1208 +1011	3·80	C. Hazard *et al.*	Siding Spring,NSW, Australia	Feb 1986[8]
12 900	92·3	QSO 0046 −293	4·01	S.J.Warren *et al.*	Siding Spring, NSW, Australia	Sept 1986[8]
12 900	92·4	QSO PC0910 +5625	4·04	M. Schmidt *et al.*	Palomar, Cal., USA	June 1987
13 000	92·6	QSO 0000 −2620	4·11	C. Hazard *et al.*	Siding Spring, NSW, Australia	Aug 1987[8]
13 100	93·4	QSO 0051 −279	4·43	S. J. Warren *et al.*	Siding Spring, NSW, Australia	Nov 1987[8]

Note: *c* is the notation for the speed of light. (see p.65). [1] *Term first utilised in March 1888.* [2] *Re-estimate by G. de Vaucouleurs in Dec 1983.* [3] *Discovered by Vesto Slipher (1875–1969) from Flagstaff, Arizona, USA 1920. Redshift, denoted by z, is the measure of the speed of recession indicated by the ratio resulting from the subtraction of the rest wavelength of an emission line from the observed wavelength divided by the rest wavelength.* [4] *In 1934 Hubble opined that the observable horizon would be 3000 m light-years.* [5] *In Dec 1963 Dr I. S. Shklovsky's (USSR) suggestion that QSO 3C2 was more distant was subsequently confirmed with a value of 0·612 c.* [6] *In Oct 1968 Dr Margaret Burbidge (GB) published a tentative redshift of 2·38 for QSO 5C 2.56.* [7] *Anglo-Australian telescope.* [8] *UK Schmidt telescope.*

The Universe

discovered RG 0058.8–2807 (see Lightest Star) which has a total luminosity only 0·000 21 that of the Sun and an absolute visual magnitude of 20·2 so that the visual brightness is less than one millionth that of the Sun.

Brightest and latest supernova ■ The brightest ever seen by historic man is believed to be SN 1006 in April 1006 near *Beta Lupi*, which flared for 2 years and attained a magnitude of −9 to −10. The remnant is believed to be the radio source G.327·6 + 14·5 nearly 3000 light-years distant. Others have occurred in 1054, 1604, 1885 and most recently on 23 Feb 1987 when Ian Shelton sighted that designated − 69 202 in the Large Magellanic Cloud 170 000 light-years distant. This supernova was visible to the naked eye when at its brightest in May 1987. Preliminary evidence suggests that the pulsar resulting from the supernova explosion is spinning at a rate of 1968·629 revolutions per sec (equivalent to a pulse period of 0·5079677 millisec) which is close to the theoretical limit of 2000 revolutions per sec when such a star is supposed to fly apart. Assuming that the pulsar has a nominal diameter of about 20 km *12 miles* then the equatorial 'surface' is moving at a velocity of 40 per cent of the speed of light. It also appears to be being orbited at a distance of 1 300 000 km *810 000 miles* by a Jupiter size object which may be a further remnant of the supernova explosion (see also Pulsars).

Constellations ■ The largest of the 89 constellations is *Hydra* (the Sea Serpent), which covers 1302·844 °² or 6·3 per cent of the hemisphere and contains at least 68 stars visible to the naked eye (to 5·5 mag.). The constellation *Centaurus* (Centaur), ranking ninth in area embraces however at least 94 such stars. The smallest constellation is *Crux Australis* (Southern Cross) with an area of only 0·16 per cent of the whole sky *viz* 68·477 deg² compared with the 41 252·96 deg² of the whole sky.

Stellar planets ■ All claims to have discovered planetary systems around other stars must be treated with suspicion since there appears to be a confusion with small, dim stellar companions known as 'brown dwarfs' which are failed stars since they are too cool to trigger the fusion of hydrogen. Of the nine possible candidates announced by Bruce Campbell, Gordon Walker, and Stephenson Yang of the University of Victoria, British Columbia, Canada, in August 1988, the most promising appears to be the inferred existence of a planet one and a half times the mass of Jupiter orbiting the bright star 36 Ursae Majoris A with an orbital period of three years.

Longest name ■ *Shurnarkabtishashutu* is the Arabic for 'under the southern horn of the bull'.

Black Holes ■ The concept of superdense bodies was first adumbrated by the Marquis de LaPlace (1749–1827). This term for a star that has undergone complete gravitational collapse was first used by Prof John Archibald Wheeler at an Institute for Space Studies meeting in New York City, USA on 29 Dec 1967.

The first tentative identification of a Black Hole was announced in December 1972 in the binary-star X-ray source Cygnus X-1. The best candidate is LMC X–3 of 10 solar masses and 180 000 light-years distant reported in Jan 1983. The critical size has been estimated to be as low as a diameter of 5·9 km *3·67 miles*. One at the centre of the Seyfert galaxy, NGC 4151 in *Canes Venatici*, was estimated by Michael Preston (GB) in Oct 1983 to be of between 50–100 million solar masses or up to 2 × 10³⁸ tonnes.

THE UNIVERSE

Outside the Milky Way galaxy, which is part of the so-called Local Group of galaxies moving at a speed of 2 300 000 km/h *1 400 000 mph* relative to the microwave background radiation in a direction offset 44° from the centre of the Virgo cluster, there exist 10 000 million other galaxies. In March 1985 David J. Batuski and Jack O. Burns of the University of New Mexico, Albuquerque, announced the discovery of the largest discrete object in the Universe—a filamentary arrangement of Abell clusters stretching

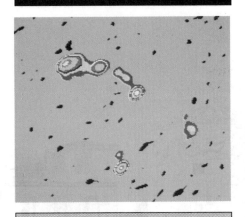

First double quasar ● This is an image-processed radio map of the double quasar 0957 +56. The first to be announced and detected by the largest terrestrial radio telescope, it is some 10 million light years away. The bending of light which produces this double image confirms a prediction made by Einstein in his General Theory of Relativity of 1916.   (Photo: Science Photo Library)

across the South Galactic Cap and measuring 1000 million light-years, 9·46 × 10²¹ km *5·88 × 10²¹ miles* in length.

Farthest visible object ■ The remotest heavenly body visible with the *naked eye* is the Great Galaxy in *Andromeda* (mag. 3·47), known as Messier 31. First noted by Simon Marius (1570–1624) from Germany It is a rotating nebula in spiral form, and its distance from the Earth is about 2 150 000 light-years which is approximately 20·3 × 10¹⁸ km or *12 600 000 000 000 000 000 miles* and is moving towards us. It is just possible however that, under ideal seeing conditions, Messier 33, the Spiral in Triangulum (mag. 5·79), can be glimpsed by the naked eye of keen-sighted people at a distance of 2 360 000 light-years.

Quasars ■ An occultation of 3C-273, observed from Australia on 5 Aug 1962, enabled the existence of quasi-stellar radio sources ('quasars' or QSOs) to be announced by Maarten Schmidt (b. Netherlands 1929). The red shift proved to be z = 0·158. Quasars have immensely high luminosity for bodies so distant and of such small diameter. It was announced in May 1983 that the quasar S5 0014 +81 had a visual luminosity 1·1 × 10¹⁵ times greater than that of the Sun. The first double quasar (0957 +56) among 1500 known quasars, was announced in May 1980.

Pulsars ■ The earliest observation of a pulsating radio source or 'pulsar' CP 1919 (now PSR 1919 +21) by Dr Jocelyn Burnell (*née* Bell, 1943) was

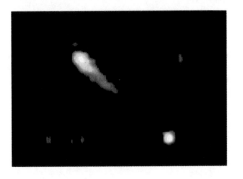

First quasar ● This photograph, recorded by the Jodrell Bank MERLIN network of radio telescopes, reveals quasar 3C-273, the nearest known to us and the first 'quasi-stellar radio source' to be detected. It is some 2100 million light years away and is receding from us at a rate of 50 000 km per sec. Its distinctive jet extends for an estimate 1·2 million light years. (Photo: Science Photo Library).

announced from the Mullard Radio Astronomy Observatory, Cambs, England, on 24 Feb 1968. It had been detected on 28 Nov 1967. For pulsars whose spin rates have been firmly established, the fastest spinning is PSR 1937 + 214 which was discovered by a group led by Donald C Backer in November 1982. It is in the minor constellation Vulpecula (the Little Fox), 16 000 light years distant, and has a pulse period of 1.557806449 millisec, which is equivalent to a spin rate of 641.9282708 revolutions per sec. In August 1986 James Imamura, Thomas Steinam-Cameron and John Middleditch obtained *tentative* evidence that the star GX 339-4 in the constellation Ara has a spin period of 885·08 revolutions per sec. *Highly preliminary* observations suggest that the new pulsar which resulted from the supernova explosion in the Large Magellanic Cloud in 1987 (see Brightest and Latest Supernova) has an initial spin period of 1968·629 revolutions per sec. The pulsar which has the slowest spin down rate and is therefore the most accurate stellar clock is PSR 1855 + 09 at only 2·1 x 10²⁰ sec/sec.

Remotest object ■ Both the interpretation of the very large redshifts exhibited by quasars and the estimation of equivalent distances remain controversial. The record red shift of $z = 4·43$ for quasar 0051-279 (see Table) was announced by Stephen Warren *et al.* on November 1987 from analysis of plates from the UK Schmidt telescope, Siding Spring, NSW, Australia. Assuming an 'observable horizon', where the speed of recession very closely approaches the speed of light approximately 14 000 million light years or 1·32 × 10²³ km *82 300 000 000 000 000 000 miles*, this quasar would be more than 13 100 million light-years distant. The 3 K background radiation or primordial hiss discovered in 1965 by Arno Penzias and Robert Wilson of Bell Laboratories appears to be moving at a velocity of 99·9998 per cent of the speed of light. Work in the near infra-red spectrum by Richard Elston and George H and Marcia J Rieke, from April 1987 at the University of Arizona's Steward Observatory, revealed two very dim, fuzzy proto–galaxies, seemingly lying beyond the most distant quasars. It was suggested in February 1988 that these might be 17 000 million light–years distant but the high red shift value of at least $Z = 6$ has not yet been confirmed.

Age of the Universe ■ For the age of the Universe a consensus value of 14 ±3 aeons or gigayears (an aeon or gigayear being 1000 million light years) is obtained from various cosmological techniques. The equivalent value of the Hubble constant based on a Friedman model of the Universe without cosmological constant is 70 ±15 km/s/Mpc. In 1973 an *ex nihilo* creation was postulated by Edward P. Tryon (US). Modified versions of the Inflationary Model, originally introduced by Alan Guth (US) in 1981, now complement the 'Big Bang' theory of creation.

TELESCOPES

Earliest ■ Although there is evidence that early Arabian scientists understood something of the magnifying power of lenses, their first use to form a telescope has been attributed to Roger Bacon (*c.* 1214–92) in England. The prototype of modern refracting telescopes was completed by Johannes Lippershey for the Netherlands government on 2 Oct 1608.

Largest reflector ■ The altazimuth mounted 6 m *236·2 in* telescope is sited on Mount Semirodriki, near Zelenchukskaya in the Caucasus Mountains, USSR, at an altitude of 2080 m *6830 ft*. Work on the 70 tonne mirror was not completed until the summer of 1974 and regular observations were begun on 7 Feb 1976 after 16 years' work. The weight of the 42 m *138 ft* high assembly is 840 tonnes. Being the most powerful of all telescopes, its range, which includes the location of objects down to the 25th magnitude, represents the limits of the observable Universe. Its light-gathering power would enable it to detect the light from a candle at a distance of 24 000 km *15 000 miles*.

On 12 Sep 1985, work started on the W. M. Keck 10 m *393·7 in* reflector for Caltech and the University of California on Mauna Kea, Hawaii, USA. It is due to be completed by 1989 and will comprise 36 independently-controlled fitting hexagonal mirrors.

Note: The attachment of an electronic charge-coupled device (CCD) increases the 'light-grasp' of a telescope by a factor up to 100 fold. Thus a 508 cm *200 in* telescope achieves the light-gathering capacity of a 25·4 m *1000 in* telescope.

Largest refractor ■ The 18·90 m *62 ft* long 101·6 cm *40 in* telescope completed in 1897 is situated at the Yerkes Observatory, Williams Bay, Wisconsin, USA and belongs to the University of Chicago, Illinois, USA. In 1900 a 125 cm *49·2 in* refractor 54·85 m *180 ft* in length was built for the Paris Exposition but its optical performance was too poor to justify attempts to use it.
Britain's largest refractor is the 71·12 cm *28 in* Great Equatorial Telescope of 1893 installed in the Old Royal Observatory, Greenwich, South east London.

Largest radio dish ■ Extra-terrestrial radio waves were first detected by Karl Jansky of Bell Telephone Laboratories, Holmdel, New Jersey, USA using a 30·48 m *100 ft* long shortwave rotatable antenna in 1932. The world's largest dish radio telescope is the partially-steerable ionospheric assembly built over a natural bowl at Arecibo, Puerto Rico, completed in November 1963 at a cost of about $9 000 000 . The dish has a diameter of 304·8 m *1000 ft* and covers 7·48 ha *18¹⁄₂ acres*. Its sensitivity was raised by a factor of 1000 and its range to the edge of the observable Universe at some 15 000 million light-years by the fitting of new aluminium plates at a cost of $8·8 million. Rededication was on 16 Nov 1974.

The world's largest trainable dish-type radio telescope is the 100 m *328 ft* diameter, 3048-tonnes *3000-ton* assembly at the Max Planck Institute for Radio Astronomy of Bonn in the Effelsberger Valley, West Germany; it became operative in May 1971. The cost of the installation, begun in November 1967, was 36 920 000 DM.

Largest radio installation ■ It was reported in October 1986 that radio astronomers first linked the NASA deep-space installation at Tidbinbilla, Australia with the tracking stations at Usuda and Kashima,

Japan and with the TDRS (Tracking and Data Relay Satellite) which is in a geosynchronous orbit. This has now been developed to create a radio telescope with an effective diameter of 2·16 Earth diameters, 27 523 km *17 102 miles*.

The world's largest terrestrial radio-telescopic installation is the US National Science Foundation VLA (Very Large Array). It is Y-shaped with each arm 20·9 km *13 miles* long with 27 mobile antennae (each of 25 m *82 ft* diameter) on rails. It is 80 km *50 miles* west of Socorro in the Plains of San Augustin, New Mexico, USA and was dedicated on 10 Oct 1980 at a cost of $78 million.

Oldest observatory ■ The oldest building extant is 'Tower of the Winds' used by Andronichus of Cyrrhus in Athens, Greece *c.* 100 BC, and equipped with sundials and clepsydra.

Highest observatory ■ The University of Denver's High Altitude Observatory is at 4297 m *14 100 ft* and was opened in 1973. The principal instrument is a 60·48 cm *24 in* Ealing Beck reflecting telescope.

Planetaria ■ The ancestor of the planetarium is the rotatable Gottorp Globe, built by Andreas Busch in Denmark between 1654 and 1664 to the orders of Olearius, court mathematician to Duke Frederick III of Holstein. It is 10·54 m *34·6 ft* in circumference, weighs nearly 3 ¹⁄₂ tonnes and is now preserved in Leningrad, USSR. The stars were painted on the inside. The earliest optical installation was not until 1923 in the Deutsches Museum, Munich, by Zeiss of Jena, East Germany. The world's largest planetarium is in Miyazaki, Japan. Construction was completed on 30 Jun 1987 and the dome has a diameter of 27 m *88 ft 7 in*.

Space telescope ■ The first space observatory was the Orbiting Solar observatory 0504 launched on 18 Oct 1967. The largest will be the $1·2 billion NASA Edwin P Hubble Space Telescope of 11 tonnes *10·8 tons* and 13·1 m *43 ft* in overall length with a 240 cm *94·5 in* reflector eventually to be placed in orbit at *c.* 480 km *300 miles* altitude aboard a US Space Shuttle. The cost of maintaining it and its staff after the launch postponement of October 1986 has been $230 000 per day.

CHAPTER 4

Highest melting point
Because of its extreme melting temperature it is difficult to utilise tungsten. This illustration made using a scanning electron microscope shows bonding between tungsten spheres in which copper acts as a 'glue'. The globules on the spheres are also of copper.
(Photo: Science Photo Library)

Science and Technology

Elements

All known matter in, on and beyond the Earth is made up of chemical elements. It is estimated that there are 10^{87} electrons in the known Universe. The total of naturally-occurring elements is 94, comprising, at ordinary temperatures, 2 liquids, 11 gases and 81 solids (including 72 metals). The so-called 'fourth state' of matter is plasma, when negatively-charged electrons and positively-charged ions are in flux.

Lightest and heaviest sub-nuclear particles ■ By April 1988 the existence was accepted of 31 'stable' particles, 64 meson resonance multiplets, and 52 baryon resonance multiplets, representing the eventual discovery of 247 particles and an equal number of anti-particles. The heaviest stable particles fully accepted is the neutral weak gauge boson, the Z°, of mass 92·4 GeV which was first detected in May 1983 by the UA1 Collaboration, CERN, Geneva, Switzerland using the 540 GeV Super Proton Synchrotron proton-antiproton beam collider. The heaviest hadron accepted is the upsilon (6S) meson resonance of mass 11·02 GeV and lifetime $8·3 \times 10^{-24}$ sec., which consists of a bottom or beauty quark and its anti-quark, and which was first identified in October 1984 by two groups using the electron storage ring facilities at Cornell University, Ithaca, New York, USA. Sub-atomic concepts require that the masses of the graviton, photon and neutrino should all be zero. Based on the sensitivities of various cosmological theories, upper limits for the masses of these particles are $7·6 \times 10^{-67}$ g for the graviton, $5·3 \times 10^{-60}$ g for the photon, and $3·2 \times 10^{-32}$ g for the neutrino (cf. electron mass $9·10939 \times 10^{-28}$ g).

Most and least stable ■ The 'grand unified' theory of the weak, electromagnetic, and strong forces predicts that the proton will not be stable. However experiments reported in 1986 indicate that the lifetime of the most likely decay mode (to a positron and a neutral pion) has a lower limit of $3·1 \times 10^{32}$ years which is over forty times longer than the maximum lifetime predicted by the theory. The least stable or shortest-lived particles are the two baryon resonances N(2220) and N(2600), both with $1·6 \times 10^{-24}$ sec although the *predicted* lifetimes of both the weak gauge bosons, the $W^{\pm}$ and Z°, are $2·6 \times 10^{-25}$ sec.

Newest particle ■ The newest particles are the chi (2P) meson resonances announced in 1987 by a joint Columbia University–State University of New York (Stony Brook) who used the electron storage

Heaviest particle ● The track seen here highlighted in white was made on the central detector of the UA1 experiment at CERN, Geneva, Switzerland by the first appearance of the boson Z° in May 1983.

Largest negative expansion ● As well as possessing the largest negative coiefficient of expansion, plutonium, which occurs in nature in only minute amounts, is radioactive in all its isotopes. The isotope plutonium-238 is used as a long-life power source and is employed to power the Pioneer 10 interplanetary probe. Here a pellet can be seen illuminated by the glow of its own radioactivity. (Photo: Science Photo Library)

ring facilities at Cornell University, Ithaca, New York, USA. The mesons consist of a mixture of a bottom quark and its anti-quark and have masses of 10·235 GeV [10], 10·255 GeV [11] and 10·269 GeV [12].

Smelliest substance ■ The most evil, of the 17 000 smells so far classified, must be a matter of opinion but ethyl mercaptan (C_2H_5SH) and butyl seleno-mercaptan (C_4H_9SeH) are pungent claimants, each with a smell reminiscent of a combination of rotting cabbage, garlic, onions, burnt toast and sewer gas.

Most expensive perfume ■ Retail prices tend to be fixed with an eye to public relations rather than levels solely dictated by the market cost of ingredients and packaging. The Chicago-based firm Jōvan marketed from March 1984 a cologne called Andron which contains a trace of the attractant pheromone androstenol which has a cost of $2750 per oz $97 per gram.

Most potent poison ■ The rickettsial disease, Q-fever, can be instituted by a *single* organism though it is fatal in only 1 in 1000 cases. About 10 organisms of *Francisella tularenesis* (formerly *Pasteurella tularenesis*) can institute tularaemia, variously called alkali disease, Francis disease or deerfly fever. This is fatal in upwards of 10 cases in 1000.

Most powerful nerve gas ■ VX, 300 times more toxic than phosgene ($COCl_2$) used in World War I, was developed at the Chemical Defence Experimental Establishment, Porton Down, Wilts in 1952. Patents were applied for in 1962 and published in February 1974 showing it to be Ethyl S-2-diisopropy-laminoethylmethylphosphonothiolate. The lethal dosage is 10 mg-minute/m³ airborne or 0·3 mg orally.

Most absorbent substance ■ The US Department of Agriculture Research Service announced on 18 Aug 1974 that 'H-span' or Super Slurper composed of one half starch derivative and one fourth each of acrylamide and acrylic acid can, when treated with iron, retain water 1300 times its own weight.

Finest powder ■ The ultimate is solid helium which was first postulated to be a monatomic powder as early as 1964.

Most lethal man-made chemical ■ TCDD (2,3,7,8-tetrachlorodibenzo-p-dioxin), discovered in 1872, is admitted to be 150 000 times more deadly than cyanide at $3·1 \times 10^{-9}$ moles/kg.

THE 109 ELEMENTS

There are 94 naturally-occurring elements. To date the discovery of a further 15 transuranic elements (Elements 95 to 109) has been claimed of which 10 are undisputed.

COMMONEST

LITHOSPHERE: Oxygen (O) 46·60% by weight. Discovered in 1771 by Scheele (Germany-Sweden).
ATMOSPHERE: Nitrogen (N) 78·09% by volume. Discovered in 1772 by Rutherford (GB).
EXTRA-TERRESTRIAL: Hydrogen (H) 90% of all matter. Discovered in 1776 by Cavendish (GB).

RAREST (OF THE 94)

Astatine 0·16 g (At) 1/1176th oz in Earth's crust. Discovered in 1940 by Corson (USA) *et al*.
The naturally-occurring isotope astatine 215 occurs only to the extent of $1·6 \times 10^{-10}$ oz 4·5 nanograms.

LIGHTEST

OVERALL: Hydrogen (H) 0·000 089 89 g/cm³ 0·005 612 lb/ft³. Discovered in 1776 by Cavendish (GB).
Metal: Lithium (Li) 0·5334 g/cm³ 33·30 lb/ft³. Discovered in 1817 by Arfwedson (Sweden).

DENSEST

Osmium (Os) 22·59 g/cm³ 1410 lb/ft³. Discovered in 1804 by Tennant (GB).

HEAVIEST GAS

Radon (Rn) 0·01005 g/cm³ 0·6274 lb/ft³ at 0°C. Discovered in 1900 by Dorn (Germany).

NEWEST

Element 108 or Unniloctium (Uno). This is a provisional IUPAC name. Discovered in 1984 by G.Munzenberg *et al*. (West Germany) and at Dubna Research Institute, Moscow, USSR.

A single atom of Unnilennium was created by bombardment of bismuth by iron ions at the GSI Laboratory Dormstadt, West Germany on 29 Aug 1982. It had the highest atomic number (element 109) and the highest atomic mass (266). There is a very tentative Soviet claim to have observed the formation of an isotope of mass 276 of element 110 (provisional name 'Ununnilium' symbol Uun).

PUREST

Helium 4(⁴He) 2 parts in 10^{15} (1978). Discovered in 1868 by Lockyer (GB) and Janssen (France). Identified on Earth by Ramsay (GB) in 1895.

HARDEST

Carbon (C) Diamond allotrope, Knoop value 8400. Prehistoric.

MOST EXPENSIVE

Californium (Cf) Sold in 1970 for $10 per microgram. Discovered in 1950 by Seaborg (USA) *et al*.

STABILITY

MOST: Tellurium 128 Double beta decay estimate. Half-life of $1·5 \times 10^{24}$ years. Discovered in 1782 by von Reichenstein (Austria).
Alpha decay record is Samarium 148 at 8×10^{15} years and beta decay record is Cadmium 113 ar 9×10^{15} years.
LEAST: Lithium 5 (^{5}Li) Lifetime of $4·4 \times 10^{-22}$ sec. Discovered in 1817 by Arfwedson (Sweden).

ISOTOPES

MOST: 36: Xenon (Xe) Discovered in 1898 by Ramsay and Travers (GB); Caesium (Cs) Discovered in 1860 by Bunsen and Kirchoff (Germany).
LEAST: 3 (confirmed); Hydrogen (H) Discovered in 1776 by Cavendish (GB)

MOST DUCTILE

Gold (Au) 1 oz drawn to 1g/2·4 km *43 miles.* Ante 3000 BC.

HIGHEST TENSILE STRENGTH

Boron (B) $3·9 \times 10^6$ lb f/in^2 26·8 GPa. Discovered in 1808 by Gay-Lussac and Thenard (France) and H. Davy (GB).

MELTING/BOILING POINT

LOWEST: Non-metallic; Helium 4 (^{4}He) $-272·375°$C under pressure 24·985 atm (2532 kPa) and $-268·928°$C. Discovered in 1868 by Lockyer (GB) and Janssen (France).
Monatomic hydrogen (H) is expected to be a non–liquefiable superfluid gas.
Metallic; Mercury (Hg) $-38·836°$ C/356·661° C. Prehistoric.
HIGHEST: Non-metallic; Carbon (carbyne 6) (C) 3530° C/3870°C. Prehistoric.
The carbyne forms of carbon were discovered by A.E. Goresy and G. Donnay (USA) and A.M. Sladkov and Yu.P. Koudrayastev (USSR) in 1968.
Metallic; Tungsten (W) 3420°C and 5860°C. Discovered in 1783 by J. J. and F. d'Elhuyar (Spain).

EXPANSION

LARGEST (negative): Plutonium (Pu) $-5·8 \times 10^{-5}$ cm/cm-deg C between 450–480°C (Delta prime allotrope discovered 1953). Discovered in 1940 by Seaborg (USA) *et al.*
LOWEST (positive): Carbon (diamond) (C) $1·0 \times 10^{-6}$ cm/cm/deg C (at 20°C). Prehistoric.
HIGHEST (metal): Caesium (Cs) $9·7 \times 10^{-5}$ cm/cm/deg C (at 20°C). Discovered in 1860 by Bunsen and Kirchoff (Germany).
HIGHEST (solid): Neon (Ne) $1·94 \times 10^{-3}$ cm/cm/deg C at $-248·59°$C. Discovered in 1898 by Ramsay and Travers (GB).

MOST TOXIC

Radium 224 (^{224}Ra) Naturally occurring isotope 17 000 x more toxic than plutonium 239. Discovered in 1898 by the Curies and Belmont (France).

Numbers

In dealing with large numbers, scientists use the notation of 10 raised to various powers to eliminate a profusion of noughts. For example, 19 160 000 000 000 miles would be written $1·916 \times 10^{13}$ miles. Similarly, a very small number, for example 0·000 015 432 4 of a gram, would be written $1·543\ 24 \times 10^{-5}$. Of the prefixes used before numbers the smallest is 'atto' from the Danish or Norwegian *atten,* for 18, symbol a, indicating 10^{-18} of a unit. The highest is 'exa' (*Greek,* hexa, *six i.e. six groups of three zeros),* symbol E, indicating 10^{18}.

Highest numbers ■ The highest lexicographically accepted named number in the system of successive powers of ten is the centillion, first recorded in 1852. It is the hundredth power of a million, or one followed by 600 noughts. The highest named number outside the decimal notation is the Buddhist *asankhyeya,* which is equal to 10^{140} and mentioned in Jaina works of *c.* 100 BC.

The number 10^{100} is designated a Googol. The term was suggested by the 9-year old nephew of Dr Edward Kasner (US) (d. 1955). Ten raised to the power of a Googol is described as a Googolplex. Some conception of the magnitude of such numbers can be gained when it is said that the number of electrons in some models of the observable Universe does not exceed 10^{87}.

The highest number ever used in a mathematical proof is a bounding value published in 1977 and known as Graham's number. It concerns bichromatic hypercubes and is inexpressible without the special 'arrow' notation, devised by Knuth in 1976, extended to 64 layers.

Largest factored number ■ Computer Scientists using more than 400 linked computers have found the factors of a 100–digit number. The calculation took 26 days, and threatens the security of many modern crytographic systems.

Prime numbers ■ A prime number is any positive integer (excluding unity 1) having no integral factors other than itself and unity, e.g. 2, 3, 5, 7 or 11. The lowest prime number is thus 2. The highest known prime number is $2^{216,091} -1$, discovered in September 1985 by analysts using a Cray X-MP/24 computer at Chevron Geosciences Co in Houston, Texas, USA. It is the 31st known Mersenne prime, and contains 65 050 digits. The lowest non-prime or composite number (excluding 1) is 4.

Perfect numbers ■ A number is said to be perfect if it is equal to the sum of its divisors other than itself, e.g. $1+2+4+7+14 = 28$. The lowest perfect number is 6 ($=1+2+3$). The highest known and the 31st so far discovered, is $(2^{216,091} -1) \times 2^{216,090}$. It is a consequence of the highest known prime (see above).

Newest mathematical constant ■ The study of turbulent water, the weather, and other chaotic phenomena has revealed the existence of a new universal constant, the Feigenbaum number, named after its discoverer. It is equal to approximately 4·669 201 609 102 990.

Most-proved theorem ■ A book published in 1940 contained 370 different proofs of Pythagoras's Theorem including one by President Garfield of the United States.

Longest proof ■ The proof of the classification of all finite simple groups is spread over more than 14 000 pages in nearly 500 papers in mathematical journals contributed by more than 100 mathematicians over a period of more than 35 years.

Oldest mathematical puzzle ■ dating from 1650 BC.

As I was going to St Ives
I met a man with seven wives,
Every wife had seven sacks,
and every sack had seven cats,
Kitten, cats, sacks and wives,
how many were going to St Ives?

Largest claimed accurate number in physics ■ Sir Arthur Eddington announced in 1938 that there are exactly 15 747 724 136 275 002 577 605 653 961 181 555 468 044 717 914 527 116 709 366 231 425 076 185 631 031 296 protons in the universe, and the same number of electrons. Unfortunately for Eddington, no one else accepted his over-precise calculation, which is now discredited.

Most prolific mathematician ■ Leonard Euler, (Switzerland) (1707–83) was so prolific that his papers were still being published for the first time more than 50 years after his death. His collected works have been printed bit by bit since 1910 and will eventually occupy more than 75 large quarto volumes.

Largest prize ever offered ■ Dr Paul Wolfskell left prize money in his will for the first person to solve Fermat's Last Theorem. This prize was worth 100 000 deutschmarks in 1908. As a result of inflation, the prize is now just over 10 000 deutschmarks.

Longest computer computation for a yes–no answer ■ The twentieth Fermat number $2^{2^{20}} + 1$, was tested on a CRAY–2 supercomputer in 1986 to see if it was a prime number. After 10 days of calculation the answer was NO.

Most innumerate ■ The Nambiquara of the north-west Matto Grosso of Brazil lack any system of numbers. They do, however, have a verb which means 'they are alike'.

Most accurate and most inaccurate version of 'pi' ■ The greatest number of decimal places to which *pi* (π) has been calculated is 201 326 000 on 27 Jan 1988 by Yasumasa Kanada of Tokyo University, Japan using a Hitachi supercomputer Hitacs-802/80. The computation took 5 hr 57 min. In 1897 the General Assembly of Indiana enacted in House Bill No. 246 that *pi* was *de jure* 4. Places 762 – 767 comprise six consecutive '9's.

In 1853 William Shanks published his calculation to π to 707 decimal places, all calculated by hand. Ninety–two years later, 1945, it was discovered that the last 180 digits were in fact all wrong.

Earliest measures ■ The earliest known measure of weight is the *beqa* of the Amratian period of Egyptian civilisation *c.* 3800 BC found at Naqada, Egypt. The weights are cylindrical with rounded ends from 188·7 to 211·2 g *6·65–7.45 oz.* The unit of length used by the megalithic tomb-builders in north western Europe *c.* 3500 BC appears to have been 82·90 cm ±0·09 cm *2·72±0·003 ft.* This was deduced by Professor Alexander Thom (1894–1985) in 1966.

Time measure ■ Owing to variations in the length of a day, which is estimated to be increasing irregularly at the average rate of about a millisecond per century due to the Moon's tidal drag, the second has been redefined. Instead of being 1/86 400th part of a mean solar day, it has, since 1960, been reckoned as 1/31 556 925 9747th part of the solar (or tropical) year at AD 1900, January 0·12 hr, Ephemeris time. In 1958 the second of Ephemeris time was computed to be equivalent to 9 192 631 770 ± 20 cycles of the radiation corresponding to the transition of caesium 133 atoms when unperturbed by exterior fields. The greatest diurnal change recorded has been 10 milliseconds on 8 Aug 1972 due to the most violent solar storm recorded in 370 years of observations.

The accuracy of the caesium beam frequency standard approaches 8 parts in 10^{14} compared to 2 parts in 10^{13} for the methane-stabilised helium-neon laser and 6 parts in 10^{13} for the hydrogen maser.

The longest measure of time is the *kalpa* in Hindu chronology. It is equivalent to 4320 million years. In astronomy a cosmic year is the period of rotation of the Sun around the centre of the Milky Way galaxy i.e. 225 million years. In the Late Cretaceous Period of *c.* 85 million years ago the Earth rotated faster so resulting in 370·3 days per year while in Cambrian times some 600 million years ago there is evidence that the year extended over 425 days.

Physical Extremes

Highest temperature ■ Those produced in the centre of a thermonuclear fusion bomb are of the order of 300 000 000 – 400 000 000° C. Of controllable temperatures the highest effective laboratory figure reported is 200 million degrees C achieved in the Tokamak Fusion Test Reactor at the Princeton Plasma Physics Laboratory, USA in June 1986.

Lowest temperature ■ The absolute zero of temperature, 0 K, on the Kelvin scale corresponds to $-273·15°$ C or $-459·67°$ F. The lowest temperature reached is 3×10^{-8} Kelvin above absolute zero attained in a two-stage nuclear demagnetisation cryostat at Espoo, Finland by the team led by Professor Olli V. Lounasmaa (b. 1930) and announced in June 1984.

Smallest thermometer ■ Dr Frederich Sachs, a biophysicist at the State University of New York at Buffalo, USA, has developed an ultra-microthermometer for measuring the temperature of single living cells. The tip is one micron in diameter, about one fiftieth the diameter of a human hair.

Largest barometer ■ A water barometer 12 m *39 ft* in height was constructed in 1987 by Bert Bolle, Curator of the Barometer Museum, Maartensdijk, Netherlands where the instrument is situated.

Highest pressures ■ A sustained laboratory pressure of 1·70 megabars (170 GPa *11 000 tons* *force/in²*) was achieved in the giant hydraulic diamond-faced press at the Carnegie Institution's Geophysical Laboratory, Washington, DC, USA and reported in June 1978. This laboratory announced solid hydrogen achieved at 57 kilobars pressure on 2 Mar 1979. If created, metallic hydrogen is expected to be silvery white but soft with a density of 1·1 g/cm³. The pressure required for the transition is estimated by H. K. Mao and P. M. Bell to be 1 megabar at 25° C. Using dynamic methods and impact speeds of up to 29000 km/h *18 000 mph,* momentary pressures of 75 000 000 atmospheres (7000 GPa *490 000 tons/in²*) were reported from the US in 1958.

Highest velocity ■ The highest velocity at which any solid visible object has been projected is 150 km/sec *335 000 mph* in the case of a plastic disc at the Naval Research Laboratory, Washington DC, USA reported in August 1980.

Finest balance ■ The Sartorius Model 4108 manufactured in Göttingen, West Germany, can weigh objects of up to 0·5 g to an accuracy of 0·01 μ g or 0·000 000 01g, equivalent to little more than one sixtieth of the weight of the ink on this full stop .

Largest bubble chamber ■ The $7 million installation, completed in October 1973 at Weston, Illinois, USA is 4·57 m *15 ft* in diameter. It contains 33 000 litres *7259 gal* of liquid hydrogen at a temperature of −247° C and has a super conducting magnet of 3 tesla.

Fastest centrifuge ■ Ultra-centrifuges were invented by Theodor Svedberg (b. 30 Aug 1884) (Sweden) in 1923. The highest man-made rotary speed ever achieved and the fastest speed of any earth-bound object is 7250 km/h *4500 mph* by a swirling tapered 15·2 cm *6 in* carbon fibre rod in a vacuum at Birmingham University, England reported on 24 Jan 1975.

Finest cut ■ The $13 million Large Optics Diamond Turning Machine at the Lawrence Livermore National Laboratory, California, USA was reported in June 1983 to be able to sever a human hair 3000 times lengthwise.

Longest echo ■ The longest in any building is one of 15 sec following the closing of the door of the Chapel of the Mausoleum, Hamilton, Lanarkshire, Scotland built 1840–55.

Most powerful electric current ■ If fired simultaneously the 4032 capacitors comprising the Zeus capacitor at the Los Alamos Scientific Laboratory, New Mexico, USA would produce, for a few microseconds, twice as much current as that generated elsewhere on Earth.

Hottest flame ■ Carbon subnitride (C₄N₂) which at one atmosphere pressure can produce a flame calculated to reach 5261 K.

Highest measured frequency ■ The highest *directly* measured is a visible yellow-green light at 520·2068085 terahertz (a terahertz being a million million hertz or cycles per second) for the o-component of the 17–1 P(62) transition line of iodine 127. The highest measured frequency determined by precision metrology is a green light at 582·491703 terahertz for the b₂₁ component of the R(15) 43–0 transition line of iodine 127. However, with the decision on 20 Oct 1983 by the Conférence Générale des Poids et Mesures (CGPM) to define exactly the metre (m) in terms of the velocity of light (*c*) such that 'the metre is the length of the path travelled by light in vacuum during a time interval of 1/299 792 458 of a second' then frequency *(f)* and wavelength λ are exactly interchangeable through the relationship *fλ = c*.

Lowest friction ■ The lowest coefficient of static and dynamic friction of any solid is 0·02, in the case of polytetrafluoroethylene ([C₂F₄]ₙ), called PTFE— equivalent to wet ice on wet ice. It was first manufactured in quantity by E. I. du Pont de Nemours & Co Inc. in 1943, and is marketed from the USA as Teflon. In the United Kingdom it is marketed by ICI as Fluon. In the centrifuge at the University of Virginia, USA a 13·60 kg *30 lb* rotor magnetically supported has been spun at 1000 rev/sec in a vacuum of 10⁻⁶ mm of mercury pressure. It loses only one revolution per second per day, thus spinning for years.

Smallest hole ■ A hole of 40 Å (4 × 10⁻⁶ mm) was shown visually using a JEM 100C electron microscope and Quantel Electronics devices at the Dept of Metallurgy, Oxford on 28 Oct 1979. To find such a hole is equivalent to finding a pinhead in a haystack with sides of 1·93 km *1·2 miles.* An electron microscope beam on a sample of sodium beta-alumina at the University of Illinois, USA, in May 1983 accidentally bored a hole 2 × 10⁻⁹ m in diameter.

Most powerful laser beams ■ The first illumination of another celestial body was achieved on 9 May 1962, when a beam of light was successfully reflected from the Moon by the use of a laser (light amplification by stimulated emission of radiation) attached to a 121·9 cm *48 in* telescope at Massachusetts Institute of Technology, Cambridge, Massachusetts, USA. The spot was estimated to be 6·4 km *4 miles* in diameter on the Moon. The device was propounded in 1958 by the American Dr Charles Hard Townes (b. 1915). Such a flash for 1/5000th of a second can bore a hole through a diamond by

vaporisation at 10 000° C, produced by 2 × 10²³ photons. The 'Shiva' laser was reported at the Lawrence Livermore Laboratory, California, USA to be concentrating 2·6 × 10¹³ watts into a pinhead-sized target for 9·5 × 10⁻¹¹ sec in a test on 18 May 1978.

Brightest light ■ The brightest artificial sources are 'laser' pulses generated at the US Los Alamos National Laboratory, New Mexico, announced in March 1987 by Dr Robert Graham. An ultra-violet flash lasting 1 picosecond (1 × 10⁻¹² sec) is intensified to an energy of 5 × 10¹⁵ watts. Of continuously burning sources, the most powerful is a 313 kW high-pressure argon arc lamp of 1 200 000 candle-power, completed by Vortek Industries Ltd of Vancouver, BC, Canada in March 1984.

The most powerful searchlight ever developed was one produced during World War II by the General Electric Company Ltd at the Hirst Research Centre in Wembley, London. It had a consumption of 600 kW and gave an arc luminance of 46 500 candelas/cm² *300 000 candles/in²* and a maximum beam intensity of 2 700 000 000 candles from its parabolic mirror (diameter 3·04 m *10 ft*).

Shortest light pulse ■ Charles Z. Shank and colleagues of the AT & T Laboratories in New Jersey, USA achieved a light pulse of 8 femtoseconds (8 × 10⁻¹⁵ sec) announced in April 1985. The pulse comprised only 4 or 5 wavelengths of visible light or 2·4 micrometres long.

Most durable light ■ The average bulb lasts for 750–1000 hr. There is some evidence that a 5 watt carbide filament bulb made by the Shelby Electric Co and presented by Mr Bernell in the Fire Department, Livermore, south Alameda County, California, USA was first shedding light in 1901.

Heaviest magnet ■ That in the Joint Institute for Nuclear Research at Dubna, near Moscow, USSR for the 10 GeV synchrophasotron measures 60 m *196 ft* in diameter, and weighs 36 000 tonnes.

Magnetic fields ■ The strongest continuous field strength achieved was a total of 35·3 ± 0·3 teslas at the Francis Bitter National Magnet Laboratory, Massachusetts Institute of Technology, USA on 26 May 1988 employing a hybrid magnet with holmium pole pieces. This had the effect of enhancing the central magnetic field generated in the heart and brain.

The weakest magnetic field measured is one of 8 × 10⁻¹⁵ tesla in the heavily shielded room at the same laboratory. It is used by Dr David Cohen for research into the very weak magnetic field generated in the heart and brain.

Most powerful microscope ■ The scanning tunnelling microscope invented at the IBM Zürich research laboratory in 1981 has the magnifying ability of 100 million and is capable of resolving down to one hundredth the diameter of an atom (3 × 10⁻¹⁰ m). The fourth generation of the scanning tunnelling microscope now being developed is said to be 'about the size of a finger tip'.

By using field ion microscopy the tips of probes of scanning tunnelling microscopes have been shaped to end in a single atom—the last three layers constituting the world's smallest man-made pyramid consisting of 7, 3 and 1 atoms. It was announced in July 1986 from AT & T Bell Laboratories, Murray Hill, New Jersey, USA that they had successfully deposited a single atom (probably of germanium) from the tungsten tip of a scanning tunnelling microscope back on to a germanium surface.

Loudest noise ■ The loudest in a laboratory has been 210 decibels or 400 000 acoustic watts reported by NASA from a 14·63 m *48 ft* steel and concrete test bed for the Saturn V rocket static with 18·3 m *60 ft* deep foundations at Marshall Space Flight Center, Huntsville, Alabama, USA in October 1965. Holes could be bored in solid material by this means, and the audible range was in excess of 161 km *100 miles.*

Smallest microphone ■ Professor Ibrahim Kavrak of Bogazici University, Istanbul, Turkey developed a microphone for a new technique of pressure measurement in fluid flow in 1967. It has a frequency response of 10 Hz to 10 KHz and measures 1·5 mm × 0·76 mm *0·06 in × 0·03 in.*

Highest note ■ A 'laser' beam striking a sapphire crystal at the Massachusetts Institute of Technology, USA in September 1964 generated a note of 60 gigahertz.

Most powerful particle accelerator ■ The 2-kilometre *6562-ft* diameter proton synchroton at the Fermi National Accelerator Laboratory east of Batavia, Illinois, USA is the highest energy 'atomsmasher' in the world. On 14 May 1976 an energy of 500 giga electron volts (5 x 10^{11}) was achieved for the first time. On 13 Oct 1985 a centre of mass energy of 1·6 tera electron volts (1·6 x 10^{11} electron volts) was achieved by colliding beams of protons and anti–protons. This involves 1000 super–conducting magnets maintained at a temperature of −268·8° C *−452° F* by means of the world's largest 4500-litre *990-gal* per hour helium liquefying plant which began operating on 18 Apr 1980.

The aim of CERN (*Conseil Européen pour la Recherche Nucléaire*) to collide beams of protons and anti-protons in their Super Proton Synchroton (SPS) near Geneva, Switzerland at 270 GeV × 2 = 540 GeV was achieved at 4.55 a.m. on 10 Jul 1981. This was the equivalent of striking a fixed target with protons at 150 TeV or 150 000 GeV.

The US Department of Energy set up a study for the $6 billion Super Superconductivity Collider (SSC) 1995 with two 20 TeV proton and anti-proton colliding beams on 16 Aug 1983 with a diameter of 83·6 km *52 miles.* White House approval was announced on 30 Jan 1987.

Quietest place ■ The 'dead room', measuring 10·67 × 8·50 m *35 ft x 28 ft* in the Bell Telephone System laboratory at Murray Hill, New Jersey, USA, is the most anechoic room in the world, eliminating 99·98 per cent of reflected sound.

Sharpest objects and smallest tubes ■ The sharpest objects yet made are glass micropipette tubes used in intracellular work on living cells. Techniques developed and applied by Professor Kenneth T. Brown and Dale G. Flaming of the Department of Physiology, University of California, San Francisco, USA achieved by 1977 bevelled tips with an outer diameter of 0·02 μm and 0·01 μm inner diameter. The latter is smaller than the smallest known nickel tubing by a factor of 340 and is 6500 times thinner than human hair.

Smallest man-made object ■ It was announced by Texas Instruments, Dallas, Texas, USA on 8 Feb 1988 that they had succeeded in making 'quantam dots' of indium and gallium arsenide only 100 millionths of a millemetre in diameter

Highest vacuum ■ Those obtained at the IBM Thomas J. Watson Research Center, Yorktown Heights, New York, USA in October 1976 in a cryogenic system with temperatures down to −269 °C *−452 °F* in scientific research are of the order of 10^{-14} torr. This is equivalent to depopulating (baseball-sized) molecules from 1 metre apart to 80 km apart or from 1 yard to 50 miles.

Lowest viscosity ■ The California Institute of Technology first announced on 1 Dec 1957 that there was no measurable viscosity, i.e. perfect flow, in liquid helium II, which exists at temperatures close to absolute zero (−273·15 °C *−459·67 °F*).

Highest voltage ■ The highest ever potential difference obtained in a laboratory has been 32 ±1·5 million volts by the National Electrostatics Corporation at Oak Ridge, Tennessee, USA on 17 May 1979.

Borings and Mines

Deepest ■ Man's deepest penetration into the Earth's crust is a geological exploratory drilling near Zapolarny, Kola peninsula, USSR, begun in 1970. By 1987 a depth of 13 km *8·07 miles or 42 650 ft* was surpassed. Progress has understandably greatly slowed to 500 m *1640 ft* per annum as the eventual target of 15 000 m *49 212 ft* in 1989–90 is neared. The drill bit is mounted on a turbine driven by a mud pump. The temperature at 11 km *6·83 miles* was already 200°C. The West Germans announced the test drilling of the Erbendorf hole, Upper Bavaria on 9 Oct 1986. The planned depth of the £150 million project is 14 km *45 900 ft 8·69 miles 392° F.*

Ocean drilling ■ The deepest recorded drilling into the sea bed by the *Glomar Challenger* of the US Deep Sea Drilling Project is one of 1740 m *5709 ft* off north-west Spain in 1976. The deepest site is now 7034 m *23 077 ft* below the surface on the western wall of the Mariana Trench (see page 54) in May 1978.

The deepest drilling in the North Sea is in 795·8 m *2611 ft* of water on 11-12 Jun 1986 by the British-built *Sovereign Explorer,* a propulsion-assisted semisubmersible drilling unit operated by Scotdrill Offshore Company, Aberdeen, Scotland and contracted to Chevron Petroleum.

Ice-core drilling ■ The deepest borehole in ice was drilled during the course of the 30th Soviet Antarctic Expedition in 1985 when a depth of 2202 m *7225 ft* was achieved at the Vostok station in central Antarctica. The 18th Expedition drilled the deepest 'dry' borehole (without antifreeze) in 1972 which reached 952·5 m *3125 ft.*

Oil fields ■ In 1988 the world's largest oil producer was the USSR with 11·9 million barrels per day, followed by the USA with 8·31 million, with the UK sixth with 2·47 million barrels.

The world's largest oil field is the Ghawar field, Saudi Arabia developed by ARAMCO, which measures 240 x 35 km *150 x 22 miles.*

The area of the designated parts of the UK Continental shelf as at mid-1987 was 651 650 km² *252 000 miles²* with proven and probable reserves of 1330 million tonnes of oil and 634 000 million m³ *22 400 000 million ft³* of gas. Gas was first discovered in the West Sole Field in October 1965 and oil in commercial quantities in the Forties Field (Block 22/17) at 3352 m *11 000 ft* from the drilling barge *Sea Quest* on 18 Sep 1970, though a small gas field was detected near Whitby, North Yorks in 1937. The most productive field is BP's Forties Field which on 3 Apr 1989 became the first oilfield in western Europe to produce a total of 2 billion barrels of oil and natural gas liquids. Production peaked for the UK's 32 oil fields at 127·5 million tonnes.

Gas deposits ■ The largest gas deposit in the world is at Urengoi, USSR with an eventual production of 261 600 million yd³ *200 000 million m³* per year through 6 pipelines from proved reserves of 9 155 600 million yd³ *7 000 000 million m³.* The trillionth (10¹²) cubic metre was produced on 23 Apr 1986.

Oil platforms ■ The world's most massive oil platform is the *Statfjord B* concrete gravity-base platform built at Stavanger, Norway owned by the Statfjord Group and operated by Mobil Exploration Norway Inc until 31 Dec 1986. Tow-out to its permanent field took place between 1 and 5 Aug 1981 and it was the heaviest object ever moved-816 000 tonnes or 803 000 long tons ballasted weight. The £1·1 billion structure was towed by 8 tugs with a combined power of 115 000 hp. The height of the concrete structure is 204 m *670 ft* and the overall height 271 m *890 ft.* It thus weighs almost three times the weight of each of the towers of the World Trade Center, New York City, USA (290 000 long tons). The world's tallest production platform is the $500 000 000 off-shore oil rig *Bullwinkle,* towed out from Corpus Christi, Texas, USA to a site 241 km *150 miles* south of New Orleans on 27 May 1988. It stands 492·2 m *1615 ft* tall.

Gusher ■ The greatest wildcat ever recorded blew at Alborz No 5 well, near Qum, Iran on 26 Aug 1956. The uncontrolled oil gushed to a height of 52 m *170 ft* at 120 000 barrels per day at a pressure of 62 055 kPa *9000 lb/in².* It was closed after 90 days' work by B. Mostofi and Myron Kinley of Texas. The Lake View No 1 gusher in California on 15 Mar 1910 may have yielded 125 000 barrels in its first 24 hours.

Largest open cast mine ● Fortuna-Garsdorf, near Bergheim, West Germany is the world's largest open cast mine. Its cut extends to 4 x 3 km *2·5 x 2 miles* and 250 m *820 ft* deep. (Photo : Zefa).

Oil spills ■ The slick from the Mexican marine blow-out beneath the drilling rig *Ixtoc I* in the Gulf of Campeche, Gulf of Mexico, on 3 Jun 1979 reached 640 km *400 miles* by 5 Aug 1979. It was eventually capped on 24 Mar 1980 after a loss of 3 000 000 barrels *526 975 tons 535 000 tons.*

The *Exxon Valdez* (Capt Joseph Hazelwood) in Prince William Sound, Alaska, USA struck a reef on 24 Mar 1989 spilling 10 million gallons of crude slick spread over 2 600 miles².

The worst oil spill in history was of 232 460 tons *236 000 tonnes* of oil from two super-tankers *Atlantic Empress* and *Aegean Captain* when they collided off Tobago on 19 Jul 1979. The worst oil spill in British waters was from the 118 285-dwt *Torrey Canyon* which struck the Pollard Rock off Land's End on 18 Mar 1967 resulting in a loss of 106 000 tons of oil.

Flare ■ The greatest gas fire was that which burnt at Gassi Touil in the Algerian Sahara from noon on 13 Nov 1961 to 9.30 a.m. on 28 Apr 1962. The pillar of flame rose 137 m *450 ft* and the smoke 182 m *600 ft.* It was eventually extinguished by Paul Neal ('Red') Adair (b. 1932), of Houston, Texas, USA using 245 kg *550 lb* of dynamite. His fee was understood to be about $1 000 000 plus expenses.

Water well ■ The world's deepest water bore is the Stensvad Water Well 11-W1 of 2231 m *7320 ft* drilled by the Great Northern Drilling Co Inc in Rosebud County, Montana, USA in October–November 1961. The Thermal Power Co geothermal steam well begun in Sonoma County, California, USA in 1955 is down to 2752 m *9029 ft.*

Great Britain ■ The deepest well in Great Britain is a water table well 866 m *2842 ft* deep in the Staffordshire coal measures at Smestow 8 km *5 miles* south-west of Wolverhampton.

The deepest artesian well in Britain is that at the White Heather Laundry, Stonebridge Park, Brent, London, bored in 1911 to a depth of 678 m *2225 ft.* The deepest known hand-dug well is one dug to a depth of 391.6 m *1285 ft* in 1858 to March 1862 on the site of Fitzherbert School, Woodingdean, Brighton, East Sussex.

MINE RECORDS

EARLIEST *World* ● 41 250 BC ± 1600 Lion Cavern, Haematite (red iron ore) at Ngwenya, Hhohho, Swaziland.
GB ● 3390 BC ± 150 Flint at Church Hill, Findon, W. Sussex.

DEEPEST *World*[1] ● 3777 m *12 391 ft (2·34 miles)* Gold, Western Deep Levels (temp 55°C *131°F*) at Carletonville, South Africa.
GB ● 1315 m *4314 ft* Coal, Plodder Seam, Bickershaw Colliery at Leigh, Lancs.
GB ● 1097 m *3600 ft* Tin, Williams Shaft at Dolcoath (1910) near Camborne, Cornwall.

FASTEST DRILLING
The most footage drilled in one month is 10 477m *34 574 ft* of a hole drilled during June 1988 by Harkins & Company Rig Number 13 while drilling four wells in McMullen County, Texas, USA.

COPPER *Deepest open pit* ● 800 m *2625 ft* Bingham Canyon (begun 1906), Location near Salt Lake City, Utah, USA.
Largest underground ● 573 km *356 miles* tunnels, San Manuel Mine, Magma Copper Co in Arizona, USA.

LEAD *Largest* ● >10 per cent of world output Viburnum Trend in south-east Missouri, USA.

GOLDMINING *Area* ● >51 per cent of world output, 38 mines of the Witwatersrand Discovery, South Africa, in 1886.

GOLD *Largest World*[2] ● 4900 ha *12 100 acres* East Rand Proprietary Mines Ltd at Boksburg, Transvaal, South Africa.
Largest, GB ● 120 000 fine oz (1854–1914), Clogau, St David's (discovered 1836) at Gwynedd, Wales.
Richest ● 49·4 million fine oz, Crown Mines (all-time yield) in Transvaal, South Africa.

IRON *Largest* ● 20 300 million tonnes *19 995 million tons rich ore* Lebedinsky (45–65% ore), Kursk region, USSR.

PLATINUM *Largest* ● 28 tonnes per annum, Rustenburg Platinum Mines Group, Rustenburg Platinum, Mine Location Western Transvaal, South Africa.

TUNGSTEN *Largest* ● 2000 tonnes per day, Union Carbide Mount Morgan mine, near Bishop, California, USA.

URANIUM *Largest* ● 5000 tons of uranium oxide, Rio Tinto Zinc open cast pit at Rössing, Namibia, South West Africa.

SPOIL DUMP *Largest, World* ● 275 million yd³ *210 million m³* New Cornelia Tailings at Ten Mile Wash, Arizona, USA.
Largest, GB ● 141 ha *348 acre* 12 million m³, Allerton Tip, near Castleford, West Yorks.

QUARRY *Largest, World* ● 7·21 km² *2·81 miles²*. *3355 million tonnes 3700 million short tons* extracted. Bingham Canyon, Utah, USA.
Largest, GB ● 150 m *500 ft* deep, 2·6 km *1·6 mile* circumference, Old Delabole Slate Quarry (since c. 1570), Cornwall.

COAL, OPEN CAST MINE ● 325 m deep 1130 ft 21 km² *8 mile²* area Fortuna-Garsdorf (lignite) (begun 1955), near Bergheim, West Germany.

COAL MINE *Oldest, UK* ● c. 1822 founded by William Stobart at Wearmouth, near Sunderland, Tyne and Wear.

---

[1] *Sinking began in Jun 1957. Scheduled to reach 3880 m 12 730 ft by 1992 with 14 000 ft or 2·65 miles regarded as the limit. No. 3 vertical ventilation shaft is the world's deepest shaft at 2948·9 m 9675 ft. This mine requires 128 050 tonnes 130 000 tons of air per day and refrigeration which uses the energy it would take to make 37 000 short tons of ice. An underground shift comprises 11 150 men. The deepest exploratory coal mining shaft is one reaching 6700 ft 2042 m near Thorez in the Ukrainian Donbas field, USSR in August 1983.*

[2] *The world's most productive gold mine may be Muruntau, Kyzyl Kum, Uzbekistan, USSR. According to one Western estimate it produces 80 tonnes of gold in a year. It has been estimated that South Africa has produced in 96 years (1886–1982) 36 400 tons or more than 31 per cent of all gold mined since 3900 BC.*

Power

Steam engines *Oldest* ■ The oldest steam engine in working order is the 1812 Boulton & Watt 26-hp 1066 mm *42 in* bore beam engine on the Kennet & Avon Canal at Great Bedwyn, Wilts. It was restored by the Crofton Society in 1971 and still runs periodically.

Largest ■ The largest single-cylinder steam engine ever built was that designed by Matthew Loam of Cornwall and made by the Hayle Foundry Co in 1849 for installation for land draining at Haarlem, Netherlands. The cylinder was 3·65 m *12 ft* in diameter such that each stroke, also of 3·65 m *12 ft*, lifted 61 096 l *13 440 gallons* or 60 tons of water.

Most efficient ■ The most efficient steam engine recorded was Taylor's engine built by Michael Loam for United Mines, Gwennap, Cornwall in 1840. It registered only 1·7 lb of coal per horsepower per hour.

Largest power plant ■ Currently, the most powerful installed power station is the Grand Coulee, Washington State, USA with 7·4 million kilowatt hours (ultimately 10 830 MW) which began operating in 1942.

The $11-billion Itaipu power station on the Paraná river by the Brazil-Paraguay border began generating power formally on 25 Oct 1984 and will attain 13 320 kW from 18 turbines. Construction began in 1975 with a workforce reaching 28 000. A 20 000-MW power station project on the Tunguska River, USSR was announced in February 1982.

The world's largest coal-fired power complex at Ekibastuz, Kazakhstan, USSR began generating in May 1982.

The power station with the greatest installed capacity in Great Britain is Drax, North Yorks, with 5 of its 660-MW sets yielding 3300-MW in mid-1986. The sixth set was operational in 1987. A 3300-MW oil-fired installation is under construction on the Isle of Grain, Kent.

The largest hydroelectric plant in the UK is the North of Scotland Hydroelectricity Board's Power Station at Loch Sloy, Dumbartonshire. The installed capacity of this station is 130 MW. The Ben Cruachan pumped storage scheme was opened on 15 Oct 1965 at Loch Awe, Argyll, Scotland. It has a capacity of 400 MW and cost £24 000 000.

The 1880-MW underground pumped storage scheme at Dinorwic, Gwynedd is the largest in Europe with a head of 530 m *1739 ft* and a capacity of 390 m³/sec *13 770 ft³/sec*. The £425-million plant was completed in 1984 with a capacity of 1681 MW.

Earliest atomic pile ■ The world's first atomic pile was built in a disused doubles squash court at Stagg Field, University of Chicago, Illinois. It went 'critical' at 3.25 p.m. on 2 Dec 1942.

Nuclear power station ■ The first nuclear power station producing electricity was the ERR-1 in the USA on 20 Dec 1951. Britain's earliest was Calder Hall (Unit 1), Cumbria on 27 Aug 1956.

The world's largest nuclear power station with 10 reactors and an output of 9096 MW is the station in Fukushima, Japan.

Nuclear reactor ■ The largest single nuclear reactor in the world is the 1450-MW (net) reactor at the Ignalina station, Lithuania, USSR, put on full power in January 1984. The largest under construction is the CHOOZ-B1 reactor in France which is scheduled for operation in 1991 and will have a net capacity of 1457 MW.

Fusion power ■ Tokamak-7, the experimental thermonuclear apparatus, was declared in January 1982 by USSR academician Velikhov to be operating 'reliably for months on end'. An economically featured thermonuclear reactor is not anticipated in 1989 until 'about 2030'. The recent temperature attained in the Joint European Torus (JET) at Culham,

Oxon was 100 million° C (180 million° F) on 10 Oct 1988. On 24 Mar 1989 Prof Martin Fleischmann (GB) and Prof Stanley Pons (USA) announced that they had succeeded in obtaining fusion energy at room temperature at the University of Utah, USA by electrolysing heavy water with a platinum anode and a palladium cathode.

Solar power plant ■ The largest solar furnace in the world is the $141-million 10 megawatt 'Solar I', 19·3 km *12 miles* south-east of Barstow, California, first tested in April 1982. It comprises 1818 mirrors in concentric circles focused on a boiler atop a 77·7 m *255-ft* high tower. Sunlight from 222 heliostats is concentrated on a target 34·7 m *114 ft* up in the power tower. The $30-million thermal solar energy system at Pakerland Packing Co, Bellevue Plant, Green Bay, Wisconsin, USA completed in January 1984 comprises 9750 1·21 x 2· 43 m *4 x 8 ft* collectors covering 28 985 m² *7·16 acres*. It will yield up to 8000 million BTUs a month.

Tidal power station ■ The world's first major station is the *Usine marémotrice de la Rance*, officially opened on 26 Nov 1966 at the Rance estuary in the Golfe de St Malo, Brittany, France. It was built in five years at a cost of 420 000 000 francs, and has a net annual output of 544 000 000 kWh. The 804 m *880 yd* barrage contains 24 turbo alternators. The $1000-million Passamaquoddy project for the Bay of Fundy in Maine, USA, and New Brunswick, Canada, remains a project. The $46-million pilot Annapolis River project for the Bay of Fundy was begun in 1981.

Largest boiler ■ The largest boilers ever designed are those ordered in the United States from Babcock & Wilcox (USA) with a capacity of 1330 MW so involving the evaporation of 4 232 000 kg *9 330 000 lb* of steam per hour. The largest installed in the United Kingdom are five 660-MW units for the Drax Power Station, designed and constructed by Babcock & Wilcox.

Largest generator ■ Generators in the 2 000 000-kW (or 2000-MW) range are now in the planning stages both in the UK and the USA. The largest operational is a turbo-generator of 1450 MW (net) being installed at the Ignalina Atomic Power Station in Lithuania .

Largest turbines ■ The largest hydraulic are those rated at 815 000 kW (equivalent to 1·1 million hp), 9·7 m *32 ft* in diameter with a 407 tonne *401 ton* runner and a 317·5 tonne *312½ ton* shaft installed by Allis-Chalmers at the Grand Coulee 'Third Powerplant', Washington State, USA.

Pump ■ The world's largest reversible pump-turbine is that made by Allis-Chalmers for the Bath County project, Virginia, USA. It has a maximum rating of 457 MW as a turbine and maximum operating head of 393 m *1289 ft*. The impeller/runner diameter is 6349 mm *20 ft 9 in* with a synchronous speed of 257·1 rpm.

Gas ■ The largest gas turbine is type GT 13 E from BBC Brown Boveri AG with a maximum output of 140MW. The first machine is being installed in Holland in order to increase the general output of a 500MW steam-powered plant (Hemweg 7) by more than 46 per cent.

Battery *Largest* ■ The 10 MW lead-acid battery at Chino, California, USA has a design capacity of 40 MWh. It will be used at an electrical sub-station for levelling peak demand loads. This $13 million project is a co-operative effort by Southern California Edison Company, Electric Power Research Institute, and International Lead Zinc Research Organization Inc.

Longest-lasting ■ The zinc foil and sulfur dry-pile batteries made by Watlin and Hill of London in 1840 have powered ceaseless tintinnabulation inside a bell jar at the Clarendon Laboratory, Oxford since that year.

Largest gasworks ■ The flow of natural gas from the North Sea is diminishing the manufacture of gas by the carbonisation of coal and the reforming process using petroleum derivatives. Britain's largest ever gasworks, 120 ha *300 acres*, were at Beckton, Newham, East London. Currently, the largest gasworks in the UK are the Breakwater Works at Oreston, Plymouth, Devon, which opened in 1966–7 and cover an area of 7·6 ha *19 acres*. They convert complex hydrocarbons into methane and produce 1 415 850 m³ *50 million ft³* per day.

Biggest black-out ■ The greatest power failure in history struck seven north-eastern US states and Ontario, Canada, on 9–10 Nov 1965. About 30 000 000 people in 207 200 km² *80 000 miles²* were plunged into darkness. Only two were killed. In New York City the power failed at 5.27 p.m. and was not fully restored for 13 ½ hr. The total consequential losses in the 52-min New York City power failure of 13 Jul 1977 including looting was put at $1 billion .

Windmill *Earliest* ■ The earliest recorded windmills are those used for grinding corn in Iran in the 7th century AD.

The earliest date attributed to a windmill in England is 1185 for one at Weedley, near Hull, Humberside.

Oldest ■ The oldest Dutch mill is the towermill at Zeddam, Gelderland built in *c.* 1450. The oldest working mill in England is the post-mill at Outwood, near Redhill, Surrey, built in 1665, though the Ivinghoe Mill in Pitstone Green Farm, Bucks, dating from 1627, has been restored. The post-mill in North Ronaldsay, Orkney Islands operated until 1905. The Netherlands' largest is the Dijkpolder in Maasland built in 1718. The sails measure 29 m *95 ¾ ft* from tip to tip.

Tallest ■ De Noord windmill in Schiedam, Netherlands, at 33·33 m *109 ft 4 in*, is the tallest in Europe.The tallest windmill still standing in Britain is the 9-storey Sutton mill, Norfolk built in 1853 which (before being struck by lightning in 1941) had sails 22·2 m *73 ft* in diameter with 216 shutters.

Largest ■ The world's first 3000-kW wind generator was the 150 m *492 ft* tall turbine, built by Grosse Windenergie–Anlage which was set up in 1982 on the Friesian coast of West Germany. The £12 million 3000-kW aerogenerator LS1 with 60 m *196 ft 10 in* blades on a 37 m *121 ft* tall tower on Burgar Hill, Evie, Orkney built by Taylor Woodrow was switched on in a gale on 10 Nov 1987. It should yield 9 million kW/h per annum. The $14·2-million GEC MOD-5A installation on the north shore of Oahu, Hawaii will produce 7300 kW when the wind reaches 51·5 km/h *32 mph* with 122-m *400-ft* rotors. Installation was started in March 1984.

Water mill ■ There has been a water-powered corn-mill at Priston Mill near Bath, Avon since pre-Norman times. The earliest recorded is dated AD 931.

Tidal Mill ■ On 1 May 1988 the Eling Tide Mill, Hants attained 15 hr 26 min rotation of the waterwheel in one day. It is the only surviving mill in the world harnessing the power of the tide for regular production of wholemeal flour.

Engineering

Oldest machinery ■ The earliest mechanisms still in use are the *dâlu*—a water-raising instrument known to have been in use in the Sumerian civilisation which originated *c.* 3500 BC in lower Iraq and which are thus even earlier than the *Saqiyas* on the Nile.

The oldest piece of machinery (excluding clocks) operating in the United Kingdom is the snuff mill driven by a water wheel at Messrs Wilson & Co's Sharrow Mill in Sheffield, South Yorks. It is known to have been operating in 1797 and more probably since 1730.

Blast furnace ■ The non-communist world's largest blast furnace has an inner volume of 5245 m³ *185 224 ft³* and a 14·9 m *49 ft* diameter hearth at ZBF at the Oita Works, (Kyūshū), Japan completed in

October 1976 with 4 314 300 tons *4 380 000 tonnes* annual capacity .

Cat cracker ■ 'The world's largest catalyst cracker is Exxon's Bayway Refinery plant at Linden, New Jersey, USA with a fresh feed rate of 19 077 000 litres *5 040 000 US gal* per day.

Conveyor belt ■ The world's longest single-flight conveyor belt is one of 29 km *18 miles* in Western Australia installed by Cable Belt Ltd of Camberley, Surrey. Great Britain's is also by Cable Belt and of 8·9 km *5 ½ miles* underground at Longannet Power Station, Fife, Scotland. The world's longest multi-flight conveyor is one of 100 km *62 miles* between the phosphate mine near Bucraa and the port of El Aaiun, Morocco, built by Krupps and completed in 1972. It has 11 flights of between 9 and 11 km *5·6–6·8 miles* and was driven at 4·5 m/sec *10·06 mph* but has since been closed down.

Most powerful crane ■ The most powerful cranes are the two aboard the semi-submersible vessel *Micoperi 7000* (190 m *623·35 ft* in length and 89 m *292 ft* in breadth) operated by Officine Meccaniche Reggiane, built by Monfalcone, Gorizia, Italy and launched 15 Dec 1986. Each has a capacity of 6895 tons *7000 tonnes.*

Gantry crane ■ The 28·14 m *92·3 ft* wide Rahco (R. A. Hanson Disc. Ltd) gantry crane at the Grand Coulee Dam Third Powerplant was tested to lift a load of 2232 long tonnes in 1975. It lowered a 1762 ton *1789 tonne* generator rotor with an accuracy of 0·8 mm *¹⁄₋₃₂ in.*

Tallest mobile crane ■ The 810-tonne Rosenkranz K10001 with a lifting capacity of 1000 tonnes, and a combined boom and jib height of 202 m *663 ft* is carried on 10 trucks each limited to a length of 23·06 m *75 ft 8 in* and an axle weight of 118 tonnes. It can lift 30 tonnes to a height of 160 m *525 ft.*

The Taklift 4 craneship of the Smit International fleet based in Rotterdam, Netherlands has boom jib reaching a height of 95 m *312 ft.*

Most powerful diesel engines ■ Five 12RTA84 type diesel engines have been constructed by Sulzer brothers of Winterthur, Switzerland, for containerships built for the American President Lines. Each 12 cylinder power unit gives a maximum continuous output of 41 920 kW *57 000 bhp* at 95 rev/min. The first of these ships, the *President Truman,* was handed over in April 1988 and the most recent in September of that year.

Dragline ■ The Ural Engineering Works at Ordzhonikidze, USSR, completed in March 1962, has a dragline known as the ES-25(100) with a boom of 100 m *328 ft* and a bucket with a capacity of 24 m³ *31·5 yd³*. The world's largest walking dragline is 'Big Muskie', the Bucyrus-Erie 4250W with an all-up weight of 11 820 tons *12 000 tonnes* and a bucket capacity of 168 m³ *220 yd³* on a 94·4 m *310 ft* boom. This is the largest mobile land machine and is now operating on the Central Ohio Coal Company's Muskingum site in Ohio, USA.

The largest dragline excavator in Britain is 'Big Geordie', the Bucyrus-Erie 1550W 6250 gross hp, weighing 3000 tonnes with a forward mast 48·7 m *160 ft* high. On open-cast coal workings at Butterwell, Northumberland in September 1975 it proved able to strip 100 tonnes of overburden in 65 sec with its 49·7 m³ *65 yd³* bucket on a 80·7 m *265 ft* boom. It is owned by Derek Crouch (Contractors) Ltd of Peterborough, Cambs.

Earthmover ■ The giant wheeled loader developed for open-air coal mining in Australia by SMEC, a consortium of 11 manufacturers in Tokyo, Japan is 16·8 m *55·1 ft* in length, weighs 180 tonnes and its rubber tyres are 3·5 m *11·5 ft* in diameter. The bucket has a capacity of 19 m³ *671 ft³.*

Escalator ■ The term was registered in the US on 28 May 1900 but the earliest 'Inclined Escalator' was installed by Jesse W. Reno on the pier at Coney Island, New York, USA in 1896. The first installation in

Britain was at Harrods department store, London in November 1898. The escalators on the Leningrad underground, USSR at Lenin Square have 729 steps and a vertical rise of 59·68 m *195 ft 9 ½ in.*

The longest escalators in Britain are the four in the Tyne Tunnel, Tyne and Wear installed in 1951. They measure 58·7 m *192 ft 8 in* between combs with a vertical lift of 25·9 m *85 ft* and a step speed of up to 2·7 km/h *1·7 mph.*

The world's longest 'moving sidewalks' are those installed in 1970 in the Neue Messe Centre, Dusseldorf, West Germany which measure 225 m *738 ft* between comb plates. The longest in Great Britain is the 114·3 m *375 ft* long Dunlop Starglide at London's Heathrow Airport Terminal 3, installed in March–May 1970.

The world's longest *ride* is on the 4-section outdoor escalator at Ocean Park, Hong Kong which has an overall length of 227 m *745 ft* and a total vertical rise of 115 m *377 ft.*

Excavator ■ The world's largest excavator is the 13 000-tonne bucket wheel excavator being assembled at the open-cast lignite mine of Hambach, West Germany with a rating of 200 000 m² *260 000 yd²* per 20 hr working day. It is 210 m *690 ft* in length and 82 m *269 ft* tall. The wheel is 67·88 m *222 ft* in circumference with 5 m *6·5 yd²* buckets.

Forging ■ The largest forging on record is one of a 204·4 tonne *450 600 lb* 16·76 m *55 ft* long generator shaft for Japan, forged by the Bethlehem Steel Corp of Pennsylvania, USA in October 1973.

Fork lift truck ■ Kalmar LMV of Sweden manufactured in 1985 ten counterbalanced fork lift trucks capable of lifting loads up to 80 tonnes at a load centre of 2300 mm *90·5 in.* They were built to handle the large-diameter pipeline in the Libyan Great Man-made River Project.

Lathe ■ The largest is the 38·4 m *126 ft* long 416·2 tonne giant lathe built by Waldrich Siegen of West Germany in 1973 for the South African Electricity Supply Commission at Rosherville with a capacity for 300 tonne work pieces and swing-over bed of 5 m *16 ft 5 in* in diameter.

Greatest lift ■ The heaviest lifting operation in engineering history was the raising of the entire 1·6 km *0·745 mile* long offshore Ekofisk complex in the North Sea owing to subsidence of the sea bed. The complex consists of eight platforms weighing some 40 000 tonne. During 17–18 Aug 1987 it was raised 6·5 m *21 ft 4 in* by 122 hydraulic jacks requiring a computer-controlled hydraulic system developed and supplied by the Dutch Mannesmann-Texroth company: Hydraudyne Systems & Engineering bv of Boxtel, Netherlands.

Slowest machine ■ A nuclear environmental machine for testing stress corrosion has been developed by Nene Instruments of Wellingborough, Northants that can be controlled at a speed as slow as one million millionth of a millimetre per minute, or one metre *3·28 ft* in about 2000 million years.

Nut ■ The largest nuts ever made weigh 4·74 tonnes *93·4 cwt* each with an outside diameter of 132 cm *52 in* and a 63·5 cm *25 in* thread. Known as 'Pilgrim Nuts', they are manufactured by Pilgrim Moorside Ltd of Oldham, Lancs for use on the columns of a large forging press.

Oil tank ■ The largest oil tanks ever constructed are the five Aramco 1 ½-million-barrel storage tanks at Ju'aymah, Saudi Arabia. They are 21·94 m *72 ft* tall with a diameter of 117·6 m *386 ft* and were completed in March 1980.

Passenger lift ■ The fastest domestic passenger lifts in the world are the express lifts to the 60th floor of the 240 m *787·4 ft* tall 'Sunshine 60' building, Ikebukuro, Tōkyō, Japan completed 5 Apr 1978. They were built by Mitsubishi Corp and operate at a speed of 609·6 m/min *2000 ft/min* or 36·56 km *22·72 mph.* Much higher speeds are achieved in the winding cages of mine shafts. A hoisting shaft 2072 m

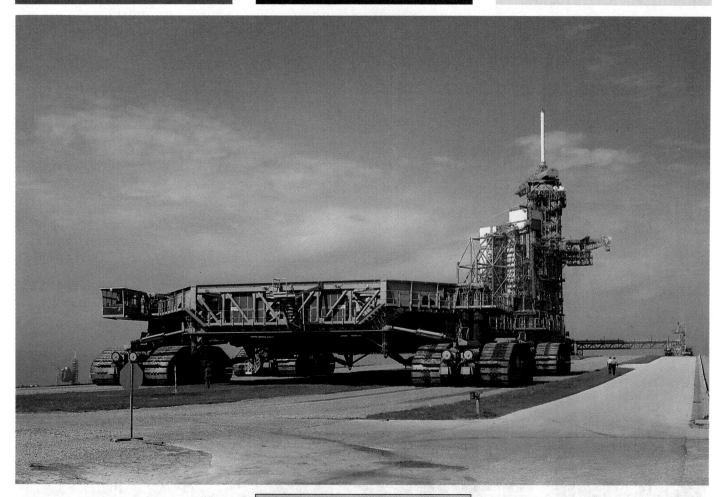

6800 ft deep, owned by Western Deep Levels Ltd in South Africa, winds at speeds of up to 65·2 km/h *40·9 mph* (1095 m *3595 ft* per min). Otitis-media (popping of the ears) presents problems much above even 16 km/h *10 mph*.

The longest lift in the United Kingdom is one 3051 m *930 ft* long inside the BBC Television Tower at Bilsdale, West Moor, North Yorks, built by J. L. Eve Construction. It runs at 39·6 m/min *130 ft/min*. The longest fast lifts are the two 15-passenger cars in the British Telecom Tower, London which travel 164 m *540 ft* at up to 304 m/min *1000 ft/min*.

Trapped in a lift ■ Graham Coates established an involuntary duration record when trapped in a lift for 62 hr in Brighton, East Sussex on 24–26 May 1986.

Pipelines *Oil* ■ The world's earliest pipeline of 5 cm *2 in* diameter cast iron, laid at Oil Creek, Pennsylvania, USA in 1863 was torn up by Luddites.

The longest crude oil pipeline in the world is the Interprovincial Pipe Line Company's installation from Edmonton, Alberta, Canada to Buffalo, New York State, USA, a distance of 2856 km *1775 miles*. Along the length of the pipe 13 pumping stations maintain a flow of 31 367 145 litres *6 900 000 gal* of oil per day. The eventual length of the Trans-Siberian Pipeline will be 3732 km *2319 miles*, running from Tuimazy through Omsk and Novosibirsk to Irkutsk. The first 48-km *30-mile* section was opened in July 1957.

Gas ■ The world's longest submarine pipeline is that of 425 km *264 miles* for natural gas from the Union Oil Platform to Rayong, Thailand opened on 12 Sep 1981. The longest North Sea pipeline is the Ekofisk–Emden line stretching 418 km *260 miles* and completed in July 1975. The deepest North Sea pipeline is that from the Cormorant Field to Firths Voe, Shetland at 162 m *530 ft*.

The longest natural gas pipeline in the world is the Trans-Canada Pipeline which by 1974 had 9099 km *5654 miles* of pipe up to 106·6 cm *42 in* in diameter. The Tyumen–Chelyabinsk–Moscow–Brandenburg gasline stretches 4330 km *2690 miles*.

Largest excavator ● The world's largest excavator is the 13 000-tonne bucket wheel excavator being assembled at the open-cast lignite mine of Hambach, West Germany with a rating of 200 000 m³ *260 000 yd³* per 20-hr working day. It is 210 m *690 ft* in length and 82 m *269 ft* tall. The wheel is 67·88 m *222 ft* in circumference with 5 m³ *6·5 yd³* buckets. (Photo: Robert Langen/Rheinbraun).

The large-calibre Urengoi-Uzhgorod line to Western Europe, begun in November 1982, stretches 4451 km *2765 miles* and was completed on 25 Jul 1983. It has a capacity of 32 000 million m³ *42 000 million yd³* per annum.

Water ■ The world's longest water pipeline runs a distance of 563 km *350 miles* to the Kalgoorlie gold fields from near Perth in Western Australia. Engineered in 1903, the system has since been extended five-fold by branches.

Most expensive ■ The world's most expensive pipeline is the Alaska Pipeline running 1284 km *798 miles* from Prudhoe Bay to Valdez. By completion of the first phase in 1977 it had cost at least $6000 million. The pipe is 1·21 m *48 in* in diameter and will eventually carry up to 2 million barrels of crude oil per day.

Press ■ The world's two most powerful production machines are forging presses in the USA. The Loewy closed-die forging press, in a plant leased from the US Air Force by the Wyman-Gordon Company at North Grafton, Massachusetts weighs 9326 tons *9469 tonnes* and stands 34·79 m *114 ft 2 in* high, of which 20·1 m *66 ft* is sunk below the operating floor. It has a rated capacity of 43 931 tons *44 600 tonnes*, and became operational in October 1955. The other similar press is at the plant of the Aluminum Company of America in Cleveland, Ohio. In January 1986 ASEA's QUINTUS Dept delivered a sheet metal forming press to BMW AG, Munich, West Germany. This press, which is the largest in the world in terms

of forming pressure and press force is a QUINTUS Fluid Cell Press with a press force of 106 000 tonnes. The Bêché and Grohs counter-blow forging hammer, manufactured in West Germany is rated at 60 000 tonnes. The most powerful press in Great Britain is the closed-die forging and extruding press installed in 1967 at the Cameron Iron Works, Livingston, West Lothian, Scotland. The press is 28 m *92 ft* tall (8·2 m *27 ft* below ground) and exerts a force of 29 550 tons *30 000 tonnes*.

Printer ■ The world's fastest printer is the Radiation Inc electro-sensitive system at the Lawrence Radiation Laboratory, Livermore, California, USA. High-speed recording of up to 30 000 lines, each containing 120 alphanumeric characters, per minute is attained by controlling electronic pulses through chemically-impregnated recording paper which is rapidly moving under closely-spaced fixed styli. It can thus print the wordage of the whole Bible (773 692 words) in 65 seconds—3306 times as fast as the world's fastest typist.

Radar installation ■ The largest of the three installations in the US Ballistic Missile Early Warning System (BMEWS) is that near Thule, in Kalaatdlit Nunaat (Greenland), 1498 km *931 miles* from the North Pole. It was completed in 1960 at a cost of $500 000 000. Its sister stations are one at Cape Clear, Alaska, USA which was completed in 1961 and the $115 000 000 radar installation at Fylingdales Moor, North Yorks which was completed in June 1963. The largest scientific radar installation is the 84 000-m² *21-acre* ground array at Jicamarca, Peru.

Ropeway or téléphérique ■ The longest ropeway in the world is the Compagnie Minière de l'Ogoouè or COMILOG installation built in 1959–62 for the Moanda manganese mine in Gabon which extends 76 km *47·2 miles*. It has 858 towers and 2800 buckets with 155 km *96·3 miles* of wire rope running over 6000 idler pulleys.

The highest and longest passenger-carrying aerial ropeway in the world is the Teleférico Mérida (Mérida téléphérique) in Venezuela, from Mérida

City (1639·5 m *5379 ft*) to the summit of Pico Espejo (4763·7 m *15 629 ft*), a rise of 3124 m *10 250 ft*. The ropeway is in four sections, involving 3 car changes in the 12·8-km *8-mile* ascent in 1 hr. The fourth span is 3069 m *10 070 ft* in length. The two cars work on the pendulum system—the carrier rope is locked and the cars are hauled by means of three pull ropes powered by a 230 hp *233 cv* motor. They have a maximum capacity of 45 persons and travel at 9·7 m *32 ft* per sec (35·08 km/h *21·8 mph*). The longest-single span ropeway is the 4114 m *13 500 ft* span from the Coachella Valley to Mt San Jacinto (3298 m *310 821 ft*), California, USA, inaugurated on 12 Sep 1963.

Britain's longest cabin lift is that at Llandudno, Wales, opened in June 1969. It has 42 cabins with a capacity of 1000 people per hour and is 1621 m *5320 ft* in length.

Shovel ■ The Marion 6360 has a reach of 72·16 m *236·75 ft*, a dumping height of 46·63 m *153 ft* and a bucket capacity of 180 yd³ *4860 ft³*. Manufactured in 1964 by the Marion Power Shovel Company, Ohio, USA, it weighs 11 million kg *24 250 000 lb* and uses 20 electric motors that generate 45 000 horse power to operate its 67·2 m *220·5 ft* long boom arm. It is operated for open-cast coal mining near Percy in Illinois, USA by the Arch Mineral Corporation .

Snow plough blade ■ A blade measuring 9·83 m *32 ft 3 in* in length was designed and constructed by Thomas Sedgwick Construction Co. Inc. of Syracuse, New York, USA for use at Hancock International Airport. With a 6 in *15·24 cm* snowfall the plough can push away 8 500 yd³ *6 499 m³* of snow in one hour.

Transformer ■ The world's largest single-phase transformers are rated at 1 500 000 kVA of which eight are in service with the American Electric Power Service Corporation. Of these, five stepdown from 765 to 345 kV. Britain's largest transformers are those rated at 1 000 000 kVA 400/275 kV built by Hackbridge & Hewittic, Walton-on-Thames, Surrey, first commissioned for the CEGB in October 1968.

Transmission lines ■ The longest span between pylons of any power line in the world is that across the Sogne Fjord, Norway, between Rabnaberg and Fatlaberg. Supplied in 1955 by Whitecross of Warrington, Cheshire, and projected and erected by A. S. Betonmast of Oslo as part of the high-tension power cable from Refsdal power station at Vik, it has a span of 4888 m *16 040 ft* and a weight of 12 tonnes. In 1967 two further high-tensile steel/aluminium lines 4878 m *16 006 ft* long, and weighing 33 tonnes, manufactured by Whitecross and BICC were erected here. The longest in Britain are the 1618 m *5310 ft* lines built by J. L. Eve across the Severn with main towers each 148 m *488 ft* high.

Highest ■ The world's highest are those across the Straits of Messina, with towers of 205 m *675 ft* (Sicily side) and 224 m *735 ft* (Calabria) and 3627 m *11 900 ft*

apart. The highest lines in Britain are those made by BICC at West Thurrock, Essex, which cross the Thames estuary suspended from 192 m *630 ft* tall towers at a minimum height of 76 m *250 ft*, with a 130 tonne breaking load. They are 1371 m *4500 ft* in apart.

Highest voltages ■ The highest voltages now carried are 1 330 000 volts 1970 km *1224 miles* on the DC Pacific Inter-tie in the United States. The Ekibastuz DC transmission lines in Kazakhstan, USSR are planned to be 2400 km *1490 miles* long with 1 500 000 volt capacity.

Valve ■ The world's largest valve is the 9·75 m *32 ft* diameter, 170 tonne butterfly valve designed by Boving & Co Ltd of London for use at the Arnold Airforce Base engine test facility in Tennessee, USA.

Wire ropes ■ The longest wire ropes in the world are the 4 made at British Ropes Ltd, Wallsend, Tyne and Wear each measuring 24 000 m *14·9 miles*. The ropes are 35 mm *1·3 in* in diameter, weigh 108·5 tonnes each and were ordered by the CEGB for use in the construction of the 2000-MW cross-Channel power cable. The thickest ever made are spliced crane strops from wire ropes 28·2 cm *11 ¼ in* thick made of 2392 individual wires in March 1979 by British Ropes Ltd of Doncaster at Willington Quay, also Tyne and Wear, designed to lift loads of up to 3000 tonnes. The heaviest ever wire ropes (4 in number) are each of 130 tonnes, made for the twin shaft system of Western Deep Levels Gold Mine, South Africa, by Haggie Rand Ltd of Johannesburg.

The suspension cables on the Seto Grand Bridge, Japan completed in 1988, are 104 cm *41 in* in diameter.

Wind tunnels ■ The world's largest wind tunnel is that on the NASA-Ames Research Centre in Mountain View, Palo Alto, California, USA reopened on 11 Dec 1987 with a 12 × 24 m *40 × 80 ft* tunnel powered by six 22 500 hp motors enabling a best speed of 555 km/h *345 mph*.

COMPUTERS

Earliest ■ The earliest programmable electronic computer was the 1500-valve Colossus formulated by Prof Max H. A. Newman FRS (1897–1985) and built by T. H. Flowers MBE. It was run in December 1943 at Bletchley Park, Bucks to break the German coding machine Enigma. It arose from a concept published in 1936 by Dr Alan Mathison Turing OBE, FRS (1912–54) in his paper *On Computable Numbers with an Application to the Entscheidungsproblem*. Colossus was declassified on 25 Oct 1975. The world's first stored-program computer was the Manchester University Mark I which incorporated the Williams storage cathode ray tube (pat. 11 Dec 1946). It ran its first program, by Prof Tom Kilburn CBE FRS (b. 1921) for 52 min on 21 Jun 1948.

Computers were greatly advanced by the invention of the point-contact transistor by John Bardeen and Walter Brattain announced in July 1948, and the junction transistor by R. L. Wallace, Morgan Sparks and Dr William Bradford Shockley (b. 1910) in early 1951. The concept of the integrated circuit, which has enabled micro-miniaturisation, was first published on 7 May 1952 by Geoffrey W. A. Dummer MBE (b. 1909) in Washington, DC, USA. The microcomputer was achieved in 1969–73 by M. E. Hoff Jr of Intel Corporation with the production of the microprocessor chip '4004'.

Most powerful and fastest ■ The world's most powerful and fastest computer is the liquid-cooled CRAY-2, named after Seymour R. Cray of Cray Research, Inc, Minneapolis, Minnesota, USA. Its memory has a capacity of 256 million 64-bit words, resulting in a capacity of 32 million bytes of main memory. (NB a 'byte' is a unit of storage comprising 8 'bits' which are collectively equivalent to one alphabetic symbol or two numericals.) It attains speeds of 250 million floating point operations per second. The cost of a mid-range system was quoted in October 1985 at $17 million. The most powerful British computer is the International Computer's Distribution Array Processor—the ICL DAP.

Sondia National Laboratory, New Mexico on 18 Mar 1988 announced a 'massively parallel' hypercube computer with 1024 parallel processors which, by breaking down problems into parts for simultaneous solution, proved 1019 times faster than a conventional mainframe computer. In May 1988 NEC (Nippon Electric Co.) announced a £1600 million research programme to attain a fifth generation computer able to read handwriting and understand speech in many languages and incorporating super conduction and Josephson functions.

Smallest word processor ■ The Easi-Text 1350 was introduced by Minimicro of Huntington, North Yorks, in April 1986. It is based on the Sharp PC-1350 computer which measures 182 ×72 ×16 mm *7.2 ×2.8 ×0.6 in* and the entire system including an A4-size Epson P-80 printer fits into an executive briefcase.

Megabits ■ The megabit barrier was broken in February 1984, with the manufacture of a 1024K-bit integrated circuit the size of a drawing pin head and as thin as a human hair, by four Japanese companies, Hitachi, NEC, NTT Atsugi Electrical Communications and Toshiba. Toshiba announced that manufacture of an 80-picosecond LSI (large scale integration) chip of gallium arsenide had started in 1985–6.

Fastest Transistor ■ A transistor capable of switching 230 000 million times per second was announced by Illinois State University, USA on 5 Oct 1986.

TIME PIECES

Clock *Oldest* ■ The earliest mechanical clock, that is, one with an escapement, was completed in China in AD 725 by I Hsing and Liang Lingtsan.

The oldest surviving working clock in the world is the faceless clock dating from 1386, or possibly earlier, at Salisbury Cathedral, Wilts, which was restored in 1956 having struck the hours for 498 years and ticked more than 500 million times. Earlier dates, ranging back to *c.* 1335, have been attributed to the weight-driven clock in Wells Cathedral, Somerset, but only the iron frame is original. A model of Giovanni de Dondi's heptagonal astronomical clock of 1348–64 was completed in 1962.

Largest ■ The world's most massive clock is the Astronomical Clock in the Cathedral of St Pierre, Beauvais, France, constructed between 1865 and 1868. It contains 90 000 parts and measures 12·1 m *40 ft* high, 6·09 m *20 ft* wide and 2·7 m *9 ft* deep. The Su Sung Clock, built in China at K'aifeng in 1088–92, had a 20·3-tonne *20-ton* bronze armillary sphere for 1· 52 tonnes *1½ tons* of water. It was removed to Beijing in 1126 and was last known to be working in its 12·1 m *40 ft* high tower in 1136.

'Timepiece', which measures 15·54 m × 15·54 m × 15·54 m *51 ft × 51 ft × 51 ft*, is suspended over five storeys in the atrium of the International Square building in Washington, DC, USA. Computer driven and accurate to within 1/100th of a second, it weighs 2 tonnes. It is lit by 122 m *400 ft* of neon tube lighting and requires 460 m *1500 ft* of cable and wiring. Twelve tubes at its base light to tell the hour and the minute. The clock, designed by the sculptor John Safer, also indicates when the sun is at its zenith in twelve international cities.

The largest clock in the United Kingdom is that on the Royal Liver Building, Liverpool (built 1908–11) with dials 7·62 m *25 ft* in diameter and the 4 minute hands each 4·26 m *14 ft* long. The mechanism and dials weigh 22 tons and are 67 m *220 ft* above street level.

Clock faces ■ The world's largest is that of the floral clock at 21 m *68 ft 10 ¾ in* in diameter, manufactured by Seiko for Koryu Fujisho Company and installed in June 1988 inside the Rose Building in the city of Hokkaido, Japan.The large hand of the clock is 8·5 m *27 ft 10 ½ in* long.

The largest four-faced clock in the world is that on the building of the Allen-Bradley Company of Milwaukee, Wisconsin, USA. Each face has a diameter of 12·28 m *40 ft 3 ½ in* with a minute hand 6·09 m *20 ft* in overall length. The largest single-faced clock is the octagonal Colgate Clock in Jersey, New Jersey, USA with a diameter of 15·24 m *50 ft* and a minute hand 8·31 m *27 ft 3 in* in length. It is being dismantled from the position it has occupied since 1908 atop the company's factory which is being redeveloped. It is planned to relocate it at another site. The tallest four-faced clock in the world is that of the Williamsburgh Savings Bank in Brooklyn, New York City, USA. It is 131 m *430 ft* above street level.

The digital, electronic, two-sided clock which revolves on top of the Texas Building in Fort Worth, Texas, USA, has dimensions of 13·4 × 13·4 × 8·5 m *44 × 44 × 28 ft*.

Most accurate ■ The Olsen Clock, completed for Copenhagen Town Hall, Denmark in December 1955 has more than 14 000 units, and took 10 years to make, and the mechanism functions in 570 000 different ways. The celestial pole motion will take 25 753 years to complete a full circle and is the slowest-moving designed mechanism in the world. The clock is accurate to 0·5 sec in 300 years—50 times more accurate than the previous record.

Longest stoppage 'Big Ben' ■ The longest stoppage of the clock in the House of Commons clock tower, London since the first tick on 31 May 1859 has been 13 days from noon on 4 Apr to noon on 17 Apr 1977. In 1945 a host of starlings slowed the minute hand by 5 minutes.

Most expensive ■ The highest price paid for any clock is £500 000 for a Thomas Tompion (1639–1713) bracket clock bought by the British Museum by private treaty on 15 Jul 1982.

Pendulum ■ The longest pendulum in the world is 22·5 m *73 ft 9 ³⁄₄ in* on the water-mill clock installed by Hattori Tokeiten Co in the Shinjuku NS building in Tokyo, Japan in 1983.

Watch *Oldest* ■ The oldest watch (portable clockwork time-keeper) is one made of iron by Peter Henlein in Nürnberg (Nüremberg), Bavaria, Germany, *c.* 1504. The earliest wrist watches were those of Jacquet-Droz and Leschot of Geneva, Switzerland, dating from 1790.

Largest ■ A 'Swatch' 162 m *531 ft 6 in* long and 20 m *65 ft 7 ¹⁄₂ in* in diameter, made by D. Tomas Feliu, was set up on the Bank of Bibao building, Madrid, Spain from 7–12 Dec 1985.

The Eta 'watch' on the Swiss pavilion at Expo 86 in Vancouver, British Columbia from May–October weighed 35 tonnes *34·4 tons* and stood 24·3 m *80 ft* high.

Smallest ■ Those produced by Jaeger le Coultre of Switzerland. Equipped with a 15-jewelled movement measure just over 1·2 cm *¹⁄₂ in* long and 0·476 cm *³⁄₁₆ in* in width. Movement and case weigh under 7 g *0·25 oz*.

Thinnest ■ The wrist watches of the Swiss Concord Delirium IV measure 0·98 mm *0·0385 in* thick and retailed for $16 000 (including 18-carat gold strap) in June 1980.

Astronomical ■ The entirely mechanical Planetarium Copernicus, made by Ulysse Nardin of Switzerland is the only wristwatch that indicates the time of the day, the date, phases of the Moon, the astronomical position of the Sun, Earth, Moon and the planets known in Copernicus' day. It also represents the Ptolemaic universe showing the astrological 'aspects' at any given time.

A special version of 65 Planetaria is being produced with the face cut from the meterorite found by Admiral R.E. Peary in Cape York, Greenland in 1897.

Most expensive ■ Excluding watches with jewelled cases, the most expensive standard man's pocket watch is *Heaven at Hand*, known to the connoisseurs as *the Packard* and made in 1922 by Patek Philippe for the American automobile magnate James Packard. The timepiece is the most outstanding example of a 'complicated' pocket watch in the world and was bought back by Patek Philippe in September 1988 for £750 000. To satisfy Packard's eccentric demands, Patek Philippe created a perfect celestial chart in enamel on the watch and housed it in one of the gold casings, to

show the heavens as they moved over Packard's hometown of Warren, Ohio, USA–in fact exactly as he could see them from his bedroom window.

The record price paid for a watch is £1 6004 392 (SwFr 4·5 million) by an anonymous South American at Habsburg Feldman, Geneva, Switzerland on 9 Apr 1989 for a Patek Philippe Calibre '89 with 1 728 separate parts.

Most accurate time measurer ■ The most accurate time-keeping devices are the twin atomic hydrogen masers installed in 1964 in the US Naval Research Laboratory, Washington, DC, USA. They are based on the frequency of the hydrogen atom's transition period of 1 420 450 751 694 cycles/sec. This enables an accuracy to within 1 sec in 1 700 000 years.

Largest sundial ■ The world's largest sundial is the Samrat Yantra with gnomon height of 27 m *88·5 ft* and a vertical height of 36 m *118 ft* built in 1724 at Jaipur, India.

TELECOMMUNICATIONS

Telephone ■ The country with the greatest number of telephone lines is the United States, with 114 349 000 lines, equivalent to 483 for every 1000 people. This compares with the British Telecom figure of 23 700 000 (December 1988) (6th largest in the world to the USA, Japan, USSR, West Germany and France), or 418 per 1000 people. The territory with fewest reported telephone lines is Pitcairn Island with 24.

The city with most access lines is New York City, NY, USA, with 4 337 890 at mid 1987. In 1983 Washington, DC, USA reached the level of 1730 telephones per 1000 people.

Longest telephone cable ■ The world's longest submarine telephone cable is ANZCAN, which runs for 15 151 km *9415 miles* (8181 nautical miles) from Port Alberni, Canada to Auckland, New Zealand and Sydney, Australia via Fiji and Norfolk Island. It cost some US$ 379 000 000 and was inaugurated by HM Queen Elizabeth II in November 1984.

Longest terrestrial call ■ A telephone call around the world, over an estimated 158 845 km *98 700 miles,* was made on 28 Dec 1985 from, and back to, the Royal Institution, London, during one of the Christmas lectures given by David Pye, Professor of Zoology, Queen Mary College, London. The international telecommunications 'rule', that only one communication satellite be used at a time, was suspended for the demonstration so that both geostationary Intelsats, one over the Indian Ocean and one over the Pacific, could be employed. The two 'telephonists', Anieka Russell and Alison Risk, experienced a delay in their conversation of 530 milliseconds.

Telephone directories ■ The world's most difficult directory to tear in half would be that for Houston, Texas which runs to 2889 pages for 939 640 listings. It is now issued in 2 sections. The easiest would be that for Knippa, Texas—221 listings on 2 pages. The directory for Anguilla in 1972 was of 26 numbers in typescript.

Largest and smallest telephone ■ The world's largest operational telephone was exhibited at the Glasgow Garden Festival, Strathclyde in May 1988. It was 3·96 m *13 ft* high and 4·57 m *15 ft* long, and weighed 3 tonnes. The handset, being 3·05 m *10 ft* long, is hydraulically operated to raise itself into a vertical position. The smallest operational telephone was created by Jeff Smith of GTE Northwest, Everett, Washington State, USA in 1988 and measured 10·48 cm × 1·90 cm × 3·81 cm *4 ¹⁄₈ in × ³⁄₄ in × 1 ¹⁄₂ in.*

Largest switchboard ■ The world's biggest switchboard is that in the Pentagon, Washington, DC, USA with 25 000 lines handling over 200 000 calls per day through 160 934 km *100 000 miles* of telephone cable. The 1988 phone bill was expected to be $11·2 million.

Optical fibre ■ The longest distance at which

signals have been transmitted without repeaters is 251·6 km *156·3 miles* at the British Telecom research laboratory at Martlesham Heath, Suffolk in February 1985. The laser wavelength was 1525 nm and the rate was 35 megabits/sec.

ROCKETRY AND MISSILES

Earliest uses ■ War rockets, which were propelled by gun-powder, charcoal saltpetre and sulfur, were described by Tseng Kung Liang of China in 1042. This early form of rocket became known in Europe by 1258.

The pioneer of military rocketry in Britain was Col Sir William Congreve, Bt, MP (1772–1828), Comptroller of the Royal Laboratory, Woolwich, London and Inspector of Military Machines. His '2·72 kg *6 lb*, rocket' was developed to a range of 1825 m *2000 yd* by 1805 and first used by the Royal Navy against Boulogne, France on 8 Oct 1806.

The first launching of a liquid-fuelled rocket (patented 14 Jul 1914) was by Dr Robert Hutchings Goddard (1882–1945) of the USA, at Auburn, Massachusetts, USA, on 16 Mar 1926, when his rocket reached an altitude of 12·5 m *41 ft* and travelled a distance of 56 m *184 ft*. The USSR's earliest rocket was the semi-liquid fuelled GIRD-IX (Gruppa Izucheniya Reaktivnogo Dvizheniya) begun, in 1931 and tested on 17 Aug 1933.

Longest ranges ■ On 16 Mar 1962, Nikita Khrushchyev, then Prime Minister of the USSR, claimed in Moscow that the USSR possessed a 'global rocket' with a range of 30 000 km *about 19 000 miles* i.e. more than the Earth's semi-circumference and therefore capable of hitting any target from either direction.

Highest velocity ■ The first space vehicle to achieve the Third Cosmic velocity sufficient to break out of the Solar System was *Pioneer 10* (see table p.83). The Atlas SLV-3C launcher with a modified Centaur D second stage and a Thiokol Te-364-4 third stage left the Earth at an unprecedented 51 682 km/h *32 114 mph* on 2 Mar 1972. The highest recorded velocity of any space vehicle has been 240 000 km/h *149 125 mph* in the case of the US–German solar probe *Helios B* launched on 15 Jan 1976.

Closest approach to the Sun by a rocket ■ The research spacecraft *Helios B* approached within 43·4 million km *27 million miles* of the Sun, carrying both US and West German instrumentation on 16 Apr 1976.

Remotest man-made object ■ Pioneer 10, launched from Kennedy Space Center, Cape Canaveral, Florida, USA crossed the mean orbit of Pluto on 17 Oct 1986 being then at a distance of 5900 million km *3670 million miles*. It was beyond the furthest extension of Pluto's orbit by April 1989 and will continue into space at 49 000 km/h *30 450 mph*. In AD 34 593 it will make its nearest approach to the Star *Ross* 248, 10·3 light-years distant. Before 1991, *Voyager 1*, travelling faster, will surpass *Pioneer 10* in remoteness from the Earth.

The spacecraft carries a plaque designed to communicate with any possible interstellar humanoids. This shows a man and a woman and, diagrammatically, where the spacecraft comes from in our Solar System and how our Sun relates to the pulsars whose rates are given in digital code.

SPACE FLIGHT

The physical laws controlling the flight of artificial satellites were first propounded by Sir Isaac Newton (1642–1727) in his *Philosophiae Naturalis Principia Mathematica* ('Mathematical Principles of Natural Philosophy'), begun in March 1686 and first published in July 1687. The first artificial satellite was successfully put into orbit at an altitude of 228·5/946 km *142/588 miles* and a velocity of more than 28 565 km/h *17 750 mph* from Baikonur, north of Tyuratam, 275 km *170 miles* east of the Aral Sea on the night of 4 Oct 1957. This spherical satellite *Sputnik* ('Fellow Traveller') 1, officially designated 'Satellite 1957 Alpha 2', weighed 83·6 kg *184·3 lb*, with a

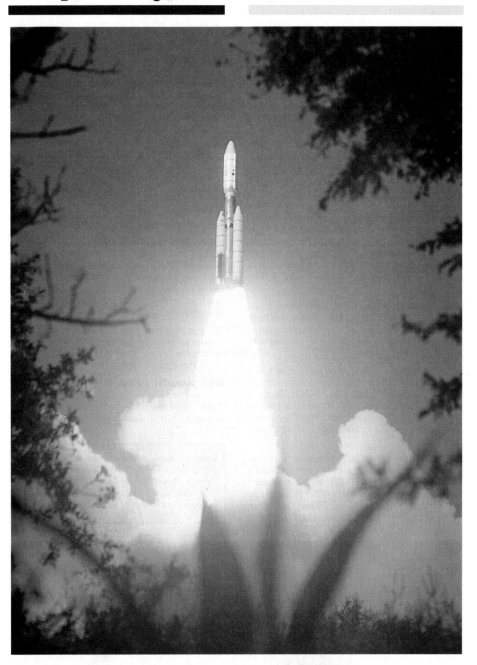

Remotest man-made object ● The launching of the space probe Voyager 1 on its mission to the outer planets. By 1991 Voyager will surpass Pioneer 10 in its remoteness from the Earth. (Photo: NASA/Science Photo Library)

diameter of 58 cm *22·8 in*, and its lifetime is believed to have been 92 days, ending on 4 Jan 1958. The 29·5 m *96 ft 8 in* SL-4 launcher was designed under the direction of former Gulag prisoner Dr Sergey Pavlovich Korolyov (1907–66).

Earliest manned satellite ■ The earliest manned space flight ratified by the world governing body, the Fédération Aéronautique Internationale (FAI founded 1905), was by Cosmonaut Flight Major (later Colonel) Yuriy Alekseyevich Gagarin (1934-68) in *Vostok 1* on 12 Apr 1961.

Details filed showed take-off to be from Baikonur at 6.07 a.m. GMT and the landing near Smelovka, near Engels, in the Saratov region, USSR, 108 minutes later. The maximum altitude during Vostok I's 40 868·6 km *25 394·5 miles* flight was listed at 327 km *203·2 miles*, with a maximum speed of 28 260 km/h *17 560 mph*.

Colonel Gagarin, invested a Hero of the Soviet Union and awarded the Order of Lenin and the Gold Star Medal, was killed in a low level jet plane crash near Moscow on 27 Mar 1968.

First woman in space ■ The first woman to orbit the Earth was Junior Lieutenant (now Lt-Col Eng) Valentina Vladimirovna Tereshkova (b. 6 Mar 1937), who was launched in *Vostok 6* from Tyuratam, USSR, at 9.30 a.m. GMT on 16 Jun 1963, and landed at 8.16 a.m. on 19 Jun, after a flight of 2 days 22 hr 50 min, during which she completed over 48 orbits (1 971 000 km *1 225 000 miles*) and passed momentarily within 4·8 km *3 miles* of Vostok 5.

Space fatalities ■ The greatest published number to perish in any of the 125 attempted space flights to date is seven (five men and two women) aboard the *Challenger* 51L on 28 Jan 1986 when an explosion occurred 73 sec after lift off, at a height of 14 326 m *47 000 ft*.

First 'walk' in space ■ Lt-Col (now Maj-Gen) Aleksey A. Leonov (b. 20 May 1934) from *Voskhod 2* was the first person to engage in 'extra-vehicular activity' on 18 Mar 1965. Capt Bruce McCandless II (b. 8 Jun 1937) USN, from the space shuttle *Challenger*, was the first to engage in untethered EVA, at

PROGRESSIVE ROCKET ALTITUDE RECORDS

HEIGHT MILES	HEIGHT KM	ROCKET	PLACE	LAUNCH DATE	
0·71	1·14	A 3 in *7·62 cm* rocket	Hackney, London, England	Apr	1750
1·24	2	Reinhold Tiling[1] (Germany) solid fuel rocket	Osnabruck, Germany	Apr	1931
3·1	5	GIRD-X semi-liquid fuel (USSR)	Moscow,USSR	25 Nov	1933
8·1	13	USSR 'Stratosphere' rocket	USSR		1935
52·46	84·42	A.4 rocket (Germany)[2]	Peenemünde, Germany	3 Oct	1942
c. 85	c. 136	A.4 rocket (Germany)[2]	Heidelager, Poland	early	1944
118	190	A.4 rocket (Germany)[2]	Heidelager, Poland	mid	1944
244	392·6	V-2/W.A.C. Corporal (2-stage) Bumper No. 5 (USA)	White Sands, NM, USA	24 Feb	1949
318	512	Geophysical rocket V-5-V (USSR)	Tyuratam, USSR		1950–52
682	1097	Jupiter C (USA)	Cape Canaveral, Florida, USA	20 Sep	1956
>800	>1300	ICBM test flight R-7 (USSR)	Tyuratam, USSR	Aug	1957
>2700	>4345	Farside No. 5 (4-stage) (USA)	Eniwetok Atoll	20 Oct	1957
70 700	113 770	Pioneer I-B Lunar Probe (USA)	Cape Canaveral, Florida, USA	11 Oct	1958
215 300 000*	346 480 000	Luna I or Mechta (USSR)	Tyuratam, USSR	2 Jan	1959
242 000 000*	389 450 000	Mars I (USSR)	USSR	1 Nov	1962
3 666 000 000[3]	5 900 000 000	Pioneer 10 (USA) (see pages 69, 82)	Kennedy Space Center, Cape Canaveral, Florida, USA	2 Mar	1972

Apogee in solar orbit.
[1] *There is some evidence that Tiling may shortly after have reached 9500 m (5·90 miles) with a solid fuel rocket at Wangerooge, East Friesian Islands, West Germany.*
[2] *The A4 was latterly referred to as the V2 rocket, a code for second revenge weapon (vergeltungswaffe) following upon the V1 'flying bomb'.*
[3] *Distance on crossing Pluto's orbit on 17 Oct 1986*

an altitude of 264 km *164 miles* above Hawaii, on 7 Feb 1984. His MMU (Manned Manoeuvering Unit) back-pack cost $15 million to develop.

Astronaut ■ The oldest of the 214 people in space has been Karl G. Henize (US), aged 58 while on the 19th Space Shuttle mission aboard the *Challenger* on 29 Jul 1985. The youngest has been Major (later Lt-Gen) Gherman Stepanovich Titov (b. 11 Sep 1935), who was aged 25 years 329 days when launched in *Vostok 2* on 6 Aug 1961.

Longest manned space flight ■ Col Vladimir Titov (b. 1 Jan 1951) and flight engineer Musa Manarov (b. 22 Mar 1951) launched to the Mir space station aboard *Soyuz* TM4 on 21 Dec 1987, landed, in *Soyuz* TM6 (with French cosmonaut Jean- Loup Chretien), at a secondary recovery site near Dzhez-kazgan, Kazakhstan, USSR, on 21 Dec 1988, after a spaceflight lasting 365 days 22 hr 39 min 47 sec. The most experienced space traveller is Col Yuri Romanenko (b. 1944) who has clocked up 430 days 18 hr 20 min on three spaceflights, in 1977–8, 1980 and 1987.

Most journeys ■ Capt John Watts Young (b. 24 Sep 1930) (USN ret) completed his sixth space flight on 8 Dec 1983 when he relinquished command of *Columbia* STS 9/Spacelab after a space career of 34 days 19 hr 42 min 13 sec.

Largest crew ■ The most crew on a single space mission is eight. This included one female and was launched on Space Shuttle STS 61A, *Challenger 9*, the 22nd shuttle mission, on 30 Oct 1985, carrying the West German Spacelab D1 laboratory. The mission, commanded by Hank Hartsfield, lasted 7 days 44 min 51 sec.

Most in space ■ The greatest number of people in space at any one time is 11: five Americans aboard a Shuttle and five Russians and an Indian aboard *Salyut 7* in April 1984; the eight STS 61A astronauts above and three Russians aboard *Salyut 7* in October 1985; and the five STS 27 astronauts and five Soviet

cosmonauts and one Frenchman aboard Mir in December 1988.

Lunar conquest ■ By FAI (Fédération Aéronautique Internationale) definition 'space' starts at an altitude of 100 km *62·137 miles* or *328 083 ft*. Neil Alden Armstrong (b. Wapakoneta, Ohio, USA of Scottish [via Ireland] and German ancestry, on 5 Aug 1930), command pilot of the *Apollo 11* mission, became the first man to set foot on the Moon, on the Sea of Tranquillity, at 02.56 and 15 sec GMT on 21 Jul 1969. He was followed out of the Lunar Module *Eagle* by Col Edwin Eugene Aldrin, Jr, USAF (b. Montclair, New Jersey, USA of Swedish, Dutch and British ancestry, on 20 Jan 1930), while the Command Module *Columbia* piloted by Lt Col Michael Collins, USAF (b. Rome, Italy, of Irish and pre-Revolutionary American ancestry, on 31 Oct 1930) orbited above.

Eagle landed at 20.17 and 42 sec GMT on 20 Jul and lifted off at 17.54 GMT on 21 Jul, after a stay of 21 hr 36 min. *Apollo 11* had blasted off from Cape Canaveral, Florida, USA at 13.32 GMT on 16 Jul and was a culmination of the US space programme which, at its peak, employed 376 600 people and attained in 1966–7 a peak budget of $5 900 000 000 .

There is evidence that Pavel Belyayev was the cosmonaut selected by the USSR for a manned circumlunar flight in *Zond 7* on 9 Dec 1968, 12 days before the *Apollo 8* flight, but no launch took place.

Most powerful rocket ■ The USSR's *Energya*, first launched on 15 May 1987 from the Baikonur Cosmodrome, when fully loaded weighs 2400 tonnes and has a thrust of over 4000 tonnes. It is capable of

> **Longest manned space flight ●** This photograph, exclusive to *The Guinness Book of Records*, shows Vladimir Titov and Musa Manarov (plus comrades) on their return flight after 365 days 22 hr 39 min 47 sec in space.

placing 140 tonnes into low Earth orbit and measures 59 m *193·56 ft* tall with a maximum diameter of 16 m *52·5 ft*. It comprises a core stage powered by four liquid oxygen and liquid hydrogen engines – the first cryogenic units flown by the Russians. There are also four strap-on boosters powered by single RD 170 engines burning liquid oxygen and kerosene. A six-strap version with an upper stage could place up to 180 tonnes into low Earth orbit, take 32 tonnes to the Moon or 27 tonnes to Venus or Mars.

Altitude ■ The greatest altitude attained by man was when the crew of the ill-fated *Apollo 13* were at apocynthion (*i.e.* their furthest point) 254 km *158 miles* above the lunar surface and 400 187 km *248 655 miles* above the Earth's surface at 1.21 am BST on 15 Apr 1970. The crew were Capt James Arthur Lovell, Jr, USN (b. Cleveland, Ohio, 25 Mar 1928), Fred Wallace Haise, Jr (b. Biloxi, Missouri, 14 Nov 1933) and John L. Swigert (1931—82).

The greatest altitude attained by a woman is 396·8 km *248 miles* by Astronaut Rhea Seddon (b. 1947) during her flight in Space Shuttle STS 51D *Discovery* in April 1985. The record in an aircraft is 24 336 m *79 842 ft* by Natalia Prokhanova (USSR) (b. 1940) in an E-33 jet, on 22 May 1965.

Speed ■ The fastest speed at which humans have travelled is 39 897 km/h *24 791 mph* when the Command Module of *Apollo 10* carrying Col (now Brig Gen) Thomas Patten Stafford, USAF (b. Weatherford, Oklahoma. 17 Sep 1930), and Cdr Eugene Andrew Cernan (b. Chicago,Illionois 14 Mar 1934) and Cdr (now Capt) John Watts Young, USN (b. San Francisco, California 24 Sep 1930), reached this maximum value at the 121·9 km *400 000 ft* altitude interface on its trans-Earth return flight on 26 May 1969.

The highest speed ever attained by a woman is 28 115 km/h *17 470 mph* by Jnr Lt (now Lt Col) Valentina Vladimirovna Tereshkova-Nikolayev (b. 6 Mar 1937) of the USSR in *Vostok 6* on 16 June 1963.

The highest speed ever achieved by a woman aircraft pilot is 2687·42 km/h *1669·89 mph* by Svetlana Savitskaya (USSR) reported on 2 Jun 1975.

Duration record on the Moon ■ The crew of *Apollo 17* collected a record 114·8 kg*253 lb* of rock and soil during their longest 'extra-vehicular activity' of 22 hr 5 min. They were Capt Eugene A. Cernan, USN (b. Chicago, Illionois 14 Mar 1934) and Dr Harrison H. (Jack) Schmitt (b. Santa Rosa, New Mexico, 3 Jul 1935) who became the 12th man on the Moon. The crew were on the lunar surface for 74 hr 59 min during this longest of lunar missions which took 12 days 13 hr 51 min on 7–19 Dec 1972.

First extra-terrestrial vehicle ■ The first wheeled vehicle landed on the Moon was *Lunakhod I* which began its Earth-controlled travels on 17 Nov 1970. It moved a total of 10·54 km *6·54 miles* on gradients up to 30° in the Mare Imbrium and did not become non-functioning until 4 Oct 1971.

The lunar speed and distance record was set by the *Apollo 16* Rover with 18km/h *11·2 mph* downhill and 33·8 km *22·4 miles*.

Heaviest and largest space object ■ The heaviest object orbited is the Saturn V third stage with *Apollo 15* (spacecraft) which, prior to trans-lunar injection in parking orbit, weighed 140 512 kg *138·29 tons*.

The 200 kg *442 lb* US RAE (Radio Astronomy Explorer) B or *Explorer 49* launched on 10 Jun 1973 had, however, antennae 415 m *1500 ft* from tip to tip.

Most expensive project ■ The total cost of the US manned space programme up to and including the lunar mission of *Apollo 17* has been estimated to be $25 541 400 000 .

The first 15 years of the USSR space programme from 1958 to September 1973 have been estimated to have cost $45 000 million. The cost of the NASA Shuttle programme was $9·9 billion to the launch of *Columbia* on 12 Apr 1981.

CHAPTER 5

Windsor castle
The largest inhabited castle in the world at New Windsor, Berkshire. It is primarily of 12th century construction and is in the form of a waisted parallelogram 576 by 164 m *1890 by 540 ft.* (Photo: All Sport: Simon Bruty)

Buildings and Structures

EARLIEST STRUCTURES

World ■ The earliest known human structure is a rough circle of loosely piled lava blocks found on the lowest cultural level at the Lower Palaeolithic site at Olduvai Gorge in Tanzania revealed by Dr Mary Leakey in January 1960. The structure was associated with artifacts and bones on a work-floor, dating from *c.* 1 750 000 BC. The earliest evidence of *buildings* yet discovered is that of 21 huts with hearths or pebble-lined pits and delimited by stake-holes found in October 1965 at the Terra Amata site in Nice, France, thought to belong to the Acheulian culture of *c.* 400 000 years ago. Excavation carried out between 28 Jun and 5 Jul 1966 revealed one hut with palisaded walls with axes of 15 m *49 ft* and 6 m *20 ft.* The remains of a stone tower 6·1 m *20 ft* high originally built into the walls of Jericho have been excavated and are dated to 5000 BC. The foundations of the walls themselves have been dated to as early as 8350 BC. The oldest free-standing structures in the world are now believed to be the megalithic temples at Mgarr and Skorba in Malta. With those at Ggantija in Gozo they date from *c.* 3250 BC.

Great Britain ■ Twelve small stone clusters, associated with broken bones and charcoal in stratum C of the early Palaeolithic site at Hoxne, near Eye, Suffolk may be regarded as Britain's earliest structural remains, dated *c.* 250 000 BC. On the Isle of Jura, Argyll, a hearth consisting of three linked stone circles has been dated to the *Mesolithic* period *6013±200* BC. The earliest surviving piece of Roman building is the bottom 4·25 m *14 ft* of their beacon at Dover, Kent dating from the 1st century AD.

Ireland ■ The earliest known evidence of human occupation in Ireland dates from the *Mesolithic* period *c. 7500* BC at the Carrowmore site in Co. Sligo. Ireland became enisled or separated from Great Britain *c.* 9050 BC. Nearby there are megalithic burials dated to *3800±80* BC.

Buildings for Working

LARGEST

Construction project ■ The Madinat Al-Jubail Al-Sinaiyah project in Saudi Arabia is believed to be the largest public works project in modern times. Construction started in 1976 for the new industrial city covering 1 015 km² *250 705 acres.* At the peak of construction, nearly 52 000 workers were employed representing 62 nationalities. The total earth moving and dredging volume by 1988 had reached 270 million m³, enough to construct a belt around the earth at the Equator 7 meters wide by 1 meter high.

The seawater colling system is believed to be the world's largest canal system bringing 10 million cubic meters (*353 million ft³*) of seawater per day to cool the industrial establishment.

The London docklands development has been described as 'the world's largest commercial development'. The first phase will cost about £3500 million.

Industrial ■ The largest industrial plant in the world is the Nizhniy Tagil Railroad Car and Tank Plant, 136 km *85 miles* north-west of Sverdlovsk, USSR which has 827 000 m² or *204·3 acres* of floor space. It has an annual capacity to produce 2500 T-72 tanks.

Commercial ■ The greatest ground area covered by any commercial building in the world under one roof is the flower auction building of the Co-operative VBA (Verenigde Bloemenveilingen Aalsmeer, Aalsmeer), Netherlands, which was built with dimensions of 776 × 547 m *2546 × 1794 ft.* The floor surface of 343 277 m² *84·82 acres* was extended in 1986 to 368 477 m² *91·05 acres.* The building with the largest cubic capacity in the world is the Boeing Company's main assembly plant at Everett, Washington State, USA ,completed in 1968 with a capacity of 5·6 million m³ *200 million ft³.*

The largest building in Britain is the Ford Parts

Centre at Daventry, Northants, which measures 602 × 237 m *1978 × 780 ft* or 14·86 ha *36·7 acres.* It was opened on 6 Sep 1972 and cost nearly £8 million. It employs 1600 people and is fitted with 14 000 fluorescent lights.

Scientific ■ The most capacious is the Vehicle Assembly Building (VAB) at Complex 39, the selected site for the final assembly and launching of the Apollo moon spacecraft on the Saturn V rocket, at the John F. Kennedy Space Center (KSC) on Merritt Island, Cape Canaveral, Florida, USA. Construction began in April 1963 by the Ursum Consortium. It is a steel-framed building measuring 218 m *716 ft* in length, 158 m *518 ft* in width and 160 m *525 ft* high. The building contains four bays, each with its own door 140 m *460 ft* high. Its floor area is 31 911 m² *343 500 ft²* and its capacity is 3 666 500 m³ *129 482 000 ft³.* The building was 'topped out' on 14 Apr 1965 at a cost of $108 700 000.

Administrative ■ The largest ground area covered by any office building is that of the Pentagon, in Arlington, Virginia, USA. Built to house the US Defense Department's offices it was completed on 15 Jan 1943 and cost an estimated $83 000 000. Each of the outermost sides is 281 m *921 ft* long and the perimeter of the building is about 1370 m *1500 yd.* Its five storeys enclose a floor area of 604 000 m² *6 500 000 ft².* The corridors measure 27 km *17 miles* in length and there are 7748 windows to be cleaned. Twenty-nine thousand people work in the building which has over 44 000 telephones connected by 257 500 km *160 000 miles* of cable. Two hundred and twenty staff handle 280 000 calls a day. Two restaurants, six cafeterias and ten snack bars and a staff of 675 form the catering department.

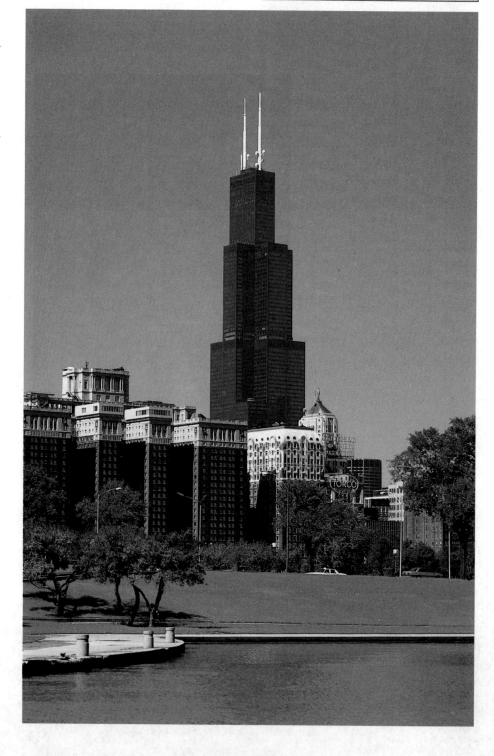

Tallest office building ● Sears Tower, national headquarters of Sears Roebuck & Co of Chicago, Illinois, USA is 110 storeys high rising to 475·18 m *1559 ft* in height after the installation of two TV antennae. The building boasts 16 700 personnel, 103 elevators 16 000 windows and 18 escalators. (Photo: Spectrum)

Office ■ Those with the largest rentable space are The World Trade Center in New York City, USA with a total of 406 000 m² *4 370 000 ft²* in each of the twin towers of which the taller Tower Two (formerly B) is 415·22 m *1362 ft 3¼ in.* The tip of the TV antenna on Tower One is 521·2 m *1710 ft* above street level and is thus 46 m *151 ft* taller than the antennae atop the Sears Tower (see below).

The largest single open plan office in the United Kingdom is that of British Gas West Midlands at Solihull, Warks built by Spooners (Hull) Ltd in 1962. It now measures 230 by 49 m *753 ft by 160 ft*, accommodating 2125 clerical and managerial staff.

TALLEST

The tallest office building in the world is the Sears Tower, national headquarters of Sears, Roebuck & Co in Wacker Drive, Chicago, Illinois, USA with 110 storeys rising to 443 m *1454 ft* and begun in August 1970. Its gross area is 408 760 m² *4 400 000 ft²*. It was 'topped out' on 4 May 1973, having surpassed the World Trade Center in New York City in height at 2.35 p.m. on 6 Mar 1973 with the first steel column reaching to the 104th storey. The addition of two TV antennae brought the total height to 475·18 m *1559 ft*. The building's population is 16 700 served by 103 elevators and 18 escalators. It has 16 000 windows. Tentative plans for a 169-storey 701 m *2300 ft* tall building, projected to cost $1250 million, for the Chicago Loop, Illinois, USA were published on 27 Oct 1981.
Demolition on the Central Place site in Brisbane, Queensland, Australia began on 9 Aug 1987 for the erection of the 120 storey world's tallest building 445 m *1460 ft* in height for completion at a cost of $A800 million by late 1990.

The Trump City Tower, on the banks of the Hudson river, New York City, USA of 559·3 m *1 835 ft* has been heralded for completion in 1999.

Great Britain ■ The tallest office block in Britain and the tallest cantilevered building in the world is the £72 million National Westminster tower block in Bishopsgate, City of London completed in 1979. It has 49 storeys and 3 basement levels, serviced by 21 lifts, and is 183 m *600 ft 4 in* tall. The gross floor area is 59 121 m² *636 373 ft²*.

The Canary Wharf development plans in London Docklands included three 50-storey office towers of up to 259 m *850 ft*. The tallest will probably be finally limited to 243·8 m *800 ft* because of air safety.

SHALLOWEST

The shallowest commercial building is the 1·8 m *6 ft* wide, 30 m *100 ft* long Sam Kee Building at 8 West Pender, Vancouver, Canada. It was erected in 1912.

HABITATIONS

Greatest altitude ■ The highest inhabited buildings in the world are those in the Indo–Tibetan border fort of Bāsisi by the Māna Pass (Lat. 31° 0 4′N; Long. 79° 24′ E) at *c.* 5988 m *19 700 ft*. In April 1961, however, a 3-room dwelling was discovered at 6600 m *21 650 ft* on Cerro Llullaillaco (6723 m *22 058 ft*), on the Argentine–Chilean border, believed to date from the late pre-Columbian period *c.* 1480. A settlement on the T'e-li-mo trail in southern Tibet is sited at an apparent altitude of 6019 m *19 800 ft*.

Northernmost ■ The Danish Scientific station set up in 1952 in Pearyland, northern Kalaalit Nunaat (Greenland), is over 1450 km *900 miles* north of the Arctic Circle. Eskimo hearths dated to before 1000 BC were discovered in Pearyland in 1969. Polar Eskimos were discovered in Inglefield Land, NW Greenland in 1818. The USSR's drifting research station 'North Pole 15' passed within 2·8 km *1¼ miles* of the North Pole in December 1967. The most northerly continuously inhabited place is the Canadian Department of National Defense outpost at Alert on Ellesmere Island, Northwest Territories in Lat. 82° 30′ N, Long. 62° W, set up in 1950.

Southernmost ■ The most southerly permanent human habitation is the United States' Amundsen–Scott South Polar Station (see Chapter 9), completed in 1957 and replaced in 1975.

EMBASSIES AND CIVIC BUILDINGS

Largest ■ The USSR embassy on Bei Xiao Jie, Beijing, China, in the north-eastern corner of the northern walled city, occupies the whole 18·2 ha *45 acre* area of the old Orthodox Church Mission (established 1728), now known as the *Bei guan*. It was handed over to the USSR in 1949.

The largest in Great Britain is the United States embassy in Grosvenor Square, London. The Chancery Building alone, completed in 1960, has 600 rooms for a staff of 700 on seven floors with a usable floor area of 236 895 m² *255 000 ft²*.

EXHIBITION CENTRES

Largest *World* ■ The International Exposition Center in Cleveland, Ohio, USA, the world's largest, is situated on a 70·8 ha *175 acre* site adjacent to Cleveland Hopkins International Airport in a building which measures 232 250 m² *2·5 million ft²*. An indoor terminal provides direct rail access and parking for 10 000 cars.

Great Britain ■ The National Exhibition Centre, Birmingham, opened in February 1976, consists of five halls which inter-connect cover 87 180 m² *938·397 ft²* with a volume of 1 168 466 m³ or *41·26 million ft³*.

INDUSTRIAL STRUCTURES

Tallest chimneys ■ The $5·5 million International Nickel Company's stack is 379·6 m *1245 ft 8 in* tall at Copper Cliff, Sudbury, Ontario, Canada, completed in 1970. It was built by Canadian Kellogg Ltd in 60 days and the diameter tapers from 35·4 m *116·4 ft* at the base to 15·8 m *51·8 ft* at the top. It weighs 39 006 tonnes *38 390 tons* and became operational in 1971. The world's most massive chimney is one of 350 m *1148 ft* at Puentes de Garcia Rodriguez, north-west Spain, built by M. W. Kellogg Co. It contains 15 750 m³ *20 600 yd³* of concrete and 1315 tonnes *2·9 million lb* of steel and has an internal volume of 189 720 m³ *6·7 million ft³*. Europe's tallest chimney serves the Zasavje thermo-power plant in Trboulje, Yugoslavia and was completed to 350 m *1181 ft* on 1 Jun 1976.

The tallest chimney in Great Britain is one of 259 m *850 ft* at Drax Power Station, North Yorks, begun in 1966 and topped out on 16 May 1969. It has an untapered diameter of 26 m *87 ft 9 in* and has the greatest capacity of any chimney. The architects were Clifford Tee & Gale of London. The oldest known industrial chimney in Britain is the Stone Edge Chimney, near Chesterfield, Derbyshire, built to a height of 16·76 m *55 ft ante* 1771.

Cooling towers ■ The largest is that adjacent to the nuclear power plant at Uentrop, West Germany, which is 179·8 m *590 ft* tall, completed in 1976. The largest in the United Kingdom are of the Ferrybridge and Didcot type and measure 114 m *375 ft* tall and 91 m *300 ft* across the base.

HANGARS

Largest ■ Hangar 375 ('Big Texas') at Kelly Air Force Base, San Antonio, Texas, USA, completed on 15 Feb 1956, has four doors each 76·2 m *250 ft* wide and 18·28 m *60 ft* high weighing 608 tonnes/ *598 tons*. The high bay area measures 609·6 ×91·4 ×27·4 m *2000 ×300 ×90 ft* and is surrounded by a 17·8 ha *44 acre* concrete apron. Delta Airlines' jet base on a 56·6 ha *140 acre* site at Hartsfield International Airport, Atlanta, Georgia, USA has 14·5 ha *36 acres* under roof.

The largest hangar building in the United Kingdom is the Britannia assembly hall at the former Bristol Aeroplane Company's works at Filton, Avon, now part of British Aerospace. The overall width of the hall is 321 m *1054 ft* and the overall depth of the centre bay is 128 m *420 ft*. It encloses a floor area of 3·0 ha *7½ acres*. The cubic capacity of the hall is 934 000 m³ *33 000 000 ft³*. The building was begun in April 1946 and completed by September 1949. (See also Largest Doors.)

GLASSHOUSE

Largest *Great Britain* ■ That owned by van Heyningen Bros at Waterham, Herne Bay, Kent covers 9·10 ha *22·5 acres* and was completed in October 1982. A crop of 160 000 tomato plants is grown under 1155 tonnes of glass.

GRAIN ELEVATOR

Largest ■ The single-unit elevator operated by the C·G·F Grain Company at Wichita, Kansas, USA, consists of a triple row of storage tanks, 123 on each side of the central loading tower or 'head house'. The unit is 828 m *2 717 ft* long and 30 m *100 ft* wide. Each tank is 37 m *120 ft* high, with an inside diameter of 9 m *30 ft* giving a total storage capacity of 7·3 million hl *20 000 000 bushels* of wheat. The largest collection of elevators in the world are the 23 at City of Thunder Bay, Ontario, Canada, on Lake Superior with a total capacity of 37·4 million hl *103·9 million bushels*.

SEWAGE WORKS

Largest ■ The West-Southwest Treatment Plant, opened in 1940 on a site of 203 ha *501 acres* in Chicago, Illinois, USA, serves an area containing 2 940 000 people. It treated an average of 3160 million litres *835 000 000 US gal* of wastes per day in 1973 and the capacity of its sedimentation and aeration tanks is 1 280 000 m³ *1·6 million yd³*. The largest full treatment works in Britain and probably in Europe is the Beckton Works, East London which serves a 2 966 000 population and handles a daily flow of 941 million litres *207 million gal* in a tank capacity of 21 400 m³ *757 000 ft³*.

WOODEN BUILDING

Largest ■ The two US Navy airship hangars built in

HIGHEST STRUCTURES IN GREAT BRITAIN

Metres	Feet		
123	404	Salisbury Cathedral Spire	c. 1305–
160	525	Lincoln Cathedral	1307–1548
149	489	St Paul's Cathedral, London	1315–1561
158·1	518·7	Blackpool Tower, Lancashire	1894
171·29	562	New Brighton Tower, Merseyside	1898–1919
250	820	GPO Radio Masts, Rugby	1925–
304·8	1000*	ITA Mast, Mendlesham, Suffolk	Jul 1959
385	1265	IBA Mast, Emley Moor, West Yorkshire	1965–1969†
385	1265	IBA Mast, Belmont, Lincolnshire	1965–
387·1	1272	IBA Mast, Belmont, Lincolnshire	Sep 1967

* ITA masts of the same height followed at Lichfield, Staffordshire; Black Hill, Strathclyde; Caldbeck, Cumbria; and Durris, Grampian.
† Severely damaged by ice and replaced.

1942–3 at Tillamook, Oregon, USA are now used by the Louisiana-Pacific Corporation as a sawmill. They measure 304·8 m long, 51·8 m high at the crown and 90·22 m wide at the base (*1000 ft × 170 ft × 296 ft*). What is believed to be the oldest complete wooden building in England was discovered in December 1986 in the Fenlands, Cambs. It measures 8 m *26·2 ft* × 2 m *6·65 ft* and was a burial chamber of the Neolithic period *c.* 5000 years ago.

AIR-SUPPORTED BUILDING

Largest ■ That of the 80 600 capacity octagonal Pontiac Silverdome Stadium, Michigan, USA was 159 m *522 ft* wide and 220 m *722 ft* long. The air pressure was 34·4 kPa *5 lb/in²* supporting the 4 ha *10 acre* translucent 'Fiberglas' roofing. The structural engineers were Geiger-Berger Associates of New York City, USA. The largest standard size air hall was one 262 m *860 ft* long, 42·6 m *140 ft* wide and 19·8 m *65 ft* high. One was first sited at Lima, Ohio, USA, made by Irvin Industries of Stamford, Connecticut.

Buildings for Living

Oldest ■ The oldest extant wooden buildings in the world are those comprising the Pagoda, Chuma-nar gate and the Temple of Horyu (Horyu-ji), at Nara,

Shallowest commercial building ● Erected in 1912 the Sam Kee at 8 West Pender, Vancouver, Canada is 1·8 m wide *6 ft* wide and 30 m *100 ft* long.

Japan, dating from *c.* AD 670 and completed in 715. The wood used were beams from 1000-year-old Hinoki trees. The nearby Daibutsuden, built in 1704–11, once measured 87 m long, 51 m wide and 46·75 m tall *285·4 ft × 167·3 ft × 153·3 ft*. Presently the dimensions are 57·3 × 50·4 × 48·6 m *188 × 165·3 × 159·4 ft*.

CASTLES

Earliest ■ The castle at Gomdan, in the Yemen, originally had 20 storeys and dates from before AD 100.

The oldest stone castle extant in Great Britain is Richmond Castle, North Yorks, built *c.* 1075. The oldest Irish castle is Ferrycarrig near Wexford, dating from *c.* 1180. The oldest castle in Northern Ireland is Carrickfergus Castle, Co. Antrim, Northern Ireland, which dates from before 1210.

Largest ■ The largest inhabited castle in the world is the royal residence of Windsor Castle at New Windsor, Berks. It is primarily of 12th century

construction and is in the form of a waisted parallelogram 576 x 164 m *1890 x 540 ft*.

The total area of Dover Castle in Kent, however, covers 13·75 ha *34 acres* with a width of 335·2 m *1100 ft* and a curtain wall of 550 m *1800 ft*, or if underground works are taken in, 700 m *2300 ft*. The overall dimensions of Carisbrooke Castle (110 x 137 m *450 ft x 360 ft*), Isle of Wight, if its earthworks are included, are 411 m x 251 m *1350 ft x 825 ft*. The largest castle in Scotland is Edinburgh Castle with a major axis of 402 m *1320 ft* and measuring 1025 m *3360 ft* along its perimeter wall including the Esplanade. The most capacious of all Irish castles is Carrickfergus (see above) but that with the most extensive fortifications is Trim Castle, Co. Meath, built *c.* 1205 with a curtain wall 443 m *1455 ft* long.

Forts ■ The largest ancient castle in the world is Hradčany Castle, Prague, Czechoslovakia, originating in the 9th century. It is an oblong irregular polygon with an axis of 570 m *1870 ft* and an average traverse diameter of 128 m *420 ft* with a surface area of 7·28 ha *18 acres*. Fort George, Ardersier, Inverness-shire, Scotland, built in 1748–69, measures 640 m *2100 ft* in length and has an average width of 189 m *620 ft*. The total site covers 17·2 ha *42½ acres*.

Thickest walls ■ Urnammu's city walls at Ur (now Muqayyar, Iraq), destroyed by the Elamites in 2006 BC, were 27 m *88½ ft* thick in mud brick. The walls of the Great Tower or Donjon of Flint Castle, built in 1277–80 are 7·0 m *23 ft* thick.

PALACES

Largest ■ The Imperial Palace (Gu gong) in the centre of Peking (Beijing, the northern capital), China, covers a rectangle 960 x 750 m *1050 yd x 820 yd*, an area of 72 ha *177·9 acres*. The outline survives from the construction of the third Ming Emperor, Yung Lo of 1402–24, but due to constant rearrangements most of the intra-mural buildings are 18th-century. These consist of 5 halls and 17 palaces of which the last occupied by the last Empress until 1924 was the Palace of Accumulated Elegance (*Chu xia gong*).

The Palace of Versailles, 23 km *14 miles* south-west of Paris, has a façade with 375 windows, 580 m *634 yds* in length. The building, completed in 1682 for Louis XIV, occupied over 30 000 workmen under Jules Hardouin-Mansert (1646–1708).

Residential ■ The palace (Istana Nurul Iman) of H.M. the Sultan of Brunei in the capital Bandar Seri Begawan and completed in January 1984 at a reported cost of £300 million is the largest in the world with 1788 rooms and 257 lavatories. The underground garage accommodates the Sultan's 110 cars.

The largest palace in the United Kingdom in royal use is Buckingham Palace, London, so named after its site, bought in 1703 by John Sheffield, the 1st Duke of Buckingham and Normanby (1648–1721). Buckingham House was reconstructed in the Palladian style between 1835 and 1836, following the design of John Nash (1752–1835). The 186 m *610 ft* long East Front was built in 1846 and refaced in 1912. The Palace, which stands in 15·8 ha *39 acres* of garden, has 600 rooms including a ballroom 34 m *111 ft* long. The largest ever royal palace has been Hampton Court, Middlesex, acquired by Henry VIII from Cardinal Wolsey in 1525 and greatly enlarged by him and later by William III, Anne and George I, whose son George II was its last resident monarch. It covers 1·6 ha *4 acres* of a 270·7 ha *669 acre* site.

Largest moat ■ From plans drawn by French sources it appears that those which surround the Imperial Palace in Beijing (see above) measure 49 m *54 yd* wide and have a total length of 3290 m *3600 yd*. The city's moats total in all 38 km *23½ miles*.

HOTELS

Largest ■ The Las Vegas Hilton, Nevada, USA, built on a 25·5 ha *63 acre* site in 1974–81, has 3174 rooms, 13 international restaurants and a staff of 3600.

It has a 2·47 ha *10 acre* rooftop recreation deck, a 4460 m² *48 000 ft²* pillar-free ballroom and 11600 m² *125 000 ft²* of convention space.

The Hotel Rossiya in Moscow opened in 1967 with 3200 rooms but owing to its proportion of dormitory accommodation, is not now internationally listed among the largest hotels. The Izmailovo Hotel complex opened in July 1980 for the XXIInd Olympic Games in Moscow, was designed to accommodate 9500 people.

Great Britain ■ The greatest sleeping capacity of any hotel in Great Britain is 1859 in the London Forum Hotel, Cromwell Road, London, which has a staff of 419 and was opened in 1973. The Regent Palace Hotel, Piccadilly Circus, London, opened 20 May 1915, has, however, 225 more rooms totalling 1140. The largest hotel is the Grosvenor House Hotel, Park Lane, London, which was opened in 1929. It is eight storeys high, covering 1 ha *2½ acres* and caters for more than 100 000 visitors per year in 470 rooms. The Great Room is the largest single hotel room measuring 55 X 40 m *181 ft X 131 ft* with a height of 7 m *23 ft*. Banquets for 1500 are frequently handled.

The Regent Hotel, Royal Leamington Spa, Warks, when first opened in 1819 with 100 bedrooms and one bathroom was acclaimed to be the largest in the world.

Largest lobby ■ The lobby at the Hyatt Regency, San Francisco, USA, is 106·6 m *350 ft* long, 48·7 m *160 ft* wide and at 51·8 m *170 ft* is the height of a 17-storey building.

Tallest ■ Measured from street level of its main entrance to the top, the 226·1 m *741·9 ft* tall 73-storey Westin Stamford in Raffles City, Singapore was topped out in March 1985. The $235 million hotel is operated by Westin Hotel Company and owned by Raffles City Pte Ltd. Their Detroit Plaza measuring from the rear entrance level is however 227·9 m *748 ft* tall.

Britain's tallest hotel is the 27-storey 132·24 m *380 ft* tall 914-bedroom London Forum Hotel .

Smallest ■ Punta Grande Hotel, Las Puntas, Hierro Island, Tenerife in the Canaries has a total area of 600 m² *6459 ft²*. There are four double bedrooms looking on to a small terrace, a lounge, a bar–

> **Most hotel rooms** ● Among the largest hotels is the Hotel Rossiya in Moscow which opened in 1967 comprising a total of 3200 rooms. (Photo: Spectrum)

restaurant and a solarium. Rebuilt in 1987, the building is more than 150 years old.

Narrowest ■ The Star Hotel in Moffat, Dumfries and Galloway, Scotland, the narrowest detached hotel, is only 6·1 m *20 ft* wide. The eight-bedroom hotel, which has two bars, is owned by Douglas and Monica House and Tim and Allison Leighfield.

Most remote ■ Garvault Hotel, by Kinbrace, Sutherland, Scotland is claimed to be the most isolated in mainland Britain being some 25·7 km *16 miles* from its nearest competitor at Forsinard, also in Sutherland.

Most expensive ■ The roof-top Royal Suite in the Marbella–Dinamar, Puerto Banus, Marbella, Spain costs 500 000 pesetas per day excluding VAT. It has 2 halls, 2 dining rooms, 5 double bedrooms, 7 bathrooms, a kitchen, a service area, a study/library/office, a lounge, an 8 metre heated swimming pool with a massage system, 2 solariums, a sauna and an 18-hole putting green.

In May 1989 the Hotel Bel-Air in Los Angeles, USA sold for a record $1·2 million (£710 900) per room to the Sekitei Kaihatsu Company of Tokyo, Japan.

Great Britain ■ The Royal Suite of the Hotel

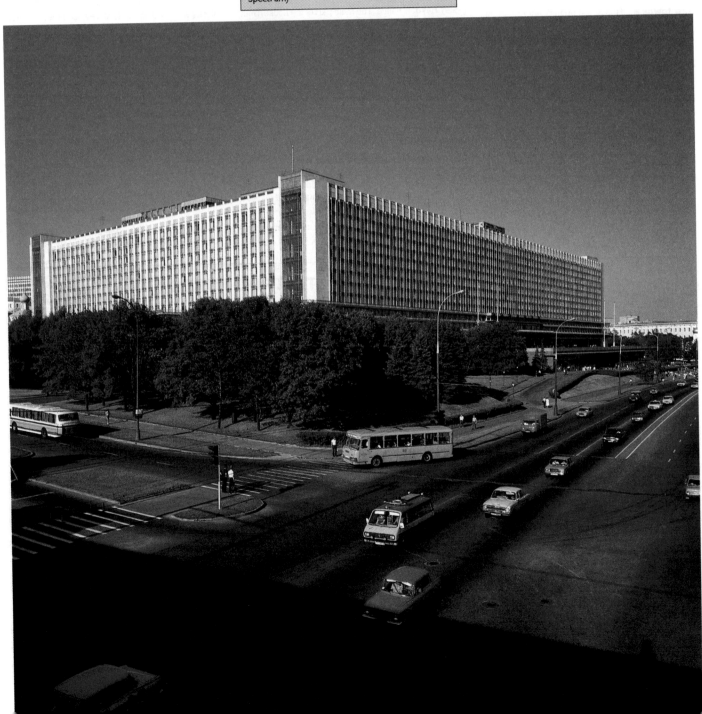

Buildings for Living

Inter-Continental, London, costs £1391 per day (incl. VAT).

Most mobile ■ The 3-storey brick Hotel Fairmount (built 1906) in San Antonio, Texas, USA, which weighed 1451 tonnes *1393 tons*, was moved on 36 dollies with pneumatic tyres over city streets approximately five blocks and over a bridge, which had to be reinforced. The move by Emmert International of Portland, Oregon, USA took four days, 30 Mar–2 Apr 1985, and cost $650 000.

Spas ■ The largest measured by number of available hotel rooms is Vichy, Allier, France, with 14 000 rooms.

Spas are named after the watering place in the Liège province of Belgium where hydropathy was developed from 1626. The highest French spa is Bareges, Hautes-Pyrénées, at 1240 m *4068 ft* above sea level.

HOUSING

Largest estate ■ In the United Kingdom the 675 ha *1670 acre* Becontree Estate is on a site of 1214 ha *3000 acres* in Barking and Redbridge, London, built between 1921 and 1929. The total number of homes is 26 822, with an estimated population of nearly 90 000.

New towns ■ Of the 32 set up in Great Britain, that with the largest eventual planned population is Milton Keynes, Bucks, with a projected 210 000 for 1992.

Largest house *World* **■** The 250-room Biltmore House in Asheville, North Carolina, USA, is owned by George and William Cecil, grandsons of George Washington Vanderbilt II (1862–1914). The house was built between 1890 and 1895 in an estate of 48 160 ha *119 000 acres*, at a cost of $4 100 000 and now valued at $55 000 000 with 4856 ha *12 000 acres*.

The most expensive private house ever built is the Hearst Ranch at San Simeon, California, USA. It was built from 1922–39 for William Randolph Hearst (1863–1951), at a total cost of more than $30 000 000. It has more than 100 rooms, a 32 m *104 ft* long heated swimming pool, an 25 m *83 ft* long assembly hall and a garage for 25 limousines. The house required 60 servants to maintain it.

The house with the most rooms is Knole, near Sevenoaks, Kent, believed to have had 365 rooms, one for each day of the year, and now in the care of the National Trust. It is built round seven courtyards, the total depth from front to back being about 120 m *400 ft*. Thomas Bourchier, Archbishop of Canterbury (1454–86), bought the estate in 1456 and commenced building. Sir Thomas Sackville, then the Earl of Dorset who leased it in 1566 put the finishing touches between 1603 –8.

Smallest house ■ In Britain the 19th-century fisherman's cottage at The Quay, Conwy, Gwynedd, Wales has a 182 cm *72 in* frontage, is 309 cm *122 in* high, and 254 cm *100 in* front to back. It has two tiny rooms and a staircase. The narrowest known house frontage is of 1·19 m *47 in* at 50 Stuart Street, Millport, Great Cumbrae, Strathclyde, Scotland.

Largest non–palatial residence ■ St Emmeram Castle, Regensburg, West Germany, valued at more than $177 million contains 517 rooms with a floor space of 21 460 m^2 *231 000 ft^2*. Only 95 rooms are personally used by its owner, Prince Johannes von Thurm und Taxis, and his family.

Great Britain **■** Wentworth Woodhouse, near Rotherham, South Yorks, formerly the seat of the Earls Fitzwilliam. is now privately owned by Wensley Haydon-Baillie. The main part of the house, built over 300 years ago, has more than 240 rooms with over 1000 windows, and its principal façade is 183 m *600 ft* long. The royal residence Sandringham House, Norfolk, has been reported to have had 365 rooms before the demolition of 73 surplus rooms in 1975. The largest house in Ireland is Castletown in Co. Kildare, owned by the Hon. Desmond Guinness, and the headquarters of the Irish Georgian Society. Scotland's largest house is Hopetoun House, West Lothian, built between 1696 and 1756 with a west façade 206 m *675 ft* long.

Most expensive private house ■ The Kenstead Hall with the adjoining Beechwood property in The Bishop's Avenue, Hampstead, London, residence of the late King of Saudi Arabia, was put on the market for £16 million in August 1982.

Oldest in Britain ■ Eastry Court near Sandwich, Kent dates from AD 603. Some of the original timbers and stone infill still survive behind its present Georgian façade.

Inhabited **■** There is evidence that Barton Manor, Barton Close, Nyetimber, Pagham, West Sussex includes the remains of a hall, or *aula*, built in Saxon times *c.* 800 AD.

Most visited stately home ■ In Great Britain in 1988 Warwick Castle, near Stratford-on-Avon, Warks, received 645 000 visitors. Built by the Beauchamp family, it dates from the 14th century.

Oldest Barracks ■ These are believed to be Collins Barracks, formerly the Royal Barracks, Dublin, Ireland, completed in 1704 and still in use.

FLATS

Tallest ■ The 218 m *716 ft* Metropolitan Tower on West 57 Street, New York, USA, is of 78 storeys of which the upper 48 are residential.

Largest ■ The private blocks which form the Barbican Estate, in the City of London, with 2011 flats occupy a 16 ha *40 acre* site with covered parking space for 2000 cars. The architects were Chamberlain, Powell and Bon.

The largest council block is Hyde Park, Sheffield, Yorks with 1300 flats in 18 storeys completed in 1964.

The tallest residential block in Great Britain is Shakespeare Tower in the Barbican in the City of London, which has 116 flats on 44 storeys and rises to a height of 127·77 m *419 ft 2½ in* above the street. The first of the three Barbican towers was 'topped out' in May 1971.

Most expensive ■ The largest of the four flats at Rutland Gate, Kensington, London, designed by YRM Architects and occupied in 1988 were reputed to be worth around £6 million. The flat has a private swimming pool and seven bedrooms, and overlooks Hyde Park.

Mobile ■ The Cudecom Building, an eight-storey apartment block in Bogota, Colombia, South America weighing 7700 tonnes *7584 tons* was moved intact 28·95 m *95 ft* by Antionio Paez–Restrepo & Cia., S. en C on 6 Oct 1974 to make way for a road.

THE WORLD'S TALLEST STRUCTURES

HEIGHT		STRUCTURE	LOCATION	MATERIAL	BUILDING OR COMPLETION
m	**ft**				**DATES**
62	*204*	Djoser step pyramid (earliest Pyramid)	Saqqâra, Egypt	Tura limestone casing	*c.* 2650 BC
91·7	*300·8*	Pyramid of Meidum	Meidum, Egypt	Tura limestone casing	*c.* 2600 BC
101·1	*331·6*	Snefru Bent pyramid	Dahshûr, Egypt	Tura limestone casing	*c.* 2600 BC
104	*342*	Snefru North Stone pyramid	Dahshûr, Egypt	Tura limestone casing	*c.* 2600 BC
146·5	*480·9* [1]	Great Pyramid of Cheops (Khufu)	El Gizeh, Egypt	Tura limestone casing	*c.* 2580 BC
160	*525* [2]	Lincoln Cathedral, Central Tower	Lincoln, England	lead sheathed wood	*c.* 1307–1548
149	*489* [3]	St Paul's Cathedral spire	City of London, England	lead sheathed wood	1315–1561
141	*465*	Minster of Notre Dame	Strasbourg, France	Vosges sandstone	1420–1439
153	*502* [4]	St Pierre de Beauvais spire	Beauvais, France	lead sheathed wood	–1568
144	*475*	St Nicholas Church	Hamburg, Germany	stone and iron	1846–1847
147	*485*	Rouen Cathedral spire	Rouen, France	cast iron	1823–1876
156	*513*	Köln Cathedral spires	Cologne, W. Germany	stone	–1880
169	*555* [5]	Washington Monument	Washington, DC, USA	stone	1848–1884
300·5	*985·9* [6]	Eiffel Tower	Paris, France	iron	1887–1889
318	*1046*	Chrysler Building	New York City, USA	steel and concrete	1929–1930
381	*1250* [7]	Empire State Building	New York City, USA	steel and concrete	1929–1930
479	*1572*	KWTV Television Mast	Oklahoma City, USA	steel	Nov 1954
490	*1610* [8]	KSWS Television Mast	Roswell, New Mexico, USA	steel	Dec 1956
493	*1619*	WGAN Television Mast	Portland, Maine, USA	steel	Sept 1959
510	*1676*	KFVS Television Mast	Cape Girardeau, Missouri, USA	steel	Jun 1960
533	*1749*	WTVM & WRBL Television Mast	Columbus, Georgia, USA	steel	May 1962
533	*1749*	WBIR-TV Mast	Knoxville, Tennessee, USA	steel	Sept 1963
628	*2063*	KTHI-TV Mast	Fargo, North Dakota, USA	steel	Nov 1963
646·38	*2120·6*	Warszawa Radio Mast	Plock, Poland	galvanised steel	22 July 1974

[1] *Original height. With loss of pyramidion (topmost stone) height now 137 m 449 ft 6 in.*
[2] *Fell in a storm.*
[3] *Struck by lightning and destroyed 4 June 1561.*
[4] *Fell April 1573, shortly after completion.*
[5] *Sinking at a rate of 0·0047 ft per annum or 12·7 cm 5 in since 1884.*
[6] *Original height. With addition of TV antenna in 1957, now 320·75 m 1052 ft.*
[7] *Original height. With addition of TV tower on 1 May 1951, now 449 m 1472 ft. Exterior is clad in limestone from the Empire Quarry, Indiana.*
[8] *Fell in gale in 1960.*

Most expensive house ● Hearst Ranch at San Simeon, California, USA. Built between 1922–39 for William Randolph Hearst (1863–1951) at a cost of more than $30 000 000. There are over 100 rooms and a 32 m *104 ft* swimming pool, a 25 m *83 ft* long assembly hall and a garage for 25 cars. 60 servants are employed to maintain it. (Photo: Spectrum)

Buildings for Entertainment

STADIUM

Largest ■ The open Strahov Stadium in Prague, Czechoslovakia was completed in 1934 and can accommodate 240 000 spectators for mass displays of up to 40 000 Sokol gymnasts.

Football ■ The Maracaña Municipal Stadium in Rio de Janeiro, Brazil, has a normal capacity of 205 000, of whom 155 000 may be seated. A crowd of 199 854 was accommodated for the World Cup final between Brazil and Uruguay on 16 Jul 1950. A dry moat, 2·13 m *7 ft* wide and more than 1·5 m *5 ft* deep, protects players from spectators and *vice versa*. Britain's most capacious football stadium is Hampden Park, Glasgow, Scotland opened on 31 Oct 1903 and once surveyed to accommodate 184 000 compared with a record attendance of 149 547 on 17 Apr 1937 and the present licensed limit of 74 400.

Covered ■ The Azteca Stadium, Mexico City, Mexico, opened in 1968, has a capacity of 107 000 nearly all are under cover. The world's largest retractable roof is the 53 000 seating-capacity of the Toronto Blue Jays baseball team new stadium near the CN Tower completed in June 1989. The diameter is 207 m *679 ft*.

The largest covered stadium in Great Britain is the Empire Stadium, Wembley, Middlesex, opened in April 1923. It was the scene of the 1948 Olympic Games and the final of the 1966 World Cup. In 1962–3 the capacity under cover was increased to 100 000 of whom 45 000 may be seated. The original cost was £1 250 000.

Largest roof ■ The transparent acryl glass 'tent' roof over the Munich Olympic Stadium, West Germany, measures 84 997·9 m² *914 940 ft²* in area resting on a steel net supported by masts. The roof of longest span in the world is the 207·2 m *680 ft* diameter of the Louisiana Superdome (see below). The major axis of the elliptical Texas Stadium completed in 1971 at Irving, Texas, USA is, however, 240 m *787 ft 4 in*.

Indoor ■ The 5·26 ha *13 acre* $173 million 83·2 m *273 ft* tall Superdome in New Orleans, Louisiana, USA was completed in May 1975. Its maximum seating capacity for conventions is 97 365 or 76 791 for football. Box suites rent for $35 000 excluding the price of admission. A gondola with six 7·92 m *312 in* TV screens produces instant replay.

Amusement resort *Largest* ■ Disney World is set in 11 332 ha *28 000 acres* of Orange and Osceola counties, 32 km *20 miles* south-west of Orlando in central Florida, USA. It was opened on 1 Oct 1971 with a $400 million investment. The attendance in 1988 was 22 500 000.

Most attended ■ The most attended resort is Disneyland, Anaheim, California (opened 1955) which received its 250 millionth visitor on 24 Aug 1985 at 9.52 a.m. Disneyland expects to welcome its 300 millionth visitor before the end of 1989.

Largest pleasure beach ■ Virginia Beach, Virginia, USA has 45 km *28 miles* of beach front on the Atlantic and 16 km *10 miles* of estuary frontage. The area embraces 600 km² *255 miles²* and 134 hotels and motels. The most visited pleasure beach in Britain is at Blackpool, Lancs which attracts 6 ½ million visitors annually.

Piers ■ A pleasure pier was completed at Great Yarmouth, Norfolk in 1808 but was washed away in 1953. The Old Pier, Weymouth, Dorset dates back to 1812. The longest pleasure pier in the world is Southend Pier at Southend-on-Sea in Essex. It is 2·15 km *1·34 miles* in length and it was first opened in August 1889 with final extensions made in 1929. In 1949–50 the pier had a peak 5 750 000 visitors. The pier railway closed in October 1978, and reopened on 2 May 1986.

The resort with most piers is Atlantic City, New Jersey with 6 pre-war and 5 currently. In Great Britain only Blackpool has as many as three–North, Central and South.

FAIRS

Earliest fair ■ The earliest major international fair was the Great Exhibition of 1851 in the Crystal Palace, Hyde Park, London which in 141 days attracted 6 039 195 admissions.

Largest ■ The site of the St Louis, Missouri, USA, Louisiana Purchase Exposition covered 514·66 ha *1271·76 acres*. It also staged the 1904 Olympic Games and drew an attendance of 19 694 855.

Record attendance ■ 64 218 770 attended Expo 70 held on a 330 ha *815 acre* site at Osaka, Japan from March to September 1970. It made a profit of 19 439 402 017 yen.

Big wheel ■ The original Ferris Wheel, named after its constructor, George W. Ferris (1859–96), was erected in 1893 at the Midway, Chicago, Illinois, USA at a cost of $385 000. It was 76 m *250 ft* in diameter, 240 m *790 ft* in circumference, weighed 1087 tonnes *1070 tons* and carried 36 cars each seating 60 people, making a total of 2 160 passengers. The structure was removed in 1904 to St Louis, Missouri, USA and was eventually sold as scrap for $1800. In 1897 a Ferris Wheel with a diameter of 86·5 m *284 ft* was erected for the Earl's Court Exhibition, London. It had ten 1st-class and 30 2nd-class cars. The largest diameter wheels now operating are 'The Giant Peter' at Himeji Central Park, Himeji City, Hyogo, and that at the city of Tsukuba, both in Japan and with a height of 85 m *278 ft 10 in*. The latter has a capacity for 384 riders.

Switchbacks *Fastest and steepest* ■ The maximum speeds claimed for switchbacks, scenic railways or roller coasters have in the past been exaggerated for commercial reasons. The $8 million Magnum XL-200 opened early 1989 at Cedar Point Park, Sandusky, Ohio, USA has a vertical drop of 58·52 m *192 ft* on which a speed of 112·65 km/h *70 mph* is reached. Cedar Point has nine coasters making its total more than any other Park.

Longest ■ The longest roller coaster in the world is *The Beast* at Kings Island near Cincinnati, Ohio, USA. Measurements at the bottom of its 42·98 m *141 ft* high drop returned a speed of 104·23 km/h *64·77 mph* on 5 Apr 1980. The run of 2·25 km *1·40 miles* incorporates 243·8 m *800 ft* of tunnels and a 540-degree banked helix.

Tallest ■ The tallest is the *Moonsault Scramble* at the Fujikyu Highland Park, near Kawaguchi Lake, Japan opened on 24 Jun 1983. It is 75 m *246 ft* tall (with a speed of 105 km/h *65·2 mph*).

Longest slide ■ The Bromley Alpine Slide on Route 11 in Peru, Vermont, USA, has a length of 1402 m *4600 ft* and a vertical drop of 250 m *820 ft*.

Largest harem ■ The Winter Harem of the Grand Seraglio at Topkapi, Istanbul, Turkey was completed in 1589 with 400 rooms. By the time of the deposing of Abdul Hamid II in 1909 the number of *carge* (those who serve) had dwindled from 1200 to 370 odalisques with 127 eunuchs.

Night club *Oldest* ■ The earliest night club (*boîte de nuit*) was 'Le Bal des Anglais' at 6 rue des Anglais, Paris, 5ᵉ, France. Founded in 1843, it closed *c.* 1960.

Largest ■ 'Gilley's Club' (formerly 'Shelly's'), built in 1955, was extended in 1971 on Spencer Highway, Houston, Texas, USA with a seating capacity of 6000 under one roof covering 1·6 ha *4 acres*. In the more classical sense the largest night club in the world is 'The Mikado' in the Akasaka district of Tokyo, Japan with a seating capacity of 2000. It is 'manned' by 1250 hostesses. Binoculars are essential to an appreciation of the floor show.

Lowest ■ The 'Minus 206' in Tiberias, Israel on the shores of the Sea of Galilee. It is 206 m *676 ft* below sea level. An alternative candidate is the oft-raided 'Outer Limits', opposite the Cow Palace, San Francisco, California, USA. It has been called "The Most

OLDEST

There are various claimants to the title of the United Kingdom's oldest inn. A foremost claimant is **'The Fighting Cocks'**, St Albans, Herts (an 11th-century structure on an 8th-century site). The timber frame of **The Royalist Hotel,** Digbeth Street, Stow-on-the-Wold, Glos. has been dated to even earlier. It was the inn 'The Eagle and the Child' in the 13th century and known to exist in AD 947. An origin as early as AD 560 has been claimed for **'Ye Olde Ferry Boat Inn'** at Holywell, Cambs. There is some evidence that it antedates the local church, built in 980, but the earliest documents are not dated earlier than 1100. There is evidence that the **'Bingley Arms'**, Bardsey, near Leeds, West Yorks, restored and extended in 1738, existed as the 'Priest's Inn', according to Bardsey Church records, dated 905.

The oldest pub in Northern Ireland is **'Grace Neill's Bar'**, Donaghadee, County Down built in 1611. An inn has stood on the site of the **'Brazen Head Inn'**, Lower Bridge Street, Dublin since the late 12th century. The present structure dates from 1668.

LARGEST

The largest public house in Great Britain is the **'Downham Tavern'**, Downham Way, Bromley, Kent built in 1930. Two large bars (counter length 13·7 m *45 ft*) accommodate 1000 customers with 18-20 staff.

SMALLEST

The **'Lakeside Inn'**, The Promenade, Southport, Merseyside as measured by floor area is 6·70 m *22 ft* in length by 4·87 m *16 ft* in width. The ground floor of **'The Nutshell'**, Bury St. Edmunds, Suffolk is 4·82 x 2·28 m *15 ft 10 in x 7ft 6 in*.

'The Smiths Arms', Godmanstone, Dorset has external dimensions of 12·04 m *39 ft 6 in* in length 3·5 m *11 ft 6 in* in width and 3·65 m *12 ft* in height.

The pub with the smallest bar room is the **'Dove Inn'**, Upper Mall, Chiswick, London measuring 127 m x 239 m *4 ft 2 in x 7 ft 10 in*. Another contender is the **'Earl Grey'**, Quenington, Glos. whose measurements are 3·73 m x 2·89 m *12 ft 3 in x 9 ft 6 in*.

The longest bar in a pub is of 31·77 m *104 ft 3 in* in **'The Horse Shoe'**, Drury Street, Glasgow. The Grand Stand Bar at Galway Racecourse, Ireland, completed in 1955, measures 64 m *210 ft*.

LONGEST PUB NAME

'The Old Thirteenth Cheshire Astley Volunteer Rifleman Corps Inn' in Astley Street, Stalybridge, Manchester has 55 letters. The contrived name of the recently opened US Bar and Grill in Fulham Road, London is 'Henry J Bean's But His Friends, Some of Whom Live Down This Way, All Call Him Hank Bar and Grill' with 74 letters.

HIGHEST

In the United Kingdom the **'Tan Hill Inn'** is 528 m *1732 ft* above sea level. It is just in North Yorks on the moorland road between Reeth, North Yorks and Brough, Cumbria. The 'Snowdon Summit' licenced bar and cafeteria is, when open, the highest at 1085 m *3560 ft*.

SUPERLATIVE PUBS & INNS OF THE BRITISH ISLES

THE HORSE SHOE BAR
GLASGOW

THE GRACE NEILLS BAR
COUNTY DOWN, DONAGHADEE

THE TAN HILL INN
KELD – DURHAM/NORTH YORKS BORDER

THE BINGLEY ARMS
LEEDS

THE LAKESIDE INN
SOUTHPORT, MERSEYSIDE

THE NUTSHELL
BURY ST. EDMUNDS, E. ANGLIA

THE BRAZEN HEAD INN
DUBLIN

THE OLD THIRTEENTH CHESHIRE ASTLEY VOLUNTEER RIFLEMAN CORPS INN
STALYBRIDGE, MANCHESTER

YE OLDE FERRY BOAT INN
HOLYWELL, CAMBRIDGESHIRE

THE ROYALIST HOTEL
STOW-ON-THE-WOLD

THE FIGHTING COCKS
ST. ALBANS

THE EARL GREY
QUENINGTON, GLOUCESTERSHIRE

THE DOVE
UPPER MALL, LONDON W6

THE DOWNHAM TAVERN
BROMLEY, KENT

THE SMITHS ARMS
GODMANSTONE, DORSET

Busted Joint' and also 'The Slowest to Get the Message'.

Restaurants *Earliest* ■ The 'Casa Botin' was opened in 1725 in Calle de Cuchilleros 17, Madrid, Spain.

Largest ■ The 'Tump Nak' Thai restaurant in Bangkok consists of 65 adjoining houses built on 4 ha *10 acres*. A thousand waiters are available to serve the 3000 potential customers.

Highest ■ The highest restaurant in the world is at the Chacaltaya ski resort, Bolivia at 5340 m *17 519 ft*. The highest in Great Britain is the 'Ptarmigan Observation Restaurant' at 1112 m *3650 ft* above sea level on Cairngorm (1244 m *4084 ft*) near Aviemore, Inverness-shire, Scotland.

PUBLIC HOUSES

See map on p.93 ■ **Largest** *World* ■ The largest beer-selling establishment in the world is the 'Mathäser', Bayerstrasse 5, Munich, West Germany, where the daily sale reaches 48 000 litres *84 470 pts*. It was established in 1829, was demolished in World War II and rebuilt by 1955, and now seats 5500 people. The through-put at the Dube beer halls in the Bantu township of Soweto, Johannesburg, South Africa may, however, be higher on some Saturdays when the average daily consumption of 27 280 litres *48 000 pts* is far exceeded.

Longest bars ■ The world's longest permanent bar is the 103·6 m *340 ft* long bar in 'Lulu's Roadhouse', Kitchener, Ontario, Canada opened on 3 Apr 1984. The 'Bar at Erickson's', on Burnside Street, Portland, Oregon, USA in its heyday (1883–1920) possessed a bar which ran continuously around and across the main saloon measuring 208·48 m *684 ft*. The chief bouncer, Edward 'Spider' Johnson, had an assistant named 'Jumbo' Reilly who weighed 23 st and was said to resemble 'an ill-natured orang-utan'. Beer was 5 cents for 16 fluid ounces. Temporary bars have been erected of greater length.

The longest bar in Grear Britain with beer pumps is the Long Bar at The Cornwall Coliseum Auditorium at Carlyon Bay, St Austell, Cornwall, measuring 31·8 m *104 ¼ ft* and having 34 dispensers (beer and lager). The longest bar in a pub is of 31·77 m *104 ⅓ ft* in 'The Horse Shoe', Drury Street, Glasgow, Scotland. The Grand Stand Bar at Galway Racecourse, Ireland, completed in 1955, measures 64 m *210 ft*.

Shortest name ■ In Great Britain the shortest name was the 'X' at Westcott, Cullompton, Devon but in October 1983 the name was changed to the 'Merry Harriers'.

Commonest name ■ There are probably about 630 called the 'Red Lion'. Arthur Amos of Bury St Edmunds, Suffolk, has recorded 21 516 differently-named pubs continuously since 1938. On his death in June 1986, his son John took over the collection which now numbers 24 387.

Most visits ■ Stanley House of Totterdown, Bristol has visited 3309 differently named pubs in Britain by way of public transport only, from 1969 to 1989. Jimmy Young GM, BEM, of Better Pubs Ltd, claims to have visited 23 752 different pubs as at 20 April 1989.

Towers and Masts

TALLEST STRUCTURES

World ■ The tallest structure in the world, the guyed Warszawa Radio mast at Konstantynow near Gabin and Plock, 96 km *60 miles* north-west of the capital of Poland, is 646·38 m *2120 ⅔ ft* tall or more than four-tenths of a mile. It was completed on 18 Jul 1974 and put into operation on 22 Jul 1974. It was designed by Jan Polak and weighs 550 tonnes. The mast is so high that anyone falling off the top would reach their terminal velocity and hence cease to be accelerating before hitting the ground. Work was

> **Largest roof** ● The transparent acryl glass 'tent' roof over the Munich Olympic Stadium West Germany measures 84 997·9 m² *914 940 ft²* in area resting on a steel net supported by masts. (Photo: All Sport).

begun in July 1970 on this tubular steel construction, with its 15 steel guy ropes. It recaptured for Europe, after 45 years, a record held in the USA since the Chrysler Building surpassed the Eiffel Tower in 1929.

The tallest structure in the Great Britain is the Independent Broadcasting Authority's mast north of Horncastle, Lincs, completed in 1965 to a height of 385 m *1265 ft* with 2·13 m *7 ft* added by meteorological equipment installed in September 1967. It serves Yorkshire TV and weighs 210 tonnes.

TALLEST TOWERS

The tallest self-supporting tower (as opposed to a guyed mast) in the world is the $44 million CN Tower in Metro Center, Toronto, Canada, which rises to 555·33 m *1822 ft 1 in*. Excavation began on 12 Feb 1973 for the 130 000 tonne *12805 ton* structure of reinforced, post-tensioned concrete topped out on 2 Apr 1975. The 416-seat restaurant revolves in the Sky Pod at 347·5 m *1140 ft* from which the visibility extends to hills 120 km *74 ½ miles* distant. Lightning strikes the top about 200 times (30 storms) per annum.

The tallest tower built before the era of television masts is the Eiffel Tower in Paris, France, designed by Alexandre Gustav Eiffel (1832–1923) for the Paris Exhibition and completed on 31 Mar 1889. It was 300·51 m *985 ft 11 in* tall, now extended by a TV antenna to 320·75 m *1052 ⅓ ft* and weighs 7340 tonnes *7224 tons*. The maximum sway in high winds is 12·7 cm *5 in*. The whole iron edifice, which has 1792 steps, took 2 years, 2 months and 2 days to build and cost 7 799 401 francs 31 centimes.

The tallest self-supported tower in Great Britain is the 329·18 m *1080 ft* tall Independent Broadcasting Authority transmitter at Emley Moor, West Yorks, completed in September 1971. The structure, which cost £900 000, has an enclosed room at the 263·65 m *865 ft* level and weighs with its foundations more than 15 000 tonnes. The tallest tower of the pre-television era was the New Brighton Tower of 171·29 m *562 ft* built on Merseyside in 1897–1900 and dismantled in 1919–21.

Bridges

Oldest ■ Arch construction was understood by the Sumerians as early as 3200 BC and a reference exists to a Nile bridge in 2650 BC. The oldest surviving datable bridge in the world is the slab stone single arch bridge over the River Meles in Smyrna (now Izmir), Turkey, which dates from *c.* 850 BC.

The clapper bridges of Dartmoor and Exmoor (e.g. the Tarr Steps over the River Barle, Exmoor, Somerset) are thought to be of prehistoric types although none of the existing examples can be certainly dated. They are made of large slabs of stone placed over boulders. The Romans built stone bridges in England and remains of these have been found at Corbridge (Roman, Corstopitum), Northumberland dating to the 2nd century AD; Chesters, Northumberland; and Willowford, Cumbria. Remains of a very early wooden bridge have been found at Aldwinkle, Northants.

LONGEST

Cable suspension ■ The world's longest bridge span is the main span of the Humber Estuary Bridge, Humberside, England at 1410 m *4626 ft*. Work began on 27 Jul 1972, after a decision announced on 22 Jan 1966. The towers are 162·5 m *533 ft 1 ⅝ in* tall from datum and are 36 mm *1 ⅜ in* out of parallel, to allow for the curvature of the Earth. Including the Hessle and the Barton side spans, the bridge stretches 2220 m or *1·37 miles*. It was structurally completed on 18 Jul 1980 at a cost of £96 million and was opened by H M the Queen on 17 Jul 1981. Tolls, ranging between 70 pence for motorcycles and £8 for heavy vehicles, are the highest in Britain.

The double-deck road Akashi-Kaikyo bridge linking Honshū and Shikoku, Japan is planned to be completed in 1998. The main span will be 1990 m *6529 ft* in length with an overall suspended length with side spans totalling 3560 m *11 680 ft*. The Seto-Ohashi double-deck road and rail bridge linking Kojima, Honshu with Sakaide, Shikoku, Japan opened on 10 Apr 1988 at a cost of £4900 million and 17 lives. The tolls for cars are £24 each way for the 12·7 km *7·9 miles* on spans and viaducts.

Work on the Messina Bridge linking Sicily with Calabria on the Italian mainland is due to start in 1991. The single span will be the world's largest by far at 3 320 m *10 892 ft*. The escalating cost of such a project was estimated by 1988 already to have passed the £10 250 million mark. Plans for a £183 million second Severn Bridge were published in July 1986 from Sudbrook, Gwent, Wales to Redwick in Avon. Completion is scheduled for *c.* 1995.

Cantilever ■ The Quebec Bridge (Pont de Québec) over the St Lawrence River in Canada has the longest cantilever truss span of any in the world—549 m *1800 ft* between the piers and 987 m *3239 ft* overall. It carries a railway track and two carriageways. Begun in 1899, it was finally opened to traffic on 3 Dec 1917 at a cost of 87 lives, and $Can.22 500 000.

The longest cantilever bridge in Great Britain is the Forth Bridge. Its two main spans are 521 m *1710 ft* long. It carries a double railway track over the Firth of Forth 47·5 m *156 ft* above the water level. Work commenced in November 1882 and the first test trains crossed on 22 Jan 1890 after an expenditure of £3 million. It was officially opened on 4 Mar 1890. Of the 4500 workers who built it, 57 were killed in various accidents.

Steel arch ■ The longest is the New River Gorge Bridge, near Fayetteville, West Virginia, USA, completed in 1977 with a span of 518·2 m *1700 ft*.

The longest steel arch bridge in Great Britain is the Runcorn to Widnes bridge, Cheshire opened on 21 Jul 1961 with a span of 329·8 m *1082 ft*.

Floating bridge ■ The longest is the Second Lake Washington Bridge, Evergreen, Seattle, Washington State, USA. Its total length is 3839 m *12 596 ft* and its

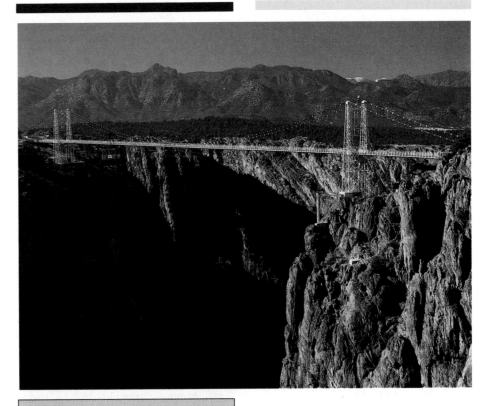

Highest bridge ● The Royal Gorge of the Arkansas River in Colorado, USA is 321 m *1053 ft* above water level. Construction was commenced on 5 Jun 1929 and it was opened to traffic on 6 Dec 1929 at a cost of $ 350 000 000. (Photo: Images Colour Library).

floating section measures 2291 m *7518 ft*. It was built at a total cost of $15 000 000 and completed in August 1963.

Covered bridge ■ The longest is that at Hartland, New Brunswick, Canada measuring 390·8 m *1282 ft* overall, completed in 1899.

Railway bridge ■ The longest is the Huey P. Long Bridge, Metairie, Louisiana, USA with a railway section 7009 m *22 996 ft (7 km 4·35 miles)* long. It was completed on 16 Dec 1935 with a longest span of 241 m *790 ft*.

The longest railway bridge in Britain is the second Tay Bridge (3552 m *11 653 ft*), across the Firth of Tay at Dundee, Scotland, opened on 20 Jun 1887. Of the 85 spans, 74 (length 3136 m *10 289 ft*) are over the waterway. The 878 brick arches of the London Bridge to Deptford Creek viaduct built in 1836 extend for 6·0 km *3 ¾ miles*.

Longest bridging ■ The Second Lake Pontchartrain Causeway was completed on 23 Mar 1969, joining Lewisburg and Mandeville, Louisiana, USA. It has a length of 38 422 m *126 055 ft*. It cost $29 900 000 and is 69 m *228 ft* longer than the adjoining First Causeway completed in 1956. The longest railway viaduct in the world is the rock-filled Great Salt Lake Railroad Trestle, carrying the Southern Pacific Railroad 19 km *11·85 miles* across the Great Salt Lake, Utah, USA. It was opened as a pile and trestle bridge on 8 Mar 1904, but converted to rock fill in 1955–60.

The longest stone arch bridging is the 1161 m *3810 ft* long Rockville Bridge north of Harrisburg, Pennsylvania, USA with 48 spans containing 196 000 tonnes *193 060 ton* of stone and completed in 1901.

Widest bridge ■ The widest long-span bridge is the 502·9 m *1650 ft* span Sydney Harbour Bridge, Australia (48·8 m *160 ft* wide). It carries two electric overhead railway tracks, eight lanes of roadway and a cycle and footway. It was officially opened on 19 Mar 1932. The Crawford Street Bridge in Providence, Rhode Island, USA has a width of 350 m *1147 ft*. The River Roch is bridged for a distance of

445 m *1460 ft* where the culvert passes through the centre of Rochdale, Manchester and this is sometimes claimed to be a breadth.

Bridge Building ■ A team of 26 Engineer Regiment of Iserlohn, West Germany constructed a bridge across an 8-metre gap using a five-bay single-storey MGB (medium girder bridge) in 8 min 59 sec at their training area on 18 Oct 1988.

A 546·13 m *1792 ft* long rope suspension bridge was erected at Spaarnwoude, Holland by 1500 boy scouts and girl guides from 28 Jul–6 Aug 1987.

HIGHEST

The highest bridge in the world is the bridge over the Royal Gorge of the Arkansas River in Colorado, USA which is 321 m *1053 ft* above the water level. It is a suspension bridge with a main span of 268 m *880 ft* and was constructed in six months, ending on 6 Dec 1929. The highest railway bridge in the world is the single-track span at Fades, outside Clermont-Ferrand, France. It was built in 1901–9 with a span of 144 m *472 ft* and is 132·5 m *435 ft* above the River Sioule. The road bridge at the highest altitude in the world, 5602 m *18 380 ft*, is the 30 m *98·4 ft* long Bailey Bridge designed and constructed by Lt Col S.G. Vombatkere and an Indian Army team in Aug 1982 near Khardung La, in Ladakh, India.

The highest railway bridge in Great Britain is the Ballochmyle viaduct over the river Ayr, Ayrshire, Scotland built 51·5 m *169 ft* over the river bed in 1846–8 with the then world's longest masonry arch span of 55·16 m *181 ft*.

AQUEDUCTS

Longest ancient ■ The greatest of ancient aqueducts was the Aqueduct of Carthage in Tunisia, which ran 141 km *87·6 miles* from the springs of Zaghouan to Djebel Djougar. It was built by the Romans during the reign of Publius Aelius Hadrianus (AD 117–138). By 1895, 344 arches still survived. Its original capacity has been calculated at 31·8 million litres *7 000 000 gal* per day.

The triple-tiered aqueduct Pont du Gard, built in AD 19 near Nîmes, France, is 48 m *160 ft* high.

The tallest of the 14 arches of Aguas Livres Aqueduct, built in Lisbon, Portugal, in 1784 is 65 m *213 ¼ ft*

Longest modern ■ The world's longest aqueduct, in the non-classical sense of water conduit, excluding irrigation canals, is the California State Water Project aqueduct, completed in 1974, to a length of 1329 km *826 miles* of which 619 km *385 miles* is canalised.

The longest bridged aqueduct in Great Britain is the Pont Cysylltau in Clwyd on the Frankton to Llantisilio branch of the Shropshire Union Canal. It is 307 m *1007 ft* long, and has 19 arches up to 36 m *121 ft* high above low water on the Dee. Designed by Thomas Telford (1757–1834) it was opened in 1805.

The original stone-built Barton Aqueduct, constructed by James Brindley in 1761 to carry the Bridgewater Canal over the river Irwell, was replaced in 1893 by the Barton Swing Aqueduct as a result of the construction of the Manchester Ship Canal which followed the course of the Irwell. Other earlier aqueducts built by James Brindley and still in use can be found on the Trent and Mersey Canal near Burton-on-Trent, where the canal crosses the river Dove, and at Rugeley where it crosses the Trent, both date from around 1772. On the adjoining Staffordshire and Worcestershire Canal near Great Haywood, Brindley, aqueducts also dating from about 1772 carry the canal over the rivers Trent and Sow.

Canals

Earliest ■ Relics of the oldest canals in the world, dated by archaeologists *c.* 4000 BC, were discovered near Mandali, Iraq early in 1968.

The earliest canals in Britain were first cut by the Romans. In the Midlands the 17 km *11 mile* long Fossdyke Canal between Lincoln and the river Trent at Torksey was built in about AD 65 and was scoured in 1122. It is still in use today. Though the Exeter Canal was cut as early as 1564–6, the first wholly artificial major navigation canal in the United Kingdom was the 29·7 km *18½ mile* long canal with 14 locks from Whitecoat Point to Newry, Northern Ireland opened on 28 Mar 1742. The Sankey Navigation Canal in Lancashire, 12·8 km *8 miles* in length, with 10 locks, was opened in November 1757.

Longest ■ The Volga–Baltic Canal opened in April 1965 runs 2300 km *1850 miles* from Astrakhan up the Volga, via Kuybyshev, Gor'kiy and Lake Ladoga, to Leningrad, USSR. The longest canal of the ancient world has been the Grand Canal of China from Peking (Beijing) to Hangchou. It was begun in 540 BC and not completed until 1327 by which time it extended (including canalised river sections) for 1781 km *1107 miles*. The estimated work force *c.* AD 600 reached 5 000 000 on the Pien section. Having been allowed by 1950 to silt up to the point that it was nowhere more than 1·8 m *6 ft* deep, it is now, however, plied by vessels of up to 2000 tonnes.

The Beloye More (White Sea) Baltic Canal from Belomorsk to Povenets, in the USSR, is 227 km *141 miles* long with 19 locks. It was completed with the use of forced labour in 1933. It cannot accommodate ships of more than 5 m *16 ft* in draught.

The world's longest big ship canal is the Suez Canal linking the Red and Mediterranean Seas, opened on 16 Nov 1869 but inoperative from June 1967 to June 1975. The canal was planned by the French diplomatist Comte Ferdinand de Lesseps (1805–94) and work began on 25 Apr 1859. It is 161·9 km *100·6 miles* in length from Port Said lighthouse to Suez Roads and 60 m *197 ft* wide. The work force consisted of 8213 men and 368 camels. The largest vessel to transit has been SS *Settebello* of 322 446 tonnes dwt (length 338·43 m *1110·3 ft*, beam 57·35 m *188·1 ft* at a maximum draft of 22·35 m *73·3 ft*). This was southbound in ballast on 6 Aug 1986. USS *Shreveport* transited southbound on 15–16 Aug 1984 in a record 7 hr 45 min.

Canals and river navigations in Great Britain amount to approximately 5630 km *3 500 miles* with 290 km *150 miles* being restored. Of this total 4000 km *2500 miles* are inter-linked. The geographical north-south extreme is Ripon, North Yorks, to Goldalming, Surrey at 670 km *415 miles*.

Panama canal ● The third busiest in the world with over 10 000 transits per year. The lock gates which have been operational since the canal opened on 15 Aug 1914 are 25 m *82 ft* high and weigh an estimated 730 to 780 tons, each gate is seven feet thick and 65 ft long. (Photo: Robert Harding)

Busiest ■ The busiest big ship canal is the Kiel Canal linking the North Sea with the Baltic Sea in West Germany with over 45 000 transits recorded in 1987. Next comes the Suez Canal with over 20 000 transits and third the Panama Canal with over 10 000 transits. Busiest in terms of tonnage of shipping using it is the Suez Canal with nearly 440 000 000 grt.

Longest seaway ■ The St Lawrence Seaway (304 km *189 miles* long) along the New York State–Ontario border from Montreal to Lake Ontario enables ships up to 222 m *728 ft* long and 8 m *26·2 ft* draught, some of which are of 26 400 tonnes *26 000 tons*, to sail 3769 km *2342 miles* from the North Atlantic up the St Lawrence estuary and across the Great Lakes to Duluth, Minnesota, USA on Lake Superior (183 m *602 ft* above sea level). The project, begun in 1954, cost $470 000 000 and was opened on 25 Apr 1959.

Longest irrigation canal ■ The Karakumskiy Kanal stretches 850 km *528 miles* from Haun-Khan to Ashkhabad, Turkmenistan, USSR. In September 1971 the 'navigable' length reached 450 km *280 miles*. The length of the £370 million project will reach 1300 km *930 miles*.

LOCKS

Largest ■ The sea lock at Zeebrugge, Belgium measures 500 × 57 × 23 m *1640 × 187 × 75·4 ft* giving a volume of 655 300 m³ *857 066 yd³*. The Berendrecht Lock, Antwerp, Belgium will have the same length but a width of 68 m *223 ft* at a depth of 21·5 m *70·5 ft* giving a volume of 731 000 m³ *956 000 yd³*.

The largest and deepest lock in the United Kingdom is the Royal Portbury Entrance Lock, Bristol which measures 366 × 42·7 m *1200 × 140 ft* and has a depth of 20·2 m *66 ft*. It was opened in August 1977.

Deepest ■ The John Day dam lock on the river Columbia, Oregon and Washington State, USA was completed in 1963. It can raise or lower barges 34·4 m *113 ft* and is served by a 998 tonne *982 ton* gate.

Highest rise and longest flight ■ The world's highest lock elevator overcomes a head of 68·58 m *225 ft* at Ronquières on the Charleroi–Brussels Canal,

Dams and Tunnels

97

Belgium. The two 236-wheeled caissons, each able to carry 1370 tonnes *1350 tons*, take 22 min to cover the 1432 m *4698 ft* long ramp. The highest rise of any boat-carrying plane in Britain was the 68·6 m *225 ft* of the 285 m *935 ft* long Hobbacott Down plane on the Bude Canal, Cornwall.

The longest flight of locks in the United Kingdom is on the Worcester and Birmingham Canal at Tardebigge, Hereford and Worcester, where in a 4 km *2¹⁄₂ mile* stretch there are the Tardebigge (30 locks) and Stoke (6 locks) flights which together drop the canal 78·9 m *259 ft*. The flight of locks on the Huddersfield Canal, closed in 1944, on the 11·6 km *7¹⁄₄ mile* stretch to Marsden, numbered 42.

Largest cut ■ The Gaillard Cut (known as 'the Ditch') on the Panama Canal is 82 m *270 ft* deep between Gold Hill and Contractor's Hill with a bottom width of 152 m *500 ft*. In one day in 1911 as many as 333 dirt trains each carrying 363 tonnes *357 tons* left this site. The total amount of earth excavated for the whole Panama Canal as of 1 Oct 1979 was 509 338 960 m³ *666 194 450 yd³* which total will be raised by the further widening of the Gaillard Cut.

Dams

Earliest ■ The earliest known dams were those uncovered by the British School of Archaeology in Jerusalem in 1974 at Jawa in Jordan. These stone-faced earth dams are dated to c. 3200 BC.

Most massive ■ Measured by volume the earth and rock filled Pati dam on the Pavaná river, Argentina has a volume of 238 180 000 m³ *311 527 000 yd³*. It is 174·9 km *108·6 miles* in length and 36 m *118 ft* high. The Chapetón, dam also on the Pavaná, is planned to have a volume of 296 200 000 m³ *387 400 000 yd³* and a crest length of 224 km *139 miles*. Both will be surpassed in volume by the Syncrude Tailings Dam in Canada with 540 000 000 m³ *706 000 000 yd³*.

The most massive dam in Britain is the Northumbrian Water Authority's Kielder Dam, a 52 m *170 ft* high earth embankment measuring 1140 m *3740 ft* in length and 5 300 000 m³ *6 932 000 yd³*. There are longer low dams or barrages of the valley cut-off type, notably the Hanningfield Dam, Essex, built from July 1952 to August 1956 to a length of 2088 m *6850 ft* and a height of 19·7 m *64 ¹⁄₂ ft*.

Largest concrete ■ The Grand Coulee Dam on the Columbia River, Washington State, USA was begun in 1933 and became operational on 22 Mar 1941. It was completed in 1942 at a cost of $56 million. It has a crest length of 1272 m *4173 ft* and is 167 m *550 ft* high with a capacity of 8 092 000 m³ *10 585 000 yd³* of concrete and weighs approximately 19 595 000 tonnes *19 285 000 tons*.

Highest ■ This will be the 335 m *1098 ft* high Rogunsky earth-fill dam across the river Vakhsh, Tadzhikistan, USSR with a crest length of only 602 m *1975 ft* and a volume of 85 million m³. Building since 1973, the completion date is still unconfirmed. Meanwhile the tallest completed is the 300 m *984 ft* high Nurek dam, USSR of 58 million m³ volume.

The rock-fill Llyn Brianne Dam, Dyfed is Great Britain's highest dam, reaching 91 m *298¹⁄₂ ft* in November 1971. It became operational on 20 Jul 1972.

Longest ■ The 41 m *134¹⁄₂ ft* high Yacyreta–Apipe dam across the Paraná on the Paraguay–Argentina borders extends for 72 km *44·7 miles*. In the early 17th century an impounding dam of moderate height was built in Lake Hungtze, Kiangsu, China, to a reputed length of 100 km *62 miles*.

The longest sea dam in the world is the Afsluitdijk stretching 32·5 km *20·195 miles* across the mouth of the Zuider Zee in two sections of 2·499 km *1·553 miles* (mainland of North Holland to the Isle of Wieringen) and 30 km *18·641 miles* from Wieringen to Friesland. It has a sea-level width of 89 m *293 ft* and a height of 7·5 m *24 ft 7 in*.

Strongest ■ This will be upon completion the 242 m *793 ft* high Sayano-Shusenskaya dam on the river Yenisey, USSR which is designed to bear a load of 18 000 000 tonnes from a fully-filled reservoir of 31 300 million m³ *41 000 million yd³* capacity .

Largest reservoir ■ The most voluminous man-made reservoir is the Kakhovskaya Reservoir, USSR, with a volume of 182 km³ *147 550 000 acre-feet*. The world's largest artificial lake measured by surface area is Lake Volta, Ghana, formed by the Akosombo Dam completed in 1965. By 1969 the lake had filled to an area of 8482 km² *3275 miles²* with a shoreline 7250 km *4500 miles* in length.

The completion in 1954 of the Owen Falls Dam near Jinja, Uganda, across the northern exit of the White Nile from the Victoria Nyanza marginally raised the level of that natural lake by adding 270 km³ *218 900 000 acre-feet*, and technically turned it into a reservoir with a surface area of 6·9 million ha *17 169 920 acres*.

The $4-billion Tucurui Dam in Brazil of 64·3 million m³, had, by 1984, converted the Tocantins River into a 1900 km *1180 mile* long chain of lakes.

The most capacious reservoir in Britain is Kielder Water in the North Tyne Valley, Northumberland, which filled to 2000 million hl *44 000 million gallons* from 15 Dec 1980 to mid-1982, and which acquired a surface area of 1086 ha *2684 acres* and a perimeter of 43·4 km *27 miles* to become England's second largest lake. Rutland Water has a lesser capacity (124 106 million l *27 300 million gallons*) and a lesser perimeter (38·6 km *24 miles*) but a greater surface area of 1254 ha *3100 acres*. The deepest reservoir in Europe is Loch Morar, Inverness-shire, Scotland, with a maximum depth of 310 m *1017 ft* (see also page 59).

The largest wholly artificial reservoir in Great Britain is the Queen Mary Reservoir, built between August 1914 and June 1925, at Littleton, near Staines, Surrey, with an available storage capacity of 369·6 million hl *8130 million gal* and a water area of 286 ha *707 acres*. The length of the perimeter embankment is 6329 m *20 766 ft* (6·32 km *3·93 miles*).

Largest polder *(Reclaimed land)* ■ Of the five great polders in the old Zuider Zee, Netherlands, will be the 60 300 ha *149 000 acre* (603 km² *232·8 miles²*) Markerwaard. Work on the 106 km *66 mile* long surrounding dyke was begun in 1957. The water area remaining after the erection of the 1927–32 dam (32 km *20 miles* in length) is called IJssel meer, which will have a final area of 1262·6 km² *487¹⁄₂ miles²*.

Largest levees ■ The most massive ever built are the Mississippi levees begun in 1717 but vastly augmented by the US Federal Government after the disastrous floods of 1927. These extend for 2787 km *1732 miles* along the main river from Cape Girardeau, Missouri, USA to the Gulf of Mexico and comprise more than 765 million m³ *1000 million yd³* of earthworks. Levees on the tributaries comprise an additional 3200 km *2000 miles*. The Pine Bluff, Arkansas to Venice, Louisiana, USA segment of 1046 km *650 miles* is continuous.

Tunnels

LONGEST

Rail ■ The 53·85 km *33·46 mile* long Seikan Rail Tunnel has been bored 240 m *787 ft* beneath sea level and 100 m *328 ft* below the sea bed of the Tsugaru Strait between Tappi Saki, Honshū, and Fukushima, Hokkaidō, Japan. Tests started on the sub-aqueous section (23·3 km *14¹⁄₂ miles*) in 1964 and construction in June 1972. It was holed through on 27 Jan 1983 after a loss of 34 lives. The cost by the finish of tunnelling after 20 years 10 months in March 1985 and subsequent maintenance to February 1987 was 800 000 million yen.The fast test run took place on 13 Mar 1988.

Great Britain's longest main-line railway tunnel is the

Severn Tunnel (7 km *4 miles 628 yd*), linking Avon and Gwent, completed with 76 400 000 bricks between 1873 and 1886.

Continuous Subway ■ The Moscow Metro underground railway line from Belyaevo to Medvedkovo is c. 30·7 km *19·07 miles* long and was completed in 1978/9.

Road tunnel ■ The 16·32 km *10·14 mile* long two-lane St Gotthard Road Tunnel from Göschenen to Airolo, Switzerland, opened to traffic on 5 Sep 1980. Nineteen lives were lost during the construction, begun in autumn 1969, at a cost of SF 686 million.

The longest road tunnel in the United Kingdom is the Mersey Tunnel, joining Liverpool and Birkenhead, Merseyside. It is 3·43 km *2·13 miles* long, or 4·62 km *2·87 miles* including branch tunnels. Work was begun in December 1925 and it was opened by HM King George V on 18 Jul 1934. The total cost was £7 ³⁄₄ million. The 11 m *36 ft* wide four-lane roadway carries nearly 7 ¹⁄₂ million vehicles a year. The first tube of the second Mersey Tunnel was opened on 24 Jun 1971.

Excavation of the projected £6000 million Eurotunnel under the English Channel between Cheriton near Folkestone, Kent and Sargatte by Calais, France began on 1 Jul 1987 and should be completed by 1993. The length of the twin rail tunnels of 7·6 m *24 ft 11 in* diameter will be 49·94 km *31·03 miles*.

Largest ■ The largest diameter road tunnel in the world is that blasted through Yerba Buena Island, San Francisco, California, USA. It is 23 m *76 ft* wide, 17 m *58 ft* high and 165 m *540 ft* long. More than 80 000 000 vehicles pass through on its two decks every year.

Water supply tunnel ■ The longest tunnel of any kind is the New York City West Delaware water-supply tunnel, begun in 1937 and completed in 1944. It has a diameter of 4·1 m *13¹⁄₂ ft* and runs for 168·9 km *105 miles* from the Rondout Reservoir into the Hillview Reservoir, on the border of Yonkers and New York City, USA.

The United Kingdom's is the Kielder Water tunnel system. These tunnels have been driven through the rock to link the Tyne Valley with the Wear Valley. A pipe then passes under the river Wear and the tunnel then proceeds to link up with the Tees Valley. The system is 32·18 km *20·2 miles* in length.

Hydro-electric, irrigation or sewerage ■ The 82·9 km *51¹⁄₂ mile* long Orange-Fish Rivers Tunnel, South Africa, begun in 1967 at an estimated cost of £60 million. The boring was completed in April 1973. The lining to a minimum thickness of 23 cm *9 in* will give a completed diameter of 5·33 m *17¹⁄₂ ft*.

The Majes project in Peru involves 98 km *60·9 miles* of tunnels for hydro-electric and water-supply purposes. The dam is at 4200 m *13 780 ft* altitude. The Chicago TARP (Tunnels and Reservoir Plan) in Illinois, USA involves 193 km *120 miles* of sewerage tunnelling.

Bridge-tunnel ■ The Chesapeake Bay Bridge-Tunnel, extending 28·40 km *17·65 miles* from Eastern Shore, Virginia Peninsula to Virginia Beach, Virginia, USA. It cost $200 000 000 and was completed after 42 months and opened to traffic on 15 Apr 1964. The longest bridged section is Trestle C (7·34 km *4·56 miles* long) and the longest tunnel is the Thimble Shoal Channel Tunnel (1·75 km *1·09 miles*).

Longest and Largest canal-tunnel ■ The Rove Tunnel on the Canal de Marseille au Rhône in the South of France was completed in 1927 and is 7120 m *23 359 ft* long, 22 m *72 ft* wide and 11·4 m *37 ft* high. Built to be navigated by sea-going ships, it was closed in 1963 following a collapse of the structure and has not been re-opened.

Oldest navigable ■ The Malpas Tunnel on the Canal du Midi in south-west France was completed in 1681 and is 161 m *528 ft* long. Its completion enabled vessels to navigate from the Atlantic Ocean to the Mediterranean Sea via the river Garonne to Toulouse and the Canal du Midi to Sete.

The longest canal tunnel in Great Britain is the Standedge (more properly Stanedge) Tunnel in West Yorks on the Huddersfield Narrow Canal built from 1794 to 4 Apr 1811. It measures 5·21 km *3 miles 418 yd* in length and was closed on 21 Dec 1944. However it is currently undergoing restoration.

The British canal system has contained 84 tunnels exceeding 27·4 m *30 yd* of which 48 are still open. The longest of these is the 2·79 km *3056 yd* long Blisworth Tunnel on the Grand Union in Northamptonshire. The now closed Huddersfield Narrow Canal is the highest in the Great Britain, at 194 m *638 ft* above sea level.

Tunnelling ■ The longest unsupported example of a machine-bored tunnel is the Three Rivers Water Tunnel driven 9·37 km *30 769 linear feet* with a 3·2 m *10·5 ft* diameter for the city of Atlanta, Georgia, USA from April 1980 to February 1982. S & M Constructors Inc of Cleveland, Ohio, USA achieved 54·5 m *179 ft* in a day through the granite, schist and gneiss.

The NCB record of 251·4 m *824·8 ft* for a 3·80 m *12½ ft* wide, 2 m *6½ ft* high roadway by a team of 35 pitmen in five days was set at West Cannock, Staffs, No. 5 Colliery from 30 Mar–3 Apr 1981.

Specialised Structures

Highest Advertising signs ■ The four Bank of Montreal logos atop the 72-storey 285 m *935 ft* tall First Canadian Place, Toronto, Canada. Each sign, built by Claude Neon Industries Ltd, measures 6·09×6·70 m *20×22 ft* and was lifted by helicopter.

Largest ■ The most conspicuous sign ever erected was the electric Citroën sign on the Eiffel Tower, Paris. It was switched on on 4 Jul 1925, and could be seen 38 km *24 miles* away. It was in six colours with 250 000 lamps and 90 km *56 miles* of electric cables. The letter 'N' which terminated the name 'Citroën' between the second and third levels measured 20·8 m *68 ft 5 in* in height was dismantled in 1936. For

the largest ground sign see Chapter 8, p. 147 Largest letter.

Neon signs ■ The letter 'M' installed on the Great Mississippi River Bridge is 548·6 m *1800 ft* long and comprises 200 high intensity lamps. The largest neon sign measures 64 × 16·7 m *210 × 55 ft* built for Marlboro cigarettes at Hung Hom, Kowloon, Hong Kong in May 1986. It contains 10 668 m *35 000 ft* of neon tubing and weighs approximately 113 tons *114·7 tonnes*.

An interior lit fascia advertising sign in Clearwater, Florida, USA completed by Adco Sign Corp in April 1983 measures 356·17 m *1168 ft 6½ in* in length.

Hoarding ■ The largest reported hoarding is one 86·56 m X 25 m *284 ft X 82 ft* and was produced by Heritage Hampers. The site is the roof of the Ayresome Park, Middlesbrough Football Club stand, North Yorks.

Britain's largest illuminated sign is the name VOLVO LEX extending 57·930 m *190 ft 1 in* installed by Herbert & Sons Signs Ltd of Surrey at Lex, a Volvo dealer in Edgware Road, Colindale, London NW9.

Animated sign ■ The world's most massive is reputed to be that outside the Circus Circus Hotel, Reno, Nevada, USA named Topsy, the Clown. It is 38·7 m *127 ft* tall and weighs over 40 tons *40·8 tonnes* with 2·25 km *1·4 miles* of neon tubing. His smile measures 4·26 m *14 ft* across.

Barn ■ The largest barn in Great Britain is one at Frindsbury, Kent. Its length is 66·7 m *219 ft* and it is still wholly roofed. The Ipsden Barn, Oxon, is 117 m *385½ ft* long but 9 m *30 ft* wide 1074 m² *(11 565 ft²)*. The longest tithe barn in Britain is one measuring 81 m *268 ft* long at Wyke Farm, near Sherborne, Dorset.

Largest Bonfire ■ This was constructed in Espel, in the Noordoost Polder, Netherlands. It stood 27·87 m *91 ft 5 in* high with a base circumference of 84·40 m *276 ft 11 in* and was lit on 19 Apr 1987.

Great Britain's was the Coronation bonfire atop Arrowthwaite Brows, Whitehaven, Cumbria, lit in 1902 with 800 tons *812 tonnes* of timber, 4546 litres *1000 gal* each of petroleum and tar. It was octagonal in shape and built to a height of 36·67 m *120 ft* with a base circumference of 47·2 m *155 ft* tapering to 6·1 m *20 ft*.

Longest breakwater ■ The world's longest breakwater is that which protects the Port of Galveston, Texas, USA. The granite South Breakwater is 10·85 km *6·74 miles* in length.

Great Britain's is the North Breakwater at Holyhead, Anglesey, which is 2395 m *(1·48 miles 7860 ft)* in length and was completed in 1873.

Buildings demolished by explosives ■ The largest has been the 21-storey Traymore Hotel, Atlantic City, New Jersey, USA on 26 May 1972 by Controlled Demolition Inc of Towson, Maryland, USA. This 600-room hotel had a cubic capacity of 181 340 m³ *6 495 500 ft³*. The tallest chimney ever demolished by explosives was the Matla Power Station chimney, Kriel, South Africa on 19 Jul 1981. It stood 275 m *902 ft* and was brought down by The Santon (Steeplejack) Co Ltd of Manchester, England.

Cemetery *Largest* ■ Leningrad contains over 500 000 of the 1 300 000 victims of the German army's siege of 1941–3. Great Britain's is Brookwood Cemetery, Brookwood, Surrey, owned by the London Necropolis Co. It is 200 ha *500 acres* in extent and has more than 225 000 interments.

Tallest ■ The permanently illuminated Memorial Cemiferio Ecurñencio, São Paulo, Brazil is 10-storeys high, occupying an area of 18 000 m² *4·448 acres*. When full the final capacity of spaces will be 20 000.

Tallest columns ■ The 36 fluted pillars 27·43 m *90 ft* tall, of Vermont marble in the colonnade of the Education Building, Albany, New York State, USA.

Their base diameter is 1·98 m *6¹/₂ ft*. The tallest load-bearing stone columns in the world are those measuring 21 m *69 ft* in the Hall of Columns of the Temple of Amun at Karnak, opposite Thebes on the Nile, the ancient capital of Upper Egypt. They were built in the 19th dynasty in the reign of Rameses II *c.* 1270 BC.

Crematorium ■ The oldest crematorium in Great Britain was built in 1879 at Woking, Surrey. The first cremation took place there on 26 Mar 1885, the practice having been found legal after the cremation of Iesu Grist Price on Caerlan Fields, Llantrisant, Mid Glamorgan on 13 Jan 1884. The total number of people cremated in Britain since has been 11 172 452.

The largest crematorium in the world is at the Nikolo-Arkhangelskoye Cemetery, East Moscow, USSR with 7 twin cremators of British design, completed in March 1972. It has several Halls of Farewell for atheists. Currently, Britain's largest is the City of London Crematorium, E.12.

Largest dome ■ The Louisiana Superdome, New Orleans, USA has a diameter of 207·26 m *680 ft*. (see p.92 for further details.) The largest dome of ancient architecture is that of the Pantheon, built in Rome in AD 112, with a diameter of 43 m *142¹/₂ ft*.

Britain's largest is that of the Bell Sports Centre, Perth, Scotland, with a diameter of 67 m *222 ft* designed by D. B. Cockburn and constructed in Baltic whitewood by Muirhead & Sons Ltd of Grangemouth, Central, Scotland.

Doors *Largest* ■ The four doors in the Vehicle Assembly Building near Cape Canaveral, Florida, USA have a height of 140 m *460 ft* (see p. 86).

Great Britain's are those to the Britannia Assembly Hall, at Filton airfield, Avon. The doors are 315 m *1035 ft* in length and 20 m *67 ft* high, divided into three bays each 105 m *345 ft* across. The largest simple hinged door in Great Britain is that of Ye Old Bull's Head, Beaumaris, Anglesey, which is 3·35 m *11 ft* wide and 3·96 m *13 ft* high.

Heaviest ■ Leading to the laser target room at Lawrence Livermore National Laboratory, California, USA. It weighs 321·4 tons *326·5 tonnes*, is up to 2·43 m *8 ft* thick and was installed by Overly.

Oldest ■ Great Britain's oldest are those of Hadstock Church, near Saffron Walden, Essex, which date from *c.* 1040 AD and exhibit evidence of Danish workmanship.

Largest dry dock ■ With a maximum shipbuilding capacity of 1 200 000 tons deadweight the Okpo No 1 Dry Dock, Chojé Island in South Korea measures 525 m *1722·4 ft* long by 131 m *430 ft* wide and was completed in 1979. The dock gates 14 m *46 ft* high and 10 m *32·8 ft* thick at the base are the world's largest.

Britain's largest is the Belfast Harbour Commission and Harland and Wolff building dock in Belfast, Northern Ireland. It was excavated by Wimpey to a length of 556 m *1825 ft* and a width of 93 m *305 ft* and can accommodate tankers of 1 000 000 tons deadweight. Work was begun on 26 Jan 1968 and completed on 30 Nov 1969 and involved the excavation of 306 000 m³ *400 000 yd³*.

Largest earthworks ■ Prior to the mechanical era were the Linear Earth Boundaries of the Benin Empire in the Bendel state of Nigeria. These were first reported in 1900 and partially surveyed in 1967. In April 1973 it was estimated by Patrick Darling that the total length of the earthworks was probably between 6400–12 800 km *4000 and 8000 miles* with the amount of earth moved estimated at from 380–460 million m³ *500 to 600 million yd³*.

The greatest prehistoric earthwork in Britain is Wansdyke, originally Wodensdic, which ran 138 km *86 miles* from Portishead, Avon to Inkpen Beacon and Ludgershall, south of Hungerford, Berks. It was built by the Belgae as their north boundary. The most extensive single site earthwork is the Dorset Cursus

near Gussage St Michael 8 km *5 miles* south-west of Cranborne, dating from *c.* 1900 BC. The workings are 9·7 km *6 miles* in length, involving an estimated 191 000 m³ *250 000 yd³* of excavations. The largest of the Celtic hill-forts is that known as Mew Dun, or Maiden Castle, 3 km *2 miles* SW of Dorchester, Dorset. It covers 46·5 ha *115 acres* and was abandoned shortly after AD 43.

Fence *Longest* ■ The dingo-proof wire fence enclosing the main sheep areas of Australia is 1·8 m *6 ft* high, 30 cm *1 ft* underground and stretches for 5531 km *3437 miles*. The Queensland State Government discontinued full maintenance in 1982 but 500 km *310 miles* is now being repaired.

Tallest ■ The world's tallest fences are security screens 20 m *65·6 ft* high erected by Harrop-Allin of Pretoria, South Africa in November 1981 to protect fuel depots and refineries at Sasolburg, South Africa.

Tallest flagstaff ■ Erected outside the Oregon Building at the 1915 Panama-Pacific International Exposition in San Francisco, California, USA, and trimmed from a Douglas fir, it stood 91 m *299 ft 7 in* in height and weighed 47 tonnes *45 tons*. The tallest unsupported flag pole in the world is the 85·95 m *282 ft* tall steel pole weighing 54 430 kg *120 000 lb* which was erected on 22 Aug 1985 at the Canadian Expo 86 exhibition in Vancouver, British Columbia and supporting a gigantic ice hockey stick 62·5 m *205 ft* in length. Mr Sherrold Haddad of Flag Chevrolet Oldsmobile Ltd was instrumental in moving and reconstructing the flagstaff where it has been relocated at the company's premises in 104th Avenue, Surrey, British Columbia, Canada.

Great Britain's is a 68 m *225 ft* tall Douglas fir staff at Kew, Richmond upon Thames, Surrey. Cut in Canada, it was shipped across the Atlantic and towed up the river Thames on 7 May 1958, to replace the old 65 m *214 ft* tall staff of 1919.

Tallest fountain ■ The Fountain at Fountain Hills, Arizona, USA built at a cost of $1 500 000 for McCulloch Properties Inc. At full pressure of 26·3 kg/cm²

375 *lb/in²* and at a rate of 26 500 litres/min *5828 imp. gal/min* the 170 m *560 ft* tall column of water weighs more than 8 tonnes. The nozzle speed achieved by the three 600 hp pumps is 236 km/h *146·7 mph*.

Britain's tallest is the Emperor Fountain at Chatsworth, Bakewell, Derbys. When first tested on 1 Jun 1844, it attained the then unprecedented height of 79 m *260 ft*. Since the war it has not been played to more than 76 m *250 ft* and rarely beyond 55 m *180 ft*.

Largest fumigation ■ Carried out during the restoration of the Mission Inn complex in Riverside, California, USA on 28 Jun–1 Jul 1987 to rid the buildings of termites. It was performed by Fume Masters Inc of Riverside with over 350 tarpaulins weighing up to 160 kg *350 lb* and involved completely covering the 6500 m² *70 000 ft²* site and buildings – domes, minarets, chimneys and balconies – some of which exceeded 30 m *100 ft* in height.

Largest garbage dump ■ Reclamation Plant No. 1, Fresh Kills, Staten Island, New York, USA, opened in March 1974, is the world's largest sanitary landfill. In its first 4 months 457 000 tonnes *450 000 tons* of refuse from New York City was dumped on the site by 700 barges.

Largest gasholder ■ The gasholders at Fontaine l'Eveque, Belgium where disused mines have been adapted to store up to 500 million m³ *17 650 million ft³* of gas at ordinary pressure. Probably the largest conventional gasholder is that at Wien-Simmering, Vienna, Austria completed in 1968, with a height of 84 m *274 ²/₃ ft* and a capacity of 300 000 m³ *10·59 million ft³*.

Great Britain's are at the East Greenwich Gas Works No 2 Holder built in 1891 with an original capacity for 346 000 m³ *12 200 000 ft³*. As constructed its capacity is 252 000 m³ *8·9 million ft³* with a water tank 92 m *303 ft* in diameter and a full inflated height of 45 m *148 ft*. The No 1 holder (capacity 243 500 m³ *8·6 million ft³*) has a height of 61 m *200 ft*. The River Tees Northern Gas Board's 361 m *1186 ft* deep underground storage in use since January 1959 has a capacity of 9300 m³ *330 000 ft³*.

Largest revolving globe ■ The 21¹/₂ tonne 8·50 m *27 ft 11 in* diameter sphere in Babson College Wellesley, Massachusetts, USA was completed at a cost of $200 000 in 1956.

Longest deep-water jetty ■ The Quai Hermann

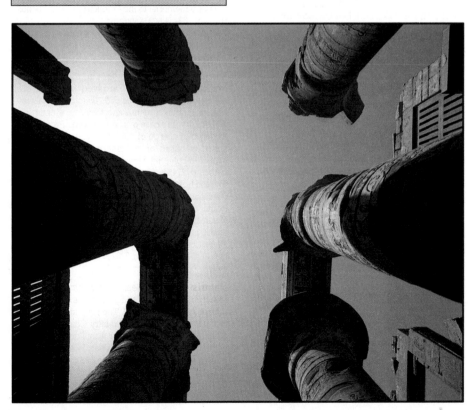

du Pasquier at Le Havre, France, with a length of 1524 m *5000 ft* is part of an enclosed basin and has a constant depth of water of 9·8 m *32 ft* on both sides.

Kitchen ■ An Indian government field kitchen set up in April 1973 at Ahmadnagar, Maharashtra a famine area, daily provided 1·2 million subsistence meals.

Tallest lamppost ■ The tallest lighting columns are the four made by Petitjean & Cie of Troyes, France and installed by Taylor Woodrow at Sultan Qaboos Sports Complex, Muscat, Oman, they stand 63·5 m *208 ft 4 in* high .

Tallest lighthouse ■ The 106 m 348 ft steel tower near Yamashita Park in Yokohama, Japan has a power of 600 000 candles and a visibility range of 32 km *20 miles*.

Bishop Rock, Isles of Scilly measures 47·8 m *156·8 ft* high to its helipad. The tallest Scottish lighthouse is the 42·3 m *139 ft* tall North Ronaldsay lighthouse, Orkney Islands.

The lights with the greatest range are those 332 m *1092 ft* above the ground on the Empire State Building, New York City, USA. Each of the four-arc mercury bulbs has a rated candlepower of 450 000 000, visible 130 km *80 miles* away on the ground and 490 km *300 miles* away from aircraft. They were switched on on 31 Mar 1956.

The lighthouse in Great Britain with the most powerful light is the shorelight at Strumble Head, near Fishguard, Dyfed, Wales It has an intensity of 6 000 000 candelas. The Irish light with the greatest intensity is Aranmore on Rinrawros Point, Co. Donegal.

Remotest lighthouse ■ Britain's is Trinity House lighthouse about 16 sea miles (18·4 statute miles *29·6 km*) off the Dyfed coast. Scotland's is Sule Skerry, 56 km *35 miles* off shore and 72 km *45 miles* northwest of Dunnet Head, Caithness and Ireland's is Blackrock, 14 km *9 miles* off the Mayo coast.

Largest marquee ■ Covering an area of 17 500 m² *188 368 ft ²* (1·7 ha *4·32 acres*) and erected by the firm of Deuter from Augsburg, West Germany, for the 1958 'Welcome Expo' in Brussels, West Belgium.

Britain's was one made by Piggot Brothers in 1951 and used by the Royal Horticultural Society at their annual show (first held in 1913) in the grounds of the Royal Hospital in Chelsea, London measuring 94 x 146 m *310 ft x 480 ft* and consisted of 30 km *18¾ miles* of 91 cm *36 in* wide canvas covering a ground area of 13 820 m² *148 800 ft ²*.

The largest single-unit tent in Britain covers a ground area of more than 12 000 m² *129 170 ft ²* and was manufactured by Clyde Canvas Ltd of Edinburgh, Scotland. Manor Marquees Ltd, of Maidstone, Kent, erected a 143 m *470 ft* long marquee in one lift on 16 May 1987.

The Offshore Europe 1983 exhibition at Bridge of Don, Aberdeenshire, Scotland was housed in 15 contiguous air tents covering 6·91 acres *28 400 m ²*.

Tallest maypole ■ The tallest reported and erected in England was one of Sitka spruce 32·12 m *105 ft 7 in* tall put up in Pelynt, Cornwall on 1 May 1974. The permanent pole at Paganhill, near Stroud, Glos, is 27·43 m *90 ft* tall.

Maze ■ The oldest datable representation of a labyrinth is that on a clay tablet from Pylos, Greece from *c.* 1200 BC.

The world's largest hedge maze is that at Longleat, near Warminster, Wilts, designed for Lord Weymouth by Greg Bright which has 2·72 km *1·69 miles* of paths flanked by 16 180 yew trees. It was opened on 6 Jun 1978 and measures 116 × 57 m *381 × 187 ft*. 'Il Labirinto' at Villa Pisani, Stra, Italy, in which Napoleon was 'lost' in 1807, had 6·4 km *4 miles* of pathways.

Menhir ■ The tallest found is the 380 tonnes Grand Menhir Brisé, now in four pieces, which originally stood 22 m *69 ft* high at Locmariaquer, Brittany, France. Recent research suggests a possible 22·8 m *75 ft* high menhir, in three pieces, weighing 250 tons also at Locmariaquer. Great Britain's tallest is one of 7·6 m *25 ft* at Rudston, Humberside.

Monuments *Tallest* ■ The stainless steel Gateway to the West Arch in St Louis, Missouri, USA, completed on 28 Oct 1965 to commemorate the westward expansion after the Lousiana Purchase of 1803 is a sweeping arch spanning 192 m *630 ft* and rising to the same height of 192 m *630 ft* and costing $29 000 000 . It was designed in 1947 by the American architect Eero Saarinen (d.1961).

Tallest column ■ Constructed from 1936–9, at a cost of $1 500 000, the tapering column which commemorates the battle of San Jacinto (21 Apr 1836), on the bank of the San Jacinto River near Houston, Texas, USA, is 173 m *570 ft* tall, 14 m *47 ft* square at the base, and 9 m *30 ft* square at the observation tower, which is surmounted by a star weighing 196·4 tons *199·6 tonnes*. It is built of concrete, and is faced with buff limestone, having a weight of 31 384 tons *31 888 tonnes*.

Great Britain's largest megalithic prehistoric monument and largest existing henge are the 11·5 ha *28½ acre* earthworks and stone circles of Avebury, Wilts, 'rediscovered' in 1646. The earliest calibrated date in the area of this Neolithic site is *c.* 4200 BC. The work is 365 m *1200 ft* in diameter with a 12 m *40 ft* ditch around the perimeter and required an estimated 15 million man-hours of work. The henge of Durrington Walls, Wilts, obliterated by road building, had a diameter of 472 m *1550 ft*. It was built from *c.* 2500 BC and required some 900 000 man-hours.

The largest trilithons exist at Stonehenge, to the south of Salisbury Plain, Wilts, with single sarsen blocks weighing over 45 tonnes and requiring over 550 men to drag them up a 9° gradient. The earliest stage of the construction of the ditch has been dated to 2800 BC. Whether Stonehenge, which required some 30 million man-years, was a lunar calendar, a temple, an eclipse-predictor or a navigation school is still debated.

The newest scheduled ancient monuments are a hexagonal pill box and 48 concrete tank traps south of Christchurch, Dorset, built in World War II and protected since 1973.

Largest artificial mound ■ The gravel mound built as a memorial to the Seleucid King Antiochus I (reigned 69–34 BC) stands on the summit of Nemrud Dagi (8205 ft *2494 m*) in south-east of Malatya, eastern Turkey. This measures 197 ft *59·8 m* tall and covers 7·5 acres *3 ha*.

Europe's is Silbury Hill, 9·7 km *6 miles* west of Marlborough, Wilts, which involved the moving of an estimated 681 000 tonnes *670 785 tons* of chalk, at a cost of 18 million man-hours to make a cone 39 m *130 ft* high with a base of 2 ha *5½ acres*. Prof. Richard Atkinson in charge of the 1968 excavations showed that it is based on an innermost central mound, similar to contemporary round barrows, and is now dated to 2745 ±185 BC. The largest long barrow in England is that inside the hill-fort at Maiden Castle near Dorchester, Dorset (see Earthwork). It originally had a length of 548 m *1800 ft* and had several enigmatic features such as a ritual pit with pottery, limpet shells and animal bones, but the date of these is not certain. The longest long barrow containing a megalithic chamber is that at West Kennet (*c.* 2200 BC), near Silbury, Wilts, measuring 117 m *385 ft* in length.

Naturist resort *Oldest and largest* ■ The oldest resort is Der Freilichtpark, Klingberg, West Germany established in 1903. The largest in area in the world is the Beau Valley Country Club, Warmbaths, South Africa extending over 4 million m² *988 acres* with up to 20 000 visitors a year. However, 100 000 people visit the smaller centre Helio-Marin at Cap d'Agde, southern France, which covers 90 ha *222 acres*. The appellation 'nudist camp' is deplored by naturists.

Largest standing obelisk (monolithic) ■ The skewer or spit (from the Gk *obeliskos,*) of Tuthmosis III brought from Aswan, Egypt by Emperor Constantius in the spring of AD 357 was repositioned in the Piazza San Giovanni in Laterane, Rome on 3 Aug 1588. Once 36 m *118·1 ft* tall, it now stands 32·81 m *107·6 ft* and weighs 455 tonnes. The unfinished obelisk, probably commissioned by Queen Hatshepsut *c.* 1490 BC, at Aswan, is 41·75 m *136·8 ft* in length and weighs 1168 tonnes.

The United Kingdom's is Cleopatra's Needle on the Embankment, London, which at 20·88 m *68 ft 5 in* is the world's 11th tallest. It weighs 186·3 tons *189·35 tonnes* and was towed up the Thames from Egypt on 21 Jan 1878 and positioned on 13 September. The longest an obelisk has remained *in situ* is that still at Heliopolis, near Cairo, erected by Senusret I *c.* 1750 BC.

Longest pier ■ The Dammam Pier, Saudi Arabia, on the Persian Gulf, with an overall length of 10·93 km *6·79 miles* was begun in July 1948 and completed on 15 Mar 1950. The area was subsequently developed by 1980 into the King Abdul Aziz Port with 39 deep-water berths. The original causeway, much widened, and the port extend for 12·8 km *7·95 miles*.

Great Britain's is the Bee Ness Jetty, completed in 1930, which stretches 2500 m *8200 ft* along the west bank of the river Medway, 5 to 8 to 9·6 km *6 miles* below Rochester, at Kingsnorth, Kent.

Largest pyramid ■ The largest pyramid, and the largest monument ever constructed, is the Quetzacóatl at Cholula de Rivadabia, 101 km *63 miles* south-east of Mexico City. It is 54 m *177 ft* tall and its base covers an area of nearly 18·2 ha *45 acres*. Its total volume has been estimated at 3 300 000 m³ *4 300 000 yd ³* compared with 2·5 million m³ *3 360 000 yd ³* for the Pyramid of Cheops (see Seven Wonders of the World). The pyramid-building era here was between the 2nd and 6th centuries AD.

Oldest pyramid ■ The Djoser step pyramid at Saqqâra, Egypt constructed by Imhotep to a height of 62 m *204 ft* originally with a Tura limestone casing *c.* 2650 BC. The largest known single block comes from the Third Pyramid (the pyramid of Mycerinus) and weighs 290 tonnes *285 tons*. The oldest New World pyramid is that on the island of La Venta in south-eastern Mexico built by the Olmec people *c.* 800 BC. It stands 30 m *100 ft* tall with a base dimension of 128 m *420 ft*.

Tallest scarecrow ■ Constructed by a team of 20 men from Ward Building Systems Ltd of Castle Howard, North Yorks measuring 27·5 m *90 ft 1 in* in height and with an arm spread of 19·8 m *65 ft* on 30 May 1988.

Snow and ice constructions ■ A snow palace 26·5 m *87 ft* high and one of four structures which spanned 214·2 m *702·7 ft* wide was unveiled on 7 Feb 1987 Asahikawa City, Hokkaido, Japan.
The world's largest ice construction is the Ice Palace built in January 1986 using 9 000 blocks of ice at St Paul, Minnesota, during the Winter Carnival. Designed by Ellerbe Associates Inc, it stood 39·24 m *128 ft 9 in* high—the equivalent of a 13-storey building.

Snowman ■ 'Super Frosty', built by a team in Anchorage, Alaska, USA led by Myron L. Ace between 20 Feb and 5 Mar 1988, stood 19·37 m *63·56 ft*.

Longest stairway ■ The service staircase for the Niesenbahn funicular rises to 2365 m *7759 ft* near Spiez, Switzerland. It has 11 674 steps and a bannister. The stone-cut T'ai Chan temple stairs of 6600 steps in the Shantung Mountains, China ascend 1428 m in 8 km *4700 ft in 5 miles*. The longest spiral staircase is one 336·2 m *1103 ft* deep with 1520 steps installed in the Mapco–White County Coal Mine, Carmi, Illinois, USA by Systems Control Inc in May 1981.

The longest stairs in Great Britain are those from the transformer gallery to the surface, 324 m *1065 ft*, in the Cruachan Power Station, Argyll, Scotland. They

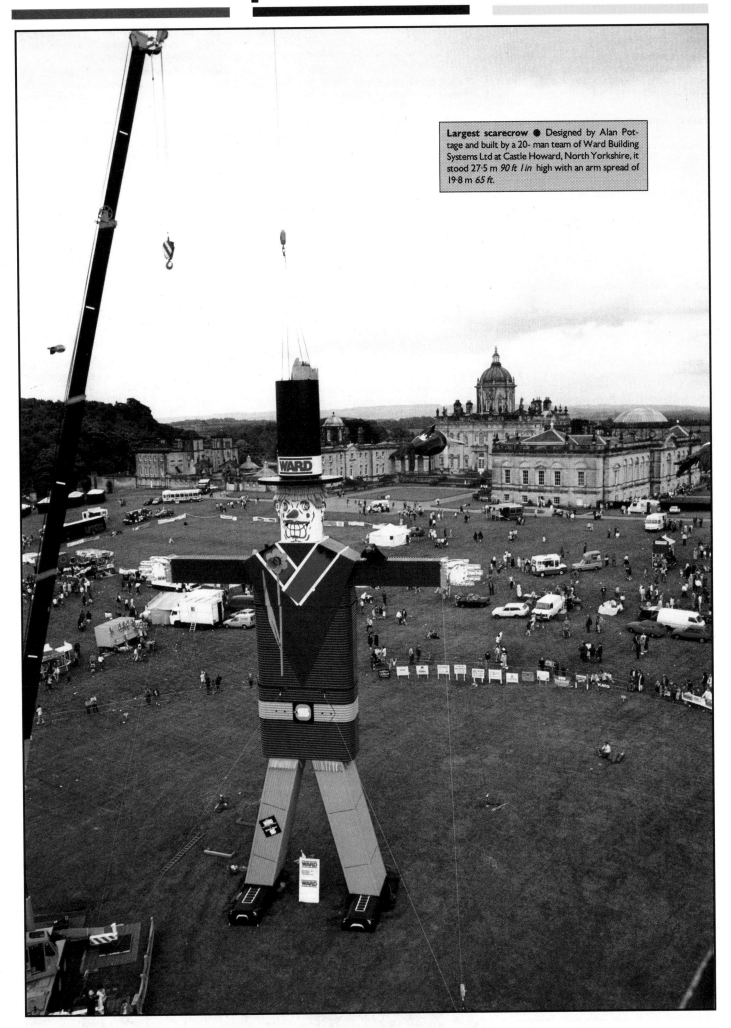

Largest scarecrow ● Designed by Alan Pottage and built by a 20- man team of Ward Building Systems Ltd at Castle Howard, North Yorkshire, it stood 27·5 m *90 ft 1 in* high with an arm spread of 19·8 m *65 ft*.

have 1420 steps and the plant's work study unit allows 27 min 41·4 sec for the ascent.

Longest statue ■ Near Bamiyan, Afghanistan there are the remains of the recumbent Sakya Buddha, built of plastered rubble, which was 'about 305 m' *1000 ft* long and is believed to date from the 3rd or 4th century AD.

Tallest statue ■ A full-figure statue, that of 'Motherland', an enormous pre-stressed concrete female figure on Mamayev Hill, outside Volgograd, USSR, designed in 1967 by Yevgeniy Vuchetich, to commemorate victory in the Battle of Stalingrad (1942–3). The statue from its base to the tip of the sword clenched in her right hand measures 82·30 m *270 ft.*

Tallest swing ■ A glider swing 9·14 m *30 ft* high was constructed by Kenneth R. Mack, Langenburg, Saskatchewan, Canada for Uncle Herb's Amusements. The swing is capable of taking its four sides 7·62 m *25 ft* off the ground.

Largest tidal river barrier ■ The Thames Barrier at Woolwich, London has 9 piers and 10 gates. There are six rising sector gates 61 m *200 ft 1 ½ in* wide and four falling radial gates 31·5 m *103 ft 4 in* wide. The site was chosen in 1971. It was opened by HM Queen on 8 May 1984.

Largest tomb ■ The Mount Li tomb, belonging to Zheng, the first Emperor of China, dates to 221 BC and is situated 40 km *25 miles* east of Xianyang. The two walls surrounding the grave measure 2173 × 974 m *7129 × 3195 ft* and 685 × 578 m *2247 × 1896 ft.* Some pits in the tomb contained an estimated 8000 life-size

SEVEN WONDERS

The Seven Wonders of the World were first designated by Antipater of Sidon in the 2nd century BC. They included the Pyramids of Giza, built by three Fourth Dynasty Egyptian Pharaohs, Khwfw (Khufu or Cheops), Kha-f-Ra (Khafre, Khefren or Chepren) and Menkaure (Mycerinus) near El Giza (El Gizeh), south-west of El Qâhira (Cairo) in Egypt.

THE GREAT PYRAMID

The 'Horizon of Khufu' was finished under Rededef *c.* 2580 BC. Its original height was 146·5 m *480 ft 11 in* (now, since the loss of its topmost stones and the pyramidion, reduced to 137 m *449 ft 6 in*) with a base line of 230 m *756 ft* and thus covering slightly more than 5 ha *13 acres.* It has been estimated that a permanent work force of 4000 required 30 years to manoeuvre into position the 2 300 000 limestone blocks averaging 2 ½ tonnes each, totalling about 5 840 000 tonnes and a volume of 2 568 000m³ *90 700 000 ft³.* Some blocks weigh 15 tons. A costing exercise published in December 1974 indicated that it would require 405 men 6 years at a cost of $1·13 billion.

FRAGMENT REMAINS OF:

The Temple of Artemis (Diana) of the Ephesians, built *c.* 350 BC at Ephesus, Turkey (destroyed by the Goths in AD 262); The Tomb of King Mausolus of Caria, at Halicarnassus, now Bodrum, Turkey, *c.* 325 BC.

NO TRACE REMAINS OF:

The Hanging Gardens of Semiramis, at Babylon, Iraq *c.* 600 BC; The statue of Zeus (Jupiter), by Phidias (5th century BC) at Olympia, Greece (lost in a fire at Istanbul) in marble, gold and ivory and 12 m *40 ft* tall ; The figure of the god Helios (Apollo), the 35 m *117 ft* tall statue by Chares of Lindus called the Colossus of Rhodes (sculptured 292–280 BC, destroyed by an earthquake in 224 BC;

The 122 m *400 ft* tall world's earliest lighthouse, built by Sostratus of Cnidus (*c.* 270 BC) as a pyra-midically-shaped tower of white marble (destroyed by earthquake in AD 1375), on the island of Pharos (Greek, pharos =lighthouse), off the coast of El Iskandariya (Alexandria), Egypt.

terracotta soldiers. A tomb housing 180 000 Second World War dead on Okinawa, Japan was enlarged in 1985 to accommodate another 9 000 bodies thought to be buried on the island.

Tallest totem pole ■ A 52·73 m *173 ft* tall pole was raised on 6 Jun 1973 at Alert Bay, British Columbia, Canada. It tells the story of the Kwakiutl and took 36 man-weeks to carve.

Largest vats ■ 'Strongbow', used by H.P. Bulmer Ltd, the English cider makers of Hereford, measures 19·65 m *64 ½ ft* in height and 23·0 m *75 ½ ft* in diameter with a capacity of 74 099 hl *1 630 000 gallons.*

The largest wooden wine cask in the world is the Heidelberg Tun, completed in 1751, in the cellar of the Friedrichsbau Heidelberg, West Germany. Its capacity is 1855 hl *40 790 gal.*

Oldest ■ The world's oldest is that in use since 1715 at Hugel et Fils (founded 1639) Riquewihr, Haut-Rhin by the most recent of the 12 generations of the family.

Longest wall ■ The Great Wall of China has a main-line length of 3460 km *2150 miles* – nearly three times the length of Britain. Completed during the reign of Ch'in Shih Huang-ti (221–210 BC), it has a further 2860 km *1780 miles* of branches and spurs. Its height varies from 4·5 m–12 m *15–39 ft* and it is up to 9·8 m *32 ft* thick. It runs from Shanhaikuan, on, the Gulf of Pohai, to Yumenkuan and Yang-kuan and was kept in repair up to the 16th century. Some 51·5 km *32 miles* have been destroyed since 1966 and part was blown up to make way for a dam in July 1979. On 6 Mar 1985 a report from China stated that a five-year-long survey proved that the total length had been 9980 km *6200 miles.*

The longest of the Roman walls in Britain was the 4 5–6 m *15–20 ft* tall Hadrian's Wall, built AD 122–126. It crossed the Tyne-Solway isthmus for 118 km *73 ½ miles* from Bowness-on-Solway, Cumbria, to Wallsend-on-Tyne, Tyne and Wear, being abandoned in AD 383.

Water tower ■ The Union at New Jersey, USA built

> **Largest vat** ● The Heidelberg Tun wooden wine cask is the largest in the world, with a capacity of 1855 hl *40 790 gal.* (Photo: Edmond von Konig).

in 1965, rises to a height of 64 m *210 ft* with a capacity of 9462 hl *250 000 gal.* It is owned and operated by the Elizabethtown Water Company.

Largest waterwheel ■ The Mohammadieh Noria wheel at Hamah, Syria has a diameter of 40 m *131 ft* and dates from Roman times. The Lady Isabella wheel at Laxey, Isle of Man was built for drainage. Completed on 27 Sep 1854 it has been disused since 1929 and has a circumference of 69 m *228 ft,* a diameter of 22 m *72 ½ ft* with an axle weighing 9 tonnes. Britain's largest working wheel is that of 15·36 m *50 ft 5 in* diameter built in 1870 at Caernarfon, Gwynedd, Wales. It worked until 1925, is 1·52 m *5 ft* in width and can be seen at the Welsh Slate Museum, Dinorwic, Llanberis, Gwynedd.

Largest window ■ The largest sheet of glass ever manufactured was one of 50 m² *538·2 ft²,* or 20 m *65 ft 7 in* by 2·5 m *8 ft 2 ¼ in,* exhibited by the Saint Gobin Company in France at the *Journées Internationales de Miroiterie* in March 1958. The largest single windows in the world are those in the Palace of Industry and Technology at Rondpoint de la Défense, Paris, France with an extreme width of 218 m *715·2 ft* and a maximum height of 50 m *164 ft.* The record for Pilkington of St Helens, Merseyside is a sheet of 2·5 × 15·2 m *8 ft 2 ¼ × 49 ft 10 ½ in* made for the Festival of Britain in 1951.

Largest wine cellar ■ The cellars at Paarl, those of the Ko-operative Wijnbouwers Vereeniging, known as KWV, near Cape Town, in the centre of the wine-growing district of South Africa, cover an area of 10 ha *25 acres* and have a capacity of 136 million litres *30 million gal.* The Cienega Winery of the Almaden Vineyards in Hollister, California, USA covers 1·6 ha *4 acres* and can house 37 300 oak barrels containing 1·83 million gallons of wine.

Largest ziggurat ■ The largest (from the Assyrian *ziqqurati,* summit, height) ever built was by the Elamite King Untash *c.* 1250 BC. known as the Ziggurat of Choga Zanbil, 30 km *18·6 miles* from Haft Tepe, Iran. The outer base was 105 × 105 m *344 ft* and the fifth 'box' 28 × 28 m *91·8 ft* nearly 50 m *164 ft* above. The largest surviving is the Ziggurat of Ur (now Muquyyar, Iraq) with a base 61 × 45·7 m *200 × 150 ft* built in the reign of Ur-nammu (*c.* 2113:2096 BC) to three storeys surmounted by a summit temple. The first and part of the second storeys now survive to a height of 18 m *60 ft .*

CHAPTER 6

Largest bus fleet
Of the London fleet of 5 100 buses, 4 550 are double deckers. Here they are seen displaying their characteristic flocking behaviour which is believed to be protection against predators. (Photo: John Freeman/Impact Photos).

Ships

Ships

EARLIEST SEA-GOING BOATS

Aborigines are thought to have been able to cross the Torres Strait from New Guinea to Australia, then at least 70 km *43½ miles* across, at least as early as 40 000 BC. They are believed to have used double canoes. The earliest *surviving* 'vessel' is a pinewood dug-out found in Pesse, Netherlands and dated to *c.* 6315 ±275 BC and now in the Provincial Museum, Assen. The earliest representation of a boat is disputed between possible rock art outlines of Mesolithic skin-boats in Høgnipen, Norway (*c.* 8000–7000 BC); Minateda, Spain (7000–3000 BC) and Kobystan, USSR (8000–6000 BC). A 45 cm *18 in* long paddle was found at the Star Carr, North Yorks site, described in 1948. It has been dated to *c.* 7600 BC and is now in the Cambridge Museum of Archaeology.

The oldest surviving boat is a 8·2 m *27ft* long 0·76 m *2½ ft* wide wooden eel-catching canoe discovered at Tybrind Vig on the Baltic Island of Fünen which is dated to *c.* 4490 BC.

The oldest surviving prehistoric boat in Britain was found in 1984 on Hasholme Hall Farm, Holme-on-Spalding Moor, North Humberside. It is 2300 years old and is 147·63 m *45 ft* long. It will require special conservation until the late 1990s.

The oldest shipwreck ever found is one of a Cycladic trading vessel located off the islet of Dhókós, near the Greek island of Hydra, reported in May 1975 and dated to 2450 BC ±250.

A wreck about 2400 years old is currently being excavated in the crater of a live volcano off the northern coast of Sicily. The cargo includes large quantities of classic Greek pottery.

Earliest power ■ Propulsion by steam engine was first achieved when in 1783 the Marquis Jouffroy d'Abbans (1751–1832) ascended a reach of the river Saône near Lyon, France, in the 180-tonne paddle steamer *Pyroscaphe*.

The tug *Charlotte Dundas* was the first successful power-driven vessel. She was a stern paddle-wheel steamer built for the Forth and Clyde Canal, Scotland in 1801–2 by William Symington (1763–1831), using a double-acting condensing engine constructed by James Watt (1736–1819). The screw propeller was invented and patented by a Kent farmer, Sir Francis Pettit Smith (1808–71) on 31 May 1836 (Brit. Pat. No 7104).

The world's oldest active steam ship is the paddle steamer *Skibladner*, which has plied Lake Mjøsa, Norway since 1856. She was built in Motala, Sweden and has had two major refits.

Oldest vessel ■ The training ship *Foudroyant*, for many years a familiar sight lying at her moorings in Portsmouth Harbour, was built, of teak, at Bombay in 1817 as HMS *Trincomalee*. In use as seamanship training ship since 1897, the *Foudroyant* was towed from Portsmouth, Hants to West Hartlepool, Tyne and Wear in 1987 to undergo repairs and restoration as a typical naval frigate of the Nelson era.

Earliest turbine ■ The *Turbinia*, built in 1894 at Wallsend-on-Tyne, Tyne and Wear, to the design of the Hon. Sir Charles Parsons OM, KCB (1854–1931), was 30·48 m *100 ft* long and of 45·2 tonnes *44½ tons* displacement with machinery consisting of three steam turbines totalling about 2000 shaft horsepower. At her first public demonstration in 1897 she reached 34·5 knots (*63·9 km/h*) and is now preserved at Newcastle-upon-Tyne.

WARSHIPS

Largest battleships ■ The 270·6 m *887 ¾ ft* long USS *New Jersey* with a full load displacement of 58 000 tonnes. was the last fire support ship on active service off the Lebanon coast with her nine 16-in guns from 14 Dec 1983 to 26 Feb 1984. The $405-million refit of USS *Iowa* was completed in May 1984. USS *Missouri* and USS *Wisconsin* were recommis-

sioned in 1986 and 1988 respectively. The 16-inch projectiles of 1225 kg *2700 lb* can be fired 39 km *23 miles*.

The Japanese battleships *Yamato* (completed on 16 Dec 1941 and sunk south-west of Kyūshū, Japan, by US planes on 7 Apr 1945) and *Musashi* (sunk in the Philippine Sea by 11 bombs and 16 torpedoes on 24 Oct 1944) were the largest battleships ever commissioned, each with a full load displacement of 72 809 tons *73 977 tonnes*. With an overall length of 263 m *863 ft*, a beam of 38·7 m *127 ft* and a full load draught of 10·8 m *35½ ft* they mounted nine 460 mm *18·1 in* guns in three triple turrets. Each gun weighed 164·6 tonnes *162 tons* and was 22·8 m *75 ft* in length firing a 1451 kg *3200 lb* projectile.
Britain's largest ever and last battleship was HMS *Vanguard* (1944–1960) with a full load displacement of 52 245 tonnes *51 420 tons* and an overall length of 248·1 m *814 ft*. She mounted eight 38 cm *15 in* guns.

Smallest Royal Navy warship ■ The *Attacker* Class Fast Patrol boats, built by Allday in 1983/4, have an overall length of 20 m *65·6 ft* and a displacement of 34 tonnes. HMS *Attacker*, one of five of these vessels, is operated by students of the Universities of Glasgow and Strathclyde for training. Under her commander, Lt Commander A. G. C. Black, she visited a total of 24 ports in the Clyde Estuary between 10 a.m. on 11 Nov 1988 and 11 a.m. on 12 Nov.

Earliest Surviving 'Ironclad' ■ HMS *Warrior*, open to the public at Portsmouth, Hants, in her restored state since 1987, was built on the Thames at Blackwall in 1860. Constructed of iron and teak, she was powered by a 932 kW *1 250 hp* steam engine as well as a full rig of sails. After her withdrawal from service the *Warrior* performed various static roles, latterly spending 50 years as an oil depot pontoon at Milford Haven. She was presented to the Maritime Trust in 1978. After the completion of extensive restoration work she was towed to Portsmouth.

Guns and armour ■ The largest guns ever mounted in any of HM ships were the 45 cm *18 in* pieces in the light battle cruiser (later aircraft carrier) HMS *Furious* in 1917. In 1918 they were transferred to the monitors HMS *Lord Clive* and *General Wolfe*. The thickest armour ever carried was in HMS *Inflexible* (completed 1881), measuring 60 cm *24 in* backed by teak up to a maximum thickness of 106·6 cm *42 in*.

Fastest warship ■ The hovercraft, the 23·7 m *78 ft* long 100 tonne US Navy test vehicle SES-100B achieved a speed of 91·9 knots *105·8 mph*. (see p. 109).

Fastest destroyer ■ The highest speed attained by a destroyer was 45·25 knots (*83·42 km/h*) by the 2830 tonne French destroyer *Le Terrible* in 1935. She was built in Blainville, France and powered by four Yarrow small tube boilers and two Rateau geared turbines giving 100 000 SHP. She was removed from the active list at the end of 1957.

AIRCRAFT CARRIERS

Largest ■ The warships with the largest full load displacement in the world are the Nimitz class US Navy aircraft carriers USS *Nimitz, Dwight D. Eisenhower, Carl Vinson, Theodore Roosevelt* and *Abraham Lincoln* at 91 487 tons. They are 322·9 m *1092 ft* in length overall with 1·82 ha *4½ acres* of flight deck and have a speed well in excess of 30 knots *56 km/h* from their 4 nuclear-powered 260 000 shp geared steam turbines. They have to be refuelled after about 1 450 000 km *900 000 miles* steaming. Their complement is 5684. The total cost of the *Abraham Lincoln*, laid down at Newport News on 3 Nov 1984, will exceed, together with the *George Washington*, $3 ¼ billion, excluding the 90-plus aircraft carried. USS *Enterprise* is, at, 335·8 m *1102 ft* still the longest warship ever built.

The Royal Navy's largest fighting ship is aircraft carrier HMS *Ark Royal*, commissioned 1 Nov 1985. She has a 167·6 m *550 ft* long flight deck and is

209·3 m *685·8 ft* long overall, and has a top speed of 28 knots being powered by 4 Rolls Royce Olympus TM3B gas turbines delivering 94 000 shp.

Most landings ■ The greatest number on an aircraft carrier in one day was 602 achieved by Marine Air Group 6 of the United States Pacific Fleet Air Force aboard the USS *Matanikau* on 25 May 1945 between 8 a.m. and 5 p.m.

SUBMARINES

Largest ■ The world's largest submarines are of the USSR Typhoon class. The launch of the first at the secret covered shipyard at Severodvinsk in the White Sea, USSR was announced by NATO on 23 Sep 1980. They are believed to have a dived displacement of 25 000 tonnes, measure 170 m *557·6 ft* overall and be armed with twenty SS NX 20 missiles with a 4800 nautical mile *8895 km* range, each with seven warheads. By late 1987 two others built in Leningrad, USSR were operational, each deploying 140 warheads.

The largest submarines ever built for the Royal Navy are the four atomic-powered nuclear missiles *Resolution, Repulse, Renown* and *Revenge* R class boats with a surface displacement of 7620 tonnes *7500 tons* and 8534 tonnes *8400 tons* submerged, a length of 129·5 m *425 ft*, a beam of 10 m *33 ft* and a draught of 9·1 m *30 ft*. The longest submarine patrol ever spent dived and unsupported is 111 days by H M Submarine *Warspite* (Cdr J. G. F. Cooke RN) in the South Atlantic from 25 Nov 1982 to 15 Mar 1983. She sailed 30 804 nautical miles *57 085 km*.

Fastest ■ The Russian Alfa-class nuclear-powered submarines have a reported maximum speed of 42 knots *77·8 km/h* plus. With use of titanium alloy they are believed to be able to dive to 762 m *2500 ft*. A US spy satellite over Leningrad's naval yard on 8 Jun 1983 showed they were being lengthened and are now 79·3 m *260·1 ft* long.

Deepest ■ The two USN vessels able to descend 3650 m *12 000 ft* are the 3-man *Trieste II* (DSV I) of 303 tons (recommissioned in November 1973) and the DSV 2 (deep submergence vessel) USS *Alvin*. The *Trieste II* was reconstructed from the record-breaking bathyscaphe *Trieste* but without the Krupp-built sphere, which enabled it to descend to 10 917 m *35 820 ft*. (See Chapter 3, Greatest ocean descent.)

PASSENGER LINERS

Largest ■ By tonnage is the 73 192 grt Norwegian cruise ship *Sovereign of the Seas*. Built at the French shipyard Chantiers de l'Atlantique at St Nazaire, she entered service from Miami in January 1988.

Britain's largest liner is RMS *Queen Elizabeth 2* at 67 139·94 gross tons, with an overall length of 293 m *963 ft*, completed for Cunard Line in 1968. She set a 'turn round' record of 5 hr 47 min at New York City, USA on 21 Nov 1983. Her original steam turbines were replaced with diesel electric units in 1987.

Longest ■ The *Norway* of 70 202 grt and 315 66 m *1035 ft 7½ in* in overall length with a capacity of 2400 passengers. She was built as the *France* in 1961 and renamed after purchase in June 1979 by Knut Kloster of Norway. Her second maiden voyage was from Southampton, Hants on 7 May 1980.
The RMS *Queen Elizabeth* (finally 82 998 but formerly 83 673 gross tons), of the Cunard fleet, was the largest passenger vessel ever built and had the largest displacement of any liner in the world. She had an overall length of 314 m *1031 ft*, was 36 m *118 ft 7 in* in breadth and was powered by steam turbines which developed 168 000 hp. Her last passenger voyage ended on 15 Nov 1968. In 1970 she was removed to Hong Kong to serve as a floating marine university and renamed *Seawise University*. She was burnt out on 9 Jan 1972 when three *simultaneous* outbreaks of fire strongly pointed to arson. The gutted hull had been cut up and removed by 1978. *Seawise* was a pun on the owner's initials — C. Y. Tung (1911–82).

MARINE CIRCUMNAVIGATION RECORDS

(Compiled by Nobby´Clarke and Richard Boehmer)

A true circumnavigation entails passing through two antipodal points which are at least 20 000 km *12 429 statute miles* apart. A non-stop circumnavigation is entirely self-maintained; no water supplies, provisions, equipment or replacements of any sort may be taken aboard en route. Vessel may anchor, but no physical help may be accepted apart from passing mail or messages.

CATEGORY	VESSEL	NAME/SKIPPER	START	FINISH
EARLIEST	*Vittoria* Expedition of Fernão de Magalhães, c. 1480–k. 1521	Juan Sebastián de Elcano or del Cano (d. 1526) and 17 crew	Seville, Spain 20 Sep 1519	San Lucar 6 Sep 1522 49 400 km *30 700 miles*
EARLIEST BRITISH	*Golden Hind* (ex *Pelican*) 100 tons	Francis Drake (c. 1540–96) (Knighted 4 Apr 1581)	Plymouth 13 Dec 1577	26 Sep 1580
EARLIEST WOMAN	*Etoile* (Storeship for Bougainville's La Boudeuse)	Crypto-female valet of M. de Commerson, named Jeanne Baret	St Malo 1766	1769 (revealed as female on Hawaii)
EARLIEST FORE-AND-AFT RIGGED VESSEL	*Union* 98 tons (Sloop)	John Boit Junior, aged 19–21, (US) and 22 crew	Newport, RI 1794 (via Cape Horn westabout)	Newport, RI 1796
EARLIEST YACHT	*Nancy Dawson* (Schooner)	Robert Shedden (British) and crew (died in Mexico, 1849)	Thames 1847	Thames 1850
EARLIEST YACHT OWNERS	*Sunbeam* 51·8 m *170 ft* 3-masted Topsail schooner	Lord and Lady Brassey (British), passengers and crew	Cowes, Isle of Wight 1876	Cowes, Isle of Wight 1877
EARLIEST SOLO	*Spray* 11·2 m *36 ¾ ft* Gaff yawl	Capt Joshua Slocum, 51, (US) (a non-swimmer)	Newport, RI, via Magellan Straits 24 Apr 1895	3 Jul 1898 74 000 km *46 000 miles* (100 mpd)
EARLIEST TRIMARAN	*Victress* 12·19 m *40 ft* Bermudan ketch	Nigel Tetley (British) (b. South Africa)	Plymouth 1968 (W–E via Cape Horn)	1969 (trimaran sank after circumnavigation was completed)
EARLIEST SOLO CATAMARAN	*Amon-Re* 7·97 m *26 ft 2 in* Bermudan sloop	Alan Butler (Canada)	Barbados 1980 (E–W via Panama)	Barbados 1986 (also smallest catamaran to circumnavigate)
EARLIEST MOTOR BOAT	*Speejacks* 29·87 m *98 ft*	Albert Y. Gowen (US) wife and crew	New York City 1921	New York City 1922
EARLIEST SOLO MOTOR BOAT	*Mabel E. Holland* 12·8 m *42 ft* (no sails)	David Scott Cowper (British)	Plymouth 1984 (via Panama Canal)	Plymouth 170 days 2 hr 15 min (165·7 mpd)
EARLIEST WOMAN SOLO	*Mazurek* 9·5 m *31 ft 2 in* Bermudan sloop	Krystyna Chojnowska-Liskiewicz (Polish)	Las Palmas 28 Mar 1976 (westabout via Panama)	Tied knot 21 Mar 1978
EARLIEST NON-STOP SOLO Port to Port	*Suhaili* 9·87 m *32·4 ft* Bermudan ketch	Robin Knox Johnston CBE	Falmouth 14 Jun 1968	22 Apr 1969 (312 days)
EARLIEST WOMAN NON-STOP SOLO	*First Lady* 11·24 m *37 ft* Bermudan sloop	Kay Cottee (Australian)	Sydney 1987 (W–E via Cape Horn)	Sydney 1988 (approx 127 mpd)
MOST NON-STOP SOLO CIRCUMNAVIGATIONS	*Parry Endeavour* 13·92 m *44 ft* Bermudan sloop	Jon Sanders (Australian)	Fremantle 25 May 1986	Fremantle 13 Mar 1988 (3 circumnavigations in 657 days)
SMALLEST BOAT	*Acrohc Australis* 3·6 m *11 ft 10 in* Bermudan sloop	Serge Testa (Australian)	Brisbane 1984	Brisbane 1987 (500 sailing days)
EARLIEST SOLO KNIGHT	*Glory* 6 m *19 ft 8 in* Junk sloop	Sir Henry Pigott Bt	Poole June 1983	Poole Feb 1986
EARLIEST SUBMERGED	*Triton* US Submarine	Capt Edward L. Beach USN plus 182 crew	New London, Connecticut 16 Feb 1960	10 May 1960 49 422 km *39 708 miles*
EARLIEST SOLO IN BOTH DIRECTIONS	*Solitaire* 10·36 m *34 ft* Bermudan sloop	Leslie Thomas Powles (British)	Falmouth 1975 (E–W) Lymington 1980 (W–E)	(via Panama) Lymington 1978 (via Cape Horn) Lymington 1981
EARLIEST SOLO IN BOTH DIRECTIONS (via Cape Horn)	*Ocean Bound* 12·52 m *41 ft 1 in* Bermudan sloop	David Scott Cowper (British)	Plymouth 1979 (W–E) Plymouth 1981 (E–W)	Plymouth 1980 Plymouth 1982
EARLIEST SOLO ROUND THREE TIMES (same yacht)	*Tarmin* 7·5 m *24 ft 7 in* Bermudan sloop	John Sowden (US)	Various ports 1966, 1974, 1983	1970, 1977, 1986
MOST SOLO CIRCUMNAVIGATIONS	*Perie Banou* 10·24 m *33 ft 7 in* and *Parry Endeavour* (see above)	Jon Sanders (Australian)	Fremantle 1981 Fremantle 1986	Fremantle 1982 (twice) Fremantle 1988 (thrice)
MOST CIRCUMNAVIGATIONS ALONE BY HUSBAND/WIFE	*Myonie* 11 m *36 ft* Gaff ketch	Al Gehrman (US), Helen (wife) (no passengers or crew)	Florida 1961, 1966, 1972, 1979	Florida 1964, 1970, 1976, 1983
FASTEST SAIL NON-STOP W–E Solo in monohull	*American Promise* 18·3 m *60 ft* cutter	Dodge Morgan (US)	Bermuda 12 Nov 1985	Bermuda (via 5 capes) 11 Apr 1986 150 days 1 hr 6 min (171·1 mpd ave.)
FASTEST SAIL WITH STOPS E–W Solo in monohull	*Ocean Bound* 12·52 m *41 ft 1 in* Bermudan sloop	David Scott Cowper (British)	Plymouth 22 Sep 1981	Plymouth (via 5 capes with 3 stops) 17 May 1982 221 days + 16 days in port
FASTEST SAIL WITH STOP W–E Clippership	*James Baines* 81·1 m *266 ft* 3-masted ship	Charles McDonnell (British)	Liverpool 10 Dec 1854	Liverpool (via Melbourne) 20 May 1855 127 days + 28 days in port + 5 days under tow
FASTEST SAIL WITH STOPS W–E Solo in monohull	*Crédit Agricole (III)* 18·3 m *60 ft* ULDB cutter	Philippe Jeantot (French)	Newport, RI (BOC) 30 Aug 1986	Newport, RI (3 stops) 7 May 1987 134 d 5 h 23 m 56 s + 115 d 17 h 26 m in port
FASTEST SAIL WITH STOPS W–E Non-solo in monohull	*UBS Switzerland* 24·4 m *80 ft* IOR sloop	Pierre Fehlmann (Swiss)	Portsmouth (WRWR) 28 Sep 1985	Portsmouth (3 stops) 9 May 1986 117 d 14 h 31 m 42 s + 105 d 5 h 49 m 58 s in port
FASTEST SAIL WITH STOPS W–E Solo in multihull	*Kriter Brut de Brut* 23·5 m *77 ft* trimaran	Philippe Monnet (French)	Brest, France 10 Dec 1986	Brest, France (3 stops) 19 Apr 1987 127 d 12 h 11 m + 2 d 7 h 6 m in Cape Town

* Eduard Roditi, author of *Magellan of the Pacific*, advances the view that Magellan's slave, Enrique, was the first circumnavigator. He had been purchased in Malacca and it was shown that he already understood the Filipino dialect Vizayan, when he reached the Philippines from the east. He 'tied the knot' off Limasawa on 28 Mar 1521. The first to circumnavigate in both directions was Capt Tobias Furneaux, RN (1735–81) as second lieutenant aboard the *Dolphin* from/to Plymouth east to west via the Magellan Straits from 1766–68 and as captain of the *Adventure* from/to Plymouth west to east via Cape Horn in 1772–4. ULDB = Ultra-light displacement boat. BOC = British Oxygen Corp. Challenge Around Alone Race. WRWR = Whitbread Round World Race. All mileages are nautical miles.

TRANS-ATLANTIC MARINE RECORDS

(Compiled by Nobby Clarke and Richard Boehmer)

CATEGORY	VESSEL	NAME/SKIPPER	START	FINISH	DURATION	DATE
EARLIEST CRUISE	Lively 140-ton Brig	Shuttleworth (British) guests + 25 crew	UK Hudson Bay	Florida UK	420 days	1783–4
EARLIEST SOLO SAILING E–W	15-ton Gaff sloop	Josiah Shackford (US)	Bordeaux, France	Suriñam (Guiana)	35 days	1786
EARLIEST ROWING	Ship's boat c. 6·1 m 20 ft	John Brown & 5 British deserters from garrison	St Helena (10 Jun)	Belmonte, Brazil (fastest ever row)	28 days (83 mpd)	1799
EARLIEST CROSSING (2 men)	Charter Oak 13·1 m 43 ft	C. R. Webb & 1 crew (US)	New York	Liverpool	35 days 15 hr	1857
EARLIEST TRIMARAN (Raft)	Non Pareil 7·62 m 25 ft	John Mikes & 2 crew (US)	New York	Southampton	51 days	1868
EARLIEST SOLO SAILING W–E	Centennial 6·09 m 20 ft	Alfred Johnson (US)	Glos., Mass.	Wales	46 days	1876
EARLIEST WOMAN (with US husband)	New Bedford 6·09 m 20 ft (Bermudan ketch)	Mrs Joanna Crapo (b. Scotland) (Thomas Crapo)	Chatham, Mass.	Newlyn, Cornwall	51 days (Earliest with Bermudan rig)	1877
EARLIEST SINGLE-HANDED RACE	Sea Serpent 4·57 m 15 ft	J. W. Lawlor (US) (winner)	Boston (21 Jun)	Coverack, Cornwall	45 days	1891
EARLIEST ROWING BY 2 MEN (fastest 2-crew)	Fox 5·58 m 18½ ft	Georg Harboe & Frank Samuelsen (Norwegian)	New York (6 Jun)	Isles of Scilly (1 Aug)	55 days (56 mpd) (see solo rows)	1897
EARLIEST MOTOR-BOAT	Abiel Abbott Low 11·58 m 38 ft (Engine: 10hp kerosene)	William C. Newman (US) Edward (son)	New York	Falmouth	36 days (83·3 mpd)	1902
EARLIEST OUTBOARD	Trans-Atlantic 7·92 m 26 ft (2·65 hp Evinrudes)	Al Grover (US) Dante (son)	St Pierre, NF (via Azores)	Lisbon	34 days (88 mpd approx)	1985
EARLIEST CANOE (with sail)	Deutscher Sport 6·55 m 21½ ft	Franz Romer (German)	Las Palmas	St Thomas	58 days (47 mpd)	1928
EARLIEST WOMAN SOLO E–W	Felicity Ann 7·01 m 23 ft	Ann Davison (British)	Portsmouth Las Palmas	Dominica (20 Nov 1952)	65 days	1952–3
EARLIEST WOMAN SOLO W–E	Lugger 5·5 m 18 ft	Gladys Gradeley (US)	Nova Scotia	Hope Cove, Devon	60 days	1903
EARLIEST WOMAN SOLO (both directions)	Ultima Ratio 10·67 m 35 ft (trimaran)	Ingeborg von Heister (German)	Las Palmas Bermuda	Barbados Gibraltar	33 days 46 days	1969 1970
EARLIEST WOMAN SOLO (across 2 oceans)	Zama Zulu 13·1 m 43 ft (ferroconcrete hull)	Anna Woolf (South African)	Cape Town	Bowling, Scotland	8920 miles in 109 days	1976
SMALLEST W–E	God's Tear 2·71 m 8 ft 11 in	Wayne Dickinson (US)	Allerton, Mass. (30 Oct)	Aranmore Is. NW Ireland (20 Mar)	142 days	1982–3
SMALLEST E–W (Southern)	Toniky-Nou 1·79 m 5 ft 10½ in (barrel)	Eric Peters (British)	Las Palmas (25 Dec)	St Francoise, Guadeloupe (8 Feb)	46 days	1982–3
OLDEST SOLO ROWING	Khaggavisana 6·02 m 19¾ ft	Sidney Genders (51 years) (British)	Penzance, Cornwall	Miami, Florida via Antigua	160 days 8 hr	1970
YOUNGEST SOLO ROWING	Finn Again 6·25 m 20 ft 6 in	Sean Crowley (25 years 306 days) (British)	Halifax, NS (17 Jun)	Co. Galway (21 Sep)	95 days 22 hr	1988
EARLIEST ROW BOTH DIRECTIONS	QE III 5·87 m 19 ft 10 in	Don Allum (British)	Canaries St John's, NF	Nevis Ireland	114 days 77 days	1986 1987
EARLIEST SOLO ROWING E–W	Britannia 6·70 m 22 ft	John Fairfax (British)	Las Palmas (20 Jan)	Ft Lauderdale, Florida (19 Jul)	180 days	1969
EARLIEST SOLO ROWING W–E	Super Silver 6·1 m 20 ft	Tom McClean (Irish)	St John's, NF	Black Sod Bay, Ireland (27 Jul)	70·7 days	1969
YOUNGEST SOLO SAILING	Sea Raider 10·67 m 35 ft	David Sandeman (British) (17 years 176 days)	Jersey, CI	Newport, RI	43 days	1976
OLDEST SOLO SAILING	Tawny Pipit 7·62 m 25 ft	Stefan Szwarnowski (British) (75 years 182 days)	Southampton (7 Jun)	New Jersey (30 Aug)	84 days	1988
SMALLEST RAFT	L'Egaré 5·2 m 17 ft (Cedar logs)	Henri Beaudout (French) & 2 crew	Halifax, NS	Falmouth	87 days	1956
FASTEST SAIL W–E Clippership	Red Jacket 76·5 m 251 ft 3-masted ship	Asa Eldridge (US)	Sandy Hook, NJ 11 Jan 1854	Liverpool Bar 23 Jan 1854	12 days (approx 275 mpd ave.)	1854
FASTEST SAIL W–E Non-solo in monohull	Phocea 74·0 m 243 ft ULDB schooner	Philippe Morinay (French)	Ambrose Light Tower 26 Jun 1988	Lizard Lighthouse 3 Jul 1988	8 days 3 hr 29 min (368·3 mpd ave.)	1988
FASTEST SAIL W–E Solo in multihull	Ericsson 22·6 m 74 ft catamaran	Bruno Peyron (French)	Ambrose Light Tower 7 Apr 1987	Lizard Lighthouse 19 Apr 1987	11 days 11 hr 4 min (261·8 mpd ave.)	1987
FASTEST SAIL W–E Non-solo in multihull	Jet Services 5 22·9 m 75 ft catamaran	Serge Madec (French)	Ambrose Light Tower 24 May 1988	Lizard Lighthouse 31 May 1988	7 days 6 hr 30 min (412·6 mpd ave.)	1988
FASTEST SAIL E–W Clippership	Andrew Jackson 67·1 m 220 ft 3-masted ship	W.S. Johnson (US)	Liverpool 3 Nov 1860	New York 18 Nov 1860	15 days (approx 210 mpd ave.)	1860
FASTEST SAIL E–W Solo in monohull	Thursday's Child 18·3 m 60 ft ULDB cutter	Warren Luhrs (US)	Plymouth (STAR) 2 Jun 1984	Newport, RI 19 Jun 1984	16 days 22 hr 27 min (171·2 mpd ave.)	1984
FASTEST SAIL E–W Non-solo in monohull	Faram Serenissima 20·3 m 67 ft ULDB sloop	Bruno Bacilieri (Italian)	Plymouth (2STAR) 6 Jun 1981	Newport, RI 22 Jun 1981	16 days 1 hr 25 min (180·6 mpd ave.)	1981
FASTEST SAIL E–W Solo in multihull	Fleury Michon (IX) 18·3 m 60 ft trimaran	Philippe Poupon (French)	Plymouth (STAR) 5 Jun 1988	Newport, RI 15 Jun 1988	10 days 9 hr 15 min 9 sec (279·2 mpd ave.)	1988
FASTEST SAIL E–W Non-solo in multihull	Royale (II) 25·9 m 85 ft catamaran	Loic Caradec (French)	Plymouth (2STAR) 8 Jun 1986	Newport, RI 21 Jun 1986	13 days 6 hr 12 min 30 sec (218·7 mpd ave.)	1986
FASTEST SAIL DAY'S RUN Solo in multihull	Laiterie Mont St Michel 18·3 m 60 ft trimaran	Olivier Moussy (French)	50° 13' N 11° 30' W 1818 GMT 6 Jun 1988	48° 18' N 23° 30' W 2117 GMT 7 Jun 1988	483·60 nm/26 hr 59 min (430 mpd)	1988
FASTEST SAIL DAY'S RUN Non-solo in multihull	Formule TAG 24·4 m 80 ft catamaran	Mike Birch (Canadian)	49·181° N 40·424° W 2259 GMT 25 Aug 1984	52·170° N 27·796° W 2241 GMT 26 Aug 1984	512·15 nm/23 hr 42 min (518 mpd)	1984
FASTEST POWER W–E	Virgin Atlantic Challenger II 22·0 m 72 ft	Richard Branson (British)	Ambrose Light Tower 1103 GMT 26 Jun 1986	Bishop Rock Light 1934 GMT 29 Jun 1986	3 days 8 hr 31 min (840 mpd ave.)	1986

N.B. ULDB = Ultra-light displacement boat. All mileages are nautical miles. STAR and 2STAR are Trans-Atlantic races.

TANKERS

Largest ■ The largest tanker and ship of any kind is the 555 051 tonnes deadweight *Hellas Foss*, a steam turbine tanker built in 1979. Of 254 582 gross registered tonnage and 227 801 net registered tonnage, she is Greek–owned by the Bilinder Marine Corporation of Athens.

CARGO VESSELS

Largest ■ Carrying dry cargo is the Norwegian ore carrier *Berge Stahl* of 364·767 tonnes dwt built in South Korea for the Norwegian owner Sig Bergesen. It has a length of 343 m *1125 ft*, a beam measuring 63·5 m *208 ft* and was launched on 5 Nov 1986. The largest British ore/oil carriers (registered in the Isle of Man) are Lombard North Central Leasing's *Rapana* and *Rimula* built in Sweden in 1973 and 1974 of 227 400 tonnes dwt, *121 165 grt* with lengths of 332·77 m *1091 ft 9 in.*

Largest whale factory ■ The USSR's *Sovietskaya Ukraina* (32 034 gross tons) with a summer deadweight of 46 738 tonnes *46 000 tons* was completed in October 1959. She is 217·8 m *714½ ft* in length and 25·8 m *84 ft 7 in* in the beam.

Barges ■ The world's largest RoRo (roll-on, roll-off) ships are four *El Rey* class barges of 16 700 tons and 176·78 m *580 ft* in length. They were built by the FMC Corp of Portland, Oregon, USA and are operated by Crowley Maritime Corp of San Francisco, USA between Florida, USA and Puerto Rico with tri-level lodging of up to 376 truck-trailers.

Largest container ship ■ Shipborne containerisation began in 1955 when the tanker *Ideal X* was converted by Malcom McLean (US). She carried containers only on deck.

The twelve built for United States Lines in Korea in 1984–5 are capable of carrying 4482 TEU (6·1 m *20ft equivalent units—20 ft* containers) and have a gross tonnage of 57 075. They were named *American Alabama, American California, Illinois, Kentucky,* etc. Following the financial collapse of United States Lines, the fleet was sold and the twelve ships now have names such as *Sea-Land Atlantic, Sea-Land Achiever, Commitment, Integrity,* etc, while others carry names either with the prefix 'Nedlloyd' (*Nedlloyd Holland*) or the suffix 'Bay' (*Galveston Bay*).

Most powerful tugs ■ The *Smit Singapore* commissioned in April 1984 by Smit Tak International, of 22 000 horsepower and 189 tons bollard pull at full power is 75·2 m *246·72 ft* long and 15·68 m *51·44 ft* wide.

Largest car ferries ■ The world's largest car and passenger ferry is the 37 800 grt M/S *Olympia* which entered service across the Baltic between Helsinki, Finland and Stockholm, Sweden in May, 1985. Built in Abo, Finland for the Viking Line, she is 177·1 m *581 ft* long, 29 m *95 ft* in the beam and can carry 2500 passengers and 600 cars or 62 trailers.

Fastest ■ The 24 065 grt gas turbine-powered *Finn-jet*. Built in 1977 operates in the Baltic between Helsinki, Finland and Travemunde, West Germany and is capable of exceeding 30 knots.

Largest rail ferry ■ The 9700-dwt 21-knot *Railship II* went into service on the Baltic run in November 1984. She can carry 8820 m *65 ft 7 in* long rail cars, is 186·5 m *611 ft 10 in* overall and was built for HM Gehrckens of Hamburg, West Germany.

Largest propeller ■ The largest propeller ever made is the triple-bladed screw of 11 m *36 ft 1 in*

diameter made by Kawasaki Heavy Industries on 17 Mar 1982 for the 208 739 ton bulk carrier *Hoei Maru* (now renamed *New Harvest*).

Largest hydrofoil ■ The 64·6 m *212 ft* long *Plainview* (314 tonnes *310 tons* full load) naval hydrofoil was launched by the Lockheed Shipbuilding and Construction Co at Seattle, Washington State, USA on 28 Jun 1965. She has a service speed of 50 knots *92 km/h*. Three 165-ton Supramar PTS 150 Mk III hydrofoils carry 250 passengers at 40 knots *74 km/h* across the Öre Sound between Malmö and Copenhagen. They were built by Westermoen.

> **Largest passenger ship** ● *Soverign of the Seas* constructed in France at the shipyard Chantiers de l'Atlantique, St. Nazaire at a of cost of $183 million, she entered service in January 1988. Her crew of 750, include Norwegian officers, deck and engine crew and international hotel staff. Passenger to crew ratio is three to one. Her gross registered tonnage is 73 192 with a crusing speed of 16–21 knots. (Photo: Gamma).

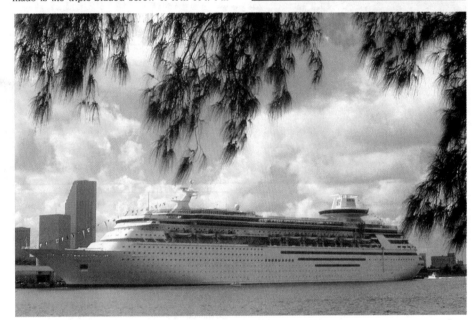

TRANS-PACIFIC MARINE RECORDS
(Compiled by Nobby Clarke and Richard Boehmer)

CATEGORY	VESSEL	NAME/SKIPPER	START	FINISH	DURATION	DATE
EARLIEST SOLO (Woman)	*Sea Sharp II* 9·45 m *31 ft*	Sharon Sites Adams (US)	Yokohama, Japan	San Diego, Cal.	75 days (5911 miles)	1969
EARLIEST ROWING	*Britannia II* 10·66 m *35 ft*	John Fairfax (British) Sylvia Cook (British)	San Francisco 26 Apr 1971	Hayman I., Australia 22 Apr 1972	362 days	1971–2
EARLIEST ROWING SOLO	*Hele-on-Britannia* 9·75 m *32 ft*	Peter Bird (British)	San Francisco 23 Aug 1982	Gt Barrier Reef, Australia 14 Jun 1983	294 days 14 480 km *9000 miles*	1982–3
EARLIEST SOLO (Totally Blind)	*Dark Star* 7·79 m *25 ft 7 in* (BM Sloop)	Hank Dekker (US)	San Francisco	Honolulu	23 days (Braille charts, compass and loran)	1983
EARLIEST RAFT (shore to shore)	*La Balsa* 12·8 m *42 ft* (Balsa logs)	Vital Alsar (Spanish) & 3 crew	Guayaquil Ecuador	Mooloolaba Australia	160 days	1970
FASTEST SAIL CALIFORNIA–HAWAII Solo in monohull	*Intense* 9·1 m *30 ft* ULDB sloop	Bill Strange (US)	San Francisco (SoloTP) 25 Jun 1988	Kauai 7 Jul 1988	11 days 15 hr 21 min (182·4 mpd ave.)	1988
FASTEST SAIL CALIFORNIA–HAWAII Non-solo in monohull	*Merlin* 20·4 m *67 ft* ULDB sloop	Bill Lee (US)	Los Angeles (TransPac) 2 Jul 1977	Honolulu 10 Jul 1977	8 days 11 hr 1 min 45 sec (264 mpd ave.)	1977
FASTEST SAIL CALIFORNIA–HAWAII Solo in multihull	*Bullfrog Sunblock* 12·2 m *40 ft* trimaran	Ian Johnston (Australian)	San Francisco (SoloTP) 14 Jun 1986	Kauai 24 Jun 1986	10 days 10 hr 3 min 43 sec (204 mpd ave.)	1986
FASTEST SAIL CALIFORNIA–HAWAII Non-solo in multihull	*Double Bullet* 19·7 m *65 ft* catamaran	Bob Hanel (US)	Los Angeles (TransPac) 2 Jul 1983	Honolulu 9 Jul 1983	7 days 7 hr 30 min 56 sec (304·2 mpd ave.)	1983
FASTEST SAIL AUSTRALIA–HORN Clippership	*Lightning* 74·4 m *243 ft* 3-masted ship	James Forbes (British)	Melbourne 20 Aug 1854	Cape Horn 8 Sep 1854	19 days (approx 315 mpd ave.)	1854

N.B.—The earliest single-handed Pacific crossings were achieved East–West by Bernard Gilboy (US) in 1882 in the 5·48 m *18 ft* double-ender *Pacific* to Australia and West–East by Fred Rebel (Latvia) in the 5·48 m *18 ft Elaine*, (from Australia) and Edward Miles (US) in the 11·2 m *36¾ ft Sturdy II* (from Japan) both in 1932, the latter via Hawaii. ULDB = Ultra-light displacement boat. All mileages are nautical miles.

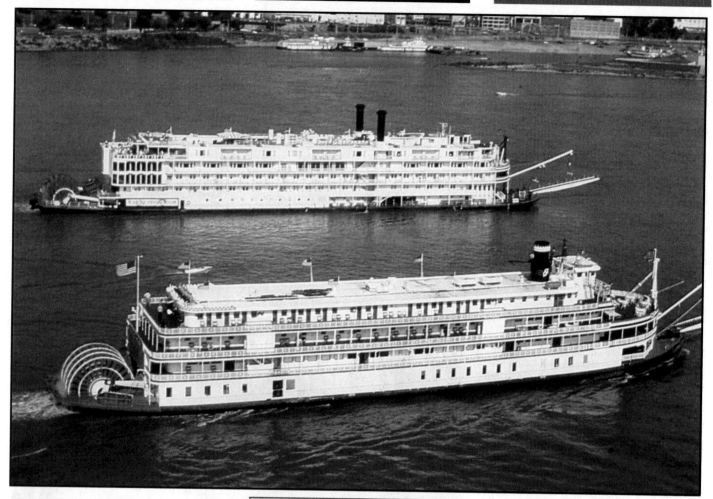

Hydrofoil Ltd of Mandal, Norway. A 500-ton wing ground effect vehicle capable of carrying 900 tons has been reported in the USSR.

River boat ■ The world's largest inland boat is the 116 m *382 ft Mississippi Queen* designed by James Gardner of London. The vessel was commissioned on 25 Jul 1976 in Cincinatti, Ohio, USA and is now in service on the Mississippi River.

Fastest building ■ The fastest times in which complete ships of more than 10 000 tons were ever built were achieved at Kaiser's Yard, Portland, Dorset during the war-time programme for building 2 742 Liberty ships in 18 yards from 27 Sep 1941. In 1942 No. 440, named *Robert E. Peary*, had her keel laid on 8 November, was launched on 12 November and was operational after 4 days 15 ½ hr on 15 November. She was broken up in 1963.

Most powerful icebreakers ■ The most powerful purpose-built icebreaker is the 25 375 tonne-*25 000 -ton* 140 m *460 ft* long *Rossiya*, powered by 55·95 kW *75 00 hp* nuclear engines, built in Leningrad, USSR and completed in 1985. A $(Can) 500 million, 74·6 kW, *100 000 hp* 194 m *636 ft* long Polar icebreaker of the Class 8 was ordered by the Canadian Government in October 1985. The largest *converted* icebreaker was the 306·9 m *1007 ft* long SS *Manhattan* (43 000 shp), which was converted by the Humble Oil Co into a 152 407 tonne *150 000 -ton* icebreaker with an armoured prow 69 ft 2 in long. She made a double voyage through the North-West Passage in arctic Canada from 24 Aug to 12 Nov 1969. The North-West Passage was first navigated by Roald Engebereth Gravning Amundsen (Norway) (1872–1928) in the sealing sloop *Gjöa* on 11 Jul 1906.

Yacht *Most expensive* ■ The fitting out of the 143·2 m *470 ft* Saudi Arabian royal yacht *Abdul Aziz*, built in Denmark, was completed on 22 Jun 1984 at Vospers Yard, Southampton, Hants. It was estimated in September 1987 to be worth more than $100 million.

Longest ■ The longest private (non-Royal) yacht is

the 85·9 m *282 ft Nabila* originally costing some $29 million. She was sold in September 1987 by the Sultan of Brunei to New York property dealer Donald Trump (b. 1946) for close to this price and renamed *Trump Princess*. Her original owner was Adnan Kashoggi who installed a helicopter pad and an operating theatre.

Dredger most powerful ■ The 142·7 m *468·4 ft* long *Prins der Nederlanden* of 10 586 grt can dredge 20 000 tonnes *19 700 tons* of sand from a depth of 35 m *115 ft* via two suction tubes in less than an hour.

Wooden ship *Heaviest* ■ The *Richelieu*, 101 70 m *333 ⅔ ft* long and of 8662 tonnes *8534 tons* was launched in Toulon, France on 3 Dec 1873. HM battleship *Lord Warden*, completed in 1869, displaced 8060 tonnes *7940 tons.*

Longest ■ Of modern wooden ships ever built the longest was the New York-built *Rochambeau* (1867–72) formerly *Dunderberg* measured 115 m *377 ft 4 in* overall. It should be noted that the biblical length of Noah's Ark was 300 cubits or, at 45·7 cm *18 in* to a cubit, 137 m 450 ft.

Largest human powered ■ The giant ship *Tessarakonteres* 3-banked catamaran galley with 4000 rowers, built for Ptolemy IV *c.* 210 BC in Alexandria, Egypt, measured 128 m *420 ft* with up to 8 men to an oar of 38 cubits (17·5 m *57 ft*) in length.

Longest canoe ■ The 35·7 m *117 ft* long 20.3 tonnes *20 ton* Kauri wood Maori war canoe *Nga Toki Matawhaorua* was built by adzes at Kerikeri Inlet, New Zealand in 1940 for a crew of 70 or more. The 'Snake Boat' *Nadubhagóm* 41·1 m *135 ft* long from

Kerala, southern India has a crew of 109 rowers and 9 'encouragers'.

Light Vessels ■ The earliest station still marked by a light vessel is the Newarp in the North Sea, off Great Yarmouth, Norfolk in 1791. A Nore light vessel was first placed in the Thames estuary in 1732.

SAILING SHIPS

Largest ■ The largest vessel ever built in the era of sail was the *France II* (5806 gross tons), launched at Bordeaux, France in 1911. The *France II* was a steel-hulled, five-masted barque (square-rigged on four masts and fore and aft rigged on the aftermost mast). Her hull measured 127·4 m *418 ft* overall. Although principally designed as a sailing vessel with a stump topgallant rig, she was also fitted with two steam engines. She was wrecked off New Caledonia on 13 Jul 1922.

The only seven-masted sailing schooner ever built was the 114·4 m *375·6 ft* long *Thomas W. Lawson* (5218 gross tons) built at Quincy, Massachusetts, USA in 1902 and wrecked off the Isles of Scilly, Cornwall on 15 Dec 1907.

Largest in service ■ Is the 117·5 m *385½ ft Sedov* launched in 1921 and used for training in the USSR. She is 14·6 m *48 ft* in width and has a sail area of 4192 m² *45 123 ft².*

The world's only surviving First Rate Ship-of-the-Line is the Royal Navy's 104-gun battleship HMS *Victory*, laid down at Chatham, Kent on 23 Jul 1759 and constructed from the wood of some 2200 oak trees. She bore the body of Admiral Nelson from Gibraltar to Portsmouth arriving 44 days after serving as his victorious flagship at the Battle of Trafalgar of 21 Oct 1805. In 1922 she was moved to No 2 dock, Portsmouth—site of the world's oldest graving dock. The length of her cordage (both standing and running rigging) is 30·77 km (*19·12 miles*).

Longest ■ The longest is the 134 m *440 ft* long French built *Wind Song* with four aluminium masts each 62·17 m *204 ft* high. The polyester sails are computer-controlled. It is operated as a Pacific cruise vessel for 150 passengers by Windstar Sail Cruises Ltd. Her two sister ships are *Wind Spirit* and *Wind Star*.

Largest junks ■ The largest on record was the sea-going *Cheng Ho*, flagship of Admiral Cheng Ho's 62 treasure ships, of *c.* 1420, with a displacement of 3150 tonnes *3100 tons* and a length variously estimated up to 164 m *538 ft* and believed to have had nine masts. A river junk 110 m *361 ft* long, with treadmill-operated paddle-wheels, was recorded in AD 1161. In *c.* AD 280 a floating fortress 182·8 m *600 ft* square, built by Wang Chün on the Yangtze, took part in the Chin-Wu river war. Present-day junks do not, even in the case of the Chiangsu traders, exceed 51·8 m *170 ft* in length.

Longest day's run under sail ■ Calculated for any commercial vessel under sail the longest day's run was one of 462 nautical miles (*856·16 km*) by the clipper *Champion of the Seas* (2722 registered tons) of the Liverpool Black Ball Line running before a north-westerly gale in the south Indian Ocean under the command of Capt Alex Newlands in 1854. The elapsed time between the fixes was 23 hr 17 min giving an average of 19·97 knots *37·00 km/h* (see Chapter 11, Yachting, for sporting record).

Largest sails ■ Sails are known to have been used for marine propulsion since 3500 BC. The largest spars ever carried were those in HM Battleship *Temeraire*, completed at Chatham, Kent, on 31 Aug 1877. She was broken up in 1921. The fore and main yards measured 35 m *115 ft* in length. The foresail contained 1555 m *5100 ft* of canvas, weighing 2·03 tonnes *2 tons* and the total sail area was 2322 m² *25 000 ft²*. HM Battleship *Sultan* was ship-rigged when completed at Chatham, Kent on 10 Oct 1871 and carried 3168 m² *34 100 ft²* of sails plus 1421 m² *15 300 ft²* of stunsails. She was broken up in 1946.

Tallest mast ■ The *Velsheda*, a J Class sailing vessel is the tallest known single masted yacht in the world. Measured from heel fitting to the mast truck she is 51·59 m *169¼ ft* in height. Built in 1933, the second of the four British J-Class yachts, she was unusual in that she was the only one ever built that was not intended to race for the America's Cup. With a displacement of 145 tonnes *143 tons* she supports a sail area of 7 500 ft² *16 140 ft²*.

Largest wreck ■ The 312 186 dwt VLCC (Very Large Crude Carrier) *Energy Determination* blew up and broke in two in the Straits of Hormuz on 12 Dec 1979. Her full value was $58 million. The largest wreck removal was carried out in 1979 by Smit Tak International who removed the remains of the French tanker *Betelgeuse*, 120 000 tons, from Bantry Bay, Ireland, within 20 months.

Most massive collision ■ The closest approach to an irresistible force striking an immovable object occurred on 16 Dec 1977, 35 km *22 miles* off the coast of southern Africa when the tanker *Venoil* (330 954 dwt) struck her sister ship *Venpet* (330 869 dwt).

OCEAN CROSSINGS

Earliest Atlantic ■ The earliest crossing of the Atlantic by a power vessel, as opposed to an auxiliary-engined sailing ship, was a 22-day voyage begun in April 1827, from Rotterdam, Netherlands, to the West Indies by the *Curaçao*. She was a 38·7 m *127 ft* wooden paddle boat of 438 tons, built as the *Calpe* in Dover, Kent in 1826 and purchased by the Dutch Government for the West Indian mail service. The earliest Atlantic crossing entirely under steam (with intervals for desalting the boilers) was by HMS *Rhadamanthus* from Plymouth, Devon to Barbados in 1832. The earliest crossing under continuous steam power was by the condenser-fitted packet ship *Sirius* (714 tonnes *703 tons*) from Queenstown (now Cóbh), Ireland, to Sandy Hook, New Jersey, USA, in 18 days 10 hr on 4–22 Apr 1838.

Fastest Atlantic ■ This was made by the *United States* (then 51 988, now 38 216 gross tons), former flagship of the United States Lines. On her maiden voyage between 3 and 7 Jul 1952 from New York, USA to Le Havre, France and Southampton, Hants, she averaged 35·39 knots, or *65·95 km/h* for 3 days 10 hr 40 min (6.36 p.m. GMT, 3 July to 5.16 a.m., 7 July) on a route of 2949 nautical miles *5465 km* from the Ambrose Light Vessel to the Bishop Rock Light, Isles of Scilly, Cornwall. During this run, on 6–7 Jul 1952, she steamed the greatest distance ever covered by any ship in a day's run (24 hr) — 868 nautical miles *1609 km*, hence averaging 36·17 knots *67·02 km/h*. The maximum speed attained from her 240 000 shp engines was 38·32 knots (*71·01 km/h*) in trials on 9–10 Jun 1952.

Fastest Pacific ■ From Yokohama to Long Beach, California, USA (4840 nautical miles *8960 km*) in 6 days 1 hr 27 min (30 Jun–6 Jul 1973) by the container ship *Sea-Land Commerce* (50 315 tons) at an average of 33·27 knots (*61·65 km/h*).

Fastest Channel crossing ■ The English Channel was crossed by a commercial ferry in 52 min 49 sec from Dover, Kent to Calais, France by Townsend Thoresen's *Pride of Free Enterprise* in a near gale of Force 7 on 9 Feb 1982.

Water speed ■ The highest speed ever achieved on water is an estimated speed 300 knots (*556 km/h*, *345 mph*) by Kenneth Peter Warby MBE (b. 9 May 1939) on the Blowering Dam Lake, New South Wales, Australia on 20 Nov 1977 in his unlimited hydroplane *Spirit of Australia*. The official world water speed record is 277·57 knots (*514·389 km/h 319·627 mph*) set on 8 Oct 1978 by Warby on Blowering Dam Lake.

MERCHANT SHIPPING

World total ■ The world total of merchant shipping, excluding vessels of less than 100 gross tonnage, sailing vessels and barges, was 75 680 vessels of 403 406 079 gross tonnage on 1 Jul 1988. The largest merchant fleet in the world as at mid-1988 was that under the flag of Liberia with 1507 ships of 49 733 615 gross tonnage. The UK figure for mid-1988 was 2142 ships of 8 260 431 gross tonnage.

Largest and busiest ports ■ Physically, the largest port in the world is the Port of New York and New Jersey, USA. The port has a navigable waterfront of 1215 km *755 miles* (474 km *295 miles* in New Jersey) stretching over 238 km² *92 miles²*. The world's busiest port and largest artificial harbour is Rotterdam-Europoort in the Netherlands which covers 100 km² *38 miles²* with 122·3 km *76 miles* of quays. It handled 272·8 million tonnes of sea-going cargo in 1988, an increase of almost 7% on its 1987 figure. Although the port of Singapore handled less tonnage, in terms of numbers of ships it was busier, with 36 000 ships calling there during 1988.

HOVERCRAFT

Earliest ■ The ACV (air-cushion vehicle) was first made a practical proposition by Sir Christopher Sydney Cockerell CBE, FRS (b. 4 June 1910), a British engineer who had the idea in 1954, published his Ripplecraft report 1/55 on 25 Oct 1955 and patented it on 12 Dec 1955. The earliest patent relating to air-cushion craft was applied for in 1877 by John I. Thornycroft (1843–1928) of Chiswick, London and the Finn Toivo Kaario developed the idea in 1935. The first flight by a hovercraft was made by the 4-tonne Saunders-Roe SR-N1 at Cowes, Isle of Wight on 30 May 1959. With a 680 kg *1500 lb* thrust Viper turbojet engine, this craft reached 68 knots *126 km/h* in June 1961. The first hovercraft public service was run across the Dee estuary, Scotland by the 60 knot *111 km/h* 24-passenger Vickers-Armstrong VA-3 between July and September 1962.

Largest ■ The SRN4 Mk III, a British-built civil hovercraft weighs 305 tons and has a capacity of 418 passengers and 60 cars. It is 56·38 m *185 ft* in length, is powered by four Bristol Siddeley Marine Proteus engines, giving a maximum speed in excess of the scheduled permitted cross-Channel operating speed of 65 knots.

Fastest ■ The world's fastest warship a hovercraft, is the 23·7 m *78 ft* long 100-tonne US Navy test vehicle SES-100B. She attained a world record 91·9 knots *105·8 mph* on 25 Jan 1980 on the Chesapeake Bay Test Range, Maryland, USA. As a result of the success of this test craft a 3000-tonne US Navy Large Surface Effect Ship (LSES) was built by Bell Aerospace under contract from the Department of Defense in 1977–81.

Longest journey ■ The longest hovercraft journey was one of 8047 km *5000 miles* under the leadership of David Smithers, through eight West African countries in a Winchester Class SRN6, between 15 Oct 1969 and 3 Jan 1970 by the British Trans-African Hovercraft Expedition.

Cross-Channel ■ The fastest scheduled crossing of the Channel was achieved by an SRN 4 Mark II Mountbatten Class Hovercraft operated by Hoverspeed on 1 Sept 1984 when *The Swift* completed the Dover–Calais run in 24 min 8·4 sec.

Highest ■ The greatest altitude at which a hovercraft is operating is on Lake Titicaca, Peru, where since 1975 an HM2 Hoverferry has been hovering 3811 m *12 506 ft* above sea level.

MODEL BOATS

Bob Lawson and Gordon Parker of the Lowestoft Model Boat crewed a radio-controlled scale model boat on 16-17 Jul 1988 at Oulton Broad, Suffolk which set a 24-hr distance record of 156·34 km *97·15 miles*.

Road Vehicles

COACHING

Before the widespread use of tarred road surfaces from 1845 coaching was slow and hazardous. The zenith was reached on 13 Jul 1888 when J. Selby Esq. drove the *Old Times* coach 173 km *108 miles* from London to Brighton and back with eight teams and 14 changes in 7 hr 50 min to average 22·19 km/h *13·79 mph*. Four-horse carriages could maintain a speed of 34 km/h *21 ⅓ mph* for nearly an hour. The *Border Union* stage coach, built *c.* 1825, ran four in hand from Edinburgh to London (632 km *393 miles*). When it ceased in 1842, due to competition from railways, the allowed schedule was 42 hr 23 min to average better than 14·9 km/h *9¼ mph*.

The record for changing a team of four horses by a team of 12 ostlers is 24·53 sec set at Olympia, London, on 18 Dec 1987, for the Norwich Union Charity Mail Coach team led by driver John Parker.

The longest horse drawn procession was a cavalcade of 68 carriages which measured 'nose to tail' 920 m *3018 ft*, organised by the Spies Travelling Company of Denmark on 7 May 1986. It carried 810 people through the woods around Copenhagen to celebrate the coming of spring.

MOTOR CARS

The number of automobiles constructed worldwide in 1987 was 14 300 000 of which 3 860 000 were made in Japan and 7 098 910 in the USA. General Motors sold 3 603 074. The UK production figure for 1988 was 1 226 835.

Earliest automobiles *Model* ■ The earliest automobile of which there is record is a two-foot-long steam-powered model constructed by Ferdinand Verbiest (d. 1687), a Belgian Jesuit priest, and described in his *Astronomia Europaea*. His model of 1668 was possibly inspired either by Giovanni Branca's description of a steam turbine, published in his *La Macchina* in 1629, or by writings on 'fire carts' or *Nan Huai-Jen* in the Chu dynasty (*c.* 800 BC).

Passenger-carrying ■ The earliest full-scale automobile was the first of two military steam tractors, completed at the Paris Arsenal in 1769 by Nicolas-Joseph Cugnot (1725–1804). This reached 3·6 km/h

2 $\frac{1}{4}$ mph. Cugnot's second, larger tractor, completed in May 1771, today survives in the *Conservatoire nationale des arts et métiers* in Paris. The world's first passenger-carrying automobile was a steam-powered road vehicle carrying eight passengers and built by Richard Trevithick (1771–1833). It first ran on 24 Dec 1801 in Camborne, Cornwall.

Internal combustion ■ The Swiss Isaac de Rivaz (d. 1828) built a carriage powered by his 'explosion engine' in 1805. The first practical internal-combustion-engined vehicle was that built by the Londoner Samuel Brown (Patent 5350, 25 Apr 1826) whose 2·9 kW *4 hp* two-cylinder atmospheric gas 88 litre engined carriage climbed Shooters Hill, Blackheath, Kent in May 1826. Britain's continuous motoring history started in November 1894 when Henry Hewetson drove his imported Benz Velo in the south-eastern suburbs of London. The first successful petrol-driven car, the Motorwagen, built by Karl-Friedrich Benz (1844–1929) of Karlsruhe, Germany ran at Mannheim, Germany, in late 1885. It was a 230 kg *3 cwt* 3-wheeler reaching 13–16 km/h *8–10 mph*. Its single-cylinder engine (bore 91·4 mm, stroke 160 mm) delivered 0·63 kW *0·85 hp* at 400 rpm. It was patented on 29 Jan 1886. Its first 1 km road test was reported in the local newspaper, the *Neue Badische Landeszeitung*, of 4 Jun 1886, under the heading 'Miscellaneous'.

Registrations *Earliest and most expensive* ■ The world's first plates were probably introduced by the Parisian police in 1893. Registration plates were introduced in Britain in 1903.

The original A1 plate was secured by the 2nd Earl Russell (1865–1931) for his 12 hp Napier. This plate, willed in September 1950 to Trevor T. Laker of Leicester, was sold in August 1959 for £2500 in aid of charity.

Licence plate No 8 was sold at a Hong Kong government auction for HK$5 million on 13 Feb 1988 to Law Ting-pong, a textile manufacturer. The number 8 is considered a lucky number.

FASTEST CARS

Land speed ■ The *official* one-mile land-speed record is 1019·467 km/h *633·468 mph* set by Richard Noble OBE (b. 1946) on 4 Oct 1983 over the Black Rock Desert, Nevada, USA, in his 17 000 lb thrust Rolls Royce Avon 302 jet-powered *Thrust 2*, designed by John Ackroyd (see also table).

The highest reputed land speed is 1190·377 km/h *739·666 mph* or Mach 1·0106 by Stan Barrett (US) in

The Budweiser Rocket, a rocket-engined 3-wheeled car at Edwards Air Force Base, California, USA on 17 Dec 1979 (see also table). The highest land speed attained in Britain is 424·74 km/h *263·92 mph* by Richard Noble in *Thrust 2* at Greenham Common, Berks on 25 Sep 1980.

The highest land speed recorded by a woman is 843·323 km/h *524·016 mph* by Mrs Kitty Hambleton *née* O'Neil (US) in the 48 000-hp rocket-powered 3-wheeled S.M.1 *Motivator* over the Alvard Desert, Oregon, USA on 6 Dec 1976. Her official two-way record was 825·126 km/h *512·710 mph* and she probably touched 965 km/h *600 mph* momentarily.

Diesel engined ■ The prototype 230 hp 3 litre Mercedes C 111/3 attained 327·3 km/h *203·3 mph* in tests on the Nardo Circuit, southern Italy on 5–15 Oct 1978, and in April 1978 averaged 314·462 km/h *195·398 mph* for 12 hours, so covering a world record 3773·55 km *2399·76 miles*.

Rocket-powered sleds ■ The highest speed recorded on ice is 399·00 km/h *247·93 mph* by *Oxygen* driven by Sammy Miller (b. 15 Apr 1945) on Lake George, New York, USA on 15 Feb 1981.

Steam car ■ On 19 Aug 1985 Robert E. Barber broke the 79-year-old record for a steam car driving No 744 *Steamin' Demon*, built by the Barber-Nichols Engineering Co, 234·33 km/h *145·607 mph* at Bonneville Salt Flats, Utah, USA.

Road cars ■ Various detuned track cars have been licensed for road use but are not for-sale production models. Manufacturers of very fast and very expensive models understandably limit speed tests to stipulated engine revs. Ferrari asserted a speed of 323·5 km/h *201 mph* for their £140 000 F40 in July 1987. The highest road-tested acceleration reported is 0–96·5 km/h *0–60 mph* in 4·1 sec for an MG Metro 6R4 International Rally Car in 1986. The fastest lap on a UK circuit by a production car was achieved by a Ferrari Testarossa at 275·19 kmh *171 mph* with a peak speed of 280·01 kmh *174 mph* at the Millbrook Proving Ground, Beds on 12 Dec 1988. The car was driven by Howard Lees of *Autocar & Motor Magazine*.

LARGEST CARS

Of cars produced for private road use, the largest has

> **First practical petrol driven car** ● The Benz Motorwagen which was patented in 1886. (Photo: Daimler-Benz Bildarchiv-Stuttgart).

been the Bugatti 'Royale' type 41, known in Britain as the 'Golden Bugatti', of which only six were assembled (although it is *believed* that seven were built) at Molsheim, France by the Italian Ettore Bugatti. First built in 1927, this machine has an 8-cylinder engine of 12·7 litres capacity, and measures over 6·7 m *22 ft* in length. The bonnet is over 2 m *7 ft* long.

Largest engines ■ The largest car ever used was the 'White Triplex', sponsored by J. H. White of Philadelphia, Pennsylvania, USA. Completed early in 1928, after two years' work, the car weighed over 4·06 tonnes *4 tons* and was powered by three Liberty V12 aircraft engines with a total capacity of 81188 cc, developing 1119 kW *1500 bhp* at 2000 rpm. It was used to break the world speed record but crashed at Daytona, Florida, USA on 13 Mar 1929.

Most powerful ■ The six-wheeled Jameson-Merlin, powered by a 27000 cc 1313 kW *1760 hp* Rolls Royce V12 Merlin aero-engine, governed down to a maximum speed of 298 km/h *185 mph*. It had a range of 480 km *300 miles* with tanks of 272 litres *60 gal* capacity. The vehicle weighed 2·69 tonnes *2·65 tons* overall, but it has now been destroyed.

Production car ■ The highest engine capacity of a production car was 13·5 litres *824 in*^{3}, for the US Pierce-Arrow 6–66 Raceabout of 1912–18, the US Peerless 6–60 of 1912–14 and the Fageol of 1918. The most powerful current production car is the Ferrari F40 which develops 356 kW *478 hp*, it is reported that approximately 770 will be built.

Heaviest ■ The heaviest car in production today (four to five made annually) appears to be the Soviet-built Zil limousine, which weighs 3 tonnes. The 'stretched' Zil used by Mikail Gorbachev weighs 6 tonnes and is made of 3-inch armour-plated steel. The 8-cylinder, 7 litre engine guzzles fuel at the rate of 6 miles to the gallon.

Longest ■ A 21·93 cm *71 ft 11 in* Cadillac Eldorado 1982 designed by Heikki Reijonen and built in the US by Walt Kurozynski, it has 18 wheels, weighs more than 7 tons, and equipped with a swimming pool, bar with space for 20 people, three telephones, television, video and solar deck.

Lowest car ■ Perry Watkins and Danny Curtis of Aylesbury, Bucks built their Hillman Imp 'Impressed', which stands 67 cm *26 $\frac{1}{2}$ in* from the highest point on its open-top roof to the road.

Most durable car ■ The highest recorded mileage for a car was 1 906 879 km *1 184 880 authenticated miles* by August 1978 for a 1957 Mercedes 180 D owned by Robert O'Reilly of Olympia, Washington State, USA. Its subsequent fate is unknown. R. L. Bender of Madison, Wisconsin, USA, claimed 1 643 206 km *1 021 041 miles* by 9 Jun 1984 for his car which he had been driving since 1958.

MOST EXPENSIVE CARS

Special ■ The most expensive car to build has been the US Presidential 1969 Lincoln Continental Executive delivered to the US Secret Service on 14 Oct 1968. It has an overall length of 6·56 m *21 ft 6·3 in* with a 4·06 m *13 ft 4 in* wheel-base and with the addition of 2·03 tonnes *2 tons* of armour plate, weighs 5·43 tonnes *5·35 tons* (5443 kg *12 000 lb*). The estimated cost of research, development and manufacture was $500 000 but it is rented at $5000 per annum. Even if all four tyres were shot out it can travel at 80 km/h *50 mph* on inner rubber-edged steel discs. Carriage House Motor Cars of New York, USA in March 1978 completed four years' work on converting a 1973 Rolls Royce including lengthening it by 76·2 cm *30 in*. The price tag was $500 000.

Standard ■ The most expensive British standard car is the Rolls-Royce 8-cylinder 6750 cc Phantom VI quoted in May 1989 at £350 000 (including tax). More expensive are custom-built models. Jack Barclay Ltd of Berkeley Square, London quote £4000 000 for an armour-plated Rolls-Royce Phantom VI.

The unrivalled collector of Rolls-Royces was Bhag-

FASTEST CARS

CATEGORY	KM/H	*MPH*	CAR	DRIVER	PLACE	DATE
JET ENGINED *official*	1019·4	*633·468*	Thrust 2	Richard Noble (GB)	Black Rock Desert Nevada, USA	4 Oct 1983
ROCKET ENGINED *official*	1001·473	*622·287*	Blue Flame	Gary Gabelich (USA)	Bonneville, Utah, USA	23 Oct 1970
unofficial*	1190·377	*739·666*	Budweiser Rocket	Stan Barrett (USA)	Edwards Air Force Base, California, USA	17 Dec 1979
WHEEL DRIVEN *turbine*	690·909	*429·311*	Bluebird	Donald Campbell (UK)	Lake Eyre, Australia	17 Jul 1964
multi piston engine	673·516	*418·504*	Goldenrod	Robert Summers (USA)	Bonneville, Utah, USA	12 Nov 1965
single piston engine	575·149	*357·391*	Herda-Knapp-Milodon	Bob Herda (USA)	Bonneville, Utah, USA	2 Nov 1967

* This published speed of Mach 1·0106 is *not* officially sanctioned by the USAF whose Digital Instrumented Radar was not calibrated or certified. The radar information was *not* generated by the vehicle directly but by an operator aiming the dish by means of a TV screen. To claim a speed to 6 significant figures appears quite unsustainable.

wan Shri Rajneesh (b. 1931), the Indian mystic lately of Rajneeshpuram, Oregon, USA. His disciples bestowed 93 of these upon him before his deportation in November 1985.

Used ■ The greatest price paid for any used car is $8·1 million for the 1931 Berline de Voyage Royale, one of six Bugatti Royales, by Thomas Monaghan of Ann Arbor, Michigan, USA. The car, formerly part of the William F. Harrah collection, was first sold to property developer Jerry Moore for $6·5 million when the collection was cut down from 1700 to 1300 cars in June 1986, then on to Mr Monaghan some months later. In Great Britain £5·5 million was paid at auction by Christie's at the Royal Albert Hall, London for a 1931 Bugatti Type 41 Royale Sports Coupé on 19 Nov 1987 by Nicholas Harley, a London dealer.

Most inexpensive ■ The cheapest car of all time was the 1922 Red Bug Buckboard, built by Briggs and Stratton Co of Milwaukee, Wisconsin, USA, listed at $150–$125. It had a 1·57 m *62 in* wheel base and weighed 111 kg *245 lb*. Early models of the King Midget cars were sold in kit form for self-assembly for as little as $100 as late as 1948. By May 1989 the cheapest quoted new car price in Britain was £2 895 for a Fiat 126, 652-cc two-door car.

Longest in production ■ The Morgan 4/4 celebrates its fifty-fourth birthday on 27 Dec 1989. Built by the Morgan Motor Car Co of Malvern, Hereford and Worcester (founded 1910), there is still a four-year waiting list.

Amongst mass-production models, both the Citroen 2cv and Volkswagen 'Beetle' date from 1938. The 20–millionth 'Beetle' came off the Mexican production line on 15 May 1981 and residual production continues. The 2cv remains in production in Portugal. Britain's champion seller has been the Mini,

designed by Sir Alec Issigonis (1906–88), which originally sold for £496 19s 2d in August 1959. Sales at April 1989 reached 5 118 447.

DRIVING

Round the world ■ The fastest circumnavigation embracing more than an equator's length of driving (40 075·0 km *24 901·47 road miles*) is one of 74 days 1 hr 11 min by Garry Sowerby (driver) and Ken

Longest fuel range ● The greatest distance driven without refuelling on a single fuel fill in a standard vehicle (135·1 litre *40·7 gal* carried in factory optional twin fuel tanks) is 2094·9 km *1300·9 miles* by a Toyota LandCruiser diesel pick-up, driven by Ewan Kennedy and Ray Barker with John Windass (Observer) from Sydney, Australia to Eyre Highway, South Australia in 31 hr 8 min in May 1988.

Langley (navigator) of Canada from 6 Sep to 19 Nov 1980 in a Volvo 245 DL westwards from Toronto, Canada through 4 continents and 23 countries. The distance covered was 43 030 km *26 738 miles* (see below for their Cape to Cape record). Between 30 Mar 1964 and 23 Apr 1984 entertainers Manfred Müller and Paul-Ernst Luhrs drove round the world in their 1963 Citroen 2cv covering 83 countries and 350 000 km *217 490 miles*. They started and finished in Bremerhaven, West Germany.

Amphibious circumnavigation ■ The only circumnavigation by an amphibious vehicle was by Ben Carlin (Australia) (d. 7 Mar 1981) in an amphibious jeep *Half-Safe*. He completed the last leg of the Atlantic crossing (the English Channel) on 24 Aug 1951. He arrived back in Montreal, Canada on 8 May 1958 having completed a circumnavigation of 62 765 km *39 000 miles* over land and 15 450 km *9600 miles* by sea and river. He was accompanied on the trans-Atlantic stage by his ex-wife Elinore (US) and on the long trans-Pacific stage (Tokyo to Anchorage) by Broye Lafayette De-Mente (b. Missouri, 1928).

One-year duration record ■ The greatest distance ever covered in one year is 573 029 km *354 257 miles* by 2 Delta Motors Opel Rekord

PROGRESSIVE SPEED RECORDS

Speed km/h	mph	Person and Vehicle	Place	Date
40	25	Sledging	Heinola, Finland	c.6500 BC
55	35	Horse-riding	Anatolia, Turkey	c.1400 BC
70	45	Mountain Sledging	Island of Hawaii (now USA)	*ante* AD 1500
80	50	Ice Yachts (earliest patent)	Netherlands	AD 1600
95	56·75	Grand Junction Railway 2–2–2: *Lucifer*	Madeley Banks, Staffs, England	13 Nov 1830
141·3	87·8	Tommy Todd, downhill skier	La Porte, California, USA	Mar 1873
144·8	90·0	Midland Railway 4–2–2 2·36 m *7 ft 9 in* single	Ampthill, Bedford, England	Mar 1897
210·2	130·61	Siemens and Halske electric engine	Marienfeld-Zossen, near Berlin	27 Oct 1903
c.257·5	c.150	Frederick H. Marriott (fl. 1957) Stanley Steamer *Wogglebug*	Ormond Beach, Florida, USA	26 Jan 1907
339	210·64	Sadi Lecointe (France) Nieuport-Delage 29	Villesauvage, France	25 Sep 1921
668·2	415·2	Flt Lt (Later Wing Cdr) George Hedley Stainforth AFC *Supermarine S.6B*	Lee-on-Solent, England	29 Sep 1931
1004	623·85	Flugkapitan Heinz Dittmar *Me. 163V–1*	Peenemunde, Germany	2 Oct 1941
1078	670	Capt Charles Elwood Yeager, USAF *Bell XS–1*	Muroc Dry Lake, California, USA	14 Oct 1947
1556	967	Capt Charles Elwood Yeager, USAF *Bell XS–1*	Muroc Dry Lake, California, USA	26 Mar 1948
4675·1	2905	Major Robert M. White, North American *X–15*	Muroc Dry Lake, California, USA	7 Mar 1961
c.28 260	c.17 560	Flt Maj Yuriy Alekseyevich Gagarin, *Vostok I*	Earth orbit	12 Apr 1961
38 988	24 226	Col Frank Borman, USAF, Capt James Arthur Lovell, Jr, USN, Major William A. Anders, USAF *Apollo VIII*	Trans-lunar injection	21 Dec 1968
39 897	24 790·8	Cdrs Eugene Andrew Cernan and John Watts Young, USN and Col Thomas P. Stafford, USAF *Apollo X*	Re-entry after lunar orbit	26 May 1969

A complete progressive table comprising entries from prehistoric times to date was published in the 1977 edition.

2-litres which both covered this distance between 18 May 1988 and the same date in 1989. The cars were driven on tar and gravel roads in the Northern Cape by a team of drivers from Delta Motor Corporation, Port Elizabeth, South Africa.

Trans-Americas ■ Garry Sowerby (Canada), with Tim Cahill (USA) as co-driver and navigator, drove a 1988 GMC Sierra K3500 four-wheel-drive pick-up truck powered by a 6·2 litre V8 Detroit diesel engine from Ushuaia, Tierra del Fuego, Argentina to Prudhoe Bay, Alaska, USA, a distance of 23 720 km *14 739 miles*, in a total elapsed time of 23 days 22 hr 43 min from 29 Sep to 22 Oct 1987. The vehicle and team were surface freighted from Cartagena, Colombia to Balboa, Panama so as to by-pass the Darien Gap. This was first traversed by the Land Rover *La Cucaracha Carinosa* (The Affectionate Cockroach) of the Trans-Darién Expedition 1959–60, crewed by former SAS man Richard E. Bevir (UK) and engineer Terence John Whitfield (Australia). They left Chepo, Panama on 3 Feb 1960 and reached Quibdó, Colombia on 17 Jun, averaging 201 m *220 yd* per hour of indescribable difficulty.

Cape to Cape ■ The first traverse of the world's greatest land mass (Afro-Eurasia) was achieved by Richard Pape, who left the North Cape in an Austin A90 on 28 Jul and arrived in Cape Town on 22 Oct 1955 with the milometer recording 28 160 km *17 500 miles* after 86 days. The speed record was set by Ken Langley and Garry Sowerby of Canada driving north in 28 days 13 hr 10 min for 20 166 km *12 531 miles* from 4 Apr–2 May 1984.

Cape to London ■ The 18 787 km *11 674 mile* road route from Cape Town, South Africa, to London is 14 days 19 hr 26 min set by husband and wife team Brig John and Dr Lucy Hemsley from 8 to 22 Jan 1983 in a Range Rover. Apart from the Channel crossing they were the first to drive entirely overland from Capetown, South Africa, to London.

Cape to Cairo ■ Brig Hemsley and his wife, in the course of establishing the above Cape to London record drove from Capetown, South Africa to Cairo, Egypt in 10 days 12 hr 16 min from 8-18 Jan 1983, a distance of 11 159 km *6934 miles*. During the course of the drive, theirs was the first car to cross the Allenby Bridge between Israel and Jordan for seven years. This bridge has not been traversed by car subsequently.

British Counties ■ Jim, June and Tony Laird of Buxton, Derbys covered all 62 mainland counties of Great Britain by car over a 2324·9 km *1444·4 mile* route on 8–9 Apr 1989 in a time of 24 hr 56 min. June and Jim Laird and Peter Riley also covered the 32 counties of Northern and Southern Ireland by car in a time of 19 hr 44 min over a 1213·8 km *754·4 mile* route on 25–6 Mar 1989.

Round Britain economy ■ A diesel-powered Ford Fiesta 1600 was driven by Rod Lambert and Ray Hancock with navigator John Taylor around the 5808 km *3609 mile* course from 14–21 Jun 1987 returning a fuel consumption of 30·16 km/litre *85·2 mpg*.

Petrol consumption ■ An experimental Japanese vehicle achieved the equivalent of 2269 km/litre, *6409 mpg* in the Shell Mileage Marathon at Silverstone, Northants on 30 Jun 1988.

Most economical ■ Amongst production cars available in the United Kingdom both Citroen AX 14DTR and the Daihatsu Charade Diesel Turbo could make this claim. The Department of Transport figures are: Citroen 54·3 mpg (urban cycle), 78·5 mpg (steady 56 mph), 56.5 mpg (steady 75 mph); Daihatsu 57.6 mpg (urban cycle) 78·5 mpg (steady 56 mph), 49·6 (steady 75 mph). *(Because of current standard practice metric figures have not been added.)*

Longest fuel range ■ The greatest distance driven without refuelling on a single fuel fill in a standard vehicle (135·1 litre *40·7 gal* carried in factory optional twin fuel tanks) is 2094·9 km

1300·9 miles by a Toyota LandCruiser diesel pick-up driven by Ewan Kennedy and Ray Barker with John Windass (Observer) from Sydney, Australia to a point on the Eyre Highway west of Wirrulla in South Australia in 31 hr 8 min in May 1988. The average speed was 67·3 km/h *41·8 mph* giving 31·9 mpg *8·8 litres/100km*.

Mountain driving ■ Vehicles have been driven up Ben Nevis, Inverness-shire, Scotland (1343 m *4406 ft*) on six occasions. The record times are 7 hr 23 min (ascent) and 1 hr 55 min (descent) by George F. Simpson in an Austin 7 on 6 Oct 1928. Henry Alexander accomplished the feat twice in May 1911 (Model T Ford) and on 13 Sep 1928 (Model A Ford). The most recent ascent was on 11 Sep 1987 when two Suzuki 4-wheel ATV Quad Runner vehicles drove from Old Inverlochy Castle to the summit in 2 hr 21 min. They were driven by Jerome Fack of Wadebridge, Cornwall, Paul Hunt of Egham, Surrey, David Kirke of London and Rod Shand of Fort William, Scotland.

Driving in reverse ■ Charles Creighton (1908–70) and James Hargis of Maplewood, Missouri, USA drove their Ford Model A 1929 roadster in reverse from New York, USA 5375 km *3340 miles* to Los Angeles, California, USA from 26 Jul–13 Aug 1930 without once stopping the engine. They arrived back in New York in reverse on 5 Sep so completing 11 555 km *7180 miles* in 42 days.

The highest average speed attained in any non-stop reverse drive exceeding 800 km *500 miles* was achieved by Gerald Hoagland who drove a 1969 Chevrolet Impala 806·2 km *501 miles* in 17 hr 38 min at Chemung Speed Drome, New York, USA on 9–10 Jul 1976 to average 45·72 km/h *28·41 mph*.

Brian 'Cub' Keene and James 'Wilbur' Wright drove their Chevrolet Blazer 14 533 km *9031 miles* in 37 days (1 Aug–6 Sep 1984) through 15 US states and Canada. Though it was prominently named 'Stuck in Reverse' law enforcement officers in Oklahoma refused to believe it and insisted they drove in reverse reverse, i.e. forwards, out of the state.

Battery-powered vehicle ■ Robert Dodds and Ian Pridding with the support of the Pontllanfraith Rotary Club travelled 1479 km *919 miles* from John O'Groats, Scotland to Land's End, Cornwall in a Sinclair C5 in 80 hr 47 min from 18–21 May 1987. David Turner and Tim Pickhard of Turners of Boscastle Ltd, Cornwall, travelled 1408 km *875 miles* from Land's End to John O'Groats in 63 hours in a Freight Rover Leyland Sherpa powered by a Lucas electric motor from 21–23 Dec 1985.

Joe Schwarzkopf-Bowers, of Watford, Herts drove his modified battery-powered Bond Equipe from Heathrow Airport, London to Crewkerne, Somerset on 16 May 1986, a distance of 212·4 km *132 miles* on a single charge costing an estimated 60p. On 5 Jul 1988 he drove a complete circuit of the M25 (195·5 km *121·5 miles*) non-stop at an average speed of 64·36 kmh *40 mph* on a single charge in his specially designed car.

Two-side-wheel driving ■ *Car* ■ Bengt Norberg (b. 23 Oct 1951) of Äppelbo, Sweden drove a Mitsubishi Colt GTi-16V on two side wheels non-stop for a distance of 310·391 km *192·873 miles* in a time of 7 hr 15 min 50 sec, he also achieved a distance of 44·805 km *30·328 miles* in one hour at Rattvik Horse Track, Sweden on 24 May 1989.

Göran Eliasson (b. 7 Dec 1946) of Boras, Sweden achieved 143·027 km/h *88·87 mph* on the two wheels of a standard Volvo 760 at Anderstorp on 24 May 1987.

Truck ■ Gilbert Bataille of Paris, France drove a Leyland T45 Road Runner Truck on two wheels for 4·60 km *2·864 miles* at the British Truck Grand Prix, Silverstone, Northants on 17 Aug 1986.

Bus ■ Bobby Ore (b. Jan 1949) drove a double-decker bus a distance of 246 m *810 ft* at North Weald Airfield, Essex on 21 May 1988.

Wheelie ■ Steve Murty drove a Multi-Part Skytrain truck on its rear wheels for 412·5 m *1353 ⅓ ft* at Mondello Park, Co. Kildare, Ireland on 23 Aug 1987. The 60-tonne truck was powered by a 373 kW *500 bhp* Cummins turbo-charged 14-litre engine and had a ZF-Ecomat hp 600 5-speed automatic gearbox.

Most durable driver ■ The Goodyear Tire and Rubber Co. test driver Weldon C. Kocich drove 5 056 470 km *3 141 946 miles* from 5 Feb 1953 to 28 Feb 1986 so averaging 153 226 km *95 210 miles* per year.

Oldest driver ■ Roy M. Rawlins (b. 10 Jul 1870) of Stockton, California, USA was warned for driving at 152 km/h *95 mph* in a 88·5 km/h *55 mph* zone in June 1974. On 25 Aug 1974 he was awarded a California State licence valid until 1978, but Mr Rawlins died on 9 Jul 1975, one day short of his 105th birthday. Mrs Maude Tull of Inglewood, California, USA who took to driving aged 91 after her husband died, was issued a renewal on 5 Feb 1976 when aged 104.

Britain's oldest known drivers have been Benjamin Kagan (1878–1988) of Leeds and the Rev Albert Thomas Humphrey (1886–1988) from Pawlett, near Bridgwater, Somerset who were both still driving at the age of 102 . The oldest age at which a man has passed the Department of Transport driving test has been 89 years 2 months by David Coupar (b. 9 Feb 1898) on 4 Mar 1987 in Perth, Perthshire. The oldest woman to pass was Mrs Gerty Edwards Land (b. 9 Sep 1897) on 27 Apr 1988 in Colne, Lancs. She was aged 90 years 229 days.

The holder of the earliest driving licence to be issued in Britain is Mr Reginald 'Gerry' Bond (b. 16 Jul 1889) of Bournemouth, Dorset whose first licence is dated October 1907.

Youngest driver ■ Instances of drivers have been recorded in HM Armed Forces much under 17 years. Mrs P. L. M. Williams (b. 3 Feb 1926), now of Risca, Gwent, as Private Patterson in the ATS, drove a 5-ton truck in 1941 aged 15. Stephen Andrew Blackbourn of Lincoln, Lincs having passed his driving test on his 17th birthday, went on to pass the advanced test less than five hours later on 20 Feb 1989.

Russell John Hutton of Hitchin, Herts, passed his test on 2 Jun 1988 aged 16 years 79 days.

Driving tests ■ The record for persistence in taking the Department of Transport's Test of Competence to Drive is held by Mrs Git Kaur Randhawa (b. 7 Feb 1937) of Hayes, Middlesex, who triumphed at her 48th attempt after more than 330 lessons on 19 Jun 1987.

The world's easiest tests have been those in Egypt in which the ability to drive 6 m *19·64 ft* forward and the same in reverse has been deemed sufficient. In 1979 it was reported that accurate reversing had been added between two rubber traffic cones. 'High cone attrition' soon led to the substitution of white lines. Mrs Fannie Turner (b. 1903) of Little Rock, Arkansas, USA passed the *written* test for drivers on her 104th attempt in October 1978.

SERVICES

Car parks ■ The world's largest is the West Edmonton Mall, Edmonton, Alberta, Canada, which can hold 20 000 vehicles. There are overflow facilities on an adjoining lot for 10 000 more cars.

The largest parking area in Great Britain is that for 15 000 cars and 200 coaches at the National Exhibition Centre, Birmingham (see p. 87).

Britain's highest capacity underground car park is under the Victoria Centre, Nottingham with a capacity of 1650 cars, opened in June 1972.

Garage ■ The largest private garage is one of two storeys built outside Bombay for the private collection of 176 cars owned by Pranlal Bhogilal (b. 1939).

The KMB Overhaul Centre operated by the Kowloon Motor Bus Co (1933) Ltd, Hong Kong, is the world's largest multi-storeyed service centre. Purpose built for double deck buses, its four floors occupy in excess of 47 000 m² *11·6 acres.*

Filling stations ■ The largest concentration of pumps are 204–96 of them are Tokheim electronic Unistar and 108 are Tokheim Explorer (Mechanical) in Jeddah, Saudi Arabia.

The largest filling station of the 20 016 in the United Kingdom is the Esso service area on the M4 at Leigh Delamere, Wilts, opened on 3 Jan 1972. It has 48 petrol and diesel pumps and extends over 17·4 ha *43 acres.* The commonest brand in the United Kingdom is Shell with 2886 retail outlets.

The highest in the world is at Leh, Ladakh, India at 3658 m *12 001 ft* operated by the Indian Oil Corporation.

Unleaded petrol ■ The first unleaded petrol to be available in the United Kingdom went on sale on 24 Jun 1986. The Minister of State for the Environment, William Waldegrave, made the first fill at Esso's Stamford Bridge Service Station, London.

As the culmination of a 'Let's get leadless' campaign organised by the *Express and Star* newspaper, 1115 cars were converted on a single site in Wolverhampton, West Midlands on 30 Apr 1989.

Tow ■ The longest on record was one of 7658 km *4759 miles* from Halifax, Nova Scotia to Canada's Pacific coast, when Frank J. Elliott and George A. Scott of Amherst, Nova Scotia, Canada, persuaded 168 passing motorists in 89 days to tow their Model T Ford (in fact engineless) to win a $1000 bet on 15 Oct 1927.

After his 1969 MGB, TJN 405H, broke down in the vicinity of Moscow, USSR Eddie McGowan of Chipping Warden, Oxon, was towed a distance of 2343 km *1456 miles* from Moscow to West Berlin on a 2 m *7 ft* single nylon tow rope on 12–17 Jul 1987.

Tyres *Largest* ■ The world's largest ever manufactured were by the Goodyear Tire & Rubber Co. for giant dumper trucks. They measure 3·65 m *12 ft* in diameter, weigh 5670 kg *12 500 lb* and cost $74 000. A tyre 5·18 m *17 ft* in diameter is believed to be the limitation of what is practical.

Fattest ■ The widest tyres in normal production are the P7 345/35 VR 15s made by Pirelli for the rear wheels of the Lamborghini Countach and De Tomaso Pantera GTS.

Skid marks ■ The longest recorded on a public road have been those 290 m *950 ft* long left by a Jaguar car involved in an accident on the M1 near Luton, Beds, on 30 Jun 1960. Evidence given in the subsequent High Court case *Hurlock* v. *Inglis et al.* indicated a speed 'in excess of 160 km/h *100 mph* before the application of the brakes'. The skid marks made by the jet-powered *Spirit of America*, driven by Norman Craig Breedlove, after the car went out of control at Bonneville Salt Flats, Utah, USA, on 15 Oct 1964, were nearly 9·6 km *6 miles* long.

VEHICLES

Largest ambulance ■ The world's largest are the 18 m *59 ft 0 ½ in* long articulated Alligator Jumbulances Mark VI, VII and VIII and IX, operated by The ACROSS Trust to convey the sick and handicapped

Petrol pumps ● Some of the 204 pumps, the largest concentration of pumps, - 96 of them are Tokheim electronic Unistar and 108 are Tokheim Explorer (Mechanical) in Jeddah, Saudi Arabia. (Photo : Tokheim)

on holidays and pilgrimages across Europe. They are built by Van Hool of Belgium with Fiat engines, cost £200 000 and convey 44 patients and staff.

Crawler ■ The most massive vehicle ever constructed is the Marion eight-caterpillar crawler used for conveying *Saturn V* rockets to their launching pads at Cape Canaveral, Florida. It measures 40 m x 34·7 m *131 ft 4 in x 114 ft* and the two built cost $12 300 000. The loaded train weight is 8036 tons *8165 tonnes.* The windscreen wipers are 106 cm *42 in* blades and are the world's largest.

Land ■ The most massive automotive land vehicle is 'Big Muskie', the 10 890-tonne *10 700-ton* mechanical shovel built by Bucyrus Erie for the Musk mine. It is 148·43 m *487 ft* long, 46·02 m *151 ft* wide and 67·66 m *222 ft* high with a grab capacity of 325 tons.

Longest ■ The Arctic Snow Train owned by the world-famous wire-walker Steve McPeak (US) has 54 wheels and is 174·3 m *572 ft* long. It was built by R.G. Le Tourneau Inc of Longview, Texas, USA for the US Army. Its gross train weight is 400 tons with a top speed of 32 km/h *20 mph* and it was driven by a crew of six when used as an 'overland train' for the military. McPeak repaired it and every punctured wheel single-handed in often sub-zero temperatures in Alaska. It generates 4680 shp and has a fuel capacity of 29 648 litres *6522 gal* .

Buses *Earliest* ■ The first municipal motor omnibus service in the world was inaugurated on 12 Apr 1903 between Eastbourne railway station and

Battery powered vehicle ● Joe Schwarzkopf-Bowers setting off on his record breaking journey of the M25 in his battery-powered car. On 5 Jul 1988 he drove a complete circuit of the M25 (195·5 km *121·5 miles)* non-stop at an average speed of 64·36 kmh *40 mph* on a single charge. (Photo: Joe Schwarzkopf-Bowers).

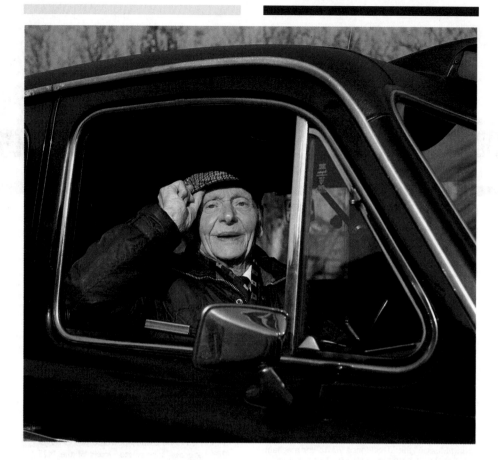

Meads, East Sussex, England. A steam-powered bus named *Royal Patent* ran between Gloucester and Cheltenham, Glos for four months in 1831.

Longest ■ The 10 870 kg *10·72 ton*, 23·16 m *76 ft* articulated buses, with 121 passenger seats and room also for 66 'strap-hangers', built by the Wayne Corporation of Richmond, Indiana, USA for use in the Middle East. The longest rigid single bus is 14·96 m *49 ft* long, carrying 69 passengers built by Van Hool of Belgium.

Largest fleet ■ The world's largest bus fleet is the 6580 single-deck buses in Rio de Janeiro, Brazil. Of the London fleet of 4 803 buses, 4 120 are double-deckers.

Longest route ■ The longest regularly scheduled bus route is by 'Across Australia Coach Lines', who inaugurated a regular scheduled service between Perth and Brisbane on 9 Apr 1980. The route is 5455 km *3389 miles* taking 75 hr 55 min. The longest route in Great Britain is 1089 km *677 miles* between Plymouth, Devon and Aberdeen, Scotland. The 806 service is operated jointly by Western National Ltd and Northern Scottish Omnibuses Ltd, each company allocating coaches on alternate days.

Caravans *Longest journey* ■ The continuous motor caravan journey of 231 288 km *143 716 miles* by Harry B. Coleman and Peggy Larson in a Volkswagen Camper from 20 Aug 1976 to 20 Apr 1978 through 113 countries. Saburo Ouchi (b. 7 Feb 1942) of Tokyo, Japan drove 270 000 km *167 770 miles* in 91 countries from 2 Dec 1969 to 10 Feb 1978.

Largest ■ Built in Britain for exhibition purposes are the £300 000 'State Super Caravans', 18 m *59 ft 0½ in* in length and 3·5 m *11 ft 5¾ in* wide built by Coventry Steel Caravans of Newport Pagnell, Bucks.

Fastest ■ The world speed record for a caravan is 201·02 km/h *124·91 mph* by an Alpha 14 towed by a Le Mans Aston Martin V8 saloon driven by Robin Hamilton at RAF Elvington, North Yorks on 14 Oct 1980.

Dumper truck ■ The world's largest is the Terex Titan 33–19 manufactured by the Terex Division of General Motors Corporation. It has a loaded weight of 548·6 tonnes *539·9 tons* and a capacity of 317·5 tonnes *312½ tons*. When tipping its height is

17·06 m *56 ft*. The 16-cylinder engine delivers 246 kW *3300 hp* and the fuel tank holds 5904·6 litres *1300 gal*.

Fire engine ■ The world's most powerful fire appliance is the 641·5 Kw *860 hp* 8-wheel Oshkosh firetruck used for aircraft fires. It can discharge 190 000 litres *41 600 gal* of foam through two turrets in just 150 sec. It weighs 60 tonnes *59 tons*.

Karting ■ The highest mileage recorded in 24 hours on a closed circuit driven by a four-man team is 1638·3 km *1018 laps of a mile* at Erbsville Kartway, Waterloo, Ontario, Canada. The 5-hp 140-cc Honda engined kart was driven by Owen Nimmo, Gary Ruddock, Jim Timmins and Danny Upshaw on 4–5 Sep 1983.

The greatest recorded in a 48-hour marathon is 2730 km *1696·3 miles* by Denis Wedes, Stephen Mantle, Len Nicholson and Janice Bennett driving a Yamaha RC100SE kart powered by a KT100J 100 cc engine at Mount Sugarloaf Circuit, Newcastle, New South Wales, Australia on 25–7 Mar 1983.

The highest mileage of the 100-cc non-gearbox solo six-hour record is 313·51 km *194·81 miles* by Emily Newman at Rye House Raceway, Hoddesdon, Hertson 25 Jul 1986.

Lawn mowers ■ The widest gang mower in the world is the 5-ton 18·28 m *60 ft* wide 27-unit 'Big Green Machine' used by the sod farmer Jay Edgar Frick of Monroe, Ohio, USA. It mows an acre in 60 sec.

The longest drive on a lawn mower was 4877 km *3031 miles* when Steve Perritt of Standlake, Oxon drove a Kubota G3HST from Windsor, Berks to Great Dunmow, Essex via Inverness, Highland, in 30 driving days from 14 Feb to 18 Mar 1988. The greatest distance covered in the annual 12-hour Lawn Mower

Race (under the rules of the BLMRA, the British Lawn Mower Racing Association) is 460·295 km *286 miles* by Andy, Barry and Trevor Stemp at Wisborough Green, West Sussex on 30–31 Jul 1988.

A 12-hour run-behind record of 162·7 km *101·15 miles* was set at Wisborough Green on 8–9 Jul 1984 by the 'Super Gnome' team.

Snowmobiles ■ Tony Lenzini of Duluth, Minnesota, USA, drove his 1986 Arctic Cat Cougar snowmobile a total of 11 604·6 km *7211 miles* in 60 riding days between 28 Dec 1985 and 20 Mar 1986.

Richard and Raymond Moore and Loren Matthews drove their snowmobile 9456 km *5876 miles* from Fairbanks, Alaska to Fenton, Michigan, USA, in 39 days from 3 Feb–13 Mar 1980.

Solar powered ■ The highest speed attained by a solely solar-powered land vehicle is 78·37 km/h *48·71 mph* by Molly Brennan driving the General Motors *Sunraycer* at Mesa, Arizona, USA on 24 Jun 1988. On the same day *Sunraycer* also attained a top speed of 129·04 km/h *80·2 mph* using both solar and battery power. In November 1987 *Sunraycer* won the 3138 km *1950 mile* solar challenge race in Australia, finishing two and a half days ahead of its nearest competitor.

Taxis ■ The largest taxi fleet is that in Mexico City, Mexico with 60 000 'normal' taxis, pesaros (communal fixed route taxis) and settas (airport taxis). Currently there are 15 232 taxis and 20 063 drivers in London.

The longest fare on record is one of 22 000 km *13 670 miles* with the meter running at a cost of £31 446. Ned Kelly and a team of five including taxi driver Guy Smith left London on 19 Aug 1988 travelling through 14 countries and arrived in Australia on 27 Oct 1988. A sum of £250 000 was raised for charities in Ireland, United Kingdom, Singapore and Australia.

Charles Kerslake (b. 27 June 1895) held a London Metropolitan cab licence from February 1922 until his retirement in May 1988.

Tractor ■ The world's largest tractor is the $459 000 US Department of Agriculture Wide Tractive Frame Vehicle completed by Ag West of Sacramento, California in June 1982. It measures 10·05 m *33 ft* between its wheels which are designed to run on permanent paths and weighs 22·22 tonnes *21·87 tons*.

The sport of tractor-pulling was put on a national US championship basis in 1967 at Bowling Green, Ohio, USA where the winner was 'The Purple Monster' built and driven by Roger E. Varns. Today there are 12 classes ranging up to '12 200 lb unlimited'.

Trams *Longest journey* ■ The longest now possible is from Krefeld St Tönis to Witten Annen Nord, West Germany. With luck at the eight interconnections the 105·5 mile *65·5 mile* trip can be achieved in 5½ hr. By late 1987 there were more than 320 tramway systems surviving of which the most extensive is that of Leningrad, USSR with 2500 cars on 53 routes. The only system in Great Britain until the £43 million Greater Manchester Rapid Transit System opens is at Blackpool, Lancs. The Glasgow system was scrapped in 1962 and that in London in 1952.

Oldest ■ In revenue service are motor cars 1 and 2 of the Manx Electric Railway dating from 1893.

Trolleybuses ■ The last trolleybus in Britain, owned by Bradford Corporation, ran in 1972. Plans have been made to reintroduce trolleybuses by both West Yorks and South Yorks Passenger Transport Executives.

Most powerful truck ■ A 1987 Ford L T L 9000 truck, owned and driven by Ken Warby of Cincinnati, Ohio, USA, is equipped with a General Electric J 79 tuned to produce 88 950 N *20 000 lbf* of thrust. Weighing 4·4 tonnes it has achieved 338·27 km/h *210·2 mph* in 7·7 sec over a quarter mile standing start.

Wrecker ■ The world's most powerful wrecker is the Twin City Garage and Body Shop's 20·6 tonne *21 ton* 10·9 m *36 ft* long 1969 International M6-23 'Hulk' stationed at Scott City, Missouri, USA. It can lift in excess of 295 tonnes *300 tons* on its short boom.

ROAD LOADS

Heaviest load ■ On 14–15 Jul 1984 John Brown Engineers & Contractors BV moved the Conoco Kotter Field production deck with a roll-out weight of 3805 tonnes for the Continental Netherlands Oil Company of Leidsenhage, Netherlands.

The heaviest road load moved in the United Kingdom has been a 1305-tonne *1284-ton* module for the semi-submersible drilling rig *Ocean Alliance 2002*. It measured 21 m *70 ft* high by 30·5 m *100 ft* long by 27·4 m *90 ft* wide and was drawn by four tractor units covering a total of 0·8 km *0·49 mile* of public road on its journey from the River Tees to the River Clyde on 5 Nov 1985.

The longest item moved has been a 83·8 m *275 ft* long high-pressure steel gas storage vessel weighing 233 tonnes *229 tons* transported to a new site at Beckton gasworks in East London on 10 Jul 1985. The overall train length was 99 m *325 ft*.

MOTORCYCLES *(see also Chapter 11)*

Earliest ■ The earliest internal combustion-engined motorised bicycle was a wooden-framed machine built at Bad Cannstatt in Oct–Nov 1885 by Gottlieb Daimler (1834–1900) of Germany and first ridden by Wilhelm Maybach (1846–1929). It had a top speed of 19 km/h *12 mph* and developed 0·373 kW *one-half of one horsepower* from its single-cylinder 264-cc four-stroke engine at 700 rpm. Known as the 'Einspur', it was lost in a fire in 1903. The first motorcycles of entirely British production were the 1046-cc Holden flat-four and the 2 ³/₄ hp Clyde single both produced in 1898. The earliest factory which made motorcycles in quantity was opened in 1894 by Heinrich and Wilhelm Hildebrand and Alois Wolfmüller at Munich, West Germany. In its first two years this factory produced over 1000 machines, each having a water-cooled 1488-cc twin-cylinder four-stroke engine developing about 2·5-bhp at 600 rpm—the highest capacity motor cycle engine ever put into production.

Fastest production road machine ■ The 93 kW *125 hp* one litre Kawasaki ZX10 has a road-tested top speed of 270 km/h *168 mph*. Its list price in May 1989 was £5 199 in the United Kingdom.

Fastest racing machine ■ There is no satisfactory answer to the identity of the fastest track machine other than to say that the current Kawasaki, Suzuki and Yamaha machines have all been geared to attain speeds marginally in excess of 300 km/h *186·4 mph* under race conditions.

Highest speeds ■ Official world speed records must be set with two runs over a measured distance made in opposite directions within a time limit—1 hr for FIM records and 2 hr for AMA records.

Donald A. Vesco (USA) (b. 8 Apr 1939), riding his 21 ft *6·4 m* long *Lightning Bolt* streamliner, powered by two 1016 cc Kawasaki engines on Bonneville Salt Flats, Utah, USA on 28 Aug 1978 set AMA and FIM absolute records with an overall average of 512·733 km/h *318·598 mph* and had a fastest run at an average of 513·165 km/h *318·66 mph*.

The highest speed achieved over two runs in the UK is 308·82 km/h *191·897 mph* by Roy Francis Daniel (b. 7 Dec 1938) on his 998 cc supercharged twin-engined RDS Triumph at Elvington, North Yorks on 29 Jul 1978. His average time for the flying 402 m *440 yd* was 4·69 sec.

The world record for 1 km *1093·6 yd* from a standing start is 16·68 sec by Henk Vink (b. 24 Jul 1939) (Netherlands) on his supercharged 984 cc four-cylinder Kawasaki, at Elvington Airfield, North Yorks on 24 Jul 1977. The faster run was made in 16·09 sec.

The world record for 402 m *440 yd* from a standing start is 8·805 sec by Henk Vink on his supercharged 1132 cc four-cylinder Kawasaki at Elvington Airfield, North Yorks on 23 Jul 1977. The faster run was made in 8·55 sec.

The fastest time for a single run over 402 m *440 yd* from a standing start is 7·08 sec by Bo O'Brechta (USA) riding a supercharged 1200 cc Kawasaki-based machine at Ontario, California, USA in 1980. The highest terminal velocity recorded at the end of a 402 m *440 yd* run from a standing start is 321·14 km/h *199·55 mph* by Russ Collins (USA) at Ontario on 7 Oct 1978.

Most expensive motorcycle ■ The Japanese Bimota YB4 750 cc is the most expensive roadgoing motorcycle available in the United Kingdom. Priced

at £15 550 it has an electronically fuel-injected Yamaha engine in a rectangular section alloy frame.

Smallest ■ Paul Ashley of Basildon, Essex has constructed a motorcycle with a wheelbase of 175 mm *6·88 in*, a seat height of 175 mm *6·88 in* and with wheels 50 mm *1·96 in* in diameter. Powered by a 3·5 cc engine he has ridden it over 120 m *400 ft* reaching a speed of 8 km/h *5 mph*.

Duration ■ The longest time a solo motorcycle has been kept in non-stop motion is 560 hr by Norberto Naummi, Foppiani Maurizio and Roberto Ghillani who covered 30 370 km *18 000 miles* at an average speed of 54·23 km/h *33·69 mph* in Varano do

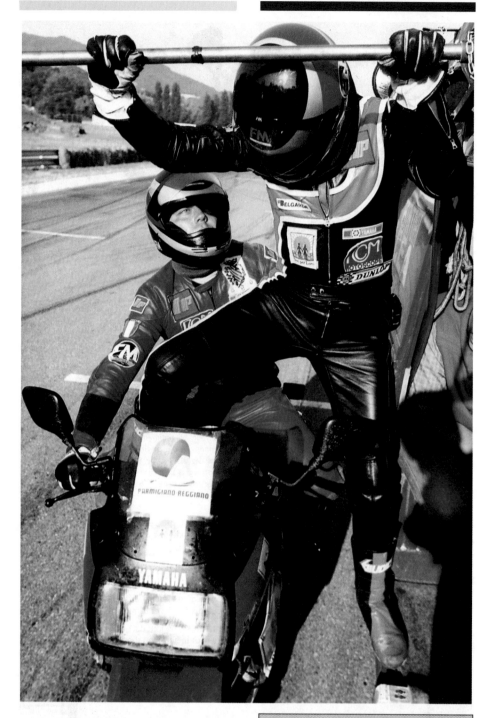

13 Jun 1895) still regularly rides his Suzuki 125 GS Special motorcycle every day.

BICYCLES

Earliest ■ The first design for a machine propelled by cranks and pedals with connecting rods has been attributed to Leonardo da Vinci (1452–1519), or one of his pupils, dated c. 1493. The earliest such design actually built was in 1839–40 by Kirkpatrick Macmillan (1810–78) of Dumfries, Scotland. It is now in the Science Museum, Kensington and Chelsea, London. The first practical bicycle was the *vélocipède* built in March 1861 by Pierre and his son Ernest Michaux of rue de Verneuil, Paris. In 1870, James Starley, in Coventry, constructed the first 'penny-farthing' or Ordinary bicycle. It had wire-spoked wheels for lightness and was available with an optional speed gear.

Bicycle parade ■ The greatest participation is one involving 2 ¾ per cent of the entire population of San Juan, Puerto Rico (1 816 300) on 17 Apr 1988. It was organised by TV personality 'Pacheco' aka Joaquín Monserrat.

Trishaw ■ The longest trishaw parade on record was when 177 trishaw pedlars rode in single convoy in Penang, Malaysia on 23 Nov 1986.

Longest ■ The longest true tandem bicycle ever built (i.e. without a third stabilising wheel) is one of 20·4 m *66 ft 11 in* for 35 riders built by the Pedaal-stompers Westmalle of Belgium. They rode c. 60 m *195 ft* in practice on 20 Apr 1979. The machine weighs 1100 kg *2425 lb*.

Terry Thessman of Pahiatua, New Zealand designed and built a bike measuring 22·24 m *72·96 ft* long, and

---

Bicycle parade ● Leading the parade is TV personality 'Pacheco' aka Joaquín Monserrat. 2·75 per cent of the entire population (1 816 300) of San Juan, Puerto Rico took part in the extravaganza on 17 Apr 1988.

Melegari, Italy from 16 Aug–8 Sep 1986. (See above and right).

Biggest pyramid ■ The White Helmets, the Royal Signals Motorcycle Display Team, successfully achieved an eight-bike, 36-man pyramid for 300 m *328 yds* on 2 Sep 1986 and also achieved a 13-man pyramid, held together by muscle and determination only, with no straps, harnesses or any other aids, mounted on three motorcycles which travelled a distance of 1 km *0·8 mile* in a time of 2 min 6·6 sec at Catterick Airfield, North Yorks on 30 Sep 1988.

Backwards riding ■ Steering a motorcycle facing backwards from the top of a 3.3 m *10 ft* ladder over a continuous period of 1 hr 30 min Signalman Dewi Jones of the Royal Signals White Helmets, covered a distance of 33 km *20·505 miles* at Catterick Airfield, North Yorkshire on 30 Nov 1988.

Wheelie ■ Doug Domokos on the Alabama International Speedway, Talladega, USA on 27 Jun 1984 covered 233·34 km *145 miles* non-stop on the rear wheel of his Honda XR 500. He stopped only when the gas ran out.

The highest speed attained on a back wheel is

Motorcyle duration record ● Two of the three riders in action during the change-over of the 560 hr solo motorcycle non-stop ride. The riders were Norberto Naummi, Foppiani Maurizio and Roberto Ghillani who covered 30 370 km *18 000 miles* at an average speed of 54·23 km/h *33·69 mph* in Varano do Melegari, Italy from 16 Aug–8 Sep 1986.

221·43 km/h *137·6 mph* by Richard Almet (France) on 15 Aug 1986 at the Multi-Part British Truck Grand Prix, Silverstone, Northants.

Two wheel side car riding ■ Graham John Martin drove a distance of 320·1 km *198·9 miles* on a Yamaha XS 1100 cc bike in a time of 3 hr 5 min at Gerotek Test Track, Pretoria, South Africa on 21 Aug 1988.

Most on one machine ■ The record for the most people on a single machine is for 46 members of the Illawarra Mini Bike Training Club, New South Wales, Australia. They rode on a 1000 cc motorcycle and travelled a distance of 1·7 km *1 mile* on 11 Oct 1987.

Oldest motorcyclist ■ Arthur Merrick Cook (b.

First pneumatic bicycle tyre ● John Boyd Dunlop, inventor, fitted the first pair of cycle tyres to the rear wheels of his son Johnnie's Edlin Quadrant tricycle on the 28 Feb 1888. (Photo: Keystone Collection).

Takayuki Koike of Kanagawa, Japan set a record for 160·9 km *100 miles* in 6 hr 44 min 21·84 sec on 9 Aug 1987.

Sprint ■ The sprint record from a standing start over 100 metres is 13·71 sec by John Foss of Westbury, New York, USA, in Tokyo, Japan on 1 Aug 1987.

Penny-farthing ■ The record for riding from John O'Groats, Scotland to Land's End, Cornwall on Ordinary bicycles, more commonly known in the 1870s as Penny-farthings, is 9 days 6 hr 52 min by police officer Clive Flint, of Manchester on a 16·4 m *5 ft* high model from 2–10 Jun 1984. He averaged 160·93 km *100 miles* on the journey raising money for The Spastics Society.

G. P. Mills (Anfield BC) rode this course in 5 days 1 hr 45 min on a 53-inch Humber from 4–10 Jul 1886.

Underwater tricycling ■ A team of 32 divers pedalled a distance of 187·7 km *116·66 miles* in 75 hr 20 min on a standard tricycle at Diver's Den, Santa Barbara, California, USA on 16–19 Jun 1988 to raise money for the Muscular Dystrophy Association.

Unicycle record ● Looking refreshed after a gruelling ride are Mike Day and Michel Arets who travelled 1450 km *901 miles* on their unicycles from Land's End to John O'Groats between 27 Aug and 10 Sep 1986.

weighing 340 kg, which was ridden a distance of 246 m *807.08 ft* on 27 Feb 1988.

Smallest ■ The world's smallest wheeled rideable bicycle is one with wheels of 1·95 cm *0·76 in* diameter which was ridden by its constructor Neville Patten of Gladstone, Queensland, Australia for a distance of 4·1 m *13 ft 5½ in* on 25 Mar 1988. Jacques Puyoou of Pau, Pyrénées–Atlantiques, France has built a tandem 36 cm *14·1 in* wheel diameter ridden by him and Madame Puyoou.

Largest ■ A classic Ordinary bicycle with wheels of 165·7 cm *65¼ in* diameter front and 45·7 cm *18 in* back was constructed by the Coventry Machinists Co in 1881. It is now owned by Paul Foulkes-Halbard of Crowborough, West Sussex.

A bicycle with an 2·50 m *8 ft 2½ in* front wheel with pedal extenders was built in 1878 for circus demonstrations.

Fastest HPV's ■ The world speed records for human-powered vehicles (HPVs) are 99·68 km/h *61·94 mph* (single rider) by John Seibert at La Garita, Colorado, USA on 27 Oct 1980; and 101·25 km/h *62·92 mph* (multiple riders) by Dave Grylls and Leigh Barczewski at the Ontario Speedway, California, USA on 4 May 1980.

A British 200 m record was set by S. Poulter in *Poppy Flyer*, in 9·10 sec at Greenham Common, Berks on 2 Aug 1981.

Endurance ■ From 10–21 July 1983, 24 City and Guilds College, London, students drove an HPV round Great Britain on a 5914 km *3675 mile* route to average 23·19 km/h *14·41 mph.*

Wheelie ■ A world duration record of 4 hr 21 min 1 sec was set by Robert Hurd at the Recreation Centre, Winchester, Hants on 18 Nov 1986.

Unicycles ■ The tallest unicycle ever mastered is one 31·01 m *101 ft 9 in* tall ridden by Steve McPeak (with a safety wire or mechanic suspended by an overhead crane) for a distance of 114·6 m *376 ft* in Las Vegas, USA in October 1980. The freestyle riding of ever taller unicycles (i.e. without any safety harness) must inevitably lead to serious injury or fatality.

Endurance ■ Deepak Lele of Maharashtra, India unicycled 6378 km *3963 miles* from New York to Los Angeles, USA from 6 Jun–25 Sep 1984. Mike Day, 21 of

Manchester and Michel Arets, (b. 9 Sep 1959) of Maidstone, Kent unicycled 1450 km *901 miles* from Land's End, Cornwall to John O'Groats, Scotland from 27 Aug to 10 Sep 1986 in 14 days 12 hr 41 min.

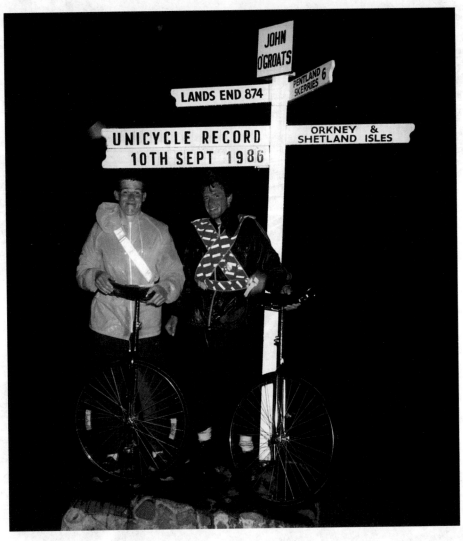

Railways

TRAINS

Earliest ■ Wagons running on wooden rails were used for mining as early as 1550 at Leberthal, Alsace, and in Britain for conveying coal at Wollaton near Nottingham from 1603–15 and at Broseley Colliery, Salop, in October 1605. Richard Trevithick (1771–1833) built his first steam locomotive for the 914 mm *3 ft* gauge iron plateway at Coalbrookdale, Salop, in 1803, but there is no evidence that it ran. His second locomotive drew wagons in which men rode on a demonstration run at Penydarren, Mid-Glamorgan, Wales, on 22 Feb 1804, but it broke the plate rails. The earliest commercially successful steam locomo-

tive worked in 1812 on the Middleton Colliery Railway to Leeds, Yorks, authorised by Britain's first Railway Act on 9 Jun 1758. The first permanent public railway to use steam traction was the Stockton & Darlington, from its opening on 27 Sep 1825 from Shildon to Stockton via Darlington, in Cleveland. The 7 tonne *Locomotion* could pull 48 tonnes at a speed

> **Fastest train ●** The TGV (Train à Grande Vitesse) inaugurated on 27 Sep 1981 and by September 1983 had reduced its scheduled time for the Paris–Lyon run of 425 km *264 miles* to 2 hr exactly, so averaging 212·5 km/h *132 mph*. The peak speed attained is 270 km/h *168 mph*.
> (Photo: Ace).

of 24 km/h *15 mph*. It was designed and driven by George Stephenson (1781–1848).

The first regular steam passenger service was inaugurated over a one-mile section (between Bogshole Farm and South Street in Whitstable), Yorks on the 10·05 km *6¼ mile* Canterbury & Whitstable Railway in Kent on 3 May 1830, hauled by the engine *Invicta*. The first practical electric railway was Werner von Siemens' oval metre-gauge demonstration track about 300 m *328 yd* long at the Berlin Trades Exhibition on 31 May 1879.

Fastest ■ The highest speed attained by a railed vehicle is 9851 km/h *6121 mph* or Mach 8 by an unmanned rocket sled over the 15·2 km *9½ mile* long rail track at White Sands Missile Range, New

Mexico, USA on 5 Oct 1982. The world's fastest speed with passengers in a non-railed vehicle is 400·7 km/h *249 mph* by the Maglev (magnetic levitation) MLU-001 test train over the 7 km *4·3 mile* long JNR experimental track at Miyazaki, Japan on 4 Feb 1987. On 1 May 1988 West Germany's Intercity Experimental train attained 405 km/h *252 mph* on a test run between Würzburg and Fulda.

The highest speed recorded on any national rail system is 380 km/h *236 mph* by the French SNCF high-speed train TGV-PSE on trial near Tonnerre on 26 Feb 1981. The TGV (Train à Grande Vitesse) inaugurated on 27 Sep 1981 by September 1983 had reduced its scheduled time for the Paris–Lyon run of 425 km *264 miles* to 2 hr exactly, so averaging 212·5 km/h *132 mph*. The peak speed attained is 270 km/h *168 mph*.

The highest speed ever ratified for a steam locomotive was 202·8 km/h *126 mph* over 402 m *440 yd* by the LNER 4-6-2 No 4468 *Mallard* (later numbered 60022) which hauled seven coaches weighing 243 tonnes *240 tons* gross down Stoke Bank, near Essendine, between Grantham, Lincs, and Peterborough, Cambs, on 3 Jul 1938. Driver Joseph Duddington was at the controls with Fireman Thomas Bray. The engine suffered some damage.

British Rail inaugurated their HST (High Speed Train) daily services between London–Bristol and South Wales on 4 Oct 1976. The electric British Rail APT-P (Advanced Passenger Train-Prototype) attained 261 km/h *162 mph* between Glasgow and Carlisle on its first revenue-earning run on 7 Dec 1981. It covered the 645 km *401 ¼ miles* from Glasgow to London in 4 ¼ hr, but was subsequently withdrawn from service because of technical problems.

British Rail set a new world speed record for diesel traction on 1 Nov 1987 when a special train testing the prototype SIG bogies for the Mk IV Inter City coaches reached 283·9 km/h *176·4 mph* between Darlington and York, with two Inter City 125 power cars.

Design of the 140 mph *237 km/h* £1 129 000 Class 91 Electra locomotive, tested in July 1988, calls for an eventual schedule for the 632 km *393 miles* London–Edinburgh route of 3 ½ hr, to average 180·6 km/h *112·28 mph*.

Longest non-stop ■ The longest run on British Rail without any advertised stop is the Night Motorail Service from Inverness to Euston. The distance is 913·7 km *567·75 miles* in a time of 11 hr 4 min.

Most powerful ■ The world's most powerful steam locomotive, measured by tractive effort, was No.700, a triple-articulated or triplex 2-8-8-8-4, six-cylinder engine built by the Baldwin Locomotive Works in 1916 for the Virginian Railroad. It had a tractive force of 75 434 kg *166 300 lb* working compound and 90 520 kg *199 560 lb* working simple.

Probably the heaviest train ever hauled by a single engine was one of 15 545 tonnes *15 300 tons* made up of 250 freight cars stretching 2·5 km *1·6 miles* by the *Matt H. Shay* (No 5014), a 2-8-8-8-2 engine which ran on the Erie Railroad from May 1914 until 1929.

On 16 Feb 1986, a single locomotive, No 59001, one of four diesels built by General Motors and privately owned by quarry company Foster Yeoman of Minehead, Somerset, hauled a 4639 tonne *4565 ton* train, the heaviest on record, during trials on Savernake Bank, Wilts.

Greatest load ■ The heaviest single pieces of freight ever conveyed by rail are limited by the capacity of the rolling stock. The world's strongest rail carrier with a capacity of 807 tonnes *749 tons* is the 336-tonne 36-axle 92 m *301 ft 10 in* long 'Schnabel' built for a US railway by Krupp, West Germany, in March 1981.

The heaviest load carried by British Rail was a 37·1 m *122 ft* long boiler drum, weighing 279 tonnes *275 tons* which was carried from Immingham Dock to Killingholme, Humberside, in September 1968.

The heaviest load ever moved on rails is the 10 860 tonnes *10 700-ton* Church of the Virgin Mary built in 1548 in the village of Most, Czechoslovakia, in October–November 1975 because it was in the way of coal workings. It was moved 730 m *800 yd* at 0·002 km/h *0·0013 mph* over 4 weeks at a cost of £9 million.

Freight trains ■ The longest and heaviest freight train on record was about 6 km *4 miles* in length. It comprised 500 coal cars with three 3600-hp diesels pulling and three more in the middle, on the Iaeger, West Virginia, to Portsmouth, Ohio, USA stretch of 252 km *157 miles* on the Norfolk and Western Railway on 15 Nov 1967. The total weight was nearly 42 674 tonnes *42 000 tons.*

British Rail's heaviest freight train began its regular run on 16 Sep 1983 from Merehead Quarry, Somerset, to Acton, West London, with 3300 tonnes *3250 tons* of limestone in 43 wagons and 2 engines stretching nearly 800 m *½ mile.* Since Feb 1986 this has been hauled by a single '59' class diesel.

TRACKS

Longest ■ The world's longest run is one of 9438 km *5864 ½ miles* on the Trans-Siberian line from Moscow to Nakhodka, USSR, in the Soviet Far East. There are 97 stops on the journey which takes 8 days 4 hr 25 min. The 3145 km *1954 mile* Baykal-Amur northern main line (BAM), begun with forced labour in 1938, was restarted in 1974 and put into service on 27 Oct 1984. A total of 382 million m³ *13 500 million ft³* of earth had to be moved and 3901 bridges built in this £8000 million project.

Longest straight ■ The Commonwealth Railways Trans-Australian line over the Nullarbor Plain from Mile 496 between Nurina and Loongana, Western Australia, to Mile 793 between Ooldea and Watson, South Australia, is 478 km *297 miles* dead straight although not level.

The longest straight on British Rail is the 29 km *18 miles* between Barlby Junction and Brough on the 'down' line on the Selby, North Yorks, to Kingston-upon-Hull, Humberside, line.

Widest and narrowest gauge ■ The widest in standard use is 1·676 m *5 ½ ft*. This width is used in Spain, Portugal, India, Pakistan, Bangladesh, Sri Lanka, Argentina and Chile. The narrowest gauge on which public services are operated is 260 mm *10¼ in* on the Wells Harbour (1·12 km *0·7 mile*) and the Wells – Walsingham Railways (6·5 km *4 miles*) in Norfolk.

Highest line ■ At 4817 m *15 806 ft* above sea level the standard gauge (1435 mm *4 ft 8 ½ in*) track on the Morococha branch of the Peruvian State Railways at La Cima is the highest in the world.
The highest point on the British Rail system is at the pass of Drumochter on the Perthshire–Inverness border, where the track reaches an altitude of 452 m *1484 ft* above sea-level. The highest railway in Britain is the Snowdon Mountain Railway, which rises from Llanberis, Gwynedd to 1064 m *3493 ft* above sea-level, just below the summit of Snowdon (*Yr Wyddfa*). It has a gauge of 800 mm *2 ft 7½ in.*

Lowest line ■ The world's lowest is in the Seikan Tunnel between Honshu and Hokkaido, Japan. The rails are 240 m *786 ft* below the Tsugaro Straits. The tunnel was opened on 13 Mar 1988. It is 53·8 km *33·4 miles* long. On British Rail the Severn Tunnel is 43·8 m *144 ft* below sea level.

Steepest gradient ■ The world's steepest standard by adhesion is 1:11 between Chedde and Servoz on the metre gauge SNCF Chamonix line, France.

The steepest sustained adhesion-worked gradient on main line in the United Kingdom is the 3·2 km *2 mile* Lickey incline of 1:37·7 just south-west of Birmingham. From the tunnel bottom to James Street, Liverpool, on the former Mersey Railway, there is a stretch of 1:27; and between Folkestone Junction and Harbour, Kent 1·6 km *1 mile* of 1:30.

Slightest gradient ■ The slightest gradient

posted on the British Rail system is one indicated as 1 in 14 400 between Pirbright Junction and Farnborough, Hants. This could be described alternatively as England's most obtuse summit.

Busiest system ■ The railway carrying the largest number of passengers is the East Japan Railway Company which at its busiest in 1986 carried 19 017 419 passengers daily. Among articles lost were 572 7000 umbrellas, 285 092 clothing items, 217 968 books and stationery items, 206 083 accessories and purses.

Greatest length of railways ■ The country with the greatest length of railway is the United States, with 296 489 km *184 235 miles* of track. The farthest anyone can get from a railway on the mainland island of Great Britain is 155·6 km *97·3 miles* by road in the case of Southend, Mull of Kintyre.

The number of journeys made on British Rail in the 12 months to 31 Mar 1989 was 727 200 000 (average 45·5 km *28·3 miles*) compared with the peak year of 1957, when 1101 million journeys (average 33 km *20·51 miles*) were made.

RAIL TRAVEL

Calling all stations ■ Alan M. Witton of Chorlton, Manchester visited every open British Rail station (2362) in a continuous tour for charity of 26 703 km *16 592 ¾ miles* in 452 hr 26 ½ min (27 136 min) from 13 Jul–28 Aug 1980.

Colin M. Mulvany and Seth N. Vafiadis of West London visited every British Rail station (2 378) embracing also the Tyne and Wear, Glasgow and London underground systems (333 stations) for charity in 31 days 5 hr 8 min 58 sec over 24 989 km *15 527·6 miles* to average 61·2 km/h *38·05 mph* from 4 Jun–5 Jul 1984.

Four points of compass ■ Carl Lombardelli of Romford, Essex traversed the extreme points of the compass for stations in Great Britain—Thurso (north), Lowestoft, Suffolk (east), Penzance, Cornwall (south) and Arisaig, Scotland (west) in 48 hr 15 min from 8–10 Sep 1985.

Most miles in 7 days ■ Derek Small of Newcastle upon Tyne, travelled 15 084 km *9373 ¼ miles* with a British Rail 7-day Rover ticket from 15–21 May 1989.

Longest journey ■ The greatest distance travelled on British Rail by InterCity within 24 hours is 2842·8 km *1766 ½ miles* on 5–6 Apr 1989 by David and Elaine Stevenson of Shepshed, Leics.

In the course of some 73 years commuting on British Rail from Kent to London, Ralph Ransome of Birchington travelled an equivalent of an estimated 39 times round the world. He retired early, aged 93, on 5 Feb 1986.

Irish rail travel ■ John Byrne of Dublin, Ireland, travelled the length of the entire Irish rail system – Iarnród Éireann in connection with the Cheeverstown Rail Marathon from Dublin to Dublin in 3 days 14 hr 50 min on 21–4 Sep 1987.

John Byrne and Lisa Shelley covered the entire passenger rail networks of Iarnrod Eireann and Northern Ireland Railways in 4 days 2 hr 47 min from 4–8 Jul 1988.

Most countries in 24 hours ■ The number of countries travelled through entirely by train in 24 hours is 10 by Aaron Kitchen on 16–17 Feb 1987. His route started in Yugoslavia and continued through Austria, Italy, Liechtenstein, Switzerland, France, Luxembourg, Belgium, Netherlands arriving in West Germany 22 hr 42 min later.

Super Traveller ■ Andrew Kendall of Moreton, Wirral, Lancs, has clocked up an amazing 116 244 miles by train in 1988 to become British Rail's Super Traveller of the year.

Handpumped railcars ■ A speed of 20 mph for a 300 m *984 ft* course was first surpassed at Port Moody, British Columbia, Canada by the 5-man team (1 pusher, 4 pumpers) from Port Moody Motors with

Moscow metro ● The world's busiest metro-seen here are a few of the 6 ½ million passengers who visit the many stations each day. The stations are colourfully decorated with paintings, mosaics and carvings and innumerable marble columns. (Photo: Intourist).

33·54 sec on 27 Jun 1982. They averaged 32·20 km/h *20·008 mph.*

STATIONS

Largest ■ The world's largest is Grand Central Terminal, Park Avenue and 43rd Street, New York City, USA built 1903–13. It covers 19 ha *48 acres* on two levels with 41 tracks on the upper level and 26 on the lower. On average more than 550 trains and 180 000 people per day use it.

The largest railway station in extent on the British Rail system is the 16-platform Clapham Junction, London, extending over 11·22 ha *27 ¾ acres* with a total face of 3243 m *10 682 ft.* The station with the largest number of platforms is London Waterloo (9·9 ha *24 ½ acres*), with 21 main and two Waterloo and City Line platforms, with a total face of 4679 m *15 352 ft.* Victoria Station (8·80 ha *21 ¾ acres*) has, however, a total face length of 5213 m *17 102 ft* for its 16 platforms.

Oldest ■ Liverpool Road Station, Manchester, England was first used on 15 Sep 1830 and now partly turned into a museum.

Busiest ■ The busiest railway junction in Great Britain is Clapham Junction, London, on the Southern Region of British Rail, with an average of 2200 trains passing through each 24 hr.

Highest ■ Condor station in Bolivia at 4786 m *15 705 ft* on the metre-gauge Rio Mulato to Potosi line. The highest passenger station on British Rail is Corrour, Inverness-shire, Scotland at an altitude of 410·5 m *1347 ft* above sea level.

Waiting rooms ■ The world's largest waiting rooms are the four in Peking Station, Chang'an Boulevard, Peking, China, opened in September 1959, with a total standing capacity of 14 000.

Platform ■ The longest railway platform in the world is the Khargpur platform, West Bengal, India, which measures 833 m *2733 ft* in length. The State Street Center subway platform staging on 'The Loop' in Chicago, Illinois, USA measures 1066 m *3500 ft* in length.

The longest in the British Rail system is the 602·69 m *1977 ft 4 in* long platform at Gloucester.

The two platforms comprising the New Misato railway station on the Musashino line, Saitama, Japan are 300 m *984 ft* apart and are connected by a bridge.

UNDERGROUND RAILWAYS

Most extensive ■ The subway with most stations in the world is the New York City Transport Authority subway, USA (first section opened on 27 Oct 1904) with a total of 372·93 km *231·73 route miles* and 1 073 000 000 passengers in 1988. The 466 stations are closer set than London's. The earliest (first section between Farringdon St and Edgware Road, opened 10 Jan 1863) and one of the most extensive underground or rapid transit railway systems of the 67 in the world is the London Underground with 408 km *254 miles* of route, of which 135 km *85 miles* is bored tunnel and 32 km *20 miles* is 'cut and cover'. The whole system is operated by a staff of 19 000 serving 273 stations. The 457 trains comprising 3875 cars carried 798 000 000 passengers in 1987/8. The greatest depth is 67·4 m *221 ft* near Hampstead on the Northern Line. The longest journey without a change is Epping to West Ruislip—54·9 km *34·1 miles.*

Travelling *London Underground* ■ The record for touring the 272 stations including Heathrow Terminal 4 station opened 12 Apr 1986 is 18 hr 41 min 41 sec set by a team of five: Robert A. Robinson, Peter D. Robinson, Timothy J. Robinson, Timothy J. Clark and Richard J. Harris on 30 Jul 1986. Peter Robinson (b. 19 Jul 1974) was the youngest to tour all stations on 22 Jul 1982 aged 8.

New York, USA subway ■ The record for travelling the whole system is 29 hr 47 min 12 sec travelling through 466 separate stations 483 km *300 miles* set by Richard Temple, Phil Vanner and Tom Murphy on 12 –13 Dec 1988.

Busiest ■ The world's busiest metro system is that in Greater Moscow, USSR with as many as 2·55 billion passengers per year. There are 132 stations (15 of which have more than one name, being transfer stations) and 212.5 km *132 miles* of track. The 5 kopeck fare has not changed since the Metro first went into operation in 1935.

Travelling record ■ The record transit on 9 Dec 1988 through all 123 named stations) was 9 hr 39 min 50 sec by Peter Altman of Edgware, Middlesex and Miss Jackie Smith of Bobblestock, Herefordshire.

MODEL RAILWAYS

Non-stop duration ■ A loco plus six coaches in 864 hr 30 min from 1 Jun–7 Jul 1978, covering 1091 km *678 miles,* organised by Roy Catton at 'Pastimes' Toy Store, Mexborough, South Yorks.

The longest recorded run by a model *steam* locomotive is 231·7 km *144 miles* in 27 hr 18 min by the 18·4 cm *7 ¼ in* gauge 'Winifred', built in 1974 by Wilf Grove at Thames Ditton, Surrey, on 8–9 Sep 1979. 'Winifred' works on 5·6 kg/cm² *80 lb/in²* pressure and is coal fired with cylinders 54 mm *2 ⅛ in* in diameter and 79 mm *3 ⅛ in* stroke.

Smallest ■ The most miniature model railway ever built is one of 1:1000 scale by Jean Damery (b. 1923) of Paris, France. The engine ran on a 4 ½ volt battery and measures 7·9 mm *⁵⁄₁₆ in* overall.

Aircraft

Note—The use of the Mach scale for aircraft speeds was introduced by Prof Ackeret of Zürich, Switzerland. The Mach number is the ratio of the velocity of a moving body to the local velocity of sound. This ratio was first employed by Dr Ernst Mach (1838–1916) of Vienna, Austria in 1887. Thus Mach 1·0 equals 1224·67 km/h *760·98 mph* at sea level at 15°C, and is assumed, for convenience, to fall to a constant 1061·81 km/h *659·78 mph* in the stratosphere, i.e. above 11 000 m *36 089 ft.*

EARLIEST FLIGHTS

The first controlled and sustained power-driven flight occurred near the Kill Devil Hill, Kitty Hawk, North Carolina, USA, at 10.35 a.m. on 17 Dec 1903, when Orville Wright (1871–1948) flew the 12-hp chain-driven *Flyer I* for a distance of 36·5 m *120 ft* at an air speed of 48 km/h *30 mph,* a ground speed of 10·9 km/h *6·8 mph* and an altitude of 2·5–3·5 m *8–12 ft* for about 12 sec watched by his brother Wilbur (1867–1912), four men and a boy. Both brothers, from Dayton, Ohio, were bachelors because, as Orville put it, they had not the means to 'support a wife as well as an aeroplane'. The *Flyer* is now in the National Air and Space Museum at the Smithsonian Institution, Washington DC, USA.

The first hop by a man-carrying aeroplane entirely under its own power was made when Clément Ader (1841–1925) of France flew in his *Eole* for about 50 m *164 ft* at Armainvilliers, France, on 9 Oct 1890. It was powered by a lightweight steam engine of his own design which developed about 20 hp (15 kW). The earliest 'rational design' for a flying machine, according to the Royal Aeronautical Society, was that published by Emanuel Swedenborg (1688–1772) in Sweden in 1717.

The first officially recognised flight in the British Isles was made by the US citizen Samuel Franklin Cody (1861–1913) who flew 423 m *1390 ft* in his own biplane at Farnborough, Hants, on 16 Oct 1908. Horatio Frederick Phillips (1845–1924) almost certainly covered 152 m *500 ft* in his Phillips II *'Venetian blind'* aeroplane at Streatham, in 1907.

The first Briton to fly was George Pearson Dickin (1881–1909), a journalist from Southport, Lancs as a passenger to Wilbur Wright at Auvóur, France on 3 Oct 1908. The first resident British citizen to fly in Britain was J. T. C. Moore-Brabazon (later Lord Brabazon of Tara PC, GBE, MC) (1884–1964) with three short but sustained flights from 30 Apr–2 May 1909.

Cross-Channel ■ The earliest was made on Sunday, 25 Jul 1909 when Louis Blériot (1872–1936) of France flew his Blériot XI monoplane, powered by a 23-hp Anzani engine, 41·8 km *26 miles* from Les Baraques, France, to Northfall Meadow near Dover Castle, Kent, in 36 ½ min, after taking off at 4.41 a.m.

Jet-engined ■ Proposals for jet propulsion date back to Captain Marconnet (1909) of France, and Henri Coanda (1886–1972) of Romania, and to the turbojet proposals of Maxime Guillaume in 1921. The earliest tested run was that of the British Power Jets Ltd's experimental WU1 (Whittle Unit) on 12 Apr 1937, invented by Flying Officer (later Air Commodore Sir) Frank Whittle OM, KBE (1907-88), who had applied for a patent on jet propulsion in 1930. The first flight by an aeroplane powered by a turbojet engine was made by the Heinkel He 178, piloted by Flug Kapitan Erich Warsitz, at Marienehe, Germany, on 27 Aug 1939. It was powered by a Heinkel He S3b engine (378 kg *834 lb* as installed with long tailpipe) designed by Dr Hans 'Pabst' von Ohain and first tested in August 1937.

The first British jet flight occurred when Fl-Lt P. E. G. 'Jerry' Sayer OBE (k. 1942) flew the Gloster-Whittle E.28/39 (wing span 8·84 m *29 ft*, length 7·70 m *25 ft 3 in*) fitted with an 390 kg *860 lb* s. t. Whittle W-1 engine for 17 min at Cranwell, Lincs, on 15 May 1941. The maximum speed was c. 560 km/h *350 mph*. This aircraft (W4041/G) is now in the Science Museum, London.

Supersonic flight ■ The first was achieved on 14 Oct 1947 by Capt (later Brig Gen) Charles ('Chuck') Elwood Yeager, (b. 13 Feb 1923), over Edwards Air Force Base, Muroc, California, in a Bell XS-1 rocket plane ('Glamorous Glennis') with Mach 1·015 (1078 km/h *670 mph*) at an altitude of 12 800 m *142 000 ft*. The first British aircraft to attain Mach 1 in a dive was the de Havilland D. H. 108 tail-less research aircraft on 6 Sep 1948, piloted by John Derry. The XS-1 is now in the National Air and Space Museum at the Smithsonian Institution, Washington DC, USA.

Trans-Atlantic ■ The first crossing of the North Atlantic by air was made by Lt-Cdr (later Rear Admiral) Albert Cushion Read (1887–1967) and his crew (Stone, Hinton, Rodd, Rhoads and Breese) in the 84 knot *155 km/h* US Navy/Curtiss flying boat NC-4 from Trepassey Harbor, Newfoundland, via the Azores, to Lisbon, Portugal, from 16–27 May 1919. The whole flight of 7591 km *4717 miles*, originating from Rockaway Air Station, Long Island, NY, USA on 8 May, required 53 hr 58 min, terminating at Plymouth, Devon, on 31 May. The Newfoundland–Azores flight of 1930 km *1200 miles* took 15 hr 18 min at 81·7 knots *151·4 km/h*.

Non-stop ■ The first non-stop trans-Atlantic flight was achieved 18 days later at 4.13 p.m. GMT on 14 Jun 1919, from Lester's Field, St John's, Newfoundland, 3154 km *1960 miles* to Derrygimla bog near Clifden, Co. Galway, Ireland, at 8.40 a.m. GMT, 15 Jun, when the pilot, Capt John William Alcock DSC (1892–1919), and the navigator Lt Arthur Whitten Brown (1886–1948) flew across in a Vickers Vimy, powered by two 360-hp Rolls-Royce Eagle VIII engines. Both men were created civil KBEs' on 21 Jun 1919 when Alcock was aged 26 years 227 days, and they shared a *Daily Mail* prize of £10 000.

Solo ■ The 79th man to achieve a trans-Atlantic flight but the first to do so solo was Capt (later Brig) Charles Augustus Lindbergh (Hon AFC) (1902–74) who took off in his 220 hp Ryan monoplane *Spirit of St Louis* at 12.52 p.m. GMT on 20 May 1927 from Roosevelt Field, Long Island, NY, USA. He landed at 10.21 p.m. GMT on 21 May 1927 at Le Bourget Airfield, Paris, France. His flight of 5810 km *3610 miles* lasted 33 hr 29 ½ min and he won a prize of $25 000. The *Spirit of St Louis* is now in the National Air and Space Museum at the Smithsonian Institution, Washington DC, USA.

Most flights ■ Between March 1948 and his retirement on 1 Sep 1984 Flight Service Manager Charles M. Schimpf logged a total of 2 880 Atlantic crossings—a rate of 6·4 per month.

Trans-Pacific ■ The first non-stop flight was by Major Clyde Pangborn and Hugh Herndon in the Bellanca cabin plane *Miss Veedol* from Sabishiro Beach, Japan 7335 km *4558 miles* to Wenatchee, Washington State, USA in 41 hr 13 min from 3–5 Oct 1931. (For earliest crossing see Circumnavigational flights below.)

Circumnavigational flights ■ Strict circumnavigation requires passing through two antipodal points thus with a minimum distance of 40 007·89 km *24 859·75 miles*.

Earliest ■ The earliest such flight of 26 345 miles *42 398 km* was by two US Army Douglas DWC amphibians in 57 'hops'. The *Chicago* was piloted by Lt Lowell H. Smith and Lt Leslie P. Arnold and the *New Orleans* by Lt Erik H. Nelson and Lt John Harding between 6 Apr and 28 Sep 1924 beginning and ending at Seattle, Washington State, USA.

Fastest ■ The fastest flight under the FAI rules which permit flights that exceed the length of the

Tropic of Cancer or Capricorn (36 787·599 km *22 858·754 miles*) was that of the 37 216 km *23 125 mile* eastabout flight of 36 hr 54 min 15 sec by the Boeing 747 SP 'Friendship One' (Capt. Clay Lacy) from Seattle, Washington State, USA with 141 passengers on 28–30 Jan 1988. The plane reached 1292 km/h *803 mph* over the Atlantic and refuelled only in Athens, Greece and T'ai-pei, Taiwan.

First without refuelling ■ Dick Rutan and Jeana Yeager in their specially constructed aircraft *Voyager*, designed by Dick's brother Burt Rutan, flew from Edwards Air Force Base, California, USA from 14–23 Dec 1986. Their flight took 9 days 3 min 44 sec and they covered a distance of 40 212·139 km *24 986·665 miles* averaging 186·1 km/h *115·64 mph*. The plane, with a wing span of 33·77 m *110·8 ft*, was capable of carrying 5636 litres *1240 gal* of fuel weighing 4052 kg *8934 lb*. It took over two years and 22 000 man-hours to construct. The pilot flew from a cockpit measuring 1·7 × 0·54 m *5·6 × 1·8 ft* and the off-duty crew member occupied a cabin 2·3 × 0·6 m *7½ × 2 ft*. *Voyager* is now in the National Air and Space Museum at the Smithsonian Institution, Washington, DC, USA.

First circum-polar ■ Achieved by Capt Elgen M. Long, 44, in a Piper Navajo from 5 Nov–3 Dec 1971. He covered 62 597 km *38 896 miles* in 215 flying hours. The cabin temperature sank to −40° C *−40° F* over Antarctica.

First single-engined flight ■ Richard Norton, an American airline captain, and Calin Rosetti, head of satellite navigation systems at the European Space Agency, made the first single-engined circum-polar flight in a Piper PA-46-310P Malibu. This began and finished at Le Bourget Airport, Paris, France from 21 Jan–15 Jun 1987. They travelled 55 266 km *34 342 miles* in a flying time of 185 hr 41 min. The so-called 'Flight of the Arctic Tern' also set 16 other point-to-point records.

Largest wing span ■ The aircraft with the largest wing span ever constructed is the $40-million Hughes H.4 Hercules flying boat ('Spruce Goose'), which was raised 21·3 m *70 ft* into the air in a test run of 914 m *1000 yd*, piloted by Howard Hughes (1905–76) off Long Beach Harbor, California, USA on 2 Nov 1947. The eight-engined 193-tonne *190-ton* aircraft had a wing span of 97·51 m *319 ft 11 in* and a length of 66·64 m *218 ft 8 in*, and never flew again. In a brilliant engineering feat she was moved bodily by Goldcoast Corp aided by the US Navy barge crane YD-171 on 22 Feb 1982 to her final resting place 9·6 km *6 miles* across the harbour under a 213·4 m *700 ft* diameter dome. Among current aircraft, the Soviet Antonov An-124 has a span of 73·3 m *240 ft 5¾ in* and the Boeing 747-400 one of 64·92 m *213 ft*. A modified six-engine version of the An-124, dubbed An-225, has a wing span of 88·4 m *290 ft 0 in*.

The $34-million Piasecki Heli-Stat, comprising a framework of light-alloy and composite materials to mount four Sikorsky SH-34J helicopters and the envelope of a Goodyear ZPG-2 patrol airship, was exhibited on 26 Jan 1984 at Lakehurst, New Jersey,

USA. Designed for use by the US Forest Service and designated Model 94-37J Logger, it had an overall length of 104·55 m *343 ft* and was intended to carry a payload of 21·4 tons. It crashed on 1 Jul 1986.

Heaviest ■ The aircraft with the highest standard maximum take-off weight is the Antonov An-225 *Myriya* (Dream) at 508 tonnes *508 tons*. This aircraft lifted a payload of 156 300 kg *344 579 lb* to a height of 12 410 m *40 715 ft* on 22 Mar 1989. This flight was achieved by Capt Alexander Galunenko with his crew of 7 pilots. The flight was made along the route Kiev-Leningrad-Kiev without landing at a range of 2100 km *1305 miles* for 3 hr 47 min. 109 world aviation records have been fixed for this flight.

Electric plane ■ The MB-E1 is the first electrically propelled aircraft. A Bosch 8-kW motor *10·7 hp* is powered by Varta FP25 nickel-cadmium 25 Ah batteries. The plane, with a wingspan of 12 m *39·4 ft* is 7 m *23 ft* long and weighs 400 kg *882 lb*. It was designed by the model aircraft constructor American Fred Militky and made its maiden flight on 21 Oct 1973.

Solar powered ■ The *Solar Challenger*, designed by a team led by Dr Paul MacCready, was flown for the first time entirely under solar power on 20 Nov 1980. On 7 Jul 1981, piloted by Steve Ptacek (USA), the *Solar Challenger* became the first aircraft of this category to achieve a crossing of the English Channel. Taking off from Pontois-Cormeilles, Paris, France the 262·3 km *163 mile* journey to Manston, Kent was completed in 5 hr 23 min at a maximum altitude of 3353 m *11 000 ft*. The aircraft has a wing span of 14·3 m *47 ft*.

Ultralight ■ On 3 Aug 1985 Anthony A. Cafaro (b. 30 Nov 1951) flew a ULA (max weight 111 kg *245 lb*, max speed 104·6 km/h *65 mph*, capacity 18·93 litre *5 US gal*) single-seater Gypsey Skycycle for 7 hr 31 min at Dart Field, Mayville, NY, USA. Nine fuel 'pick-ups' were completed during the flight.

Smallest ■ The smallest plane ever flown is the *Baby Bird*, designed and built by Donald R. Stits. It is 3·35 m *11 ft* long, with a wing span of 1·91 m *6 ft 3 in*, and weighs 114·3 kg *252 lb* empty. It is powered by a 55-hp 2-cylinder Hirth engine, giving a top speed of 177 km/h *110 mph*. It was first flown by Harold Nemer on 4 Aug 1984 at Camarillo, California, USA. The smallest jet is the 450 km/h *280 mph* Silver Bullet weighing 196 kg *432 lb* with a 5·18 m *17 ft* wing span built by Bob Bishop (USA).

Bombers *Heaviest* ■ The eight-jet swept-wing Boeing B-52H Stratofortress, which has a maximum take-off weight of 220 tonnes has a wing span of 56·38 m *185 ft* and is 48·02 m *157 ft 6¾ in* in length, with a speed of over 1046 km/h *650 mph*. The B-52 can carry twelve SRAM thermonuclear short-range attack missiles or twenty-four 340 kg *750 lb* bombs

First non-stop trans-Atlantic flight ● A Vickers *Vimy* similar to the one flown by Alcock and Brown. (Photo: K.J.A. Brookes)

under its wings and eight more SRAMs or eighty-four 226 kg *500 lb* bombs in the fuselage. The 10-engined Convair B-36J, weighing 185 tonnes *183 tons*, had a greater wing span, at 70·10 m *230 ft* but it is no longer in service. Its top speed was 700 km/h *435 mph*.

Fastest ■ The world's fastest operational bombers are the French Dassault Mirage IV, which can fly at Mach 2·2 2333 km/h *1450 mph* at 11 000 m *36 000 ft*. The American General Dynamics FB-111A has a maximum speed of Mach 2·5; and the Soviet swing-wing Tupolev Tu-22M known to NATO as 'Backfire' has an estimated over-target speed of Mach 2·0 but which may be as fast as Mach 2·5.

Largest airliner ■ The highest capacity jet airliner is the Boeing 747 'Jumbo Jet', first flown on 9 Feb 1969 (see Heaviest aircraft) and has a capacity of from 385 to more than 500 passengers with a maximum speed of 969 km/h *602 mph*. Its wing span is 59·64 m *231·8 ft* and its length 70·7 m *195·7 ft*. It entered service on 22 Jan 1970. The first 747-400 was rolled out on 26 Jan 1988 for service with Northwest Airlines with a wing span of 64·92 m *213 ft* and a range exceeding 12 875 km *8000 miles* and a capacity for 422 passengers. Theoretical accommo-dation is available for 516 passengers seated 10-abreast in the main cabin plus up to 69 in the stretched upper deck in the 747-300. A version of the McDonnell Douglas MD-11 airliner is being studied with accommodation for 515 passengers in the main cabin and up to 96 in a lower so-called panorama deck forward of the wing.

The greatest passenger load recorded was one of 306 adults, 328 children and 40 babies (total 674) from the cyclone-devastated Darwin to Sydney, New South Wales, Australia on 29 Dec 1974.

The largest ever British aircraft was the experimen-tal Bristol Type 167 Brabazon, which had a maximum take-off weight of 131·4 tonnes *129·4 tons*, a wing span of 70·10 m *230 ft* and a length of 53·94 m *177 ft*. This eight-engined aircraft first flew on 4 Sep 1949. Concorde has a maximum take-off weight of 185 065 kg *408 000 lb*.

Fastest airliner ■ The supersonic BAC/Aérospatiale Concorde, first flown on 2 Mar 1969, with a designed capacity of 128 passengers, cruises at up to Mach 2·2 (2333 km/h *1450 mph*). It flew at Mach 1·05 on 10 Oct 1969, exceeded Mach 2 for the first time on 4 Nov 1970 and became the first supersonic airliner used on passenger services on 21 Jan 1976. The New York–London record is 2 hr 55 min 15 sec set on 6 Feb 1988.

Most capacious ■ The Aero Spacelines Super Guppy has a cargo hold with a usable volume of 1410 m³ *49 790ft³* and a maximum take-off weight of 79·38 tonnes *78·12 tons*. Wing span is 47·62 m *156 ft 3 in*, length 43·05 m *141 ft 3 in*. Its cargo compartment measures 33·17 m *108 ft 10 in* in length with a cylindrical section of 7·62 m *25 ft* in diameter. The Soviet Antonov An-124 Ruslan has a cargo hold with a usable volume of 1014 m³ *35 800 ft³* and a maximum take-off weight of 405 tonnes *398·6 tons*. It is powered by four Lotarev D-18T turbofans giving a cruising speed of up to 850 km/h *528 mph* at 12 000 m *39 370 ft* and a range of 4500 km *2796 miles*. A special-purpose heavy-lift version of the An-124, dubbed An-225 has been developed with a stretched fuselage providing as much as 1 190 m³ *42 000 ft³* usable volume. A new wing centre section carries an additional two engines, providing an estimated total 310 000 lb thrust. Having flown first on 21 Dec 1988, the aircraft was expected to be used to ferry large parts of the Soviet Energia launch vehicle on a complete Buran space shuttle.

Largest propeller ■ The largest ever used was the 6·9 m *22 ft 7½ in* diameter Garuda propeller, fitted to the Linke-Hofmann R II built in Breslau, Germany (now Wroclaw, Poland), which flew in 1919. It was driven by four 193 kW *260-hp* Mercedes engines and turned at only 545 rpm.

Scheduled flights *Longest* ■ The non-stop flight of United Airlines and Qantas Los Angeles–Sydney is

Concorde ● The supersonic BAC/Aérospatiale Concorde first flown on 2 Mar 1969, with a capacity of 128 passengers, it cruised up to Mach 2·2(2333 km/h *1450 mph*). The New York–London record is 2 hr 55 min 15 sec set on 6 Feb 1988. (Photo: Roger Perry/Impact Photos).

14 hr 50 min in a Boeing 747 SP (Special Perform-ance), over 12 050 km *7487 miles*. The longest delivery flight by a commercial jet is 8936 nautical miles or 16 560 km *10 290 miles* from Seattle, Wash-ington State, USA to Cape Town, South Africa by the South African Airways' Boeing 747 SP (Special Per-formance) 'Matroosberg' using 178 400 kg *175·5 tons* of pre-cooled fuel in 17 hr 22 ½min on 23–24 Mar 1976. The Boeing 747-400, which was entering ser-vice in early 1988, has a range of more than 13 500 km *8 406 miles* at long-range cruising speed with 412 passengers. Claimed ferry range is more than 15 500 km *9 650 miles*.

Shortest ■ The scheduled flight by Loganair between the Orkney Islands of Westray and Papa Westray which has been flown with Britten-Norman Islander twin-engined 10-seat transports since Sept-ember 1967. Though scheduled for 2 min, in favour-able wind conditions it has been accomplished in 58 sec by Capt Andrew D. Alsop.

United Airlines provide the shortest scheduled flight by jet, a Boeing 727 between San Francisco and Oakland, California, USA. There are three flights daily and return, the flight time averaging 5 minutes for the 19·3 km *12 mile* journey.

Gary W. Rovetto of Island Air on 21 Mar 1980 flew on the scheduled flight from Center Island to Decatur Island, Washington State, USA in 41 sec.

Most flights in 24 hours ■ Paula Scrimshaw of Guernsey, Channel Islands, made 24 scheduled passenger flights in Trislanders of Aurigny Air Services between Jersey and Guernsey in 11 hr 50 min on 18 Nov 1988.

Fastest intercontinental scheduled airline ■ GB Airways have, since 1931, been operating a scheduled service from Gibraltar in Europe to Tangier in Africa on an almost daily basis. The flight by Vickers Viscount averages 15 minutes and covers a distance of 60 km *37 miles*.

Round the world ■ The fastest time for a trip on scheduled flights for a circumnavigation is 44 hr 6 min by David J. Springbett (b. 2 May 1938) of Taplow, Bucks. His route took him from Los Angeles eastabout via London, Bahrain, Singapore, Bangkok, Manila, Tokyo and Honolulu from 8–10 Jan 1980 over a 37 124 km *23 068 mile* course.

Paris–London ■ The fastest time to travel the 344 km *214 miles* from central Paris, France to central London (BBC TV centre) is 38 min 58 sec by David Boyce of Stewart Wrightson (Aviation) Ltd on 24 Sep 1983 by motorcycle and helicopter to Le Bourget; Hawker Hunter jet (piloted by the late Michael Carlton) to Biggin Hill, Kent; helicopter to the TV centre car park.

London–New York ■ From central London to downtown New York City, USA by helicopter and Concorde the record is 3 hr 59 min 44 sec and the return in 3 hr 40 min 40 sec, both by David J. Spring-bett and David Boyce on 8 and 9 Feb 1982.

John O'Groats–Land's End ■ The record time for an End to End over Great Britain where supersonic overflying is banned is 46 min 44 sec by a Phantom Jet (Wing-Cdr John Brady and Flt Lt Mike Pugh) on 24 Feb 1988.

HIGHEST SPEED

Official record ■ The air speed record is 3529·56 km/h *2193·167 mph* by Capt Eldon W. Joersz and Maj George T. Morgan, Jr, in a Lockheed SR-71A near Beale Air Force Base, California, USA over a 25 km *15½ mile* course on 28 Jul 1976.

Air-launched record ■ The fastest fixed-wing aircraft in the world was the US North American Aviation X-15A-2, which flew for the first time (after modification from X-15A) on 25 Jun 1964 powered by a liquid oxygen and ammonia rocket propulsion system. Ablative materials on the airframe once enabled a temperature of 3000°F to be withstood. The landing speed was momentarily 389·1 km/h *242 mph*. The highest speed attained was 7274 km/h *4520 mph* (Mach 6·7) when piloted by Maj William J. Knight, USAF (b. 1930), on 3 Oct 1967. An earlier version piloted by Joseph A. Walker (1920–66) reached 107 960 m *354 200 ft* (67·08 miles) also over Edwards Air Force Base, California, USA on 22 Aug 1963. The programme was suspended after the final flight of 24 Oct 1968.

The US NASA Rockwell International Space Shuttle Orbiter *Columbia* was launched from the Kennedy Space Center, Cape Canaveral, Florida, USA commanded by Cdr John W. Young USN and piloted by Robert L. Crippen on 12 Apr 1981 after expen-diture of $9900 million since 1972. *Columbia* broke all records for space by a fixed-wing craft with 26 715 km/h *16 600 mph* at main engine cut-off. After re-entry from 122 km *400 000 ft*, experiencing tem-peratures of 2160° C *3920° F*, she glided home weighing 97 tonnes *95 tons* with a landing speed of 347 km/h *216 mph* on Rogers Dry Lake, California, USA on 14 Apr 1981. Under a new FAI (Fédération Aéronautique Internationale) Category P for Aerospacecraft, the *Columbia* is holder of the cur-rent absolute world record for duration of 10 days 7 hr 47 min 23 sec to main touchdown when launched on its sixth mission, STS 9 Spacelab 1, with six crewmen on 28 Nov 1983. *Challenger* was destroyed soon after launch from Cape Canaveral on 28 Jan 1986 (see Chapter 4). *Atlantis* holds the Shuttle altitude record of 515 km *320 miles* achieved on 3

Oct 1985 on its maiden flight STS 51J. The greatest mass lifted by Shuttle and placed in orbit was 118 697 kg *261 679 lb* by *Discovery* on STS 51A, launched on 8 Nov 1984.

Fastest jet ■ The USAF Lockheed SR-71, a reconnaissance aircraft, is the world's fastest jet (See Official Record above). First flown on 22 Dec 1964, it is reportedly capable of attaining an altitude ceiling of close to 30 480 m *100 000 ft*. It has a wing span of 16·94 m *55·6 ft* and a length of 32·73 m *107·4 ft* and weighs 75·9 tons *170 0000 lb* at take-off. Its reported range is 4800 km *2982 miles* at Mach 3 at 24 000 m *78 750 ft*. At least 30 are believed to have been built.

It was reported on 15 Jan 1988 that the US Air Force was developing secretly a Mach 5 *6115 km/h 3800 mph* high altitude (above 30 480 m *100 000 ft*) stealth aircraft.

Fastest combat jet ■ The USSR Mikoyan MiG-25 fighter (NATO code name 'Foxbat'). The reconnaissance 'Foxbat-B' has been tracked by radar at about Mach 3·2 (3395 km/h *2110 mph*). When armed with four large underwing air-to-air missiles known to NATO as 'Acrid', the fighter 'Foxbat-A' is limited to Mach 2·8 (2969 km/h *1845 mph*). The single-seat 'Foxbat-A' spans 13·95 m *45 ft 9 in*, is 3·82 m *278 ft 2 in* long and has an estimated maximum take-off weight of 37 421 kg *82 500 lb*.

Fastest biplane ■ The Italian Fiat CR42B, with a 753 kW *1010-hp* Daimler-Benz DB601A engine, which attained 520 km/h *323 mph* in 1941. Only one was built.

Fastest piston-engined aircraft ■ The fastest speed is for a cut-down privately-owned Hawker Sea Fury which attained 836 km/h *520 mph* in level flight over Texas, USA, in August 1966. It was piloted by Mike Carroll (k. 1969) of Los Angeles, USA. The FAI accredited record for a piston-engined aircraft is 832·12 km/h *517·055 mph* over Mojave, California, USA by Frank Taylor (US) in a modified North American P-51D Mustang powered by a 3000-hp Packard Merlin, over a 25 km *15½ mile* course, on 30 Jul 1983.

Fastest propeller-driven aircraft ■ The Soviet Tu-114 turboprop transport achieved a recorded speed of 877·212 km/h *545·076 mph* carrying heavy payloads over measured circuits. It is developed from the Tupolev Tu-95 bomber, known in NATO as the 'Bear', and has four 14,795-hp engines. The turboprop-powered Republic XF-84H prototype US Navy fighter which flew on 22 Jul 1955 had a top *design* speed of 1078 km/h *670 mph* but was abandoned. McDonnell Douglas expects its projected MD-91X, powered by counter-rotating multi-bladed fans, to cruise at about Mach 0·78 814 km/h *514 mph*. Testing during 1987–8 with an MD-80 experimentally fitted with a General Electric GE36 engine driving two fans (in place of one of the two standard Pratt & Whitney JT8D turbofans) attained a maximum speed of Mach 0·865.

Fastest trans-Atlantic flight ■ The flight record is 1 hr 54 min 56.4 sec by Maj James V. Sullivan, 37, and Maj Noel F. Widdifield, 33, flying a Lockheed SR-71A eastwards on 1 Sep 1974. The average speed, slowed by refuelling by a KC-135 tanker aircraft, for the New York–London stage of 5570·80 km *3461·53 miles* was 2908·026 km/h *1806·963 mph*. The solo record (Gander to Gatwick) is 8 hr 47 min 32 sec by Capt John J. A. Smith in a Rockwell 685 on 12 Mar 1978.

Altitude ■ The official record by an aircraft taking off from the ground under its own power is 37 650 m *(123 524 ft)* by Aleksandr Fedotov (USSR) in a Mikoyan E.266M (MiG-25) aircraft, powered by two 14 000 kg *30 865 lb* thrust turbojet engines, on 31 Aug 1977.

In the same aircraft he established the fastest climb record on 17 May 1975 reaching 30 000 m *98 425 ft* in 4 min 11·7 sec after take off.

Duration ■ The record is 64 days 22 hr 19 min and 5 sec, set up by Robert Timm and John Cook in a

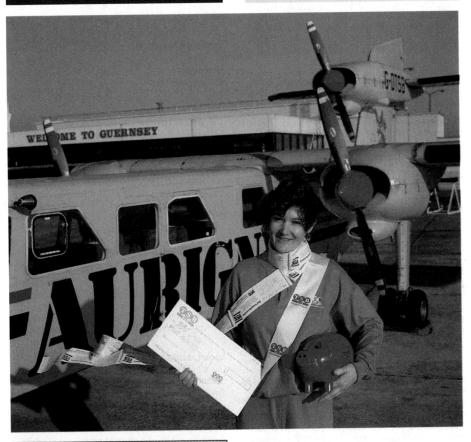

Most flights in one day ● Paula Scrimshaw of Guernsey, Channel Islands made 24 scheduled passenger flights between Jersey and Guernsey in a time of 11 hr 50 min on 18 Nov 1988.

Cessna 172 'Hacienda'. They took off from McCarran Airfield, Las Vegas, Nevada, USA just before 3.53 p.m. local time on 4 Dec 1958, and landed at the same airfield just before 2.12 p.m. on 7 Feb 1959. They covered a distance equivalent to six times round the world with continued refuellings, without landing.

AIRPORTS

Largest *World* ■ The world's £2100-million King Khalid International Airport outside Riyadh, Saudi Arabia covers an area of 221 km² *86 miles²*. It was opened on 14 Nov 1983. It also has the world's largest control tower, 74 m *243 ft* in height. The Hajj Terminal at the £2800-million King Abdul-Aziz airport near Jeddah is the world's largest roofed structure covering 1·5 km² *370 acres.* The present six runways and 5 terminal buildings of Dallas/Fort Worth Airport, Texas, USA are planned to be extended to nine runways and 13 terminals with 260 gates with an ultimate capacity for 150 million passengers. The world's largest airport terminal is Hartsfield Atlanta International Airport, Georgia, USA, opened on 21 Sep 1980 with floor space covering 20·43 ha *50½ acres.* It has 138 gates handling nearly 50 million passengers a year but has a capacity for 75 million. The new airport planned for Denver, Colorado, USA was expected to occupy an area of 116·5 km² *45 miles²* and in early 1988 was the only new major airport being planned. It was to have 12 runways. Construction of new homes within the expected 60 dB noise 'contour' was banned.

United Kingdom ■ Sixty-nine airline companies from 61 countries operate scheduled services into Heathrow Airport, London (1197 ha *2958 acres*). Between 1 Apr 1988 and 31 Mar 1989 there were 355 120 air transport movements, including 330 376 passenger flights, handled by a staff of 48 600 employed by the various companies, government departments and Heathrow Airport Ltd, a subsidiary of the BAA plc. The total number of passengers, both incoming and outgoing, was 38 053 432 including transit passengers. The most flights yet handled by Heathrow in a day was 1 121 on 16 Sep 1988 and the largest number of passengers yet handled in a day was 136 738 on 4 Sep 1988. A record 12 446 passengers were handled in one hour (1100–1200 hrs GMT) on 31 Jul 1988. The Airport's busiest single hour for aircraft movements was 1000–1100 hours GMT on 5 Jul 1984 when 81 flights were handled using two active runways. 66 airlines fly direct scheduled passenger services to 213 destinations in 84 countries. Heathrow Airport is the UK's No.2 busiest port behind Dover in terms of visible trade, handling £21 805·5 million worth of imports and exports.This represents some 13·7 per cent of visible trade through all UK ports and 72·8 per cent of that through all airports.

Busiest ■ The Chicago International Airport, O'Hare Field, Illinois, with a total of 56 281 000 passengers in the year 1988 or Atlanta's Hartsfield Airport Georgia, USA with 766 200 aircraft movements, compared with Chicago O'Hare's 753 400 movements. This represents a take-off or landing every 39·66 sec round the clock.

Heathrow Airport, London handles more *international* traffic than any other, having 34 742 100 international passengers in 1988. London, Gatwick Airport is now the second busiest international airport with 18 248 000 passengers. In terms of freight operations, New York's Kennedy International Airport handled 1 072 600 tonnes in 1988, while Tokyo International Airport at Narita handled 1 018 600 tonnes of *international* freight.

Non-airline airport ■ Among airports served by very few airlines, Van Nuys in southern California, USA is the busiest. In 1987, the airport saw 492 936 movements, of which less than one per cent were scheduled airline. Santa Ana, also in southern California, recorded 526 798 movements but at least 17 per cent were airline operations. Non-airline civil aircraft movements at the two airports were 488 567 and 436 808, respectively. This equates to more than 55 non-airline take-offs or landings at Van Nuys per hour throughout the year.

The busiest landing area ever has been Bien Hoa Air Base, South Vietnam, which handled approximately 1 000 000 take-offs and landings in 1970.

The world's largest 'helipad' was An Khe, South Vietnam. The heliport at Morgan City, Louisiana, USA, one of a string used by helicopters flying energy-related offshore operations into the Gulf of Mexico, has pads for 46 helicopters.

Highest and lowest ■ The highest is La Sa (Lhasa) Airport, People's Republic of China at 4363 m *14 315 ft* .

The lowest landing field is El Lisan on the east shore of the Dead Sea, 360 m *1180 ft* below sea level, but during World War II BOAC Short C-class flying boats operated from the surface of the Dead Sea 394 m *1292 ft* below sea level. The lowest international airport is Schiphol, Amsterdam, at 4·5 m *15 ft* below sea level.

Farthest and nearest to city or capital centres ■ The airport farthest from the city centre it allegedly serves is Viracopos, Brazil, which is 96 km *60 miles* from São Paulo.
Gibraltar Airport is a mere 800 m *880 yd* from the city centre.

Longest runway ■ The longest runway in the world is the 11 km *7 miles* in length (of which 4572 m *15 000 ft* is concreted) at Edwards Air Force Base on the bed of Rogers Dry Lake at Muroc, California, USA. The whole test centre airfield extends over 168km² *65 miles²*. In an emergency an auxiliary 19 km *12 mile* strip is available along the bed of the Dry Lake. The *Voyager* aircraft, taking off on its round-the-world unrefuelled flight (see Circumnavigational flights) used 4328 m *14 200 ft* of concrete runway at Edwards AFB. The world's longest civil airport runway is one of 4·89 km *3·04 miles* at Pierre van Ryneveld Airport, Upington, South Africa, constructed in five months from August 1975 to January 1976. A paved runway 6·24 km *3·88 miles* long appears on maps of Jordan at Abu Husayn. The longest runway normally available to civil aircraft in the United Kingdom is No.1 at Heathrow Airport, London, measuring 3·90 km *2·42 miles*. The most southerly major runway (2·57 km *1·6 miles*) in the world is at Mount Pleasant, East Falkland (Lat 51° 50'S), built in 16 months to May 1985.

Busiest airline ■ The country with the busiest airlines system is the United States where 404 307 784 000 revenue passenger miles were flown on larger US certificated air carriers in domestic operations in 1987. This was equivalent to an annual trip of 2685 km *1668 miles* for every one of the inhabitants. United Kingdom airlines flew 705 424 000 km *438 330 086 miles* and carried 87 517 397 passengers on all services excluding air taxi operations in 1987.

Longest air ticket ■ This was one of 12 m *39 ft 4½ in* issued for $4500 to M. Bruno Leunen of Brussels, Belgium in December 1984 for an 85 623 km *53 203 mile* trip on 80 airlines with 109 stopovers.

HELICOPTERS

Earliest ■ Leonardo da Vinci (1452-1519) proposed the idea of a helicopter-type craft although it is believed that the Chinese had built helicopter toys before this time. Igor Sikorsky built a helicopter in Russia in 1909 but the first practical machine was the Focke-Achgellis first flown in 1936.

Fastest ■ Trevor Eggington, 53, averaged 400·87 km/h *249·10 mph* over Somerset, on 11 Aug 1986 in a Westland Lynx company demonstrator helicopter.

Largest ■ The Soviet Mil Mi-12 (NATO codename 'Homer'), also known as the V-12 is powered by four 6500-hp turboshaft engines and has a span of 67 m *219 ft 10 in* over its rotor tips with a length of 37·00 m *121 ft 4½ in* and it weighs 103·3 tonnes.

Greatest load ■ On 3 Feb 1982 at Podmoscovnoé in the USSR, a Mil Mi-26 heavy-lift helicopter, crewed by G. V. Alfeurov and L. A. Indeyev (co-pilot), lifted a total mass of 56·77 tonnes *55·87 tons* to 2000 m *6560 ft*.

Smallest ■ The Aerospace General Co one-man rocket-assisted minicopter weighs about 72·5 kg *160 lb* cruising 400 km *250 miles* at 37 km/h *185 mph*.

Highest altitude ■ The record for helicopters is 12 442 m *40 820 ft* by an Aérospatiale SA315B *Lama*, over France on 21 Jun 1972. The highest recorded landing has been at 7000 m *23 000 ft* below the south-east face of Everest in a rescue sortie in May 1971.

Circumnavigation ■ H. Ross Perot and Jay Coburn, both of Dallas, Texas, USA made the first helicopter circumnavigation in 'Spirit of Texas' on 1–30 Sep 1982. The first solo round-the-world flight in a helicopter was completed by Dick Smith (Australia) on 22 Jul 1983. Flown from and to the Bell Helicopter facility at Fort Worth, Texas, in a Bell Model 206L *Long Ranger III*, his unhurried flight began on 5 Aug 1982 and covered a distance of 56 742 km *35 258 miles*.

AUTOGYROS

Earliest ■ The autogyro or gyroplane, a rotorcraft with an unpowered rotor turned by the airflow in flight, preceded the practical helicopter with engine-driven rotor. Juan de la Cierva (Spain) made the first successful autogyro flight with his model C.4 (commercially named an *Autogiro*) at Getafe, Spain, on 9 Jan 1923.

Speed, altitude and distance records ■ Wing-Cdr Kenneth H. Wallis (GB) holds the straight-line distance record of 874·32 km *543·27 miles* set in his WA-116F autogyro on 28 Sep 1975 non-stop from Lydd, Kent to Wick, Caithness, Scotland. Wing-Cdr Wallis flew his WA-116, with a 72-hp McCulloch engine, to a record speed of 193·9 km/h *120½ mph* over a 3 km *1·86 mile* straight course on 18 Sep 1986. On 20 Jul 1982, flying from Boscombe Down, Wilts, he established a new autogyro altitude record of 5643·7 m *18 516 ft* in his WA-121/Mc. It was reported that on 8 Apr 1931 Amelia Earhart (US) reached a height in excess of 5791 m *19 000 ft* at Pitcairn Aviation Field, Pennsylvania, USA.

FLYING-BOAT

Fastest ■ The fastest flying-boat ever built has been the Martin XP6M-1 Seamaster, the US Navy four-jet-engined minelayer flown in 1955–9 with a top speed of 1040 km/h *646 mph*. In September 1946 the Martin JRM-2 Mars flying-boat set a payload record of 30 992 kg *68 327 lb*. The official flying-boat speed record is 912 km/h *566·69 mph*, set up by Nikolay Andreyevskiy and crew of two in a Soviet Beriev M-10, powered by two AL-7 turbojets, over a 15-25 km *9·3 to 15½ mile* course on 7 Aug 1961. The M-10 holds all 12 records listed for jet-powered flying-boats, including an altitude of 14 962 m *49 088 ft* set by Georgiy Buryanov and crew over the Sea of Azov on 9 Sep 1961.

AIRSHIPS

Earliest ■ The earliest flight in an airship was by Henri Giffard from Paris in his steam-powered coal-gas 2500 m³ *88 300 ft³* 43·8 m *144 ft* long airship on 24 Sep 1852. The earliest British airship was a 566 m³ *20 000 ft³* 22·8 m *75 ft* long craft built by Stanley Spencer whose maiden flight was from Crystal Palace, London on 22 Sep 1902. The latest airship to be built in Britain is the 6666 m³ *235 400 ft³* 59 m *193·6 ft* long Skyship 500 HL designed and built by Airship Industries. This 20-passenger dirigible (G-SKSB) was flown for the first time at RAE Cardington, Beds on 6 Mar 1984.

Largest *Rigid* ■ The 213·9-tonne *210½-ton* German *Graf Zeppelin II* (LZ 130), with a length of 245 m *803·8 ft* and a capacity of 199 981 m³ *7 062 100 ft³*. She made her maiden flight on 14 Sep 1938 and in May and August 1939 made radar spying missions in British air space. She was dismantled in April 1940. Her sister ship *Hindenburg* was 1·70 m *5·6 ft* longer.

The largest British airship was the R101 built by the Royal Airship Works, Cardington, Beds, which first flew on 14 Oct 1929. She was 236·8 m *777 ft* in length and had a capacity of 155 995 m³ *5 508 800 ft³*. She crashed near Beauvais, France, killing 48 aboard, on 5 Oct 1930.

Non-rigid ■ The largest ever constructed was the US Navy ZPG 3-W which had a capacity of 42 937 m³ *1 516 300 ft³*, was 122·9 m *403· ft* long and 25·93 m *85·1 ft* in diameter, with a crew of 21. She first flew on 21 Jul 1958, but crashed into the sea in June 1960.

Hot-air ■ The world altitude, duration and distance records, of 3159 m *10 365 ft*, 1 hr 26 min 52 sec, and 37·07 km *23·03 miles* respectively, are held by the Cameron D-38 hot-air airship flown at Cunderdin, Western Australia on 27 Aug 1982 by R. W. Taaffe (Australia).

Oscar Lindstrom in a Colt AS 56 Hotair airship achieved a distance and duration record of 93 033 km *57·8 miles* in a time of 3 hr 41 min 55 sec from Stockholm to Tobo, Sweden on 20 Mar 1988.

Greatest passenger load ■ The most people ever carried in an airship was 207 in the US Navy *Akron* in 1931. The trans-Atlantic record is 117 by the German *Hindenburg* in 1937.

The largest airship currently certified for the public transport of passengers (13) is the 6666 m³ *235 400 ft³* 59 m *193·6 ft* non-rigid Skyship 600 series built by Airship Industries.

Distance records ■ The FAI (Fédération Aéronautique Internationale) accredited straight-line distance record for airships is 6384·5 km *3967·1 miles*, set up by the German *Graf Zeppelin*, captained by Dr Hugo Eckener, between 29 Oct and 1 Nov 1928. The German Zeppelin L59 flew from Yambol, Bulgaria to south of Khartoum, Sudan and returned from 21–25 Nov 1917 to cover a minimum of 7250 km *4500 miles*.

Duration record ■ The longest recorded flight by a non-rigid airship (without refuelling) is 264 hr 12 min by a US Navy Goodyear-built ZPG-2 class ship (Cdr J. R. Hunt USN) from South Weymouth NAS, Massachusetts, USA from 4–15 Mar 1957 landing back at Key West, Florida, USA having flown 15 205 km *9448 miles*.

BALLOONING

Earliest ■ The earliest recorded ascent was by a model hot-air balloon invented by Father Bartolomeu de Gusmão (né Lourenço) (1685–1724), which was flown indoors at the Casa da India, Terreiro do Paço, Portugal on 8 Aug 1709.

Distance record *(Great-circle distance between take-off and first landing point)* ■ The record distance travelled by a balloon is 8382·54 km *5208·68 miles* by the Raven experimental helium-filled balloon *Double Eagle V* (capacity 11 300 m³ *399·053 ft³*) from 9–12 Nov 1981, from Nagashima, Japan to Covello, California, USA. The crew for this first manned balloon crossing of the Pacific Ocean were Ben L. Abruzzo, 51, Rocky Aoki, 43 (Japan), Ron Clark, 41 and Larry M. Newman, 34.

Ex-USAF Colonel Joe Kittinger (see Parachuting) became the first man to complete a solo trans-Atlantic crossing by balloon.
Accomplished in the 3000 m³ helium-filled balloon *Rosie O'Grady* between 14–18 Sep 1984, Kittinger lifted off from Caribou, Maine, USA and completed a distance of approximately 5701 km *3543 miles* before landing at Montenotte, Italy in 86 hr. The first balloon crossing of the North Atlantic had been made during 12–17 Aug 1978 (137 hr 6 min) in the gas balloon *Double Eagle II* crewed by Ben L. Abruzzo, Maxie L. Anderson and Larry M. Newman.

The first crossing of the United States was by the helium-filled balloon *Super Chicken III* (pilots Fred Gorell and John Shoecraft) from Costa Mesa, California, 4047 km *2515 miles* to Blackbeard's Island, Georgia from 9–12 Oct 1981.

Highest *Unmanned* ■ The altitude attained by an unmanned balloon was 51 815 m *170 000 ft* by a

Parachuting ● The largest free fall formation was achieved on 11 Jul 1988 over Quincy, Illinois, USA, when 144 parachutists formed a diamond which they held for 8·8 sec. (Photos: Gamma)

Winzen balloon of 1·35 million m³ *47·8 million ft³* launched at Chico, California, USA in October 1972.

Manned ■ The greatest altitude reached in a manned balloon is an unofficial 37 735 m (*123 800 ft*) by Nicholas Piantanida (1933–66) of Bricktown, New Jersey, USA from Sioux Falls, South Dakota, USA on 1 Feb 1966. He landed in a cornfield in Iowa but did not survive. The official record is 34 668 m *113 740 ft* by Cdr Malcolm D. Ross, USNR and the late Lt-Cdr Victor A. Prother, USN in an ascent from the deck of USS *Antietam* on 4 May 1961, over the Gulf of Mexico in a balloon of 339 804 m³ *12 million ft².* Owing to an oversight, Harold Froelich and Keith Lang, scientists from Minneapolis, USA ascended in an open gondola and without the protection of pressure suits to a height of 12·84 km *42 150 ft,* just under 8 miles, on 26 Sep 1956. During their 6 ½ hour flight, the temperature at maximum altitude (measured with a laboratory thermometer) was −57·7°C *−72°F.*

MILESTONES IN ABSOLUTE HUMAN ALTITUDE RECORDS

Altitude					
m	**ft**	**Pilot**	**Vehicle**	**Place**	**Date**
24*	*80*	Jean François Pilâtre de Rozier (1757–85) (France)	Hot Air Balloon (tethered)	Fauxbourg, Paris	15 & 17 Oct 1783
c.100	*c.330*	de Rozier and the Marquis d'Arlandes (1742–1809) (France)	Hot Air Balloon (free flight)	LaMuette, Paris¹	21 Nov 1783
c.900	*c.3000*	Dr Jacques-Alexandre-César Charles (1746–1823) and Ainé Robert (France)	Charlière Hydrogen Balloon	Tuileries, Paris	1 Dec 1783
c.2750	*c.9000*	Dr J.-A.-C. Charles (France)	Hydrogen Balloon	Nesles, France	1 Dec 1783
c.4000	*c.13 000*	James Sadler (GB)	Hydrogen Balloon	Manchester	May 1785
7740²	*25 400*	James Glaisher (1809–1903) (GB)	Hydrogen Balloon	Wolverhampton	17 Jul 1862
9615	*31 500*	Prof A. Berson (Germany)	Hydrogen Balloon Phoenix	Strasbourg, France	4 Dec 1894
11 145	*36 565*	Sadi Lecointe (France)	Nieuport Aircraft	Issy-les-Moulineaux, France	30 Oct 1923
15 837	*51 961*	Prof Auguste Piccard and Paul Kipfer (Switzerland)	FNRS I Balloon	Augsburg, Germany	27 May 1931
22 066	*72 395*	Capts Orvill A. Anderson and Albert W. Stevens (US Army Air Corps)	US Explorer II Helium Balloon	Rapid City, South Dakota, USA	11 Nov 1935
24 262	*79 600*	William Barton Bridgeman (USA)	US Douglas D558—II *Skyrocket*	California, USA	15 Aug 1951
38 465	*126 200*	Capt Iven C. Kincheloe, Jr (USAF)	US Bell X-2 Rocket plane	California, USA	7 Sep 1956
51 694	*169 600*	Joseph A. Walker (USA)	US X-15 Rocket plane	California, USA	30 Mar 1961
km	**Statute miles**				
327	*203·2*	Flt-Major Yuriy A. Gagarin (USSR) (1934–68)	USSR *Vostok I* Capsule	Orbital flight	12 Apr 1961
377 657	*234 672*	Col Frank Borman, USAF, Capt James Arthur Lovell, Jr, USN and Major William A. Anders, USAF	US *Apollo VIII* Command Module	Circum-lunar flight	25 Dec 1968
400 171	*248 655*	Capt James Arthur Lovell Jr, USN, Frederick Wallace Haise Jr and John L. Swigert Jr (1931–82)	US *Apollo XIII*	Abortive lunar landing mission	15 Apr 1970

* There is some evidence that Father Bartolomeu de Gusmo flew in his hot-air balloon in his 4th experiment post August 1709 in Portugal.

¹ Duration c.1.54 to 2.16 pm from Château de LaMuette to Butte aux Cailles, Paris 13e. Volume of the 21·3 m 70 ft high balloon was 60 000 'piedcubes' c.1700 m³.

² Glaisher, with Henry Tracey Coxwell (1819–1900) claimed 11 275 m 37 000 ft from Wolverhampton on 5 Sep 1862. Some writers accept 9145 m 30 000 ft.

A complete progressive table comprising entries from 1783 to date was published in the 1977 edition.

Largest ■ The largest balloons built have an inflatable volume of 2 million m³ *70 million ft³* by Winzen Research Inc, Minnesota, USA. These stand 300 m *1000 ft* tall and are unmanned.

Hot-air ■ The modern revival in this form of ballooning began in the USA in 1961 and the first World Championships were held in Albuqerque, New Mexico, USA on 10–17 Feb 1973.

The greatest mass ascent of hot-air balloons from a single site took place when 128 participants at the 9th Bristol International Balloon Festival at Ashton Court, Bristol, Avon on 15 Aug 1987 took off within 1 hour.

First to cross Atlantic and duration ■ Richard Branson (GB) with his pilot Per Lindstrand (GB), were the first to cross the Atlantic in a hot-air balloon, on 2–3 Jul 1987 from Sugarloaf, Maine, USA to Limavady, Co. Londonderry, N. Ireland, a distance of 4947 km *3075 miles* in 31 hours 41 minutes. Their balloon, *Virgin Atlantic Challenger*, of 65 000 m³ *2·3 million ft³* capacity, was the largest ever flown and reached speeds in excess of 209 km/h *130 mph*.

Altitude ■ Per Lindstrand (GB) achieved the altitude record of 19 811 m *64 996 ft* in a Colt 600 hot-air balloon over Laredo, Texas, USA on 6 Jun 1988.

The FAI endurance and distance record for a gas and hot-air balloon is 96 hr 24 min and 3339·086 km *2074·817 miles* by *Zanussi* crewed by Donald Allan Cameron (GB) and Major Christopher Davey which failed by only 166 km *103 miles* to achieve the first balloon crossing of the Atlantic on 30 Jul 1978.

Miss Champagne a balloon of 73 625 m³ *2·6 million ft³* capacity was built by Tom Handcock of Portland, Maine, USA. Tethered, it rose to height of 12 ·25 m *50 ft* with 61 passengers on board on 19 Feb 1988.

The Dutch balloonist Henk Brink made a free flight of 200 m *656 ft* in the 24 000 m³ *850 000 ft³* *Nashua Number One* carrying a total of 50 passengers and crew. The flight, on 17 Aug 1988, lasted 25 min, commenced from Lelystad airport, the Netherlands, and reached an altitude of 100 m *328 ft*.

PERSONAL AVIATION RECORDS

Oldest and youngest passengers ■ Airborne births are reported every year. The oldest person to fly has been Mrs Jessica S. Swift (b. Anna Stewart 17 Sep 1871), aged 110 yrs 3 months, from Vermont to Florida, USA in Dec 1981. The oldest Briton to fly is Charlotte Hughes of Marske-by-the-Sea, Cleveland, North Yorks (b. 1 Aug 1877) on a Concorde flight to New York on 4 Aug 1987 as a 110th birthday present. She returned four days later.

Most experienced passenger ■ Edwin A. Shackleton has flown as a passenger in 314 different types of aircraft. His first flight was in March 1943 in an R9548; other aircraft have included helicopters, gliders, microlights, gas and hot air balloons.

Youngest and oldest pilots ■ The youngest age at which anyone has ever qualified as a military pilot is 15 years 5 months in the case of Sgt Thomas Dobney (b. 6 May 1926) of the RAF. He had overstated his age (14 years) on entry. A wholly untutored James A. Stoodley aged 14 years 5 months took his 13-year-old brother John on a 29-minute joy ride in an unattended US Piper Cub trainer aircraft near Ludgershall, Wilts in December 1942.

The world's oldest pilot is Ed McCarty (b. 18 Sep 1885) of Kimberly, Idaho, USA who in 1979 was flying his rebuilt 30-year-old Ercoupe, aged 94. The oldest British pilot is Air Commodore Harold 'Daddy' Probyn (b. 8 Dec 1891), who first flew with the RFC in 1916 and last flew on 8 Dec 1983 a Rheims Rocket No. 5Y A.Y.F in Kenya.

Longest interval between trans-Atlantic flights ■ Wing-Cdr A. G. Evenden first flew the Atlantic as a crew member on the British airship R-34 on the first airship crossing between 2–6 Jul 1919. 60 years later he made the crossing on 2 Jul 1979 by Concorde.

PARACHUTING RECORDS

It is estimated that the human body reaches 99 per cent of its low-level terminal velocity after falling 573 m *1880 ft*, which takes 13–14 sec. This is 188–201 km/h *117–125 mph* at normal atmospheric pressure in a random posture, but up to 298 km/h *185 mph* in a head-down position.

FIRST ● Tower[1] ● Louis-Sébastien Lenormand (1757–1839), quasi-parachute, Montpellier, France, 1783.

Balloon ● André-Jacques Garnerin (1769–1823), 680 m *2230 ft* Monceau Park, Paris, France, 22 Oct 1797.

Aircraft ● *Man*; 'Captain' Albert Berry, an aerial exhibitionist, St. Louis, Missouri, USA, 1 Mar 1912. *Woman*; Mrs Georgina 'Tiny' Broadwick (b. 1893), Griffith Park, Los Angeles, USA, 21 Jun 1913.

LONGEST DURATION FALL ● Lt Col Wm H. Rankin, USMC, 40 min due to thermals, North Carolina, USA, 26 Jul 1956.

LONGEST DELAYED DROP ● World ● *Man*; Capt Joseph W. Kittinger[2], 25 816 m *84 700 ft 16·04 miles*, from balloon at 31 333 m *102 800 ft*, Tularosa, New Mexico, USA, 16 Aug 1960. *Woman*; E. Fomitcheva (USSR) 14 800 m *48 556 ft* over Odessa, USSR, 26 Oct 1977.

Over UK ● *Man (Civilian)*; M. Child, R. McCarthy, 10 180 m *33 400 ft* from balloon at 10 851 m *35 600 ft*, Kings Lynn, Norfolk, 18 Sep 1986. *Woman (Civilian)*; Francesca Gannon and Valerie Slattery, 6520 m *21 391 ft* from aircraft at 7600 m *24 934 ft*, Netheravon, Wilts, 11 Mar 1987. *Group*; S/Ldr J. Thirtle AFC, Fl Sgt A. K. Kidd AFM, Sgts L. Hicks (d. 1971), P. P. Keane AFM BEM, K. J. Teesdale AFM, 11 943 m *39 183 ft* from aircraft at 12 613 m *41 383 ft*, Boscombe Down, Wilts, 16 Jun 1967.

BASE JUMP[3] **● Longest (Spire) ●** Carl Ronald Boenische and Jean K. Campbell Boenische, 1763 m *5784 ft*, Trollveggan Spire, Romsdal, Norway, 4 Jul 1984.

Bridge ● Donald R. Boyles, 320 m *1053 ft*, Royal Gorge, Colorado, USA, 7 Sep 1970.

Tower ● Herbert Leo Schmidtz (USA), KTUL-TV mast 604 m *1984 ft*, Tulsa, Oklahoma, USA, 4 Oct 1970.

MID-AIR RESCUE ● Earliest ● Miss Dolly Shepherd brought down Miss Louie May on her single 'chute from balloon at 3350 m *11 000 ft*, Longton, Staffs, 9 Jun 1908.

Lowest ● Gregory Robertson saved Debbie Williams (unconscious), collision at 2750 m *9000 ft*, pulled her ripcord at 1065 m *3500 ft*— 10 secs from impact, Coolidge, Arizona, USA, 18 Apr 1987.

HIGHEST ESCAPE ● Flt Lt J. de Salis, RAF and Fg Off P. Lowe, RAF, 17 068 m *56 000 ft*, Moynash, Derby, 9 Apr 1958.

Lowest ● S/Ldr Terence Spencer DFC, RAF, 9–12 m *30–40 ft*, Wismar Bay, Baltic, 19 Apr 1945.

[1] *The king of Ayutthaya, Siam in 1687 was reported to have been diverted by an ingenious athlete parachuting with two large umbrellas. Faustus Verancsis is reputed to have descended in Hungary with a framed canopy in 1617.*

[2] *Maximum speed in rarefied air was 1006 km/h*

HIGHEST LANDING ● Ten USSR parachutists[4], 7133 m *23 405 ft*, Lenina Peak, May 1969.

LOWEST INDOOR JUMP ● Andy Smith and Phil Smith, 58·5 m *192 ft*, Houston Astrodome, Texas, USA, 16–17 Jan 1982.

MOST SOUTHERLY ● T/Sgt Richard J. Patton (d. 1973), Operation Deep Freeze, South Pole, 25 Nov 1956.

MOST NORTHERLY ● Dr Jack Wheeler (US); pilot Capt Rocky Parsons, −31·6° C (−25° F), in Lat. 90° 00' N, 15 Apr 1981.

CROSS-CHANNEL (LATERAL FALL) ● Sgt Bob Walters with three soldiers and two Royal Marines, 35·4 km *22 miles* from 7600 m *25 000 ft*, Dover, Kent to Sangatte, France, 31 Aug 1980.

TOTAL SPORT PARACHUTING DESCENTS ● *Man*; Roch Charmet (France, d. 20 Feb 1989), 14 650, various locations. *Woman*; Valentina Zakoretskaya (USSR), 8000, over USSR, 1964–Sep 1980.

24-HOUR TOTAL ● Dale Nelson (USA), 301 (in accordance with United States Parachute Association rules), Pennsylvania, USA, 26–27 May 1988.

MOST TRAVELLED ● Kevin Seaman from a Cessna Skylane (pilot Charles E. Merritt), 19 611 km *12 186 miles*, jumps in all 50 US States, 26 Jul–15 Oct 1972.

HEAVIEST LOAD ● US Space Shuttle *Columbia*, external rocket retrieval, 80 ton capacity, triple array, each 36·5 m *120 ft* diameter, Atlantic, off Cape Canaveral, Florida, USA, 12 Apr 1981.

HIGHEST COLUMN ● 24 Royal Marine Team, Dunkeswell, Devon, 20 Aug 1986.

LARGEST FREE FALL FORMATION ● 144, held for 8·8 sec, from 4876 m *16 000 ft*, Quincy, Illinois, USA, 11 Jul 1988.

OLDEST ● *Man*; Edwin C. Townsend (d. 7 Nov 1987), 89 years, Vermillion Bay, Louisiana, USA, 5 Feb 1986. *Woman*; Mrs Sylvia Brett (GB), 80 years 166 days, Cranfield, Beds, 23 Aug 1986.

LONGEST FALL WITHOUT PARACHUTE ● **World ●** Vesna Vulovic (Yugoslavia), air hostess in DC-9 which blew up at 10 160 m *33 330 ft* over Serbska Kamenice, Czechoslovakia, 26 Jan 1972. **UK ●** Flt-Sgt Nicholas Stephen Alkemade (d. 22 Jun 1987), from blazing RAF *Lancaster* bomber, at 5485 m *18 000 ft* over Germany (near Oberkürchen), 23 Mar 1944.

625·2 mph 27 430 m 90 000 ft—*marginally supersonic.*

[3] *'Base' is an acronym for jumping from fixed objects — Building, Antenna, Span and Earth. Carl Boenische was killed on 7 Jul 1984.*

[4] *Four were killed.*

Most flying hours *Pilot* ■ Max Conrad (1903–79) (USA) between 1928 and mid-1974 totalled 52 929 hr 40 min logged flight more than six years airborne. He completed 150 trans-Atlantic crossings in light aircraft.

Passenger ■ The record as a supersonic passenger is held by Fred Finn who made his 654th Concorde crossing to May 1989.

Since September 1970 Maisie Muir of Orkney, Scotland has flown over 8000 times with Loganair.

Most take-offs and landings ■ Al Yates and Bob Phoenix of Texas, USA made 193 take-offs and daylight landings at unduplicated airfields in 14 hr 57 min in a Piper Seminole, on 15 Jun 1979.

E. K. Coventry (pilot) and D. Bullen (navigator) made full-stop landings in a Piper Arrow in all of England's 45 counties between dawn and dusk on 24 Jul 1984.

Human-powered flight ■ The first man-powered Channel crossing was achieved on 12 Jun 1979 by Bryan Allen (US) in the *Gossamer Albatross*, designed by Dr Paul MacCready. The 35·82 km *22·26 mile* long flight from Folkestone England to Cape Gris Nez, France set the duration record of 2 hr 49 min.

The Daedalus Project, centred on the Massachusetts Institute of Technology, achieved its goal of human-powered flight from Crete to the island of Santorini 119 km *74 miles* distant on 23 Apr 1988 when Kanellos Kanellopoulos (b. 25 Apr 1957) averaged 29·7 km/h *18·5 mph* in his 34·1 m *112 ft* wingspan machine.

MODEL AIRCRAFT

Altitude, speed and duration ■ Maynard L. Hill (US) flying radio-controlled models established the world record for altitude of 8208 m *26 929 ft* on 6 Sep 1970 and on 4 Jul 1983 set a closed-circuit distance record of 765 km *1231 miles*. The free-flight speed record is 343·92 km/h *213·70 mph* by V. Goukoune and V. Myakinin (both USSR) with a radio-controlled model at Klementyeva, USSR, on 21 Sep 1971. The record duration flight is one of 32 hr 7 min 40 sec by Eduard Svoboda (Czechoslovakia), flying a radio-controlled glider on 23–24 Aug 1980. An indoor model with a rubber motor designed by J. Richmond (USA) set a duration record of 52 min 14 sec on 31 Aug 1979.

Cross-Channel ■ The first model helicopter flight was achieved by an 5 kg *11 lb* model Bell 212 radio controlled by Dieter Zeigler for 52 km *32 miles* between Ashford, Kent and Ambleteuse, France on 17 Jul 1974.

Smallest ■ The smallest to fly is one weighing 0·1 g *0·004 oz* powered by attaching a horsefly and designed by insectonaut Don Emmick of Seattle, Washington State,. USA on 24 Jul 1979. One flew for 5 minutes at Kirkland, Washington State, USA.

Paper aircraft ■ The flight duration record for a paper aircraft is 16·89 sec by Ken Blackburn in the Reynolds Coliseum, North Carolina State University on 29 Nov 1983. The indoor record with a 3·65 m *12 ft* ceiling is 1 min 33 sec set in the Fuji TV studios, Tōkyō, Japan on 21 Sep 1980. A paper plane was reported and witnessed to have flown 2 km *1¼ miles* by 'Chick' C. O. Reinhart from a 10th-storey office window at 60 Beaver Street, New York Ciyt, USA across the East River to Brooklyn in August 1933, helped by a thermal from a coffee-roasting plant. An indoor distance of 58·82 m *193 ft* was recorded by Tony Felch at the La Crosse Center, Wisconsin on 21 May 1985.

The largest flying paper aeroplane was constructed on 26 Apr 1986 by Grahame Foster, David Broom and Andrew Barkas at the Old Warden Aerodrome, Biggleswade, Beds. With a wing span of 1·8 m *6 ft* it was launched from a platform of height 3·04 m *10 ft* and flew for 16·4 m *54 ft* during the course of the BBC television programme *The Great Egg Race*.

Roads

Traffic volume *Highest* ■ The highest traffic volume of any point in the world is at the East Los Angeles interchange (Santa Ana, Pomona, Golden State, Santa Monica, Hollywood and San Bernardino Freeways), California, USA with a 24-hr average on weekdays of 522 020 vehicles—363 per minute. The most heavily travelled stretch of road is Route 101 Junction Route 405 Sherman Oaks and Haverhurst Ave, Encino, Los Angeles, California, with a weekday traffic volume of 288 000 vehicles.

The territory with the highest traffic density in the world is Hong Kong. By 1 Jan 1984 there were 302 118 motor vehicles on 1253 km *778·9 miles* of serviceable roads giving a density of 4·14 m *4·53 yd* per vehicle. The comparative figure for the United Kingdom in 1984 was 19·60 m *21·44 yd*. The world's busiest bridge is the Howrah Bridge across the river Hooghly in Calcutta. In. addition to 57 000 vehicles a day it carries an incalculable number of pedestrians across its 457 m *1500 ft* long 21·9 m *72 ft* wide span.

The greatest traffic density at any one point in Great Britain is at Hyde Park Corner, London. The flow (including the underpass) for 24 hours in 1983 was 214 000 vehicles. The busiest Thames bridge is Twickenham Bridge, with a 24-hr average of 62 000 vehicles compared with 73 000 for the Dartford Tunnels. Britain's busiest and most heavily travelled motorway is the M25 between junctions 10 and 13 (towards Staines), which carries 160 000 vehicles a day or 58 400 000 per year.

Largest traffic jams ■ The longest ever reported was that of 16 Feb 1980 which stretched northwards from Lyon 176 km *109·3 miles* towards Paris, France.

The longest in Britain were 2 of 64·3 km *40 miles* on the M1 from Junction 13 (Milton Keynes) to Junction 18 (Rugby) on 5 Apr 1985, and on the M6 between Charnock Richard and Carnforth, Lancs on 17 Apr 1987 involving 200 000 people and a tailback of 50 000 cars and coaches.

Most complex interchange ■ The most complex interchange on the British road system is that at Gravelly Hill, north of Birmingham on the Midland Link Motorway section of the M6, opened on 24 May 1972. Popularly known as 'Spaghetti Junction', it includes 18 routes on six levels together with a diverted canal and river, which consumed 26 000 tonnes of steel, 250 000 tonnes of concrete and 300 000 tonnes of earth, and cost £8 200 000.

Longest bypass ■ The M25 6-lane London Orbital Motorway at 195·5 km *121½ miles* commenced in 1972 and was completed on 29 Oct 1986 at an estimated cost of £909 million or £8 million per mile. The first circumnavigation was by Terence Whelan, editor of *Ideal Home*, and Peter Cracknell (navigator).

Longest viaduct ■ The longest elevated road viaduct on the British road system is the 4779 m *2·97 mile* Gravelly Hill to Castle Bromwich section of the M6 in the West Midlands. It was completed in May 1972.

Square *Largest* ■ The Tian an men (Gate of Heavenly Peace) square in Beijing (Peking),

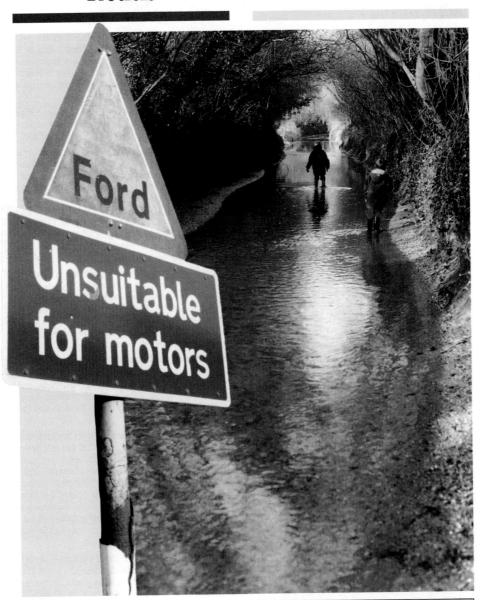

Longest ford ● The longest ford in any classified road in England is in Violet's Lane, north of Furneux Pelham, Herts which measures 903 m *987½ yd* in length. (Photos: David Roberts)

described as the navel of China, extends over 39·6 ha *98 acres*. The Maiden e Shah in Isfahan, Iran extends over 8·1 ha *20·1 acres*.

Oldest ■ The oldest London square is Lincoln's Inn Fields, dating to the mid-17th century. The largest is the 2·82 ha *6·99 acre* Ladbroke Square (open to residents only), constructed in 1842–5, while Lincoln's Inn Fields measures 2·76 ha *6·84 acres*.

Traffic lights ■ Semaphore-type traffic *signals* had been set up in Parliament Square, London in 1868 with red and green gas lamps for night use. It was not an offence to disobey traffic signals until assent was given to the 1930 Road Traffic Bill. Traffic *lights* were introduced in Great Britain with a one-day trial in Wolverhampton on 11 Feb 1928. They were first permanently operated in Leeds, West Yorks on 16 Mar and in Edinburgh, Scotland on 19 Mar 1928. The first vehicle-actuated lights were installed by Plessey at the Cornhill–Gracechurch junction, City of London, in April 1932.

Parking meters ■ The earliest ever installed, put in the business district of Oklahoma City, Oklahoma, USA on 19 Jul 1935, were the invention of Carl C. Magee (US) and reached London in 1958.

Worst driver ■ It was reported that a 75-year-old male driver received ten traffic tickets, drove on the wrong side of the road four times, committed four hit-and-run offences and caused six accidents, all within 20 minutes, in McKinney, Texas, USA on 15 Oct 1966.

The most heavily banned driver in Britain was John Hogg, 28, who, in the High Court, Edinburgh on 27 Nov 1975, received 5¾ years in gaol and his 3rd, 4th and 5th life bans for drunken driving in a stolen car while disqualified. For his previous 40 offences he had received bans of 71½ years plus two life bans.

Milestone ■ Britain's oldest milestone *in situ* is a Roman stone dating from AD 150 on the Stanegate, at Chesterholme, near Bardon Mill, Northumberland.

Longest ford ■ The longest ford in any classified road in England is in Violet's Lane, north of Furneux Pelham, Herts which measures 903 m *987½ yd* in length.

Street *Longest* ■ The longest designated street in the world is Yonge Street running north and west from Toronto, Canada. The first stretch, completed on 16 Feb 1796, ran 55·783 km *34 miles 53 chains.* Its official length now extended to Rainy River at the Ontario–Minnesota border is 1896·2 km *1178·3 miles.*

Commonest name ■ In Greater London it is High Street (122), followed by Station Road (100).

Narrowest ■ The world's narrowest street is in the village of Ripatransone in the Marche region of Italy. It is called Vicolo della Virilita (Virility Alley) and is 43 cm *16·9 in* wide.

Shortest ■ The title of 'The Shortest Street in the World' is claimed by Bacup in Lancashire where 'Elgin Street', situated by the old market ground, measures just 5·18 m *17 ft 0 in.* It is not a carriageway, but a railed close.

Steepest ■ The steepest street in the world is Baldwin Street, Dunedin, New Zealand which has been surveyed to have a maximum gradient of 1 in 1·266. Britain's steepest motorable road is the unclassified Chimney Bank at Rosedale Abbey, North Yorks which is signposted '1 in 3'. The county surveyor states it is 'not quite' a 33 per cent gradient. Of the five unclassified roads with 1 in 3 gradients the most severe is Hard Knott Pass between Boot and Ambleside, Cumbria.

The longest steep hill on any classified road in the United Kingdom is the Bealach na Ba ('the pass of the cattle') on the road from Kishorn to Applecross in Highland, Scotland. In 9·6 km *6 miles* this single-track road rises from sea level to 626 m *2054 ft* with gradients of 1 in 4 and several hairpin bends. A sign warns that it is not suitable for 'inexperienced drivers'.

Road *Mileages* ■ The country with the greatest

length of road is the United States (all 50 states), with 6 263 210 km *3 891 781 miles* of graded roads at 31 Dec 1986. Regular driving licences are issuable at 15 without a driver education course only in Hawaii and Mississippi. Thirteen US states issue restricted juvenile licences at 14.

Great Britain has 352 292 km *218 904 miles* of road including 2980 km *1851 miles* of motorway at June 1988, and 22 151 831 vehicles as at December 1987.

The first sod on Britain's first motorway, the M6 Preston bypass, was cut by bulldozer driver Fred Hackett on 12 Jun 1956 on the section between junctions 29 and 32 opened in December 1958. Britain's longest uninterrupted dual carriageway is from Plymouth to Exeter (A38) and thence by the M5 and M6 for 829 km *515 miles* terminating at Dunblane Fourways Restaurant, Stirling, Scotland. The oldest of the 46 motorway service stations is Watford Gap on the M1, opened on 2 Nov 1959.

Oldest ■ The oldest known trackway in England is the Sweet Way in the Somerset levels, dated to *c.* 4000 BC. The oldest in Ireland are near Lanesborough, County Longford where prehistoric tracks made of oak and ash logs which have been carbon-dated to *c.* 2500–2300 BC have been discovered at Corlea and Derryoghill bogs.

Longest motorable road ■ The Pan-American Highway, from north-west Alaska to Santiago, Chile, thence eastward to Buenos Aires, Argentina and terminating in Brasilia, Brazil. There remains a gap known as the Tapon del Darién, in Panama and the Atrato Swamp, Colombia.

The longest designated road in Great Britain is the A1 from London to Edinburgh, of 650 km *404 miles.* The longest Roman roads were Watling Street, from Dubrae (Dover), 346 km *215 miles* through Londinium (London) to Viroconium (Wroxeter), and Fosse Way, which ran 350 km *218 miles* from Lindum (Lincoln) through Aquae Sulis (Bath) to Isca Dumnoniorum (Exeter). However, a 16 km *10 mile* section of Fosse Way between Ilchester and Seaton remains indistinct.

Lowest roads ■ The road along the Israeli shores of the Dead Sea, 393 m *1290 ft* below sea level. The world's lowest 'pass' is Rock Reef Pass, Everglades National Park, Florida, USA which is 91 cm *3 ft* above sea level.

> **Widest road** ● The central reservation and intersection of the Monumental Axis running for 2·4 km *1½ miles* from the Municipal Plaza to the Plaza of the Three Powers in Brasilia, the capital of Brazil. The 6-lane boulevard was opened in April 1960 and is 250 m *273·4 yd* wide. (Photo: Lupe A Cunha).

The lowest surface roads in Great Britain are just below sea level in the Holme Fen area of Cambridgeshire.

Highest roads ■ The highest trail in the world is a 13 km *8 mile* stretch of the Kang-ti-suu between Khaleb and Hsin-chi-fu, Tibet which in two places exceeds 6080 m *20 000 ft.* The highest carriageable road in the world is one 1180 km *733·2 miles* long between Tibet and south-western Sinkiang, completed in October 1957, which takes in passes of an altitude up to 5632 m *18 480 ft* above sea level.

Europe's highest pass (excluding the Caucasian passes) is the Col de Restefond (2802 m *9193 ft*), completed in 1962 with 21 hairpins between Jausiers and Saint Etienne-de-Tinée, France. It is usually closed between early October and early June. The highest motor road in Europe is the Pico de Veleta in the Sierra Nevada, southern Spain. The shadeless climb of 36 km *22·4 miles* brings the motorist to 3469 m *11 384 ft* above sea level and became, on completion of a road on its southern side in 1974, arguably Europe's highest 'pass'.

The highest road in the United Kingdom is the A6293 unclassified tarmac private extension at Great Dun Fell, Cumbria (847 m *2780 ft*) leading to a Ministry of Defence and Air Traffic Control installation. A permit is required to use it. The highest public classified road in England is the A689 at Killhope Cross (626 m *2056 ft*) on the Cumbria–Durham border near Nenthead. The highest classified road in Scotland is the A93 road over the Grampians through Cairnwell, a pass between Blairgowrie, Perthshire and Braemar, Aberdeenshire, which reaches a height of 670 m *2199 ft.* The highest classified road in Wales is the Rhondda-Afan inter-valley road (A4107), which reaches 533 m *1750 ft* 4 km *2½ miles* east of Abergwynfi, Mid Glamorgan. An estate track exists to the summit of Ben a'Bhuird (1176 m *3860 ft*) in Grampian, Scotland. The highest motorway in Great Britain is the trans-Pennine M62, which, at the Windy Hill interchange, reaches an altitude of 371 m *1220 ft.* Its Dean Head cutting is the deepest roadway cutting in Europe at 55·7 m *183 ft.*

Widest roads ■ The Monumental Axis running for 2·4 km *1½ miles* from the Municipal Plaza to the Plaza of the Three Powers in Brasilia, the capital of Brazil. The 6-lane boulevard was opened in April 1960 and is 250 m *273·4 yd* wide. The San Francisco-Oakland Bay Bridge Toll Plaza has 23 lanes (17 west-bound) serving the Bridge in Oakland, California, USA.

The only instance of 17 carriageway lanes side by side in Britain occurs on the M61 at Linnyshaw Moss, Worsley, Greater Manchester.

CHAPTER 7

Largest shopping centre
The world's largest shopping centre is the $1·1 billion West Edmonton Mall, Alberta, Canada first opened on 15 Sept 1981 and completed four years later. It covers 483 080 m² *5·2 million ft²* on a 44·5 ha *110 acre* site. It encompasses 828 stores and services as well as five amusement areas including this Waterpark, 11 major department stores, 19 cinemas, 110 restaurants, a night club, a bingo hall, a chapel and a number of aviaries and aquariums. Parking is provided for 20 000 vehicles.
(Photo: Images)

Commerce

Commerce

Oldest industry ■ The oldest known industry is flint knapping, involving the production of chopping tools and hand axes, dating from 2·5 million years ago in Ethiopia. The earliest evidence of trading in exotic stone and amber dates from *c.* 28 000 BC in Europe. Agriculture is often described as 'the oldest industry in the world', whereas in fact there is no firm evidence yet that it was practised before *c.* 11 000 BC. Recent excavations at La Tolita, Ecuador, have shown that platinum was already extensively extracted by the 2nd century BC. The earliest evidence for zinc mining is from Zawar in Rajasthan and dates to 2000 or more years ago, as shown by dating of timbers from the mines.

Oldest company ■ The Faversham Oyster Fishery Co is referred to in the Faversham Oyster Fishing Act 1930 as existing 'from time immemorial', i.e. in English law, from before 1189.

Stora Kopparbergs Bergslags of Falun, Sweden is Sweden's oldest industrial enterprise, in continuous operation since the 11th century. It is first mentioned in historical records in the year 1288, when a Swedish Bishop bartered an eighth share in the enterprise. Originally concerned with the mining and processing of copper, it is today the largest privately-owned power producer in Sweden.

The Royal Mint has origins going back to AD 287. The Oxford University Press celebrated a 500th anniversary in 1978 not of itself but of the earliest origin of printing in Oxford in 1478. The Shore Porters' Society of Aberdeen, a haulier, shipping and warehouse partnership, is known to have been established before 4 Jun 1498. The Whitechapel Bell Foundry of Whitechapel Road, east London, has been in business since *c.* 1570. It has, through Master Founder Thomas Mears II, indirect successions, since 1810, via Rudhalls of Gloucester back to 1270.

The retail business in Britain with the oldest history is the Oxford ironmonger Gill & Co of 127–8, High Street founded by Abel Smythe *c.* 1530. R. Durtnell & Sons, builders, of Brasted, Kent, has been run by the same family since 1591. Mr Richard Durtnell is of the 12th

> **Oldest company** ● Stora Kopparbergs Bergslags of Falun, Sweden is Sweden's oldest industrial enterprise, in continuous operation since the 11th century. It is first mentioned in historical records in the year 1288 (see the Deed of exchange below), when a Swedish Bishop bartered an eighth share in the enterprise. Originally concerned with the mining and processing of copper, it is today the largest privately-owned power producer in Sweden. (Photo: Stora Foto)

generation. The first bill of adventure, signed by the English East India Co was dated 21 Mar 1601.

Greatest assets ■ The business with the greatest amount in physical assets was the Bell System, which comprised the American Telephone and Telegraph Company and its subsidiaries. The Bell System's total assets on the consolidated balance sheet at the time of its divestiture and break-up into 8 companies on 31 Dec 1983 reached $149 529 million. The plant involved included more than 142 million telephones. The number of employees was 1 036 000. The company's market value of $59 392 million was held among 3 000 000 common share-holders.

A total of 20 109 shareholders had attended the Annual Meeting in April 1961, thereby setting a world record.

Currently the largest assets of any manufacturing corporation are the $74 293 000 000 of Exxon Corporation, the world's largest oil company, on 1 Jan 1988. They have 101 000 employees. The first company to have assets in excess of $1 billion was the United States Steel Corporation (now USX Corporation) with $1400 million at the time of its creation by merger in 1917.

The net assets of Shell Transport and Trading Company PLC at 31 Dec 1988 were £10 071 million comprising mainly its 40 per cent share in the net assets of the Royal Dutch Shell Group of Companies which stood at £25 151 million. Group companies employ some 134 000. Shell Transport was formed in 1897 by Marcus Samuel (1853–1927), later the 1st Viscount Bearsted.

The largest recorded rights issue was one of £921 million by Barclays Bank announced on 7 Apr 1988.

The biggest British manufacturing company is Imperial Chemical Industries PLC with assets of £9400 million at 1 Jan 1989. Its staff and payroll averaged 130 000 during the year. The company, which has more than 400 UK and overseas subsidiaries, was formed on 7 Dec 1926 by the merger of 4 concerns—British Dyestuffs Corporation Ltd; Brunner, Mond & Co Ltd; Nobel Industries Ltd and United Alkali Co Ltd. The first chairman was Sir Alfred Moritz Mond (1868–1930), later the 1st Lord Melchett.

Greatest profit ■ The greatest net profit ever made by any corporation in 12 months is $7647 million by American Telephone and Telegraph Co from 1 Oct 1981 to 30 Sep 1982.

Greatest loss ■ The Argentine petroleum company YPF (Yacimientos Petrolíferos) (government owned) made a trading record loss of US $4 643 995 000 in 1983. The loss for the National Coal

Board (now British Coal) in the tax year ending on 31 Mar 1985 was £2225 million.

Largest employer ■ The world's largest employer is Indian Railways with 1 617 613 staff in 1987/8. Europe's largest employer is the UK's National Health Service with 1 225 995 staff as at 30 Sep 1987.

Greatest sales ■ The first company to surpass the $1 billion (US) mark in annual sales was the United States Steel Corporation in 1917. Now there are 570 corporations with sales exceeding £1000 million including 272 from the United States. The *Fortune 500 List* of April 1989 is headed by the General Motor Corporation of Detroit with sales of $121 085·4 million for 1988.

The world's largest private company is Cargill Inc, the Minneapolis, Minnesota grain-trading company, with sales of $32 000 million in 1985/86.

The top gross profits in the United Kingdom in *The Times 1000 1987–88* were those of British Petroleum with £3883 million.

Largest take-over ■ The highest bid in a corporate takeover was $21 000 million for RJR Nabisco Inc by the Wall Street leveraged buyout firm Kohlberg Kravis Roberts who offered $90 a share on 24 Oct 1988. By 1 Dec 1988 the bid led by Henry Kravis, 44 reached $109 per share to aggregate $25 000 million.

The greatest acquisition by a British company was that achieved in stages by British Petroleum of American Standard Oil (formerly Sohio). BP offered $7·7 billion for the unacquired 45 per cent of shares by 13 May 1987. The Guinness PLC takeover of the Distillers Company PLC on 18 Apr 1986 was £2·695 billion.

Greatest bankruptcy ■ Rajendra Sethia (b. 1950) was arrested in New Delhi on 2 Mar 1985 on charges including criminal conspiracy and forgery. He had been declared bankrupt by the High Court in London on 18 Jan 1985 when Esal Commodities was stated to be in debt for a record £170 million. His personal debts were estimated at £140 million.

William G. Stern (b. Hungary, 1936) of Golders Green, north London, a US citizen since 1957, who set up Wilstar Group Holding Co in the London property market in 1971, was declared bankrupt for £104 390 248 in February 1979. This figure rose to £142 978 413 by February 1983. He was discharged for £500 000 suspended for 2 ½ years on 28 Mar 1983.

Companies ■ The number of companies on the register in Great Britain at 31 Mar 1989 was 1 132 951 of which 10 264 were plcs and the balance private.

Most directorships ■ The record for directorships was set in 1961 by Hugh T. Nicholson (1914–85), formerly senior partner of Harmood Banner & Sons, London who, as a liquidating chartered accountant, became director of all 451 companies of the Jasper group in 1961 and had seven other directorships.

Accountancy firms ■ The world's largest firm of accountants is Ernst & Young International with a merged worldwide fee income of $4300 million, a total og 6000 partners and a total staff of 70 000 in May 1989.

Advertising agency ■ The largest advertising agency group in the world is Saatchi & Saatchi PLC of London. *Advertising Age* lists the group's billings for 1988 at about $13 529 million.

Biggest advertiser ■ The world's biggest advertiser is Sears, Roebuck and Co, spending $1 186 800 000 in 1988 excluding its catalogue.

Aerospace company ■ The world's largest aerospace company is Boeing with 1988 sales of $16 962 000 000 and a workforce of 155 000 worldwide. Cessna Aircraft Company of Wichita, Kansas, USA, in 1988, had total sales of $453·7 million. The company has produced more than 177 000 aircraft since Clyde Cessna's first was built in 1911.

Airline ■ The largest airline in the world is the

USSR state airline 'Aeroflot', so named since 1932. This was instituted on 9 Feb 1923, with the title of Civil Air Fleet of the Council of Ministers of the USSR, abbreviated to 'Dobrolet'. It operates 1650 aircraft over 1 000 000 km *620 000 miles* of routes, employs 500 000 people and carried 119 million passengers and 3 million tonnes of freight in 1987. Seventy per cent of its routes are international and it serves 160 passenger routes and five cargo routes outside the country, and makes regular flights to 98 countries. Its domestic network covers 3600 towns. The commercial airline carrying the greatest number of passengers (Dec 1984) was United Airlines Inc. of Illinois with 41 273 000 passengers. The company had 47 900 employees and a fleet of 319 jet planes. On 1 Apr 1987 British Airways operated a fleet of 165 aircraft. Staff employed on airline activities totalled 39 000 and 19 681 000 passengers were carried in 1986–7 on 550 000 km *341 754 miles* of unduplicated routes.

The oldest existing national airline is Koninklijke-Luchtvaart-Maatschappij NV (KLM) of the Netherlands, which opened its first scheduled service (Amsterdam–London) on 17 May 1920, having been established on 7 Oct 1919. One of the original constituents of British Airways, Handley-Page Transport Ltd, was founded in May 1919 and merged into Imperial Airways in 1924. Delag (Deutsche Luftschiffahrt AG) was founded at Frankfurt am Main on 16 Nov 1909 and started a scheduled airship service in June 1910. Chalk's International Airline has been flying amphibian planes from Miami, Florida to the Bahamas since July 1919. Albert 'Pappy' Chalk flew from 1911 to 1975.

Aluminium producer ■ The world's largest producer of primary aluminium is Alcan Aluminium Ltd of Montreal, Canada with its affiliated companies. The company shipped 2 278 000 tonnes *2 197 000 tons* in 1987.

Art auctioneering ■ The largest and oldest firm of art auctioneers in the world is the Sotheby Group of London and New York, founded in 1744 although their trading until 1778 was primarily in books. Christie's held their first art auction in 1766. Sotheby's turnover in 1988 was a record £1 billion. A single session record of £61 600 000 million was set at Sotheby's, New York in November 1987.

Bank ■ The International Bank for Reconstruction and Development (founded 27 Dec 1945), the 'World Bank', the world's largest multilateral development bank, at 1818 H Street NW, Washington DC, had an authorised share capital of $171·4 billion at 31 Dec 1988. There were 151 members with a subscribed capital of $102·0 billion at 31 Dec 1988 at which time the World Bank also had reserves and accumulated net income, unallocated, of $9·2 billion. The International Monetary Fund also in Washington DC, USA had 151 members with total quotas of SDR 89 987·6 million (*£66 974·99 million* or *$117 967·44 million*) as at Feb 1989.

The world's biggest commercial bank is Dai-Ichi Kangyo Bank Ltd of Japan with assets on 31 Mar 1988 of $371 100 million.

The UK's oldest independent bank is C. Hoare & Co started in 1633 by Lawrence Hoare, a goldsmith, in London. The bank with most branches is the State Bank of India with 11 883 on 1 Jan 1989 with assets of £19 280 million. The bank with the largest network in the United Kingdom is the National Westminster with consolidated total assets of £98 642 000 000 and 3077 branches as at 31 Dec 1988.

Banquet ■ It was estimated that some 30 000 attended a military feast at Radewitz, Poland on 25 Jun 1730 thrown by King August II (1709–33).

The greatest number of people served indoors at a single sitting was 18 000 municipal leaders at the Palais de l'Industrie, Paris on 18 Aug 1889. At the wedding of cousins Menachem Teitelbaum, and Brucha Sima Melsels, both 18, conducted by their grandfather Grand Rabbi Moses at Uniondale, Long Island, New York on 5 Dec 1984, the attendance of the Satmar sect of Hasidic Jews was estimated at between 17 000 and 20 000. Meal Mart of Brooklyn, a kosher caterer, provided the food including 2 tons of gefilte fish.

The most expensive menu ever served was for the main 5½-hr banquet at the Imperial Iranian 2500th Anniversary gathering at Persepolis in October 1971. It comprised quail eggs stuffed with Iranian caviar, a mousse of crayfish tails in Nantua sauce, stuffed rack of roast lamb, with a main course of roast peacock stuffed with *foie gras*, fig rings and raspberry sweet champagne sherbet, with wines including *Château Lafite-Rothschild* 1945 at £40 (now £235) per bottle from Maxime's, Paris.

Bicycle manufacturers ■ The world's biggest manufacturer of bicycles is Hero Cycles of Ludhiana, Punjab, India founded in 1956 by the Munjal brothers. In 1988 they turned out 2 641 914 units. China is estimated to have 210 million bicycles.

Book shop ■ The book shop with most titles and the longest shelving (48 km *30 miles*) in the world is W. & G. Foyle Ltd, London. First established in 1904 in a small shop in Islington, the company is now at 113–119 Charing Cross Road. The area on one site is 7044 m² *75 825 ft²*. The most capacious individual bookstore in the world measured by square footage is Barnes & Noble Bookstore of Fifth Ave at 18th Street, New York City, USA with 14 330 m² *154 250 ft²* and with 20·71 km *12·87 miles* of shelving.

Brewer ■ The oldest brewery in the world is the Weihenstephan Brewery, Freising, near Munich, West Germany, founded in AD 1040.

The largest single brewing organisation in the world is Anheuser-Busch Inc. of St Louis, Missouri, USA, with 12 breweries in the USA. In 1988 the company sold 78 500 000 US barrels, equivalent to *9213 million litres*, the greatest annual volume ever produced by a brewing company. The company's St Louis plant covers 40·5 ha *100 acres* and after completion of current modernisation projects will have an annual capacity in excess of 13 000 000 US barrels *1525·183 million litres*. The largest brewery on a single site is Coors Brewing Company of Golden, Colorado, USA where 16 534 000 barrels *1 940 264 900 litres* were sold in 1988.

The largest brewing company in the United Kingdom, based on its 7102 public houses, 638 off-licences and the 291 hotels it owns, licenses and operates in 54 countries is Bass plc. The company has net assets of £3 262 500 000, it controls 13 breweries and has 84 843 employees. Its turnover for the year ending 30 Sep 1988 was £3 734 300 000.

Brickworks ■ The largest brickworks in the world is the London Brick Company Limited plant at Stewartby, Bedfordshire. The works, established in 1898, now cover 90 ha *221 acres* and have a production capacity of 10·5 million bricks and brick equivalent each week.

Building contractor ■ The largest construction company in the United Kingdom is George Wimpey plc (founded 1880).The turnover of work was £1726 million in 1988 with 17 000 staff in 20 countries.

Building societies ■ The world's biggest lender is the Japanese government-controlled House Loan Corporation. The biggest building society in the world is the Halifax Building Society of Halifax, West Yorkshire. Established in 1853 it has total assets of £40 400 000 000 in 1988. Lending during 1988 was £10 600 000 000. It has 16 390 employees and over 2692 offices.

Chemist store chain ■ The largest chain of chemist stores in the world is Boots The Chemists, which has 1050 retail stores. The firm was founded by Jesse Boot (b. Nottingham, 1850), later the 1st Baron Trent, who died in 1931.

Chocolate factory ■ The largest chocolate and confectionery factory is that built by Hershey Chocolate Company in Hershey, Pennsylvania, USA in 1903–5. It has 185 800 m² *2 000 000 ft²* of floor space.

Computer company ■ The world's largest computer firm is International Business Machines (IBM) Corporation of New York. In December 1988 assets were $73 037 000 000 and gross income was $59 681 000 000. In October 1979 it made the largest borrowing in corporate history with $1 billion. Its world-wide employees number 389 348 and there are 787 988 stockholders.

Department stores ■ F. W. Woolworth, which celebrated its centenary year in 1979, now operates a total of 7739 stores world-wide. Frank Winfield Woolworth opened his first store 'The Great Five Cent Store' in Utica, New York State on 22 Feb 1879. The 1988 income was $288 million.

The world's largest department store is R. H. Macy & Co Inc. at Broadway and 34th Street, New York. It covers 20·3 ha *50·5 acres* and employs 14 000 who handle 400 000 items. The sales of the company and its subsidiaries in 1987–8 were $5 729 000 000. Mr Rowland Hussey Macy's sales on his first day at his fancy goods store on 6th Avenue, on 27 Oct 1858, were recorded as $11·06.

The largest department store in the United Kingdom is Harrods Ltd of Knightsbridge, London named after Henry Charles Harrod (1800–85), who opened a grocery in Knightsbridge Village in 1849. It has a total selling floor space of 8·09 ha *20 acres*, (49 lifts and 36 escalators) employs between 4000 and 6000 people depending on the time of year, and achieved record sales of over £312 million for the year ending 1 Feb 1987. The record for a day is £7·0 million in the January 1987 sale. The January 1986 sale generated a record £38 600 000.

Highest sales per unit area ■ The department store with the fastest-moving stock in the world is the Marks & Spencer premier branch, at Marble Arch, London. The figure of £1600-worth of goods per square foot of selling space per year is believed to be an understatement. The selling area is 12 025 m² *129 300 ft²*. The company has 282 branches in the UK and operates on over 761 780 m² *8·2 million ft²* of selling space and has stores on the Continent and in Canada and the United States.

Longest wait for a sale ■ Kevin Mellish (b. 2 Aug 1948) queued for a carpet reduced in price by more than 86 per cent for 20 days outside Arding and Hobbs, Clapham, London, from 7 to 27 Dec 1986.

Distillery ■ The world's largest distilling company is the Seagram Company Ltd, of Canada. Its sales in the year ending 31 Jan 1989 totalled US $5 055 671 000. The group employs about 16 200 people.

The largest blender and bottler of Scotch whisky is United Distillers' Shieldhall plant in Glasgow, with a capacity to fill an estimated 144 million bottles of Scotch a year, equivalent to approximately 24 million gallons most of which is exported.

The world's largest-selling brand of gin is Gordon's. Old Bushmills Distillery, County Antrim, Northern Ireland, licensed in 1608, claims to have been in production in 1276.

Employment agency ■ The world's largest employment group became Blue Arrow when on 5 Sep 1987 it bid successfully for the US company Manpower at £825 million.

Fisheries ■ The greatest catch ever recorded with a single throw is 2471 tonnes by the purse seine-net boat M/S *Flømann* from Hareide, Norway in the Barents Sea on 28 Aug 1986. It was estimated that more than 120 million fish were caught in this shoal. The catch record of a single trawler is £278 798 from a 37 300 ton catch by the Icelandic *Videy* at Hull, England on 11 Aug 1987.

Grocery stores ■ The largest grocery chain in the world is the Kroger Co of the United States with 1988 sales of $19·1 billion, and total current assets valued at $4·46 billion. Kroger operates 1235 supermarkets and 958 convenience stores, and employs 170 000 people.

Hotelier ■ The top revenue-earning hotel business is Holiday Corporation with a total revenue of $5·4 billion, from 1863 hotels (358 532 rooms), at 1 Jan 1989, in 53 countries. The business was founded by Charles Kemmons Wilson with his first Holiday Inn hotel on Summer Avenue, Memphis, Tennessee, USA in 1952.

Insurance ■ The company with the highest volume of insurance in force in the world is the Prudential Insurance Company of America of Newark, New Jersey with $756·7 billion at 31 Dec 1988. The total consolidated assets are $153·0 billion.

The largest single association in the world is the Blue Cross and Blue Shield Association, the US-based hospital insurance organisation, with a membership of 74 million on 31 Dec 1988. Benefits paid out in 1988 totalled $48·4 billion.

The largest life assurance group in the United Kingdom is the Prudential Corporation plc. At 1 Jan 1989 the tangible assets were £30 837 600 000.

The largest life-assurance policy ever written was one for $44 million for a Calgary land developer Victor T. Uy in February 1982 by Transamerica Occidental Life Assurance Co. The salesman was local manager Lorenzo F. Reyes. The highest payout on a single life has been some $18 million to Mrs Linda Mullendore, wife of an Oklahoma rancher, reported on 14 Nov 1970. Her murdered husband had paid $300 000 in premiums in 1969.

The largest ever marine insurance loss was aproximately $836 million for the Piper Alpha Oil Field in the North Sea. On 6 Jul 1988 a leak from a gas compression chamber underneath the living quarters ignited and triggered a series of explosions which blew Piper Alpha apart. Of the 232 people on board only 65 survived.

The largest sum claimed for consequential losses is £890 million against owning, operating and building corporations and Claude Phillips resulting from the 66-million-gallon oil spill from M. T. *Amoco Cadiz* on the Brittany coast on 16 Mar 1978.

Jewellery auction ■ The world's largest jewellery auction, which included the Van Cleef and Arpels 1939 ruby and diamond necklace, brought £31 380 197 on 3 Apr 1987 when the Duchess of Windsor's (1896–1986) collection was auctioned at Sotheby's, Geneva, Switzerland.

Landowner ■ The world s largest landowner is the United States Government, with a holding of 294 371 500 ha *727 400 000 acres* which is bigger than the world's 8th largest country, Argentina, and 12 times larger than the United Kingdom. It has been suggested that the USSR Government constitutionally owned all the land in the entire country excepted perhaps that on which foreign embassies stand. The world's largest *private* landowner is reputed to be International Paper Co with 3·64 million ha *9 million acres*. The United Kingdom's greatest ever private landowner was the 3rd Duke of Sutherland, George Granville Sutherland-Leveson-Gower KG (1828–92), who owned 549 560 ha *1 358 000 acres* in 1883. Currently the largest landholder in Great Britain is the Forestry Commission (instituted 1919) with 1 149 400 ha *2 840 198 acres*. The landowner with the largest known acreage is the 9th Duke of Buccleuch (b. 1923) with 136 035 ha *336 000 acres*.

The longest tenure is that by St Paul's Cathedral of land at Tillingham, Essex, given by King Ethelbert before AD 616.

The world's most expensive piece of property quoted in October 1988 by the Japanese National Land Agency is around the central Tokyo retail food store Mediya Building at 33·3 million yen per m² (then equivalent to $248 000).

The record price per acre for agricultural land in Great Britain is £12 000 at Elm Road, March, Cambs. It was sold by J. Collingwood & Son of March on 31 Dec 1973.

The highest rentals in the world for prime offices, according to *World Rental Levels* by Richard Ellis of

London, are in Tokyo, Japan at £1035·41 per m² *£96·19 per ft²* p.a. (October 1988). With added service charges and rates Tokyo is also top at £106·55.

Greatest auction ■ The greatest auction was of the Hughes Aircraft Co for $5000 million by General Motors of Detroit, Michigan, USA on 5 Jun 1985.

Greatest barter deal ■ The biggest barter in trading history was 36 million barrels of oil valued at £900 million exchanged for ten Boeing 747s for the Royal Saudi Airline in July 1984.

Menswear store ■ The world's largest store selling only men's suits and accessories is Slater Menswear of Howard Street, Glasgow, Strathclyde with a weekly turnover in excess of 2000 suits per week. The premises cover 3740 m² *40 250 ft²* and carry a stock of over 17 000 suits at any one time.

Mineral water ■ The world's largest mineral water firm is Source Perrier, near Nîmes, France with an annual production of more than 2 500 000 000 bottles, of which 1 000 000 000 now come from Perrier. The French drink about 72 litres *152 pints* of mineral water per person per year.

Motor car manufacturer ■ The largest manufacturing company in the world is General Motors Corporation of Detroit, Michigan, USA with operations throughout the world. Apart from its core business of motor vehicles and components, it produces defence and aerospace materials and provides computer and communication services. During 1988 worldwide sales totalled $110 228 500. Its assets at 31 Dec 1988 were valued at $90 570 800 000. Its total 1988 payroll was $27 548 600 000 to an average of 765 700 employees. Dividends paid in 1988 were $1 657 500 000.

Great Britain ■ The largest British manufacturer was the Rover Group plc with 520 000 vehicles produced in 1988 and a sales turnover of £3224 million of which £908 million were overseas sales. The company produced 4 out of every 10 cars built in Britain and accounted for nearly 7 out of 10 cars exported from the UK.

Largest plant ■ The largest single automobile plant in the world is the Volkswagenwerk, Wolfsburg, West Germany, with 60 000 employees and a capacity for 4000 vehicles daily. The surface area of the factory buildings is 150 ha *371 acres* and that of the whole plant 1980 ha *4892 acres* with 70 km *43·5 miles* of rail sidings.

Salesmanship ■ The all-time record for automobile salesmanship in units sold individually is 1425 in 1973 by Joe Girard of Michigan. His lifetime total of one-at-a-time 'belly to belly' selling was 13 001 sales, all retail with a record 174 in a month. His third best selling book *How To Close Every Sale* was published in 1989.

Oil refineries ■ The world's largest refinery has been the Amerada Hess refinery in St Croix, Virgin Islands producing on average 379 000 barrels per day in 1988.

Great Britain ■ The largest oil refinery in the United Kingdom is the Esso Refinery at Fawley, near Southampton. Opened in 1921 and much expanded in 1951, it has a capacity of 15·6 million tonnes per year. The total investment, together with the associated chemical plant, on the 1295 ha *3200 acre* site is in excess of £1·7 billion on a replacement cost basis. The area occupied by the Shell Stanlow Refinery at Ellesmere Port, Cheshire, founded in 1922 and now with a capacity of 18 million tonnes per year, is 810 ha *2000 acres*.

Paper company ■ The world's largest company in paper, fibre and wood products is Georgia-Pacific of Atlanta, Georgia, USA with sales in 1988 of $9509 billion employing 44 000 workers. The largest uncoated woodfree paper machine in the United Kingdom is PM6 at New Thames Paper Company, located at Kemsley near Sittingbourne, Kent with a capacity in excess of 135 000 tonnes a year. The paper manufacturing and converting complex covers an area of 60·7 ha *150 acres*.

Pharmaceuticals ■ The world's largest health care products company is Johnson & Johnson of New Brunswick, New Jersey, USA with sales of $9 billion in 1988.

Britain's largest pharmaceutical turnover in 1987–88 was by Glaxo with £2059 million.

Photographic store ■ The photographic store with the largest selling area is Jessop of Leicester Ltd's Photo Centre, Hinckley Road, Leicester opened in June 1979 with an area now of 2508 m² *27 000 ft²*.

Public relations ■ The world's largest public relations firm is Burson Marsteller with headquarters in New York and a 1988 net fee income of $154 300 000. Hill and Knowlton Inc. have most offices world wide with 56 including one in Beijing, China.

The world's pioneer public relations publication is *Public Relations News*, founded by Mrs Denny Griswold in 1944 and which now circulates in 91 countries.

Publishing ■ The world's largest publisher is Bertelsmann of West Germany which owns Doubleday and Bantam Books and RCA Records. Its estimated sales in 1987 were $6200 million.

Record store ■ HMV opened the world's largest record store at 150 Oxford Street, London on 24 Oct 1986. Its trading area measures 3407·9 m² *36 684 ft²*.

Restaurateurs ■ The largest restaurant chain in the world is that operated by McDonald's Corporation of Oak Brook, Illinois, USA founded on 15 Apr 1955 in Des Plaines, Chicago by Ray A. Kroc BH (Bachelor of Hamburgerology) (1902–84), after buying out the McDonald brothers' restaurants. 'Mac' McDonald, who with his brother Dick opened his first fast food drive-in outlet in Pasadena, California in 1937, died in 1971. By 3 Apr 1989 the number of McDonald's restaurants licensed and owned in 50 countries and territories around the world reached 10 500, serving 22 million customers per day, with an aggregate throughput of 70 billion 100 per cent pure beef hamburgers. Sales system-wide in 1988 surpassed $16·1 billion.

Britain's largest hotel and catering group is Trusthouse Forte with over 800 hotels worldwide. It employs 63 800 full and part-time staff in the UK, 16 000 overseas, and which had a turnover of £2 044 000 000 in 1987–88.

Fish and chip restaurant ■ The world's largest fish and chip shop is Harry Ramsden's, White Cross, Guiseley, West Yorkshire, England with 140 staff serving 1 000 000 customers per annum, who consume 210 tons of fish and 350 tons of potatoes. On 30 Oct 1988, between 11.30 am and 10.00 pm, Harry Ramsden's celebrated their Diamond Jubilee by serving 10 182 servings of fish and chips at 1928 prices.

Retailer ■ The largest retailing firm in the world is Sears, Roebuck and Co (founded by Richard Warren Sears in North Redwood railway station, Minnesota, USA in 1886) of Chicago, Illinois, USA. World-wide revenues were $30·26 billion in the year ending 31 Dec 1988 when Sears Merchandise Group had 824 retail stores, 1649 sales offices and 1700 independent catalogue merchants in the USA. Total assets stood at $23·71 billion.

Shipbuilding ■ In 1988 there was 10 909 340 gross tonnage of ships, excluding sailing ships, non-propelled vessels and vessels of less than 100 gross tonnage, completed throughout the world. The figures for the USSR, Romania and the People's Republic of China are incomplete. Japan completed 4 040 199 gross tonnage (37 per cent of the world total). The world's leading shipbuilder in 1988 was Hyundai of South Korea, which completed 25 vessels of 1 715 534 gross tonnage. Physically the largest shipyard in the United Kingdom is Harland and Wolff of Queen's Island, Belfast, which covers some 120 ha *300 acres*. The United Kingdom completions totalled 59 975 gross tonnage in 1988.

Shipping line ■ The largest shipping owners and

operators are Exxon Corporation (see p. 130) whose fleets of owned/managed and chartered tankers in 1987 totalled a daily average of 8 997 000 deadweight tons.

Shopping centre ■ The world's largest shopping centre is the $1·1 billion West Edmonton Mall, Alberta, Canada first opened on 15 Sep 1981 and completed four years later which covers 483 080 m² *5·2 million ft²* on a 44·5 ha *110 acre* site. It encompasses 828 stores and services as well as 11 major department stores. Parking is provided for 20 000 vehicles for more than 500 000 shoppers per week. The world's first shopping centre was Roland Park Shopping Center, Baltimore, Maryland, USA built in 1896. The world's largest wholesale merchandise mart is the Dallas Market Center, located on Stemmons Freeway, Dallas, Texas, USA with nearly 864 000 m² *9·3 million ft²* in eight buildings. The complex covers 60 ha *150 acres* with some 3400 permanent showrooms displaying merchandise of more than 26 000 manufacturers. The Center attracts 600 000 buyers each year to its 38 annual markets and trade shows.

The largest covered city centre shopping complex in Britain is Manchester's Arndale Centre which has a floor area of 208 672 m² *2 246 200 ft²* including a 44 713 m² *481 300 ft²* car park for 1800 cars. It was built from 1976–79, has a gross shopping area of 110 270 m² *1 187 000 ft²* and is the first such centre in Europe with its own radio station called 'Centre Sound' Radio, which broadcasts daily into eight Arndale Centres around the UK.

The longest mall in the world can be found at the £40 million shopping centre at Milton Keynes, Bucks. It measures 650 m *710 yd 2 ft.*

Soft drinks ■ The world's most popular soft drink is Coca-Cola with over 419 000 000 drinks sold per day by late 1988 in more than 160 countries. Coke was launched as a tonic by Dr John S. Pemberton of Atlanta, Georgia, USA in 1886. The Coca-Cola Company was formed in 1892. Coca-Cola is the number one soft drink in the USA and Independent Beverage Industry statistics estimate that it has a market share of 20·1 per cent of the $28 billion market to Pepsi's 18·3 per cent.

Steel company ■ The non-communist world's largest producer of steel is Nippon Steel Corporation of Japan, which produced 28·34 million tons of crude steel in 1989. Its workforce is 59 500. The Mizushima works of Kawasaki Steel produced 7 775 020 tons of crude steel during 1988, the highest amount produced in a single integrated steel works in Japan.

Sugar mill ■ The highest recorded output for any sugar mill was set in 1966–67 by Ingenio de San Cristobal y Anexas, S.A., Veracruz, Mexico with 247 900 tonnes refined from 2 886 074 tonnes of cane ground. The world's largest cane sugar plant is that of the California & Hawaiian Sugar Co founded in 1906 at Crockett, California, USA with an output of 8 million lb per day.

Largest supermarket ■ The world's largest supermarkets (self-service with check-outs) were the Piggly Wiggly chain started in 1916 by Clarence Saunders (1881–1953) in Memphis, Tennessee, USA. Above 2500 m² *25 000 ft²* net shopping area, stores are usually termed superstores, and above 5000 m² *50 000 ft²*—hypermarkets.

The largest such in Britain is the 8392 m² *90 337 ft²* Tesco hypermarket at Weston Favell, Northants opened in October 1974 with parking for 1300 cars.

Tobacco plant ■ The world's largest and most automated cigarette plant is R. J. Reynolds Tobacco Co.'s $1-billion facility at Tobaccoville, North Carolina, USA opened in September 1986 which produces more than 110 billion cigarettes p.a..

Toy shop ■ The world's biggest toy shop is Hamleys, founded in 1760 in Holborn, London and removed to Regent Street, London W1 in 1901. It has selling space of 4180 m² *45 000 ft²* on six floors with over 400 employees during the Christmas season.

Undertaker (or Mortician) ■ The world's largest undertaking business is SCI (Service Corporation International), Houston, Texas, USA with 502 funeral homes and 73 flower shops with associated limousine fleets and cemeteries. Its annual revenue in this most recession-proof of industries in the year ending 31 Dec 1988 was $692 817 000.

Vintners ■ The oldest champagne firm is Ruinart Père et Fils founded in 1729. The oldest cognac firm is Augier Frères & Cie, established in 1643.

Economics

MONETARY AND FINANCIAL

Largest budget ■ The greatest governmental expenditure ever made by any country has been $1004·6 billion by the United States Government for the fiscal year 1987. The highest ever revenue figure was $854·1 billion in this same US fiscal year.

The greatest fiscal surplus ever was $8 419 469 844 in the United States in 1947–8. The worst deficit was the $237·9 billion in the US fiscal year 1987.

The greatest general UK government expenditure is £183·0 billion planned for the fiscal year 1988–89. The highest general government receipts are expected to be £184·9 billion for the same fiscal

Inflation ● On 6 Nov 1923 the circulation of Reichsbank marks in Germany reached 400 338 326 350 700 000 000 and inflation was 755 700 million fold on 1913 levels. Banknotes for five million marks were printed and money bills were used as waste paper. This 1923 picture shows children playing with stacks of practically worthless money. (Photos: Keystone & Mary Evans)

year. The Public Sector Borrowing Requirement, running at a peak £11 628 million in 1983, was reduced to –£0·6 billion in May 1988.

Foreign aid ■ The total net foreign aid given by the United States Government between 1 Jul 1945 and 1 Jan 1986 was $256 516 million. The country receiving most US aid in 1987 was Israel with $3808 million. US foreign aid began with $50 000 to Venezuela for earthquake relief in 1812.

Least taxed ■ The lowest income-taxed sovereign countries in the world are Bahrain, Brunei, Kuwait and Qatar where the rate, regardless of income, is nil. No tax is levied on the Sarkese (inhabitants of Sark) in the Channel Islands or on the inhabitants of Tristan da Cunha.

Highest taxation rates ■ The country with the most confiscatory taxation is Norway where in

January 1974 the Labour Party and Socialist Alliance abolished the 80 per cent limit. Some 2000 citizens were then listed in the *Lignings Boka* as paying more than 100 per cent of their taxable income. The shipping magnate Hilmar Reksten (1897–1980) was assessed at 491 per cent. In the United Kingdom until 1979 the former top earned and unearned rates were 83 per cent and 98 per cent. The standard rate of tax was reduced to 25 per cent and the higher rate ot 40 per cent in the 1988 budget. The all-time record was set in 1967–68, when a 'special charge' of up to 9s. (45p) in the £ additional to surtax brought the top rate to 27s. 3d. (or 136 per cent) in the £ on investment income.

Balance of payments ■ The record deficit for any country for a fiscal year is $140 569 million in 1986 by the USA. The record surplus was $96 400 million in 1987 by Japan.

The most favourable current balance of payments figure for the United Kingdom has been a surplus of £7272 million in 1981 (best quarter Jan–Mar £2698 million). The worst figure was a deficit of £3591 million in 1974. Monthly figures are regarded as too erratic to be of great significance.

Highest tax demands ■ The highest recorded personal tax demand is one for $336 million on 70 per cent of the estate of Howard Hughes. The highest disclosed UK personal income tax demand raised is one for £5 371 220 against international merchant·banker Nicholas van Hoogstraten, then 34, for 1981.

Highest and lowest rates in Great Britain ■ Income tax was first introduced in Great Britain in 1799 for incomes above £60 per annum. It was discontinued in 1815, only to be reintroduced in 1842 at the rate of 7d. (2·91p) in the £. It was at its lowest at 2d. (0·83p) in the £ in 1875, gradually climbing to 1s. 3d. (6·24p) by 1913. From April 1941 until 1946 the record peak of 10s. (50p) in the £ was maintained to assist in the financing of the war effort.

National debt ■ The largest national debt of any country in the world is that of the United States, where the gross federal public debt of the federal government surpassed the 'trillion' (10^{12}) dollar mark on 30 Sep 1981. By the end of 1987 it had reached $2355·3 billion with net interest payments on the debt of $138·6 billion.

The national debt in Great Britain was less than £1 million during the reign of James II in 1687. It was £197 295 million or £3464 per person at 31 Mar 1988. This, placed in a pile of brand new £5 notes, would be 3·28 km *2·03 miles* in height.

Most foreign debt ■ The country most heavily in overseas debt at 1 Jan 1989 was Brazil with $120·1 billion.

Gross national product ■ The country with the largest gross national product is the United States which, having reached $3 trillion ($3 \times 10^{12}$) in 1981, was running at $4598 billion at the end of the fiscal year 1987. The GNP of the United Kingdom at factor cost in 1987 was £352 205 million.

National wealth ■ The richest territory in the 1988 World Bank rankings is Bermuda with $20 420 measured by average per caput. The USA, which had taken the lead in 1910, was 3rd behind Switzerland. The United Kingdom stood 23rd with $8920. It has been estimated that the value of all physical assets in the USA on 1 Jan 1983 was $12·5 trillion ($12·5 \times 10^{12}$) per caput. The latest estimated figure for private wealth in the UK is £1 172 000 million or £53 000 per household.

Poorest country ■ The lowest published annual income per caput of any country in the world is that of Chad at $59 in 1983, but the World Bank has no publishable data for 17 marxist countries.

Gold and foreign currency reserves ■ The country with the greatest monetary gold reserve is the United States, whose Treasury had 263·90 million fine oz of the world's 949·86 million fine oz on hand in March 1987. Valued at $400 per fine oz, these amounts would translate to $105 560 million and $379 944 million respectively. The United States Bullion Depository at Fort Knox, 48 km *30 miles* south-west of Louisville, Kentucky, USA, has been the principal federal depository of US gold since December 1936. Gold is stored in 446 000 standard mint bars of 12·4414 kg *400 troy ounces* measuring 17·7 × 9·2 × 4·1 cm *7 × 3⅝ × 1⅝ in*. Gold's peak price was $850 on 21 Jan 1980.

The lowest published figure for the sterling area's gold and convertible currency reserves was $298 000 000 on 31 Dec 1940. The valuation in July 1987 was a peak $34 915 million and the peak figure for gold was $7334 million on 31 Dec 1981.

Minimum Lending Rate ■ The highest ever figure for the British bank rate (since 13 Oct 1972, the Minimum Lending Rate) has been 17 per cent from 15 Nov 1979 to 3 Jul 1980. The longest period without a change was the 12 years 13 days from 26 Oct 1939 to 7 Nov 1951, during which time the rate stayed at 2 per cent. This lowest ever rate had been first attained on 22 Apr 1852.

Richest man ● *Forbes* Magazine estimated on 8 Jul 1988 that Yoshiaki Tsutsumi, chairman of the Seibu Group, was the world's richest man, from 70 real-estate and transport companies, with assets of $18 900 million. (Photo: Gamma)

Worst inflation ■ The world's worst inflation occurred in Hungary in June 1946, when the 1931 gold pengö was valued at 130 million trillion (1·3 × 10^{20}) paper pengös. Notes were issued for 'Egymillard billion' (one milliard billion or 10^{21}) pengös on 3 Jun and withdrawn on 11 Jul 1946. Vouchers for 1000 billion billion (10^{27}) pengös were issued for taxation payment only.

On 6 Nov 1923 the circulation of Reichsbank marks reached 400 338 326 350 700 000 000 and inflation was 755 700 million fold on 1913 levels.

The country with the highest rate of inflation in recent times was Bolivia, with 8274 per cent for the year 1985 and an annual rate in August 1985 of 23 000 per cent.

The United Kingdom's worst rate in a year has been for August 1974 to August 1975 when inflation ran at a rate of 26·9 per cent. The Tax and Price Index (allowing for tax reliefs) was 2·1 per cent for the 12 months to May 1988. The peak TPI extrapolated figure was 31·9 per cent in August 1975.

Least inflation ■ For 1987 Japan's inflation rate averaged 0·1 per cent.

WEALTH AND POVERTY

The comparison and estimations of extreme personal wealth are beset with intractable difficulties. Quite apart from reticence and the element of approximation in the valuation of assets, as Jean Paul Getty (1892–1976) once said: 'If you can count your millions you are not a billionaire.' The term millionaire was invented *c.* 1740 and billionaire (in the original American sense of one thousand million) in 1861. The earliest dollar centi-millionaire was Cornelius Vanderbilt (1794–1877) who left $100 million in 1877. The earliest billionaires were John Davison Rockefeller (1839–1937); Henry Ford (1863–1947) and Andrew William Mellon (1855–1937). In 1937, the last year in which all 3 were alive, a billion US dollars were worth £205 million, but that amount of sterling would today have a purchasing power exceeding £5000 million.

Richest men ■ Many of the riches of most of the world's 29 remaining monarchs are national rather than personal assets. The least fettered and most monarchical is HM Sir Muda Hassanal Bolkiah Mu'izzaddin Waddaulah Hon GCMG (b. 15 Jul 1946) of Brunei. He appointed himself Prime Minister, Finance and Home Affairs Minister on 1 Jan 1984. *Fortune* Magazine reported in September 1988 that his fortune was $25 000 million.

Forbes Magazine estimated on 8 Jul 1988 that Yoshiaki Tsutsumi, chairman of the Seibu Group, was the world's richest man, from 70 real-estate and transport companies, with assets of $18 900 million.

Institutional Investor Magazine reported in its May 1989 issue that the richest man in the United States was Ronald Perelman of New York City, with a personal fortune of $5 billion. Aged 46, Perelman has largely accumulated his fortune over the last ten years.

The richest man in Great Britain is reputed to be the 6th Duke of Westminster (b. 22 Dec 1951), whose assets were estimated in April 1989 to be worth £3·2 billion.

Highest incomes ■ The greatest incomes derive from the collection of royalties per barrel by rulers of oil-rich sheikhdoms who have not abrogated personal entitlement. Shaikh Zayid ibn Sultan an-Nuhayan (b. 1918), head of state of the United Arab Emirates, arguably has title to some $9000 million of the country's annual gross national product.

The highest gross income ever achieved in a single year by a private citizen is an estimated $105 000 000 in 1927 (equals some $600 000 000 in 1987—see Highest salary, p. 135) by the Neapolitan-born Chicago gangster Alphonse ('Scarface Al') Capone (1899–1947). This was derived from illegal liquor trading and alky-cookers (illicit stills), gambling establishments, dog tracks, dance halls, 'protection' rackets and vice from 1925–27. There were no convictions from 915 murders by his 'Italian Mob' in south Chicago. On his business card the former 'bouncer' and brothel-keeper described himself as a 'second-hand furniture dealer'.

Proved wills and death duties ■ Sir John Reeves Ellerman, 2nd Bt (1909–73) left £53 238 370 on which all-time record death duties were payable. This is the highest-valued will ever proved in the United Kingdom. On 29 Apr 1985 the estate of Sir Charles Clore (1904–79) was agreed at £123 million. The Inland Revenue claimed £84 million but settled for £67 million. The greatest will proved in Ireland was that of the 1st Earl of Iveagh (1847–1927), who left £13 486 146.

Richest women ■ The title of the world's wealthiest woman has been wrongly conferred upon the recluse Hioleko (b. 1930), widow since October 1986 of Kenji Osano. The US press first estimated her wealth at $25 000 million. In fact much of her husband's wealth was diverted from her. HM the Queen is asserted by some to be the wealthiest woman but few of her assets under the perpetual succession of the Crown are either personal or disposable. The largest amount proved in the will of a woman in the United Kingdom has been the £7 607 168 of the Rt Hon. Countess of Sefton in 1981. Mrs Anna Dodge (later Mrs Hugh Dillman), who was born in Dundee, Scotland, died on 3 Jun 1970 in the United States, aged 103, and left an estate of £40 million.

The cosmetician Madame C. J. Walker *née* Sarah Breedlove (b. Delta, Louisiana, USA 23 Dec 1867, d. 1919) is reputed to have become the first self-made millionairess. She was an uneducated Negro orphan whose fortune was founded on a hair straightener.

The youngest person ever to accumulate a million dollars was the child film actor Jackie Coogan (b. Los Angeles, USA 26 Oct 1914), co-star with Sir Charles Chaplin (1889–1977) in *The Kid*, made in 1920. Shirley Temple (b. Santa Monica, California, USA 23 Apr 1928), formerly Mrs John Agar Jr, now Mrs Charles Black, accumulated wealth exceeding $1 000 000 before she was 10. Her child acting career spanned the years 1934–39.

Richest families ■ It has been tentatively estimated that the combined value of the assets nominally controlled by the du Pont family of some 1600 members may be of the order of $150 000 million. The family arrived in the USA from France on 1 Jan 1800. Capital from Pierre du Pont (1730–1817) enabled his son Eleuthère Irénée du Pont to start his explosives company in the United States.

Largest dowry ■ The largest recorded dowry was that of Elena Patiño, daughter of Don Simón Iturbi Patiño (1861–1947), the Bolivian tin millionaire, who in 1929 bestowed £8 000 000 from a fortune at one time estimated to be worth £125 000 000.

Greatest miser ■ If meanness is measurable as a ratio between expendable assets and expenditure then Henrietta (Hetty) Howland Green (*née* Robinson) (1835–1916), who kept a balance of over $31 400 000 in one bank alone, was the all-time world champion. Her son had to have his leg amputated because of her delays in finding a *free* medical clinic. She herself ate cold porridge because she was too thrifty to heat it. Her estate proved to be of $95 million.

Return of cash ■ The largest amount of *cash* ever found and returned to its owners was $500 000 (US) found by Lowell Elliott, 61, on his farm at Peru, Indiana, USA. It had been dropped in June 1972 by a parachuting hijacker. Jim Priceman, 44, assistant cashier at Doft & Co Inc., returned an envelope containing $37·1 million in *negotiable* bearer certificates found outside 110 Wall Street to A. G. Becker Inc. of New York, USA on 6 Apr 1982. In announcing a reward of $250 Beckers were acclaimed as 'being all heart'.

Greatest bequests ■ The greatest bequests in a lifetime of a millionaire were those of Ryoichi Sasakawa, chairman of the Japanese Shipbuilding Industry Foundation, who made total donations of 405 732 907 012 yen during the years 1962–84, and the late John Davison Rockefeller (1839–1937), who gave away sums totalling $750 million. The greatest benefactions of a British millionaire were those of William Richard Morris, later the Viscount Nuffield GBE, CH (1877–1963), which totalled more than £30 000 000 between 1926 and his death on 22 Aug 1963. The Scottish-born US citizen Andrew Carnegie (1835–1919) is estimated to have made benefactions totalling £70 million during the last 18 years of his life. These included 7689 church organs and 2811 libraries. He had started life in a bobbin factory at $1·20 per week.

The largest bequest in the history of philanthropy was the $500 000 000 gift, announced on 12 Dec 1955, to 4157 educational and other institutions by the Ford Foundation (established 1936) of New York, USA.

Highest salary ■ It was reported by the US government that Michael Milken, the 'junk bond king' at Drexel Burnham Lambert Inc., was paid $550 million in salary and bonuses in 1987.

Britain's highest paid man is William Brown, a Lloyd's broker, whose annual salary was reported in February 1989 as being £2 000 000.

Highest fees ■ The highest-paid investment consultant in the world is Harry D. Schultz, who operates from Monte Carlo. His standard consultation fee for 60 minutes is $2400 on weekdays and $3400 at weekends. His quarterly retainer permitting calls on a daily basis is $28 125. His 'International Harry Schultz Letter', instituted in 1964, now sells at $50 per copy. A life subscription costs $2400.

Golden handshake ■ *Business Week* magazine reported in May 1989 that the largest golden handshake ever given was one of $53·8 million, to F. Ross Johnson, who left RJR Nabisco as chairman in February 1989.

In the United Kingdom, Robert Noonan was reported on 25 Apr 1989 to stand to receive £2 270 000 in a pay-off under the £82 million terms of a bid for Marler Estates, of which he was chairman, by Conrad Holdings.

PAPER MONEY

Earliest ■ Paper money is an invention of the Chinese, first tried in AD 812 and prevalent by AD 970. The world's earliest bank-notes (*banco-sedler*) were issued in Stockholm, Sweden in July 1661, the oldest survivor being one of 5 dalers dated 6 Dec 1662. The oldest surviving printed Bank of England note is one for £555 to bearer, dated 19 Dec 1699, 11·4 × 19·6 cm *4½ × 7½ in.*

Largest and smallest ■ The largest paper money ever issued was the 1-kwan note of the Chinese Ming dynasty issue of 1368–99, which measured 22·8 × 33·0 cm *9 × 13 in.* In October 1983 one sold for £340. The smallest national note ever issued was the 10-bani note of the Ministry of Finance of Romania, in 1917. It measured (printed area) 27·5 × 38 mm *1·09 × 1·49 in.* Of German *Notgeld* the smallest are the 1–3 pfg of Passau (1920–21) measuring 18 × 18·5 mm *0·70 × 0·72 in.*

Highest denominations ■ The highest denomination notes in circulation are US Federal Reserve bank-notes for $10 000. They bear the head of Salmon Portland Chase (1808–73). None has been printed since July 1944 and the US Treasury announced in 1969 that no further notes higher than $100 would be issued. Only 348 $10 000 bills remain in circulation or unretired.

Two Bank of England notes for £1 000 000 still exist, dated before 1812, but these were used only for internal accounting. In November 1977 the existence of a Treasury £1-million note dated 30 Aug 1948 came to light and it was sold by private treaty for $A18 500 in Australia. On 19 Feb 1987 a 50-tickal overprinted on a 1-tickal dark grey on grey Siamese note of 25 Jun 1918 was sold at an auction at Spinks in Singapore for $51 000 to Jan Olav Aamlid of Oslo Mynthandel A/S, Norway.

The highest issued denominations have been £1000 notes, first printed in 1725, discontinued on 22 Apr 1943 and withdrawn on 30 Apr 1945. At least 16 of these notes were still unretired up to November 1979 (last data to be published). Of these perhaps 10 are in the hands of collectors or dealers.

Lowest denomination ■ The lowest denomination legal tender bank-note is the 1-sen (or 1/100th of a rupiah) Indonesian note. Its exchange value in mid-1984 was 140 to the new penny.

The lowest denomination Bank of England notes ever printed were the black on pale blue half-crown (now 12½p) notes in 1941, signed by the late Sir Kenneth Peppiatt. Very few examples have survived and they are now valued at from £750.

Highest circulation ■ The highest ever Bank of England note circulation in the United Kingdom was £14 400 million worth on 24 Dec 1986 — equivalent to a pile 230·34 km *143·13 miles* high in £5 notes.

Banknote collection ■ R. Aguilar-Bolaños of the United Nations Industrial Development Organisation in Vienna has amassed 173 banknotes, each from a different country, since he started collecting in 1965.

CHEQUES AND COINS

Largest ■ The greatest amount paid by a single cheque in the history of banking was one for Rs. 16 640 000 000, equivalent to £852 791 660, handed over by the Hon. Daniel P. Moynihan, US Ambassador to India in New Delhi, on 18 Feb 1974. An internal US Treasury cheque for $4 176 969 623·57 was drawn on 30 Jun 1954. The largest cheque drawn in Britain was one for £753 000 000 drawn on 1 Jan 1989, signed by Graeme Odgers of British Telecom, payable to the Inland Revenue as part of its corporation tax payments.

Collection—record price ■ The highest price paid for a coin collection has been $18 000 000 for 100 484 gold coins of Norwegian, Swedish, Danish and Finnish origin from the period 1873–1926. They were purchased by Jan Olav Aamlid of Oslo Mynthandel A/S, Norway through Spink & Son in London in June 1988.

Largest hoards ■ The largest hoard was one of about 80 000 aurei in Brescello near Modena, Italy in 1814, believed to have been deposited c. 37 BC. The numerically largest hoard ever found was the Brussels hoard of 1908 containing c. 150 000 coins. A hoard of 56 000 Roman coins was found at Cunetio near Marlborough, Wilts on 15 Oct 1978.

On 10 Dec 1986 the Irish High Court ruled that Michael Webb, farmer of Clonmel, Tipperary, have a hoard discovered by him in 1980 returned by the National Museum or be paid £5 225 000 in lieu. He had been offered £9500 for the Christian Derrynaflan chalice and 3 other pieces.

On 20 Jul 1985 two sons of Mel Fisher found the main cargo of the Spanish *Nuestra Senhora de Atocha* sunk off Key West, Florida, USA in 1622. The value of the cargo already recovered has been $80 million but is now expected to be close to $400 million, mainly in silver bars.

The greatest discovery of treasure is the estimated $2000 million of gold coins and platinum ingots from the sunken Tsarist battleship *Admiral Nakhimov* (8524 tonnes) 60 m *200 ft* down off the Japanese island of Tsushima. She sank on 27 May 1905. A figure of $2000 million has also been ascribed to the *San Jose* which sank in 210–365 m *700–1200 ft* of water off Colombia in 1708. Diving began in August 1984.

Largest mint ■ The largest mint in the world is the US Treasury's mint built from 1965–9 on Independence Mall, Philadelphia, covering 4·65 ha *11½ acres* with an annual production capacity on a 3-shift 7-day week of 8000 million coins. A single stamping machine can produce coins at a rate of 10 000 per hour.

Charity fund raising ■ The globally televised 'Live Aid' concerts, organised by Bob Geldof and Bill Graham, with 60 rock acts in Philadelphia and London on 13 Jul 1985, raised £35 million within 2 weeks. The estimated viewership, via a record 12 satellites, was 1·6 billion or one-third of the world's population. The 'Sport Aid' event, conceived by Chris Long and organised by Bob Geldof (Hon. KBE), took place in 277 cities in 78 countries on 25 May 1986 and raised a world-wide figure of over £67 million.

The greatest recorded amount raised by a charity walk or run is (Can)$24.7 million by Terry Fox (1958–81) of Canada who ran with an artificial leg from St John's, Newfoundland to Thunder Bay, Ontario in 143 days from 12 Apr–2 Sep 1980. He covered 5373 km *3339 miles*.

Column of coins ■ The most valuable column of coins amassed for charity was worth £13 628 and was knocked over by Frankie Vaughan at Mecca's Club, Bolton, Lancashire on 18 Aug 1984.

Line of coins ■ The highest-valued line of coins was 16·12 km (*10 miles 5 ft 7 in*) made up of 662 353 US quarters to a value of $165 788 on 16 Mar 1985 at Central City Park, Atlanta, Georgia, USA, and sponsored by the National Kidney Foundation of Georgia Inc. A carpet of 1 945 223 Belgian one franc coins (21 mm *0·83 in* in diameter) and thus with a total length of 40·849 km *25·384 miles* was laid in Geel, Belgium by members of Mepp-Stegeta on 25 Jun 1988. The longest line of coins laid in Britain was 23·55 km *14·63 miles* long, achieved by friends and pupils of Brumby Comprehensive School, Scunthorpe, South Humberside with 1·3 million 1p coins on 29 Mar 1987. The Copper Mountain, devised by Terry Pitts Fenby for the NSPCC at Self-

ridges, Oxford Street, London consisted of over 3 million coins in 350 days (24 May 1984–7 May 1985), with a total value of £57 051·34.

LABOUR

Oldest trade union ■ The oldest of the 84 trade unions affiliated to the Trades Union Congress (founded 1868) is the Educational Institute of Scotland (EIS), founded in Edinburgh on 18 Sep 1847, with 44 596 members.

Largest trade union ■ The world's largest union has been Solidarność (Solidarity), founded in Poland in November 1980, which by October 1981 was reported to have 8 000 000 members at the time it was outlawed.

United Kingdom ■ The largest union in the United Kingdom is the Transport and General Workers' Union, with 1 348 712 members at 1 Jan 1988. Its peak membership was 2 086 281 in 1979.

Smallest trade union ■ The ultimate in small unions was the Jewelcase and Jewellery Display Makers Union (JJDMU) founded in 1894. It was dissolved on 31 Dec 1986 by its general secretary, Charles Evans. The motion was seconded by Fergus McCormack, its only surviving member.

Longest name ■ The union with the longest name is the International Association of Marble, Slate and Stone Polishers, Rubbers and Sawyers, Tile and Marble Setters' Helpers and Marble Mosaic and Terrazzo Workers' Helpers, or the IAMSSPRSTMSHMMTWH of Washington DC, USA.

Earliest labour dispute ■ A labour dispute concerning monotony of diet and working conditions was recorded in 1153 BC in Thebes, Egypt. The earliest recorded strike was one by an orchestra leader named Aristos from Greece, in Rome c. 309 BC. The cause was meal breaks.

Largest labour dispute ■ The most serious single labour dispute in the United Kingdom was the General Strike of 4–12 May 1926, called by the Trades Union Congress in support of the Miners' Federation. During the 9 days of the strike 1 580 000 people were involved and 14 220 000 working days were lost.

During the year 1926 a total of 2 750 000 people were involved in 323 different labour disputes and the working days lost during the year amounted to 162 300 000, the highest figure ever recorded. Provisional figures for 1987 were 2 260 000 working days lost involving 785 stoppages with 597 000 workers involved.

Longest strike ■ The world's longest recorded strike ended on 4 Jan 1961, after 33 years. It concerned the employment of barbers' assistants in Copenhagen, Denmark. The longest recorded major strike was that at the plumbing fixtures factory of the Kohler Co in Sheboygan, Wisconsin, USA, between April 1954 and October 1962. The strike is alleged to have cost the United Automobile Workers' Union about $12 000 000 to sustain.

Britain's most protracted national strike was called by the National Union of Mineworkers from 8 Mar 1984 to 5 Mar 1985. HM Treasury estimated the cost to be £2625 million or £118·93 per household.

Highest unemployment ■ The highest recorded percentage unemployment in Great Britain was on 23 Jan 1933, when the total of unemployed persons on the Employment Exchange registers was 2 903 065, representing 22·8 per cent of the insured working population. The peak figure for the post-war period has been 12·3 per cent (3 407 729) on 9 Jan 1986, falling to 9 per cent by the summer of 1988.

Lowest unemployment ■ In Switzerland in December 1973 (pop. 6·6 million), the total number of unemployed was reported to be 81. The lowest recorded peace-time level of unemployment in Britain was 0·9 per cent on 11 Jul 1955, when 184 929 persons were registered. The peak figure for the

employed labour force in the United Kingdom has been 25 520 000 in December 1979.

ASSOCIATION

Oldest club ■ Britain's oldest gentleman's club is White's, St James's, London, opened c. 1697 by Francis White (d. 1711) as a Chocolate House, and moved to its present site in 37 St James's in 1755. This has been described as an 'oasis in a desert of democracy'. Britain's oldest known dining club is the Charterhouse School Founder's Day Dinner held each twelfth of December.

London clubland's most senior member is Sir Walter Howard MBE who joined the United Oxford and Cambridge University Club in 1912 and who was born in 1888.

ENERGY CONSUMPTION

To express the various forms of available energy (coal, liquid fuels and water power, etc., but omitting vegetable fuels and peat), it is the practice to convert them all into terms of coal.

The highest consumption in the world is in the United States, with an average of 13 011 kg *255·6 cwt* per person per annum. With only 5·3 per cent of the world's population, the USA consumes 28·6 per cent of the world's gasoline and 32·9 per cent of the world's electric power. The United Kingdom average was 5956 kg *117·2 cwt* per person in 1987. The lowest recorded average was in 1974 at 13 kg *28·6 lb* per person in Rwanda.

STOCK EXCHANGES

The oldest Stock Exchange of the 138 listed throughout the world is that of Amsterdam, in the Netherlands, founded in 1602 with dealings with printed shares of the United East India Company of the Netherlands in the Oude Zijds Kapel. The largest in trading volume in 1987 was Tokyo with $1750 billion moving ahead of New York City with $1590 billion.

Most bargains ■ The highest number of equity bargains in one day on the London Stock Exchange was 114 973 on 22 Oct 1987. The record for a year was 13 021 337 bargains in the year ending 31 Dec 1987. There were 7145 securities (cf. 9749 peak in June 1973) listed at 31 Dec 1988. Their total nominal value was £365 860 million (gilt-edged £137 784 million) with a market value of £1 633 123 million (gilt-edged £139 814 million).

The highest closing figure for the FT–SE Share Index was 2443·4 on 16 Jul 1987. The greatest rise in a day has been 142·2 points to 1943·8 on 21 Oct 1987 and the greatest fall in a day was 250·7 to 1801·6 on 20 Oct 1987.

Most highly valued UK company ■ The market capitalisation of British Petroleum as at 31 Mar 1987 was £16 749·4 million.

Highest par value ■ The highest denomination of any share quoted in the world is a single share in Moeara Enim Petroleum worth £42 846 (*143 000 Dutch florins*) on 8 Apr 1987.

US records ■ The highest index figure on the Dow Jones average (instituted 8 Oct 1896) of selected industrial stocks at the close of a day's trading was 2722·42 on 25 Aug 1987. The record day's trading was 608 148 710 shares on 20 Oct 1987. The old record trading volume in a day on the New York Stock Exchange of 16 410 030 shares on 29 Oct 1929, the 'Black Tuesday' of the famous 'crash', was unsurpassed until April 1968. The Dow Jones industrial average, which reached 381·71 on 3 Sep 1929, plunged 30·57 points on 29 Oct 1929, on its way to the Depression's lowest point of 41·22 on 8 Jul 1932. The largest decline in a day, 508·00 points (22·6 per cent), occurred on 19 Oct 1987. The total lost in security values from 1 Sep 1929 to 30 Jun 1932 was $74 000 million. The greatest paper loss in a year was $209 957 million in 1974. The record daily increase of 69·89 on 3 Apr 1986 was most recently bettered on 21

Tokyo Stock Exchange ● The largest Stock Exchange in trading volume in 1987 was Tokyo with $1750 billion moving ahead of New York City with $1590 billion. (Photo: Zefa)

Oldest Stock Exchange ● Right: The oldest Stock Exchange of the 138 listed throughout the world is that of Amsterdam, in the Netherlands, founded in 1602 with dealings with printed shares of the United East India Company of the Netherlands in the Oude Zijds Kapel. (Photo: Gamma)

New York Stock Exchange ● The largest stock trade in the history of the New York Exchange was a 48 788 800-share block of Navistar International Corporation stock at $10 in a $487 888 000 transaction on 10 Apr 1986. The highest price paid for a seat on the NY Stock Exchange was $1 150 000 in 1987. The lowest 20th-century price was $17 000 in 1942. The market value of stocks listed on the New York Stock Exchange reached an all-time high at the end of Aug 1987—$2 945 883 381 839. (Photo: Zefa)

Oct 1987 with 186·84 points to 2027·85. The percentage record was 15·34 per cent between 3 Mar (53·84) and the next opening on 15 Mar 1933 (62·10). The largest stock trade in the history of the New York Exchange was a 48 788 800-share block of Navistar International Corporation stock at $10 in a $487 888 000 transaction on 10 Apr 1986. The highest price paid for a seat on the NY Stock Exchange was $1 150 000 in 1987. The lowest 20th-century price was $17 000 in 1942. The market value of stocks listed on the New York Stock Exchange reached an all-time high at the end of Aug 1987—$2 945 883 381 839.

Largest and smallest equity ■ The greatest aggregate market value of any corporation at year end was £26 million for IBM on 31 Dec 1985.

Britain's smallest company ever was Frank Davies Ltd, incorporated on 22 Aug 1924 with ½d share capital divided into two ¼d shares. Converting to decimal coinage (£0·002 divided into two shares of £0·001), it was finally dissolved in 1978 without ever having increased its share capital.

Greatest personal loss ■ The highest recorded personal paper losses on stock values have been those of the late Ray A. Kroc, chairman of McDonald's Corporation, with $64 901 718 on 8 Jul 1974 (see page 132).

Largest flotation ■ The largest ever flotation in stock-market history has been that of British Gas plc with an equity offering producing proceeds of £7750 million to 4 ½ million shareholders. Allotment letters were dispatched on 15 Dec 1986.

Largest investment house ■ The largest securities company in the USA, and once the world's largest partnership with 124 partners, before becoming a corporation in 1959, is Merrill, Lynch, Pierce, Fenner & Smith Inc. (founded 6 Jan 1914) of New York. Its parent, Merrill, Lynch and Co., Inc., has assets of over $64·4 billion, approximately 42 000 employees, more than 470 branch offices and 7·2 million customer accounts.

Names ■ The longest name on the British Index of Company Names is The Australian Academy of the Humanities for the Advancement of Scholarship in Language, Literature, History, Philosophy and the Fine Arts, a company incorporated by Royal Charter. The longest name on the Index registered under the Companies Acts is The Liverpool and Glasgow Association for the Protection of Commercial Interest

as Respects Wrecked and Damaged Property Ltd, company number 15147. The shortest names on the Index are G Ltd, company number 1656906, and U Ltd, company number 1910886.

POSTAL SERVICES

Largest mail ■ The country with the largest mail in the world is the United States, whose population posted 140·1 billion letters and packages in 1985 when the US Postal Service employed 744 490 people, with the world's largest civilian vehicle fleet of 200 811 cars and trucks. The United Kingdom total was 13 500 million letters and 197·1 million parcels in the year ending 31 Mar 1988. The record day was 15 Dec 1986 with 120 million items when Christmas cards coincided with the British Gas flotation. The United States also takes first place in the average number of letters which each person posts during one year. The figure was 589 in 1985. The United Kingdom figure was 209 per head in 1986.

Postal address—highest numbering ■ The practice of numbering houses began on the Pont Notre Dame, Paris, France in 1463. The highest-numbered house in Britain is No. 2679 Stratford Road, Hockley Heath, West Midlands, owned since 1964 by Mr and Mrs Howard Hughes. The highest-numbered house in Scotland is No. 2629 London Road, Mount Vernon, Glasgow, which is part of the local police station.

Oldest pillar boxes ■ A cast iron posting box dating from c. 1690 was found at the White Hart coaching inn, Spilsby, Lincolnshire in January 1988. The oldest pillar box still in service in the British Isles

is one dating from 8 Feb 1853 in Union Street, St Peter Port, Guernsey. It was cast by John Vaudin in Jersey and was restored to its original maroon livery in October 1981. The oldest box in mainland Britain is at Barnes Cross, Holwell (postally in Bishop's Caundle), Dorset, dating from probably later in 1853. In Ireland, the hexagonal-roofed pillar box in Kent Railway Station, Glanmire, County Cork dates from 1857.

Post offices ■ The Post Office's northernmost post office is at Haroldswick, Unst, Shetland Islands. The most southerly in the British Isles is at Samarès, Jersey. The oldest is at Sanquhar, Dumfries and Galloway, which was first referred to in 1763. In England the post office at Shipton-under-Wychwood, Oxon dates back to April 1845. The highest post office in England is at Flash, Staffs at 462·6 m *1518 ft*. The longest counter in Britain was one of 56·38 m *185 ft* with 33 positions when opened in 1962 at Trafalgar Square, London. Currently the longest is at George Square, Glasgow, being 47·8 m *157 ft* long with 27 positions.

Highest priced stamp ● The highest price paid for a stamp at an auction in the UK was £105 925 (including the buyer's premium and VAT on the premium) for this Neapolitan Provinces ½ tornese stamp, issued in 1861, which was black instead of the intended green. It was sold at Phillips, London on 20 Oct 1988. (Photo: Phillips Fine Art Auctioneers)

Agriculture

Origins ■ It has been estimated that about 21 per cent of the world's land surface is cultivable and that only 7·6 per cent is actually under cultivation. In the UK there are 18 889 715 ha *46 677 000 acres* of farmland on nearly 240 300 holdings. Evidence adduced in 1971 from Nok Nok Tha and Spirit Cave, Thailand tends to confirm that plant cultivation was part of the Hoabinhian culture *c.* 11 000 BC but it is still likely that hominids (humans and their human-like ancestors) probably survived for 99·93 per cent of their known history without cultivating plants or domesticating animals. It has been suggested that Reindeer (*Rangifer tarandus*) may have been domesticated as early as 18 000 BC, but definite proof remains lacking.

The earliest known domesticated *food* animals were probaly descendants of the Wild goat or Bezoar (*Capra*

aegagrus = hircus), which were herded at Asiah, Iran *c.*7700 BC. Sheep (*Ovis aries*) have been dated *c.*7200 BC at Argissa Magula, Thessaly, Greece and pigs (*Sus domestica*) and cattle (*Bos primigenius = taurus*) *c.*7000 BC at the same site.

The earliest definite date for the horse (*Equus caballus*) is *c.*4350 BC from Dereiska, Ukraine, USSR, but cribbiting evidence from southern France indicates that horses may have been tethered earlier than 30 000 BC.

Chickens were domesticated before 6000 BC in Indochina and by 5900–5400 BC had spread to North China, as shown by radiocarbon dating from a Neolithic site at Peiligan, near Zhengzou and also Cishan and Beixin. Chickens did not reach Britain until *c.* 150 BC.

FARMS

Earliest ■ The earliest dated British farming site is Neolithic and is enclosed within the Iron-Age hill fort at Hembury, Devon, excavated during 1934–5 and now dated to 4210–3990 BC. Pollen analysis from two sites, Oakhanger, Hampshire and Winfrith Heath, Dorset (Mesolithic *c.* 5000 BC), indicates that Mesolithic man may have had deer herds which were fed on ivy during the winter months.

Largest ■ The largest farms in the world are collective farms (*sovkhozes*) in the USSR. These have been reduced in number from 235 500 in 1940 to only 18 000 in 1980 and have been increased in size so that units of over 25 000 ha *60 000 acres* are not uncommon. The pioneer farm owned by Laucidio Coelho near Campo Grande, Mato Grosso, Brazil *c.* 1901 was 8700 km² *3358 miles²* with 250 000 head of cattle at the time of his death in 1975.

The largest farms in the British Isles are Scottish hill farms in the Grampians. The largest arable farm is that at Elveden, Suffolk, farmed by the Earl of Iveagh. Here 4513·1 ha *11 151·9 acres* are farmed on an estate of 9112·45 ha *22 517 acres*, the greater part of which was formerly derelict land. The 1988 production included 9117 tonnes *8973 tons* of grain and 57 000 tonnes *56 102 tons* of sugar beet. The livestock includes 1030 ewes and 5724 pigs.

Cattle station ■ The world's largest cattle station is the Anna Creek station of 30 113·5 km² *11 626·8 miles²*, South Australia owned by the Kidman family. It is thus 23 per cent of the size of England. The biggest component is Strangway at 14 114 km² *5449 miles²*. Until 1915 the Victoria River Downs Station, Northern Territory had an area of 22 400 000 acres (90 650 km² *35 000 miles²*), the same as England's 20 largest counties put together.

Sheep station ■ The largest sheep station in the world is Commonwealth Hill, in the north-west of South Australia. It grazes between 60 000 and 70 000 sheep and 54 000 uninvited kangaroos in an area of 10 567 km² *4080 miles²*, i.e. larger than the combined area of Norfolk and Suffolk. The head count on Sir William Stevenson's 12 140 ha *30 000 acre* Lochinver Station in New Zealand was 133 231 on 1 Jan 1989 on 10 319 ha *25 500 acres*. The largest sheep move on record occurred when 27 horsemen moved a flock of 43 000 sheep 64 km *40 miles* from Barcaldine to Beaconsfield Station, Queensland, Australia in 1886.

Rice farming ■ The largest contiguous wild rice (*Zizania aquatica*) farm in the world is Clearwater Rice Inc. at Clearbrook, Minnesota, USA with 809 ha *2000 acres*. In 1986 it yielded 261 727 kg *577 000 lb*, the largest to date.

Turkey farm ■ The world's largest turkey farm is that of Bernard Matthews plc, at Great Witchingham, Norfolk, England with 2600 staff tending 8 500 000 turkeys.

Chicken ranch ■ The Croton Egg Farm in Ohio, USA has 4·8 million hens laying some 3·7 million eggs daily.

Piggery ■ The world's largest piggery is the Sljeme pig unit in Yugoslavia which is able to process 300 000 pigs in a year.

Cow shed ■ The longest cow shed in Britain is that

of the Yorkshire Agricultural Society at Harrogate, North Yorkshire. It is 139 m *456 ft* in length with a capacity of 686 cows. The National Agricultural Centre, Kenilworth, Warwickshire, completed in 1967, has, however, capacity for 782 animals.

Foot-and-mouth disease ■ The worst outbreak of foot-and-mouth disease in Great Britain was that from Shropshire on 25 Oct 1967 to 25 Jun 1968 in which there were 2364 outbreaks and 429 632 animals slaughtered at a direct and consequential loss of £150 000 000. The outbreak of 1871, when farms were much smaller, affected 42 531 farms. The disease first appeared in Britain at Stratford, east London in August 1839.

Sheep shearing ■ The highest speed for sheep shearing in a working day was that recorded for John Fagan who machine-sheared 804 lambs (average 89·3 per hour) in 9 hr at Hautora Rd, Pio Pio, New Zealand on 8 Dec 1980. Peter Casserly of Christchurch, New Zealand achieved a solo blade (i.e. hand-shearing) record of 353 lambs in 9 hours on 13 Feb 1976. Four men machine-sheared 2519 sheep in 9 hr at Stewarts Trust, Waikaia, Southland, New Zealand on 11 Feb 1982. In a 24-hour shearing marathon, Alan MacDonald and Keith Wilson machine-sheared 2220 sheep at Warkworth, Auckland Province on 26 Jun 1988.

Mr Lavor Taylor (1896–1989) of Ephraim, Utah claimed to have sheared 515 000 sheep to May 1984.

British records for 9 hr have been set at 706 by David Galloway (373) and Andrew Muirhead (333) on 25 Jun 1988 (sheep caught *by* shearers). At the Royal Highland Show held at Dundee, Scotland, in June 1957 Godfrey Bowen (New Zealand) sheared a Cheviot ewe in 46 sec.

Sheep survival ■ On 24 Mar 1978 Alex Maclennan dug out 16 sheep buried in a snowdrift for 50 days near the River Skinsdale on Mrs Tyser's Gordonbush Estate, Sutherland, Scotland, after the great January blizzard. One ewe was found alive. The sheeps' hot breath creates air-holes in the snow, and they gnaw their own wool for protein.

Mushroom farm ■ The largest single mushroom farm in the world is that of Moonlight Mushroom Inc., founded in 1937 in a disused limestone mine near Worthington, Pennsylvania, USA. It employs over 900 in a maze of underground galleries 177 km *110 miles* long, producing over 20 412 000 kg *20 090 tons* of mushrooms per year. The French annual consumption is unrivalled at 3·17 kg *7 lb* per caput.

Wheat field ■ The largest single fenced field sown with wheat was one of 14 160 ha *35 000 acres* sown in 1951 south-west of Lethbridge, Alberta, Canada.

Hop field ■ The largest is one of 695 ha *1717 acres* near Toppenish, Washington State, USA. It is owned by John I. Haas Inc., the world's largest hop growers, with hop farms in Idaho, Oregon, Washington State, Tasmania and Kent, England, with a total net area of 1724·7 ha *4262 acres*.

Community garden ■ The largest such project is that operated by the City Beautiful Council, and the Benjamin Wegerzyn Garden Center at Dayton, Ohio, USA. It comprises 1173 allotments each of 74·45 m² *812¼ ft²*.

CROP YIELDS

Wheat ■ Crop yields for highly tended small areas are of little significance. The British record is 13·99 tonnes/ha *111·4 cwt/acre* at 15·5 per cent moisture on a field of 17·49 ha *43·24 acres* by Gordon Rennie of Clifton Mains, Newbridge, Midlothian.

Barley ■ A yield of 11·76 tonnes/ha *93·7 cwt/acre* of Gerbel Winter Barley was achieved in August 1984 by the Brewster family farm at Kirknewton, Midlothian from a 8·29 ha *20·48 acre* field.

Potato ■ The greatest number of US barrels picked in a 9½ hr day is 235 by Walter Sirois (b. 1917) of Caribou, Maine on 30 Sep 1950.

Corn ■ A yield of 352·64 US bushels (15 ½ per cent moisture) from an acre, using De Kalb XL-54, was achieved by Roy Lynn Jr near Kalamazoo, Michigan, USA on 30 Sep 1977.

Sugar beet ■ The highest recorded yield for sugar beet is 139·9 tonnes/ha *55·71 tons per acre* by Andy Christensen and Jon Giannini in the Salinas Valley, California, USA.

Two one-pound loaves (1 white, 1 wholemeal) and 115 gm *4·05 oz* of butter (from 9 litres *15·8 pints* of milk produced by 'Daffodil') were produced in 29 min 37 sec at Thriplow Farm, Cambridgeshire, England on 18 Apr 1986.

Ploughing ■ The world championship (instituted 1953) has been staged in 18 countries and won by ploughmen of 12 nationalities of which the United Kingdom has been most successful with ten championships. The only man to take the title three times has been Hugh B. Barr of Northern Ireland in 1954–5–6.

The fastest recorded time for ploughing an acre *0·404 ha* (minimum 32 right-hand turns and depth 22 cm *9 in*) is 11 min 21·8 sec by Robert Dee using a Fiat 180-90 DT tractor at Hodstock Priory Farm, Blythe, Notts, England on 1 Nov 1984.

Frank Allinson of Leyburn, North Yorkshire, ploughed for 250 hr 9 min 50 sec from 14–24 Nov 1981. DMI Inc of Goodfield, Illinois, USA marketed a 'Hydrawide' plough with 21 furrows in 1978.

The greatest recorded acreage ploughed with a six-furrow plough to a depth of 22·86 cm *9 in* in 24 hr is 63·43 ha *156·74 acres* by Christiaan Mauritius Van Den Heever using a 158-hp Fiat 160/90DT tractor at Swerwerskraal No. 733 farm, Potgietersrus, South Africa on 8–9 Jan 1988.

Rick ■ A rick of 40 400 bales of straw was completed from 22 Jul to 3 Sep 1982 by Nick and Tom Parsons with a gang of eight at Cuckoo-pen Barn Farm, Birdlip, Glos. It measured 45·7 × 9·1 × 18·2 m *150 × 30 × 60 ft* high and weighed some 711 tonnes *700 tons*. They baled, hauled and ricked 24 200 bales in seven consecutive days from 22–29 Jul.

Field mouse ■ 'Kernel Mickey Mouse' covering 210·4 ha *520 acres* was cultivated by the Pitzenberger family on a farm owned by the Buehlje family in Sheffield, Iowa, USA as part of Mickey Mouse's 60th birthday celebrations in August 1988. The 89 hectares *220 acres* of corn and the 121·4 hectares *300 acres* of oats can be seen from a height of 9144 m *30 000 ft*.

LIVESTOCK

Note: Some exceptionally high livestock auction prices are believed to result from collusion between buyer and seller to raise the ostensible price levels of the breed concerned. Others are marketing and publicity exercises with little relation to true market prices.

Highest priced *Bull* ■ The highest price has been $2 500 000 for the beefalo (a ⅜Bison, ⅜Charolais, ¼ Hereford) 'Joe's Pride' sold by D. C. Basalo of Burlingame, California to the Beefalo Cattle Co of Canada, of Calgary on 9 Sep 1974. A young 14-month-old Canadian Holstein bull 'Pickland Elevation B. ET' was bought by Premier Breeders of Stamfordham, Northumberland, England for £233 000 in Sep 1982.

> **Field mouse** ● 'Kernel Mickey Mouse' covering 210·4 ha *520 acres* was cultivated by the Pitzenberger family on a farm owned by the Buehlje family in Sheffield, Iowa, USA as part of Mickey Mouse's 60th birthday celebrations in August 1988. The 89 hectares *220 acres* of corn and the 121·4 hectares *300 acres* of oats can be seen from a height of 9144 m *30 000 ft*. (Photo: Walt Disney Company)

The highest price paid for a bull in Britain is 60 000 guineas (£63 000) for 'Lindertis Evulse', an Aberdeen-Angus owned by Sir Torquil and Lady Munro of Lindertis, Kirriemuir, Angus. The bull was bought by James R. Dick (1928–74), co-manager of Black Watch Farms on 5 Feb 1963. It failed a fertility test in August 1963 when 20 months old, thus becoming the world's most expensive piece of beef.

Cow ■ The highest price ever paid for a cow is $1 300 000 for a Holstein at auction in East Monpelier, Vermont, USA in 1985. The British record is £33 600 for 'Ullswater Beatexus 8th', a British Friesian sold to the British Livestock Embryo Syndicate of Royston, Herts by Sir Keith and Lady Showering of West Horrington, Wells, Somerset on 9 May 1981.

Goat ■ On 25 Jan 1985 an Angora buck bred by Waitangi Angoras, Waitangi, New Zealand was sold to Elliott Brown Limited, Waipu, New Zealand for NZ$140 000.

Sheep ■ The highest price ever paid for a sheep is $A215 000 for the Merino ram 'Bicentenary 88' sold by the Collinsville Stud, South Australia reported in October 1987.

The British auction record is £30 000 paid on 29 Oct 1987 by Mr B. Lawson of Whashton, North Yorks for a Swaledale Shearling ram owned by Mr Ronnie Metcalfe of Stainton, North Yorks.

Wool ■ The highest price ever paid for wool was $A320 per kg greasy for a bale of Tasmania superfine at the wool auction in Tasmania, Australia on 25 Feb 1988 by Fujii Keori Ltd of Osaka, Japan — top bidders since 1973.

A Merino wether lost in the Benambra State Forest, NSW, Australia for five years produced 24·5 kg *54 lb* of wool. Its fleece was 45·7 cm *18 in* long.

©DISNEY

Pig ■ The highest price ever paid for a pig is $56 000 for a cross-bred barrow named 'Bud' owned by Jeffrey Roemisch of Hermleigh, Texas, USA and bought by E. A. 'Bud' Olson and Phil Bonzio on 5 Mar 1983. The UK record is 3300 guineas (£3465), paid by Malvern Farms for a Swedish Landrace gilt 'Bluegate Ally 33rd' owned by Davidson Trust in a draft sale at Reading, Berks on 2 Mar 1955.

Horse ■ The highest price paid for a draught horse is $47 000 by C. G. Good of Ogden, Iowa, USA (see page 30) for the seven-year-old Belgian stallion 'Farceur' at Cedar Falls, Iowa, USA on 16 Oct 1917. A Welsh mountain pony stallion named 'Coed Cock Bari' was sold to an Australian bidder in Wales in September 1978 for 21 000 guineas (then £22 050).

Donkey ■ The lowest price ever realised for livestock was at a sale at Kuruman, Cape Province, South Africa in 1934 where donkeys were sold for less than 2p each.

Cattle *Heaviest* ■ The heaviest on record was a Holstein-Durham cross named 'Mount Katahdin' exhibited by A. S. Rand of Maine, USA from 1906–10 and frequently weighed at an even 2267 kg *5000 lb*. He was 1·88 m *6 ft 2 in* at the shoulder with a 3·96 m *13 ft* girth and died in a barn fire *c.* 1923.

The British record is the 2032 kg *4480 lb* of 'The Bradwell Ox' owned by William Spurgin of Orpland Farm, Bradwell-on-Sea, Essex. This colossus measured 4·57 m *15 ft* from nose to tail and had a maximum girth of 3·35 m *11 ft* in 1830 when six years. The famous Shorthorn 'Durham' or 'Wonderful Ox' bred by Charles and Robert Colling of Teeswater, Yorks, weighed 1727 kg *3808 lb* at the age of ten years. It was finally slaughtered in 1807 after dislocating a hip. The 'Airedale Heifer' of East Riddlesdon, nr Keighley, South Yorkshire, weighed 1197·5 kg *2640 lb* in *c.* 1820 and was 3·62 m *11 ft 10½ in* long.

The heaviest breed of cattle is the Chianini, brought to the Chiana Valley, central-west Italy, from the Middle East in pre-Roman times. Four types of the breed exist, of which the largest is the Val di Chianini, found on the plains and low hills of Arezzo and Sienna. Mature bulls average 1·73 m *5 ft 8 in* at the forequarters and weigh 1300 kg *2865 lb* (cows 850 kg *1873 lb*), but Chianini oxen have been known to attain heights up to 1·9 m *6 ft 2¾ in*. The sheer expense of feeding such huge cattle has put the breed under threat of extinction in Italy, but farmers in North America, Mexico and Brazil are still enthusiastic buyers of the breed. Britain's largest breed of heavyweight cattle is the South Devon, mature bulls measuring up to 1·55 m *5 ft 1 in* at the withers and weighing about 1250 kg *2755 lb* (cows 1·35 m *4 ft 5 in* and 675 kg *1488 lb*). The heaviest example on record scaled 1678 kg *3700 lb*.

Smallest ■ The smallest breed of domestic cattle is the Ovambo of Namibia, West Africa. Mature bulls and cows weigh 225 kg *496 lb* and 160 kg *353 lb* respectively on average. The smallest British breed is the Miniature Dexter. Mature bulls weigh 450 kg *992 lb* (height at withers 1·1 m *3 ft 3⅓ in*). In May 1984 a height of 86·3 cm *34 in* was reported for an adult Miniature Dexter cow named 'Mayberry' owned by Mr R. Hillier of Church Farm, South Littleton, Evesham, Worcs.

Calf *Heaviest* ■ The heaviest recorded live birthweight for a calf is 102 kg *225 lb* from a British Friesian cow at Rockhouse Farm, Bishopston, Swansea, West Glamorgan, in 1961. On 28 May 1986 a Holstein cow owned by Sherlene O'Brien of Simitar Farms, Henryetta, Oklahoma, USA gave birth to a perfectly formed still-born calf weighing 122·4 kg *270 lb*. The sire was an Aberdeen-Angus bull which had 'jumped the fence'.

Lightest ■ The lowest live birthweight recorded for a calf is 8 kg *17 lb 10 oz* for a bull (breed not identified) born on Jan van Rensberg's farm at Kankus, Orange Free State, South Africa, in August 1972. It stood 40 cm *15·74 in* at the hindquarters and measured 55 cm *21·6 in* overall.

Pigs *Heaviest* ■ The heaviest pig ever recorded was a Poland-China hog named 'Big Bill' who was so obese that his belly dragged along the ground. In 1933 he was being driven by his owner, W. J. Chappall, to the Chicago World Fair for exhibition purposes when the truck he was travelling in had to brake suddenly and he suffered a broken leg. As a result the giant hog's owner decided to put the animal out of his misery and drove him to a local garage in Jackson, Tennessee, USA where he was given a lethal dose of chloroform. Before he died, however, 'Big Bill' was weighed and measured. He scaled an astonishing 1157·5 kg *2552 lb*, and other statistics included a shoulder height of 1·52 m *5 ft* and a length of 2·74 m *9 ft*. At Mr Chappall's request his prize possession was mounted and put on display in Weekly County, Tennessee until 1946 when he was acquired by a travelling carnival. On the death of the carnival's proprietor his family allegedly donated 'Big Bill' to a museum, but no trace has been found of him since.

The heaviest pig ever bred in Britain was the now extinct Rudgewick, which scaled about 453 kg *1000 lb* at the age of two years. In 1798 a weight of 739·3 kg *1630 lb* was recorded for a boar bred in Middlesex. Another one bred at Godstone, Surrey, scaled 660·4 kg *1456 lb* in 1805. The only other British breed of pig known to exceed 635 kg *1400 lb* was the Gloucester Old Spot. One huge boar bred by Joseph Lawton of Astbury, Cheshire (and possibly owned by Joseph Bradbury of Little Hay Wood, Staffs) weighed 639·5 kg *1410 lb* in 1774. It stood 1·43 m *4 ft 8¼ in* at the shoulder and was 2·94 m *9 ft 8 in* long.

Smallest breed ■ The smallest breed of pig is the 'Mini Maialino' developed by Stefano Morini of St Golo d'Enza, northern Italy, after ten years of experimentation with Vietnam pot-bellied pigs. The piglets weigh 400 g *14 oz* at birth and 9 kg *20 lb* at maturity.

Piglets ■ The average birthweight for a piglet is 1·36 kg *3 lb*. A Hampshire × Yorkshire sow belonging to the Rev. John Schroeder of Mountain Grove, Missouri, USA farrowed a litter of 18 on 26 Aug 1979. Five of them were stillborn including one male which weighed 2·38 kg *5·25 lb*.

The highest recorded weight for a piglet at weaning (eight weeks) is 36·7 kg *81 lb* for a boar, one of nine piglets farrowed on 6 Jul 1962 by the Landrace gilt 'Manorport Ballerina 53rd', *alias* 'Mary', and sired by a Large White named 'Johnny' at Kettle Lane Farm, West Ashton, Trowbridge, Wilts. In Nov 1957 a total weight of 514·3 kg *1134 lb* was reported at weaning for a litter of 18 piglets farrowed by an Essex sow owned by Mrs B Ravell of Seaton House, Thorugumbald, Hull.

Sheep *Heaviest* ■ The heaviest sheep ever recorded was an old Leicester Longwool ram which scaled 214 kg *472 lb*.

Smallest ■ The smallest breed of sheep is the Soay, which is now confined to the island of Hirta in the St Kilda group, Outer Hebrides, Scotland. Adults weigh 25–27·2 kg *55–60 lb*.

Lambs ■ The highest recorded birthweight for a lamb is 17·2 kg *38 lb* at Clearwater, Sedgwick County, Kansas, USA in 1975, but neither lamb nor ewe survived. Another lamb of the same weight was born on 7 Apr 1975 on the Gerald Neises Farm, Howard, South Dakota, USA but died soon afterwards. The British record is 11·79 kg *26 lb* for a lamb born on 9 Feb 1967 by Alan F. Baldry from an ewe belonging to J. L. Arkwright of Winkleigh, Devon. A four-year-old Suffolk ewe owned by Gerry H. Watson of Augusta, Kansas, USA gave birth to two live sets of triplets on the 30/31 Jan 1982. The total weight of the lambs was 22·4 kg *49½ lb*. A Suffolk × Border Leicester ewe owned by Major P. Cazenove of Cottesbroke, Northants gave birth to live quadruplets totalling 19·5 kg *43 lb* were produced by a Suffolk x half-breed ewe owned by Dr S. Yuill-Walker of Lower Court, Chadlington, Oxon, in 1968.

The lowest live birthweight recorded for a lamb is

1·02 kg *2 lb 4 oz* for a ram named 'Tiny' owned by Jeanette Fox of Daisy Bank Farm, Barthomley, Cheshire, in April 1980. It was nursed to full health.

Oldest ■ A crossbred sheep owned by Griffiths & Davies, Dolclettwr Hall, Taliesin, near Aberystwyth, Wales gave birth to a healthy lamb in the spring of 1988 at the grand old age of 28 after lambing successfully more than 40 times. She died on 24 Jan 1989 just one week away from her 29th birthday.

Goats *Largest* ■ The largest goat ever recorded was a British Saanen named 'Mostyn Moorcock' owned by Miss Pat Robinson of Ewyas Harold, Herefordshire, which reached a weight of 181·4 kg *400 lb* (shoulder height 111·7 cm *44 in* and overall length of 167·6 cm *66 in*). He died in 1977 aged four years. Some Pygmy goats only weigh 15–20 kg *33–44 lb*.

Oldest ■ The oldest goat on record is a Toggenburg feral cross named 'Hongi' (b. August 1971) belonging to Miss April J. Koch of Glenorchy, near Otago, New Zealand, who was still alive mid-March 1989 aged 17 years 8 months. The oldest goat currently living in Britain is 'Emmahazelina' (b. 20 Apr 1972) a British Toggenburg type, owned by Michael C. Johnston of Farrington, Blandford Forum, Dorset.

Turkey *Heaviest and most expensive* ■ The greatest dressed weight recorded for a turkey is 37·59 kg *82 lb 14⅜ oz* for a stag reared by British United Turkeys of Chester, Cheshire. It won the annual 'heaviest turkey' competition held in London on 8 Dec 1987 and was bought for a record £4200 by Dewhurst the butchers. Stags of this size have been so over-developed for meat production that they are unable to mate because of their shape and the hens have to be artificially inseminated.

Chicken *Heaviest* ■ The heaviest breed of chicken is the White Sully, which Mr Grant Sullens of West Point, California, USA developed over a period of seven years by crossing and recrossing large Rhode Island Reds with other varieties. One monstrous rooster named 'Weirdo' reportedly weighed 10 kg *22 lb* in January 1973, and was so aggressive that he had already killed two cats and crippled a dog which came too close.

The heaviest chicken recorded in Britain is a White Ross I rooster named 'Bruno' reared by John Steele of Kirk Hills Farms, White Hills, Banff, Scotland. This outsized bird recorded a weight of 8·07 kg *17 lb 12½ oz* on 6 Mar 1989.

Eggs ■ The heaviest egg reported is one of 454 g *16 oz*, with double yolk and double shell, laid by a White Leghorn at Vineland, New Jersey, USA on 25 Feb 1956. The largest recorded was one of 'nearly 12 oz' for a five-yolked egg 31 cm *12¼ in* around the long axis and 22·8 cm *9 in* around the short, laid by a Black Minorca at Mr Stafford's Damsteads Farm, Mellor, Lancs, England in 1896.

The lightest egg is one of 1·47 g *0·05 oz* (27 ×22 mm *1·06 × 0·86 in*) laid by a Leghorn/Ranger cross named 'Obedience' owned by Miss Verity Nicholson of Adstock Fields Farm House, Buckingham, Bucks on 12 Mar 1986.

Most yolks ■ The highest claim for the number of yolks in a chicken's egg is nine reported by Mrs Diane Hainsworth of Hainsworth Poultry Farms, Mount Morris, New York in July 1971 and also from a hen in Kirgizya, USSR in August 1977.

Chicken flying ■ 'Sheena', a barnyard bantam owned by Bill and Bob Knox, flew 192·07 m *630 ft 2 in* at Parkesburg, Pennsylvania, USA on 31 May 1985.

Goose *Heaviest egg* ■ The heaviest egg on record is one of 680 g *24 oz* which measures 34 cm *13·5 in* round the long axis and has a maximum circumference of 24 cm *9·5 in*. It was laid on 3 May 1977 by a white goose named 'Speckle' owned by Donny Brandenberg, of Goshen, Ohio, USA. The average weight is 283–340 g *10–12 oz*.

Largest 'geometry set' ● This 60 tonne monument has been built in Jeddah as a reminder of the importance of engineering and planning in the developments taking place in Saudi Arabia. The compass stands 37.25 m *122 ft 2½ in* above ground level. (Photo: Al Makeaba Stores).

Largest golf club ● This golf club is 3.75 m *12 ft 3¾in* long and weighs 40 kg *88.1 lb*. It was made by Gunnar Bäckström (seen here supporting Håkan Hansson the skiier on his shoulders) of Sälen, Sweden.

Largest teapot ● This giant teapot exhibited at the 1988 Glasgow Garden Festival measured 3.6 m (*12ft*) high and had a diameter of 5.03 m (*16½ft*). It was produced for Stoke-on-Trent City Council by the manufactures ANMAC of Nottingham. The decoration on the teapot was an adaptation of the Chinese willow pattern and conveyed the story of Stoke-on-Trent for example the three traditional Chinese characters crossing the bridge became a miner, a steelworker and a potter representing Stoke industries, the boat became a canal narrow boat and the two birds were replaced by two Spitfire fighter planes to commemorate Stoke man Reginald Mitchell who designed the aircraft. (Photo: Rex Features)

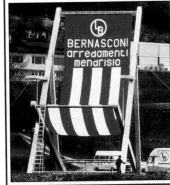

Largest chair ● This 12.71 m *41 ft 8½ in* tall, 7.26 m *23 ft 9½ in* wide deck-chair was constructed by Luigi Bernasconi & Co of Mendrisio, Switzerland and was exhibited from 11-13 Apr 1987.

Largest coathanger ● The world's largest coathanger measures 4.6 m x 2.06 m x 0.5 m (*15 ft x 6.75 ft x 1.6 ft*) and weighs 200 kg (*440 lb*). It was made of Oregon pine and plywood by Stefan Geir Karlsson of Reykjavik, Iceland.

Largest windsock
● This wine-bottle shaped windsock had an overall length of 16.8 m *55 ft* and was made by The Monterey Vineyard, California, USA in June 1988.

Prolificacy *Cattle* ■ On 25 Apr 1964 it was reported that a cow named 'Lyubik' had given birth to seven calves at Mogilev, USSR. Five short-lived and one still born calf were recorded from a Friesian at Te Puke, North Island, New Zealand on 27 Jul 1980. A case of five live calves at one birth was reported in 1928 by T. G. Yarwood of Manchester. The life time prolificacy record is 39 in the case of 'Big Bertha' (b. 17 Mar 1944), a Dremon owned by Jerome O'Leary of Blackwatersbridge, Co. Kerry, Ireland.

'Soender Jylland's Jens', a Danish black and white bull, left 220 000 surviving progeny by artificial insemination when he was put down aged 11 in Copenhagen in September 1978. 'Bendalls Adema', a Friesian bull, died aged 14 at Clondalkin, County Dublin, Ireland on 8 Nov 1978 having sired an estimated 212 000 progeny by artificial insemination.

Pigs ■ The highest recorded number of piglets in one litter is 34, farrowed on 25–26 Jun 1961 by a sow owned by Aksel Egedee of Denmark. In February 1955 a Wessex sow belonging to Miss E. C. Goodwin of Paul's Farm, Leigh, near Tonbridge, Kent also had a litter of 34, of which 30 were still-born. A litter of 32 piglets (eight still-born) was farrowed in February 1971 by a British Saddleback owned by Mr R. Spence of Toddington, Glos. The highest number of live births in Britain is 30 from a White Wessex sow reported by W. Ives of Dane End Fruit Farm, near Ware, Herts in September 1979. A Large White owned by H. S. Pedlingham farrowed 385 pigs in 22 litters (Dec 1923–Sep 1934). During the period 1940–52 a Large Black sow belonging to A. M. Harris of Lapworth, Birmingham, farrowed 26 litters. A Newsham Large White × Landrace sow of Meeting House Farm, Staintondale, near Scarborough, Yorks, had farrowed 189 piglets (seven still-born) in nine litters up to 22 Mar 1988. Between 6 May 1987 and 9 Feb 1988 she gave birth to 70 piglets. A breeding sow will live 12 years or more before it is slaughtered, but the maximum potential lifespan is 20 years.

Sheep ■ A case of eight lambs at a birth was reported by D. T. Jones of Priory Farm, Gwent, in June 1956 and by Ken Towse of Buckton near Bridlington in March 1981 but none lived. A Border Leicester × Merino sheep owned by Roger Saunders gave birth to 4 ram and 3 ewe live lambs at Strathdownie, Victoria, Australia on 19 Jun 1984. Seven live lambs (4 rams and 3 ewes) were also reported for a Finn × Targhoe ewe owned by Elsward Meine of Crookston, Minnesota, USA on 24 Mar 1980.

Goats ■ According to the British Goat Society at least one or two cases of quintuplets are recorded annually out of the 10 000 goats registered, but some breeders only record the females born. On 14 Jan 1980 a Nanny named 'Julie' owned by Galen Cowper of Nampah, Idaho, USA gave birth to septuplets, but they all died including the mother.

Chickens ■ The highest authenticated rate of egg-laying is by a White Leghorn chicken hen, No. 2988 at the College of Agriculture, University of Missouri, USA, with 371 eggs in 364 days in an official test conducted by Professor Harold V. Biellier ending on 29 Aug 1979. The UK record is 353 eggs in 365 days in a National Laying Test at Milford, Surrey in 1957 by a Rhode Island Red 'Wonderful Lady' owned by W. Lawson of Welham Grange, Retford, Nottinghamshire.

The highest recorded annual average per bird for a flock is 313 eggs in 52 weeks from a flock of 1000 Warren-Stadler SSL layers (from 21 weeks of age) by Eric Savage, White Lane Farm, Albury, Surrey, England in 1974–5.

Duck ■ An Aylesbury duck belonging to Annette and Angela Butler of Princes Risborough, Bucks, England laid 457 eggs in 463 days including an unbroken run of 375 in as many days. The duck died on 7 Feb 1986. Another duck of the same breed owned by Edmond Walsh of Gormanstown, Co Kildare, Ireland laid eggs every year right up to her 25th birthday. She died on 3 Dec 1978 aged 28 years 6 months.

Milk yields *Cows* ■ The highest recorded world lifetime yield of milk is 211 025 kg (*465 224 lb*) by the unglamorously named cow No. 289 owned by M. G. Maciel & Son of Hanford, California to 1 May 1984. The greatest yield of any British cow was that given by 'Winton Pel Eva 2' owned by John Waring of Glebe House, Kilnwick near Pocklington, Humberside, with 165 000 kg. The greatest recorded yield for one lactation (maximum 365 days) is 25 247 kg *55 661 lb* by the Holstein 'Beecher Arlinda Ellen' owned by Mr and Mrs Harold L. Beecher of Rochester, Indiana in 1975. The British lactation record (305 days) was set by 'Michaelwood Holm Emoselle 25' (b. 1 Aug 1973), a Friesian, owned by Mr and Mrs M. T. Holder of Aylesmore Farm, Newent, Glos with 19 400 kg *42 769 lb* in 1984–5.

The Irish lactation record (305 days) is held by 'Oriel Freda 10' (b. 21 Feb 1978), a Friesian owned by Mellifont Abbey Trust, Collon, Co. Louth, Ireland with 21 513 kg in 1986. The highest reported milk yield in a day is 109·3 kg *241 lb* by 'Urbe Blanca' in Cuba on or about 23 Jun 1982.

Hand milking ■ Andy Faust at Collinsville, Oklahoma, USA in 1937 achieved 99·92 UK gal in 12 hr.

Goats ■ The highest recorded milk yield for any goat is 3499 kg *7714 lb* in 365 days by 'Osory Snow-Goose' owned by Mr and Mrs G. Jameson of Leppington, NSW, Australia in 1977. A 15-year-old goat owned by Mrs Nanbui Meghani of Bhuj, Gujarat, India was reported in November 1984 to have lactated continuously for 12 years.

Butter fat yield ■ The world record lifetime yield is 7425 kg *16 370 lb* by the US Holstein 'Breezewood Patsy Bar Pontiac' in 3979 days.

The world record for 365 days is 1418 kg *3126 lb* by 'Roybrook High Ellen', a Holstein owned by Yashuhiro Tanaka of Tottori, Japan.

The British record butter fat yield in a lifetime is 5518 kg *12 166 lb* by the Ayrshire cow 'Craighead

Welma' owned by W. Watson Steele from 123 865 kg *273 072 lb* at 4·45 per cent.

The British record for 365 days is 852 kg *1878 lb* by 'Michaelwood Holm Emoselle 25', a Friesian owned by Mick and Linda Holder of Aylesmore Farm, Newent, Glos. 'Michaelwood Holm Emoselle 25' went on to milk for a total of 395 days in her 8th lactation, producing an incredible 1012 kg *2231 lb* of butterfat.

The British record for butter fat in one day is 4·53 kg *10 lb* by British Friesian 'Michaelwood Holm Emoselle 25'.

Cheese ■ The most active cheese-eaters are the people of France, with an annual average in 1983 of 19·8 kg *43·6 lb* per person. The world's biggest producer is the United States with a factory production of 4 773 500 000 lbs (2 200 000 tonnes *2 165 000 tons*) in 1980. The UK cheese consumption where 67 per cent is Cheddar in 1988 was 7·87 kg *16·02 lb* per head.

The oldest and most primitive cheeses are the Arabian *kishk*, made of dried curd of goats' milk. There are today 450 named cheeses in 18 major varieties, but many are merely named after different towns and differ only in shape or the method of packing. France has 240 varieties.

The world's most expensive cheese in its home market is Le Leruns made from ewes' milk at 90FF per kilo. Cheese made to the Liederkranz formula in Van Wert, USA retails for $2·25 per 4 oz; equivalent to $9·00 per lb. Britain's most costly cheese is Lanark Blue which is obtainable from some shops for £7·50 per lb.

Oldest goat ● 'Emmahazelina' (b. 20 Apr 1972) owned by Michael Johnston of Farrington, Blandford Forum, Dorset is currently the oldest goat living in Britain. (Photo: Michael Johnston)

CHAPTER 8

Largest ballet company
The world's largest ballet company is The Bolshoi Ballet of Moscow, USSR. The company was established in 1776 performing primarily at the mansion of Count R. I. Vorontsov. In 1780 the Petrovsky Theatre was opened as the company's home but it burned down in 1805. The present Bolshoi Theatre was opened on 19 January 1825, and it accommodates an audience of more than 2000. In 1924 an affiliate auditorium was added to the theatre complex and in 1961 the 6000-seat Palace of Congresses in the Kremlin was acquired as a third performing stage. Today The Bolshoi Ballet has a 2000-strong workforce including 260 dancers. The photgraph shows Yuri Vasyuchenko in The Bolshoi Ballet's production of 'Spartacus'. (Photo: David Tack. By arrangement with The Entertainment Corporation)

The Arts and Entertainment

Painting

Oldest ■ Evidence of Palaeolithic art was first found in 1833 at Veyrier, 5 km *3 miles* south-west of Geneva, Switzerland, when François Mayor (1779–1854) found two harpoon-like objects decorated with geometric figures. Recently discovered pieces of bone with geometric engraved marks on them from an Old Stone Age site at Bilzingsleben, near Erfurt, East Germany, could possibly be the world's oldest examples of art. They are dated to *c.* 350 000 years ago. The oldest known dated examples of representational art come from La Ferrassie, near Les Eyzies in the Périgord, France in layers dated to *c.* 25 000 BC. Blocks of stone were found with engraved animals and female symbols; some of the blocks also had symbols painted in red ochre. Pieces of ochre with ground facets have been found at Lake Mungo, NSW, Australia in a context *ante* 30 000 BC but there is no evidence whether these were used for body-painting or pictorial art.

Largest ■ *Panorama of the Mississippi*, completed by John Banvard (1815–91) in 1846, showing the river for 1930 km *1200 miles* in a strip probably 1524 m *5000 ft* long and 3·66 m *12 ft* wide, was the largest painting in the world, with an area of more than 5575 m *60 000 ft²*. The painting is believed to have been destroyed when the rolls of canvas, stored in a barn at Cold Spring Harbor, Long Island, New York State, USA, caught fire shortly before Banvard's death on 16 May 1891.

The Battle of Gettysburg, completed in 1883, after 2½ years of work, by Paul Philippoteaux (France) and 16 assistants, was 125 m *410 ft* long, 21·3 m *70 ft* high and weighed 5·45 tonnes *5·36 tons.* It depicts the climax of the battle, in southern Pennsylvania, USA, on 3 Jul 1863. In 1964 it was bought by Joe King of Winston-Salem, North Carolina, USA after being stored by E. W. McConnell in a Chicago warehouse since 1933 but, owing to deterioration, the sky was trimmed so decreasing the area.

Jackson Bailey's *Life of Christ* exhibited by Religious Art Institute of America Inc. of Atlanta, Georgia, USA comprises 50 panels 3·35 × 6·09 m *11 × 20 ft* and was complete by 1971 with an area of 1022 m² *11 000 ft²*.

Kimiko Hibino (b. 1942) painted over 800 species of the animal kingdom on a canvas 3 km *1·86 miles* long and 2·2 m *7·2 ft* wide. On 27 Oct 1985, it was unveiled with the help of 3000 volunteers along the bank of the Tamagawa River in Tokyo, Japan.

'Old Master' ■ The largest 'Old Master' is *Il Paradiso*, by Jacopo Robusti, *alias* Tintoretto (1518–94), and his son Domenico (1565–1637) on the east wall of the Sala del Maggior Consiglio in the Palazzo Ducale (Doge's Palace) in Venice, Italy between 1587 and 1590. The work is 22 m *72 ft 2 in* long and 7 m *22 ft 11½ in* high and contains some 350 human figures.

GB ■ The oval *Triumph of Peace and Liberty* by Sir James Thornhill (1676–1734), on the ceiling of the Painted Hall in the Royal Naval College, Greenwich. It measures 32·3 m × 15·4 m *106 ft × 51 ft* and took 20 years (1707–27) to complete.

Auction ■ The largest painting ever auctioned was Carl Larsson's *Midvinterblot* painted in Stockholm, Sweden in 1911–15 and sold at Sotheby's, London on 25 Mar 1988 for £880 000 to the Umeda Gallery of Japan.

Most valuable ■ The 'Mona Lisa' (*La Gioconda*) by Leonardo da Vinci (1452–1519) in the Louvre, Paris, France was assessed for insurance purposes at $100 000 000 for its move to Washington, DC, USA and New York City, USA for exhibition from 14 Dec 1962 to 12 Mar 1963. However, insurance was not concluded because the cost of the closest security precautions was less than that of the premiums. It was painted *c.* 1503–7 and measures 77 × 53 cm *30·5 × 20·9 in.* It is believed to portray either Mona (short for Madonna) Lisa Gherardini, the wife of Francesco del Giocondo of Florence, or Constanza

d'Avalos, coincidentally nicknamed La Gioconda, mistress of Giuliano de Medici. Francis I, King of France, bought the painting for his bathroom in 1517 for 4000 gold florins or 15·3 kg *92 oz* of gold.

Most prolific painter ■ Pablo Diego José Francisco de Paula Juan Nepomuceno Crispin Crispiano de la Santisima Trinidad Ruiz y Picasso (1881–1973) of Spain was the most prolific of all painters in a career which lasted 78 years. It has been estimated that Picasso produced about 13 500 paintings or designs, 100 000 prints or engravings, 34 000 book illustrations and 300 sculptures or ceramics. His life-time *oeuvre* has been valued at £500 million.

Commercial ■ Morris Katz (b. 1932) of Greenwich Village, New York City, USA is the most prolific painter of saleable paintings in the world. His sales total as of 5 Mar 1986 was 153 629. On the NBC 'Today' TV programme in November 1985 Katz demonstrated he could paint at a rate of 0·25 m² *2·64 ft²* per min.

Most repetitious painter ■ William Allen Bixler (1876–1961) of Andersen, Indiana, USA reproduced his painting *The Old Swimmin' Hole* over 5000 times between the years 1912–18. The painting was inspired by James Whitcomb Riley's poem of the same name.

Oldest RA ■ The oldest ever Royal Academician has been (Thomas) Sidney Cooper CVO, who died on 8 Feb 1902 aged 98 yr 136 days, having exhibited 266 paintings over the record span of 69 consecutive years (1833–1902).

Youngest RA ■ Mary Moser (1744–1819) (later Mrs Hugh Lloyd), was elected on the foundation of the Royal Academy in 1768 when aged 24.

Youngest exhibitor ■ The youngest ever exhibitor at the Royal Academy of Arts Annual Summer Exhibition was Lewis Melville 'Gino' Lyons (b. 30 Apr 1962). His *Trees and Monkeys* was painted on 4 Jun 1965, submitted on 17 Mar 1967 and exhibited to the public on 29 Apr 1967.

Largest galleries ■ The world's largest art gallery is the Winter Palace and the neighbouring Hermitage in Leningrad, USSR. One has to walk 24 km *15 miles* to visit each of the 322 galleries, which house nearly 3 000 000 works of art and objects of archaeological interest.

Modern art ■ The Georges Pompidou National

Centre for Art and Culture, Beauborg, opened in Paris, France in 1977 with 17 700 m² *183 000 ft²* of floor space.

Most heavily endowed ■ The most heavily endowed is the J. Paul Getty Museum, Malibu, California, USA with an initial £700 000 000 in January 1974 and now £104 million p.a. for acquisitions. It has 38 galleries.

Finest brush ■ The finest standard brush sold is the 000 in Series 7 by Winsor and Newton known as a 'triple goose'. It is made of 150–200 Kolinsky sable hairs weighing 15 mg *0·000529 oz.*

MURALS

Earliest ■ The earliest known murals on man-made walls are the clay relief leopards at Catal Hüyük in southern Anatolia, Turkey, discovered by James Malaart at level VII in 1961 and dating from *c.* 6200 BC.

Largest ■ A mural on the 23-storey Vegas World Hotel, Las Vegas, Nevada, USA covers an area of 8866·56 m² *95 442 ft².*

The longest recorded continuous mural is one stretching 497·7 m *1633 ft* on the walls of the Royal Liverpool Children's Hospital, Alder Hey, Liverpool. It covers an area of 1668·7 m² *17 963 ft². Future entries for this category will be assessed on overall area only.*

Largest mosaic ■ The world's largest mosaic is on the walls of the central library of the Universidad Nacional Autónoma de Mexico, Mexico City, Mexico. There are four walls, the two largest measuring 1203 m² *12 949 ft²* each representing the pre-Hispanic past.

Britain ■ The largest Roman mosaic in Britain is the Woodchester Pavement, Glos of *c.* AD 325, excavated in 1793, now re-covered with protective earth. It measured 14·3 m² *47 ft²* comprising 1·6 million tesserae. A total reconstruction carried out by Robert and John Woodward of Stroud, Glos was completed in June 1987.

'WORK OF ART'

Largest ■ The largest work of art was the wrapping in 1983 of 11 islands in Biscayne Bay, Florida, USA in flamingo pink plastic tutus for Christo's work entitled *Surrounded Islands.* The amount of plastic sheeting used was 603 000 m² *6 500 000 ft².*

HIGHEST PRICE

Most expensive painting ■ *Irises* by Vincent Van Gogh (b. 30 Mar 1853, Zundert, Netherlands–d. 29 Jul 1890, Auvers-sur-Oise, France) was sold for a record $53·9 million (including buyer's premium) at Sotheby's, New York on 11 Nov 1987. It took less than four minutes to sell the 71·7 cm × 92·7 cm *28 in × 36½ in* canvas which Van Gogh had painted in 1889 whilst a voluntary patient at the Saint Remy Mental Asylum in Provence, France. The successful bid was made by telephone from Europe.

Abstract ■ The auction record for an abstract painting is $11·55 million for a large drip painting entitled *Number 8, 1950* by Jackson Pollock (1912–1956) at Sotheby's, New York, USA on 2 May 1989. It was purchased by art consultant Jeffrey Deitch on behalf of a client.

Miniature portrait ■ The highest price ever is the £352 000 paid by the Alexander Gallery, New York, USA at a sale held by Christie's, London on 7 Nov 1988 for a 54 mm *2⅛ in* high miniature of George Washington, painted by John Ramage (*c.* 1784–1802), an Irish-American miniaturist in 1789.

20th century painting ■ The record bid at auction for a 20th century painting is $47·8 million for Picasso's (1881–1973) 1901 self-portrait *Yo Picasso* at Sotheby's, New York on 9 May 1989.

Living artist ■ The highest price at auction for a work by a living artist was $17·05 million for *False Start* by Jasper Johns at Sotheby's, New York, USA on 10 Nov 1988. It was bought by a New York dealer.

UK ■ The highest price for any painting by a living United Kingdom-born artist has been $6·27 million for *Triptych May–June* by Francis Bacon (b. Dublin, Ireland, 1909, then part of the United Kingdom), sold on 2 May 1989 at Sotheby's, New York, USA.

Print ■ The record price for a print at auction was £561 600 for a 1655 print of *Christ Presented to the People* by Rembrandt at Christie's, London on 5 Dec 1985, sold by Chatsworth Settlement Trustees.

Drawing ■ The highest price ever paid for any drawing is £3 546 000 for a study of an apostle's head and hand for the Transfiguration in the Vatican by Raphael (Raffaello Santi 1483–1520) and sold for the 11th Duke of Devonshire (b. 1920) at Christie's, London on 3 Jul 1984.

Poster ■ The record price for a poster is £62 000 for an advertisement for the 1902 Vienna Exhibition by Koloman Moser (b. Vienna 30 Mar 1868—d. 18 Oct 1918), sold at Christie's, South Kensington, London on 1 Apr 1985.

Largest ■ A poster measuring 100 m × 100 m *328 ft × 328 ft* (10 000 m² *107 642 ft²*) was constructed by 10 000 citizens of Obihiro, Hokkaido, Japan on 26 Jul 1987 for the Obihiro Green Frontier Festival.

Sculpture

Earliest ■ A piece of ox rib found in 1973 at Pech de l'Aze, Dordogne, France in an early Middle Palaeolithic layer of the Riss glaciation *c.* 105 000 BC has several engraved lines on one side, thought to be possibly intentional. A churingo or curved ivory plaque rubbed with red ochre from the Middle Palaeolithic Mousterian site at Tata, Hungary has been dated to 100 000 BC by the thorium/uranium method. The earliest known examples of sculpture date from the Aurignacian culture *c.* 28 000–22 000 BC and include the so-called Venus figurines from Austria and the numerous figurines from northern Italy and central France. A carving in mammoth ivory from the Magdalenian culture of a horse 6·3 cm *2½ in* long was found in the Vogelherd cave in south-west Germany.

Britain ■ The earliest example of an engraving found in Britain is of a horse's head on a piece of rib-bone from Robin Hood Cave, Creswell Crag, Derbys. It dates from the Upper Palaeolithic period (*c.* 15 000 to 10 000 BC). The earliest Scottish rock carving from Lagalochan, Argyll dates from *c.* 3000 BC. Geometric carvings on the tomb at Newgrange, Co. Meath, Ireland are also between 3000–2500 years.

Most expensive ■ The record price paid for a sculpture at auction is $10·12 million for *Petite danseuse de quatorze ans* by Edgar Degas (1834–1917), by an anonymous European bidder at Sotheby's, New York, USA on 10 May 1988. This ballerina is the most famous of the Degas bronzes and the only sculpture he exhibited in his lifetime.

The highest price paid for the work of a sculptor during his lifetime is the $1 265 000 given at Sotheby Parke Bernet, New York on 21 May 1982 for the 190·5 cm *75 in* long elmwood *Reclining Figure* by Henry Moore, OM, CH (b. 30 Jul 1898 d. 31 Aug 1986).

Largest ■ The mounted figures of Jefferson Davis (1808–89), Gen. Robert Edward Lee (1807–70) and Gen. Thomas Jonathan (Stonewall) Jackson (1824–63), cover 0·5 ha *1·33 acres* on the face of Stone Mountain, near Atlanta, Georgia, USA. They are 27·4 m *90 ft* high. Roy Faulkner was on the mountain face for 8 years 174 days with a thermo-jet torch working with the sculptor Walker Kirtland Hancock and other helpers from 12 Sep 1963 to 3 Mar 1972.

If completed, the world's largest sculpture will be that of the Indian chief Tashunca-Uitco (*c.* 1849–77), known as Crazy Horse, of the Oglala tribe of the Dakota or Nadowessioux (Sioux) group, on horseback. The sculpture was begun on 3 Jun 1948 near Mount Rushmore, South Dakota, USA. A projected 171·6 m *563 ft* high and 195 m *641 ft* long, it was the uncompleted life work of one man, Korczak Ziólkowski (1908–82). The horse's nostril is 15·2 m

Largest sculpture ● The mounted figures of Jefferson Davis (1808–89), Gen. Robert Edward Lee (1807–70) and Gen. Thomas Jonathan (Stonewall) Jackson (1824–63), cover 0·5 ha *1·33 acres* on the face of Stone Mountain, near Atlanta, Georgia, USA. They are 27·4 m *90 ft* high. Roy Faulkner was on the mountain face for 8 years 174 days with a thermo-jet torch working with the sculptor Walker Kirtland Hancock and other helpers from 12 Sep 1963 to 3 Mar 1972. (Photo: Photo Source)

50 ft deep and 10·7 m *35 ft* in diameter. In 1985–6 another 400 000 tons of granite blasted off the mountain face brought the total to 8·2 million tons.

Ground figures ■ In the Nazca Desert, 300 km *185 miles* south of Lima, Peru there are straight lines (one more than 11·2 km *7 miles* long), geometric shapes and shapes of plants and animals drawn on the ground some time between 100 BC and AD 600 for an uncertain but probably religious, astronomical, or even economic purpose by a imprecisely identified civilisation. They were first detected from the air *c.* 1928 and have also been described as the world's longest works of art.

Hill figures ■ In August 1968, a 100 m *330 ft* tall figure was found on a hill above Tarapacá, Chile.

The largest human hill carving in Britain is the 'Long Man' of Wilmington, East Sussex, 68 m *226 ft* in length. The oldest of all White Horses in Britain is the Uffington White Horse in Oxfordshire, dating from the late Iron Age (*c.* 150 BC) and measuring 114 m *374 ft* from nose to tail and 36 m *120 ft* high.

Most massive mobile ■ *White Cascade* weighing 8 tonnes and measuring 30·48 m *100 ft* from top to bottom was installed on 24–25 May 1976 at the Federal Reserve Bank of Philadelphia, Pennsylvania, USA. It was designed by Alexander Calder (1898–1976), whose first mobiles were exhibited in Paris, France in 1932 and whose *Big Crinkley* sold for a record £555 572 at Sotheby's, New York, USA on 10 May 1984.

ANTIQUE PRICE RECORDS

ANCIENT SCULPTURE

An 8 in 6000-year-old neolithic sculpture of a seated goddess from the estate of James Johnson Sweeney was sold for $1·32 million, at auction by Sotheby's, New York, USA on 24 Nov 1986. The purchaser was Mrs Shelby White Levy, a New York, USA financial writer.

ART NOUVEAU

The highest auction price for any piece of art nouveau is $360 000 for a spider-web leaded glass mosaic and bronze table lamp by L. C. Tiffany at Christie's, New York, USA on 8 Apr 1980.

BED

A 1930 black lacquer kingsize bed made by Jean Durand was auctioned at Christie's, New York, USA on 2 Oct 1983 for £49 668.

BLANKET

The most expensive blanket was a Navajo Churro hand-spun serape of *c.* 1852 sold for $115 500 with premium at Sotheby's, New York, USA on 22 Oct 1983.

CARPET

In 1946 the Metropolitan Museum, New York, USA privately paid $1 million for the 807 × 414 cm *26·5 × 13·6 ft* Anhalt Medallion carpet made in Tabriz or Kashan, Persia *c.* 1590. The highest price ever paid at auction for a carpet is £231 000 for a 17th-century 'Polonaise' silk and metal thread carpet at Sotheby's, London on 13 Oct 1982.

CERAMICS

The highest auction price for any ceramic is HK$22 million £1 726 845 for a rare Chinese guanyao brushwasher. It was bought by a Los Angeles collector at Sotheby's, Hong Kong on 16 May 1989.

CHAMBER POT

A 935 g *33 oz* silver pot, made by David Willaume and engraved for the 2nd Earl of Warrington, made £9500 at Sotheby's, London on 14 Jun 1984.

CIGARETTE CARD

The most valuable card is one of the six known baseball series cards of Honus Wagner, who was a non-smoker, which was sold in New York, USA in December 1981 for $25 000.

DOLLS

The highest price at auction for a doll is £90 200 for a 1909 bisque Kämmer and Reinhardt doll at Sotheby's, London on 16 Feb 1989. It was purchased by Mme Dina Vierny who plans to open a Museum of Childhood in France.

FURNITURE

The highest price ever paid for a single piece of furniture is $12·1 million at Christie's, New York, USA on 3 Jun 1989 for a mahogany desk cum bookcase made in the 1760's by master craftsman John Goddard of Newport, Rhode Island for the eminent statesman Nicholas Brown. It was bought by Israel Sack, one of New York's leading dealers in American furniture. The English furniture record was set by a black-japanned bureau-bookcase of c. 1705. Formerly owned by Queen Mary, it made $860 000 at Christie's, New York, USA on 18 Oct 1981. The record in the UK is £407 000 paid for a George II bombe commode at Christie's, London on 7 Jul 1988.

GLASS

The auction record is £520 000 for a Roman glass cage-cup of c. AD 300 measuring 17·78 cm 7 in in diameter and 10·16 cm 4 in in height, sold at Sotheby's, London, on 4 Jun 1979 to Robin Symes.

GOLD PLATE

The highest price for any gold artefact is £950 400 for the 22-carat font made by Paul Storr to the design of Humphrey Repton in 1797. It was sold at Christie's by Lady Anne Cavendish-Bentinck and bought by Armitage of London on 11 Jul 1985.

GUNS

The highest price ever paid for a single gun is £125 000 given by the London dealers F. Partridge for a French flintlock fowling piece made for Louis XIII c. 1615 and attributed to Pierre le Bourgeoys of Lisieux, France (d. 1627). This piece was included in the collection of the late William Goodwin Renwick of the United States sold by Sotheby's, London on 21 Nov 1972. It is now in the Metropolitan Museum of Art, New York, USA.

HAT

The highest price ever paid for a hat is $66 000 by the Alaska State Museum at a New York City, USA auction in November 1981 for a Tlingit Kiksadi ceremonial frog helmet from c. 1600.

ICON

The record auction price for an icon is $150 000 paid at Christie's, New York on 17 Apr 1980 for the *Last Judgement* (from the George R. Hann collection, Pittsburgh, USA) made in Novgorod, USSR in the 16th century.

JADE

The highest price ever paid for an item in jade is $396 000 (with premium) at Sotheby's, New York, USA on 6 Dec 1983 for a mottled brownish-yellow belt-hook and pendant mask of the Warring States Period of Chinese history.

JEWELS

The highest auction price for any jewels is £2 825 000 (or £3·1 million with the buyer's premium) for two pear-shaped diamond drop earrings of 58·6 and 61 carats at Sotheby's, Geneva on 14 Nov 1980. Neither the buyer nor seller was disclosed.

MECHANICAL TOY

The auction record for a toy is £25 500 for a model train set of Stephenson's *Rocket* made by Marklin of Germany in tin plate in 1909 sold at Sotheby's, London on 29 May 1984.

MUSICAL BOX

The highest price paid for a musical box is £20 900 (with premium) for a Swiss-made example made for a Persian prince in 1901, sold at Sotheby's, London on 23 Jan 1985.

PAPERWEIGHT

The highest price ever paid for a glass paperweight is $143 000 (with premium) at Sotheby's, New York, USA on 2 Dec 1983 for a blue glass weight made at Pantin, Paris, France *post* 1850.

Most expensive doll ● Mme Dina Vierny paid £90 200 for a 1909 Kämmer and Reinhardt bisque character doll at Sotheby's, London on 16 Feb 1989. (Photo: Sotheby's)

PISTOL

The highest price paid at auction for a pistol is £242 000 at Christie's, New York, USA on 14 May 1987 for a .45 calibre Colt single-action army revolver, Serial No. 1 for 1873.

PLAYING CARDS

The highest price paid for a deck of playing cards is $143 352 (with premium) by the Metropolitan Museum of Art, New York, USA at Sotheby's, London on 6 Dec 1983.

POT LID

The highest price paid for a pot lid is £3960 for one depicting 'Eastern Lady with Black Attendant', sold at Phillips, London on 7 Jan 1987.

ENGLISH SILVER

The record for a single piece of English silver is £770 000 for an epergne by de Lamerie sold at Christie's, London by the Earl of Portarlington and bought by Jacques Koopman on 17 Dec 1986. The Treasury inkstand of Sir Robert Walpole, Prime Minister from 1715 to 1742, sold for £770 000 to the London dealers Spink and Armitage at Christie's, London on 14 Dec 1988. The 100-piece Paul de Lamerie service made for the 7th Earl of Thanet c. 1745 was sold by Lord Hothfield at Sotheby's, London on 22 Nov 1984 for £825 000 (with premium).

SCIENTIFIC INSTRUMENT

The highest auction price for a scientific instrument is £385 000 for a 34·29 cm 13 ½ in Dutch gilt-brass astrolabe of 1559 by Walter Arsenius at Christie's, South Kensington on 29 Sep 1988.

SNUFF BOX

The highest price ever paid for a snuff box is £764 826 in a sale at Christie's, Geneva on 11 Nov 1986 for a pale-green chrysoprase and diamond gold box once owned by Frederick the Great of Prussia. It was purchased by a London dealer.

SPOONS

A Wiener werkstaffe spoon by Josef Hoffmann, Austria c. 1905 was sold at Sotheby's, London for £17 600 (with premium) on 28 Apr 1983. A set of 13 Henry VIII Apostle spoons owned by Lord Astor of Hever was sold for £120 000 on 24 Jun 1981 at Christie's, London.

STUFFED BIRD

The highest price ever paid for a stuffed bird is £9000. This was given on 4 Mar 1971 at Sotheby's, London by the Iceland Natural History Museum for a specimen of the Great Auk (*Alca impennis*) in summer plumage, which

was taken in Iceland c. 1821; it stood 57 cm 22 ½ in high. The Great Auk was a flightless North Atlantic seabird which was finally exterminated on Eldey, Iceland in 1844, becoming extinct through hunting. The last British sightings were at Co. Waterford, Ireland in 1834 and St Kilda, Western Isles c. 1840.

SWORD

The highest price paid for a sword is £823 045 for the Duke of Windsor's Royal Navy officer's sword (presented to him by King George V in 1913) at Sotheby's, Geneva on 3 Apr 1987.

TAPESTRY

The highest price paid for a tapestry is £550 000 for a Swiss medieval tapestry frieze in two parts dated 1468–1476 at Sotheby's, Geneva, on 10 Apr 1981 by the Basle Historische Museum.

THIMBLE

The record auction price for a thimble is £8000 paid by London dealer Winifred Williams at Christie's, London on 3 Dec 1979 for a Meissen dentil-shaped porcelain piece of c. 1740.

TOY SOLDIER

The highest price paid for a single toy soldier is £1200 for an extremely rare 70 mm scale figure of the Colonel–in–Chief, the Welsh Guards at Phillips, London on 9 Sep 1987.

TYPEWRITER

The highest price paid for an antique machine is £3000 for an 1886 Daw and Tait machine auctioned at Sotheby's, London on 12 Dec 1980.

WALKING STICK

The highest auction price for a walking stick has been $24 200 at Sotheby Parke Bernet, New York, USA in 1983 for an octagonal whale ivory nobbed stick decorated by Scrimshanders in 1845.

Language and Literature

Earliest ■ The ability to speak is believed to be dependent upon physiological changes in the height of the larynx between *Homo erectus* and *Homo sapiens sapiens* as developed c. 45 000 BC. The earliest written language discovered has been on Yangshao culture pottery from Paa-t'o, near Xi'an (Sian) in the Shaanxi (Shensi) province of China found in 1962. This bears proto-characters for the numbers 5, 7 and 8 and has been dated to 5000–4000 BC. The earliest dated pictographs are on clay tablets from Nippur, southern Iraq, from one of the lowest excavation levels equivalent to Uruk V/VI and dated in 1979 to c. 3400 BC. Tokens or tallies from Tepe Asiab and Ganji-I-Dareh Tepe in Iran have however been dated to 8500 BC. The earliest known piece of writing from the British Isles (c. AD 630) is a fragment of Irish uncial script in an ecclesiastical history sold for £75 000 by the Folger Shakespeare Library, Washington, DC, USA to the British Rail Pension Fund at Sotheby's, London on 25 Jun 1985.

British ■ Fragments of Roman wooden writing tablets found in the 1970s at Vindolandia near Newcastle-upon-Tyne have been shown to make up the earliest known substantial written records in British history. These contain letters and a quotation from the Roman poet Virgil and are dated to c. AD 100.

Oldest English words ■ It was first suggested in 1979 that languages ancestral to English and to Latvian (both Indo-European) split c. 3500 BC. About 40 words of a pre-Indo-European substrate survive in English e.g. apple (apal), bad (bad), gold (gol) and tin (tin) according to researches completed in 1988.

Commonest language ■ Today's world total of languages and dialects still spoken is about 5000 of which some 845 come from India. The language spoken by more people than any other is Mandarin, by an estimated 68 per cent of China's population, hence 715 million people in 1988. The so-called national language (*Guóyǔ*) is a standardised form of Northern Chinese (*Běifanghuà*) as spoken in the Peking area. This was alphabetised into *zhùyīn fúhào* of 37 letters in 1913 by Wa Chih-hui (1865–1953). On 11 Feb 1938 the *Hanyu-Pinyin-Fang'an* system, which is a phonetic pronunciation guide, was introduced. The next most commonly spoken language, and the most widespread, is English, with an estimated 330 000 000 as a mother tongue and nearly twice as many using it as a second or third language.

British Isles ■ In Great Britain and Ireland there are six indigenous tongues: English, Cornish, Scots Gaelic, Welsh, Irish Gaelic and Romany (Gipsy). Mr Edward (Ned) Maddrell (1877–1974) of Glen Chass, Port St Mary, Isle of Man died as the last islander whose professed tongue was Manx. Cornish, of which there are now some 300 students, came within an ace of extinction. A dictionary was published in 1887, four years before the death of the then last fluent speaker John Davey. A Cornish novel by Melville and Kitty Bennetto, *An Gurun Wosek a Geltya*, was published in November 1984. In the Channel Islands, apart from Jersey and Guernsey *normand*, there survive words of Sarkese or *Sèrtchais* in which the Parable of the Sower, as recited by some fishermen, was noted and published by Prince Louis Lucien Bonaparte (1813–91) in 1862.

Most languages ■ The former Australian territory of Papua New Guinea has, owing to so many isolated valleys, the greatest concentration of separate languages in the world, with more than 10 per cent of the world's total of 5000.

Most complex ■ The following extremes of complexity have been noted: Chippewa, the North American Indian language of Minnesota, USA, has the most verb forms with up to 6000; Haida, the North American Indian language, has the most prefixes with 70; Tabassaran, a language in Daghestan, USSR, uses the most noun cases with 48, while Eskimos use 63 forms of the present tense and simple nouns have as many as 252 inflections. In Chinese the 40-volume *Chung-wén Tà Tz'u-tiĕn* dictionary lists 49 905 characters. *The Dictionary of Chinese Characters* (Sichuan and Huber) in eight volumes will contain 20 million characters when completed in 1989. The fourth tone of 'i' has 84 meanings, varying as widely as 'dress', 'hiccough' and 'licentious'. The written language provides 92 different characters of 'i''. The most complex written character in Chinese is that representing *xiè* consisting of 64 strokes, meaning 'talkative'. The most complex in current use is *nang* with 36 strokes, meaning a blocked-up nose.

Least irregular verbs ■ Esperanto was first published by its inventor Dr Ludwig Zamenhof (1859–1917) of Warsaw in 1887 without irregular verbs and is now estimated (by text book sales) to have a million speakers. The even earlier interlanguage Volapük, invented by Johann Martin Schleyer (1831–1912), also has absolutely regular configuration. The Turkish language has a single irregular verb—*olmak*, to be.

Most irregular verbs ■ According to *The Morphology and Syntax of Present-day English* by Professor Olu Tomori, English has 283 irregular verbs of which 30 are merely formed with prefixes.

Rarest sounds ■ The rarest speech sound is probably the sound written ř in Czech which occurs in very few languages and is the last sound mastered by Czech children. In the southern Bushman language !xo there is a click articulated with both lips, which is written ☉. The *l* sound in the Arabic word *Allah*, in some contexts, is pronounced uniquely in that language.

Commonest sound ■ No language is known to be without the vowel *a* (as in the English father).

Vocabulary ■ The English language contains about 490 000 words plus another 300 000 technical terms, the most in any language, but it is doubtful if any individual uses more than 60 000. Those in Great Britain who have undergone a full 16 years of education use perhaps 5000 words in speech and up to 10 000 words in written communications. The membership of the International Society for Philosophical Enquiry (no admission for IQs below 148) have an average vocabulary of 36 250 words. Shakespeare employed a vocabulary of *c.* 33 000 words.

Greatest linguist ■ If the yardstick of ability to speak with fluency and reasonable accuracy is adhered to, it is doubtful whether any human could maintain fluency in more than 20–25 languages concurrently or achieve fluency in more than 40 in a lifetime.

Historically the greatest linguists have been proclaimed as Cardinal Mezzofanti (1774–1849) of Italy (fluent in 26 or 27); Professor Rask (1787–1832) of Denmark, Sir John Bowring (1792–1872) and Dr Harold Williams of New Zealand (1876–1928), who were all fluent in 28 languages.

The most multi-lingual living person is Georges Henri Schmidt (b. Strasbourg, France, 28 Dec 1914), the Chief of the UN Terminology Section in 1965–71. The 1975 edition of *Who's Who in the United Nations* listed 'only' 19 languages because he was then unable to find time to 'revive' his former fluency in 12 others. Powell Alexander Janulus (b. 1939) has worked with 41 languages in the Provincial Court of British Columbia, Vancouver, Canada.

Britain ■ Britain's greatest linguist is George Campbell (b. 9 Aug 1912), who is retired from the BBC Overseas Service where he *worked* with 54 languages.

ALPHABET

Earliest ■ The earliest example of alphabetic writing has been found at Ugarit (now Ras Sharma), Syria, dated to *c.* 1450 BC. It comprised a tablet of 32 cuneiform letters.

Oldest letter ■ The letter 'O' is unchanged in shape since its adoption in the Phoenician alphabet *c.* 1300 BC.

Newest letters ■ The newest letters added to the English alphabet are 'j' and 'v' which are of post-Shakespearean use *c.* 1630. Formerly they were used only as variants of 'i' and 'u'. There are 65 alphabets now in use.

Longest ■ The language with most letters is Cambodian with 72 (including useless ones).

Shortest ■ Rotokas in central Bougainville Island has least letters with 11 (a, b, e, g, i, k, o, p, ř, t and u).

Most and least consonants ■ The language with most distinct consonantal sounds is that of the Ubykhs in the Caucasus, with 80–85, and that with the least is Rotokas, which has only six consonants. The English word 'latchstring' has six consecutive letters which are consonants, but the Georgian word *gvprtskvnis* (he is feeling us) has eight separately pronounced consonants.

Most and least vowels ■ The language with the most vowels is Sedang, a central Vietnamese language with 55 distinguishable vowel sounds, and that with the least is the Caucasian language Abkhazian with two. The record in written English for consecutive vowels is six in the musical term *euouae*. The Estonian word *jäääärne*, meaning the edge of the ice, has the same four consecutively. The name of a language in Pará State, Brazil consists solely of seven vowels—*uoiauai*.

Largest letters ■ The largest permanent letters in the world are giant 183 m *600 ft* letters spelling READYMIX on the ground in the Nullarbor Plain near East Balladonia, Western Australia. These were constructed in December 1971.

Smallest letters ■ The 16 letters MOLECULAR DEVICES have been etched into a salt crystal by an electron beam so that the strokes were only 2 to 3 nm (10^{-9}) wide—the width of 20 hydrogen atoms. This was done by Michael Isaacson at Cornell University, Ithaca, New York, USA in February 1982.

WORDS

Longest ■ Lengthy concatenations and some compound or agglutinative words or nonce words are or have been written in the closed-up style of a single word e.g. the 182-letter fricassee of 17 sweet and sour ingredients in Aristophanes' comedy *The Ecclesiazusae* in the 4th century BC. A compound 'word' of 195 sanskrit characters (which transliterates into 428 letters in the Roman alphabet) describing the region near Kanci, Tamil Nadu, India appears in a 16th-century work by Tirumalāmbā, Queen of Vijayanagara.

English ■ The longest real word in the Oxford English Dictionary is *floccipaucinihilipilification* (alternatively spelt in hyphenated form with 'n' in

Most languages ● The former Australian territory of Papua New Guinea has, owing to so many isolated valleys, the greatest concentration of separate languages in the world, with more than 10 per cent of the world's total of 5000. This photograph shows the Purewi Wig men of Papua New Guinea. (Photo: Compix)

seventh place), with 29 letters, meaning 'the action of estimating as worthless', first used in 1741, and later by Sir Walter Scott (1771–1832). The longest factitious word in the Oxford English Dictionary is *pneumonoultramicroscopicsilicovolcanoconiosis (–koniosis)* with 45 letters – alleged to mean 'a lung disease caused by the inhalation of very fine silica dust'. Webster's Third International Dictionary lists among its 450 000 entries: *pneumonoultramicroscopic-silicovolcanoconiosises* (47 letters), the plural of the above-mentioned disease.

The longest regularly formed English word is *praetertranssubstantiationalistically* (37 letters) used by Mark McShane in his 1963 novel *Untimely Ripped*. The medical term *hepaticocholangiocholecystenterostomies* (39 letters) refers to the surgical creations of new communications between gallbladders and hepatic ducts and between intestines and gallbladders. The longest words in common use are *disproportionableness* and *incomprehensibilities* (21 letters). *Interdenominationalism* (22 letters) is found in Webster's Dictionary and hence perhaps *interdenominationalistically* (28 letters) is permissible. Simon Proctor of Maidstone, Kent has compiled 15 592 lesser words (excluding plurals) from its 28 letters.

Longest palindromes ■ The longest known palindromic word is *saippuakivikauppias* (19 letters), Finnish for a dealer in lye (i.e. caustic soda). The longest in English is *redivider* (nine letters). The nine-letter word *Malayalam* is a proper noun given to the language of the Malayali people in Kerala, southern India, while *Kanakanak* near Dillingham, Alaska is a nine-lettered palindromic place-name. The contrived chemical term *detartrated* has 11 letters. Some baptismal fonts in Greece and Turkey bear the circular 25-letter inscription NIΨONANOMH-MATAMHMONANOΨIN meaning 'wash (my) sins not only (my) face'. This appears at St Mary's Church, Nottingham, St Paul's, Woldingham, Surrey and other churches. The longest palindromic composition devised is one of 80 000 words completed by Edward Benbow of Bewdley, Hereford & Worcs in September 1988. It begins 'Al, sign it, "Lover"! . . .' and hence predictably ends '. . . . revolting, Isla'. The longest palindromic novel, *Dr Awkward and Olson in Oslo* contains 31 594 words and was written by Lawrence Levine, New York, USA in 1986.

Longest scientific name ■ The systematic name for deoxyribonucleicacid of the human mitochondria contains 16 569 nucleotide residues and is thus *c.* 207 000 letters long. It was published in key form in *Nature* on 9 Apr 1981.

Longest anagrams ■ The longest non-scientific English words which can form anagrams are the 18-letter transpositions *conservationalists* and *conversationalists*. The longest scientific transposals are *hydroxydesoxycorticosterone* and *hydroxydeoxycorticosterones*, with 27 letters.

Longest abbreviation ■ The longest known abbreviation is S.K.O.M.K.H.P.K.J.C.D.P.W.B., the initials of the Syarikat Kerjasama Orang-orang Melayu Kerajaan Hilir Perak Kerana Jimat Cermat Dan Pinjam-meminjam Wang Berhad. This is the Malay name for The Cooperative Company of the Lower State of Perak Government's Malay People for Money Savings and Loans Ltd, in Teluk Anson, Perak, West Malaysia (formerly Malaya). The abbreviation for this abbreviation is Skomk. The 55-letter full name of Los Angeles (El Pueblo de Nuestra Señora la Reina de los Angeles de Porciuncula) is abbreviated to LA or 3·63 per cent of its length.

Longest acronym ■ The longest acronym is NII-

LONGEST WORDS

JAPANESE[1]
Chi-n-chi-ku-ri-n (12 letters)
a very short person (slang)

SPANISH
Superextraordinarisimo (22 letters)
extraordinary

FRENCH
Anticonstitutionnellement (25 letters)
anticonstitutionally

CROATIAN
Prijestolonasljednikovica (25 letters)
wife of an heir apparent

ITALIAN
Precipitevolissimevolmente (26 letters)
as fast as possible

PORTUGUESE
Inconstitucionalissimamente (27 letters)
with the highest degree of unconstitutionality

ICELANDIC
Haecstaréttarmálaflutningsmaður (29 letters)
supreme court barrister

RUSSIAN
Ryentgyenoelyektrokardiografichyeskogo (33 Cyrillic letters, transliterating as 38)
of the radioelectrocardiographic

HUNGARIAN
Megszentségtelenithetetlenségeskedéseitekért (44 letters)
for your unprofanable actions

TURKISH[4]
Cekoslovakyalılastıramadıklarımızdanmıymıssınız (47 letters)
'are you not of that group of persons that we were said to be unable to Czechoslovakianise?'

DUTCH[4]
Kindercarnavalsoptochtvoorbereidingswerkzaamheden (49 letters)
preparation activities for a children's carnival procession

MOHAWK[2]
Tkanuhstasrihsranuhwe'tsraaksahsrakaratattsrayeri' (50 letters)
the praising of the evil of the liking of the finding of the house is right

GERMAN[3],[4]
Donaudampfschiffahrtselectrizitaetenhauptbetriebswerkbauunterbeamtengesellschaft (80 letters)
The club for subordinate officials of the head office management of the Danube steamboat electrical services (name of a pre-war club in Vienna)

SWEDISH[4]
Nordösterssjökustartilleriflygspaningssimulatoranläggningsmaterielunderhållsuppföljningssystemdiskussionsinläggsförberedelsearbeten (130 letters)
Preparatory work on the contribution to the discussion on the maintaining system of support of the material of the aviation survey simulator device within the north-east part of the coast artillery of the Baltic

[1] Patent applications sometimes harbour long compound 'words'. An extreme example is one of 13 kana which transliterates to the 40-letter Kyūkitsūrohekimenfuchakunenryōsekisanryō meaning 'the accumulated amount of fuel condensed on the wall face of the air intake passage'.
[2] Lengthy concatenations are a feature of Mohawk. Above is an example.
[3] The longest dictionary word in everyday usage is Rechtsschutzversicherungsgesellschaften (39 letters) meaning 'insurance companies which provide legal protection'.
[4] Agglutinative words are limited only by imagination and are not found in standard dictionaries. The first 100-letter such word was published in 1975 by the late Eric Rosenthal in Afrikaans.

OMTPLABOPARMBETZHELBETRABSBOMONIM-ONKONOTDTEKHSTROMONT with 56 letters (54 in Cyrillic) in the *Concise Dictionary of Soviet Terminology*, meaning: the laboratory for shuttering, reinforcement, concrete and ferroconcrete operations for composite-monolithic and monolithic constructions of the Department of the Technology of Building–assembly operations of the Scientific Research Institute of the Organisation for building mechanisation and technical aid of the Academy of Building and Architecture of the USSR.

Commonest words and letters ■ In written English the most frequently used words are, in order: the, of, and, to, a, in, that, is, I, it, for and as. The most used in conversation is I. The commonest letter is 'e' and the commonest initial letter is 'T'.

Most meanings ■ The most over-worked word in English is the word *set* which has 58 noun uses, 126 verbal uses and ten as a participial adjective.

Most succinct word ■ The most challenging word for any lexicographer to define briefly is the Fuegian (southernmost Argentina and Chile) word *mamihlapinatapai* meaning 'looking at each other hoping that either will offer to do something which both parties desire but are unwilling to do'.

Most synonyms ■ The condition of being inebriated has more synonyms than any other condition or object. Delacourt Press of New York City, USA has published a selection of 1224 from 2241 compiled by Paul Dickson of Garrett Park, Maryland, USA.

Most homophones ■ The most homophonous sounds in English are *air* and *sol* which, according to the researches of Dora Newhouse of Los Angeles, USA, both have 38 homophones. The homonym with most variant spellings is *air* with Aire, are, Ayer, Ayr, Ayre, err, e'er, ere, eyre and heir.

Most accents ■ Accents were introduced in French in the reign of Louis XIII (1601–43). The word with most accents is *újjáépítésére*, the Hungarian word meaning 'for its reconstruction'. Two runners up each with 5 accents are the French *hétérogénéité*, meaning heterogeneity, and an atoll in the Pacific Ocean 516 km *320 miles* east-southeast of Tahiti which is named Héréhérétué.

PERSONAL NAMES

Earliest ■ The earliest personal name which has survived is seemingly that of a predynastic king of Upper Egypt *ante* 3050 BC, who is indicated by the hieroglyphic sign for a scorpion. It has been suggested that the name should be read as Sekhen. The earliest known name of any resident of Britain is Divitiacus, King of the Suessiones, the Gaulish ruler of the Kent area *c.* 100 BC under the name Prydhain. Scotland, unlike England, was never fully conquered by the Roman occupiers (AD 43–410). Calgacus (b. *c.* AD 40), who led the final resistance in Scotland, was the earliest native whose name has been recorded.

Longest pedigree ■ The only non-royal English pedigree that can with certainty show a clear pre-Conquest descent is that of the Arden family. Shakespeare's mother was a Mary Arden. It is claimed on behalf of the Clan Mackay that their clan can be traced to Loarn, the Irish invader of south-west Pictland, now Argyll, *c.* AD 501.

Longest surname ■ A six-barrelled surname was borne by the late Major L.S.D.O.F. (Leone Sextus Denys Oswolf Fraudatifilius) Tollemache-Tollemache de Orellana-Plantagenet-Tollemache-Tollemache, who was born on 12 Jun 1884 and died of pneumonia in France on 20 Feb 1917. At school he was known as Tolly.

The current record is for four-barrelled names examples include the family names of Lord Thurlow (Hovell-Thurlow-Cumming-Bruce) and the Earl of Wharncliffe (Montagu-Stuart-Wortley-Mackenzie). Of non-repetitious surnames, the last example of a five-barrelled one was that of the Lady Caroline Jemima Temple-Nugent-Chandos-Brydges-Grenville (1858–1946). The longest single English surname is Featherstonehaugh (17 letters), variously pronounced Featherstonehaw or Festonhaw or Fessonhay or Freestonhugh or Feerstonhaw or Fanshaw. In Scotland the surname Nin (feminine of Mac) Achinmacdholicachinskerray (29 letters) was recorded in an 18th-century parish register.

Most Christian names ■ The great-great-grandson of Carlos III of Spain, Don Alfonso de Borbón y Borbón (1866–1934) had 94 Christian names of which several were lengthened by hyphenation.

John and Margaret Nelson of Chesterfield, Derbys gave their daughter Tracy Nelson (b. 31 Dec 1985) a total of 139 other Christian names. In Nov 1986 the Registrar agreed that the names would have to be accommodated on a document separate from the birth certificate.

Shortest ■ The commonest single-letter surname is O, prevalent in Korea but with 52 examples in US phone books (1973–81) and 12 in Belgium. This name causes most distress to those concerned with the prevention of cruelty to computers. Every other letter, except Q, has been traced in US phone books (used as a surname) by A. Ross Eckler. There are two one-lettered Burmese names: E (calm), pronounced aye, and U (egg), pronounced Oo. U *before* the name means 'uncle'.

British ■ There exist among the 47 000 000 names on the Dept of Health & Social Security index six examples of a one-lettered surname. Their identity has not been disclosed, but they are 'A', 'B', 'J', 'N', 'O' and 'X'. Two-letter British surnames include By and On and have recently been joined by Oy, Za and others. The Christian name 'A' has been used for five generations in the Lincoln Taber family of Fingringhoe, Essex.

Commonest family name ■ The Chinese name Chang is borne, according to estimates, by between 9·7 and 12·1 per cent of the Chinese population, so indicating even on the lower estimate that there are at least some 104 million Changs—more than the entire population of all but seven of the 170 other sovereign countries of the world.

The commonest surname in the English-speaking world is Smith. The most recent published count showed 659 050 nationally insured Smiths in Great Britain, of whom 10 102 were plain John Smith and another 19 502 were John (plus one or more given names) Smith. Including uninsured persons there were over 800 000 Smiths in England and Wales alone, of whom 81 493 were called A. Smith. There were an estimated 2 382 509 Smiths in the USA in 1973. It is no secret that by 1984 there were some 90 000 Singhs in Britain—the name means 'in secret'.

'Macs' ■ There are estimated to be 1 600 000 persons in Britain with M', Mc or Mac (Gaelic genitive of 'son') as part of their surnames. The commonest of these is Macdonald which accounts for about 55 000 of the Scottish population.

Most versions ■ Mr Edward A. Nedelcov of Regina, Saskatchewan, Canada has collected 1131 versions of the spelling of his family name since January 1960. Mzilikazi of Zululand (b. c. 1795) had his name chronicled in 325 spellings, according to researches by Dr R. Kent Rasmussen.

Most changed ■ Excluding members of the royal family the living monogamous woman who has most times changed her name is Lady Home of the Hirsel, formerly Lady Douglas-Home; Countess of Home; Lady Dunglass, and originally Miss Elizabeth Alington.

Most contrived ■ In the United States the determination to derive commercial or other benefit from being the last listing in the local telephone book has resulted in self-given names, starting with up to 9 Z's—an extreme example being Zachary Zzzzzzzzzra in the San Francisco book. The alpha and omega of Britain's 82 directories are Mrs Maude E. Aab of Hull, Humberside and the Zzzzzz Coffee Shop in Gray's Inn Road, London WC1.

PLACE-NAMES

Earliest ■ The world's earliest known place-names are pre-Sumerian e.g. Kish, Ur and Attara and therefore earlier than c. 3500 BC.

British ■ The earliest recorded British place-name is Belerion, the Penwith peninsula of Cornwall, referred to as such by Pytheas of Massilia c. 308 BC. The name Salakee on St Mary's, Isles of Scilly is however arguably of a pre-Indo-European substrate, meaning *tin island*. There are reasons to contend that Leicester (Roman, Ligora Castrum) contains an element reflecting its founding by the western Mediterranean navigators, the Ligurians, as early as c. 1200 BC. The earliest distinctive name for what is now Great Britain was Albion by Himilco c. 500 BC. The oldest name among England's 46 counties is Kent, first mentioned in its Roman form of Cantium (from the Celtic *canto*, meaning a rim, i.e. a coastal district), from the same circumnavigation by Pytheas. The earliest mention of England is the form *Angelcymn*, which appeared in the Anglo-Saxon Chronicle in AD 880.

Longest ■ The official name for Bangkok, the capital city of Thailand, is Krungthep Mahanakhon. The full name is however: Krungthep Mahanakhon Bovorn Ratanakosin Mahintharayutthaya Mahadilokpop Noparatratchathani Burirom Udomratchanivetmahasathan Amornpiman Avatarnsathit Sakkathattiyavisnukarmprasit (167 letters), which in its most scholarly transliteration emerges with 175 letters. Cauaiauaia in Angola has nine consecutive vowel letters.

The longest place-name now in use in the world is Taumatawhakatangihangakoauauotamateaturipukakapikimaungahoronukupokaiwhenuakitanatahu, the unofficial 85-letter version of the name of a hill (305 m *1002 ft* above sea level) in the Southern Hawke's Bay district of North Island, New Zealand. The Maori translation means 'The place where Tamatea, the man with the big knees, who slid, climbed and swallowed mountains, known as landeater, played his flute to his loved one.'

Great Britain ■ The longest place-name in the United Kingdom is the concocted 58-letter version of Llanfairpwllgwyngyllgogerychwyrndrobwllllantysiliogogogoch, which is translated: 'St Mary's Church by the pool of the white hazel trees, near the rapid whirlpool, by the red cave of the Church of St Tysilio'. This is the name used for the reopened (April 1973) village railway station in Anglesey, Gwynedd, Wales, and was coined by a local bard, Y Bardd Cocos–John Evans (1827–95) as a hoax. The *official* name consists of only the first 20 letters. The longest Welsh place-name listed in the Ordnance Survey Gazetteer is Lower Llanfihangel-y-Creuddyn (26 letters), a village near Aberystwyth, Dyfed. For commercial rather than toponymic reasons the proprietors of the Fairbourne Steam Railway, near

Barmouth, North Wales have posted a 67-letter-long name on a station board 19·5 m *64 ft* long. It reads Gorsafawddachaidraigddanheddogleddollonpenrhynarefrdraethceredigion though the 'll' should read 'l' making 66 letters or 65 if 'ch' is regarded as a single letter.

England ■ The longest single-word (unhyphenated) place-name in England is Blakehopeburnhaugh, a hamlet between Byrness and Rochester in Northumberland, of 18 letters.

The nearby Cottonshopeburnfoot (19 letters) is locally rendered as one word though not by the Ordnance Survey.

The hyphenated Sutton-under-Whitestonecliffe, North Yorks has 27 letters on the Ordnance Survey but with the insertion of 'the' and the dropping of the final 'e' it has 29 letters in the Post Office list.

The longest parish name is Saint Mary le More and All Hallows with Saint Leonard and Saint Peter, Wallingford (68 letters) in Oxfordshire, formed on 5 Apr 1971.

Scotland ■ The longest single-word place-name in Scotland is Coignafeuinternich in Inverness-shire. Kirkcudbrightshire (also 18 letters) became merged into Dumfries and Galloway on 16 May 1975. A hill in the Loch More area, just north of Aultanrynie, Highland region is named Meallan Liath Coire Mhic Dhubhghaill (32 letters).

Ireland ■ The longest place-name in Ireland is Muckanaghederdauhaulia (22 letters), 6 km *4 miles* from Costello in Camus Bay, Co. Galway. The name means 'soft place between two seas'.

Shortest ■ The shortest place-names in the world are the French village of Y (population 143), so named since 1241, the Danish village Å on the island Fyn, the Norwegian village of Å (pronounced 'Aw'), the Swedish place Å in Vikholandet, U in the Caroline Islands, Pacific Ocean, and the Japanese town of Sosei which is alternatively called Aioi or O. There was once a '6' in West Virginia, USA.

Great Britain ■ The shortest place-names in Great Britain are the two-lettered places of Ae (population 199 in 1961), Dumfries and Galloway; Oa on the island of Islay, Strathclyde, and Bu on Wyre, Orkney Islands. In Gaelic the name of the island of Iona is I. In the Shetland Islands there are skerries called Ve and two stacks called Aa. The River E flows into the southern end of Loch Mhór, Inverness-shire, and O Brook flows on Dartmoor, Devon.

The shortest place-name in Ireland is Ta (or Lady's Island) Lough, a sea inlet on the coast of Co. Wexford. Tievelough, in Co. Donegal, is also called Ea.

Most spellings ■ The spelling of the Dutch town of Leeuwarden has been recorded in 225 versions since AD 1046.

Bromesberrow, Hereford & Worcs, is recorded in 161 spellings since the 10th century as reported by local historian Lester Steynor.

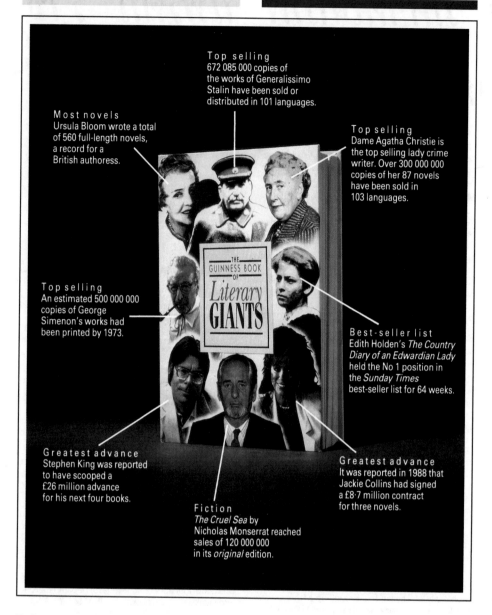

Most novels
Ursula Bloom wrote a total of 560 full-length novels, a record for a British authoress.

Top selling
672 085 000 copies of the works of Generalissimo Stalin have been sold or distributed in 101 languages.

Top selling
Dame Agatha Christie is the top selling lady crime writer. Over 300 000 000 copies of her 87 novels have been sold in 103 languages.

Top selling
An estimated 500 000 000 copies of George Simenon's works had been printed by 1973.

THE GUINNESS BOOK OF *Literary* GIANTS

Best-seller list
Edith Holden's *The Country Diary of an Edwardian Lady* held the No 1 position in the *Sunday Times* best-seller list for 64 weeks.

Greatest advance
Stephen King was reported to have scooped a £26 million advance for his next four books.

Greatest advance
It was reported in 1988 that Jackie Collins had signed a £8·7 million contract for three novels.

Fiction
The Cruel Sea by Nicholas Monserrat reached sales of 120 000 000 in its *original* edition.

Literature

Oldest ■ The oldest surviving printed work is the Dharani scroll or *sutra* from wooden printing blocks found in the foundations of the Pulguk Sa pagoda, Kyŏngju, South Korea on 14 Oct 1966. It has been dated to no later than AD 704. It was claimed in November 1973 that a 28-page book of Tang dynasty poems at Yonsei University, Korea was printed from metal type *c.* 1160. The oldest medical literature, a small clay tablet in the Sumerian script from Nippur (now in Iraq), is dated to *c.* 2100 BC. It is now in the University Museum of Philadelphia, Pennsylvania, USA and gives details of various ointments and plasters made of crushed turtle shell, nagasi plant, salt and mustard. Beer formed an ingredient of some of the ointments. Paper dating to between 71 BC and AD 21 have been found in north-west China, i.e. 100 years earlier than the previous presumed date for paper's invention.

Oldest mechanically printed ■ It is widely accepted that the earliest mechanically printed full-length book was the 42-line per page Gutenberg Bible, printed in Mainz, West Germany, *c.* 1454 by Johann Henne zum Gensfleisch zur Laden, called 'zu Gutenberg' (*c.* 1398– 1468). Work on water marks published in 1967 indicates a copy of a surviving printed 'Donatus' Latin grammar was made from paper of *c.* 1450. The earliest exactly dated printed work is the Psalter completed on 14 Aug 1457 by Johann Fust (*c.* 1400–66) and Peter Schöffer (1425–1502), who had been Gutenberg's chief assistant. The earliest printing by William Caxton (*c.* 1422–1491) though undated would appear to be *The Recuyel of*

the *Historyes of Troye* in Cologne in late 1473 to spring 1474.

Largest book ■ The *Super Book* measuring 2·74 × 3·07 m *9 ft × 10 ft 2⅛ in* was published in Denver, Colorado, USA in 1976. It consisted of 300 pages and weighed 252·6 kg *557 lb*.

Largest publication ■ The 1112-volume set of *British Parliamentary Papers* was published by the Irish University Press in 1968–72. A complete set weighs 3·3 tonnes *3¼ tons*, costs £50 000 and would take six years to read at ten hours per day. The production involved the death of 34 000 Indian goats, and the use of £15 000 worth of gold ingots. The total print is 500 sets and the price per set in 1987 was £49 500.

Largest dictionary ■ Deutsches Wörterbuch started by Jacob and Wilhelm Grimm in 1854 was completed in 34 519 pages and 33 volumes in 1971. Today's price is DM5425. The largest English-language dictionary is the 20-volume *Oxford English Dictionary*, with 21 728 pages. The first edition, edited by Sir James Murray, was published between 1884 and 1928. A first Supplement of 964 pages appeared in 1932, and a second one in four volumes, edited by R. W. Burchfield, between 1972 and 1986. Work on the Second Edition prepared by J. A. Simpson and E. S. C. Weiner, began in 1984 and the work involved represented 500-person years. Published in March 1989, it defines a total of 616 500 word-forms, with 2 412 400 illustrative quotations, and approximately 350 million letters and figures. Now computerised, the Dictionary required 625 million bytes to store the text in machine-readable

form. The longest entry in the Second Edition is that for the verb *set*, with over 75 000 words of text. The greatest outside contributor has been Marghanita Laski (1915–88) with a reputed 250 000 quotations from 1958 until her death.

The *New Grove Dictionary of Music and Musicians* edited by Stanley Sadie CBE (b. 30 Oct 1930), published in 20 volumes by Macmillan in February 1981, contains over 22 million words and 4500 illustrations and is the largest specialist dictionary. The price in 1987 was £1100.

Smallest book ■ The smallest marketed bound printed book is one printed on 22 gsm paper measuring 1 mm × 1 mm *¼₂₅ × ¼₂₅ in*, comprising the children's story *Old King Cole!* and published in 85 copies in March 1985 by The Gleniffer Press of Paisley, Renfrew, Scotland. The pages can be turned (with care) only by the use of a needle.

Longest novel ■ The longest important novel ever published is *Les hommes de bonne volonté* by Louis Henri Jean Farigoule (1885–1972), *alias* Jules Romains, of France, in 27 volumes in 1932–46. The English version *Men of Good Will* was published in 14 volumes in 1933–46 as a 'novel-cycle'. The 4959-page edition published by Peter Davies Ltd has an estimated 2 070 000 words excluding a 100-page index. The novel *Tokuga-Wa Ieyasu* by Sohachi Yamaoka has been serialised in Japanese daily newspapers since 1951. Now completed, it will require nearly 40 volumes.

Earliest encyclopaedias ■ The earliest known encyclopaedia was compiled by Speusippus (*post* 408–*c.* 338 BC), a nephew of Plato, in Athens *c.* 370 BC. The earliest encyclopaedia compiled by a Briton was *Liber exerptionum* by the Scottish monk Richard (d. 1173) at St Victor's Abbey, Paris *c.* 1140.

Largest encyclopaedia ■ The largest encyclopaedia is *La Enciclopedia Universal Ilustrada Europeo-Americana* (J. Espasa & Sons, Madrid and Barcelona) totalling 105 000 pages and an annual supplement since 1935 comprising 165 200 000 words. The number of volumes in the set in August 1983 was 104, and the price $2325.

The largest encyclopaedia ever compiled was the Yung-lo ta tien (the great thesaurus of the Yung-lo reign) of 22 937 manuscript chapters (370 still survive) in 11 095 volumes. It was written by 2000 Chinese scholars in 1403–08.

Most comprehensive encyclopaedia ■ The most comprehensive English-language encyclopaedia is *The New Encyclopaedia Britannica*, first published in Edinburgh, Scotland in December 1768. A group of booksellers in the United States acquired reprint rights in 1898 and completed ownership in 1899. The current 32-volume 15th edition contains 32 330 pages and 44 000 000 words from more than 4000 contributors. It is now edited in Chicago, Illinois, USA.

Longest index ■ The Tenth Collective Index of *Chemical Abstracts* completed in June 1983 contains 23 948 253 entries in 131 445 pages and 75 volumes, and weighs 172·3 kg *380 lb*.

Who's Who ■ The longest entry in *Who's Who* (founded 1848) was that of the Rt Hon. Sir Winston Leonard Spencer Churchill KG, OM, CH, TD (1874–1965), who appeared in 67 editions from 1899 (18 lines) and had 211 lines by the 1965 edition. Currently the longest entry in its wider format is that of Barbara Cartland, the romantic novelist, with 143 lines. Apart from those who qualify for inclusion by hereditary title, the youngest entry has been Sir Yehudi Menuhin OM, KBE (b. New York City, USA, 22 Apr 1916), the concert violinist, who first appeared in the 1932 edition aged 15. The longest entry of the 66 000 entries in *Who's Who in America* is that of Dr Glenn T. Seaborg (b. 19 Apr 1912) with an all-time record of 100 lines.

Literary luncheons ■ Literary luncheons were inaugurated by Christina Foyle (Mrs Ronald Batty) in October 1930 at the Old Holborn Restaurant, London. Attendances were over 1500 at the Grosvenor

House, Park Lane, London at lunches for Mistinguett (1873–1956) and Dr Edvard Benes (1884–1948) both in 1938.

MAPS

Oldest ■ A clay tablet depicting the river Euphrates flowing through northern Mesopotamia, Iraq, dates to *c.* 2250 BC. The earliest surviving product of English map-making is the Anglo-Saxon *mappa mundi*, known as the Cottonian manuscript, from the late 10th century. The earliest printed map in the world is one of western China dated to 1115. The earliest printed map of Britain was Ptolemy's outline printed in Bologna, Italy in 1477.

Largest ■ A *Giant Relief Map of California*, by Reuben Hall, weighing 39 tonnes *38·4 tons*, was displayed in the Ferry Building, San Francisco, USA from 1924 until 1960. Now in storage in Hamilton Air Force Base, Novato, California, USA it measures 137·1 × 5·48 m *450 × 18 ft*. Known as *Paradise in Panorama* it required 29 man years and $147 000 to build.

HIGHEST PRICES

Most expensive book ■ The highest price paid for any book has been £8 140 000 for the 226-leaf manuscript *The Gospel Book of Henry the Lion, Duke of Saxony* at Sotheby's, London on 6 Dec, 1983. The book, 34·3 × 25·4 cm *13½ × 10 in*, was illuminated by the monk Herimann *c.* 1170 at Helmershansen Abbey with 41 full-page illustrations, and was bought by Hans Kraus for the Hermann Abs consortium.

Printed book ■ The highest price ever paid for a printed book has been $5 390 000 for an Old Testament (Genesis to the Psalms) of the Gutenberg Bible printed in 1455 in Mainz, Germany. It was bought by the Maruzen Co Ltd, Tokyo booksellers, at Christie's, New York, USA on 22 Oct 1987. The most expensive new book is the reproduction of the full set of ornithological prints *The Birds of America* by John James Audubon (1785–1851) by Abbeville Press, at $15 000.

Broadsheet ■ The highest price ever paid for a broadsheet was £412 500 for one of the 22 known copies of *The Declaration of Independence*, printed in Philadelphia, Pennsylvania, USA in 1776 by Samuel T. Freeman & Co, and sold to the Chapin Library, Williams College, Williamstown, Massachusetts, USA at Christie's, New York, USA on 22 Apr 1983.

Manuscript ■ The highest price ever paid for a complete manuscript has been £2·2 million by Armand Hammer at Christie's, London on 12 Dec 1980 for Leonardo da Vinci's 36-page Codex Leicester illustrated manuscript on cosmology compiled *c.* 1507. It was sold by the trustees of the Holkham estate.

British ■ London dealer Quaritch paid £1 540 000 at Sotheby's, London on 21 Jun 1988 for the 14th-century elaborately illuminated Hours and Psalter of Elizabeth de Bohun, Countess of Northampton.

Musical ■ The auction record for a musical manuscript (including buyer's premium) is £2 585 000 for a 508-page 21·6 × 16·5 cm *8½ × 6½ in* bound volume of nine complete symphonies in Mozart's hand by London dealer James Kirkman at Sotheby's, London on 22 May 1987. The seller was an anonymous European.

Earliest ■ The earliest known manuscript written in Britain is a bifolium of Eusebius' *Historia Ecclesiastica* from *c.* AD 625, possibly from the Jarrow library.

Atlas ■ The highest price paid for an atlas has been £340 000 for a Gerardus Mercator atlas of *c.* 1571 of Europe, sold at Sotheby's, London on 13 Mar 1979.

BIBLE

Oldest ■ The earliest biblical texts are from two silver amulets found under the Scottish Church, Jerusalem in 1979 bearing Numbers Ch. 6 v. 22–27 dated to *c.* 587 BC. In 1945 various papyrus texts were dicovered at Nag Hammodi, upper Egypt; they include gnostic gospels or secret books (apocrypha) ascribed to Thomas, James, John, Peter and Paul. They were buried *c.* 350 AD but the originals are thought to have been written *c.* AD 120–150. The oldest known bible is the *Codex Vaticanus* written in Greek *ante* AD 350 and preserved in the Vatican Museum, Rome. The earliest complete bible *printed* in English was one edited by Miles Coverdale, Bishop of Exeter (*c.* 1488–1569), while living in Antwerp, and printed in 1535. William Tyndale's New Testament in English had, however, been printed in Cologne and in Worms, Germany in 1525 while John Wycliffe's first manuscript translation dates from 1382.

Longest book ■ The longest book in the Authorised Version of the Bible is the Book of Psalms, while the longest book including prose is the Book of the Prophet Isaiah, with 66 chapters.

Shortest book ■ The Third Epistle of John has only 294 words in 14 verses. The Second Epistle of John has only 13 verses but 298 words.

Longest and shortest psalm ■ Of the 150 psalms, the longest is the 119th, with 176 verses, and the shortest is the 117th, with two verses.

Longest and shortest verse ■ The shortest verse in the Authorised Version (King James) of the Bible is verse 35 of Chapter XI of the Gospel according to St John, consisting of the two words 'Jesus wept'. The longest is verse 9 of Chapter VIII of the Book of Esther, which extends to a 90-word description of the Persian empire.

Total letters and words ■ The total number of letters in the Bible is 3 566 480. The total number of words depends on the method of counting hyphenated words, but is usually given as between 773 692 and 773 746. The word 'and' according to Colin McKay Wilson of the Salvation Army appears 46 227 times.

Longest name ■ The longest actual name in English language bibles is the 18-letter Maher-shalal-hash-baz, the symbolic name of the second son of Isaiah (Isaiah, Chapter VIII, verses 1 and 3). The caption of Psalm 22, however, contains a Hebrew title sometimes rendered Al-Ayyeleth Hash-Shahar (20 letters).

DIARIES AND LETTERS

Longest kept diary ■ Col. Ernest Loftus CBE of Harare, Zimbabwe began his daily diary on 4 May 1896 at the age of 12 and continued it until his death on 7 Jul 1987 aged 103 years 178 days.

George C. Edler (b. 13 Dec 1889) of Bethesda, Maryland, USA, has kept a diary with no breaks since 1 Jan 1912.

The diary of T. C. Baskerville of Chorlton-cum-Hardy, Manchester, maintained since 1939, comprises an estimated 5 650 000 words in 163 volumes occupying 36 000 pages.

Longest and most letters ■ The longest personal letter based on a word count is one of 1 402 344 words started on 3 Jan 1982 by Alan Foreman of New Barn, Dartford, Kent, England and posted to his wife Janet on 25 Jan 1984.

Vichi Noda, former Vice Minister of Treasury and Minister of Construction in Japan, from July 1961 until his bedridden wife Mitsu's death in March 1985, wrote her 1307 letters amounting to 50 000 characters during his overseas trips. These letters have been published in 25 volumes totalling 12 404 pages.

The Rev Canon Bill Cook and his fiancée/wife Helen of Diss, Norfolk, exchanged 6000 love letters during their 4½ year separation from March 1942–May 1946.

Longest letter to an editor ■ The *Upper Dauphin Sentinel* of Pennsylvania, USA published a letter of 25 513 words over eight issues from August to November 1979, written by John Sultzbaugh of Lykens, Pennsylvania.

Most letters to an editor ■ David Green, a solicitor, of Castle Morris, Dyfed, Wales had 121 letters published in the main correspondence columns of *The Times* by 15 Mar 1989. His record year was 1972 with 12.

Shortest correspondence ■ The shortest correspondence on record was that between Victor Marie Hugo (1802–85) and his publisher Hurst and Blackett in 1862. The author was on holiday and anxious to know how his new novel *Les Misérables* was selling. He wrote '?'. The reply was '!'.

The shortest letter to *The Times* comprised the single abbreviated symbol 'Dr²?' in the interrogative from R. S. Cookson of London NW11, on 30 Jul 1984, in a correspondence on the correct form of recording a plurality of academic doctorates. On 8 Jan 1986 a letter was sent to *The Times* by a seven-year-old girl from the Isle of Man. It read 'Sir, Yours faithfully Caroline Sophia Kerenhappuch Parkes'. The brief epistle was intended to inform readers of her unusual name, Kerenhappuch, mentioned in a letter the previous week from the Rev. John Ticehurst on the subject of uncommon 19th-century names.

Most personal mail ■ The highest confirmed mail received by any private citizen in a year is 900 000 letters by the baseball star Hank Aaron (b. 1934) reported by the US Postal Department in June 1974. About a third were letters of hate engendered by his bettering of 'Babe' Ruth's career record for 'home runs' set in 1927. (See Chapter 11.)

Pen pals ■ The longest sustained correspondence on record is one of 75 years from 11 Nov 1904 between Mrs Ida McDougall of Tasmania, Australia and Miss R. Norton of Sevenoaks, Kent until Mrs McDougall's death on 24 Dec 1979.

Christmas card exchange ■ Scots born Leonard Moran, of Maenclochog, Dyfed, Wales and his brother James of Deal, Kent have exchanged the same Christmas card since 1934 (excluding the war years).

Christmas cards ■ The greatest number of personal Christmas cards sent out is believed to be 62 824 by Mr Werner Erhard of San Francisco, California, USA in December 1975. Many must have been to unilateral acquaintances. The earliest known Christmas card was sent out by Sir Henry Cole (1808–82) in 1843 but did not become an annual ritual until 1862.

AUTOGRAPHS AND SIGNATURES

Earliest ■ The earliest surviving examples of an autograph are those made by scribes on cuneiform clay tablets from Tell Abu Salābīkh, Iraq dated to the early Dynastic III A *c.* 2600 BC. A scribe named 'a-du' has added 'dub-sar' after his name thus translating to 'Adu, scribe'. The earliest surviving signature on a papyrus is that of the scribe Amen-'aa dated to the Egyptian middle kingdom which began *c.* 2130 BC and which is in the Leningrad Museum, USSR. A signum exists for William I (the Conqueror) *c.* 1070. The earliest English sovereign whose handwriting is known to have survived is Edward III (1327–77). The earliest full signature extant is that of Richard II (dated 26 Jul 1386). The Magna Carta does not bear even the mark of King John (reigned 1199–1216), but carries only his seal affixed on 19 Jun 1215.

Most expensive ■ The highest price ever paid on the open market for a single autograph letter signed has been $360 000 paid on 29 Oct 1986 at Sotheby's, New York, USA for a letter by Thomas Jefferson condemning prejudice against Jews in 1818. It was sold by Charles Rosenbloom of Pittsburgh, Pennsylvania, USA. The highest price paid for an autograph letter signed by a living person is $12 500 at the Hamilton Galleries on 22 Jan 1981 for a letter from President Ronald Reagan praising Frank Sinatra.

A record $4250 was paid at a Hamilton sale on 12 Aug 1982 by Barry D. Hoffman for the signed portrait of Al Capone (1899–1947).

Rarest and most valuable ■ Only one example of the signature of Christopher Marlowe (1564–93) is known. It is in the Kent County Archives on a will of 1583. It is estimated that a seventh Shakespearean signature, should it ever come to light would realise more than £1 million at auction.

The only known document which bears 10 US presidential signatures is a letter sent by President F. D. Roosevelt to Mr Richard C. Corbyn, then of Dallas (now of Amarillo), Texas, USA dated 26 Oct 1932. It was subsequently signed by Herbert Hoover, Harry Truman, General Eisenhower, Gerald Ford, Lyndon Johnson, Jimmy Carter, Ronald Reagan and George Bush. Nixon's first signature was signed with an auto-pen but he later re-signed it.

AUTHORS

Most prolific ■ The champion of the goose quill era was Józef Ignacy Kraszewski (1812–87) of Poland who produced more than 600 volumes of novels and historical works.

A lifetime output of 72–75 million words has been calculated for Charles Harold St John Hamilton, *alias* Frank Richards (1876–1961), the creator of Billy Bunter. In his peak years (1915–26) he wrote up to 80 000 words a week for the boys' school weeklies *Gem* (1907–39); *Magnet* (1908–40) and Boys' Friend.

Soho Tokutomi (1863–1957) wrote the history *Kinsei Nippon Kokuminshi* in 100 volumes of 42 468 pages and 19 452 952 letters in 35 years.

Most novels ■ The greatest number of novels published by an authoress is 904 by Kathleen Lindsay (Mrs Mary Faulkner) (1903–73) of Somerset West, Cape Province, South Africa. She wrote under two other married names and eight pen names. Baboorao Arnalkar (b. 9 Jun 1907) of Maharashtra State, India between 1936 and 1984 has published 1092 short mystery stories in book form and several non-fiction books.

After receiving a probable record 743 rejection slips the British novelist John Creasey MBE (1908–73), under his own name and 25 *noms de plume*, had 564 books totalling more than 40 000 000 words published from 1932 to his death. The British authoress with the greatest total of full-length titles was Ursula Harvey Bloom (Mrs A. C. G. Robinson, formerly Mrs Denham-Cookes, (1892–1984), who reached 560 in 1976, starting in 1924 with *The Great Beginning* and including the best sellers *The Ring Tree* (novel) and *The Rose of Norfolk* (non-fiction). Enid Mary Blyton (1898–1968) (Mrs Darrell Waters) completed 700 titles of children's stories, many of them brief, with 59 in 1955.

Most text books ■ Britain's most successful writer of text books is ex-schoolmaster Ronald Ridout (b. 23 Jul 1916) who between 1948 and April 1989 had 515 titles published with sales of 89 250 000. His *The First English Workbook* has sold 5 284 000 copies.

Highest paid ■ In 1958 Mrs Deborah Schneider of Minneapolis, Minnesota, USA wrote 25 words to complete a sentence in a competition for the best blurb for Plymouth cars. She won from about 1 400 000 entrants the prize of $500 every month for life. On normal life expectations she should collect $12 000 per word. No known anthology includes Mrs Schneider's deathless prose but it is in her deed box at her bank 'Only to be opened after death'. She passed $6000 a word by 1983.

Greatest advance ■ The greatest advance paid for any book is $5 000 000 for *Whirlwind* to James Clavell at auction in New York City, USA on 11 Jan 1986 by William Morrow & Co and Avon Books.

On 5 May 1988 Mary Higgins Clark (USA) signed a contract for $10 100 000 for four novels and a book of short stories.

It was reported on 19 Aug 1988 that Jackie Collins had signed a £8·7 million contract for three books for publishers Simon & Schuster, New York, USA.

Top selling ■ It was announced on 13 Mar 1953 that 672 058 000 copies of the works of Generalissimo

Stalin (born Yózef Vissarionovich Dzhugashvili) (1879–1953), had been sold or distributed in 101 languages.

Currently the top-selling authoress is Barbara Cartland with global sales of over 500 000 000 for 493 titles in 27 languages. She has averaged 23 titles per year for the last 13 years. She received 'La Medaille de Vermeil de la Ville de Paris' for selling 25 000 000 books in France.

The all-time estimate of book sales by Erle Stanley Gardner (1889–1970) (US) to 1 Jan 1989 is 320 802 493 copies in 37 languages. The top-selling lady crime writer has been Dame Agatha Christie (*née* Miller) (later Lady Mallowan) (1890–1976) whose 87 crime novels sold an estimated 300 000 000 in 103 languages. *Sleeping Murder* was published posthumously in 1977. An estimated 500 000 000 copies of Georges Simenon's works had been printed by 1973.

Longest biography ■ The longest biography in publishing history is that of Sir Winston Churchill by his son Randolph (4832 pages) and Martin Gilbert (16 745 pages) to date comprising some 9 244 000 words. Georges Simenon (b. 1903) wrote 22 autobiographical books from 1972.

Interviewer ■ The writer who has interviewed most heads of state and heads of government in the world is Brian Rossiter Crozier (GB) (b. 4 Aug 1918) with 64 in the period 1948–89.

Most rejections ■ The greatest recorded number of publishers' rejections for a manuscript is 242 (by March 1988) for the 150 000-word manuscript *World Government Crusade* written in 1966 by Gilbert Young (b. 1906) of Bath. The record for rejections before publication is from 176 publishers (and non-acknowledgement from many others) in the case of Bill Gordon's *How Many Books Do You Sell in Ohio?* from 19 Oct 1983 to 20 Nov 1985. Mr Gordon then spoiled his record by himself rejecting a publisher's written offer from Aames-Allen.

Oldest authoress ■ The oldest authoress in the world was Mrs Alice Pollock (*née* Wykeham-Martin) (1868–1971), of Haslemere, Surrey, whose book *Portrait of My Victorian Youth* (Johnson Publications) was published in March 1971 when she was aged 102 years 8 months.

Longest literary gestation ■ The standard German dictionary *Deutsches Wörterbuch*, begun by the brothers Grimm in 1854, was finished in 1971. *Acta Sanctorum*, begun by Jean Bolland in 1643, arranged according to saints' days, reached the month of November in 1925 and an introduction for December was published in 1940. Oxford University Press received back their proofs of *Constable's Presentments* from the Dugdale Society in December 1984. They had been sent out for correction 35 years earlier in December 1949.

Youngest Poet Laureate ■ Laurence Eusden (1688–1730) 'received the bays' on 24 Dec 1718 at the age of 30 years and 3 months.

Oldest Poet Laureate ■ The greatest age at which a poet has succeeded is 73 in the case of William Wordsworth (1770–1850) on 6 Apr 1843. The longest-lived Laureate was John Masefield, OM, who died on 12 May 1967, aged 88 years 345 days. The longest any poet has worn the laurel is 41 years 322 days, in the case of Alfred (later the 1st Lord) Tennyson (1809–92), who was appointed on 19 Nov 1850 and died in office on 6 Oct 1892.

Longest Poem ■ The lengthiest poem ever published has been the Kirghiz folk epic *Manas*, which appeared in printed form in 1958 but which has never been translated into English. It runs to 'more than 500 000 lines'. Short translated passages appear in *The Elek Book of Oriental Verse*. The longest poem ever written in the English language is one on the life of King Alfred by John Fitchett (1766–1838) of Liverpool which ran to 129 807 lines and took 40 years to write. His editor Robert Riscoe added the concluding 2585 lines.

Roger Brien's (b. Montreal, 1910) *Prométhée-*

dialogue des vivants et des morts runs to 456 047 lines written from 1964–81. Brien has written another 497 000 lines of French poetry in over 90 published works.

Most successful poem ■ *If* by Joseph Rudyard Kipling (1865–1936), first published in 1910, has been translated into 27 languages and, according to Kipling, 'anthologised to weariness'.

HIGHEST PRINTINGS

The world's most widely distributed book is the Bible, which has been translated into 310 languages and portions of it into a further 1597 languages. This compares with 222 languages for Lenin. It has been estimated that between 1815 and 1975 some 2 500 000 000 copies were printed of which 1 500 000 000 were handled by Bible Societies. In the period 1976–1987 combined world-wide sales of Today's English Version (*Good News*) New Testament and Bible (which is copyright of the Bible Societies) exceeded 104 000 000 copies.

Apart from the King James version (averaging some 13 million copies printed annually) there are at least 14 other copyrights on other versions of the Bible. The oldest publisher of bibles is the Cambridge University Press which began with the Geneva version in 1591.

It has been reported that 800 000 000 copies of the red-covered booklet *Quotations from the Works of Mao Tse-tung* were sold or distributed between June 1966, when possession became virtually mandatory in China, and September 1971 when its promoter Marshal Lin Piao died in an air crash.

It is believed that in the USA, Van Antwerp Bragg and Co printed some 60 million copies of the 1879 edition of *The McGuffey Reader*, compiled by Henry Vail in the pre-copyright era for distribution to public schools.

The total disposal through non-commercial channels by Jehovah's Witnesses of *The Truth that Leads to Eternal Life* published by the Watchtower Bible and Tract Society of Brooklyn, New York, USA on 8 May 1968, reached 106 865 672 in 117 languages by March 1989.

BEST-SELLING BOOKS

Excluding versions of the Bible, the world's all-time best-selling book is *The Guinness Book of Records*, first published in October 1955 by the Guinness Brewery and edited by Norris Dewar McWhirter (b. 12 Aug 1925) and his twin brother Alan Ross McWhirter (k. 27 Nov 1975). Global sales in 31 languages surpassed 61 million by early 1989.

Best-seller lists ■ The longest duration on the *New York Times* best-seller list (founded 1935) has been for *The Road Less Traveled* by M. Scott Peck which on 2 Oct 1988 had its 258th week on the lists.

The Country Diary of an Edwardian Lady (Michael Joseph, Webb & Bower) by Edith Holden (1871–1920) held the No. 1 position in the *Sunday Times* best-seller list (which excludes books published annually) for 64 weeks. Its global sales in 13 languages reached 2 870 231 copies by January 1989.

Fiction ■ The novel with the highest sales has been *Valley of the Dolls* (first published Mar 1966) by Jacqueline Susann (Mrs Irving Mansfield) (1921–74) with a world-wide total of 28 712 000 to 30 March 1987. In the first 6 months Bantam sold 6·8 million. In the United Kingdom the highest print order has been 3 000 000 by Penguin Books Ltd for their paperback edition of *Lady Chatterley's Lover*, by D. H. (David Herbert) Lawrence (1885–1930). The total sales to Apr 1989 were 4 790 000. Alistair Stuart MacLean (1922–87) wrote 30 books of which 28 each sold over a million in the United Kingdom alone. His books have been translated into 28 languages and 13 have been filmed. It has been estimated that a 'MacLean' novel is purchased every 18 seconds. *The Cruel Sea* by Nicholas Monsarrat (1910–79), published in 1951 by Cassell, reached sales of 1 200 000 in its original edition.

Fastest publisher ■ The ITN Election Factbook published by Michael O'Mara was printed by Hazell, Watson & Viney in less than 24 hours of the general election date of 11 Jun 1987 being announced.

Slowest seller ■ The accolade for the world's slowest-selling book (known in US publishing as slooow sellers) probably belongs to David Wilkins's translation of the New Testament from Coptic into Latin, published by Oxford University Press in 1716 in 500 copies. Selling an average of one each 20 weeks, it remained in print for 191 years.

PUBLISHERS AND PRINTERS

Oldest publisher ■ Cambridge University Press has a continuous history of printing and publishing since 1584. The University received Royal Letters Patent to print and sell all manner of books on 20 Jul 1534.

In 1978 the Oxford University Press celebrated the 500th anniversary of the printing of the first book in the City of Oxford in 1478. This was before OUP was itself in existence.

Most prolific publisher ■ In terms of new titles per annum Britain's most prolific publisher in 1988 was Oxford University Press with 1608. The UK published a record 62 062 book titles in 1988 of which a record 14 593 were reprints. Progress Publishers of Moscow, USSR prints over 750 titles in 50 languages annually. The company was founded in 1931 as Publishing Association of Foreign Workers in the USSR and is now the largest publishing house in the USSR with a staff of 1500.

Largest printer ■ The largest printers in the world are R. R. Donnelley & Sons Co of Chicago, Illinois, USA. The company, founded in 1864, has plants in 24 main centres, turning out $2 878 000 000 worth of work per year. More than 2 000 000 short tons of paper are consumed every year. The largest printer under one roof is the United States Government Printing Office (founded 1861) in Washington, DC, USA. Encompassing 13·92 ha *34·4 acres* of floor space the central office processes an average of 2249 print orders daily, and consumes 47 625 tonnes *105 million lb* of paper annually. The Superintendent of Documents sells approximately $71·1 million worth of US government publications every year and maintains an inventory of over 26 000 titles in print, receiving 5600 mail orders each day.

Largest print order ■ The initial print order for the 55th Automobile Association *Members' Handbook* (1987–8) was 4 820 000 copies—stacked one on top of another, 35 times the height of Ben Nevis. The total print since 1908 has been 91 520 000. It is currently printed by web offset by Petty & Sons of Leeds, West Yorks. The aggregate print of *The Highway Code* (instituted 1931) reached 107 539 339 in April 1989.

LIBRARIES

Earliest ■ One of the earliest known collections of archival material was that of King Ashurbanipal at Nineveh (668–627 BC). He had clay tablets referring to events and personages as far back as the Dynasty of Agade *c.* 23rd century BC.

Largest ■ The United States Library of Congress (founded on 24 Apr 1800), on Capitol Hill, Washington, DC, USA contains 88 million items, including 26 million volumes and pamphlets. The buildings contain 26·14 ha *64·6 acres* of floor space and 856 km *532 miles* of shelving.

The largest non-statutory library in the world is the New York Public Library (founded 1895) on Fifth Avenue, New York, USA with a floor space of 48 800 m² *525 276 ft²* and 141·6 km *88 miles* of shelving. Its collection including 82 branch libraries embraces 13 887 774 volumes, 18 349 585 manuscripts and 381 645 maps.

The greatest personal library ever amassed was that of Sir Thomas Phillipps. Dispersal began in 1886. The residue was bought largely unseen by the brothers

Highest printings ● It has been reported that 800 000 000 copies of the red-covered booklet *Quotations from the Works of Mao Tse-tung* were sold or distributed between June 1966, when possession became virtually mandatory in China, and September 1971 when its promoter Marshal Lin Piao (who can be seen with Mao Tse-Tung in the main picture) died in an air crash. (Photos: Keystone Collection)

Lionel Robinson CBE, MC and Philip Robinson for £100 000. Sales began on 1 Jul 1946.

UK ■ The largest library in the United Kingdom is the British Library, dispersed among 18 buildings in London and a 24·3 ha *60 acre* site at Boston Spa, West Yorks, with a total staff of some 2500. The Library contains over 18 million volumes. Stock increases involve over 12·8 km *8 miles* of new shelving annually. The Newspaper Library at Colindale, north London, opened in 1932, has 562 300 volumes and parcels comprising 70 000 different titles on 35·4 km *22 miles* of shelving. The Document Supply Centre in West Yorks (shelf capacity 157·7 km *98 miles*) runs the largest library inter-lending operation in the world; it handles annually nearly 3 million requests from other libraries (UK and overseas) for items they do not hold in stock. The National Sound Archive holds 1 000 000 discs and 50 000 hours of recorded

tape. The largest public reference library in Europe is the extended Mitchell Library, North Street, Glasgow, Scotland with a floor area of 50·00 m² *538 200 ft²* or 4·9 ha *12·3 acres* and an ultimate capacity for 4 000 000 volumes.

Overdue books ■ The record for an unreturned and overdue library book was set when a book in German on the Archbishop of Bremen, published in 1609, was borrowed from Sidney Sussex College, Cambridge by Colonel Robert Walpole in 1667–68. It was found by Professor Sir John Plumb in the library of the then Marquess of Cholmondeley at Houghton Hall, Norfolk and returned 288 years later. No fine was exacted.

Oldest museum ■ The oldest museum still extant in the world is the Ashmolean Museum in Oxford built from 1679–83 and named after the collector Elias Ashmole (1617–92). Since 1924 it has housed an exhibition of historic scientific instruments.

Largest museum ■ The Smithsonian Institution comprises 14 museums with 6000 employees. It contains over 135 million objects and specimens. The largest and most visited museum in the United Kingdom is the British Museum (founded in 1753), which was opened to the public in 1759. The main building in Bloomsbury, London was begun in 1823 and has a total floor area of 8·7 ha *21·5 acres.* In 1988, 3 838 848 people passed through its doors.

The American Museum of Natural History is situated between 77th and 81st Streets and Central Park West and Columbus Avenue in New York City, USA. It was founded in 1869 and comprises 22 interconnected buildings. The buildings of the Museum and the Planetarium contain an area of 139 350 m² *1·5 million ft²* of floor space accommodating more than 36 million artifacts and specimens. Its exhibits are viewed by more than 2·6 million visitors each year.

Most popular ■ The highest attendance for any museum is that at the Smithsonian's National Air and Space Museum, Washington, DC, USA opened in July 1976. The record-setting day in 1984 required the doors to be temporarily closed with an attendance of 118 437.

NEWSPAPERS

Oldest ■ A copy has survived of a news pamphlet published in Cologne, West Germany in 1470. The oldest existing newspaper in the world is the Swedish official journal *Post och Inrikes Tidningar*, founded in 1645. It is published by the Royal Swedish Academy of Letters. The oldest existing commercial newspaper is the *Haarlems Dagblad/Oprechte Haarlemsche Courant*, published in Haarlem in the Netherlands. First issued as the *Weeckelycke Courante van Europa* on 8 Jan 1656, a copy of issue No. 1 survives.

UK ■ The newspaper with the earliest origins is *Berrow's Worcester Journal* (originally the *Worcester Post Man*), published in Worcester. It was traditionally founded in 1690 and has appeared weekly since June 1709. No complete file exists. The earliest date of foundation for any British newspaper published under the same title is the *Stamford Mercury*, printed since 1712 and traditionally even 1695. The *London Gazette* (originally the *Oxford Gazette*) was first published on 16 Nov 1665. The oldest Sunday newspaper is *The Observer*, first issued on 4 Dec 1791. The earliest known edition of the Belfast-based *News Letter* was dated 6 Mar 1738 and has been a daily since 1855. *The Daily Universal Register* was founded in 1785 and changed its name to *The Times* in 1788.

Largest newspapers ■ The most massive single issues of a newspaper have been of the *Sunday New York Times* which by August 1987 had reached 6·35 kg *14 lb* with a prediction that 7·7 kg *17 lb* was a probability. The largest page size ever used has been 130 cm × 89 cm *51 in × 35 in* for *The Constellation*, printed in 1859 by George Roberts as part of the 4 Jul celebrations in New York City, USA. The *Worcestershire Chronicle* was the largest British newspaper. A surviving issue of 16 Feb 1859 measures 82 cm × 57 cm *32¼ in × 22½ in*.

Smallest newspapers ■ The smallest original page size has been the 7·6 × 9·5 cm *3 × 3¾ in* of the *Daily Banner* (25 cents per month) of Roseberg, Oregon, USA, issues of which, dated 1 and 2 Feb 1876, survive. The *Answers to Correspondents* published by Messrs Carr & Co, Paternoster Square, London in 1888 was 9 × 11 cm *3½ × 4½ in*. The British Library Newspaper Library has the *Watford News and Advertiser* of 1 Apr 1899 measuring 7·5 × 10 cm *2·9 × 3·9 in*.

Most expensive ■ Britain's most expensive papers are *The Observer* and *The Sunday Times* at 60p–more than double the price of the 1955 *Guinness Book of Records*.

Most ■ The United States had 1657 English-language daily newspapers at 30 Sep 1986 with a combined net paid circulation of 62 766 232 copies per day. The peak year for US newspapers was 1910, when there were 2202. The leading newspaper readers in the world are the people of Sweden, where 580 newspapers are sold for each 1000 compared with the UK figure of 410.

Longest editorship ■ Sir Etienne Dupuch OBE (b. 16 Feb 1899) of Nassau, Bahamas, Editor-in-Chief of *The Tribune* since 1 Apr 1919 to 1972, and Contributing Editor to the present time, entered his 70th year as an editor on 1 Apr 1988. The longest editorship of any United Kingdom national newspaper has been more than 59 years by C. P. Scott (1846–1932) of the *Manchester Guardian*, who was appointed, aged 26, in 1872 and who died on 1 Jan 1932.

Most durable feature ■ Eric Hardy of Liverpool is now in his 62nd year as a regular natural history contributor to the *Daily Post* of Liverpool with a weekly 'Countryside' feature. Albert E. Pool (b. 1909) was a part-time journalist for the *Lincolnshire and South Humberside* (formerly *Hull*) *Times* from March 1923 until the demise of the paper on 26 Jul 1985.

Most syndicated columnist ■ In 1978 Ann Landers (*née* Eppie Lederer) appeared in over 1200 newspapers with an estimated readership of 90 million. Her only serious rival was 'Dear Abby' (Mrs Pauline Phillips) her identical twin sister (b. 1920) based in Beverly Hills, California.

Longest-lived strip ■ The most durable newspaper comic strip has been the 'Katzenjammer Kids' (Hans and Fritz) created by Rudolph Dirks and first published in the *New York Journal* on 12 Dec 1897.

Earliest cartoon strip ■ 'The Yellow Kid' first appeared in the *New York Journal* on 18 Oct 1896.

Most widely syndicated cartoon strip ■ 'Peanuts' by Charlie Schulz of Santa Rosa, California, USA has appeared in more than 2000 newspapers in 68 countries in 26 languages since October 1950. In 1986 his income was estimated at $1 million per month.

Most misprints ■ The record for misprints in *The Times* was set on 22 Aug 1978 when on page 19 there were 97 in 5½ single column inches. The passage concerned 'Pop' (Pope) Paul VI.

Most durable advertiser ■ The Jos Neel Co, a clothing store in Macon, Georgia, USA (founded 1880) has run an 'ad' in the *Macon Telegraph* every day in the upper left corner of page 2 since 22 Feb 1889 or 35 760 times to March 1987.

CIRCULATION

Earliest 1 000 000 ■ The first newspaper to achieve a circulation of 1 000 000 was *Le Petit Journal*, published in Paris, France, which reached this figure in 1886, when selling at 5 centimes. The *Daily Mail* first reached a million on 2 Mar 1900.

Highest ■ The *Yomiuri Shimbun* newspaper (founded 1874) of Japan which attained a figure of 14 996 303 copies on 1 Apr 1989. This is achieved by totalling the figures for editions published in various centres with a morning figure of 9 847 338 and an

evening figure of 4 748 965. It reaches 24·6 per cent of Japan's 40 million households. It has a staff of 7998 and 128 bureaux. In Japan 569 newspapers are printed for each 1000 people. *Trud*, the Soviet trade union daily, is printed in 62 cities in 20·35 million copies of which only 70 000 are bought at news-stands. The eight-page weekly newspaper *Argumenty I Fakty* (founded 1978) of Moscow, USSR attained a figure of 21 294 069 copies on 10 Mar 1989. It has an estimated readership of 64 000 000.

Britain ■ *The News of the World* has attained sales of 9 000 000 copies with an estimated readership of more than 19 000 000. The paper first appeared on 1 Oct 1843, and surpassed the million mark in 1905. The latest sales figure is 5 237 000 copies per issue (mid May 1989), with an estimated readership of 13 546 000.

The highest net sale of any daily newspaper in the United Kingdom is that of *The Sun*, founded in London in 1964. The latest sales figure is 3 909 246 (May 1989), with an estimated readership of 11 596 000. The record number of entrants received for a newspaper competition was by *The Sun* for its game entitled 'Lotto'. In the period January to February 1988, a total of 4 367 382 entries were registered — equivalent to to 3000 full-to-the-brim standard pillar boxes.

Most read ■ The national newspaper which achieves the closest to a saturation circulation is the *Sunday Post*, established in Glasgow in 1914. In 1988 its estimated readership in Scotland of 2 359 000 represented 57 per cent of the entire population aged 15 and over. The *Arran Banner* (founded March 1974) has a readership of 97 + per cent on Britain's 7th largest offshore island.

PERIODICALS

Oldest ■ The oldest continuing periodical in the world is *Philosophical Transactions of the Royal Society*, published in London, which first appeared on 6 Mar 1665.

The bi-monthly *Gospel Magazine* has been published since 1766. Curtis's *Botanical Magazine* has been in continuous publication since 1 Feb 1787, as several 'parts' a year forming a series of continuously numbered volumes. Britain's oldest weekly periodical is *The Lancet*, first published in 1823. The *Scots Magazine* began in 1739 and ran until 1826, and

---

Highest circulation ● In its 39 basic international editions *Reader's Digest* (established February 1922) circulates 28 000 000 copies monthly in 15 languages, including a United States edition of more than 16 250 000 copies and a United Kingdom edition (established 1939) of 1 555 791 copies (ABC Jul–Dec 1987). (Photo: Reader's Digest)

---

with only three breaks has been produced since 1924.

Largest circulations ■ The peak circulation of any weekly periodical has been that of *TV Guide* (USA) which in 1974 became the first magazine in history to sell a billion (1000 million) copies in a year. The world's highest circulation magazine currently is *Modern Maturity* (US) with a figure in Jan–Jul 1988 of 17 924 783. In its 39 basic international editions *Reader's Digest* (established February 1922) circulates 28 000 000 copies monthly in 15 languages, including a United States edition of more than 16 250 000 copies and a United Kingdom edition (established 1939) of 1 547 904 copies (ABC July–December 1988). *Parade*, the American syndicated Sunday newspaper colour magazine, is distributed with 319 newspapers every Sunday. The current circulation is 33 217 317 (April 1989).

Great Britain ■ The highest circulation of any periodical is that of the *Radio Times* (instituted on 28 Sept 1923). The average weekly sale for July–Dec 1988 was 3 119 129 copies with a readership of 9 264 000. The highest sale of any issue was 11 220 666 copies for the Christmas issue of 1988. *TV Times* averaged sales of 3 032 343 in the period January–December 1988 with an estimated readership of 9 104 000 (January–December 1988).

Weightiest ■ The heaviest magazine ever published was the September 1987 issue of American *Vogue* which ran to 828 hernia-inducing pages.

Annual ■ *Old Moore's Almanack* has been published annually since 1697, when it first appeared as a broadsheet by Dr Francis Moore (1657–1715) of Southwark, London to advertise his 'physiks'. The annual sale certified by its publishers W. Foulsham & Co Ltd of Slough, Berks is one million copies and its aggregate sale is estimated to be in excess of 108 million.

CROSSWORDS

First ■ The earliest known crossword was a 9 by 9 Double Diamond published in *St Nicholas* for September 1875 in New York City. This was discovered by Dr Kenneth Miller of Newcastle-upon-Tyne, England, inventor of the colour crossword in 1983. The first crossword published in a British newspaper was one furnished by C. W. Shepherd in the *Sunday Express* of 2 Nov 1924. However, a 25-letter acrostic of Roman provenance was discovered on a wall in Cirencester, Glos in 1868.

Largest published crossword ■ In July 1982 Robert Turcot of Québec, Canada compiled a crossword comprising of 82 951 squares. It contained 12 489 clues across, 13 125 down and covered 3·55 m² *38·28 ft²*.

Fastest solution ■ The fastest recorded time for completing *The Times* crossword under test conditions is 3 min 45·0 sec by Roy Dean of Bromley, Kent in the BBC *Today* radio studio on 19 Dec 1970. Dr John Sykes won *The Times* championship eight times between 1972 and 1985.

Slowest solution ■ In May 1966 *The Times* of London received an announcement from a Fijian woman that she had just succeeded in completing their crossword No. 673 in the issue of 4 Apr 1932.

Most durable compilers ■ Adrian Bell (1901–1980) of Barsham, Suffolk contributed a record 4520 crosswords to *The Times* from 2 Jan 1930 until his death. The most prolific compiler is Roger F. Squires of Ironbridge, Shropshire, who compiles 37 published puzzles single-handedly each week. His total output to September 1989 was over 33 400, equivalent to over one million clues.

ADVERTISING RATES

The highest ever price for a single page was $436 300 for a four-colour back cover in *Parade* (circulation 33·2 million per week) in January 1989 (see above). The record for a four-colour inside page is $379 400 in *Parade*. The advertising revenue from the November 1982 US edition of *Reader's Digest* was a peak $14 716 551.

The highest expenditure ever incurred on a single advertisement in a periodical has been $3 200 000 by Gulf and Western Industries on 5 Feb 1979 for insertions in *Time* magazine (US and selected overseas editions).

The British record is some £100 000 for a 20-page colour supplement by Woolworths in the *Radio Times* of 16 Nov 1972 (approximately £493 000 at today's prices). The rate for a single page in the *News of the World SunDay* magazine is £28 500, and £57 000 for a centre spread (April 1987). The world's highest newspaper advertising rate is 41 550 000 yen for a full page in the morning edition and 32 370 000 yen for the evening edition of the *Yomiuri Shimbun* of Tokyo (April 1989).

The highest rate in Britain is a full page in colour in the *Sunday Times* at £60 000 (March 1988).

Music

Whistles and flutes made from perforated phalange bones have been found at Upper Palaeolithic sites of the Aurignacian period (*c.* 25 000–22 000 BC) e.g. at Istallóskö, Hungary and in Molodova, USSR. The world's earliest surviving musical notation dates from *c.* 1800 BC. A heptatonic scale deciphered from a clay tablet by Dr Duchesne-Guillemin in 1966–7 was found at a site in Nippur, Sumer, now Iraq. An Assyrian love song, also *c.* 1800 BC, to an Ugaritic god from a tablet of notation and lyric was reconstructed for an 11-string lyre at the University of California, Berkeley, USA on 6 Mar 1974. Musical history can, however, be traced back to the 3rd millennium BC, when the yellow bell (*huang chung*) had a recognised standard musical tone in Chinese temple music.

INSTRUMENTS

Earliest piano ■ The earliest pianoforte in existence is one built in Florence, Italy in 1720 by Bartolommeo Cristofori (1655–1731) of Padua, and now preserved in the Metropolitan Museum of Art, New York City, USA.

Grandest piano ■ The grandest grand piano was one of 1¼ tonnes 3·55 m *11 ft 8 in* in length made by Chas H. Challen & Son Ltd of London in 1935. The longest bass string measured 3·02 m *9 ft 11 in* with a tensile strength of 30 tonnes.

Most expensive piano ■ The highest price ever paid for a piano has been $390 000 at Sotheby Parke Bernet, New York, USA on 26 Mar 1980 for a Steinway grand of *c.* 1888 sold by the Martin Beck Theater. It was bought by a non-pianist.

Smallest piano ■ The smallest playable piano is a ⅛th scale model of a 1910 Knabe. It measures 19·05 × 8·57 × 16·5 cm *7½ × 3⅜ × 6½ in* and was built by Emil J. Cost.

Largest organ ■ The largest and loudest musical instrument ever constructed is the now only partially functional Auditorium Organ in Atlantic City, New Jersey, USA. Completed in 1930, this heroic instrument had two consoles (one with seven manuals and another movable one with five), 1477 stop controls and 33 112 pipes ranging in tone from 4·7 mm *³⁄₁₆ of an inch* to the 19·5 m *64 ft* tone. It had the volume of 25 brass bands, with a range of seven octaves. The world's largest fully functional organ is the six manual 30 067 pipe Grand Court Organ installed in the Wanamaker Store, Philadelphia, Pennsylvania, USA in 1911 and enlarged between then and 1930. It has a 19·5 m *64 ft* tone gravissima pipe. The world's largest church organ is that in Passau Cathedral, West Germany. It was completed in 1928 by D. F. Steinmeyer & Co and has 16 000 pipes and five manuals. The world's most powerful electronic organ is Robert A. Nye's 6000-watt 'Golden Spirit' organ, designed by Henry N. Hunsicker. It has 600 speakers and made its public concert debut in Trump's Castle, Atlantic City, New Jersey, USA on 9 Dec 1988. The chapel organ at West Point US Military Academy, NY, USA has, since 1911, been expanded from 2406 to 18 200 pipes.

Great Britain ■ The largest organ in Great Britain is that completed in Liverpool Anglican Cathedral on 18 Oct 1926, with two five-manual consoles of which only one is now in use, and 9704 speaking pipes (originally 10 936) ranging from tones 1·9 cm to 9·75 m ¾ *in to 32 ft*.

Loudest organ stop ■ The Ophicleide stop of the Grand Great in the Solo Organ in the Atlantic City Auditorium (see above) is operated by a pressure of water 24 kPa (3½ lb/in²) and has a pure trumpet note of ear-splitting volume, more than six times the volume of the loudest locomotive whistles.

Largest pan pipes ■ The world's largest pan pipes created by Simon Desorgher and Lawrence Casserley consist of five contra-bass pipes, each 100 mm in diameter with lengths of 4790 mm, 4160 mm, 3606 mm, 3104 mm and 2666 mm respectively and five bass pipes of 50 mm diameter with lengths of 2395 mm, 2080 mm, 1803 mm, 1522 mm and 1333 mm. Their first public appearance was at Jubilee Gardens, London on 9 Jul 1988.

Most durable musicians ■ Elsie Maude Stanley Hall (1877–1976) gave piano recitals for 90 years, giving her final concert in Rustenburg, Transvaal, South Africa aged 97. Charles Bridgeman (1779–1873) of All Saints Parish Church, Hertford, who was appointed organist in 1792, was still playing 81 years later in 1873. Norwegian pianist Reidar Thommesen (1889–1986) played over 30 hours a week in theatre cafés when a nonagenarian.

Largest brass instrument ■ The largest recorded brass instrument is a tuba standing 2·28 m

Largest PA system ● On Aug 20th 1988 at the Castle Donington 'Monsters of Rock' Festival a total of 360 Turbosound cabinets offering a potential 523 kW of programme power, formed the largest front-of-house PA. The average Sound Pressure Level at the mixing tower was 118 dB, peaking at a maximum of 124 dB during Iron Maiden's set. It took five days to set up the system. (Photo: Nik Milner)

$7^{1}/_{2}$ ft tall, with 11·8 m 39 ft of tubing and a bell 1 m 3 ft 4 in across. This contrabass tuba was constructed for a world tour by the band of American composer John Philip Sousa (1854–1932), c. 1896–8. It is now owned by a circus promoter in South Africa.

Largest stringed instrument ■ The largest movable stringed instrument ever constructed was a pantaleon with 270 strings stretched over 4·6 m² 50 ft² used by George Noel in 1767. The greatest number of musicians required to operate a single instrument was the six required to play the gigantic orchestrion, known as the Apollonican, built in 1816 and played until 1840.

Largest guitar ■ The largest and presumably also the loudest guitar in the world is one 4·35 m 14 ft 3¼ in tall, and 140 kg 309 lb in weight, built by Joe Kovacic of Lado Musical Inc, Scarborough, Ontario, Canada.

Most expensive standard sized guitar ■ The German chittara battente by Jacob Stadler, dated 1624, was sold for £10 500 at Christie's, London on 12 Jun 1974.

Largest double bass ■ A double bass measuring 4·26 m 14 ft tall, was built in 1924 in Ironia, New Jersey, USA by Arthur K. Ferris, allegedly on orders from the Archangel Gabriel. It weighed 590 kg 11·6 cwt with a sound box 2·43 m 8 ft across, and had leathern strings totalling 31·7 m 104 ft. Its low notes could be felt rather than heard. On 27 Jun 1984 five members of 'Bass Ten' from Bournemouth, Dorset bowed and six-fingered a double bass simultaneously in a rendition of Monti's Czardas at Hever Castle, Kent.

Most valuable 'cello ■ The highest ever auction price for a violoncello or any musical instrument is £682 000 at Sotheby's, London on 22 Jun 1988 for a Stradivarius known as 'The Cholmondeley' made in Cremona, Italy c. 1698.

Most valuable violin ■ The Lady Blunt Stradivarius violin of 1721 failed at £820 000 to reach its undisclosed 'reserve' at Sotheby's, London on 14 Nov 1985. The highest price ever paid at auction for a violin is £572 000 for one made by Joseph Guarneri del Gesu of Cremona in 1743 at Sotheby's, London on 23 Nov 1988. Stradivarius's (1644–1737) Alard violin was confirmed by Jacques Français to have been sold by private treaty by W. E. Hill for $1·2 million to a Singaporean.

Most durable fiddlers ■ Rolland S. Tapley retired as a violinist from the Boston Symphony Orchestra after reputedly playing for an unrivalled 58 years from February 1920 to 27 Aug 1978. Otto E. Funk, 62, walked 6702 km 4165 miles from New York City to San Francisco, California, USA playing his Hopf violin every step of the way westward. He arrived on 16 Jun 1929 after 183 days on the road.

Largest drum ■ A drum with a 3·96 m 13 ft diameter, was built by the Supreme Drum Co, London, and played at the Royal Festival Hall, London on 31 May 1987.

Largest drum kit ■ A drum kit consisting of 81 pieces–45 drums, including six bass drums, 15 cymbals, five temple blocks, two triangles, two gongs, two sets of wind chimes, one solid bar chime, six assorted cowbells, a drum set tambourine, a vibra slap and an icebell, is owned by Darreld MacKenzie of Calgary, Alberta, Canada.

Longest alphorn ■ A 35·96 m 118 ft (excluding mouthpiece) weighing 83 kg 183 lb was built by Swiss-born Peter Wutherich, of Boise, Idaho, USA. The sound takes 105·7 milliseconds to emerge from the bowl after entry into the mouthpiece.

Highest and lowest notes ■ The extremes of orchestral instruments (excluding the organ) range between a handbell tuned to g^v (6272 cycles/sec) and the sub-contrabass clarinet, which can reach C_{11} or 16·4 cycles/sec. The highest note on a standard pianoforte is c^v (4186 cycles/sec), which is also the violinist's limit. In 1873 a sub double bassoon able to reach B_{11} ± or 14·6 cycles/sec was constructed but

no surviving specimen is known. The extremes for the organ are g^{vi} (the sixth G above middle C) (12·544 cycles/sec) and C_{111} (8·12 cycles/sec) obtainable from 1·9 cm ¾ in and 19·5 m 64 ft pipes respectively.

Easiest and most difficult instruments ■ The American Music Conference announced in September 1977 that the easiest instrument is the ukulele, and the most difficult are the French horn and the oboe, which latter has been described as 'the ill woodwind that no one blows good'.

Fastest bagpipe playing ■ Sgt Mick Maitland, Pipe Major of No. 111 RAF Fighter Squadron played 'Scotland the Brave' on his pipes at a speed of Mach 2·0 and a height of 12 190 m 40 000 ft. He was flown in a Phantom XV 574 by Wing Commander Phil W. Roser, the Squadron Commander. This supersonic performance was given 64·3 km 40 miles south of RAF Akrotiri, Cyprus on 3 Jun 1986.

SONG

Oldest song ■ The shaduf chant has been sung since time immemorial by irrigation workers on the man-powered pivoted-rod bucket raisers of the Nile water mills (or saqiyas) in Egypt. The oldest known harmonised music performed today is the English song Sumer is icumen in which dates from c. 1240.

National anthems ■ The oldest national anthem is the Kimigayo of Japan, in which the words date from the 9th century, whilst the oldest music belongs to the Netherlands. The anthem of Greece constitutes the first two verses of the Solomos poem, which has 158 stanzas. The shortest anthems are those of Japan, Jordan and San Marino, each with only four lines. Of the 11 wordless national anthems the oldest is that of Spain dating from 1770.

Longest rendering ■ 'God Save the King' was played non-stop 16 or 17 times by a German military band on the platform of Rathenau railway station, Brandenburg, Germany on the morning of 9 Feb 1909. The reason was that King Edward VII was struggling inside the train with the uniform of a German field-marshal before he could emerge.

Top songs ■ The most frequently sung songs in English are Happy Birthday to You (based on the original Good Morning to All), by Mildred and Patty S. Hill of New York, USA (published in 1935 and in copyright until 2010); For He's a Jolly Good Fellow (originally the French Malbrouk), known at least as early as 1781, and Auld Lang Syne (originally the Strathspey I Fee'd a Lad at Michaelmass), some words of which were written by Robert Burns (1759–96). Happy Birthday was sung in space by the Apollo IX astronauts on 8 Mar 1969.

Top-selling sheet music ■ Sales of three non-copyright pieces are known to have exceeded 20 000 000, namely The Old Folks at Home by Stephen Foster (1855), Listen to the Mocking Bird (1855) and The Blue Danube (1867). Of copyright material the two top sellers are Let Me Call You Sweetheart (1910 by Whitson and Friedman) and Till We Meet Again (1918, by Egan and Whiting) each with some 6 000 000 by 1967. Other huge sellers have been St Louis Blues, Stardust and Tea for Two.

Most successful songwriters ■ The songwriters responsible for the most number one singles are John Lennon and Paul McCartney. In the United States McCartney is credited as writer on 32 number one hits, six more than Lennon. In Great Britain Lennon authored 28 number ones, McCartney 27. In America 23 of their number ones were jointly written, in Great Britain, 24.

After Lennon/McCartney the most successful songwriters in terms of number one hits in Great Britain are Benny Andersson and Bjorn Ulvaeus of the group ABBA, who have written ten.

In the United States Barry Gibb of the Bee Gees has written or co-written 16 number ones.

The most successful female songwriter in America is Carole King with eight number ones – in Great Britain it is Madonna with six.

HYMNS

Earliest ■ There are more than 950 000 Christian hymns in existence. The music and parts of the text of a hymn in the Oxyrhynchus Papyri from the 2nd century are the earliest known hymnody. The earliest exactly datable hymn is the Heyr Himna Smióur (Hear, the maker of heaven) from 1208 by the Icelandic bard and chieftain Kolbeinn Tumason (1173–1208).

Longest ■ The Hora novissima tempora pessima sunt; vigilemus by Bernard of Cluny (12th century), runs to 2966 lines. In English the longest is The Sands of Time are Sinking by Mrs Anne Ross Cousin, née Cundell (1824–1906), which is in full 152 lines, though only 32 lines in the Methodist Hymn Book.

Shortest ■ The shortest hymn is the single verse in long metre Be Present at our Table Lord, anon., but attributed to 'J. Leland'.

Most prolific hymnists ■ Mrs Frances (Fanny) Jane van Alstyne, née Crosby (1820–1915) (USA) wrote 8500 hymns although she had been blinded at the age of six weeks. She is reputed to have knocked off one hymn in 15 minutes. Charles Wesley (1707–88) wrote about 6000 hymns. In the 7th (1950) edition of Hymns Ancient and Modern the works of John Mason Neale (1818–66) appear 56 times.

BELLS

Oldest ■ The tintinnabulum found in the Babylonian Palace of Nimrod in 1849 by Mr (later Sir) Austen Henry Layard (1817–94) dates from c. 1100 BC. The oldest known tower bell is one in Pisa, Italy dated MCVI (1106).

Great Britain ■ The fragile hand bell known as the Black or Iron Bell of St Patrick is dated c. AD 450. The oldest tower bell in Great Britain is one of 50 kg 1 cwt at St Botolph, Hardham, Sussex, still in use but dated ante 1100. The oldest inscribed bell is the Gargate bell at Caversfield church, Oxfon and is dated c. 1200–1210. The oldest dated bell in England is one hanging in Lissett church, near Bridlington, Humberside discovered in October 1972 to bear the date MCCLIIII (1254).

Heaviest ■ The Tsar Kolokol, cast on 25 Nov 1735 in Moscow weighs 196 tonnes 193 tons, measures 5·9 m 19 ft 4½ in in diameter and 5·87 m 19 ft 3 in high, and its greatest thickness is 60 cm 24 in. The bell is cracked, and a fragment, weighing about 11 tonnes was broken from it. The bell has stood, unrung, on a platform in the Kremlin in Moscow since 1836. The heaviest bell in use is the Mingun bell, weighing 90·52 tons with a diameter of 5·09 m 16 ft 8½ in at the lip, in Mandalay, The Union of Myanma, which is struck by a teak boom from the outside. It was cast at Mingun late in the reign of King Bodawpaya (1782–1819). The heaviest swinging bell in the world is the Petersglocke in the south-west tower of Cologne Cathedral, West Germany, cast in 1923 with a diameter of 3·40 m 11 ft 1¾ in weighing 25·4 tonnes 25 tons.

Great Britain ■ The heaviest bell hung in Great Britain is 'Great Paul' in the south-west tower of St Paul's Cathedral, London, cast in 1881. It weighs 17 002 kg 16 tons 14 cwt 2 qrs 19 lb, has a diameter of 2·9 m 9 ft 6½ in and sounds note E-flat. 'Big Ben', the hour bell in the clock tower of the House of Commons, was cast in 1858 and weighs 13 761 kg 13 tons 10 cwt 3 qrs 15 lb. It is the most broadcast bell in the world and is note E.

Peals ■ A ringing peal is defined as a diatonic 'ring' of five or more bells hung for full-circle change ringing. Of 5500 rings so hung only 70 are outside the United Kingdom and Ireland. The heaviest ring in the world is that of 13 bells cast in 1938–9 for the Anglican Cathedral, Liverpool. The total bell weight is 16·76 tonnes 16½ tons of which Emmanuel, the tenor bell note A, weighs 4170·8 kg 82 cwt 11 lb.

Largest carillon ■ The largest carillon (minimum of 23 bells) in the world is the Laura Spelman

Rockefeller Memorial Carillon in Riverside Church, New York, USA with 74 bells weighing 102 tons. The bourdon, giving the note lower C, weighs 18 563 kg *40 926 lb*. This 18·27 ton bell, cast in England, with a diameter of 3·09 cm *10 ft 2 in* is the largest *tuned* bell in the world.

Great Britain ■ The carillon in St Nicholas Church, Aberdeen, Scotland consists of 48 bells, the total weight of which is 25 838 kg *25 tons 8 cwt 2 qrs 13 lb*. The bourdon bell weighs 4571 kg *4 tons 9 cwt 3 qrs 26 lb* and is the note G-sharp.

Bell ringing ■ Eight bells have been rung to their full 'extent' (40 320 unrepeated changes of Plain Bob Major) only once without relays. This took place in a bell foundry at Loughborough, Leicestershire, beginning at 6.52 a.m. on 27 Jul 1963 and ending at 12.50 a.m. on 28 Jul, after 17 hr 58 min. The peal was composed by Kenneth Lewis of Altrincham, Manchester, and the eight ringers were conducted by Robert B. Smith, aged 25, of Marple, Manchester. Theoretically it would take 37 years 355 days to ring 12 bells (maximus) to their full extent of 479 001 600 changes. The greatest number of peals (minimum of 5040 changes, all in tower bells) rung in a year is 209 by Mark William Marshall of Ashford, Kent in 1973. The late George E. Fearn rang 2666 peals from 1928 to May 1974. Matthew Lakin (1801–1899) was a regular bell-ringer at Tetney Church near Grimsby, Humberside for 84 years.

ORCHESTRAS

Largest orchestra ■ On 17 Jun 1872, Johann Strauss the younger (1825–99) conducted an orchestra of 987 pieces supported by a choir of 20 000, at the World Peace Jubilee in Boston, Massachusetts, USA. The number of first violinists was 400.

Largest band ■ The most massive band ever assembled was one of 20 100 bandsmen at the Ullevaal Stadium, Oslo, Norway from Norges Musikkorps Forbund bands on 28 Jun 1964. On 17 Apr 1982, 6179 'musicians' congregated at Bay Shore Mall, Milwaukee, Wisconsin, USA for a rendering of Sousa's 'Stars and Stripes Forever'. According to one music critic, the 'instruments' included 'kazoos, 7-Up bottles, one-man-band contraptions, coffee cans, bongo drums and anything-you-can-thump-on'. 'At times' the report concludes, 'you could almost tell what they were playing.'

Largest marching band ■ The largest marching band was one of 4524 including 1342 majorettes under the direction of Danny Kaye (1913–87) at Dodger Stadium, Los Angeles on 15 Apr 1985.

Most durable conductor ■ The Cork Symphony Orchestra performed under the baton of Dr Aloys Fleischmann for 54 seasons (1935–88).

Most successful bands ■ Most British Open Brass Band Championship titles (inst. 1853) have been won by the Black Dyke Mills Band which has won 22 times from 1862 to 1974 including three consecutive wins in 1972–4. The most successful pipe band is the Shotts & Dykehead Caledonian Pipe Band with their 10th world title in August 1980. The City of Wellington Pipe Band Incorporated has won 26 Grade 1 New Zealand Championship titles since 1955.

ATTENDANCES

Classical ■ An estimated 800 000 attended a free open-air concert by the New York Philharmonic conducted by Zubin Mehta, on the Great Lawn of Central Park, New York, USA on 5 Jul 1986, as part of the Statue of Liberty Weekend.

Pop festival ■ The greatest attendance has been 725 000 for Steve Wozniak's 1983 US Festival. The attendance at the 3rd Pop Festival at East Afton Farm, Freshwater, Isle of Wight on 30 Aug 1970 was claimed by its promoters, Fiery Creations, to be 400 000.

Solo performer ■ The largest paying audience ever attracted by a solo performer was an estimated 175 000 in the Maracaña Stadium, Rio de Janeiro,

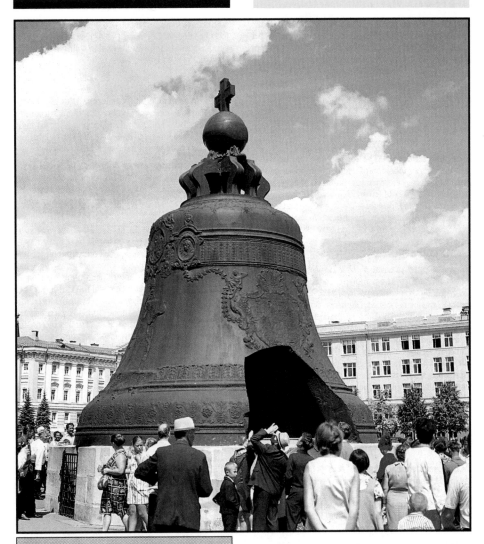

Heaviest bell ● The heaviest bell in the world is the Tsar Kolokol, cast on 25 Nov 1735 in Moscow. It weighs 196 tonnes, measures 5·9 m *19 ft 4½ in* in diameter and 5·87 m *19 ft 3 in* high, and its greatest thickness is 60 cm *24 in*. The bell is cracked, and a fragment, weighing about 11 tonnes was broken from it. The bell has stood, unrung, on a platform in the Kremlin in Moscow since 1836. (Photo: Spectrum)

Brazil to hear Frank Sinatra (b. 1915) on 26 Jan 1980. Jean-Michel Jarre entertained an estimated 1·3 million at downtown Houston, Texas, USA at a free concert on 5 Apr 1986.

Greatest choir ■ Excluding 'sing alongs' by stadium crowds, the greatest choir is one of 60 000 which sang in unison as a finale of a choral contest among 160 000 participants in Breslau, Germany on 2 Aug 1937.

Most successful concert tour ■ Bruce Springsteen's tour, which began in April 1984, grossed an estimated $117 million. He played 158 dates in 61 cities spread over 11 countries and was seen by 4 767 854 people.

Wembley Stadium ■ Michael Jackson sold out seven nights at Wembley Stadium in the summer of 1988. The Stadium has a capacity of 72 000 so a total of 504 000 people saw Jackson perform on 14, 15, 16, 22, 23 Jul and 26, 27 Aug 1988.

COMPOSERS

Most prolific ■ The most prolific composer of all time was probably Georg Philipp Telemann (1681–1767) of Germany. He composed 12 complete sets of services (one cantata every Sunday) for a year, 78 services for special occasions, 40 operas, 600 to 700 orchestral suites, 44 Passions, plus concertos and chamber music. The most prolific symphonist was Johann Melchior Molter (c. 1695–1765) of Germany who wrote 169. Joseph Haydn (1732–1809) of Austria wrote 108 numbered symphonies, many of which are regularly played today.

Most rapid ■ Among composers of the classical period the most prolific was Wolfgang Amadeus Mozart (1756–91) of Austria, who wrote c. 1000 operas, operettas, symphonies, violin sonatas, divertimenti, serenades, motets, concertos for piano and many other instruments, string quartets, other chamber music, masses and litanies, of which only 70 were published before he died aged 35. His opera *La Clemenza di Tito* (1791) was written in 18 days, and three symphonic masterpieces, *Symphony No. 39 in E flat major, Symphony No. 40 in G minor* and the *Jupiter Symphony No. 41 in C major*, were reputedly written in the space of 42 days in 1788. His overture *Don Giovanni* was written in full score at one sitting in Prague in 1787 and finished on the day of its opening performance.

Longest symphony ■ The longest of all single classical symphonies is the orchestral symphony No. 3 in D minor by Gustav Mahler (1860–1911) of Austria. This work, composed in 1896, requires a contralto, a women's and a boys' choir in addition to a full orchestra. A full performance requires 1 hr 40 min, of which the first movement alone takes between 30 and 36 min. The Symphony No. 2 (the Gothic), composed from 1919–22 by William Havergal Brian (1876–1972), was played by over 800 performers (four brass bands) in the Victoria Hall, Hanley, Staffs on 21 May 1978 (conductor Trevor Stokes). A recent broadcast required 1 hr 45½ min. Brian wrote an even vaster work based on Shelley's 'Prometheus Unbound' lasting 4 hr 11 min but the full score has been missing since 1961. The symphony *Victory at Sea* written by Richard Rodgers and arranged by Robert Russell Bennett for NBC TV in 1952 lasted for 13 hours.

Longest piano composition ■ The longest continuous non-repetitive piano piece ever published has been *The Well-Tuned Piano* by La Monte Young, first presented by the Dia Art Foundation at the Concert Hall, Harrison St, New York, USA on 28 Feb 1980. The piece lasted 4 hr 12 min 10 sec. *Symphonic Variations*, composed in the 1930s for piano and orchestra by the British born Kaikhosru Shapurji Sorabji (1892–1988) on 500 pages of close manuscript in three volumes, would last for six hours at the prescribed tempo.

Longest silence ■ The longest interval between the known composition of a major composer and its performance in the manner intended is from 3 Mar 1791 until 9 Oct 1982 (over 191 years), in the case of Mozart's *Organ Piece for a Clock*, a fugue fantasy in F minor (K 608), arranged by the organ builders Wm Hill & Son and Norman & Beard Ltd at Glyndebourne, East Sussex.

PERFORMERS

Highest-paid pianist ■ Wladziu Valentino Liberace (1917–87) earned more than $2 million each 26-week season with a peak of $138 000 for a single night's performance at Madison Square Garden, New York in 1954. The highest-paid classical concert pianist was Ignace Jan Paderewski (1860–1941), Prime Minister of Poland (1919–20), who accumulated a fortune estimated at $5 000 000, of which $500 000 was earned in a single season in 1922–3. The *nouveau riche* wife of a US industrialist once required him to play in her house behind a curtain. For concerts Artur Rubinstein (1887–1982), between 1937 and 1976, commanded 70 per cent of the gross.

Greatest span ■ Sergey Vasiliyevich Rachmaninov (1873–1943) had a span of 12 white notes and could play a left-hand chord of C, E♭, G, C, G.

Most successful singer ■ Of great fortunes earned by singers, the highest on record are those of Enrico Caruso (1873–1921), the Italian tenor, whose estate was about $9 000 000 and the Italian-Spanish coloratura soprano Amelita Galli-Curci (1889–1963),

who received about $3 000 000. The Irish tenor Count John Francis McCormack (1884–1945) gave up to ten concerts to capacity audiences in a single season in New York.

David Bowie drew a fee of $1·5 million for a single show at the US Festival in Glen Helen Regional Park, San Bernardino County, California, USA on 26 May 1983. The four-man Van Halen rock band attracted a matching fee. The total attendance at Michael Jackson's world tour, Sep 1987–Dec 1988, brought in a tour gross revenue in excess of $124 million.

Singer's pulling power ■ In 1850, up to $653 was paid for a single seat at the US concerts of of Johanna ('Jenny') Maria Lind (1820–87), the 'Swedish nightingale'. She had a range from g to e''' of which the middle register is still regarded as unrivalled.

Worst singer ■ While no agreement exists as to the identity of history's greatest singer, there is unanimity on the worst. The excursions of the soprano Florence Foster Jenkins (1868–1944) into lieder and even high coloratura culminated on 25 Oct 1944 in her sell-out concert at the Carnegie Hall, New York, USA. The diva's (already high) high F was said to have been made higher in 1943 by a crash in a taxi. It is one of the tragedies of musicology that Madame Jenkins' *Clavelitos*, accompanied by Cosme McMoon, was never recorded for posterity.

OPERA

Longest ■ The longest of commonly performed operas is *Die Meistersinger von Nürnberg* by Wilhelm Richard Wagner (1813–83) of Germany. A normal uncut performance of this opera as per-

> **Largest opera house ●** The Metropolitan Opera House, Lincoln Center, New York, completed in September 1966 at a cost of $45 700 000, has a capacity of 3800 seats in an auditorium 137 m *451 ft* deep. The stage is 71 m *234 ft* wide and 44·5 m *146 ft* deep. (Photo: Images)

formed by the Sadler's Wells company between 24 Aug and 19 Sep 1968 entailed 5 hr 15 min of music. *The Heretics* by Gabriel von Wayditch (1888–1969), a Hungarian-American, is orchestrated for 110 pieces and lasts 8 ½ hr.

Shortest ■ The shortest opera published was *The Deliverance of Theseus* by Darius Milhaud (1892–1972), first performed in 1928, which lasted for 7 min 27 sec.

Longest aria ■ The longest single aria, in the sense of an operatic solo, is Brünnhilde's immolation scene in Wagner's *Gotterdammerung*. A well-known recording of this has been precisely timed at 14 min 46 sec.

Largest opera houses ■ The Metropolitan Opera House, Lincoln Center, New York, USA completed in September 1966 at a cost of $45 700 000, has a capacity of 3800 seats in an auditorium 137 m *451 ft* deep. The stage is 71 m *234 ft* wide and 44·5 m *146 ft* deep.

The tallest opera house is one housed in a 42-storey building on Wacker Drive in Chicago, Illinois, USA. The Teatro della Scala (La Scala) in Milan, Italy shares with the Bolshoi Theatre in Moscow, USSR the distinction of having the greatest number of tiers. Each has six, with the topmost being nicknamed the *Galiorka* by Russians.

Youngest opera singers ■ Ginetta Gloria La Bianca, born in Buffalo, New York State, USA on 12 May 1934, sang Rosina in *The Barber of Seville* at the Teatro dell'Opera, Rome, Italy on 8 May 1950 aged 15 years 361 days, having appeared as Gilda in *Rigoletto* at Velletri 45 days earlier. Ginetta La Bianca was taught by Lucia Carlino and managed by Angelo Carlino.

Oldest opera singer ■ The tenor Giovanni Martinelli sang Emperor Altoum in *Turandot* in Seattle, Washington State, USA on 4 Feb 1967 when aged 81.

Danshi Toyotake (b. 1 Aug 1891) has been singing *Musume Gidayu* for 91 years.

Longest encore ■ The longest operatic encore, listed in the *Concise Oxford Dictionary of Opera*, was of the entire opera Cimarosa's *Il Matrimonio Segreto* at its première in 1792. This was at the command of the Austro-Hungarian Emperor Leopold II (reigned 1790–2).

Most curtain calls ■ On 24 Feb 1988 Luciano Pavarotti received 165 curtain calls and was applauded for 1 hr 7 min after singing the part of Nemorino in Gaetano Donizetti's *L'elisir d'amore* at the Deutsche Oper in West Berlin, Germany.

BALLET

Fastest 'entrechat douze' ■ In the *entrechat* (a vertical spring from the fifth position with the legs extended criss-crossing at the lower calf), the starting and finishing position each count as one such that in an *entrechat douze* there are *five* crossings and uncrossings. This was performed by Wayne Sleep for the BBC *Record Breakers* programme on 7 Jan 1973. He was in the air for 0·71 sec.

Grands jetés ■ On 28 Nov 1988, Wayne Sleep completed 158 grands jetés along the length of Dunston Staiths, Gateshead, Tyne & Wear in two minutes.

Most turns ■ The greatest number of spins called for in classical ballet choreography is 32 *fouettés rond de jambe en tournant* in *Swan Lake* by Pyotr Ilyich Chaykovskiy (Tschaikovsky) (1840–93).

Miss Rowena Jackson (later Chatfield) MBE (b. Invercargill, NZ, 1925) achieved 121 such turns at her class in Melbourne, Victoria, Australia in 1940.

Most curtain calls ■ The greatest recorded number of curtain calls ever received is 89 by Dame Margaret Evelyn Arias DBE, *née* Hookham (born Reigate, Surrey, 18 May 1919) *alias* Margot Fonteyn, and Rudolf Hametovich Nureyev (born on a train near Irkutsk, USSR, 17 Mar 1938) after a performance of *Swan Lake* at the Vienna Staatsoper, Austria in October 1964.

Largest cast ■ The largest number of ballet dancers used in a production in Britain has been 2000 in the London Coster Ballet of 1962, directed by Lillian Rowley, at the Royal Albert Hall, London.

Theatre

Oldest ■ Theatre in Europe has its origins in Greek drama performed in honour of a god, usually Dionysus. The earliest amphitheatres date from the 5th century BC. The first stone-built theatre in Rome erected in 55 BC could accommodate 40 000 spectators.

Oldest indoor theatre ■ The oldest indoor theatre in the world is the Teatro Olimpico in Vicenza, Italy. Designed in the Roman style by Andrea di Pietro, *alias* Palladio (1508–80), it was begun three months before his death and finished by his pupil Vicenzo Scamozzi (1552–1616) in 1583. It is preserved today in its original form.

Great Britain ■ The earliest London theatre was James Burbage's 'The Theatre', built in 1576 near Finsbury Fields, London. In 1989 archaeologists found the remains of the Elizabethan Rose theatre at Bankside in Southwark; it was built in 1587 by Philip Henslowe. The oldest theatre still in use in Great Britain is The Royal, Bristol. The foundation stone was laid on 30 Nov 1764, and the theatre was opened on 30 May 1766 with a 'Concert of Musick and a Specimen of Rhetorick'. The City Varieties Music Hall, Leeds was a singing room in 1762 and so claims to outdate the Theatre Royal. Actors had the legal status of rogues and vagabonds until the passing of the Vagrancy Act in 1824. The oldest amateur dramatic society is the Old Stagers inaugurated in Canterbury, Kent in 1841. They have performed in every year except the years of World Wars I and II.

Largest ■ The world's largest building used for theatre is the National People's Congress Building (*Ren min da hui tang*) on the west side of Tian an men Square, Peking, China. It was completed in 1959 and covers an area of 5·2 ha *12·9 acres*. The theatre seats 10 000 and is occasionally used as such, as in 1964 for the play *The East is Red*. The highest capacity purpose-built theatre is the Perth Entertainment Centre, Western Australia completed at a cost of $A8·3 million in November 1976 with 8003 seats. The stage area is 1148 m² *12 000 ft²*.

Great Britain ■ The highest capacity theatre is the Odeon, Hammersmith, London, with 3483 seats. The largest theatre stage in Great Britain is the Opera House in Blackpool, Lancs. It was rebuilt in July 1939 and has seats for 2975 people. Behind the 14 m *45 ft* wide proscenium arch, the stage is 33 m *110 ft* high, 18 m *60 ft* deep and 30 m *100 ft* wide, and there is dressing-room accommodation for 200 artistes.

Smallest ■ The smallest regularly operated professional theatre in the world is the Piccolo in Juliusstrasse, Hamburg, West Germany. It was founded in 1970 and has a maximum capacity of 30 seats.

Largest amphitheatre ■ The Flavian amphitheatre or Colosseum of Rome, Italy, completed in AD 80, covers 2 ha *5 acres* with a capacity of 87 000. It has a maximum length of 187 m *612 ft* and a maximum width of 175 m *515 ft*.

Largest stage ■ The largest stage in the world is in the Ziegfeld Room, Reno, Nevada, USA with 53·6 m *176 ft* passerelle, three main lifts each capable of raising 1200 show girls (65·3 tonnes *64¼ tons*), two 19·1 m *62½ ft* circumference turntables and 800 spotlights.

Longest runs ■ The longest continuous run of any show in the world is *The Mousetrap* by Dame Agatha Mary Clarissa Christie DBE (*née* Miller, later Lady Mallowan) (1890–1976). This thriller opened on 25 Nov 1952, at the Ambassadors Theatre (capacity 453) and moved after 8862 performances to the St Martin's Theatre next door on 25 Mar 1974. The 36th anniversary performance on 25 Nov 1988 was the 14 989th. The 15 000th performance was on 9 Dec 1988 and the Box Office reached £14 million from more than 7 ½ million attenders. The Vicksburg Theater Guild, Mississippi, USA has been playing the melodrama *Gold in the Hills* by J. Frank Davis discontinuously but every season since 1936.

Revue ■ The greatest number of performances of any theatrical presentation is 47 250 (to April 1986) in the case of *The Golden Horseshoe Revue*–a show staged at Disneyland Park, Anaheim, California, USA. It started on 16 Jul 1955, closed on 12 Oct 1986 and has been seen by 16 million people. The three main performers were Fulton Burley, Dick Hardwick and Betty Taylor who played as many as five houses a day in a routine that lasted 45 minutes.

Broadway ■ *A Chorus Line* which opened on 25 Jul 1975 entered its 13th year in August 1987. It was created by Michael Bennet (b. 1943) who died of AIDS, aged 44, in Arizona, USA on 2 Jul 1987.

Musical shows ■ The off-Broadway musical show *The Fantasticks* by Tom Jones and Harvey Schmidt opened on 3 May 1960 and the total number of performances to 3 May 1987 is 11 240 at the Sullivan Street Playhouse, Greenwich Village, New York, USA.

Britain ■ The longest-running musical show ever performed in Britain was *The Black and White*

Minstrel Show, later *Magic of the Minstrels*. The aggregate but discontinuous number of performances was 6464 with a total attendance of 7 794 552. The show opened at the Victoria Palace, London on 25 May 1962 and closed on 4 Nov 1972. It reopened for a season in June 1973 at the New Victoria and finally closed on 8 Dec 1973.

London ■ The Andrew Lloyd Webber musical *Cats* surpassed *Jesus Christ Superstar* on its eighth birthday at the New London Theatre, Drury Lane on 12 May 1989 (3358 performances) when it was being played in ten centres simultaneously. The aggregate gross was estimated at 250 million.

Comedy ■ The British record for long-running comedy is held by *No Sex Please We're British* by Anthony Marriott and Alistair Foot and presented by John Gale, which opened at the Strand Theatre on 3 Jun 1971, transferred to the Duchess Theatre on 2 Aug 1986, and finally ended its run on 5 Sep 1987 after 17 years and 6761 performances. Its director Allan Davis had his name in lights from the start.

Christmas seasons ■ The record for the longest run of consecutive Christmas seasons at the same theatre is held by *The Sooty Show*. It has been running annually at The Mayfair Theatre, London since 1966.

Shortest runs ■ The shortest run on record was that of *The Intimate Revue* at the Duchess Theatre, London, on 11 Mar 1930. Anything which could go wrong did. With scene changes taking up to 20 min apiece, the management scrapped seven scenes to get the finale on before midnight. The run was described as 'half a performance'.

The greatest loss sustained by a theatrical show was by the Royal Shakespeare Company's musical *Carrie* which closed after five performances on Broadway on 17 May 1988 at a cost of $7 million.

Lowest attendance ■ The ultimate in low attendances was in December 1983 when the comedy *Bag* in Grantham, Lincs opened to a nil attendance.

Youngest Broadway producer ■ Margo Feiden (Margo Eden) (b. New York, 2 Dec 1944) produced the musical *Peter Pan*, which opened on 3 Apr 1961, when she was 16 years 5 months old. She wrote *Out Brief Candle*, which opened on 18 Aug 1962. She is now a leading art dealer.

One-man shows ■ The longest run of one-man shows is 849 by Victor Borge (b. Copenhagen, 3 Jan 1909) in his *Comedy in Music* from 2 Oct 1953 to 21 Jan 1956 at the Golden Theater, Broadway, New York City, USA. The world aggregate record for one-man shows is 1700 performances of *Brief Lives* by Roy Dotrice (b. Guernsey, 26 May 1923) including 400 straight at the Mayfair Theatre, London ending on 20 Jul 1974. He was on stage for more than 2 ½ hr per performance of this 17th-century monologue and required 3 hr for make-up and 1 hr for removal of make-up so aggregating 40 weeks in the chair.

Most durable actors and actresses ■ Kanmi Fujiyama (b. 1929) played the lead role in 10 288 performances by the comedy company Sochiku Shikigeki from November 1966 to June 1983. Dame Anna Neagle DBE (1904–86) played the lead role in *Charlie Girl* at the Adelphi Theatre, London for 2062 of 2202 performances between 15 Dec 1965 and 27 Mar 1971. She played the role a further 327 times in 327 performances in Australasia. Frances Etheridge has played Lizzie, the housekeeper, in *Gold in the Hills* (see Longest runs) more than 660 times over a span of 47 years since 1936. David Raven played Major Metcalfe in *The Mousetrap* on 4575 occasions between 22 Jul 1957 and 23 Nov 1968. Jack Howarth MBE (1896–1984) was an actor on the stage and in television for 76 years from 1907 until his last appearance after 23 years as Albert Tatlock in *Coronation Street* on 25 Jan 1984.

Advance sales *Broadway* ■ The Broadway record for advance sales was set in 1987 by *Phantom of the Opera* at $19 000 000.

Least insecure ■ Ben Vereen was given a 20-week guarantee of $52 500 per week plus a cut of

the 'box office' in the Broadway production *Pippin* in 1986.

Most roles ■ The greatest recorded number of theatrical, film and television roles is 3385 from 1951 to March 1989 by Jan Leighton (US).

Most theatrical roles ■ Kanzaburo Nakamura (b. July 1909) has performed in 806 Kabuki titles from November 1926 to January 1987. As each title in this classical Japanese theatrical form lasts 25 days, he has therefore played 20 150 performances.

Shakespeare ■ The first all-amateur company to have staged all 37 plays was The Southsea Shakespeare Actors, Hants (founded 1947) in October 1966 when, under K. Edmonds Gateley MBE, they presented *Cymbeline*. The longest is *Hamlet* with 4042 lines and 29 551 words. Of Shakespeare's 1277 speaking parts the longest is Hamlet with 11 610 words.

Longest chorus line ■ The longest chorus line in performing history numbered up to 120 in some of the early Ziegfeld's Follies. In the finale of *A Chorus Line* on the night of 29 Sep 1983 when it broke the record as the longest-running Broadway show ever, 332 top-hatted 'strutters' performed on stage.

Highest cabaret fee ■ Dolly Parton received up to $400 000 per live concert. Johnny Carson's fee for the non-televised Sears Roebuck Centenary Gala in October 1984 was set at $1 million.

Ice shows ■ Holiday on Ice Production Inc., founded by Morris Chalfen in 1945, stages the world's most costly live entertainment with up to seven productions playing simultaneously in several of 75 countries. By 8 Mar 1988 the show had been seen by 250 000 000 spectators. The total skating and other staff exceeds 900. The most prolific producer of ice shows was Gerald Palmer (1908–83) with 137 since 1945 including 34 consecutive shows at the Empire Pool, Wembley, London with attendances up to 850 000. Hazel Wendy Jolly (b. 1933) has appeared in the Wembley Winter Pantomime for 27 years.

Most ardent theatre-goers ■ Dr H. Howard Hughes (b. 1902), Professor Emeritus of Texas Wesleyan College, Fort Worth, Texas, USA has attended 6136 shows in the period 1956–87. Britain's leading 'first nighter' Edward Sutro MC (1900–78) saw 3000 first-night productions from 1916–56 and possibly more than 5000 in his 60 years of theatre-going. The highest precisely recorded number of theatre attendances in Britain is 3687 shows in 33 years from 28 Mar 1953 to his death on 10 Sep 1986 by John Iles of Salisbury, Wilts.

Arts festival ■ The world's largest arts festival is the annual Edinburgh Festival Fringe (instituted in 1947). In 1985, 510 groups gave 9424 performances of 1091 shows between 9 and 31 Aug. Professor Gerald Berkowitz of Northern Illinois University attended a record 145 separate performances at the 1979 Festival from 15 Aug–8 Sep.

Fashion shows ■ The most prolific producer of fashion shows is Adalene Ross of San Francisco, California, USA with totals over 4721 to April 1989.

Recorded Sound

Origins ■ The gramophone (phonograph) was first conceived by Charles Cros (1842–88), a French poet and scientist, who described his idea in sealed papers deposited in the French Academy of Sciences on 30 Apr 1877. However, the realisation of a practical device was first achieved by Thomas Alva Edison (1847–1931) of the USA. The first successful wax cylinder machine was constructed by his mechanic, John Kruesi, on 4–6 Dec 1877, demonstrated on 7 Dec and patented on 19 Feb 1878. The horizontal disc was introduced by Emile Berliner (1851–1929) and first demonstrated in Philadelphia on 18 May 1888.

Earliest recordings ■ The earliest birthdate of anyone whose voice is recorded is that of Lajos Kossuth (b. 9 Sep 1802 d. 24 Mar 1894), former Governor of Hungary whose speech in Torino, Italy on 20 Sep 1890 is still preserved on a wax cylinder in the National Széchényi Library in Budapest, Hungary. The earliest-born recorded singer was Peter Schram, the Danish baritone of whom a cylinder was made in the role of Don Giovanni on his 70th birthday on 5 Sep 1889.

Tape recording ■ Magnetic recording was invented by Valdemar Poulsen (1869–1942) of Denmark with his steel wire Telegraphone in 1898 (US Pat. No. 661619). Fritz Pfleumer (German Patent 500900) introduced tape in 1928.

Tapes were first used at the Blattner Studios, Elstree, Herts in 1929. Plastic tapes were devised by BASF of Germany in 1932–5, but were not marketed until 1950 by Recording Associates of New York. In April 1983 Olympic Optical Industry Co of Japan marketed a

micro-cassette recorder 10·7 × 5·1 × 1·4 cm *4·2 × 2 × 0·55 in* weighing 125 g *4·4 oz.*

Oldest records ■ The BBC record library contains over 1 000 000 records, including 5250 with no known matrix. The oldest records in the library are white wax cylinders dating from 1888. The earliest commercial disc recording was manufactured in 1895. The world's largest private collection is believed to be that of Stan Kilarr (b. 1915) of Klamath Falls, Oregon, USA with some 500 000.

Smallest functional record ■ Six titles of 33·3 mm *1⁵/₁₆ in* diameter were recorded by HMV's studio at Hayes, Middlesex on 26 Jan 1923 for Queen Mary's Dolls' House. Some 92 000 of these miniature records were pressed including 35 000 of 'God Save The King' (Bb 2439).

Phonographic identification ■ Dr Arthur B. Lintgen (b. 1932) of Rydal, Pennsylvania, USA, has an as yet unique and proven ability to identify the music on phonograph records purely by visual inspection without hearing a note.

Earliest jazz records ■ *Indiana* and *The Dark Town Strutters Ball* were recorded for the Columbia label in New York on or about 30 Jan 1917, by the Original Dixieland Jazz Band, led by Dominick (Nick) James La Rocca (1889–1961). This was released on 31 May 1917. The first jazz record to be released was the ODJB's *Livery Stable Blues* (recorded 26 Feb),

THE GUINNESS JUKEBOX OF RECORDS

Earliest ● The first jukebox was the result of an idea by Louis Glass, the general manager of the Pacific Phonograph Co. As an experiment he fitted a coin slot on an Edison battery-operated phonograph and hired it out to the Palais Royale Saloon, San Francisco, USA on 23 Nov 1889. Louis Glass installed four listening tubes and for a 'Nickel-in-the-slot' the customer received about two minutes of musical entertainment. The idea was an enormous success and by 1939 an estimated 300000 juke-boxes

were in use, absorbing 30 million discs per year. **Most popular ●** The most popular jukebox of all time is the Model 1015 (see artwork) produced by Paul Fuller for Wurlitzer. During 1946-47, to accompany

the shipment of more than 56000 models, Wurlitzer devised the largest promotional campaign in jukebox history. Magazine advertisements, and billboards across the USA proclaimed, and persuaded America, that 'Wurlitzer is Jukebox'.

Artwork: Peter Harper

US TOP 10 JUKEBOX SINGLES OF ALL TIME	3. Rock Around the Clock Bill Haley & the Comets. 1955	6. Mack the Knife Bobby Darin. 1959	9. Old Time Rock & Roll Bob Seger. 1979
1. Hound Dog/Don't Be Cruel Elvis Presley 1956	4. The Dock of the Bay Otis Redding. 1968	7. Light My Fire The Doors. 1967	10. My Girl The Temptations. 1965
2. Crazy Patsy Cline. 1961	5. I Heard It Through the Grapevine Marvin Gaye. 1968	8. Blueberry Hill Fats Domino. 1956	© 1988 Amusement & Music Operators Association

backed by *The Dixie Jass Band One-Step* (recorded 26 Feb), released by Victor on 7 Mar 1917.

Most successful singer ■ The most successful singer is Madonna (Madonna Louise Veronica Ciccone, Mrs Sean Penn, b. 16 Aug 1959). Her album *True Blue*, with sales of over 11 million, was a number one LP in 28 countries – a totally unprecedented achievement. Up to March 1989 she had a total of 17 British Top Ten hits. *Like a Prayer* gave her her sixth No. 1 single, increasing her lead over her nearest female rival, Sandie Shaw, who has three. Her first three albums together sold 3 million copies in Britain. In 1986 she became the first woman ever to top the annual sales tabulations for both singles and albums, massively outselling all other recording artists. Two of her albums *Like a Virgin* (1985), and *True Blue* (1986) have contained 5 Top Five singles.

Most successful solo recording artist ■ No independently audited figures have ever been published for Elvis Aron Presley (1935–77). In view of Presley's world-wide tally of over 170 major hits on singles and over 80 top-selling albums from 1956 continuing after his death, it may be assumed that it was he who must have succeeded Bing Crosby as the top-selling solo artist of all time.

On 9 Jun 1960 the Hollywood Chamber of Commerce presented Harry Lillis (*alias* Bing) Crosby Jr (1904–77) with a platinum disc to commemorate the alleged sale of 200 000 000 records from the 2600 singles and 125 albums he had recorded. On 15 Sep 1970 he received a second platinum disc when Decca claimed a sale of 300 650 000 discs. No independently audited figures of his global lifetime sales have ever been published and figures are considered exaggerated.

Most successful group ■ The singers with the greatest sales of any group have been The Beatles. This group from Liverpool, Merseyside comprised George Harrison MBE (b. 25 Feb 1943), John Ono (formerly John Winston) Lennon MBE (b. 9 Oct 1940–k. 8 Dec 1980), James Paul McCartney MBE (b. 18 Jun 1942)

and Richard Starkey MBE *alias* Ringo Starr (b. 7 Jul 1940). The all-time Beatles sales by May 1985 have been estimated by EMI at over 1000 million discs and tapes.

All four ex-Beatles sold many million further records as solo artists. Since their break-up in 1970, it is estimated that the most successful group in the world in terms of record sales is the Swedish foursome ABBA (Agnetha Faltskog, Anni-Frid Lyngstad, Bjorn Ulvaeus and Benny Andersson) with total sales of 215 million discs and tapes by May 1985.

Most successful all-girl group *UK* ■ The most successful all-girl group in the history of the UK singles chart is Bananarama. Between 1982 and 1988 the group, comprising Keren Woodward, Sarah Dallin and Siobhan Fahey, scored 15 consecutive hits on their own, and a further two in partnership with the Funboy Three. Fahey left the group to pursue a solo career after marrying Eurythmics' Dave Stewart in 1988, and was replaced by Jacqui O'Sullivan.

Earliest golden discs ■ The earliest recorded piece eventually to aggregate a total sale of a million copies was performances by Enrico Caruso (b. Naples, Italy, 1873, d. 2 Aug 1921) of the aria 'Vesti la giubba' ('On with the Motley') from the opera *I Pagliacci* by Ruggiero Leoncavallo (1858–1919), the earliest version of which was recorded with piano on 12 Nov 1902.

The first single recording to surpass the million mark was Alma Gluck's *Carry Me Back to Old Virginny* on the Red Seal Victor label on the twelve-inch *30·48 cm* single faced (later backed) record 74420.

The first actual golden disc was one sprayed by RCA

Victor for the US trombonist and band-leader Alton 'Glenn' Miller (1904–44) for his *Chattanooga Choo Choo* on 10 Feb 1942.

Most golden discs ■ The only *audited* measure of gold, platinum and multiplatinum singles and albums within the United States is certification by the Recording Industry Association of America introduced 14 Mar 1958. Out of the 2582 RIAA awards made to 1 Jan 1985, The Beatles with 47 (plus one with Billy Preston) have most for a group. Paul McCartney has 27 more awards outside the group and with Wings (including one with Stevie Wonder and one with Michael Jackson).

The most awards to an individual is 51 to Elvis Presley (1935–77) spanning the period 1958 to 1 Jan 1986. Globally, however, Presley's total of million-selling singles has been authoritatively placed at 'approaching 80'.

Most recordings ■ Miss Lata Mangeshkar (b. 1928) between 1948 and 1987 has reportedly recorded not less than 30 000 solo, duet and chorus-backed songs in 20 Indian languages. She frequently had five sessions in a day and has 'backed' in excess of 2000 films.

In the period between February 1987 and May 1989, Genesis P. Orridge and his band Psychic TV released 14 live albums on Temple Records. The albums are part of a series of 23.

Biggest sellers (Singles) ■ The greatest seller of any gramophone record to date is *White Christmas* by Irving Berlin (b. Israel Bailin, at Tyumen, Russia, 11 May 1888) and recorded by Bing Crosby on 29 May 1942. It was announced on Christmas Eve 1987 that North American sales alone reached 170 884 207 copies by 30 Jun 1987.

The highest claim for any 'pop' record is an unaudited 25 000 000 for *Rock Around the Clock*, copyrighted in 1953 by James E. Myers under the name Jimmy DeKnight and the late Max C. Freedmann and recorded on 12 Apr 1954 by Bill Haley (1927–1981) and the Comets.

The top-selling British record of all time is *I Want to Hold Your Hand* by The Beatles, released in 1963, with world sales of over 13 000 000.

The top selling single of all time in the UK is *Do They Know It's Christmas*, written and produced by Bob Geldof and Midge Ure, with 3·6 million by May 1987 with a further 8·1 million world-wide. The profits were in aid of the Ethiopian Famine Relief Fund and are now estimated to be over £90 million.

The only female solo artist to have a million-selling single in the UK is Jennifer Rush, whose single *The Power of Love* was certified in 1985. Forty-five other singles by groups, duos or male soloists have sold a million copies in the UK. The best-selling female duet in the UK is *I Know Him So Well* by Elaine Page and Barbara Dickson with sales of over 820 000 to May 1987.

Biggest sellers (Albums) ■ The best selling album of all time is *Thriller* by Michael Jackson (b. Gary, Indiana, USA 29 Aug 1958) with global sales of 40 million copies by May 1988.

The best selling album by a group is Fleetwood Mac's *Rumours* with over 20 million sales to May 1987.

The best selling album by a British group is *Dark Side of the Moon* by Pink Floyd with sales audited at 19·5 million to December 1986.

The best-selling album in Britain is Dire Straits' *Brothers in Arms*, with over three million sold by May 1988.

The best-selling album by a woman is *Whitney Houston* by Whitney Houston released in 1985. It had sold over 14 million copies by May 1987, including over 9 million in America, one million in the UK, and a further million in Canada. This is also the best-selling debut album of all time.

The best-selling movie soundtrack is *Saturday Night Fever* with sales of over 26·5 million to May 1987.

The charts (US Singles) ■ Singles record charts were first published by *Billboard* on 20 Jul 1940 when the No. 1 was *I'll Never Smile Again* by Tommy Dorsey (1905–56). *Near You* by Francis Craig stayed at the No. 1 spot for 17 weeks in 1947. *Tainted Love* by Soft Cell stayed on the chart for 43 consecutive weeks from January 1982.

The Beatles have had the most No. 1s (20), Conway Twitty the most Country No. 1s (35) and Aretha Franklin the most Black No. 1s (20). Aretha Franklin is also the female solo artist with the most million-selling singles with 14 between 1967 and 1973. Elvis Presley has had the most hit singles on *Billboard*'s Hot 100–149 from 1956 to April 1989.

The charts (US Albums) ■ Billboard first published an album chart on 15 Mar 1945 when the No. 1 was *King Cole Trio* featuring Nat 'King' Cole

(1919–65). *South Pacific* was No. 1 for 69 weeks (non-consecutive) from May 1949. *Dark Side of the Moon* by Pink Floyd (see above) enjoyed 730 weeks on the *Billboard* charts to April 1989.

The Beatles had the most No. 1s (15), Elvis Presley was the most successful male soloist (9), and Simon and Garfunkel the top duo with three. Elvis Presley has had the most hit albums (94 from 1956 – April 1989).

The woman with the most No. 1 albums (6), and most hit albums in total (40 between 1963 and April 1989), is Barbra Streisand, 30 of which have been certified gold (500 000 sales) or platinum (1 million sales) by the RIAA, making Streisand the best-selling female singer of all time.

The charts (UK Singles) ■ Singles record charts were first published in Britain on 14 Nov 1952 by *New Musical Express*. *I Believe* by Frankie Laine (b. 30 Mar 1913) held No. 1 position for 18 weeks (non-consecutive) from April 1953, with *Rose Marie* by Slim Whitman (b. 20 Jan 1924) the consecutive record holder with 11 weeks from July 1955.

The longest stay has been the 122 weeks of *My Way* by Francis Albert Sinatra (b. 12 Dec 1915) in ten separate runs from 2 Apr 1969 to 1972.

The record for most consecutive weeks on the chart is 56 weeks for Engelbert Humperdinck's *Release Me* from 26 Jan 1967. The Beatles and Presley hold the record for most No. 1 hits with 17 each, with Presley having an overall record of 106 hits in the UK singles chart from 1956 to May 1987.

The charts (UK Albums) ■ The first British album chart was published on 8 Nov 1958 by *Melody Maker*. The first No. 1 LP was the film soundtrack *South Pacific* which held the position for a record 70 consecutive weeks and eventually achieved a record 115 weeks at No. 1.

The album with the most total weeks on chart is *Rumours* by Fleetwood Mac with 420 weeks by May 1988. The Beatles have had most No 1 albums—12; and Elvis Presley the most hit albums—91.

The youngest female soloist to have a No. 1 album in Britain is Kylie Minogue (b. Melbourne, Australia, 28 May 1968), who was 20 years old when her debut album *Kylie* topped the chart in July 1988. Kylie also holds the record for the best-ever start to a singles chart career, with her first five singles peaking at No. 1, 2, 2, 2 and 2 respectively.

Fastest-selling non-pop albums ■ The fastest-selling non-pop record of all time is *John Fitzgerald Kennedy—A Memorial Album* (Premium Albums), recorded on 22 Nov 1963, the day of Mr Kennedy's assassination, which sold 4 000 000 copies at 99 cents in six days (7–12 Dec 1963), thus ironically beating the previous speed record set by the satirical LP *The First Family* in 1962–3.

The fastest-selling British record is the Beatles' double album *The Beatles* (Apple) with 'nearly 2 million' in its first week in November 1968.

Advance sales ■ The greatest advance sale for a single world-wide is 2 100 000 for *Can't Buy Me Love* by the Beatles. Released 21 Mar 1964, it also holds the British record of 1 million jointly with another Beatles single, *I Want to Hold Your Hand*, released 29 Nov 1963. The UK record for advance sales of an album is 1 100 000 for *Welcome to the Pleasure Dome*, the debut album by Frankie Goes To Hollywood from 1984.

Fastest live recording to retail ■ A limited edition of Midge Ure's *Dear God* single including two live tracks *All Fall Down* and *Strange Brew* on the B-side was delivered to retail 81 hrs 15 min after the live performance at The Venue, Edinburgh on 21 Nov 1988 at which the tracks were recorded.

Most song titles - DJ challenge ■ On 10 Mar 1989, disc-jockey John Murray played 26 song titles from two decks in two minutes at Viewforth High School, Kirkcaldy, Fife, Scotland.

Compact discs ■ Announced by Philips in 1978, and introduced by the same company in 1982, the compact disc (CD) increasingly challenges the LP and cassette as a recording medium.

The first CD to sell a million copies world-wide was Dire Straits' *Brothers in Arms* in 1986. It subsequently topped a million sales in Europe alone including over 250 000 in Britain–both records.

Most Grammy awards ■ The all time record of

28 awards is held by Sir Georg Solti KBE the British conductor born in Budapest, Hungary 22 Oct 1912 which he has won since 1958.

The greatest number won in a year is eight by Michael Jackson in 1984.

Photography

CAMERAS

Earliest ■ The earliest veiled reference to a photograph on glass taken in a camera was in a letter dated 19 Jul 1822 from Joseph Nicéphore Niépce (1765–1833), a French scientist. It was a photograph of a copper engraving of Pope Pius VII taken at Gras, near Chalon-sur-Saône, France and it was rediscovered in London in February 1952 by the photohistorian Helmut Gernsheim after 6 years' research. The earliest photograph taken in England was one of a diamond-paned window in Laycock (or Lacock) Abbey, Wilts taken in August 1835 by William Henry Fox Talbot, MP (1800–77), the inventor of the negative-positive process. The negative of this was donated to the Science Museum, London in 1937 by his grand–daughter Matilda. The world's earliest aerial photograph was taken in 1858 by Gaspard Félix Tournachon (1820–1910), *alias* Nadar, from a balloon near Villacoublay, on the outskirts of Paris.

Largest ■ The largest and most expensive industrial camera ever built is the 27 tonne Rolls Royce camera now owned by Maxwell Data Management of Derby commissioned in 1956. It measures 2·69 m *8 ft 10 in* high, 2·51 m *8 ¼ ft* wide and 14·02 m *46 ft* in length. The lens is a 160 cm *63 in* f 16 Cooke Apochromatic, the bellows were made by Camera Bellows Ltd of Birmingham. In 1989 it was still in full use.

Smallest ■ Apart from cameras built for intra-cardiac surgery and espionage, the smallest that has been marketed is the circular Japanese 'Petal' camera with a diameter of 2·9 cm *1·14 in* and a thickness of 1·65 cm *0.65 in*. It has a focal length of 12 mm *0·47 in*. The BBC TV programme *Record Breakers* showed prints from this camera on 3 Dec 1974.

Fastest ■ A camera built for research into high-power lasers by The Blackett Laboratory of Imperial College of Science and Technology, London, registers images at a rate of 33 000 million per sec.

Most expensive ■ The most expensive complete range of camera equipment in the world is that of Nikon Corporation of Tokyo, Japan, who marketed in April 1989 their complete range of 29 cameras with 83 lenses and 657 accessories. Fox Talbot of London quoted £132 673·69 excluding VAT. The highest auction price for an antique camera is £21 000 for a J. B. Dancer stereo camera, patented in 1856 and sold at Christie's, South Kensington on 12 Oct 1977.

Longest negative ■ On 1 Jul 1988 Christopher Creighton of Port Hope, Ontario, Canada using a 24 in focal length Turner-Reich lens, fitted to a Kodak 8 Cirkut camera, made a portrait of an estimated 1500 inhabitants of Port Hope achieving a 355 degree view in a single shot. The resulting negative measured 362 cm × 19·7 cm *11 ft 10½ in × 7¾ in.*

Most expensive photograph ■ A photograph taken by Edward Weston in 1927 of a nautilus shell was sold at Sotheby's New York, USA, in April 1989 for $115 000 (£66 500).

Cinema

FILMS

The earliest motion pictures ever taken were by Louis Aimé Augustin Le Prince (1842–90). He was attested to have achieved dim moving outlines on a whitewashed wall at the Institute for the Deaf, Washington Heights, New York, USA as early as 1885–87. The earliest surviving film (sensitised 53·9 mm *2⅛ in* wide paper roll) is from his camera,

Most expensive personal movie prop ● These ruby slippers, worn by Judy Garland in the 1939 film *The Wizard of Oz*, were sold on 2 Jun 1988 to a mystery buyer at Christie's, New York, USA for $165 000. (Photo: Christie's)

patented in Britain on 16 Nov 1888, taken in early October 1888 of the garden of his father-in-law, Joseph Whitley, in Roundhay, Leeds, West Yorks at 10 to 12 frames per second. The first commercial presentation of motion pictures was at Holland Bros' Kinetoscope Parlor at 1155 Broadway, New York City, USA on 14 Apr 1894. Viewers could see five films for 25 cents or 10 for 50 cents from a double row of Kinetoscopes developed by William Kennedy Laurie Dickson (1860–1935), assistant to Thomas Alva Edison (1847–1931) in 1889–91. The earliest publicly presented film on a *screen* was *La Sortie des Ouvriers de l'Usine Lumière* probably shot in August or September 1894 in Lyon, France. It was exhibited at 44 rue de Rennes, Paris, France on 22 Mar 1895 by the Lumière brothers, Auguste Marie Louis Nicholas (1862–1954) and Louis Jean (1864–1948).

Earliest 'talkie' ■ The earliest sound-on-film motion picture was achieved by Eugene Augustin Lauste (1857–1935) who patented his process on 11 Aug 1906 and produced a workable system using a string galvanometer in 1910 at Benedict Road, Stockwell, London. The earliest public presentation of sound on film was by the Tri-ergon process at the Alhambra cinema, Berlin, Germany on 17 Sep 1922.

Largest output ■ Indian production of feature length films was a record 807 in 1987.

Most expensive film ■ The highest ever budgeted film has been $69 million for *Rambo III* released in May 1988 starring Sylvester Stallone. He thereby became history's highest paid actor with receipts of £10 500 000 (see opposite).

Least expensive full–length feature film ■ The total cost of production for the 1927 film *The Shattered Illusion*, by Victorian Film Productions, was £300. It took twelve months to complete and

included spectacular scenes of a ship being overwhelmed by a storm.

Most expensive film rights ■ The highest price ever paid for film rights was $9 500 000 announced on 20 Jan 1978 by Columbia for *Annie*, the Broadway musical by Charles Strouse starring Andrea McCardle, Dorothy Loudon and Reid Shelton.

Longest film ■ The longest film ever made was the 85-hr *The Cure for Insomnia* in 1987. It was directed by John Henry Timmis IV and premièred in its entirety at the School of Art Institute, Chicago, USA on 31 Jan 1987.

Longest-running film ■ *Emmanuelle* opened on 26 Jun 1974 at the Paramount City, Paris, France and closed on 26 Feb 1985 – the longest continuous run of any one film at one cinema.

Highest box office gross ■ The box office gross champion is Steven Spielberg's *ET:The Extra-Terrestrial*, released on 11 Jun 1982, which has earned a gross $700 million. On 27 May 1989 *Indiana Jones and the Last Crusade* (Paramount) grossed $11 200 000 for a single day record. The highest opening day gross was scored by *Return of the Jedi* on 25 May 1983 with a take of $6 219 629 at 1002 sites.

Largest loss ■ Michael Cimino's 1980 production *Heaven's Gate* took $1·5 million in North American rentals against an estimated negative cost of $44 million and a total cost, including distribution and overheads, of $57 million.

Most violent ■ The National Coalition on Television Violence has listed 123 deaths and 245 separate acts of violence in 109 minutes of *Rambo III*. Sylvester Stallone, as a one man fighting machine, fends off the Soviet Army single-handedly.

Most destructive chase sequence ■ Over 150 vehicles including two Cadillac Eldorados, two Chrysler Magnums, numerous boats, trucks and motorcycles and two Pitts high-performance aeroplanes were wrecked in H. B. Halicki's 1982 film *The Junkman*.

Highest earnings ■ The highest rate of pay in cinema history is that paid to Sylvester Stallone (b. New York, USA 6 Jul 1946). Having received $12 million each for *Cobra* and *Over the Top* plus, shares of box office, Stallone received $19 500 000 for *Rambo III* (see left) which surpassed the $18·5 million received by Marlon Brando for his nine minutes of screen time in *Superman*. The highest-paid actresses are Meryl Streep (b. Summit, NJ, USA 1949) with $4 million for *Out of Africa* and the same for *Heartburn*, and Barbra Streisand with $5 million for *Nuts*.Stuntman Dar Robinson was paid $100 000 for the 335 m *1100 ft* leap from the CN Tower, Toronto, Canada in November 1979 for *High Point*. His parachute opened just 91 m *300 ft* above ground. He died 21 Nov 1986 (aged 39).

Longest series still continuing ■ Japan's *Tora-San* films have now stretched from *Tora-San I* in August 1969 to *Tora-San XL* in 1988 with Kiyoshi Atsumi (b. 1929) starring in each for Shochiku Co.

LONGEST MAKE-UP JOBS

Name of Film	Actor	Time (hours)
THE ILLUSTRATED MAN (USA, 1969)	Rod Steiger	20
AN AMERICAN WEREWOLF IN LONDON (GB, 1981)	David Naughton	10
A NIGHTMARE ON ELM ST IV (USA, 1989)	Robert Englund	7½
THE BRIDE OF FRANKENSTEIN (USA, 1935)	Boris Karloff	7
THE ELEPHANT MAN (GB, 1980)	John Hurt	7
KRULL (GB, 1983)	Francesca Annis	6½
THE HUNCHBACK OF NOTRE DAME (USA, 1939)	Charles Laughton	5½
THE PLANET OF THE APES (USA, 1968)	Roddy McDowall*	5
LITTLE BIG MAN (USA, 1970)	Dustin Hoffman	5
NOSFERATU (WEST GERMANY, 1979)	Klaus Kinski	5

*and other principal apes.

Most portrayed character ■ The character most frequently recurring on the screen is Sherlock Holmes, created by Sir Arthur Conan Doyle (1859–1930). He has been portrayed by 70 actors in 197 films between 1900 and 1988.

In horror films the character most often portrayed is Count Dracula, created by the Irish writer Bram Stoker (1847–1912). Representations of the Count or his immediate descendants outnumber those of his closest rival, Frankenstein's monster, by 155 to 109.

Largest number of extras ■ It is believed that over 300 000 extras appeared in the funeral scene of Sir Richard Attenborough's *Gandhi* (1982).

Largest studios ■ The largest complex of film studios in the world is that at Universal City, Los Angeles, California, USA. The Back Lot contains 561 buildings and there are 34 sound stages on the 170 ha *420 acre* site.

Largest studio stage ■ The world's largest studio stage is the 007 stage at Pinewood Studios, Bucks. It was designed by Ken Adam and Michael Brown and built in 1976 for the James Bond film *The Spy Who Loved Me*. It measures 102 × 42 × 12 m *336 × 139 × 41 ft* and accommodated 4·54 million litres *1·2 million gallons* of water, a full–scale 600 000–ton oil tanker and three nuclear submarines.

Largest film set ■ The largest film set ever built was the 400 × 230 m *(1312 × 754 ft)* Roman Forum designed by Veniero Colosanti and John Moore for Samuel Bronston's production of *The Fall of the Roman Empire* (1964). It was built on a 22·25 ha *55 acre* site outside Madrid, Spain. 1100 workmen spent 7 months laying the surface of the Forum with

Largest number of costume changes by one person ● Here are just five of the 65 costumes worn by Elizabeth Taylor in the 1963 film *Cleopatra*. The costumes were designed by Irene Sharaff and cost $130 000. (Photo: Keystone, Popper, National Film Archive, Rex Features)

170 000 cement blocks, erecting 6705 m *22 000 ft* of concrete stairways, 601 colums and 350 statues, and constructing 27 full-size buildings.

The largest indoor set was the UFO landing site built for the climax of Steven Spielberg's *Close Encounters of the Third Kind*. The 137 × 786 × 27 m *450 × 250 × 90 ft* set was constructed inside a 3·53 million m³ *10 million ft³* dirigible hangar at Mobile, Alabama, USA. The structure included 6·4 km *4 miles* of scaffolding, 1570 m² *16 900 ft²* of fibreglass, 2740 m² *29 500 ft²* of nylon canopy and 'enough concrete to make a full-scale replica of the Washington monument'.

Longest directorial career ■ The directorial career of King Vidor (1894–1982) lasted for 66 years, beginning with the two-reel comedy *The Tow* and culminating in another short, a documentary called *The Metaphor*.

Oldest director ■ Joris Ivens (b. Netherlands 1898) directed the Franco-Italian co-production *Le Vent* in 1988 at the age of 89. He made his directorial debut with the Dutch film *De Brug* in 1928.
George Cukor (1899–1983) was Hollywood's oldest director. In October 1980, at 81 years old, he was signed by MGM to direct the film *Rich and Famous* starring Jacqueline Bisset and Candice Bergen.

Most generations of screen actors in a family ■ There are four generations of screen actors in the Redgrave family. Roy Redgrave (1872–1922) made his screen debut in 1911 and continued to appear in Australian films until 1920. Sir Michael Redgrave married actress Rachel Kempson and their two daughters Vanessa and Lynn and son Corin all went into films. Vanessa's two daughters Joely and Natasha and Corin's daughter Jemma are already successful actresses with films such as *Wetherby*, *A Month in the Country* and *The Dream Demon* to their respective credit.

Largest number of costumes ■ The largest number of costumes for any one film was 32 000 for the 1951 film *Quo Vadis*.

Largest number of costume changes by one person ■ Elizabeth Taylor changed costume 65 times in *Cleopatra* (1963). The costumes were designed by Irene Sharaff and cost $130 000.

Most expensive costume ■ Constance Bennett's sable coat in *Madam X* was valued at $50 000. The most expensive costume designed and made specially for a film was Edith Head's mink and sequins dance costume worn by Ginger Rogers in *Lady in the Dark*. It cost Paramount $35 000.

Most expensive personal movie prop ■ The ruby slippers, worn by Judy Garland in the 1939 film *The Wizard of Oz*, were sold on 2 Jun 1988 to a mystery buyer at Christie's, New York, USA for $165 000.

Most Oscars ■ Walter (Walt) Elias Disney (1901–66) won more 'Oscars' – the awards of the United States Academy of Motion Picture Arts and

Sciences, instituted on 16 May 1929 and named after Mr Oscar Pierce of Texas, USA – than any other person. The physical count comprises 20 statuettes and 12 other plaques and certificates including posthumous awards. The only person to win four Oscars in a starring role has been Miss Katharine Hepburn, formerly Mrs Ludlow Ogden Smith (b. Hartford, Conn., USA, 9 Nov 1909) in *Morning Glory* (1932–3), *Guess Who's Coming to Dinner* (1967), *The Lion in Winter* (1968) and *On Golden Pond* (1981). She has been nominated 12 times. Only four actors have won two Oscars in starring roles—Frederic March in 1931/32 and 1946, Spencer Tracy in 1937 and 1938, Gary Cooper in 1941 and 1952, and Marlon Brando in 1954 and 1972. Edith Head (Mrs Wiard B. Ihnen) (1907–81) won eight individual awards for costume design. The film with most awards has been *Ben Hur* (1959) with 11. That with the highest number of nominations was *All About Eve* (1950) with 14. It won six (Best Supporting Actor: George Sanders, Best Picture, Best Costume Design: Edith Head, Charles Le Maire, Best Director: Joseph L. Mankiewicz, Best Sound Recording, Best Screenplay: Joseph L. Mankiewicz). The youngest ever winner was Shirley Temple (b. 24 Apr 1928) aged five with her honorary Oscar, and the oldest George Burns (b. 20 Jan 1896) aged 80 for *The Sunshine Boys* in 1976.

Versatility show-business awards ■ The only three performers to have won Oscar, Emmy, Tony and Grammy awards have been Helen Hayes (b. 1900) in 1932–1976; Richard Rodgers (1902–1979), composer of musicals, and Rita Moreno (b. 1931) in 1961–1977. Barbra Streisand (b. 24 Apr 1942 in Brooklyn, New York, USA) received Oscar, Grammy and Emmy awards in addition to a special 'Star of the Decade' Tony award.

Most honoured entertainer ■ The most honoured entertainer in history is Bob Hope (né Leslie Townes Hope, Eltham, London; 29 May 1903). He has been uniquely awarded the USA's highest civilian honours – the Medal of Freedom (1969); Congressional Gold Medal (1963); Medal of Merit (1966); Distinguished Public Service Medal (1973); Distinguished Service Gold Medal (1971) and is also an Hon. CBE (1976) and was appointed Hon. Brigadier of the US Marine Corps. He also has 44 honorary degrees.

CINEMAS

Earliest ■ The earliest structure designed and exclusively used for exhibiting projected films is believed to be one erected at the Atlanta Show, Georgia, USA in October 1895 to exhibit C. F. Jenkins' phantoscope. The earliest attempt at establishing a cinema in Britain was made by Birt Acres, whose Kineopticon opened at 2 Piccadilly Mansions at the junction of Piccadilly Circus and Shaftesbury Avenue on 21 Mar 1896. After only a few weeks, the cinema was gutted by fire.

Largest ■ The largest cinema in the world is the Radio City Music Hall, New York City, USA, opened on 27 Dec 1932 with 5945 (now 5874) seats. Cineplex, opened at the Toronto Eaton Centre, Canada on 19 Apr 1979, has 18 separate theatres with an aggregate capacity of 1700.

Great Britain **■** The Odeon, Leicester Square, London, has 1983 seats.

Most and least cinemas ■ The country with the largest number of cinemas in relation to population is San Marino, with one cinema for every 3190 inhabitants (a total of seven). In comparison the USA has one cinema for every 11 000 inhabitants and the UK has one cinema for every 45 000 inhabitants. Saudi Arabia (population 8 million) has no cinemas, the public presentation of films being illegal as contrary to strict Islamic belief.

Highest cinema-going ■ The Chinese Ministry of Culture reported in September 1987 that there were 21 000 million cinema attendances in 1986—or nearly 21 per person per annum.

Biggest screen ■ The permanently installed cinema screen with the largest area is one of 28·28 ×

21·48 m *92³/₄ ft × 70¹/₂ ft* in the Keong Emas Imax Theatre, Taman Mini Park, Jakarta, Indonesia opened on 20 Apr 1984. It was made by Harkness Screens Ltd at Borehamwood, Herts. A temporary screen 90·5 m × 10 m *297 ft × 33 ft* was used at the 1937 Paris Exposition.

Most films seen ■ Albert E. van Schmus (b. 1921) saw 16 945 films in 32 years (1949–1982) as a rater for Motion Picture Association of America Inc.

Radio

The earliest patent for telegraphy without wires (wireless) was received by Dr Mahlon Loomis (USA) (1826–86). It was entitled 'Improvement in Telegraphy' and was dated 20 Jul 1872 (US Pat. No. 129 971). He in fact demonstrated only potential differences on a galvanometer between two kites 22 km *14 miles* apart in Loudoun County, Virginia, USA in October 1866.

Earliest patent ■ The first patent for a system of communication by means of electro-magnetic waves, numbered No. 12039, was granted on 2 Jun 1896 to the Italian-Irish Marchese Guglielmo Marconi (1874–1937). A public demonstration of wireless transmission of speech was, however, given in the town square of Murray, Kentucky, USA in 1892 by Nathan B. Stubblefield. He died destitute on 28 Mar 1928. The first permanent wireless installation was at The Needles on the Isle of Wight, by Marconi's Wireless Telegraph Co Ltd, in November 1897.

Earliest broadcast ■ The world's first advertised broadcast was made on 24 Dec 1906 by the Canadian-born Professor Reginald Aubrey Fessenden (1868–1932) from the 128 m *420 ft* mast of the National Electric Signalling Company at Brant Rock, Massachusetts, USA. The transmission included Handel's *Largo*. Fessenden had achieved the broadcast of speech as early as November 1900 but this was highly distorted.

The first experimental broadcasting transmitter in Great Britain was set up at the Marconi Works in Chelmsford, Essex in December 1919, and broadcast a news service in February 1920. The earliest regular broadcast was made from the Marconi transmitter '2MT' at Writtle, Essex on 14 Feb 1922.

Transatlantic transmissions ■ The earliest claim to have received wireless signals (the letter S in Morse Code) across the Atlantic was made by Marconi, George Stephen Kemp and Percy Paget from a 10 kW station at Poldhu, Cornwall, to Signal Hill, St John's, Newfoundland, Canada, at 12.30 p.m. on 12 Dec 1901. Human speech was first heard across the Atlantic in November 1915 when a transmission from the US Navy station at Arlington, Virginia was received by US radio-telephone engineers on the Eiffel Tower.

Earliest radio-microphones ■ The radio-microphone, which was in essence also the first 'bug', was devised by Reg Moores (GB) in 1947 and first used on 76 MHz in the ice show *Aladdin* at Brighton Sports Stadium, East Sussex, England in September 1949.

Longest BBC national broadcast ■ The reporting of the Coronation of Queen Elizabeth II on 2 Jun 1953 began at 10.15 a.m. and finished at 5.30 p.m., after 7 hr 15 min.

Longest continuous broadcast ■ The longest continuous broadcast (excluding disc-jockeying) has been one of 484 hr (20 days 4 hr) by Larry Norton of WGRQ FM Buffalo, New York State, USA from 19 Mar–8 Apr 1981. *No further claims for the above category will be entertained.* Radio Telefís Éireann transmitted an unedited reading of *Ulysses* by James Joyce (1882–1941) for 29 hr 38 min 47 sec on 16–17 Jul 1982.

Topmost prize ■ Mary Buchanan, 15, on WKRQ, Cincinnati, USA won a prize of $25 000 for 40 years (*viz* $1 million) on 21 Nov 1980.

Brain of Britain quiz ■ The youngest person to

become 'Brain of Britain' on BBC radio was Anthony Carr, 16, of Anglesey in 1956. The oldest contestant has been the author and translator Hugh Merrick (1898–1980) in his 80th year in August 1977. The record score is 35 by the 1981 winner Peter Barlow of Richmond, Surrey and Peter Bates of Taunton, Somerset who won the title in 1984.

Most durable programmes ■ CKNW's 'Roving Mike' programme with Bill Hughes has been broadcast six days a week in New Westminster, British Columbia, Canada since 1944. On 8 Oct 1987, the programme celebrated its 13 000th consecutive broadcast. The weekly sports report 'The Tenpin Tattler' was first broadcast on WCFL, Chicago, Illinois, USA on 24 Aug, 1935. Fifty three-years and 2756 broadcasts later, it still continues on WGN, Chicago.

BBC **■** The longest-running BBC radio series is *The Week's Good Cause* which began on 24 Jan 1926. The St Martin-in-the-Fields Christmas appeal by Canon Geoffrey Brown on 14 Dec 1986 raised a record £138 039. *Daily Service* began with an experimental broadcast on 2 Jan 1928 but it was transmitted only on Daventry 5XX. By December 1929 it was broadcast from all BBC transmitters.

The longest running record programme is *Desert Island Discs* which began on 29 Jan 1942 and on which programme only one guest, Arthur Askey CBE (1900–82), has been stranded a fourth time (on the 1572nd show on 20 Dec 1980). The programme was originally presented by its creator, Roy Plomley OBE, who died on 28 May 1985 having presented 1791 editions.

The longest-running solo radio feature is *Letter from America* by (Alfred) Alistair Cooke, Hon. KBE (b. Salford 20 Nov 1908), first broadcast on 24 Mar 1946. That on his 80th birthday was No. 2074. The longest-running radio serial is *The Archers* which was created by Godfrey Baseley and was first broadcast on 1 Jan 1951. On 26 May 1989 the 10 000th episode was transmitted – a total of 2500 hours plus an additional 1689 hours of omnibus. To coincide with this, the Post Office issued a Commemorative Cover to celebrate this milestone of broadcasting. Up to May 1989 the signature tune *Barwick Green* had been played approximately 43 000 times. The only role which has been played without interruption from the start has been that of Philip Archer by Norman Painting OBE (b. Leamington Spa, Warwicks 23 Apr 1924).

Earliest antipodal reception ■ Frank Henry Alfred Walker (b. 11 Nov 1904), on the night of 12 Nov 1924 at Crown Farm, Cuttimore Lane, Walton-on-Thames, Surrey, received on his home-made 2-valve receiver on 75 metres, signals from Marconi's yacht *Electra* (call sign ICCM) in Australian waters.

Most assiduous radio ham ■ The late Richard C. Spenceley of KV4AA at St Thomas, Virgin Islands built his contacts (QSOs) to a record level of 48 100 in 365 days in 1978.

Most stations ■ The country with the greatest number of radio broadcasting stations is the United States, where there were 9512 authorised broadcast stations as at April 1985 made up of both AM (amplitude modulation) and FM (frequency modulation).

Highest listening ■ The peak recorded listenership on BBC Radio was 30 000 000 adults on 6 Jun 1950 for the boxing match between Lee Savold (US) and Bruce Woodcock (GB) (b. Doncaster, South Yorks, 1921).

Highest response ■ The highest recorded response from a radio show occurred on 27 Nov 1974 when, on a 5-hr talk show on WCAU, Philadelphia, Pennsylvania, USA, astrologer Howard Sheldon registered a call count of 388 299 on the *Bill Corsair Show*.

Smallest set ■ The Toshiba AM-FM RP-1070 with inbuilt loudspeaker measures 9·0 × 5·4 × 1·3 cm *3·5 × 2·1 × 0·5 in* and with battery weighs 70 g *2·5 oz*.

Television

Invention ■ The invention of television, the instantaneous viewing of distant objects by electrical transmissions, was not an act but a process of successive and interdependent discoveries.

The first commercial cathode ray tube was introduced in 1897 by Karl Ferdinand Braun (1850–1918), but was not linked to 'electric vision' until 1907 by Professor Boris Rosing (disappeared 1918) of Russia in St Petersburg (Leningrad). A. A. Campbell Swinton FRS (1863–1930) published the fundamentals of television transmission on 18 Jun 1908 in a brief letter to *Nature* entitled 'Distant Electric Vision'.

The earliest public demonstration of television was given on 27 Jan 1926 by John Logie Baird (1888–1946) of Scotland, using a development of the mechanical scanning system patented by Paul Gottlieb Nipkow (1860–1940) on 6 Jan 1884. He had achieved the transmission of a Maltese Cross over 3·05 m *10 ft* at 8 Queen's Arcade, Hastings, East Sussex, England by February 1924 and the first facial image (of William Taynton, 15) at 22, Frith Street, London on 30 Oct 1925. Taynton had to be bribed with 2s6d. A patent application for the Iconoscope had been filed on 29 Dec 1923 by Dr Vladimir Kosma Zworykin (1889–1982) but was not issued until 20 Dec 1938. Kenjiro Takayanagi (b. 20 Jan 1899) succeeded in transmitting a 40-line electronic picture on 25 Dec 1926 with a Braun cathode ray tube and a Nipkow disc at Hamamatsu Technical College, Japan.

Baird launched his first television 'service' via a BBC transmitter on 30 Sep 1929 and marketed the first sets, Baird Televisors, at 26 guineas in May 1930.

Public transmissions on 30 lines were made from 22 Aug 1932 until 11 Sep 1935. It has been estimated that 6 million billion (6×10^{15}) electrons traverse a television tube each second.

Earliest service ■ The world's first high-definition (i.e. 405 lines) television broadcasting service was opened from Alexandra Palace, north London, on 2 Nov 1936, when there were about 100 sets in the United Kingdom. The chief engineer was Mr Douglas Birkinshaw. A television station in Berlin, Germany made a low-definition (180-line) transmission from 22 Mar 1935 but the transmitter burnt out in August that year.

Transatlantic transmission ■ On 9 Feb 1928 the image of J. L. Baird and of a Mrs Howe was transmitted from Station 2 KZ at Coulsdon, Surrey, England to Station 2 CVJ, Hartsdale, New York State, USA. The earliest transatlantic transmission by satellite was achieved at 1 a.m. on 11 Jul 1962, via the active satellite *Telstar 1* from Andover, Maine, USA to Pleumeur Bodou, France. The picture was of Frederick R. Kappell, chairman of the American Telephone and Telegraph Company, which owned the satellite. The first 'live' broadcast was made on 23 Jul 1962 and the first woman to appear was the *haute couturière* Ginette Spanier, directrice of Balmain, the next day.

Longest telecast ■ The longest pre-scheduled telecast on record was a continuous transmission for 163 hr 18 min by GTV 9 of Melbourne, Australia covering the Apollo XI moon mission from 19–26 Jul 1969. The longest continuous TV transmission under a single director was a show hosted by Scott Winters on TV-23, Wyoming, Michigan, USA from 31 Mar–2 Apr for 36 hr under the direction of Melissa Prusi.

Earliest video-tape recording ■ Alexander M. Poniatoff first demonstrated video-tape recording known as Ampex (his initials plus 'ex' for excellence) in 1956. The earliest demonstration of a home video recorder was on 24 Jun 1963 at the BBC News Studio at Alexandra Palace, London of the Telcan developed by Norman Rutherford and Michael Turner of the Nottingham Electronic Valve Co.

Fastest video production ■ Tapes of the Royal Wedding of HRH Prince Andrew and Miss Sarah Ferguson on 23 Jul 1986 were produced by Thames Video Collection. Live filming ended with the depar-

Longest-running domestic drama serial ● Wetherfield residents have spent many a cosy evening at *Coronation Street's* local, the Rover's Return. The serial has run twice weekly since 9 Dec 1960 with an additional omnibus edition every Sunday since 26 Jan 1989. (Photo: Popperfoto)

ture of the honeymoon couple from Chelsea Hospital by helicopter at 4.42 p.m. The first fully edited and packaged VHS tapes were purchased 5 hr 41 min later by Fenella Lee and Lucinda Burland of West Kensington at the Virgin Megastore in Oxford Street, London at 10.23 p.m.

Most durable shows ■ The world's most durable TV show is NBC's *Meet the Press*, first transmitted on 6 Nov 1947 and weekly since 12 Sep 1948, originated by Lawrence E. Spivak, who appeared weekly as either moderator or panel member until 1975. On 1 Jun 1986 Joe Franklin presented the 21 700th version of his show started in 1951. Since 1949 over 150 000 individual episodes of the TV show *Bozo the Clown*, by Larry Harmon Pictures, have been aired daily on 150 stations in the US and abroad. The greatest number of hours on camera on US national commercial television is 10 037 ½ by the TV personality Hugh Downs in over 43 years to 15 Apr 1988.

Great Britain ■ *Andy Pandy* was first transmitted on 11 Jul 1950 but consisted of repeats of a cycle of 26 shows until 1970. *Come Dancing* was first transmitted on 29 Sep 1950 but is seasonal. *Sooty* was first presented on BBC by its deviser Harry Corbett (b. 1918) in 1952. In 1968, *Sooty* moved to Thames Television and when Harry retired in 1975, the show was, and is continued to this day by his son Matthew. *The Good Old Days* ran from 20 Jul 1953 to 31 Dec 1983. Barney Colehan MBE produced all 244 programmes. The *BBC News* was inaugurated in vision on 5 Jul 1954. Richard Baker OBE read the news from 1954 to Christmas 1982. Of current affairs programmes BBC's weekly *Panorama* was first transmitted on 11 Nov 1953 but has summer breaks, whereas Granada's *What the Papers Say* was transmitted weekly from 5 Nov 1956 until September 1988. The monthly *Sky at Night* has been presented by Patrick Moore CBE without a break or a miss since 24 Apr 1957. The BBC's *Farming* programme was transmitted weekly from 3 Oct 1957 until its end in late spring 1988. The longest-serving TV quizmaster is Bamber Gascoigne of Granada's *University Challenge* which ran from 21 Sep 1962 until 31 Dec 1987. The longest-running domestic drama serial is Granada's *Coronation Street* which has run twice weekly since 9 Dec 1960. William Roache had played Ken Barlow without a break since the outset for 28 years by 9 Dec 1988.

Most sets ■ The USA had, by January 1988, 88·6 million TV households, with 42·29 million on cable TV. The number of homes with colour sets was 85 030 000 (96 per cent) by January 1988. More than 60 per cent of the total homes own two or more TV sets. The proportion of households in Great Britain with colour sets was 90 per cent in 1987. Just over half (51 per cent) of all households had two or more sets.

The number of licences current in the United Kingdom was 19 406 183 on 28 Feb 1989 of which 17 429 226 were for colour sets. Black and white licences have declined since 1979. On 15 Feb 1988 the new China News Agency announced that China's number of TV viewers had risen to 600 million from 100 million sets.

TV watching ■ In June 1988 it was reported that the average US child sees at least 26 000 murders on TV by his or her 18th birthday. Between the ages of 2 and 11 the average viewing time is 31 hours 52 minutes per week. The global total of homes with television surpassed 500 million in 1987 led by the USA with 89·13 million. There are 8250 TV transmitting stations world-wide of which 1241 are in the USA. There are 364 TV sets per 1000 people in the USA compared with 348 in Sweden and 330 in Britain. In 1988 the average British viewer watched 25 hr 21 min of television per week.

Greatest audience ■ The greatest estimated number of viewers worldwide for a televised event is 2500 million for the live and recorded transmissions of the XXIIIrd Olympic Games in Los Angeles, California, USA from 27 Jul to 13 Aug 1984. The American Broadcasting Co airing schedule comprised 187 ½ hours of coverage on 56 cameras. The estimated viewership for the 'Live Aid' concerts organised by Bob Geldof and Bill Graham, via a record 12 satellites, was 1·6 billion or nearly one third of the world's population.

The programme which attracted the highest ever viewership was the *Goodbye, Farewell and Amen* final episode of M*A*S*H (the acronym for Mobile Army Surgical Hospital 4077) transmitted by CBS on 28 Feb 1983 to 60·3 per cent of all households in the United States. It was estimated that some 125 million people tuned in, taking a 77 per cent share of all viewing.

The UK record is 39 million for the wedding of TRH the Prince and Princess of Wales in London on 29 Jul 1981.

Most expensive production ■ *The Winds of War*, a seven-part Paramount World War II saga aired by ABC, was the most expensive ever TV production costing $42 million over 14 months' shooting. The final episode on 13 Feb 1983 attracted a rating of 41 per cent (percentage of total number of viewers), and a share of 56 per cent (percentage of total sets turned on that were tuned in).

Largest contracts ■ The highest paid television performer currently is Bill Cosby, who was reported in September 1988 to have earned $92 million during the two-year period 1987–8 for his TV shows, concerts, albums and endorsements. John William Carson (b. 23 Oct 1925), the host of *The Tonight Show* has a contract with NBC reportedly calling for annual payment of $5 000 000 for his one-hour evening show aired four times weekly. The highest-paid current affairs or news performer is Dan Rather of CBS who reportedly signed an $8 million contract for five years from 1982.

Marie Osmond signed a contract worth $7 million for seven hours of transmission, paid by NBC on 9 Mar 1981. The figure includes talent and production costs.

Great Britain ■ The largest contract in British television was one of a reported £9 000 000, inclusive of production expenses, signed by Tom Jones (b. Thomas Jones Woodward, 7 Jun 1940) of Treforest, Mid Glamorgan, Wales in June 1968 with ABC-TV of the United States and ATV in London for 17 one-hour shows per annum from January 1969 to January 1974.

Highest-paid entertainer ■ The highest paid newscaster and journalist is Dan Rather of the CBS' *Nightly News*, reported in February 1986 to be paid $2 500 000 per annum.

It was reported by *Forbes* magazine in September 1988 that the world's highest-paid entertainer is Michael Jackson earning $97 million over a period of two years.

Largest TV prizes ■ On 24 Jul 1975 WABC-TV, New York City, USA transmitted the first televised Grand Tier draw of the State Lottery in which the winner took the grand prize of $1 000 000. This was, however, taxable.

Most successful telethon ■ The Jerry Lewis

Labor Day Telethon on 2 Sep 1984 raised $32 074 566 in pledges for the Muscular Dystrophy Association. The Victims of Famine in East Africa and the Sahel appeal raised a record £9 518 736 from 17 Jul 1984 to 6 Feb 1985.

Biggest sale ■ The greatest number of episodes of any TV programme ever sold has been 1144 episodes of *Coronation Street* by Granada Television to CBKST Saskatoon, Saskatchewan, Canada, on 31 May 1971. This constituted 20 days 15 hr 44 min continuous viewing. A further 728 episodes (Jan 1974–Jan 1981) were sold to CBC in August 1982.

Most rented video *UK* ■ The video which in 1987 attracted most home viewers was *Ghostbusters* with an audience of 13 100 000. The percentage of families hiring videos rose to 46 per cent.

Top-selling video ■ CBS/Fox Video's *Crocodile Dundee* (Australia 1986) is the top-selling feature film in Britain.

Most prolific scriptwriter ■ The most prolific television writer in the world is the Rt Hon. Lord Willis (b. 13 Jan 1918), who from 1949–87 has created 37 series, including the first seven years and 2 250 000 words of *Dixon of Dock Green* which ran on BBC television from 1955 to 1976, 32 stage plays and 39 feature films. He has had 24 plays produced. His total output since 1942 is estimated at 19 300 000 words.

'Mastermind' records ■ Mrs Jennifer Keaveney (on 'The life and work of E. Nesbit') scored a record 40 points in a 1986 semi-final and equalled her semi-final score of 40 points when she won the 1986 final with 'The life and works of Elizabeth Gaskell' of this BBC TV series which began on 11 Sep 1972. Mary Elizabeth Raw also scored 40 points in the first programme of the 1989 series. Sir David Hunt KCMG, OBE won the 'Mastermind Champions' contest on 3 May 1982.

TV producer ■ Aaron Spelling (b. 1928) has produced more than 1770 TV episodes totalling 2250 hours of air time, as well as 207 $\frac{1}{2}$ hours of TV movies and eight feature films. The total 2467 broadcast hours is equal to 3688 km *13·7 million ft* of film and, projected 24 hours a day, it would take 103·9 days – just 3 $\frac{1}{2}$ months – to screen it all. The average American TV is turned on six hours per day. At that rate, Spelling has produced enough film to last 374 days.

Highest TV advertising rates ■ The highest TV advertising rate has been $600 000 per $\frac{1}{2}$ min for NBC network prime time during the transmission of Super Bowl XXI on 25 Jan 1987, watched by a record 127 million viewers. In Great Britain the maximum peak-time (8.00–11.20 p.m.) weekday 60-sec spot rate on Thames Television is £75 250 +VAT (January 1989). The longest run was 7 min 10 sec by Great Universal Stores on TV-am's *Good Morning Britain* for £100 000 on 20 Jan 1985.

Most takes ■ The highest number of 'takes' for a TV commercial is 28 in 1973 by Pat Coombs, the comedienne. Her explanation was 'Every time we came to the punch line I just could not remember the name of the product'.

Commercial records ■ It was reported in March 1988 that Pepsi Cola had paid Michael Jackson £7 million to do four TV commercials for them.

Largest and smallest sets ■ The Sony Jumbo Tron colour TV screen at the Tsukuba International Exposition '85 near Tokyo in March 1985 measured 24·3 m ×45·7 m *80 ft ×150 ft*.

The largest cathode ray tubes for colour sets are 94 cm *37 in* models manufactured by Mitsubishi Electric of Japan.

The Seiko TV-Wrist Watch launched on 23 Dec 1982 in Japan has a 30·5 mm *1·2 in* screen and weighs only 80 g *2·8 oz*. Together with the receiver unit and the headphone set the entire black and white system, costing 108 000 yen, weighs only 320 g *11·3 oz*. The smallest single-piece set is the Casio-Keisanki TV-10 weighing 338 g *11·9 oz* with a 6·85 cm *2·7 in* screen, launched in Tokyo in July 1983. The smallest colour set is the liquid crystal display (LCD) Japanese Epson launched in 1985 with dimensions of 7·6 ×17·1 ×2·8 cm *3 ×6 $\frac{3}{4}$ ×1 $\frac{1}{8}$ in* weighing, with batteries and its 52 800 crystals, only 453 g *16 oz*.

Pole sitting
There being no international rules, the
'standards of living' at the top of poles vary
widely. Mellissa Sanders lived in a 1·8 m x 2·1 m
6 ft x 7 ft 'house' at the top of a pole in
Indianapolis, Indiana, USA from 26 Oct 1986 to
24 Mar 1988, a total of 516 days. In spite of the
lack of space, she did find room for a television,
an exercise bike and two telephones.
(Photos: Retna).

Human Achievements

Endurance and Endeavour

Most travelled ■ The world's most travelled men are Parke G. Thompson, from Akron, Ohio, USA, and Giorgio Ricatto, from Turin, Italy, both of whom have visited all of the 170 sovereign countries and 62 of the 63 non-sovereign or other territories (see heading COUNTRIES, in Chapter 10, p. 194). Both men still have to go to the Heard & McDonald Islands, an island group in the southern Indian Ocean.

The most travelled man in the horseback era was probably the Methodist preacher Bishop Francis Asbury (b. Handsworth, West Midlands, 1745), who travelled 424 850 km *264 000 miles* in North America from 1771 to 1815. During this time he preached some 16 000 sermons and ordained nearly 3 000 ministers.

Most isolated ■ The farthest any human has been removed from his nearest living fellow man is 3596·4 km *2233·2 miles* in the case of the Command Service Module pilot Alfred M. Worden on the US *Apollo 15* lunar mission of 30 Jul–1 Aug 1971.

Longest walks ■ The first person reported to have 'walked round the world' was George Matthew Schilling (USA) from 3 Aug 1897 to 1904, but the first verified achievement was by David Kunst (b. 1939, USA) from 20 Jun 1970 to 5 Oct 1974. Tomas Carlos Pereira (b. Argentina, 16 Nov 1942) spent 10 years, 6 Apr 1968 to 8 Apr 1978, walking 48 000 km *29 825 miles* around four continents. Steven Newman of Bethal, Ohio, USA spent 4 years walking 36 200 km *22 500 miles* around the world, 1 Apr 1983 to 1 Apr 1987, covering 20 countries and five continents. Rick Hansen (b. Canada, 1957), who was paralysed from the waist down in 1973 as a result of a motor accident, wheeled his wheelchair over 40 074·06 km *24 901·55 miles* through four continents and 34 countries. He started his journey from Vancouver on 21 Mar 1985 and arrived back on 22 May 1987. George Meegan (b. 2 Oct 1952) from Rainham, Kent walked 30 431 km *19 019 miles* from Usuaia, the southern tip of South America, to Prudhoe Bay in northern Alaska, taking 2426 days from 26 Jan 1977 to 18 Sep 1983, and thus completed the first traverse of the western hemisphere. Sean Eugene Maguire (b. USA, 15 Sep 1956) walked 11 791 km *7327 miles* from the Yukon River, north of Livengood, Alaska, to

Key West, Florida, in 307 days, 6 Jun 1978 to 9 Apr 1979. The trans-Canada (Halifax to Vancouver) record walk of 6057 km *3764 miles* is 96 days by Clyde McRae, 23, from 1 May to 4 Aug 1973. John Lees (b. 23 Feb 1945) of Brighton, East Sussex between 11 Apr and 3 Jun 1972 walked 4628 km *2876 miles* across the USA from City Hall, Los Angeles, California to City Hall, New York in 53 days 12 hr 15 min (average 86·49 km *53·75 miles* a day).

Britain ■ The longest continuous walk in Britain is one of 11 341 km *7047 miles* around the British coast by Ron Bullen of Binbrook, Lincs from 1 Apr 1986 to 7 Feb 1987. Cathryn Townsend set a record for the longest continuous female walk in Britain by walking for a total distance of 8714 km *5416 miles* around the British coast, between 26 Oct 1986 and 2 Aug 1987, starting and finishing at the Palace Pier, Brighton, East Sussex.

North Pole conquest ■ The claim of neither of the two US Arctic explorers, Dr Frederick Albert Cook (1865–1940) and Cdr (later Rear-Ad.) Robert Edwin Peary (1856–1920), of the US Naval Civil Engineering branch, in reaching the North Pole is subject to positive proof. On excellent pack ice and modern sledges Wally Herbert's 1968–9 expedition (see heading 'Arctic crossing') attained a best day's route mileage of 37 km *23 miles* in 15 hr. Cook claimed 41·8 km *26 miles* twice while Peary claimed a surely unsustainable average of 61 km *38 miles* over eight consecutive days.

The first people definitely to have reached the North Pole on ground level — the exact point Lat. 90° 00′ 00″ N (± 300 metres) — were Pavel Afanasyevich Geordiyenko, Pavel Kononovich Sen'ko, Mikhail Mikhaylovich Somov and Mikhail Yemel'yenovich Ostrekin (all USSR), on 23 Apr 1948. They arrived and departed by air.

The earliest indisputable attainment of the North Pole by surface travel over the sea-ice was at 3 p.m. (Central Standard Time) on 19 Apr 1968 by Ralph Plaisted (US) and 3 companions after a 42-day trek in four Skidoos (snow-mobiles). Their arrival was independently verified 18 hr later by a US Air Force weather aircraft. The party returned by aircraft. The sea bed is 4087 m *13 410 ft* below the North Pole.

Naomi Uemura (1941–84), the Japanese explorer and mountaineer, became the first person to reach the North Pole in a solo trek across the Arctic ice cap at 4.45 a.m. GMT on 1 May 1978. He had travelled 725 km *450 miles* setting out on 7 Mar from Cape Edward, Ellesmere Island in northern Canada. He averaged nearly 13 km *8 miles* per day with his sled 'Aurora' drawn by 17 huskies. He also left by aircraft.

Dr Jean-Louis Etienne, 39, was the first to reach the Pole solo and without dogs, on 11 May 1986 after 63 days. On 20 Apr 1987 Fukashi Kazami, 36, of Tokyo, Japan reached the North Pole from Ward Hunt Island, northern Canada in 44 days having started on his 250-cc motorcycle on 8 Mar. Both left by aircraft.

The first woman to set foot on the North Pole was Mrs Fran Phipps on 5 Apr 1971. Galina Aleksandrovna Lastovskaya (b. 1941) and Lilia Vladislavovna Minina (b. 1959) were crew members of the USSR atomic icebreaker *Arktika* which reached the Pole on 17 Aug 1977.

South Pole conquest ■ The first men to cross the Antarctic circle (Lat. 66° 33′ S) were the 193 crew of the *Resolution* (462 tonnes) (Capt James Cook, RN (1728–79)) and *Adventure* (336 tonnes) (Lt Tobias Furneaux) on 17 Jan 1773 in 39° E. The first person known to have sighted the Antarctic ice shelf was Capt. Thaddeus Thaddevich Bellingshausen (Russia) (1778–1852) on 27 Jan 1820 from the vessels *Vostock* and *Mirnyi*. The first known to have sighted the mainland of the continent was Capt. William Smith (1790–1847) and Master Edward Bransfield, RN, in the brig *Williams*. They saw the peaks of Trinity Land 3 days later on 30 Jan 1820.

The South Pole (alt. 2779 m *9186 ft* on ice and 102 m *336 ft* bed rock) was first reached at 11 a.m. on 14 Dec 1911 by a Norwegian party of five men led by Capt. Roald Engebereth Gravning Amundsen (1872–1928), after a 53-day march with dog sledges from the Bay of Whales, to which he had penetrated in the *Fram*. Subsequent calculations showed that

Walking round the world ● The first verified walk round the world was by David Kunst (b. 1939) who left his home town of Waseca, Minnesota, USA on 20 Jun 1970 and arrived back there on 5 Oct 1974. His walk took him through America, Europe, Asia and Australia. At the start he was accompanied by his brother, John, but John was killed by bandits in Afghanistan and an other brother, Peter, replaced him. Among the places that they visited were New York, in the USA (left), Lisbon, in Portugal (right), New Delhi, in India (bottom left) and Perth, in Australia (bottom right). A total of four mules walked with them, one of which (Willie Makeit II) can be seen below with David and in the New Delhi picture. (Photos: David Kunst and Spectrum)

Olav Olavson Bjaaland (the last survivor) and Helmer Hanssen probably passed within 400–600 m *1310–1970 ft* of the exact pole. The other 2 members were Sverre H. Hassell (d. 1928) and Oskar Wisting (d. 1936).

The first woman to set foot on Antarctica was Mrs Karoline Mikkelsen on 20 Feb 1935. No woman stood on the South Pole until 11 Nov 1969. On that day Lois Jones, Eileen McSaveney, Jean Pearson, Terry Lee Tickhill (all US), Kay Lindsay (Australia) and Pam Young (NZ) arrived by air.

First to see both poles ■ The first people to see both poles were Roald Engebereth Amundsen and Oskar Wisting when they flew aboard the airship *Norse* over the North Pole on 12 May 1926, having previously been to the South Pole on 14 Dec 1911.

First to land on both poles ■ Dr Albert P. Crary (US) (1911–87) reached the North Pole in a Dakota aircraft on 3 May 1952. On 12 Feb 1961 he arrived at the South Pole by Sno Cat on a scientific traverse party from the McMurdo Station.

Arctic crossing ■ The first crossing of the Arctic sea-ice was achieved by the British Trans-Arctic Expedition which left Point Barrow, Alaska on 21 Feb 1968 and arrived at the Seven Island archipelago north-east of Spitzbergen 464 days later on 29 May 1969 after a haul of 4699 km *2920 statute miles* and a drift of 1126 km *700 miles* compared with the straight-line distance of 2674 km *1662 miles.* The team comprised Wally Herbert (leader), 34, Major Ken Hedges, 34, RAMC, Allan Gill, 38, and Dr Roy Koerner, 36 (glaciologist), and 40 huskies. The only crossing achieved in a single season was that by Fiennes and Burton (see heading 'Polar circumnavigation') from Alert via the North Pole to the Greenland Sea in open snowmobiles. Both of these reached the North Pole and returned by land.

Antarctic crossing ■ The first surface crossing of the Antarctic continent was completed at 1.47 p.m. on 2 Mar 1958, after a trek of 3473 km *2158 miles* lasting 99 days from 24 Nov 1957, from Shackleton Base to Scott Base via the Pole. The crossing party of 12 was led by Dr (now Sir) Vivian Ernest Fuchs (b. 11 Feb 1908). The 4185 km *2600 mile* trans-Antarctic leg from Sanae to Scott Base of the 1980–82 Trans-Globe Expedition was achieved in 66 days from 26 Oct 1980 to 11 Jan 1981 having passed through the South Pole on 23 Dec 1980. The 3-man party on snowmobiles comprised Sir Ranulph Fiennes, Bt (b. 1944), Oliver Shepard and Charles Burton.

Polar circumnavigation ■ The first polar circumnavigation was achieved by Sir Ranulph Fiennes, Bt and Charles Burton of the British Trans-Globe Expedition who travelled south from Greenwich (2 Sep 1979), via the South Pole (17 Dec 1980) and the North Pole (11 Apr 1982), and back to Greenwich arriving after a 56 325 km *35 000 mile* trek on 29 Aug 1982.

Longest sledge journeys ■ The longest totally self-supporting Polar sledge journey ever made was one of 1738 km *1080 miles* from west to east across Greenland (now Kalaallit Nunaat) from 18 Jun to 5 Sep 1934 by Capt. M. Lindsay (1905–1981) (later Sir Martin Lindsay of Dowhill, Bt, CBE, DSO), Lt Arthur S. T. Godfrey, RE (later Lt. Col., k. 1942), Andrew N. C. Croft (later Col., DSO) and 49 dogs. The Ross Sea Party of 10 (3 died) sledged over 3220 km *2000 miles* in 300 days from 6 May 1975.

Greatest ocean descent ■ The record ocean descent was achieved in the Challenger Deep of the Marianas Trench, 400 km *250 miles* south-west of Guam, in the Pacific Ocean, when the Swiss-built US Navy bathyscaphe *Trieste*, manned by Dr Jacques Piccard (b. 1914) (Switzerland) and Lt Donald Walsh, USN reached 10 916 m *(35 813 ft 6·78 miles)* down, at 1.10 p.m. on 23 Jan 1960 (see p. 54). The pressure of the water was 1183 kgf/cm² *16 883 lbf/in²* and the temperature 3° C *37·4° F.* The descent took 4 hr 48 min and the ascent 3 hr 17 min.

Deep diving records ■ The record depth for the

extremely dangerous activity of breath-held diving is 105 m *344 ft* by Jacques Mayol (France) off Elba, Italy, in December 1983. He descended on a sled in 104 seconds and ascended in 90 seconds. The record for women is 75 m *246 ft ¾ in* by Rossana Majorca (Italy) off Syracuse, Sicily on 31 Jul 1987.

The record dive with scuba (self-contained underwater breathing apparatus) is 133 m *437 ft* by John J. Gruener and R. Neal Watson (US) off Freeport, Grand Bahama on 14 Oct 1968. For women it is 105·16 m *345 ft* by Marty Dunwoody (US) off Bimini, Bahama Islands on 20 Dec 1987. The record dive utilising gas mixtures (nitrogen, oxygen and helium) is a simulated dive of 685·8 m *2250 ft* in a dry chamber by Stephen Porter, Len Whitlock and Erik Kramer at Duke University Medical Center in Durham, North Carolina, USA on 3 Feb 1981 in a 43-day trial in a sphere of 2·43 m *8 ft.* A team of 6 divers (4 Comex and 2 French Navy) descended and worked efficiently during a period of 6 days to a depth of 520 m *1706 ft* off Marseilles, France as part

of the Hydro VIII operation in ths spring of 1988. This involved the use of 'hydreliox', a synthetic breathing mixture containing a high percentage of hydrogen.

Deepest underwater escapes ■ The deepest underwater rescue achieved was of the *Pisces III* in which Roger R. Chapman, 28, and Roger Mallinson, 35, were trapped for 76 hr when it sank to 480 m *1575 ft,* 240 km *150 miles* south-east of Cork, Ireland on 29 Aug 1973. She was hauled to the surface by the cable ship *John Cabot* after work by *Pisces V, Pisces II* and the remote control recovery vessel US CURV on 1 Sep. The greatest depth of an actual escape without any equipment has been from 68·58 m *225 ft* by Richard A. Slater from the rammed submersible *Nekton Beta* off Catalina Island, California, USA on 28 Sep 1970. The record for an escape with equipment was by Norman Cooke and Hamish Jones on 22 Jul 1987. During a naval exercise they escaped from a depth of 183 m *601 ft* from the submarine HMS *Otus* in Bjornefjorden, off Bergen, Norway, wearing standard suits with a built-in life-jacket, from which air expanding during the ascent passes into a hood over the escaper's head.

Deepest salvage ■ The greatest depth at which salvage has been achieved is 5029 m *16 500 ft* by the bathyscaphe *Trieste II* (Lt Cdr Mel Bartels, USN), to attach cables to an 'electronic package' on the sea bed 645 km *400 miles* north of Hawaii on 20 May 1972.

Flexible dress divers ■ The deepest salvage operation ever achieved with divers was on the wreck of HM cruiser *Edinburgh* sunk on 2 May 1942 in the Barents Sea off northern Norway inside the Arctic Circle in 244·7 m *803 ft* of water. Twelve divers dived on the wreck in pairs using a bell from the *Stephaniturm* (1446 tonnes) over 32 days under the direction of former RN officer Michael Stewart from 17 Sep to 7 Oct 1981. A total of 460 gold ingots (the only 100 per cent salvage to date) was recovered and was divided thus: £16 million to the USSR, £7·9 million to HM Government and some £20 million to the salvage contractors, Jessop Marine Recoveries Ltd (10 per cent) and Wharton Williams Ltd (90 per cent), giving a total of £43·9 million. John Rossier, 28, was the first to touch the gold. The longest decompression time was 7 days 10 hr 27 min.

The record recovery in terms of gold ingots was that from the White Star Liner HMS *Laurentic,* which was mined in 40·2 m *132 ft* of water off Fanad

Head, Donegal, Ireland in 1917. Since 1917, 43 tonnes of gold (3191 of the 3211 ingots) have been recovered by the Royal Navy, Cossum Diving Syndicate and Consortium Recovery Ltd.

Greatest penetration into the earth ■ The deepest penetration made into the ground by man is in the Western Deep Levels Mine at Carletonville, Transvaal, South Africa where a record depth of 3777 m (*12 391 ft 2·34 miles*) was attained, temperature 55° C *131° F*.

Longest on a raft ■ The longest recorded survival alone on a raft is 133 days (4 ¹/₂ months) by Second Steward Poon Lim (b. Hong Kong) of the UK Merchant Navy, whose ship, the SS *Ben Lomond*, was torpedoed in the Atlantic 910 km *565 miles* west of St Paul's Rocks in Lat. 00° 30′ N Long. 38° 45′ W at 11.45 a.m. on 23 Nov 1942. He was picked up by a Brazilian fishing boat off Salinópolis, Brazil on 5 Apr 1943 and could walk ashore. In July 1943 he was awarded the BEM and now lives in New York City.

Maurice and Maralyn Bailey of Derby survived 118 ¹/₃ days in an inflatable dinghy 1·37 m *4 ¹/₂ ft* in diameter in the Pacific from 4 Mar to 30 Jun 1973.

Shaft-sinking record ■ The one-month (31 days) world record is 381·3 m *1251 ft* for a standard shaft 7·92 m *26 ft* in diameter at Buffelsfontein Mine, Transvaal, South Africa, in March 1962. The British record of 131·2 m *430 ft* of 7·92 m *26 ft* diameter shaft was set in No. 2 Shaft of the NCB's Whitemoor Mine near Selby, North Yorks in 31 days (15 Nov–16 Dec 1982).

Most marriages ■ The greatest number of marriages accumulated in the monogamous world is 27 by former Baptist minister Glynn 'Scotty' Wolfe (b. 25 Jul 1908) of Blythe, California, USA, who first married in 1927. His latest wife is Daisy Delgado (b. 29 Dec 1970), a Filipino from Liloan, Cebu. His previous oldest wife was 38. His total number of children is, he believes, 41.

The greatest number of monogamous marriages by a woman is 21 by Linda Lou Essex of Anderson, Indiana, USA. She has been married to 15 different men since 1957, divorcing the last one in 1988.

The record for bigamous marriages is 104 by Giovanni Vigliotto, one of some 50 aliases used by either Fred Jipp (b. New York City, 3 Apr 1936) or Nikolai Peruskov (b. Siracusa, Sicily, 3 Apr 1929)

during 1949–81 in 27 US states and 14 other countries. Four victims were aboard one ship in 1968 and two in London. On 28 Mar 1983 in Phoenix, Arizona, USA he received 28 years for fraud, 6 for bigamy and was fined $336 000.

In Britain, the only monogamous citizen who married eight men is Olive Joyce Wilson of Marston Green, Birmingham. She has consecutively been Mrs John Bickley; Mrs Don Trethowan; Mrs George Hundley; Mrs Raymond Ward; Mrs Harry Latrobe; Mrs Leslie Harris; Mrs Ray Richards, and now Mrs John Grassick. All were divorced except Mr Hundley, who died.

Oldest bride and bridegroom ■ The oldest recorded bridegroom has been Harry Stevens, 103, who married Thelma Lucas, 84, at the Caravilla Retirement Home, Wisconsin, USA on 3 Dec 1984.

The British record was set by Sir Robert Mayer CH, KCVO (1879–1985) who married Jacqueline Noble, 51, in London on 10 Nov 1980 when aged 101 years. Mrs Winifred Clark (b. 13 Nov 1871) became Britain's oldest recorded bride when she married Albert Smith, 80, at St Hugh's Church, Cantley, South Yorks the day before her 100th birthday.

Longest engagement ■ The longest engagement on record was between Octavio Guillen and Adriana Martinez. They finally took the plunge after 67 years in June 1969 in Mexico City, Mexico. Both were then aged 82.

Longest marriage ■ The longest recorded marriages are of 86 years, one between Sir Temulji Bhicaji Nariman and Lady Nariman from 1853 to 1940 resulting from a cousin marriage when both were 5. Sir Temulji (b. 3 Sept 1848) died, aged 91 years 11 months, in August 1940 at Bombay. Lazarus Rowe (b. Greenland, New Hampshire, USA, 1725) and Molly Webber were recorded as marrying in 1743. He died first in 1829 after 86 years of marriage.

The British record is for a marriage of 82 years, between James Frederick Burgess (b. 3 Mar 1861,

d. 27 Nov 1966) and his wife Sarah Ann, *née* Gregory (b. 11 Jul 1865, d. 22 Jun 1965) who were married on 21 Jun 1883 at St James's, Bermondsey, London.

Golden weddings ■ The greatest number of golden weddings in a family is ten, the six sons and four daughters of Joseph and Sophia Gresl of Manitowoc, Wisconsin, USA all celebrating golden weddings between April 1962 and September 1988. The most in Britain is seven, the three sons and four daughters of Mr and Mrs J. Stredwick of East Sussex all celebrating their golden weddings between May 1971 and April 1981.

Most married ■ Jack V. and Edna Moran of Seattle, Washington State, USA have married each other 40 times since the original and only really necessary occasion on 27 Jul 1937 in Seaside, Oregon, USA. Subsequent ceremonies have included those at Banff, Canada (1952), Cairo, Egypt (1966) and Westminster Abbey, London (1975).

Youngest married ■ It was reported in 1986 that an 11-month-old boy was married to a 3-month-old girl in Bangladesh to end a 20-year feud between two families over a disputed farm.

Mass ceremony ■ The largest mass wedding ceremony was one of 6516 couples officiated over by Sun Myung Moon (b. 1920) of the Holy Spirit Association for the Unification of World Christianity at a factory near Seoul, South Korea on 30 Oct 1988.

Most expensive wedding ■ The wedding of Mohammed, son of Shaik Rashid Bin Saeed Al Maktoum, to Princess Salama in Dubai in May 1981 lasted 7 days and cost an estimated £22 million in a purpose-built stadium for 20 000.

Oldest divorced ■ On 2 Feb 1984 a divorce was granted in Milwaukee, Wisconsin, USA between Ida Stern, aged 91, and her husband Simon, 97. The British record age is 101 years by Harry Bidwell at Brighton, East Sussex. He divorced on 21 Nov 1980 from a younger wife.

Dining out ■ The world champion for eating out has been Fred E. Magel of Chicago, Illinois, USA who since 1928 has dined out 46 000 times in 60 nations as a restaurant grader. He asserts the one which served largest helpings was Zehnder's Hotel, Frankenmuth, Michigan, USA. Mr Magel's favourite dishes were South African rock lobster and mousse of fresh English strawberries.

Party giving ■ The 'International Year of the Child' children's party in Hyde Park, London was attended by the royal family and 160 000 children on 30–31 May 1979.

The world's largest birthday party was attended by 8534 people on 8 Dec 1987 in Indianapolis, Indiana, USA. The party was held to mark the 100th birthday of the United Way.

The largest Christmas Party ever staged was that thrown by the Boeing Company in the 65 000-seat Kingdome, Seattle, Washington State, USA, in two shows totalling 103 152 people on 15 Dec 1979. During St Patrick's week of 11–17 Mar 1985, Houli-han's Old Place hosted St Pat's Parties at the 48 Kansas City, Missouri-based Gilbert/Robinson restaurants for a total of 206 854 documented guests.

Toastmasters ■ Toasting is generally believed to date back to the 17th century. Originally toastmas-ters wore a black tail coat together with a sash, which is still required uniform in the City of London. William Knight-Smith (d. 1932), is thought to be the first red-coated toastmaster (c. 1900) and also the first recorded professional toastmaster.

Lecture fees ■ Dr Ronald Dante was paid $3 080 000 for lecturing students on hypnotherapy at a 2-day course held in Chicago, USA on 1–2 Jun 1986. He was teaching for eight hours each day, and thus earned $192 500 per hour.

Working week ■ A case of a working week of 142 hours (with an average each day of 3 hr 42 min 51 sec for sleep) was recorded in June 1980 by Dr Paul Ashton, 32, the anaesthetics registrar at Birken-head General Hospital, Merseyside. He described the week in question as 'particularly bad but not untypical'. Some non-consultant doctors are con-tracted to work 110 hours a week or be available for 148 hours. Some contracts for fully salaried univer-sity lecturers call for a 3-hr week or a 72-hr year spread over 24 weeks.

Working career ■ The longest working life has been that of 98 years by Mr Izumi (see p. 13) who began work goading draft animals at a sugar mill at Isen, Tokunoshima, Japan in 1872. He retired as a sugar cane farmer in 1970 aged 105.

The longest working life recorded in the UK was that of Susan O'Hagan (1802–1909) who was in dom-estic service with 3 generations of the Hall family of Lisburn, near Belfast, Northern Ireland for 97 years from the age of 10 to light duties at 107.

The longest recorded industrial career in one job in Britain was that of Miss Polly Gadsby who started work with Archibald Turner & Co of Leicester aged 9. In 1932, after 86 years' service, she was still at her bench wrapping elastic, at the age of 95. Theodore C. Taylor (1850–1952) served 86 years with J.T. & T. Taylor of Batley, West Yorks including 56 years as chairman. The longest serving chairman (appointed July 1926) of any board of directors was Mrs Mary Henrietta Anne Moody (b. 7 Apr 1881) of Mark & Moody Ltd, printers and booksellers of Stourbridge, West Midlands. She had completed 59 years at the time of her death on 5 Aug 1985. Edward William Beard (1878–1982), a builder of Swindon, Wilts retired in October 1981 from the firm he had founded in 1896 after 85 years. Commissioner Cath-erine Bramwell-Booth (b. 20 Jul 1883, d. 4 Oct 1987) had been serving the Salvation Army since 1903. Richard John Knight (b. 2 Apr 1881) was company secretary to seven companies at the time of his death on 12 Nov 1984 aged 103 years.

Most durable coal miner ■ George Stephenson (b. 21 Apr 1833) worked at William Pit, a Whitehaven colliery, Cumbria from 1840 (aged 7) for 82 years until his retirement in 1922. He died on 18 Mar 1926 aged 92 years 10 months having received a testimonial of £54 12s.

Longest pension ■ Miss Millicent Barclay, daughter of Col. William Barclay, was born post-humously on 10 Jul 1872 and became eligible for a Madras Military Fund pension to continue until her

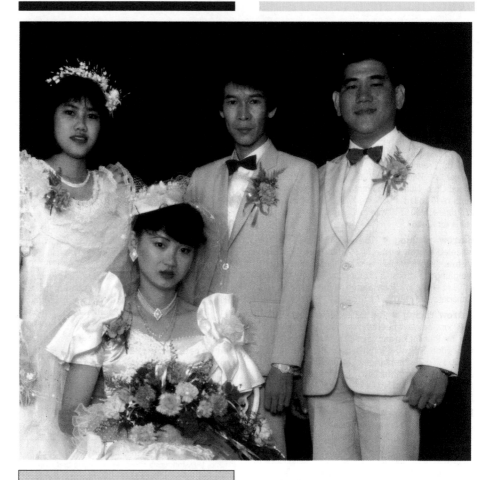

Best man ● The world champion 'best man' is Ting Ming Siong (right), from Sibu, Sarawak, in Malaysia, who officiated for the 465th time since 1976 in March 1989.

marriage. She died unmarried on 26 Oct 1969 having drawn the pension for every day of her life of 97 years 3 months.

Medical families ■ The four sons and five daughters of Dr Antonio B. Vicencio of Los Angeles, California USA all qualified as doctors during 1964–82. Eight sons of John Robertson of Benview, Dumbarton, Strathclyde graduated as medical doctors between 1892 and 1914. Henry Lewis Lut-terloh and Elizabeth Grantham of Chatham County, North Carolina, USA were the grandparents of 19 medical doctors. From 1850 to 1962 they practised a total of 704 man-years. The Maurice family of Marl-borough, Wilts have had the same practice for six generations since 1792.

Miscellaneous Endeavours

Accordion playing ■ Pieter van Loggerenberg of Hoedspruit, Transvaal, South Africa played an accordion for 85 hr from 7–10 Jul 1987 as part of the Wildlife Festival of Hoedspruit.

Apple peeling ■ The longest single unbroken apple peel on record is one of 52·51 m *172 ft 4 in* peeled by Kathy Wafler of Wolcott, NY, USA in 11 hr 30 min at Long Ridge Mall, Rochester, NY, USA on 16 Oct 1976. The apple weighed 567 g *20 oz*.

Apple picking ■ The greatest recorded perform-ance is 7180·33 kg *15 830 lb* picked in 8 hr by George Adrian of Indianapolis, Indiana, USA on 23 Sept 1980.

Auctioneering ■ The longest one-man auction on record is one of 60 hr by Reg Coates at Gosport, Hants from 9–11 Sept 1988.

Bag-carrying ■ The greatest non-stop bag-carrying feat carrying 50·8 kg *1 cwt* of household coal in an open bag is 54·7 km *34 miles* by Neil Sulli-van, 37, of Small Heath, Birmingham, in 12 hr 45 min on 24 May 1986.

The record for the 1012·5 m *1107·2 yd* course annual Gawthorpe, West Yorks race is 4 min 19 sec by Terry Lyons on 16 Apr 1979.

Bagpipes ■ The duration record pipe is one of 120 hr by Jordon Anderson, William Scannell, Frederick Côté and Andrew Belson at the Old Fort on St Helens' Island, Quebec, Canada, playing two at a time in shifts from 6–11 Aug 1988.

Balancing on one foot ■ The longest recorded duration for balancing on one foot is 34 hr by Shri N. Ravi in Sathyamangalam City, Tamil Nadu, India on 17–18 Apr 1982. The disengaged foot may not be rested on the standing foot nor may any object be used for support or balance.

Balloon release ■ The largest mass balloon release ever was one of 1 429 643 balloons at Public Square in Cleveland, Ohio, USA on 27 Sep 1986.

The British record was 115 000 helium balloons released simultaneously on 30 May 1988 from Castle Howard, near Malton, North Yorks.

Band marathon ■ The longest recorded 'blow-in' is 102 hr 43 min 43 sec by the Band of the West Mid-lands Fire Service, at the National Exhibition Centre in Birmingham from 22–26 Oct 1986.

Band, one-man ■ Eugenio Soler of Barcelona, Spain has developed a tricycle with moving parts which he has called 'Tricimelotocus Orquestralis', on which he can play 50 different instruments simul-taneously. He demonstrated this in Barcelona on 21 Jun 1988, which had been designated the Interna-tional Day of Music. Rory Blackwell played 314 instruments in a single rendition in 1 min 23·07 sec at Dawlish, Devon on 27 May 1985. Dave Sheriff (b. David Adams) of Garve, Highland played his one-man band (which must include at least three instruments played simultaneously) for 199 hr from 17–25 Feb 1989 at the Eastgate Shopping Centre, Inverness, Highland. Nicki Clarke of Chester, Cheshire created the women's record of 100 hr

20 min from 24–28 Mar 1986 at the Hotel Leofric, Coventry, West Midlands.

Barrel jumping on ice skates ■ The official distance record is 8·99 m *29 ft 5 in* over 18 barrels by Yvon Jolin at Terrebonne, Quebec, Canada on 25 Jan 1981. The feminine record is 6·21 m *20 ft 4½ in* over 11 barrels by Janet Hainstock in Michigan, USA on 15 Mar 1980.

Barrel rolling ■ The record for rolling a full 36-gallon metal beer barrel over a measured mile is 8 min 7·2 sec by Phillip Randle, Steve Hewitt, John Round, Trevor Bradley, Colin Barnes and Ray Glover of Haunchwood Collieries Institute and Social Club, Nuneaton, Warwicks on 15 Aug 1982. A team of 10 rolled a 63½ kg *140 lb* barrel 240·35 km *150 miles* in 30 hr 31 min in Chlumcany, Czechoslovakia on 27–28 Oct 1982.

Barrow pushing ■ The heaviest loaded one-wheeled barrow pushed for a minimum 60·96 level metres *200 level feet* is one loaded with bricks weighing a gross 3·753 tonnes *8275 lb* through 74·06 m *243 ft* by John Sarich at London, Ontario, Canada on 19 Feb 1987.

Barrow racing ■ The fastest time attained in a 1·609 km *1 mile* wheel-barrow race is 4 min 48·51 sec by Piet Pitzer and Jaco Erasmus at the Transvalia High School, Vanderbijlpark, South Africa on 3 Oct 1987. Brothers-in-law Malcolm Shipley and Adrian Freeburg pushed each other from John O'Groats to Land's End for charity in 30 days from 28 Jul to 26 Aug 1981.

Bath tub racing ■ The record for a 57·9 km *36 mile* bath tub race is 1 hr 22 min 27 sec by Greg Mutton at the Grafton Jacaranda Festival, NSW, Australia on 8 Nov 1987. Tubs are limited to 1·90 m *75 in* and 6-hp motors. The greatest distance for paddling a hand-propelled bath tub in 24 hr is 145·6 km *90·5 miles* by 13 members of Aldington Prison Officers Social Club, nr Ashford, Kent on 28–29 May 1983.

Baton twirling ■ Victor Cerda, Sol Lozano, Harry Little III (leader) and Manuel Rodriguez twirled batons for 122½ hours from 24–29 Jun 1984 in El Seveno, California, USA.

The greatest number of complete spins done between tossing a baton into the air and catching it is 10, by Donald Garcia, on the BBC *Record Breakers* programme on 9 Dec 1986. The record for women is seven, by Lisa Fedick on the same programme, Joanne Holloway, at the UK National Baton Twirling Association Championships in Paignton, Devon on 29 Oct 1987 and Rachel Hayes on 18 Sep 1988, also later shown on the BBC *Record Breakers* programme.

Bed making ■ The record time set under the rigorous rules of the Australian Bedmaking Championships is 28·2 sec solo by Wendy Wall, 34, of Hebersham, Sydney, NSW on 30 Nov 1978. The British pair record with 1 blanket, 2 sheets, an undersheet, an uncased pillow, 1 counterpane and 'hospital' corners is 19·0 sec by Sisters Jill Bradbury and Chris Humpish of Hammersmith Hospital, London on 8 Oct 1985 on BBC TV's *Record Breakers* programme.

Bed of nails ■ The Reverend Ken Owen, 48, of Pontypridd, Mid Glamorgan lay on a bed of nails for a total of 300 hr, including 132 hr 30 min without a break, from 3–14 May 1986 starting at Bridgend Hotel, Pontygwaith and concluding at the The Three Horse Shoes, Tonteg, Pontypridd. Much longer dur-

> **Most on a bike** ● 19 members of the Jago Sport Club, Java, Indonesia mounted a bicycle and managed to ride it a distance of 200 m *656 ft 2 in* at Semarang, Java on 30 Jun 1988.

ations are claimed by uninvigilated *fakirs* — the most extreme case being *Silki* who claimed 111 days in São Paulo, Brazil ending on 24 Aug 1969.

Bed pushing ■ The longest recorded push of a normally sessile object is of 5204 km *3233 miles 1150 yd* in the case of a wheeled hospital bed by a team of nine employees of Bruntsfield Bedding Centre, Edinburgh from 21 Jun to 26 Jul 1979.

Bed race ■ The record time for the annual Knaresborough Bed Race (established 1966) in North Yorks is 12 min 25 sec for the 3·27 km *2 mile 63 yd* course crossing the River Nidd by the Bebra Beavers' team on 11 Jun 1988. The course record for the 16·09 km *10 mile* Chew Valley Lake race (established 1977) in Avon is 50 min by the Westbury Harriers' 3-man bed team.

Beer keg lifting ■ Tom Caskin raised a keg of beer weighing 62·5 kg *137·79 lb* above his head 360 times in the space of 6 hr in Newry, Co. Down, Northern Ireland on 20 Aug 1988.

Beer mat flipping ■ Dean Gould of Felixstowe, Suffolk flipped and caught a pile of 102 mats (1·2 mm-thick 490 gsm wood pulp board) through 180 degrees in Hamburg, West Germany on 18 Mar 1988.

Beer stein carrying ■ Barmaid Rosie Schedelbauer covered a distance of 15 m *49 ft 2½ in* in 4 sec with five full steins in each hand in a televised contest at Königssee, West Germany on 29 Jun 1981.

Best man ■ The world champion 'best man' is Ting Ming Siong, from Sibu, Sarawak, in Malaysia, who officiated for the 465th time since 1976 in March 1989.

Bicycle, most mounting simultaneously ■ On 30 Jun 1988 at Semarang, Central Java, Indonesia 19 members of the Jago Sport Club mounted and rode a single bicycle a distance of 200 m *656 ft 2 in*.

Boat trot ■ The 'City of Dublin' Appeal Committee of the Royal National Lifeboat Institution organised 329 sailing boats belonging to members of Dublin sailing clubs to be moored into a double ring pattern in the shape of a sunflower in Dun Laoghaire Harbour, Dublin, Ireland on 14 Jun 1987.

Boomerang throwing ■ The earliest mention of a word similar to *boomerang* is *wo-murrang* in Collins *Acct. N.S. Wales Vocab.* 1798. The earliest certain Australian account of a returning boomerang (term established 1827) was in 1831 by Major (later Sir Thomas) Mitchell.

The greatest number of consecutive two-handed catches is 653 by Bob Croll (Australia) on 7 Apr 1984 at Albury, Australia. The longest out and return distance is one of 121 m *397 ft* by Christian Jabet (France) near Lyon, France on 5 Apr 1986. The longest flight duration (with self-catch) is one of 2 min 59·94 sec by Dennis Joyce (USA) at Bethlehem, Pennsylvania, USA on 25 Jun 1987. John Flynn (USA) caught 70 boomerang throws in 5 min at Geneva, Switzerland on 20 Aug 1988. The juggling record is 69 by Bob Burwell (Australia) at Fairfax, Virginia, USA on 11 Jun 1982.

Brick carrying ■ The greatest distance achieved for carrying a brick 4·08 kg *9 lb* in a nominated ungloved hand in an uncradled downward pincher grip is 99·37 km *61¾ miles* by Reg Morris of Walsall, West Midlands on 16 Jul 1985.

The feminine record for a 4·422 kg *9 lb 12 oz* brick is 36·2 km *22½ miles* by Wendy Morris of Walsall, West Midlands on 28 Apr 1986. The British feminine record for a 2·97 kg *6 lb 9 oz* smooth-sided brick is 9·6 km *6 miles* by Karen Stevenson of Wallasey, Merseyside on 17 Aug 1984.

Bricklaying ■ Tony Gregory of Horndon on the Hill, Essex laid 747 bricks, each weighing 2·00 kg *4·41 lb*, in 60 min at Grays, Essex on 18 Apr 1987. This was achieved in accordance with the rules of the Brick Development Association and the Guild of Bricklayers.

Bricklifting ■ Geoff Capes lifted 26 bricks in Brockley, south London on 16 Jun 1988, and also at the BBC *Record Breakers* studios on 9 Nov 1988. Before a standardised set of rules had been drawn up, Geoff had lifted 28 bricks, on 18 Sep 1987.

Brick throwing ■ The greatest reported distance for throwing a standard 2·268 kg *5 lb* building brick is 44·54 m *146 ft 1 in* by Geoff Capes at Braybrook School, Orton Goldhay, Cambs on 19 Jul 1978.

Bubble ■ David Stein of New York, USA created a 15·24 m *50 ft* long bubble on 6 Jun 1988. He made the bubble using a bubble wand, washing-up liquid and water.

Bubble gum blowing ■ The greatest reported diameter for a bubble gum bubble under the strict rules of this highly competitive activity is 55·8 cm *22 in* by Susan Montgomery Williams of Fresno, California, USA in June 1985. The British record is 42 cm *16¹⁄₂ in* by Nigel Fell, 13, from Derriaghy, Northern Ireland in November 1979. This was equalled by John Smith of Willingham, Cambs on 25 Sep 1983.

Burial alive ■ Voluntary burial alive claims (of which claims up to 217 days have been published) are inadmissible unless the depth of the coffin is a minimum 2 m *6 ft 6³⁄₄ in* below ground; the coffin has a maximum cubic capacity of 1·5 million cc *54 ft³*, and the single aperture for communication and feeding has a maximum dimension of 10 cm *4 in.* 'Country' Bill White, 50, was so buried from 31 Jul to 19 Dec 1981 (141 days) in Killeen, Texas, USA.

Camping out ■ The silent Indian *fakir* Mastram Bapu ('contented father') remained on the same spot by the roadside in the village of Chitra for 22 years from 1960–82.

Canal jumping (dyke vaulting) ■ In the sport of Fierljeppen at Winsam, Friesland, Netherlands, the record is 18·61 m *61 ft 0³⁄₄ in* across the water with a 12·2 m *40 ft* aluminium pole set by Aarth de Wit in August 1983.

Card throwing ■ Kevin St Onge threw a standard playing card 56·41 m *185 ft 1 in* at the Henry Ford Community College Campus, Dearborn, Michigan, USA on 12 Jun 1979.

Carriage driving ■ The only man to drive 48 horses in a single hitch is Dick Sparrow of Zearing, Iowa, USA from 1972–7. The lead horses were on reins 41 m *135 ft* long.

Card wrecking ■ The greatest number of cars wrecked in a stunting career is 1997 to 1 Jun 1989 by Dick Sheppard of Gloucester, England.

Catapulting ■ The greatest recorded distance for a catapult shot is 415 m *1362 ft* by James M. Pfotenhauer using a patented 5·22 m *17 ft 1¹⁄₂ in* 'Monarch IV Supershot' and a 53-calibre lead musket ball on Ski Hill Road, Escanaba, Michigan, USA on 10 Sep 1977.

Champagne cork flight ■ The longest distance from an untreated and unheated bottle 1·22 m *4 ft* from level ground is 54·18 m *177 ft 9 in* by Professor Emeritus Heinrich Medicus, RPI, at the Woodbury Vineyards Winery, New York, USA on 5 Jun 1988.

Champagne fountain ■ The greatest number of storeys achieved in a champagne fountain, successfully filled from the top and using 10 404 traditional long-stem glasses, is 44 (height 7·52 m *24·7 ft*), achieved by Pascal Leclerc at the Biltmore Hotel, Los Angeles, California USA on 18 Jun 1984.

Cigar box balancing ■ Bruce Block balanced 211 King Edward boxes on his chin for 9 sec in the Hilton Hotel, Akron, Ohio, USA on 28 Jul 1988.

Clapping ■ The duration record for continuous clapping (sustaining an average of 160 claps per min audible at 109·7 m *120 yd*) is 58 hr 9 min by V. Jeyaraman of Tamil Nadu, India from 12–15 Feb 1988.

Club swinging ■ Albert Rayner set a world record of 17 512 revolutions (4·9 per sec) in 60 min at Wakefield, West Yorks on 27 Jul 1981. M. Dobrilla swung continuously for 144 hr at Cobar, NSW, Australia finishing on 15 Sept 1913.

Circus Records

The world's largest permanent circus is Circus Circus, Las Vegas, Nevada, USA opened on 18 Oct 1968 at a cost of $15 000 000. It covers an area of 11 984 m² *129 000 ft²* capped by a tent-shaped flexiglass roof 27·43 m *90 ft* high. The largest travelling circus is the Circus Vargas in the USA which can accommodate 5000 people under its Big Top.

Flying trapeze ■ Downward circles or 'muscle grinding'—1350 by Sarah Denu (aged 14) (US) Madison, Wisconsin, USA, 21 May 1983. Single-heel hang on swinging bar, Angela Revelle (Angelique), Australia, 1977.

Highest aerial act ■ Ian Ashpole (b. 15 Jan 1956) of Ross-on-Wye, Hereford and Worcester performed a trapeze act suspended from a hot-air balloon between St Neots, Cambs and Newmarket, Suffolk at 5004·8 m *16 420 ft* on 16 May 1986.

Triple twisting double somersault ■ Tom Robin Edelston to catcher John Zimmerman, Circus World, Florida, USA, 20 Jan 1981.

Full twisting triple and the quadruple ■ Vasquez Troupe. Miguel Vasquez to catcher Juan Vasquez at Ringling Bros, Amphitheater, Chicago, Illinois, USA in November 1981. On 20 Sep 1984 he performed a triple somersault in a layout position (no turn) to catcher Juan Vasquez at the Sports Arena, Los Angeles, California, USA.

Triple back somersault with 1¹⁄₂ twists ■ Terry Cavaretta Lemus (now Mrs St Jules). At Circus Circus, Las Vegas, Nevada, USA in 1969.

Trampoline ■ Septuple twisting back somersault to bed and quintuple twisting back somersault to shoulders by Marco Canestrelli to Belmonte Canestrelli at Madison Square Gardens, New York, USA on 5 Jan and 28 Mar 1979. Richard Tison (France) performed a triple twisting triple back somersault for television near Berchtesgaden, West Germany on 30 Jun 1981.

Flexible pole ■ Double full twisting somersault to a 5·08 cm *2 in* diameter pole by Roberto Tabak (aged 11) in Sarasota, Florida, USA in 1977. Triple full twisting somersault by Corina Colonelu Mosoianu (aged 13) at Madison Square Garden, New York, USA on 17 Apr 1984.

Human pyramid (or tuckle) ■ Twelve (3 high) supported by a single under-stander. Weight 771 kg *1700 lb* or *121·4 stone* by Tahar Douis of the Hassani Troupe at BBC TV Pebble Mill Studio, Birmingham on 17 Dec 1979.

Nine high by top-mounter Josep-Joan Martínez Lozano, aged 10, of the Colla Vella dels Xiquets, 12 m *39 ft* tall on 25 Oct 1981 in Valls, Spain.

Oldest clown ■ Charlie Revel (b. Andrea Lassere, Spain, 24 Apr 1896) performed for 82 years (1899–1981).

JUGGLING RECORDS

7 clubs ■ Albert Petrovski (USSR), 1963; Sorin Munteanu (Romania), 1975; Jack Bremlov (Czechoslovakia), 1985; Albert Lucas (US), 1985; Anthony Gatto (US), 1988.

8 plates ■ Enrico Rastelli (Italy), 1896–1931; Albert Lucas (US), 1984.

10 balls ■ Enrico Rastelli (Italy), 1896–1931; Albert Lucas (US), 1984.

12 rings ■ Albert Lucas (US), 1985.

Pirouettes with 3 cigar boxes ■ Kris Kremo (Switzerland) (quadruple turn with 3 boxes in mid-air), 1977.

Duration 5 clubs ■ 37 min 10 sec, Albert Lucas (US), 1984.

3 objects while running—joggling ■ Owen Morse (US), 100 m in 11·9 sec, 1988. Kirk Swenson (US), 1·6 km *1 mile* in 4 min 43 sec, 1986 and 5 km *3·1 miles* in 16 min 55 sec, 1986.

5 objects while running—joggling ■ Owen Morse (US), 100 m in 13·8 sec, 1988.

7 ping-pong balls with mouth ■ Tony Ferko (Czechoslovakia), 1987.

5 balls inverted ■ Bobby May (US), since 1953.

3 objects without a drop ■ Dave Pope and Jas Angelo (both GB), both 6 hr 26 min 31 sec, 1989.

Coal cutting ■ The individual record is 221·5 tonnes in a week of 5 shifts by Jim Marley (b. 1914) at East Walbottle Colliery, Tyne and Wear in 1949. This included 48·3 tonnes in 6 hr. The NCB record for a week's production by a 48-man team is 32 333 tonnes at the biggest pit at Kellingley Colliery, Knottingley, West Yorks in the pre-Christmas 'Bull Week' in December 1982.

Coal shovelling ■ The record for filling a 508 kg *1120 lb* hopper with coal is 29·4 sec by Piet Groot at the Inangahua A and P Show, New Zealand on 1 Jan 1985.

Coin balancing ■ The tallest column of coins ever stacked on the edge of a coin is 205 Canadian 25-cent pieces on top of a Canadian Olympic commemorative coin which was freestanding vertically on the base of a coin flat on the surface, by Bruce McConachy (b. 1963) of West Vancouver, BC, Canada for Fuji-TV in Tokyo, Japan on 24 Feb 1985.

Alex Chervinsky (b. 22 Feb 1908) of Lock Haven, Pennsylvania, USA achieved a pyramid of 390 coins on his 75th birthday.

Coin snatching ■ The greatest number of 10p pieces clean caught from being flipped from the back of a forearm into the same downward palm is 140 by Dean Gould in Hamburg, West Germany on 19 Mar 1988.

Competition winnings ■ The largest individual competition prize win on record is $307 500 by Herbert J. Idle, 55, of Chicago in an encyclopaedia contest run by Unicorn Press Inc., on 20 Aug 1953. The highest value first prize offered in Britain has been a £172 950 new house in a £491 000 competition run by the *London Evening Standard* in April and May 1987.

Cow chip tossing ■ The record distances in the country sport of throwing dried cow chips depend on whether or not the projectile may be 'moulded into a spherical shape'. The greatest distance achieved under the 'non-sphericalisation and 100 per cent organic' rule (established in 1970) is 81·07 m *266 ft* by Steve Urner at the Mountain Festival, Tehachapi, California, USA on 14 Aug 1981.

Cardiopulmonary resuscitation ■ Roger Frisby and Trevor Toogood completed a 110 hr CPR marathon (cardiopulmonary resuscitation—15 compressions alternating with two breaths) between 14–19 Nov 1988 in Shaftesbury, Dorset.

Crawling ■ The longest continuous voluntary crawl (progression with one or other knee in unbroken contact with the ground) on record is 45·87 km *28½ miles* by Reg Morris of Brownhills, West Midlands on 29 Jul 1988. The crawl took place on a measured course 2·41 km *1½ miles* long. It took 9½ hours and 19 laps of the track to gain the record. Over a space of 15 months ending on 9 Mar 1985 Jagdish Chander, 32, crawled 1400 km *870 miles* from Aligarh to Jamma, India to propitiate his favourite Hindu goddess, Mata.

Crochet ■ Mrs Barbara Jean Sonntag (b. 1938) of Craig, Colorado, USA crocheted 330 shells plus five stitches (equivalent to 4412 stitches) in 30 min at a rate of 147 stitches a minute on 13 Jan 1981. Miss Ria van der Honing of Wormerveer, Netherlands, completed a crochet chain 62·50 km *38·83 miles* in length on 14 Jul 1986. Mrs Sybille Anthony completed a 120-hr crochet marathon at Toombul Shopping-town, Queensland, Australia on 7 Oct 1977.

Cucumber slicing ■ Norman Johnson of Blackpool College, Lancs set a record of 13·4 sec for slicing a 30·48 cm *12 in* cucumber, 3·81 cm *1½ in* in diameter, at 22 slices to the inch (total 244 slices) at *West Deutscher Rundfunk* in Cologne, West Germany on 3 Apr 1983.

Custard pie throwing ■ The most times champion in the annual World Custard Pie Championships, now at Ditton, Maidstone, Kent (instituted 1968) have been 'The Birds' ('The Bashers') and the 'Coxheath Men' ('Custard Kings') each with three wins. The target (face) must be 2·53 m *8 ft 3⅞ in* from the thrower who must throw a pie no more than 26·03 cm *10¼ in* in diameter. Six points are scored for a square hit full in the face.

Dancing dragon ■ The longest dancing dragon, created by members of the Hawaii Chinese Community, Hawaii, USA in January 1989, was 188·24 m *617 ft 7 in* long. It was made from silk, bamboo and papier mâché among other things, and decorated with gold scales. 53 people then brought it to life in dance as part of the celebrations to mark the Chinese bicentennial in Hawaii.

Greatest omnivore ● Michel Lotito of Grenoble, France — known as Monsieur Mangetout — has been eating metal and glass since 1959, and since 1966 his diet has included 10 bicycles. (Photo: Rex Features)

Debating ■ Students at University College, Dublin, Ireland debated the motion that 'Every Dog should have its Day' for 503 hr 45 min, from 16 Nov–7 Dec 1988.

Demolition work ■ Fifteen members of the Black Leopard Karate Club demolished a seven-room wooden farmhouse west of Elnora, Alberta, Canada in 3 hr 18 min by foot and empty hand on 13 Jun 1982.

Domino stacking ■, David Coburn successfully stacked 291 dominoes on a single supporting domino on 19 Aug 1988 in Miami, Florida, USA.

Domino toppling ■ The greatest number set up single-handed and toppled is 281 581 out of 320 236 by Klaus Friedrich, 22, in Bayern, West Germany on 27 Jan 1984. The dominoes fell within 12 min 57·3 sec having taken 31 days (10 hours daily) to set up.

30 students at Delft, Eindhoven and Twente Technical Universities in the Netherlands set up 1 500 000 dominoes depicting all of the EC member countries. Of these, 1 382 101 were toppled by one push on 2 Jan 1988.

Drink round ■ Liam Fallon treated 1613 people to a free drink at a charity fund-raising gathering on 4 Jul 1987 at Lord Byron's Wine Bar, Solihull, Warwicks.

Drumming ■ The world duration drumming record is 44 days 1 hr by Trevor Mitchell at the Brown Cow Hotel, Scunthorpe, Humberside from 5 Jul to 18 Aug 1986.

Four hundred separate drums were played in 31·78 sec by Rory Blackwell at Finlake Country Park, Chudleigh, Devon on 30 May 1988.

Ducks and drakes ■ The best is 29 skips (14 plinkers and 15 pitty-pats) by Arthur Ring, 69, at Midway Beach, California, USA on 4 Aug 1984 and Jerdone 'Jerry' McGhee, 42, at Wimberley, Texas, USA on 18 Nov 1986.

Eating ■ Michel Lotito (b. 15 Jun 1950) of Grenoble, France, known as Monsieur Mangetout, has been eating metal and glass since 1959. Gastroenterologists have X-rayed his stomach and have described his ability to consume 900 g *2 lb* of metal per day as unique. His diet since 1966 has included 10 bicycles, a supermarket trolley in 4½ days, 7 TV sets, 6 chandeliers and a low-calorie Cessna light

Dancing

Marathon dancing must be distinguished from dancing mania, or tarantism, which is a pathological condition. The worst outbreak of this was at Aachen, Germany in July 1374, when hordes of men and women broke into a frenzied and compulsive choreomania in the streets. It lasted for many hours until injury or complete exhaustion ensued.

Largest and longest dances ■ An estimated 25 000 attended a 'Moonlight Serenade' outdoor evening of dancing to the music of the Glenn Miller Orchestra in Buffalo, New York, USA on 20 Jul 1984. An estimated total of 20 000 dancers took part in the National Square Dance Convention at Louisville, Kentucky, USA on 26 Jun 1983.

The most severe marathon dance staged as a public spectacle was one by Mike Ritof and Edith Boudreaux who logged 5148 hr 28½ min to win $2000 at Chicago's Merry Garden Ballroom, Belmont and Sheffield, Illinois, USA from 29 Aug 1930 to 1 Apr 1931. Rest periods were progressively cut from 20 to 10 to 5 to nil minutes per hour with 10-inch steps and a maximum of 15 seconds for closure of eyes.

Will Kemp in 1599 Morris-danced his way from London to Norwich in 9 days.

'Rosie Radiator' (Rose Marie Ostler) on 16 Aug 1986 claimed a mileage of 9·6 km *6 miles* in leading a column of 17 tap dancers across San Francisco.

Ballroom *Marathon* ■ The individual continuous world record for ballroom dancing is 126 hr by Scott Michael, 31, a dancing instructor of Huntington Beach, California, USA, on 20–25 Jun 1986 at the Dance Masters Ballroom Studio, Stanton, California, USA. 27 girls worked shifts as his partner.

Champions ■ The world's most successful professional ballroom dancing champions have been Bill Irvine MBE and Bobbie Irvine MBE, who won 13 world titles between 1960 and 1968. The oldest competitive ballroom dancer is Albert J. Sylvester CBE, JP (b. 24 Nov 1889) of Corsham, Wilts who retired aged 94.

Belly dancing ■ The longest recorded belly dancing marathon was one of 106 hr by Eileen Foucher at Rush Green Hospital, Romford, Essex from 30 Jul–3 Aug 1984.

Charleston ■ The charleston duration record is 110 hr 58 min by Sabra Starr of Lansdowne, Pennsylvania, USA from 15–20 Jan 1979.

Conga ■ The longest recorded conga was the Miami Super Conga, held in conjunction with Calle Ocho — a party to which Cuban-Americans invite the rest of Miami for a celebration of life together. Held on 13 Mar 1988, the conga consisted of 119 986 people.

The longest one in Britain comprised a 'snake' of 8659 people from the South Eastern Region of the Camping and Caravanning Club of Great Britain and Ireland on 4 Sep 1982 at Brands Hatch, Kent.

Country dancing ■ The most complex Scottish country dance ever held was a 256-some reel, choreographed by Ian Price, which took place on 24 Apr 1988 in Vancouver, Canada.

Disco ■ The longest recorded disco dancing marathon is one of 462½ hr by Alfie Turner of Romford, Essex from 28 Apr–17 May 1985.

Flamenco ■ The fastest flamenco dancer ever measured is Solero de Jerez, aged 17, who in Brisbane, Australia in September 1967 in an electrifying routine attained 16 heel taps per second.

Jiving ■ The duration record for non-stop jiving is 97 hr 42 min by Richard Rimmer (with a relay of partners) of Caterham, Surrey from 11–16 Nov 1979. Under the strict rules of the European Rock 'n' Roll Association the duration pair record is 24 hr 5 min by 5 couples at the Clayton Community Festival, Victoria, Australia from 11–12 Oct 1986.

Tap ■ The fastest *rate* ever measured for tap dancing is 28 taps per second by Michael Flatley of Palos Park, Illinois, USA on 9 May 1989. Roy Castle, the presenter of the BBC TV *Record Breakers* programme, achieved one million taps in 23 hr 44 min at the *Guinness World of Records* exhibition, London on 31 Oct–1 Nov 1985. The greatest ever assemblage of tap dancers in a single routine is 4497 outside Macy's Store in New York City, USA on 28 Aug 1988, subsequently shown on the BBC TV *Record Breakers* programme.

aircraft which he ate in Caracas, Venezuela. He is said to have provided the only example in history of a coffin (handles and all) ending up inside a man.

In an 'Outrageous Contest' organised by WKQX Chicago from 11–15 Sep 1980, Jay Gwaltney, 19, ate a birch tree that was 3·35 m *11 ft* in length and had a 12 cm *4·7 in* diameter trunk. It took him 89 hr.

Egg and spoon racing ■ Chris Riggio of San Francisco, California, USA completed a 45·86 km *28·5 mile* fresh egg and dessert spoon marathon in 4 hr 34 min on 7 Oct 1979.

Egg dropping ■ The greatest height from which fresh eggs have been dropped (to earth) and remained intact is 198 m *650 ft* by David S. Donoghue from a helicopter on 2 Oct 1979 on a golf course in Tokyo, Japan.

Egg hunt ■ The greatest egg hunt on record involved 72 000 hard-boiled eggs and 40 000 candy eggs at the 26th annual Garrison Egg Hunt at Homer, Georgia, USA on 7 Apr 1985.

Egg shelling ■ Two kitchen hands, Harold Witcomb and Gerald Harding, shelled 1050 dozen eggs in a 7¼ hr shift at Bowyers, Trowbridge, Wilts on 23 Apr 1971. Both were blind.

Egg throwing ■ The longest authenticated distance for throwing a fresh hen's egg without breaking it is 96·90 m *317 ft 10 in* by Risto Antikainen to Jyrki Korhonen at Siilinjarvi, Finland on 6 Sep 1981.

Escalator riding ■ The record for travelling a pair of 'up' and 'down' escalators is 84 hr, by a team of nine from Metro Theatres Alberton, Johannesburg, South Africa, from 5–8 Dec 1987. The total distance travelled was 164·54 km *102¼ miles*.

Escapology ■ The most renowned of all escape artists has been Ehrich Weiss *alias* Harry Houdini (1874–1926), who pioneered underwater escapes from locked, roped and weighted containers while handcuffed and shackled with irons.

A manufacturer of strait-jackets acknowledges that an escapologist 'skilled in the art of bone and muscle manipulation' could escape from a standard jacket in seconds. There are, however, methods by which such circumvention can itself be circumvented. Nick Janson of Benfleet, Essex has escaped from handcuffs locked on him by more than 1300 different police officers since 1954.

Family tree ■ The farthest back the lineage of any family has been traced is that of K'ung Ch'iu or Confucius (551–479 BC). His 4 greats grandfather K'ung Chia is known from the 8th century BC. This man's 85th lineal descendants Wei-yi (b. 1939) and Wei-ning (b. 1947) live today in Taiwan (Formosa).

Fashion show ■ The longest distance covered by girl models is 114·4 km *71·1 miles* from 19–21

Feminine beauty ● The shortest reign as Miss World was 18 hours by Miss Germany (Gabriella Brum) in 1980. (Photo: Rex Features)

Sep 1983 by Roberta Brown and Lorraine McCourt at Parke's Hotel, Dublin, Ireland. Male model Eddie Warke covered a further 19·1 km *11·9 miles* on the catwalk. The compère was Marty Whelan of Radio 2.

Faux pas ■ If measured by financial consequence, the greatest *faux pas* on record was that of the young multi-millionaire James Gordon Bennett, committed on 1 Jan 1877 at the family mansion of his demure fiancée one Caroline May, in Fifth Avenue, New York, USA. Bennett arrived in a two-horse cutter late and obviously in wine. By dint of intricate footwork, he gained the portals to enter the withdrawing room where he was the cynosure of all eyes. He mistook the fireplace for a plumbing fixture more usually reserved for another purpose. The May family broke the engagement and Bennett (1841–1918) was obliged to spend the rest of his foot-loose and fancy-free life based in Paris with the resultant non-collection of millions of tax dollars by the US Treasury.

Feminine beauty ■ Female pulchritude, being qualitative rather than quantitative, does not lend itself to records. It has been suggested that, if the face of Helen of Troy (*c.* 1200 BC) was capable of

launching 1000 ships, a unit of beauty sufficient to launch one ship should be a millihelen.

The earliest international beauty contest was staged by P. T. Barnum (with the public to be the judges) in the USA in June 1855. The Miss America contest was staged at Atlantic City, New Jersey, USA in 1921 and was won by a thin blue-eyed blonde with a 76·2 cm *30 in* chest, Margaret Gorman. The world's largest annual beauty pageants are the Miss World (inaugurated 1951) and Miss Universe (1952) contests. The most successful country in the latter contest has been the USA with winners in 1954–56–60–67–70–80. The number of countries represented has reached 80. The country which has produced the most winners in the Miss World contest is the United Kingdom, with five. They were Rosemarie Frankland (1961); Ann Sidney (1964); Lesley Langley (1965); Helen Morgan (1974), who resigned, and Sarah-Jane Hutt (1983). The maximum number of contestants was 84 in November 1988. The shortest reign was 18 hours by Miss Germany (Gabriella Brum) in 1980.

Field gun pull ■ Three teams of eight members from 55 Ordnance Company (Volunteers) Royal Army Ordnance Corps pulled a 25-pounder field gun over a distance of 137·92 km *85·7 miles* in 24 hours in Hounslow, Middx on 15–16 Apr 1988.

Field to loaf ■ The fastest time for producing loaves from growing wheat is 40 min 8 sec at Bartley

Mill, Bells Yew Green, near Frant, East Sussex on 19 Aug 1988.

Fire pumping ■ The greatest gallonage stirrup-pumped by a team of eight in an 80-hr charity pump is 97 050 litres *21 348 gal* by firefighters representing Ilkeston Fire Station from 17–20 Aug 1988 at the Market Place in Ilkeston, Derbyshire.

Fire pump manhandling ■ The longest unaided tow of a fire appliance in excess of 508 kg *10 cwt* in 24 hr on a closed circuit is 358·8 km *223 miles* by a 32-man team of the Dublin Fire Brigade with an 520 kg *1144 lb* fire pump on 20–21 Jun 1987.

Flute marathon ■ The longest recorded marathon by a flautist is 61 hr by Joseph Shury of the Sri Chinmoy Marathon Team, Toronto, Ontario, Canada from 21–23 Mar 1986.

Flying disc throwing (formerly frisbee) ■ The World Flying Disc Federation indoor records are, men: 121·6 m *398·9 ft* by Van Miller (US) at Flagstaff, Arizona, USA on 18 Sep 1982; and women: 69·8 m *229 ft* by Suzanne Fields (US) at Cedar Falls, Iowa, USA on 26 Apr 1981. The outdoor records are, men: 190·07 m *623·6 ft* by Sam Ferrans (US), 2 Jul 1988 at La Habra, California, USA; and women: 125·09 m *410·4 ft* by Chris O'Cleary (US), 22 Jul 1988 at San Francisco, California, USA. The throw, run and catch records are, men: 92·64 m *303·9 ft* by Hiroshi Oshima (Japan), 20 Jul 1988 at San Francisco, California, USA; and women: 60·02 m *196·91 ft* by Judy Horowitz (US), 29 Jun 1985 at La Mirada, California, USA. The group marathon record is 1198 hr by Prince George's Community College Club from 1 Jun–21 Jul 1981 at Largo, Maryland, USA (see Throwing p. 186).

Footbag ■ The world record for keeping a footbag airborne is 36 230 consecutive kicks or hacks by Andy Linder (US) in Palatine, Illinois, USA on 24 Aug 1986. The feminine record is held by Tricia Sullivan with 12 838 on 31 Jul 1985 at Golden, Colorado, USA. The sport originated in Oregon, USA in 1972 and was invented by John Stalberger (US).

Girning ■ The only girner to have won six national titles is Ron Looney of Egremont, Cumbria from 1979–84.

Gladiatorial combat ■ Emperor Trajan of Rome (AD 98–117) staged a display involving 4941 pairs of gladiators over 117 days. Publius Ostorius, a freed-man, survived 51 combats in Pompeii.

Gold panning ■ The fastest time for 'panning' eight planted gold nuggets in a 25·4 cm *10 in* diameter pan is 9·23 sec by Bob Box of Ahwahnee, California, USA, and the female record is 10·03 sec by Susan Bryeans of Fullerton, California, both in the 23rd World Gold Panning Championship on 6 Mar 1983 at Knotts Berry Farm, Buena Park, California, USA.

Golf ball balancing ■ Lang Martin balanced seven golf balls vertically without adhesive at Charlotte, North Carolina, USA on 9 Feb 1980.

Grape catching ■ The greatest distance at which a grape thrown from level ground has been caught in the mouth is 97·43 m *319 ft 8 in* by Arden Chapman at Northeast Louisiana University, Monroe, USA on 18 Jul 1980.

Grave digging ■ It is recorded that Johann Heinrich Karl Thieme, sexton of Aldenburg, Germany, dug 23 311 graves during a 50-year career. In 1826 his understudy dug *his* grave.

Guitar playing ■ The longest recorded solo guitar-playing marathon is one of 300 hr by Vincent Paxton at the Lord Nelson public house, Winterslow, Wilts from 23 Nov–6 Dec 1986.

Gum boot throwing ■ The longest recorded distance for 'Wellie wanging' (size 8 Challenger Dunlop Boot) is 52·73 m *173 ft* by Tony Rodgers of Warminster, Wilts on 9 Sep 1978. Rosemary Payne established the feminine record at Cannon Hill Park, Birmingham on 21 Jun 1975 with 39·60 m *129 ft 11 in*.

FOOD

APPLE PIE

The largest apple pie ever baked was that by ITV chef Glynn Christian in a 12 m × 7 m *40 ft × 23 ft* dish at Hewitts Farm, Chelsfield, Kent from 25–27 Aug 1982. Over 600 bushels of apples were included in the pie which weighed 13·66 tonnes *30 115 lb*. It was cut by Rear Admiral Sir John Woodward.

BANANA SPLIT

The longest banana split ever made was one of 7·32 km *4·55 miles* in length made by residents of Selinsgrove, Pennsylvania, USA on 30 Apr 1988.

BARBECUE

The record attendance at a one-day barbecue was 35 072, at the Iowa State Fairgrounds, Des Moines, Iowa, USA on 21 Jun 1988. The greatest meat consumption at a one-day barbecue was at the same event — 9131 kg *20 130 lb* of pork in five hours.

The greatest quantity of meat consumed at any barbecue was 9576 kg *21 112 lb* of beef at the Sertoma Club Barbecue, New Port Richey, Florida, USA from 7–9 Mar 1986.

CAKES

The largest cake ever created weighed 40·82 tonnes *90 000 lb*, included 13·61 tonnes *30 000 lb* of vanilla icing, was 33·5 × 24·3 m *110 × 80 ft* in size and was baked in 32 hours by Chef Franz Eichenauer at the City Coliseum, Austin, Texas, USA on 20 Feb 1986. It was cut by HRH the Prince of Wales and the Governor of Texas, Mark White Jr. The tallest cake was 23·68 m *77 ft 8 in* high, created by Mrs Nilasari with assistance from a team of 121 in Surabaya, Indonesia. Work started on the cake on 16 Feb 1989 and it was finished on 9 Apr 1989. The 'Alimentarium', a museum of food in Vevey, Switzerland, has on display the world's oldest cake, which was sealed and 'vacuum-packed' in the grave of Pepionkh, who lived in Ancient Egypt around 2200 BC. The 11 cm *4·3 in* wide cake has sesame on it and honey inside, and possibly milk too.

CHEESE

The largest cheese ever created was a cheddar of 18 171 kg *40 060 lb*, made on 13–14 Mar 1988 at Simon's Specialty Cheese, Little Chute, Wisconsin, USA. It was subsequently taken on tour in a specially designed, refrigerated 'Cheesemobile'.

CHERRY PIE

The largest cherry pie ever made was one weighing a total of 12 861·82 kg *28355·17 lb* and containing 11 754·06 kg *25 890 lb* of cherry filling. It measured 5·33 m *17 ft 6 in* in diameter, 66·04 cm *26 in* in depth, and was baked by Chef Pierre Bakeries in conjunction with the Michigan Cherry Committee in Traverse City, Michigan, USA on 25 Jul 1987.

CHOCOLATE MODEL

The largest chocolate model was one weighing 1800 kg *3968·3 lb*, of the 1992 Olympic Centre, Barcelona, Spain. It was made by Gremi Provincial de Pastigeria i Confiteria School, Barcelona in November 1985 and measured 10 × 5 m × 73 cm *32 ft 9½ in × 16 ft 4⅓ in × 28·7 in*.

CHRISTMAS PUDDING

The largest was one of 1390 kg *3064·42 lb*, made by employees of Herbert Adams in Kensington, Victoria, Australia. They started preparing it on 16 Nov 1987 and finished the decorating on 9 Dec 1987.

COCKTAIL

The largest cocktail on record was one of 1363·83 litres *300 gal* created by Bacardi Imports in Miami, Florida, USA on 9 Mar 1989, and named 'Cuba Libre'.

CONDIMENT RAREST

The world's most prized condiment is Cà Cuong, a secretion recovered in minute amounts from beetles in North Vietnam. Owing to war conditions, the price had risen to $100 per 28 g *1 oz* before supplies virtually ceased in 1975.

CUSTARD PIE

The largest custard pie made was one of 203·2 kg *448 lb* made in the kitchen of Jury's Hotel, Dublin, Ireland under the supervision of Derek McLoughlin and John Clancy on 6 Feb 1987.

DISH

The largest menu item in the world is roasted camel, prepared occasionally for Bedouin wedding feasts. Cooked eggs are stuffed into fish, the fish stuffed into cooked chickens, the chickens stuffed into a roasted sheep's carcass and the sheep stuffed into a whole camel.

EASTER EGGS

The heaviest Easter egg ever made was one weighing 3430 kg *7561 lb 13½ oz*, measuring 3·04 m *10 ft* high, by Siegfried Berndt at 'Macopa' Patisserie, Leicester, and completed on 7 Apr 1982. An egg 5·78 m *18 ft 11½ in* tall was constructed by Tobler Suchard of Bedford, on 10 Apr 1987.

FOOD MOST EXPENSIVE

The most expensively priced food (as opposed to spice) is First Choice Black Périgord truffle (*Tuber melanosporum*), retailed at £8·50 per 12·5 g *0·44 oz* tin. However, in January 1985 in the Hafr El-Baten market, Riyadh, Saudi Arabia local truffles sold for SR 5000 for 3 kg, equivalent to £50·16 for 12·5 g.

FRUIT MOST EXPENSIVE

On 5 Apr 1977 John Synnott of Ashford, County Wicklow, Ireland sold 453 g *1 lb* of strawberries (a punnet of 30 berries) to the restaurateur Leslie Cooke, at auction by Walter L. Cole Ltd in the Dublin Fruit Market for £530 or £17·70 a berry.

HAGGIS

The largest haggis (encased in eight ox stomach linings) on record was one weighing 273·5 kg *603 lb* made for the ASDA Superstore, Corby, Northants by David A. Hall Ltd of Broxburn, Lothian on 6 Nov 1986.

HAMBURGER

The largest hamburger on record was one of 2270·66 kg *5005 lb 13·8 oz* made on 13 Oct 1985 by Spur Steak Ranches (Pty) Ltd at Three Anchor Bay, Cape Town, South Africa. The burger had a diameter of 7·10 m *23 ft 3½ in* and was cut into over 15 750 portions after grilling.

ICE CREAM SUNDAE

The largest ice cream sundae was one weighing 24 908·8 kg *54 914·8 lb* made by Palm Dairies Ltd under the supervision of Mike Rogiani in Edmonton, Alberta, Canada on 24 Jul 1988. It consisted of 20 270·7 kg *44 689·5 lb* of ice-cream, 4394·4 kg *9688·1 lb* of syrup and 243·7 kg *537·2 lb* of topping.

JELLY

The world's largest jelly, a 35 000 litre *7700 gal* watermelon flavoured pink jelly made by Paul Squires and Geoff Ross, worth $14 000, was set at Roma Street Forum, Brisbane, Queensland, Australia on 5 Feb 1981 in a tank by Pool Fab.

KEBAB

The longest kebab ever made was one 270 m *885 ft 10 in* long, under the leadership of Karel Sobota in Velké Březno, Czechoslovakia on 17 Sep 1988.

LOAF

The longest loaf ever baked was a rosca de Reyes 649·90 m *2132 ft 2½ in* in length and 1173 kg *2586 lb* in weight at the Exelaris Hyatt Regency Hotel, Acapulco, Mexico on 6 Jan 1985. If a consumer of the rosca (twisted loaf) finds the embedded bread doll he has to throw the next rosca party.

The largest pan loaf baked was one of 1435 kg *3163 lb 10 oz* measuring 3 × 1·25 × 1·1 m *9 ft 10 in × 4 ft 1 in × 3 ft 7 in* by staff of Sasko in Johannesburg, South Africa on 18 Mar 1988.

LOLLIPOP

The world's largest iced lollipop was one of 2608 kg *5750 lb* constructed for the Westside Assembly of God Church, Davenport, Iowa, USA on 7 Sep 1975. The largest 'regular' lollipop was one of 931 kg *2052·5 lb* made by the Hyatt Regency Memphis Hotel, Tennessee, USA on 20 Feb 1986.

MEAT PIE

The largest meat pie on record weighed 9030 kg *19 908 lb* and was the 9th in the series of Denby Dale, West Yorks pies. It was baked on 3 Sep 1988 to mark the bicentenary of Denby Dale pie making, the first one in 1788 having been made to celebrate King George III's return to sanity. The 4th (Queen Victoria's Jubilee, 1887) went a bit 'off' and had to be buried in quick-lime.

MILK SHAKE

The largest milk shake was a chocolate one of 4682·5 litres *1030 gal*, made by Lotta Rock Dairy, Inc., of Littleton, New Hampshire, USA on 12–13 Aug 1988.

MINCE PIE

The largest mince pie recorded was one of 1025 kg *2260 lb*, measuring 6·09 × 1·52 m *20 × 5 ft*, baked at Ashby-de-la-Zouch, Leics on 15 Oct 1932.

OMELETTE

The largest omelette in the world was one made of 54 763 eggs with 240 kg *531 lb* cheese in a skillet 9·1 m *30 ft* in diameter cooked by Michael McGowan assisted by his staff and the Sunrise Jaycees of Las Vegas, Nevada, USA on 25 Oct 1986.

A Spanish omelette weighing 300 kg *660 lb* was made by Jose Antonio Rivera Casal at Caracacia, Padron, Spain on 17 May 1987 and consisted of 5000 eggs, 500 kg *1102 lb* of potatoes, 80 kg *176 lb* of red peppers, 10 kg *22 lb* of salt and 150 litres *33 gal* of oil.

PAELLA

The largest paella measured 16 m *52·48 ft* in diameter and was made by Josep Gruges 'Pepitu' on 25 Aug 1987 in the Playa de Aro, Gerona, Spain. The ingredients included 3700 kg *8140 lb* of rice, 3000 kg *6600 lb* of meat, 1500 kg *3300 lb* of mussels, 700 kg *1540 lb* each of beans and peppers, 200 kg *440 lb* of garlic and 400 litres *88 gal* of oil. The paella was eaten by 40 000 people who washed it all down with 8000 bottles of Catalan champagne.

PANCAKE

Members of the Lefaivre Lions Club made and flipped a pancake 9·14 m *30 ft* in diameter and 2·54 cm *1 in* deep at Lefaivre, Ontario, Canada on 26 Jun 1988. The pancake weighed 907·18 kg *2000 lb*.

PASTRY

The longest pastry in the world was the 'record' pastry 513·04 m *1683 ft 2½ in* in length made by chefs at the Hyatt Regency Ravinia, Atlanta, Georgia, USA on 26 Jul 1986.

PIZZA PIE

The largest pizza ever baked was one measuring 30·51 m *100 ft 1 in* in diameter, organised by Lorenzo Amato and Louis Piancone and completed at Highway 27, Havana, Florida, USA on 11 Oct 1987.

POPCORN

The largest container of popcorn was a box measuring 7·62 m × 7·62 m *25 ft × 25 ft* which was filled at Jones High School, Orlando, Florida, USA on 15–17 Dec 1988. After popping, the average depth of the corn was 1·85 m *6·06 ft*, giving a total volume of 107·26 m³ *3787·5 ft³*.

POTATO CRISPS

Charles Chip Inc. of Mountville, Pennsylvania, USA, produced crisps 10 × 17·5 cm *4 × 7 in* from outsize potatoes in February 1977.

POTATO MASH

A single serving of 8·26 tonnes *18 260 lb* of potato mash was prepared in a concrete mixer for the 17th Annual Potato Bowl at Grand Forks, North Dakota, USA on 4 Sep 1982.

SALAMI

The longest salami on record was one 17·9 m *58 ft 9 in* long with a circumference of 52·7 cm *20¾ in*, weighing 391·6 kg *863·5 lb*, made by Kutztown Bologna Company, Pennsylvania, USA on 21 Aug 1986.

SAUSAGE (SEE ALSO GRILL, P. 190)

The longest continuous sausage ever made was one of 21·12 km *13·125 miles* made at the premises of Keith Boxley at Wombourne, near Wolverhampton in 15 hr 33 min on 18–19 Jun 1988.

SPICE MOST EXPENSIVE

Prices for wild ginseng (root of *Panax quinquefolius*), from the Chan Pak Mountain area of China, thought to have aphrodisiac qualities, were reported in November 1977 to be as high as $23 000 per ounce in Hong Kong. Total annual shipments from Jilin Province do not

exceed 4 kg *140 oz* a year. A leading medical journal in the USA has likened its effects to 'corticosteroid poisoning'.

SPICE 'HOTTEST'

The hottest of all spices is claimed to be Siling labuyo from the Philippines.

The chili pepper or capsicum known as Tepin, of southwest USA, comes in pods 7 mm *⅜ in* in diameter. A single dried gram will produce detectable 'heat' in 31 kg *68·3 lb* of bland sauce.

STICK OF ROCK

The mightiest piece was a stick weighing more than 305 kg *673·5 lb*, 3·6 m *12 ft* long and 40·6 cm *16 in* thick made by Carshalton Confectionery Company of St. Annes-on-Sea, Lancs on 21 May 1987.

STRAWBERRY BOWL

The largest strawberry bowl ever picked was by children from various schools at Hewitts Farm, Chelsfield, Kent on 7 Jul 1988, having a net weight of 1218·0 kg *2685·2 lb*.

SWEET TOP-SELLING

The world's top-selling sweets (candies) are Life Savers with 33 431 236 300 rolls between 1913 and May 1987. A tunnel formed by the holes in the middle placed end to end would stretch to the Moon and back more than three times. Thomas Syta of Van Nuys, California, USA made one last 7 hr 10 min (with hole intact) on 15 Jan 1983.

TRIFLE

The largest sherry trifle on record was one weighing 1140 kg *2513 lb* including 100 litres *22 gal* of sherry made on 1 Feb 1989 by students of Seale-Hayne College, Newton Abbot, Devon.

Ice cream sundae ● The largest ice cream sundae weighed 24 908·8 kg *54 914·8 lb* and was made by Palm Dairies Ltd under the supervision of Mike Rogiani in Edmonton, Alberta, Canada on 24 Jul 1988. It took 5 hours to construct, with the help of 25 people.

YORKSHIRE PUDDING

The largest was one measuring 21·37 m² *230 ft²* made by Willie Johnston of Hope Valley Round Table, South Yorks and students from Castle College, Sheffield in conjunction with BBC Radio Sheffield, with 720 eggs, 68·04 kg *150 lb* of flour and 136·4 litres *30 gal* of milk on 18 Nov 1988.

--- DRINK ---

As from 1 Jan 1981 the strength of spirits has been expressed only in terms of percentage volume of alcohol at 20° C. Absolute or '100 per cent vol' alcohol was formerly expressed to be 75·35° over proof or 75·35°OP. In the USA proof is double the actual percentage of alcohol by volume at 15·6° C *60° F* such that absolute alcohol is 200 per cent proof spirit. 'Hangovers' are said to be aggravated by the presence of such toxic congenerics as amyl alcohol ($C_5H_{11}OH$).

BEER

Strongest ■ As measured by volume of alcohol, Roger & Out brewed at the Frog & Parrott in Sheffield, South Yorks, from a recipe devised by W.R. Nowill and G.B. Spencer, has an alchol volume is 16·9 per cent with an original gravity of 1125°. It was first brewed in July 1985 and has been on sale ever since. The strongest as measured by original gravity is Domesday Ale brewed by the Cornish Brewery Company Ltd, Redruth, Cornwall with an alcohol content of 15·86 per cent by volume. It has an original gravity of 1143·5°. The strongest lager is Samichlaus Dark 1987 brewed by Brauerei Hürlimann of Zürich, Switzerland. It has an original gravity of 1123° and is 14·93 per cent alcohol by volume at 20° C.

Weakest ■ A sweet ersatz beer brewed in Germany by Sunner, Colne-Kalk, in 1918 had an original gravity of 1000·96° and a strength 1/30th that of the weakest beer now obtainable in the UK.

BOTTLES

Largest ■ One measuring 1·83 m *6 ft* tall and 1·46 m *4 ft 9½ in* in circumference was unveiled at the *Guinness World of Records*, Piccadilly, London on 31 Mar 1987. The bottle, built by independent family whisky company William Grant & Sons as part of its centenary celebrations, contained 40·7 gal *185 litres* of William Grant's Family Reserve Finest Scotch Whisky.

The largest bottles normally used in the wine and spirit trade are the Jeroboam (equal to 4 bottles of champagne or, rarely, of brandy and from 5–6 ¹/₂ bottles of claret according to whether blown or moulded) and the double magnum (equal, since *c.* 1934 to 4 bottles of claret or, more rarely, red Burgundy). A complete set of champagne bottles would consist of a quarter bottle, through the half bottle, bottle, magnum, Jeroboam, Rehoboam, Methuselah, Salmanazar and Balthazar, to the Nebuchadnezzar, which has a capacity of 16 litres *28·14 pt,* and is equivalent to 20 bottles.

A bottle containing 33 litres of Chateau La Rose Marechale 1985 equal in volume to 44 whole wine bottles was auctioned on 11 Oct 1988 in Copenhagen, Denmark.

Martell Cognac is available in a range of 21 bottle sizes from 3 cl *0·05 pt* to 3·78 l *6·6 pt.*

Smallest ■ The smallest bottles of liquor now sold are of Whyte and Mackay Scotch Whisky. Standing just over 5 cm *2 in* high and containing 1·3 ml *22 minims.* A mini case of 12 bottles costs £5.50 including VAT and measures 4·67 × 3·33 × 2·69 cm *1·84 × 1·31 × 1·06 in* the distributors are Cumbrae Supply Co. Paisley, Scotland.

MOST ALCOHOLIC DRINKS
During independence (1918–40) the Estonian Liquor Monopoly marketed 98 per cent potato alcohol (196 proof US). In 31 US states *Everclear,* 190 proof or 95 per cent vol alcohol, is marketed by the American Distilling Co 'primarily as a base for home-made cordials'. Royal Navy rum, introduced in 1655, was 40° OP (79 per cent vol) before 1948, but was reduced to 4·5° UP (under proof) or 46 per cent vol before its abolition on 31 July 1970. The Royal New Zealand Navy still issues Navy Rum at 4·5 under proof and is the only Navy in the world that does. Full strength Pusser's naval rum is currently distributed by I. D.V.(UK)Ltd of Harlow, Essex.

SPIRITS
Most expensive ■ A 60-year-old bottle of 'The Macallan' was sold by the Rotary Club of Elgin, Grampian, for £6000 on 2 Jun 1988. The purchaser was Sheraton Caltrust of Glasgow, Strathclyde.

In Britain *Hennessy Private Reserve Grande Champagne* retails for £120 (including VAT) for a standard bottle.

WINE
Oldest ■ Two bottles from Xinyang, Hunan, China in 1980 from a tomb dated to 1300 BC. A wine jar recovered in Rome has been found to bear the label 'Q. Lutatio C. Mario Cos' meaning that it was produced in the consulship of Q. Lutatius and C. Marius i.e. in 102 BC. A bottle of 1748 Rudesheimer Rosewein was auctioned at Christie's, London for £260 on 6 Dec 1979.

Most expensive ■ £105 000 was paid for a bottle of 1787 Château Lafite claret sold to Christopher Forbes (USA) at Christie's, London on 5 Dec 1985. The price was affected insofar as the bottle was initialled by Thomas Jefferson (1743–1826), 3rd President of the United States. In Nov 1986 its cork, dried out by exhibition lights, slipped thus making the wine undrinkable.

A bottle of white wine – Château d'Yquem of 1784 and also initialled by Thomas Jefferson – was sold at auction by Christie's, London on 4 Dec 1986 for £36 900 to Iyad Shiblaq, Jordan, a teetotaller.

A half bottle of 1784 Château Margaux bearing the initials of Thomas Jefferson was sold by Christie's, at Vinexpo, in Bordeaux, France for FF180 000. In April 1989 it was accidentally knocked over and broken into pieces where it was on display at a restaurant in New York, USA, thereby making it the most expensive carpet to be cleaned.

Auction ■ The largest single sale of wine was conducted by Christie's of London on 10–11 Jul 1974 at Quaglino's Ballroom, London when 2325 lots comprising 432 000 bottles realised £962 190.

Tasting ■ The largest ever reported was that staged by the Wine Institute at St Francis Hotel, San Francisco, California, USA on 17 Jul 1980 with 125 pourers, 90 openers and a consumption of 3000 bottles.

Gum wrapper chain ■ The longest gum wrapper chain on record was made by Cathy Ushler of Redmond, Washington State, USA. When measured in October 1987, it was 1819·9 m *5967 ft* long.

Gun running ■ The record for the Royal Tournament Naval Field Gun Competition (instituted 1907, with present rules since 1913) is 2 min 40·6 sec by the Portsmouth Command Field Gun crew at Earl's Court, London on 19 Jul 1984. The barrel alone weighs 406 kg *8 cwt.* The wall is 1·52 m *5 ft* high and the chasm 8·53 m *28 ft* across.

Haggis hurling ■ The longest recorded distance for throwing a haggis (min. weight 680 g *1 lb 8 oz*) is 55·11 m *180 ft 10 in* by Alan Pettigrew on Inchmurrin, Loch Lomond, Strathclyde on 24 May 1984.

Hairdressing ■ Elie Algranti cut, set and styled hair continuously for 415 hr from 4–21 Feb 1989 in Mossel Bay, South Africa.

Hair splitting ■ The greatest reported achievement in hair splitting has been that of the former champion cyclist and craftsman Alfred West (1901–85) who succeeded in splitting a human hair 17 times into 18 parts on eight occasions.

Handbell ringing ■ The longest recorded handbell-ringing recital has been one of 56 hr 3 min by 12 handbell ringers of Ecclesfield School, Sheffield, South Yorks from 21–23 Jul 1985.

Handshaking ■ Rainer Vikström of Turku, Finland shook 19 592 different hands in 8 hours on 15 May 1988 during Turku's Fourth Annual Spring Market 'Manun Markkinat'. The record number of hands shaken by a public figure at an official function was 8513 by President Theodore Roosevelt (1858–1919) at a New Year's Day White House presentation in Washington, DC, USA on 1 Jan 1907.

Hay bale rolling ■ 'Cressy Rangers' Mark Eastoe and Paul Bowles rolled a 400 kg *882 lb* round bale over a 50 m *164 ft* course in 20·53 sec to win the Hay Bale Rolling Championship held at Cressy, Tasmania, Australia on 12 Mar 1988.

Hedge laying ■ John Williams of Sennybridge and David James of Llanwern, both Brecon, hedged by the 'stake and pleach' method a total of 241·4 m *264 yd* in 11 hr 24 min on 28 Apr 1986.

High diving ■ The highest regularly performed head-first dives are those of professional divers from La Quebrada ('the break in the rocks') at Acapulco, Mexico, a height of 26·7 m *87¹/₂ ft.* The base rocks, 6·4 m *21 ft* out from the take-off, necessitate a leap of 8·22 m *27 ft* out. The water is 3·65 m *12 ft* deep.

The world record high dive is 53·9 m *176 ft 10 in* by Olivier Favre (Switzerland) at Villers-le-Lac, France on 30 Aug 1987. The feminine record is 36·57 m *120 ft* by Lucy Wardle (US) at Ocean Park, Hong Kong on 6 Apr 1985. The highest witnessed in Britain is one of 32·9 m *108 ft* into 2·43 m *8 ft* of water at the Aqua Show at Earl's Court, London on 22 Feb 1946 by Roy Fransen (1915–85).

On 8 May 1885, Sarah Ann Henley, 24, jumped from the Clifton Suspension Bridge, which crosses the Avon. Her 76 m *250 ft* fall was slightly cushioned by her voluminous dress and petticoat acting as a parachute. She landed, bruised and bedraggled, in the mud on the north bank and was carried to hospital by 4 policemen. On 11 Feb 1968 Jeffrey Kramer, 24, leapt off the George Washington Bridge 76 m *250 ft* above the Hudson River, New York City, USA, and survived. Of the 696 identified people who have made 73 m *240 ft* suicide dives from the Golden Gate Bridge, San Francisco, California, USA since 1937, 12 survived of whom Todd Sharratt was the only one who managed to swim ashore unaided.

Col. Harry A. Froboess (Switzerland) jumped 110 m *360 ft* into the Bodensee from the airship *Graf Hindenburg* on 22 Jun 1936.

The greatest height reported for a dive into an air bag is 99·36 m *326 ft* by stuntman Dan Koko from the top of Vegas World Hotel and Casino into a 6·1 × 12·2 × 4·2 m *20 × 40 × 14 ft* target on 13 Aug

1984. His impact speed was 141 km/h *88 mph.* Kitty O'Neill dived 54·8 m *180 ft* from a helicopter over Northridge, California, USA on 9 Sep 1979 on to an air cushion measuring 9·14 × 18·28 m *30 × 60 ft* for a TV film stunt.

High kicking ■ The world record for high kicks (heel to ear level) is 12 360 in 5 ¹/₂ hr by Chung Kwun Ying at Guangzhou, China on 26 Mar 1989. Tony Higo holds heel to ear level high kick records of 94 in 10 seconds and 190 in 25 seconds, both achieved on Yorkshire TV's Telethon 1988, in Leeds, West Yorks on 30 May 1988, while the record for one minute is 217 by Scott Reeves, at the Pleasure Dome, Huddersfield, West Yorks on 10 Dec 1988. *Please note that this category will not be included in future editions of the book.*

High-wire act ■ The greatest height above street level of any high-wire performance has been a 42·6 m *140 ft* long wire between the 411 m *1350 ft* tall twin towers of the World Trade Center, New York, USA, by Philippe Petit, 24, of Nemours, France on 7 Aug 1974. He was charged with criminal trespass after a 75 min display of at least seven crossings. The police psychiatrist opined 'Anyone who does this 110 storeys up can't be entirely right.'

Hitch-hiking ■ The title of world champion hitch-hiker is claimed by Bill Heid of Allen Park, Michigan, USA who from 1964 to 1985 obtained free rides of 492 248 km *305 870 miles.* Stephen Burns of Melbourne, Australia hitched round all 48 co-terminous states of the USA in 26 days 6 hr in an 18 407 km *11 438 mile* trip in 56 vehicles from 8 Sep to 4 Oct 1984.

The hitch-hiking record for the 1406 km *874 miles* from Land's End, Cornwall to John O'Groats, Caithness, is 17 hr 8 min by Martin Clark and Graham Beynon of Guildford, Surrey on 14–15 Sep 1987. The time before the first 'hitch' on the first day is excluded. The fastest time recorded for the round trip is 41 hr 42 min by Anthony D. Sproson of Wolverhampton from 17–19 Sep 1984.

Hod carrying ■ Jim Ford of Bury, Lancs carried bricks totalling 161 kg *355 lb* up the minimum 3·65 m *12 ft* ladder (17 rungs) on 28 Jun 1984 at Hever Castle, Kent on the *International Guinness TV Show* presented by David Frost. Eric Stenman of Jakobstad, Finland carried 74 bricks of 4 kg *8·8 lb* each, so totalling 296 kg *651 lb,* in a 4 kg *8·8 lb* hod 5 metres *16·4 ft* on the flat before ascending a runged ramp to a height of 2·13 m *7 ft* on 25 Jul 1939.

Homework — longest on ice ■ In 1967, Thomas Litz, a teacher in Switzerland, set some homework which he marked but forgot to return. It was only in 1988, while sorting through old papers, that he came across the exercises. One of the pupils, Mark Johnson, had by this time himself become a teacher at the school, and on 1 Feb 1988 was given his homework back, 21 years late.

Hoop rolling ■ In 1968 it was reported that Zolilio Diaz (Spain) had rolled a hoop 965 km *600 miles* from Mieres to Madrid, Spain and back in 18 days.

Hop-scotch ■ The longest recorded hop-scotch marathon is one of 101 hr 15 min by Mark Harrison and Tony Lunn at the Studio Night Club, Leicester from 30 Sep to 4 Oct 1985.

House of cards ■ The greatest number of storeys achieved in building freestanding houses of standard playing cards is 68 to a height of 3·9 m *12 ft 10 in* built by John Sain, 15, of South Bend, Indiana, USA in May 1984.

Hula hooping ■ The highest claim for sustaining gyrating hoops between shoulders and hips is 81 by William Kleeman 'Chico' Johnson (b. 8 Jul 1939) on BBC TV's *Record Breakers* on 18 Sep 1983. Three complete gyrations are mandatory. The women's record is 75 by Desai Kehaiovi of the Kehaiovi Troupe of Bulgaria on Wellington Pier, Great Yarmouth, Norfolk on 12 Jul 1987.

The longest marathon for a single hoop is 90 hr by Roxann Rose of Pullman, Washington State, USA from 2–6 Apr 1987.

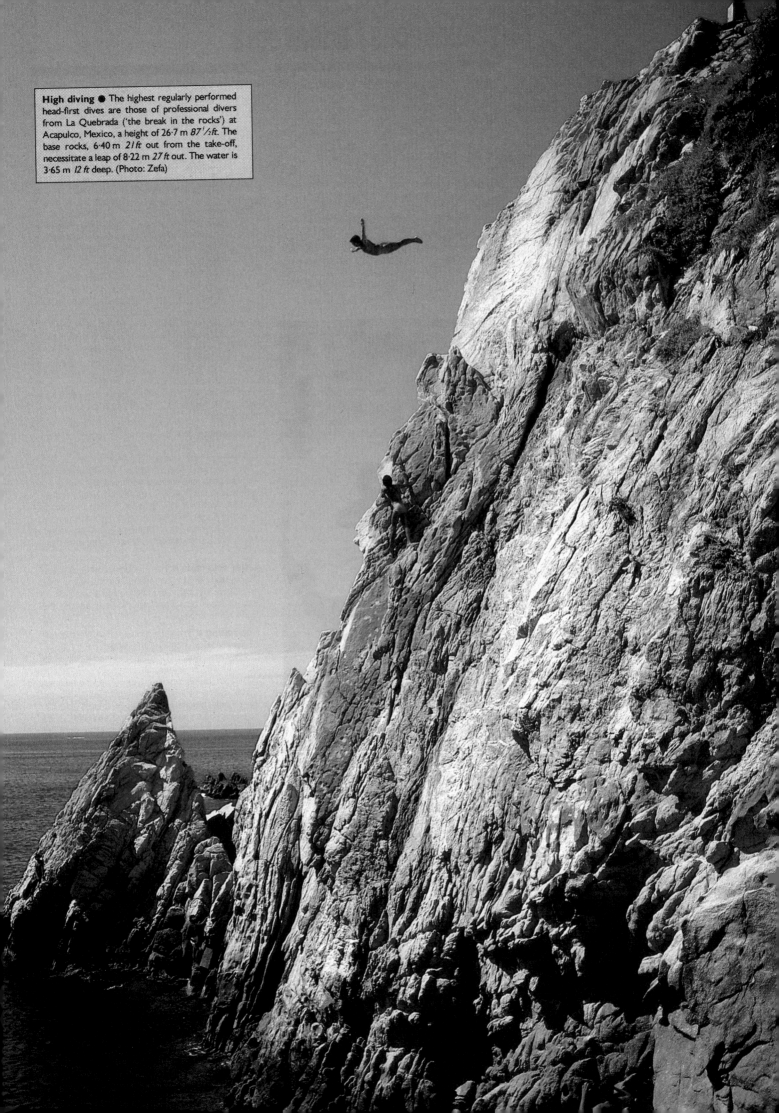

High diving ● The highest regularly performed head-first dives are those of professional divers from La Quebrada ('the break in the rocks') at Acapulco, Mexico, a height of 26·7 m *87½ft*. The base rocks, 6·40 m *21 ft* out from the take-off, necessitate a leap of 8·22 m *27 ft* out. The water is 3·65 m *12 ft* deep. (Photo: Zefa)

Human cannonball ■ The first human cannonball was Emilio Onra *né* Maîtrejean at Cirque d'Hiver, Paris, France on 21 Nov 1875. The record distance for firing a human from a cannon is 53·3 m *175 ft* in the case of Emanuel Zacchini, son of the pioneer Hugo Zacchini in the Ringling Bros and Barnum & Bailey Circus, Madison Square Gardens, New York City, USA in 1940. His muzzle velocity has been estimated at 86·9 km/h *54 mph*. On his retirement the management were fortunate in finding that his daughter Florinda was of the same calibre. An experiment on Yorkshire TV on 17 Aug 1978 showed that when Miss Sue Evans, 17, was fired she was 9·5 mm *⅜ in* shorter on landing.

Human centipede ■ The largest 'human centipede' to move 30 m *98 ft 5 in* (with ankles firmly tied together) consisted of 490 people. Not one single person fell over in the course of the walk, which took place on 13 Mar 1989 at Pocklington School, in York.

Human fly ■ The longest climb achieved on the vertical face of a building occurred on 26 Jun 1986 when Daniel Goodwin, 30, of California, USA climbed a record 342·9 m *1125 ft* up the outside of the 555·33 m *1822 ft* CN Tower in Toronto, Canada (the tallest self-supporting tower in the world) using neither climbing aids nor safety equipment. Lead climber Jean-Claude Droyer (b. 8 May 1946) of Paris, France, and Pierre Puiseux (b. 2 Dec 1953) of Pau, France climbed up the outside of the Eiffel Tower to a height of 300 m *984 ft* with no dynamic mechanical assistance on 21 Jul 1980. Jean-Claude took 2 hr 18 min 15 sec to complete the climb.

Ironing ■ The duration record for ironing is 128 hr by Nigel Towning of Grantham, Lincs from 3–8 Oct 1988.

Joke cracking ■ Felipe Carbonell of Lima, Peru told jokes for 72 hr at the Alfa Hotel, Lisbon, Portugal from 18–21 Mar 1988. The duo record is 60 hr by Derek Denniss and John Evans at Sandton City, Johannesburg, South Africa from 8–10 Sep 1988.

Jumble sale ■ The Cleveland Convention Center, Ohio, USA White Elephant Sale (instituted 1933) on 18–19 Oct 1983 raised $427 935·21. The greatest amount of money raised at a one-day sale is $170 139·76 at the 56th one-day rummage sale organised by the Winnetka Congregational Church, Illinois, USA on 12 May 1988.

Britain's largest jumble sale was 'Jumbly '79' sponsored by *Woman's Own* at Alexandra Palace, London from 5–7 May 1979 in aid of the Save the Children Fund. The attendance was 60 000 and the gross takings in excess of £60 000.

Kissing ■ The most prolonged osculatory marathon in cinematic history is one of 185 sec by Regis Toomey and Jane Wyman (b. Sarah Jane Faulks 4 Jan 1914, later Mrs Ronald Reagan) in *You're in the Army Now* released in 1940. Eddie Levin and Delphine Crha celebrated the breaking of the record for the longest ever kiss of 17 days 10 ½ hr in Chicago, Illinois, USA on 24 Sep 1984 with a kiss. James Whale kissed 4525 women in 8 hr at the *Yorkshire TV* Telethon garden party in Leeds, West Yorks on 30 May 1988, a rate of 1 every 6·36 sec.

Kite flying ■ The longest kite flown was 705 m *2313 ft* in length, which was made and flown by Michel Trouillet, Pierre Agniel and Philippe Bertron, at Nîmes, France on 15 Nov 1987. The classic record height is 9740 m *31 955 ft* by a train of eight kites over Lindenberg, Germany on 1 Aug 1919.

The fastest speed attained by a kite was 180·24 km/h *112 mph* for a kite flown by Tony Wolfenden at Melbourne, Victoria, Australia on 16 Oct 1988. The greatest lift by a single kite was one of 330·21 kg *728 lb*, achieved by a kite flown by G. William Tyrrell Jr in Ocean City, Maryland, USA on 23 Sep 1984. The longest recorded flight is one of 180 hr 17 min by the Edmonds Community College team at Long Beach, Washington State, USA from 21–29 Aug 1982. Managing the flight of the J-25 parafoil was Harry N. Osborne.

Knitting ■ The world's most prolific hand-knitter of all time has been Mrs Gwen Matthewman of Featherstone, West Yorks. She attained a speed of 111 stitches per min in a test at Phildar's Wool Shop, Central Street, Leeds, West Yorks on 29 Sep 1980. Her technique has been filmed by the world's only Professor of Knitting — a Japanese.

The Exeter Spinners — Audrey Felton, Christine Heap, Eileen Lancaster, Majorie Mellis, Ann Sandercock and Maria Scott — produced a jumper by hand from raw fleece in 1 hr 55 min 50·2 sec on 25 Sep 1983 at BBC Television Centre, London.

Knot-tying ■ The fastest recorded time for tying the six Boy Scout Handbook Knots (square knot, sheet bend, sheep shank, clove hitch, round turn and 2 half hitches and bowline) on individual ropes is 8·1 sec by Clinton R. Bailey Sr, 52, of Pacific City, Oregon, USA on 13 Apr 1977.

Knitting ● Mrs Gwen Matthewman of Featherstone, West Yorks is the world's fastest knitter, achieving a speed of 111 stitches per minute in September 1980.

Laundry ■ The greatest quantity of laundry washed in a nine hour working day is 63 596 kg *140 204 lb*, by staff at Central Linen Service, Kilkenny, South Australia, Australia on 18 May 1989.

Leap-frogging ■ The greatest distance covered was 1429·2 km *888·1 miles* by 14 members of The Class of 1988 of Hanover High School, in Hanover, New Hampshire, USA, who started leap-frogging on 10 Jun 1988 and stopped 189 hrs 49 mins later, on 18 Jun 1988.

Life saving ■ In November 1974 the city of Galveston, Texas, USA and the Noon Optimist Club unveiled a plaque to the deaf-mute lifeguard Leroy Colombo (1905–74) who saved 907 people from drowning in the waters around Galveston Island from 1917 to his death. The greatest single rescue in Britain was on 17 Mar 1907 when four lifeboats lifted 456 shipwreck survivors to safety off The Lizard, Cornwall.

Lightning, most times struck ■ The only man in the world to be struck by lightning seven times is ex-park ranger Roy C. Sullivan (US), the human lightning conductor of Virginia, USA. His attraction for lightning began in 1942 (lost big toe nail), and was resumed in July 1969 (lost eyebrows), in July 1970 (left shoulder seared), on 16 Apr 1972 (hair set on fire), on 7 Aug 1973 (new hair refired and legs seared), on 5 Jun 1976 (ankle injured), and he was sent to Waynesboro Hospital with chest and stomach burns on 25 Jun 1977 after being struck while fishing. In September 1983 he died by his own hand, reportedly rejected in love.

Limbo ■ The lowest height for a bar (flaming) under which a limbo dancer has passed is 15·5 cm *6⅛ in* off the floor by Marlene Raymond, 15, at the Port of Spain Pavilion, Toronto, Canada on 24 Jun 1973. Junior J. Renaud (b. 7 Jun 1954), Australia became the first Official World Limbo Champion at the inaugural International Limbo Competition on 19 Feb 1974 at Port of Spain, Trinidad.

The record on roller skates is 13·33 cm *5¼ in*, first achieved by Denise Culp of Rock Hill, South Carolina, USA on 22 Jan 1984. This has since been equalled by Tracey O'Callaghan on 2 Jun 1984 and Sandra Siviour on 30 Mar 1985, both at Bexley North, NSW, Australia, Jessie Ball on 27 Jun 1985 at Beverley Hills, NSW, Australia, and Kelly Foley on 22 May 1987, Magdalena Petrik and Meegan Anderson, both on 13 Apr 1988, and Michelle Boyle, Donna Bray and Jessica McLeish, on 21 May 1988, all at Parramatta, NSW, Australia. On 28 Jun 1988 Erika Howell of Brunswick, Georgia, USA also equalled this height.

Lion-taming ■ The greatest number of lions mastered and fed in a cage by an unaided lion-tamer was 40, by 'Captain' Alfred Schneider in 1925. Clyde Raymond Beatty handled more than 40 'cats' (mixed lions and tigers) simultaneously. Beatty (b. Bainbridge, Ohio, USA, 10 Jun 1903, d. Ventura, California, USA, 19 Jul 1965) was the featured attraction at every show he appeared with for more than 40 years. He insisted upon being called a lion-trainer. More than 20 lion-tamers have died of injuries since 1900.

Litter collection ■ The greatest number of volunteers involved in collecting litter on one day is 3510, who filled 3641 bags and 25 skips on 4 Sep 1988 as part of the 'Clean Forth' project to clean up the Forth River, Scotland.

Log rolling ■ The record number of International Championships is 10 by Jubiel Wickheim (of Shawnigan Lake, British Columbia, Canada) between 1956 and 1969. At Albany, Oregon, USA on 4 Jul 1956 Wickheim rolled on a 35·5 cm *14 in* log against Chuck Harris of 'Kelso, Washington State, USA for 2 hr 40 min before losing. The youngest international log-rolling champion is Cari Ann Hayer (b. 23 Jun 1977), who won her first championship on 15 Jul 1984 at Hayward, Wisconsin, USA.

Magician, fastest ■ Paul Ricksecker performed 91 different tricks in 2 min 12·5 sec at the 57th Annual Magi-Fest, Columbus, Ohio, USA on 6 Feb 1988.

Mantle of bees ■ Danielle Goullet was covered by a mantle of an estimated 141 000 bees weighing 19·01 kg *41·89 lb* at Darra, Australia on 24 Sep 1988.

Merry-go-round ■ The longest merry-go-round marathon on record is one of 312 hr 43 min by Gary Mandau, Chris Lyons and Dana Dover in Portland, Oregon, USA from 20 Aug–2 Sep 1976.

Message in a bottle ■ The longest recorded interval between drop and pick-up is 73 years in the case of a message thrown from the SS *Arawatta* out of Cairns, Queensland, Australia on 9 Jun 1910 in a lotion bottle and reported to be found on Moreton Island on 6 Jun 1983.

Meteorological balloon inflation ■ The inflation of a standardised 1000-gramme meteorological balloon to a diameter of 2·43 m *8 ft* against time was achieved by Nicholas Berkeley Mason in 57 min 7 sec for a Fuji TV programme in Tokyo, Japan on 9 Mar 1986.

Milk bottle balancing ■ The greatest distance walked by a person continuously balancing a full pint milk bottle on the head is 52·9 km *32·9 miles* by

Ashrita Furman of New York, USA at Phuket, Thailand on 23 Jan 1989.

Morse ■ The highest recorded speed at which anyone has received Morse code is 75·2 words per minute — over 17 symbols per second. This was achieved by Ted R. McElroy of the USA in a tournament at Asheville, North Carolina, USA on 2 Jul 1939.

The highest speed recorded for hand key transmitting is 175 symbols a minute by Harry A. Turner of the US Army Signal Corps at Camp Crowder, Missouri, USA on 9 Nov 1942. Thomas Morris, a GPO operator, is reputed to have been able to send at 39–40 wpm *c*. 1919 but this is not verifiable.

Musical chairs ■ The largest game on record was one starting with 6500 participants, ending with Christine Rick on the last chair, which was held on the beach at Weymouth, Dorset on 30 May 1988.

Musical march ■ The longest recorded musical march was one of 63·4 km *39·4 miles* in Caney, Kansas, USA by Caney Valley USD 436 Pride of Caney Marching Band in 12 hr 13 min on 17 Sep 1988. 18 of 51 members completed the full march.

Needle threading ■ The record number of times that a strand of cotton has been threaded through a number 13 needle (eye 12·7 mm × 1·6 mm *¹/₂ in × ¹/₁₆ in*) in 2 hr is 5370, set by Diane Sharp on 1 Aug 1987 at the Charitable Union's centenary event, Battle Creek, Michigan, USA.

Noodle making ■ Mark Pi of the China Gate Restaurant, Columbus, Ohio, USA made 2048 noodle strings (over 1·52 m *5 ft*) in 34·5 sec on 12 Feb 1983.

Omelette making ■ The greatest number of two-egg omelettes made in 30 min is 315 by John Elkhay at the City Lights Restaurant in Providence, Rhode Island, USA on 29 Jun 1985.

Onion peeling ■ The record for peeling 22·67 kg *50 lb* of onions is 3 min 18 sec by Alan St Jean in Plainfield, Connecticut, USA on 6 Jul 1980. Under revised rules stipulating a minimum of 50 onions, Alfonso Salvo of York, Pennsylvania, USA peeled 22·67 kg *50 lb* of onions (52 onions) in 5 min 23 sec on 28 Oct 1980.

Organ ■ The longest recorded electric organ marathon is one of 440 hr by Tony Peters at Sheppey Beach Social Club, Isle of Sheppey, Kent from 20 Apr–8 May 1987.

The longest church organ recital ever sustained has been 119 hr by Martin Stanley at St. Mary the Virgin, Brixham, Devon from 25–30 Aug 1986.

Oyster opening ■ The record for opening oysters is 100 in 2 min 22·17 sec by Mike Racz in Invercargill, New Zealand on 25 Aug 1987.

Paddle boating ■ The longest recorded voyage is 3582 km *2226 miles* in 103 days by the foot power of Mick Sigrist and Brad Rud down the Mississippi River from the headwaters in Minnesota to the Gulf of Mexico from 4 Aug to 11 Nov 1979.

Pancake tossing ■ The greatest number of times a pancake has been tossed in 2 minutes is 262 by Philip Artingstall on 28 Apr 1989 at Fordyce School, Fordyce, Grampian.

Piano playing ■ The record for piano playing is 1218 hr (50 days 18 hr) playing 22 hr every day (with 5 min intervals each playing hour) from 7 May to 27 Jun 1982 by David Scott at Wagga Wagga League Football Club, NSW, Australia. *The non-stop category is now discontinued.*

Piano smashing ■ The record time for demolishing an upright piano and passing the entire wreckage through a circle 22·8 cm *9 in* in diameter is 1 min 37 sec by six members of the Tinwald Rugby Football Club, Ashburton, New Zealand led by David Young on 6 Nov 1977.

Messrs Anthony Fukes, Mike Newman and Terry Cullington smashed a piano with bare hands and feet in 2 min 53 sec in Nottingham on 25 Aug 1979. All wreckage was passed through the circle.

Piano tuning ■ The record time for pitch raising (one semi-tone or 100 cents) and then returning a piano to a musically acceptable quality is 4 min 20 sec by Steve Fairchild at the Piano Technicians Guild contest at the Dante Piano Co factory, NY, USA on 5 Feb 1980.

Pillar box mounting ■ The record number to pile on top of or hang from a standard double pillar box (oval top of 0·55 m² *6 ft²*) is 32, all students of Wentworth College, York University in Parliament St, York on 27 Feb 1985.

Pipe smoking ■ The duration record for keeping a pipe (3·3 g *0·1 oz* of tobacco) continuously alight with only an initial match under IAPSC (International Association of Pipe Smokers Clubs) rules is 126 min 39 sec by 5-time champion William Vargo of Swartz Creek, Michigan, USA at the 27th World Championships in 1975.

Milk bottle balancing ● Ashrita Furman of New York, USA walked 52·9 km *32·9 miles* whilst balancing a full pint milk bottle on his head at Phuket, Thailand on 23 Jan 1989.

The only other 5-time champion is Paul T. Spaniola (US) (1951–66–70–73–77). On 18 Aug 1984 Joe Oetli achieved 130 min 11 sec at the 15th Iowa State Fair contest using *two* matches. Longer durations have been recorded in less rigorously invigilated contests in which the foul practices of 'tamping' and 'gardening' are not unknown.

Plane pulling ■ Dave Gauder single-handedly pulled Concorde 12·19 m *40 ft* across the tarmac at Heathrow Airport, London on 11 Jun 1987.

Plate spinning ■ The greatest number of plates spun simultaneously is 84 by Dave Spathaky on BBC TV's *Record Breakers* on 21 Oct 1986.

Pogo stick jumping ■ The greatest number of jumps achieved is 130 077 by Gary Stewart in Reading, Ohio, USA on 8–9 Mar 1985.

Ashrita Furman of New York, USA set a distance record of 18·68 km *11·53 miles* in 8 hr 21 min on 8 Jan 1986. His 'route' up and down the foothills of Mt Fuji, Japan was from the Gotemba railroad station, west along the Gotembaguchi Tozando Road, to an elevation of 90 m *295·28 ft*, and return.

Pole sitting ■ Modern records do not, in fact, compare with that of St Simeon the Younger (*c.* AD 521–597), called Stylites, a monk who spent his last

45 years up a stone pillar on the Hill of Wonders, near Antioch, Syria.

There being no international rules, the 'standards of living' at the top of poles vary very widely. Mellissa Sanders lived in a shack on the top of a pole in Indianapolis, Indiana, USA from 26 Oct 1986 to 24 Mar 1988, a total of 516 days.

Pat Bowen stayed in a barrel (max. capacity 150 gallons) atop a pole (5·48 m *18 ft*) outside the Bull Hotel, Ludlow, Salop for 40 days 1 hr from 28 May to 7 Jul 1986.

Pop/rock group ■ The duration record for a four-man group is 147 hr by the 'Dekorators' at Becketts Bar, Bexhill-on-Sea, East Sussex from 8–14 Jan 1984.

Potato peeling ■ The greatest amount of potatoes peeled by five people to an institutional cookery standard with standard kitchen knives in 45 min is 310·84 kg *685 lb 4 oz* (net) by Lia Sombroek, Marlene Guiamo, Walijem Kertoidjojo, Judith van Druenen and Wijna Scheringa at Emmeloord, Netherlands on 17 Sept 1987.

Pram pushing ■ The greatest distance covered in pushing a pram in 24 hr is 563·62 km *350·23 miles* by 60 members of the Oost-Vlaanderen branch of Amnesty International at Lede, Belgium on 15 Oct 1988. A 10-man Royal Marine team from the Commando Training Centre, Lympstone, Devon, with an adult 'baby', covered 406·60 km *252·65 miles* in 24 hr from 31 Mar to 18 Apr 1984.

'Psychiatrist' fastest ■ The world's fastest 'psychiatrist' was Dr Albert L. Weiner of Erlton, New Jersey, USA, trained solely in osteopathy but who dealt with up to 50 psychiatric patients a day in four treatment rooms. He relied heavily on narcoanalysis, muscle relaxants and electro-shock treatments. In December 1961 he was found guilty on 12 counts of manslaughter from using unsterilised needles.

Quizzes ■ The highest number of participants was 80 977 in the All-Japan High School Quiz Championship televised by NTV on 31 Dec 1983. The most protracted contest was that lasting 110 hr in Long Hanborough, Oxon from 27 Mar to 1 Apr 1986. The 2 teams answered correctly 22 483 of the 37 310 questions.

Quoit throwing ■ The world record for rope quoit throwing is an unbroken sequence of 4002 pegs by Bill Irby Sr of Australia in 1968.

Ramp jumping ■ The longest distance ever achieved for motorcycle long jumping is 74·98 m *246 ft* by Todd Seeley at a World of Wheels show in Tampa, Florida, USA on 28 Feb 1988.

The pioneer of this form of exhibition — Evel Knievel (b. Robert Craig Knievel, 17 Oct 1938 at Butte, Montana, USA) — had suffered 433 bone fractures by his 1975 season. His abortive attempt to cross the 485 m *1600 ft* wide and 180 m *600 ft* deep Snake River Canyon, Idaho, USA on 8 Sep 1974 in a rocket reputedly increased his lifetime earnings by $6 million.

The longest ramp jump in a car by a professional stunt driver is 70·73 m *232 ft* by Jacqueline De Creed (*née* Creedy) in a 1967 Ford Mustang at Santa Pod Raceway, Beds on 3 Apr 1983.

Rappeling (or Abseiling) ■ The west face of Thor Peak, Baffin Island, northern Canada allowed an abseiling or rappeling record of 990 m *3250 ft* by a team of 16 led by Steve Holmes (US) in July 1982. The longest descent down the side of a skyscraper is one of 245·5 m *805 ft 5 in* by Sgt Mick Herrick down the north tower of the Rialto Building in Melbourne, Victoria, Australia on 27 Nov 1988.

Riding in armour ■ The longest ride in armour is one of 288·47 km *179·25 miles* by Gary Bourne and Derek Ward, from 10–14 Jul 1988, around Kent. Their riding time was 41 hr 5 min.

Riveting ■ The world's record for riveting is 11 209 in 9 hr by John Moir at the Workman Clark Ltd shipyard, Belfast, Northern Ireland, in June 1918.

Ramp jumping ● The longest distance ever achieved for motorcycle long jumping is 74·98 m *246 ft* by Todd Seeley at a World of Wheels show in Tampa, Florida, USA on 28 Feb 1988. (Photo: St Petersburg Times)

His peak hour was his 7th with 1409, an average of nearly 23 ½ per min.

Rocking chair ■ The longest recorded 'Rockathon' is 453 hr 40 min by Robert McDonald at Mariposa, California, USA from 14 Mar–2 Apr 1986.

Rolling pin ■ The record distance for a woman to throw a 907 g *2 lb* rolling pin is 53·4 m *175 ft 5 in* by Lori La Deane Adams, 21, at Iowa State Fair, Iowa, USA on 21 Aug 1979.

Sand castle ■ A castle 8·37 km *5·2 miles* long was made by staff and pupils of Ellon Academy, near Aberdeen, Grampian, on 24 Mar 1988.

Sand sculpturing ■ The longest sand sculpture ever made — with a water-saturated mound of sand mechanically piled up and the sculpture meticulously carved out — was a 3279 m *10 760 ft* long 'Millerpede' which meandered along South Padre Island, Texas, USA on 18 Mar 1987, organised by Walter McDonald and Lucinda Wierenga and built by college students and local members of the Sons of the Beach organisation. The tallest was the 'Lost City of Atlantis' which was 16·08 m *52 ft 9 in* tall and was built by Sand Sculptors International of California on Treasure Island, Florida, USA from 21–26 Apr 1986.

Scooter riding ■ The greatest distance covered by a team of 25 in 24 hr is 540·93 km *336·11 miles* by Wimmera Young Farmers, Victoria, Australia on 22–23 Mar 1980.

See-saw ■ George Partridge and Tamara Marquez of Auburn High School, Washington, USA on a suspension see-saw completed 1101 hr 40 min (indoor) from 28 Mar–13 May 1977. Georgia Chaffin and Tammy Adams of Goodhope Junior High School, Cullman, Alabama, USA completed 730 hr 30 min (outdoor) from 25 Jun–25 Jul 1975.

Sermon ■ The longest sermon on record was delivered by the Reverend Ronald Gallagher at the Baptist Temple, Appomattox, Virginia, USA for 120 hr from 26 Jun–1 Jul 1983. From 31 May to 10 June 1969 the 14th Dalai Lama (b. 6 Jul 1934 as Tenzin Gyalto), exiled ruler of Tibet, completed a sermon on Tantric Buddhism for 5–7 hr per day to total 60 hr, in India.

Shaving ■ The fastest barbers on record are Denny Rowe, who shaved 1994 men in 60 min with a retractor safety razor in Herne Bay, Kent on 19 Jun 1988, taking on average 1·8 sec per volunteer, and drawing blood four times, and Gerry Harley, of Gillingham, Kent, who on 13 Aug 1984 shaved 235 even braver volunteers with a cut-throat razor, averaging 15·3 sec per face. He drew blood only once.

Sheaf tossing ■ The world's best performance for tossing a 3·63 kg *8 lb* sheaf for height is 19·77 m *64 ft 10¼ in* by Trond Ulleberg of Skolleborg, Norway on 11 Nov 1978. Such pitchfork contests date from 1914.

Sheep to shoulder ■ At the International Wool Secretariat Development Centre, Ilkley, West Yorks, a team of eight using commercial machinery produced a jumper from shearing sheep to the finished article in 2 hr 28 min 32 sec on 3 Sep 1986.

Shoe-shining ■ In this category (limited to a team of 4 teenagers; duration of 8 hr; shoes 'on the hoof') the record is 11 651 pairs by four members of the London Church of Christ at Covent Garden, London on 18 Mar 1989.

Shorthand fastest ■ The highest recorded speeds ever attained under championship conditions are: 300 words per min (99·64 per cent accuracy) for 5 minutes and 350 wpm (99·72 per cent accuracy, that is, two insignificant errors) for 2 minutes by Nathan Behrin (US) in tests in New

Plane pulling ● Dave Gauder single-handedly pulled Concorde (weighing 102·6 tonnes *101 tons*) 12·19 m *40 ft* across the tarmac at Heathrow Airport, London on 11 Jun 1987. (Photo: Peter Brooker/Rex Features)

York in December 1922. Behrin (b. 1887) used the Pitman system invented in 1837. Morris I. Kligman, official court reporter of the US Court House, New York has taken 50 000 words in 5 hr (a sustained rate of 166·6 wpm). Rates are much dependent upon the nature, complexity and syllabic density of the material. Mr G. W. Bunbury of Dublin, Ireland held the unique distinction of writing at 250 wpm for 10 minutes on 23 Jan 1894.

Mr Arnold Bradley achieved a speed of 309 wpm without error using the Sloan-Duployan system with 1545 words in 5 minutes in a test in Walsall, West Midlands on 9 Nov 1920.

Showering ■ The most prolonged continuous shower bath on record is one of 340 hr 40 min by Kevin McCartney of State University College at Buffalo, New York, USA, from 29 Mar to 12 Apr 1985. The feminine record is 121 hr 1 min by Lisa D'Amato from 5–10 Nov 1981 at Harpur College, Binghamton, also New York, USA. Desquamation can be a positive danger.

Singing ■ The longest recorded solo-singing marathon is one of 200 hr 20 min by Jorge António Hidalgo Chamorro at the Piano Bar, Barcelona, Spain, from 7–15 Nov 1985. The marathon record for a choir is 80 hr 1 min by the Young Spirit of the Apache Junction High School, Arizona, USA from 2–5 Feb 1989. Acharya Prem Bhikuji (d. 18 Apr 1970) started chanting the Akhand Rama-Dhoon at Jamnagar, Gujarat, India on 31 Jul 1964 and devotees were continuing in January 1988.

Skate boarding ■ 'World' championships have been staged intermittently since 1966. David Frank, 25, covered 435·3 km *270·5 miles* in 36 hr 43 min 40 sec in Toronto, Canada on 11–12 Aug 1985.

The highest speed recorded on a skate board under USSA rules is 115·53 km/h *71·79 mph* on a course at Mt Baldy, California, USA in a prone position by Richard K. Brown, 33, on 17 Jun 1979. The stand-up record is 86·01 km/h *53·45 mph* by John Hutson, 23, at Signal Hill, Long Beach, California, USA on 11 Jun 1978. The high-jump record is 1·67 m *5 ft 5·7 in* by Trevor Baxter (b. 1 Oct 1962) of Burgess Hill, East Sussex at Grenoble, France on 14 Sep 1982. At the 4th US Skateboard Association Championship, at Signal Hill on 25 Sept 1977, Tony Alva, 19, jumped 17 barrels (5·18 m *17 ft*).

Slinging ■ The greatest distance recorded for a sling-shot is 437·13 m *1434 ft 2 in* using a 129·5 cm *51 in* long sling and a 56·5 g *2 oz* stone by Lawrence L. Bray at Loa, Utah, USA on 21 Aug 1981.

Smoke ring blowing ■ The highest recorded number of smoke rings formed from the lips from a single pull of a cigarette (cheek-tapping is disallowed) is 355 by Jan van Deurs Formann of

Copenhagen, Denmark, achieved in Switzerland in August 1979.

Snow shoeing ■ The USSA record for covering 1609·34 m *1 mile* is 7 min 56 sec by Mark Lessard at Corinth, New York, USA in 1979.

Spear throwing ■ The greatest distance achieved throwing a spear with the aid of a woomera is 99·51 m *326 ft 6 in* by Bailey Bush on 27 Jun 1982 at Camden, NSW, Australia.

Spike driving ■ In the World Championship Professional Spike Driving Competition held at the Golden Spike National Historic Site in Utah, USA, Dale C. Jones, 49, of Lehi, drove six 7-in railroad spikes in a time of 26·4 sec on 11 Aug 1984. He incurred no penalty points under the official rules.

Spinning by hand ■ The duration record for spinning a clock-balance wheel by unaided hand is 5 min 26·8 sec by Philip Ashley, 16, of Leigh, Lancs on 20 May 1968. The record using 91·4 cm *36 in* of string with a 205·5 g *7¼ oz* top is 58 min 20 sec by Peter Hodgson at Southend-on-Sea, Essex on 4 Feb 1985.

Spitting ■ The greatest distance achieved at the Annual Tobacco Spitting Classic (instituted 1955) at Raleigh, Mississippi, USA is 10·24 m *33 ft 7½ in* by Jeff Barber on 25 Jul 1981. (In 1980 he reached 13·71 m *45 ft* at Fulton, Missouri, USA, and on 29 Jun 1985 he won a record 13th National Spitting title at Raleigh.) In the 3rd International Spittin', Belchin' and Cussin' Triathlon, Harold Fielden reached 10·36 m *34 ft 0¼ in* at Central City, Colorado, USA, on 13 Jul 1973. Distance is dependent on the quality of salivation, absence of cross wind, the two-finger pucker and coordination of the back arch and neck snap. Sprays or wads smaller than a dime are not measured. Randy Ober of Bentonville, Arkansas, USA spat a tobacco wad 14·50 m *47 ft 7 in* at the Calico 5th Annual Tobacco Chewing and Spitting Championships north of Barstow, California, USA on 4 Apr 1982. The record for projecting a melon seed under WCWSSCA rules is 19·91 m *65 ft 4 in* by John Wilkinson in Luling, Texas, USA, on 28 Jun 1980. The furthest recorded distance for a cherry stone is 22·14 m *72 ft 7½ in* by Rick Krause, at Eau Claire, Michigan, USA on 2 Jul 1988.

Square dance calling ■ Alan Covacic called for 26 hr 2 min for the Wheelers and Dealers Square Dance Club at RAF Halton, Aylesbury, Bucks from 18–19 Nov 1988.

Stair climbing ■ The 100-storey record for stair climbing was set by Dennis W. Martz in the Detroit Plaza Hotel, Detroit, Michigan, USA on 26 Jun 1978 at 11 min 23·8 sec. Dale Neil, 22, ran a vertical mile on the stairs of the Peachtree Plaza Hotel, Atlanta, Georgia, USA in continuous action of 2 hr 1 min 24 sec on 9 Mar 1984. *These records can only be attempted in buildings with a minimum of 70 storeys.*

The record for the 1760 steps (vertical height 342 m *1122 ft*) in the world's tallest free-standing structure, Toronto's CN Tower, Canada, is 8 min 28 sec by George Kapenyes on 27 Oct 1985. Robert C. Jezequel ran 17 round trips in 11 hr 20 min on 18 Oct 1985 without use of the elevator for a vertical height of 11 627·5 m *38 148 ft.*

Pete Squires raced up the 1575 steps of the Empire State Building, New York, USA on 12 Feb 1981 in 10 min 59 sec.

In the line of duty Bill Stevenson mounted 334 of the 364 steps of the tower in the Houses of Parliament 4000 times in the 15 years 1968–83 — equivalent to 24·9 ascents of Everest.

A team of 200 ran up the 1336 stairs of the world's tallest hotel, the Westin Stamford, Singapore, on 3 May 1987. The fastest time was recorded by Kenneth Keng at 7 min 20 sec.

Stamp licking ■ Ian Thomas of Brisbane, Australia licked and affixed 204 stamps in 4 min at the Sunpex '85 Exhibition, Brisbane on 5 Oct 1985.

Standing ■ The longest period on record that anyone has continuously stood is for more than 17 years in the case of Swami Maujgiri Maharij when performing the *Tapasya* or penance from 1955 to November 1973 in Shahjahanpur, Uttar Pradesh, India. When sleeping he would lean against a plank. He died aged 85 in September 1980.

Stilt-walking ■ Hop stringers use stilts up to 4·57 m *15 ft*. In 1892 M. Garisoain of Bayonne stilt-walked 8 km *4·97 miles* into Biarritz in 42 min to average 11·42 km/h *7·10 mph*. In 1891 Sylvain Dornon stilt-walked from Paris, France to Moscow, USSR via Vilno in 50 stages for the 2945 km *1830 miles*. Another source gives his time as 58 days. Even with a safety or Kirby wire very high stilts are *extremely* dangerous — 25 steps are deemed to constitute 'mastery'. Eddy Wolf ('Steady Eddy') of Loyal, Wisconsin, USA mastered stilts measuring 12·36 m *40 ft 6½ in* from ground to ankle over a distance of 27 steps without touching his safety handrail wires, at Yokohama Dreamland Park, Yokohama on 9 Mar 1986. His aluminium stilts weighed 25 kg *55 lb* each. Joe Long (b. Kenneth Caesar), who has suffered 5 fractures, mastered 25·4 kg *56 lb* 7·31 m *24 ft* stilts at BBC Television Centre, London on 8 Dec 1978. The endurance record is 4804 km *3008 miles* from Los Angeles, California, USA to Bowen, Kentucky, USA, from 20 Feb to 26 Jul 1980 by Joe Bowen. Masaharu Tatsushiro, 28 (Japan), ran 100 m *328 ft* on 30·48 cm *1 ft* high stilts in 14·15 sec in Tokyo, Japan on 30 Mar 1980.

Stowaway ■ The most rugged stowaway was Socarras Ramirez who escaped from Cuba on 4 Jun 1969 by stowing away in an unpressurised wheel well in the starboard wing of a Douglas DC8 from Havana, Cuba to Madrid, Spain in a 9010 km *5600 mile* Iberian Airlines flight.

Stretcher bearing ■ The longest recorded carry of a stretcher case with a 63·5 kg *10 st* 'body' is 229 km *142·3 miles* in 38 hr 39 min by two four-man teams from 1 Field Ambulance, Canadian Forces Base, Calgary, Canada from 5–7 Apr 1989.

The record limited to Youth Organisations (under 20 years of age) and 8-hr carrying is 67·62 km *42·02 miles* by 8 members of the Henry Meoles School, Moreton, Wirral, Cheshire on 13 Jul 1980.

String ball largest ■ The largest ball of string on record is one of 3·88 m *12 ft 9 in* in diameter, 12·19 m *40 ft* in circumference and weighing 10 tonnes, amassed by Francis A. Johnson of Darwin, Minnesota, USA between 1950–78.

Submergence ■ The *continuous* duration record (*i.e.* no rest breaks) for 'scuba' (*i.e.* self-contained and without surface air hoses) is 212 hr 30 min by Michael Stevens of Birmingham in a Royal Navy tank at the National Exhibition Centre, Birmingham from 14–23 Feb 1986. Measures have to be taken to reduce the risk of severe desquamation in such endurance trials.

Suggestion boxes ■ The most prolific example on record of the use of any suggestion box scheme is that of John Drayton (1907–87) of Newport, Gwent who plied the British rail system with a total of 31 400 suggestions from 1924 to August 1987 of which over one in seven were adopted and 100 were accepted by London Transport. In 1983 he was presented with a chiming clock by British Rail to mark almost 60 years of suggestions.

Swinging ■ The record duration for continuous swinging in a hammock is 240 hr by John David Joyce of Bryan, Texas, USA from 29 Jul to 8 Aug 1986.

Switchback riding ■ The endurance record for rides on a roller coaster is 503 hr by M. M. Daniel Glada and Normand St-Pierre at Parc Belmont, Montreal, Canada from 18 Jul to 10 Aug 1983. The minimum qualifying average speed required is 40 km/h *25 mph*.

Tailoring ■ The highest speed in which the manufacture of a 3-piece suit has been executed from sheep to finished article is 1 hr 34 min 33·42 sec by 65 members of the Melbourne College of Textiles, Pascoe Vale, Victoria, Australia on 24 Jun 1982. Catching and fleecing took 2 min 21 sec, and

carding, spinning, weaving and tailoring occupied the remaining time.

Talking ■ The world record for talking is 260 hours by R Meenakshisundaram at Madurai, Tamil Nadu, India from 24 Mar–4 Apr 1989. The women's non-stop talking record was set by Mrs Mary E. Davis, who on 2 Sep 1958 started at a radio station in Buffalo, New York, USA and did not draw breath until 110 hr 30 min 5 sec later on 7 Sep in Tulsa, Oklahoma, USA. (See also Filibusters, Chapter 10.)

The longest recorded after-dinner speech was one of 34 hr 16 min by Paul Egan at University College, Dublin, Ireland from 19–21 Nov 1988. Historically the longest recorded after-dinner speech with *unsuspecting* victims was one of 3 hr by the Reverend Henry Whitehead (d. March 1896) at the Rainbow Tavern, Fleet Street, London on 16 Jan 1874.

T-bone dive ■ The so-called T-bone dives or Dive Bomber crashes by cars off ramps over and on to parked cars are often measured by the number of cars, but owing to their variable size and that their purpose is purely to cushion the shock, distance is more significant.

Stuart Cameron drove a Datsun 240Z for a record leap of 64·01 m *210 ft* at Bovingdon Airfield, Herts on 4 Sep 1988.

Teeth-lifting ■ Joe Ponder of Love Valley, North Carolina, USA raised a pumpkin weighing 274·9 kg

Tree climbing ● The fastest speed climb up a 30·4 m *100 ft* fir spar pole and back down to the ground is one of 24·82 sec by Guy German of Sitka, Alaska, USA on 3 Jul 1988 at the Albany World Championship Timber Carnival in Albany, Oregon, USA. German is seen here on his way down to a new record. (Photo: Terry Gleason)

606 lb 45·7 cm *18 in* off the ground with his teeth at Circleville, Ohio, USA on 19 Oct 1985. 'Hercules' John Massis (b. Wilfried Oscar Morbée, 4 Jun 1940, d. 11 Jul 1988) of Oostakker, Belgium prevented a helicopter from taking off using only a tooth bit harness in Los Angeles, California, USA on 7 Apr 1979 for a *Guinness Spectacular* TV show.

Throwing ■ The longest independently authenticated throw of any inert object heavier than air is 383·13 m *1257 ft*, for a flying ring, by Scott Zimmerman on 8 Jul 1986 at Fort Funston, California, USA.

Tightrope walking ■ The greatest 19th-century tightrope walker was Jean François Gravelet, *alias* Charles Blondin (1824–97), of France, who made the earliest crossing of the Niagara Falls on a 76 mm *3 in* rope, 335 m *1100 ft* long, 48·75 m *160 ft* above the Falls on 30 Jun 1859. He also made a crossing with Harry Colcord pick-a-back on 15 Sep 1860. Though other artistes still find it difficult to believe, Colcord was his agent. The oldest wirewalker was 'Professor' William Ivy Baldwin (1866–1953), who crossed the South Boulder Canyon, Colorado, USA on a 97·5 m *320 ft* wire with a 38·1 m *125 ft* drop on his 82nd birthday on 31 Jul 1948.

The world tightrope endurance record is 185 days by Henri Rochetain (b. 1926) of France on a wire 120 m *394 ft* long, 25 m *82 ft* above a supermarket in Saint Etienne, France from 28 Mar–29 Sep 1973. His ability to sleep on the wire has left doctors puzzled. Ashley Brophy, of Neilborough, Victoria, Australia, walked 11·57 km *7·18 miles* on a wire 45 m *147·64 ft* long 10 m *32·81 ft* high at the Adelaide Grand Prix, Australia on 1 Nov 1985 in 3 ½ hr.

Steve McPeak (b. 21 Apr 1945) of Las Vegas, Nevada, USA ascended the 46·6 mm *1·83 in* diameter Zugspitzbahn cable for a vertical height of 705 m *2313 ft* in 3 stints aggregating 5 hr 4 min on 24/25/28 Jun 1981. The maximum gradient over the stretch of 2282 m *7485 ft* was above 30 degrees.

The greatest drop over which anyone has walked on a tightrope is 1008 m *3304 ft* by Michel Menin, of France, above the Angel Falls, Venezuela on 1 Mar 1988. He repeated this feat the following day.

The first crossing of the River Thames was achieved by Charles Elleano (b. 1911) of Strasbourg, France

on a 320 m *1050 ft* wire 18·2 m *60 ft* above the river in 25 min on 22 Sep 1951.

Top spinning ■ A team of 25 from the Mizushima Plant of Kawasaki Steel Works in Okayama spun a giant top 2 m *6 ft 6¾ in* tall and 2·6 m *8 ft 6¼ in* in diameter weighing 360 kg *793·6 lb* for 1 hr 21 min 35 sec on 3 Nov 1986.

Train spotting ■ Bill Curtis of Clacton-on-Sea, Essex is acknowledged as the world champion train spotter — or 'gricer' (after Richard Grice, the first champion). His totals include some 60 000 locomotives, 11 200 electric units and 8 300 diesel units, clocked up over a period of 40 years in a number of different countries.

Tree climbing ■ The fastest speed climb up a 30·5 m *100 ft* fir spar pole and return to the ground is one of 24·82 sec by Guy German of Sitka, Alaska, USA on 3 Jul 1988 at the World Championship Timber Carnival in Albany, Oregon, USA.

The fastest time up a 9 m *29·5 ft* coconut tree barefoot is 4·88 sec by Fuatai Solo, 17, in Sukuna Park, Fiji on 22 Aug 1980.

Tree sitting ■ The duration record for sitting in a tree is 431 days by Timothy Roy at Golf n'Stuff Amusement Park, Norwalk, California, USA from 4 Jul 1982–8 Sep 1983.

Tree topping ■ Guy German climbed a 30·5 m *100 ft* spar and sawed off the top in a record time of 58·95 sec at Albany, Oregon, USA on 3 Jul 1988.

Typewriting ■ The world duration record for typewriting on an electric machine is 264 hr by Violet Gibson Burns at the Royal Easter Show, Sydney, Australia from 29 Mar–9 Apr 1985.

The longest duration in a typing marathon on a manual machine is 123 hr by Shambhoo Govind Anbhawane of Bombay, India from 18–23 Aug 1986 on a Godrej Prima manual machine, aggregating 806 000 strokes.

Les Stewart of Mudjimba Beach, Queensland, Australia has typed the numbers 1 to 584 000 in *words* on 11 570 quarto sheets as of 23 Feb 1989. His target is to become a 'millionaire'.

The highest recorded speeds attained with a ten-word penalty per error on a manual machine are:

Five Min: 176 wpm net Mrs Carole Forristall Waldschlager Bechen at Dixon, Illinois, USA on 2 Apr 1959. One Hour: 147 wpm net Albert Tangora (US) (Underwood Standard), 22 Oct 1923.

The official hour record on an electric machine is

9316 words (40 errors) on an IBM machine, giving a net rate of 149 words per min, by Margaret Hamma, now Mrs Dilmore (US), in Brooklyn, New York, USA on 20 Jun 1941. In an official test in 1946 Stella Pajunas, now Mrs Garnard, attained a rate of 216 words in a minute on an IBM machine.

Mary Ann Morel (South Africa) set a numerical record at the CABEX '85 Exhibition in Johannesburg, South Africa on 6 Feb 1985 by typing spaced numbers from 1 to 781 in 5 min.

Tyre supporting ■ The greatest number of motor tyres supported in a free-standing 'lift' is 96 by Gary Windebank of Romsey, Hants in February 1984. The total weight was 653 kg *1440 lb*. The tyres used were Michelin XZX 155 × 13.

Unsupported circle ■ The highest recorded number of people who have demonstrated the physical paradox of all being seated without a chair is an unsupported circle of 10 323 employees of the Nissan Motor Company at Komazawa Stadium, Tokyo, Japan on 23 Oct 1982.

The British record is 7402 participants at Goodwood Airfield, West Sussex on 25 May 1986, as part of a Sport Aid event.

Walking on hands ■ The duration record for walking on hands is 1400 km *871 miles* by Johann Hurlinger, of Austria, who in 55 daily 10-hr stints, averaged 2·54 km/h *1·58 mph* from Vienna to Paris in 1900. Shin Don-mok of South Korea completed a 50 m *54·68 yd* inverted sprint in 17·44 sec at the Toda Sports Centre, Saitama, Japan on 14 Nov 1986.

A four-man team of David Lutterman, Brendan Price, Philip Savage and David Scannel covered 1·609 km *1 mile* in 24 min 48 sec on 15 Mar 1987 at Knoxville, Tennessee, USA. This compares with the record of 3 min 2 sec the right way up.

Walking on water ■ Wearing 3·36 m *11 ft* water ski shoes, called Skijaks, and using a twin-bladed paddle, David Kiner walked 249·44 km *155 miles* on the Hudson River from Albany to Battery Park, New York, USA. His walk took him 57 hr, from 22–27 Jun 1987.

Wall of death ■ The greatest endurance feat on a wall of death was 6 hr 7 min 38 sec by Hugo Dabbert (b. Hildesheim, 24 Sep 1938) at Rüsselsheim, West Germany on 14 Aug 1980. He rode 6841 laps on the 10 m *32·8 ft* diameter wall on a Honda CM 400T averaging 35·2 km/h *21·8 mph* for the 214·8 km *133·4 miles*.

Whip cracking ■ The longest stock whip ever 'cracked' (*i.e.* the end made to travel above the speed of sound — 1223 km/h *760 mph*) is one of 42·67 m *140 ft* (excluding the handle) wielded by Garry Brophy at Adelaide, Australia on 31 Oct 1985.

Whistling ■ Roy Lomas achieved 122·5 decibels at 2½ m *8·20 ft* in the Deadroom at the BBC studios in Manchester on 19 Dec 1983. The marathon record is held by David Frank of Toronto, Canada, who completed 35 hr non-stop at the Washington Monument, Washington, DC, USA on 17–18 Jul 1987.

Window cleaning ■ Donald Young cleaned three standard 1040 × 1153 mm *40·94 × 45·39 in* office windows with a 300 mm *11·8 in* long squeegee and 9 litres *1·98 gal* of water in 14·90 sec on 28 Jan 1989 at Lubbock, Texas, USA.

Wing walking ■ Helen Tempest flew on the wing of an aircraft for 2 hr 40 mins on 31 Aug 1988, taking off from Stapleford Airfield, Essex and landing at Shoreham Airport, East Sussex.

Winkling ■ Mrs B. Charles picked 50 shells (with a straight pin) in 3 min 15 sec at Eastbourne, East Sussex on 4 Aug 1982.

Wire slide ■ The greatest distance recorded in a wire slide is from the London Weekend TV building to the barge *Driftwood* 112·7 m *370 ft* below and 281·9 m *925 ft* distant on the Thames on 27 Oct 1986. This 'death slide' set up by the Royal Marines was traversed by Lady Nourse *née* Lavinia Malim for charity. The estimated run length was 305 m *1000 ft*.

Wood cutting ■ The first recorded lumberjack

sports competition was held in 1572 in the Basque region of Spain. The records set at the Lumberjack World Championships at Hayward, Wisconsin, USA (founded 1960) are:

Power Saw	8·71 sec	
Ron Johnson (US)	1986	
One-Man Bucking	18·96 sec	
Rolin Eslinger (US)	1987	
Standing Block Chop	22·05 sec	
Melvin Lentz (US)	1988	
Underhand Block Chop	17·84 sec	
Laurence O'Toole (Australia)	1985	
Two-Man Bucking	7·27 sec	
Jim Colbert (US), Mike Sullivan (US)	1988	
Springboard Chopping	1 min 18·45 sec	
Bill Youd (Australia)	1985	

Writing minuscule ■ In 1926 an account was published of Alfred McEwen's pantograph record in which the 56-word version of the Lord's Prayer was written by diamond point on glass in the space of 0·04 × 0·02 mm *0·0016 × 0·0008 in.* Frederick C. Watts of Felmingham, Norfolk demonstrated for photographers on 24 Jan 1968 his ability, without mechanical or optical aid, to write the Lord's Prayer 34 times (9452 letters) within the size of a definitive UK postage stamp *viz* 21·33 × 18·03 mm *0·84 × 0·71 in.* Surendra Apharya of Jaipur, India demonstrated the ability to write 241 characters (names of various countries and regions) on a single grain of rice on 25 Feb 1989. Tsutomu Ishii of Tokyo wrote TOKYO JAPAN on a human hair in April 1983.

Writing under handicap ■ The ultimate feat in 'funny writing' appears to be the ability to write extemporaneously and decipherably backwards, upside down, laterally inverted (mirror-style), while blindfolded, with both hands simultaneously. Three claims to this ability, with both hands and feet simultaneously, by Mrs Carolyn Webb of Thirlmere, NSW, Australia, Mrs Judy Hall of Chesterfield, Virginia, USA, and Robert Gray of Toronto, Ontario, Canada, are outstanding.

Yard of ale ■ Peter Dowdeswell of Earls Barton, Northants drank a yard of ale (1·42 litres *2 ½ pints*) in 5·0 sec at RAF Upper Heyford, Oxon on 4 May 1975.

Yodelling ■ The most protracted yodel on record was that of Errol Bird for 26 hr in Lisburn, Northern Ireland on 27–28 Sep 1984. Yodelling has been defined as 'repeated rapid changes from the chest-voice to falsetto and back again'. The most rapid recorded is fiev tones (three falsetto) in 1·9 sec by Donn Reynolds of Canada on 25 Jul 1984.

Yo-yo ■ A yo-yo was a toy in Grecian times and is depicted on a bowl dated 450 BC. It was also a Filipino jungle fighting weapon recorded in the 16th century weighing 1·81 kg *4 lb* with a 6 m *20 ft* thong. The word means 'come-come'. Though illustrated in a book in 1891 as a bandalore the craze did not begin until it was started by Donald F. Duncan of Chicago, Illinois, USA in 1926. The most difficult modern yo-yo trick is the 'whirlwind' incorporating both inside and outside horizontal loop-the-loops. The individual continuous endurance record is 121 hr 10 min by Bob Brown of Boston, Massachusetts, USA from 24–29 Jun 1985. Dr Allen Bussey in Waco, Texas, USA on 23 Apr 1977 completed 20 302 loops in 3 hr, and on 5 Nov 1988 Luis Salamanca of Bogota, Colombia set a one hour speed record of 7 574 loops at the *Channel 9* Studios in Artarmon, Sydney, Australia. The largest yo-yo ever constructed was one by Dr Tom Kuhn weighing 116·11 kg *256 lb* test launched from a 52·2 m *150 ft* crane in San Francisco, California, USA on 13 Oct 1979.

Manufactured Articles

Amplifier ■ The largest working guitar amplifier is 2·75 m *9·04 ft* high, weighs 325·68 kg *718 lb*, houses 32 25·4 cm *10 in* speakers driven by 600 watts of all tube power. However, it can handle 1400 watts output. This Ampeg Mega SVT Bass Amp System was unveiled at the NAMM EXPO in Chicago, Illinois by St Louis Music of St Louis, Missouri, USA.

Antique ■ The largest antique ever sold was London Bridge in March 1968. The sale was made by Ivan F. Luckin of the Court of Common Council of the Corporation of London to the McCulloch Oil Corporation of Los Angeles, California, USA for £1 029 000. The 10 000 tonnes of façade stonework were re-assembled, at a cost of £3 million, at Lake Havasu City, Arizona, USA and 're-dedicated' on 10 Oct 1971.

Armour ■ The highest auction price paid for a suit of armour was £1 925 000 by B. H. Trupin (US) on 5 May 1983 at Sotheby's, London for a suit made in Milan by Giovanni Negroli in 1545 for Henri II of France. It came from the Hever Castle Collection in Kent.

Basket ■ The biggest basket ever made was 4·57 m *15 ft* tall, woven by Nineteenth Century Basket Company, Warren, Ohio, USA in 1986.

Beds ■ In Bruges, Belgium, Philip, Duke of Burgundy had a bed 3·81 m wide and 5·79 m long *12½ m × 19 ft* erected for the perfunctory *coucher officiel* ceremony with Princess Isabella of Portugal in 1430.

The largest bed in Great Britain is the Great Bed of Ware, dating from *c.* 1580, from the Crown Inn, Ware, Herts, now preserved in the Victoria and Albert Museum, London. It is 3·26 m wide, 3·37 m long and 2·66 m tall *10 ft 8½ in × 11 ft 1 in × 8 ft 9 in*. The largest bed marketed in the United Kingdom was the Super Size Diplomat bed, 2·74 m wide × 2·74 m long, *9 ft × 9 ft* from The London Bedding Centre, Sloane Street. It costs more than £4000. A promotional 1500 kg *1½ ton* 6 m × 4·40 m *19 ft 8 in × 14 ft 5 in* pinewood bed accommodating 39 people was exhibited by a French company in August 1986.

Beer cans ■ Beer cans date from a test marketing by Krueger Beer of Newark, New Jersey, USA at Richmond, Virginia, USA in 1935. The largest collection has been made by John F. Ahrens of Mount Laurel, New Jersey, USA with nearly 15 000 different cans. A Rosalie Pilsner can sold for $6000 in the USA in April 1981.

Beer labels (Labology) ■ Jan Solberg of Oslo, Norway has amassed 317 800 different labels from around the world.

The greatest collection of different British beer labels is 30 722 (to April 1987) by Keith Osborne, Hon. Sec. of The Labologists' Society (founded by Guinness Exports Ltd in 1958). His oldest is one from A. B. Walker & Co, Warrington, Cheshire of *c.* 1846.

Beer mats (Tegestology) ■ The world's largest collection of beer mats is owned by Leo Pisker of Vienna, who had collected over 126 700 different mats from 152 countries by April 1989. The largest collection of British mats is 41 750 formed by Timothy Stannard of Birmingham, West Midlands.

Beer tankard ■ The largest tankard was made by the Selangor Pewter Co, Kuala Lumpur, Malaysia and unveiled on 30 Nov 1985. It measures 198·7 cm *6½ ft* in height and has a capacity of 2796 litres *615 gal*.

Blanket ■ The largest blanket measured 21·3 × 46·3 m *70 × 152 ft* (988·45 m² *10 640 ft²*) and consisted of 1100 squares. It was made by Adolph Coors Company Volunteers, Denver, Colorado, USA and took 13 000 hours to complete. It was displayed at the Denver Broncos practice stadium on 12 Dec 1987.

Bottle caps ■ Since 1950 Helge Friholm (b. 1910) of Søborg, Denmark has amassed 53 320 different bottle caps (to April 1989) from 159 countries.

Pyramid ■ A pyramid consisting of 223 300 bottle caps was constructed by 16 students of the Economische Hogeschool Saint-Aloysius, Brussels, Belgium from 22 Feb–3 Mar 1988.

Bottle collections ■ David L. Maund of Upham, Hampshire, has a collection of unduplicated miniature Scotch whisky bottles amounting to 7014. Over the past 30 years he has also collected 323 different miniature Guinness bottles.

George E. Terren of Southboro, Massachusetts, USA, has a collection of 29 508 miniature and distilled spirit and liquor bottles as at 1 Mar 1988.

At 12 May 1989 Ted Shuler of Germantown, Tennessee, USA, had a collection of 2018 different bottled beers with specimens from 89 countries.

The world's greatest collection of whisky bottles is one of 3100 unduplicated assembled by Sig Edward Giaccone at his whiskyteca, Salo, Lake Garda, Italy.

The collection of unduplicated labels by Ian Boasman of Bistro French, Preston, Lancs had reached 2067 by April 1988.

Cans ■ A Colosseum-shaped structure consisting of 1 250 000 empty beverage cans was built in Coccaglio, Brescia, Italy by members of AVIS–AIDO with the co-operation of Rail (producers of aluminium cans). It was completed on 18 Oct 1987 after 1500 hours of work.

Candle ■ A candle 24·38 m *80 ft* high and 2·59 m *8½ ft* in diameter was exhibited at the 1897 Stockholm Exhibition by the firm of Lindahls. The overall height was 38·70 m *127 ft*. Currently the largest is that made by the Atletiek-en Trimvereniging Tegelen Sportsclub of Tegelen, Netherlands on 1 Jun 1986. It stands 27·15 m *89 ft 1 in* high.

Card ■ The world's largest greeting card was produced by students of Drake University, Des Moines, Iowa, USA. It measured 14·3 m × 8·76 m *47 ft*

Antique ● The largest antique ever sold was London Bridge in March 1968. The sale was made by Ivan F. Luckin of the Court of Common Council of the Corporation of London to the McCulloch Oil Corporation of Los Angeles, California, USA for £1 029 000. The 10 000 tonnes of façade stonework were re-assembled, at a cost of £3 million, at Lake Havasu City, Arizona, USA and 're-dedicated' on 10 Oct 1971.

COLLECTIONS

Matchbox label collection ● (right) Teiichi Yoshizawa (b. 1904) of Chiba-Ken, Japan has amassed 712 118 matchbox labels (including advertising labels) from 150 countries since 1925.

Credit card collection ● (left) The largest collection of valid credit cards at April 1988 is one of 1 199 (all different) by Walter Cavanagh, USA. The cost of aquisition to 'Mr Plastic Fantastic' was nil, and he keeps them in the world's longest wallet - 76.2 m *250 ft* long, weighing 15.87 kg 35 lb and worth more than $1.40 million in credit.

Cigarette rolling paper booklets ● The largest collection of cigarette rolling paper booklets is one of 2 366 owned by Peter Emmens of Kenley, Surrey. (Photo: Ronald Chapman for Guinness Publishing)

× 28 ft 9 in. It was delivered by the United States Postal Service to Michael Ferrari, President of Drake University on 27 Sep 1988. The largest greeting card delivered by the Royal Mail in the UK measured 25·6 × 2·4 m *84 × 8 ft*. It was constructed by members of Leeds City Council's 'Give for Life' campaign and was sent to HRH The Princess Royal at Buckingham Palace.

Carpets and rugs ■ The earliest carpet known is a Seythian woollen pile-knotted carpet measuring 1·8 m² (*6 ft²*) and dating from the 4th-3rd centuries BC. It was discovered by the Russian archaeologist Sergey Ivanovich Rudenko in 1947 in the Pazyryk Valley in southern Siberia and is now preserved in the Hermitage, Leningrad, USSR.

Of ancient carpets the largest was a gold-enriched silk carpet of Hashim (dated AD 743) of the Abbasid caliphate in Baghdad, Iraq. It is reputed to have measured 54·86 by 91·44 m *180 × 300 ft*. A 4851 m² *52 225 ft²* or 28 ton red carpet was laid on 13 Feb 1982, by the Allied Corporation, from Radio City Music Hall to the New York Hilton along the Avenue of the Americas, New York City, USA.

The most finely woven carpet known is one having 576 knots per cm² *3716 per in²* woven by five women, selected from 3000 weaving specialists, for Ozipek Halicilik A.S. of Hereke, Turkey. The project took five years to complete and the finished product, named *Hereke Treasure* was sold to Gandhara Carpet Japan Ltd, Tokyo in March 1988. The most magnificent carpet ever made was the Spring carpet of Khusraw made for the audience hall of the Sassanian palace at Ctesiphon, Iraq. It was about 650 m² *7000 ft²* of silk and gold thread, and encrusted with emeralds. It was cut up as booty by looters in AD 635 and from the known realisation value of the pieces must have had an original value of some £100 000 000.

Chair ■ The largest chair is a 12·71 m *41 ft 8½ in* tall, 7·26 m *23 ft 9½ in* wide deck-chair constructed by Luigi Bernasconi & Co, Mendrisio, Switzerland. It was exhibited from 11–13 Apr 1987.

Chandelier ■ The largest set of chandeliers was built for the palace of HM Sir Muda Hassanal Bolkiah of Brunei in 1983. His palace or Istana Nurul Iman is in the capital, Bandar Seri Begawan. Britain's largest chandelier measures 9·1 m *30 ft* and is in the Chinese Room at the Royal Pavilion, Brighton, East Sussex. It was made in 1818 and weighs 1 tonne.

Christmas cracker ■ The largest functional cracker ever constructed was one measuring 33·07 m *108½ ft* long built by Don Cameron Balloons of Bristol for Christmas 1988.

Cigars ■ The largest cigar ever made measures 5·095 m *16 ft 8½ in* in length and weighs 262 kg *577 lb 9 oz* (over ¼ ton) taking 243 hours and using 3330 full tobacco leaves. It was made by Tinus Vinke and Jan Weijmer in February 1983 and is in the Tobacco Museum in Kampen, Netherlands. The largest marketed cigar in the world is the 35·5 cm *14 in* Valdez Emperado manufactured by Fábrica de Puros Santa Clara of San Andrés Tuxtla, Veracruz, Mexico and exclusively distributed by Tabacos San Andrés.

The most expensive standard cigar in the world is the 23·5 cm *9¼ in* long Montecristo 'A' which retails in Britain at £16·50.

Joseph Hruby of Lyndhurst, Ohio, USA has the largest known collection of cigar bands with 198 525 different examples dating from c. 1895.

Cigarettes ■ World production in 1985 was 9873 billion cigarettes. The people of China were estimated to consume 1180 million in 1985. In Senegal 80 per cent of urban males smoke. The peak consumption in the United Kingdom was 3230 cigarettes per adult in 1973. The peak volume was 110·2 million kg *243 100 000 lb* in 1961, compared with 79·4 million kg *175 million lb* in 1987 when 95 000 million cigarettes were sold. In the United Kingdom in 1987 44 per cent of adult males were smokers, averaging 136 cigarettes per week each. Of women 34 per cent smoked. Of the 151 brands most recently analysed for the

Can structure ● A Colosseum-shaped structure consisting of 1 250 000 empty beverage cans was built in Coccaglio, Brescia, Italy by members of AVIS-AIDO with the co-operation of Rail (producers of aluminium cans). It was completed on 18 Oct 1987 after 1500 hours of work.

Dept of Health and Social Security, the one with highest tar/nicotine content is *Capstan Full Strength* with 24/2·4 mg per cigarette. *Silk Cut Ultra Low King Size*, *Embassy Ultra Mild King Size* and *John Player King Size Ultra Mild* with < 4/0·3 are at the lower risk end of the league table. In the Philippines there is a brand with 71 mg nicotine per cigarette.

The world's most popular cigarette is *Marlboro*, a filter cigarette made by Philip Morris, which sold 237 000 million units in 1982. The largest-selling British cigarette in 1987 *Benson and Hedges Special Filter*. The oldest brand still available on the British market is *Wills Woodbine*, introduced in 1888.

The longest cigarettes ever marketed were *Head Plays*, each 27·9 cm *11 in* long and sold in packets of five in the United States in about 1930, to save tax. The shortest were *Lilliput* cigarettes, each 31·7 mm *1¼ in* long and 3 mm *⅛ in* in diameter, made in Great Britain in 1956.

The world's largest collection of cigarettes is that of Robert E. Kaufman MD, of New York, USA. In April 1989 he had 8320 different cigarettes made in 172 countries. The oldest brand represented is *Lone Jack*, made in the USA c. 1885. Both the longest and shortest (see above) are represented.

Cigarette cards ■ The earliest known tobacco card is 'Vanity Fair' dated 1876, issued by Wm S. Kimball & Co, Rochester, New York, USA. The earliest British example appeared c. 1883 in the form of a calendar issued by Allen & Ginter, of Richmond, Virginia, trading from Holborn Viaduct, City of London. The largest known collection is that of Mr Edward Wharton-Tigar MBE (b. 1913) of London with a collection of more than 1 000 000 cigarette and trade cards in about 45 000 sets. This collection has been accepted as a bequest by the British Museum where it will eventually be available for public study.

On 30 Jul 1987, a complete set of Taddy's Clowns and Circus Artistes was sold at Phillips, London for £15 500 (£17 050 including buyer's premium of £1550), a record price for cigarette cards at auction. Only a handful of complete sets of 20 are known. James Taddy & Co, a small London tobacco firm

founded c. 1740, was renowned for its beautifully produced cards.

Cigarette lighter ■ The Leader Lighthouse Table Lighter is made in 18-ct gold—designed in the shape of a lighthouse set on an island base of amethyst which alone weighs 50 kg *1 cwt*. It weighs 1600 g *51·4 oz troy* and the windows on the lighthouse stem are amethyst. Priced at £37 500, it was sold by Alfred Dunhill, St James's, London in 1986.

Since 1970, Bent Hansen of Præstø, Denmark has collected 7564 cigarette lighters from all over the world.

Cigarette packets ■ The earliest surviving cigarette packet is a Finnish *Petit Canon* packet for 25, made by Tollander & Klärich in 1860, from the Ventegodt Collection. The rarest is the Latvian 700-year anniversary (1201–1901) *Riga* packet, believed to be unique, from the same collection. The largest verified private collection was one of 62 837 from over 150 countries owned by Vernon Young of Farnham, Surrey.

Cigarette rolling paper booklets ■ The largest collection of cigarette rolling paper booklets is one of 2366 owned by Peter Emmens of Kenley, Surrey.

Coathanger ■ The world's largest coathanger measures 4·6 × 2·06 × 0·5 m (*15 × 6·75 × 1·6 ft*) and weighs 200 kg (*440 lb*). It was made of Oregon pine and plywood by Stefan Geir Karlsson of Reykjavik, Iceland.

Credit card collection ■ The largest collection of valid credit cards at May 1989 is one of 1208 (all different) by Walter Cavanagh (b. 1943) of Santa Clara, California, USA. The cost of acquisition to 'Mr Plastic Fantastic' was nil, and he keeps them in the world's longest wallet—76·2 m *250 ft* long weighing 15·87 kg *35 lb* and worth more than $1·5 million in credit.

Curtain ■ The largest curtain ever built was a bright orange-red 4064 kg *4 ton* 56 m *185 ft* high curtain suspended 411 m *1350 ft* across the Rifle Gap, Grand Hogback, Colorado, USA by Bulgarian-born sculptor Christo (*né* Javacheff) on 10 Aug 1971. It blew apart in a 80 km/h *50 mph* gust 27 hr later. The total cost involved in displaying this work of art was $750 000.

The world's largest functional curtain is one 167·6 m long × 19·8 m high *550 ft × 65 ft* in the Brabazon hangar at British Aerospace, Filton, Bristol, used to enclose aircraft in the paint-spraying bay. It is electrically drawn.

Dress ■ The dress with the highest price tag ever

Largest firework ● *Universe I Part II* exploded for the Lake Toya Festival, Hokkaido, Japan on 15 Jul 1988. The 700 kg *1543 lb* shell was 139 cm *54·7 in* in diameter and burst to a diameter of 1200 m *3937 ft.*

exhibited by a Paris fashion house was one in the Schiaparelli spring/summer collection on 23 Jan 1977. 'The Birth of Venus' designed by Serge Lepage with 512 diamonds was priced at FFr. 7 500 000.

A robe for Emperor Field-Marshal Jean-Bédel Bokassa with a 11·8 m *39 ft* long train was encrusted with 785 000 pearls and 1 220 000 crystal beads by Guiselin of Paris for £77 125. It was for his coronation at Bangui, Central African Empire (now Republic) on 4 Dec 1977 (see also Shoes).

The world's longest wedding dress train measured 26·2 m *86 ft.* The dress was created by Manjit Singh, Mohinder Kaur and their two daughters Gulneider and Kamaljit Kaur of Leicester. It was made of red silk, gold lace, beads and sequins and was displayed at the City Health and Yoga Centre, Leicester in January 1989.

Electric bulb ■ The smallest electric bulb is one 3 mm *0·12 in* long by 0·5 mm *0·02 in* in diameter made by the Hamai Electric Lamp Co, Tokyo, Japan.

Fabrics ■ The oldest surviving fabric discovered from Level VI A at Çatal Hüyük, Turkey has been radio-carbon dated to 5900 BC.

The most expensive fabric is Vicuña cloth manufactured by Fujii Keori Ltd of Osaka, Japan at £4450 per metre in January 1988. The most expensive evening wear fabric was that designed by Alan Hershman of Duke Street, London at £850 per metre. Each square metre, despite 155 000 hand-sewn sequins, weighs less than 198 g *7 oz.*

The most expensive cloth, the brown-grey throat hair of Indian goats, is Shatoosh (or Shatusa), finer and more expensive than Vicuña. It was sold by Neiman-Marcus of Dallas, Texas, USA at $1000 per yard but supplies have now dried up.

Fan ■ An intricately carved, wooden fan measuring 3·3 m *10·9 ft* when unfolded and 1·8 m *6 ft* high was completed by Wang Xianbao of Shanghai, China in January 1987.

Firework ■ The largest firework ever produced has been *Universe I Part II* exploded for the Lake Toya Festival, Hokkaido, Japan on 15 Jul 1988. The 700 kg *1543 lb* shell was 139 cm *54·7 in* in diameter and burst to a diameter of 1200 m *3937 ft.*

The longest firecracker display was produced by the Johor Tourism Department, the United Malaysian Youth Movement and Mr Yap Seng Hock, and took place on 20 Feb 1988 at Pelangi Garden, Johor Bahru, Johor, Malaysia. The total length of the display was 5723·3 m (*18 777 ft*) and consisted of 3 338 777 firecrackers and 666 kg (*1468 lb*) of gunpowder. It burned for 9 hr 27 min.

Flags ■ The oldest known flag is one dated to *c.* 3000 BC found in 1972 at Khabis, Iran. It is of metal and measures 23 ×23 cm *9 ×9 in* and depicts an eagle, two lions and a goddess, three women and a bull.

The oldest national flags are claimed by Austria, Denmark, Malta, Japan, Sri Lanka and Mali.

The largest flag in the world, the 'Great American Flag', was displayed at Evansville, Indiana, USA on 22 Mar 1980 measuring 125 m *411 ft* by 64 m *210 ft* with a weight of 7 tonnes. It was donated to the White House and was the brainchild of Len Silverfine. The largest Union Flag (or Union Jack) was one 73·15 × 32·91 m *240 × 108 ft* displayed at the Royal Tournament, Earl's Court, London in July 1976. It weighed more than a ton and was made by Form 4Y at Bradley Rowe School, Exeter, Devon. The largest flag *flown* from a flagstaff is a Brazilian national flag measuring 70 × 100 m *229 ft 8 in × 328 ft 1 in* in Brasilia. The study of flags is known as vexillology from Latin *vexillum,* a flag, and was coined by Dr Whitney Smith of Winchester, Massachusetts, USA.

Float ■ The largest float was the 47·24 m *155 ft* long, 7·32 m *24 ft* wide 'Merry Christmas America' float bearing three double arches, a 5·18 m *17 ft* Christmas tree, two 4·57 m *15 ft* peppermint candy sticks and 500 m² *5380 ft²* of wrapping paper, used at the 40th Annual Christmas Parade, Baton Rouge, Louisiana, USA on 5 Dec 1986.

Football ■ The world's largest football measures 2·36 m *7 ¾ ft* in diameter, weighs 36·28 kg *80 lb* and has 8640 stitches requiring 129·54 m *425 ft* of thread. It was made by Mitre Sports of Huddersfield, West Yorks and it is hoped that the football will eventually be signed by each of the 92 Football League Clubs.

Furniture ■ The largest item of furniture in the world is a wooden bench along the Masuhoura Beach, Ishikawa, Japan which can seat over 1400 people and measures 460·9 m *1512 ft* long. It was completed by a team of 800 on 9 Mar 1987.

Garden gnome ■ The earliest recorded garden gnome was one placed in the rockery at Lamport Hall, Northants in 1847 by Sir Charles Isham, Bt (1819–1903) who believed they were real people.

Glass ■ The most priceless example of the art of glass-making is usually regarded as the glass Portland Vase which dates from late in the 1st century BC or 1st century AD. It was made in Italy, and was in the possession of the Barberini family in Rome from at least 1642. It was eventually bought by the Duchess of Portland in 1792 but smashed while in the British Museum by William Lloyd on 7 Feb 1845. The thinnest glass, type D263, has a minimum thickness of 0·035 mm *0·00137 in* and a maximum thickness of 0·055 mm *0·0021 in.* It is made by Deutsche Spezialglas AG, Grünenplan, West Germany for use in electronic and medical equipment.

Gold ■ The gold coffin of the 14th-century BC Pharaoh Tutankhamun discovered by Howard Carter on 16 Feb 1923 in the Valley of the Kings, western Thebes, Egypt weighed 110·4 kg *243 lb.* The exhibition at the British Museum from 30 Mar to 30 Dec 1972 attracted 1 656 151 people (of whom 45·7 per cent bought catalogues), resulting in a profit of £657 731·22.

Grill ■ A 493·94 m *1620 ½ ft* long grill was made by the Fedéracio de Colles de Lleida for a snail

Gold ● The gold coffin of the 14th-century BC Pharaoh Tutankhamun discovered by Howard Carter on 16 Feb 1923 in the Valley of the Kings, western Thebes, Egypt weighed 110·4 kg *243 lb.* The exhibition at the British Museum from 30 Mar to 30 Dec 1972 attracted 1 656 151 people (of whom 45·7 per cent bought catalogues), resulting in a profit of £657 731·22. (Photo: Spectrum)

barbecue at Lérida, Spain on 8 May 1988. 207 000 snails were cooked on it.

Hammock ■ A 44·4 m *145½ ft* long hammock was woven by members of the Åboland Crafts Guild, Pargas, Finland in July 1988. The completed hammock was suspended between large oak trees and accommodated 21 people.

Jigsaw ■ The earliest jigsaws were made as 'dissected maps' by John Spilsbury (1739–69) in Russell Court off Drury Lane, London *c.* 1762. The largest jigsaw ever made is one measuring 767·35 m² *8260 ft²* with 1908 pieces made by the pupils of the Drawing School of Centelles, Barcelona, Spain and assembled on 23 Apr 1989.

In July 1986 'L'Association l'Arbre aux Mille Sources' constructed a jigsaw consisting of 150 000 pieces and measuring 25 × 14·64 m *82 × 48 ft*. Fujisankei Communications Group of Japan commissioned Yanoman Co to produce a puzzle 3·24 × 5·88 m *10·63 × 19·29 ft* wide with 61 752 pieces. Each piece was sold for charity. Custom-made Stave puzzles made by Steve Richardson of Norwich, Vermont, USA of 2640 pieces cost $7355 in March 1989.

Kettle ■ The largest antique copper kettle was one standing 0·9 m *3 ft* high with a 1·8 m *6 ft* girth and a 90 litre *20 gal* capacity, built in Taunton, Somerset, for the hardware merchants Fisher and Son *c.* 1800.

Lantern ■ The largest lantern was 7 m *23 ft* high and 2·5 m *8·2 ft* wide, and was made in February 1989 by staff of the Sheraton Towers Hotel, Singapore.

Matchbox labels ■ The oldest match label of accepted provenance is that of Samuel Jones *c.* 1830. The finest collection of trade mark labels (excluding any bar or other advertising labels) is some 280 000 pieces collected by the phillumenist Robert Jones of Indianapolis, USA. Teiichi Yoshizawa (b. 1904) of Chiba-Ken, Japan has amassed 712 118 matchbox labels (including advertising labels) from 150 countries since 1925. The greatest British prize is a Lucifer & Congreve label of *c.* 1835.

Matchstick ■ The longest matchstick, made by Stichting 'De Langste Daag' at Tegelen, Netherlands on 25 Jun 1988, measured 18·80 m *61 ft 8 in*, weighed 1000 kg *2204 lb* and burnt for 6 hr 45 min 1 sec.

Needles ■ Needles made of bone have been found in sites of the Upper Palaeolithic Aurignacian period in France dated *c.* 28 000–24 000 BC. The longest is one 185·5 cm *6 ft 1 in* long made by George Davies of Thomas Somerfield, Bloxwich, West Midlands for stitching on mattress buttons lengthways. One is preserved in the National Needle Museum at Forge Mill, Redditch, Worcs.

Nylon ■ The lowest denier nylon yarn ever produced is the 6 denier used for stockings exhibited at the Nylon Fair in London in February 1956.

The sheerest stockings normally available are 9 denier. A hair from the average human head is about 50 denier.

Penknife ■ The penknife with the greatest number of blades is the Year Knife made by cutlers Joseph Rodgers & Sons, of Sheffield, South Yorks, whose trade mark was granted in 1682. The knife was made in 1822 with 1822 blades and a blade was added every year until 1973 when there was no further space. It was acquired by Britain's largest hand tool manufacturers, Stanley Works (Great Britain) Ltd of Sheffield, South Yorks, in 1970.

Pens ■ The most expensive writing pen is the 5003.002 CARAN D'ACHE 18-carat solid gold Madison slimline ballpoint pen incorporating white diamonds of 6.35 carats, exclusively distributed by Jakar International Limited, London. Its recommended retail price is £20 950 (incl. VAT).

A Japanese collector paid 1·3 million French francs in Feb 1988 for the 'Anémone' fountain pen made by Réden, France. It was encrusted with 600 precious stones including emeralds, amethysts, rubies, sapphires and onyx and took skilled craftsmen over a year to complete.

The world's leading pen is the BiC Crystal with 14 000 000 being manufactured daily by the BiC organisation world-wide. More than 500 000 are sold daily in the UK, which, if used, would offer a write-out length of at least 1 250 000 km *776 735·2 miles* – the equivalent of drawing a line around the world 31 times or alternatively to the Moon and back and back to the Moon again.

Pistol ■ In Dec 1983 it was reported that Ray Bily (US) owned an initialled gold pistol made for Hitler which was valued for insurance at $375 000.

The pistol with the largest magazine capacity is the .22LR M.100P with 103 rounds of continuous firepower, manufactured by Calico, Bakersfield, California, USA.

Photographs with stars ■ During the past five years, Barbara Ann Thomas of Fredericksburg, Virginia, USA has had her photograph taken with 168 Hollywood stars. Husband John acts as photographer whilst they holiday at film locations in Hollywood, Los Angeles, California, USA.

Postcards ■ Deltiology is claimed to be the third largest collecting hobby next only to stamps and coins. Austria issued the first cards in 1869 followed by Britain in 1872. The highest price paid for a postcard was $4400 for one of the five known Mucha Waverly Cycle postcards. It was sold by Susan Brown Nicholson of Lisle, Illinois, USA in September 1984. The world's largest postcard collection is owned by Mario Morby, 12, of Streetly, West Mid-

lands, consisting of 1 000 265 postcards. *No further claims for the above category will be entertained.*

Quilt ■ The world's largest quilt was made by 7000 citizens of North Dakota for the 1989 centennial of North Dakota. It measured 25·9 × 40·8 m *85 × 134 ft*.

Ropes ■ The largest rope ever made was a coir fibre launching rope with a circumference of 119 cm *47 in* made in 1858 for the British liner *Great Eastern* by John and Edwin Wright of Birmingham, West Midlands. It consisted of four strands, each of 3780 yarns. The longest fibre rope ever made without a splice was one of 10 000 fathoms or 18 288 m *11·36 miles* of 16·5 cm *6½ in* circumference manila by Frost Brothers (now British Ropes Ltd) in London in 1874. (See also Wire ropes, Chapter 4.)

The strongest cable-laid wire rope strop made is one 282 mm *11·1 in* in diameter with a breaking strain of 3250 tonnes.

Longest scarf ■ The longest scarf ever knitted measured an amazing 32 km 3·9 m *20 miles 13 ft* long. It was knitted by residents of Abbeyfield Houses for the Abbeyfield Society and was completed on 29 May 1988.

Shoes ■ James Smith, founder of James Southall & Co of Norwich, Norfolk introduced sized shoes in 1792. The firm began making 'Start-rite' children's shoes in 1923.

Emperor Bokassa of the Central African Empire (now Republic) commissioned pearl-studded shoes from the House of Berluti, Paris, France for his self-coronation on 4 Dec 1977 at a cost of $85 000.

The most expensive shoes are mink-lined golf shoes with 18-carat gold embellishments and ruby-tipped spikes made by Stylo Matchmakers International of Northampton, Northants, which retail for $16 846 (£9895) per pair in the USA.

A pair of women's cream kid and braid high-heeled shoes *c.* 1660 sold by Lord Hereford at Sotheby's, London in September 1987 to Mrs Sonia Bata fetched £21 000.

Excluding cases of elephantiasis, the largest shoes ever sold are a pair size 42 built for the giant Harley Davidson of Avon Park, Florida, USA. The normal limit is size 14. For advertising and display purposes facsimiles of shoes weighing up to 1·5 tonnes have been constructed.

Silver ■ The largest single pieces of silver are a pair of water jugs of 242·7 kg *10 408 troy oz 4·77 cwt* made in 1902 for the Maharaja of Jaipur (1861–1922). They are 160 cm *5 ft 3 in* tall, with a circumference of 2·48 m *8 ft 1½ in*, and have a capacity of 8182 litres *1800 gallons*. They are now in the City Palace, Jaipur, India. The silversmith was Gorind Narain.

Snuff ■ The most expensive snuff obtainable in Britain is 'Café Royale' sold by G. Smith and Sons (est. 1869) of 74, Charing Cross Road, London. The price was £2·35 per oz in April 1989.

Sofa ● The longest standard sofa manufactured for market is the Augustus Rex Sofa, 3·74 m *12 ft 3 in* in length made by Dodge & Son of Sherborne, Dorset. (Photo: Farquharson Murless)

Sofa ■ The longest standard sofa manufactured for market is the Augustus Rex Sofa, 3·74 m *12¼ ft* in length made by Dodge & Son of Sherborne, Dorset. William L. Maclean, furniture manufacturers of Brighton, East Sussex received a commission for a 4·63 m *15 ft 2·43 in* long sofa from an international hotel chain in April 1989.

Suit ■ EVA suits for extra-vehicular activity worn by Space Shuttle crews from 1982 had a unit cost of $3·6 million.

Table ■ The longest table was set up in Pesaro, Italy on 20 Jun 1988 by the US Libertas Scavolini Basketball team. It was 3070 m *3357 yd* long and was used to seat 12 000 people.

Table cloth ■ The world's largest table cloth is one 300·5 m *328·6 yd* long by 184 cm *72 in* wide made of damask by Tonrose Limited of Manchester in June 1988.

Tapestry ■ The earliest known examples of tapestry woven linen are three pieces from the tomb of the Egyptian pharaoh Thutmose IV and dated to 1483–1411 BC.

The largest tapestry ever woven is the *History of Irak*, with an area of 1242·1 m² *13 370·7 ft²*. It was designed by the Yugoslavian artist Frane Delale and produced by the Zivtex Regeneracija Workshop in Zabok, Yugoslavia. The tapestry was completed in 1986 and it now adorns the wall of an amphitheatre in Baghdad, Iraq.

Britain's largest single piece of tapestry is *Christ in His Majesty*, measuring 21·94 × 11·88 m *72 × 39 ft* designed by Graham Vivian Sutherland OM (1903–80) for an altar hanging in Coventry Cathedral, West Midlands. It cost £10 500, weighs 760 kg *¾ ton* and was delivered from Pinton Frères of Felletin, France on 1 Mar 1962.

The famous Bayeux *Telle du Conquest, dite tapisserie de la reine Mathilde*, a hanging 49·5 cm *19½ in* wide by 70·40 m *231 ft* in length depicts events of 1064–6 in 72 scenes and was probably worked in Canterbury, Kent, *c.* 1086. It was 'lost' for 2½ centuries from 1476 until 1724.

The Overlord Embroidery of 34 panels each 2·43 × 0·91 m *8 × 3 ft*, commissioned by Lord Dulverton CBE, TD (b. 1915) from the Royal School of Needlework in London, was completed in 1979 after 100 man-years of work and is 12·49 m *41 ft* longer than the Bayeux. It has the largest area of any embroidery with 75·8 m² *816 ft²*.

An uncompleted 20·3 cm *8 in* deep 407·82 m *1338 ft* long embroidery of scenes from C. S. Lewis's *Narnia* children's stories has been worked by Mrs Margaret S. Pollard of Truro, Cornwall to the order of Michael Maine.

Tartan ■ The earliest evidence of tartan is the so-called Falkirk tartan, found stuffed in a jar of coins in Bells Meadow, Falkirk, Stirlingshire, Scotland. It is of a dark and light brown pattern and dates from *c.* AD 245.

The earliest reference to a specific named tartan is to a Murray tartan in 1618 although Mackay tartan was probably worn earlier.

There are 1300 tartans known to the Museum of Scottish Tartans at Comrie, Perthshire. HRH Prince of Wales is eligible to wear 11 including the Balmoral which has been exclusive to the royal family since 1852.

Ticket ■ The smallest ticket was one measuring 3 × 7 × 1 mm for admission to the Asian-Pacific Exposition Fukuoka '89, Fukuoka, Japan. It was made of ceramic on which letters of 85–280 microns were printed.

Whisky collection ● The world's greatest collection of whiskies is one of 3100 unduplicated labels assembled at the 'Whiskyteca in Salo', Lake Garda, Italy. Here, the proprietor, Sig Edward Giaccone, surveys 'the water of life' revealing a particular penchant for Islay malts..

Time capsule ■ The world's largest time capsule is the Tropico Time Tunnel of 283 m³ *10 000 ft³* in a cave in Rosamond, California, USA sealed by the Kern Antelope Historical Society on 20 Nov 1966 and intended for opening in AD 2866.

Toy ■ 'Lots-a-Lots-a-Legggggggs', the 1000-legged pink caterpillar, measures 76·2 m *250 ft* and weighs 136·08 kg *300 lb*. It was created by Commonwealth Toy & Novelty Co, Inc, New York, USA.

Toy construction ■ The tallest Lego tower ever constructed, 15·01 m *49 ft 2⅛ in*, was built in the forecourt of Waterloo Station, London on 29–30 Oct 1985.

Typewriters ■ The first patent for a typewriter was by Henry Mill in 1714 but the earliest known working machine was made by Pellegrine Turri (Italy) in 1808.

Vase ■ The largest vase on record is one 2·78 m *8 ft* in height, weighing 294·8 kg *650 lb*, thrown by Sebastiano Maglio at Haeger Potteries of Dundee, Illinois, USA (founded 1872) during August 1976.

The Chinese ceramic authority Chingwah Lee of San Francisco was reported in August 1978 to have appraised a unique 99 cm *39 in* Kang Hsi four-sided vase then in a bank vault in Phoenix, Arizona, USA at '$60 million'.

Wallet ■ The most expensive wallet ever made is a platinum-cornered, diamond-studded crocodile creation made by Louis Quatorze of Paris and Mikimoto of Tokyo selling in September 1984 at £56 000.

Wreath ■ The most expensive wreath on record was that presented to Sri Chinmoy in New York on 11 Jul 1983 by Ashrita Furman and Pahar Meltzer. It was handled by the Garland of Divinity's Love Florist, contained 10 000 flowers, and cost $3500.

Zip-fastener ■ The world's longest zip-fastener is 632·45 m *2074 ft* long made for covers of aquatic cables by RIRI of Mendrisio, Italy in January 1985. It has 119 007 nylon teeth.

C H A P T E R   10

Youngest monarch
The country with the youngest monarch is
Swaziland, where King Mswati III was crowned at
the age of 18 years 6 days. The picture shows the
coronation celebrations on 25 Apr 1986.
(Photo: Comma/Barritt)

Political and Social

Largest political division ■ The British Commonwealth of Nations, a free association of 48 sovereign independent states together with 17 non-sovereign states and dependencies administered by them, covers an area of 27 171 608 km² *10 491 016 miles²* with a population estimated in 1988 to be 1 213 601 000. Fiji declared itself a Republic on 1 Oct 1987 and also severed links. The British Empire began to expand when Henry VII patented trade monopolies to John Cabot in March 1496 and when the East India Co. was incorporated on 31 Dec 1600.

COUNTRIES

The world comprises 170 sovereign countries and 63 separately administered non-sovereign or other territories, making a total of 233.

The United Nations still lists the *de jure* territories of East Timor (now incorporated into Indonesia), Western Sahara (now in Morocco), the former mandated territory of Palestine and the uninhabited Canton and Enderbury Islands (now disputed between the USA and Kiribati) but does not list the three Baltic states of Estonia, Latvia and Lithuania though their forcible incorporation into the USSR in 1940 has never been internationally recognised. Neither does it list the *de facto* territories of Taiwan, Mayotte or Spanish North Africa, the four Antarctic Territories or the Australian Territory of Coral Sea Islands and Heard and McDonald Islands. The USA's renunciation of the Pacific Islands' trusteeship on 3 Nov 1986 is resulting in the creation of Micronesia, Marshall Islands, Northern Mariana Islands and Palau as separate entities.

Largest ■ The country with the greatest area is the Union of Soviet Socialist Republics (the Soviet Union), comprising 15 Union (constituent) Republics with a total area of 22 402 200 km² *8 649 500 miles²*, or 15 per cent of the world's total land area, and a total coastline (including islands) of 106 360 km *66 090 miles*. The country measures 8980 km *5580 miles* from east to west and 4490 km *2790 miles* from north to south and is 91·8 times the size of the United Kingdom. Its population on 1 Jul 1987 was an estimated 284 000 000.

The United Kingdom covers 244 110 km² *94 251 miles²* (including 3100 km² *1197 miles²* of inland water), or 0·16 per cent of the total land area of the world. Great Britain is the world's eighth largest island, with an area of 218 040 km² *84 186 miles²* and a coastline 7930 km *4928 miles* long, of which Scotland accounts for 4141 km *2573 miles*, Wales 685 km *426 miles* and England 3104 km *1929 miles*.

Smallest ■ The smallest independent country in the world is the State of the Vatican City or Holy See (Stato della Città del Vaticano), which was made an enclave within the city of Rome, Italy on 11 Feb 1929. The enclave has an area of 44 ha *108·7 acres*. The maritime sovereign country with the shortest coastline is Monaco with 5·61 km *3·49 miles* excluding piers and breakwaters. The world's smallest republic is Nauru, less than 1 degree south of the equator in the western Pacific, which became independent on 31 Jan 1968. It has an area of 2129 ha *5263 acres* and a population of 8100 (latest estimate 1987).

The smallest colony in the world is Gibraltar (since 1969, the City of Gibraltar) with an area of 5·8 km² *2½ miles²*. However, Pitcairn Island, the only inhabited (59 people at 1 Jan 1987) island of a group of four (total area 48 km² *18½ miles²*), has an area of 388 ha *960 acres/1½ miles²*. It was named after Midshipman Robert Pitcairn of HMS *Swallow* in July 1767.

The official residence, since 1834, of the Grand Master of the Order of the Knights of Malta, totalling 1·2 ha *3 acres* and comprising the Villa del Priorato di Malta on the lowest of Rome's seven hills, the 46 m *151 ft* Aventine, retains certain diplomatic privileges as does 68 via Condotti. The Order has

WORLD POPULATION

Date	Millions	Date	Millions
8000 BC	c. 6	1960	3049
AD 1	c. 255	1970	3678
1000	c. 254	1975	4033
1250	416	1980	4415
1500	460	1981	4530
1600	579	1982	4607
1700	679	1983	4685
1750	770	1984	4763
1800	954	1985	4837
1900	1633	1986	4917
1920	1862	1987 (mid)	5000*
1930	2070	1988	5081
1940	2295	1990	5246
1950	2513	2050†	14 000

* Population Institute of Washington, DC, USA declared this landmark was reached on 7 Jul 1986 whereas the UN nominated 11 Jul 1987 'Baby Five Billion Day'.

† In May 1988 it was estimated that the likely world population in 2050 would be as high as 14 000 million. Note The all-time peak annual increase of 2 per cent c. 1958–62 had declined by 1·73 per cent by 1975–80. By 1990 this should decline to 1·5 per cent. This, however, now produces an annual increment of 87 million peaking to 90 million in the 1990s.

On the estimates of the French demographer Biraben, A. R. Thatcher has calculated that 63 800 million people died between 40 000 BC and AD 1980. This indicates that there have thus been some 68 700 million specimens of Homo sapiens sapiens who ever lived i.e. the present population is about one thirteenth of those who have ever lived.

World population ● Matej Gaspar, b. 11 Jul 1987 in Zagreb, Yugoslavia, was symbolically named the world's 5 billionth inhabitant by the United Nations Secretary-General, Javier Pérez de Cuellar. After visiting the baby in hospital, he gave a speech hailing scientific and economic progress that have enabled the world to accommodate its rapidly growing masses. However, he also called for the implementation of family-planning programmes and for a 'determined attack' on poverty. It is predicted that without such measures the population will double during the next century. (See also graph below)

accredited representatives to foreign governments and is hence sometimes cited as the world's smallest 'state'.

Flattest and most elevated ■ The country with the lowest highest point is the Republic of the Maldives which attains 2·4 m *8 ft*. The country with the highest lowest point is Lesotho. The egress of the Senqu (Orange) riverbed is 1381 m *4530 ft* above sea level.

Most impenetrable boundary ■ The 'Iron Curtain' (1380 km *858 miles*) dividing the Federal Republic of Germany (West) and the German Democratic Republic (East) utilises 2 230 000 land mines and 80 500 km *50 000 miles* of barbed wire, much of it of British manufacture, in addition to many watch-towers containing detection devices. The whole strip, 246 m *270 yd*, wide occupies 344 km² *133 miles²* of East German territory and cost an estimated $7000 million to build and maintain. It reduced the westward flow from more than 200 000 in 1961 to a trickle of 30 (including eight guards) in 1985. The death toll has been 184 since 1962. Construction of the second wall, 165·7 km *103 miles* in length, began in East Berlin in March 1984.

Longest and shortest frontier ■ The longest *continuous* frontier in the world is that between Canada and the United States, which (including the Great Lakes boundaries) extends for 6416 km *3987 miles* (excluding 2547 km *1538 miles* with Alaska).

The frontier which is crossed most frequently is that between the United States and Mexico. It extends for 3110 km *1933 miles* and there are more than 120 000 000 crossings every year. The Sino-Soviet frontier, broken by the Sino-Mongolian border, extends for 7240 km *4500 miles*, with no reported figure of crossings. The 'frontier' of the Holy See in Rome measures 4·07 km *2·53 miles*. The land frontier between Gibraltar and Spain at La Linea, closed between June 1969 and February 1985, measures 1·53 km *1672 yd*. Zambia, Zimbabwe, Botswana and Namibia (South West Africa) almost merge.

The United Kingdom's frontier with the Republic of Ireland measures 358 km *223 miles*.

Most frontiers ■ China has the most land frontiers with 13 — Mongolia, USSR, North Korea, Hong Kong, Macau, Vietnam, Laos, Burma, India, Bhutan, Nepal, Pakistan and Afghanistan. These extend for 24 000 km *14 900 miles*. France, if all her *départements d'outre-mer* are included, may, on extended territorial waters, have 20.

POPULATIONS

World ■ The daily increase in the world's population is 223 285, or 155 per minute. For past, present and future estimates see table.

Matej Gaspar, born 11 Jul 1987 in Yugoslavia, was symbolically named the world's 5 billionth inhabitant by the United Nations Secretary-General.

Most populous country ■ The most populated country is China, which in *pinyin* is written Zhongguo (meaning, central land). The census of July 1982 was 1 008 175 288 while the mid-1987 estimate was 1 085 000 000. The rate of natural increase in the People's Republic of China is now estimated to be 35 068 a day or 12·8 million per year. The census of July 1982 required 5 100 000 enumerators to work for 10 days. India is set to overtake China in size of population by AD 2050 with 1590 million against 1554 million.

Least populous ■ The independent state with the smallest population is the Vatican City or the Holy See (see Smallest country, above), with 750 inhabitants in 1987 and a nil return for births.

Most densely populated ■ The most densely populated territory in the world is the Portuguese province of Macau (or Macao), on the southern coast of China. It has an estimated population of 392 000 (mid-1986) in an area of 16·05 km² *6·2 miles²*, giving a density of 24 423 per km² *63 225 per mile²*.

The principality of Monaco, on the south coast of France, has a population of 27 000 (mid-1985) in an area of just 191·4 ha *473 acres,* a density equal to 14 750 people per km² *38 179 people per mile²*.

Of territories with an area of more than 1000 km², Hong Kong (1037 km² *400·5 miles²*) contains 5 533 000 (1986), giving the territory a density of 5169/km² *13 390/mile²*. Hong Kong is now the most populous of all colonies. The transcription of the name is from a local pronunciation of the Peking dialect version of Xiang gang (a port for incense). The 1976 by-census showed that the west area of the urban district of Mong Kok on the Kowloon Peninsula had a density of 252 090/km² *652 910/mile²*. In 1959, at the peak of the housing crisis, it was reported that in one house designed for 12 people the number of occupants was 459, including 104 in one room and four living on the roof.

Of countries over 2589 km² *1000 miles²* the most densely populated is Bangladesh with a population of 103 200 000 (1986) living in 142 775 km² *55 126 miles²* at a density of 727/km² *1882/mile²*. The Indonesian island of Java (with an area of 126 295 km² *48 763 miles²*) had a population of 100 300 000 (1987), giving a density of 793/km² *2056/mile²*.

The United Kingdom (244 110 km² *94 251 miles²*) had an estimated population of 56 930 200 000 at mid-1987, giving a density of 233 persons/km² *604/mile²*. The mid-1986 population density for the Royal Borough of Kensington and Chelsea, London was 11 262/km² *29 168/mile²*.

Most sparsely populated ■ Antarctica became permanently occupied by relays of scientists from October 1956. The population varies seasonally and reaches 2000 at times.

The least populated territory, apart from Antarctica, is Kalaallit Nunaat (formerly Greenland), with a population of 53 406 (1986) in an area of 2 175 000 km² *840 000 miles²*, giving a density of one person to every 40·72 km² *15·72 miles²*. Some 84·3 per cent of the island comprises an ice-cap.

The lowest population densities in the United Kingdom are in the Highlands and Islands of Scotland with 13·1/km² *33·9/mile²*. The most sparsely populated county in England is Northumberland with 60·40/km² *156·45/mile²*.

Emigration ■ More people emigrate from Mexico than from any other country. An estimated 800 000 illegally entered the USA in 1980 alone. The Soviet invasion of Afghanistan in December 1979 caused an influx of 2 900 000 refugees into Pakistan and a further 2 200 000 into Iran. A total of 108 000 emigrated from the UK in 1985. Her largest number of emigrants in any one year was 360 000 in 1852, mainly from Ireland.

Immigration ■ The country which regularly receives the most legal immigrants is the United States. It has been estimated that between 1820 and 1985 the USA received 52 520 358 *official* immigrants. One in 24 of the US population is, however, an *illegal* immigrant. In 1986, 629 000 aliens were arrested by US patrol on the Mexican border.

The peak year for immigration into the United Kingdom was the 12 months from 1 Jul 1961 to 30 Jun 1962, when about 430 000 Commonwealth citizens arrived. The number of immigrants in the year 1987 was 45 500. The estimated total of 'non-whites' for Great Britain was 2 430 000 or 4·5 per cent of the population, averaged over surveys in 1984–6.

Biggest demonstration ■ A figure of 2·7 million was published from China for the demonstration against the USSR in Shanghai on 3–4 Apr 1969 following the border clashes.

Most patient 'Refusenik' ■ The USSR citizen who waited longest for an exit visa was Benjamin Bogomolny (b. 7 Apr 1946) who first applied in 1966. He arrived in Vienna on 14 Oct 1986. Vladimir Slepak (b. 29 Oct 1927) became the new champion, having waited since June 1970.

Tourism ■ The record influx of tourists into the United Kingdom was 15 600 000 in 1987 and their record spending was £6300 million plus £1500 on British carriers in 1987.

Birth rate *Highest and lowest* ■ The rate for the whole world was 28 per 1000 in 1987. The highest estimated by the UN is 55·1 per 1000 for Kenya for 1980–5. A worldwide survey published in 1985 showed no country with a rising birth rate—the last being Nepal.

Excluding Vatican City, where, the rate is negligible, the lowest recorded rate is 9·3 per 1000 (1985) for San Marino.

The crude birth rate — the number of births per thousand population—for the United Kingdom was 13·6 in 1987 (13·6 for England and Wales, 12·9 for Scotland and 17·7 for Northern Ireland), whilst for the Republic of Ireland it was 16·6 registered live births per thousand population. (All figures for 1987 are provisional.) The annual number of births in England and Wales was highest this century in 1920 at 957 782 (since the first full year of 463 787) and lowest in 1977 at 569 259. After falling each year since 1964 when there were 875 972 births, the number started to rise again in 1978. In 1987 there were 681 511 births (on average 1867 per day or 78 per hour), of which 23·2 per cent were illegitimate.

Death rate ■ The death rate for the whole world was 10 per 1000 in 1987. The estimated death rate in Kampuchea of 40·0 per 1000 from 1975–80 subsided to 19·7 from 1980–5. The estimated figure for Sierra Leone from 1980–5 was 29·7.

The lowest of the latest available recorded rates is 3·5 deaths/1000 in Tonga in 1985.

The crude death rate—the number of deaths per thousand population of all ages—for the United Kingdom was 11·3 in 1987 (11·3 for England and Wales, 12·1 for Scotland and 9·7 for Northern Ireland). The local authority district with the highest SMR (Standard Mortality Ratio, where the national average is 100) was Castle Morpeth, Northumberland where the SMR was 135 in 1986. Wealden, East Sussex had the lowest SMR in 1986 at 75. The provisional 1987 rate for the Republic of Ireland was 8·8 registered deaths per 1000.

Natural increase ■ The rate of natural increase for the whole world is estimated to be 28 − 10 = 18 per 1000 in 1987 compared with a peak 22 per 1000 in 1965. The highest of the latest available recorded rates is 41·1 (55·1 − 14) from Kenya in 1980–5.

The 1986 rate for the United Kingdom was 1·5 (1·5 in England and Wales, 0·5 in Scotland and 7·4 in Northern Ireland). The rate for the first time in the first quarter of 1975 became temporarily one of natural decrease. The figure for the Republic of Ireland was 7·9/1000 in 1986.

The lowest rate of natural increase in any major independent country is in the Federal Republic of Germany with a negative figure of −1·3 per 1000 (10·2 births and 11·5 deaths) for 1986. On the Isle of Man the figure is −3·8 (11·0 births and 14·8 deaths).

Marriage ages ■ The lowest average age for marriage is India, with 20 years (males) and 14 ½ years (females). At the other extreme is Ireland, with 26·8 (males) and 24·7 (females). In the mid 16th century the average age for first marriages by women in England was 26·7 years. In the People's Republic of China the *recommended* age for marriage for men has been 28 and for women 25. In England and Wales the average (modal) age at marriage in 1987 was 27 years (bridegrooms) and 24·7 years (brides).

Divorces ■ The country with most divorces is the United States with a total of 1 157 000 in 1987 — a rate of 4·8 per cent per thousand marriages. The all-time high rate was 49·75 per cent in 1981. In 1986 some 2 per cent of all *existing* marriages in the USA broke up. In the United Kingdom more than one in seven marriages end in divorce before a fifth anniversary. By 1985, 13 per cent of families had one parent.

Sex ratio ■ There were estimated in 1981 to be 1006·7 males in the world for every 1000 females. The country with the largest recorded shortage of males is the USSR, with 1132·1 females to every 1000 males (1985 census). The country with the largest recorded woman shortage is Pakistan, with 906 to every 1000 males in 1981. The figures are, however, probably under-enumerated due to *purdah*. The ratio in the United Kingdom was 1053 females to every 1000 males at mid-1986, and is expected to be 1034/1000 by AD 2000.

Infant mortality ■ The world rate in 1987 was 80 per 1000 live births. Based on deaths before one year of age, the lowest of the latest recorded rates is 4·9 in Japan in 1987.

In Ethiopia the infant mortality rate was unofficially estimated to be nearly 550/1000 live births in 1969. The highest rate recently estimated is 180/1000 in Sierra Leone (1980-85).

The rate of infant mortality — the number of deaths at ages under one year per thousand live births — for the United Kingdom was 9·1 in 1987 (9·2 for England and Wales, 8·5 for Scotland and 8·6 for Northern Ireland). The corresponding rate in 1986 for the Republic of Ireland was 8·7.

Expectation of life at birth ■ World expectation of life is rising from 47·4 years (1950–5) towards 64 ½ years (1995–2000). There is evidence that life expectation in Britain in the 5th century AD was 33 years for males and 27 years for females. In the decade 1890–1900 the expectation of life among the population of India was 23·7 years.

Based on data published by WHO in April 1989, the highest average expectation of life is in Japan, with 82·1 years for women. A figure of 75·61 years for men was published in 1988.

The lowest recorded expectation of life at birth is 36·6 years for males and 37·3 years for females in Afghanistan.

The latest available figures for England and Wales (1983–5) are 71·8 years for males and 77·7 years for females, 70·1 and 76·3 in Scotland, 70·1 and 76·3 in Northern Ireland, (1984–86). For the Republic of Ireland, the figure (1980) was 69 ½ years for males and 75 for females. The British figure for 1901–10 was 48 ½ years (males) and 52·4 years (females).

5 billion figure passed
● 1987

● 2 billion - 1920 s

● 1 billion - early 1800 s

llion

● ½ billion

|1500 |1600 |1700 |1800 |1900

WORST DISASTERS IN THE WORLD

DISASTER	NUMBER KILLED	LOCATION	DATE
Pandemic	75 000 000	Eurasia: The Black Death (bubonic, pneumonic and septicaemic plague)	1347–51
Genocide	c. 35 000 000	Mongol extermination of Chinese peasantry	1311–40
Famine	c. 30 000 000[1]	Northern China	1959–61
Influenza	21 640 000	Worldwide	1918–19
Earthquake[2]	1 100 000	Near East and E. Mediterranean (see p. 60)	c. July 1201
Circular Storm[2]	1 000 000	Ganges Delta Islands, Bangladesh	12–13 Nov 1970
Flood	900 000	Hwang-ho River, China	Oct 1887
Landslides (Triggered off by single earthquake)	180 000	Kansu Province, China	16 Dec 1920
Atomic Bomb	155 200	Hiroshima, Japan (including radiation deaths within a year)	6 Aug 1945
Conventional Bombing[3]	c. 140 000	Tokyo, Japan	10 Mar 1945
Volcanic Eruption	92 000	Tambora Sumbawa, Indonesia	5–7 Apr 1815
Avalanches	c. 18 000[4]	Yungay, Huascarán, Peru	31 May 1970
Marine (Single Ship)	c. 7700	Wilhelm Gustloff (25 892 tonnes) German liner torpedoed off Danzig by USSR submarine S-13 (only 903 survivors)	30 Jan 1945
Dam Burst	c. 5000[5]	Manchhu River Dam, Morvi, Gujaret, India	11 Aug 1979
Panic	c. 4000[6]	Chungking (Zhong qing) China, air raid shelter	c. 8 Jun 1941
Industrial (Chemical)	3350	Union Carbide methylisocyanate plant, Bhopal, India	2–3 Dec 1984
Smog	2850	London fog, England (excess deaths)	5–13 Dec 1952
Tunnelling (Silicosis)	c. 2500	Hawk's Nest hydroelectric tunnel, W. Virginia, USA	1931–35
Explosion	1963[7]	Halifax, Nova Scotia, Canada	6 Dec 1917
Fire[8] (Single Building)	1670	The Theatre, Canton, China	May 1845
Mining[9]	1572	Hinkeiko Colliery, China (coal dust explosion)	26 Apr 1942
Tornado	c. 1300	Shaturia, Bangladesh	26 Apr 1989
Riot	c. 1200	New York anti-conscription riots	13–16 Jul 1863
Road[10]	c. 1100	Petrol tanker explosion inside Salang Tunnel, Afghanistan	2 or 3 Nov 1982
Mass Suicide[11]	913	People's Temple cult by cyanide, Jonestown, Guyana	18 Nov 1978
Crocodiles	c. 900	Japanese soldiers, Ramree I., Burma (disputed)	19–20 Feb 1945
Railway	>800	Bagmati River, Bihar, India	6 Jun 1981
Fireworks	>800	Dauphin's wedding, Seine, Paris	16 May 1770
Aircraft (Civil)[12]	583	KLM-Pan Am Boeing 747 ground crash, Tenerife	27 Mar 1977
Man-eating Animal	436	Champawat district, India, tigress shot by Col. Jim Corbet (d. 1955)	1907
Terrorism	329	Bomb aboard Air-India Boeing 747, crashed into Atlantic south-west of Ireland. Sikh extremists suspected	23 Jun 1985
Bacteriological & Chemical Warfare	c. 300	Novosibirsk B & CW plant, USSR	Apr–May 1979
Hail	246	Moredabad, Uttar Pradesh, India	20 Apr 1888
Offshore Oil Platform	167	Piper Alpha oil production platform, North Sea	6 Jul 1988
Submarine	130	Le Surcouf rammed by US merchantman Thomas Lykes in Caribbean	18 Feb 1942
Helicopter	54	Israel, military 'Sea Stallion', West Bank	10 May 1977
Ski Lift (Cable Car)	42	Cavalese resort, northern Italy	9 Mar 1976
Mountaineering	40[13]	USSR expedition on Mount Everest	Dec 1952
Nuclear Reactor	31[14]	Chernobyl No. 4, Ukraine, USSR	26 Apr 1986
Elevator (Lift)	23	Vaal Reefs gold mine lift fell 1·93 km 1·2 miles	27 Mar 1980
Lightning	21	Hut in Chinamasa Krael nr Mutari, Zimbabwe (single bolt)	23 Dec 1975
Yacht Racing	19	28th Fastnet Race—23 boats sank or abandoned in Force 11 gale	13–15 Aug 1979
Space Exploration	7	US Challenger 51L Shuttle, Cape Canaveral, Florida, USA	28 Jan 1986
Nuclear Waste Accident	high but undisclosed[15]	Venting of plutonium extraction wastes, Kyshtym, USSR	c. Dec 1957

FOOTNOTES

[1] It has been estimated that more than 5 million died in the post-World War I famine of 1920–1 in the USSR. The USSR government in July 1923 informed Mr (later President) Herbert Hoover that the ARA (American Relief Administration) had since August 1921 saved 20 million lives from famine and famine-related diseases.

[2] This figure published in 1972 for the Bangladeshi disaster was from Dr Afzal, Principal Scientific Officer of the Atomic Energy Authority Centre, Dacca. One report asserted that less than half of the population of the 4 islands of Bhola, Charjabbar, Hatia and Ramagati (1961 Census 1·4 million) survived. The most damaging hurricane recorded was Hurricane Gloria from 26-28 Sep 1985 with estimated insurance losses of £3500 million.

[3] The number of civilians killed by the bombing of Germany has been put variously at 593 000 and 'over 635 000' including some 35 000 deaths in the raids on Dresden, Germany from 13–15 Feb 1945. Total Japanese fatalities were 600 000 (conventional) and 220 000 (nuclear).

[4] A total of 18 000 Austrian and Italian troops was reported to have been lost in the Dolomite valleys of northern Italy on 13 Dec 1916 in more than 100 snow avalanches. Some of the avalanches were triggered by gun-fire.

[5] The dynamiting of a Yangtze Kiang dam at Huayuan Kow by the KMT during the Sino-Japanese war in 1938 is reputed to have resulted in 900 000 deaths.

[6] It was estimated that some 5000 people were trampled to death in the stampede for free beer at the coronation celebration of Czar Nicholas II in Moscow in May 1896.

[7] Some sources maintain that the final death toll was over 3000 on 6–7 Dec. Published estimates of the 11 000 killed at the BASF chemical plant explosion at Oppau, West Germany on 21 Sep 1921 were exaggerated. The best estimate is 561 killed.

[8] >200 000 killed in the sack of Moscow, as a result of fires started by the invading Tatars in May 1571. Worst ever hotel fire 162 killed, Hotel Daeyungak, Seoul, South Korea 25 Dec 1971. Worst circus fire 168 killed Hartford, Conn., USA 6 Jul 1944.

[9] The worst gold mining disaster in South Africa was when 182 were killed in Kinross gold mine on 16 Sep 1986.

[10] Some estimates ran as high as 2700 victims from carbon monoxide asphyxiation after Soviet military sealed both ends of the 2·7 km 1·7 mile long tunnel. The worst ever years for road deaths in the USA and the UK have been respectively 1969 (56 400) and 1941 (9169). The global aggregate death toll was put at 25 million by September 1975. The world's highest death rate is 29 per 100 000 in 1978 in Luxembourg and Portugal. The greatest pile-up on British roads was on the M6 near Lymm Interchange, near Thelwall, Cheshire, involving 200 vehicles on 13 Sep 1971 with 11 dead and 60 injured.

[11] 22 000 Japanese civilians jumped off a cliff to their deaths in June 1943 during the US Marines assault of the island of Tarawa (now in Kiribati). An unknown proportion may have been under duress of the defending troops.

[12] The crash of JAL's Boeing 747, flight 123, near Tokyo on 12 Aug 1985, in which 520 passengers and crew perished, was the worst single plane crash in aviation history.

[13] According to Polish sources, not confirmed by the USSR. Also 23 died on Mount Fuji, Japan in blizzard and avalanche on 20 Mar 1972.

[14] Explosion at 0123 hrs Soviet European time 26 Apr 1986. The estimates for the eventual death toll vary between 200 and 600 by AD 2026 (per Nikolay Romanenko, Ukrainian Health Minister, on 4 Apr 1987) and 75 000 (per Dr Robert Gale, US bone transplant specialist). Izvestia published an estimate of consequential loss at 8000 million roubles to date on 4 Mar 1988.

[15] More than 30 small communities in a 1200 km² 460 mile² area eliminated from USSR maps since 1958. Possibly an ammonium nitrate-hexone explosion.

Housing ■ For comparison, dwelling units are defined as a structurally separated room or rooms occupied by private households of one or more people and having separate access or a common passageway to the street.

The first country to surpass 100 000 000 housing units was India in 1972. In 1981 the figure was 142 954 921.

Great Britain had a stock of 22 272 000 dwellings as at 1 Dec 1987. The record number of permanent houses built in a year has been 413 715 in 1968. By March 1988 66·5 per cent of dwellings in England were owner-occupied.

Physicians ■ The country with the most physicians is the USSR, with 831 300, or one to every 307 persons. China had an estimated 1·4 million para-medical personnel, known as 'barefoot doctors', by 1981. There were 128 983 doctors on the General Medical Council's Principal List, and therefore entitled to practise in the United Kingdom as at 1 Jan 1988.

Dentists ■ The country with the most dentists is the United States, where 145 800 were registered members of the American Dental Association in 1987. The number of dentists registered in the United Kingdom as at 1 Jan 1988 was 25 286.

Psychiatrists ■ The country with the most psychiatrists is the United States. The registered membership of the American Psychiatric Association (inst. 1894) was 32 000 in 1987. The membership of the American Psychological Association (inst. 1892) was 60 000 in 1987. The No. 1 city in the 1987 couch rankings is Boston, Massachusetts with 1 shrink for 328 heads.

Largest hospital World ■ The largest mental hospital in the world is the Pilgrim State Hospital, West Brentwood, Long Island, NY, USA, with 3618 beds. It formerly contained 14 200 beds. The largest psychiatric institute is at the University of California, Los Angeles, USA.

The busiest maternity hospital in the world has been the Mama Yemo Hospital, Kinshasa, Zaïre with 41 930 deliveries in 1976. The record 'birthquake' occurred on a day in May 1976 with 175 babies born. The hospital had 599 beds.

Great Britain ■ The largest hospitals of any kind in Great Britain are Hartwood Hospital near Shotts, Lanarkshire with 1600 staffed beds for mentally ill patients.

The largest acute hospital in Great Britain is the St James's University Hospital (which is also a teaching hospital), Leeds, West Yorks, with 1432 staffed beds.

The largest maternity hospital in Great Britain is the Simpson Memorial Maternity Pavilion, Edinburgh with 218 staffed beds.

The largest children's hospital in Great Britain is Queen Mary's Hospital for Children, at Carshalton, Sutton, Surrey, with 340 staffed beds.

TOWNS AND CITIES

Oldest ■ The oldest known walled town in the world is Arihā (Jericho). The Radio-carbon dating on specimens from the lowest levels reached by archaeologists indicates habitation there by perhaps 3000 people as early as 7800 BC. The settlement of Dolní Věstonice, Czechoslovakia, has been dated to the Gravettian culture c. 27 000 BC. The oldest capital city in the world is Dimashq (Damascus), Syria. It has been continuously inhabited since c. 2500 BC.

The oldest town in Great Britain is often cited as Colchester, the old British Camulodunum, headquarters of Belgic chiefs in the 1st century BC. However, the name of the tin trading post Salakee, St Mary's, Isles of Scilly is derived from pre-Celtic roots and hence ante 550 BC. The oldest borough in Britain is reputed to be Barnstaple, Devon whose charter was granted by King Athelstan (927–939) in AD 930.

The only one of the United Kingdom's 58 cities with a Saxon charter is Ripon, North Yorks which was a bishopric in 672 and had a charter dated 886.

Most populous ■ The most populous 'urban agglomeration' in the world is the 'Keihin Metropolitan Area' (Tokyo-Yokohama Metropolitan Area) of 2800 km² *1081 miles²* containing an estimated 29 272 000 people in 1985. The municipal population of Greater Tokyo in 1985 was 11 903 900. The population of the metropolitan area of Greater Mexico City in 1985 was published as 17 321 800 with the city proper at 10 499 000 in 1984.

The most populous conurbation in Britain is London, with a population of 6 775 500 (mid-1986). The residential population of the City of London (274 ha *677·3 acres* plus 24·9 ha *61·7 acres* foreshore) is 5750 (1987 estimate) compared with 128 000 in 1801. The daytime figure is 330 000. The peak figure for London was 8 615 050 in 1939.

Largest in area ■ The world's largest town, in area, is Mount Isa, Queensland, Australia. The area administered by the City Council is 40 978 km² *15 822 miles²*. The largest conurbation in the United Kingdom is Greater London with an area of 1579·5 km² *609·8 miles²*.

Towns, villages and hamlets *Great Britain* ■ The smallest place with a town council is Llanwrtyd Wells, Powys (pop. 528 at 1981 census). The smallest town with a Royal Charter (granted in 1290) is Caerwys, Clwyd, Wales with a civil parish population of 1040. The strongest claimant to be Britain's oldest village is Thatcham, Berks. The earliest Mesolithic settlement there has been dated to 7720 BC. Kidlington, Oxon (population 17 200) claimed to be 'England's largest village' until 1987 when it ceased to be run by a parish council.

Highest ■ The highest capital in the world, before the domination of Tibet by China, was Lhasa, at an elevation of 3684 m *12 087 ft* above sea level. La Paz, administrative and *de facto* capital of Bolivia, stands at an altitude of 3631 m *11 916 ft* above sea level. El Alto airport is at 4080 m *13 385 ft*. The city was founded in 1548 by Capt. Alonso de Mendoza on the site of an Indian village named Chuquiapu. It was originally called Ciudad de Nuestra Señora de La Paz (City of Our Lady of Peace), but in 1825 was renamed La Paz de Ayacucho, its present official name. Sucre, the legal capital of Bolivia, stands at 2834 m *9301 ft* above sea level. The new town of Wenchuan, founded in 1955 on the Chinghai–Tibet road, north of the Tangla range, is the highest in the world at 5100 m *16 732 ft* above sea level.

The highest village in Britain is Flash, north Staffs at 462·6 m *1518 ft* above sea level. The highest in Scotland is Wanlockhead, in Dumfries and Galloway, at 420 m *1380 ft* above sea level.

Lowest ■ The settlement of Ein Bokek, which has a synagogue, on the shores of the Dead Sea is the lowest in the world at 393·5 m *1291 ft* below sea level.

Northernmost ■ The world's most northerly town with a population of more than 10 000 is the Arctic port of Dikson, USSR in 73° 32′ N, so named in 1875 after a Swedish brewer. The northernmost village is Ny Ålesund (78° 55′ N), a coalmining settlement on King's Bay, Vest Spitsbergen, in the Norwegian territory of Svalbard, inhabited only during the winter season. The northernmost capital is Reykjavik, Iceland in 64° 08′ N. Its population was estimated to be 91 394 in 1986.

Southernmost ■ The world's southernmost village is Puerto Williams (population about 350) on the north coast of Isla Navarino, in Tierra del Fuego, Chile, 1090 km *680 miles* north of Antarctica. Wellington, North Island, New Zealand, with a 1987 population of 325 700, is the southernmost capital city on 41° 17′ S. The world's southernmost administrative centre is Port Stanley, with a population of 1200, (51° 43′ S) in the Falkland Islands.

Most remote from the sea ■ The largest town most remote from the sea is Wu-lu-mu-chi (formerly Ürümqi) in Xinjiang (formerly Tihwa, Sinkiang), capital of the Uighur autonomous region of China, at a distance of about 2250 km *1400 miles* from the nearest coastline. Its population was estimated to be 947 000 in 1987.

Royalty and Heads of State

Oldest ruling house ■ The Emperor of Japan, Akihito (b. 23 Dec 1933), is the 125th in line from the first Emperor, Jimmu Tenno or Zinmu, whose reign was traditionally from 660 to 581 BC, but more probably from *c.* 40 BC to *c.* 10 BC.

Her Majesty Queen Elizabeth II (b. 21 Apr 1926)

WORST DISASTERS IN THE BRITISH ISLES

DISASTER	NUMBER KILLED	LOCATION	DATE
Famine	1 500 000 [1]	Ireland (famine and typhus)	1846–51
Pandemic (The Black Death)	800 000		1347–50
Influenza	225 000		Sep–Nov 1918
Circular Storm	*c.* 8000	'The Channel Storm'	26 Nov 1703
Smog	2850	London fog	5–13 Dec 1952
Flood	*c.* 2000 [2]	Severn Estuary	20 Jan 1606
Bombing	1436	London	10–11 May 1941
Marine (Single Ship)	*c.* 800 [3]	HMS *Royal George* off Spithead	29 Aug 1782
Riot	565 (min)	London anti-Catholic Gordon riots	2–13 Jun 1780
Mining	439	Universal Colliery, Senghenydd, Mid Glamorgan	14 Oct 1913
Terrorism (Aircraft)	270 [4]	Bomb aboard Pan Am Boeing 747, crashed over Lockerbie, Dumfries & Galloway	21 Dec 1988
Dam Burst	250	Bradfield Reservoir, Dale Dyke, near Sheffield, South Yorks (embankment burst)	12 Mar 1864
Railway	227 [5]	Triple collision, Quintins Hill, Dumfries & Galloway	22 May 1915
Fire (Single building)	188 [6]	Theatre Royal, Exeter	5 Sep 1887
Panic (After outbreak of fire)	183	Victoria Hall, Sunderland, Tyne and Wear	16 Jun 1883
Offshore Oil Platform	167	Piper Alpha oil production platform, North Sea	6 Jul 1988
Landslide	144	Pantglas coal tip No. 7, Aberfan, Mid Glamorgan	21 Oct 1966
Explosion	134 [7]	Chilwell, Notts (explosives factory)	1 Jul 1918
Submarine	99	HMS *Thetis*, during trials, Liverpool Bay	1 Jun 1939
Tornado	75	Tay Bridge collapsed under impact of 2 tornadic vortices	28 Dec 1879
Helicopter	45	Chinook, off Sumburgh, Shetland Islands	6 Nov 1986
Nuclear Reactor	39	cancer deaths to 1977 Windscale (now Sellafield), Cumbria	10 Oct 1957
Road	33	Coach crash, River Dibb, nr Grassington, North Yorks	27 May 1975
Lightning	31	(Annual total) Worst year on record (annual av. 12)	1914
Yacht Racing	19	28th Fastnet Race — 23 boats sank or abandoned in Force 11 gale. Of 316 starters only 128 finished	13–15 Aug 1979
Avalanches	8	Lewes, East Sussex	27 Dec 1836
Mountaineering	6	On Cairngorm, near Braemar (1245 m)	21 Nov 1971
Earthquake	2	London earthquake, Christ's Hospital (Newgate)	6 Apr 1580

FOOTNOTES

[1] *Based on the net rate of natural increase between 1841 and 1851, a supportable case for a loss of population of 3 million can be made out if rates of under-enumeration of 25 per cent (1841) and 10 per cent (1851) are accepted. Potato rot (Phytophthora infestans) was first reported on 13 Sep 1845.*

[2] *Death tolls of 100 000 were reputed in England and Holland in the floods of 1099, 1421 and 1446.*

[3] *c. 4000 were lost on HM Troopship Lancastria, 16 503 tonnes, off St Nazaire on 17 Jun 1940. The Princess Alice collision in the Thames with the Bywell Castle off Woolwich on 3 Sep 1878 killed 786.*

[4] *The worst crash by a UK operated aircraft was that of a Dan-Air Boeing 727 from Manchester which crashed into a mountain on the Canary Islands on 25 Apr 1980 killing 146 people. There were no survivors.*

[5] *The 194·7 m 213 yd long troop train was telescoped to 61·2 m 67 yd. Signalmen Meakin and Tinsley were sentenced for manslaughter. Britain's worst underground train disaster was the Moorgate Tube disaster of 28 Feb 1975 when 43 persons were killed.*

[6] *In July 1212, 3000 were killed in the crush, burned or drowned when London Bridge caught fire at both ends. The death toll in the Great Fire of London of 1666 was only 8. History's first 'fire storm' occurred in the Quebec Yard, Surrey Docks, Southwark, London during the 300-pump fire in the Blitz on 7–8 Sep 1940. Dockland casualties were 306 killed. Britain's most destructive fire was that leading to a £165-million loss at the Army Ordnance depot, Donnington, Salop in June 1982.*

[7] *HM armed cruiser Natal blew up off Invergordon killing 428 on 30 Dec 1915.*

WORLD'S MOST POPULOUS URBAN SETTLEMENTS

Population	Name	Country	Date
>100	**Dolní Věstonice**	Czechoslovakia	*c.* 27000 BC
c. 150	**Chemi Shanidar**	Iraq	8900 BC
27 000	**Jericho (Arīhā)**	Occupied Jordan	7800 BC
c. 5000	**Çatal Huyuk, Anatolia**	Turkey	*c.* 6800 BC
>5000	**Hierakonopolis (Nekhen)**	Egypt	*c.* 3200 BC
50 000	**Uruk (Erech) (now Warka) from 3800 BC**	Iraq	3000 BC
250 000	**Greater Ur (now Tell Muqayyar)**	Iraq	2200 BC
350 000	**Babylon (now al-Hillah)**	Iraq	600 BC
500 000	**Pataliputra (Patna) Bihār**	India	400–185 BC
600 000	**Seleukia (near Baghdad)**	Iraq	300 BC–165 AD
1 100 000	**Rome (founded c. 510 BC)**	Italy	133 BC
1 500 000	**Angkor**	Cambodia	900 BC
1·0–1·5 million	**Hangchow (now Hangzhou)**	China	1279
707 000	**Peking (Cambaluc) (now Beijing)**	China	1578
1 117 290	**London**	United Kingdom	1801
8 615 050	**London (peak)**	United Kingdom	1939
11 903 900	**Tokyo**	Japan	1985

Note: The UN projection for AD 2000 for Greater Mexico City is 31 616 000.

Longest serving leader ● Marshal Kim Il Sung (*né* Kim Sung Chu) (b. 15 Apr 1912) has been political leader (Head of Government or Head of State) of the Democratic People's Republic of Korea (North Korea) since 25 Aug 1948. (Photo: Gamma)

BRITISH MONARCHY RECORDS

LONGEST REIGN OR TENURE

Kings
59 years 96 days[1] George III 1760–1820

Queens Regnant
63 years 216 days Victoria 1837–1901

Queens Consort
57 years 70 days Charlotte 1761–1818 (Consort of George III)

SHORTEST REIGN OR TENURE

Kings
77 days[2] Edward V 1483

Queens Regnant
13 days[3] Jane, 6–19 Jul 1553

Queens Consort
154 days Yoleta (1285–6) (Second Consort of Alexander III)

LONGEST LIVED

Kings
81 years 239 days[4] George III (b. 1738–d. 1820)

Queens Regnant
81 years 243 days Victoria (b. 1819–d. 1901)

Queens Consort
87 years Lady Elizabeth Bowes Lyon, Queen Elizabeth, the Queen Mother: (b. 4 Aug 1900)

MOST CHILDREN (LEGITIMATE)[5]

Kings
18 Edward I 1272–1307

Queens Regnant
9[6] Victoria (b. 1819–d. 1901)

Queens Consort
15 Eleanor (c. 1244–90) and Charlotte (b. 1744–d. 1818)

OLDEST TO START REIGN OR CONSORTSHIP

Kings
64 years 10 months William IV 1830–7

Queens Regnant
37 years 5 months Mary I 1553–8

Queens Consort
56 years 53 days Alexandra (b. 1844–d. 1925) (Consort of Edward VII)

YOUNGEST TO START REIGN OR CONSORTSHIP

Kings
269 days Henry VI in 1422

Queens Regnant
6 or 7 days Mary, Queen of Scots in 1542

Queens Consort
6 years 11 months Isabella (Second Consort of Richard II in 1396)

MOST MARRIED

Kings
6 times Henry VIII 1509–47

Queens Regnant
3 times Mary, Queen of Scots 1542–67 (Executed 1587)

Queens Consort
4 times Catherine Parr (b. c. 1512–d. 1548) (Sixth Consort of Henry VIII)

MOST ALIVE SIMULTANEOUSLY

Between 30 Oct 1683 (birth of George Augustus of Hanover, later George II) and 6 Feb 1685 (death of Charles II) there were eight heads of state living simultaneously (Charles II, James II, William and Mary, Anne, George I and II) and also Richard Cromwell (d. 1712), the 2nd Lord Protector and *de facto* head of state in 1658–59.

Notes (Dates are of reigns or tenures unless otherwise indicated)
[1] James Francis Edward, the Old Pretender, known to his supporters as James III, styled his reign from 16 Sep 1701 until his death 1 Jan 1766 (i.e. 64 years 109 days).
[2] There is the probability that in pre-Conquest times Sweyn 'Forkbeard', the Danish King of England, reigned for only 40 days in 1013–14.
[3] She accepted the allegiance of the Lords of the Council (9 Jul) and was proclaimed on 10 Jul so is often referred to as the '9 (or 10) day Queen'.
[4] Richard Cromwell (b. 4 Oct 1626), the 2nd Lord Protector from 3 Sep 1658 until his abdication on 24 May 1659, lived under the alias John Clarke until 12 Jul 1712 aged 85 years 9 months and was thus the longest lived head of state.
[5] Henry I (b. 1068–d. 1135) in addition to one (possibly two) legitimate sons and a daughter had at least 20 bastard children (9 sons, 11 daughters), and possibly 22, by six mistresses.
[6] Queen Anne (b. 1665–d. 1714) had 17 pregnancies, which produced only five live births.

Oldest ruling house ● Forty-six of the world's 170 sovereign states are not republics. Seen here is the Emperor of Japan, Akihito (b. 23 Dec 1933), who is the 125th in line from the first Emperor, Jimmu Tenno or Zinmu, whose reign was traditionally from 660 to 581 BC, but was more probably from c. 40 BC to c. 10 BC. (Photo: Gamma/Kogure)

represents dynasties historically traceable back at least to the 4th century AD in the case of Tegid, great grandfather of Cunedda, founder of the House of Gwynedd in Wales; she is 54th in the line. If the historicity of some early Scoto-Irish and Pictish kings were acceptable, the lineage could be extended to about 70 generations.

Reigns *Longest all-time* ■ The longest recorded reign of any monarch is that of Phiops II or Neferkare, a Sixth Dynasty Pharaoh of ancient Egypt. His reign began c. 2281 BC, when he was aged 6, and is believed to have lasted c. 94 years. Minhti, King of Arakan (Burma), is reputed to have reigned for 95 years between 1279 and 1374. Musoma Kanijo, chief of the Nzega district of western Tanganyika (now part of Tanzania), reputedly reigned for more than 98 years from 1864, when aged 8, until his death on 2 Feb 1963. The longest reign of any European monarch was that of Afonso I Henrigues of Portugal who ascended the throne on 30 Apr 1112 and died on 6 Dec 1185 after a reign of 73 years 220 days, first as a Count and then as King.

Roman occupation ■ During the 369-year-long Roman occupation of England, Wales and parts of southern Scotland there were 40 sole and 27 co-emperors of Rome. Of these the longest reigning was Constantinus I (The Great) from 31 Mar 307 to 22 May 337 — 30 years 2 months.

Shortest ■ The Crown Prince Luis Filipe of Portugal was mortally wounded at the same time that his father was killed by a bullet which severed his carotid artery, in the streets of Lisbon on 1 Feb 1908. He was thus technically King of Portugal (Dom Luis III) for about 20 minutes.

Highest post-nominal numbers ■ The highest post-nominal number ever used to designate a

member of a royal house was 75, briefly enjoyed by Count Heinrich LXXV Reuss (1800–1). All male members of this branch of the German family are called Heinrich and are successively numbered from I upwards *each* century.

British regnal numbers date from the Norman Conquest. The highest is 8, used by Henry VIII (1509–1547) and by Edward VIII (1936) who died as HRH the Duke of Windsor on 28 May 1972. Jacobites liked to style Henry Benedict, Cardinal York (b. 1725), the grandson of James II, as Henry IX in respect of his 'reign' from 1788 to 1807 when he died as last survivor in the male line of the House of Stuart.

Longest-lived 'royals' ■ The longest life among the blood royal of Europe has been that of the Princess Pauline Marie Madeleine of Croy, who uniquely celebrated her 100th birthday in her birthplace of Le Roeulx, Belgium on 11 Jan 1987. The greatest age among European royal consorts is the 101 years 268 days of HSH Princess Leonilla Bariatinsky (b. Moscow, 9 Jul 1816), who married HSH Prince Louis of Sayn-Wittgenstein-Sayn and died in Ouchy, Switzerland on 1 Feb 1918. The longest-lived Queen on record was Empress Zita of Austria and Hungary, whose husband reigned as Emperor Charles I of Austria and King Charles IV of Hungary from 1916–18; she died on 14 Mar 1989 aged 96 years 309 days.

HRH Princess Alice Mary VA, GCVO, GBE, Countess of Athlone (b. 25 Feb 1883) became the longest

Youngest queen ● The country which currently has the youngest sovereign queen is Denmark, with Queen Margrethe II (b. 16 Apr 1940). (Photo: Keystone)

First female President ● Isabel Perón of Argentina became the world's first female President when she succeeded her husband Juan Perón on his death on 1 Jul 1974. She held office until deposed in a military coup on 24 Mar 1976. (Photo: Gamma)

ever lived British 'royal' on 15 Jul 1977 and died aged 97 years 313 days on 3 Jan 1981. She fulfilled 20 000 engagements, including the funerals of five British monarchs.

Youngest king and queen ■ Forty-six of the world's 170 sovereign states are not republics. They are headed by 1 emperor, 12 kings, 3 queens, 4 princely rulers, 3 sultans, 3 amirs, the Pope, a sheik, a ruler and one elected monarch. Queen Elizabeth II is head of state of 16 other Commonwealth countries. That with the youngest king is Swaziland where King Mswati III was crowned on 25 Apr 1986 aged 18 years 6 days. He was born Makhosetive, the 67th son of King Subhusa II. That with the youngest queen is Denmark with Queen Margrethe II (b. 16 Apr 1940).

Heaviest monarch ■ The world's heaviest monarch is the 1·9 m *6 ft 3 in* tall King Taufa'ahau of Tonga who in September 1976 was weighed on the only adequate scales in the country at the airport, recording 209·5 kg *(33 st/462 lb)*. By 1985 he was reported to have slimmed down to 139·7 kg *(22 st/308 lb)*. His embassy car in London has the number plate '1 TON'.

Most prolific ■ The most prolific monogamous 'royals' have been Prince Hartmann of Liechtenstein (1613–86) who had 24 children, of whom 21 were liveborn, by Countess Elisabeth zu Salm-Reifferscheidt (1623–88). HRH Duke Roberto I of Parma (1848–1907) also had 24 children but by two wives. One of his daughters, HIM Empress Zita of Austria (1892–1989), was exiled on 23 Mar 1919 but visited Vienna, her titles intact, on 17 Nov 1982 reminding republicans that her father succeeded to the throne of Parma in 1854.

Head of state *Oldest and youngest* ■ The oldest head of state in the world is Olaf V, King of Norway (b. 2 Jul 1903). The youngest is King Mswati III of Swaziland (b. 19 Apr 1968).

First female ■ Isabel Perón (b. 1931) of Argentina became the world's first female president when she succeeded her husband on his death on 1 Jul 1974. She held office until she was deposed in a bloodless coup on 24 Mar 1976. President Vigdis Finnbogadottir (b. 1930) of Iceland became the world's first democratically-elected female head of state on 30 Jun 1980.

Legislatures

PARLIAMENTS — WORLD

Earliest and oldest ■ The earliest known legislative assembly or *ukkim* was a bicameral one in Erech, Iraq *c.* 2800 BC. The oldest legislative body is the *Althing* of Iceland founded in AD 930. This body, which originally comprised 39 local chieftains at Thingvellir, was abolished in 1800, but restored by Denmark to a consultative status in 1843 and a legislative status in 1874. The legislative assembly with the oldest continuous history is the Court of Tynwald in the Isle of Man, which celebrated its millennium in 1979.

Largest ■ The largest legislative assembly in the world is the National People's Congress of the People's Republic of China. The sixth congress, when convened in June 1983, had 2978 members. Its standing committee has 197 members.

Smallest quorum ■ The House of Lords has the smallest quorum, expressed as a percentage of eligible voters, of any legislative body in the world, namely less than one-third of 1 per cent. The number of peers in 1988 was 1244. To transact business there must be three peers present, including the Lord Chancellor or his deputy. The House of Commons' quorum of 40 MPs, including the Speaker or his deputy, is 20 times as exacting.

Highest-paid legislators ■ The most highly paid of all the world's legislators are members of the US Congress whose basic annual salary is $89 500 with limited honoraria of $20 940. In addition, up to

$1 021 167 per annum is allowed for office help, with a salary limit of $50 000 for any one staff member (limited to 16 in number). Senators are allowed up to $143 000 per annum for an official office expense account from which official travel, telegram, long-distance telephone, air mail, postage, stationery, subscriptions to newspapers and office expenses in home state are paid. They also command very low rates for filming, speech and radio transcriptions and, in the case of women senators, beauty treatment. When abroad they have access to 'counterpart funds'. The President of the USA has a salary of $200 000 taxable plus $170 000 non-taxable for travel or entertainment, and a lifetime pension of $69 630 per annum.

Longest membership ■ The longest span as a legislator was 83 years by József Madarász (1814–1915). He first attended the Hungarian Parliament in 1832–6 as *oblegatus absentium* (*i.e.* on behalf of an absent deputy). He was a full member in 1848–50 and from 1861 until his death on 31 Jan 1915.

Longest UN speech ■ The longest speech made in the United Nations has been one of 4 hr 29 min on 26 Sep 1960 by President Dr Fidel Castro Ruz (b. 13 Aug 1927) of Cuba.

Filibusters ■ The longest continuous speech in the history of the United States Senate was that of Senator Wayne Morse (1900–74) of Oregon on 24–25 Apr 1953, when he spoke on the Tidelands Oil Bill for 22 hr 26 min without resuming his seat. Interrupted only briefly by the swearing-in of a new senator, Senator Strom Thurmond (b. 1902) (South Carolina, Democrat) spoke against the Civil Rights Bill for 24 hr 19 min on 28–29 Aug 1957. The US national duration record is 43 hr by Texas State Senator Bill Meier against non-disclosure of industrial accidents in May 1977.

Oldest treaty ■ The Anglo-Portuguese Treaty of Alliance was signed in London over 614 years ago on 16 Jun 1373. The text was confirmed 'with my usual flourish' by John de Banketre, Clerk.

Constitutions ■ The world's oldest constitution is that of the United States of America ratified by the necessary Ninth State (New Hampshire) on 21 Jun 1788 and declared to be in effect on 4 Mar 1789. The only countries without one-document constitutions are Israel, Libya, New Zealand, Oman and the United Kingdom.

Women's suffrage ■ The earliest legislature with female voters was the Territory of Wyoming, USA in 1869, followed by the Isle of Man in 1881. The earliest country to have universal suffrage was New Zealand in 1893. The vote of Mrs Lily Maxwell in Manchester on 26 Nov 1867 was declared illegal on 9 Nov 1868.

PARLIAMENTS — UNITED KINGDOM

Earliest ■ The earliest known use of the term 'parliament' is in an official royal document, in the meaning of a summons to the King's (Henry III's) Council, dating from 19 Dec 1241.

The Houses of Parliament of the United Kingdom in the Palace of Westminster, London had 1843 members (House of Lords 1193 of whom *c.* 610 are active, House of Commons 650) in late 1988.

Longest ■ The longest English Parliament was the 'Pensioners' Parliament of Charles II, which lasted from 8 May 1661 to 24 Jan 1679, a period of 17 years 8 months and 16 days. The longest United Kingdom Parliament was that of George V, Edward VIII and George VI, lasting from 26 Nov 1935 to 15 Jun 1945, a span of 9 years 6 months and 20 days.

Shortest ■ The parliament of Edward I, summoned to Westminster for 30 May 1306, lasted only 1 day. That of Charles II at Oxford lasted 7 days from 21–28 Mar 1681. The shortest United Kingdom Parliament was that of George III, lasting from 15 Dec 1806 to 29 Apr 1807, a period of only 4 months and 14 days.

Longest sittings ■ The longest sitting in the House of Commons was one of 41½ hr from 4 p.m. on 31 Jan 1881 to 9.30 a.m. on 2 Feb 1881, on the question

of better Protection of Person and Property in Ireland. The longest sitting of the Lords has been 19 hr 16 min from 2.30 p.m. on 29 Feb to 9.46 a.m. on 1 Mar 1968 on the Commonwealth Immigrants Bill (committee stage). The longest sitting of a standing committee occurred from 10.30 a.m. on 11 May to 12.08 p.m. on 13 May 1948 when Standing Committee D considered the Gas Bill through two nights for 49 hr 38 min.

Longest speeches ■ The longest recorded continuous speech in the Chamber of the House of Commons was that of Henry Peter Brougham (1778–1868) on 7 Feb 1828, when he spoke for 6 hr on Law Reform. He ended at 10.40 p.m. and the report of this speech occupied 12 columns of the next day's *Times*. Brougham, created the 1st Lord Brougham and Vaux on 22 Nov 1830, then set the House of Lords record, also with 6 hours, on 7 Oct 1831, when speaking on the second reading of the Reform Bill, 'fortified by 3 tumblers of spiced wine'.

The longest back-bench speech under present, much stricter standing orders has been one of 4 hr 23 min by Ivan John Lawrence QC, MP (b. 24 Dec 1936), Conservative Member for Burton, opposing the Water (Fluoridation) Bill on 6 Mar 1985. John Golding MP (b. 9 Mar 1931) (then Labour, Newcastle-under-Lyme) spoke for 11 hr 15 min in committee on small amendments to the British Telecommunications Bill on 8–9 Feb 1983.

The longest speech in Stormont, Northern Ireland was one of 9 hr 26 min by Thomas Gibson Henderson MP (1887–1970) on the Appropriations Bill from 6.32 p.m. on 26 to 3.58 a.m. on 27 May 1936.

Greatest parliamentary petition ■ The greatest petition has been supposed to be the Great Chartist Petition of 1848 but of the 5 706 000 'signatures' only 1 975 496 were valid. The largest of all time was for the abolition of Entertainment Duty with 3 107 080 signatures, presented on 5 Jun 1951. Since 1974, the signatures have not been counted at all.

Most and least time-consuming legislation ■ The most profligate use of parliamentary time was on the Government of Ireland Bill of 1893–4, which required 82 days in the House of Commons of which 46 days were in committee. The record for a standing committee is 59 sittings for the Police and Criminal Evidence Bill from 17 Nov 1983 to 29 Mar 1984.

The Abdication Bill (of King Edward VIII) passed all its stages in the Commons (2 hr) and the Lords (8 min) on 11–12 Dec 1936 and received the Royal Assent at 1.52 a.m. on the latter date. Several bills have gone through the Commons without debate — most notably the Protection of Birds (Amendment) Bill 1976, which took just 67 sec in July 1976.

Private Members' Bills ■ Balloting by private members for parliamentary time was in being at least as early as 1844. The highest recorded number of public Bills introduced by private members was 226 in 1908 but the highest number to receive Royal Assent was 27 in the Commons and 7 in the Lords in 1963–4. The worst session was 1973–4 with nil from 42 presented in the Commons and nil from 10 in the Lords.

Divisions ■ The record number of divisions in the House of Commons is 64 on 23–24 Mar 1971 including 57 in succession between midnight and noon. The largest division was one of 350–310 on the vote of no confidence on 11 Aug 1892.

ELECTIONS — WORLD

Largest ■ The largest elections in the world were those beginning on 24 Dec 1984 for the Indian *Lok Sabha* (Lower House) which has 542 elective seats. The government of Rajiv Gandhi was returned in polls in which 379 000 000 electors were eligible to vote for 5301 candidates at 480 000 polling stations manned by 2½ million staff. In Maduranthkam (electorate 120 021) there were 90 candidates.

Closest ■ The ultimate in close general elections occurred in Zanzibar (now part of Tanzania) on 18 Jan 1961, when the Afro-Shirazi Party won by a single seat, after the seat of Chake-Chake on Pemba Island had been gained by a single vote.

The narrowest recorded percentage win in an election would seem to be for the office of Southern District Highway Commissioner in Mississippi, USA on 7 Aug 1979. Robert E. Joiner was declared the winner over W. H. Pyron with 133 587 votes to 133 582. The loser got more than 49·9999 per cent of the votes.

Most decisive ■ North Korea recorded a 100 per cent turn-out of electors and a 100 per cent vote for the Workers' Party of Korea in the general election of 8 Oct 1962. The next closest approach was in Albania on 14 Nov 1982 when a single voter spoiled national unanimity for the official (and only) Communist candidates, who thus obtained only 99·99993 per cent of the poll in a 100 per cent turn-out of 1 627 968.

Most bent ■ In the Liberian presidential election of 1927 President Charles D. B. King (1875–1961) was returned with a majority over his opponent, Mr Thomas J. R. Faulkner of the People's Party, officially announced as 234 000. President King thus claimed a 'majority' more than 15½ times greater than the entire electorate.

Highest personal majority ■ The highest ever personal majority by any politician has been 424 545 by Ram Bilas Paswan, 30, the Janata candidate for Hajipur in Bihar, India in March 1977. The electorate was 625 179. In 1956 W. R. D. Bandaranaike achieved 91·82 per cent of the poll with 45 016 votes in Attanagalla constituency of Sri Lanka (then Ceylon).

Communist parties ■ The largest national Communist party outside the USSR (18 500 000 members in 1987) and communist states has been the Partito Comunista Italiano, with a membership of 2 300 000 in 1946. The total was 1 600 000 in 1986. The membership in mainland China was estimated to be 44 000 000 in 1987. The Communist Party of Great Britain, formed on 31 Jul 1920 in Cannon Street Station Hotel, London, attained its peak membership of 56 000 in December 1942, compared with 20 599 in 1979 and 8378 in 1988. The decline has been caused by doctrinal disputes and divisions over relations with the USSR leading to expulsions and the formation of new parties or groups within the Labour movement.

Largest ballot paper ■ On 5 Mar 1985 in the State Assembly (Vidhan Sabha) elections in Karnataka, India there were 301 candidates for Belgaum City.

Most mature electorate ■ The eligibility for voting in Andorra is 25 years.

Most coups ■ Statisticians contend that Bolivia, since it became a sovereign country in 1825, had its

---

PRIME MINISTERIAL RECORDS

Though given legal warrant in the instrument of the Congress of Berlin in 1878 and an established place in the Orders of Precedence in England and Scotland in 1904, the office of Prime Minister was not statutorily recognised until 1917. All previous acknowledged First Ministers had tenure as First Lords of the Treasury with the exception of No 12, William Pitt, Earl of Chatham, who controlled his ministers as Secretary of State of the Southern Department or as Lord Privy Seal. The first to preside over his fellow King's ministers was Walpole from 1721, and undisputedly from 15 May 1730.

LONGEST SERVING	17 years 47 days	17th	Hon. William Pitt (1759–1806)	19 Dec 1783–3 Feb 1801
LONGEST SERVING (*20th century*)	>10 years	52nd	Margaret Thatcher (*née* Roberts) (b. 13 Oct 1925)	from 3 May 1979
MOST MINISTRIES	5 times	41st	Earl Baldwin KG (1867–1947)	22 May 1923–28 May 1937
SHORTEST SERVICE IN OFFICE	120 days	22nd	George Canning (1770–1827)	10 Apr–8 Aug 1827
YOUNGEST TO ASSUME OFFICE	24 years 205 days	17th	Hon. William Pitt (1759–1806)	19 Dec 1783 (declined when 23 yr 275 days)
OLDEST FIRST TO ASSUME OFFICE	70 years 109 days	31st	Viscount Palmerston KG, GCB (1784–1865)	6 Feb 1855
GREATEST AGE IN OFFICE	84 years 64 days	33rd	William Gladstone (1809–1898)	3 Mar 1894 (elected at 82 yr 171 days)
LONGEST LIVED	92 years 322 days	47th	Earl of Stockton OM (1894–1986)	from 6 Apr 1984 (so surpassing No 44)
LONGEST SURVIVAL AFTER OFFICE	41 years 45 days	13th	Duke of Grafton KG (1735–1811)	from 28 Jan 1770
SHORTEST LIVED	44 years	7th	Duke of Devonshire (1720–1764)	d. 2 Oct 1764 (exact birth date unknown)
SHORTEST MINISTRY	22 days	24th	Duke of Wellington KG, GCB, GCH (1769–1852)	17 Nov–9 Dec 1834
SHORTEST POSSESSION OF SEALS	c. 48 hours	4th	Earl of Bath (1684–1764)	10–12 Feb 1746
SHORTEST PRIOR SERVICE AS MP	2 years 11 months	17th	Hon. William Pitt (1759–1806)	–19 Dec 1783
LONGEST PRIOR SERVICE AS MP	47 years	31st	Viscount Palmerston KG, GCB (1784–1865)	1807–6 Feb 1855
LONGEST SUBSEQUENT SERVICE AS MP	22 years 156 days	39th	Earl Lloyd George OM (1863–1945)	22 Oct 1922–26 Mar 1945
LONGEST SPAN AS MP	63 years 360 days	44th	Sir Winston Churchill KG, OM, CH (1874–1965)	1 Oct 1900–25 Sep 1964
RICHEST	£7¼million (now say £200 million)	29th	Earl of Derby KG, GCMG (1799–1869)	Annual rent roll in 1869 £170 000
POOREST	£40 000 (now >£1 million) in debt	17th	Hon. William Pitt (1759–1806)	Level of personal debt by 1800
TALLEST	1·85 m 6 ft 1 in.	51st	Lord Callaghan KG (b. 27 Mar 1912)	
SHORTEST	1·64 m 5 ft 4¾ in.	28th	Lord John Russell KG, GCMG (1792–1878)	Seven-month baby: max. wt. 50·7 kg 8 stone
MOST CHILDREN (*fathered*)	15 or 16	13th	Duke of Grafton KG (1735–1811)	Twice married
MOST CHILDREN (*uniquely mothered*)	2	52nd	Margaret Thatcher (b. 13 Oct 1925)	Twins born 21 Aug 1953
MOST LIVING SIMULTANEOUSLY	19	8th, 11th–26th, 29th–30th	from birth of Peel (26th) to death of Chatham (11th)	5 Feb–11 May 1788
	19	12th, 14th–31st	from birth of Disraeli (31st) to death of Shelburne (14th)	21 Dec 1804–7 May 1805
MOST LIVING EX PRIME MINISTERS	5	9th, 13–16th	Bute, Grafton, North, Shelburne, Portland (Pitt) till Bute died	19 Dec 1783–10 Mar 1792
	5	46–50th	Eden, Macmillan, Home, Wilson, Heath (Callaghan) till Eden died	5 Apr 1976–14 Jan 1977
	5	47–51st	Macmillan, Home, Wilson, Heath, Callaghan (Thatcher) till Macmillan died	4 May 1979–29 Dec 1986
MOST PRINCIPAL OFFICES	4	51st	Lord Callaghan KG uniquely served also as Foreign and Home Secretary and as Chancellor of the Exchequer	16 Oct 1964–4 May 1979

191st coup on 30 Jun 1984 when President Hernan Siles Zuazo, 70, was kidnapped from his official residence by more than 60 armed men.

PRIME MINISTERS AND STATESMEN

Oldest ■ The longest-lived prime minister of any country was Dr Willem Drees (Social Democrat), Prime Minister of the Netherlands in 1948–58. He was born on 5 Jul 1886 and died on 13 May 1988, aged 101 years 313 days.

El Hadji Muhammad el Mokri, Grand Vizier of Morocco, died on 16 Sep 1957 at a reputed age of 116 Muslim (*Hijri*) years, equivalent to 112 ½ Gregorian years. The oldest age of first appointment has been 81 by Morarji Ranchhodji Desai of India (b. 29 Feb 1896) in March 1977.

Longest term of office ■ The longest serving current prime minister is Lee Kuan Yew, Hon. GCMG, Hon. CH (b. 16 Sep 1923) of Singapore, who has been 6 times re-elected and remains in office after 29 years.

Marshal Kim Il Sung (*ne* Kim Sung Chu) (b. 15 Apr 1912) has been Head of Government or Head of State of the Democratic People's Republic of Korea since 25 Aug 1948.

Andrey Andreyevich Gromyko (b. 6 Jul 1909) had been Minister of Foreign Affairs of the USSR since 15 Feb 1957, having been Deputy Foreign Minister since 1946, when he was elected President of the USSR on 2 Jul 1985. Pyotr Lomako (b. 1904) has served in the government of the USSR as Minister for Non-Ferrous Metallurgy from 1940. He was relieved of his post after 46 years on 1 Nov 1986, aged 82, having served on the Central Committee of the CPSU since 1952.

Woman ■ Sirimavo Bandaranaike (b. 1916) of Ceylon (now Sri Lanka) became the first woman prime minister when her party, the Sri Lanka (Blessed Ceylon) Freedom Party, won the general election in July 1960.

EUROPEAN PARLIAMENT ELECTION RECORDS

In the European Parliament elections of 15 Jun 1989 the highest majority in the 81 UK constituencies was 108 488 (L. T. Smith, Lab) in Wales South East. Lowest was 518 (Ms A. J. Pollack, Lab) in London South West. Largest and smallest electorates were 615 135 in Dorset East and Hampshire West and 317 129 in Highlands and Islands. Highest turn-out was 46.8 per cent in Wales North. Lowest was 27.6 per cent in London North East. Northern Ireland voted by proportional representation. At the Hampshire Central by-election on 15 Dec 1988 there was a record low turn-out for a Euro-election in the UK, when only 14.11 per cent of the eligible electorate voted.

MAJORITIES — UNITED KINGDOM

Party ■ The largest single party majority was that of the Liberals in 1832, of 307 seats, with a record of 66.7 per cent of the vote. In 1931 the Coalition of Conservatives, Liberals and National Labour candidates had a majority of 491 seats and 60.5 per cent of the vote. The narrowest party majority was that of the Whigs in 1847, with a single seat. The highest popular vote for a single party was 13 948 883 for Labour in 1951.

The largest majority on a division was one of 463 (464 votes to 1), on a vote of confidence in the conduct of World War II, on 29 Jan 1942. Since the war the largest has been one of 461 (487 votes to 26) on 10 May 1967, during the debate on the government's application for Britain to join the European Economic Community (the 'Common Market').

HOUSE OF LORDS

Oldest member ■ The oldest member ever was the Rt Hon. Lord Shinwell PC, CH (1884–1986) who first sat in the Lower House in November 1922 and lived to be 101 years 202 days. The oldest peer to make a maiden speech was Lord Maenan (1854–1951) aged 94 years 123 days (see Peerage, p. 204).

Youngest member ■ The youngest potential member of the House of Lords is currently the Earl of Hardwicke (b. 3 Feb 1971). The youngest current member to have taken his seat is Viscount Goschen (b. 16 Nov 1965).

POLITICAL OFFICE HOLDERS

Chancellorship *Longest and shortest tenures* ■ The Rt Hon. Sir Robert Walpole KG, later the 1st Earl of Orford (1676–1745), served 22 years 5 months as Chancellor of the Exchequer, holding office continuously from 12 Oct 1715 to 12 Feb 1742, except for the period from 16 Apr 1717 to 2 Apr 1721. The briefest tenure of this office was 26 days in the case of the Baron (later the 1st Earl of) Mansfield (1705–93), from 11 Sep to 6 Oct 1767. The only man with four terms was the Rt Hon. William Ewart Gladstone (1809–98).

The longest budget speech was that of the Rt Hon. David (later Earl) Lloyd George PC, OM (1863–1945) on 29 Apr 1909 which lasted 4 hr 51 min but was interrupted by a 30-min laryngeal tea break. He announced *inter alia* the introduction of car tax and petroleum duty. Mr Gladstone spoke for 4¾ hours on 18 Apr 1853.

Foreign Secretaryship *Longest tenures* ■ The longest continuous term of office of any Foreign Secretary has been the 10 years 359 days of Sir Edward Grey KG, MP (later Viscount Grey of Fallodon) from 11 Dec 1905 to 5 Dec 1916. The Rt Hon.

Sir Henry John Temple, 3rd Viscount Palmerston KG, PC, GCB, in three spells in 1830–34, 1835–41 and 1846–51, aggregated 15 years 296 days.

Speakership *Longest* ■ Arthur Onslow (1691–1768) was elected Mr Speaker on 23 Jan 1728, aged 36. He held the position for 33 years 43 days, until 18 Mar 1761, allowing for the 'lost' 11 days (3–13 Sep 1752).

MPs *Youngest* ■ The youngest ever woman MP has been Josephine Bernadette Devlin, now Mrs Michael McAliskey (b. 23 Apr 1947), elected for Mid Ulster (Ind. Unity) aged 21 years 359 days on 17 Apr 1969. Henry Long (1420–90) was returned for an Old Sarum seat at the age of 15. His precise date of birth is unknown. Minors were debarred in law in 1695 and in fact in 1832.

Oldest ■ Sir Francis Knollys (c. 1550–1648), 'the ancientest Parliament man in England', was elected for Reading in 1640 when apparently aged 90 and was probably 97 or 98 at the time of his death.

The oldest of 20th-century members has been Samuel Young (b. 14 Feb 1822), Nationalist MP for East Cavan (1892 to 1918), who died on 18 Apr 1918, aged 96 years 63 days. The oldest 'Father of the House' in parliamentary history was the Rt Hon. Charles Pelham Villiers (b. 3 Jan 1802), member for Wolverhampton South when he died on 16 Jan 1898, aged 96 years 13 days. He was a member for 63 years 6 days, having been returned at 17 elections. The oldest current member is Robert Edwards MP (Lab) for Wolverhampton South-East (b. 16 Jan 1905).

Longest span ■ Sir Francis Knollys (c. 1550–1648) was elected for Oxford in 1575 and died a sitting member for Reading 73 years later in 1648.

The longest span of service of any 20th-century MP is 63 years 11 months (1 Oct 1900 to 25 Sep 1964) by the Rt Hon. Sir Winston Leonard Spencer Churchill KG, OM, CH, TD (1874–1965), with breaks only in 1908 and 1922–4. The longest continuous span was that of C. P. Villiers (see above). The longest span in the Palace of Westminster (both Houses of Parliament) has been 72 years by the 10th Earl of Wemyss and March GCVO, who, as Sir Francis Wemyss-Charteris-Douglas, served as MP for East Gloucestershire (July 1841–1846) and Haddingtonshire (1847–83) and then took his seat in the House of Lords, dying on 30 Jun 1914 aged 95 years 330 days. The longest living of all parliamentarians was Theodore Cooke Taylor (1850–1952), Liberal MP for Batley 1910–18.

Briefest span ■ There are two 18th-century examples of posthumous elections. Capt. the Hon. Edward Legge, RN (1710–47) was returned unopposed for Portsmouth on 15 Dec 1747. News came later that he had died in the West Indies 87 days before polling. In 1780 John Kirkman, standing for the City of London, expired before polling had ended but was nonetheless duly returned. A. J. Dobbs (Lab, Smethwick), elected on 5 Jul 1945, was killed on the way to take his seat.

Women ■ The first woman to be elected to the House of Commons was Mme Constance Georgine Markievicz (*née* Gore Booth). She was elected as member (Sinn Fein) for St Patrick's Dublin, on 28 December 1918. The first woman to take her seat was the Viscountess Astor CH (1879–1964) (née Nancy Witcher Langhorne at Danville, Virginia, USA; formerly Mrs Robert Gould Shaw), who was elected Unionist member for the Sutton division of Plymouth, Devon on 28 Nov 1919, and took her seat 3 days later. The first woman to take her seat from the island of Ireland was Lady Fisher (*née* Patricia Smiles) as unopposed Ulster Unionist for North Down on 15 Apr 1953, as Mrs Patricia Ford.

The first woman cabinet minister was the Rt Hon. Margaret Grace Bondfield PC, CH (1873–1953), appointed Minister of Labour in 1929.

Heaviest and tallest ■ The heaviest MP of all time is believed to be Sir Cyril Smith MBE, Liberal

member for Rochdale since October 1972, when in January 1976 his peak reported weight was 189·6 kg *29 st 12 lb*.

Sir Louis Gluckstein GBE, TD, QC (1897–1979), Conservative member for East Nottingham (1931–45), was an unrivalled 2·02 m *6 ft 7½ in*. Currently the tallest is the Hon. Archie Hamilton, Conservative member for Epsom and Ewell, at 1·98 m *6 ft 6 in*.

Mayoralties ■ The longest recorded mayoralty was that of Edmond Mathis (1852–1953), *maire* of Ehuns, Haute-Saône, France for 75 years (1878 to 1953). The mayoralty of the City of London dates from 1192 with the 20-year term of Henry Fitz Ailwyn until 1212. The most elections, since these became annual in 1215, has been eight by Gregory de Rokesley (1274/5 to 1280/1). The earliest recorded mayor of the City of York, Nigel, dates from 1142. Alderman G. T. Paine served as Mayor of Lydd, Kent for 29 consecutive years from 1931 to 1961. Cllr Denis Martineau took office as Lord Mayor of Birmingham on 20 May 1986 following in office his father, grandfather, great grandfather and great great grandfather.

Local government service duration records ■ The oldest local office was that of reeve to supervise villeins. First mentioned in AD 787, it evolved to that of shire reeve, hence sheriff.

Major Sir Philip Barber Bt, DSO, TD, DL (1876–1961) served as county councillor for Nottinghamshire for 63 years 41 days from 8 Mar 1898 to 18 Apr 1961. Matthew Anderson was a member of the Borough Council of Abingdon, Oxon for 69 years 4 months from April 1709 until August 1778. Henry Winn (1816–1914) served as parish clerk for Fulletby near Horncastle, Lincs for 76 years.

Clifford Tasker (1906–1980) of Pontefract, West Yorks was appointed as presiding officer for elections in 1921 when aged 15, and served for 59 years until March 1980.

Weight of legislation ■ The greatest amount of legislation in a year has been 11 453 pages (83 Public General Acts and 2251 Statutory Instruments) in 1975. This compares with 46 Acts and 1130 Instruments of 1998 pages in 1928. The most Acts were 123 in 1939 and the fewest 39 in 1929 and 1942. The peak for Statutory Instruments was 2916 in 1947.

Honours, Decorations and Awards

Oldest order ■ The earliest honour known was the 'Gold of Honour' for extraordinary valour awarded in the 18th dynasty c. 1440–1400 BC. A statuette was found at Qan-el-Kebri, Egypt. The order which can trace its origins furthest back is the Military and Hospitaller Order of St Lazarus of Jerusalem founded by St Basil the Great in the 4th century AD. A date as early as AD 809 has been attributed to the Most Ancient Order of the Thistle, but is of doubtful provenance. The Order of St John in Scotland, founded in 1124, was suppressed in the 16th century but revived in 1947. The prototype of the princely Orders of Chivalry is the Most Noble Order of the Garter founded by King Edward III c. 1348.

Most titles ■ The most titled person in the world is the 18th Duchess of Alba (Alba de Tormes), Doña Maria del Rosario Cayetana Fitz-James Stuart y Silva. She is eight times a duchess, 15 times a marchioness, 21 times a countess and is 19 times a Spanish grandee.

Versatility ■ The only person to win a Victoria Cross and an Olympic Gold Medal has been Lt Gen. Sir Philip Neame VC, KBE, CB, DSO (1888–1978). He won the VC in 1914 and was an Olympic gold medallist for Britain for rifle shooting in 1924 though under the illusion at the time that he was shooting for the British Empire. The only George

Cross holder who was also a Fellow of the Royal Society was Professor Peter Victor Danckwerts GC, MBE, FRS F Eng (1916–85) who defused 16 parachute mines in under 48 hr in the London docks during the Battle of Britain as a Sub Lt RNVR in August 1940.

Victoria Cross *Double awards* ■ The only three men ever to have been awarded a bar to the Victoria Cross (instituted 29 Jan 1856) are:

Surg.-Capt. (later Lt-Col.) Arthur Martin-Leake VC*, VD, RAMC (1874–1953) (1902 and bar 1915).
Capt. Noel Godfrey Chavasse VC*, MC, RAMC (1884–1917) (1916 and bar posthumously 31 Jul–2 Aug 1917).
Second Lt (later Capt.) Charles Hazlitt Upham VC*, NZMF (b. 21 Sep 1908) (1941 and bar 1942).

The most VCs awarded in a war were the 634 in World War I (1914–18). The greatest number won in a single action was 11 at Rorke's Drift in the Zulu War on 22–23 Jan 1879. The school with most recipients is Eton College, Col. H. H. Jones being the 36th (posthumously in the Falklands campaign).

Youngest ■ The lowest established age for a VC is 15 years 100 days for hospital apprentice Andrew (wrongly gazetted as Arthur) Fitzgibbon (born at Peteragurh, northern India, 13 May 1845) of the Indian Medical Services for bravery at the Taku Forts in northern China on 21 Aug 1860. The youngest living VC is Capt. Rambahadur Limbu (b. 1 Nov 1939, Chyangthapu, Nepal) of the 10th Princess Mary's Own Gurkha Rifles. The award was for his courage as a L/Cpl while fighting in the Bau district of Sarawak, east Malaysia on 21 Nov 1965. He retired on 25 Mar 1985 as Lieutenant.

Oldest ■ Capt. William Raynor was the oldest person to receive the medal. It was awarded when he was 62, for the part he played in blowing up an arms store besieged by insurgents on 11 May 1857, the second day of the Indian Mutiny. The medal was retrieved on behalf of the family at a London auction in 1987, and is displayed at the RAOC Museum, Camberley, Surrey.

Longest lived ■ The longest lived of all the 1351 winners of the Victoria Cross has been Lt Col. Harcus Strachan VC. He was born in Bo'ness, West Lothian, Scotland on 7 Nov 1884 and died in Vancouver, British Columbia, Canada on 1 May 1982 aged 97 years 175 days.

Most highly decorated ■ The six living persons to have been twice decorated with any of the United Kingdom's topmost decorations are Capt. C. H. Upham VC and bar; the Viscount de l'Isle VC, KG; HM the Queen Mother CI, GCVO, GBE, who is a Lady of the Garter and a Lady of the Thistle; HRH the Duke of Edinburgh KG, KT, OM, GBE; HRH Prince Charles KG, KT, GCB and HM King Olaf V of Norway KG, KT, GCB, GCVO. Lord De L'Isle is the only person who has both the highest military and highest civil honour. Britain's most highly decorated woman is the World War II British agent Mrs Odette Hallowes GC, MBE, Légion d'Honneur, Ordre St George (Belge), who survived imprisonment and torture at the hands of the Gestapo from 1943–5. Violette Reine Elizabeth Szabo (*née* Bushnell) GC (1921–45) lost her husband in the French Legion at El Alamein in 1942. He was Etienne Szabo, Médaille Militaire, Légion d'Honneur and Croix de Guerre.

Top jet ace ■ The greatest number of kills in jet to jet battles is 16 by Capt. Joseph Christopher McConnell, Jr USAF (b. Dover, New Hampshire, USA, 30 Jan 1922) in the Korean war (1950–3). He was killed on 25 Aug 1954. It is possible that an Israeli ace may have surpassed this total in the period 1967–70 but the identity of pilots is subject to strict security.

Top woman ace ■ The record score for any woman fighter pilot is 12 by Jnr Lt Lydia Litvak (USSR) (b. 1921) on the Eastern Front between 1941 and 1943. She was killed in action on 1 Aug 1943.

Top-scoring air aces (World Wars I and II) ■ The 'scores' of air aces in both wars are *still* hotly disputed. The highest figures officially attributed have been:

World	United Kingdom
World War I	
75[1] Col. René Paul Fonck (France) Gr Cordon Ld'H, C de G (26 palms), Méd. Mil., MC*, C de G (Belge) (d. 1953)	73 Major Edward Mannock VC, DSO**, MC*
World War II	
352 Major Erich Hartmann (Germany)	38 Wg Cdr (now AVM) James Edgar Johnson CB, CBE, DSO**, DFC*[2]

[1] A total of 80 was attributed to Rittmeister Manfred Freiherr (Baron) von Richthofen (Germany) but more than 20 of these are not fully verifiable from German records, leaving Col.-Gen. Ernst Udet (d. 1941) Ordre pour le Mérite, Iron Cross with the highest number of unquestioned victories at 62.

[2] The greatest number of successes against flying bombs (V1s) was by Sqn Ldr Joseph Berry DFC** (b. Nottingham, 1920, k. 2 Oct 1944) who brought down 60 in 4 months. The most successful fighter pilot in the RAF was Sqn Ldr Marmaduke Thomas St John Pattle DFC*, of South Africa, with a known total of at least 40. In the Battle of Leyte Gulf, Cdr David McCampbell, USN shot down nine aircraft in one mission on 24 Oct 1944.

Youngest award ■ The youngest age at which an official gallantry award has ever been won is 8 years in the case of Anthony Farrer who was given the Albert Medal on 23 Sep 1916 for fighting off a cougar at Cowichan Lake, Vancouver Island, Canada to save Doreen Ashburnham. She was also awarded the AM, which, in 1971, was exchanged for the George Cross.

Most lifeboat medals ■ Sir William Hillary (1771–1847), founder of the Royal National Lifeboat Institution in 1824, was personally and uniquely awarded four RNLI Gold Medals, in 1825, 1828 and 1830 (twice). The only triple award this century has been to Coxswain Henry Blogg GC, BEM (1876–1954) of Cromer, Norfolk, who also had four Silver Medals. The record for Silver Medals is five by Sydney Harris of Great Yarmouth and Gorleston, both Norfolk (1905 (twice), 1909, 1912 and 1916).

Most mentions in despatches ■ The record number of 'mentions' is 24 by Field Marshal the Rt Hon. Sir Frederick Sleigh Roberts Bt, the Earl Roberts VC, KG, PC, KP, GCB, OM, GCSI, GCIE, VD (1832–1914).

Most post-nominal letters ■ Lord Roberts, who was also a privy counsellor, was the only non-royal holder of eight sets of *official* post-nominal letters. Currently the record number is seven by Marshal of the RAF the Rt Hon. Lord Elworthy KG, GCB, CBE, DSO, LVO, DFC, AFC (b. 23 Mar 1911) of New Zealand. HRH the Duke of Windsor (1894–1972) when Prince of Wales had 10 sets and was also a privy counsellor *viz* KG, PC, KT, KP, GCB, GCSI, GCMG, GCIE, GCVO, GBE, MC. He later appended the ISO but never did so in the cases of the OM, CH or DSO of which orders he had also been sovereign.

Civilian gallantry ■ Reginald H. Blanchford of Guernsey received the MBE for gallantry in 1950; the Queen's Commendation in 1957; the George Medal in 1958; the OBE for gallantry in 1961 for saving life from cliff tops. He was also awarded the Life Saving Medal in Gold 1957 with golden bar 1963 and was made a Knight of Grace of the Order of St John in 1970.

USSR ■ The USSR's highest award for valour is the Gold Star of a Hero of the Soviet Union. Over 10 000 were awarded in World War II. Among the 109 awards of a second star were those to Marshal Iosif Vissarionovich Dzhugashvili, *alias* Stalin (1879–

1953), and Lt-General Nikita Sergeyevich Khrushchyov (1894–1971). The only war-time triple awards were to Marshal Georgiy Konstantinovich Zhukov, Hon. GCB (1896–1972) (subsequently awarded a fourth Gold Star) and to the leading air aces Guards Colonel (later Marshal of Aviation) the late Aleksandr Ivanovich Pokryshkin and Aviation Maj. Gen. Ivan Nikitovich Kozhedub (b. 8 Jun 1920) (Order of the Red Banner, seven times). Zhukov also uniquely had the Order of Victory (twice), the Order of Lenin (six times) and the Order of the Red Banner (thrice). Leonid Ilich Brezhnev (1907–1982) was four times Hero of the Soviet Union and Hero of Socialist Labour, Order of Victory, Order of Lenin (eight times) and Order of the Red Banner (twice).

Germany ■ The Knight's Cross of the Iron Cross with swords, diamonds and golden oak-leaves was uniquely awarded to Col. Hans Ulrich Rudel (1916–82) for 2530 operational flying missions on the Eastern Front in the period 1941–5. He destroyed 519 Soviet armoured vehicles.

USA ■ The highest US military decoration is the Medal of Honor. Five marines received both the Army and Navy Medals of Honor for the same acts in 1918 and 14 officers and men received the medal on two occasions between 1864 and 1915. General Douglas MacArthur (1880–1964) is the most highly decorated American soldier, having received 59 decorations with 16 Oak Leaf clusters, plus 18 campaign stars. He was awarded the Medal of Honor in World War II.

Record price ■ The highest price ever paid for a VC group has been £110 000 for the medals of the Battle of Britain fighter pilot Wing Cdr J. B. Nicholson VC, DFC (k. 1945), one of only three men ever to win the VC actually defending Britain. The auction was at Glendining & Co, London on 27 Apr 1983.

The record for a George Cross is £20 250 at Christie's on 14 Mar 1985, for that of Sgt Michael Willets (3rd Battalion Parachute Regiment), killed by an IRA bomb in Ulster in 1971.

Order of Merit ■ The Order of Merit (instituted on 23 Jun 1902) is limited to 24 members. The longest lived of the 153 holders has been the Rt Hon. Bertrand Arthur William Russell, 3rd Earl Russell, who died on 2 Feb 1970 aged 97 years 260 days.

> **Most valuable annual prize** ● The value of each of the 1989 Nobel Prizes was Sw Kr 3 000 000, which at the time of printing was equivalent to nearly £292 000. The ceremonial presentations for physics, chemistry, physiology or medicine, literature and economics take place in Stockholm, Sweden and that for peace is in Oslo, Norway. (Photo: Gamma/Sica)

The oldest recipient was Admiral of the Fleet the Hon. Sir Henry Keppel GCB, OM (1809–1904), who received the Order aged 93 years 56 days on 9 Aug 1902. The youngest recipient has been HRH the Duke of Edinburgh KG, PC, KT, OM, GBE, who was appointed on his 47th birthday on 10 Jun 1968.

Anti-submarine successes ■ The highest number of U-boat kills attributed to one ship in the 1939–45 War was 15 to HMS *Starling* (Capt. Frederic John Walker CB, DSO***, RN). Captain Walker was in command at the sinking of a total of 25 U-boats between 1941 and the time of his death on 9 Jul 1944. The US Destroyer Escort *England* sank six Japanese submarines in the Pacific between 18 and 30 May 1944.

Most successful submarine captains ■ The most successful of all World War II submarine commanders was Leutnant Otto Kretschmer, captain of the U.23 and U.99 who up to March 1940 sank one destroyer and 44 allied merchantmen totalling 270 895 gross registered tonnes.

In World War I Kapitän-Leutnant (later Vizeadmiral) Lothar von Arnauld de la Perière, in the U.35 and U.139, sank 195 allied ships totalling 466 198 gross tonnes. The most successful boats were U.35, which in World War I sank 54 ships of 90 350 grt in a single voyage and 224 ships of 539 711 grt all told, and U.48, which sank 51 ships of 310 007 grt in World War II. The largest target ever sunk by a submarine was the Japanese aircraft carrier *Shinano* (59 994 tonnes) by USS *Archerfish* (Cdr Joseph F. Enright, USN) on 29 Nov 1944.

— NOBEL PRIZES —

Earliest 1901 for Physics, Chemistry, Physiology or Medicine, Literature and Peace

Most Prizes USA outright or shared 192 including most for Physiology or Medicine (65); Physics (51); Chemistry (33), Peace (18); Economics (15). France has most for Literature (12). The United Kingdom total is 88 outright or shared, comprising Chemistry (23); Physiology or Medicine (22); Physics (20); Peace (10); Literature (8); Economics (5).

Oldest Laureate Professor Francis Peyton Rous (US) (1879–1970) in 1966 shared in Physiology or Medicine prize aged 87

Youngest Laureates *At time of award:* Professor Sir Lawrence Bragg CH, OBE, MC, FRS (1890–1971) 1915 Physics prize at 25 *At time of work:* Bragg, and Theodore W. Richards (US) (1868–1928) 1914 Chemistry prize at 23 *Literature:* Rudyard Kipling (UK) (1865–1936) 1907 prize at 41 *Peace:* Mrs Mairead Corrigan-

Maguire (Northern Ireland) (b. 27 Jan 1944) 1976 prize (shared) at 32

Most 3 Awards: International Committee of the Red Cross, Geneva (founded 1863) Peace 1917, 1944 and 1963 (shared); 2 Awards: Dr Linus Carl Pauling (US) (b. 28 Feb 1901) Chemistry 1954 and Peace 1962; Mme Marja Sklodowska Curie (Polish-French) (1867–1934) Physics 1903 (shared) and Chemistry 1911; Professor John Bardeen (US) (b. 23 May 1908) Physics 1956 (shared) and 1972 (shared); Professor Frederick Sanger OM, CBE, FRS (b. 13 Aug 1918) Chemistry 1958 and 1980 (shared); Office of the United Nations' High Commissioner for Refugees, Geneva (founded 1951) Peace 1954 and 1981.

Highest Prize Sw Kr 3 000 000 (for 1989) equivalent to £292 000

Lowest Prize Sw Kr 115 000 (1923) equivalent to £6620

AWARDS

Most valuable annual prize ■ The value of each of the 1989 Nobel Prizes (see also p. 203) was Sw Kr 3 000 000, which at the time of printing was equivalent to nearly £292 000. The ceremonial presentations for physics, chemistry, physiology or medicine, literature and economics take place in Stockholm, Sweden and that for peace is in Oslo, Norway.

Most statues ■ The world record for raising statues to oneself was set by Generalissimo Dr Rafael Leónidas Trujillo y Molina (1891–1961), former President of the Dominican Republic. In March 1960 a count showed that there were 'over 2000'. The country's highest mountain was named Pico Trujillo (later Pico Duarte). One province was called Trujillo and another Trujillo Valdez. The capital was named Ciudad Trujillo (Trujillo City) in 1936, but reverted to its old name of Santo Domingo de Guzmán on 23 Nov 1961. Trujillo was assassinated in a car ambush on 30 May 1961, and 30 May is now celebrated as a public holiday. The man to whom most statues have been raised is Buddha. The 20th-century champion is Vladimir Ilyich Ulyanov, *alias* Lenin (1870–1924), busts of whom have been mass-produced, as also has been the case with Mao Tse-tung (1893–1976) and Ho Chi Minh (1890–1969).

PEERAGE

Most ancient ■ The oldest extant peerage is the premier Earldom of Scotland, held by the Rt Hon. Margaret of Mar, the Countess of Mar and 31st holder of this Earldom (b. 19 Sep 1940), who is the heir-at-law of Roderick or Rothri, 1st Earl (or Mormaer) of Mar, who witnessed a charter in 1114 or 1115 as 'Rothri *comes*'.

Oldest creation ■ The greatest age at which any person has been raised to the peerage is 93 years 337 days in the case of Sir William Francis Kyffin Taylor GBE, KC (b. 9 Jul 1854), created Baron Maenan of Ellesmere, Salop, on 10 Jun 1948, and died, aged 97, on 22 Sep 1951. The oldest elevation to a life peerage has been that of Emanuel Shinwell PC, CH (b. 18 Oct 1884) on 2 Jun 1970 when aged 85 years 227 days. He died on 8 May 1986 aged 101.

Longest-lived peer ■ The longest-lived peer ever recorded was the Rt Hon. Emanuel Shinwell PC, CH (b. 18 Oct 1884), created a life baron in 1970. The oldest peeress recorded was the Countess Desmond, who was alleged to be 140 when she died in 1604. This claim is patently exaggerated but it is accepted that she may have been 104. Currently the oldest peer is the Rt Hon. Major the Earl of Southesk of Kinnaird Castle, Brechin, Angus (b. 23 Sep 1893).

Youngest peers ■ Twelve Dukes of Cornwall became (in accordance with the grant by the

Crown in Parliament) peers at birth as the eldest sons of a sovereign; and the 9th Earl of Chichester inherited his earldom at his birth on 14 Apr 1944, 54 days after his father's death. The youngest age at which a person has had a peerage conferred on him is 7 days old in the case of the Earldom of Chester on HRH the Prince George (later George IV) on 19 Aug 1762. The youngest to be created a life peer or peeress is Baroness Masham of Ilton, Countess of Swinton (b. 19 Apr 1935) aged 34, in 1970.

Longest and shortest peerages ■ The longest tenure of a peerage has been 87 years 10 days in the case of Charles St Clair, Lord Sinclair, born 30 Jul 1768, succeeded 16 Dec 1775 and died aged 94 years 243 days on 30 Mar 1863.

The shortest enjoyment of a peerage was the 'split second' by which the law assumes that the Hon. Wilfrid Carlyl Stamp (b. 28 Oct 1904), the 2nd Baron Stamp, survived his father, Sir Josiah Charles Stamp GCB, GBE, the 1st Baron Stamp, when both were killed as a result of German bombing of London on 16 Apr 1941. Apart from this legal fiction, the shortest recorded peerage was one of 30 min in the case of Sir Charles Brandon KB, the 3rd Duke of Suffolk, who died, aged 13 or 14, just after succeeding his brother, Henry, when both were suffering a fatal illness, at Buckden, Cambs on 14 Jul 1551.

Highest numbering ■ The highest succession number borne by any peer is that of the present 35th Baron Kingsale (John de Courcy, b. 27 Jan 1941), who succeeded to the then 746-year-old Barony on 7 Nov 1969. His occupations have included barman, bingo-caller and plumber.

Most creations ■ The largest number of new hereditary peerages created in any year was the 54 in 1296. The record for all peerages (including 40 life peerages) is 55 in 1964. The greatest number of extinctions in a year was 16 in 1923 and the greatest number of deaths was 44 in 1935.

Most prolific ■ The most prolific peers of all time are believed to be the 1st Earl Ferrers (1650–1717) and the 3rd Earl of Winchilsea (*c.* 1627–89), each with 27 legitimate children. In addition, the former reputedly fathered 30 illegitimate children. Currently the peer with the largest family is the Rt Hon. Bryan Walter Guinness, 2nd Baron Moyne (b. 27 Oct 1905) with six sons (one now deceased) and five daughters. The most prolific peeress is believed to be Mary Fitzgerald, wife of Patrick, 19th Baron Kingsale, who bore 23 children (no twins) who survived to baptism. She died in 1663.

Baronets ■ The greatest age to which a baronet has lived is 101 years 188 days, in the case of Sir Fitzroy Donald Maclean, 10th Bt KCB (1835–1936). He was the last survivor of the Crimean campaign of 1853–56. Capt. Sir Trevor Wheler, 13th Baronet (b. 20 Sep 1889) entered his 83rd year as a baronet on 11 Aug 1984 but died aged 96 on 14 Jan 1986. The only baronetess is Dame Maureen Dunbar of Hempriggs, who succeeded in her own right as 8th in line of a 1706 baronetcy in 1965. There are some 1350 baronets.

Knights *Youngest and oldest* ■ The youngest age for the conferment of a knighthood is 29 days for HRH the Prince George (b. 12 Aug 1762) (later George IV) by virtue of his *ex officio* membership of the Order of the Garter (KG) consequent upon his creation as Prince of Wales on 17 or 19 Aug 1762. The greatest age for the conferment of a knighthood is on a 100th birthday, in the case of the Knight Bachelor Sir Robert Mayer CH (1879–1985), who was additionally made a KCVO by the Queen at the Royal Festival Hall, London on 5 Jun 1979.

Most brothers ■ George and Elizabeth Coles of Australia had five sons knighted — Sir George CBE (1885–1977); Sir Arthur (b. 1892); Sir Kenneth (b. 1896); Sir Edgar (b. 1899) and Sir Norman (b. 1907).

Most freedoms ■ Probably the greatest number of freedoms ever conferred on any man was 57 in

the case of Andrew Carnegie (1835–1919), who was born in Dunfermline, Fife but emigrated to the United States in 1848. The most freedoms conferred upon any citizen of the United Kingdom is 42, for Sir Winston Churchill (1874–1965).

Most honorary degrees ■ The greatest number of honorary degrees awarded to any individual is 111, given to Reverend Father Theodore M. Hesburgh (b. 1918), president of the University of Notre Dame, Indiana, USA. These were accumulated from 1954 to June 1987.

Greatest vote ■ The largest monetary vote made by Parliament to a subject was the £400 000 given to the 1st Duke of Wellington (1769–1852) on 12 Apr 1814. He received in all £864 000. The total received by the 1st, 2nd and 3rd Dukes to January 1900 was £1 052 000.

The Royal Society (founded 1662) ■ The longest term as an FRS (Fellow of the Royal Society) has been 61 years in the case of Bertrand Russell, 3rd Earl (1872–1970), who had been elected in 1908. The longest-lived FRS has been Sir Rickard Christophers CIE, OBE (1873–1978) aged 104 years 84 days. John Lubbock (1834–1913), later 1st Baron Avebury, was elected at the age of 23 in 1857.

Erasmus Darwin was elected on 9 Apr 1761 and was followed by his son Robert (1788 to 1848), *his* son Charles (1879 to 1881), his sons Sir George (1879 to 1912), Francis (1882 to 1925) and Horace (1903 to 1928) and Sir George's son Sir Charles (1922 to 1962), so spanning over 200 years with five generations.

Oxford and Cambridge Unions ■ Four brothers were presidents of the Union in the case of the sons of the Rt Hon. Isaac Foot: Sir Dingle Foot (Balliol, 1927–8); John (Lord Foot) (Balliol, 1930–1) and the Rt Hon. Michael (Wadham, 1933–4) at Oxford and Hugh (Lord Caradon) (St John's, 1929) at Cambridge. The last named's son, the Hon. Paul, was president at Oxford (University College, 1960–1).

Military and Defence

WAR

Earliest conflict ■ The oldest known offensive weapon is a broken wooden spear found in April 1911 at Clacton-on-Sea, Essex by S. Hazzledine Warren. This is much beyond the limit of carbon-dating but is estimated to have been fashioned before 200 000 BC.

Longest ■ The longest war was the 'Hundred Years' War' between England and France, which lasted from 1338 to 1453 (115 years), although it may be said that the nine Crusades from the First (1096–1104) to the Ninth (1270–91), extending over 195 years, comprised a single holy war. The Swiss Jean-Jacques Babel estimated that since *c.* 3500 BC there have been only 292 years in which warfare was unrecorded.

Shortest ■ The shortest war on record was that between the United Kingdom and Zanzibar (now part of Tanzania) from 9.02 to 9.40 a.m. on 27 Aug 1896. The UK battle fleet under Rear-Admiral (later Admiral Sir) Harry Rawson (1843–1910) delivered an ultimatum to the self-appointed Sultan Sa'íd Khalid to evacuate his palace and surrender. This was not forthcoming until after 38 minutes of bombardment. Admiral Rawson received the Brilliant Star of Zanzibar (first class) from Hamud ibn Muhammad, the new Sultan. It was proposed at one time that elements of the local populace should be compelled to defray the cost of the broadsides fired.

Bloodiest ■ By far the most costly war in terms of human life was World War II (1939–45), in which the total number of fatalities, including battle deaths and civilians of all countries, is estimated to have been 54 800 000 assuming 25 million USSR fatalities and 7 800 000 Chinese civilians killed. The country which suffered most was Poland with 6 028 000 or 17·2 per cent of her population of 35 100 000 killed. The total combatant death toll from World War I was 9 700 000 compared with the 15 600 000 of World War II.

In the case of the United Kingdom, however, the heavier armed forces fatalities occurred in World War I (1914–18), with 765 399 killed out of 5 500 000 engaged (13·9 per cent), compared with 265 000 out of 5 896 000 engaged (4·49 per cent) in World War II.

In the Paraguayan war of 1864–70 against Brazil, Argentina and Uruguay, their population was reduced from 1 400 000 down to 220 000 survivors of whom only 30 000 were adult males.

Surgeon Major William Brydon CB (1811–1873) was the sole survivor of the 7-day retreat of 16 000 soldiers and camp followers from Kabul, Afghanistan. His horse died 2 days after his arrival at Jellalabad, India on 13 Jan 1842.

Bloodiest civil ■ The bloodiest civil war in history was the T'ai-p'ing ('Great Peace') rebellion, in which peasant sympathisers of the southern Ming dynasty fought the Manchu government troops in China from 1851 to 1864. The rebellion was led by the deranged Hung Hsiu-ch'üan (executed) who imagined himself to be a younger brother of Jesus Christ. His force was named T'ai-p'ing T'ien Kuo (Heavenly Kingdom of Great Peace). According to the best estimates, the loss of life was some 30 000 000 including more than 100 000 killed by government forces in the sack of Nanking on 19–21 Jul 1864.

Most costly ■ The material cost of World War II far transcended that of the rest of history's wars put together and has been estimated at $1·5 million million. The total cost to the Soviet Union was estimated in May 1959 at 2 500 000 000 000 roubles while a figure of $530 000 million has been estimated for the USA. In the case of the United Kingdom the cost of £34 423 million was over 5 times as great as that of World War I (£6700 million) and 158·6 times that of the Boer War of 1899–1902 (£217 million).

Last battle on British soil ■ The last pitched land battle in Britain was at Culloden Field, Drummossie Moor, near Inverness on 16 Apr 1746. The last clan battle in Scotland was between Clan Mackintosh and Clan MacDonald at Mulroy, Inverness-shire in 1689. The last battle on English soil was the Battle of Sedgemoor, Somerset on 6 Jul 1685, when the forces of James II defeated the supporters of Charles II's illegitimate son, James Scott (formerly called Fitzroy or Crofts), the Duke of Monmouth (1649–85). During the Jacobite rising of 1745–6, there was a skirmish at Clifton Moor, Cumbria on 18 Dec 1745, when forces under Prince William, the Duke of Cumberland (1721–65), brushed with the rebels of Prince Charles Edward Stuart (1720–88) with about 12 killed on the King's side and five highlanders. This was a tactical victory for the Jacobites under Lord George Murray.

Bloodiest battle *Modern* ■ The battle with the greatest recorded number of *military* casualties was the first Battle of the Somme, France from 1 Jul to 19 Nov 1916, with 1 043 896 — of these 623 907 were Allied (including 419 654 British) and the rest German. The published German figure of c. 670 000 is not now accepted. Gunfire was heard on Hampstead Heath, London. The greatest death toll in a battle has been estimated at c. 2 100 000 in the Battle of Stalingrad ending with the German surrender on 31 Jan 1943 by Field Marshal Friedrich von Paulus (1890–1957). The Soviet garrison commander was Gen. Vasiliy Chuikov. Additionally, only 1515 civilians from a pre-war population of more than 500 000 were found alive after the battle. The final investment of Berlin by the Red Army from 16 Apr–2 May 1945 involved 3 500 000 men; 52 000 guns and mortars; 7750 tanks and 11 000 aircraft on both sides.

Ancient ■ Modern historians give no credence, on logistic grounds, to the casualty figures attached to ancient battles, such as the 250 000 reputedly killed at Plataea (Greeks v. Persians) in 479 BC or the 200 000 allegedly killed in a single day at Châlons, France (Huns v. Romans) in AD 451.

British ■ The bloodiest battle fought on British soil was the battle of Towton, near Tadcaster, North Yorks on 29 Mar 1461, when 36 000 Yorkists defeated 40 000 Lancastrians. The total loss has been estimated at between 28 000 and 38 000 killed. A figure of 80 000 British dead was attributed by Tacitus to the battle of AD 61 between Queen Boudicca (Boadicea) of the Iceni and the Roman Governor of Britain Suetonius Paulinus, for the reputed loss of only 400 Romans in an army of 10 000. The site of the battle is unknown but may have been near Borough Hill, Daventry, Northants, or more probably near Hampstead Heath, London. Prior to this battle the Romans had lost up to 70 000 in Colchester and London.

Greatest naval battle (See also p. 206) ■ The greatest number of ships and aircraft ever involved in a sea–air action was 231 ships and 1996 aircraft in the Battle of Leyte Gulf, in the Philippines. It raged from 22 to 27 Oct 1944, with 166 Allied and 65 Japanese warships engaged, of which 26 Japanese and six US ships were sunk. In addition, 1280 US and 716 Japanese aircraft were engaged. The greatest purely naval battle of modern times was the Battle of Jutland on 31 May 1916, in which 151 Royal Navy warships were involved against 101 German warships. The Royal Navy lost 14 ships and 6097 men and the German fleet 11 ships and 2545 men. The death toll at the Battle of Lepanto on 7 Oct 1571 has been estimated at 33 000.

Greatest invasion *Seaborne* ■ The greatest invasion in military history was the Allied land, air and sea operation against the Normandy coasts of France on D-day, 6 Jun 1944. Thirty-eight convoys of 745 ships moved in on the first 3 days, supported by 4066 landing craft, carrying 185 000 men, 20 000 vehicles and 347 minesweepers. The air assault comprised 18 000 paratroopers from 1087 aircraft. The 42 available divisions possessed an air support from 13 175 aircraft. Within a month 1 100 000 troops, 200 000 vehicles and 750 000 tons of stores were landed. The Allied invasion of Sicily from 10–12 Jul 1943 involved the landing of 181 000 men in 3 days.

Airborne ■ The largest airborne invasion was the Anglo-American assault of three divisions (34 000 men), with 2800 aircraft and 1600 gliders, near Arnhem, in the Netherlands, on 17 Sep 1944.

Last on the soil of Great Britain ■ The last invasion of Great Britain occurred on 12 Feb 1797, when

Most costly war ● The material cost of World War II far transcended that of the rest of history's wars put together and has been estimated at $1·5 million million. In the case of the United Kingdom the cost of £34 423 million was over 5 times as great as that of World War I (£6700 million). Sights such as this one, of bombed buildings in London, were commonplace. (Photo: Keystone)

the Irish-American adventurer General Tate landed at Carreg Gwastad with 1400 French troops. They surrendered near Fishguard, Dyfed to Lord Cawdor's force of the Castlemartin Yeomanry and some local inhabitants armed with pitchforks. The UK Crown Dependency of the Falkland Islands was invaded by Argentine troops on 2 Apr 1982. British troops re-landed at San Carlos on 21 May and accepted the surrender of Brig. Gen. Mario Menéndez 24 days later on 14 Jun 1982.

Greatest evacuation ■ The greatest evacuation in military history was that carried out by 1200 Allied naval and civil craft from the beach-head at Dunkerque (Dunkirk), France between 27 May and 4 Jun 1940. A total of 338 226 British and French troops were taken off.

Worst sieges ■ The worst siege in history was the 880-day siege of Leningrad, USSR by the German Army from 30 Aug 1941 until 27 Jan 1944. The best estimate is that between 1·3 and 1·5 million defenders and citizens died. The longest recorded siege was that of Azotus (now Ashdod), Israel which according to Herodotus was invested by Psamtik I of Egypt for 29 years in the period 664–610 BC.

DEFENCE SPENDING

In May 1988 it was estimated that the world's spending on armaments was running at the annual rate of some $660 000 million. This represents £72 per person per annum, or 10 per cent of the world's total production of goods and services. In 1987 there were 28 123 000 full-time armed force regulars or conscripts plus 40 289 400 reservists to total 68 412 400.

The budgeted expenditure on defence by the US Government for the fiscal year 1988 was $283 159 million.

The defence burden on the USSR has been estimated by official sources in the USA and the UK as a percentage of GNP (Gross National Product) to be between 13 and 17 per cent, and thus may be nearly treble the rate of that of the USA (5·9 per cent of GNP in 1988).

The UK defence estimate for 1988–9 was £19 200 million.

THE BATTLE OF SALAMIS

The greatest of ancient naval battles, involving nearly 200 000 men, and perhaps the most significant naval battle ever, was the Battle of Salamis in September 480 BC. Through their victory the Athenians and their allies were able to force back the invading Persians and retain their independence, thus paving the way for the subsequent flourishing of Greek civilisation. This artist's impression of the scene of the battle shows the anguish of the Persian King, Xerxes, watching the battle from Mount Aegaleos on the Greek mainland, as his fleet (grey ships) fail to achieve the breakthrough he was seeking. As

long as the Greek fleet remained undefeated, Persian mastery of Greece could not be achieved, and although wave upon wave of Persian ships moved into the narrow strait in the course of the day—see map—the Greeks managed to hold out. The Persians lost about five times as many ships as the Greeks during the battle, in spite of their great superiority in numbers (an estimated 800 ships as opposed to some 380 for the Athenians and their allies). This was a setback which signalled the beginning of the decline of Persian sea power in the Mediterranean. (Artwork: Chris Forsey)

North

▲ Mt Aegaleos

Island of Salamis

Piraeus

Greeks
Persians

MEDITERRANEAN

ARMED FORCES

Largest ■ Numerically the largest regular armed force in the world is that of the USSR with 5 225 000 (1987). China's People's Liberation Army's strength in 1987 was estimated to be 3 200 000 (comprising land, sea and air forces), with reductions continuing. Her reserves number around 4·4 million and her para-military forces of armed and unarmed militias are estimated by the International Institute of Strategic Studies at 'some 12 million'. The USA's military manpower is 2 158 000 (1987) and that of the United Kingdom 318 700 (1987/88).

Navies *Largest* ■ The largest navy in the world in terms of manpower is the United States Navy, with a manpower of 583 800 and 199 600 Marines in mid-1987. The active strength in 1987 included 5 nuclear-powered aircraft carriers, with 10 others, 3 battleships, 92 nuclear attack submarines and 4 diesel attack submarines, 36 cruisers, 68 destroyers, 115 frigates and 60 amphibious warfare ships. The USSR's navy has a larger submarine fleet of 375 vessels (including 127 nuclear attack). The Red Fleet has 6 aircraft carriers, 37 cruisers and 63 destroyers.

The strength of the Royal Navy in mid-1987 included 3 *Invincible* class carriers, 4 nuclear submarines with strategic atomic missiles, 15 other nuclear and 12 diesel attack submarines, 14 guided weapon destroyers and 35 frigates. The uniformed strength was 66 500 including Royal Naval Air Service and Royal Marines (7700) in 1987–8. In 1914 the Royal Navy had 542 warships including 72 capital ships with 16 building, thus being the largest navy in the world.

Longest-serving admiral ■ Admiral of the Fleet Sir Provo Wallis GCB (1791–1892) first served on HMS *Cleopatra* in October 1804. Because of his service on HMS *Cleopatra* in 1805 against the French he was kept on the active list in 1870 for life. He thus became 87 years 4 months on paid active service though he was earlier on the books as a volunteer from 1795–1804 for a further 9 years — a system by which even infants could gain seniority on joining.

Armies *Oldest* ■ The oldest army in the world is the 80-90 strong Pontifical Swiss Guard in the Vatican City, with a regular foundation dating back to 21 Jan 1506. Its origins extend back before 1400.

Largest ■ Numerically, the world's largest army is that of the People's Republic of China, with a total strength of some 2 300 000 in mid-1987. The total size of the USSR's army in mid-1987 was estimated by the International Institute of Strategic Studies at 2 000 000 men (including 28 500 Spetsnaz), believed to be organised into 209 divisions. The strength of the British Army was 158 700 in 1987–8. The basic strength maintained in Northern Ireland in 1988 is 11 400. Between 1969 and mid-1988, 1829 civilians and 827 armed forces and police personnel had been killed in the province.

Oldest soldiers ■ The oldest old soldier of all time was probably John B. Salling of the army of the Confederate States of America and the last accepted survivor of the US Civil War (1861–5). He died in Kingsport, Tennessee, USA on 16 Mar 1959, aged 113 years 1 day. The oldest Chelsea pensioner, based *only* on the evidence of his tombstone, was 111-year-old William Hiseland (b. 6 Aug 1620, d. 7 Feb 1732). The longest-serving British soldier has been Field Marshal Sir William Gomm GCB (1784–1875), who was an ensign in 1794 and Constable of the Tower of London at his death aged 91.

Youngest soldiers ■ Marshal Duke of Caxias (b. 25 Aug 1803, d. 7 May 1880), Brazilian military hero and statesman, entered his infantry regiment at the age of 5 in 1808.

Dr Kenneth Vernon Bailey MC (b. 14 Dec 1897) served as a 2nd lieutenant in the 2/8th Btn Manchester Regt for some 6 weeks before his 17th birthday. Probably the youngest enlistment in the 20th century was of William Frederick Price (b. 1 Jun 1891), who was enlisted into the army at Aldershot on 23 May 1903, aged 11 years 356 days.

Youngest conscripts ■ President Francisco Macias Nguema of Equatorial Guinea (deposed in August 1979) decreed in March 1976 compulsory military service for all boys aged between 7 and 14. The edict stated that any parent refusing to hand over his or her son 'will be imprisoned or shot'.

Tallest soldiers ■ The tallest soldier of all time was Väinö Myllyrinne (1909–63) who was inducted into the Finnish Army when he was 2·21 m *7 ft 3 in* and later grew to 2·51 m *8 ft 3 in*. The British Army's tallest soldier was Benjamin Crow who was signed on at Lichfield in November 1947 when he was 2·15 m *7 ft 1 in* tall. Edward Evans (1924–58), who later grew to 2·35 m *7 ft 8½ in*, was in the army when he was 2·08 m *6 ft 10 in*.

British regimental records ■ The oldest regular regiment in the British Army is the Royal Scots, raised in French service in 1633, though the Buffs (Royal East Kent Regiment) can trace back their origin to independent companies in Dutch pay as early as 1572. The Coldstream Guards, raised in 1650, were, however, placed on the establishment of the British Army before the Royal Scots and the Buffs. The oldest armed body in the United Kingdom is the Queen's Bodyguard of the Yeomen of the Guard formed in 1485. The Honourable Artillery Company, senior regiment of the Territorial Army, formed from the Fraternity of St George, Southwark, received its charter from Henry VIII in 1537 but this lapsed until re-formed in 1610. The infantry regiment with most battle honours is the Queen's Lancashire Regiment with 188. The most senior regiment of the Reserve Army is the Royal Monmouthshire Royal Engineers (Militia) formed on 21 Mar 1577 and never disbanded, with battle honours at Dunkirk, 1940 and Normandy, 1944.

Greatest mutiny ■ In the 1914–18 War 56 French divisions comprising some 650 000 men and their officers refused orders on the Western Front sector of General Robert Nivelle in April 1917 after the failure of his offensive.

Longest march ■ The longest march in military history was the famous Long March by the Chinese Communists in 1934–5. In 368 days, of which 268 days were days of movement, from October to October, their force of 90 000 covered 9650 km *6000 miles* from Kiangsi to Yenan in Shensi via Yünnan. They crossed 18 mountain ranges and six major rivers and lost all but 22 000 of their force in continual rear-guard actions against nationalist Kuo-min-tang (KMT) forces.

On the night of 12–13 Sep 1944 a team of nine from B Company 4th Infantry Battalion of the Irish Army made a night march of 67·59 km *42 miles* in full battle order carrying 18·1 kg *40 lb* in 11 hr 49 min.

A team of the 29 Commando Regiment, each man carrying a 18·14 kg *40 lb* pack, including a rifle, covered the Plymouth Marathon in 4 hr 35 min 47·28 sec on 1 Nov 1987.

Army drill ■ On 8–9 Jul 1987 a 90-man squad of the Queen's Colour Squadron, RAF, performed a total of 2 722 662 drill movements (2 001 384 rifle and 721 278 foot) at RAF Uxbridge, Middx from memory and without a word of command in 23 hr 55 min.

Air forces *Oldest* ■ The earliest autonomous air force is the Royal Air Force which owes its origins to the Corps of Royal Engineers Balloon Section (founded 1878), to the Air Battalion of the Royal Engineers (1 Apr 1911) and to the Royal Flying Corps (13 May 1912). The RAF took its place alongside the Navy and the Army as a separate service with its own ministry on 1 Apr 1918. The Prussian Army used a balloon near Strasbourg, France as early as 24 Sep 1870.

Largest ■ The greatest air force of all time was the United States Army Air Corps (now the US Air Force), which had 79 908 aircraft in July 1944 and 2 411 294 personnel in March 1944. The US Air Force including strategic air forces had 605 805 personnel and 4887 combat aircraft in mid-1986. The USSR Air Force had 453 000 men in mid-1986. It had 5150 combat aircraft. In addition, the USSR's Offensive Strategic Rocket Forces had about 298 000 operational personnel in mid-1986. The strength of the Royal Air Force was 93 300 with 50 operational squadrons in 1988.

BOMBS

Heaviest ■ The heaviest conventional bomb ever used operationally was the Royal Air Force's 'Grand Slam', weighing 9975 kg *22 000 lb* and measuring 7·74 m *25 ft 5 in* long, dropped on Bielefeld railway viaduct, Germany on 14 Mar 1945. In 1949 the United States Air Force tested a bomb weighing 19 050 kg *42 000 lb* at Muroc Dry Lake, California, USA. The heaviest known nuclear bomb was the MK 17 carried by US B-36s in the mid-1950s. It weighed 19 050 kg *42 000 lb* and was 7·37 m *24½ ft* long.

Atomic ■ The first atom bomb dropped on Hiroshima, Japan by the United States at 8.16 a.m. on 6 Aug 1945 had an explosive power equivalent to that of 12·5 kilotons *12 500 short tons* of trinitrotoluene ($C_7H_5O_6N_3$), called TNT. Code-named 'Little Boy' it was 3·04 m *10 ft* long and weighed 4080 kg *9000 lb* and burst 580 ± 15 m *c. 1900 ft* above the city centre. The most powerful thermonuclear device so far tested is one with a power equivalent to 57 000 000 short tons of TNT, or 57 megatons, detonated by the USSR in the Novaya Zemlya area at 8.33 a.m. GMT on 30 Oct 1961. The shock wave circled the world three times, taking 36 hr 27 min for the first circuit. Some estimates put the power of this device at between 62 and 90 megatons. The largest US H-Bomb tested was the 18–22 megaton 'Bravo' at Bikini Atoll, Marshall Islands on 1 Mar 1954. On 9 Aug 1961, Nikita Khrushchev, then the Chairman of the Council of Ministers of the USSR, declared that the Soviet Union was capable of constructing a 100-megaton bomb, and announced the possession of one in East Berlin, East Germany on 16 Jan 1963. Such a device could make a crater in rock 107 m *355 ft* deep and 2·9 km *1·8 miles* wide and a fireball 13·9 km *8·7 miles* in diameter.

Largest nuclear weapons ■ The most powerful ICBM (inter-continental ballistic missiles) are the USSR's SS–18s (Model 5), believed to be armed with 10 750-kiloton MIRVs (multiple independently targetable re-entry vehicles). Earlier models had a single 20-megaton warhead. The US Titan II carrying a W-53 warhead was rated at 5 to 9 megatons but is now withdrawn leaving the 1–2 megaton W-56 as the most powerful US weapon.

Largest 'conventional' explosion ■ The largest use of conventional explosive was for the demolition of the fortifications and U-boat pens at Helgoland on 18 Apr 1947. A net charge of 4061 tonnes (7122 tonnes gross) was detonated by Commissioned Gunner E. C. Jellis of the naval team headed by Lt F. T. Woosnam RN aboard HMS *Lasso* lying 14·5 km *9 miles* out to sea.

TANKS

Earliest ■ The first tank was 'No. 1 Lincoln' modified to become 'Little Willie' built by William Foster & Co Ltd of Lincoln. It first ran on 6 Sep 1915. Tanks were first taken into action by the Heavy Section, Machine Gun Corps, which later became the Royal Tank Corps, at the battle of Flers-Courcelette in France on 15 Sep 1916. The Mark I Male tank, armed with a pair of 6-pounder guns and four machine guns, weighed 28·4 tonnes and was driven by a motor developing 105 hp which gave it a maximum road speed of 4·8–6·4 km/h *3–4 mph*.

Heaviest and fastest ■ The heaviest tank ever constructed was the German Panzer Kampfwagen Maus II, which weighed 192 tonnes. By 1945 it had reached only the experimental stage and was not

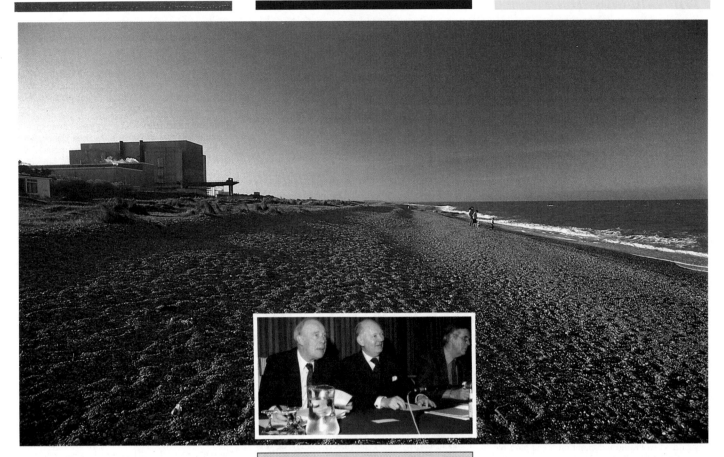

Longest inquiry ● Britain's longest and most expensive public inquiry has been that over the projected £1200 million Sizewell B nuclear power station, Suffolk under Sir Frank Layfield QC (seated centre). It began on 11 Jan 1983 and finished after 340 days of hearings on 7 Mar 1985 in the Snape Maltings, Aldeburgh. The cost to public funds was £20 million and the 3000-page 8-volume report weighed 13·6 kg *30 lb* and cost £30. (Photos: Images Colour Library and CEGB)

proceeded with. The heaviest operational tank used by any army was the 75·2 tonne 13-man French Char de Rupture 2C bis of 1922. It carried a 155-mm howitzer and had two 250 hp engines giving a maximum speed of 12 km/h *8 mph*. The world's most heavily armed tank since 1972 has been the Soviet T-72 with a 125 mm *4·92 in* high velocity gun. The British AVRE 'Centurion' has a 165 mm *6·5 in* low-velocity demolition gun. The world's fastest tank is the British Scorpion AFV which can touch 80·5 km/h *50 mph* with 75 per cent payload.

The heaviest British armoured vehicle ever built was the 79-tonne prototype 'Tortoise'. With a crew of seven and a designed speed of 19 km/h *12 mph*, this tank had a width 5 cm *2 in* less than that of the one-time operational 66-tonne 'Conqueror'.

GUNS

Earliest ■ Although it cannot be accepted as proven, the best opinion is that the earliest guns were constructed in both China and in north Africa in *c.* 1250. The earliest representation of an English gun is contained in an illustrated manuscript dated 1326 at Oxford. The earliest anti-aircraft gun was an artillery piece on a high-angle mounting used in the Franco-Prussian War of 1870 by the Prussians against French balloons.

Largest ■ The two most massive guns ever constructed were used by the Germans in the siege of Sevastopol on the Eastern Front in July 1942. They were of a calibre of 800 mm *31 ¹/₂ in* with barrels 28·87 m *94 ft 8¹/₂ in* long and named *Dore* and *Gustav*. Their remains were discovered, one near Metzenhof, Bavaria in August 1945 and the other in the Soviet zone. They were built by Krupp as railway guns carried on 24 cars, two of which had 40 wheels each. The whole assembly of the gun was 42·9 m *141 ft* long and weighed 1344 tonnes with a crew of 1500. The range for an 8·1 tonne projectile was 46·67 km *29 miles*.

During the 1914–18 War the British Army used a gun of 457 mm *18 in* calibre. The barrel alone weighed 127 tonnes. In World War II the 'Bochebuster', a train-mounted howitzer with a calibre of 457 mm *18 in* firing a 1133 kg *2500 lb* shell to a maximum

range of 20 850 m *22 800 yd*, was used from 1940 onwards as part of the Kent coast defences.

Greatest range ■ The greatest range ever attained by a gun was achieved by the HARP (High Altitude Research Project) gun consisting of two 419 mm *16·5 in* calibre barrels in tandem 36·4 m *119·4 ft* long weighing 150 tonnes at Yuma, Arizona, USA. On 19 Nov 1966 an 84 kg *185 lb* projectile was fired to an altitude of 180 km *111·8 miles* or *590 550 ft*. The static V3 underground firing tubes built in 50-degree shafts near Mimoyècques, near Calais, France to bombard London were never operative.

The famous long-range gun which shelled Paris in World War I was the 'Kaiser Wilhelm Geschütz' with a calibre of 220 mm *8·66 in*, a designed range of 127·9 km *79¹/₂ miles* and an achieved range of 122 km *76 miles* from the Forest of Crépy in March 1918. The 'Big Berthas' were mortars of 420 mm *16·53 in* calibre and with a range of less than 14 500 m *9 miles*.

Mortars ■ The largest mortars ever constructed were Mallets mortar (Woolwich Arsenal, London, 1857), and the 'Little David' of World War II, made in the USA. Each had a calibre of 920 mm *36¹/₄ in*, but neither was ever used in action. The heaviest mortar used was the tracked German 600 mm *23·6 in* siege piece known as 'Karl' before Stalingrad, USSR.

Largest cannon ■ The highest-calibre cannon ever constructed is the 'Tsar Puchka' (King of Cannons), now housed in the Kremlin, Moscow, USSR. It was built in the 16th century with a bore of 920 mm *36·2 in* and a barrel 3·18 m *10 ft 5 in* long. It weighs 40 tonnes or 2400 *pouds* (*sic*). The Turks

fired up to seven shots per day from a bombard 7·92 m *26 ft* long, with an internal calibre of 1066 mm *42 in* against the walls of Constantinople (now Istanbul) from 12 Apr to 29 May 1453. It was dragged by 60 oxen and 200 men and fired a 543 kg *1200 lb* stone cannon ball.

Military engines ■ The largest military catapults, or onagers, could throw a missile weighing 27 kg *60 lb* a distance of 457 m *500 yd*.

Conscientious objector *Most obdurate* ■ The only conscientious objector to be six times court-martialled in World War II was Gilbert Lane of Wallington, Surrey. He served 31 months' detention and 183 days' imprisonment.

Nuclear delivery vehicles ■ As of mid-1987 the USSR deployed 2511 strategic nuclear delivery vehicles while the USA on the same date deployed 1957 vehicles or 340 below the 2250 SALT II limit. The comparative number of warheads has been estimated by the International Institute for Strategic Studies at USSR 11 044 and USA 13 873.

Judicial

LEGISLATION AND LITIGATION

Statutes *Oldest* ■ The earliest surviving judicial code was that of King Ur-Hammu during the third dynasty of Ur, Iraq, *c.* 2110 BC. The oldest English statute in the Statute Book is a section of the Statute of Marlborough of 1267, retitled in 1948 'The Distress Act, 1267' and last cited in the High Court in 1986. Some statutes enacted by Henry II (d. 1189) and earlier kings are even more durable as they have been assimilated into the Common Law. An extreme example is Ine's Law concerning the administration of shires. Ine reigned AD 689–726.

Longest in the United Kingdom ■ The weightiest piece of legislation ever written is the Income and Corporation Taxes bill of more than 1000 pages and weighing 2·5 kg *5¹/₂ lb*. Lord Houghton of Sowerby appealed to fellow peers in November 1987 'not to walk about with it' for fear of ruptures. Lord Houghton was 89. Of old statutes, 31

George III XIV, the Land Tax Act of 1791, written on parchment, consists of 780 skins forming a roll 360 m *1170 ft* long.

Shortest ■ The shortest statute is the Parliament (Qualification of Women) Act 1918, which runs to 27 operative words: 'A woman shall not be disqualified by sex or marriage from being elected to or sitting or voting as a Member of the Commons House of Parliament.' Section 2 contains a further 14 words giving the short title.

Most inexplicable ■ Certain passages in several Acts have always defied interpretation and the most inexplicable must be a matter of opinion. A judge of the Court of Session of Scotland once sent the Editor his candidate which reads: *'In the Nuts (unground), (other than ground nuts) Order, the expression nuts shall have reference to such nuts, other than ground nuts, as would but for this amending Order not qualify as nuts (unground) (other than ground nuts) by reason of their being nuts (unground).'*

Earliest English patent ■ The earliest of all known English patents was that granted by Henry VI in 1449 to Flemish-born John of Utyman for making the coloured glass required for the windows of Eton College. The peak number of applications for patents filed in the United Kingdom in any one year was 63 614 in 1969. The shortest, concerning a harrow attachment, of 48 words was filed on 14 May 1956 while the longest, comprising 2318 pages of text and 495 pages of drawings, was filed on 31 Mar 1965 by IBM to cover a computer.

Most protracted litigation ■ The longest contested law suit ever recorded ended in Poona, India on 28 Apr 1966, when Balasaheb Patloji Thorat received a favourable judgment on a suit filed by his ancestor Maloji Thorat 761 years earlier in 1205. The points at issue were rights of presiding over public functions and precedences at religious festivals.

The dispute over the claim of the Prior and Convent (now the Dean and Chapter) of Durham Cathedral to administer the spiritualities of the diocese during a vacancy in the See grew fierce in 1283. It flared up again in 1672 and 1890; an attempt in November 1975 to settle the issue, then 692 years old, was unsuccessful. Neither side admits the legitimacy of writs of appointment issued by the other even though identical persons are named.

Fastest trial ■ The law's shortest delay occurred in *Duport Steel and Others* v. *Sirs and Others* heard in the High Court on 25 Jan 1980; the appeal was heard on 26 Jan and the appeal heard in the House of Lords on 1 Feb (a.m.) with the decision given p.m.

Longest trial ■ The longest jury trial in legal history is *Kemner* v. *Monsanto Co.* which started on 6 Feb 1984. The trial, at St Clair County Court House, Belleville, Illinois, USA before Circuit Judge Richard P. Goldenhersh, ended on 26 Aug 1987 after 657 days and jury deliberation of two months. The verdict was returned on 22 Oct when the plaintiffs secured sums of $1 nominal compensatory damage and $16 250 000 punitive damage in a case concerning an alleged toxic spill in Sturgeon, Illinois in 1979.

Longest British trials ■ The longest trial in the annals of British justice was the Tichborne personation case. The civil trial began on 11 May 1871, lasted 103 days and collapsed on 6 Mar 1872. The criminal trial went on for 188 days, resulting in a sentence on 28 Feb 1874 for two counts of perjury (two 7-year consecutive terms of imprisonment with hard labour) on London-born Arthur Orton, *alias* Thomas Castro (1834–98), who claimed to be Roger Charles Tichborne (1829–54), the elder brother of Sir Alfred Joseph Doughty-Tichborne, 11th Bt (1839–66). The whole case thus spanned 1025 days. The jury were out for only 30 minutes.

The impeachment of Warren Hastings (1732–1818), which began in 1788, dragged on for 7 years until 23 Apr 1795, but the trial lasted only 149 days. He was appointed a member of the Privy Council in 1814.

The fraud case *R* v. *Bouzaglo and Others* ended

before Judge Brian Gibbens (1912–85) on 1 May 1981 having lasted 274 days. They appealed on 10 Dec 1981. Trial costs were estimated at £2·5 million.

The fluoridation case *McColl* v. *Strathclyde Regional Council* lasted 204 days ending on 27 Jul 1982 before Lord Jauncey, whose judgment in the £1 million case ran to 400 pages.

The longest case in the House of Lords was *Armstrong Patents* v. *British Leyland* — seven weeks ending on 27 Feb 1986.

Murder ■ The longest murder trial in Britain was that at the Old Bailey, London of Reginald Dudley, 51, and Robert Maynard, 38, in the Torso Murder of Billy Moseley and Micky Cornwall which ran before Mr Justice Swanwick from 11 Nov 1976 to 17 Jun 1977 with 136 trial days. Both men were sentenced to life imprisonment (minimum 15 years). Costs were estimated to exceed £500 000 and the evidence amounted to 3 500 000 words.

Longest tribunal *Divorce* ■ The longest trial of a divorce case in Britain was *Gibbons* v. *Gibbons and Roman and Halperin*. On 19 Mar 1962, after 28 days, Mr Alfred George Boyd Gibbons was granted a decree *nisi* against his wife Dorothy for adultery with Mr John Halperin of New York City, NY, USA.

Shortest trials ■ The shortest recorded British murder hearings were *R.* v. *Murray* on 28 Feb 1957 and *R.* v. *Cawley* at Winchester assizes on 14 Dec 1959. Proceedings occupied only 30 seconds on each occasion.

Litigants in person ■ Since the Union of the Parliaments in 1707 the only Scot to win an appeal in person before the House of Lords has been Mr Jack Malloch, an Aberdeen schoolmaster. In 1971 he was restored to his employment with costs under the dormant but operative Teachers Act 1882 securing also a professional status in law for all qualified Scottish teachers.

Dr Mark Feldman, a podiatric surgeon, of Lauderhill, Florida, USA became the first litigant in person to secure 7 figures ($1 million) before a jury in compensatory and punitive damages in September 1980. The case concerned conspiracy and fraud alleged against 6 other doctors.

Longest address ■ The longest address in a British court was in *Globe and Phoenix Gold Mining Co Ltd* v. *Amalgamated Properties of Rhodesia*. Mr William Henry Upjohn KC (1853–1941) concluded his speech on 22 Sep 1916, having addressed the court for 45 days.

Highest bail ■ The world record for bail was set at $5000 million by Judge J. Dominique Olcomendy of San Francisco Municipal Court, California, USA on Dorothy M. Toines, 25, for soliciting prostitution on 8 Feb 1988. She was unable to pay the 10 per cent or $500 million necessary for her release after repeated failures to appear in court. The bail figure was reduced on 25 Feb by a Superior Court judge to a more affordable $500 but she was re-arrested on 21 Mar 1988 for a fifth time. The Assistant District Attorney's comment was 'See what happens when you reduce a $5 billion bail'.

The highest bail figure in a British court is £1·2 million in the case of *Inland Revenue* v. *Piggott* at Newmarket, Cambs on 19 Dec 1986 which was reduced to £500 000 on 23 Dec 1986. This amount was subsequently equalled in the Guinness PLC affair at Bow Street Court, London in the cases of Ernest Walter Saunders, former chief executive (7 May 1987); Sir Isidore (Jack) Lyons (9 Oct 1987); Gerald Ronson (14 Oct 1987); Roger Seelig (16 Oct 1987); Lord (3rd Baron) Spens (11 Mar 1988); Anthony Parnes (24 Mar 1988) and David Mayhew (8 Apr 1988). Shabtai Kalmanowitch, who was charged with dishonestly procuring $2 030 000, was also allowed £500 000 bail at Bow Street Magistrates Court, London on 3 Jul 1987, and the same amount was set for Peter Clowes, Peter Naylor and Guy von Cramer on 8 Dec 1988 at the Guildhall Justice rooms, following the collapse of Barlow Clowes.

Longest inquiry ■ The longest and most expen-

sive public inquiry has been that over the projected £1200 million Sizewell B nuclear power station, Suffolk under Sir Frank Layfield QC. It began on 11 Jan 1983 and finished after 340 days of hearings on 7 Mar 1985 in the Snape Maltings, Aldeburgh. The cost to public funds was £20 million and the 3000-page eight-volume report weighed 13·6 kg *30 lb* and cost £30.

Best attended trial ■ The greatest attendance at any trial was that of Major Jesús Sosa Blanco, aged 51, for an alleged 108 murders. At one point in the 12 ¹/₂ hr trial (5.30 p.m. to 6 a.m., 22–23 Jan 1959), 17 000 people were present in the Havana Sports Palace, Cuba. He was executed on 18 Feb 1959.

Greatest damages *Personal injury* ■ The greatest personal injury damages ever awarded were $78 million to the model Maria Hanson, 26, on 29 Sep 1987 whose face was slashed with razors in Manhattan, New York City, USA in June 1987. The three men convicted and now serving 5–15 years have no assets and Miss Hanson is entitled to 10 per cent of their post-prison earnings.

On 18 Jul 1986 a Bronx Supreme Court Jury awarded $65 086 000 to Mrs Agnes Mae Whitaker against the New York City Health and Hospitals Corporation for medical malpractice.

The compensation for the disaster in 1984 at the Union Carbide Corporation plant in Bhopal, India was agreed on 14 Feb 1989 at $470 million, following a settlement between the corporation and the Indian Government.

Samer Aboul-Hosn, 23, was awarded £1 032 000 by Mr Justice Hirst in the High Court, London on 10 Jul 1987 against the Italian Hospital, Norman Grant, Peter Crawford and Zuhair Nouri for post-operative medical negligence.

Civil damages ■ The largest damages awarded in legal history were $11 120 million to Pennzoil Co against Texaco Inc. concerning the latter's allegedly unethical tactics in January 1984 to break up a merger between Pennzoil and Getty Oil Co, by Judge Solomon Casseb Jr in Houston, Texas on 10 Dec 1985. The two leading counsels were Joe Jamail (Pennzoil) and Richard Miller (Texaco). An out-of-court settlement of $5 500 million was reached after a 48-hour negotiation on 19 Dec 1987.

Breach of promise ■ The largest sum involved in a breach of promise suit in the United Kingdom was £50 000, accepted in 1913 by Miss Daisy Markham, *alias* Mrs Annie Moss (d. 20 Aug 1962, aged 76), in settlement against the 6th Marquess of Northampton DSO (1885–1978).

Defamation and libel ■ A sum of $16 800 000 was awarded to Dr John J. Wild, 58, at the Hennepin District Court, Minnesota, USA on 30 Nov 1972 against The Minnesota Foundation and others for defamation, bad-faith termination of a contract, interference with a professional business relationship, along with $10·8 million in punitive damages. The Supreme Court of Minnesota granted an option of a new trial or a $1·5 million *remittitur* to Dr Wild on 10 Jan 1975. There was a no-disclosure clause in the settlement. The $39·6 million awarded in Columbus, Ohio, USA on 1 Mar 1980 to Robert Guccione, publisher of *Penthouse*, for defamation against Lowry Flynt, publisher of *Hustler*, was reduced by Judge Craig Wright to $4 million on 17 Apr 1980. The hearing ended in May 1982 with *Penthouse* being cleared of libel.

The greatest damages for libel ever awarded in Great Britain was the £1 million settlement to Elton John against *The Sun* for articles published in December 1988. The record award by a jury was the £600 000 settlement to Sonia Sutcliffe against *Private Eye* in May 1989 for articles published in 1981, 1983 and 1989.

The most expensive defamation trial in Great Britain has been the 87-day-long case of *Gee* v. *British Broadcasting Corporation* which ran before Lord Justice Croom-Johnson from 22 Oct 1984 to 2 May 1985. The costs have been estimated at £1·5 million excluding the BBC's internal costs over the 681 days from the offending transmission of *That's Life* on 26 Jun 1983. Dr Gee, who was in the witness stand for 27 days, received a record settlement of £100 007.

A $640 million libel suit was brought by the California resort La Costa against *Penthouse* in March 1975. In May 1982 a jury exonerated the magazine of libel, but in July their verdict was set aside by a Californian judge, who was then removed from the case. Costs exceeded $10 million.

Greatest compensation for wrongful imprisonment ■ Isadore Zimmerman (1917–83) of New York City, USA accepted an award of $1 000 000 in 1982 for wrongful imprisonment for 24 years following a false conviction for slaying a policeman. After deduction of legal fees and expenses he took home some $600 000 or some $25 000 for each year in jail. He died some 14 months later.

The greatest Crown compensation in Britain for wrongful imprisonment has been £17 500 paid to Laszlo Virag, 35, who had been sentenced to 10 years' imprisonment at Gloucester assizes in 1969 for theft and shooting and wounding a police officer. His acceptance of this sum was announced on 23 Dec 1974 after he was released in April 1974 on grounds of mistaken identity.

Greatest alimony suit ■ Belgian-born Sheika Dena Al-Fassi, 23, filed the highest ever alimony claim of $3000 million against her former husband Sheik Mohammed Al-Fassi, 28, of the Saudi Arabian royal family, in Los Angeles, California, USA in February 1982. Mr Marvin Mitchelson, explaining the size of the settlement claim, alluded to the Sheik's wealth which included 14 homes in Florida alone and numerous private aircraft. On 14 Jun 1983 she was awarded $81 million and declared she would be 'very very happy' if she was able to collect.

Greatest divorce settlement ■ The reported settlement achieved by the lawyers of Soraya Khashóggi was £500 million plus property from her husband Adnan. Mrs Anne Bass, former wife of Sid Bass of Texas, USA was reported to have rejected $535 million as inadequate to live in the style to which she had been made accustomed.

The highest High Court divorce award received was £700 000 on 13 Nov 1980 for 'Mrs P' after 23 years of marriage, against her former husband from Jersey from whom she had been receiving £6000 per annum. In *Edgar* v. *Edgar* in 1980, £750 000 was awarded but this was set aside on appeal when Mrs Edgar accepted a much lesser figure.

Patent case ■ On 13 Mar 1986 Hughes Tool Co of Houston, Texas was awarded $205 381 259·40 in a suit involving Smith International Inc. over an infringement of their patent for the 'O' ring seal used in drilling. The inventor was Edward M. Galle.

Largest suit ■ The highest amount of damages ever sought to date is $675 000 000 000 000 (then equivalent to 10 times the US national wealth) in a suit by Mr I. Walton Bader brought in the US District Court, New York City, USA on 14 Apr 1971 against General Motors and others for polluting all 50 states.

Largest law firm ■ The world's largest law firm is Baker & McKenzie with 920 lawyers in 37 offices in 25 countries. It was founded in Chicago, Illinois, USA in 1949.

Highest costs ■ The 119-day trial of seven servicemen from Cyprus under the Official Secrets Act 1911 ending at the Old Bailey, London on 29 Oct 1985 cost an estimated £3½–£5 million. All the defendants were acquitted.

The most expensive man-hunt in police history was one costing £4 million terminating on 13 Jun 1981 with the arrest of Peter William Sutcliffe (the 'Yorkshire Ripper'), in Sheffield, South Yorks. His trial at the Old Bailey, London cost £250 000 and resulted in his being sentenced to a minimum of 30 years for 13 murders and seven attempted murders which orphaned 25 children.

Longest lease ■ There is a lease concerning a plot for a sewage tank adjoining Columb Barracks, Mullingar, County Westmeath, Ireland, which was signed on 3 Dec 1868 for 10 000 000 years. It is to be assumed that a future civil servant will bring up the matter for review early in AD 10 001 868. Leases in Ireland lasting 'for ever' are quite common.

Greatest lien ■ The greatest lien by a court is 40 000 million lire on 9 Apr 1974 upon Vittorio and Ida Riva in Milan for back taxes allegedly due on a chain of cotton mills around Turin, Italy.

Wills *Shortest and longest* ■ The shortest valid will in the world is 'Vše zene', the Czech for 'All to wife', written and dated 19 Jan 1967 by Herr Karl Tausch of Langen, Hessen, West Germany. The shortest will contested but subsequently admitted to probate in English law was the case of *Thorne* v. *Dickens* in 1906. It consisted of the three words 'All for mother' in which 'mother' was not his mother but his wife. The smallest will preserved by the Record Keeper is an identity disc 3·8 cm $1\frac{1}{2}$ *in* in diameter belonging to A.B. William Skinner, killed aboard HMS *Indefatigable* at Jutland in 1916. It had 40 words engraved on it including the signatures of two witnesses and was proved on 24 Jun 1922.

The longest will on record was that of Mrs Frederica Evelyn Stilwell Cook, proved at Somerset House, London on 2 Nov 1925. It consisted of four bound volumes containing 95 940 words.

Most durable judges ■ The oldest recorded active judge was Judge Albert R. Alexander (1859–1966) of Plattsburg, Missouri, USA. He was the magistrate and probate judge of Clinton County until his retirement aged 105 years 8 months on 9 Jul 1965.

The greatest recorded age at which any British judge has sat on a bench was 93 years 9 months in the case of Sir William Francis Kyffin Taylor GBE, KC (later Lord Maenan), who was born on 9 Jul 1854 and retired as presiding judge of the Liverpool Court of Passage in April 1948, having held that position since 1903. Sir Salathiel Lovell (1619–1713) was, however, still sitting when he died on 3 May 1713 in his 94th or 95th year. The greatest age at which a House of Lords judgment has been given is 92 in the case of the 1st Earl of Halsbury (b. 3 Sep 1823) in 1916. Lord Chief Baron of Exchequer in Ireland, the Rt Hon. Christopher Palles (1831–1920) served for 42 years from 17 Feb 1874 until 1916.

Master of the Rolls ■ The longest tenure of the Mastership of the Rolls since the office was inaugurated in 1286 has been 24 years 7 months by David de Wollore from 2 Jul 1346 to 27 March 1371. The longest tenure since the Supreme Court Judicature Act of 1881 has been that of 20 years by the Rt Hon. Lord Denning PC (b. 23 Jan 1899) from 1962 to 30 Sep 1982. He had been first appointed a high court judge in 1944. William Morland held the office for 77 days, while in 1629 Sir Humphrey May died 'soon after' his appointment on 10 Apr.

Youngest judge ■ No collated records on the ages of judicial appointments exist. However, David Elmer Ward had to await the legal age of 21 before taking office after nomination in 1932 as Judge of the County Court at Fort Myers, Florida, USA.

The youngest certain age at which any English judge has been appointed is 28, in the case of Sir Ernest Wild KC (b. 1 Jan 1869) who was appointed Judge of the Norwich Guildhall Court of Record in 1897 at that age. The lowest age of appointment this century has been the 42 years 2 months of Lord Hodson in 1937.

Most judges ■ Lord Balmerino was found guilty of treason by 137 of his peers on 28 Jul 1746. In *R* v. *Canning* at the Old Bailey in 1754 Elizabeth Canning was deported to Connecticut, USA for wilful perjury by 19 judges voting 10 to 9. In *Young, James and Webster* v. *United Kingdom*, the British Rail 'closed shop' case, before the European Court of Human Rights in Strasbourg on 3–4 Mar 1981, Mr David Calcutt QC won a judgment for the railwaymen by 18 to 3.

Most offices ■ The most high judicial offices held by one man has been by Alexander Wedderburn (1733–1805), later Lord Loughborough and Earl of Rosslyn, who was Solicitor General in 1771, Attorney General in 1778, Chief-Justice of common pleas 1780–93 and Lord Chancellor from 27 Jan 1793 until he resigned in 1801.

Youngest English QC ■ The earliest age at which a barrister has taken silk this century is 33 years 8 months in the case of Mr (later the Rt Hon. Sir) Francis Raymond Evershed (1899–1966) in April 1933. He was later Lord Evershed, Master of the Rolls. Buller was nepotistically given silk aged 31, being a nephew of the then Lord Chancellor, Lord Bathurst.

Most successful ■ Sir Lionel Luckhoo KCMG, CBE, senior partner of Luckhoo and Luckhoo of Georgetown, Guyana, succeeded in getting his 245th successive murder charge acquittal by 1 Jan 1985.

Most durable solicitors ■ William George (1865–1967), brother of Prime Minister David Lloyd George, passed his preliminary law examination in May 1880 and was practising until December 1966 aged 101 years 9 months. The most durable firm is Thomson, Snell & Passmore of Tonbridge, Kent, begun by the Reverend Nicholas Hooper, a part-time scrivener, in 1570.

CRIME

Mass killings *China* ■ The greatest massacre ever imputed by the government of one sovereign nation against the government of another is that of 26 300 000 Chinese during the regime of Mao Tse-tung between 1949 and May 1965. This accusation was made by an agency of the USSR government in a radio broadcast on 7 Apr 1969. The broadcast broke down the figure into four periods: 2·8 million (1949–52); 3·5 million (1953–57); 6·7 million (1958–60); and 13·3 million (1961–May 1965).

The Walker Report published by the US Senate Committee of the Judiciary in July 1971 placed the parameters of the total death toll within China since 1949 between 32·25 and 61·7 million. An estimate of 63·7 million was published by Jean-Pierre Dujardin in *Figaro* magazine of 19–25 Nov 1978.

USSR ■ The total death toll in the Great Purge, or *Yezhovshchina*, in the USSR from 1936–8 has never been published. Evidence of its magnitude may be found in population statistics which show a deficiency of males from *before* the outbreak of the 1941–45 war.

Prof. Igor Bestuzhev-Lada published an estimate of Stalin's victims in 1929–53 in the *Nedelya* supplement to *Izvestia* of 16 Apr 1988 of 50 million dead. Nobel prizewinner Alexander Solzhenitsyn estimated the loss of life from state repression and terrorism from October 1917 to December 1959 under Lenin, Stalin and Khrushchev at 66 700 000.

Nazi Germany ■ The best estimate of the number of Jewish victims of the Holocaust or the genocidal 'Final Solution' or *Endlösung* ordered by Adolf Hitler (1889–1945) in April 1941 and continuing into May 1945 is 5·8 million.

At the SS (*Schutzstaffel*) extermination camp (*Vernichtungslager*) known as Auschwitz-Birkenau (Oświecim-Brzezinka), near Oświecim (Auschwitz) in southern Poland, where a minimum of 920 000 people (Soviet estimate is 4 000 000) were exterminated from 14 Jun 1940 to 18 Jan 1945, the greatest number killed in a day was 6000.

Cambodia ■ As a percentage of a nation's total population the worst genocide appears to have been that in Cambodia, formerly Kampuchea. According to the Khmer Rouge Foreign Minister, Ieng Sary, more than a third of the 8 million Khmers were killed between 17 Apr 1975 and January 1979. The highest 'class' ideals induced indifference to individual suffering to the point of serving as a warrant for massacre. Under the rule of Saloth Sar *alias* Pol Pot, a founder member of the CPK (Communist Party of Kampuchea, formed in September 1960) towns, money and property were abolished and economical execution by bayonet and club introduced for such offences as falling asleep during the day, asking too many questions, playing non-communist music, being old and feeble, being the offspring of an 'undesirable' or being too well educated. Deaths at the Tuol Sleng interrogation centre reached 582 in a day.

In Chinese history of the 13th–17th centuries there were three periods of wholesale massacre. The numbers of victims attributed to these events are assertions rather than reliable estimates. The figure put on the Mongolian invasions of northern China from 1210–19 and from 1311–40 are both of the order of 35 million, while the number of victims of the bandit leader Chang Hsien-chung (c. 1605–47), known as the 'Yellow Tiger', from 1643–7 in the Zechuan province has been put at 40 million.

Saving of life ■ The greatest number of people saved from extinction by one man is an estimated 90 000 Jews in Budapest, Hungary from July 1944 to January 1945 by the Swedish diplomat Raoul Wallenberg (b. 4 Aug 1912). After escaping an assassination attempt by the Nazis, he was imprisoned without trial in the Soviet Union. On 6 Feb 1957 Mr Gromyko said prisoner 'Wallenberg' had died in a cell in Lubyanka Jail, Moscow on 16 Jul 1947. Sighting reports within the Gulag system have persisted for 42 years since his disappearance. He was made an Honorary Citizen of the USA on 5 Oct 1981 and on 7 May 1987 a statue was unveiled to him in Budapest to replace an earlier one which had been removed.

Largest criminal organisation ■ The largest syndicate of organised crime is the Mafia or La Cosa Nostra, which has infiltrated the executive, judiciary and legislature of the United States. It consists of some 3000 to 5000 individuals in 25 'families' federated under 'The Commission', with an annual turnover in vice, gambling, protection rackets, tobacco, bootlegging, hijacking, narcotics, loan-sharking and prostitution which was estimated by *US News & World Report* in December 1982 at $200 billion and a profit estimated in March 1986 by the Attorney Rudolph Giuliani at $75 billion. Its origin in the USA dates from 1869 in New Orleans. The biggest Mafia (derived from an arabic expression connoting beauty and excellence allied with bravery) killing was from 11–13 Sep 1931 when 40 mafiosi were liquidated following the murder in New York of Salvatore Maranzano, *Il Capo di Tutti Capi*, on 10 Sep. The greatest breaches of *omerta* (the vow of silence) were by Joseph Valachi who 'sang like a canary' in 1963, and by the much bereaved Tommaso Buschetta, 56, in 1984. The latter's information led to 329 convictions and 2655 years' imprisonment, and $9·6 million in fines plus 19 life sentences in the Sicilian Mafia or Cupola trial in Palermo from 10 Feb 1986 to 16 Dec 1987. Michele 'the Pope' and his brother Salvatore 'the Senator' Greco had been accused of slaying the Carabinieri General Dalla Chiesa in Palermo on 3 Sep 1982.

Murder rate *Highest and lowest* ■ The country with the highest recorded murder rate is Brazil, with 104 homicides for each 100 000 of the population in 1983, or 370 per day. A total of 592 deaths was attributed to one Colombian bandit leader, Teófilo ('Sparks') Rojas, aged 27, between 1948 and his death in an ambush near Armenia, Colombia on 22 Jan 1963. Some sources attribute 3500 slayings to him during *La Violencia* of 1945–62.

The highest homicide rates recorded in New York City, USA have been 58 in a week in July 1972 and 13 in a day in August 1972. In 1973 the total for Detroit, Michigan, USA (pop. then 1·5 million) was 751. The Chicago Crime Commission, Illinois, USA published in March 1983 a list of 1081 unsolved gang slayings since 1919.

In the Indian state of Sikkim, in the Himalayas, murder is practically unknown, while in the Hunza area of Kashmir, in the Karakoram, only one definite case by a Hunzarwal has been recorded since 1900.

Genocide ● The highest recorded genocide as a percentage of an independent nation's total population appears to have occurred in Cambodia, formerly Kampuchea. According to the Khmer Rouge Foreign Minister, Ieng Sary, more than a third of the 8 million Khmers were killed between 1975 and 1979. Under the rule of Saloth Sar *alias* Pol Pot, people were executed for such offences as falling asleep during the day, asking too many questions, playing non-communist music, being old and feeble, being the offspring of an 'undesirable' or being too well educated. Towns, property and money were abolished, leading to the unusual sight of wads of unwanted banknotes just lying around in the streets. This picture was taken *c.* 1979. (Photo: Keystone Collection)

In Great Britain the total number of homicides and deaths from injuries purposely inflicted by other persons in the year 1986 was 826. This figure compares with a murder total of 124 in 1937 and 125 in 1958.

Most prolific murderers ■ It was established at the trial of Behram, the Indian Thug, that he had strangled at least 931 victims with his yellow and white cloth strip or *ruhmal* in the Oudh district between 1790 and 1840. It has been estimated that at least 2 000 000 Indians were strangled by Thugs (*burtotes*) during the reign of the Thugee (pronounced tugee) cult from 1550 until its final suppression by the British raj in 1853.

The greatest number of victims ascribed to a murderess has been 650 in the case of Countess Erzsebet Bathory (1560–1614) of Hungary. At her trial, which began on 2 Jan 1611, a witness testified to seeing a list of her victims in her own handwriting totalling this number. All were alleged to be young girls from near her castle at Csejthe where she died on 21 Aug 1614. She had been walled up in her room for 3½ years after being found guilty.

20th century ■ Pedro Alonso López (b. Colombia, 1949) known as the 'Colombian Monster', was reported captured by the villagers of Ambato, Ecuador in early March 1980. He admitted to more than 300 murders of pre-teenage girls in Colombia, Peru and Ecuador since 1973. The remains of 53 victims

of the 110 admitted to in Ecuador were rapidly detected after his confession.

In a drunken rampage lasting 8 hours on 26–27 Apr 1982 policeman Wou Bom-Kon, 27, killed 57 people and wounded 35 with 176 rounds of rifle ammunition and hand grenades in the Kyong Sang-Namdo province of South Korea. He blew himself up with a grenade.

Six men were each charged with 21 murders at Lancaster Crown Court on 9 Jun 1975 concerning the bombing of the two Birmingham public houses Mulberry Bush and Tavern in the Town on 21 Nov 1974. They were John Walker, Patrick Hill, Robert Hunter, Noel McIlkenny, William Power and Hugh Callaghan. These convictions were sent on 20 Jan 1987 by the Home Secretary to the Court of Appeal which unanimously confirmed the verdicts on 28 Jan 1988. The self-confessed arsonist Bruce Lee was sent to a mental hospital by Leeds Crown Court in January 1981 but on 14 Mar 1982 he retracted his confessions to starting fires in which 26 perished. On 2 Dec 1983 the Court of Appeal quashed charges of causing 11 of the deaths.

Judith Minna Ward, 25, of Stockport, Cheshire was convicted on 11 separate murder charges on 4 Nov 1974 making 12 in all arising from the explosion in an army coach on the M62 near Drighlington, West Yorks on 4 Feb 1974. Mary Ann Cotton (*née* Robson) (b. 1832, East Rainton, County Durham), hanged in Durham Jail on 24 Mar 1873, is believed to have poisoned 14, possibly 20, people.

Dennis Andrew Nilsen (b. 1948), then of 23 Cranley Gardens, Muswell Hill, north London, admitted to 15 one-at-a-time murders between December 1978 and February 1983. He was sentenced to life imprisonment with a 25-year minimum on 4 Nov 1983 at the Old Bailey by the Rt Hon. Lord Justice Croom-Johnson PC, DSC for six murders and two attempted murders.

Dominic McGlinchey (b. 1955) in November 1983 admitted in a press interview to at least 30 killings in Northern Ireland. He was jailed for 10 years at Dublin's Special Criminal Court on 11 Mar 1986 for shooting with intent to resist arrest in County Clare on 17 Mar 1984.

On 7 May 1981 John Thompson of Hackney, London was found guilty at the Old Bailey of the 'specimen' murder by arson of Archibald Campbell and jailed for life. There were 36 other victims at the Spanish Club, Denmark St, London.

The worst armed rampage in Britain was at Hungerford, Berks on 19 Aug 1987 during which Michael Ryan, 27, shot dead 15 people and wounded 15 others before shooting himself.

Suicide ■ The estimated daily rate of suicides throughout the world surpassed 1000 in 1965. The country with the highest suicide rate is the USSR with a rate of 30 per 100 000 in 1985. The number in China rose to 382 per day, or 16 per hour, in 1987–88. The country with the lowest recorded rate is Jordan with just a single case in 1970 and hence a rate of 0·04 per 100 000. In England and Wales there were 4315 suicides in 1984 — equivalent to 11·7 per day.

Mass suicide ■ The total number of victims of the mass cyanide poisoning of the People's Temple cult near Port Kaituma, Guyana on 18 Nov 1978 was 913. The leader was the paranoid 'Rev' Jim Jones of San Francisco, who had deposited 'millions of dollars' overseas.

The volcanic crater of Mt Mihara on an island in Sagami Bay, south of Yokohama was the scene of more than 1000 suicides from 1933–6.

Mass poisoning ■ On 1 May 1981 the first of more than 600 victims of the Spanish cooking oil scandal died. On 12 Jun it was discovered that this 8-year-old boy's cause of death was the use of 'denatured' industrial colza from rape seed. The trial of 38 defendants including the manufacturers Ramón and

Elias Ferrero lasted from 30 Mar 1987 to 28 Jun 1988 on 586 counts on which the prosecution demanded jail sentences totalling 60 000 years.

Robbery ■ The greatest robbery on record was that of the Reichsbank following Germany's collapse in April/May 1945. The Pentagon in Washington described the event, first published in the *Guinness Book of Records* in 1957, as 'an unverified allegation'. *Nazi Gold* by Ian Sayer and Douglas Botting, published in 1984, however, finally revealed full details and estimated the total haul at current values as £2500 million.

The robbery in the Knightsbridge Safety Deposit Centre, London on 12 Jul 1987 was estimated at £30 million, the property being stolen from 113 of the 126 boxes that were broken into. The managing director Parvez Latiff, 30, was among those charged on 17 Aug 1987.

At 6.40 a.m. on 26 Nov 1983 six masked men raided the Brinks Mat Unit 7 warehouses at the Heathrow Trading Estate, removing 6 800 bars of gold and platinum together with diamonds and travellers' cheques worth £26 369 778. Michael McAvoy, 32, of East Dulwich and Brian Robinson, 41, of Lewisham were each sentenced to 25 years at the Old Bailey on 3 Dec 1984. Others were found guilty of related offences while further cases were pending in 1988.

Art ■ It is arguable that the *Mona Lisa*, though never valued, is the most valuable object ever stolen. It disappeared from the Louvre, Paris on 21 Aug 1911. It was recovered in Italy in 1913 when Vincenzo Perrugia was charged with its theft.

On 12 Dec 1988 three paintings by Van Gogh, valued at an estimated 100–150 million Dutch florins (approximately £28–42 million), were stolen from a museum in Otterlo, Netherlands. One of the paintings was later found in a stolen car parked in front of the museum director's house as a token of 'goodwill' from the thieves, and as evidence that they also had the other two.

On 25 Dec 1985 140 'priceless' gold, jade and obsidian artifacts were stolen from the National Anthropology and History Institute, Mexico City, Mexico.

Bank ■ During the extreme civil disorder prior to 22 Jan 1976 in Beirut, Lebanon a guerilla force blasted the vaults of the British Bank of the Middle East in Bab Idriss and cleared out safe deposit boxes with contents valued by former Finance Minister, Lucien Dahadah, at \$50 million and by another source at an 'absolute minimum' of \$20 million.

Train ■ The greatest recorded train robbery occurred between about 3.03 a.m. and 3.27 a.m. on 8 Aug 1963, when a General Post Office mail train from Glasgow, Scotland was ambushed at Sears Crossing and robbed at Bridego Bridge near Mentmore, Bucks. The gang escaped with about 120 mailbags containing £2 631 784 worth of bank notes being taken to London for destruction. Only £343 448 was recovered.

Jewels ■ The greatest recorded theft of jewels was from the bedroom of the 'well-guarded' villa of Prince Abdel Aziz bin Ahmed Al-Thani near Cannes, France on 24 Jul 1980 valued at £16 000 000. The haul from Bond Jewellers, Conduit St, London on 20 Jun 1983 was estimated to be worth £6 million.

Greatest kidnapping ransom ■ Historically the greatest ransom paid was that for Atahualpa by the Incas to Francisco Pizarro in 1532–33 at Cajamarca, Peru which constituted a hall full of gold and silver, worth in modern money some \$170 million.

The greatest ransom ever reported in modern times is 1500 million pesos for the release of the brothers Jorge Born, 40, and Juan Born, 39, of Bunge and Born, paid to the left-wing urban guerilla group Montoneros in Buenos Aires, Argentina on 20 Jun 1975.

The youngest person kidnapped has been Carolyn Wharton, born at 12.46 p.m. on 19 Mar 1955 in the Baptist Hospital, Texas, USA and kidnapped, by a woman disguised as a nurse, at 1.15 p.m. aged 29 minutes.

Greatest hijack ransom ■ The highest amount ever paid to aircraft hijackers has been \$6 million by the Japanese government in the case of a JAL DC-8 at Dacca Airport on 2 Oct 1977 with 38 hostages. Six convicted criminals were also exchanged. The Bangladesh government had refused to sanction any retaliatory action.

Largest narcotics haul ■ In October 1983 it was estimated that the narcotics crime in the USA was running at \$80 000 million per annum with cocaine dealers turning a profit of \$35 000 million and illegal domestic 'green collar' marijuana growers netting \$13 900 million.

The greatest drug haul ever achieved was 1320·8 kg *1·3 tons* of top-grade heroin inside bales of natural rubber at the docks in Bangkok, Thailand, on 13 Feb 1988, registered for shipment to New York City, USA on 25 Feb. The value was put at \$2000 million by the Thai authorities.

The bulkiest haul was 2 903 000 kg *2850 long tons* of Colombian marijuana in the 14-month-long 'Operation Tiburon' concluded by the DEA with the arrest of 495 people and the seizure of 95 vessels announced on 5 Feb 1982.

In Britain, the Home Office disclosed on 23 Dec 1977 that 13 million LSD tablets with a street value approaching £100 million had been destroyed on the conclusion of 'Operation Julie'. The largest amount of drugs seized in one operation by weight was from the *Salton Sea*, a Honduras-registered cargo ship, at Ramsgate, Kent between 4–9 Sep 1988, when 10 tonnes of cannabis was recovered.

Greatest banknote forgery ■ The greatest forgery was the German Third Reich government's forging operation, code name 'Bernhard', engineered by SS Sturmbannführer Alfred Naujocks of the Technical Dept of the German Secret Service Amt VI F in Berlin in 1940–1. It involved £150 000 000 worth of £5 notes.

Biggest bank fraud ■ The largest amount of money named in a defalcation case has been a gross SwFr 222 million at the Lugano branch of Lloyd's Bank International in Switzerland on 2 Sep 1974. Mark Colombo and Egidio Mombelli were tried and found guilty in Lugano on 30 Oct 1975 on charges of mismanagement and falsification of accounting documents.

Computer fraud ■ Between 1964 and 1973, 64 000 fake insurance policies were created on the computer of the Equity Funding Corporation in the USA, involving \$2000 million.

Stanley Mark Rifkin (b. 1946) was arrested in Carlsbad, California, USA by the FBI on 6 Nov 1978 charged with defrauding a Los Angeles bank of \$10·2 million by manipulation of a computer system. He was sentenced to 8 years' imprisonment in June 1980.

Theft ■ It was estimated in November 1983 that the greatest theft in the world is running at \$160 000 million per annum. This is the value of 'bosses' time' paid for but not worked in the United States in 1983/84.

The government of the Philippines announced on 23 Apr 1986 that they had succeeded in identifying \$860·8 million 'salted' by the former President Ferdinand Edralin Marcos (b. 11 Sep 1917) and his wife Imelda. It was asserted that the total since November 1965 was believed to be between \$5 and \$10 billion.

Largest object stolen by a single man ■ On a moonless night at dead calm high water on 5 Jun 1966, armed with only a sharp axe, N. William Kennedy slashed away the mooring lines at Wolfe's Cove, St Lawrence Seaway, Canada of the 10 639-dwt SS *Orient Trader* owned by Steel

Factors Ltd of Ontario. The vessel drifted to a waiting blacked-out tug thus escaping a ban on any shipping movements during a violent wild-cat waterfront strike. She sailed for Spain.

Maritime fraud ■ A cargo of 180 000 tonnes of Kuwaiti crude oil on the supertanker *Salem* at Durban was sold without title to the South African government in December 1979. The ship mysteriously sank off Senegal on 17 Jan 1980 leaving the government to pay £148 million to Shell International, who owned the shipment.

CAPITAL PUNISHMENT

Capital punishment is known to date at least from the Iron Age, as evidenced by the finding of Tollund man in Denmark. The countries in which capital punishment is still prevalent include China (hundreds of shootings per annum); South Africa (about 100 hangings for rape, robbery and murder); Turkey; Iran; USA (reintroduced in 38 states since January 1983 for the most heinous murders); USSR (23 capital offences including profiteering, speculation and currency offences for which some 400 persons have been reportedly shot annually).

Capital punishment was first abolished *de facto* in 1798 in Liechtenstein. The death penalty for murder was formally abolished in Britain on 18 Dec 1969.

Capital punishment in the British Isles dates from AD 450, but was abolished by William I and reimposed by Henry I, reaching a peak in the reign of Edward VI (1547–53), when an average of 560 persons were executed annually at Tyburn alone. Even into the 19th century there were 223 capital crimes, but these resulted in only 25 hangings. Between 1830 and 1964 the most murderers hanged in a year was 27 (24 men, 3 women) in 1903. In 1956 there were no executions.

Largest hanging ■ The most people hanged from one gallows were 38 Sioux Indians by William J. Duly outside Mankato, Minnesota, USA for the murder of unarmed citizens on 26 Dec 1862. The Nazi Feldkommandant simultaneously hanged 50 Greek resistance men as a reprisal in Athens on 22 Jul 1944.

Last hangings ■ The last public execution in England took place outside Newgate Prison, London at 8 a.m. on 26 May 1868, when Michael Barrett was hanged for his part in the Fenian bomb outrage on 13 Dec 1867, when 12 were killed outside the Clerkenwell House of Detention, London. The earliest non-public execution was of the murderer Thomas Wells on 13 Aug 1868. The last public hanging in Scotland was that of the murderer Robert Smith outside Dumfries Gaol on 12 May 1868 by the hangman Mr Askern. The last in the United States occurred at Owensboro, Kentucky in 1936. The last hangings in the United Kingdom were those of Peter Anthony Allen (b. 4 Apr 1943), hanged at Walton Prison, Liverpool by Robert L. Stewart, and John Robson Walby (b. 1 Apr 1940), *alias* Gwynne Owen Evans, at Strangeways Gaol, Manchester, both on 13 Aug 1964. They had been found guilty of the capital murder of John Alan West, on 7 Apr 1964. The 15th, youngest and last woman executed this century was Mrs Ruth Ellis (*née* Neilson), 28, for the murder of David Blakely, 25, shot outside the Magdala, Hampstead on 10 Apr 1955. She was executed on 13 Jul at Holloway Prison, London. The last hanging in the Republic of Ireland took place in 1954.

Last from yard-arm ■ The last naval execution at the yard-arm was the hanging of Private John Dalliger, Royal Marines, aboard HMS *Leven* in Victoria Bay near Lu-ta, China, on 13 Jul 1860. Dalliger had been found guilty of two attempted murders.

Youngest ■ On 26 Jun 1885 James Arcene was executed for a crime he committed when aged 10. In Britain the hanging of persons under 18 was expressly excluded in the Children's and Young Persons' Act 1933 (Sec. 33). No person under that age was, in fact, executed more recently than 1887.

The lowest satisfactorily recorded age was of a boy aged 8 'who had malice, cunning and revenge' in firing two barns and who was hanged at Abingdon, Oxon in the 17th century. The youngest persons hanged since 1900 have been six 18-year-olds, the most recent of whom was Francis Robert George ('Flossie') Forsyth on 10 Nov 1960.

Oldest ■ The oldest person hanged in the United Kingdom since 1900 was a man of 71 named Charles Frembd (*sic*) at Chelmsford Gaol on 4 Nov 1914, for the murder of his wife at Leytonstone, London. In 1822 John Smith, said to be 80, of Greenwich, south-east London, was hanged for the murder of a woman.

Last guillotinings ■ The last person to be publicly guillotined in France was the murderer Eugene Weidmann before a large crowd at Versailles, near Paris at 4.50 a.m. on 17 Jun 1939. The executioner was Henri Desfourneaux, who was succeeded by his nephew André Obrecht (1897–1983) in 1951, who was in turn succeeded by his niece's husband Marcel Chevalier in January 1978. Dr Joseph Ignace Guillotin (1738–1812) died a natural death. He had advocated the use of the machine designed by Dr Antoine Louis in 1789 in the French constituent assembly. The last use before abolition on 9 Sep 1981 was on 10 Sep 1977 at Baumettes Prison, Marseille for torturer and murderer Hamida Djandoubi, 28.

Death Row ■ The longest sojourn on Death Row was the 39 years of Sadamichi Hirasawa (1893–1987) in Sendai Jail, Japan. He was convicted in 1948 of poisoning 12 bank employees with potassium cyanide to effect a theft of £100, and died aged 94. Willie Jasper Darden, 54, survived a record six death warrants in 14 years on Death Row for the murder of a shopkeeper in 1973. His final TV interview was interrupted by a power failure caused by a test of the Florida electric chair in which he died on 15 Mar 1988. On 31 Oct 1987 Liong Wie Tong, 52, and Tan Tian Tjoen, 62, were executed for robbery and murder by firing squad in Jakarta, Indonesia after 25 years on Death Row.

Executioners ■ The longest period of office of a public executioner was that of William Calcraft (1800–79), who was in action from 1828 to 25 May 1874 and officiated at nearly every hanging outside and later inside Newgate Prison, London. On 2 Apr 1868 he hanged the murderess Mrs Frances Kidder, 25, outside Maidstone Jail, Kent — the last public execution of a woman.

For 56 years from 1900 to the retirement of Albert in February 1956, the Pierrepoint family largely monopolised the task of executing murderers and war criminals. Henry Albert (1876–1922) officiated from 1900–1911 with a record 20 executions in Britain in 1909 and the last double female execution (the baby farmers Mrs Amelia Sachs and Mrs Annie Walters) on 3 Feb 1903. The longest-serving executioner has been his eldest brother Thomas Pierrepoint from 1903 to 1948. Albert Pierrepoint, son of Henry Albert, officiated at the hanging of 530 men and 20 women in his career in nine countries including a record 27 war criminals in one day in Germany. Britain's 9th and last chief prison hangman was Henry B. Allen who was on call until the abolition of hanging for murder in 1969.

Lynching ■ The worst year in the 20th century for lynchings in the United States has been 1901, with 130 lynchings (105 Negroes, 25 Whites), while the first year with no reported cases was 1952. The last lynching case recorded in Britain was that of *R* v. *Caskie and Stevenson* on 29 Dec 1922. The accused were discharged after a verdict of not proven for murder by assault of Robert Alexander Stewart, 32, at Dalmarnock Bridge, Glasgow on 11 Sep 1922. Stewart was falsely thought by a tram conductor to be kidnapping Alistair John Sinclair, 5, who gave evidence not under oath standing on a seat.

Corporal punishment ■ The last use of corporal punishment in one of HM Prisons was on 26 Jun 1962 and it was abolished in the United Kingdom by the Criminal Justice Act 1967. The treadmill which 14 prisons operated in 1878 was finally suspended on 1 Apr 1902. Men on the 36-man wheel at Northallerton, North Yorks raised themselves 2937 m *9639 ft* in an 8-hour day, equivalent to reaching within 33·8 m *111 ft* of the summit of Everest in 3 days.

PRISON SENTENCES

Longest sentences ■ A 10 000-year sentence was imposed on Deuel Wilhelm Davies, 40, on 4 Dec 1981 in Tuscaloosa, Alabama, USA for a triple murder (including his mother-in-law) in 1976. A sentence of 384 912 years was *demanded* at the prosecution of Gabriel March Grandos, 22, at Palma de Mallorca, Spain on 11 Mar 1972 for failing to deliver 42 768 letters, or 9 years per letter.

Juan Corona, a Mexican-American, was sentenced to 25 consecutive life terms, for murdering 25 farm workers in 1970–1 around Feather River, Yuba City, California, USA at Fairfield on 5 Feb 1973. His 20th-century record was surpassed by Dean Corll (27) in 1974 and John Wayne Gacy (33 victims) in 1980.

Kevin Mulgrew from the Ardoyne district of Belfast was sentenced on 5 Aug 1983 to life imprisonment for the murder of Sergeant Julian Connolley of the UDR. In addition he was given a further 963 years to be served concurrently on 84 other serious charges including 13 conspiracies to murder and 8 attempted murders.

The longest single period served by a reprieved murderer in Great Britain this century was 40 years 11 months by John Watson Laurie, the Goat Fell or Arran murderer, who was reprieved on the grounds of insanity in November 1889. He died in Perth Penitentiary on 4 Oct 1930.

The longest specific minimum period recommended by a judge under the Murder (Abolition of Death Penalty) Act 1965 has been 45 years in the case of Jordanian terrorist Nezar Hindawi for his abortive bomb plot against an El Al airliner on 24 Oct 1986.

The longest single sentence passed on a woman under English law was 20 years for Mrs Lona Teresa Cohen *née* Petra (b. 1913) at the Old Bailey on 2 Mar 1961 for conspiring to commit a breach of the Official Secrets Act 1911. The sentence of this KGB agent was remitted by the Foreign Secretary on no known lawful authority on 24 Jul 1969. Ward (see Most prolific murderers) was sentenced to 20 years for a single offence and an aggregate 30 years on 4 Nov 1974.

Longest time served ■ Paul Geidel (b. 21 Apr 1894) was convicted of second degree murder on 5 Sep 1911 as a 17-year-old porter in a New York, USA hotel. He was released from the Fishkill Correctional Facility, Beacon, New York aged 85 on 7 May 1980 having served 68 years 8 months and 2 days — the longest recorded term in US history. He first refused parole in 1974. Rudolph Hess, formerly Hitler's deputy, was captured at Eaglesham on 10 May 1941 and died in Spandau Prison on 17 Aug 1987 aged 93, having entered his 47th year in prison.

Longest in Broadmoor Special Hospital ■ The longest period for which any person has been detained in Broadmoor Hospital, Crowthorne, Berks, which provides conditions of maximum security for patients with criminal, violent or dangerous propensities, is 76 years in the case of William Giles. He had been charged with arson but found insane and was admitted to Broadmoor Hospital in May 1885 at the age of 10 and died there in March 1962, at the age of 87.

The longest escape from Broadmoor was one of 39 years, by James Kelly, who got away on 23 Jan 1888, using a pass key made from a corset spring. After an adventurous life in Paris, France, in New York, USA and at sea he returned in April 1927 to ask for readmission. After some difficulties this was arranged. He died in Broadmoor in September 1929.

Most appearances ■ A record for arrests was set by Tommy Johns (1922–88) in Brisbane, Queens-land, Australia on 9 Sep 1982 when he faced his 2000th conviction for drunkenness since 1957. His total at the time of his last drink on 30 Apr 1988 was 'nearly 3000'.

Greatest mass arrests ■ The greatest mass arrest reported in a democratic country was of 15 617 demonstrators on 11 Jul 1988, rounded up by South Korean police to ensure security in advance of the 1988 Olympic Games in Seoul. The largest in the United Kingdom occurred on 17 Sep 1961, when 1314 demonstrators supporting unilateral nuclear disarmament were arrested for obstructing highways leading to Parliament Square, London by sitting down. As a consequence of the 1926 General Strike there were 3149 prosecutions: incitement (1760) and violence (1389).

FINES

Heaviest ■ The largest fine ever was one of $650 million, which was imposed on the US securities house Drexel Burnham Lambert in December 1988 for insider trading. This figure represented $300 million in direct fines, with the balance to be put into an account to satisfy claims of parties that could prove that they were defrauded by Drexel's actions.

The heaviest fine ever imposed by a United Kingdom court is £525 000 on 10 Dec 1983 on the National Graphical Association (NGA) for illegal picketing of the *Messenger* newspaper plant, Warrington, Cheshire owned by Mr Eddie Shah.

On 6 Feb 1985 Lloyd's of London fined Peter Dixon, chairman of the PCW (Peter Cameron-Webb) Syndicate, £1 000 000 in connection with alleged misappropriation of £38·17 million. A High Court judgment of £8·2 million against Mr Dixon was also made in chambers.

The highest fine ever imposed on a UK company is 10 million ECUs (equivalent to £5·7 million) on ICI by the EEC for irregular trading concerning polypropylene from 1977–83, on 24 Apr 1986.

PRISONS

Largest ■ The most capacious prison in Great Britain is Wandsworth, south London, with a certified normal accommodation of 1266. Peak occupation of 1519 was reached on 30 Apr 1988. The highest prison walls in Great Britain are those of Lancaster Prison, measuring 11–15·85 m *36–52 ft*. The Maze Prison, near Lisburn, Northern Ireland, opened in 1974, covers 53·8 ha *133 acres* with eight 100-cell blocks surrounded by a 9·1 m *30 ft* wall.

The largest prison in Scotland is Barlinnie, Glasgow, with 750 single cells. Ireland's largest prison is Mountjoy Prison, Dublin, with 808 cells.

Highest population ■ The peak average prison population, including police cell occupation, for England and Wales was the figure for the week beginning 17 Jul 1987 with 51 239. In Scotland the prison population record was 5400 in 1972 and in Northern Ireland 2934 on 16 Nov 1975.

Most secure prison ■ After it became a maximum security federal prison in 1934, no convict was known to have lived to tell of a successful escape from the prison of Alcatraz Island in San Francisco Bay, California, USA. A total of 23 men attempted it but 12 were recaptured, 5 shot dead, one drowned and 5 presumed drowned. On 16 Dec 1962, just before the prison was closed on 21 Mar 1963, one man reached the mainland alive, only to be recaptured on the spot. John Chase held the record with 26 years there.

Most expensive prison ■ Spandau Prison, Berlin, originally built in 1887 for 600 prisoners, was used solely for the Nazi war criminal Rudolf Hess (b. 26 Apr 1894, d. 17 Aug 1987) for the last twenty years of his life. On 19 Aug 1987 it was announced that he had strangled himself with a piece of electrical flex and that he had left a note in old German script. He remained in lone confinement at Spandau for a total of forty years. The cost of maintenance of the staff of 105 was estimated at $415 000 per annum in 1987.

Longest escape ■ The longest recorded escape by a recaptured prisoner was that of Leonard T. Fristoe, 77, who escaped from Nevada State Prison, USA on 15 Dec 1923 and was turned in by his son on 15 Nov 1969 at Compton, California. He had had 46 years of freedom under the name of Claude R. Willis. He had killed two sheriff's deputies in 1920. The longest period of freedom achieved by a British gaol breaker is more than 32 years by Irish-born John Patrick Hannan, who escaped from Verne Open Prison at Portland, Dorset on 22 Dec 1955. He had served only 1 month of a 21-month term for car stealing and assaulting two policemen.

Greatest gaol break ■ In February 1979 a retired US Army colonel, Arthur 'Bull' Simons, led a band of 14 to break into Gasre prison, Tehran, Iran to rescue two fellow Americans. Some 11 000 other prisoners took advantage of this and the Islamic revolution in what became history's largest ever gaol break.

In July 1971, Raoul Sendic and 105 other Tupamaro guerillas escaped from a Uruguayan prison through a tunnel 91 m *298 ft* long.

The greatest gaol break in the United Kingdom was that from the Maze Prison on 25 Sep 1983, when 38 IRA prisoners escaped from Block H-7. By June 1988 10 were still at large. The Provisional IRA had been first set up in Ballinamore, County Leitrim, Ireland in 1967.

Education

Compulsory education was first introduced in 1819 in Prussia. It became compulsory in the United Kingdom in 1870.

University *Oldest* ■ The Sumerians had scribal schools or *É-Dub-ba* soon after 3500 BC. The oldest existing educational institution in the world is the University of Karueein, founded in AD 859 in Fez, Morocco. The University of Bologna was founded in 1088.

The oldest university in the United Kingdom is the University of Oxford, which came into being *c.* 1167. The oldest of the existing colleges is probably University College (1249), though its foundation is less well documented than that of Merton in 1264. The earliest college at Cambridge University is Peterhouse, founded in 1284. The largest college at either university is Trinity College, Cambridge, founded in 1546. The oldest university in Scotland is the University of St Andrews, Fife. Established as a university in 1411, theology and medicine may have been taught there since *c.* AD 900.

Greatest enrolment ■ The university with the greatest enrolment in the world is the University of Rome, Italy (founded 1930) which reported 180 000 students in June 1987. Britain's largest university is the University of London with 51 296 internal students and 24 856 external students (1987) so totalling 76 152. The Open University, first called the University of the Air (Royal Charter 30 May 1969), at Walton Hall near Milton Keynes, Bucks has 5209 part-time tutors and 133 198 students.

Largest ■ The largest existing university building in the world is the M. V. Lomonosov State University on the Lenin Hills, south of Moscow, USSR. It stands 240 m *787 ft 5 in* tall, has 32 storeys and 40 000 rooms. It was constructed from 1949–53.

Professor *Youngest* ■ The youngest at which anybody has been elected to a chair in a university is 19 years in the case of Colin MacLaurin (1698–1746), who was elected to Marischal College, Aberdeen as Professor of Mathematics on 30 Sep 1717. In 1725 he was made Professor of Mathematics at Edinburgh University on the recommendation of Sir Isaac Newton, who was a professor at Cambridge aged 26. Henry Phillpotts (1778–1869) became a don at Magdalen College, Oxford on 25 Jul 1795 aged 17 years 80 days.

Most durable ■ Dr Joel Hildebrand (1881–1983), Professor Emeritus of Physical Chemistry at the University of California, Berkeley, USA, first became an

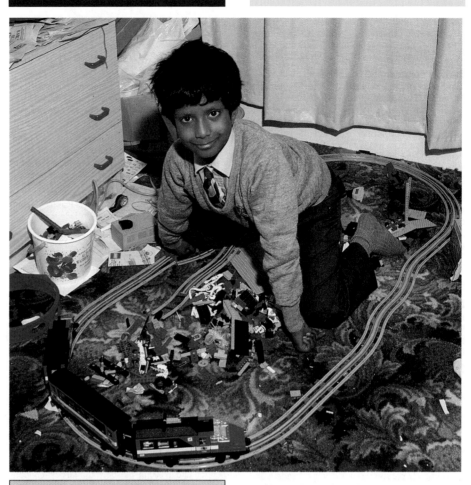

assistant professor in 1913 and published his 275th research paper 68 years later in 1981. The longest period for which any professorship has been held in Britain is 63 years in the case of Thomas Martyn (1735–1825), Professor of Botany at Cambridge University from 1762 until his death. The last professor-for-life was the pathologist Professor Henry Roy Dean (1879–1961) for his last 39 years at Cambridge.

Most graduates in family ■ Mr and Mrs Albert Kunz of Bloomington, Indiana, USA saw all their eight daughters and five sons graduate from Indiana University between 1932 and 1956.

Youngest undergraduate and graduate ■ The most extreme recorded case of undergraduate juvenility was that of William Thomson (1824–1907), later Lord Kelvin OM, GCVO, who entered Glasgow University aged 10 years 4 months in October 1834 and matriculated on 14 Nov the same year. Adragon Eastwood De Mello (b. 5 Oct 1976) of Santa Cruz, California, USA obtained his BA in Mathematics from the University of California in Santa Cruz on 11 Jun 1988 at the age of 11 years 8 months. Ruth Lawrence (b. 1971) of Huddersfield, West Yorkshire became Britain's youngest undergraduate when she was accepted for entrance to Oxford at the age of 12. She had passed Pure Mathematics O level at the age of 9 and Pure Mathematics A level and Grade 1 S level in June 1981, aged 10, and graduated from St Hugh's in Oxford with a first-class degree, top of 191 entrants, on 4 Jul 1985.

Ganesh Sittampalam (b. February 1979) of Surbiton, Surrey is the youngest person to have passed an A level, achieving grade A's at both Mathematics and

Further Mathematics in June 1988, when aged 9 years 4 months.

Youngest doctorate ■ On 13 Apr 1814 the mathematician Carl Witte of Lochau was made a Doctor of Philosophy of the University of Giessen, Germany when aged 12.

School *Oldest in Britain* ■ The title of the oldest existing school in Britain is contested. It is claimed that King's School in Canterbury, Kent was a foundation of Saint Augustine, some time between his arrival in Kent in AD 597 and his death *c.* 604. Cor Tewdws (College of Theodosius) at Llantwit Major, South Glamorgan, reputedly burnt down in AD 446, was refounded, after an elapse of 62 years, by St Illtyd in 508, and it flourished into the 13th century. Winchester College was founded in 1382. Lanark Grammar School claims to have been referred to in a papal bull drawn up in 1183 by Lucius III.

Largest ■ In 1983/84 South Point High School, Calcutta, India (founded 1954) had an enrolment of 12 350 regular students.

The school with the most pupils in Great Britain was Exmouth Comprehensive, Devon with 2599 (1983/84). The highest enrolment in Scotland has been at Our Lady's Roman Catholic High School, Motherwell, Lanarkshire with a peak of 2325 in August 1977. The total in Holy Child School, Belfast, Northern Ireland reached 2752 in 1973 before being split up. The highest enrolment in 1986/87 is 2212 at the Methodist College, Belfast.

Most expensive ■ The annual cost of keeping a pupil at the Oxford Academy (founded 1906), Westbrook, Connecticut, USA for 1987/88 was $23 500.

In the academic year 1987/88 St Andrew's Private Tutorial Centre, Cambridge (co-founders W. A. Duncombe and C. T. Easterbrook) charged £13 359 for full-time science students (tuition and accommodation). The most expensive school in Great Britain is the American Community school in Cobham, Surrey (headmaster J. E. Page). The maximum annual fee for boarding entries in 1988/89 was £9940.

The most expensive girls' school in 1988/89 was Marymount International School, in Kingston-upon-Thames, south London (principal Sister Breda Shelly), with annual fees of £8525 for boarders.

Earliest comprehensive school ■ Lakes School, Cumbria, formed from an intake from Windermere Grammar School and other Westmorland schools, adopted the non-selective comprehensive principle as early as 1945. Calder High School was established after formal rejection of the 11-plus examinations from two West Riding schools in 1950. The earliest purpose built was Kidbrooke Comprehensive for Girls, in south-east London, opened in 1954.

Oldest PTA ■ The parent–teacher association with the earliest known foundation date in Britain is that for Lawrence Sheriff School, Rugby, Warwicks, formed in 1908.

Most schools ■ The greatest documented number of schools attended by a pupil is 265 by Wilma Williams, now Mrs R. J. Horton, from 1933–43 when her parents were in show business in the USA.

Most O and A levels ■ Dr Francis L. Thomason of Hammersmith, London had by August 1986 accumulated 70 O and O/A, 16 A and 1 S levels making a total of 87, of which 36 were in the top grade. A. F. Prime, a prisoner in HM Open Prison, Sudbury, accumulated a total of 1 S, 14 As and 34 Os between 1968 and 1982. Environmental difficulties tend to make study harder in prison than elsewhere.

The highest number of top grade A levels attained at one sitting is seven, by Stephen Murrell of Crown Woods School, Eltham in June 1978, out of eight passes. Robert Pidgeon (b. 7 Feb 1959) of St Peter's School, Bournemouth secured 13 O level passes at grade A at one sitting in the summer of 1975, and subsequently passed three A levels at grade A and two S levels with firsts. Nicholas Barberis achieved a total of 27 top grades whilst at Eltham College, London passing 20 O/AO levels and 7 A levels, all at grade A, between 1984 and 1988.

Youngest headmaster ■ The youngest headmaster of a major public school was Henry Montagu Butler (b. 2 Jul 1833), appointed Headmaster of Harrow School on 16 Nov 1859, when aged 26 years 137 days. His first term in office began in January 1860.

Most durable don ■ Dr Martin Joseph Routh (b. Sept 1755) was President of Magdalen College, Oxford from April 1791 for 63 years 8 months, until his death in his 100th year on 22 Dec 1854. He had previously been a fellow for 16 years and was thus a don for a span of 79 years.

Most durable teachers ■ David Rhys Davies (1835–1928) taught as a pupil teacher and subsequently a teacher and headmaster for a total of 76 years. Most of his teaching was done at Talybont-on-Usk School near Brecon, Powys (1856–79) and at Dame Anna Child's School, Whitton, Powys. Col. Ernest Achey Loftus CBE, TD, DL (1884–1987) served as a teacher over a span of 73 years from May 1901 in York, England until 18 Feb 1975 in Zambia, retiring as the world's oldest civil servant aged 91 years 38 days. His father William was born in Hull in the reign of William IV in 1832.

Elsie Marguerite Touzel (1889–1984) of Jersey, Channel Islands began her teaching career aged 16 in 1905 and was teaching at Les Alpes School, Faldonet until her retirement 75 years later on 30 Sep 1980.

Highest endowment ■ The greatest single gift in the history of higher education has been $125 million to Louisiana State University by C. B. Pennington in 1983.

Religions

Oldest ■ Human burial, which has religious connotations, is known from c. 60 000 BC among *Homo*

sapiens neanderthalensis in the Shanidar cave, northern Iraq. The earliest named prophet was Zoroaster (Zarathustra) dated to c. 600 BC. He has 250 000 followers today.

Largest ■ Religious statistics are necessarily only approximate. The test of adherence to a religion varies widely in rigour, while many individuals, particularly in the East, belong to two or more religions.

Christianity is the world's prevailing religion, with some 1 619 272 560 adherents in 1987, or 32·9 per cent of the world's population. In 1988 there were 864 379 000 Roman Catholics, or 17 per cent of the world's population in the same year.

The largest non-Christian religion is Islam (Muslim) with some 880 555 000 followers in 1988.

In the United Kingdom the Anglicans comprise members of the Established Church of England, the Dis-established Church in Wales, the Episcopal Church in Scotland and the Church of Ireland. The Church of England has 2 provinces (Canterbury and York), 44 dioceses, 10 649 full-time diocesan clergymen and 13 369 parishes (mid-1987).

In Scotland the most numerous group is the Church of Scotland (12 synods, 47 presbyteries), which had 854 311 members as at 1 Jan 1987.

Largest clergies ■ The world's largest religious organisation is the Roman Catholic Church, with 157 cardinals, 737 archbishops, 3138 bishops, 402 886 priests and 908 158 nuns in 1988.

Jews ■ The total of world Jewry is estimated to be 16 million. The highest concentration is in the USA with 5 834 650 of whom 1 742 500 are in the New York area. The total in Israel is 3 537 000. The total of British Jewry is 330 000 of whom 201 000 are in London and 11 000 in Glasgow, the largest concentration in Scotland. The total in Tokyo, Japan is only 750.

PLACES OF WORSHIP

Earliest ■ Many archaeologists are of the opinion that the decorated Upper Palaeolithic caves of Europe (c. 30 000–10 000 BC) were used as places of worship or religious ritual. Claims have been made that the El Juyo cave, northern Spain contains an actual shrine, dated to c. 12 000 BC. The oldest surviving Christian church in the world is a converted house in Douro-Europos (now Qal'at es Salihiye) in eastern Syria, dating from AD 232.

Oldest *Great Britain* ■ The oldest ecclesiastical building in the United Kingdom is a 6th-century cell built by St Brendan in AD 542 on Eileachan Naoimh (pronounced Noo), Garvelloch Islands, Argyllshire. The church in Great Britain with the oldest origins is St Martin's Church in Canterbury, Kent. It was built in AD 560 on the foundations of a 1st-century Roman church. The chapel of St Peter on the Wall, Bradwell-on-Sea, Essex was built from AD 654–660. The oldest church in Ireland is the Gallerus Oratory, built c. 750 at Ballyferriter, near Kilmalkedar, County Kerry. Britain's oldest nunnery is St Peter and Paul Minster, on the Isle of Thanet, Kent. It was founded c. 748 by the Abbess Eadburga of Bugga. The oldest catholic church is St Etheldreda, Ely Place, Holborn, London, founded in 1251. The oldest non-conformist chapel is the thatched chapel at Horningsham, Wilts, dated 1566.

Largest temple ■ The largest religious structure ever built is Angkor Wat (City Temple), enclosing 162·6 ha *402 acres* in Cambodia (formerly Kampuchea), south-east Asia. It was built to the Hindu god Vishnu by the Khmer King Suryavarman II in the period 1113–50. Its curtain wall measures 1280 × 1280 m *4199 × 4199 ft* and its population, before it was abandoned in 1432, was 80 000. The whole complex of 72 major monuments, begun c. AD 900, extends over 24 × 8 km *15 × 5 miles*. The largest Buddhist temple in the world is Borobudur, near Jogjakarta, Indonesia, built in the 8th century. It is 31·5 m *103 ft* tall and 123 m *403 ft* square.

The largest Mormon temple is the Salt Lake Temple, Utah, USA dedicated on 6 Apr 1893 and with a floor area of 23 505 m² *253 015 ft²* or *5·80* acres.

Largest cathedral ■ The world's largest cathedral is the cathedral church of the Diocese of New York, St John the Divine, with a floor area of 11 240 m² *121 000 ft²* and a volume of 476 350 m³ *16 822 000 ft³*. The cornerstone was laid on 27 Dec 1892, and work on the Gothic building was stopped in 1941. Work restarted in earnest in July 1979. In New York it is referred to as 'Saint John the Unfinished'. The nave is the longest in the world at 183·18 m *601 ft* in length, with a vaulting 37·79 m *124 ft* in height.

The cathedral covering the largest area is that of Santa Mariá de la Sede in Sevilla (Seville), Spain. It was built in Spanish Gothic style between 1402 and 1519 and is 126·18 m *414 ft* long, 82·60 m *271 ft* wide and 30·48 m *100 ft* high to the vault of the nave.

The largest cathedral in the British Isles is the Cathedral Church of Christ in Liverpool. Built in modernised Gothic style, work was begun on 18 Jul 1904, and it was finally consecrated on 25 Oct 1978 after 74 years (cf. Exeter 95 years) using ½ million stone blocks and 12 million bricks at an actual cost of some £6 million. The building encloses 9687 m² *104 275 ft²* and has an overall length of 193·85 m *636 ft*. The Vestey Tower is 100·88 m *331 ft* high. It contains the highest vaulting in the world — 53·34 m *175 ft* maximum at undertower, and the highest Gothic arches ever built, being 32·61 m *107 ft* at apices.

Smallest ■ The smallest church in the world designated as a cathedral is that of the Christ Catholic Church, Highlandville, Missouri, USA. Consecrated in July 1983 it measures 4·26 × 5·18 m *14 × 17 ft* and has seating for 18 people.

The smallest cathedral in use in the United Kingdom (of old foundation) is the Cathedral of the Isles on the Isle of Cumbrae, Strathclyde which was built 1849–51. The nave measures only 12·19 × 6·09 m *40 × 20 ft* and the total floor area is 197·3 m² *2124 ft²*. Oxford Cathedral in Christ Church (College) is 47·24 m *155 ft* long.

Largest church ■ The largest church in the world is the basilica of St Peter, built between 1492 and 1612 in the Vatican City, Rome, Italy. Its length, measured from the apse, is 186·33 m *611 ft 4 in*. The area is 15 142 m² *162 990 ft²*. The inner diameter of the famous dome is 41·98 m *137 ft 9 in* and its centre is 119 m *390 ft 5 in* high. The external height is 139·52 m *457 ft 9 in*.

The elliptical Basilique of St Pie X at Lourdes, France, completed in 1957 at a cost of £2 000 000, has a capacity of 20 000 under its giant span arches and a length of 200 m *656 ft*.

The crypt of the underground Civil War Memorial Church in the Guadarrama Mountains, 45 km *28 miles* from Madrid, Spain, is 260 m *853 ft* in length. It took 21 years (1937–58) to build, at a reported cost of £140 000 000, and is surmounted by a cross 150 m *492 ft* tall.

The largest Church in the United Kingdom is the Collegiate Church of St Peter at Westminster built AD 1050–1745. Its maximum dimensions are overall: length 161·5 m *530 ft*; breadth across transept 61·87 m *203 ft* and internal height 30·98 m *101 ft 8 in*. The largest parish church is the Parish Church of the Most Holy and Undivided Trinity at Kingston-upon-Hull, covering 2530 m² *27 235 ft²* and with an external length and width of 87·7 × 37·7 m *288 ft × 124 ft*. It is also believed to be the country's oldest brick building serving its original purpose, dating from c. 1285. Both the former Cathedral of St Mungo, Glasgow and Beverley Minster, Humberside are now used as parish churches. The largest school chapel is that of the 45·7 m *150 ft* high Lancing College, West Sussex with a capacity of 600.

Smallest church ■ The world's smallest church

is the Union Church at Wiscasset, Maine, USA, with a floor area of 2·92 m² *31½ ft²* (2·13 × 1·37 m *7 × 4½ ft*). St Gobban's Church, Portbradden, County Antrim, Northern Ireland measures 3·7 × 2·0 m *12 ft 1½ in × 6ft 6 in*.

The smallest church in use in England is Bremilham Church, Cowage Farm, Foxley near Malmesbury, Wilts which measures 3·65 × 3·65 m *12 × 12 ft* and is used for service once a year. The smallest completed mediaeval English church in regular use is that at Culbone, Somerset, which measures 10·66 × 3·65 m *35 × 12 ft*. The smallest Welsh chapel is St Trillo's Chapel, Rhôs-on-Sea (Llandrillo-yn-Rhos), Clwyd, measuring only 3·65 × 1·83 m *12 × 6 ft*. The smallest chapel in Scotland is St Margaret's, Edinburgh, measuring 5·02 × 3·20 m *16½ × 10½ ft*, giving a floor area of 16·09 m² *173¼ ft²*.

Largest synagogue ■ The largest synagogue in the world is the Temple Emanu-El on Fifth Avenue at 65th Street, New York City, NY, USA. The temple, completed in September 1929, has a frontage of 45·72 m *150 ft* on Fifth Avenue and 77·11 m *253 ft* on 65th Street. The sanctuary proper can accommodate 2500 people, and the adjoining Beth-El Chapel seats 350. When all the facilities are in use, more than 6000 people can be accommodated.

The largest synagogue in Great Britain is the Edgware Synagogue, Barnet, London, completed in 1959, with a capacity of 1630 seats. That with the highest registered membership is Ilford Synagogue with 2492 at 1 Jan 1983.

Largest mosque ■ The largest mosque ever built was the now ruinous al-Malawiya mosque of al-Mutawakil in Samarra, Iraq built from AD 842–52 and measuring 3·72 ha *9·21 acres* with dimensions of 238·9 × 156·0 m *784 × 512 ft*. The world's largest mosque in use is the Umayyad Mosque in Damascus, Syria built on a 2000-year-old religious site measuring 157 × 97 m *515 × 318 ft* thus covering an area of 1·52 ha *3·76 acres*.

Tallest minaret ■ The tallest minaret in the world is that for the £218 million Great Hassan II Mosque, Casablanca, Morocco measuring 175·6 m *576 ft*. The Qutb Minar, south of New Delhi, India, built in 1194, is 72·54 m *238 ft* tall.

Tallest and oldest pagoda ■ The world's tallest pagoda is the Phra Pathom Chedi at Nakhon Pathom, Thailand, which was built for King Mongkut from 1853–70. It rises to 115 m *377 ft*. The oldest pagoda in China is Sung-Yo Ssu in Honan built with 15 12-sided storeys in AD 523, though the 99·3 m *326 ft* tall Shwedagon Pagoda, Yangon (formerly Rangoon), The Union of Myanma (formerly Burma) is built on the site of a 8·2 m *27 ft* tall pagoda of 585 BC.

Sacred object ■ The sacred object with the highest intrinsic value is the 15th-century gold Buddah in Wat Trimitr Temple in Bangkok, Thailand. It is 3·04 m *10 ft* tall and weighs an estimated 5½ tonnes. At the June 1989 price of £230 per fine ounce, its intrinsic worth was £20·8 million. The gold under the plaster exterior was found only in 1954.

Longest nave ■ The longest nave in the United Kingdom is that of St Albans Cathedral, which is 86·86 m *285 ft* long. The central tower of Liverpool's Anglican Cathedral (internal overall length 193·85 m *636 ft*) interrupts the nave with an under-tower space.

Tallest spire ■ The tallest cathedral spire in the world is that of the Protestant Cathedral of Ulm in West Germany. The building is early Gothic and was begun in 1377. The tower, in the centre of the west façade, was not finally completed until 1890 and is 160·90 m *528 ft* high. The world's tallest church spire is that of the Chicago Temple of the First Methodist Church on Clark Street, Chicago, Illinois, USA. The building consists of a 22-storey skyscraper (erected in 1924) surmounted by a parsonage at 100·5 m *330 ft*, a 'Sky Chapel' at 121·92 m *400 ft* and a steeple cross at 173·12 m *568 ft* above street level.

The highest spire in Great Britain is that of the church of St Mary, called Salisbury Cathedral, Salisbury, Wilts. The Lady Chapel was built in the years 1220–5 and the main fabric of the cathedral was finished and consecrated in 1258. The spire was added later, *ante* 1305, and reaches a height of 123·13 m *404 ft*. The central spire of Lincoln Cathedral, completed *c.* 1307 and which fell in 1548, was 160·02 m *525 ft* tall.

Stained glass *Oldest* ■ Pieces of stained glass dated before AD 850, some possibly even to the 7th century, excavated by Professor Rosemary Cramp, were placed into a window of that date in the nearby St Paul's Church, Jarrow, County Durham. The oldest complete stained glass in the world represents the Prophets in a window of the Cathedral of Augsburg, Bavaria, West Germany, dating from the second half of the 11th century. The oldest datable stained glass in the United Kingdom has been represented by a figure of St Michael in All Saints Church, Dalbury, Derbyshire of the late 11th century.

Largest ■ The largest stained-glass window is the complete mural of the Resurrection Mausoleum in Justice, Illinois, USA, measuring 2079 m² *22 381 ft²* in 2448 panels, completed in 1971. The back-lit glass mural installed in 1979 in the atrium of the Ramada Hotel, Dubai is 41·14 m *135 ft* high. The largest single stained-glass window in Great Britain is the East Window in Gloucester Cathedral measuring 21·94 × 11·58 m *72 × 38 ft*, set up to commemorate the Battle of Crécy (1346), while the largest area of stained glass comprises the 128 lights, totalling 2322 m² *25 000 ft²*, in York Minster.

> **Largest non-Christian religion** ● The largest non-Christian religion is Islam (Muslim) with some 880 555 000 followers in 1988. This shot shows the Ka'bah, the holiest shrine of Islam, in Mecca, Saudi Arabia, the most holy city of Islam. (Photo: Camerapix)

Brasses ■ The world's oldest monumental brass is that commemorating Bishop Yso von Wölpe in Andreaskirche, Verden, near Hanover, West Germany, dating from 1231. An engraved coffin plate of St Ulrich (d. 973), laid in 1187, was found buried in the Church of SS Ulrich and Afra, Augsburg, West Germany in 1979. The oldest brass in Great Britain is of Sir John D'Abernon (d. 1277) at Stoke D'Abernon, near Leatherhead, Surrey, dating from *c.* 1320.

A dedication brass dated 24 Apr 1241 in Ashbourne Church, Derbyshire has been cited as the earliest arabic writing extant in Britain.

CHURCH PERSONNEL

There are 1848 'registered' saints (including 60 St Johns) of whom 628 are Italians, 576 French and 271 from the United Kingdom and Ireland. Of these, eight came from Cambridge and seven from Oxford between 1535 and 1645, but none from the House of Commons. Britain's first Christian martyr was St Alban, executed *c.* AD 209. The first US-born saint was Mother Elizabeth Ann Bayley Seton (1774–1821), canonised 14 Sep 1975. The total includes 79 popes.

Most rapidly canonised ■ The shortest interval that has elapsed between the death of a saint and his canonisation was in the case of St Anthony of Padua, Italy, who died on 13 Jun 1231 and was canonised 352 days later on 30 May 1232. For the other extreme of 857 years see papal table.

Bishopric *Longest tenure* ■ The longest tenure of any Church of England bishopric is 57 years in the case of the Rt Reverend Thomas Wilson, who was consecrated Bishop of Sodar and Man on 16 Jan 1698 and died in office on 7 Mar 1755. Of English bishoprics the longest tenures, if one excludes the unsubstantiated case of Aethelwulf, reputedly Bishop of Hereford from 937 to 1012, are those of 47 years by Jocelin de Bohun (Salisbury) 1142–89 and Nathaniel Crew or Crewe (Durham) 1674–1721.

Bishop *Oldest* ■ The oldest serving bishop (excluding suffragans and assistants) in the Church of England as at June 1987 was the Right Reverend

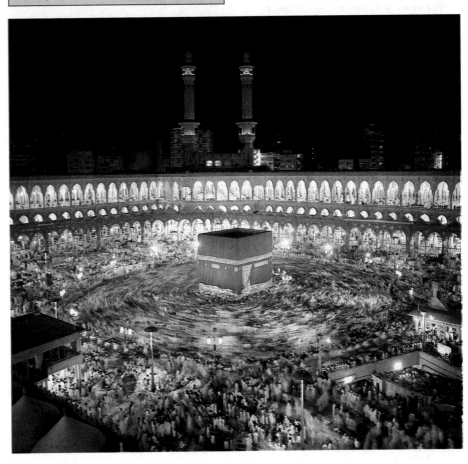

POPES & CARDINALS

LONGEST PAPAL REIGN
Pius IX—Giovanni Maria Mastai-Ferretti (1846–1878). 31 years 236 days

SHORTEST PAPAL REIGN
Stephan II (752). 2 days

LONGEST-LIVED POPE
St Agatho (d. 681) (probably exaggerated). ?106 years. Leo XIII—Gioacchino Pecci (1810–1903). 93 years 140 days

YOUNGEST ELECTED
Benedict IX—Theophylact (c. 1020–1056) in 1032. 11 or 12 years

LAST MARRIED
Adrian II (pre-celibacy rule). Elected 867

LAST WITH CHILDREN
Gregory XIII—Ugo Buoncompagni (1502–1585) had a son. Elected 1572

LAST NON-CARDINAL
Urban VI—Bartolomeo Prignano (1318–89), Archbishop of Bari. 8 Apr 1378

LAST BRITON
Adrian IV—Nicholas Breakspear (c. 1100–59) (b. Abbots Langley, Herts). Elected 4 Dec 1154

LAST PREVIOUS NON-ITALIAN
Adrian VI—Adrian Florenz Boeyens (Netherlands). Elected 31 Aug 1522

SLOWEST ELECTION
Gregory X—Teobaldi Visconti, 31 months. Feb 1269–1 Sep 1271

FASTEST ELECTION
Julius II—on first ballot, 21 Oct 1503

SLOWEST CANONISATION
St Leo III—over span of 857 years, 816–1673

OLDEST CARDINAL
(*all-time*)
Georgio da Costa (b. Portugal, 1406, d. Rome, Italy aged 102 years). Elected 18 Sep 1508
(*current*)
Julijans Vaivods (b. Latvia 18 Aug 1895)

YOUNGEST CARDINAL
(*all-time*)
Luis Antonio de Bourbon (b. 25 Jul 1727) aged 8 years 147 days. Elected 19 Dec 1735
(*current*)
Alfonso Lopez Trujillo of Colombia (b. 18 Nov 1935). 47 years 76 days

LONGEST-SERVING CARDINAL
Cardinal Duke of York, grandson of James VII of Scotland and II of England, 60 years 10 days, 1747–1807

LONGEST-SERVING BISHOP
Bishop Louis François de la Baume de Suze (1603–1690). 76 years 273 days from 6 Dec 1613

Richard David Say, Bishop of Rochester, who was born on 4 Oct 1914.

The oldest Roman Catholic bishop in recent years has been Bishop Angelo Teutonico, formerly Bishop of Aversa (b. 28 Aug 1874), who died aged 103 years 276 days on 31 May 1978. He had celebrated mass about 24 800 times. Bishop Herbert Welch of the United Methodist Church, who was elected a Bishop for Japan and Korea in 1916, died on 4 Apr 1969 aged 106.

Youngest ■ The youngest bishop of all time was HRH the Duke of York and Albany KG, GCB, GCH, the second son of George III, who was elected Bishop of Osnabrück, through his father's influence as Elector of Hanover, at the age of 196 days on 27 Feb 1764. He resigned after 39 years' enjoyment. The youngest serving bishop (excluding suffragans and assistants) in the Church of England is the Reverend Dr David Hope (b. 14 Apr 1940) whose appointment to the See of Wakefield was announced on 2 Jul 1985. When suffragens and assistants are counted, the youngest is Canon Michael Scott-Joynt, Bishop of Stafford, who was appointed on 21 Apr 1987 aged 44.

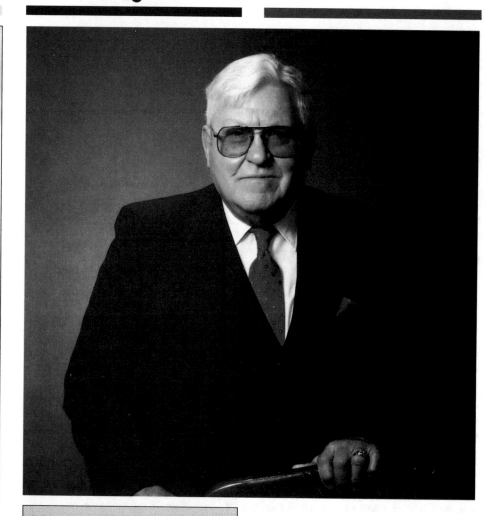

Sunday school ● Roland E. Daab (b. 25 Mar 1914) now of St Paul United Church of Christ, Columbia, Illinois, USA has attended Sunday school for 3675 consecutive Sundays without a miss for over 70 years to 30 Apr 1989.

Oldest parish priest ■ Father Alvaro Fernandez (b. 8 Dec 1880, d. 6 Jan 1988) served as a parish priest at Santiago de Abres, Spain from 1919 continuing into his 108th year. The oldest Anglican clergyman, the Reverend Clement Williams (b. 30 Oct 1879), died aged 106 years 3 months on 3 Feb 1986. He lined the route at Queen Victoria's funeral and was ordained in 1904.

Longest service ■ Rev K. M. Jacob (b. 10 Jul 1880) was made a deacon in the Marthoma Syrian Church of Malabar in Kerala, southern India in 1897. He served his church until his death on 28 Mar 1984, 87 years later.

The longest Church of England incumbency on record is one of 75 years 357 days by the Reverend Bartholomew Edwards, Rector of St Nicholas, Ashill, Norfolk from 1813 to 1889. There is some doubt as to whether the Reverend Richard Sherinton was installed at Folkestone from 1524 or 1529 to 1601. If the former is correct it would surpass the Norfolk record. The parish of Farrington, Hants had only two incumbents in a 122-year period *viz* Reverend J. Benn (28 Mar 1797 to 1857) and Reverend T. H. Massey (1857 to 5 Apr 1919). From 1675 to 1948 the incumbents of Rose Ash, Devon were from eight generations of the family of Southcomb.

Longest-serving chorister ■ John Love Vokins (b. 19 Jun 1890) has been a chorister for 94 years. He joined the choir of Christ Church, Heeley, Sheffield in 1895 and that of St Michael's, Hathersage 35 years later.

Oldest warden ■ Having become a chorister in 1876 at the age of 9, Thomas Rogers was appointed vicar's warden in 1966 at Montacute, Somerset, aged 99.

Sunday school ■ Sunday schools were established by Congregationalists in Neath and Tirdwyn-cyn, Wales in 1697. Roland E. Daab (b. 25 Mar 1914) now of St Paul United Church of Christ, Columbia, Illinois, USA has attended for 3675 consecutive Sundays without a miss for over 70 years to 30 Apr 1989.

Largest and smallest parishes ■ The smallest parish in the United Kingdom is The Scares, which consists of rocky islets in Luce Bay with an area of 0·44 ha *1·10 acres* and is included in Wigtown, Dumfries and Galloway. In 1982 the parish of Dallinghoo Wield, Suffolk boasted a population of nil and an area of 14·6 ha *38 acres*. The largest parish is Kilmonivaig in Inverness-shire with an area of 108 145·46 ha *267 233·03 acres*.

Oldest parish register ■ The oldest part of any parish register surviving in England contains entries from the summer of 1538. There is a sheet from that of Alfriston, East Sussex recording a marriage on 10 Jul 1504 but this is amid entries from 1547. Scotland's oldest surviving register is that for Anstruther-Wester, Fife, with burial entries from 1549.

Largest crowds ■ The greatest recorded number of human beings assembled with a common purpose was an estimated 15 000 000 at the Hindu festival of Kumbh mela, which was held at the confluence of the Yamuna (formerly called the Jumna), the Ganges and the invisible 'Saraswathi' at Allahabad, Uttar Pradesh, India on 6 Feb 1989.

Largest funerals ■ The funeral of the charismatic C. N. Annadurai (d. 3 Feb 1969), Madras Chief Minister, was, according to a police estimate, attended by 15 million. The longest funeral in Britain was probably that of Vice Admiral Viscount Nelson on 9 Jan 1806. Ticket-holders were seated in St Paul's Cathedral by 8.30 a.m. Many were unable to leave until after 9 p.m. The queue at the grave of the Russian chansonnier and guitarist Vladimir Visotsky (d. 28 Jul 1980), stretched 10 km *6·2 miles*.

P T E R   11

Most prolific scorer
Michael Jordan (b. 17 Feb 1963) of the Chicago Bulls is the current scoring ace in the National Basketball Association and his career average points per game 32·6 (11 263 points in 345 games, 1984-9) is the highest for all players who have scored 10 000 + points, although his career is unfinished. During the 1986-7 season, Jordan scored the 3rd highest ever season total of 3041 points with a 5th highest ever season average of 37·1. Both these records have only been surpassed by one person, Wilt Chamberlain, whose overall career average was 30·1 points. Chamberlain was the fastest to score 10 000 points taking 236 games and Jordan was second fastest, scoring his 10 000th point on 25 Jan 1989 during his 303rd game. (Photo: All-Sport/Rick Stewart)

General Records

Origins ■ Sport stems from the time when self-preservation ceased to be the all-consuming human preoccupation. Archery, although a hunting skill in Mesolithic times (by *c.* 8000 BC), did not become an organised sport until later, possibly as early as *c.* 1150 BC, as an archery competition is described in Homer's *Iliad*, and certainly by *c.* AD 300, among the Genoese. The earliest dated evidence is *c.* 2750–2600 BC for wrestling. Ball games by girls depicted on Middle Kingdom murals at Beni Hasan, Egypt have been dated to *c.* 2050 BC.

Fastest ■ The highest speed reached in a non-mechanical sport is in sky-diving, in which a speed of 298 km/h *185 mph* is attained in a head-down free-falling position, even in the lower atmosphere. In delayed drops speeds of 1005 km/h *625 mph* have been recorded at high, rarefied altitudes. The highest projectile speed in any moving ball game is *c.* 302 km/h *188 mph* in pelota. This compares with 273 km/h *170 mph* (electronically timed) for a golf ball driven off a tee.

Slowest ■ In wrestling, before the rules were modified towards 'brighter wrestling', contestants could be locked in holds for so long that a single bout once lasted for 11 hr 40 min. In the extreme case of the 2 hr 41 min pull in the regimental tug o' war in Jubbulpore, India, on 12 Aug 1889, the winning team moved a net distance of 3·6 m *12 ft* at an average speed of 0·00135 km/h *0·00084 mph*.

Longest ■ The most protracted human-powered sporting event is the *Tour de France* cycling race. In 1926 this was over 5743 km *3569 miles*, lasting 29 days, but the duration is now reduced to 21 days.

Largest pitch ■ For any ball game, is that of polo, with 12·4 acres *5 ha*, or a maximum length of 300 yd *274 m* and a width, without side boards, of 200 yd *182 m*. With boards the width is 160 yd *146 m*. Twice a year in the Parish of St Columb Major, Cornwall, a game called hurling (not to be confused with the Irish game) is played on a 'pitch' which consists of the entire parish, approximately 25 square miles *64·7 km²*.

World record breakers *Youngest* ■ The youngest at which anybody has broken a non-mechanical world record is 12 yr 298 days for Gertrude Caroline Ederle (USA) (b. 23 Oct 1906) with 13 min 19·0 sec for women's 880 yd freestyle swimming at Indianapolis, USA on 17 Aug 1919.

Oldest ■ Gerhard Weidner (West Germany) (b. 15 Mar 1933) set a 20-mile walk record on 25 May 1974, aged 41 yr 71 days, the oldest to set an official world record recognised by an international governing body. Lee Chin-yong (South Korea) (b. 15 Aug 1925) was 62 yr 273 days when he broke the consecutive chins record on 14 May 1988.

Most prolific ■ Between 24 Jan 1970 and 1 Nov 1977 Vasiliy Alekseyev (USSR) (b. 7 Jan 1942) broke 80 official world records in weightlifting.

Champion *Youngest* ■ The youngest successful competitor in a world title event was a French boy, whose name is not recorded, who coxed the Netherlands' Olympic pair at Paris on 26 Aug 1900. He was not more than ten and may have been as young as seven. The youngest individual Olympic winner was Marjorie Gestring (USA) (b. 18 Nov 1922), who took the springboard diving title at the age of 13 yr 268 days at the Olympic Games in Berlin on 12 Aug 1936.

Oldest ■ Oscar Gomer Swahn (Sweden) (1847–1927) was aged 64 yr 258 days when he won a gold medal in the 1912 Olympic Running Deer team shooting competition.

Youngest international ■ The youngest at which any person has won international honours is aged eight in the case of Joy Foster, the Jamaican singles and mixed doubles table tennis champion in 1958.

British ■ Diver Beverley Williams (b. 5 Jan 1957) was 10 yr 268 days old when she competed against the USA at Crystal Palace, London on 30 Sep 1967.

Oldest competitor at major games ■ William Edward Pattimore (b. 1 Mar 1892) competed for Wales at bowls at the 1970 Commonwealth Games in Edinburgh at the age of 78, the oldest competitor at such an international event open to competitors of all ages.

Britain's oldest Olympian was Hilda Lorna Johnstone (b. 4 Sep 1902) who was 70 yr 5 days when she was placed twelfth in the Dressage competition at the 1972 Olympic Games.

Most versatile ■ Charlotte 'Lottie' Dod (1871–1960) won the Wimbledon singles tennis title five times between 1887 and 1893, the British Ladies' Golf Championship in 1904, an Olympic silver medal for archery in 1908, and represented England at hockey in 1899. She also excelled at skating and tobogganing.

Mildred 'Babe' Zaharias (*née* Didrikson) (1914–56) (USA) won two gold medals (80 m hurdles and

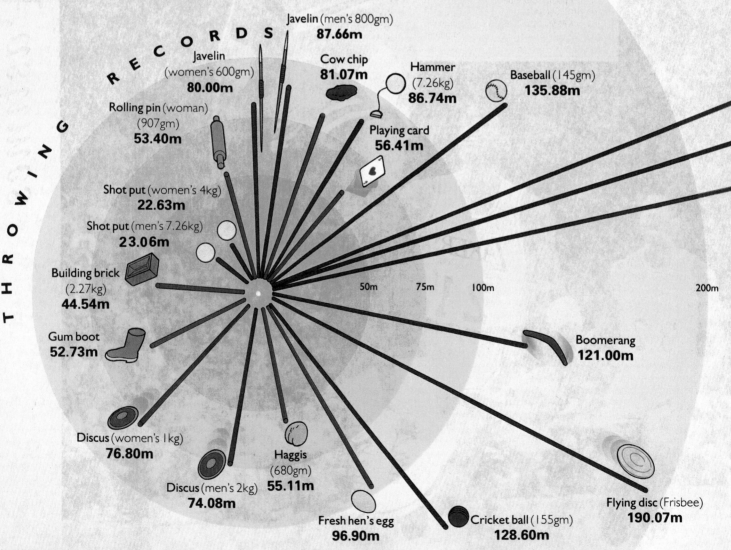

THROWING RECORDS

Javelin (men's 800gm)
87.66m

Javelin (women's 600gm)
80.00m

Cow chip
81.07m

Hammer (7.26kg)
86.74m

Baseball (145gm)
135.88m

Rolling pin (woman) (907gm)
53.40m

Playing card
56.41m

Shot put (women's 4kg)
22.63m

Shot put (men's 7.26kg)
23.06m

Building brick (2.27kg)
44.54m

Gum boot
52.73m

Boomerang
121.00m

50m   75m   100m   200m

Discus (women's 1kg)
76.80m

Haggis (680gm)
55.11m

Discus (men's 2kg)
74.08m

Fresh hen's egg
96.90m

Cricket ball (155gm)
128.60m

Flying disc (Frisbee)
190.07m

Artwork: Drawing Attention - Rhoda & Robert Burns

javelin) and a silver (high jump) at the 1932 Olympic Games. She set world records at those three events in 1930-2. She was an All-American basketball player for three years and set the world record for throwing the baseball 90·22 m *296 ft*. Switching to golf she won the US Women's Amateur title in 1946 and the US Women's Open in 1948, 1950 and 1954. She also excelled at several other sports.

Charles Burgess Fry (GB) (1872-1956) was probably the most versatile male sportsman at the highest level. On 4 Mar 1893 he equalled the world long jump record of 7·17 m *23 ft 6½ in*. He represented England v. Ireland at soccer (1901) and played first-class rugby for the Barbarians. His greatest achievements, however, were at cricket, where he headed the English batting averages in six seasons and captained England in 1912. He was also an excellent angler and tennis player.

Longest reign ■ Jacques Edmond Barre (France) (1802-73) was a world champion for 33 years (1829-62) at real tennis. Although archer Alice Blanche Legh (1855-1948) did not compete every year, she was a British champion for a span of 41 years (1881-1922), during which she won 23 national titles, the last when she was aged 67.

Heaviest sportsman ■ Professional wrestler William J. Cobb of Macon, Georgia, USA, who in

Olympic ■ The total attendance at the 1984 Summer Games was given as 5 797 923 for all sports, including 1 421 627 for soccer and 1 129 465 for track and field athletics.

Single sporting venue ■ 'More than 400 000' travel to the annual *Grand Prix d'Endurance* motor race on the Sarthe circuit near Le Mans, France.

Stadium ■ A crowd of 199 854 attended the Brazil v. Uruguay soccer match, in the Maracaña Municipal Stadium, Rio de Janeiro, Brazil on 16 Jul 1950.

Most participants ■ The Examiner Bay to Breakers 12·2 km *7·6 mile* race in San Francisco, California, USA is contested annually by 100 000 runners. Including unregistered athletes, an estimated 110 000 took part on 15 May 1988. The 1988 Women's International Bowling Congress Championship tournament attracted 77 735 bowlers for the 96-day event held 31 Mar-4 Jul at Reno/Carson City, Nevada, USA.

Gymnastics/Aerobics display ■ The annual Czechoslovak Spartakiad features gymnastics displays by about 180 000 participants. Held at the Strahov Stadium, Prague, there are 200 000 spectators for each of the four days. On the six hectare infield there are markers for 13 824 gymnasts at a time.

Worst disasters ■ In recent history, an estimated

Aerobatics

Origins ■ The first aerobatic 'manoeuvre' is generally considered to be the sustained inverted flight in a Bleriot of Célestin-Adolphe Pégoud (1889 – 1915), at Buc, France on 21 Sep 1913, but Lt Peter Nikolayevich Nesterov (1887-1914), of the Imperial Russian Air Service, performed a loop in a Nieuport Type IV monoplane at Kiev, USSR on 27 Aug 1913.

World Championships ■ Held biennially since 1960 (except 1974), scoring is based on the system devised by Col. José Aresti of Spain. The competition consists of two compulsory and two free programmes. The men's team competition has been won a record six times by the USSR. Petr Jirmus (Czechoslovakia) is the only man to become world champion twice, in 1984 and 1986. Betty Stewart (USA) won the women's competition in 1980 and 1982. Lyubov Nemkova (USSR) won a record five medals: first in 1986, second in 1982 and 1984 and third in 1976 and 1978. The only medal achieved by Britain has been a bronze in the team event at Kiev, USSR in 1976. The highest individual placing by a Briton is fourth by Neil Williams (1935-77) in 1976.

Inverted flight ■ The duration record is 4 hr 9 min 5 sec by John 'Hal' McClain in a Swick Taylorcraft on 23 Aug 1980 over Houston International Raceways, Texas, USA.

Loops ■ On 21 Jun 1980, R. Steven Powell performed 2315 ⅝ inside loops in a Bellanca Decathalon over Almont, Michigan, USA. John McClain achieved 180 outside loops in Bellanca Super Decathalon on 2 Sep 1978 over Houston, Texas, USA.

·Brian Lecomber completed 180 consecutive inside loops in a Jaguar Extra 230 on 29 Jul 1988 over Plymouth, Devon.

American Football

Origins ■ American football, a direct descendant of the British games of soccer and rugby, evolved at American universities in the 19th century. The first match under the Harvard Rules was played by Harvard against McGill University of Montreal at Cambridge, Massachusetts, USA in 1874. The Intercollegiate Football Association was founded in 1876. The professional game dates from August 1895 when Latrobe played Jeanette at Latrobe, Pennsylvania, USA. The American Professional Football Association was formed in 1919. This became the National Football League (NFL) in 1922. The American Football League (AFL) was formed in 1960; the NFL and AFL merged in 1970.

Super Bowl ■ First held in 1967 between the winners of the NFL and the AFL. Since 1970 it has been contested by the winners of the National and American Conferences of the NFL. Pittsburgh Steelers have most wins, four, 1975-6 and 1979-80. The highest aggregate score was in 1979 when Pittsburgh beat Dallas Cowboys 35-31. The highest team score and record victory margin was when the Chicago Bears beat the New England Patriots 46-10 at New Orleans, Louisiana on 26 Jan 1986. In their 42-10 victory over the Denver Broncos on 31 Jan 1988, the Washington Redskins scored a record 35 points in the second quarter. The Green Bay Packers won a record 11 NFL titles between 1929 and 1967.

Highest team score ■ Georgia Tech, Atlanta, Georgia scored 222 points, including a record 32 touchdowns, against Cumberland University, Lebanon, Tennessee (nil) on 7 Oct 1916.

In Britain ■ The premier competition is the Budweiser Bowl which was inaugurated in 1986. It has been won a record two times by the London Ravens, 1986 and 1987.

Highest score ■ The East Kent Cougars, based in Folkestone, beat the Maidstone M20's, 148-6 at Mote Park, Maidstone, Kent on 15 May 1988.

Flying ring
383.13m

Catapult shot
415.00m

Sling-shot (56.5gm)
437.13m

300m

400m

1962 was billed as 'Happy Humphrey', weighed 363 kg (*802 lb 57 st 4 lb*). The heaviest player of a ball-game was Bob Pointer, the 221 kg *487 lb* US Football tackle formerly on the 1967 Santa Barbara High School Team, California, USA.

Largest contract ■ In March 1982, the National Football League concluded a deal worth $2000 million for five years' coverage of American Football by the three major TV networks, ABC, CBS and NBC. This represented $14·2 million for each League team.

Largest crowd ■ The greatest number of live spectators for any sporting event is the estimated 2 500 000 who have lined the route of the New York Marathon. However, spread over three weeks, it is estimated that more than 10 000 000 see the annual *Tour de France* cycling race along the route.

604 were killed after stands at the Hong Kong Jockey Club racecourse collapsed and caught fire on 26 Feb 1918. During the reign of Antoninus Pius (AD 138-161) the upper wooden tiers in the Circus Maximus, Rome collapsed during a gladiatorial combat killing some 1112 spectators.

Britain ■ On 15 Apr 1989, 95 people were killed and 170 injured, at the Leppings Lane end of Hillsborough Stadium, Sheffield, South Yorkshire, through overcrowding just after the start of the FA Cup semi-final between Liverpool and Nottingham Forest.

GUINNESS HAVE PUBLISHED **THE ENCYCLOPAEDIA OF SPORTS RECORDS & RESULTS** PETER MATTHEWS AND IAN MORRISON **£9.95**

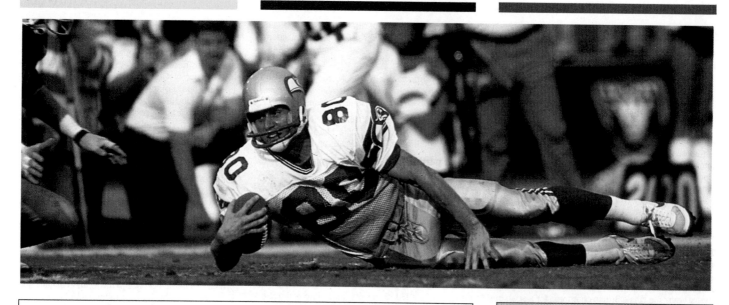

SUPER BOWL INDIVIDUAL RECORDS

POINTS 18	Roger Craig (San Francisco 49ers) 1985
TOUCHDOWNS 3	Roger Craig (San Francisco 49ers) 1985
YARDS GAINED RUSHING 204	Timmy Smith (Washington Redskins) 1988
YARDS GAINED PASSING 357	Joe Montana (San Francisco 49ers) 1989
YARDS GAINED RECEIVING 215	Jerry Rice (San Francisco 49ers) 1989
PASSES COMPLETED 29	Dan Marino (Miami Dolphins) 1985
PASS RECEPTIONS 11	Dan Ross (Cincinnati Bengals) 1982
	Jerry Rice (San Francisco 49ers) 1989
FIELD GOALS 4	Don Chandler (Green Bay Packers) 1968
	Ray Wersching (San Francisco 49ers) 1982

GUINNESS HAVE PUBLISHED **AMERICAN FOOTBALL:
RECORDS, FACTS AND CHAMPIONS** (5th EDITION)
PETER ROWE £8.95

Pass receptions ● (Above) Steve Largent of the Seattle Seahawks has made a career record 791 pass receptions, 1976–88. He also holds the record for having made a pass reception in the most consecutive games, 167, 1976–88. (Photo: All-Sport / Mike Powell)

Super Bowl XXIII ● (Below) The success of the San Francisco 49ers in beating the Cincinnati Bengals, 20–16 in Super Bowl XXIII at Miami on 22 Jan 1989, was mainly due to Joe Montana (b. 11 June 1956) (16) and Jerry Rice (b. 13 Oct 1962) (80). Rice caught a Super Bowl record equalling 11 pass receptions for a record 215 yards gained from Montana, who in total, threw for a record 357 passing yards. (Photo: All-Sport / Rick Stewart)

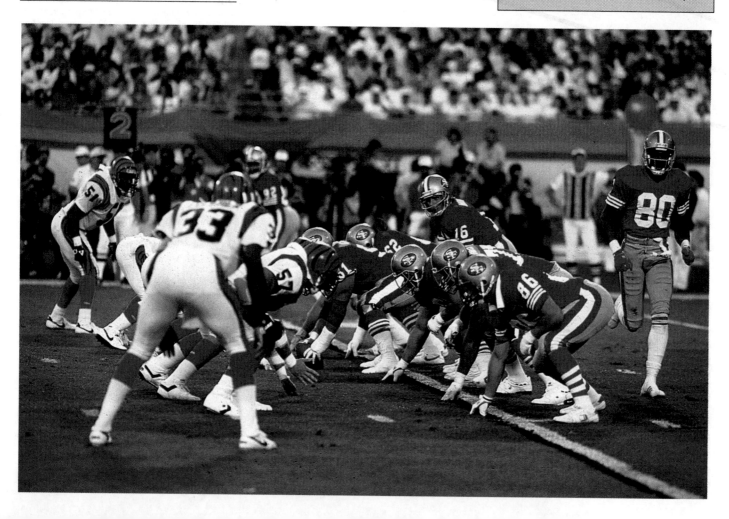

PROFESSIONAL RECORDS
(NFL 1920–87, AFL 1960–9)

MOST POINTS

Career 2002, George Blanda (Chicago Bears, Baltimore Colts, Houston Oilers, Oakland Raiders), 1949–75. **Season** 176, Paul Hornung (Green Bay Packers), 1960. **Game** 40, Ernie Nevers (Chicago Cardinals), 28 Nov 1929.

MOST TOUCHDOWNS

Career 126, Jim Brown (Cleveland Browns), 1957–65. **Season** 24, John Riggins (Washington Redskins), 1983. **Game** 6: Ernie Nevers (Chicago Cardinals), 28 Nov 1929; William 'Dub' Jones (Cleveland Browns) 25 Nov 1951; Gale Sayers (Chicago Bears), 12 Dec 1965.

MOST YARDS GAINED RUSHING

Career 16 726, Walter Payton (Chicago Bears), 1975–88. **Season** 2105, Eric Dickerson (Los Angeles Rams), 1984. **Game** 275, Walter Payton (Chicago Bears), 20 Nov 1977.

MOST YARDS GAINED PASSING

Career 47 003, Fran Tarkenton (Minnesota Vikings, New York Giants), 1961–78. **Season** 5084, Dan Marino (Miami Dolphins), 1984. **Game** 554, Norm Van Brocklin (Los Angeles Rams), 28 Sep 1951.

MOST PASSES COMPLETED

Career 3686, Fran Tarkenton (Minnesota Vikings, New York Giants), 1961–78. **Season** 378, Dan Marino (Miami Dolphins), 1986. **Game** 42, Richard Todd (New York Jets), 21 Sep 1980.

PASS RECEPTIONS

Career 759, Steve Largent (Seattle Seahawks), 1975–88. **Season** 106, Art Monk (Washington Redskins), 1984. **Game** 18, Tom Fears (Los Angeles Rams), 3 Dec 1950.

FIELD GOALS

Career 373, Jan Stenerud (Kansas City Chiefs, Green Bay Packers, Minnesota Vikings), 1967–85. **Season** 35, Ali Haji-Sheikh (New York Giants), 1983. **Game** 7, Jim Bakken (St Louis Cardinals), 24 Sep 1967.

Angling

Oldest existing club ■ The Ellem fishing club was formed by a number of Edinburgh and Berwickshire gentlemen in 1829. Its first annual general meeting was held on 29 Apr 1830.

Largest single catch ■ The largest officially ratified fish ever caught on a rod was a man-eating Great white shark (*Carcharodon carcharias*) weighing 1208 kg *2664 lb* and measuring 5·13 m *16 ft 10 in* long, caught on a 58 kg *130 lb* test line by Alf Dean at Denial Bay, near Ceduna, South Australia on 21 Apr 1959. A Great white shark weighing 1537 kg *3388 lb* was caught by Clive Green off Albany, Western Australia on 26 Apr 1976 but will remain unratified as whale meat was used as bait. The biggest ever rod-caught fish by a British angler is a 571·5 kg *1260 lb* Black marlin, by Edward A. Crutch off Cairns, Queensland, Australia on 19 Oct 1973.

In June 1978 a Great white shark measuring 6·2 m *20 ft 4 in* in length and weighing over 2268 kg *5 000 lb* was harpooned and landed by fishermen in the harbour of San Miguel, Azores.

The largest marine animal killed by *hand* harpoon was a Blue whale 29·56 m *97 ft* in length, by Archer Davidson in Twofold Bay, New South Wales, Australia in 1910. Its tail flukes measured 6·09 m *20 ft* across and its jaw bone 7·11 m *23 ft 4 in.*

The largest fish ever taken underwater was an 804 lb *364 kg* Giant black grouper or jewfish by Don Pinder of the Miami Triton Club, Florida, USA in 1955. The British spear-fishing record is 89 lb *40·36 kg* for an Angler fish by James Brown (Weymouth Association Divers) in 1969.

World Freshwater Championship ■ The *Confédération Internationale de la Pêche Sportive* (CIPS) championships were inaugurated as European championships in 1953 and recognised as World Championships in 1957. France won 12 times between 1956 and 1981 and Robert Tesse (France) took the individual title uniquely three times, in 1959–60, 1965. The record weight (team) is 34·71 kg *76·52 lb* in 3 hr by West Germany on the Neckar at Mannheim, West Germany on 21 Sep 1980. The individual record is 16·99 kg *37·45 lb* by Wolf-Rüdiger Kremkus (West Germany) at Mannheim on 20 Sep 1980. The most fish caught is 652 by Jacques Isenbaert (Belgium) at Dunajvaros, Yugoslavia on 27 Aug 1967.

Like father, like son ● Tony Pawson became the first Briton to win the World fly fishing championships at Salamanca, Spain in 1984. His son John emulated his fathers achievement in the 1988 championships. (Photo: Peter Gathercole)

Fly fishing ■ World fly fishing championships were inaugurated by the CIPS in 1981. The first British winner was Henry Anthony 'Tony' Pawson (b. 22 Aug 1921) at Salamanca, Spain in 1984. He also played amateur soccer for England and captained Oxford University at cricket.

British Championship ■ The National Angling Championship (instituted 1906) has been won seven times by Leeds (1909–10, 1914, 1928, 1948–9, 1952). James H. R. Bazley (Leeds) won the individual title twice (1909, 1927). Since 1972 the event has been split into divisions. Eddie Townsin (Cambridge) won the national title in 1967 and Div. 4 in 1982; Charlie Hibbs (Leigh) won Div. 2 in 1974 and 1984. The record catch is 34·72 kg *76 lb 9 oz* by David Burr (Rugby) in the Huntspill, Somerset in 1965. The largest single fish caught in the Championships is a carp of 6·41 kg *14 lb 2 oz* by John C. Essex on 13 Sep 1975 on the River Nene, Peterborough. The heaviest total produced by Division 1

BRITISH RECORDS—NATIONAL COARSE FISH
As recognised by the National Association of Specialist Anglers

Species	lb	oz	dr	kg	Name of Angler	Location	Date
BARBEL	14	6	–	6·52	A. D. Tryon	Royalty Fishery, Hampshire Avon	1934
BLEAK		4	4	0·12	B. Derrington	River Monnow, Wye Mouth	1982
BREAM, COMMON	16	6	–	7·43	Anthony Bromley	Private water, Staffordshire	1986
CARP	51	8	–	23·36	C. Yates	Redmire Pool, Herefordshire	1980
CARP, CRUCIAN	5	10	8	2·56	G. Halls	Lake near Kings Lynn, Norfolk	1976
CARP, GRASS	16	–	–	7·26	K. Crow	Lake near Canterbury, Kent	1986
CATFISH (WELS)	43	8	–	19·73	R. J. Bray	Wilstone Reservoir, Tring, Hertfordshire	1970
CHUB	8	4	–	3·74	G. F. Smith	Royalty Fishery, Hampshire Avon	1913
DACE	1	4	4	0·57	J. L. Gasson	Little Ouse, Thetford, Norfolk	1960
EEL	11	2	–	5·04	S. Terry	Kingfisher Lake, Ringwood, Hampshire	1978
GUDGEON		4	4	0·12	M. J. Brown	Fish Pond, Ebbw Vale, Gwent	1977
ORFE, GOLDEN	5	6	–	2·44	M. Foot	Kingsley, Hampshire	1978
PERCH	5	9	–	2·52	J. Shayler	Private water, Kent	1985
PIKE	44	14	–	20·35	Michael Linton	Ardleigh Reservoir, Essex	1987
ROACH	4	1	–	1·84	R. G. Jones	Gravel pit, Nottinghamshire	1975
RUDD *	4	8	–	2·04	Rev. E. C. Alston	Thetford, Norfolk	1933
RUFFE		5	4	0·148	R. J. Jenkins	West View Farm, Cumbria	1980
TENCH	14	3	–	6·43	Philip Gooriah	Wraysbury No.1 Reservoir, Berkshire	1987
WALLEYE	11	12	–	5·33	F. A. Adams	The Delph, Welney, Norfolk	1934
ZANDER	18	8	–	8·39	D. Litton	Cambridge stillwater	1988

Superior weight recognised by National Anglers' Council:
4 lb 10 oz, Dennis Webb at Pitsford Reservoir, Northamptonshire, 1986.

FRESHWATER GAME FISH
As recognised by the National Anglers' Council

	lb	oz	dr	kg	Name	Location	Date
SALMON	64	–	–	29·03	Miss G. W. Ballantine	River Tay, Scotland	1922
TROUT, AMERICAN BROOK	5	13	8	2·65	A. Pearson	Avington Fishery, Hampshire	1981
TROUT, BROWN	19	9	4	8·88	J. A. F. Jackson	Loch Quoich, Inverness	1978
TROUT, RAINBOW	21	4	4	9·64	D. Graham	Loch Awe, Argyll	1986
TROUT, SEA	20	2	–	9·13	V. R. Townsend	River Esk, Whitby, North Yorkshire	1986

WORLD RECORDS; FRESHWATER AND SALTWATER
A selection of All-Tackle records ratified by the International Game Fish Association as at January 1989

Species	Weight lb	oz	kg	Name of Angler	Location	Date	
BARRACUDA, GREAT	83	0	37·64	K. J. W. Hackett	Lagos, Nigeria	13 Jan	1952
BASS, EUROPEAN	20	11	9·40	Jean Baptiste Bayle	Stes Maries de la Mer, France	6 May	1986
BASS, LARGEMOUTH	22	4	10·09	George W. Perry	Montgomery Lake, Georgia, USA	2 Jun	1932
BASS, SMALLMOUTH	11	15	5·41	David L. Hayes	Dale Hollow Lake, Kentucky, USA	9 Jul	1955
BASS, STRIPED	78	8	35·60	Albert R. McReynolds	Atlantic City, New Jersey, USA	21 Sep	1982
BLUEFISH	31	12	14·40	James M. Hussey	Hatteras, North Carolina, USA	30 Jan	1972
BONEFISH	19	0	8·61	Brian W. Batchelor	Zululand, South Africa	26 May	1962
CATFISH, FLATHEAD	98	0	44·45	William O. Stephens	Lewisville, Texas, USA	2 Jun	1986
COD, ATLANTIC	98	12	44·79	Alphonse J. Bielevich	Isle of Shoals, New Hampshire, USA	8 Jun	1969
DOLPHIN	87	0	39·46	Manuel Salazar	Papagallo Gulf, Costa Rica	25 Sep	1976
HALIBUT (Pacific)	350	0	158·76	Vern S. Foster	Homer, Alaska, USA	30 Jun	1982
JACK, CREVALLE	54	7	24·69	Thomas F. Gibson Jr	Port Michel, Gabon	15 Jan	1982
JEWFISH	680	0	308·44	Lynn Joyner	Fernandina Beach, Florida, USA	20 May	1961
MACKEREL, KING	90	0	40·82	Norton I. Thomton	Key West, Florida, USA	16 Feb	1976
MARLIN, BLACK	1560	0	707·61	Alfred C. Glassell Jr	Cabo Blanco, Peru	4 Aug	1953
MARLIN, BLUE (Atlantic)	1282	0	581·51	Larry Martin	St Thomas, Virgin Islands	6 Aug	1977
MARLIN, BLUE (Pacific)	1376	0	624·14	Jay Wm de Beaubien	Kaaiwi Point, Kona Coast, Hawaii, USA	31 May	1982
MARLIN, STRIPED	494	0	224·10	Bill Boniface	Tutukaka, New Zealand	16 Jan	1986
MARLIN, WHITE	181	14	82·50	Evandro Luiz Coser	Vitoria, Brazil	8 Dec	1979
MUSKELLUNGE	69	15	31·72	Arthur Lawton	St Lawrence River, New York, USA	22 Sep	1957
PIKE, NORTHERN	55	1	25·00	Lothar Louis	Lake of Grefeern, West Germany	16 Oct	1986
SAILFISH (Atlantic)	128	1	58·10	Harm Steyn	Luanda, Angola	27 Mar	1974
SAILFISH (Pacific)	221	0	100·24	C. W. Stewart	Santa Cruz Island, Ecuador	12 Feb	1947
SALMON, ATLANTIC	79	2	35·89	Henrik Henriksen	Tana River, Norway		1928
SALMON, CHINOOK	97	4	44·11	Les Anderson	Kenia River, Alaska, USA	17 May	1985
SALMON, COHO	31	0	14·06	Mrs Lee Halberg	Cowichan Bay, BC, Canada	11 Oct	1947
SHARK, HAMMERHEAD	991	0	449·50	Allen Ogle	Sarasota, Florida, USA	30 May	1982
SHARK, MAKO	1115	0	505·76	Patrick Guillanton	Black River, Mauritius	16 Nov	1988
SHARK, PORBEAGLE	465	0	210·92	Jorge Potier	Padstow, Cornwall, England	23 Jul	1976
SHARK, THRESHER	802	0	363·80	Dianne North	Tutukaka, New Zealand	8 Feb	1981
SHARK, TIGER	1780	0	807·40	Walter Maxwell	Cherry Grove, South Carolina, USA	14 Jun	1964
SHARK, WHITE	2664	0	1208·38	Alfred Dean	Ceduna, South Australia	21 Apr	1959
SNAPPER, CUBERA	121	8	55·11	Mike Hebert	Cameron, Louisiana, USA	5 Jul	1982
SNOOK	53	10	24·32	Gilbert Ponzi	Parasmina Ranch, Costa Rica	18 Oct	1978
STURGEON	468	0	212·28	Joey Pallotta III	Benicia, California, USA	9 Jul	1983
SWORDFISH	1182	0	536·15	L. Marron	Iquique, Chile	7 May	1953
TARPON	283	0	128·36	M. Salazar	Lake Maracaibo, Venezuela	19 Mar	1956
TROUT, BROOK	14	8	6·57	Dr W. J. Cook	Nipigon River, Ontario, Canada	Jul	1916
TROUT, BROWN	35	15	16·30	Eugenio Cavaglia	Nahuel Huapi, Argentina	16 Dec	1952
TROUT, LAKE	65	0	29·48	Larry Daunis	Great Bear Lake, NWT, Canada	8 Aug	1970
TROUT, RAINBOW	42	2	19·10	David Robert White	Bell Island, Alaska, USA	22 Jun	1970
TUNA, BIGEYE (Pacific)	435	0	197·31	Dr Russel V. A. Lee	Cabo Blanco, Peru	17 Apr	1957
TUNA, BLUEFIN	1496	0	679·00	Ken Fraser	Aulds Cove, Nova Scotia, Canada	26 Oct	1979
TUNA, YELLOWFIN	388	12	176·35	Curt Wiesenhutter	San Benedicto Island, Mexico	1 Apr	1977
WAHOO	149	0	67·58	John Pirovano	Cat Cay, Bahamas	15 Jun	1962
WALLEYE	25	0	11·34	Mabry Harper	Old Hickory Lake, Tennessee, USA	1 Apr	1960

team champions is 63·99 kg *141·07 lb* by the 12-angler team from Nottingham Federation.

Casting ■ The longest freshwater cast ratified under ICF (International Casting Federation) rules is 175·01 m *574 ft 2 in* by Walter Kummerow (West Germany), for the Bait Distance Double-Handed 30 g event held at Lenzerheide, Switzerland in the 1968 Championships. The British national record is 148·78 m *488 ft 1 in* by Andy Dickison on the same occasion. At the currently contested weight of 17·7 g, known as 18 g Bait Distance, the longest Double-Handed cast is 139·31 m *457 ft ¹/₂ in* by Kevin Carriero (USA) at Toronto, Canada on 24 Jul 1984. The British National records are: Fixed spool reel, 138·79 m *455 ft 3 in* by Hugh Newton at Peterborough, Cambridgeshire on 21 Sep 1985; and Multiplier reel, 108·97 m *357 ft 6 in* by James Tomlinson at Torrington, Devon on 27 Apr 1985. The longest Fly Distance Double-Handed cast is 97·28 m *319 ft 1 in* by Wolfgang Feige (West Germany) at Toronto, Canada on 23 Jul 1984. Hywel Morgan set a

Britsh national record of 91·22 m *299 ft 2 in* at Torrington, Devon on 27 Apr 1985.

The UK Surfcasting Federation record (150 g *5¹/₄oz* weight) is 257·32 m *844 ft 3 in* by Neil Mackellow at Peterborough, Cambridgeshire on 1 Sep 1985.

IGFA World Records ■ The International Game Fish Association (IGFA) recognises world records for game fish—both freshwater and saltwater—for a large number of species of fish. Their thousands of categories include all-tackle, various line classes and tippet classes for fly fishing. New records recognised by the IGFA reached an annual peak of 1074 in 1984.

The heaviest freshwater category recognised by the IGFA is for the sturgeon - record weight of 212·28 kg *468 lb* caught by Joey Pallotta on 9 Jul 1983 off Benicia, California, USA.

Longest fight ■ The longest recorded individual fight with a fish is 32 hr 5 min by Donal Heatley

(New Zealand) (b. 1938) with a Black marlin (estimated length 6 m *20 ft* and weight 680 kg *1500 lb*) off Mayor Island off Tauranga, North Island, New Zealand on 21–22 Jan 1968. It towed the 12 tonne launch 80 km *50 miles* before breaking the line.

GUINNESS HAVE PUBLISHED **SEA FISHING** (2nd EDITION) BRIAN HARRIS £12.95

Archery

Origins ■ Though the earliest pictorial evidence of the existence of bows is seen in the Mesolithic cave paintings in Spain, archery as an organised sport appears to have developed in the 3rd century AD. Competitive archery may however date back to the 12th century BC. The oldest archery body in the British Isles is the Society of Archers in Yorkshire, formed on 14 May 1673, though the

Society of Kilwinning Archers, in Scotland, has contested the Pa-pingo Shoot since 1488. The world governing body is the *Fédération Internationale de Tir à l'Arc* (FITA), founded in 1931.

World Archery Records — Single FITA rounds

Event	Points	Name and Country	Possible	Year
MEN				
FITA	1341	Darrell Pace (USA)	1440	1979
90 m	329	Yuriy Leontyev (USSR)	360	1988
70 m	343	Tomi Poikolainen (Finland)	360	1988
50 m	345	Richard McKinney (USA)	360	1982
30 m	357	Takayoshi Matsushita (Japan)	360	1986
Team	3957	USA (Richard McKinney, Edwin Eliason, Jay Barrs)	4320	1988
WOMEN				
FITA	1352	Kim Soo-nyung (S. Korea)	1440	1988
70 m	330	Yelena Marfel (USSR)	360	1987
	330	Kim Soo-nyung (S. Korea)	360	1988
60 m	342	Lessia Schan (USSR)	360	1988
50 m	336	Kim Soo-nyung (S. Korea)	360	1988
30 m	356	Kim Soo-nyung (S. Korea)	360	1987
Team	3981	S. Korea (Kim Soo-nyung, Lee Hae-young, Kyung Wook-kim)	4320	1988

Indoor Double FITA rounds at 25 m

			Possible	Year
MEN	589	Darrell Pace (USA)	600	1985
WOMEN	588	Yelena Marfel (USSR)	600	1985

Indoor FITA round at 18 m

MEN	591	Vladimir Yescheyev (USSR)	600	1989
WOMEN	587	Denise Parker (USA)	600	1989

Highest championship scores ■ The highest scores achieved in either a World or Olympic championship for Double FITA rounds are: men, 2617 points (possible 2880) by Darrell Pace (USA) (b. 23 Oct 1956) and Richard McKinney (USA) (b. 20 Oct 1963) at Long Beach, California, USA on 21–22 Oct 1983; and women, 2683 points by Kim Soo-nyung (South Korea) (b. 5 Apr 1971) at Seoul, South Korea on 27–30 Sep 1988.

British records ■ York round – possible 1296 pts: Single round, 1168 Keith Muspratt at Cheshire Championships on 7 Aug 1988; Double round, 2254 Steven Hallard (b. 22 Feb 1965) at Lichfield, Staffordshire 8–9 Aug 1987.

Hereford (Women) – possible 1296 pts: Single round, 1202 Joanne Franks (b. 1 Oct 1967) in 1987; Double round, 2380 Joanne Franks on 8 Sep 1987.

FITA round (Men): Single round, 1312 Richard Priestman (b. 16 Jul 1955) at Hesperange, Luxembourg on 26 Jun 1988; Double round, 2604 Steven Hallard at Milan, Italy on 6 Sep 1988.

FITA round (Women): Single round, 1294 Joanne Franks at Geneva, Switzerland on 24 May 1988; Double round, 2571 Pauline Edwards on 27–30 Aug 1987.

Most titles *World (instituted 1931)* ■ The most ever won by a man is four by Hans Deutgen (Sweden) (b. 28 Feb 1917) in 1947–50 and by a woman is seven by Janina Spychajowa-Kurkowska (Poland) (b. 8 Feb 1901) in 1931–4, 1936, 1939 and 1947. Oscar Kessels (Belgium) (1904–68) participated in 21 world championships.

Olympic ■ Hubert van Innis (Belgium) (1866–61) won six gold and three silver medals at the 1900 and 1920 Olympic Games.

British ■ The greatest number is 12 by Horace Alfred Ford (1822–80) in 1849–59 and 1867, and 23 by Alice Blanche Legh (1855–1948) in 1881, 1886–92, 1895, 1898–1900, 1902–9, 1913 and 1921–2. Miss Legh was inhibited from winning from 1882 to 1885 – because her mother was champion – and for 4 further years 1915–18 because there were no Championships during World War I.

Greatest draw ■ Gary Sentman, of Roseberg,

British records ● Joanne Franks (b. 1 Oct 1967) holds numerous British archery records. (Photo: All-Sport/Russell Cheyne)

FLIGHT SHOOTING

CROSSBOW: 1871·84 m *2047 yd 2 in*, Harry Drake (USA) (b. 7 May 1915), 'Smith Creek' Flight Range near Austin, Nevada, USA, 30 Jul 1988.
UNLIMITED FOOTBOW: *Men*; 1854·40 m *1 mile 268 yd*, Harry Drake, Ivanpah Dry Lake, California, USA, 24 Oct 1971. *Female*; 1018·48 m *1113 yd 2 ft 6 in*, Arlyne Rhode (USA) (b. 4 May 1936), Wendover, Utah, USA, 10 Sep 1978.
HANDBOW: *Men*; 1222·01 m *1336 yd 1 ft 3 in*, Don Brown (USA), 'Smith Creek' Flight Range, 2 Aug 1987. *Women*; 950·39 m *1039 yd 1 ft 1 in*, April Moon (USA), Wendover, 13 Sep 1981.
CONVENTIONAL FOOTBOW: 1410·87 m *1542 yd 2 ft 10 in*, Harry Drake, Ivanpah Dry Lake, 6 Oct 1979.
COMPOUND BOW: *Men*; 1060·55 m *1159 yd 2 ft 6 in*, Bert McCune Jnr (USA), 'Smith Creek' Flight Range, 2 Aug 1987. *Women*; 738·30 m *807 yd 1 ft 3 in*, April Moon (USA), 'Smith Creek' Flight Range, 1 Aug 1987.
BROADHEAD FLIGHT BOWS: *Men*; 490·21 m *536 yd*, Arlan Reynolds (USA), Salt Lake City, Utah, USA, 27 Jun 1987. *Women*; 368·43 m *402 yd 2 ft 9 in*, April Moon (USA), Salt Lake City, 28 Jun 1987.

Oregon, USA drew a longbow weighing a record 79·83 kg *176 lb* to the maximum draw on the arrow of 72 cm *28¼ in* at Forksville, Pennsylvania, USA on 20 Sep 1975.

24 hours – target archery ■ The highest recorded score over 24 hours by a pair of archers is 65 055 during 60 Portsmouth Rounds (60 arrows per round at 20 yd at 60 cm FITA targets) by Mick Brown and Les Powici at Guildford, Surrey on 25–26 Mar 1989. Campbell Duffurn set an individual record of 31 355 in 58 Portsmouth Rounds at Evesham, Worcestershire on 28–29 Jan 1989.

Badminton

Origins ■ A similar game was played in China in the 2nd millennium BC. The modern game may have evolved c. 1870 at Badminton Hall in Avon,

the seat of the Dukes of Beaufort, or from a game played in India. The first modern rules were codified in Pune in 1876.

World team championships ■ The most wins at the men's International Championship for the Thomas Cup (instituted 1948) is eight by Indonesia (1958, 1961, 1964, 1970, 1973, 1976, 1979 and 1984). The most wins at the ladies' International Championship for the Uber Cup (instituted 1956) is five by Japan (1966, 1969, 1972, 1978 and 1981).

Most titles ■ The All-England Championships were instituted in 1899. The men's singles have been won eight times by Rudy Hartono Kurniawan (Indonesia) (b. 18 Aug 1948) in 1968–74 and 1976. The greatest number of titles won (including doubles) is 21 by George Alan Thomas (1881-1972) between 1903 and 1928. The women's singles were won ten times by Judy Hashman (*née* Devlin) (USA) (b. 22 Oct 1935) in 1954, 1957–8, 1960–4, 1966–7. She also equalled the greatest number of titles won of 17 by Meriel Lucas (later Mrs King Adams) from 1899 to 1910.

Shortest game ■ In the 1969 Uber Cup in Tokyo, Japan, Noriko Takagi (later Mrs Nakayama) (Japan) beat Poppy Tumengkol (Indonesia) in 9 min.

Longest rallies ■ In the men's singles final of the 1987 All-England Championships between Morten Frost (Denmark) and Icuk Sugiarto (Indonesia) there were two successive rallies of over 90 strokes.

Most shuttles ■ In the final of the Indian National Badminton Championships 1986, when Syed Modi beat Vimal Kumar 15–12, 15–12, 182 shuttles were used in the 66-minute period.

Baseball

Origins ■ The Reverend Thomas Wilson of Maidstone, Kent, wrote disapprovingly, in 1700, of baseball being played on Sundays. The earliest

Most scoreless innings ● Orel Leonard Hershiser IV (b. 16 Sep 1958) of the 1988 World Series winners, the Los Angeles Dodgers, pitched for a record 59 consecutive scoreless innings at the end of the regular season, 30 Aug–30 Sep 1988. Ironically the streak ended in the first innings of his first game of the 1989 season against the Cincinnatti Reds on 5 Apr 1989. (Photo: All-Sport/Budd Symes)

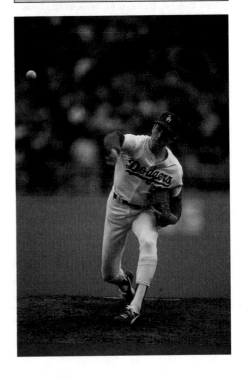

Baseball

US MAJOR LEAGUE RECORDS
AL American League
NL National League

BATTING

AVERAGE, Career, ·367 Tyrus Raymond Cobb (Detroit AL, Philadelphia AL) 1905–28. **Season**, ·438 Hugh Duffy (Boston NL) 1894.

RUNS, Career, 2245 Tyrus Raymond Cobb 1905–28.

HOME RUNS, Career*[1], 755 Henry 'Hank' Aaron (Milwaukee NL, Atlanta NL, Milwaukee AL) 1954–76. **Season**, 61 Roger Eugene Maris (New York NL) 1961.

RUNS BATTED IN, Career, 2297 Henry 'Hank' Aaron 1954–76. **Season**, 190 Lewis Rober 'Hack' Wilson (Chicago NL) 1930. **Game**, 12 James LeRoy Bottomley (St Louis NL) 16 Sep 1924. **Innings**, 7 Edward Cartwright (St Louis AL) 23 Sep 1890.

BASE HITS, Career, 4256 Peter Edward Rose (Cincinnati NL, Philadelphia NL) 1963–86. **Season**, 257 George Harold Sisler (St Louis AL) 1920.

TOTAL BASES, Career, 6856 Henry 'Hank' Aaron 1954–76. **Season**, 457 George Herman 'Babe' Ruth (New York AL) 1921.

HITS, Consecutive, 12 Michael Franklin 'Pinky' Higgins (Boston AL) 19–21 Jun 1938; Walter 'Moose' Dropo (Detroit AL) 14–15 Jul 1952.

CONSECUTIVE GAMES BATTED SAFELY, 56 Joseph Paul DiMaggio (New York AL) 15 May–16 Jul 1941.

STOLEN BASES, Career*[2], 938 Louis Clark Brock (Chicago NL, St Louis NL) 1961–79. **Season**, 130 Rickey Henley Henderson (Oakland AL) 1982.

CONSECUTIVE GAMES PLAYED*[3], 2130 Henry Louis 'Lou' Gehrig (New York AL) 1 Jun 1925–30 April 1939.

PITCHING

GAMES WON, Career, 511 Denton True 'Cy' Young (Cleveland NL, St Louis NL, Boston AL, Cleveland AL) 1890–1911. **Season**, 60 Charles Gardner Radbourn (Providence NL) 1884.

CONSECUTIVE GAMES WON, 24 Carl Owen Hubbell (New York NL) 1936–7.

SHUTOUTS, Career, 110 Walter Perry Johnson (Washington NL) 1907–27. **Season**, 16 George Washington Bradley (St Louis NL) 1876; Grover Cleveland Alexander (Philadelphia NL) 1916.

STRIKEOUTS, Career, 4919 Lynn Nolan Ryan (New York NL, California AL, Houston NL, Texas AL) 1968–89. **Season**, 383 Lynn Nolan Ryan (California AL) 1973. **Game (9 innings)**, 20 Roger Clemens (Boston AL) v. Seattle 29 Apr 1986.

NO-HIT GAMES, Career, 5 Lynn Nolan Ryan 1966–81.

EARNED RUN AVERAGE, Season, 0·90 Ferdinand Schupp (140 inns) (New York NL) 1916; 1·01 Hubert 'Dutch' Leonard (222 inns) (Boston AL) 1914; 1·12 Robert Gibson (305 inns) (St Louis NL) 1968.

COMPLETE GAMES, Career, 751 Denton True 'Cy' Young 1890–1911.

* *Japanese League records that are superior to those in the US major leagues;*
[1] *868 Sadaharu Oh (Yomiuri) 1959–80.*
[2] *1059 Yutaka Fukumoto (Hankyu) 1969–87.*
[3] *2215 Sachio Kinugasa (Hiroshima) 1970–87.*

baseball game under the Cartwright (Alexander Joy Cartwright Jr, 1820–92) rules was at Hoboken, New Jersey, USA on 19 Jun 1846, with the New York Nine beating the Knickerbockers 23–1 in four innings.

There are two major leagues in the USA: the National League (NL), formed on 2 Feb 1876 at the Grand Central Hotel, New York, and the American League (AL), formed on 28 Jan 1901.

Most home runs ■ Henry Louis 'Hank' Aaron (Milwaukee and Atlanta Braves) (b. 5 Feb 1934) holds the major league career home run record of 755, from 1954 to 1976. George Herman 'Babe' Ruth (1895–1948) has the highest home run percentage, 8·5 per cent for 714 home runs from 8399 times at bat, 1914–38. Joshua Gibson (1911–47) of Homestead Grays and Pittsburgh Crawfords, Negro League clubs, achieved a career total of nearly 800 homers including an unofficial total of 75 in 1931.

The US major league record for home runs in a season is 61 by Roger Eugene Maris (1934–85) for New York Yankees in 162 games in 1961. 'Babe' Ruth hit 60 in 154 games in 1927 for the New York Yankees. The most official home runs in minor leagues is 72 by Joe Bauman of Rosewell, New Mexico, USA in 1954.

Longest home run ■ In a minor league game at Emeryville Ball Park, California, USA on 4 Jul 1929, Roy Edward 'Dizzy' Carlyle (1900–56) hit a home run measured at 188·4 m *618 ft*. In 1919 'Babe' Ruth hit a 178·9 m *587 ft* homer in a Boston Red Sox v. New York Giants exhibition match at Tampa, Florida, USA.

Longest throw *(Ball weighs 141–148 g 5–5¼ oz)*: Men ■ Glen Edward Gorbous (b. Canada 8 Jul 1930) threw 135·88 m *445 ft 10 in* on 1 Aug 1957.

Women ■ Mildred Ella 'Babe' Didrikson (later Mrs Zaharias) (USA) (1914–56) threw 90·2 m *296 ft* at Jersey City, New Jersey, USA on 25 Jul 1931.

Fastest base runner ■ The fastest time for circling bases is 13·3 sec by Ernest Evar Swanson (1902–73) at Columbus, Ohio, USA in 1932, at an average speed of 29·70 km/h *18·45 mph*.

Fastest pitcher ■ Lynn Nolan Ryan (then of the California Angels) (b. 31 Jan 1947) was measured to pitch at 162·3 km/h *100·9 mph* at Anaheim Stadium, California, USA on 20 Aug 1974.

Youngest player ■ The youngest major league player of all time was the Cincinnati pitcher Joseph Henry Nuxhall (b. 30 Jul 1928), who played one game in June 1944, aged 15 yr 314 days. He did not play again in the NL until 1952.

Record attendances ■ The World Series record attendance is 420 784 (six games) when the Los Angeles Dodgers beat the Chicago White Sox 4–2 between 1 and 8 Oct 1959. The single game record is 92 706 for the fifth game at the Memorial Coliseum, Los Angeles, California, USA on 6 Oct 1959. The all-time season record for attendances for both leagues was 52 957 752 in 1988, including a record 28 497 310 for the American League.

An estimated 114 000 spectators watched a game between Australia and an American Services team in a demonstration event during the Olympic Games at Melbourne on 1 Dec 1956.

WORLD SERIES RECORDS
AL American League, NL National League

Most wins	**22** New York Yankees (AL)	1923–78
Most series played	**14** Lawrence Peter 'Yogi' Berra (New York, AL)	1947–63
Most home runs in a game	**3** George Herman 'Babe' Ruth (New York, AL)	6 Oct 1926
	3 Reginald Martinez Jackson (New York, AL)	18 Oct 1977
Only perfect pitch (in 9 innings)	Donald James Larson (New York, AL) v Brooklyn	8 Oct 1956

Basketball

Origins ■ The game of 'Pok-ta-Pok' was played in the 10th century BC, by the Olmecs in Mexico, and closely resembled basketball in its concept. 'Olla-malitzli' was a variation of this game played by the Aztecs in Mexico as late as the 16th century. If the solid rubber ball was put through a fixed stone ring the player was entitled to the clothing of all the spectators. Modern basketball (which may have been based on the German game *Korbball*) was devised by the Canadian-born Dr James A. Naismith (1861–1939) at the Training School of the International YMCA College at Springfield, Massachusetts, USA in mid-December 1891. The first game played under modified rules was on 20 Jan 1892. The International Amateur Basketball Federation (FIBA) was founded in 1932; it has now dropped the word Amateur from its title.

Most titles *Olympic* ■ The USA have won nine men's Olympic titles. From the time the sport was introduced to the Games in 1936 until 1972 they won 63 consecutive matches in the Olympic Games until they lost 50–51 to the USSR in the disputed Final match in Munich. They won eighth and ninth titles in 1976 and 1984. The women's title was won by the USSR in 1976 and 1980 and by the USA in 1984 and 1988.

World ■ The USSR has won most titles at both the men's World Championships (instituted 1950) with three (1967, 1974 and 1982) and women's (instituted 1953) with six (1959, 1964, 1967, 1971, 1975 and 1983).

European ■ The most wins in the European Nations Championships for men is 14 by the USSR, and in the women's event 20, also by the USSR, winning all but the 1958 championship since 1950, in this biennial contest. The most European Champions Cup (instituted 1957) wins is seven by Real Madrid, Spain 1964–5, 1967–8, 1974, 1978 and 1980. The women's title has been won 18 times by Daugawa Riga, Latvia, USSR between 1960 and 1982.

American professional ■ The most National Basketball Association (NBA) titles (instituted 1947), played for between the leading professional teams in the United States, have been won by the Boston Celtics with 16 victories between 1957 and 1986.

English ■ The most English National Championship titles (instituted 1936) have been won by London Central YMCA, with eight wins in 1957–8, 1960, 1962–4, 1967 and 1969. The English National League title has been won seven times by Crystal Palace 1974, 1976–8, 1980 and 1982–3. The most English Women's Cup titles (instituted 1965) have been won by the Tigers with eight wins, 1972–3, 1976–80 and 1982.

Highest score ■ In a senior international match Iraq scored 251 against Yemen (33) at New Delhi in November 1982 at the Asian Games. The highest in a British Championship is 125 by England v. Wales (54) on 1 Sep 1978. England beat Gibraltar 130–45 on 31 Aug 1978.

NBA ■ The highest aggregate score in an NBA match is 370 when the Detroit Pistons (186) beat the Denver Nuggets (184) in Denver on 13 Dec 1983. Overtime was played after a 145–145 tie in regulation time. The record in regulation time is 318, when Denver Nuggets beat San Antonio Spurs, 163–155 on 11 Jan 1984.

US College ■ The NCAA aggregate record is 331 when Loyola Marymount Lions (181) beat US International Gulls (150) on 31 Jan 1989. The highest score in a US college match is 210 by Essex County (Community) College when beating Englewood Cliffs College (67) on 20 Jan 1979.

United Kingdom ■ The highest score recorded in a match is 250 by the Nottingham YMCA Falcons v. Mansfield Pirates at Nottingham on 18 Jun 1974. It was a handicap competition and Mansfield received 120 points towards their total of 145. The highest score in a senior National League match is 167 by West Bromwich Kestrels *v.* Milton Keynes (69) on 13 Feb 1983. The highest in the National Cup is 146 by Doncaster *v.* Cleveland (109) on 11 Feb 1976.

Individual ■ Mats Wermelin, 13 (Sweden), scored all 272 points in a 272–0 win in a regional boys' tournament in Stockholm, Sweden on 5 Feb 1974. The highest single game score in an NBA game is 100 points by Wilton Norman Chamberlain (b. 21 Aug 1936) for Philadelphia *v.* New York on 2 Mar 1962. The record score by a woman is 156 points by Marie Boyd (now Eichler) of Central HS, Lonaconing, Maryland, USA in a 163–3 defeat of Ursaline Academy, Cumbria on 25 Feb 1924.

The highest score by a British player is 124 points by Paul Ogden for St Albans School, Oldham (226) *v.* South Chadderton (82) on 9 Mar 1982. The highest individual score in a league match in Britain is 108 by Lewis Young for Forth Steel in his team's 154–74 win over Stirling in the Scottish League Division One at Stirling on 2 Mar 1985. The record in an English National League (Div. One) or Cup match is 73 points by Terry Crosby (USA) for Home Spare Bolton in his team's 120–106 defeat by Cottrills Manchester Giants at Altrincham, Cheshire on 26 Jan 1985 and by Billy Hungrecker in a semi-final play-off for Worthing *v.* Plymouth at Worthing, West Sussex on 20 Mar 1988.

Most points ■ Kareem Abdul-Jabbar (formerly Lewis Ferdinand Alcindor) (b. 16 Apr 1947) scored an NBA career record 38 387 points, including a record 15 837 field goals, in a record 1560 games from 1969 to end of 1989 season for the Milwaukee Bucks and Los Angeles Lakers. He has also played a record 237 play-off games, scoring a record 5762 points including a record 2356 field goals.

The previous record holder, Wilt Chamberlain, had a record average of 30·1 points per game for his total of 31 419. He set a season's record 4029 for Philadelphia in 1962.

The records for the most points scored in a college career are (women): 4061, Pearl Moore of Francis Marion College, Florence, South Carolina, USA, 1975–9; (men): 4045 by Travis Grant for Kentucky State, USA in 1969–72. In the English National League, Ian Day (b. 16 May 1953) scored 3456 points in 203 games, 1973–84.

Tallest players ■ Suleiman Ali Nashnush (b. 1943) was reputed to be 2·45 m *8 ft* when he played for the Libyan team in 1962. Aleksandr Sizonenko of Kuibyshev Stroitel and USSR is 2·39 m *7 ft 10 in* tall.

The tallest woman player was Iuliana Semenova (USSR) (b. 9 Mar 1952) at a reported 2·18 m *7 ft 2 in* and weighing 127 kg *281 lb.*

British ■ Christopher Greener of London Latvians was 2·29 m *7 ft 6¼ in* and made his international debut for England *v.* France on 17 Dec 1969.

Shooting speed ■ The greatest goal-shooting demonstration has been by Ted St Martin of Jacksonville, Florida, USA who, on 25 Jun 1977, scored 2036 consecutive free throws.

In 24 hours Robert Browning scored 16 093 free throws from a total of 23 194 taken (69·38 per cent) at St Mark's School, Dallas, Texas, USA on 21–22 Nov 1987.

Steve Bontrager (USA) (b. 1 Mar 1959) of Polycell Kingston scored 21 points in a minute from seven positions in a demonstration for BBC TV's *Record Breakers* on 29 Oct 1986.

Longest goal ■ Bruce Morris scored a field goal, measured at 28·17 m *92 ft 5¼ in,* for Marshall University *v.* Appalachian State University at Huntington, West Virginia, USA on 8 Feb 1985.

British ■ A distance of 23·10 m *75 ft 9½ in* is claimed by David Tarbatt (b. 23 Jan 1949) of Altofts Aces *v.* Harrogate Demons at Featherstone, West Yorkshire on 27 Jan 1980.

NBA career ● Kareem Abdul-Jabbar retired at the end of the 1988/9 season and during his career with the Milwaukee Bucks (1969–75) and the Los Angeles Lakers (1975–89) set numerous NBA records. He retired on a high note taking part in his 10th NBA Finals series against the Detroit Pistons. (Photo: All-Sport/Mike Powell)

Billiards

Origins ■ The earliest recorded mention of billiards was in France in 1429, and Louis XI, King of France 1461–83, is reported to have had a billiard table. The first recorded public billiards room in England was the Piazza, Covent Garden, London, in the early part of the 19th century. Rubber cushions were introduced in 1835 and slate beds in 1836.

Most titles *Professional* ■ The greatest number of World Championships (instituted 1870) won by one player is eight by John Roberts Jr (GB) (1847–

1919) in 1870 (twice), 1871, 1875 (twice), 1877 and 1885 (twice). The greatest number of United Kingdom titles (instituted 1934) won is seven (1934–9 and 1947) by Joe Davis (1901–78), who also won four world titles (1928–30 and 1932).

Amateur ■ The record for world amateur titles is four by Robert James Percival Marshall (Australia) (b. 10 Apr 1910) in 1936, 1938, 1951 and 1962. The greatest number of English Amateur Championships (instituted 1888) won is 15 by Norman Dagley (b. 27 Jun 1930) in 1965–6, 1970–5, 1978–84. The record number of women's titles is eight by Vera Selby (b. 13 Mar 1930), 1970–8.

Professional and Amateur ■ Uniquely, Norman Dagley has won the English Amateur Championships (1965–6, 1970–5, 1978–84), World Amateur Championships (1971, 1975), United Kingdom Professional Championship (1987) and World Professional Championship (1987).

Highest breaks ■ Tom Reece (1873–1953) made an unfinished break of 499 135, including 249 152 cradle cannons (two points each) in 85 hr 49 min against Joe Chapman at Burroughes' Hall, Soho Square, London between 3 Jun and 6 Jul 1907. This was not recognised because press and public were not continuously present. The highest certified break made by the anchor cannon is 42 746 by William Cook (England) from 29 May to 7 Jun 1907. The official world record under the then baulk-line rule is 1784 by Joe Davis in the United Kingdom Championship on 29 May 1936. Walter Albert Lindrum (Australia) (1898–1960) made an official break of 4137 in 2 hr 55 min against Joe Davis at Thurston's on 19–20 Jan 1932, before the baulk-line rule was in force. Davis had an unofficial personal best of 2502 (mostly pendulum cannons) in a match against Tom Newman (England) (1894–1943) in Manchester in 1930. The highest break recorded in amateur competition is 1149 by Michael Ferreira (India) at Calcutta, India on 15 Dec 1978. Under the more stringent 'two pot' rule, restored on 1 Jan 1983, the highest break is Ferreira's 962 unfinished in a tournament at Bombay, India on 29 Apr 1986.

Fastest century ■ Walter Lindrum made an unofficial 100 break in 27·5 sec in Australia on 10 Oct 1952. His official record is 100 in 46·0 sec set in Sydney, Australia in 1941.

3 CUSHION

Origins ■ This pocketless variation dates back to 1878. The world governing body, the *Union Mondiale de Billiard* (UMB), was formed in 1928.

Most titles ■ William F. Hoppe (USA) (1887–1959) won 51 billiards championships in all forms spanning the pre- and post- international era from 1906 to 1952.

UMB ■ Raymond Ceulemans (Belgium) (b. 12 Jul 1935) has won 19 (1963–6, 1968–73, 1975–81, 1983, 1985).

BAR BILLIARDS

Scoring rates ■ Keith Sheard scored 28 530 in

19 min 5 sec in a league game at the Crown and Thistle, Headington, Oxford on 9 Jul 1984. Sheard scored 1500 points in a minute on BBC TV's *Record Breakers* on 23 Sep 1986.

The highest score in 24 hours by a team of five is 1 506 570 by John Burrows, Kent Murray, Ray Hussey, Roy Buckle and Brian Ray of The Hour Glass, Sands, High Wycombe, Buckinghamshire on 26–27 Nov 1983.

Board Games

Origins ■ Forerunners of the game have been traced back to a dice and a board game found in excavations at Ur, dated to 3000 BC. Later the Romans played a game remarkably similar to the modern one. The name 'backgammon' is variously ascribed · to Welsh 'little battle', or Saxon 'back game'.

Shortest game ■ Alan Malcolm Beckerson (b. 21 Feb 1938) devised a game of just 16 throws in 1982.

CHESS

Origins ■ The game originated in ancient India under the name Chaturanga (literally 'four-corps' – an army game). The name chess is derived from the Persian word *shah* (a king or ruler). The earliest reference is from the Middle Persian Karnamak (*c.* AD 590–628), though in December 1972, two ivory chessmen were found in the Uzbek Soviet Republic datable to AD 200. It reached Britain in *c.* 1255. The *Fédération Internationale des Echecs* (FIDE) was established in 1924.

World Championships ■ World champions have been generally recognised since 1886. The longest undisputed tenure was 26 yr 337 days by Dr Emanuel Lasker (1868–1941) of Germany, from 1894 to 1921. The women's world championship title was held by Vera Francevna Menchik-Stevenson (USSR, later GB) (1906–44) from 1927 until her death, and was successfully defended a record seven times. Nona Terentievna Gaprindashvili (USSR) (b. 3 May 1941) held the title from 1962 to 1978 and defended successfully four times.

Team ■ The USSR has won the men's team title (Olympiad) a record 17 times and the women's title 11 times (every time entered) to 1988.

Youngest ■ Gary Kimovich Kasparov (USSR) (b. 13 Apr 1963) won the title on 9 Nov 1985 at 22 yr 210 days. Maya Grigoryevna Chiburdanidze (USSR) (b. 17 Jan 1961) won the women's title in 1978 when only 17.

Oldest ■ Wilhelm Steinitz (Austria) (1836–1900) was 58 yr 10 days when he lost his title to Lasker on 26 May 1894.

Most active ■ Anatoliy Yevgenyevich Karpov (USSR) (b. 23 May 1951) in his tenure as champion, 1975–85, averaged 45·2 competitive games per year, played in 32 tournaments and finished first in 26.

Most British titles ■ The most British titles have been won by Dr Jonathan Penrose (b. 7 Oct 1933) with ten titles in 1958–63, 1966–9. Rowena Mary Bruce (*née* Dew) (b. 15 May 1919) won 11 women's titles between 1937 and 1969. The first British player to attain official International Grand Master status was Anthony John Miles (b. 23 Apr 1955), on 24 Feb 1976.

Highest rating ■ Robert James 'Bobby' Fischer (USA) (b. 9 Mar 1943) is reckoned on the officially adopted Elo System to be the greatest Grand Master of all time with a 2785 rating. Gary Kasparov (USSR) at 2775 is currently the highest-rated player. The highest-rated woman player is Judit Polgar (Hungary) (b. 25 Jul 1976), at 2555. The top British player on the Elo list is Nigel David Short (b. 1 Jun 1965) on 2650. The top British woman is Susan Kathryn Arkell (*née* Walker) (b. 28 Oct 1965) on 2310.

Least games lost by a world champion ■ José Raúl Capablanca (Cuba) (1888–1942) lost only 34 games in his adult career, 1909–39. He was unbeaten from 10 Feb 1916 to 21 Mar 1924 and was world champion 1921–7.

Most opponents ■ The record for most consecutive games played is 663 by Vlastimil Hort (Czechoslovakia) (b. 12 Jan 1944) over 32 1/2 hours at Porz, West Germany on 5–6 Oct 1984. He played 60–100 opponents at a time, scoring over 80 per cent wins and averaging 30 moves per game. He also holds the record for most games simultaneously, 201 during 550 consecutive games of which he only lost ten, in Seltjarnes, Iceland on 23–24 Apr 1977. Eric G. J. Knoppert (Netherlands) (b. 20 Sep 1959) played 500 games of 10-minute chess against opponents averaging 2002 on the Elo scale on 13–16 Sep 1985. He scored 413 points (1 for win, 1/2 for draw), a success rate of 82·6 per cent.

Slowest and longest games ■ The slowest reported moving (before modern rules) in an official event is reputed to have been by Louis Paulsen (Germany) (1833–91) against Paul Charles Morphy (USA) (1837–84) on 29 Oct 1857. The game ended in a draw on move 56 after 15 hours of play of which Paulsen used most of the allotted time. Grand Master Friedrich Sämisch (Germany) (1896–1975) ran out of the allotted time (2 hr 30 min for 45 moves) after only 12 moves, in Prague, Czechoslovakia, in 1938.

The slowest move played, since time clocks were introduced, was at Vigo, Spain in 1980 when Francisco Trois (b. 3 Sep 1946) took 2 hr 20 min for his seventh move *v.* Luis M. C. P. Santos (b. 30 Jun 1955).

The Master game with most moves on record was one of 194 moves, when Eugene Martinovsky (USA) (b. 3 Oct 1931) drew with Vlastimil Jansa (Czechoslovakia) (b. 27 Nov 1942) at the Gausdal International, Norway in August 1987.

DRAUGHTS

Origins ■ Draughts, known as checkers in North America, has origins earlier than chess. It was played in Egypt in the second millennium BC. The earliest book on the game was by Antonio Torquemada of Valencia, Spain in 1547.

World champions ■ Walter Hellman (USA) (1916–75) won a record eight world titles during his tenure as world champion 1948–75. Dr Marion Tinsley (USA) (b. 3 Feb 1927), the current world champion, has been internationally undefeated in matchplay from 1947 to 1988.

British titles ■ The British Championship (biennial) was inaugurated in 1886 and has been won six times by Samuel Cohen (London) (1905–72), 1924, 1927, 1929, 1933, 1937 and 1939. John McGill (Kilbride) (b. 1936) won six Scottish titles between 1959 and 1974. William Edwards (b. 28 Jan 1915) of Abercynon, Wales won the English open title on a record five successive occasions – 1979, 1981, 1983, 1985 and 1987. In 1986, Andrew Knapp (b. 19 Oct 1966), on his first attempt, became at 19 yr 322 days the youngest ever winner of the English Amateur Championship (instituted 1910).

Youngest and oldest national champion ■ Asa A. Long (b. 20 Aug 1904) became the youngest US national champion, aged 18 yr 64 days, when he won in Boston, Massachusetts, USA on 23 Oct 1922. He became the oldest, aged 79 yr 334 days, when he won his sixth title in Tupelo, Mississippi, USA on 21 Jul 1984.

Most opponents ■ Charles Walker played a record 201 games simultaneously, winning 189 and drawing 12, at New Orleans Center, Louisiana, USA on 5 Nov 1988. Newell W. Banks (1887–1977) played 140 games simultaneously, winning 133 and drawing seven, in Chicago, Illinois in 1933. His playing time was 145 min, so averaging about one move per sec. In 1947 he played blindfold for 4 hr per day for 45 consecutive days, winning 1331 games, drawing 54 and losing only two, while playing six games at a time.

Longest and shortest games ■ In competition the prescribed rate of play is not less than 30 moves per hour with the average game lasting about 90 min. In 1958 a game between Dr Marion Tinsley (USA) and Derek Oldbury (GB) lasted 7 hr 30 min (played under the 5-minutes-a-move rule). The shortest possible game is one of 20 moves composed by Alan Malcolm Beckerson (GB) in 1977.

SCRABBLE® Crossword Game

Origins ■ The crossword game was invented by Alfred M. Butts in 1931 and was developed, refined and trademarked as Scrabble® Crossword Game by James Brunot in 1948.

Highest scores ■ The highest competitive game

score is 979 by Clive Spate (b. 16 Jan 1952) in December 1988. His opponent scored 274 and the margin of victory, 705 points, is also a record. His score included a single turn of 320 for the word 'WALTZING'. The highest competitive single turn score recorded, however, is 392 by Dr Saladin Karl Khoshnaw (of Kurdish origin) in Manchester in April 1982. He laid down 'CAZIQUES', which means 'native chiefs of West Indian aborigines'.

Most titles ■ British National Championships were instituted in 1971. Olive Behan, 1972 and 1975, and Philip Nelkon, 1978 and 1981, have won twice. The highest score in the Championship has been 1863 (three-game total) by Nigel Ingham in 1987.

SOLITAIRE

The shortest time taken to complete the game is 13·22 sec by Dorothy Clark at Williamwood High School, Clarkston, Glasgow on 10 Mar 1989.

BIGGEST BOARD GAME

The world's biggest board game, called Heartopoly, involved 4317 participants and stretched around the 403 m *440 yd* Flagler Dog Track in Miami, Florida, USA on 14–15 Sep 1985.

Bobsleigh and Tobogganing

Origins ■ The oldest known sledge is dated *c.* 6500 BC and came from Heinola, Finland. The

first known bobsleigh race took place at Davos, Switzerland in 1889. The International Federation of Bobsleigh and Tobogganing was formed in 1923, followed by the International Bobsleigh Federation in 1957.

Most titles *Olympic* **■** The Olympic four-man bob title (instituted 1924) has been won five times by Switzerland (1924, 1936, 1956, 1972 and 1988). The USA (1932, 1936), Switzerland (1948, 1980), Italy (1956, 1968), West Germany (1952, 1972) and GDR (1976, 1984) have won the Olympic two-man bob (instituted 1932) event twice. The most gold medals won by an individual is three by Meinhard Nehmer (GDR) (b. 13 Jun 1941) and Bernhard Germeshausen (GDR) (b. 21 Aug 1951) in the 1976 two-man, 1976 and 1980 four-man events. The most medals won is six (two gold, two silver, two bronze) by Eugenio Monti (Italy) (b. 23 Jan 1928), 1956 to 1968. The only British victory was at two-man bob in 1964 by the Hon. Robin Thomas Valerian Dixon (b. 21 Apr 1935) and Anthony James Dillon Nash (b. 18 Mar 1936).

World and Olympic **■** The world four-man bob title (instituted 1924) has been won 18 times by Switzerland (1924, 1936, 1939, 1947, 1954–7, 1971–3, 1975, 1982–3, 1986–9). Italy won the two-man title 14 times (1954, 1956–63, 1966, 1968–9, 1971 and 1975). Eugenio Monti was a member of eleven world championship crews, eight two-man and three four-man in 1957–68.

TOBOGGANING

Origins ■ The word toboggan comes from the Micmac American Indian word *tobaakan*. The St Moritz Tobogganing Club, Switzerland, founded in 1887, is the oldest toboggan club in the world. It is notable for being the home of the Cresta Run, which dates from 1884, and for the introduction of the one-man skeleton racing toboggan.

Cresta Run ■ The course is 1212·25 m *3977 ft* long with a drop of 157 m *514 ft* and the record is

50·91 sec (av. 85·72 km/h *53·27 mph*) by Franco Gansser of Switzerland on 22 Feb 1987. On 21 Feb 1986 Nico Baracchi (Switzerland) set a record from Junction (890·2 m *2920 ft*) of 41·58 sec.

The greatest number of wins in the Grand National (instituted 1885) is eight by the 1948 Olympic champion Nino Bibbia (Italy) (b. 9 Sep 1924) in 1960-4, 1966, 1968 and 1973. The greatest number of wins in the Curzon Cup (instituted 1910) is eight by Bibbia in 1950, 1957-8, 1960, 1962-4, and 1969. He thus won the double in 1960 and 1962-4.

LUGEING

In lugeing the rider adopts a sitting, as opposed to a prone, position. Official international competition began at Klosters, Switzerland in 1881. The first European championships were at Reichenberg, Germany in 1914 and the first World Championships at Oslo, Norway in 1953. The International Luge Federation was formed in 1957. Lugeing became an Olympic sport in 1964.

Most titles *World and Olympic* ■ The most successful riders in the World Championships have been Thomas Köhler (GDR) (b. 25 Jun 1940), who won the single-seater title in 1962, 1964 (Olympic), 1966 and 1967 and shared the two-seater title in 1967 and 1968 (Olympic), and Hans Rinn (GDR) (b. 19 Mar 1953), Olympic champion two-seater 1976 and 1980 and world champion at single-seater 1973 and 1977, two-seater 1977 and 1980. Margit Schumann (GDR) (b. 14 Sep 1952) has won five women's titles, 1973-5, 1976 (Olympic) and 1977. Steffi Walter *née* Martin (GDR) (b. 17 Sep 1962) became the first rider to win two Olympic single-seater luge titles, with victories at the women's event in 1984 and 1988.

Fastest speed ■ The highest recorded, photo-timed speed is 137·4 km/h *85·38 mph* by Asle Strand (Norway) at Tandådalens Linbana, Sälen, Sweden on 1 May 1982.

Bowling (Tenpin)

Origins ■ The ancient German game of nine-pins (*Heidenwerfen* – knock down pagans) was exported to the United States in the early 17th century. In 1841 the Connecticut State Legislature prohibited the game and other states followed. Eventually a tenth pin was added to evade the ban; but there is some evidence of ten pins being used in Suffolk about 300 years ago. The first body to standardise rules was the American Bowling Congress (ABC), established in New York on 9 Sep 1895.

World Championships ■ The World (*Fédération Internationale des Quilleurs*) Championships were instituted for men in 1954 and for women in 1963. The highest pinfall in the individual men's event is 5963 (in 28 games) by Ed Luther (USA) at Milwaukee, Wisconsin, USA on 28 Aug 1971. For the current schedule of 24 games the men's record is 5261 by Richard Clay 'Rick' Steelsmith (b. 1 Jun 1964) and women's record is 4894 by Sandra Jo Shiery (USA), both at Helsinki, Finland in June 1987.

Highest scores *World* ■ The highest individual score for three sanctioned games (possible 900) is 899 by Thomas Jordan (USA) (b. 27 Oct 1966) at Union, New Jersey, USA on 7 Mar 1989. The record by a woman is 864 by Jeanne Maiden (b. 10 Nov 1957) at Solon, Ohio, USA on 23 Nov 1986. The maximum 900 for a three-game series was achieved by Glenn Richard Allison (b. 22 May 1930) at the La Habra Bowl in Los Angeles, California, USA on 1 Jul 1982, but this was not recognised by the ABC due to the oiling patterns on the boards. It has been recorded five times in unsanctioned games – by Leon Bentley at Lorain, Ohio, USA on 26 Mar 1931; by Joe Sargent at Rochester, New York, USA in 1934; by Jim Murgie in Philadelphia, Pennsylvania, USA on 4 Feb 1937; by Bob Brown at Roseville Bowl, California, USA on 12 Apr 1980 and by John Strausbaugh at York, Pennsylvania, USA on 11 Jul 1987.

Such series must have consisted of 36 consecutive strikes (i.e. all pins down with one ball).

The record for consecutive strikes in sanctioned match play is 33, first achieved by John Pezzin (b. 1930) at Toledo, Ohio, USA on 4 Mar 1976. The highest number of sanctioned 300 games is 31 (to Apr 1988) by John Henry Wilcox (b. 19 Jan 1947) of Lewisburg, Pennsylvania, USA and James Johnson Jr (b. 17 Aug 1960) of Wilmington, Delaware, USA; the women's record is 14 by Jeanne Maiden.

The highest average for a season attained in sanctioned competition is 244 by Robert Learn Jr (b. 11 Apr 1962) of Erie, Pennsylvania, USA in 1987/8. The women's record is 232 by Patty Ann of Bloomington, Illinois, USA in 1983/4.

Great Britain ■ The British record for a three-game series is 806 by Philip Anthony Scammell (b. 8 May 1962) at Worthing, West Sussex on 26 Sep 1986. Army Sergeant Michael Langley scored 835 at S.H.A.P.E., Belgium on 15 Apr 1985. The maximum score for a single game of 300 has been achieved on several occasions. The first man to do so was Albert Kirkham (b. 1931) of Burslem, Staffordshire on 5 Dec 1965. The first woman was Georgina Wardle (b. 24 Jul 1948) at the Sheffield Bowl, South Yorkshire on 20 Jan 1985. The first person to achieve the feat twice is Patrick Duggan (b. 26 May 1944), in 1972 and 1986, both at Bexleyheath Bowl, Kent. The three-game series record for a woman player is 740 by Elizabeth Cullen at the Astra Bowl, RAF Brize Norton, Oxfordshire on 15 Mar 1983.

PBA records ■ Mark S. Roth (b. 10 Apr 1951) won a record $1 360 056 in Professional Bowlers Association (PBA) competition, with 36 PBA titles to 1988. Earl Roderick Anthony (b. 27 Apr 1938) was the first to win $1 million and won a record 41 PBA titles to 1986. The season's record earnings is $225 485 by Brian Voss (b. 4 Aug 1958) in 1988.

Largest bowling centre ■ The Fukuyama Bowl, Osaka, Japan has 144 lanes. The Tokyo World Lanes Centre, Japan, now closed, had 252 lanes.

Highest score – 24 hours ■ A team of six from Goulburn Ten Pin Bowling Alley scored 83 021 in 24 hours at Goulburn, Australia on 5-6 Nov 1988.

Bowls

Origins ■ Whilst bowling games date back some 7000 years, the game of bowls in recognisable form can be traced back to the 13th century in England. The Southampton Town Bowling was formed in 1299. A green dating back to 1294 is claimed by the Chesterfield Bowling Club. After falling into disrepute, the game was rescued by the bowlers of Scotland who, headed by William W. Mitchell (1803-84), framed the modern rules in 1848-9.

Most titles *World* ■ The only man to win two or more singles titles is David John Bryant (England) (b. 27 Oct 1931), who won in 1966, 1980 and 1988. With the triples 1980, and the Leonard trophy 1984 and 1988, he has won six World Championship gold medals. At Johannesburg, South Africa, in February 1976, the South African team achieved an unprecedented clean sweep of all four titles plus the team competition (Leonard Trophy). The Leonard Trophy has been won on a record three occasions by England: 1972, 1984 and 1988.

Elsie Wilke (New Zealand) won two women's singles titles, 1969 and 1974. Two Australian women have won three gold medals: Merle Richardson: fours 1977, singles and pairs 1985; and Dorothy Roche: triples 1985 and 1988, fours 1988.

English & British ■ The record number of English Bowls Association (founded 8 Jun 1903) championships is 16 won or shared by David Bryant, including six singles (1960, 1966, 1971-3, 1975), three pairs (1965, 1969, 1974), three triples (1966, 1977, 1985) and four fours championships (1957, 1968, 1969 and 1971). He has also won seven British Isles titles (four singles, one pairs, one triple, one fours) in the period 1957-86. The youngest ever EBA singles champion was David A. Holt (b. 9 Sep 1966) at 20 yr 346 days in 1987.

Highest score ■ In an international bowls match, Swaziland beat Japan by 63-1 during the World Championships at Melbourne, Australia on 16 Jan 1980.

Most eights ■ Freda Ehlers and Linda Bertram uniquely scored three consecutive eights in the Southern Transvaal pairs event at Johannesburg, South Africa on 30 Jan 1978.

International appearances ■ By any bowler is 78 by Syd Thompson (b. 29 Aug 1912) for Ireland, 1947-73 and David Bryant for England, 1958-87. Bryant also had 50 indoor caps. The youngest bowler to represent England was Gerard Anthony Smyth (b. 29 Dec 1960) at 20 yr 196 days on 13 Jul 1981.

INDOOR

The English Indoor Bowling Association became an autonomous body in 1971. Prior to that it was part of the English Bowling Association.

Championships ■ The four-corner international championship was first held in 1936. England has won a record 23 titles. The National Singles title (instituted 1960) has been won most often by David Bryant with nine wins between 1964 and 1983. David Bryant has won the World Indoor singles (instituted 1979) three times, 1979-81 and with Tony Allcock (b. 11 Jun 1955) has won the doubles (instituted 1986) three times, 1986-7, 1989.

The youngest EIBA singles champion, John Dunn (b. 6 Oct 1963), was 17 yr 117 days when he won in 1981.

Highest score ■ Joan Eggleton, Brenda King, Maureen Smith and Patricia Bain of Eastbourne & District Indoor Bowls Club beat a four from Egerton Park, 59-2 over 21 ends at Eastbourne, East Sussex on 7 Feb 1989. The greatest 'whitewash' is 55-0 by C. Hammond and B. Funnell against A. Wise and C. Lock in the second round of the EIBA National Pairs Championships on 17 Oct 1983 at The Angel, Tonbridge, Kent.

Boxing

Origins ■ The earliest prize-ring code of rules was formulated in England on 16 Aug 1743 by the champion pugilist Jack Broughton (1704–89), who reigned from 1734 to 1750. Boxing, which had in 1867 come under the Queensberry Rules formulated for John Sholto Douglas, 8th Marquess of Queensberry (1844–1900), was not established as a legal sport in Britain until after the ruling, *R. v. Roberts and Others*, of Mr Justice Grantham, following the death of Billy Smith (Murray Livingstone) due to a fight on 24 Apr 1901.

Longest fights ■ The longest recorded fight with gloves was between Andy Bowen of New Orleans (1867–94) and Jack Burke at New Orleans, Louisiana, USA on 6–7 Apr 1893. It lasted 110 rounds, 7 hr 19 min (9.15 p.m.–4.34 a.m.), and was declared a no contest (later changed to a draw). Bowen won an 85-round bout on 31 May 1893. The longest bare-knuckle fight was 6 hr 15 min between James Kelly and Jack Smith at Fiery Creek, Dalesford, Victoria, Australia on 3 Dec 1855. The greatest number of rounds was 276 in 4 hr 30 min when Jack Jones beat Patsy Tunney in Cheshire in 1825.

Shortest fights ■ There is a distinction between the quickest knock-out and the shortest fight. A knock-out in 10½ sec (including a 10 sec count) occurred on 23 Sep 1946, when Al Couture struck Ralph Walton while the latter was adjusting a gum shield in his corner at Lewiston, Maine, USA. If the time was accurately taken it is clear that Couture must have been more than half-way across the ring from his own corner at the opening bell. The shortest fight on record appears to be one in a Golden Gloves tournament at Minneapolis, Minnesota, USA on 4 Nov 1947, when Mike Collins floored Pat Brownson with the first punch and the contest was stopped, without a count, 4 sec after the bell.

The shortest world title fight was 45 sec, when Lloyd Honeyghan (b. 22 Apr 1960) beat Gene Hatcher in an IBF welterweight bout at Marbella, Spain on 30 Aug 1987. The shortest ever heavyweight world title fight was the James J. Jeffries (1875–1953)–Jack Finnegan bout at Detroit, USA on 6 Apr 1900, won by Jeffries in 55 sec. The shortest ever British title fight was one of 40 sec (including the count), when Dave Charnley knocked out David 'Darkie' Hughes in a lightweight championship defence in Nottingham on 20 Nov 1961.

Eugene Brown, on his professional debut, knocked out Ian Bockes of Hull at Leicester on 13 Mar 1989. The fight was officially stopped after '10 seconds of the first round'. Bockes got up after a count of six but the referee stopped the contest.

Most British titles ■ The most defences of a British heavyweight title is 14 by 'Bombardier' Billy Wells (1889–1967) from 1911 to 1919. The only British boxer to win three Lonsdale Belts outright was heavyweight Henry William Cooper (b. 3 May 1934). He retired after losing to Joe Bugner (b. Hungary, 13 Mar 1950), having held the British heavyweight title from 12 Jan 1959 to 28 May 1969 and from 24 Mar 1970 to 16 Mar 1971.

The fastest time to win a Lonsdale Belt, for three successive championship wins, is 203 days by Robert Dickie (b. 23 Jun 1964) at featherweight, 9 Apr–29 Oct 1986. The longest time for winning a Lonsdale belt outright is 8 yr 236 days by Kirkland Laing, 4 Apr 1979–26 Nov 1987.

Tallest ■ The tallest boxer to fight professionally was Gogea Mitu (b. 1914) of Romania in 1935. He was 2·33 m *7 ft 4 in* and weighed 148 kg *327 lb*. John Rankin, who won a fight in New Orleans, Louisiana, USA in November 1967, was reputedly also 2·33 m *7 ft 4 in*. Jim Culley, 'The Tipperary Giant', who fought as a boxer and wrestled in the 1940's is also reputed to have been 2·33 m *7 ft 4 in*.

Most fights without loss ■ Edward Henry (Harry) Greb (USA) (1894–1926) was unbeaten in a sequence of 178 bouts, but these included 117 'no

decision', of which five were unofficial losses, in 1916–23. Of boxers with complete records, Packey McFarland (USA) (1888–1936) had 97 fights (5 draws) in 1905–15 without a defeat. Pedro Carrasco (Spain) (b. 7 Nov 1943) won 83 consecutive fights from 22 April 1964 to 3 Sep 1970, drew once and had a further nine wins before his loss to Armando Ramos in a WBC lightweight contest on 18 Feb 1972.

Most knock-outs ■ The greatest number of finishes classed as 'knock-outs' in a career (1936–63) is 145 (129 in professional bouts) by Archie Moore (USA) (b. Archibald Lee Wright, 13 Dec 1913 or 1916). The record for consecutive KO's is 44 by Lamar Clark (USA) (b. 1 Dec 1934) from 1958 to 11 Jan 1960. He knocked out six in one night (five in the first round) at Bingham, Utah, USA on 1 Dec 1958.

Largest purse ■ The total purse for the world heavyweight fight between Mike Gerard Tyson (USA) (b. 30 Jun 1966) and Michael Spinks (USA) (b. 22 Jul 1956) at Convention Hall, Atlantic City, New Jersey, USA on 27 Jun 1988, was estimated as at least $35·8 million, $22 m for Tyson and $13·8 m for Spinks,

Earliest depiction of boxing ● Boxing with gloves was depicted on a fresco, from the Isle of Thera, Greece, which has been dated to 1520 BC. (Photo: Ancient Art & Architecture Collection)

who was knocked out after 1 min 31 sec of the first round.

Highest earnings in career ■ The greatest fortune amassed in a fighting career is an estimated $69 million by Muhammad Ali (USA) (b. 17 Jan 1942) from October 1960 to December 1981. This was from 61 fights (including exhibitions) comprising a total of 551 rounds.

Attendances *Highest* ■ The greatest paid attendance at any boxing fight has been 120 757 (with a ringside price of $27·50) for the Tunney v. Dempsey world heavyweight title fight at the Sesquicentennial Stadium, Philadelphia, Pennsylvania, USA on 23 Sep 1926.

The indoor record is 63 350 at the Ali v. Leon Spinks (b. 13 Jul 1956) fight in the Superdrome, New Orleans, Louisiana, USA on 15 Sep 1978. The British attendance record is 82 000 at the Len Harvey v. Jock McAvoy fight at White City, London on 10 Jul 1939.

The highest non-paying attendance is 135 132 at the Tony Zale v. Billy Pryor fight at Juneau Park, Milwaukee, Wisconsin, USA on 16 Aug 1941.

Lowest ■ The smallest attendance at a world heavyweight title fight was 2434 at the Clay v. Liston fight at Lewiston, Maine, USA on 25 May 1965.

WORLD HEAVYWEIGHT CHAMPIONS

Earliest title fight ■ The first world heavyweight title fight, with gloves and 3-min rounds, was that between John Lawrence Sullivan (1858–1918) and 'Gentleman' James John Corbett (1866–1933) in New Orleans, Louisiana, USA on 7 Sep 1892. Corbett won in 21 rounds.

Reign *Longest* ■ Joe Louis (USA) (b. Joseph Louis Barrow, 1914–81) was champion for 11 years 252 days, from 22 Jun 1937, when he knocked out James Joseph Braddock in the eighth round at Chicago, Illinois, USA, until announcing his retirement on 1 Mar 1949. During his reign Louis made a record 25 defences of his title.

Shortest ■ 83 days for WBA champion James 'Bonecrusher' Smith (USA) (b. 3 Apr 1955), 13 Dec 1986 to 7 Mar 1987, and for Ken Norton (USA) (b. 9 Aug 1945), recognised by the WBC as champion from 18 Mar–9 Jun 1978. Tony Tucker (USA) (b. 28 Dec 1958) was IBF champion for 64 days, 30 May–2 Aug 1987.

Most recaptures ■ Muhammad Ali (b. Cassius Marcellus Clay Jr, 17 Jan 1942) is the only man to regain the heavyweight championship twice. Ali first won the title on 25 Feb 1964 defeating Sonny Liston. He defeated George Foreman on 30 Oct 1974 having been stripped of the title by the world boxing authorities on 28 Apr 1967. He won the WBA title from Leon Spinks on 15 Sep 1978 having previously lost to him on 15 Feb 1978.

Undefeated ■ Rocky Marciano (b. Rocco Francis Marchegiano) (1923–69) is the only world heavyweight champion to have been undefeated during his entire professional career (1947–56). He won all his 49 fights, 43 by knock-outs or stoppages. Currently, Mike Tyson is undefeated, having won all 36 fights to June 1989.

Oldest ■ Jersey Joe Walcott (USA) (b. Arnold Raymond Cream, 31 Jan 1914) was 37 yr 168 days, when he knocked out Ezzard Mack Charles (1921–75) on 18 Jul 1951 in Pittsburgh, Pennsylvania, USA. He was also the oldest holder at 38 yr 236 days, losing his title to Rocky Marciano on 23 Sep 1952.

Youngest ■ Mike Tyson (USA) was 20 yr 144 days when he beat Trevor Berbick (USA) to win the WBC version at Las Vegas, Nevada, USA on 22 Nov 1986. He added the WBA title when he beat James 'Bonecrusher' Smith on 7 Mar 1987 at 20 yr 249 days. He became universal champion on 2 Aug 1987 when he beat Tony Tucker (USA) for the IBF title.

Heaviest ■ Primo Carnera (Italy) (1906–67), the 'Ambling Alp', who won the title from Jack Sharkey in New York City, NY, USA on 29 Jun 1933, scaled 118 kg *260½ lb* for this fight but his peak weight was 122 kg *270 lb*. He had an expanded chest

measurement of 137 cm *54 in* and the longest reach at 217 cm *85½ in* (fingertip to fingertip).

Lightest ■ Robert James 'Bob' Fitzsimmons (1863–1917), from Helston, Cornwall weighed 75 kg *167 lb*, when he won the title by knocking out James J. Corbett at Carson City, Nevada, USA on 17 Mar 1897.

Tallest ■ There is uncertainty as to the tallest world champion. Ernest Terrell (USA) (b. 4 Apr 1939), WBA champion 1965–7, was reported to be 1·98 m *6 ft 6 in*. Slightly higher figures had been given for earlier champions, but, according to measurements by the physical education director of the Hemingway Gymnasium, Harvard University, Primo Carnera was 1·966 m *6 ft 5·4 in*, although widely reported and believed to be up to 2·04 m *6 ft 8½ in*. Jess Willard (1881–1968), who won the title in 1915, often stated to be 1·99 m *6 ft 6¼ in*, was in fact 1·96 m *6 ft 5¼ in*.

Shortest ■ Tommy Burns, world champion from 23 Feb 1906 to 26 Dec 1908, stood 1·70 m *5 ft 7 in* and weighed between 76–81 kg *168–180 lb*.

Longest lived ■ Jack Dempsey, champion from 4 Jul 1919 to 23 Sep 1928, died aged 87 yr 341 days on 31 May 1983.

WORLD CHAMPIONS Any weight

Longest reign ■ Joe Louis's heavyweight duration record of 11 yr 252 days stands for all divisions.

Youngest ■ Wilfred Benitez (b. New York, 12 Sep 1958) of Puerto Rico, was 17 yr 176 days when he won the WBA light welterweight title in San Juan, Puerto Rico on 6 Mar 1976.

Oldest ■ Archie Moore, who was recognised as a light heavyweight champion up to 10 Feb 1962 when his title was removed, was then believed to be between 45 and 48.

Longest career ■ Bob Fitzsimmons had a career of over 31 years from 1883 to 1914. He had his last world title bout on 20 Dec 1905 at the age of 42 yr 208 days.

Longest fight ■ The longest world title fight (under Queensberry Rules) was that between the lightweights Joe Gans (1874–1910), of the USA, and Oscar Matthew 'Battling' Nelson (1882–1954), the 'Durable Dane', at Goldfield, Nevada, USA on 3 Sep 1906. It was terminated in the 42nd round when Gans was declared the winner on a foul.

Most different weights ■ The first to have won world titles at four weight categories was Thomas Hearns (USA) (b. 18 Oct 1958), WBA welterweight in 1980, WBC super welterweight in 1982, WBC light heavyweight in 1987 and WBC middleweight in 1987. He added a fifth weight division when he won the super middleweight title recognised by the newly created World Boxing Organisation (WBO) on 5 Nov 1988. Winning titles recognised by the two senior authorities, the WBA and WBC, Sugar Ray Leonard (USA) (b. 17 May 1956) won world titles at his fourth and fifth weight catego-

ries, when he beat Donny Lalonde (Canada) on 8 Nov 1988, to annex both WBC light heavyweight and super middleweight titles. He had previously won the WBC welterweight in 1979 and 1980, WBA junior middleweight in 1981 and WBC middleweight in 1987.

The only man to hold world titles at three weights *simultaneously* was Henry 'Homicide Hank' Armstrong (USA) (1912–88), at featherweight, lightweight and welterweight from August to December 1938.

Most recaptures ■ The only boxer to win a world title five times at one weight is 'Sugar' Ray Robinson (USA) (b. Walker Smith Jr, 1921–89), who beat Carmen Basilio (USA) in the Chicago Stadium on 25 Mar 1958, to regain the world middleweight title for the fourth time. The record number of title bouts in a career is 37, of which 18 ended in 'no decision', by three-time world welterweight champion Jack Britton (USA) (1885–1962) in 1915–22.

Greatest weight difference ■ When Primo Carnera (Italy) 122 kg *270 lb* fought Tommy Loughran (USA) 83 kg *184 lb* for the world heavyweight title at Miami, Florida, USA on 1 Mar 1934, there was a weight difference of 39 kg *86 lb* between the two fighters. Carnera won the fight on points.

Greatest 'tonnage' ■ The greatest 'tonnage' recorded in any fight is 317 kg *700 lb* when Claude 'Humphrey' McBride (Oklahoma), 154 kg *340 lb*, knocked out Jimmy Black (Houston), who weighed 163 kg *360 lb* in the third round at Oklahoma City on 1 Jun 1971. The greatest 'tonnage' in a world title fight was 221·5 kg *488 ¾ lb*, when Carnera, then 117·5 kg *259 ½ lb* fought Paolino Uzcudun (Spain) 104 kg *229 ¼ lb* in Rome, Italy on 22 Oct 1933.

Most knock-downs in title fights ■ Vic Toweel (South Africa) (b. 12 Jan 1929) knocked down Danny O'Sullivan of London 14 times in ten rounds in their world bantamweight fight at Johannesburg on 2 Dec 1950, before the latter retired.

Twins ■ When Khaokor Galaxy (Thailand) won the WBA bantamweight title on 8 May 1988, he and his twin brother, Khaosai, were the first twins ever to be world boxing champions. Khaosai Galaxy had been WBA super flyweight champion since 21 Nov 1984.

AMATEUR

Most Olympic titles ■ Only two boxers have won three Olympic gold medals: southpaw László Papp (Hungary) (b. 25 Mar 1926), middleweight 1948, light-middleweight 1952 and 1956; and Teofilo Stevenson (Cuba) (b. 23 Mar 1952), heavyweight 1972, 1976 and 1980. The only man to win two titles in one celebration was Oliver L. Kirk (USA), who won both bantam and featherweight titles in St Louis, Missouri, USA in 1904, but he needed only one bout in each class.

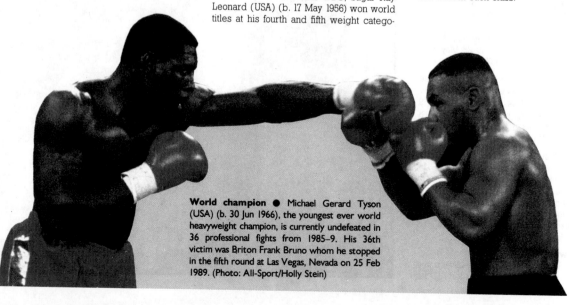

World champion ● Michael Gerard Tyson (USA) (b. 30 Jun 1966), the youngest ever world heavyweight champion, is currently undefeated in 36 professional fights from 1985–9. His 36th victim was Briton Frank Bruno whom he stopped in the fifth round at Las Vegas, Nevada on 25 Feb 1989. (Photo: All-Sport/Holly Stein)

Oldest gold medallist ■ Richard Kenneth Gunn (GB) (1871–1961) won the Olympic featherweight gold medal on 27 Oct 1908 in London aged 37 yr 254 days.

World Championships ■ Two boxers have won three world championships (instituted 1974): Teofilo Stevenson (Cuba), heavyweight 1974, 1978 and super-heavyweight 1986, and Adolfo Horta (Cuba) (b. 3 Oct 1957) bantam 1978, feather 1982 and light-weight 1986.

Most British titles ■ The greatest number of ABA titles won by any boxer is eight by John Lyon (b. 9 Mar 1962) at light-flyweight 1981–4 and at flyweight 1986–9. Alex 'Bud' Watson (b. 27 May 1914) of Leith, Scotland won the Scottish heavyweight title in 1938, 1942–3, and the light-heavyweight championship 1937–9, 1943–5 and 1947, making ten in all. He also won the ABA light-heavyweight title in 1945 and 1947.

Longest span ■ The greatest span of ABA title-winning performances is that of the heavyweight Hugh 'Pat' Floyd (b. 23 Aug 1910), who won in 1929 and gained his fourth title 17 years later in 1946.

Canoeing

The acknowledged pioneer of canoeing as a modern sport was John Macgregor (1825–92), a British barrister, in 1865. The Canoe Club was formed on 26 Jul 1866.

Most titles *Olympic* ■ Gert Fredriksson (Sweden) (b. 21 Nov 1919) won a record six Olympic gold medals, 1948–60. He added a silver and a bronze for a record eight medals. The most by a woman is three by Lyudmila Pinayeva (*née* Khvedosyuk) (USSR) (b. 14 Jan 1936), 1964–72 and Birgit Schmidt (*née* Fischer) (GDR) (b. 25 Feb 1962), one in 1980 and two in 1988. The most gold medals at one Games is three by Vladimir Parfenovich (USSR) (b. 2 Dec 1958) in 1980 and by Ian Ferguson (New Zealand) (b. 20 Jul 1952) in 1984.

World ■ Including the Olympic Games a women's record 22 titles have been won by Birgit Schmidt, 1978–88. The men's record is 13 by Gert Fredriksson, 1948–60, Rüdiger Helm (GDR) (b. 6 Oct 1956), 1976–83, and Ivan Patzaichin (Romania) (b. 26 Nov 1949), 1968–84. The most individual titles by a British canoeist is four by Richard Fox at K1 slalom in 1981, 1983, 1985 and 1989. Fox also won four gold medals at K1 team, between 1981 and 1987.

Highest speed ■ The Hungarian four-man kayak Olympic champions in 1988 at Seoul, South Korea covered 1000 m in 3 min 00.20 sec. This represents an average speed of 19.98 km/h *12.41 mph*. The USSR K4 during a 1000 m heat of the 1980 Olympics title achieved 21.15 km/h *13.14 mph* for the first 250 m.

Longest journey ■ Father and son Dana and Donald Starkell paddled from Winnipeg, Manitoba, Canada by ocean and river to Belem, Brazil, a distance of 19 603 km *12 181 miles* from 1 Jun 1980 to 1 May 1982. All portages were human powered.

Without portages or aid of any kind the longest is one of 9820 km *6102 miles* by Richard H. Grant and Ernest 'Moose' Lassy circumnavigating the eastern USA via Chicago, New Orleans, Miami, New York and the Great Lakes from 22 Sep 1930 to 15 Aug 1931.

Longest open sea voyage ■ Beatrice and John Dowd, Ken Beard and Steve Benson (Richard Gillett replaced him mid-journey) paddled 3491 km *2170 miles* (of a total 3527 km *2192 miles*) from Venezuela to Miami, Florida, USA, via the West Indies, 11 Aug 1977–29 Apr 1978 in two Klepper Aerius 20 kayaks.

English Channel ■ The singles record crossing is 3 hr 33 min 47 sec by Andrew William Dougall Samuel (b. 12 Jul 1937) of Glasgow, from Shakespeare Bay, Dover to Wissant, France on 5 Sep 1976. The doubles record is 2 hr 28 min 18 sec by Shaun

Rice (Ireland) and Colin Simpkins (South Africa) in a K2 on 19 Jul 1986 from Shakespeare Bay, Dover to Cap Gris Nez, France.

North Sea ■ On 22–23 Jun 1986, a team of five in the 'Canadian Club Challenge' paddled K1s from Zeebrugge, Belgium to Felixstowe, Suffolk, over 177 km *110 miles* across open sea, in 28 hr 56 min 12 sec.

Devizes–Westminister ■ The Senior Class record for the annual Challenge Cup race (instituted officially 1949) over 201 km *125 miles* with 76 locks on the River Thames is 15 hr 34 min 12 sec by Brian R. Greenham and Timothy J. Cornish (Reading/Leighton Park/Richmond) to win the 1979 race.

Loch Ness ■ The fastest time from Fort Augustus to Lochend (36.5 km *22.7 miles*) is 2 hr 58 min 48 sec by Colin Simpkins (South Africa) in a Jaguar K1 on 26 Jul 1987.

River Rhine ■ The fastest time, solo and unsupported, is 10 days 12 hr 9 min by Frank Palmer, 15–25 May 1988. The 'Rhine Challenge', as organised by the International Long River Canoeists Club, begins from an official marker post in Chur, Switzerland and ends at Willemstad, Holland, a distance of 1149 km *714 miles*.

Longest race ■ The Canadian Government Centennial Voyageur Canoe Pageant and Race from Rocky Mountain House, Alberta to the Expo 67 site at Montreal, Quebec was 5283 km *3283 miles*. Ten canoes represented Canadian provinces and territories. The winner of the race, which took from 24 May to 4 Sep 1967, was the Province of Manitoba canoe *Radisson*.

24 hours *Men* ■ Zdzislaw Szubski paddled 252.9 km *157.1 miles* in a Jaguar K1 canoe on the Vistula River, Wlocklawek to Gdansk, Poland on 11–12 Sep 1987.

Women ■ Lydia Formentin paddled 156.4 km *97.2 miles* on the Swan River, Western Australia in 1979.

Flat water ■ Thomas J. Mazuzan paddled, without benefit of current, 199.53 km *123.98 miles* on the Barge Canal, New York State, USA on 24–25 Sep 1986.

Open sea ■ Randy Fine (USA) paddled 194.1 km *120.6 miles* along the Florida coast on 26–27 Jun 1986.

Greatest lifetime distance ■ Fritz Lindner of Berlin, West Germany, totalled 103 444 km *64 278 miles* from 1928 to 1987.

Highest altitude ■ In September 1976 Dr Michael Leslie Jones (1951–78) and Michael Hopkinson of the British Everest Canoe Expedition canoed down the River Dudh Kosi, Nepal from an altitude of 5334 m *17 500 ft*.

Eskimo rolls *With paddle* ■ Ray Hudspith (b. 18 Apr 1960) achieved 1000 rolls in 34 min 43 sec at the Elswick Pool, Newcastle-upon-Tyne on 20 Mar 1987. Julian Dean completed 1555 continuous rolls at Casterton Swimming Pool, Cumbria, taking 1 hr 49 min 45 sec, on 6 Dec 1983.

'Hand rolls' ■ Colin Brian Hill (b. 16 Aug 1970) achieved 1000 rolls in 31 min 55.62 sec at Consett, Co. Durham on 12 Mar 1987. He also achieved 100 rolls in 2 min 39.2 sec at Crystal Palace, London on 22 Feb 1987. He completed 3700 continuous rolls at Durham City Swimming Baths, Co. Durham on 1 May 1989.

Canoe raft ■ A raft of 302 kayaks and canoes, held together by hands only, while free floating for 30 seconds, was established on the Regatta Lake at Holme Pierrepont, Nottinghamshire on 15 Sep 1986.

Card Games

Origins ■ Bridge (a corruption of Biritch, a now obsolete Russian word whose meanings include

'declarer') is thought either to be of Levantine origin, similar games having been played there in the early 1870s, or to have come from India.

Auction bridge (highest bidder names trump) was invented *c.* 1902. The contract principle, present in several games (notably the French game *Plafond, c.* 1917), was introduced to Bridge by Harold Sterling Vanderbilt (USA) on 1 Nov 1925 during a Caribbean voyage aboard the SS *Finland*. It became a world-wide craze after the USA *v.* Great Britain challenge match between Romanian-born Ely Culbertson (1891–1955) and Lt-Col Walter Thomas More Buller (1887–1938) at Almack's Club, London in September 1930. The USA won the 200-hand match by 4845 points.

Biggest tournament ■ The Epson World Bridge Championship, held on 3 Jun 1988, was contested by 84 352 players playing the same hands at more than 1731 centres. It was won by Jan Horwitz and Barbara Norante of Butler, Pennsylvania, USA, with 76.33 per cent.

Most world titles ■ The World Championship (Bermuda Bowl) has been won a record 13 times by Italy's Blue Team (*Squadra Azzura*), 1957–9, 1961–3, 1965–7, 1969, 1973–5 and by the USA, 1950–1, 1953–4, 1970–1, 1976–7, 1979, 1981, 1983, 1985, 1987. Italy also won the Olympiad in 1964, 1968 and 1972. Giorgio Belladonna (b. 7 Jun 1923) was in all the Italian winning teams. The USA have a record four wins in the women's world championship for the Venice Trophy: 1974, 1976, 1978 and 1987 and three wins at the World Team Olympiad: 1976, 1980 and 1984.

Most world championship hands ■ In the 1987 Bermuda Bowl in Ocho Rios, Jamaica, Tony Forrester, from Bradford, played a record 720 out of a possible 784 boards.

Most master points ■ In the latest ranking list based on Master Points awarded by the World Bridge Federation during the last ten years, the leading players in the world are (men) Robert Hamman (b. 1938) of Dallas, Texas, USA with 597 and (women) Sandra Landy (GB) with 284. The all-time leading Master Point winner was Giorgio Belladonna (Italy) with 1821 1/4 points. The world's leading woman player is Jacqui Mitchell (USA) with 347 points.

Barry Crane of Los Angeles, California, USA led the American Contract Bridge League rankings from 1968 to his murder in 1985. He amassed a record total of 35 137.6 Master Points. The current leader is Paul Soloway with 29 153 to June 1988. The most master points scored in a year is 3270 by Grant Baze (USA) in 1984.

The first man to win 10 000 Master Points was Oswald Jacoby (USA) (1902–84) in October 1967. He had been a member of the winning World Championship team in 1935 and on 4 Dec 1983 became the oldest member of a winning team of a major open team championship, in the Curtis Reisinger Trophy.

Rika 'Rixi' Markus (Austria, later GB) (b. 27 Jun 1910), one of the world leading players, has won numerous titles during an illustrious career and became the first woman World Grand Master in 1974.

Youngest Life Master ■ Dougie Hsieh (b. 23 Nov 1969) of New York City became the world's youngest ever Life Master in 1981 at 11 yr 306 days. The youngest ever female Master is Patricia Thomas (b. 10 Oct 1968) at 14 yr 28 days in 1982.

Perfect deals ■ The mathematical odds against dealing 13 cards of one suit are 158 753 389 899 to 1, while the odds against a named player receiving a 'perfect hand' consisting of all 13 spades are 635 013 559 599 to 1. The odds against each of the four players receiving a complete suit (a 'perfect deal') are 2 235 197 406 895 366 368301 559 999 to 1.

Possible auctions ■ The number of possible auctions with North as dealer is 128 745 650 347 030 683 120 231 926 111 609 371 363 122 697 557.

CRIBBAGE

Origins ■ The invention of the game (once called Cribbidge) is credited to the English dramatist Sir John Suckling (1609–42).

Rare hands ■ Four maximum 29 point hands have been achieved by William E. Johnson of Waltham, Massachusetts, USA, 1974–81 and by Mrs Mary Matheson of Springhill, Nova Scotia, Canada, 1974–85. Paul Nault of Athol, Massachusetts, USA had two such hands within eight games in a tournament on 19 Mar 1977.

Most points in 24 hours ■ The most points scored by a team of four, playing singles in two pairs, is 111 201 by Christine and Elizabeth Gill, Jeanette MacGrath and Donald Ward at Grannie's Healin' Hame, Embo, Highland Region on 2–3 May 1987.

Cricket

Origins ■ The earliest evidence of a game similar to cricket is from a drawing depicting two men playing with a bat and ball dated *c.* 1150. The game was played in Guildford, Surrey, at least as early as 1550. The earliest major match of which the full score survives was one in which a team representing England (40 and 70) was beaten by Kent (53 and 58 for 9) by one wicket at the Artillery Ground in Finsbury, London on 18 Jun 1744. Cricket was played in Australia as early as 1803. The first international match was played between Canada and the USA in 1844. Fifteen years later those countries were host to the first English touring team. The first touring team to visit England was an Australian Aborigine XI in 1868.

FIRST–CLASS CRICKET RECORDS

BATTING RECORDS Teams

Highest innings ■ Victoria scored 1107 runs in 10 hr 30 min against New South Wales in an Australian Sheffield Shield match at Melbourne on 27–28 Dec 1926.

Test ■ England scored 903 runs for seven wickets declared in 15 hr 17 min, *v.* Australia at The Oval, London on 20, 22 and 23 Aug 1938.

County Championship ■ Yorkshire scored 887 in 10 hr 50 min, *v.* Warwickshire at Edgbaston, Birmingham on 7–8 May 1896.

Lowest innings ■ The traditional first-class record is 12 by Oxford University (who batted a man short) *v.* the Marylebone Cricket Club (MCC) at Cowley Marsh, Oxford on 24 May 1877, and by Northamptonshire *v.* Gloucestershire at Gloucester on 11 Jun 1907. However, 'The Bs' scored 6 in their second innings *v.* England at Lord's, London on 12–14 Jun 1810 in one of the major matches of that era.

Test ■ 26 by New Zealand *v.* England at Auckland on 28 Mar 1955.

Aggregate for two innings ■ 34 (16 and 18) by Border *v.* Natal in the South African Currie Cup at East London on 19 and 21 Dec 1959. In an early match, Leicestershire totalled 23 (15 and 8) *v.* Nottinghamshire (61) at Leicester on 25 Aug 1800.

Greatest victory ■ A margin of an innings and 851 runs was recorded, when Pakistan Railways (910 for 6 wickets declared) beat Dera Ismail Khan (32 and 27) at Lahore on 2–4 Dec 1964.

In England ■ England won by an innings and 579 runs (also the record for a Test) against Australia at The Oval on 20–24 Aug 1938 when Australia scored 201 and 123 with two men short in both innings. The most one-sided county match was when Surrey (698) defeated Sussex (114 and 99) by an innings and 485 runs at The Oval on 9–11 Aug 1888.

Most runs in a day ■ Australia scored 721 all out (ten wickets) in 5 hr 48 min against Essex at Southchurch Park, Southend-on-Sea on 15 May 1948.

Test ■ 588 at Old Trafford, Manchester on 27 Jul 1936 when England added 398 and India were 190 for 0 in their second innings by the close.

BATTING RECORDS Individuals

Highest innings ■ Hanif Mohammad (b. 21 Dec 1934) scored 499 in 10 hr 35 min for Karachi against Balawalpur at Karachi, Pakistan on 8, 9 and 11 Jan 1959.

In England ■ Archibald Campbell MacLaren (1871–1944) scored 424 in 7 hr 50 min for Lancashire *v.* Somerset at Taunton, Somerset on 15–16 Jul 1895.

Test ■ Sir Garfield St Aubrun Sobers (b. 28 Jul 1936) scored 365 not out in 10 hr 14 min for West Indies *v.* Pakistan at Sabina Park, Kingston, Jamaica on 27 Feb–1 Mar 1958. The English Test record is 364 by Sir Leonard Hutton (b. 23 Jun 1916) against Australia at The Oval on 20, 22 and 23 Aug 1938.

Longest innings ■ Hanif Mohammad (Pakistan) batted for 16 hr 10 min for 337 runs against the West Indies at Bridgetown, Barbados on 20–23 Jan 1958. The English record is 13 hr 17 min by Len Hutton in his record Test score of 364 (see above).

Most runs off an over ■ The first batsman to score 36 runs off a six ball over was Sir Garfield Sobers off Malcolm Andrew Nash (b. 9 May 1945) for Nottinghamshire *v.* Glamorgan at Swansea on 31 Aug 1968. His feat was emulated by Ravishankar Jayadritha Shastri (b. 27 May 1962) for Bombay *v.* Baroda at Bombay, India on 10 Jan 1985 off the bowling of Tilak Raj (b. 15 Jan 1960).

Most runs off a ball ■ Albert Neilson Hornby (1847–1925) scored ten off James Street (1839–1906) for Lancashire *v.* Surrey at The Oval on 14 Jul 1873, and equalled by Samuel Hill Wood (later Sir Samuel Hill Hill-Wood) (1872–1949) off Cuthbert James Burnup (1875–1960) for Derbyshire *v.* MCC at Lord's on 26 May 1900.

Most sixes in an innings ■ John Richard Reid (b. 3 Jun 1928) hit 15 in an innings of 296, lasting 3 hr 40 min, for Wellington *v.* Northern Districts in a Plunket Shield match at Wellington, New Zealand on 14–15 Jan 1963.

Test ■ Walter Hammond hit ten in an innings of 336 not out for England *v.* New Zealand at Auckland on 31 Mar and 1 Apr 1933.

Double hundreds ■ The only batsman to score double hundreds in both innings is Arthur Edward Fagg (1915–77), who made 244 and 202 not out for Kent *v.* Essex at Colchester, Essex from 13–15 Jul 1938. Sir Donald Bradman scored a career record 37 double hundreds, 1927–49.

Fastest scoring ■ The fastest 50 was completed off 13 balls in 8 min (1.22 to 1.30 p.m.) in 11 scoring strokes by Clive Clay Inman (b. 29 Jan 1936) in an innings of 57 not out for Leicestershire *v.* Nottinghamshire at Trent Bridge, Nottingham on 20 Aug 1965. Full tosses were bowled to expedite a declaration.

Fastest 100 ■ Completed in 35 min off between 40 and 46 balls by Percy George Herbert Fender (1892–1985), when scoring 113 not out for Surrey *v.* Northamptonshire at Northampton on 26 Aug 1920. Steven Joseph O'Shaughnessy (b. 9 Sep 1961) also scored a hundred in 35 min for Lancashire *v.* Leicestershire at Old Trafford off 54 balls on 13 Sep 1983. In all he scored 105 and with Graeme Fowler (b. 20 Apr 1957) put on 201 runs for the first wicket in 45 mins. The match was 'dead' and irregular bowlers were used.

The hundred in fewest recorded deliveries was by David William Hookes (b. 3 May 1955) in 34 balls, in 43 min, for South Australia *v.* Victoria at Adelaide on 25 Oct 1982. In all he scored 107 from 40 balls in this the second innings, following 137 in the first innings. The most prolific scorer of hundreds in an hour or

less was Gilbert Laird Jessop (1874–1955), with 14 between 1897 and 1913. The fastest Test hundred was one off 56 balls by Isaac Vivian Alexander Richards (b. 7 Mar 1952) for the West Indies *v.* England at St John's, Antigua on 15 Apr 1986. His final score was 110 in 81 minutes. Edwin Boaler Alletson (1884–1963) scored 189 runs in 90 min for Nottinghamshire *v.* Sussex at Hove, East Sussex on 20 May 1911.

Fastest 200 ■ Scored in 113 min by Ravi Shastri off 123 balls for Bombay *v.* Baroda on 10 Jan 1985 (see most runs off an over). Clive Hubert Lloyd (b. 31 Aug 1944), for West Indians *v.* Glamorgan at Swansea on 9 Aug 1976, and Gilbert Jessop (286), for Gloucestershire *v.* Sussex at Hove on 1 Jun 1903, both scored 200 in 120 min. Lloyd received 121 balls, but the figure for Jessop is not known.

Fastest 300 ■ Completed in 181 min by Denis Compton, who scored 300 for the MCC *v.* North-Eastern Transvaal at Benoni, South Africa on 3–4 Dec 1948.

Slowest scoring ■ The longest time a batsman has ever taken to score his first run is 1 hr 37 min by Thomas Godfrey Evans (b. 18 Aug 1920), who scored 10 not out for England *v.* Australia at Adelaide on 5–6 Feb 1947. The longest innings without scoring is 87 min by Vincent Richard Hogg (b. 3 Jul 1952) for Zimbabwe–Rhodesia 'B' *v.* Natal 'B' at Pietermaritzburg in the South African Castle Bowl competition on 20 Jan 1980.

The slowest hundred on record is by Mudassar Nazar (b. 6 Apr 1956) for Pakistan *v.* England at Lahore on 14–15 Dec 1977. He required 9 hr 51 min for 114, reaching the 100 in 9 hr 17 min. The slowest double hundred is one of 12 hr 56 min (518 balls) by Don Sardha Brendon Priyantha Kuruppu (b. 5 Jan 1962) during an innings of 201 not out for Sri Lanka *v.* New Zealand at Colombo on 16–19 Apr 1987.

Highest partnership ■ For any wicket is the fourth–wicket stand of 577 by Gulzar Mahomed (b. 15 Oct 1921), 319, and Vijay Samuel Hazare (b. 11 Mar 1915), 288, for Baroda *v.* Holkar at Baroda, India on 8–10 Mar 1947.

In England ■ 555, for the first-wicket by Percy Holmes (1886–1971) (224 not out) and Herbert Sutcliffe (1894–1978) (313) for Yorkshire *v.* Essex at Leyton, Essex on 15–16 Jun 1932.

Test ■ 451, for the second wicket by William Harold Ponsford (b. 19 Oct 1900) (266) and Sir Donald Bradman (244) for Australia *v.* England at The Oval on 18 Aug 1934, and for the third wicket by Mudassar Nazar (231) and Javed Miandad Khan (b. 12 Jun 1957) (280 not out) for Pakistan *v.* India at Hyderabad, Pakistan on 14–15 Jan 1983.

BOWLING

Most wickets *In an innings* ■ Only one bowler has taken all ten wickets in an innings on three occasions – Alfred 'Tich' Freeman of Kent, 1929–31. The fewest runs scored off a bowler taking all ten wickets is ten, off Hedley Verity (1905–43) for Yorkshire *v.* Nottinghamshire at Leeds on 12 Jul 1932. The only bowler to bowl out all ten was John Wisden (1826–84) for North *v.* South at Lord's in 1850.

In a match ■ James Charles Laker (1922–86) took 19 wickets for 90 runs (9–37 and 10–53) for England *v.* Australia at Old Trafford from 27–31 Jul 1956.

Most consecutive wickets ■ No bowler in first-class cricket has yet achieved five wickets with five consecutive balls. The nearest approach was that of Charles Warrington Leonard Parker (1882–1959) (Gloucestershire) in his own benefit match against Yorkshire at Bristol on 10 Aug 1922, when he struck the stumps with five successive balls but the second was called as a no-ball. The only man to have taken four wickets with consecutive balls more than once is Robert James Crisp (b. 28 May 1911) for Western Province *v.* Griqualand West at Johannesburg, South Africa on 24 Dec 1931 and against Natal at Durban, South Africa on 3 Mar 1934.

Patrick Ian Pocock (b. 24 Sep 1946) took five wickets in six balls, six in nine balls and seven in eleven balls for Surrey v. Sussex at Eastbourne, East Sussex on 15 Aug 1972. In his own benefit match at Lord's on 22 May 1907, Albert Edwin Trott (1873–1914) of Middlesex took four Somerset wickets with four consecutive balls and then later in the same innings achieved a 'hat trick'.

Most consecutive maidens ■ Hugh Joseph Tayfield (b. 30 Jan 1929) bowled 16 consecutive eight-ball maiden overs (137 balls without conceding a run) for South Africa v. England at Durban on 25–26 Jan 1957. The greatest number of consecutive

ENGLISH ONE–DAY RECORDS

GC/NWT : Gillette Cup (1963–1980); NatWest Trophy (1981–) (60-over matches).

SL (Sunday League) : John Player (1969–1986); Refuge Assurance (1987–) (40-over matches).

B & H : Benson & Hedges Cup (1972–) (55-over matches).

MOST WINS

GC/NWT 4, Lancashire 1970–2, 1975; Sussex 1963–4, 1978, 1986; Middlesex 1977, 1980, 1984, 1988. **SL** 3, Kent 1972–3, 1976; Essex 1981, 1984–5; Hampshire 1975, 1978, 1986; Worcestershire 1971, 1987–8. **B & H** 3, Kent 1973, 1976, 1978; Leicestershire 1972, 1975, 1985.

HIGHEST INNINGS TOTAL

GC/NWT 404–3 Worcestershire v. Devon, Worcester, 1987. **SL** 310–5 Essex v. Glamorgan, Southend, 1983. **B & H** 350–3 Essex v. Oxford & Cambridge Universities, Chelmsford, 1979.

LOWEST INNINGS TOTAL

GC/NWT 39 Ireland v. Sussex, Hove, 1985. **SL** 23 Middlesex v. Yorkshire, Headingley, 1974. **B & H** 56 Leicestershire v. Minor Counties, Wellington, 1982.

HIGHEST INDIVIDUAL INNINGS

GC/NWT 206 Alvin Isaac Kallicharran (b. 21 Mar 1949), Warwickshire v. Oxfordshire, Edgbaston, 1984. **SL** 176 Graham Alan Gooch (b. 23 Jul 1953), Essex v. Glamorgan, Southend, 1983. **B & H** 198* Graham Gooch, Essex v. Sussex, Hove, 1982.

BEST INDIVIDUAL BOWLING

GC/NWT 8–21 Michael Anthony Holding (b. 16 Feb 1954), Derbyshire v. Sussex, Hove, 1988. **SL** 8–26 Keith David Boyce (b. 11 Oct 1943), Essex v. Lancashire, Old Trafford, 1971; Alan Ward (b. 10 Aug 1947) took 4 wickets in 4 balls, Derbyshire v. Sussex, Derby, 1970. **B & H** 7–12 Wayne Wendell Daniel (b. 16 Jan 1956), Middlesex v. Minor Counties (East), Ipswich, 1978.

MOST DISMISSALS IN INNINGS

GC/NWT 6, Robert William Taylor (b. 17 Jul 1941), Derbyshire v. Essex, Derby, 1981; Terry Davies (b. 25 Oct 1960), Glamorgan v. Staffordshire, Stone, 1986. **SL** 7, Bob Taylor, Derbyshire v. Lancashire, Old Trafford, 1975. **B & H** 8, Derek John Somerset Taylor (b. 12 Nov 1942), Somerset v. Combined Universities, Taunton, 1982.

RUNS IN CAREER

GC/NWT 1950, Dennis Leslie Amiss (b. 7 Apr 1943), Warwickshire 1963–87. **SL** 7040, Dennis Amiss, Warwickshire 1969–87. **B & H** 3405, Graham Gooch, Essex 1973–88.

WICKETS IN CAREER

GC/NWT 81, Geoffrey Graham Arnold (b. 3 Sep 1944), Surrey, Sussex 1963–80. **SL** 365, John Kenneth Lever (b. 24 Feb 1949), Essex 1969–88. **B & H** 143, John Lever, Essex 1972–88.

DISMISSALS IN CAREER

GC/NWT 66, Bob Taylor, Derbyshire 1963–84. **SL** 243, David Bairstow, Yorkshire 1972–88. **B & H** 118, David Bairstow, Yorkshire 1972–88.

* Not out

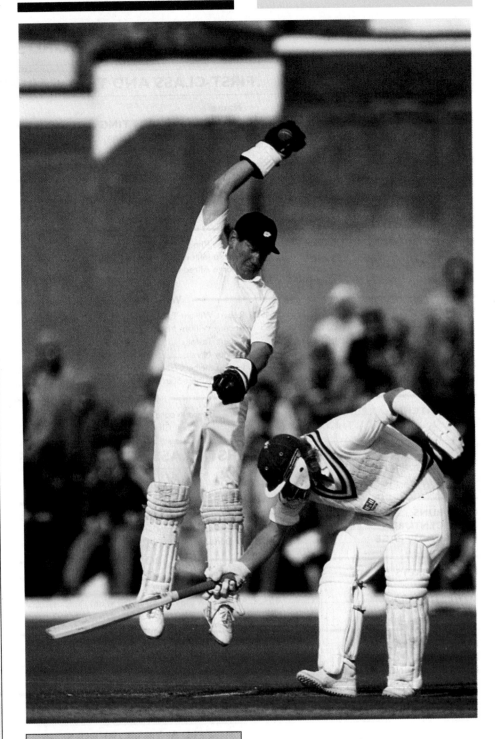

Most dismissals ● Wicket-keeper David Bairstow, of Yorkshire, has taken a record number of dismissals behind the stumps in both the Sunday League and in Benson and Hedges Cup games. He made his debut in 1972. (Photo: All-Sport / Adrian Murrell)

six-ball maiden overs bowled is 21 (131 balls) by Rameshchandra Gangaram 'Bapu' Nadkarni (b. 4 Apr 1932) for India v. England at Madras on 12 Jan 1964. Alfred Shaw (1842–1907) of Nottinghamshire bowled 23 consecutive 4-ball maiden overs (92 balls) for North v. South at Trent Bridge on 17 Jul 1876.

Most balls ■ The most balls bowled in a match is 917 by Cottari Subbanna Nayudu (b. 18 Apr 1914), 6–153 and 5–275, for Holkar v. Bombay at Bombay on 4–9 Mar 1945. The most balls bowled in a Test match is 774 by Sonny Ramadhin (b. 1 May 1929) for the West Indies v. England, 7–49 and 2–179, at Edgbaston on 29 May–4 Jun 1957. In the second innings he bowled a world record 588 balls (98 overs).

Most expensive bowling ■ The greatest number of runs hit off one bowler in an innings is 362, off Arthur Alfred Mailey (1886–1967) of New South Wales by Victoria at Melbourne on 24–28 Dec 1926. The most runs conceded by a bowler in a match is 428 by Cottari Subbanna Nayudu in the Holkar v. Bombay match above. The most runs conceded in a Test innings is 298 by Leslie O'Brien 'Chuck' Fleetwood-Smith (1910–71) for Australia v. England at The Oval on 20–23 Aug 1938.

Fastest ■ The highest electronically measured speed for a ball bowled by any bowler is 160·45 km/h *99·7 mph* by Jeffrey Robert Thomson (Australia) (b. 16 Aug 1950) against the West Indies in December 1975.

ALL-ROUNDERS

The double ■ The 'double' of 1000 runs and 100 wickets in the same season was performed a record number of 16 times by Wilfred Rhodes between 1903 and 1926. The greatest number of consecutive seasons in which a player has performed the

INDIVIDUAL RECORDS

FIRST-CLASS AND TEST CAREER

		Name	Team	Year
BATTING				
MOST RUNS	First-Class 61 237	Sir John Berry 'Jack' Hobbs (1882–1963) (av. 50·65)	Surrey/England	1905–34
	Test 10 122	Sunil Manohar Gavaskar (b. 10 Jul 1949) (av. 51·12)	India (125 Tests)	1971–87
MOST CENTURIES	First-Class 197	Sir Jack Hobbs (in 1315 innings)	Surrey/England	1905–34
	Test 34	Sunil Gavaskar (in 214 innings)	India	1971–87
HIGHEST AVERAGE	First-Class 95·14	Sir Donald George Bradman (b. 28 Aug 1908)	NSW/South Australia/Australia	1927–49
		(28 067 runs in 338 innings, including 43 not outs)		
	Test 99·94	Sir Donald Bradman (6996 runs in 80 innings)	Australia (52 Tests)	1928–48
BOWLING				
MOST WICKETS	First-Class 4187	Wilfred Rhodes (1877–1973) (av. 16·71)	Yorkshire/England	1898–1930
	Test 396	Richard John Hadlee (b. 3 Jul 1951) (av. 22·21)	New Zealand (79 Tests)	1973–89
LOWEST AVERAGE	Test 10·75	George Alfred Lohmann (1865–1901) (112 wkts)	England (18 Tests)	1886–96
(min 15 wkts)				
WICKET-KEEPING				
MOST DISMISSALS	First-Class 1649	Robert William Taylor (b. 17 Jul 1941)	Derbyshire/England	1960–88
	Test 355	Rodney William Marsh (b. 11 Nov 1947)	Australia (96 Tests)	1970–84
MOST CATCHES	First-Class 1473	Robert Taylor	Derbyshire/England	1960–88
	Test 343	Rodney Marsh	Australia	1970–84
MOST STUMPINGS	First-Class 418	Leslie Ethelbert George Ames (b. 3 Dec 1905)	Kent/England	1926–51
	Test 52	William Albert Stanley Oldfield (1894–1976)	Australia (54 Tests)	1920–37
FIELDING				
MOST CATCHES	First-Class 1018	Frank Edward Woolley (1887–1978)	Kent/England	1906–38
	Test 122	Gregory Stephen Chappell (b. 7 Aug 1948)	Australia (87 Tests)	1970–84

IN A FIRST-CLASS SEASON IN ENGLAND

		Name	Team	Year
BATTING				
MOST RUNS	3816	Denis Charles Scott Compton (b. 23 May 1918) (av. 90·85)	Middlesex/England	1947
MOST CENTURIES	18	Denis Compton (in 50 innings with 8 not outs)	Middlesex/England	1947
HIGHEST AVERAGE	115·66	Sir Donald Bradman (2429 runs in 26 innings, with 5 not outs)	Australians	1938
BOWLING				
MOST WICKETS	304	Alfred Percy 'Tich' Freeman (1888–1965) (1976·1 overs) (av. 18·05)	Kent	1928
LOWEST AVERAGE	8·54	Alfred Shaw (1842–1907) (186 wkts)	Nottinghamshire	1880
(min 100 wkts)				
WICKET-KEEPING				
MOST DISMISSALS	128	Leslie Ames (79 caught, 49 stumped)	Kent	1929
MOST CATCHES	96	James Graham Binks (b. 5 Oct 1935)	Yorkshire	1960
MOST STUMPINGS	64	Leslie Ames	Kent	1932
FIELDING				
MOST CATCHES	78	Walter Reginald Hammond (1903–65)	Gloucestershire	1928

IN A TEST SERIES

		Name	Team	Year
BATTING				
MOST RUNS	974	Sir Donald Bradman (av. 139·14)	Australia v. England (5 Tests)	1930
MOST CENTURIES	5	Clyde Leopold Walcott (b. 17 Jan 1926)	West Indies v. Australia (5 Tests)	1954–5
HIGHEST AVERAGE	563·00	Walter Reginald Hammond (563 runs, 2 inns, 1 not out)	England v. New Zealand (2 Tests)	1932–3
BOWLING				
MOST WICKETS	49	Sydney Francis Barnes (1873–1967) (av. 10·93)	England v. South Africa (4 Tests)	1913–14
LOWEST AVERAGE	5·80	George Alfred Lohmann (35 wkts)	England v. South Africa (3 Tests)	1895–6
(min 20 wkts)				
WICKET-KEEPING				
MOST DISMISSALS	28	Rodney Marsh (all caught)	Australia v. England (5 Tests)	1982–3
MOST STUMPINGS	9	Percy William Sherwell (1880–1948)	South Africa v. Australia (5 Tests)	1910–11
FIELDING				
MOST CATCHES	15	Jack Morrison Gregory (1895–1973)	Australia v. England (5 Tests)	1920–1
ALL-ROUND				
400 RUNS/ 30 WICKETS	475/34	George Giffen (1859–1927)	Australia v. England (5 Tests)	1894–5

–class cricket, v. Lancashire at Old Trafford on 26 Jun 1946.

Test cricket ■ The best all-round Test career record is that of Ian Terence Botham (b. 24 Nov 1955) with 5057 runs (av 34·87), 373 wickets (av 27·86) and 109 catches in 94 matches, 1977–87. Botham is the only player to score a hundred and take eight wickets in an innings in the same Test, with 108 and 8–34 for England v. Pakistan at Lord's on 15–19 Jun 1978. He scored a hundred (114) and took more than ten wickets (6–58 and 7–48) in a Test, for England v. India in the Golden Jubilee Test at Bombay on 15–19 Feb 1980. This feat was emulated by Imran Khan Niazi (b. 25 Nov 1952) with 117, 6–98 and 5–82 for Pakistan v. India at Faisalabad on 3–8 Jan 1983. Botham completed the double of 1000 runs and 100 wickets in the fewest Test matches (21) on 30 Aug 1979. Kapil Dev Nikhanj (India) (b. 6 Jan 1959) achieved his double in the shortest time span, 1 year 107 days, and at the youngest age, 21 yr 27 days, in his 25th Test. The double of 2000 runs and 200 wickets was achieved in fewest matches (42) by Botham and at the youngest age by Kapil Dev at 24 yr 68 days. The double of 3000 runs and 300 wickets was achieved in fewest matches, 71, by Botham and at the youngest age by Kapil Dev at 28 yr 1 day.

WICKET-KEEPING

Most dismissals *Innings* ■ The most dismissals is eight (all caught) by Arthur Theodore Wallace 'Wally' Grout (1927–68) for Queensland v. Western Australia at Brisbane on 15 Feb 1960 and by David Edward East (b. 27 Jul 1959) for Essex v. Somerset at Taunton on 27 Jul 1985. The most stumpings in an innings is six by Henry 'Hugo' Yarnold (1917–74) for Worcestershire v. Scotland at Broughty Ferry, Tay-

> **Most centuries** ● Desmond Leo Haynes (West Indies) (b. 15 Feb 1956) has scored a record 14 centuries in one day internationals, having played 158 matches, 1977–89. (Photo: All-Sport/David Cannon)

'double' is 11 (1903–13) by George Herbert Hirst (1871–1954), of Yorkshire and England. Hirst is also the only player to score 2000 runs (2385) and take 200 wickets (208) in the same season (1906).

Century and wicket on debut ■ Frederick William Stocks (b. 6 Nov 1918) of Nottinghamshire achieved the unique feat of scoring a century on his first –class debut, v. Kent at Trent Bridge on 13 May 1946, and of taking a wicket with his first ball in first-

> **Most wins** ● Phil Neale of Worcestershire holds aloft the Refuge Assurance League Trophy for the second successive year in 1988. It was Worcestershire's third success in the Sunday League having previously won the then John Player League in 1971. (Photo: All-Sport/Adrian Murrell)

> **Most Test wickets** ● Richard Hadlee (New Zealand) (b. 3 Jul 1951) has taken a record 396 Test wickets at an average of 22·22 runs per wicket in 79 Test matches, 1973–89. (Photo: All-Sport/Simon Bruty)

side on 2 Jul 1951. The Test record is seven (all caught) by Wasim Bari (b. 23 Mar 1948) for Pakistan v. New Zealand at Auckland on 23 Feb 1979, and by Bob Taylor for England v. India at Bombay on 15 Feb 1980.

Match ■ The most dismissals is 12 by: Edward Pooley (1838–1907), eight caught, four stumped, for Surrey v. Sussex at The Oval on 6–7 Jul 1868; nine caught, three stumped by both Donald Tallon

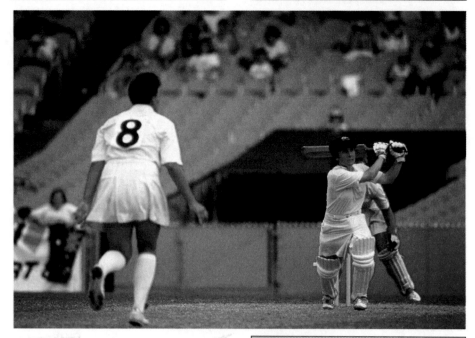

(1916–84) for Queensland v. New South Wales at Sydney, Australia on 2–4 Jan 1939, and by Hedley Brian Taber (b. 29 Apr 1940) for New South Wales v. South Australia at Adelaide on 13–17 Dec 1968. The record for catches is 11 by: Arnold Long (b. 18 Dec 1940), for Surrey v. Sussex at Hove on 18 and 21 Jul 1964, by Rodney Marsh for Western Australia v. Victoria at Perth on 15–17 Nov 1975; and by David Leslie Bairstow (b. 1 Sep 1951) for Yorkshire v. Derbyshire at Scarborough on 8–10 Sep 1982. The most stumpings in a match is nine by Frederick Henry Huish (1869–1957) for Kent v. Surrey at The Oval on 21–23 Aug 1911. The Test record for dismissals is ten, all caught, by Bob Taylor for England v. India at Bombay, 15–19 Feb 1980.

FIELDING

Most catches *Innings and Match* ■ The greatest number of catches in an innings is seven, by Michael James Stewart (b. 16 Sep 1932) for Surrey v. Northamptonshire at Northampton on 7 Jun 1957; and by Anthony Stephen Brown (b. 24 Jun 1936) for Gloucestershire v. Nottinghamshire at Trent Bridge on 26 Jul 1966.

The most catches in a Test match is seven by Greg Chappell for Australia v. England at Perth on 13–17 Dec 1974; and by Yajurvindra Singh (b. 1 Aug 1952) for India v. England at Bangalore on 28 Jan–2 Feb 1977.

Match ■ Walter Hammond held ten catches (four in the first innings, six in the second) for Gloucestershire v. Surrey at Cheltenham on 16–17 Aug 1928.

Longest throw ■ A cricket ball (155 g *5½ oz*) was reputedly thrown 128·6 m *140 yd 2 ft* by Robert Percival, a left-hander, on Durham Sands racecourse on Easter Monday, 18 Apr 1882.

TEST CRICKET

Origins ■ The first match, now considered as a Test match, was played at Melbourne on 15–19 Mar 1877 between Australia and England, represented by James Lillywhite's touring party. Neither side was representative of their countries and indeed such was the case for many matches, now accepted as Test matches, played over the next fifty years or so. The first match in England was against Australia at The Oval on 6–8 Sep 1880. Eight nations have played Test cricket; Australia, England, India, New Zealand, Pakistan, South Africa, Sri Lanka and West Indies.

OTHER TEST RECORDS

Test appearances ■ Sunil Gavaskar played in a record 125 Tests, 1975–87, including a record 106

consecutive Tests. The English record for most Tests is 114 by Michael Colin Cowdrey (b. 24 Dec 1932) and for consecutive Tests is 65 by Alan Philip Eric Knott (b. 9 Apr 1946), 1971–7 and Ian Botham, 1978–84.

Longest match ■ The lengthiest recorded cricket match was the 'timeless' Test between England and South Africa at Durban on 3–14 Mar 1939. It was abandoned after ten days (eighth day rained off) because the ship taking the England team home was due to leave. The total playing time was 43 hr 16 min and a record Test match aggregate of 1981 runs was scored.

Largest crowds ■ The greatest attendance at a cricket match is about 394 000 for the Test between India and England at Eden Gardens, Calcutta on 1–6 Jan 1982. The record for a Test series is 933 513 for Australia v. England (five matches) in 1936–37. The greatest recorded attendance at a cricket match on one day was 90 800 on the second day of the Test between Australia and the West Indies at Melbourne on 11 Feb 1961. The English match record is 159 000 for England v. Australia at Headingley, Leeds on 22–27 Jul 1948, and the record for one day probably a capacity of 46 000 for Lancashire v. Yorkshire at Old Trafford on 2 Aug 1926. The English record for a Test series is 549 650 for the series against Australia in 1953. The highest attendance for a limited-overs game is 84 153 at the Benson and Hedges World Series Cup match between Australia and England at Melbourne on 23 Jan 1985.

Most successful Test captain ■ Clive Hubert Lloyd (b. 31 Aug 1944) led the West Indies in a record 74 Test matches from 22 Nov 1974 to 2 Jan 1985. Of these, 36 were won, 12 lost and 26 were drawn. His team set records for most successive Test wins, 11 in 1984, and most Tests without defeat, 27, between losses to Australia in December 1981 and January 1985 (through injury Lloyd missed one of those matches, when the West Indies were captained by Vivian Richards).

Most extras ■ The most extras conceded in a Test innings is 71 by the West Indies in Pakistan's 1st innings at Georgetown, Guyana on 3–4 Apr 1988.

The figure consisted of 21 byes, 8 leg byes, 4 wides and 38 no-balls.

ONE-DAY INTERNATIONALS

The first 'limited overs' international was played at Melbourne Cricket Ground on 5 Jan 1971 between Australia and England. The Prudential (now Texaco) Trophy series of one-day internationals began in England in 1972, matches being of 55 overs per side. The Benson and Hedges World Cup Series has been held annually in Australia since 1979–80.

World Cup ■ The World Cup was held in England in 1975, 1979 and 1983, and in India and Pakistan in 1987. The West Indies are the only double winners, in 1975 and 1979. Matches were played at 60 overs per side (except at 50 overs in 1987).

One-day international records *Team* ■ The highest innings score by a team is 360–4 (50 overs) by the West Indies v. Sri Lanka at Karachi, Pakistan on 13 Oct 1987. The lowest completed innings total is 45 by Canada v. England at Old Trafford, Lancashire on 14 Jun 1979. The largest victory margin is 232 by Australia v. Sri Lanka (323–2 to 91), at Adelaide, Australia on 28 Jan 1985.

Individual ■ The highest individual score is 189 not out by Isaac Vivian Alexander Richards (b. 7 Mar 1952) for the West Indies v. England at Old Trafford, Lancashire on 31 May 1984. The best bowling analysis is 7–51 by Winston Walter Davis (b. 18 Sep 1958) for the West Indies v. Australia at Headingley, Yorkshire on 12 Jun 1983. The best partnership is 224 by Dean Mervyn Jones (b. 24 Mar 1961) and Allan Robert Border (b. 27 Jul 1955) for Australia v. Sri Lanka at Adelaide, Australia on 28 Jan 1985

Career ■ The most matches played is 187 by Allan Border (Australia), 1979–89. The most runs scored is 6200 (av. 49·60) by Vivian Richards (West Indies) in 165 matches, 1975–89. He has also taken most catches by a fielder, 85. The most wickets taken is 160 (av. 26·85) by Kapil Dev (India) in 138 matches, 1978–89. The most dismissals is 168 (150 ct, 18 st) by Peter Jeffrey Leroy Dujon (West Indies) (b. 28 Mar 1956) in 138 matches, 1981–9.

Most extras ■ West Indies conceded 59 extras (8 byes, 10 leg byes 4 no balls and 37 wides) against Pakistan at Brisbane on 7 Jan 1989.

ENGLISH COUNTY CHAMPIONSHIP

The greatest number of victories since 1890, when the Championship was officially constituted, has been by Yorkshire with 29 outright wins (the last in 1968), and one shared (1949). The record number of consecutive title wins is seven by Surrey from 1952 to 1958. The greatest number of appearances in County Championship matches is 763 by Wilfred Rhodes for Yorkshire between 1898 and 1930, and the greatest number of consecutive appearances is 423 by Kenneth George Suttle (b. 25 Aug 1928) for Sussex between 1954 and 1969. James Graham 'Jimmy' Binks (b. 5 Oct 1935) played in all 412 County Championship matches for Yorkshire between his debut in 1955 and his retirement in 1969.

The seven sons of the Reverend Henry Foster, of Malvern, uniquely all played county cricket for Worcestershire between 1899 and 1934.

OLDEST AND YOUNGEST

First-class ■ The oldest player in first-class cricket was the Governor of Bombay, Raja Maharaj Singh (India) (1878–1959), aged 72 yr 192 days, when he batted, scoring 4, on the opening day of the match played on 25–27 Nov 1950 at Bombay for his XI v. Commonwealth XI. The youngest is reputed to be Alim-ud-din (Pakistan) (b. 15 Dec 1930) for Rajputna v. Baroda at Baroda, India on 26 Feb 1943, aged 12 yr 73 days. The oldest Englishman was Benjamin Aislabie (1774–1842) for MCC (of whom he was the secretary) v. Cambridge University at Lord's on 1 and 2 Jul 1841, when he was aged 67 yr 169 days. The youngest English first-class player was Charles Robertson Young for Hampshire v. Kent at Gravesend on 13 Jun 1867, aged 15 yr 131 days.

Test ■ The oldest man to play in a Test match was Wilfred Rhodes, aged 52 yr 165 days, for England v. West Indies at Kingston, Jamaica on 12 April 1930. Rhodes made his Test debut in the last Test of William Gilbert Grace (1848–1915), who at 50 yr 320 days at Nottingham on 3 Jun 1899 was the oldest ever Test captain. The youngest Test captain was the Nawab of Pataudi (later Mansur Ali Khan) at 21 yr 77 days on 23 Mar 1962 for India v. West Indies at Bridgetown, Barbados. The youngest Test player was Mushtaq Mohammad (b. 22 Nov 1943), aged 15 yr 124 days, for Pakistan v. West Indies at Lahore on 26 March 1959. England's youngest player was Dennis Brian Close (b. 24 Feb 1931) aged 18 yr 149 days v. New Zealand at Old Trafford on 23 Jul 1949.

WOMEN'S CRICKET

Earliest ■ The first recorded women's match took place at Gosden Common, Surrey on 26 Jun 1745. *Circa* 1807 Christina Willes is said to have introduced the roundarm bowling style. The first Test match was Australia v. England at Brisbane on 28–31 Dec 1934. The International Women's Cricket Council was formed in 1958.

Batting *Individual* ■ The highest individual innings recorded is 224 not out by Mabel Bryant for Visitors v. Residents at Eastbourne, East Sussex in August 1901. The highest innings in a Test match is 193 by Denise Annetts (b. 30 Jan 1964), in 381 minutes, for Australia v. England at Collingham, Nottinghamshire on 23–24 Aug 1987 in a four-day Test. With Lindsay Reeler (b. 18 Mar 1961), 110 not out, she added 309 for the third wicket, the highest Test partnership. The highest in a three-day Test is 189 (in 222 minutes) by Elizabeth Alexandra 'Betty' Snowball (1907–88) for England v. New Zealand at Christchurch, New Zealand on 16 Feb 1935. Rachael Flint (*née* Heyhoe) (b. 11 Jun 1939) has scored the most runs in Test cricket with 1814 (av. 49·02) in 25 matches from December 1960 to July 1979.

Team ■ The highest innings score by any team is 567 by Tarana v. Rockley, at Rockley, New South Wales, Australia in 1896. The highest Test innings is 503 for five wickets declared by England v. New Zealand at Christchurch, New Zealand on 16 and 18 Feb 1935. The most in a Test in England is 379 by Australia v. England at The Oval on 26–27 Jul 1976. The highest innings total in England is 410 for two wickets declared by the South v. East at Oakham, Leicestershire on 29 May 1982. The lowest innings in a Test is 35 by England v. Australia at St Kilda, Melbourne, Australia on 22 Feb 1958. The lowest in a Test in England is 63 by New Zealand at Worcester on 5 Jul 1954.

Bowling ■ Mary Beatrice Duggan (England) (1925–73) took a record 77 wickets (av. 13·49) in 17 Tests from 1949 to 1963. She recorded the best Test analysis with seven wickets for six runs for England v. Australia at St Kilda, Melbourne on 22 Feb 1958. Rubina Winifred Humphries (b. 19 Aug 1915), for Dalton Ladies v. Woodfield SC, at Huddersfield, West Yorkshire on 26 Jun 1931, took all ten wickets for no runs. (She also scored all her team's runs.) This bowling feat was equalled by Rosemary White (b. 22 Jan 1938) for Wallington LCC v. Beaconsfield LCC in July 1962.

World Cup ■ Four women's World Cups have been staged. Australia won in 1978, 1982 and 1988 and England in 1973. The highest individual score in this series is 138 not out by Janette Ann Brittin (b. 4 Jul 1959) for England v. International XI at Hamilton, New Zealand on 14 Jan 1982.

MINOR CRICKET RECORDS

(where excelling those in first-class cricket)

Highest individual innings ■ In a Junior House match between Clarke's House (now Poole's) and North Town, at Clifton College, Bristol, 22–23, 26–28 Jun 1899, Arthur Edward Jeune Collins (1885–1914) scored an unprecedented 628 not out in 6 hr 50 min, over five afternoons' batting, carrying his bat through the innings of 836. The scorer, E. W. Pegler, gave the score as '628–plus or minus 20, shall we say'.

Highest partnership ■ During a Harris Shield match at Sassanian Ground, Bombay, India, Vinod Kambli (b. 18 Jan 1972) (349 not out) and Sachin Tendulkar (b. 24 Apr 1973) (326 not out) put on an unbeaten partnership of 664 runs for the third wicket for Sharadashram Vidyamandir v. St Xavier's High School.

Fastest individual scoring ■ Stanley Keppel 'Shunter' Coen (South Africa) (1902–67) scored 50 runs (11 fours and one six) in 7 min for Gezira v. the RAF in 1942. The fastest hundred by a prominent player in a minor match was by Vivian Frank Shergold Crawford (1879–1922) in 19 min at Cane Hill, Surrey on 16 Sep 1899. Lindsay Martin scored 100 off 20 deliveries (13 sixes, 5 fours and 2 singles) for Rosewater v. Warradale on 19 Dec 1987. David Michael Roberts Whatmore (b. 6 Apr 1949) scored 210 (including 25 sixes and 12 fours) off 61 balls for Alderney v. Sun Alliance at Alderney, Channel Islands on 19 Jun 1983. His first 100 came off 33 balls and his second off 25 balls.

Successive sixes ■ Cedric Ivan James Smith (1906–79) hit nine successive sixes for a Middlesex XI v. Harrow and District at Rayner's Lane, Harrow in 1935. This feat was repeated by Arthur Dudley Nourse (1910–81) in a South African XI v. Military Police match at Cairo, Egypt in 1942–3. Nourse's feat included six sixes in one over.

Fastest scoring rate ■ In the match Royal Naval College, Dartmouth v. Seale Hayne Agricultural College in 1923, Kenneth Anderson Sellar (b. 11 Aug 1906) and Leslie Kenneth Allen Block (1906–80) were set to score 174 runs in 105 min but achieved this total in 33 min, so averaging 5·27 runs per min.

Most runs off a ball ■ A scoring stroke of 11 (all run, with no overthrows) was achieved by Lt (later Lt-Col.) Philip Mitford (1879–1946), Queens Own Cameron Highlanders, in a Malta Governor's Cup match on 28 May 1903.

Most runs off an over ■ H. Morley scored 62, nine sixes and two fours, off an eight-ball over from R. Grubb which had four no-balls, in a Queensland country match in 1968–9.

Bowling ■ Nine wickets with nine consecutive balls were taken by: Stephen Fleming, for Marlborough College 'A' XI v. Bohally Intermediate at Blenheim, New Zealand in December 1967; and by Paul Hugo for Smithfield School v. Aliwal North, South Africa in February 1931. In the Inter-Divisional Ships Shield at Purfleet, Essex on 17 May 1924, Joseph William Brockley (b. 9 Apr 1907) took all ten wickets, clean bowled, for two runs in 11 balls–including a triple hat trick. Jennings Tune took all ten wickets, all bowled, for 0 runs in five overs for Cliffe v. Eastrington in the Howden and District League at Cliffe, Yorkshire on 6 May 1922.

In 1881 Frederick Robert Spofforth (1853–1926) at Bendigo, Victoria, Australia clean bowled all ten wickets in *both* innings. J. Bryant for Erskine v. Deaf Mutes in Melbourne on 15 and 22 Oct 1887, and Albert Rimmer for Linwood School v. Cathedral GS at Canterbury, New Zealand in December 1925, repeated the feat. In the 1910 season, H. Hopkinson, of Mildmay CC, London, took 99 wickets for 147 runs.

Maurice Hanes bowled 107 consecutive balls (17 overs and five balls) for Bedworth II v. A P Leamington II at Bedworth, Warwickshire on 16 Jun 1979, without conceding a run.

Wicket-keeping ■ Welihinda Badalge Bennett (b. 25 Jan 1933) caught four and stumped six batsmen in one innings, on 1 March 1953 for Mahinda College v. Galle CC, at the Galle Esplanade, Sri Lanka.

Fielding ■ In a Wellington, New Zealand secondary schools 11-a-side match on 16 Mar 1974, Stephen Lane, 13, held 14 catches in the field (seven in each innings) for St Patrick's College, Silverstream v. St Bernard's College, Lower Hutt.

GUINNESS HAVE PUBLISHED **CRICKET FACTS & FEATS** (2nd EDITION) BILL FRINDALL **£11.95**
CRICKET FIRSTS PETER MATTHEWS & ROBERT BROOKE **£8.95**

Croquet

Origins ■ Its exact origins are obscure, but croquet was probably derived from the French game *Jeu de Mail* first mentioned in the 12th century. A game resembling croquet, possibly of foreign origin, was played in Ireland in the 1830s, and was introduced to Hampshire 20 years later. The first club was formed in the Steyne Gardens, Worthing, West Sussex in 1865.

Most championships ■ The greatest number of victories in the Open Croquet Championships (instituted at Evesham, Worcestershire, 1867) is ten by John William Solomon (b. 1931) (1953, 1956, 1959, 1961, 1963–8). He also won ten Men's Championships (1951, 1953, 1958–60, 1962, 1964–5, 1971–2), ten Open Doubles (with Edmond Patrick Charles Cotter) (1954–5, 1958–9, 1961–5 and 1969) and one Mixed Doubles (with Freda Oddie) in 1954, making a total of 31 titles. Solomon has also won the President's Cup (instituted 1934, an invitation event for the best eight players) on nine occasions (1955, 1957–9, 1962–4, 1968 and 1971), and was Champion of Champions on all four occasions that this competition has been run (1967–70). G. Nigel Aspinall (b. 1946) has won the President's Cup a record 11 times, 1969–70, 1973–6, 1978, 1980, 1982, 1984–5.

Dorothy Dyne Steel (1884–1965), fifteen times winner of the Women's Championship (1919–39), won the Open Croquet Championship four times (1925, 1933, 1935–36). She had also five Doubles and seven Mixed Doubles for a total of 31 titles.

International trophy ■ The MacRobertson International Shield (instituted 1925) has been won a record seven times by Great Britain, 1925, 1937, 1956, 1963, 1969, 1974 and 1982). A record six appearances have been made by John G. Prince (New Zealand) in 1963, 1969, 1975, 1979, 1982 and 1986; on his debut he was the youngest ever international at 17 yr 190 days.

Cross-country Running

Origins ■ The earliest recorded international cross-country race took place over 14·5 km *9 miles 18 yd* from Ville d'Avray, outside Paris, France on 20 Mar 1898 between England and France (England won by 21 points to 69).

World Championships ■ The inaugural International Cross-Country Championships took place at the Hamilton Park Racecourse, Scotland on 28 Mar 1903. The greatest margin of victory is 56 sec or 356 m *390 yd* by John 'Jack' Thomas Holden (England) (b. 13 Mar 1907) at Ayr Racecourse, Scotland on 24 Mar 1934. Since 1973 the events have been official world championships under the auspices of the International Amateur Athletic Federation.

Most wins ■ The greatest number of team victories has been by England with 45 for men, 11 for junior men and seven for women. The USA have a record eight women's team victories. The greatest team domination was by Kenya at Auckland, New Zealand on 26 March 1988. Their senior men's team finished eight men in the first nine, with a low score of 23 (six to score) and their junior men's team set a record low score, 11 (four to score) with six in the first seven.

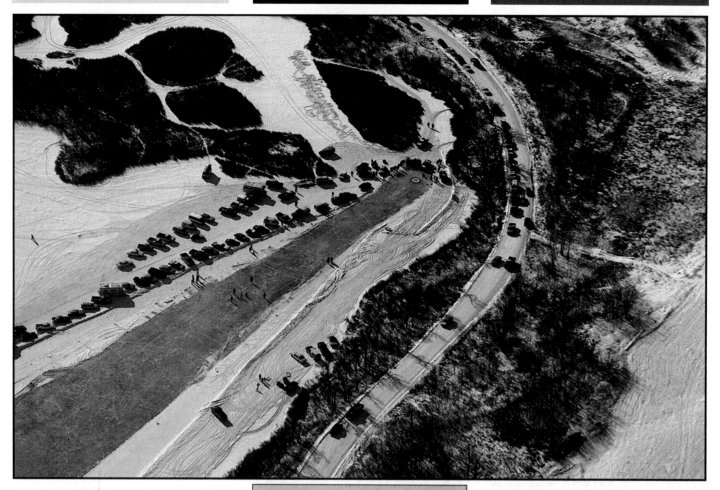

The greatest number of men's individual victories is four by: Jack Holden (England) in 1933–5 and 1939; by Alain Mimoun-o-Kacha (France) (b. 1 Jan 1921) in 1949, 1952, 1954 and 1956; by Gaston Roelants (Belgium) (b. 5 Feb 1937) in 1962, 1967, 1969 and 1972 and by John Ngugi (Kenya) (b. 10 May 1962), 1986–9. The women's race has been won five times by: Doris Brown-Heritage (USA) (b. 17 Sep 1942), 1967–71; and by Grete Waitz (*née* Andersen) (Norway) (b. 1 Oct 1953), 1978–81 and 1983.

Most appearances ■ Marcel van de Wattyne (Belgium) (b. 7 Jul 1924) ran in a record 20 races, 1946–65. The women's record is 16 by Jean Lochhead (Wales) (b. 24 Dec 1946), 1967–79, 1981, 1983–4.

English Championship ■ The National Cross-Country Championship was inaugurated at Roehampton, London in 1877. The most individual titles won is four by Percy H. Stenning (1854–92) (Thames Hare and Hounds) in 1877–80 and Alfred E. Shrubb (1878–1964) (South London Harriers) in 1901–4. The most successful club in the team race has been Birchfield Harriers from Birmingham with 28 wins and one tie between 1880 and 1988. The largest field was the 2006 finishers in the senior race in 1987 at Luton, Bedfordshire.

Largest field ■ The largest recorded field in any cross-country race was 11 763 starters (10 810 finished) in the 30 km *18·6 miles* Lidingöloppet, near Stockholm, Sweden on 3 Oct 1982.

Curling

Origins ■ Although a 15th-century bronze figure in the Florence Museum appears to be holding a curling stone, the earliest illustration of the sport was in one of the Flemish painter Pieter Bruegel's winter scenes *c.* 1560. The game was probably introduced into Scotland by Flemings in the 15th century. The earliest documented club is Muthill, Tayside, formed in 1739. Organised administration began in 1838 with the formation in Edinburgh of the Grand (later Royal) Caledonian Curling Club, the

Longest sheet ● This sheet of specially prepared curling ice at Park Lake, Neepawa, Manitoba, Canada is a record 1200 ft *365·76 m* long and not suprisingly is the location of the longest throw of a stone.

international legislative body until the foundation of the International Curling Federation in 1966. Curling was first played indoors in Montreal, Canada in 1807, and in Britain at Southport, Merseyside in 1878.

The USA won the first Gordon International Medal series of matches, between Canada and the USA, at Montreal in 1884. Curling has been a demonstration sport at the Olympic Games of 1924, 1932, 1964 and 1988.

Most titles ■ Canada has won the men's World Championships (instituted 1959) 19 times, 1959–64, 1966, 1968–72, 1980, 1982–3, 1985–7, 1989. The most Strathcona Cup (instituted 1903) wins is seven by Canada (1903, 1909, 1912, 1923, 1938, 1957, 1965) against Scotland. The most women's World Championships (instituted 1979) is seven by Canada (1980, 1984–9).

'Perfect' Game ■ Stu Beagle, of Calgary, Alberta, Canada, played a perfect game (48 points) against Nova Scotia in the Canadian Championships (Brier) at Fort William (now Thunder Bay), Ontario on 8 Mar 1960. Bernice Fekete, of Edmonton, Alberta, Canada, skipped her rink to two consecutive eight-enders on the same ice at the Derrick Club, Edmonton on 10 Jan and 6 Feb 1973. Two eight-enders in one bonspiel were scored at the Parry Sound Curling Club, Ontario, Canada from 6–8 Jan 1983.

Fastest game ■ Eight curlers from the Burlington Golf and Country Club curled an eight-end game in 47 min 24 sec, with time penalties of 5 min 30 sec, at Burlington, Ontario, Canada on 4 Apr 1986, following rules agreed with the Ontario Curling Association. The time is taken from when the first rock crosses the near hogline until the game's last rock comes to a complete stop.

Longest throw ■ The longest throw of a curling stone was a distance of 175·66 m *576 ft 4 in* by Eddie Kulbacki (Canada) at Park Lake, Neepawa, Manitoba, Canada on 29 Jan 1989. The attempt took place on a specially prepared sheet of curling ice on frozen Park Lake, a record 1200 ft *365·76 m* long.

Largest bonspiel ■ The largest bonspiel in the world is the Manitoba Curling Association Bonspiel held annually in Winnipeg, Canada. In 1988 there were 1424 teams of four men, a total of 5696 curlers, using 187 sheets of curling ice.

Largest rink ■ The world's largest curling rink is the Big Four Curling Rink, Calgary, Alberta, Canada, opened in 1959. Ninety–six teams and 384 players are accommodated on two floors each with 24 sheets of ice.

Cycling

Origins ■ The earliest recorded bicycle race was a velocipede race over 2 km *1·24 miles* at the Parc de St Cloud, Paris on 31 May 1868, won by Dr James Moore (GB) (1847–1935) (later Chevalier de la Légion d'Honneur).

Highest speed ■ The highest speed ever achieved on a bicycle is 245·077 km/h *152·284 mph* by John Howard (USA) behind a wind-shield at Bonneville Salt Flats, Utah, USA on 20 Jul 1985. It should be noted that considerable help was provided by the slipstreaming effect of the lead vehicle. The British speed record is 158·05 km/h *98·21 mph* over 200 metres by David Le Grys (b. 10 Aug 1955) on a closed section of the M42 at Alvechurch, Warwickshire on 28 Aug 1985. Fred Markham, 29, recorded an official unpaced 6·832 sec for 200 m (105·386 km/h *65·484 mph*) on a streamlined bicycle on Highway 120, California, USA on 11 May 1986.

The greatest distance ever covered in one hour is 122·771 km *76 miles 504 yd* by Leon Vanderstuyft (Belgium) (1890–1964) on the Montlhéry Motor

WORLD RECORDS

Records are recognised by the Union Cycliste Internationale (UCI) for both professionals and amateurs on open air and indoor tracks for a variety of distances at unpaced flying and standing starts and for motor-paced. In this list only the best are shown, with a † to signify those records set by a professional rather than an amateur.

OPEN-AIR TRACKS

MEN

Distance	hr:min:sec	Name and country	Venue	Date	

Unpaced standing start

1 km	1:02·091	Maic Malchow (GDR)	Colorado Springs, USA	28 Aug	1986
4 km	4:31·160	Gintautas Umaras (USSR)	Seoul, South Korea	18 Sep	1987
5 km	5:44·700	Gregor Braun (W. Germany)†	La Paz, Bolivia	12 Jan	1984
10 km	11:39·720	Francesco Moser (Italy)†	Mexico City	19 Jan	1984
20 km	23:21·592	Francesco Moser (Italy)†	Mexico City	23 Jan	1984
100 km	2:11:21·428	Beat Meister (Switzerland)	Zürich, Switzerland	14 Jul	1986
1 hour	51·151 km	Francesco Moser (Italy)†	Mexico City	23 Jan	1984

Unpaced flying start

200 metres	10·118	Michael Hübner (GDR)	Colorado Springs, USA	27 Aug	1986
500 metres	26·776	Philippe Boyer (France)†	La Paz, Bolivia	June	1989
1 km	58·269	Dominguez Rueda Efrain (Colombia)†	La Paz, Bolivia	13 Dec	1986

Motor-paced

50 km	35:21·108	Aleksandr Romanov (USSR)	Tbilisi, USSR	6 May	1987
100 km	1:10:50·940	Aleksandr Romanov (USSR)	Tbilisi, USSR	6 May	1987
1 hour	84·710 km	Aleksandr Romanov (USSR)	Tbilisi, USSR	6 May	1987

WOMEN

Unpaced standing start

1 km	1:14·249	Erika Salumyae (USSR)	Tashkent, USSR	17 May	1984
3 km	3:49·780	Rebecca Twigg (now Whitehead) (USA)	Barcelona, Spain	29 Aug	1984
5 km	6:41·75	Amanda Jones (GB)	Leicester, England	31 Jul	1982
10 km	13:19·019	Jeannie Longo (France)	Colorado Springs, USA	20 Sep	1987
20 km	26:41·013	Jeannie Longo (France)	Colorado Springs, USA	23 Sep	1987
100 km	2:28:26·259	Francesca Galli (Italy)	Milan, Italy	26 Oct	1987
1 hour	44·933km	Jeannie Longo (France)	Colorado Springs, USA	23 Sep	1987

Unpaced flying start

200 metres	11·383	Isabelle Gautheron (France)	Colorado Springs, USA	16 Aug	1986
500 metres	30·59	Isabelle Gautheron (France)	Cali, Colombia	14 Sep	1986
1 km	1:10·463	Erika Salumyae (USSR)	Tashkent, USSR	15 May	1984

Many of the above venues, such as La Paz, Colorado Springs, Cali and Mexico City, are at high altitude. The UCI recognises separate world records for the classic one-hour event at venues below 600 metres. These are: MEN 49·80193 km Francesco Moser on 3 Oct 1986, WOMEN 43·58789 km Jeannie Longo on 29 Sep 1986, both at Milan.

INDOOR TRACKS

MEN

Unpaced standing start

1 km	1:02·955	Lothar Thoms (GDR)	Moscow, USSR	22 Jul	1980
4 km	4:25·530	Gintautas Umaras (USSR)	Moscow, USSR	26 Aug	1988
5 km	5:43·514	Vyachselav Yekimov (USSR)	Moscow, USSR	21 Aug	1987
10 km	11:31·968	Vyachselav Yekimov (USSR)	Moscow, USSR	7 Jan	1989
20 km	23:52·098	Vyachselav Yekimov (USSR)	Moscow, USSR	27 Oct	1986
100 km	2:11:47·255	Beat Meister (Switzerland)	Stuttgart, W. Germany	30 Oct	1987
4 km team	4:11·301	USSR	Moscow, USSR	15 Aug	1987
1 hour	50·644 km	Francesco Moser (Italy)	Stuttgart, W. Germany	21 May	1988

Unpaced flying start

200 metres	10·117	Nikolay Kovch (USSR)	Moscow, USSR	5 Feb	1988
500 metres	26·649	Aleksandr Kirichenko (USSR)	Moscow, USSR	Oct	1988
1 km	57·764	Aleksandr Kirichenko (USSR)	Moscow, USSR	Oct	1988

Motor-paced

50 km	32:56·746	Aleksandr Romanov (USSR)	Moscow, USSR	21 Feb	1987
100 km	1:05:58·031	Aleksandr Romanov (USSR)	Moscow, USSR	21 Feb	1987
1 hour	91·131km	Aleksandr Romanov (USSR)	Moscow, USSR	21 Feb	1987

WOMEN

Unpaced standing start

1 km	1:13·377	Erika Salumyae (USSR)	Moscow, USSR	21 Sep	1983
3 km	3:43·490	Jeannie Longo (France)†	Paris (Bercy), France	14 Nov	1986
5 km	6:22·713	Jeannie Longo (France)†	Grenoble, France	2 Nov	1986
10 km	13:29·395	Jeannie Longo (France)†	Grenoble, France	7 Nov	1986
20 km	26:58·152	Jeannie Longo (France)†	Grenoble, France	7 Nov	1986
100 km	2:31:30·043	Mieke Havik (Netherlands)	Rotterdam, Netherlands	19 Sep	1983
1 hour	44·718 km	Jeannie Longo (France)†	Grenoble, France	7 Nov	1986

Unpaced flying start

200 metres	11·210	Erika Salumyae (USSR)	Moscow, USSR	24 Aug	1988
500 metres	29·655	Erika Salumyae (USSR)	Moscow, USSR	6 Aug	1987
1 km	1:05·232	Erika Salumyae (USSR)	Moscow, USSR	30 May	1987

LONG DISTANCE BESTS (unpaced)

24 hr	830·79 km	Michael L. Secrest (USA)	Montreal, Canada	13–14 Mar	1985
1 000 km	32 hr 4 min	Herman de Munck (Belgium)	Keerbergen, Belgium	23–24 Sep	1983
1 000 miles	51:12:32	Herman de Munck (Belgium)	Keerbergen, Belgium	23–25 Sep	1983

Circuit, France, on 30 Sep 1928, achieved from a standing start paced by a motorcycle. The 24 hr record behind pace is 1384·367 km *860 miles 367 yd* by Hubert Ferdinand Opperman (later the Hon. Sir) (b. 29 May 1904) in Melbourne, Australia on 23 May 1932.

Most titles *Olympic* ■ The most gold medals won is three by Paul Masson (France) (1874–1945) in 1896, Francisco Verri (Italy) (1885–1945) in 1906; and Robert Charpentier (France) (1916–66) in 1936. Daniel Morelon (France) won two in 1968, and a third in 1972; he also won a silver in 1976 and a bronze medal in 1964. In the 'unofficial' 1904 cycling programme, Marcus Hurley (USA) (1884–1950) won four events.

World ■ World Championships are contested annually. They were first staged for amateurs in 1893 and for professionals in 1895. The most wins at a particular event is ten by Koichi Nakano (Japan) (b. 14 Nov 1955), professional sprint 1977–86. The most wins at a men's amateur event is seven by; Daniel Morelon (France) (b. 28 Jul 1944), sprint 1966–7, 1969–71, 1973, 1975; and Leon Meredith (GB) (1882–1930), 100 km motor paced 1904–5, 1907–9, 1911, 1913. The most women's titles is seven by; Beryl Burton (GB) (b. 12 May 1937), pursuit 1959–60, 1962–3, 1966 and road 1960, 1967; and by Yvonne Reynders (Belgium), pursuit 1961, 1964–5 and road 1959, 1961, 1963, 1966.

British ■ Beryl Burton, 25 times British all-round time trial champion (1959–83), won 72 individual road TT titles, 14 track pursuit titles and 12 road race titles to 1986. Ian Hallam (b. 24 Nov 1948) won a record 25 men's titles, 1969–82.

Tour de France ■ The greatest number of wins in the *Tour de France* (inaugurated 1903) is five by Jacques Anquetil (France) (1934–1987), 1957, 1961–4; Eddy Merckx (Belgium) (b. 17 Jun 1945), 1969–72 and 1974; and Bernard Hinault (France) (b. 14 Nov 1954); 1978–9, 1981–2 and 1985. The closest race ever was in 1968 when after 4665 km *2898·7 miles* over 25 days (27 Jun–21 Jul) Jan Janssen (Netherlands) (b. 19 May 1940) beat Herman van Springel (Belgium) in Paris by 38 sec. The fastest average speed was 38·88 km/h *24·16 mph* by Pedro Delgado (Spain) in 1988. The longest race was 5745 km *3569 miles* in 1926. The longest ever stage was the 486 km from Les Sables d'Olonne to Bayonne in 1919.

Tour of Britain (Milk Race) ■ Four riders have won the Tour of Britain twice each–Bill Bradley (GB) (1959–60), Les West (GB) (1965, 1967), Fedor den Hertog (Netherlands) (1969, 1971) and Yuriy Kashurin (USSR) (1979, 1982). The closest race ever was in 1976 when after 1665·67 km *1035 miles* over 14 days (30 May–12 Jun) Bill Nickson (GB) (b. 30 Jan 1953) beat Joe Waugh (GB) by 5 sec. The fastest average speed is 42·185 km/h *26·213 mph* by Joey McLoughlin (GB) (b. 3 Dec 1964) in the 1986 race (1714 km *1065 miles*). Malcolm Elliott (b. 1 Jul 1961) won a record six stages in 1983 and had taken his total to 15 by 1987, after winning a record four in succession. The longest Milk Race was in 1969 (2438·16 km *1515 miles*) although the longest ever Tour of Britain was in 1953 (2624·84 km *1631 miles* starting and finishing in London).

Six-day races ■ The most wins in six-day races is 88 out of 233 events by Patrick Sercu (b. 27 Jun 1944), of Belgium, 1964–83.

Longest one-day race ■ The longest single-day 'massed start' road race is the 551–620 km *342–385 miles* Bordeaux–Paris, France, event. Paced over all or part of the route, the highest average speed was in 1981 with 47·186 km/h *29·32 mph* by Herman van Springel (Belgium) (b. 14 Aug 1943) for 584·5 km *363·1 miles* in 13 hr 35 min 18 sec.

Land's End to John O' Groats ■ The 'end to end' record for the 1363 km *847 miles* is 1 day 21 hr 3 min 16 sec (average speed 30·25 km/h *18·80 mph*) by John Woodburn (b. 22 Dec 1936) on 14–15 Aug 1982. The women's record is 2 days 11 hr 7 min by

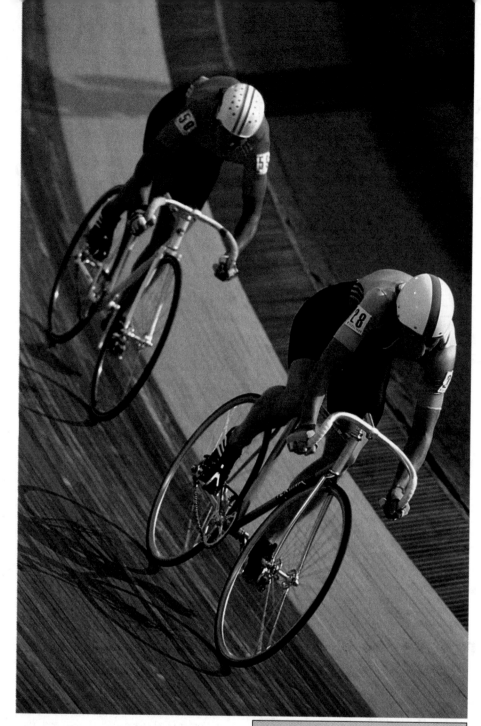

Eileen Sheridan (b. 18 Oct 1923) on 9–11 Jul 1954. She completed 1609 km *1000 miles* in 3 days 1 hr.

Cross-America ■ The trans-America solo records recognised by the Ultra-Marathon Cycling Association are: men, Pete Penseyres 8 days 9 hr 47 min; women, Elaine Mariolle 10 days 2 hr 4 min, both in the McDonald's Race Across America, Huntingon Beach, California to Atlantic City, New Jersey, 5000 km *3107 miles*, starting on 6 Jul 1986.

The trans-Canada record is 13 days 15 hr 4 min by Ronald J. Dossenbach of Windsor, Ontario, 6115 km *3800 miles* from Vancouver, BC to Halifax, Nova Scotia on 30 Jul–13 Aug 1988.

Daniel Buettner, Bret Anderson, Martin Engel and Anne Knabe cycled the length of the Americas, from Prudhoe Bay, Alaska, USA to the Beagle Channel, Ushuaia, Argentina from 8 Aug 1986–13 Jun 1987. They cycled a total distance of 24 568 km *15 266 miles*.

Endurance ■ Thomas Edward Godwin (GB) (1912–75) in the 365 days of 1939 covered 120 805 km *75 065 miles* or an average of 330·96 km *205·65 miles* per day. He then completed 160 934 km *100 000 miles* in 500 days to 14 May 1940.

Jay Aldous and Matt DeWaal cycled 22 997 km *14 290 miles* on a round-the-world trip from Place Monument, Salt Lake City, Utah, USA in 106 days, 2 Apr–16 Jul 1984.

Nicholas Mark Sanders (b. 26 Nov 1957) of Glossop, Derbyshire, circumnavigated the world (20 977·8 km *13 035 road miles*) in 78 days 3 hr 30 min between 5 Jul and 21 Sep 1985. He cycled 7728 km *4802 miles* around Britain in 22 days, 10 Jun–1 Jul 1984.

Cycle touring ■ The greatest mileage amassed in a cycle tour was more than 643 700 km *402 000 miles* by the itinerant lecturer Walter Stolle (b. Sudetenland, 1926) from 24 Jan 1959 to 12 Dec 1976. He visited 159 countries starting from Romford, Essex. From 1922 to 25 Dec 1973 Tommy Chambers (1903–84) of Glasgow, rode a verified total of 1 286 517 km *799 405 miles*.

Visiting every continent, John W. Hathaway (b. England, 13 Jan 1925) of Vancouver, Canada covered 81 300 km *50 600 miles* from 10 Nov 1974 to

6 Oct 1976. Veronica and Colin Scargill, of Bedford, travelled 29 000 km *18 020 miles* around the world on a tandem, 25 Feb 1974–27 Aug 1975.

The most participants in a bicycle tour was 31 678 in the 90 km *56 mile* London to Brighton Bike Ride on 19 Jun 1988. The most participants in a tour in an excess of 1000 km is 2037 (from 2157 starters) for the Australian Bicentennial Caltex Bike Ride from Melbourne to Sydney from 26 Nov–10 Dec 1988.

Highest ■ Mark Merrony from Tenby, Dyfed cycled at an altitude of 6410 m *21 030 ft*, for approximately thirty minutes, close to the relatively flat south summit of Mera Peak, Nepal on 7 May 1989.

CYCLO-CROSS

The greatest number of World Championships (instituted 1950) has been won by Eric de Vlaeminck (Belgium) (b. 23 Aug 1945) with the Amateur and Open in 1966 and six Professional titles in 1968–73. British titles (instituted 1955) have been won most often by John Atkins (b. 7 Apr 1942) with five Amateur (1961–2, 1966–8), seven Professional (1969–75) and one Open title in 1977.

Pennine Way ■ John North (b. 18 Aug 1943) of Rawtenstall, Lancashire, cycled or carried his machine along the 271 miles *436 km* Pennine Way from Edale, Derbyshire to Kirk Yetholm, Borders in 2 days 8 hr 45 min on 9–11 Jun 1978.

Three Peaks ■ Stuart and Neil Shipley, Adrian Scholes and Richard Day, all of Derbyshire, cycled from sea level at Caernarvon, Gwynedd, via the peaks of Snowdon, Scafell Pike and Ben Nevis, to sea level Fort William, Inverness-shire in 74 hr 47 min, from 30 Apr–3 May 1988.

CYCLE SPEEDWAY

First mention of the sport is at Coventry in 1920 and it was first organised in 1945. The sport's governing body, the Cycle Speedway Council, was formed in 1973. Most British Senior Team Championships (instituted 1950) is six by; Wednesfield, Wolverhampton (1974, 1976–8, 1981 and 1983); and by Offerton, Cheshire (1962, 1964–5, 1969, 1972–3). The most individual titles is four by Derek Garnett (b. 16 Jul 1937) (1963, 1965, 1968 and 1972); he also won the inaugural British Veterans' Championship in 1987.

ROLLER CYCLING

James Baker (USA) achieved a record speed of 246·5 km/h *153·2 mph* at El Con Mall, Tucson, Arizona, USA on 28 Jan 1989.

STATIONARY CYCLING

Rudi Jan Jozef De Greef (b. 28 Dec 1955) stayed stationary without support for 10 hr at Meensel-Kiezegem, Belgium on 19 Nov 1982.

Darts

Origins ■ Darts can be dated from the use by archers of heavily weighted ten-inch throwing arrows for self-defence in close quarters fighting. The 'dartes' were used in Ireland in the 16th century and darts was played on the *Mayflower* by the Plymouth pilgrims in 1620. The modern game dates from at least 1896 when Brian Gamlin of Bury, Lancashire, is credited with inventing the present numbering system on the board. The first recorded score of 180 was by John Reader at the Highbury Tavern in Sussex in 1902.

Most titles ■ Eric Bristow (b. 25 Apr 1957) has most wins in the World Masters Championship (instituted 1974) with five, 1977, 1979, 1981 and 1983–4, the World Professional Championship (instituted 1978) with five, 1980–1 and 1984–6, and the World Cup Singles (instituted 1977), two, 1983 and 1985. Seven men have won the annual *News of* the *World* Individual Championship twice; most recently by Mike Gregory (b. 16 Dec 1956) in 1987 and 1988. John Lowe (b. 21 Jul 1945) is the only other man to have won each of the four major titles: World Masters, 1976 and 1980; World Professional, 1979 and 1987; World Cup Singles, 1981; and *News of the World*, 1981.

World Cup ■ The first World Cup was held at the Wembley Conference Centre, London in 1977. England has a record five wins at this biennial tournament. A World Cup for women was instituted in 1983 and has been won twice by England.

Record prize ■ John Lowe won £102 000 for achieving the first 501 scored with the minimum nine darts in a major event on 13 Oct 1984 at Slough in the quarter-finals of the World Match-play Championships. His darts were six successive treble 20s, treble 17, treble 18 and double 18.

Speed records ■ The fastest time taken to complete three games of 301, finishing on doubles, is 1 min 47 sec by Keith Deller on BBC TV's *Record Breakers* on 22 Oct 1985.

The record time for going round the board clockwise in 'doubles' at arm's length is 9·2 sec by Dennis Gower at the Millers Arms, Hastings, East Sussex on 12 Oct 1975 and 14·5 sec in numerical order by Jim Pike (1903–60) at the Craven Club, Newmarket, Suffolk in March 1944. The record for this feat at the 9 ft 2·7 m throwing distance, retrieving own darts, is 2 min 13 sec by Bill Duddy (b. 29 Sep 1932) at The Plough, Haringey, London on 29 Oct 1972.

Least darts ■ Scores of 201 in four darts, 301 in six darts, 401 in seven darts and 501 in nine darts, have been achieved on various occasions. Roy Edwin Blowes (Canada) (b. 8 Oct 1930) was the first person to achieve a 501 in nine darts, 'double-on, double-off', at the Widgeons pub, Calgary, Canada at 9 Mar 1987. His scores were; Bull, treble 20, treble 17, five treble 20s and a double 20 to finish. The lowest number of darts thrown for a score of

1001 is 19 by Cliff Inglis (b. 27 May 1935) (160, 180, 140, 180, 121, 180, 40) at the Bromfield Men's Club, Devon on 11 Nov 1975. A score of 2001 in 52 darts was achieved by Alan Evans (b. 14 Jun 1949) at Ferndale, Mid Glamorgan on 3 Sep 1976. 3001 in 73 darts was thrown by Tony Benson at the Plough Inn, Gorton, Manchester on 12 Jul 1986. Linda Batten (b. 26 Nov 1954) set a women's 3001 record of 117 darts at the Old Wheatsheaf, Enfield, London on 2 Apr 1986. 100 001 was achieved in 3732 darts by Alan Downie of Stornoway on 21 Nov 1986.

Equestrian Sports

Origins ■ Evidence of horse-riding dates from a Persian engraving dated *c.* 3000 BC. Pignatelli's academy of horsemanship at Naples dates from the 16th century. The earliest jumping competition was at the Agricultural Hall, Islington, London, in 1869. Equestrian events have been included in the Olympic Games since 1912.

SHOW JUMPING

Olympic Games ■ The greatest number of Olympic gold medals is five by Hans-Günter Winkler (West Germany) (b. 24 Jul 1926), four team in 1956, 1960, 1964 and 1972 and the individual Grand Prix in 1956. The most team wins in the Prix des Nations is six by Germany in 1936, 1956, 1960, 1964 and as West Germany in 1972 and 1988. The lowest score obtained by a winner is no faults by Frantisek Ventura (Czechoslovakia) (1895–1969) on *Eliot*, 1928

and Alwin Schockemöhle (West Germany) (b. 29 May 1937) on *Warwick Rex*, 1976. Pierre Jonquères d'Oriola (France) (b. 1 Feb 1920) uniquely won the individual gold medal twice, 1952 and 1964. Richard John Hannay Meade (GB) (b. 4 Dec 1938) is the only British rider to win three gold medals – as an individual in 1972 with team titles in 1968 and 1972, all in the three-day event.

World Championships ■ The men's World Championships (instituted 1953) have been won twice by Hans-Günter Winkler (West Germany) (1954–5) and Raimondo d'Inzeo (Italy) (1956 and 1960). The women's title (1965–74) was won twice by Jane 'Janou' Tissot (*née* Lefebvre) (France) (b. Saigon, 14 May 1945) on *Rocket* (1970 and 1974).

President's Cup ■ The World team championship (instituted 1965) has been won a record twelve times by Great Britain, 1965, 1967, 1970, 1972–4, 1977–9, 1983, 1985–6.

World Cup ■ Instituted in 1979, the only double winner is Conrad Homfeld (USA) (b. 25 Dec 1951), 1980 and 1985.

King George V Gold Cup and Queen Elizabeth II Cup ■ David Broome (b. 1 Mar 1940) has won

Two golds ● Mark Todd (New Zealand) and *Charisma* won the Three-Day Event gold at the 1988 Olympics, repeating their success of 1984. This equalled the record of Charles Pahud de Mortanges (Netherlands) and *Marcroix* in 1928 and 1932. (Photo: All-Sport)

the King George V Gold Cup (first held 1911) a record five times, 1960 on *Sunsalve*, 1966 on *Mister Softee*, 1972 on *Sportsman*, 1977 on *Philco* and 1981 on *Mr Ross*. The Queen Elizabeth II Cup (first held 1949), for women, has been won five times by his sister Elizabeth Edgar (b. 28 Apr 1943), 1977 on *Everest Wallaby*, 1979 on *Forever*, 1981 and 1982 on *Everest Forever*, 1986 on *Everest Rapier*. The only horse to win both these trophies is *Sunsalve* in 1957 (with Elisabeth Anderson) and 1960.

Jumping records ■ The official *Fédération Equestre Internationale* records are: high jump 2·47 m *8 ft 1¼ in* by *Huasó*, ridden by Capt Alberto Larraguibel Morales (Chile) at Viña del Mar, Santiago, Chile on 5 Feb 1949; long jump over water 8·40 m *27 ft 6¾ in* by *Something*, ridden by André Ferreira (South Africa) at Johannesburg, South Africa on 25 Apr 1975.

The British high jump record is 2·32 m *7 ft 7¼ in* by the 16·2 hands *167 cm* grey gelding *Lastic* ridden by Nick Skelton (b. 30 Dec 1957) at Olympia, London on 16 Dec 1978. On 25 Jun 1937, at Olympia, the Lady Wright (*née* Margery Avis Bullows) set the best recorded height for a British equestrienne on her liver chestnut *Jimmy Brown* at 2·23 m *7 ft 4 in*. The greatest recorded height reached on bareback is 2·13 m *7 ft* by Michael Whitaker (b. 17 Mar 1960) on *Red Flight* at Dublin, Eire on 14 Nov 1982.

GUINNESS HAVE PUBLISHED **SHOW JUMPING: RECORDS FACTS AND CHAMPIONS** JUDITH DRAPER £14.95

THREE-DAY EVENT

Olympic Games and World Championships ■ Charles Ferdinand Pahud de Mortanges (Netherlands) (1896–1971) won a record four Olympic gold medals, team 1924 and 1928, individual (riding *Marcroix*) 1928 and 1932, when he also won a team silver medal. Bruce Davidson (USA) (b. 13 Dec 1949) is the only rider to have won two world titles (instituted 1966), on *Irish Cap* in 1974 and *Might Tango* in 1978. Richard Meade is the only British rider to win three gold medals, individual 1972 and team 1968 and 1972.

Badminton ■ The Badminton Three-Day Event

(instituted 1949) has been won six times by Lucinda Green (*née* Prior-Palmer) (b. 7 Nov 1953), in 1973 (on *Be Fair*), 1976 (*Wide Awake*), 1977 (*George*), 1979 (*Killaire*), 1983 (*Regal Realm*) and 1984 (*Beagle Bay*).

Ian Stark (GB) became the first ever rider to ride first (*Sir Wattie*) and second (*Glenburnie*) in the same year at Badminton in May 1988.

DRESSAGE

Henri St Cyr (Sweden) (1904–79) won a record four Olympic gold medals, both team and individual in 1952 and 1956. Germany (West Germany post-1968) have won a record seven team gold medals, 1928, 1936, 1964, 1968, 1976, 1984 and 1988, and have most team wins, five, at the World Championships (instituted 1966). Dr Reiner Klimke (West Germany) (b. 14 Jan 1936) is the only rider to win two world titles, on *Mehmed* in 1974 and *Ahlerich* in 1982.

CARRIAGE DRIVING

World Championships were first held in 1972. Three team titles have been won by Great Britain, 1972, 1974 and 1980, and Hungary 1976, 1978 and 1986. Two individual titles have been won by György Bárdos (Hungary), 1978 and 1980 and by Tjeerd Velstra (Netherlands), 1982 and 1986.

LONGEST RIDE ■ Henry G. Perry, a stockman from Mollongghip, Victoria, Australia rode *22 565 km 14 021 miles* around Australia in 157 days, 1 May to 4 Oct 1985, with six horses.

Fencing

Origins ■ 'Fencing' (fighting with single sticks) was practised as a sport, or as a part of a religious ceremony, in Egypt as early as *c.* 1360 BC. The first governing body for fencing in Britain was the Corporation of Masters of Defence founded by Henry VIII before 1540, and fencing has been practised as sport, notably in prize fights, since that time. The modern foil was introduced in France as a practice weapon for the short court sword in the mid-17th century. In the late 19th century the épée was developed in France and the light fencing sabre in Italy.

Most titles *World* ■ The greatest number of individual world titles won is five by Aleksandr Romankov (USSR) (b. 7 Nov 1953), at foil 1974, 1977, 1979, 1982 and 1983, but Christian d'Oriola (France) won four world foil titles, 1947, 1949, 1953–4 as well as two individual Olympic titles. Four women foilists have won three world titles: Hélène Mayer (Germany) (1910–53), 1929, 1931, 1937; Ilona Schacherer-Elek (Hungary) (b. 17 May 1907), 1934–5, 1951; Ellen Müller–Preis (Austria) (b. 6 May 1912), 1947, 1949–50; and Cornelia Hanisch (West Germany) (b. 12 Jun 1952), 1979, 1981, 1985. Of these only Ilona Schacherer-Elek also won two individual Olympic titles (1936 and 1948).

Olympic ■ The most individual Olympic gold medals won is three by Ramón Fonst (Cuba) (1883–1959) in 1900 and 1904 (two) and by Nedo Nadi (Italy) (1894–1952) in 1912 and 1920 (two). Nadi also won three team gold medals in 1920 making a then unprecedented total of five gold medals at one celebration. Edoardo Mangiarotti (Italy) (b. 7 Apr 1919) with six gold, five silver and two bronze, holds the record of 13 Olympic medals. He won them for foil and épée from 1936 to 1960. The most gold medals by a woman is four (one individual, three team) by Elena Novikova (*née* Byelova) (USSR) (b. 28 Jul 1947) from 1968 to 1976, and the record for all medals is seven (two gold, three silver, two bronze) by Ildikó Sági (formerly Ujlaki, *née* Retjö) (Hungary) (b. 11 May 1937) from 1960 to 1976.

British ■ The only British fencer to win a gold medal is Gillian Mary Sheen (b. 21 Aug 1928) in the 1956 foil. A record three Olympic medals were won by Edgar Seligman (1867–1958) with silver medals in the épée team event in 1906, 1908 and 1912.

Henry William Furse Hoskyns (b. 19 Mar 1931) has competed most often for Great Britain with six Olympic appearances, 1956–76.

Amateur Fencing Association titles ■ The most won at one weapon is ten at women's foil by Gillian Sheen (now Donaldson), 1949, 1951–8, 1960.

Field Sports

Hunting the fox in Britain became popular from the second half of the 18th century, though it is mentioned very much earlier. Prior to that time hunting was confined principally to the deer and the hare.

Pack *Earliest* ■ The Old Charlton Hunt (later the Goodwood) in West Sussex (now extinct), the Duke of Monmouth and Lord Grey of Werke at Charlton, Sussex, and the Duke of Buckingham in North Yorkshire owned packs which were entered to fox only during the reign (1660–85) of Charles II.

Largest ■ The pack with the greatest number of hounds has been the Duke of Beaufort's hounds maintained at Badminton, Avon since 1786. At times hunting six days a week, this pack once had 120 couples at hounds. It now meets four days a week.

Longest mastership ■ The 10th Duke of Beaufort (1900–84) was Master of Foxhounds from 1924 until his death in 1984 and hunted his hounds on 3895 days from 1920–67.

Longest hunt ■ The longest recorded hunt was one held by Squire Sandys which ran from Holmbank, northern Lancashire to Ulpha, Cumbria, a total of nearly 80 miles *128 km* in reputedly only 6 hr, in January or February 1743. The longest duration hunt was one of 10 hr 5 min by Charlton Hunt of West Sussex, which ran from East Dean Wood at 7.45 a.m. to a kill over 57 $\frac{1}{4}$ miles *92 km* away at 5.50 p.m. on 26 Jan 1738.

Most widespread hunting ■ Between 1969 and 1989, J. N. P. Watson, hunting correspondent to *Country Life*, hunted with 267 different packs of foxhounds, staghounds and harehounds in Britain, Ireland, USA and Europe.

BEAGLING

Longest mastership ■ Betty McKeeven (*née* Davies) has been Master of the Blean Beagles in Kent since 1909. She was given her first pack by her father at the age of eight and remains the sole Master.

GAME SHOOTING

Record heads ■ The world's finest head is the 23-pointer stag in the Maritzburg collection, East Germany. The outside span is 191 cm *75 $\frac{1}{2}$ in*, the length 120 cm *47 $\frac{1}{2}$ in* and the weight 18·824 kg *41 $\frac{1}{2}$ lb*. The greatest number of points is probably 33 (plus 29) on the stag shot in 1696 by Frederick III (1657–1713), the Elector of Brandenburg, later King Frederick I of Prussia.

Largest tally to a single sportsman ■ 556 813 head of game fell to the guns of the 2nd Marquess of Ripon between 1867 and when he dropped dead on a grouse moor after shooting his 52nd bird on the morning of 22 Sep 1923. This figure included 241 234 pheasants, 124 193 partridge and 31 900 hares. (His game books are held by the gunmakers James Purdey and Sons.)

Thomas, 6th Baron Walsingham, bagged 1070 grouse, a one-day record for a single gun, in Yorkshire on 30 Aug 1888.

Fives

A handball game against the buttress of Eton College Chapel was first recorded in 1825. New courts were built at Eton in 1840, the rules were codified in 1877, rewritten laws were introduced three times and last amended in 1981.

Most titles ■ One pair has won the amateur championship (Kinnaird Cup) nine times–Brian C.

Matthews (b. 15 Aug 1957) and John P. Reynolds (b. 9 Aug 1961), 1981–9. Anthony Hughes won nine titles but not with the same partner, eight with Arthur James Gordon Campbell, 1958, 1965–8, 1971, 1973 and 1975, and in 1963 with D. Guilford.

RUGBY FIVES

As now known, this game dates from *c.* 1850 with the first inter-public school matches recorded in the early 1870s. The Oxford *v.* Cambridge contest was inaugurated in 1925 and the Rugby Fives Association was founded in the home of Dr Edgar Cyriax (1874–1954), in Welbeck Street, London on 29 Oct 1927. The dimensions of the standard rugby fives court were approved by the Association in 1931.

Most titles ■ The greatest number of Amateur Singles Championships (instituted 1932) ever won is 15 by Wayne Enstone in 1973–8 and 1980–8. The record for the Amateur Doubles Championship (instituted 1925) is nine by David Hebden and Ian Fuller in 1980–5 and 1987–9.

The invitation World Championships were first held in 1983. On the first three occasions Wayne Enstone won the singles and Enstone and Steve Ashton the doubles.

Football (Association)

Origins ■ A game with some similarities termed *Tsu-chu* was played in China in the 4th and 3rd centuries BC. One of the earliest references to the game in England is a Royal Proclamation by Edward II in 1314 banning the game in the City of London. The earliest clear representation of football is an Edinburgh print dated 1672–3. The game was standardised with the formation of the Football Association in England on 26 Oct 1863. The oldest club is Sheffield FC, formed on 24 Oct 1857. The oldest in the Football League is Notts County, founded in 1862. Eleven per side became standard in 1870.

PROFESSIONAL

Longest match ■ The duration record for first-class fixtures is 3 hr 30 min (with interruptions), in the Copa Libertadores in Santos, Brazil, on 2–3 Aug 1962, when Santos drew 3–3 with Penarol FC of Montevideo, Uruguay.

The longest British match on record was one of 3 hr 23 min between Stockport County and Doncaster Rovers in the second leg of the Third Division (North) Cup at Edgeley Park, Stockport, Greater Manchester on 30 Mar 1946.

Longest unbeaten run ■ Nottingham Forest were undefeated in 42 consecutive First Division matches from 20 Nov 1977 to 9 Dec 1978. In Scottish Football Glasgow Celtic were undefeated in 62 matches (49 won, 13 drawn), 13 Nov 1915–21 April 1917.

Most postponements ■ The Scottish Cup tie between Inverness Thistle and Falkirk during the winter of 1978–9 was postponed a record 29 times due to weather conditions. Finally Falkirk won the game 4–0.

GOAL SCORING

Teams ■ The highest score recorded in a first-class match is 36. This occurred in the Scottish Cup match between Arbroath and Bon Accord on 5 Sep 1885, when Arbroath won 36–0 on their home ground. But for the lack of nets and the consequent waste of retrieval time the score must have been even higher. Seven further goals were disallowed for offside.

The highest margin recorded in an international match is 17, when England beat Australia 17–0 at Sydney on 30 Jun 1951. This match is not listed by England as a *full* international. The highest in the

British Isles was when England beat Ireland 13–0 at Belfast on 18 Feb 1882.

The highest score between English clubs in any major competition is 26, when Preston North End beat Hyde 26–0 in an FA Cup tie at Deepdale, Lancashire on 15 Oct 1887. The biggest victory in an FA Cup Final is six when Bury beat Derby County 6–0 at Crystal Palace on 18 Apr 1903, in which year Bury did not concede a single goal in their five Cup matches.

The highest score by one side in a Football League (First Division) match is 12 goals when West Bromwich Albion beat Darwen 12–0 at West Bromwich, West Midlands on 4 Apr 1892; when Nottingham Forest beat Leicester Fosse by the same score at Nottingham on 21 Apr 1909; and when Aston Villa beat Accrington 12–2 at Perry Barr, West Midlands on 12 Mar 1892.

The highest aggregate in League Football was 17 goals when Tranmere Rovers beat Oldham Athletic 13–4 in a Third Division (North) match at Prenton Park, Merseyside, on Boxing Day, 1935. The record margin in a League match has been 13 in the Newcastle United 13, Newport County 0 (Second Division) match on 5 Oct 1946 and in the Stockport County 13, Halifax 0 (Third Division (North)) match on 6 Jan 1934.

The highest number of goals by any British team in a professional league in a season is 142 in 34 matches by Raith Rovers (Scottish Second Division in the 1937/8 season. The English League record is 134 in 46 matches by Peterborough United (Fourth Division) in 1960/1.

Individual ■ The most scored by one player in a first-class match is 16 by Stephan Stanis (*né* Stanikowski, b. Poland, 15 Jul 1913) for Racing Club de Lens *v.* Aubry-Asturies, in Lens, France, in a wartime French Cup game on 13 Dec 1942.

The record number of goals scored by one player in an international match is ten by Sofus Nielsen (1888–1963) for Denmark *v.* France (17–1) in the 1908 Olympics and by Gottfried Fuchs (1889–1972) for Germany who beat Russia 16–0 in the 1912 Olympic tournament (consolation event) in Sweden.

Most in a season ■ The most goals in a League season is 60 in 39 games by William Ralph 'Dixie' Dean (1907–80) for Everton (First Division) in 1927/8 and 66 in 38 games by James Smith (1902–76) for Ayr United (Scottish Second Division) in the same season. With three more in Cup ties and 19 in representative matches Dean's total was 82.

Career ■ Artur Friedenreich (Brazil) (1892–1969) scored an undocumented 1329 goals in a 43 year first-class football career. The most goals scored in a specified period is 1216 by Edson Arantes do Nascimento (Brazil) (b. 23 Oct 1940), known as Pelé, from 7 Sep 1956 to 2 Oct 1974 in 1254 games. His best year was 1959 with 126, and the *Milesimo* (1000 th) came from a penalty for his club Santos in

CELTIC v. RANGERS

These two most famous clubs have dominated Scottish football titles (League, Cup and League Cup). Celtic and Rangers have won nearly two-thirds of Scottish titles (League, Cup and League Cup) to the end of the 1988/9 season. Most remarkably, between them, they have won 80% of the Scottish League titles since it was first contested in 1890/1 and in only one season (1964/5) has either of them failed to finish in the first three.

	WINS	
	CELTIC	RANGERS
LEAGUE	35	39
SCOTTISH CUP	29	24
LEAGUE/SKOL CUP	9	16

Rangers (below left) celebrate their record 16th League Cup success and later went on to win the League. However they were denied the treble for the 1988/9 season when they were beaten 1–0 in the Scottish Cup final on 20 May 1989 by Celtic (scorer Joe Miller). Captain Jim Aitken and his team-mates celebrate another Scottish Cup success for Celtic (below right). (Photos: All-Sport)

the Maracaña Stadium, Rio de Janeiro on 19 Nov 1969 when playing his 909th first-class match. He later played for New York Cosmos and on his retirement on 1 Oct 1977 his total had reached 1281, in 1363 games. He later added two more goals in special appearances. Franz 'Bimbo' Binder (b. 1 Dec 1911) scored 1006 goals in 756 games in Austria and Germany between 1930 and 1950. The international career record for England is 49 goals by Robert 'Bobby' Charlton (b. 11 Oct 1937). His first was *v.* Scotland on 19 Apr 1958 and his last on 20 May 1970 *v.* Colombia.

The greatest number of goals scored in British first-class football is 550 (410 in Scottish League matches) by James McGrory of Glasgow Celtic (1922–38). The most scored in League matches is 434, for West Bromwich Albion, Fulham, Leicester City and Shrewsbury Town, by George Arthur Rowley (b. 21 Apr 1926) between 1946 and April 1965. Rowley also scored 32 goals in the F.A. Cup and one for England 'B'.

Fastest goals ■ The fastest Football League goals on record were scored in 6 sec by Albert E. Mundy (b. 12 May 1926) (Aldershot) in a Fourth Division match v. Hartlepool United at Victoria Ground, Hartlepool, Cleveland on 25 Oct 1958, by Barrie Jones (b. 31 Oct 1938) (Notts County) in a Third Division match v. Torquay United on 31 Mar 1962, by Keith Smith (b. 15 Sep 1940) (Crystal Palace) in a Second Division match v. Derby County at the Baseball Ground, Derby on 12 Dec 1964 and by Tommy W. Langley (b. 8 Feb 1958) (Queen's Park Rangers) in a Second Division match v. Bolton Wanderers on 11 Oct 1980.

The fastest confirmed hat-trick is in 2 ½ minutes by Ephraim 'Jock' Dodds (b. 7 Sep 1915) for Blackpool v. Tranmere Rovers on 28 Feb 1942, and Jimmy Scarth (b. 26 Aug 1920) for Gillingham v. Leyton Orient in Third Division (Southern) on 1 Nov 1952. A hat-trick in 1 min 50 sec is claimed for Maglioni of Independiente v. Gimnasia y Escrima de la Plata in Argentina on 18 Mar 1973. John McIntyre (Blackburn Rovers) scored four goals in 5 min v. Everton at Ewood Park, Blackburn, Lancashire on 16 Sep 1922. William 'Ginger' Richardson (West Bromwich Albion) scored four goals in 5 min from the kick-off against West Ham United at Upton Park on 7 Nov 1931. Frank Keetley scored six goals in 21 min in the second half of the Lincoln City v. Halifax Town league match on 16 Jan 1932. The international record is three goals in 3 ½ min by Willie Hall (Tottenham Hotspur) for England against Ireland on 16 Nov 1938 at Old Trafford, Greater Manchester.

Fastest own goal ■ Torquay United's Pat Kruse (b. 30 Nov 1953) equalled the fastest goal on record when he headed the ball into his own net only 6 sec after kick-off v. Cambridge United on 3 Jan 1977.

GOALKEEPING

The longest that any goalkeeper has succeeded in preventing any goals being scored past him in international matches is 1142 min for Dino Zoff (Italy), from September 1972 to June 1974.

Closest win ● The 1988/9 League Championship was decided by the fact that Arsenal had scored more goals (73 to 65) than Liverpool, after both teams finished level on points and goal difference. The two teams had met in the last game of the season with Arsenal having to win 2–0 to take the Championship. This they achieved with a goal from Michael Thomas with virtually the last kick of the game. Here from left to right, Kevin Richardson, Steve Bould, Paul Merson and Alan Smith (who had scored the first goal) celebrate Arsenal's success. (Photo: All-Sport)

The British club record in all competitive matches is 1196 min by Chris Woods (b. 14 Nov 1959) for Glasgow Rangers from 26 Nov 1986 to 31 Jan 1987.

FA CHALLENGE CUP AND SCOTTISH FA CUP

Most wins ■ The greatest number of FA Cup wins is seven by: Aston Villa, 1887, 1895, 1897, 1905, 1913, 1920 and 1957 (nine Final appearances); and Tottenham Hotspur, 1901, 1921, 1961, 1962, 1967, 1981 and 1982 (eight appearances). Newcastle United and Arsenal have been in the final 11 times. The highest aggregate scores have been 6–1 in 1890 and 4–3 in 1953.

The greatest number of Scottish FA Cup wins is 29 by Celtic in 1892, 1899, 1900, 1904, 1907–8, 1911–12, 1914, 1923, 1925, 1927, 1931, 1933, 1937, 1951, 1954, 1965, 1967, 1969, 1971–2, 1974–5, 1977, 1980, 1985 and 1988–9.

Youngest player ■ The youngest player in an FA Cup Final was Paul Allen (b. 28 Aug 1962) for West Ham United v. Arsenal on 10 May 1980, aged 17 yr 256 days. Derek Johnstone (Rangers) (b. 4 Nov 1953) was 16 yr 11 months old when he played in the Scottish League Cup Final against Celtic on 24 Oct 1970. The youngest goal scorer in the FA Cup Final was Norman Whiteside (b. 7 May 1965) for Manchester United v. Brighton at 18 yr 19 days on 26

May 1983. The youngest player ever in the FA Cup competition was full back Andrew Awford (b. 14 Jul 1972) at 15 yr 88 days for Worcester City in a qualifying round tie at Borehamwood, Hertfordshire on 10 Oct 1987.

Most medals ■ Three players have won five FA Cupwinners' medals: James Forrest with Blackburn Rovers (1884–6, 1890–1); the Hon. Sir Arthur Fitzgerald Kinnaird KT with Wanderers (1873, 1877–8) and Old Etonians (1879, 1882); and Charles H. R. Wollaston with Wanderers (1872–3, 1876–8).

The most Scottish Cupwinners' medals won is eight by Charles Campbell (Queen's Park) in 1874–6, 1880–2, 1884 and 1886.

Longest tie ■ The most protracted FA Cup tie in the competition proper was that between Stoke City and Bury in the third round, with Stoke winning 3–2 in the fifth meeting after 9 hr 22 min of play in January 1955. The matches were at Bury (1–1) on 8 Jan; Stoke-on-Trent on 12 Jan (abandoned after 22 min of extra time with the score 1–1); Goodison Park (3–3) on 17 Jan; Anfield (2–2) on 19 Jan; and finally at Old Trafford on 24 Jan. In the 1972 final qualifying round Alvechurch beat Oxford City after five previous drawn games (total playing time 11 hours).

FOOTBALL LEAGUE/MILK CUP/ LITTLEWOODS CUP

Instituted in 1960/1, the most wins is four by Liverpool, 1981–4.

SCOTTISH LEAGUE/SKOL CUP

Instituted in 1946/7, the most wins is 16 by Rangers between 1947 and 1988.

LEAGUE CHAMPIONSHIPS

The record number of successive national league championships is nine by: Celtic (Scotland) 1966–74; CSKA, Sofia (Bulgaria) 1954–62; and MTK Budapest (Hungary) 1917–25. The Sofia club holds a European post-war record of 25 league titles, including two under its new name CFKA Sredets.

English ■ The greatest number of League Championships (First Division) is 17 by Liverpool in 1901, 1906, 1922-3, 1947, 1964, 1966, 1973, 1976-7, 1979-80, 1982-4, 1986 and 1988. The record number of wins in a season is 33 from 42 matches by Doncaster Rovers in Third Division (North) in 1946/7. The First Division record is 31 wins from 42 matches by Tottenham Hotspur in 1960/1. In 1893/4 Liverpool won 22 and drew 6 in 28 Second Division games. They also won the promotion match. The most points in a season under the current scoring system is 102 from 46 matches by Swindon in Fourth Division in 1985/6. Under the new system the First Division record would have been Liverpool's 98 in 1978/9, when they won 30 and drew 8 of their 42 matches.

'Double' ■ The only FA Cup and League Championship 'doubles' are those of Preston North End in 1889, Aston Villa in 1897, Tottenham Hotspur in 1961, Arsenal in 1971 and Liverpool in 1986. Preston won the League without losing a match and the Cup without having a goal scored against them throughout the whole competition.

Scottish ■ Glasgow Rangers have won the Scottish League Championship 39 times (one shared 1891) between 1891 and 1989. Their 76 points in the Scottish First Division in 1920/1 represent a record in any division.

Closest win ■ In 1923/4 Huddersfield won the First Division Championship over Cardiff by 0·02 of a goal with a goal average of 1·81.

THE FIFA WORLD CUP

Fédération Internationale de Football Association (FIFA), which was founded on 21 May 1904, instituted the first World Cup on 13 Jul 1930, in Montevideo, Uruguay. It is now held quadrennially. Three wins have been achieved by Brazil 1958, 1962 and 1970, and Italy 1934, 1938 and 1982. Brazil, uniquely, have taken part in all 13 finals tournaments.

Appearances ■ Antonio Carbajal (Mexico) (b. 1923) is the only player to have appeared in five World Cup finals tournaments, keeping goal for Mexico in 1950, 1954, 1958, 1962 and 1966, playing 11 games in all. The most appearances in finals tournaments is 21 by: Uwe Seeler (West Germany) (b. 5 Nov 1936), 1958-70; and by Wladyslaw Zmuda (Poland) (b. 6 Jun 1954), 1974-86. Pelé is the only player to have been with three World Cup-winning teams, in 1958, 1962 and 1970. The youngest ever to play in the World Cup is Norman Whiteside, who played for Northern Ireland v. Yugoslavia aged 17 yr 42 days on 17 Jun 1982.

Goal scoring ■ Just Fontaine (b. Marrakesh, Morocco, 18 Aug 1933) of France scored 13 goals in six matches in the final stages of the 1958 competition in Sweden. Gerd Müller (West Germany) (b. 3 Nov 1945) scored 10 goals in 1970 and four in 1974 for the highest aggregate of 14 goals. Fontaine, Jairzinho (Brazil) and Alcide Ghiggia (Uruguay) are the only three players to have scored in every match in a final series. Jairzinho scored seven in six games in 1970 and Ghiggia, four in four games in 1950 .

The most goals scored in a final is three by Geoff Hurst (b. 8 Dec 1941) for England v. West Germany on 30 Jul 1966. Three players have scored in two finals: Vava (real name Edwaldo Izito Neto) (Brazil) in 1958 and 1962, Pelé in 1958 and 1970; and Paul Breitner (West Germany) in 1974 and 1982. The fastest goal in World Cup competition was one in 27 sec by Bryan Robson (b. 11 Jan 1957) for England v. France in Bilbao on 16 Jun 1982.

The highest score in a World Cup match occurred in a qualifying match in Auckland on 15 Aug 1981 when New Zealand beat Fiji 13-0. The highest score during the final stages is 10, scored by Hungary in a 10-1 win over El Salvador at Elche, Spain on 15 Jun 1982. The highest match aggregate in the finals tournament is 12, when Austria beat Switzerland, 7-5, in 1954.

The highest scoring team in a finals tournament has been West Germany who scored 25 in six matches in 1954, for the highest average of 4·17 goals per game.

The best defensive record belongs to England, who in six matches in 1966 conceded only three goals. Curiously, no team has ever failed to score in a World Cup Final.

TOURNAMENT RECORDS

World Club Championship ■ This club tournament was started in 1960 between the winners of the European Cup and the Copa Libertadores, the South American equivalent. The most wins is three by Peñarol, Uruguay in 1961, 1966 and 1982. Independiente, Argentina won in 1973 and 1984 and reached the Final in 1975, but couldn't agree dates for the matches with Bayern Munich.

European Championship (Nations Cup) ■ Held every four years from 1958. West Germany are the only country to have won twice, in 1972 and 1980. They also lost in the 1976 final, to Czechoslovakia.

Major cup finals ● Marco Van Basten, seen here in the colours of AC Milan, has scored in finals of three major European competitions: European Cup Winners Cup for Ajax v. Lokomotiv Leipzig at Athens, Greece on 13 May 1987; European Championship for the Netherlands v. USSR at Münich, West Germany on 25 June 1988; and European Cup for AC Milan (when he scored twice) v. Steaua Bucharest at Barcelona, Spain on 24 May 1989. On each occasion Van Basten ended up on the winning side. (Photo: All-Sport/David Cannon)

European Champion Clubs Cup ■ The European Cup for the league champions of the respective nations was approved by FIFA on 8 May 1955 and was run by the European governing body UEFA (Union of European Football Associations) which came into being in the previous year. Real Madrid won the first final, and have won a record six times 1956-60, 1966. The highest score in a Final was Real Madrid's 7-3 win over Eintracht Frankfurt at Hampden Park, Glasgow on 18 May 1960.

Glasgow Celtic became the first British club to win the Cup, beating Inter-Milan 2-1 in Lisbon, Portugal on 25 May 1967. They also became the first British club to win the European Cup and the two senior domestic tournaments (League and Cup) in the same season. Liverpool, winners in 1977, 1978, 1981 and 1984, have been the most successful British club and in 1983/4 emulated Celtic by also winning two domestic competitions – League and Milk Cup.

European Cup Winners Cup ■ A tournament

for national cup winners started in 1960/1. Barcelona have won a record three times, 1979, 1982 and 1989. Tottenham Hotspur were the first British club to win the trophy, when they set a record score for the final beating Atlético Madrid 5-1 in Rotterdam, Netherlands on 15 May 1963.

UEFA Cup ■ Originally known as the International Inter-City Industrial Fairs Cup, this club tournament began in 1955. The first competition lasted three years, the second two years. In 1960/1 it became an annual tournament and since 1971/2 has been for the UEFA Cup. The most wins is three by Barcelona in 1958, 1960 and 1966. The first British club to win the trophy was Leeds United in 1968.

PLAYERS

Most durable ■ Peter Leslie Shilton (b. 18 Sep 1949) has made a record 1201 senior UK appearances, including a record 864 League appearances, 286 for Leicester City (1966-74), 110 for Stoke City (1974-7), 202 for Nottingham Forest (1977-82), 188 for Southampton (1982-7) and 79 for Derby County (1987-9), 79 FA Cup, 83 League Cup, 109 internationals, 13 Under-23, 4 Football League XI and 49 various European and other club competitons. Norman John Trollope (b. 14 Jun 1943) made 770 League appearances for one club, Swindon Town, between 1960 and 1980. Shilton also holds the record for the most senior UK appearances, 1201, in addition to his 864 League matches, he has played 122 internationals (including Under-23), 162 FA and League Cup games and 53 others.

Transfer fees ■ The highest transfer fee quoted for a player is 15 895 million lire by Napoli in 1984 for Diego Maradona (Argentina) (b. 30 Oct 1960) from Barcelona. This exceeded the *c.* £5 million that Barcelona paid for Maradona in 1982.

The record fee between two British clubs is £2 million (including VAT and other levies) paid by Tottenham Hotspur to Newcastle United for Paul Gascoigne (b. 27 May 1967) on 7 Jul 1988 and by Everton to West Ham United for Antony Richard Cottee (b. 11 Jul 1965) on 25 Jul 1988. The highest transfer fee for a British player is the estimated £3·2 million paid by Juventus of Italy to Liverpool for Ian Rush (b. 20 Oct 1961) in June 1986.

Heaviest goalkeeper ■ The biggest goalkeeper in representative football was the England international Willie J. 'Fatty' Foulke (1874-1916), who stood 1·90 m *6 ft 3 in* and weighed 141 kg *22 st 3 lb*. His last games were for Bradford City, by which time he was 165 kg *26 st.* He once stopped a game by snapping the cross bar.

INTERNATIONAL CAPS

Oldest ■ The oldest international has been William Henry 'Billy' Meredith (1874-1958) (Manchester City and United) who played outside right for Wales v. England at Highbury, London on 15 Mar 1920 when aged 45 yr 229 days. He played internationally for a record span of 26 years (1895-1920).

Youngest ■ The youngest British international was Norman Whiteside, who played for Northern Ireland v. Yugoslavia at 17 yr 42 days on 17 Jun 1982.

England's youngest international was Duncan Edwards (1936-58) (Manchester United) v. Scotland at Wembley on 2 Apr 1955, at 18 yr 183 days. The youngest Welsh cap was John Charles (b. 27 Dec 1931) (Leeds United), v. Ireland at Wrexham on 8 Mar 1950, aged 18 yr 71 days. Scotland's youngest international has been Johnny Lambie (Queen's Park), at 17 yr 2 days v. Ireland on 20 Mar 1886. The youngest for the Republic of Ireland was James Holmes (b. 11 Nov 1953) (Coventry City), at 17 yr 200 days v. Austria in Dublin on 30 May 1971.

Most international appearances ■ The greatest number of appearances for a national team is 150 by Hector Chumpitaz (Peru) (b. 12 Apr 1943) from 1963 to 1982. This includes all matches played by the national team. The record for full internationals against other national teams is 119 by Pat Jennings of Northern Ireland (as above).

Most wins ● Gary Lineker (b. 30 Nov 1960) of Barcelona celebrates beating Sampdoria, 2-0, in the final of the European Cup Winners Cup at Lausanne, Switzerland on 10 May 1989. It was Barcelona's third success, a record. (Photo: All-Sport/Simon Bruty)

The most international appearances by a woman is 56 (49 as captain) by Carol Thomas (b. 5 Jun 1955) for England, 1974–86.

ATTENDANCES

Greatest crowds ■ The greatest recorded crowd at any football match was 205 000 (199 589 paid) for the Brazil v. Uruguay World Cup match in the Maracaña Municipal Stadium, Rio de Janeiro, Brazil on 16 Jul 1950. The record attendance for a European Cup match is 136 505 at the semi-final between Glasgow Celtic and Leeds United at Hampden Park, Glasgow on 15 Apr 1970.

The British record paid attendance is 149 547 at the Scotland v. England international at Hampden Park, Glasgow on 17 Apr 1937. It is, however, probable that this total was exceeded (estimated 160 000) at the FA Cup Final between Bolton Wanderers and West Ham United at Wembley Stadium on 28 Apr 1923, when the crowd spilled onto the pitch and the start was delayed 40 min until it was cleared. The counted admissions were 126 047.

The Scottish Cup record attendance is 146 433 when Celtic played Aberdeen at Hampden Park on 24 Apr 1937. The record attendance for a League match in Britain is 118 567 for Rangers v. Celtic at Ibrox Park, Glasgow on 2 Jan 1939.

The highest attendance at an amateur match has been 120 000 in Senayan Stadium, Jakarta, Indonesia on 26 Feb 1976 for the Pre-Olympic Group II Final, North Korea v. Indonesia.

Smallest crowd ■ The smallest crowd at a full home international was 2315 for Wales v. Northern Ireland on 27 May 1982 at the Racecourse Ground, Wrexham, Clwyd. The smallest paying attendance at a Football League fixture was for the Stockport County v. Leicester City match at Old Trafford, Greater Manchester on 7 May 1921. Stockport's own ground was under suspension and the 'crowd' numbered 13 but an estimated 2000 gained free admission. When West Ham beat Castilla of Spain (5–1) in the European Cup Winners Cup at Upton Park, Greater London on 1 Oct 1980 and when Aston Villa beat Besiktas of Turkey (3–1) in the European Cup at Villa Park, Birmingham on 15 Sep 1982, there were no paying spectators due to disciplinary action by the European Football Union.

PENALTIES

The greatest number of penalty kicks taken to decide a cup game under the jurisdiction of the Football League occurred in a Freight Rover Trophy, Southern Section quarter–final between Aldershot and Fulham on 10 Feb 1987, at the Recreation Ground, Aldershot, Hampshire. After 90 minutes play the score was 1–1. A further 30 minutes of extra time produced no further scoring. It needed 28 penalty kicks, of which only seven were missed, before Aldershot won 11–10.

The record number of penalties awarded in a League match is five during the Crystal Palace v. Brighton & Hove Albion Second Division game on 27 Mar 1989. Palace missed three of their spot kicks and each side was successful once. Palace eventually won 2–1.

In the Cyprus First–Division match in which Omonia beat Olympiakos 6–4 in Nicosia on 15 February 1987, FIFA referee Stafanos Hadjistefanou awarded six penalties, three to each side, all of which were converted by George Savvides (Omonia) and Sylvester Vernon (Olympiakos).

OLYMPIC GAMES

The only country to have won the Olympic football title three times is Hungary in 1952, 1964 and 1968. The United Kingdom won the unofficial tournament in 1900 and the official tournaments of 1908 and 1912. The highest Olympic score is 17 by Denmark *v.* France 'A' (1) in 1908.

OTHER MATCHES

Highest scores *Teams* ■ Drayton Grange Colts beat Eldon Sports Reserves 49–0 in a Daventry and District Sunday League match at Grange Estate, Northamptonshire on 13 Nov 1988. Every member of the side including the goalkeeper scored at least one goal.

In an Under-14 League match between Midas FC and Courage Colts, in Kent, on 11 Apr 1976, the full-time score after 70 minutes play was 59–1. Top scorer for Midas was Kevin Graham with 17 goals. Courage had scored the first goal.

Needing to improve their goal 'difference' to gain promotion in 1979, Ilinden FC of Yugoslavia, with the collusion of the opposition, Mladost, and the referee, won their final game of the season by 134–1. Their rivals in the promotion race won their match, under similar circumstances, by 88–0.

Individual ■ Dean Goodliff scored 26 goals for Deleford Colts *v.* Iver Minors in the Slough Boys Soccer Combination Under-14 League at Iver, Buckinghamshire in his team's 33–0 win on 22 Dec 1985. The women's record is 22 goals by Linda Curl of Norwich Ladies in a 40–0 league victory over Milton Keynes Reserves at Norwich on 25 Sep 1983.

Season ■ The greatest number of goals in a season reported for an individual player in junior professional league football is 96 by Tom Duffy (b. 7 Jan 1937), for Ardeer Thistle FC, Strathclyde in 1960–1. Paul Anthony Moulden (b. 6 Sep 1967) scored 289 goals in 40 games for Bolton Lads Club in Bolton Boys Federation intermediate league and cup matches in 1981–2. An additional 51 goals scored in other tournaments brought his total to 340, the highest season figure reported in any class of competitive football for an individual. He made his Football League debut for Manchester City on 1 Jan 1986 and has played for the England Youth team.

Fastest goals *Individual* ■ Wind-aided goals in 3 sec after kick-off have been scored by a number of players. Damian Corcoran (b. 25 Nov 1976) scored three goals within a minute for 7th Fulwood Cubs *v* 4th Fulwood Cubs on 1 Feb 1987.

Own goal ■ The fastest own goals on record have been in 5 sec 'scored' by Peter Johnson of Chesham United *v.* Wycombe Wanderers on 21 Feb 1976 and by John Smythe of Vernon Carus *v.* Duke Williams Reserves in March 1986.

Team ■ The shortest time for a semi-professional team to score three goals from the start of a game is 122 sec by Burton Albion *v.* Redditch United in a Beazer Homes League Premier Division match on 2 Jan 1989.

Longest ties ■ In the Hertfordshire Intermediate Cup, London Colney beat Leavesden Hospital after 12 hr 41 min play and seven ties from 6 Nov to 17 Dec 1971.

Largest tournament ■ The Metropolitan Police 5-a-side Youth Competition in 1981 attracted an entry of 7008 teams, a record for an FA sanctioned competition.

Most and least successful teams ■ Winlaton West End FC, Tyne and Wear, completed a run of 95 league games without defeat between 1976 and 1980. Penlake Junior Football Club remained unbeaten for 153 games (winning 152 including 85 in succession) in the Warrington Hilden Friendly League from 1981 until defeated in 1986. Stockport United FC, of the Stockport Football League, lost 39 consecutive League and Cup matches, September 1976 to 18 Feb 1978.

Most indisciplined ■ In the local cup match between Tongham Youth Club, Surrey and Hawley, Hampshire, on 3 Nov 1969, the referee booked all 22 players including one who went to hospital, and one of the linesmen. The match, won by Tongham 2–0, was described by a player as 'a good, hard game'.

In a Gancia Cup match at Waltham Abbey, Essex on 23 Dec 1973, the referee, Michael J. Woodhams, sent off the entire Juventus-Cross team and some club officials. Glencraig United, Faifley, near Clydebank, had all 11 team members and two substitutes for their 2–2 draw against Goldenhill Boys' Club on 2 Feb 1975 booked in the dressing room before a ball was kicked. The referee, Mr Tarbet of Bearsen, took exception to the chant which greeted his arrival. It was not his first meeting with Glencraig.

Ball control ■ Allan Abuto Nyanjong (Kenya) juggled a regulation soccer ball for 16 hr 27 min 52 sec non-stop with feet, legs and head without the ball ever touching the ground at the Hyatt Regency Crystal City, Arlington, Virginia, USA on 16 Jan 1988. Tomas Lundman (Sweden) headed a ball for 5 hr 12 min at Märsta, Sweden on 20 May 1989. Janusz Chomontek of Gdanieck, Poland kept a football up while he travelled a distance of 30 km *18·641 miles* in 8 hr 25 min 20 sec on 19 Sep 1987.

GUINNESS HAVE PUBLISHED:
SOCCER: RECORDS, FACTS AND CHAMPIONS (2nd EDITION) JACK ROLLIN **£8.95**
SOCCER QUIZ BOOK JULIAN FARINO **£4.95**
SOCCER WHO'S WHO JACK ROLLIN **£5.95**

Gaelic Football

Origins ■ The game developed from inter-parish 'free for all' with no time-limit, specific playing area or rules. The earliest reported match was Meath *v.* Louth, at Slane in 1712. Standardisation came with the formation of the Gaelic Athletic Association in Thurles, Ireland on 1 Nov 1884.

All-Ireland Championships ■ The greatest number of All-Ireland Championships won by one team is 30 by Ciarraidhe (Kerry) between 1903 and 1986. The greatest number of successive wins is four by Wexford (1915–18) and Kerry twice (1929–32, 1978–81).

The most finals contested by an individual is eleven, including eight wins by the Kerry players Pat Spillane, Michael Sheehy, Paudie O'Shea, Ger Power and Denis Moran, 1975–86.

The highest team score in a final was when Dublin, 27 (5 goals, 12 points) beat Armagh, 15 (3 goals, 6 points) on 25 Sep 1977. The highest combined score was 45 points when Cork (26) beat Galway (19) in 1973. A goal equals three points. The highest individual score in an All-Ireland final has been 2 goals, 6 points by Jimmy Keaveney (Dublin) *v.* Armagh in 1977, and by Michael Sheehy (Kerry) *v.* Dublin in 1979.

Largest crowd ■ The record crowd is 90 556 for the Down *v.* Offaly final at Croke Park, Dublin in 1961.

Gambling

Biggest win ■ The biggest individual gambling win is $40 million by Mike Wittkowski in the Illinois State 'Lottery, announced on 3 Sep 1984. From $35 worth of 'Lotto' tickets bought by his family, the winning six numbers bring him $2 million for the next 20 years.

Largest casino ■ The Burswood Island Casino, Perth, Western Australia opened on 30 Dec 1985 has an area of 7500 m² *80 729 ft²* and contains 200 video games and 142 gaming tables.

BINGO

Bingo is a lottery game which, as Keno, was developed in the 1880s from Lotto, whose origin is thought to be the 17th-century Italian game *tumbule*. It has long been known in the British Army (called Housey-Housey) and the Royal Navy (called Tombola). The winner was the first to complete a random selection of numbers from 1 to 90. The USA version called Bingo differs in that the selection is from 1 to 75. There are an estimated six million players in the United Kingdom.

Largest house ■ The largest 'house' in Bingo sessions was 15 756 at the Canadian National Exhibition, Toronto on 19 Aug 1983. Staged by the Variety Club of Ontario Tent Number 28, there was total prize money of $C250 000 with a record one-game payout of $C100 000.

Earliest and latest Full House ■ A 'Full House' call occurred on the 15th number by Norman A. Wilson at Guide Post Working Men's Club, Bedlington, Northumberland on 22 Jun 1978, by Anne Wintle of Brynrethin, Mid-Glamorgan, on a coach trip to Bath on 17 Aug 1982 and by Shirley Lord at Kahibah Bowling Club, New South Wales, Australia on 24 Oct 1983. 'House' was not called until the 86th number at the Hillsborough Working Men's Club, Sheffield, South Yorkshire on 11 Jan 1982. There were 32 winners.

FOOTBALL POOLS

The winning dividend paid out by Littlewoods Pools in their first week in February 1923 was £2 12s 0d . In 1987/8 the three British Pools companies which comprise the Pool Promoters Association (Littlewoods, Vernons and Zetters) had a total record turnover of £661 165 000 of which Littlewoods contributed over 70 per cent.

Biggest win ■ Two unnamed punters won *c.* £1·5 million each in November 1972 on the state-run Italian pools.

British ■ The record individual payout, which is also the biggest ever prize paid in any British competition, is £1 339 358.30 paid by Littlewoods Pools to Jim Anderson, 51, of Anderton, Northamptonshire for matches on 11 Jul 1987.

The record double payout is £1 988 510 by Littlewoods on 13 Feb 1988 to John Clark of Bristol, Avon (£991 656) and an anonymous Strathclyde woman (£996 854). Littlewoods' record total payout for a single week is £3 229 599 on 8 Apr 1989.

HORSE RACING

Highest ever odds ■ The highest secured odds were 1 670 759 to 1 by George Rhodes of Aldershot, Hampshire. For a 5p bet, with a 10 per cent bonus for the ITV Seven, less tax, he was paid £86 024.42 by the William Hill Organisation on 30 Sep 1984. Edward Hodson of Wolverhampton, West Midlands landed a 3 956 748 to 1 bet for a 55p stake on 11 Feb 1984, but his bookmaker had a £3000 payout limit. The world record odds on a 'double' are 31 793 to 1 paid by the New Zealand Totalisator Agency Board on a five shilling tote ticket on *Red Emperor* and *Maida Dillon* at Addington, Christchurch in 1951.

Greatest payout ■ Anthony A. Speelman and Nicholas John Cowan (both Great Britain) won $1 627 084·40, after federal income tax of $406 768·00 was withheld, on a $64 nine-horse accumulator at Santa Anita racecourse, California, USA on 19 Apr 1987. Their first seven selections won and the payout was for a jackpot, accumulated over 24 days. The largest payout by a British bookmaker is £227 812·50 by William Hill, paid to a Mr.'X' for three winners, all coupled in three £2000 doubles and a £9000 treble on 1 Aug 1985.

Biggest tote win ■ The best recorded tote win was one of £341 2s 6d to 2s representing odds of 3410¼ to 1, by Catharine Unsworth of Blundellsands, Liverpool, Merseyside at Haydock Park on a race won by *Coole* on 30 Nov 1929. The highest odds in Irish tote history were £289.64 for a 10p unit on *Gene's Rogue* at Limerick on 28 Dec 1981.

Largest bookmaker ■ The . world's largest bookmaker is Ladbrokes with a turnover from gambling in 1988 of £1608 million. The largest chain of betting shops is that of Ladbrokes with 1825 shops in the United Kingdom and the Republic of Ireland at the end of 1988, as well as 1099 in Belgium and The Netherlands.

Topmost tipster ■ The only recorded instance of a racing correspondent forecasting ten out of ten winners on a race card was at Delaware Park, Wilmington, Delaware, USA on 28 Jul 1974 by Charles Lamb of the *Baltimore News American*.

The best performance by a British correspondent is seven out of seven winners for a meeting at York on 12 May 1988 by Fred Shawcross of the *Today* newspaper.

SLOT MACHINES

The biggest beating handed to a 'one-armed bandit' was $6 814 823.48 by Cammie Brewer, 61, at the Club Cal-Neva, Reno, Nevada, USA on 14 Feb 1988.

Gliding

Origins ■ Research by Isadore William Deiches has shown evidence of the use of gliders in Ancient Egypt *c.* 2500–1500 BC. Emanuel Swedenborg (1688–1772) of Sweden made sketches of gliders *c.* 1714. The earliest man-carrying glider was designed by Sir George Cayley (1773–1857) and carried his coachman (possibly John Appleby) about 457 m *500 yd* across a valley in Brompton Dale, North Yorkshire in the summer of 1853.

Most titles *World* ■ The most World Individual Championships (instituted 1948) won is four by Ingo Renner (Australia) in 1976 (Standard class), 1983, 1985 and 1987 (Open).

British ■ The British National Championship (instituted 1939) has been won eight times by Ralph Jones (b. 29 Mar 1936). The first woman to win this title was Anne Burns (b. 23 Nov. 1915) of Farnham, Surrey on 30 May 1966.

Altitude records *Women* ■ The women's single-seater world record for absolute altitude is 12 637 m *41 449 ft* by Sabrina Jackintell (USA) in an Astir GS on 14 Feb 1979. The height gain record is 10 212 m *33 506 ft* by Yvonne Loader (New Zealand) at Omarama, New Zealand on 12 Jan 1988. The British single-seater absolute altitude record is 10 550 m *34 612 ft* by Anne Burns in a Skylark 3B over South Africa on 13 Jan 1961, when she set a then world record and still a British record for height gain of 9119 m *29 918 ft*.

HANG GLIDING

Origins ■ In the eleventh century the monk, Eilmer, is reported to have flown from the 18·3 m *60 ft* tower of Malmesbury Abbey, Wiltshire. The earliest modern pioneer was Otto Lilienthal (1848–96) (Germany) with about 2500 flights in gliders of his own construction between 1891 and 1896. In the 1950s Professor Francis Rogallo of the National Space Agency, USA, developed a flexible 'wing' from his space capsule re-entry researches.

World Championships ■ The World Team Championships (officially instituted 1976) have been won most often by Great Britain (1981 and 1985).

WORLD RECORDS ■ The *Fédération Aéronautique Internationale* recognises world records for rigid-wing, flexwing and multiplace flexwing. These records are the greatest in each category–all by flexwing gliders.

MEN
Greatest distance in straight line: 391·56 km *243·31 miles* Larry Tudor (USA), Owens Valley, California, USA, 3 Jul 1988. Height gain: 4343·4 m *14 250 ft* Larry Tudor (USA), Owens Valley, 4 Aug 1985.
Declared goal distance: 348·70 km *216·67 miles* Larry Tudor (USA), Owens Valley, 30 Jan 1988.
Out and return distance: 310·302 km *192·818 miles* Larry Tudor (USA) and Geoffrey Lyons (GB), Owens

Valley, 26 Jun 1988. Triangular course distance: 112·949 km *70·185 miles* Palle Jensen (Denmark), Corriddeery, Australia, 6 Jan 1988.

WOMEN
Greatest distance: 233·9 km *145·34 miles* Judy Leden (GB), Owens Valley, 13 Jul 1983.
Height gain: 3291·84 m *10 800 ft* Page Pfieffer (USA), Owens Valley, 12 Jul 1979.
Out and return distance: 118·09 km *73·38 miles* Valerie Wallington (Australia), Australia, 4 Jan 1985.
Declared goal distance: 124·52 km *77·37 miles* Judy Lori (USA), Owens Valley, 15 Jul 1983.
Triangular course distance: Jenny Canderton (GB), 68·75 km *42·72 miles*, St Andre-les-Alpes, France, 23 Jun 1987.

BRITISH RECORDS
The British record for distance is held by Geoffrey Lyons, 312·86 km *194·40 miles*, in Flagstaff, Arizona, USA on 11 Jul 1988. The best in Britain is 244 km *151·62 miles* by Gordon Rigg from Lords Seat to Witham Friary, Somerset on 4 Jun 1989.

The British height gain record is 4145·33 m *13 600 ft* by Colin Rider at Wether Fell, North Yorkshire on 4 Jul 1987.

Greatest descent ■ John Bird piloted a hang glider from a height of 39 000 ft *11 887·2 m* when he was released from a hot-air balloon, to the ground, landing in Edmonton, Alberta, Canada on 29 Aug 1982. He touched down 80·4 km *50 miles* from his point of departure.

Golf

Origins ■ Although a stained glass window in Gloucester Cathedral, dating from 1350, portrays a golfer-like figure, the earliest mention of golf occurs in a prohibiting law passed by the Scottish Parliament in March 1457 under which 'goff be utterly cryit doune and not usit'. The Romans had a cognate

GLIDING WORLD RECORDS
(Single-seaters)

	DISTANCE	NAME	TYPE OF GLIDER	LOCATION	DATE
STRAIGHT DISTANCE	1460·8 km *907·7 miles*	Hans-Werner Grosse (West Germany)	ASW-12	Lübeck, W. Germany to Biarritz, France	25 Apr 1972
DECLARED GOAL DISTANCE	1254·26 km *779·4 miles*	Bruce Drake (New Zealand)	Nimbus 2	Te Anau to Te Araroa, New Zealand	14 Jan 1978
		David Speight (New Zealand)	Nimbus 2	Te Anau to Te Araroa, New Zealand	14 Jan 1978
		S. H. 'Dick' Georgeson (New Zealand)	Nimbus 2	Te Anau to Te Araroa, New Zealand	14 Jan 1978
GOAL AND RETURN	1646·68 km *1023·2 miles*	Tom Knauff (USA)	Nimbus 3	Williamsport, Pa to Knoxville, Tn, USA	25 Apr 1983
ABSOLUTE ALTITUDE	14 938 m *49 009 ft*	Robert R. Harris (USA)	Grob G102	California, USA	17 Feb 1986
HEIGHT GAIN	12 849 m *42 303 ft*	Paul Bikle (USA)	Schweitzer SGS1-23E	Mojave, California, USA	25 Feb 1961

SPEED OVER TRIANGULAR COURSE

DISTANCE	SPEED KM/H	MPH	NAME	TYPE OF GLIDER	PLACE	DATE
100 km	195·3	*121·35*	Ingo Renner (Australia)	Nimbus 3	Australia	14 Dec 1982
300 km	169·49	*105·32*	Jean-Paul Castel (France)	Nimbus 3	South Africa	15 Nov 1986
500 km	164·11	*101·97*	Jean-Paul Castel (France)	Nimbus 3	South Africa	10 Dec 1986
750 km	158·40	*98·43*	Hans-Werner Grosse (West Germany)	ASW-22	Australia	8 Jan 1985
1000 km	145·32	*90·29*	Hans-Werner Grosse (West Germany)	ASW-17	Australia	3 Jan 1979
1250 km	133·24	*82·79*	Hans-Werner Grosse (West Germany)	ASW-17	Australia	9 Jan 1980

BRITISH RECORDS

	DISTANCE	NAME	TYPE OF GLIDER	LOCATION	DATE
STRAIGHT DISTANCE	949·7 km *589·9 miles*	Karla Karel	LS-3	Australia	20 Jan 1980
DECLARED GOAL DISTANCE	859·2 km *534 miles*	M. T. Alan Sands	Nimbus 3	Ridge soaring to Chilhowee, Va, USA	23 Apr 1986
GOAL AND RETURN	1127·68 km *700·72 miles*	M. T. Alan Sands	Nimbus 3	Lock Haven, Pa to Bluefield, Va, USA	7 May 1985
ABSOLUTE ALTITUDE	11 500 m *37 729 ft*	H. C. Nicholas Goodhart	Schweitzer 1-23	California, USA	12 May 1955
HEIGHT GAIN	10 065 m *33 022 ft*	David Benton	Nimbus 2	Portmoak, Scotland	18 Apr 1980

SPEED OVER TRIANGULAR COURSE

DISTANCE	SPEED KM/H	MPH	NAME	TYPE OF GLIDER	PLACE	DATE
100 km	143·3	*88·99*	E. Paul Hodge	Standard Cirrus	Rhodesia	30 Oct 1976
300 km	146·8	*91·2*	Edward Pearson	Nimbus 2	S. W. Africa	30 Nov 1976
500 km	141·3	*87·8*	Bradley James Grant Pearson	ASW-20	South Africa	28 Dec 1982
750 km	109·8	*68·2*	Michael R. Carlton	Kestrel 19	South Africa	5 Jan 1975
1250 km	109·01	*67·73*	Robert L. Robertson	Ventus A	USA	2 May 1986

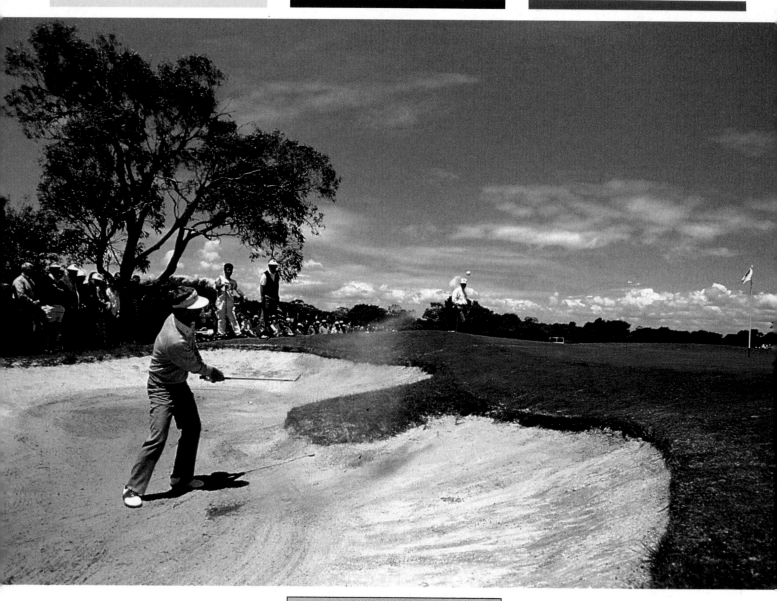

World Cup ● The USA, with Ben Crenshaw and Mark McCumber, won the World Cup (formerly Canada Cup) for a record 17th time at Royal Melbourne GC, Australia in 1988. Crenshaw (above) won the individual title with a score of 275. (Photo: All-Sport)

game called *paganica* which may have been carried to Britain before AD 400. The Chinese Nationalist Golf Association claims the game is of Chinese origin (*Ch'ui Wan*–the ball hitting game) in the 3rd or 2nd century BC. There were official ordinances prohibiting a ball game with clubs in Belgium and Holland from 1360. Gutta percha balls succeeded feather balls in 1848 and by 1902 were in turn succeeded by rubber-cored balls, invented in 1899 by Coburn Haskell (USA). Steel shafts were authorised in the USA in 1925 and in Britain in 1929.

Oldest club ■ The oldest club of which there is written evidence is the Gentlemen Golfers (now the Honourable Company of Edinburgh Golfers) formed in March 1744–ten years prior to the institution of the Royal and Ancient Club of St Andrews, Fife. However, the Royal Burgess Golfing Society of Edinburgh claims to have been founded in 1735.

Highest course ■ The Tuctu Golf Club in Morococha, Peru, is 4369 m *14 335 ft* above sea level at its lowest point. Golf has, however, been played in Tibet at an altitude of over 4875 m *16 000 ft*.

Great Britain ■ The nine hole course at Leadhills, Strathclyde is 457 m *1500 ft* above sea level.

Highest shot, on Earth ■ Timothy J. Ayers played a shot from the summit of McKinley (6194 m *20 320 ft*), Alaska, USA on 23 May 1984.

Longest hole ■ The longest hole in the world is the 7th hole (par-7) of the Sano Course, Satsuki GC, Japan, which measures 831 m *909 yd*. The longest hole on a championship course in Great Britain is the sixth at Troon, Strathclyde, which stretches 528 m *577 yd*.

Largest green ■ Probably the largest green in the world is that of the par-6 635 m *695 yd* fifth hole at International GC, Bolton, Massachusetts, USA, with an area greater than 2600 m² *28 000 ft²*.

Biggest bunker ■ The world's biggest bunker (called a trap in the USA) is Hell's Half Acre on the 535 m *585 yd* seventh hole of the Pine Valley course, Clementon, New Jersey, USA, built in 1912 and generally regarded as the world's most trying course.

Longest course ■ The world's longest course is the par-77 7612 m *8325 yd* International GC (see also above) from the 'Tiger' tees, remodelled in 1969 by Robert Trent Jones.

Floyd Satterlee Rood used the United States as a course, when he played from the Pacific surf to the Atlantic surf from 14 Sep 1963 to 3 Oct 1964 in 114 737 strokes. He lost 3511 balls on the 5468 km *3397·7 mile* trail.

Longest drives ■ In officially regulated long driving contests over level ground the greatest distance recorded is 358 m *392 yd* by William Thomas 'Tommie' Campbell (b. 24 Jul 1927) (Foxrock Golf Club) at Dun Laoghaire, Co. Dublin, Ireland in July 1964.

On an airport runway Liam Higgins (Ireland) drove a Spalding Top Flite ball 579·8 m *634·1 yd* at Baldonnel military airport, Dublin, Ireland on 25 Sep 1984. The women's record is held by Helen Dobson (GB) who drove a Titleist Pinnacle 469·1 m *531 yd* at RAF Honnington, Suffolk on 31 Oct 1987. The greatest recorded drive on an ordinary course is one of 471 m *515 yd* by Michael Hoke Austin (b. 17 Feb 1910) of Los Angeles, California, USA, in the US National Seniors Open Championship at Las Vegas, Nevada on 25 Sep 1974. Austin, 1·88 m *6 ft 2 in* tall and weighing 92 kg *210 lb* drove the ball to within a yard of the green on the par-4 412 m *450 yd* fifth hole of the Winterwood Course and it rolled 59 m *65 yd* past the flagstick. He was aided by an estimated 56 km/h *35 mph* tailwind.

A drive of 2414 m *2640 yd (1½ miles)* across ice was achieved by an Australian meteorologist named Nils Lied at Mawson Base, Antarctica in 1962. Arthur Lynskey claimed a drive of 182 m *200 yd* horizontal and 3200 m *2 miles* vertical off Pikes Peak, Colorado (4300 m *14 110 ft*) on 28 Jun 1968. On the Moon the energy expended on a mundane 274 m *300 yd* drive would achieve, craters permitting, a distance of 1·6 km *1 mile*.

Longest putt ■ The longest recorded holed putt in a major tournament was one of 26 m *86 ft* on the vast 13th green at the Augusta National, Georgia by Cary Middlecoff (USA) (b. 6 Jan 1921) in the 1955 Masters' Tournament. Robert Tyre 'Bobby' Jones Jr, (1902–71) was reputed to have holed a putt in excess of 30 m *100 ft* at the fifth green in the first round of the 1927 Open at St Andrews. Bob Cook (USA) sank a putt measured at 42·74 m *140 ft 2³⁄₄ in* on the 18th at St Andrews in the International Fourball Pro Am Tournament on 1 Oct 1976.

SCORES

Lowest 9 holes ■ Nine holes in 25 (4, 3, 3, 2, 3, 3, 1, 4, 2) was recorded by A. J. 'Bill' Burke in a round in 57 (32 +25) on the 5842 m *6389 yd* par-71 Normandie course at St Louis, Missouri, USA on 20 May 1970. The tournament record is 27 by Mike Souchak (USA) (b. 10 May 1927) for the second nine (par-35), first round of the 1955 Texas Open (see 72 holes); Andy North (USA) (b. 9 Mar 1950) second nine (par-34), first round, 1975 BC Open at En-Joie GC, Endicott, NY; José Maria Canizares (Spain) (b. 18 Feb 1947), first nine, third round, in the 1978 Swiss Open on the 6228 m *6811 yd* Crans-Sur course; and Robert Lee (GB) (b. 12 Oct 1961) first nine, first round, in the Monte Carlo Open on the 5714 m *6249 yd* Mont Agel course on 28 Jun 1985.

Lowest 18 holes *Men* ■ At least four players have played a long course (over 6000 m *6561 yd*) in a score of 58, most recently Monte Carlo Money (USA) (b. 3 Dec 1954), the par-72, 6041 m *6607 yd* Las Vegas Municipal GC, Nevada, USA on 11 Mar 1981. Alfred Edward Smith (1903–85) achieved an 18-hole score of 55 (15 under bogey 70) on his home course on 1 Jan 1936. The course measured 3884 m *4248 yd.* The detail was 4, 2, 3, 4, 2, 4, 3, 4, 3 =29 out, and 2, 3, 3, 3, 3, 2, 5, 4, 1 =26 in.

The United States PGA Tournament record for 18 holes is 59 (30 +29) by Al Geiberger (b. 1 Sep 1937) in the second round of the Danny Thomas Classic, on the 72-par 6628 m *7249 yd* Colonial GC course, Memphis, Tennessee on 10 Jun 1977. Other golfers to have recorded 59 over 18 holes in major non-PGA tournaments include: Samuel Jackson Snead (b. 27 May 1912) in the third round of the Sam Snead Festival at White Sulphur Springs, West Virginia, USA on 16 May 1959; Gary Player (South Africa) (b. 1 Nov 1935) in the second round of the Brazilian Open in Rio de Janeiro on 29 Nov 1974; David Jagger (GB) (b. 9 Jun 1949) in a Pro-Am tournament prior to the 1973 Nigerian Open at Ikoyi Golf Club, Lagos; and Miguel Martin (Spain) in the Argentine Southern Championship at Mar de Plata on 27 Feb 1987.

Women ■ The lowest recorded score on an 18-hole course (over 5486 m *6000 yd*) for a woman is 62 (30 +32) by Mary 'Mickey' Kathryn Wright (USA) (b. 14 Feb 1935) on the Hogan Park Course (par-71, 5747 m *6286 yd*) at Midland, Texas, USA, in November 1964. Wanda Morgan (b. 22 Mar 1910) recorded a score of 60 (31 +29) on the Westgate and Birchington Golf Club course, Kent, over 18 holes (4573 m *5002 yd*) on 11 Jul 1929.

Great Britain ■ The lowest score recorded in a first-class professional tournament on a course of more than 5486 m *6000 yd* in Great Britain is 61 (29 +32), by Thomas Bruce Haliburton (1915–75) of Wentworth GC in the Spalding Tournament at Worthing, West Sussex in June 1952, and 61 (32 +29) by Peter J. Butler (b. 25 Mar 1932) in the Bowmaker Tournament at Sunningdale, Berkshire on 4 Jul 1967.

Lowest 36 holes ■ The record for 36 holes is 122 (59 +63) by Sam Snead in the 1959 Sam Snead Festival on 16–17 May 1959. Horton Smith (1908–63), twice US Masters Champion, scored 121 (63 +58) on a short course on 21 Dec 1928 (see 72 holes). The lowest score by a British golfer has been 124 (61 +63) by Alexander Walter Barr 'Sandy' Lyle (b. 9 Feb 1958) in the Nigerian Open at the 5508 m *6024 yd* (par-71) Ikoyi Golf Club, Lagos in 1978.

Lowest 72 holes ■ The lowest recorded score on a first-class course is 255 (29 under par) by Leonard Peter Tupling (b. 6 Apr 1950) in the Nigerian Open at Ikoyi Golf Club, Lagos in February 1981, made up of 63, 66, 62 and 64 (average 63.75 per round).

The lowest 72 holes in a US professional event is 257 (60, 68, 64, 65) by Mike Souchak in the 1955 Texas Open at San Antonio.

The 72 holes record on the European tour is 258 (64, 69, 60, 65) by David Llewellyn (b. 18 Nov 1951) in the Biarritz Open on 1–3 Apr 1988. The lowest 72

holes in an open championship in Europe is 262 (67, 66, 66, 63) by Percy Alliss (GB) (1897–1975) in the 1932 Italian Open at San Remo, and by Lu Liang Huan (Taiwan) (b. 10 Dec 1935) in the 1971 French Open at Biarritz. Kelvin D. G. Nagle (b. 21 Dec 1920) of Australia shot 261 in the Hong Kong Open in 1961. The lowest for four rounds in a British first-class tournament is 262 (66, 63, 66 and 67) by Bernard Hunt in the Piccadilly Tournament on the par-68 5655 m *6184 yd* Wentworth East course, Virginia Water, Surrey on 4–5 Oct 1966.

Trish Johnson scored 242 (64, 60, 60, 56) (21 under par) in the Bloor Homes Eastleigh Classic at the Fleming Park Course (4025 m *4402 yd*) at Eastleigh, Hampshire on 22–25 1987. Horton Smith scored 245 (63, 58, 61 and 63) for 72 holes on the 4297 m *4700 yd* course (par-64) at Catalina Country Club, California, USA, to win the Catalina Open on 21–23 Dec 1928.

World one-club record ■ Thad Daber (USA), with a 6-iron, played the 5520 m *6037 yd* Lochmore GC, Cary, North Carolina, USA in 73 on 10 Nov 1985 to win the world one-club championship.

Highest score ■ It is recorded that Chevalier von Cittern went round 18 holes in 316, averaging 17.55 per hole, at Biarritz, France in 1888. Steven Ward took 222 strokes for the 5680 m *6212 yd* Pecos course, Reeves County, Texas, USA on 18 Jun 1976, but he was aged only 3 years 286 days.

Most shots for one hole ■ A woman player in the qualifying round of the Shawnee Invitational for Ladies at Shawnee-on-Delaware, Pennsylvania, USA, *c.* 1912, took 166 strokes for the short 118 m *130 yd* 16th hole. Her tee shot went into the Binnie-kill River and the ball floated. She put out in a boat with her exemplary but statistically-minded husband at the oars. She eventually beached the ball 2.4 km *1½ miles* downstream but was not yet out of the wood. She had to play through one on the home run. In a competition at Peacehaven, East Sussex in 1890, A. J. Lewis had 156 putts on one green without holing out.

The highest score for a single hole in the British Open is 21 by a player in the inaugural meeting at Prestwick in 1860. Double figures have been recorded on the card of the winner only once, when Willie Fernie (1851–1924) scored a ten at Musselburgh, Lothian in 1883. Ray Ainsley of Ojai, California, took 19 strokes for the par-4 16th hole during the second round of the US Open at Cherry Hills Country Club, Denver, Colorado on 10 Jun 1938. Most of the strokes were used in trying to extricate the ball from a brook. Hans Merell of Mogadore, Ohio took 19 strokes on the par-3 16th (203 m *222 yd*) during the third round of the Bing Crosby National Tournament at Cypress Point Club, Del Monte, California, USA on 17 Jan 1959.

Fastest rounds *Individual* ■ With such variations in lengths of courses, speed records, even for rounds under par, are of little comparative value. The fastest round played when the golf ball comes to rest before each new stroke is 27 min 9 sec by James Carvill (b. 13 Oct 1965) at Warrenpoint Golf Course, Co. Down, Northern Ireland (18 holes, 5628 m *6154 yd*) on 18 Jun 1987.

Team ■ Forty-eight players completed the 18-hole 6500 m *7108 yd* Kyalami course, near Johannesburg, South Africa in 9 min 51 sec on 23 Feb 1988 using only one ball. They scored 73!

Slowest rounds ■ The slowest stroke-play tournament round was one of 6 hr 45 min taken by South Africa in the first round of the 1972 World Cup at the Royal Melbourne GC, Australia. This was a four-ball medal round; everything holed out.

Most holes in 24 hours *On foot* ■ Ian Colston, 35, played 22 rounds and five holes (401 holes) at Bendigo GC, Victoria, Australia (par-73, 5542 m *6061 yd*) on 27–28 Nov 1971. The British record is 360 holes by Antony J. Clark at Childwall GC, Liverpool on 18 Jul 1983.

Using golf carts ■ Charles Stock played 783 holes at Acacia Country Club, Lyndhurst, Ohio, USA (9

holes, 2844 m *3110 yd*) on 20 Jul 1987. Terry Zachary played 391 holes in 12 hours on the 6132 m *6706 yd* course at Connaught Golf Club, Alberta, Canada on 16 Jun 1986.

Most holes played in a week ■ Steve Hylton played 1128 holes at the Mason Rudolph Golf Club (5541m *6060 yd*), Clarkesville, Tennessee, USA from 25–31 Aug 1980. Using a buggy for transport, Colin Young completed 1260 holes at Patshull Park Golf Club (5863 m *6412 yd*), Pattingham, Shropshire from 2–9 Jul 1988.

Throwing the golf ball ■ The lowest recorded score for throwing a golf ball round 18 holes (over 5500 m *6000 yd*) is 82 by Joe Flynn (USA), 21, at the 5694 m *6228 yd* Port Royal course, Bermuda on 27 Mar 1975.

Most balls hit in one hour ■ The most balls driven in one hour, over 100 yds and into a target area, is 1100 (from 1509 attempts) by Max Szuca at Tilsworth Golf Centre, Bedfordshire on 4 Sep 1988.

CHAMPIONSHIP RECORDS
LOWEST SCORES

The Open (inaugurated 1860, Prestwick, Strathclyde) *First nine holes* ■ 28 by Denis Durnian (b. 30 Jun 1950), at Royal Birkdale, Southport, Lancashire in the second round on 15 Jul 1983.

Any round ■ 63 by: Mark Stephen Hayes (USA) (b. 12 Jul 1949) at Turnberry, Strathclyde on 7 Jul 1977; Isao Aoki (Japan) (b. 31 Aug 1942) at Muirfield, East Lothian on 19 Jul 1980; and Gregory John Norman (Australia) (b. 10 Feb 1955) at Turnberry on 18 Jul 1986.

First 36 holes ■ Thomas Henry Cotton (1907–1987) at Royal St George's, Sandwich, Kent completed the first 36 holes in 132 (67 +65) on 27 Jun 1934.

Total aggregate ■ 268 (68, 70, 65, 65) by Thomas Sturges Watson (USA) (b. 4 Sep 1949) at Turnberry in July 1977.

US Open (inaugurated in 1895) *Any round* ■ 63 by: Johnny Miller (b. 29 Apr 1947) on the 6328 m *6921 yd* par-71 Oakmont Country Club course, Pennsylvania on 17 Jun 1973; by Jack Nicklaus and Tom Weiskopf (USA) (b. 9 Nov 1942), both on 12 Jun 1980.

First 36 holes ■ 134 by: Jack Nicklaus (63, 71) at Baltusrol Country Club, Springfield, New Jersey, 12–13 Jun 1980; and Tze-Chung Chen (Taiwan) (65, 69) at Oakland Hills, Birmingham, Michigan in 1985.

Total aggregate ■ 272 (63, 71, 70, 68) by Jack Nicklaus (b. 21 Jan 1940) on the lower course (6414 m *7015 yd*) at Baltusrol Country Club, 12–15 Jun 1980.

US Masters (inaugurated on 6382 m *6980 yd* Augusta National Golf Course, Georgia, 1934) *Any round* ■ 63 by Nicholas Raymond Leige Price (Zimbabwe) (b. 28 Jan 1957) in 1986.

First 36 holes ■ 131 (65, 66) by Raymond Loran Floyd (b. 4 Sep 1942) in 1976.

72-hole total ■ 271 by: Jack Nicklaus (67, 71, 64, 69) in 1965 and Raymond Floyd (65, 66, 70, 70) in 1976.

TEAM COMPETITONS

World Cup (formerly Canada Cup) ■ The World Cup (instituted as the Canada Cup in 1953) has been won most often by the USA with 17 victories between 1955 and 1988. The only men to have been on six winning teams have been Arnold Palmer (b. 10 Sep 1929) (1960, 1962–4, 1966–7) and Jack Nicklaus (1963–4, 1966–7, 1971 and 1973). Only Nicklaus has taken the individual title three times (1963–4, 1971). The lowest aggregate score for 144 holes is 544 by Australia, Bruce Devlin (b. 10 Oct 1937) and Anthony David Graham (b. 23 May 1946), at San Isidro, Buenos Aires, Argentina from 12–15 Nov 1970. The lowest individual score has been 269 by Roberto de Vicenzo (Argentina) (b. 14 Apr 1923), also in 1970.

Ryder Cup ■ The biennial Ryder Cup professional match between the USA and Europe (British Isles or Great Britain prior to 1979) was instituted in 1927. The USA have won 21 ½ to 5 ½ to date. William Earl 'Billy' Casper (b. San Diego, California, USA 24 Jun 1931) has the record of winning most matches in the Trophy with 20 in 1961–75. Christy O'Connor,Sr (Ireland) (b. 21 Dec 1924) played in ten matches, 1955–73.

Walker Cup ■ The series was instituted in 1921 (for the Walker Cup since 1922 and now held biennially). Joseph Boynton Carr (GB & I) (b. 18 Feb 1922) played in ten contests, 1947–67. The USA have won 28, Great Britain & Ireland 2 (in 1938 and 1971) and the 1965 match was tied.

Curtis Cup ■ The biennial ladies' Curtis Cup match between the USA and Great Britain and Ireland was first held in 1932. The USA have won 19, GB & I 4 (1952, 1956, 1986 and 1988) and 2 matches have been tied. Mary McKenna (GB & I) (b. 29 Apr 1949) played in a record ninth match in 1986, when for the first time she was on the winning team.

INDIVIDUAL RECORDS

Richest prize ■ The greatest first place prize money ever won is $1 000 000 by the winners of the Sun City Challenge, Bophuthatswana, South Africa in 1987, Ian Woosnam (Wales) (b. 2 Mar 1958), and 1988, Fulton Allem (South Africa). The greatest total prize money is $2 000 000 (including $360 000 first prize) for the Nabisco Championship of Golf at Pebble Beach, California, USA on 10–13 Nov 1988.

Highest earnings *US PGA and LPGA circuits* ■ The all-time professional money-winner is Tom Watson, with $5 106 697, to 13 Jun 1989. The record for a year on the US PGA circuit was set by Curtis Northup Strange (USA) (b. 20 Jun 1955) in 1988 with $1 147 644. The record career earnings for a woman is by Pat Bradley (b. 24 Mar 1951) with $2 661 046 to

25 Jun 1989, including a season's record $492 021 in 1986.

European circuit ■ Severiano Ballesteros (Spain) (b. 9 Apr 1957) won a European record £451 559 in

Greatest European earnings ● The 1988 British Open winner, Severiano Ballesteros (Spain) (b. 9 Apr 1957), playing the 9th at Royal Lytham and St Annes during his last round. It was his third Open success having previously won in 1979 and 1984 and contributed to him being the leading money winner for European Order of Merit tournaments in 1988. (Photo: All-Sport / David Cannon)

European Order of Merit tournaments in 1988. In all events world-wide in 1987 Ian Woosnam won £1 042 662.76.

Most tournament wins ■ John Byron Nelson (USA) (b. 4 Feb 1912) won a record 18 tournaments (plus one unofficial) in one year, including a record 11 consecutively from 8 Mar to 4 Aug 1945. Sam Snead won 84 official US PGA tour events 1936–65, and has been credited with a total 134 tournament victories since 1934. The ladies' PGA record is 88 by Kathy Whitworth (b. 27 Sep 1939) from 1962 to 1985.

Biggest winning margin ■ The greatest margin of victory in a major tournament is 21 strokes by Jerry Pate (USA) (b. 16 Sep 1953), who won the Colombian Open with 262 from 10–13 Dec 1981. Cecilia Leitch won the Canadian Ladies' Open Championship in 1921 by the biggest margin for a major title, 17 up and 15 to play.

Youngest and oldest champions ■ The youngest winner of The Open was Tom Morris Jr (1851–75) at Prestwick, Strathclyde in 1868 aged 17 yr 249 days. The oldest Open champion was 'Old Tom' Morris (1821–1908), aged 46 yr 99 days when he won at Prestwick in 1867. In recent times the 1967 champion, Roberto de Vicenzo, was aged 44 yr 93 days. The oldest US Open champion was Raymond Floyd (b. 4 Sep 1942) at 43 yr 284 days on 15 Jun 1986. Isabella 'Belle' Robertson (b. 11 Apr 1936) won the 1986 Scottish Women's Championship aged 50 yr 43 days.

Most club championships ■ Marjorie Edey (1913–81) was ladies champion at Charleswood Golf Club, Winnipeg, Manitoba, Canada 36 times between 1937 and 1980. The men's record is 34 by Bernard Charles Cusack (b. 24 Jan 1920), including 33 consecutively, at the Narembeen GC, Western Australia, between 1943 and 1982. At different clubs, Peter Toogood (Australia) (b. 11 Apr 1930) has won 35 championships: 2 at Huntingdale GC, Victoria, 5 at Riverside GC, 9 at Kingston Beach GC and 19 at Royal Hobart GC, all Tasmania. The British record is

MOST TITLES *World's major championships:*

The Open	Harry Vardon (1870–1937)	6	1896, 1898–9, 1903, 11, 14
The Amateur	John Ball (1861–1940)	8	1888, 90, 92, 94, 99, 1907, 1910, 12
US Open	Willie Anderson (1880–1910)	4	1901, 03–5
	Robert Tyre Jones Jr (1902–71)	4	1923, 26, 29–30
	William Ben Hogan (b. 13 Aug 1912)	4	1948, 50–1, 53
	Jack William Nicklaus (b. 21 Jan 1940)	4	1962, 67, 72, 80
US Amateur	Robert Tyre Jones Jr (1902–71)	5	1924–25, 27–8, 30
PGA Championship (USA)	Walter Charles Hagan (1892–1969)	5	1921, 24–7
	Jack William Nicklaus	5	1963, 71, 73, 75, 80
Masters Championship (USA)	Jack William Nicklaus	6	1963, 65–6, 72, 75, 86
US Women's Open	Elizabeth 'Betsy' Earle-Rawls (b. 4 May 1928)	4	1951, 53, 57, 60
	'Mickey' Wright (b. 14 Feb 1935)	4	1958–59, 61, 64
US Women's Amateur	Glenna C. Vare (*née* Collett) (b. 20 Jun 1903)	6	1922, 25, 28–30, 35
British Women's	Charlotte Cecilia Pitcairn Leitch (1891–1977)	4	1914, 20–1, 26
	Joyce Wethered (b. 17 Nov 1901) (Now Lady Heathcoat-Amory)	4	1922, 24–5, 29

Note: Nicklaus is the only golfer to have won 5 different major titles (The Open, US Open, Masters, PGA and US Amateur titles) twice and a record 20 all told (1959–86). His remarkable record in the US Open is 4 firsts, 8 seconds and 2 thirds. In 1930 Bobby Jones achieved a unique 'Grand Slam' of the US and British Open and Amateur titles.

32 by Helen Gray at Todmorden GC, Lancashire between 1952 and 1986. Patricia Shepherd (b. 7 Jan 1940) has won 30 consecutive championships at Turriff GC, Grampian, 1959–88.

Largest tournament ■ The Volkswagen Grand Prix Open Amateur Championship in the United Kingdom attracted a record 321 779 (206 820 men and 114 958 women) competitors in 1984.

HOLES IN ONE

Longest ■ The longest straight hole ever holed in one shot was, appropriately, at the tenth (408 m *447 yd*) at Miracle Hills Golf Club, Omaha, Nebraska, USA by Robert Mitera (b. 1944) on 7 Oct 1965. Mitera stood 1·68 m *5 ft 6 in* tall and weighed 75 kg *165 lb* (11 st 11 lb). He was a two handicap player who normally drove 224 m *245 yd*. A 80 km/h *50 mph* gust carried his shot over a 265 m *290 yd* drop-off. The longest 'dog-leg' hole achieved in one is the 439 m *480 yd* fifth at Hope Country Club, Arkansas, USA by L. Bruce on 15 Nov 1962. The women's record is 359 m *393 yd* by Marie Robie on the first hole of the Furnace Brook Golf Club, Wollaston, Massachusetts, USA on 4 Sep 1949. The longest hole in one performed in the British Isles is the seventh (par-4, 359 m *393 yd*) at West Lancashire GC by Peter Richard Parkinson (b. 26 Aug 1947) on 6 Jun 1972.

Consecutive ■ There are at least 16 cases of 'aces' being achieved in two consecutive holes, of which the greatest was Norman L. Manley's unique 'double albatross' on the par-4 301 m *330 yd* seventh and par-4 265 m *290 yd* eighth holes on the Del Valle Country Club course, Saugus, California, USA on 2 Sep 1964. The first woman to record consecutive 'aces' was Sue Prell, on the 13th and 14th holes at Chatswood Golf Club, Sydney, Australia on 29 May 1977.

The closest to achieving three consecutive holes in one were the late Dr Joseph Boydstone on the 3rd, 4th and 9th at Bakersfield GC, California, USA, on 10 Oct 1962 and the Rev Harold Snider (b. 4 Jul 1900) who aced the 8th, 13th and 14th holes of the par-3 Ironwood course, Arizona, USA on 9 Jun 1976.

Youngest and oldest ■ The youngest golfer recorded to have shot a hole-in-one is Coby Orr (5 years) of Littleton, Colorado on the 94 m *103 yd* fifth at the Riverside Golf Course, San Antonio, Texas, USA in 1975. The British record was set by Derek Guthrie, aged 8 yr 277 days, on the 142 m *155 yd* ninth at the Forfar Golf Club, Tayside on 20 May 1986. The youngest girl to score an ace is Stephanie Coverley, aged 12 yr 297 days on the 131 m *143 yd* fourth at Longley Park Golf Club, West Yorkshire on 7 May 1989. The oldest golfers to have performed this feat are: (men) 99 yr 244 days Otto Bucher

(Switzerland) (b. 12 May 1885) on the 100 m *130 yd* 12th at La Manga GC, Spain on 13 Jan 1985; (women) 95 yr 257 days Erna Ross (b. 9 Sep 1890) on the 102 m *112 yd* 17th at The Everglades Club, Palm Beach, Florida, USA on 23 Apr 1986. The British records: (men) was set by Samuel Richard Walker (b. 6 Jan 1892) at the 143 m *156 yd* 8th at West Hove GC, East Sussex at the age of 92 yr 169 days on 23 Jun 1984; (women) Dorothy Huntley-Flindt (b. 19 Jun 1898) at the 102 m *112 yd* 13th at Barton-on-Sea GC, Hampshire at the age of 90 yr 236 days on 10 Feb 1989.

The oldest player to score his age is C. Arthur Thompson (1869–1975) of Victoria, British Columbia, Canada, who scored 103 on the Uplands course of 5682 m *6215 yd* aged 103 in 1973.

GUINNESS HAVE PUBLISHED **GOLF: RECORDS, FACTS AND CHAMPIONS** DONALD STEEL **£12.95**

Greyhound Racing

Origins ■ The first greyhound meeting was staged at Hendon, north London with a railed hare operated by a windlass, in September 1876. Modern greyhound racing originated with the perfecting of the mechanical hare by Owen Patrick Smith at Emeryville, California, USA, in 1919. St Petersburg Kennel Club, located in St Petersburg, Florida, USA, which opened on 3 Jan 1925, is the oldest greyhound track in the world still in operation on its original site. The earliest greyhound race behind a mechanical hare in the British Isles was at Belle Vue, Manchester, opened on 24 Jul 1926.

Derby ■ The only two greyhounds to have won the English Greyhound Derby twice (instituted 1927, now over 500 m *546 yd*) are *Mick the Miller* on 25 Jul 1929, when owned by Albert H. Williams, and on 28 Jun 1930 when owned by Mrs Arundel H. Kempton, and *Patricia's Hope* on 24 Jun 1972 when owned by Gordon and Basil Marks and Brian Stanley and 23 Jun 1973 when owned by G. & B. Marks and J. O'Connor. The highest prize was £35 000 to *Indian Joe* for the Derby on 28 Jun 1980. The only greyhounds to win the English, Scottish and Welsh Derby 'triple' are *Trev's Perfection*, owned by Fred Trevillion, in 1947, *Mile Bush Pride*, owned by Noel W. Purvis, in 1959, and *Patricia's Hope* in 1972. The only two greyhounds to have won the American Derby, at Taunton, Massachusetts, twice are *Real Huntsman* in 1950–1 and *Dutch Bahama* in 1984–5.

Grand National ■ The only greyhound to have won the Grand National (instituted 1927 over 480 m *525 yd*, now 500 m *546 yd* and five flights) three times is *Sherry's Prince* (1967–78) owned by Mrs Joyce Mathews of Sanderstead, Surrey, in 1970–2.

Most consecutive wins ● *Ballyregan Bob*, owned by Cliff Kevern and seen here with his trainer George Curtis, won a record 32 consecutive races between 1985 and December 1986. (Photo: All-Sport/Simon Bruty)

Fastest greyhound ■ The highest speed at which any greyhound has been timed is 67·14 km/h *41·72 mph* (374 m *410 yd* in 20·1 sec) by *The Shoe* on the then straightaway track at Richmond, New South Wales, Australia on 25 Apr 1968. It is estimated that he covered the last 91·44 m *100 yd* in 4·5 sec or at 73·14 km/h *45·45 mph*. The highest speed recorded for a greyhound in Great Britain is 62·97 km/h *39·13 mph* by *Beef Cutlet*, when covering a straight course of 457 m *500 yd* in 26·13 sec at Blackpool, Lancashire, on 13 May 1933. The fastest automatically timed speed recorded for a full four-bend race is 62·59 km/h *38·89 mph* at Brighton, East Sussex by *Glen Miner* on 4 May 1982 with a time of 29·62 sec for 515 m *563 yd*. The fastest over hurdles is 60·58 km/h *37·64 mph* at Brighton by *Wotchit Buster* on 22 Aug 1978.

Most wins ■ The most career wins is 143 by the American greyhound, *JR's Ripper* in 1982–6. The most consecutive victories is 32 by *Ballyregan Bob*, owned by Cliff Kevern and trained by George Curtis from 1985 to 8 Dec 1986, including 16 track record times. His race wins were by an average of more than nine lengths.

Highest earnings ■ The career earnings record is held by *Homespun Rowdy* with $297 000 in the USA, 1984–7. The richest first prize for a greyhound race is $125 000 won by *Ben G Speedboat* in the Great Greyhound Race of Champions at Seabrook, New Hampshire, USA on 23 Aug 1986.

Longest odds ■ *Apollo Prince* won at odds of 250–1 at Sandown GRC, Springvale, Victoria, Australia on 14 Nov 1968.

Gymnastics

Origins ■ A primitive form of gymnastics was practised in ancient Greece and Rome during the period of the ancient Olympic Games (776 BC to AD 393) but Johann Friedrich Simon was the first teacher of modern gymnastics at Basedow's School, Dessau, Germany in 1776.

World Championships *Women* ■ The greatest number of titles won in the World Championships (including Olympic Games) is 12 individual wins and five team by Larissa Semyonovna Latynina (b. 27 Dec 1934) of the USSR, between 1956 and 1964. The USSR has won the team title on 18 occasions (out of 21 titles since 1952).

Men ■ Boris Shakhlin (USSR) (b. 27 Jan 1932) won ten individual titles between 1954 and 1964. He also had three team wins. Japan has won the team title a record ten times between 1960 and 1978.

Youngest champions ■ Olga Bicherova (USSR) (b. 26 Oct 1966) won the women's world title at 15 yr 33 days on 28 Nov 1981. The youngest male world champion was Dmitriy Belozerchev (USSR) (b. 17 Dec 1966) at 16 yr 315 days at Budapest, Hungary on 28 Oct 1983.

Olympics ■ Japan (1960, 1964, 1968, 1972 and 1976) has won the men's team title most often. The USSR has won the women's title nine times (1952–80, 1988).

The most men's individual gold medals is six by: Boris Shakhlin (USSR), one in 1956, four (two shared) in 1960 and one in 1964; and Nikolay Andrianov (USSR) (b. 14 Oct 1952), one in 1972, four in 1976 and one in 1980.

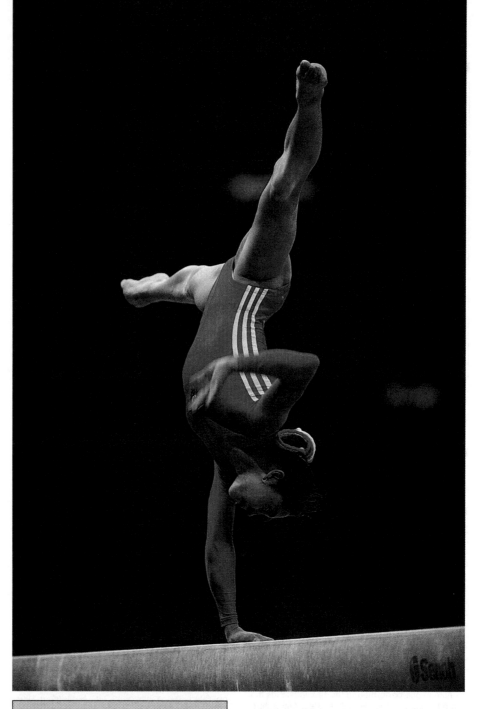

Most Olympic team titles ● The USSR won the women's gymnastics team title for a record ninth occasion at Seoul in 1988. Shown in action on the beam is Yelena Shushunova, winner of the individual Combined Exercises title. (Photo: All-Sport/David Leah)

Vera Caslavska-Odlozil (b. 3 May 1942) (Czechoslovakia) has won most individual gold medals with seven, three in 1964 and four (one shared) in 1968. Larissa Latynina won six individual gold medals and was in three winning teams from 1956–64, making nine gold medals. She also won five silver and four bronze making 18 in all—an Olympic record.

The most medals for a male gymnast is 15 by Nikolay Andrianov (USSR), seven gold, five silver and three bronze from 1972–80.

Aleksandr Ditiatin (USSR) (b. 7 Aug 1957) is the only man to win a medal in all eight categories in the same Games, with three gold, four silver and one bronze at Moscow in 1980.

Highest score ■ Nadia Comaneci (Romania) (b. 12 Nov 1961) was the first to achieve a perfect score (10·00) and achieved seven in all at the Montreal Olympics in July 1976.

British Championships ■ The British Gymnastic Championship was won ten times by Arthur John Whitford (b. 2 Jul 1908) in 1928–36 and 1939. He was also in four winning teams. Wray 'Nik' Stuart (b. 20 Jul

1927) equalled the record of nine successive wins, 1956–64. The women's record is eight by Mary Patricia Hirst (b. 18 Nov 1918) (1947, 1949–50 and 1952–6). The most overall titles in Modern Rhythmic Gymnastics is by Sharon Taylor with five successive, 1977–81.

World Cup ■ Gymnasts who have won two World Cup (instituted 1975) overall titles are three men: Nikolay Andrianov (USSR), Aleksandr Ditiatin (USSR) and Li Ning (China) (b. 8 Sep 1963), and one woman: Maria Filatova (USSR) (b. 19 Jul 1961).

Youngest international ■ Pasakevi 'Voula' Kouna (b. 6 Dec 1971) was aged 9 yr 299 days at the start of the Balkan Games at Serres, Greece on 1 Oct 1981, when she represented Greece.

Modern Rhythmic Gymnastics ■ The most overall individual titles in Modern Rhythmic Gymnastics is three by Maria Gigova (Bulgaria) in 1969, 1971 and 1973 (shared). Bulgaria has a record six team titles 1969, 1971, 1973, 1983, 1985 and 1987. Bianka Panova (Bulgaria) (b. 27 May 1960) won all four apparatus gold medals all with maximum scores, and won a team gold in 1987. Marina Lobatch (USSR) won the 1988 Olympic title with perfect scores for all events. Lilia Ignatova (Bulgaria) has won both the individual World Cup titles that have been held, 1983 and 1986.

Somersaults ■ Ashrita Furman performed 8341 forward rolls in 10 hr 30 min over 19·67 km *12 miles 390 yards* from Lexington to Charleston, Massachusetts, USA on 30 Apr 1986. Shigeru Iwasaki (b. 1960) backwards somersaulted 50 m *54·68 yd* in 10·8 sec at Tokyo, Japan on 30 Mar 1980.

Static wall 'sit' (or Samson's Chair) ■ Kevin DeWitt stayed in an unsupported sitting position against a wall for 76 min 12 sec in Kennewick, Washington, USA on 31 Jul 1986.

Handball

Origins ■ Handball was first played *c.* 1895 in Germany. It was introduced into the Olympic Games at Berlin in 1936 as an 11-a-side outdoor game, with Germany winning, but when re-introduced in 1972 it was an indoor game with seven-a-side, the standard size of team since 1952.

The International Handball Federation was founded in 1946. The first international match was held at Halle/Saale on 3 Sep 1925 when Austria beat Germany 6–3.

Most championships *Olympic* ■ The USSR have won four titles – men 1976 and 1988, women 1976 and 1980. Yugoslavia have also won a record two men's titles, 1972 and 1984.

World Championship (instituted 1938) ■ Romania have won four men's and three women's titles from 1956 to 1974. The GDR also have three women's titles, 1971, 1975 and 1978.

European Champions' Cup ■ Spartak Kiev, USSR have won 13 women's titles between 1970 and 1988. VfL Gummersbach have won a record five men's titles, 1967, 1970–1, 1974, 1983. They are also the only club team to win all three European trophies; European Champions' Cup, European Cup Winners' Cup and IHF Cup.

Highest score ■ The highest score in an international match was recorded when the USSR beat Afghanistan 86–2 in the 'Friendly Army Tournament' at Miskolc, Hungary in August 1981.

Britain *Most titles* ■ The most men's national championship titles is seven by Brentwood '72 (British Championship, 1974; English National League, 1979–83; British League, 1985). The most women's titles is seven by Wakefield Metros (English National League, 1982–87; British League, 1988).

Highest score ■ The highest score in a men's league match is by Glasgow University, who beat Claremont, 69–5 at Glasgow, Strathclyde in March 1984. The record in a women's match is 45–0 by Dunfermline College when beating Satellites Strikers at Dunfermline, Fife in December 1985.

Highest score by an individual ■ Rolv Erichsen (b. 23 Aug 1963) scored 22 for Glasgow University (63) against Claremont (3) at Claremont, East Kilbride, Strathclyde in November 1983. The women's record is 14 by Jacqueline Swain (b. 16 Jan 1963) for Wakefield Metros (40) against Kirkby Ladies (8) at Featherstone, West Yorkshire in October 1985.

Harness Racing

Origins ■ Trotting races were held in Valkenburg, Netherlands in 1554. In England the trotting gait (the simultaneous use of the diagonally opposite

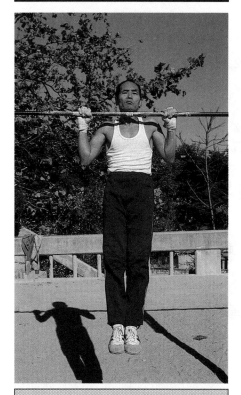

Consecutive chins ● Lee Chin-yong (South Korea) (b. 15 Aug 1925) performed 370 consecutive chins at Backyon Gymnasium, Seoul, South Korea on 14 May 1988.

legs) was known in the 16th century. The sulky first appeared in 1829. Pacers thrust out their fore and hind legs simultaneously on one side.

Most successful driver ■ In North American harness racing history has been Herve Filion (b. 1 Feb 1940) of Québec, Canada, who had achieved 11 426 wins to the end of April 1989, including a record 798 wins in a year, 1988. John D. Campbell (USA) (b. 8 Apr 1955) has the highest career earnings of $71 975 734 from 4329 wins, to April 1989. This includes a year record of $11 148 565 in 1988 when he won 480 races.

Highest price ■ For a pacer is $19·2 million for *Nihilator* who was syndicated by Wall Street Stable and Almahurst Stud Farm in 1984. The highest price paid for a trotter is $6 million for *Mack Lobell* by John Erik Magnusson of Vislanda, Sweden in 1988.

Greatest winnings ■ For any harness horse is $3 225 653 by the pacer *Nihilator*, who won 35 of 38 races in 1984–5. The greatest amount won by a trotting horse is $2 753 666 by *Idéal du Gazeau* (France) to July 1983. The single season record is $1 864 286 by *Nihilator* in 1985.

The largest ever purse was $2 161 000 for the Woodrow Wilson two-year-old race over 1 mile at the Meadowlands, New Jersey, USA on 16 Aug 1984. Of this sum a record $1 080 500 went to the winner *Nihilator*, driven by William O'Donnell (b. 4 May 1948).

Hockey

Origins ■ A representation of two players with curved snagging sticks apparently in an orthodox 'bully' position was found in Tomb No. 17 at Beni Hasan, Egypt and has been dated to *c.* 2050 BC. There is a British reference to the game in Lincolnshire in 1277. The modern game evolved in south London in the 1870s. An English Hockey Association was founded in 1875, but the current English men's governing body, the Hockey Association, was formed on 18 Jan 1886. The All-England Women's Hockey Association was founded in 1895. The *Fédération Internationale de Hockey* was formed on 7 Jan 1924.

Most Olympic medals ■ The Indians were Olympic champions from the re-introduction of Olympic hockey in 1928 until 1960, when Pakistan beat them 1–0 at Rome. They had their eighth win in 1980. Of the seven Indians who have won three Olympic team gold medals two have also won a silver medal – Leslie Walter Claudius (b. 25 Mar 1927) in 1948, 1952, 1956 and 1960 (silver) and Udham Singh (b. 4 Aug 1928) in 1952, 1956, 1964 and 1960 (silver). A women's tournament was added in 1980 when Zimbabwe were the winners. The Netherlands won in 1984 and Australia in 1988.

World Cup ■ The World Cup for men was first held in 1971, and for women in 1974. The most wins are, (men) three by Pakistan, 1971, 1978 and 1982; (women) four by the Netherlands, 1974, 1978, 1983 and 1986.

Champions' Trophy ■ First held in 1978 and contested annually since 1980 by the top six men's teams in the world; the most wins is three by Australia 1983–5 and West Germany 1986–8. The first women's Champions' Trophy was won by the Netherlands in 1987.

MEN

The first organised club was the Blackheath Rugby and Hockey Club founded in 1861. The oldest club with a continuous history is Teddington HC formed in the autumn of 1871. They played Richmond on 24 Oct 1874 and used the first recorded circle *versus* Surbiton at Bushey Park, London on 9 Dec 1876. The first international match was the Wales *v.* Ireland match at Rhyl, Clywd on 26 Jan 1895. Ireland won 3–0.

Highest international score ■ The highest score was when India defeated the USA 24–1 at Los Angeles, California, USA in the 1932 Olympic Games. The greatest number of goals in an international in Britain was when England defeated France 16–0 at Beckenham, Kent on 25 Mar 1922.

Most international appearances ■ Michael Peter (b. 7 May 1949) represented West Germany over 250 times between 1969 and 1984, indoors and out. The most by a player from the British Isles is 161 by Richard Leman (b. 13 Jul 1959), 118 for England and 43 for Great Britain, 1980–8. H. David Judge (b. 19 Jan 1936) played a record 124 times for Ireland, 1957–78. The first player to achieve 100 international appearances for England was Norman Hughes (b. 30 Sep 1952) on 21 Sep 1986.

Greatest scoring feats ■ The greatest number of goals scored in international hockey is 267 by Paul Litjens (Netherlands) (b. 9 Nov 1947) in 177 games. M. C. Marckx (Bowden 2nd XI) scored 19 goals against Brooklands 2nd XI (score 23–0) on 31 Dec 1910. He was selected for England in March 1912 but declined due to business priorities. Between 1923 and 1958, Fred H. Wagner scored 1832 goals for Beeston HC, Nottingham Casuals and the Nottinghamshire county side. David Ashman has scored 1647 goals for one club, Hamble Old Boys, Southampton, Hampshire, 1958–89. Ron Waterman has made 730 1st XI appearances for the same club, 1958–89.

Fastest goal in an international ■ John French scored 7 sec after the bully-off for England *v.* West Germany at Nottingham on 25 Apr 1971.

HARNESS RACING MILE RECORDS

TROTTING

World mile record	1:52·2	*Mack Lobell* (driver, John Campbell)	Springfield, USA	21	Aug	1987
British record	2:06·1	*Ghandy's Chance* (driver, Steve Lees)	York	25	Jun	1988

PACING

World	1:48·4	*Matt's Scooter* (driver, Michel Lachance)	Lexington, USA	23	Sep	1988
World race record	1:49·6	*Nihilator* (driver, William O'Donnell)	East Rutherford, USA	3	Aug	1985
	1:49·6	*Call For Rain* (driver, Clint Albraith)	Lexington, USA	1	Oct	1988
British record	2:02·1	*Lydia M* (driver, James Pickard)	York	10	Jul	1982

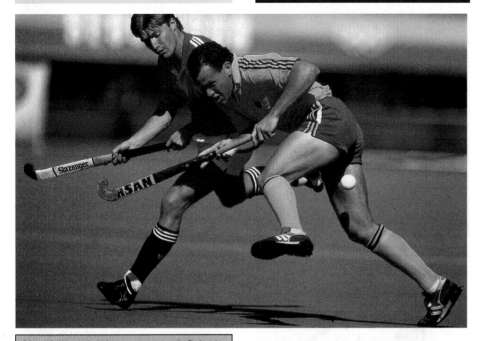

Most international appearances ● Richard Leman (b. 13 Jul 1959) has made a British Isles record number of international appearances including 45 for Great Britain. Here he is in action for Great Britain (red jersey) against Australia during the Olympic semi-final at Seoul in 1988 which Great Britain won 3-1. (Photo: All-Sport/David Cannon)

Greatest goalkeeping ■ Richard James Allen (India) (b. 4 Jun 1902) did not concede a goal during the 1928 Olympic tournament and a total of only three in the following two Olympics of 1932 and 1936. In these three Games India scored a total of 102 goals.

Longest game ■ The longest international game on record was one of 145 min (into the sixth period of extra time), when the Netherlands beat Spain 1-0 in the Olympic tournament at Mexico City on 25 Oct 1968. Club matches of 205 min have twice been recorded: the Hong Kong Football Club beat Prison Sports Dept as the first to score in a 'sudden death' play-off after 2-2 at full time on 11 Mar 1979, and Gore Court beat Hampstead in the first round of the English Club Championships in 1983.

WOMEN

The earliest women's club was East Molesey in Surrey, England formed *c.* 1887. Two ladies' hockey clubs, Wimbledon and Ealing, each founded one year later, are still in existence. The first national association was the Irish Ladies' Hockey Union founded in 1894. The All England Women's Hockey Association held its first formal meeting in Westminster Town Hall, London on 23 Nov 1895. The first international match was an England *v.* Ireland game in Dublin in 1896. Ireland won 2-0.

Most international appearances ■ Valerie Robinson made a record 144 appearances for England, 1963-84.

Highest scores ■ The highest score in an international match was when England beat France 23-0 at Merton, Greater London on 3 Feb 1923. In club hockey, Ross Ladies beat Wyeside, at Ross-on-Wye, Herefordshire 40-0 on 24 Jan 1929, when Edna Mary Blakelock (1904-89) scored a record 21 goals.

Highest attendance ■ The highest attendance was 65 165 for the match between England and the USA at Wembley, London on 11 Mar 1978.

Horse Racing

Origins ■ Horsemanship was an important part of the Hittite culture of Anatolia, Turkey dating from 1400 BC. The 33rd ancient Olympic Games of 648 BC in Greece featured horse racing. The earliest races recorded in England were those held in about AD 200 at Netherby, Cumbria between Arab horses imported by the Romans.

Largest prizes ■ The highest prize money for a day's racing is $10 million for the Breeders' Cup series of seven races staged annually in the USA since 1984. Included each year is a record $3 million for the Breeders' Cup Classic.

Most runners ■ The most horses in a race has been 66 in the Grand National on 22 Mar 1929. The record for the Flat is 58 in the Lincolnshire Handicap at Lincoln on 13 Mar 1948.

HORSES

Most successful ■ The horse with the best win-loss record was *Kincsem*, a Hungarian mare foaled in 1874, who was unbeaten in 54 races (1876-9) throughout Europe, including the Goodwood Cup of 1878.

Longest winning sequence ■ *Camarero*, foaled in 1951, was undefeated in 56 races in Puerto Rico from 19 Apr 1953 to his first defeat on 17 Aug 1955 (in his career to 1956, he won 73 of 77 races).

Career ■ *Galgo Jr* (foaled 1928) won 137 of 159 starts in Puerto Rico between 1930 and 1936; in 1931 he won a record 30 races in one year.

Same race ■ *Doctor Syntax* (foaled 1811) won the Preston Gold Cup on seven successive occasions, 1815-21.

Triple Crown winners ■ The English Triple Crown (2000 Guineas, Derby, St Leger) has been won 15 times, most recently by *Nijinsky* in 1970. The fillies' equivalent (1000 Guineas, Oaks, St Leger) has been won nine times, most recently by *Oh So Sharp* in 1985. Two of these fillies also won the 2000 Guineas: *Formosa* (in a dead-heat) in 1868 and *Sceptre* in 1902. The American Triple Crown (Kentucky Derby, Preakness Stakes, Belmont Stakes) has been achieved 11 times, most recently by *Affirmed* in 1978.

Highest price ■ Enormous valuations placed on potential stallions may be determined from sales of a minority holding, but such valuations would, perhaps, not be reached on the open market. The most paid for a yearling is $13·1m on 23 Jul 1985 at

Greatest earnings ● *Desert Orchid* has won a British record prizemoney during his career, 1983-9. Here, ridden by Simon Sherwood, he leads during his success in the 1989 Gold Cup at Cheltenham on 16 Mar 1989. (Photo: All-Sport/David Cannon)

Keeneland, Kentucky, USA by Robert Sangster and partners for *Seattle Dancer*.

Greatest winnings ■ The career earnings record is $6 679 242 by the 1987 Kentucky Derby winner *Alysheba* (foaled 1984), trained by Jack Van Berg, from 1986–8. He also earned a one year record of $3 808 600 from seven wins out of nine races in 1988, including $1 350 000 in his final race, the Breeders' Cup Classic, on 5 Nov 1988. The leading money-winning mare is *Lady's Secret* (foaled 1982) with

$3 021 325 in the USA, 1984–87. The one race record is $2·6 million by *Spend A Buck* (USA) for the Jersey Derby, Garden State Park, New Jersey, USA on 27 May 1985, of which $2 million was a bonus for having previously won the Kentucky Derby and two prepa-ratory races at Garden State Park.

Biggest weight ■ The biggest weight ever carried is 190 kg *30 stone* by both Mr Maynard's mare and Mr Baker's horse in a match won by the former over a mile at York on 21 May 1788.

Oldest winners ■ The oldest horses to win on the Flat have been the 18-year-olds *Revenge* at Shrews-bury in September 1790, *Marksman* at Ashford, Kent in September 1826 and *Jorrocks* at Bathurst, Australia in February 1851. At the same age *Wild Aster* won three hurdle races in six days in March 1919 and *Sonny Somers* won two steeplechases in February 1980.

World speed records ■ The highest race speed recorded is 69·62 km/h *43·26 mph* by *Big Racket*,

MAJOR RACE RECORDS

RACE (instituted)	RECORD TIME	MOST WINS			LARGEST FIELD
		Jockey	Trainer	Owner	
FLAT					
Derby (1780) 1½ miles *2414 m* Epsom, Surrey	2 min 33·8 sec *Mahmoud* 1936 2 min 33·84 sec *Kahyasi* 1988 (Electronically timed)	9–Lester Piggott 1954, 57, 60, 68, 70, 72, 76, 77, 83	7–Robert Robson 1793, 1802, 09, 10, 15, 17, 23 7–John Porter 1868, 82, 83, 86, 90, 91, 99 7–Fred Darling 1922, 25, 26, 31, 38, 40, 41	5–3rd Earl of Egremont 1782, 1804, 05, 07, 26 5–HH Aga Khan III 1930, 35, 36, 48, 52	34 (1862)
2000 Guineas (1809) 1 mile *1609 m* Newmarket, Suffolk	1 min 35·8 sec *My Babu* 1948	9–Jem Robinson 1825, 28, 31, 33, 34, 35, 36, 47, 48	7–John Scott 1842, 43, 49, 53, 56, 60, 62	5–4th Duke of Grafton 1820, 21, 22, 26, 27 5–5th Earl of Jersey 1831, 34, 35, 36, 37	28 (1930)
1000 Guineas (1814) 1 mile *1609 m* Newmarket	1 min 36·85 sec *Oh So Sharp* 1985	7–George Fordham 1859, 61, 65, 68, 69, 81, 83	9–Robert Robson 1818, 19, 20, 21, 22, 23, 25, 26, 27	8–4th Duke of Grafton 1819, 20, 21, 22, 23, 25, 26, 27	29 (1926)
Oaks (1779) 1½ miles *2414 m* Epsom	2 min 34·21 sec *Time Charter* 1982	9–Frank Buckle 1797, 98, 99, 1802, 03, 05, 17, 18, 23	12–Robert Robson 1802, 04, 05, 07, 08, 09, 13, 15, 18, 22, 23, 25	6–4th Duke of Grafton 1813, 15, 22, 23, 28, 31	26 (1848)
St Leger (1776) 1 m 6 f 127 yd *2932 m* Doncaster, Yorkshire	3 min 01·6 sec *Coronach* 1926 *Windsor Lad* 1934	9–Bill Scott 1821, 25, 28, 29, 38, 39, 40, 41, 46	16–John Scott 1827, 28, 29, 32, 34, 38, 39, 40, 41, 45, 51, 53, 56, 57, 59, 62	7–9th Duke of Hamilton 1786, 87, 88, 92, 1808, 09, 14	30 (1825)
King George VI and Queen Elizabeth Diamond Stakes (1951) 1½ miles *2414 m* Ascot, Berkshire	2 min 26·98 sec *Grundy* 1975	7–Lester Piggott 1965, 66, 69, 70, 74, 77, 84	4–Dick Hern 1972, 79, 80, 85	2–Nelson Bunker Hunt 1973, 74	19 (1951)
Prix de l'Arc de Triomphe (1920) 2400 metres *1 mile 864 yd* Longchamp, France	2 min 26·3 sec *Trempolino* 1987	4–Jacques Doyasbère 1942, 44, 50, 51 4–Frédéric 'Freddy' Head 1966, 72, 76, 79 4–Yves Saint-Martin 1970, 74, 82, 84 4–Pat Eddery 1980, 85, 86, 87	4–Charles Semblat 1942, 44, 46, 49 4–Alec Head 1952, 59, 76, 81 4–François Mathet 1950, 51, 70, 82	6–Marcel Boussac 1936, 37, 42, 44, 46, 49	30 (1967)
VRC Melbourne Cup (1861) 3200 metres *1 mile 1739 yd* Flemington, Victoria, Australia	3 min 19·1 sec *Rain Lover* 1968	4–Bobby Lewis 1902, 15, 19, 27 4–Harry White 1974, 75, 78, 79	7–Bart Cummings 1965, 66, 67, 74, 75, 77, 79	4–Etienne de Mestre 1861, 62, 67, 78	39 (1890)
Kentucky Derby (1875) 1¼ miles *2012 m* Churchill Downs, USA	1 min 59·4 sec *Secretariat* 1973	5–Eddie Arcaro 1938, 41, 45, 48, 52 5–Bill Hartack 1957, 60, 62, 64, 69	6–Ben Jones 1938, 41, 44, 48, 49, 52	8–Calumet Farm 1941, 44, 48, 49, 52, 57, 58, 68	23 (1974)
Irish Derby (1866) 1½ miles *2414 m* The Curragh	2 min 28·8 sec *Tambourine* 1962	6–Morny Wing 1921, 23, 30, 38, 42, 46	6–Vincent O'Brien 1953, 57, 70, 77, 84, 85	5–HH Aga Khan III 1925, 32, 40, 48, 49	24 (1962)
JUMPING					
Grand National (1839) 4½ miles *7242 m* Aintree, Liverpool, Merseyside	9 min 01·9 sec *Red Rum* 1973	5–George Stevens 1856, 63, 64, 69, 70	4–Fred Rimell 1956, 61, 70, 76	3–James Machell 1873, 74, 76 3–Sir Charles Assheton-Smith 1893, 1912, 13 3–Noel Le Mare 1973, 74, 77	66 (1929)
Cheltenham Gold Cup (1924) 3¼ miles *5230 m* Cheltenham, Gloucestershire	6 min 23·4 sec *Silver Fame* 1951	4–Pat Taaffe 1964, 65, 66, 68	5–Tom Dreaper 1946, 64, 65, 66, 68	7–Dorothy Paget 1932, 33, 34, 35, 36, 40, 52	22 (1982)
Champion Hurdle (1927) 2 miles *3218 m* Cheltenham	3 min 51·7 sec *See You Then* 1985	4–Tim Molony 1951, 52, 53, 54	5–Peter Easterby 1967, 76, 77, 80, 81	4–Dorothy Paget 1932, 33, 40, 46	24 (1964)

20·8 sec for ¼mile *409·26 m*, at Mexico City, Mexico on 5 Feb 1945. The 4-year-old carried 51·7 kg *114 lb*. The record for 1½ miles *2414 m* is 60·76 km/h *37·76 mph* by *Fiddle Isle* (carrying 56·2 kg *124 lb*) on 21 Mar 1970 and by *John Henry* (carrying 57·1 kg *126 lb*) on 16 Mar 1980, both at Santa Anita Park, Arcadia, California, USA in a time of 2 min 23 sec.

JOCKEYS

Most successful ■ William Lee 'Bill' Shoemaker (USA) (b. weighing 1·1 kg *2½ lb*, 19 Aug 1931), now weighing 44 kg *97 lb* and standing 1·50 m *4 ft 11 in*, has ridden a record 8801 winners from over 40 100 mounts from his first ride on 19 Mar 1949 and first winner on 20 Apr 1949 to start of 1989. Laffit Pincay (b. 29 Dec 1946, Panama City) has earned a career record $136 385 215 from 1966 to the start of 1989.

The most races won by a jockey in a year is 546 from 2199 rides by Chris McCarron (USA) (b. 1955) in 1974. The greatest amount won in a year is $14 877 298 by José Santos (USA) in 1988.

Wins *One day* ■ The most winners ridden in one day is nine by Chris Antley (USA) on 31 Oct 1987. They consisted of four in the afternoon at Aqueduct, New York, USA and five in the evening at The Meadowlands, New Jersey, USA.

One card ■ The most winners ridden on one card is eight by Hubert S. Jones, 17, from 13 rides at Caliente, California, USA on 11 Jun 1944; Oscar Barattuci, at Rosario City, Argentina on 15 Dec 1957; Dave Gall, from ten rides at Cahokia Downs, East St Louis, Illinois, USA on 18 Oct 1978; Chris Loseth, from ten rides at Exhibition Park, Vancouver, BC, Canada on 9 Apr 1984; and Robert Williams from ten rides at Lincoln, Nebraska, USA on 29 Sep 1984.

Consecutive ■ The longest winning streak is 12 by: Sir Gordon Richards (1904–86) (one race at Nottingham on 3 Oct, six out of six at Chepstow on 4 Oct and the first five races next day at Chepstow) in 1933; and by Pieter Stroebel at Bulawayo, Southern Rhodesia (now Zimbabwe), 7 Jun–7 Jul 1958.

TRAINERS

Jack Van Berg (USA) has the greatest number of wins in a year, 496 in 1976, and in a career, 5266 from 1955 to start of 1989. The greatest amount won in a year is $17 842 358 by D. Wayne Lukas (USA) in 1988.

The only trainer to saddle the first five finishers in a championship race is Michael Dickinson in the 1983 Cheltenham Gold Cup; on 27 Dec 1982 he won a record 12 races in one day.

OWNERS

The most lifetime wins by an owner is 4775 by Marion Van Berg in North America in the 35 years up to his death in 1971. The most wins in a year is 494 by Dan R. Lasater (USA) in 1974. The greatest amount won in a year is $5 858 168 by Ogden Phipps (USA) in 1988.

BRITISH TURF RECORDS

FLAT RACING

Most successful horses ■ *Eclipse* (foaled 1764) still has the best win-loss record, being unbeaten in a career of 18 races between May 1769 and October 1770. The longest winning sequence is 21 races by *Meteor* (foaled 1783) between 1786 and 1788. The most races won in a season is 23 by three-year-old *Fisherman* in 1856. *Catherina* (foaled 1830) won a career record 79 out of 176 races, 1832–41. The most successful sire was *Stockwell* (foaled 1849) whose progeny won 1153 races (1858–76) and who in 1866 set a record of 132 races won. The greatest amount ever won by an English-trained horse is

$1 182 140 by the filly *Pebbles* (foaled 1981) in 1983–5. In 1985 she won a record $1 012 611 in one season, including the Breeders' Cup Turf in New York, USA. The biggest winning margin in a Classic is 20 lengths by *Mayonaise* in the 1000 Guineas in 1859.

Most successful jockeys ■ Sir Gordon Richards won 4870 races from 21 815 mounts from his first mount at Lingfield Park, Surrey on 16 Oct 1920 to his last at Sandown Park, Surrey on 10 Jul 1954. His first win was on 31 Mar 1921. In 1953, at his 28th and final attempt, he won the Derby, six days after his knighthood. He was champion jockey 26 times between 1925 and 1953 and won a record 269 races in 1947. Lester Piggott (b. 5 Nov 1935) won 4349 races in Great Britain, 1948–85, but his global total exceeded 5200.

The most Classic races won by a jockey is 29 by Lester Piggott from his first on *Never Say Die* in the 1954 Derby to the 1985 2000 Guineas on *Shadeed*. (Derby—9, St Leger—8, Oaks—6, 2000 Guineas—4, 1000 Guineas—2.)

Most successful trainers ■ The record prize money earned in a season is £1 896 689 by Henry Richard Amherst Cecil (b. 11 Jan 1943) from a record 180 winners (446 runners) in 1987. Michael Ronald Stoute (b. 22 Oct 1945) set a record for worldwide earnings of £2 778 405 in 1986. The most Classics won by a trainer is 40 by John Scott (1794–1871) of Malton, Yorkshire between 1827 and 1863. James Croft of Middleham, Yorkshire trained the first four horses in the 1822 St Leger. Alec Taylor of Manton, Wiltshire headed the trainers' list for a record 12 seasons between 1907 and 1925.

Most successful owners ■ H H Aga Khan III (1877–1957) was leading owner a record 13 times between 1924 and 1952. The record prize money won in a season is £1 693 202 by Sheikh Mohammed bin Rashid al Maktoum in 1988; in 1987 his horses won a record 126 races. The most Classics won is 20 by the 4th Duke of Grafton (1760–1844) between

1813 and 1831 and by the 17th Earl of Derby (1865–1948) between 1910 and 1945.

The Derby ■ The greatest of England's five Classics is the Derby Stakes, inaugurated on 4 May 1780, and named after the 12th Earl of Derby (1752–1834). The distance was increased in 1784 from a mile to 1½miles *2·414 km*. The race has been run at Epsom Downs, Surrey, except for the two war periods, when it was run at Newmarket, Suffolk, and is for three-year-olds only. Since 1884 the weights have been: colts 57 kg *9 st*, fillies 55 kg *8 st 9 lb*. Geldings were eligible until 1904.

Largest and smallest winning margins ■ *Shergar*, ridden by Walter Swinburn, won the Derby by a record 10 lengths in 1981. There have been two dead-heats: in 1828 when *Cadland* beat *The Colonel* in the run-off, and in 1884 between *St Gatien* and *Harvester* (stakes divided).

Longest and shortest odds ■ Three winners have been returned at odds of 100–1: *Jeddah* (1898), *Signorinetta* (1908) and *Aboyeur* (1913). The shortest-priced winner was *Ladas* (1894) at 2–9 and the hottest losing favourite was *Surefoot*, fourth at 40–95 in 1890.

Largest prize ■ The richest prize on the British Turf was £296 500 in the 209th Derby on 1 Jun 1988, won by H H Aga Khan IV's *Kahyasi*.

JUMPING

Most successful horses ■ Triple Champion Hurdler *Sir Ken* (foaled 1947), who won in 1952–4, won a record 16 hurdle races in succession, April 1951 to March 1953. Three other horses have also won a record three Champion Hurdles; *Hatton's Grace* 1949–51; *Persian War* 1968–70; *See You Then* 1985–7. The greatest number of Cheltenham Gold Cup wins is five by *Golden Miller*, 1932–6.

The greatest amount earned by a British or Irish-trained jumper is £408 108 in 1983–9 by *Desert Orchid* (27 wins, 9 seconds, 5 thirds in 55 races). The

previous record holder, the mare *Dawn Run* (k. 1986), uniquely won both the Champion Hurdle (1984) and Cheltenham Gold Cup (1986).

Most successful jockeys ■ John Francome (b. 13 Dec 1952) won a career record 1138 races over jumps (from 5072 mounts) from 1970 to 1985.

The record number of wins in a season is 221 (from 663 rides) by Peter Michael Scudamore (b. 13 Jun 1958) in 1988/9. The most wins in a day is six by amateur Charlie Cunningham at Rugby, Warwickshire on 29 Mar 1881. The record number of successive wins is ten by: John Alnam 'Johnny' Gilbert (b. 26 Jul 1920), 8–30 Sep 1959; and by Phil Tuck (b. 10 Jul 1956), 23 Aug–3 Sep 1986. The record number of championships is seven by: Gerald 'Gerry' Wilson (1903–68) 1933–8 and 1941; and by John Francome (one shared) in 1976, 1979, 1981–5.

Most successful trainers ■ The most first-prize money earned in a season is £683 654 by Martin Charles Pipe (b. 29 May 1945) in 1988/9, when from 566 runners his horses had a record 208 wins. Frederick Thomas Winter (b. 20 Sep 1926) won a record eight trainers' championships, 1971–5, 1977–8 and 1985.

Grand National ■ The first Grand National Steeple Chase may be regarded as the Grand Liverpool Steeple Chase of 26 Feb 1839 though the race was not given its present name until 1847. It became a handicap in 1843. Except for 1916–18, and 1941–5 the race has been run at Aintree, near Liverpool, over 30 fences.

Most wins ■ The only horse to win three times is *Red Rum* (foaled 1965) in 1973, 1974 and 1977, from

five runs. He came second in 1975 and 1976. *Manifesto* ran a record eight times (1895–1904). He won in 1897 and 1899, came third three times and fourth once.

Highest prize ■ The highest prize and the richest ever over jumps in Great Britain was £68 740.50 won by *Rhyme 'N' Reason* on 9 Apr 1988.

Highest weight ■ The highest weight ever carried to victory is 79·4 kg *12 st 7 lb* by *Cloister* (1893), *Manifesto* (1899), *Jerry M.* (1912) and *Poethlyn* (1919).

Hurling

Origins ■ A game of very ancient origin, hurling was included in the Tailteann Games (instituted 1829 BC). It only became standardised with the formation of the Gaelic Athletic Association in Thurles, Ireland on 1 Nov 1884. The Irish Hurling Union was formed on 24 Jan 1879.

Most titles *All-Ireland* ■ The greatest number of All-Ireland Championships won by one team is 26 by Cork between 1890 and 1986. The greatest number of successive wins is four by Cork (1941–4).

Inter-provincials ■ Munster holds the greatest number of inter-provincial (Railway Cup) championships with 34 (1928–77).

Most appearances ■ The most appearances in All-Ireland finals is ten shared by Christy Ring (Cork and Munster) and John Doyle (Tipperary). They also share the record of All-Ireland medals won with eight each. Ring's appearances on the winning side were in 1941–4, 1946 and 1952–4, while Doyle's were in 1949–51, 1958, 1961–2 and 1964–5. Ring also played in a record 22 inter-provincial finals (1942–63) and was on the winning side 18 times.

Highest and lowest scores ■ The highest score in an All-Ireland final (60 min) was in 1896 when Tipperary (8 goals, 14 points) beat Dublin (no goals,

4 points). The record aggregate score was when Cork (6 goals, 21 points) defeated Wexford (5 goals, 10 points) in the 80-minute final of 1970. A goal equals three points. The highest recorded individual score was by Nick Rackard (Wexford), who scored 7 goals and 7 points against Antrim in the 1954 All-Ireland semi-final. The lowest score in an All-Ireland final was when Tipperary (1 goal, 1 point) beat Galway (nil) in the first championship at Birr in 1887.

Longest hit ■ The greatest distance for a 'lift and stroke' is one of 117 m *129 yd* credited to Tom Murphy of Three Castles, Kilkenny, in a 'long puck' contest in 1906.

Largest crowd ■ The largest crowd was 84 865 for the All-Ireland final between Cork and Wexford at Croke Park, Dublin in 1954.

Ice Hockey

Origins ■ There is pictorial evidence that a hockey-like game (*kalv*) was played on ice in the early 16th century in The Netherlands. The game was probably first played in North America on 25 Dec 1855 at Kingston, Ontario, Canada, but Halifax also lays claim to priority. The International Ice Hockey Federation was founded in 1908. The National Hockey League (NHL) of North America was inaugurated in 1917.

World Championships and Olympic Games ■ World Championships were first held for amateurs in 1920 in conjunction with the Olympic Games, which were also considered as world championships up to 1968. From 1977 World Championships have been open to professionals. The USSR won 21 world titles between 1954 and 1989, including the Olympic titles of 1956, 1964 and 1968. They have a record seven Olympic titles with a further four, 1972, 1976, 1984 and 1988. The longest Olympic career is that of Richard Torriani (Switzerland) (b. 1 Oct 1911) from 1928 to 1948. The most gold medals won by any player is three, achieved by USSR players Vitaliy Davidov, Anatoliy Firssov, Viktor Kuzkin and Aleksandr Ragulin in 1964, 1968 and 1972, and by Vladislav Tretyak in 1972, 1976 and 1984.

Stanley Cup ■ The Stanley Cup, presented by the Governor-General, Lord Stanley (original cost $48·67), became emblematic of National Hockey League supremacy 33 years after the first contest at Montreal in 1893. It has been won most often by the Montreal Canadiens with 23 wins in 1916, 1924, 1930–1, 1944, 1946, 1953, 1956–60, 1965–6, 1968–9, 1971, 1973, 1976–9, 1986.

British competitions ■ The English National (later British) League Championship (instituted 1935) has been won by the Wembley Lions four times, in 1936–7, 1952 and 1957 and by Streatham (now Redskins) in 1950, 1953, 1960 and 1982. Murrayfield Racers have won the Northern League (instituted 1966) seven times, 1970–2, 1976, 1979–80 and 1985. The Icy Smith Cup (first held 1966), the premier British club competition until 1981, was won by Murrayfield Racers nine times, 1966, 1969–72, 1975 and 1979–81. The Heineken Championship (instituted 1982) has been won a record three times by Dundee Rockets, 1982–4. The Heineken League title has been won three times by Durham Wasps, 1985, 1988–9.

Most goals *Team* ■ The greatest number of goals recorded in a world championship match was when Australia beat New Zealand 58–0 at Perth on 15 Mar 1987. The NHL record is 21 goals when Montreal Canadiens beat Toronto St Patrick's, 14–7, at Montreal on 10 Jan 1920, and Edmonton Oilers beat Chicago Black Hawks, 12–9, at Chicago on 11 Dec 1985. The NHL single team record is 16 by Montreal Canadiens *v.* Quebec Bulldogs 3, at Quebec City on 3 Nov 1920.

Most goals and points *Individual* ■ The most goals scored in a season in the NHL is 92 in the

1981/2 season by Wayne Gretzky (b. 26 Jan 1961) for the Edmonton Oilers. He scored a record 215 points, including a record 163 assists in 1985/6. In 1981/2 in all games, adding Stanley Cup play-offs and for Canada in the World Championship, he scored 238 points (103 goals, 135 assists). The North American career record for goals is 1071 (including in the NHL records for 801 goals as well as 1850 points) by Gordie Howe (b. 31 Mar 1928) (Detroit Red Wings, Houston Aeros, New England Whalers and Hartford Whalers) from 16 Oct 1946 in 32 seasons ending in 1979/80. He took 2204 games to achieve the 1000th goal, but Robert Marvin 'Bobby' Hull (b. 3 Jan 1939) (Chicago Black Hawks and Winnipeg Jets) scored his 1000th in 1600 games on 12 Mar 1978.

Wayne Gretzky (Edmonton Oilers 1979–88, Los Angeles Kings 1988–9) has the NHL record for assists of 1200 and overall records for NHL and Stanley Cup play-offs for assists, 1388 and total points, 2111 (1837 NHL, 274 Stanley Cup). His 723 goals (637 + 86) have come from 905 games, a record breaking pace.

British ■ The highest score and aggregate in a British League match was set when Medway Bears beat Richmond Raiders 48–1 at Gillingham in a Second Division fixture on 1 Dec 1985, when Kevin McNaught scored a record 25 points from seven goals and 18 assists.

The most individual goals scored in a senior game is 14 by Ron Halpin (Canada) (b. 18 Oct 1955) for Dundee Rockets in a 24–1 win over Durham Wasps at Dundee on 4 Apr 1982. Steve Moria (Canada) (b. 1960) achieved the highest number of assists, 13, for Fife Flyers at Cleveland on 28 Mar 1987. Rick Fera (Canada) (b. 1964) set British season's records of 165 goals and 318 points for Murrayfield Racers in 48 games in 1986/7. Tim Salmon (Canada) (b. 27 Nov 1964) achieved a season's record 183 assists in 47 games for Ayr Bruins in 1985/6. The highest career points for the Heineken League is 1043 (475 goals, 568 assists) by Tony Hand (GB) (b. 15 Aug 1967) in 205 games to end of the 1988/9 season.

Most points one game ■ The North American major league record for most points scored in one game is ten by Jim Harrison (b. 9 Jul 1947) (three goals, seven assists) for Alberta, later Edmonton Oilers in a World Hockey Association match at Edmonton on 30 Jan 1973, and by Darryl Sittler (b. 18 Sept 1950) (six goals, four assists) for Toronto Maple Leafs *v.* Boston Bruins in an NHL match at Toronto on 7 Feb 1976.

Fastest scoring *World* ■ In the NHL the fastest goal was after 4 sec by Joseph Antoine Claude Provost (b. 17 Sept 1933) (Montreal Canadiens) *v.* Boston Bruins in the second period at Montreal on 9 Nov 1957, and by Denis Joseph Savard (b. 4 Feb 1961) (Chicago Black Hawks) *v.* Hartford Whalers in the third period at Chicago on 12 Jan 1986. From the opening whistle, the fastest is 5 sec by Doug Smail (b. 2 Sep 1957) (Winnipeg Jets) *v.* St Louis at Winnipeg on 20 Dec 1981, and by Bryan John Trottier (b. 17 Jul 1956) (New York Islanders) *v.* Boston Bruins at Boston on 22 Mar 1984. Canadian Bill Mosienko (b. 2 Nov 1921) (Chicago Black Hawks) scored three goals in 21 sec *v.* New York Rangers on 23 Mar 1952. Toronto scored eight goals in 4 min 52 sec *v.* New York Americans on 19 Mar 1938.

In minor leagues, Kim D. Miles scored in 3 seconds for University of Guelph *v.* University of W. Ontario on 11 Feb 1975. Three goals in 12 seconds was achieved by Steve D'Innocenzo for Holliston *v.* Westwood in a high school match in Massachusetts, USA on 9 Jan 1982. The Skara Ishockeyclubb, Sweden, scored three goals in 11 seconds against Örebro IK at Skara on 18 Oct 1981. The Vernon Cougars scored five goals in 56 seconds against Salmon Arm Aces at Vernon, BC, Canada on 6 Aug 1982. The Kamloops Knights of Columbus scored seven goals in 2 min 22 sec *v.* Prince George Vikings on 25 Jan 1980.

Great Britain ■ The fastest goal in the Heineken League was scored by Steve Johnson for Durham

Wasps after four seconds *v.* Ayr Bruins at Ayr, Strathclyde on 6 Nov 1983. Kenny Westman (Nottingham Panthers) scored a hat–trick in 30 seconds *v.* Brighton Tigers on 3 Mar 1955.

In an English Junior League (under-16) game Jonathan Lumbis scored a hat-trick in 13 seconds for Nottingham Cougars *v.* Peterborough Jets on 4 Nov 1984.

Most successful goaltending ■ The most matches played by a goaltender in an NHL career without conceding a goal is 103 by Terrance 'Terry' Gordon Sawchuck (1929–70) of Detroit, Boston, Toronto, Los Angeles and New York Rangers, between 1949 and 1970. Gerry Cheevers (b. 2 Dec 1940) (Boston Bruins) went a record 32 successive games without a defeat in 1971–2.

Longest match ■ The longest match was 2 hr 56 min 30 sec (playing time) when Detroit Red Wings beat Montreal Maroons 1–0 in the sixth period of overtime at the Forum, Montreal, at 2.25 a.m. on 25 Mar 1936. Norm Smith, the Red Wings goaltender, turned aside 92 shots for the NHL's longest single shutout.

Ice Skating

Origins ■ The earliest reference to ice skating is in early Scandinavian literature referring to the 2nd century though its origins are believed, on archaeological evidence, to be ten centuries earlier still. The earliest English account of 1180 refers to skates made of bone. The earliest skating club was the Edinburgh Skating Club formed in about 1742.

The first recorded race was from Wisbech to Whittlesey, Cambridgeshire in 1763. The earliest artificial rink in the world was opened at the Baker Street Bazaar, Portman Square, London on 7 Dec 1842, although the surface was not of ice. The first artificial ice rink was opened in the King's Road, Chelsea, London on 7 Jan 1876.

The National Skating Association of Great Britain was founded in 1879. The International Skating Union was founded at Scheveningen, Netherlands in 1892.

FIGURE SKATING

Most titles *Olympic* ■ The most Olympic gold medals won by a figure skater is three by: Gillis Grafström (1893–1938) of Sweden in 1920, 1924 and 1928 (also silver medal in 1932); by Sonja Henie (1912–69) of Norway in 1928, 1932 and 1936; and by Irina Rodnina (USSR) (b. 12 Sep 1949) with two different partners in the Pairs in 1972, 1976 and 1980.

World ■ The greatest number of individual world figure skating titles (instituted 1896) is ten by Ulrich Salchow (1877–1949) of Sweden, in 1901–5 and 1907–11. The women's record (instituted 1906) is also ten individual titles by Sonja Henie between 1927 and 1936. Irina Rodnina won ten pairs titles (instituted 1908), four with Aleksey Ulanov (b. 4 Nov 1947), 1969–72, and six with her husband Aleksandr Zaitsev (b. 16 Jun 1952), 1973–8. The most ice dance titles (instituted 1952) won is six by Lyudmila Pakhomova (1946–86) and her husband Aleksandr Gorshkov (USSR) (b. 8 Oct 1946), 1970–4 and 1976. They also won the first ever Olympic ice dance title in 1976.

British ■ The most individual British titles are: (men) 11 by Jack Ferguson Page (1900–47) (Manchester SC) in 1922–31 and 1933; and (women) six by Cecilia Colledge (b. 28 Nov 1920) (Park Lane FSC, London) in 1935–6, 1937 (two), 1938 and 1946. Page and Ethel M. Muckelt (1885–1953) won nine pairs titles, 1923–31. The most by an ice dance couple is six by Jayne Torvill (b. 7 Oct 1957) and Christopher Dean (b. 27 Jul 1958), 1978–83.

Triple Crown ■ The only British skaters to win the 'Grand Slam' of World, Olympic and European titles in the same year are John Anthony Curry (b. 9 Sep 1949) in 1976 and the ice dancers Jayne Torvill

SPEED SKATING WORLD RECORDS

MEN

Metres	min sec	Name (Country)	Place	Date	
500	36·45	Uwe-Jens Mey (GDR)	Calgary, Canada	14 Feb	1988
	36·23 u	Nick Thometz (USA)	Medeo, USSR	26 Mar	1987
1000	1:12·58	Igor Zhelozovsky (USSR)	Heerenveen, Netherlands	25 Feb	1989
	1:12·58 A	Pavel Pegov (USSR)	Medeo, USSR	25 Nov	1983
	1:12·05 u	Nick Thometz (USA)	Medeo, USSR	27 Mar	1987
1500	1:52·06	André Hoffmann (GDR)	Calgary, Canada	20 Feb	1988
3000	3:59·27	Leo Visser (Netherlands)	Heerenveen, Netherlands	19 Mar	1987
	3:56·65 u	Sergeuy Martyuk (USSR)	Medeo, USSR	11 Mar	1977
5000	6:43·59	Geir Karlstad (Norway)	Calgary, Canada	6 Dec	1987
10 000	13:48·20	Tomas Gustafson (Sweden)	Calgary, Canada	21 Feb	1988

u *unofficial.* A *set at high altitude.*

WOMEN

Metres	min sec	Name (Country)	Place	Date	
500	39·10	Bonnie Blair (USA)	Calgary, Canada	22 Feb	1988
1000	1:17·65	Christa Rothenberg (now Luding) (GDR)	Calgary, Canada	26 Feb	1988
1500	1:59·30	Karin Kania (GDR)	Medeo, USSR	22 Mar	1986
3000	4:11·94	Yvonne van Gennip (Netherlands)	Calgary, Canada	23 Feb	1988
5000	7:14·13	Yvonne van Gennip (Netherlands)	Calgary, Canada	28 Feb	1988
10 000†	15:25·25	Yvonne van Gennip (Netherlands)	Heerenveen, Netherlands	19 Mar	1988

† Record not officially recognised for this distance.

WORLD SHORT TRACK SPEED SKATING RECORDS

MEN

Metres	min sec	Name (Country)	Place	Date	
500	44·46	Orazio Fagone (Italy)	Budapest, Hungary	16 Jan	1988
1000	1:32·83	Peter van der Velde (Netherlands)	Budapest, Hungary	16 Jan	1988
1500	2:25·25	Michel Daignault (Canada)	Calgary, Canada	22 Feb	1988
3000	5:04·24	Tatsuyoshi Ishihara (Japan)	Amsterdam, Netherlands	17 Mar	1985

WOMEN

Metres	min sec	Name (Country)	Place	Date	
500	47·77	Christina Sciolla (Italy)	Budapest, Hungary	16 Jan	1988
1000	1:39·00	Yan Li (China)	Calgary, Canada	25 Feb	1988
1500	2:34·85	Yan Li (China)	Calgary, Canada	23 Feb	1988
3000	5:18·33	Maria-Rosa Candido (Italy)	Budapest, Hungary	17 Jan	1988

BRITISH SHORT TRACK SPEED SKATING RECORDS

MEN

Metres	min sec	Name	Place	Date	
500	44·80	Wilfred O'Reilly	Calgary, Canada	23 Feb	1988
1000	1:33·44	Wilfred O'Reilly	Calgary, Canada	24 Feb	1988
1500	2:31·51	Wilfred O'Reilly	Calgary, Canada	17 Oct	1988
3000	5:17·47	Wilfred O'Reilly	Chamonix, France	6 Apr	1986

WOMEN

Distance	min sec	Name	Place	Date	
500	51·78	Kim Ferran	Brugge, Belgium	18 Mar	1984
1000	1:46·63	Nicky Bell	Chamonix, France	5 Apr	1986
1500	2:46·88	Amanda Worth	Tokyo, Japan	8 Apr	1983
3000	5:59·08	Amanda Worth	Richmond, London	1 Mar	1985

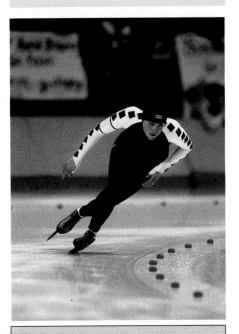

Fastest skater ● Yvonne van Gennip (Netherlads) is the current world record holder for 3000 m, 5000 m and 10 000 m. The first two were set at the 1988 Olympics when she won a third gold for 1500 m. (Photo: All-Sport / Mike Powell)

competition-a toe loop in the World Championships at Budapest, Hungary on 25 Mar 1988. Midori Ito (Japan) (b. 13 Aug 1969) was the first woman to complete a jump exceeding three turns – a triple axel in the World Championships at Paris, France on 18 Mar 1989.

Distance ■ Robin Cousins (GB) (b. 17 Aug 1957) achieved 5·81 m *19 ft 1 in* in an axel jump and 5·48 m *18 ft* with a back flip at Richmond Ice Rink, Surrey on 16 Nov 1983.

Largest rink ■ The world's largest indoor ice rink is in the Moscow Olympic arena which has an ice area of 8064 m² *86 800 ft²*. The five rinks at Fujikyu Highland Skating Centre, Japan total 26 500 m² *285 243 ft²*.

SPEED SKATING

Most titles *Olympic* ■ The most Olympic gold medals won in speed skating is six by Lidiya Skoblikova (b. 8 Mar 1939) of Chelyabinsk, USSR, in 1960 (two) and 1964 (four). The male record is by Clas Thunberg (Finland) (1893–1973) with five gold (including one tied), and also one silver and one tied bronze, in 1924 and 1928. Eric Heiden (USA) (b. 14 Jun 1958) also won five gold medals, uniquely at one Games at Lake Placid, New York, USA in 1980.

World ■ The greatest number of world overall titles (instituted 1893) won by any skater is five; by Oscar Mathisen (Norway) (1888–1954) in 1908–9 and 1912–14; and Clas Thunberg in 1923, 1925, 1928–9 and 1931. The most titles won in the women's events (instituted 1936) is five by Karin Kania (*née* Enke) (GDR) (b. 20 Jun 1961) in 1982, 1984, 1986–8. Kania also won a record six overall titles at the World Sprint Championships 1980–1, 1983–4, 1986–7.

The record score achieved for the world overall title is 159·356 points by Nikolay Gulyayev (USSR) at Heerenveen, Netherlands on 14–15 Feb 1987. The record low women's score is 171·760 points by Andrea Schöne (GDR) (b. 1 Dec 1960) at Medeo, USSR on 23–24 Mar 1984.

Longest race ■ The 'Elfstedentocht' ('Tour of the Eleven Towns') was held in the Netherlands from the 1800s to 1963 and again in 1985, covering 200 km *124 miles 483 yd*. It was transferred first to Lake Vesijärvi, near Lahti, Finland and in 1984 to Canada as the International Race of 11 Cities on the Ottawa River. The record time for 200 km is 6 hr 5 min 12 sec by Jan-Roelof Kruithof (Netherlands) (b.

and Christopher Dean in 1984. Karl Schäfer (Austria) (1909–76) and Sonja Henie achieved double 'Grand Slams', both in the years 1932 and 1936.

Highest marks ■ The highest tally of maximum six marks awarded in an international championship was 29 to Jayne Torvill and Christopher Dean (GB) in the World Ice Dance Championships at Ottawa, Canada on 22–24 Mar 1984. This comprised seven in the compulsory dances, a perfect set of nine for presentation in the set pattern dance and 13 in the free dance, including another perfect set from all nine judges for artistic present-

ation. They previously gained a perfect set of nine sixes for artistic presentation in the free dance at the 1983 World Championships in Helsinki, Finland and at the 1984 Winter Olympic Games in Sarajevo, Yugoslavia. In their career Torvill and Dean received a record total of 136 sixes.

The most by a soloist is seven: by Donald Jackson (Canada) (b. 2 Apr 1940) in the World Men's Championship at Prague, Czechoslovakia in 1962; and by Midori Ito (Japan) (b. September 1969) in the World Championships at Paris, France in 1989.

Most turns ■ Kurt Browning (Canada) (b. 18 Jun 1966) was the first to achieve a quadruple jump in

1936) on 25 Feb 1979 at Oulu, Finland. Kruithof won the race eight times, 1974, 1976–7, 1979–83. An estimated 16 000 skaters took part in 1986.

24 hours ■ Martinus Kuiper (Netherlands) skated 546·650 km *339·681 miles* in 24 hr in Alkmaar, Netherlands on 12–13 Dec 1988.

Ice and Sand Yachting

Origins ■ The sport originated in the Low Countries from the year 1600 (earliest patent granted) and along the Baltic coast. The earliest authentic record is Dutch, dating from 1768. Land or sand yachts of Dutch construction were first reported on beaches (now in Belgium) in 1595. The earliest international championship was staged in 1914.

Largest yacht ■ The largest ice yacht was *Icicle*, built for Commodore John E. Roosevelt for racing on the Hudson River, New York in 1869. It was 21 m *68 ft 11 in* long and carried 99 m² *1070 ft²* of canvas.

Highest speeds *Ice* ■ The highest speed officially recorded is 230 km/h *143 mph* by John D. Buckstaff in a Class A stern-steerer on Lake Winnebago, Wisconsin, USA in 1938. Such a speed is possible in a wind of 115 km/h *72 mph.*

Sand ■ The official world record for a sand yacht is 107 km/h *66·48 mph* set by Christian-Yves Nau (France) (b. 1944) in *Mobil* at Le Touquet, France on 22 Mar 1981, when the wind speed reached 120 km/h *75 mph.* A speed of 142·26 km/h *88·4 mph* was attained by Nord Embroden (USA) in *Midnight at the Oasis* at Superior Dry Lake, California, USA on 15 Apr 1976.

Jaï Alaï *(Pelota Vasca)*

Origins ■ The game, which originated in Italy as *longue paume* and was introduced into France in the 13th century, is said to be the fastest of all ball

> **Highest speed** ● The highest official speed for an icesurfer is 102 km/h *63·4 mph* by Joop Nederpelt (Netherlands) on Lake Ontario, Canada on 20 Mar 1987.

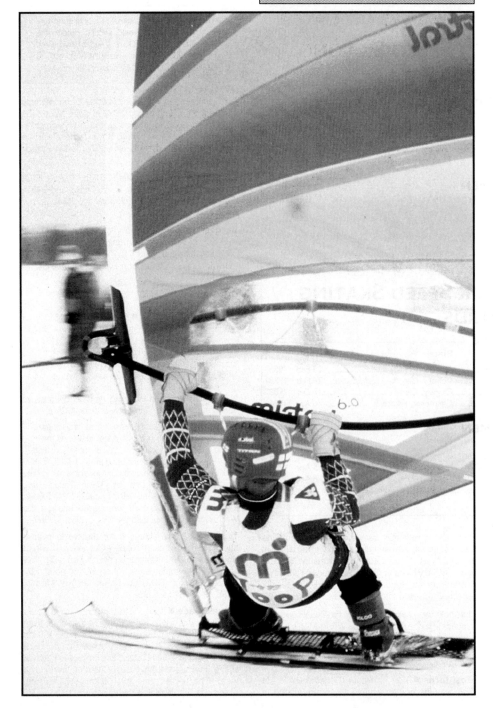

games. The glove or *gant* was introduced *c.* 1840 and the *chistera* was invented by Jean 'Gantchiki' Dithurbide of Ste Pée, France. The *grand chistera* was invented by Melchior Curuchague of Buenos Aires, Argentina in 1888. The world's largest *frontón* (enclosed stadium) is the World Jaï Alaï at Miami, Florida, USA, which had a record attendance of 15 052 on 27 Dec 1975.

World Championships ■ The *Federacion Internacional de Pelota Vasca* stage World Championships every four years (first in 1952). The most successful pair have been Roberto Elias and Juan Labat (Argentina), who won the *Trinquete Share* four times, 1952, 1958, 1962 and 1966. Labat won a record seven world titles in all. The most wins in the long court game *Cesta Punta* is three by Hamuy of Mexico, with two different partners, 1958, 1962 and 1966.

Highest speed ■ An electronically-measured ball velocity of 302 km/h *188 mph* was recorded by José Ramon Areitio at the Newport Jai Alai, Rhode Island, USA on 3 Aug 1979.

Longest domination ■ The longest domination as the world's No. 1 player was enjoyed by Chiquito de Cambo (*né* Joseph Apesteguy) (France) (1881–1955) from the beginning of the century until succeeded in 1938 by Jean Urruty (France) (b. 19 Oct 1913).

Judo

Origins ■ Judo is a modern combat sport which developed out of an amalgam of several old Japanese fighting arts, the most popular of which was jujitsu (jiu-jitsu), which is thought to be of Chinese origin. Judo has greatly developed since 1882, when it was first devised by Dr Jigoro Kano (1860–1938). The International Judo Federation was founded in 1951.

Most titles *World and Olympic* ■ World Championships were inaugurated in Tokyo, Japan in 1956. Women's championships were first held in 1980 in New York, USA. Yashiro Yamashita (b. 1 Jun 1957) won nine consecutive Japanese titles 1977–85, four world titles; Over 95 kg 1979, 1981 and 1983, Open 1981, and the Olympic Open category in 1984. He retired undefeated after 203 successive wins, 1977–85. Two other men have won four world titles, Wilhelm Ruska (Netherlands) (b. 29 Aug 1940), Over 93 kg 1967, 1971 and 1972 Olympic and Open titles, and Shozo Fujii (Japan) (b. 12 May 1950), Under 80 kg 1971, 1973 and 1975, Under 75 kg 1979. The only men to have won two Olympic gold medals are Wilhelm Ruska (Netherlands), Over 93 kg and Open in 1972; Peter Seisenbacher (Austria) (b. 25 Mar 1960), 86 kg 1984 and 1988; and Hitoshi Saito (Japan) (b. 2 Jan 1961), Over 95 kg 1984 and 1988. Ingrid Berghmans (Belgium) (b. 24 Aug 1961) has won a record five women's world titles (first held 1980): Open 1980, 1982, 1984 and 1986 and Under 72 kg in 1984. She has also won three silver medals and a bronze. She also won the Olympic 72 kg title in 1988, when women's judo was introduced as a demonstration sport.

Karen Briggs (b. 11 Apr 1963) is the most successful British player, with three women's world titles, Under 48 kg in 1982, 1984 and 1986.

British ■ The greatest number of titles (instituted 1966) won is nine by David Colin Starbrook (b. 9 Aug 1945) (6th dan): Middleweight 1969–70, Light-heavyweight 1971–5 and the Open division 1970–1. A record six titles in the women's events (instituted 1971) were won by Christine Gallie (*née* Child) (b. 1946) (6th dan): Heavyweight in 1971–5 and the Open division in 1973. Neil Adams (b. 27 Sep 1958) has the most successful international record of any British player. He won two junior (1974 and 1977) and five senior (1979–80, 1983–5) European titles; four World Championships medals (one gold, one silver, two bronze) and two Olympic silver medals. He also won eight British senior titles.

Highest grades ■ The efficiency grades in judo are divided into pupil (*kyu*) and master (*dan*) grades. The highest awarded is the extremely rare red belt *Judan* (10th dan), given to only 13 men so far. The Judo protocol provides for an 11th dan (*Jui-chidan*) who also would wear a red belt, a 12th dan (*Junidan*) who would wear a white belt twice as wide as an ordinary belt, and the highest of all, *Shihan* (ductor), but these have never been bestowed, save for the 12th dan to the founder of the sport Dr Jigoro Kano. The highest British native Judo grade is 8th dan by Charles Stuart Palmer (b. 1930). Christine Gallie was awarded her 6th dan in 1983.

10 hours ■ The brothers Carl and Peter Udry completed 18 779 judo throwing techniques in a ten-hour period at Hendra Sports Field, Truro, Cornwall on 29 Aug 1987.

Jiu-Jitsu ■ The World Council of Jiu-Jitsu Organisations have staged two World Championships, in 1984 and 1986. The Canadian team were the team winners on each occasion.

Karate

Origins ■ Based on techniques devised from the 6th century Chinese art of Shaolin boxing (Kempo), Karate was developed by an unarmed populace in Okinawa as a weapon against armed Japanese oppressors *c.* 1500. Transmitted to Japan in the 1920s by Funakoshi Gichin, this method of combat was refined into karate and organised into a sport with competitive rules. The five major styles of karate in Japan are: *Shotokan, Wado-ryu, Goju-ryu, Shito-ryu* and *Kyokushinkai*, each of which places different emphasis on speed and power, etc. Other styles include *Sankukai, Shotokai* and *Shukokai. Wu shu* is a comprehensive term embracing all Chinese martial arts. *Kung fu* is one aspect of these arts popularised by the cinema.

The governing body for the sport in Britain is the Martial Arts Commission, upon which all the martial arts are represented.

Most Olympic golds ● Peter Seisenbacher (Austria) (b. 25 Mar 1960) is one of only three men to have won two Olympic judo golds. Having won the 86 kg class in 1984, he successfully defended his title in 1988, defeating Vladimir Chestakov (USSR). The picture shows action from the final with Seisenbacher nearest the floor. (Photo: All-Sport / Mike Powell)

World Championships ■ Great Britain have won a record five world titles (instituted 1970) at the Kumite team event, 1975, 1982, 1984, 1986 and 1988. Two men's individual kumite titles have been won by: Pat McKay (GB) at Under 80 kg, 1982 and 1984; Emmanuel Pinda (France) at Open, 1984 and Over 80 kg, 1988 and Theirry Masci (France) at Under 70

Most international appearances ● Barbara Dootson (second from left, back row) has made a large number of international appearances and here lines up for England against the USA at the Oval, Surrey in 1985. (All-Sport / Adrian Murrell)

kg, 1986 and 1988. Three women's kumite titles have been won by Guus van Mourik (Netherlands) at Over 60 kg, 1982, 1984 and 1986. Three individual kata titles have been won by men: Tsuguo Sakumoto (Japan) 1984, 1986 and 1988; women: Mie Nakayama (Japan) 1982, 1984 and 1986.

Top exponents ■ The leading exponents among karateka are a number of 10th dans in Japan. The leading exponents in the United Kingdom are Tatsuo Suzuki (8th dan, *Wado-ryu*) (b. 27 Apr 1928), Keinosuke Enoeda (8th dan, *Shotokan*), Steve Arneil (8th dan, *Kyokushinkai*), Shiro Asano (7th dan, *Shokotan*), Thomas Morris (7th dan, *Shito-ryu*), David Donovan (7th dan, *Ishin-ryu*) and James Rosseau (6th dan, *Goju-ryu*).

Lacrosse

Origins ■ The game is of American Indian origin, derived from the inter-tribal game *baggataway*, and was played before 1492 by Iroquois Indians in lower Ontario, Canada and upper New York State,

USA. The French named it after their game of *chouler à la crosse*, known in 1381. It was introduced into Great Britain in 1867. The English Lacrosse Union was formed in 1892. Lacrosse was included in the Olympic Games of 1904 and 1908 and featured as an exhibition sport in the 1928, 1932 and 1948 Games.

Most titles *World* ■ The USA have won four of the five World Championships, in 1967, 1974, 1982 and 1986. Canada won the other world title in 1978 beating the USA 17–16 after extra time—this was the first drawn international match.

English ■ The English Club Championship (Iroquois Cup instituted 1890), has been won most often by Stockport with 17 wins between 1897 and 1989. The record score in a final is 33 by Stockport *v.* London University (4) on 9 May 1987.

Most international appearances ■ The record number of international representations is 33 for England by James Michael 'Mike' Roberts (Urmston) (b. 22 Feb 1946), to 1982. He is the only Englishman to play in four World Championships.

Highest scores ■ The highest score in an international match is the USA's 32–8 win over England at Toronto, Canada in 1986. England's highest score was their 19–11 win over Canada at Melbourne, Australia in August 1974.

Fastest scoring ■ Rod Burns scored only 4 seconds into the game for South Manchester and Wythenshawe *v.* Sheffield University on 6 Dec 1975.

WOMEN

The first reported playing of lacrosse by women was in 1886. The All-England Women's Lacrosse Association was formed in 1912. The game has evolved seperately from the men's game so that the rules now differ considerably.

World Championships/World Cup ■ The first World Cup was held in 1982, when the winners were the USA, and Australia won in 1986.

Most international appearances ■ Caro Macintosh (b. 18 Feb 1932) played in 56 internationals (52 for Scotland and four for Great Britain) and Barbara Dootson (b. 24 Aug 1955) in 54 (41 England, 13 Great Britain), 1974–86.

Highest score ■ The highest score by an international team was by Great Britain and Ireland with their 40–0 defeat of Long Island during their 1967 tour of the USA.

Marbles

Origins ■ The name derives from the practice in the 18th century of making the ball from marble chips. However, marbles dates from ancient times and may have been a children's game in ancient Egypt, where pebbles or nuts were used. It was introduced into Britain by the Romans in the 1st century AD. It became a competitive sport under the British Marbles Board of Control at the Greyhound Hotel, Tinsley Green, Crawley, West Sussex in 1926.

Most championships ■ The British Championship (established 1926) has been won most often by the Toucan Terribles with 20 consecutive titles (1956–75). Three founder members, Len Smith, Jack and Charlie Dempsey, played in every title win. They were finally beaten in 1976 by the Pernod Rams, captained by Len Smith's son, Paul. Len Smith (b. 13 Oct 1917) won the individual title 15 times (1957–64, 1966, 1968–73) but lost in 1974 to his son Alan.

Speed record ■ The record for clearing the ring (between 1·75 and 1·9 m *5¾–6¼ ft* in diameter) of 49 marbles is 2 min 56 sec by the Black Dog Boozers of Crawley, West Sussex at BBC Television Centre, London for BBC Television's *Record Breakers* on 14 Sep 1987.

Microlighting

The *Fédération Aéronautique Internationale* have established two classes of aircraft for which records are accepted, C1 a/o and R 1-2-3, and the following, the overall best of the two classes, are all in the C1 a/o class.

WORLD RECORDS

Distance in a straight line: 1627·78 km *1011·48 miles* Wilhelm Lischak (Austria), Volsau to Brest, France, 8 Jun 1988.

Distance in a closed circuit: 2702·16 km *1679·09 miles* Wilhelm Lischak (Austria), Wels, Austria, 18 Jun 1988.

Altitude: 7906·5 m *25 939·64 ft* Richard J. Rowley (USA), 17 Sep 1983.

Speed over a 100 km closed circuit: 297·72 km/h *185 mph* C. T. Andrews (USA), 3 Aug 1982

Speed over a 500 km closed circuit: 293·04 km/h *182 mph* C. T. Andrews (USA), 3 Aug 1982.

Bob Calvert set a British altitude record of 5791·27 m *19 000 ft* on 19 Feb 1983 at Middleton Sands, Lancashire.

Endurance ■ Eve Jackson flew from Biggin Hill, Kent to Sydney, Australia from 26 Apr 1986 to 1 Aug 1987. The flight took 279 hr 55 min and covered 26 553 km *16 500 miles*. From 1 Dec 1987 to 29 Jan 1988, Brian Milton (GB) flew from London to Sydney with a flying time of 241 hr 20 min and covered 21 898 km *13 607 miles*. Vijaypat Singhania (India) flew from Biggin Hill to Delhi, India, a distance of 8724 km *5420 miles* in 87 hr 55 min, from 18 Aug to 10 Sep 1988.

Modern Pentathlon & Biathlon

Points scores in riding, fencing, cross country and hence overall scores have no comparative value between one competition and another. In shooting and swimming (300 m) the scores are of record significance and the best achievements are shown.

The Modern Pentathlon (Riding, Fencing, Swimming, Shooting and Running) was inaugurated into the Olympic Games at Stockholm in 1912. The Modern Pentathlon Association of Great Britain was formed in 1922. *L'Union Internationale de Pentathlon Moderne* (UIPM) was founded at Aldershot, Hampshire on 3 Aug 1948. The administration of Biathlon (cross-country skiing and shooting) was added in 1957, and the name modified accordingly, *L'Union Internationale de Pentathlon Moderne et Biathlon* (UIPMB).

MODERN PENTATHLON

Most titles *World* ■ András Balczó (Hungary) (b. 16 Aug 1938) won the record number of world titles (instituted 1949), six individual and seven team. He won the world individual title in 1963, 1965–7 and 1969 and the Olympic title in 1972. His seven team titles (1960–70) comprised five world and two Olympic. The USSR has won a record 12 world and four Olympic team titles. Hungary have also won a record four Olympic team titles and nine world titles.

Women's World Championships were first held in 1981. Great Britain won three team titles 1981–3, with Sarah Parker (b. 16 Jul 1956) a member of each of those teams. The only double individual champion has been Irina Kiselyeva (USSR), 1986–7. Wendy Johana Norman (b. 20 Feb 1965) won the individual title in 1982 and team golds in 1981–2. She also won the individual World Cup title in 1980 and Great Britain won three World Cup team titles, 1978–80.

Olympic ■ The greatest number of Olympic gold medals won is three by András Balczó, a member of the winning team in 1960 and 1968 and the 1972 individual champion. Lars Hall (Sweden) (b. 30 Apr 1927) has uniquely won two individual championships (1952 and 1956). Pavel Lednyev (USSR)

(b. 25 Mar 1943) won a record seven medals (two gold, two silver, three bronze), 1968–80. The best British performance is the team gold medal in 1976 by Jim Fox, Adrian Philip Parker and Daniel Nightingale. The best individual placing is fourth by Jeremy Robert 'Jim' Fox (b. 19 Sep 1941) in 1972.

Probably the greatest margin of victory was by William Oscar Guernsey Grut (Sweden) (b. 17 Sep 1914) in the 1948 Games, when he won three events and was placed fifth and eighth in the other two.

British ■ The pentathlete with most British titles is Jim Fox, with ten (1963, 1965–8, 1970–4). Wendy Norman won a record seven women's titles, 1978–80, 1982, 1986–8.

BIATHLON

The biathlon, which combines cross-country skiing and rifle shooting, was first included in the Olympic Games in 1960, and World Championships were first held in 1958.

Most titles *Olympic Games* ■ Two Olympic individual titles have been won by: Magnar Solberg (Norway) (b. 4 Feb 1937), in 1968 and 1972; and by Franz-Peter Rötsch (GDR) at both 10 km and 20 km in 1988. The USSR has won all six 4 × 7·5 km relay titles, 1968–88. Aleksandr Tikhonov (b. 2 Jan 1947) who was a member of the first four teams also won a silver in the 1968 20 km.

World ■ Frank Ullrich (GDR) (b. 24 Jan 1958) has won a record six individual world titles, four at 10 km, 1978–81, including the 1980 Olympics, and two at 20 km, 1982–3. Aleksandr Tikhonov was in ten winning USSR relay teams, 1968–80 and won four individual titles.

The Biathlon World Cup (instituted 1979) was won three times by Frank Ullrich, 1980–2. He was second in 1979 and third in 1983.

Motorcycle Racing

Earliest race ■ The first motorcycle race was held over a mile *1·6 km* on an oval track at Sheen House, Richmond, Surrey on 29 Nov 1897, won by Charles Jarrott (1877–1944) on a Fournier. The oldest motorcycle races in the world are the Auto-Cycle Union Tourist Trophy (TT) series, first held on the 25·44 km *15·81 mile* 'Peel' (St John's) course in the Isle of Man on 28 May 1907, and still run in the island on the 'Mountain' circuit.

Fastest circuits ■ The highest average lap speed attained on any closed circuit is 257·958 km/h *160·288 mph* by Yvon du Hamel (Canada) (b. 1941) on a modified 903 cc four-cylinder Kawasaki Z1 at the 31-degree banked 4·02 km *2·5 mile* Daytona International Speedway, Florida, USA in March 1973. His lap time was 56·149 sec.

The fastest road circuit was the Francorchamps circuit near Spa, Belgium, then 14·12 km *8·74 miles* in length. It was lapped in 3 min 50·3 sec (average speed 220·721 km/h *137·150 mph*) by Barry Stephen Frank Sheene (GB) (b. 11 Sep 1950) on a 495 cc 4-cylinder Suzuki during the Belgian Grand Prix on 3 Jul 1977. On that occasion he set a record time for this ten-lap (141·20 km *87·74 mile*) race of 38 min 58·5 sec (average speed 217·370 km/h *135·068 mph*).

United Kingdom ■ The lap record for the outer circuit (4·453 km *2·767 miles*) at the Brooklands Motor Course, near Weybridge, Surrey (open between 1907 and 1939) was 80 sec (average speed 200·37 km/h *124·51 mph*) by Noel Baddow 'Bill' Pope (later Major) (GB) (1909–71) on a Brough Superior powered by a supercharged 996 cc V-twin '8-80' JAP engine developing 110 bhp, on 4 Jul 1939.

The fastest circuit in current use is that over public roads at Dundrod, Co Antrim over which Eddie Laycock set a lap record of 195·35 km/h *121·39 mph* and a nine lap race record of 193·34 km/h

120·14 mph on 30 Jul 1988, riding a 500 cc Honda in the Ulster Grand Prix.

Longest race ■ The longest race was the Liège 24 hr, run on the old Francorchamps circuit. The greatest distance ever covered is 4444·8 km *2761·9 miles* (average speed 185·20 km/h *115·08 mph*) by Jean-Claude Chemarin and Christian Leon, both of France, on a 941 cc 4-cylinder Honda on the Francorchamps circuit on 14–15 Aug 1976.

Longest circuit ■ The 60·72 km *37·73 mile* 'Mountain' circuit on the Isle of Man, over which the principal TT races have been run since 1911 (with minor amendments in 1920), has 264 curves and corners and is the longest used for any motorcycle race.

Most successful riders *Tourist Trophy* ■ The record number of victories in the Isle of Man TT races is 14 by Stanley Michael Bailey Hailwood (1940–81) between 1961 and 1979. The first man to win three consecutive TT titles in two events was James A. Redman (Rhodesia) (b. 8 Nov 1931). He won the 250 cc and 350 cc events in 1963–5. Mike Hailwood won three events in one year, in 1961 and 1967, and this feat was repeated by William Joseph Dunlop (Ireland) (b. 25 Feb 1952) in 1985 and 1988, and Steve Hislop (Scotland) in 1989.

World championships ● Eric Geboers (Belgium) has uniquely won all three categories of the Moto-Cross World Championships, at 125 cc in 1983, 250 cc in 1987 and 500 cc in 1988. Here he is in action (no. 3) during the final race of the 1988 season, the Belgian Grand Prix. (Photo: All-Sport/Simon Bruty)

The Isle of Man TT circuit speed record is 195·27 km/h *121·34 mph* by Steve Hislop (Scotland) on 4 Jun 1989. He also set the race speed record 1 hr 53 min 47·4 sec for an average speed of 192·08 km/h *119·36 mph* to win the 1989 Formula One TT on his 750 cc Honda.

World championships ■ The most World Championship titles (instituted by the *Fédération Internationale Motocycliste* in 1949) won is 15 by Giacomo Agostini (Italy) (b. 16 Jun 1942), seven at 350 cc, 1968–74, and eight at 500 cc in 1966–72, 1975. He is the only man to win two World Championships in five consecutive years (350 cc and 500 cc titles 1968–72).

Agostini won 122 races (68 at 500 cc, 54 at 350 cc) in the World Championship series between 24 Apr 1965 and 25 Sep 1977, including a record 19 in 1970, also achieved by Mike Hailwood in 1966.

Angel Roldan Nieto (Spain) (b. 25 Jan 1947) won a record seven 125 cc titles, 1971–2, 1979, 1981–4 and Klaus Enders (West Germany) (b. 1937) won six world side-car titles, 1967, 1969–70, 1972–4.

In 1985 Freddie Burdette Spencer (USA) (b. 20 Dec 1961), riding for Honda, became the first man ever to win the 250 cc and 500 cc titles in the same year.

Trials ■ A record three World Trials Championships have been won by Yrjö Vesterinen (Finland), 1976–8; Eddie Lejeune (Belgium), 1982–4 and Thierry Michaud (France), 1985–6 and 1988.

Moto-cross ■ Joël Robert (Belgium) (b. 11 Nov 1943) won six 250 cc Moto-cross World Championships (1964, 1968–72). Between 25 Apr 1964 and

18 Jun 1972 he won a record fifty 250 cc Grand Prix. The youngest moto-cross world champion was Dave Strijbos (Netherlands) (b. 9 Nov 1968), who won the 125 cc title aged 18 yr 296 days on 31 Aug 1986.

Most successful machines ■ Italian MV-Agusta machines won 37 World Championships between 1952 and 1973, and 276 World Championship races between 1952 and 1976.

Youngest and oldest world champions ■ Alberto 'Johnny' Cecotto (Venezuela) (b. 25 Jan 1956) is the youngest to win a World Championship. He was 19 yr 211 days when he won the 350 cc title on 24 Aug 1975. The oldest was Hermann-Peter Müller (1909–76) of West Germany, who won the 250 cc title in 1955 aged 46.

Motor Racing

Earliest races ■ There are various conflicting claims, but the first automobile race was the 323 km *201 mile* Green Bay to Madison, Wisconsin, USA run in 1878 won by an Oshkosh steamer. In 1887 Count Jules Félix Philippe Albert de Dion de Malfiance (1856–1946) won the *La Vélocipéde* 31 km *19·3 miles* race in Paris in a De Dion steam quadricycle in which he is reputed to have exceeded 59 km/h *37 mph*. The first 'real' race was from Paris to Bordeaux and back (1178 km *732 miles*) on 11–13 Jun 1895. The first to finish was Emile Levassor (1844–97) of France, in a Panhard-Levassor two-seater, with a 1·2-litre Daimler engine developing 3 $\frac{1}{2}$hp. His time was 48 hr 47 min (average speed 24·15 km/h *15·01 mph*). The first closed circuit race was held over five laps of a mile *1·6 km* dirt track at Narragansett Park, Cranston, Rhode Island, USA on 7 Sep 1896, won by A. H. Whiting, driving a Riker electric.

The oldest race in the world still regularly run, is the RAC Tourist Trophy, first staged on 14 Sep 1905, in the Isle of Man. The oldest continental race is the French Grand Prix, first held on 26–27 Jun 1906. The Coppa Florio, in Sicily, has been irregularly held since 1906.

Fastest circuits ■ The highest average lap speed attained on any closed circuit is 403·878 km/h *250·958 mph* in a trial by Dr Hans Liebold (Germany) (b. 12 Oct 1926) who lapped the 12·64 km *7·85 mile* high-speed track at Nardo, Italy in 1 min 52·67 sec in a Mercedes-Benz C111-IV experimental coupé on 5 May 1979. It was powered by a V8 engine with two KKK turbochargers with an output of 500 hp at 6200 rpm.

The fastest road circuit was the Francorchamps circuit near Spa, Belgium, then 14·10 km *8·76 miles* in length which was lapped in 3 min 13·4 sec (average speed 262·461 km/h *163·086 mph*) on 6 May 1973, by Henri Pescarolo (France) (b. 25 Sep 1942) driving a 2993-cc V12 Matra-Simca MS670 Group 5 sports car. The race lap average speed record at Berlin's AVUS track was 276·38 km/h *171·75 mph* by Bernd Rosemeyer (Germany) (1909–38) in a 6-litre V16 Auto Union in 1937.

Fastest pit stop ■ Robert William 'Bobby' Unser (USA) (b. 20 Feb 1934) took 4 seconds to take on fuel on lap 10 of the Indianapolis 500 on 30 May 1976.

Fastest race ■ The fastest race is the Busch Clash at Daytona, Florida, USA over 80·5 km *50 miles* on a 4 km *2½ mile* 31-degree banked track. In 1987 Bill Elliott (b. 8 Oct 1955) averaged 318·322 km/h *197·802 mph* in a Ford Thunderbird. Bill Elliott set the world record for a 805 km *500 mile* race in 1985 when he won at Talladega, Alabama, USA at an average speed of 299·793 km/h *186·288 mph*. The NASCAR (National Association for Stock Car Automobile Racing) qualifying record is 342·482 km/h *212·809 mph* by Bill Elliott in a Ford Thunderbird at Alabama International Motor Speedway, Talladega, Alabama, USA, a 4·28 km *2·66 mile* oval speedway with 33-degree banked turns, on 30 Apr 1987.

NASCAR records ■ Richard Lee Petty (USA) (b.

2 Jul 1937) won 200 NASCAR Winston Cup races in 1024 starts from 1958 to 1 May 1988. His best season was 1967 with 27 wins. Petty, on 1 Aug 1971, was the first driver to pass $1 million career earnings. The NASCAR career money record is $8 602 028 to 20 Nov 1988 by Darrell Waltrip (b. 5 Feb 1949). Bill Elliott won a year's record $2 383 187 in NASCAR events in 1985. Geoff Bodine (b. 18 Apr 1949) won 55 races in NASCAR Modified racing in 1978.

WORLD CHAMPIONSHIP GRAND PRIX MOTOR RACING

Most successful Drivers ■ The World Drivers' Championship, inaugurated in 1950, has been won a record five times by Juan-Manuel Fangio (Argentina) (b. 24 Jun 1911) in 1951 and 1954–7. He retired in 1958, after having won 24 Grand Prix races (two shared) from 51 starts.

Alain Prost (France) (b. 24 Feb 1955) holds the records for both the most Grand Prix points in a career, 540·5 and the most Grand Prix victories, 36 from 142 Grand Prix races, 1980–89. The most Grand Prix victories in a year is eight by Ayrton Senna (Brazil) (b. 21 Mar 1960) in 1988. The most Grand Prix starts is 182 by Ricardo Patrese (Italy) (b. 17 Apr 1954) from 1977 to 18 Jun 1989.

Oldest and youngest ■ The youngest world champion was Emerson Fittipaldi (Brazil) (b. 12 Dec 1946) who won his first World Championship on 10 Sep 1972 aged 25 yr 273 days. The oldest world champion was Juan-Manuel Fangio who won his last World Championship on 18 Aug 1957 aged 46 yr 55 days.

The youngest Grand Prix winner was Bruce Leslie McLaren (1937–70) of New Zealand, who won the United States Grand Prix at Sebring, Florida on 12 Dec 1959, aged 22 yr 104 days. Troy Ruttman (USA) was 22 yr 80 days when he won the Indianapolis 500 on 30 May 1952, which was part of the World Championships at the time. The oldest Grand Prix winner (in pre-World Championship days) was Tazio Giorgio Nuvolari (Italy) (1892–1953), who won the Albi Grand Prix at Albi, France on 14 Jul 1946, aged 53 yr 240 days. The oldest Grand Prix driver was Louis Alexandre Chiron (Monaco) (1899–1979), who finished sixth in the Monaco Grand Prix on 22 May 1955, aged 55 yr 292 days. The youngest driver to qualify for a Grand Prix was Michael Christopher Thackwell (New Zealand) (b. 30 Mar 1961) at the Canadian GP on 28 Sep 1980, aged 19 yr 182 days.

Manufacturers ■ Ferrari have won a record eight manufacturers' World Championships, 1961, 1964, 1975–7, 1979, 1982–3. Ferrari have 95 race wins in 446 Grand Prix, 1950–89.

The greatest dominance by one team was by McLaren in 1988 when they won 15 of the 16 Grands Prix. Ayrton Senna had eight wins and three seconds, Alain Prost had seven wins and seven seconds. The McLarens, powered by Honda engines, amassed over three times the points of their nearest rivals, Ferrari.

Fastest race ■ The fastest overall average speed for a Grand Prix race on a circuit in current use is 235·421 km/h *146·284 mph* by Nigel Mansell (GB) in a Williams-Honda at Zeltweg in the Austrian Grand Prix on 16 Aug 1987. The qualifying lap record was set by Keke Rosberg (Finland) at 1 min 05·59 sec, an average speed of 258·803 km/h *160·817 mph*, in a Williams-Honda at Silverstone in the British Grand Prix on 20 Jul 1985.

Closest finish ■ The closest finish to a World Championship race was when Ayrton Senna (Brazil) in a Lotus beat Nigel Mansell (GB) in a Williams by 0·014 sec in the Spanish Grand Prix at Jerez de la Frontera on 13 Apr 1986. In the Italian Grand Prix at Monza on 5 Sep 1971, 0·61 sec separated winner Peter Gethin (GB) from the fifth placed driver.

BRITISH GRAND PRIX
First held in 1926 as the RAC Grand Prix, and held annually with the above name since 1949. The venues have been Aintree, Merseyside; Brands

Hatch, Kent; Brooklands, Surrey; Donington, Leicestershire and Silverstone, Northamptonshire.

Fastest speed ■ The fastest race time is 1 hr 18 min 10·436 sec, average speed 235·405 km/h *146·274 mph*, when Alain Prost won in a McLaren at Silverstone on 21 Jul 1985.

Most wins ■ The most wins by a driver is five by Jim Clark, 1962–5 and 1967, all in Lotus cars. Ferrari have most wins with nine, 1951–4, 1956, 1958, 1961, 1976 and 1978.

LE MANS

The greatest distance ever covered in the 24-hour *Grand Prix d'Endurance* (first held on 26–27 May 1923) on the old Sarthe circuit at Le Mans, France is 5333·724 km *3314·222 miles* by Dr Helmut Marko (Austria) (b. 27 Apr 1943) and Gijs van Lennep (Netherlands) (b. 16 Mar 1942) in a 4907-cc flat-12 Porsche 917K Group 5 sports car, on 12–13 Jun 1971. The record for the greatest distance ever covered for the current circuit is 5332 km *3313·241 miles* (av speed 221·63 km/h *137·718 mph*) by Jan Lammers (Holland), Johnny Dumfries and Andy Wallace (both GB) in a Jaguar XJR9 on 11–12 Jun 1988.

The race lap record (now 13·535 km *8·410 mile* lap) is 3 min 21·27 sec (average speed 242·093 km/h *150·429 mph* by Alain Ferté (France) in a Jaguar XJR-9 on 10 Jun 1989. Hans Stück (West Germany) set the practice lap record of 3 min 14·8 sec (av. speed 252·05 km/h *156·62 mph*) on 14 Jun 1985.

Most wins ■ The race has been won by Porsche cars twelve times, in 1970–1, 1976–7, 1979, 1981–7. The most wins by one man is six by Jacques Bernard 'Jacky' Ickx (Belgium) (b. 1 Jan 1945), 1969, 1975–7 and 1981–2.

INDIANAPOLIS 500
The Indianapolis 804 km *500 mile* race (200 laps) was inaugurated in the USA on 30 May 1911. Two drivers have four wins: Anthony Joseph 'A.J.' Foyt, Jr (USA) (b. 16 Jan 1935) in 1961, 1964, 1967 and 1977; and Al Unser, Snr (USA) (b. 29 May 1939) in 1970–1, 1978 and 1987. The record time is 2 hr 55 min 42·48 sec (average speed 274·743 km/h *170·722 mph*) by Bobby Rahal (USA) driving a Penske March-Cosworth on 31 May 1986. The record average speed for four laps in qualifying is 360·298 km/h *223·885 mph* by Rick Mears (USA) (b. 3 Dec 1951) in a Penske-Chevrolet V8 on 14 May 1989. On the same day he set the one-lap record of 360·891 km/h *224·254 mph* as well as 363·911 km/h *226·130 mph* in pre-qualifying. The record prize fund is $5 714 725 and the individual prize record is $1 001 604 by Emerson Fittipaldi (Brazil), both in 1989.

RALLYING

The earliest long rally was promoted by the Parisian daily *Le Matin* in 1907 from Peking, China to Paris over about 12 000 km *7500 miles* on 10 Jun. The winner, Prince Scipione Borghese (1872–1927) of Italy, arrived in Paris on 10 Aug 1907 in his 40-hp Itala accompanied by his chauffeur, Ettore, and Luigi Barzini.

Longest ■ The longest ever rally was the *Singapore Airlines* London–Sydney Rally over 31 107 km *19 329 miles* from Covent Garden, London on 14 Aug 1977 to Sydney Opera House, won on 28 Sept 1977 by Andrew Cowan, Colin Malkin and Michael Broad in a Mercedes 280E. The longest held annually is the Safari Rally (first run in 1953 as the Coronation Rally, through Kenya, Tanzania and Uganda, but is now restricted to Kenya). The race has covered up to 6234 km *3874 miles*, as in the 17th Safari held from 8–12 Apr 1971. It has been won a record five times by Shekhar Mehta (b. Uganda 1945) in 1973, 1979–82.

Monte Carlo ■ The Monte Carlo Rally (first run 1911) has been won a record four times by: Sandro Munari (Italy) (b. 1940) in 1972, 1975, 1976 and 1977; and Walter Röhrl (West Germany) (b. 7 Mar 1947) (with co-driver Christian Geistdorfer) in 1980,

Most Successful Drivers
Since the first Formula One World Championships in 1950

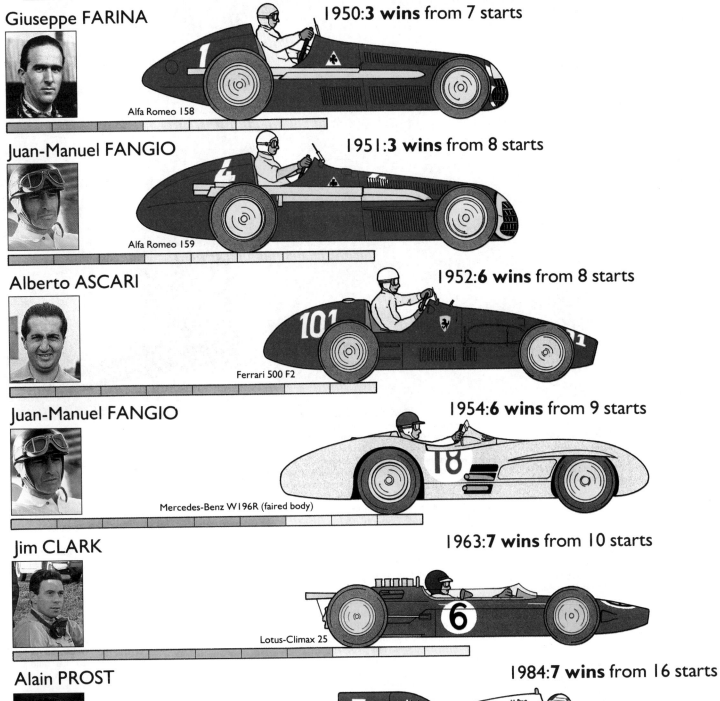

Giuseppe FARINA

1950: **3 wins** from 7 starts

Alfa Romeo 158

Juan-Manuel FANGIO

1951: **3 wins** from 8 starts

Alfa Romeo 159

Alberto ASCARI

1952: **6 wins** from 8 starts

Ferrari 500 F2

Juan-Manuel FANGIO

1954: **6 wins** from 9 starts

Mercedes-Benz W196R (faired body)

Jim CLARK

1963: **7 wins** from 10 starts

Lotus-Climax 25

Alain PROST

1984: **7 wins** from 16 starts

McLaren-Tag MP4/2

Ayrton SENNA

1988: **8 wins** from 16 starts

McLaren-Honda MP4/4

Artwork: Drawing Attention - Rhoda & Robert Burns

1982–4, each time in a different car. The smallest car to win was an 851-cc Saab driven by Erik Carlsson (Sweden) (b. 5 Mar 1929) and Gunnar Häggbom (Sweden) on 25 Jan 1962, and by Carlsson and Gunnar Palm on 24 Jan 1963.

Britain ■ The RAC Rally (first held 1932) has been recognised by the FIA since 1957. Hannu Mikkola (Finland) (b. 24 May 1942) (with co-driver Arne Hertz) has a record four wins, in a Ford Escort, 1978–9 and an Audi Quatro, 1981–2.

World Championship ■ Two World Drivers' Championships (instituted 1979) have been won by Walter Röhrl, 1980 and 1982 and by Juha Kankkunen (Finland) (b. 2 Apr 1959), 1986–7. The most wins in World Championship races is 19 by Hannu Mikkola and Markku Alen (Finland) to November 1988.

DRAG RACING

Piston engined ■ The lowest elapsed time recorded by a piston-engined dragster from a standing start for 440 yd *402 m* is 4·936 sec by Eddie Hill (USA) at Baytown, Texas, USA on 9 Oct 1988, although the official National Hot Rod Association (NHRA) record is noted as 4·990 sec by Eddie Hill at the same event. The highest terminal velocity recorded at the end of a 440 yd run is 469·17 km/h *291·54 mph* by Connie Kalitta (USA) at Pomona, California, USA on 4 Feb 1989. For a petrol-driven piston-engined car the lowest elapsed time is 7·256 sec by Bob Glidden (USA), driving a Ford Probe at Houston, Texas, USA on 5 Mar 1989 and the highest terminal velocity is 307·87 km/h *191·31 mph* by Glidden in a Ford Thunderbird at Indianapolis, USA on 4 Sep 1987. The lowest elapsed time and highest terminal velocity for a petrol-driven piston-engined motorcycle are 7·829 sec and 275·03 mph *170·90 mph* respectively, set by John Mafaro (USA) on a Suzuki at Houston on 5 Mar 1989.

The world record for two runs in opposite directions over 440 yd *402 m* from a standing start is 6·70 sec by Dennis Victor Priddle (b. 1945) of

> **Toughest** ● Generally recognised as the toughest motoring event is the Paris-Dakar Rally. It was first held in 1978 with 26 competitors. The 11th race was held 1988–9 and attracted 927 participants. The course started in Paris, France and passed through Tunisia, Libya, Niger, Mali, Guinea and ended in Dakar, Sénegal – a distance of 10 831 km *6730 miles*. (Photo: All-Sport/ Vandystadt)

Yeovil, Somerset driving his 6424-cc supercharged Chrysler dragster developing 1700 bhp using nitromethane and methanol, at Elvington Airfield, North Yorkshire on 7 Oct 1972. The faster run was made in 6·65 sec.

Rocket or jet engined ■ The highest terminal velocity recorded by any dragster is 631·732 km/h *392·54 mph* by Kitty O'Neil (USA) at El Mirage Dry Lake, California, USA on 7 Jul 1977. The lowest elapsed time is 3·58 sec by Sammy Miller in a Pontiac 'Funny Car' in 1986.

Highest speeds *See also p. 110* ■ The most successful land speed record breaker was Sir Malcolm Campbell (GB) (1885–1948). He broke the official record nine times between 25 Sep 1924, with 235·216 km/h *146·157 mph* in a Sunbeam, and 3 Sep 1935, when he achieved 480·620 km/h *301·129 mph* in the Rolls–Royce-engined *Bluebird*.

GUINNESS HAVE PUBLISHED **MOTOR RACING: THE RECORDS** IAN MORRISON **£8.95**

Mountaineering

Although bronze-age artifacts have been found on the summit of the Riffelhorn, Switzerland (2927 m *9605 ft*), mountaineering as a sport has a continuous history dating back only to 1854. Isolated instances of climbing for its own sake exist back to the 13th century. The Atacamenans built sacrificial platforms near the summit of Llullaillaco (6723 m *22 058 ft*) in

late pre-Columbian times *c.* 1490. The earliest recorded rock climb in the British Isles was of Stac na Biorrach, St Kilda (71·9 m *236 ft*) by Sir Robert Moray in 1698.

Everest ■ Everest (8848 m *29 028 ft*) was first climbed at 11.30 a.m. on 29 May 1953, when the summit was reached by Edmund Percival Hillary (b. 20 Jul 1919), created KBE, of New Zealand, and Sherpa Tenzing Norgay (1914–86, formerly called Tenzing Khumjung Bhutia), who was awarded the GM. The successful expedition was led by Col. (later Hon. Brigadier) Henry Cecil John Hunt CBE, DSO (b. 22 Jun 1910), who was created a Knight Bachelor in 1953, a life Baron on 11 Jun 1966 and KG on 23 Apr 1979.

Most conquests ■ Sherpa Sundare (or Sungdare) (b. 1955) has climbed Everest a record five times in 1979, 1981, 1982, 1985 and 1988. Ang Rita Sherpa (b. 1939), with ascents in 1983, 1984, 1985, 1987 and 1988, has also scaled Everest five times but without the use of bottled oxygen.

Solo ■ Reinhold Messner (Italy) (b. 17 Sep 1944) was the first to make the entire climb solo on 20 Aug 1980. Also Messner, with Peter Habeler (Austria) (b. 22 Jul 1942), made the first entirely oxygen-less ascent on 8 May 1978.

First Britons ■ Douglas Scott (b. 29 May 1941) and Dougal Haston (1940–77) successfully completed the climb on 24 Sep 1975.

First an ■ Junko Tabei (Japan) (b. 22 Sep 1939) reached the summit on 16 May 1975.

Oldest ■ Richard Daniel Bass (USA) (b. 21 Dec 1929) was aged 55 yr 130 days when he reached the summit on 30 Apr 1985.

Most successful expedition ■ The Norwegian Everest Expedition, led by Arne Naess (Norway), in 1985 succeeded in putting the greatest number of people on the summit, 17, from 21–30 Apr 1985, including eight on 29 April which is a record for one day. It was during this expedition that Richard Bass

(USA) became the oldest man to climb Everest and Sherpa Sundare completed the fourth of his record five ascents (see above).

All continents ■ The first person to climb the highest mountain in each of the seven continents (Africa; Kilimanjaro 5895 m *19 340 ft*: Antarctica; Vinson Massif 5140 m *16 863 ft*: Asia; Everest 8848 m *29 029 ft*: Europe; El'brus 5642 m *18 510 ft*: North and Central America; McKinley 6194 m *20 320 ft*: South America; Aconcagua 6960 m *22 834 ft* and Australasia; Carstensz Pyramid 5030 m *16 502 ft*) was Patrick Morrow (Canada) (b.18 Oct 1952). He completed the last of the seven mountains, with his successful conquest of Carstensz Pyramid on 7 May 1986.

Mountaineer ■ Reinhold Messner has successfully scaled all 14 of the world's mountains of over 8000 m *26 250 ft*, all without oxygen. With his ascent of Kanchenjunga in 1982, he became the first person to climb the world's three highest mountains, having earlier reached the summits of Everest and K2.

Greatest walls ■ The highest final stage in any wall climb is that on the south face of Annapurna I (8091 m *26 545 ft*). It was climbed by the British expedition led by Christian John Storey Bonington (b. 6 Aug 1934) when from 2 Apr to 27 May 1970, using 5500 m *18 000 ft* of rope, Donald Whillans (1933–85) and Dougal Haston scaled to the summit. The longest wall climb is on the Rupal-Flank from the base camp at 3560 m *11 680 ft* to the South Point 8042 m *26 384 ft* of Nanga Parbat – vertical ascent of 4482 m *14 704 ft*. This was scaled by the Austro-German-Italian expedition led by Dr Karl Maria Herrligkoffer (b. 13 Jun 1916) in April 1970.

Europe's greatest wall is the 2000 m *6600 ft* north face of the Eigerwand (Ogre wall) first climbed by Heinrich Harrer and Fritz Kasparek of Austria and Anderl Heckmair and Wiggerl Vörg of Germany from 21–24 Jul 1938. The north-east face of the Eiger had been climbed on 20 Aug 1932 by Hans Lauper, Alfred Zurcher, Alexander Graven and Josef Knubel. The greatest alpine solo climb was that of Walter Bonatti (Italy) (b. 22 Jun 1930) of the South-West Pillar of the Dru, Montenvers, now called the Bonatti Pillar, with five bivouacs in 126 hr 7 min from 17–22 Aug 1955.

The most demanding free climbs in the world are those rated at 5·13, the premier location for these being in the Yosemite Valley, California, USA. The top routes in Britain are graded E7·7b, which relates closely to 5·13.

Highest bivouac ■ Douglas Scott and Dougal Haston bivouacked in a snow hole at 8747 m *28 700 ft* on the south summit of Everest on the night of 24 Sep 1975. Two Japanese, Hironobu Kamuro (1951–83) and Hiroshi Yoshino (1950–83), bivouacked at 8800 m *28 870 ft* on Everest on the night of 8–9 Oct 1983, but neither survived beyond the following day.

Oldest ■ Teiichi Igarashi (Japan) (b. 21 Sep 1886) climbed Mount Fuji (3776 m *12 388 ft*) at the age of 99 years 302 days on 20 Jul 1986.

MOUNTAIN RACING

Mount Cameroun ■ Reginald Esuke (Cameroun) descended from the summit 4095 m *13 435 ft* to Buea at 915 m *3002 ft* in 1 hr 2 min 15 sec on 24 Jan 1988, achieving a vertical rate of 51 m *167·5 ft* per min. Timothy Leku Lekunze (Cameroun) set the record for the race to the summit and back of 3 hr 46 min 34 sec on 25 Jan 1987, when the temperature varied from 35°C at the start to 0°C at the summit. The record time for the ascent is 2 hr 25 min 20 sec by Jack Maitland (GB) in 1988. The women's record for the race is 4 hr 42 min 31 sec by Fabiola Rueda (Colombia) in 1989.

Ben Nevis ■ The record time for the race from Fort William Town Park to the cairn on the summit of Ben Nevis 1346·6 m *4418 ft* and return is 1 hr 25 min 34 sec by Kenneth Stuart (b. 25 Feb 1957), and the feminine record is 1 hr 43 min 25 sec by Pauline Haworth (b. 1 Aug 1956), both on 1 Sep 1984.

The full course by the bridle path is about 22 km *14 miles* but distance is saved by crossing the open hillside. The mountain was first climbed *c.* 1720 and the earliest run, by William Swan in 2 hr 41 min, was in 1895.

Snowdon ■ The Snowdon Race (Ras Yr Wyddfa) has been run annually since 1976 from Llanberis to the summit of Snowdon and back. The fastest time is 1 hr 2 min 29 sec by Kenny Stuart in 1985. Carol Marie Haigh (b. 15 Mar 1966) set a women's record of 1 hr 14 min 36 sec in 1986.

Yorkshire Three Peaks ■ The record for the current 24-mile course from Horton-in-Ribblesdale is 2 hr 51 min 45 sec by Sean Livesey of Rossendale on 30 Apr 1989. On the same day Vanessa Brindle set a women's record of 3 hr 32 min 46 sec.

MOUNTAIN ENDURANCE RUNNING

The record for the Bob Graham Round of 42 lakeland peaks covering a total distance of 99 km *62 miles* and 7900 m *26 000 ft* of ascent and descent, is 13 hr 54 min by Billy Bland, 34, on 19 Jun 1982. Ernest Roger Baumeister (b. 17 Dec 1941) (Dark Peak Fell Runners Club) ran the double Bob Graham Round in 46 hr 34 ½ min on 30 Jun–1 Jul 1979. The women's single round record is 20 hr 17 min by Helen Diamantides on 11 Jun 1988.

The Lakeland 24-hr record is 76 peaks (approximately 11 900 m *39 000 ft* of ascents and descents) from Braithwaite achieved by Mark McDermott on 19–20 Jun 1988.

The Scottish 24-hr record is 28 Munro (mountains over 914 m *3000 ft*) summits achieved by Jon Broxap on 30–31 Jul 1988. He covered 128 km *80 miles*, with 10 700 m *35 000 ft* of ascents and descents in 23 hr 20 min from Cluanie Inn.

The record for traversing the 136·79 km *85 mile* cross-country route of the nine 1219·2 m *4000 ft* Scottish peaks form Glen Nevis to Glen More is 21 hr 39 min by Martin Stone (Dark Peak Fell Runners) on 4 Jul 1987

The 'Three Thousander' record over the 15 Welsh peaks of over 914 m *3000 ft* is 4 hr 19 min 56 sec, from Snowdon Summit to Foel Fras by Colin Donnelly on 11 Jun 1988.

Everest Base Camp to Kathmandu ■ The record is 3 days 10 hr 8 min by Helene Diamantides and Alison Wright, both 22, from 8–10 Oct 1987. They covered 288 km *180 miles*, climbed 9800 m *32 000 ft* and descended 14 000 m *46 000 ft*.

British Three Peaks record ■ The Three Peaks route from sea level at Fort William, Inverness-shire, to sea level at Caernarvon, via the summits of Ben Nevis, Scafell Pike and Snowdon, was walked by Arthur Eddleston (1939–84) (Cambridge H) in 5 days 23 hr 37 min from 11–17 May 1980. Peter and David Ford, David Robinson, Kevin Duggan and John O'Callaghan, of Luton and Dunstable, ran the distance in relay in 54 hr 39 min 14 sec from 7–9 Aug 1981. The fastest individual total time for climbing the three mountains is 4 hr 16 min by Joss Naylor from 8–9 Jul 1971.

On 23 Jun 1984 a team of 3 from the Greater Manchester Police Tactical Aid Group covered the distance in 8 hr 22 min, being transported between the peaks by helicopter. Their running time was 5 hr 4 min.

A total climbing time of 7 hr 47 min was achieved by Brian Stadden from 13–15 Aug 1982 for Five Peaks, adding the highest points in Northern Ireland—Slieve Donard (852 m *2796 ft*) and in the Republic of Ireland—Carrauntoohil (1041 m *3414 ft*) to the Three Peaks.

A team of four from West Midlands Police climbed the Three peaks and the highest peaks in the Isle of Skye and the Isle of Man; Sgurr Alasdair 992 m

3257 ft and Snaefell 620 m *2036 ft*, travelling by bicycle, ferry and helicopter in a time of 77 hr 43 min (climbing time; 17 hr 57 min and cycling time; 58 hr 6 min) from 7–12 May 1988. They took short rests between climbing and cycling and slept overnight.

Pennine Way ■ The record for traversing the 436 km *271 mile* long Pennine Way is 2 days 21 hr 55 min by Michael Cudahy, 43, from 1–3 Jun 1984. The club relay record for a team of 24 is 29 hr 7 min 58 sec by Holmfirth Harriers from 28–29 Jun 1986.

Multiple peaks ■ Three members of the 'Climathon' team, Mick Cottam, Matthew Beresford and Andrew Curson, completed a climb of all 349 peaks in England over 609·6 m *2000 ft* (walking a distance of 647·76 km *402·5 miles*) from 21 Jul–11 Aug 1985.

Craig Caldwell took 377 days to cycle, walk and climb to the top of the 277 Munros (mountains over 914 m *3000 ft*) and the 222 Corbetts (762-914 m *2500-3000 ft*) in Scotland. In all he cycled 6682 km *4152 miles*, walked 4876 km *3030 miles* and climbed 252 542 m *828 491 ft*.

Top to bottom ■ Clive Johnson and Les Heaton of 'Mountain Adventure' climbed the highest peaks and descended the deepest caves in each of England, Scotland and Wales in 16 hr 14 min from 16–18 Sep 1986.

Netball

The game was invented in the USA in 1891 and introduced into England in 1895 by Dr Toles. The All England Women's Netball Association was formed in 1926. The oldest club in continuous existence is the Polytechnic Netball Club of London founded in 1907.

Most titles *World* ■ Australia has won the World Championships (instituted 1963) a record five times, 1963, 1971, 1975, 1979 and 1983.

English ■ The National Club's Championships (instituted 1966) have been won eight times by Sudbury Netball Club (1968–70; 1971 (shared), 1973, 1983–5). Surrey has won the County Championships (instituted 1932) a record 19 times (1949–64, 1966, 1981; 1969 and 1986 (both shared).

Most international appearances ■ The record number of internationals is 100 by Jillean Hipsey of England, 1978–87.

Highest scores ■ The World Tournament record score was in Auckland, New Zealand in 1975 when England beat Papua New Guinea 114 goals to 16. The record number of goals in the World Tournament is 402 by Judith Heath (England) (b. 1942) in 1971.

Olympic Games

These records include the Games held at Athens in 1906.

The earliest celebration of the ancient Olympic Games of which there is a certain record is that of July 776 BC, when Coroibos, a cook from Elis, won the foot race, though their origin dates from perhaps as early as *c.* 1370 BC. The ancient Games were terminated by an order issued in Milan in AD 393 by Theodosius I, 'the Great' (*c.* 346–95), Emperor of Rome. At the instigation of Pierre de Fredi, Baron de Coubertin (1863–1937), the Olympic Games of the modern era were inaugurated in Athens on 6 Apr 1896.

Ever present ■ Five countries have never failed to be represented at the 22 celebrations of the Summer Games: Australia, France, Greece, Great Britain and Switzerland. Of these only Great Britain has been present at all Winter celebrations as well.

Most participants ■ The greatest number of competitors at a celebration is 9302 (6892 men, 2410 women), who represented a record 160 nations, for the 1988 Summer Games at Seoul, South Korea.

Largest Crowd ■ The largest crowd at any Olympic site was 150 000 at the 1952 ski–jumping at the Holmenkøllen, outside Oslo, Norway. Estimates of the number of spectators of the marathon race through Tokyo, Japan on 21 Oct 1964 ranged from 500 000 to 1 500 000. The total spectator attendance at Los Angeles in 1984 was given as 5 797 923 (see General Records).

Olympic Torch relay ■ The longest journey of the torch within the host country, was for the XV Winter Games in Canada in 1988. The torch arrived at St John's, Newfoundland on 17 Nov 1987 and was transported 18 060 km *11 222 miles* (8188 km *5088 miles* by foot, 7111 km *4419 miles* by aircraft / ferry, 2756 km *1712 miles* by snowmobile and 5 km *3 miles* by dogsled) until its arrival at Calgary on 13 Feb 1988.

Most medals ■ In ancient Olympic Games victors were given a chaplet of wild olive leaves. Leonidas of Rhodos won 12 running titles 164–152 BC. The most individual gold medals won by a male competitor in the modern Games is ten by Raymond Clarence Ewry (USA) (1874–1937) (see Track and Field Athletics). The female record is seven by Vera Caslavska–Odlozil (Czechoslovakia) (see Gymnastics). The most gold medals won by a British competitor is four by: Paul Radmilovic (1886–1968) in water polo, 1908, 1912 and 1920 and 4 × 200 m freestyle relay in 1908; and swimmer Henry Taylor (1885–1951) in 1906 and 1908. The Australian swimmer Iain Murray Rose, who won four gold medals, was born in Birmingham, West Midlands on 6 Jan 1939.

The only Olympian to win four consecutive individual titles in the same event has been Alfred A. Oerter (USA) (b. 19 Sep 1936), who won the discus, in 1956–68. However, Raymond Clarence Ewry (USA) won both the standing long jump and the standing high jump at four games in succession, 1900, 1904, 1906 and 1908. This is if the Intercalated Games of 1906, which were staged officially by the International Olympic Committee, are included. Also Paul B. Elvström (Denmark) (b. 24 Feb 1928) won four successive gold medals at monotype yachting events, 1948–60, but there was a class change (1948 Firefly class, 1952–60 Finn class).

Swimmer Mark Andrew Spitz (USA) (b. 10 Feb 1950)

won a record seven golds at one celebration, at Munich in 1972, including three in relays. The most won in individual events at one celebration is five by speed skater, Eric Heiden (USA) (b. 14 Jun 1958) at Lake Placid, New York, USA in 1980.

The only man to win a gold medal in both the Summer and Winter Games is Edward F. Eagan (USA) (1898–1967) who won the 1920 light-heavyweight boxing title and was a member of the winning four-man bob in 1932. Christa Luding (*née* Rothenburger) (GDR) (b. 4 Dec 1959) became the first woman to win a medal at both the Summer and Winter Games when she won a silver in the cycling sprint event in 1988. She had previously won medals for ice skating, 500 m gold in 1984, and 1000 m gold and 500 m silver in 1988.

Gymnast Larissa Latynina (USSR) (b. 27 Dec 1934) won a record 18 medals (see Gymnastics). The

Modern Olympic Games ● The Olympic Games of the modern era were inaugurated in Athens on 6 Apr 1896 at the instigation of Pierre de Fredi, Baron de Coubertin (1863–1937). The picture shows the final of the 100 metres on 10 April, won by Thomas Burke (USA), second from left. (Photo: All-Sport)

record at one celebration is eight by gymnast Aleksandr Ditatin (USSR) (b. 7 Aug 1957) in 1980.

Youngest and oldest gold medallist ■ The youngest ever winner was a French boy (whose name is not recorded) who coxed the Netherlands pair in 1900. He was 7–10 years old and he substituted for Dr Hermanus Brockmann, who coxed in the heats but proved too heavy. The youngest ever female champion was Marjorie Gestring (USA) (b. 18 Nov 1922, now Mrs Bowman), aged 13 yr 268 days, in the 1936 women's springboard event. Oscar Swahn (see p.220) was in the winning Running Deer shooting team in 1912 aged 64 yr 258 days.

Youngest and oldest British competitor ■ The youngest competitor to represent Britain in the Olympic Games was Magdalena Cecilia Colledge (b. 28 Nov 1920), aged 11 yr 73 days when she skated in the 1932 Games. The oldest was Hilda Lorna Johnstone (b. 4 Sep 1902), aged 70 yr 5 days, in the equestrian dressage in the 1972 Games.

Longest Span ■ The longest span of an Olympic competitor is 40 years by: Dr Ivan Osiier (Denmark) (1888–1965) in fencing, 1908–32 and 1948; and Magnus Konow (Norway) (1887–1972) in yachting, 1908–20 and 1936–48. The longest feminine span is 24 years (1932–56) by the Austrian fencer Ellen Müller-Preis (b. 6 May 1912). Raimondo d'Inzeo (b. 8 Feb 1925) competed for Italy in equestrian events at a record eight celebrations from 1948–76, gaining one gold, two silver and three bronze medals. The women's record is six Games contested by Janice Lee York Romary (b. 6 Aug 1928), the US fencer, all six Games from 1948–1968; Lia Manoliu (Romania) (b. 25 Apr 1932) from 1952–72 winning the discus in 1968; and by Kerstin Palm (Sweden) in fencing from 1964–84. The longest span of any British competitor is 28 years by Enoch Jenkins (b. 6 Nov 1892) who appeared in the 1924 and the 1952 Games in the clay pigeon shooting event, and the longest feminine span is 20 years by Dorothy Jennifer Beatrice Tyler (*née* Odam) (b. 14 Mar 1920) who high-jumped from 1936–56. The record number of appearances for Great Britain is six by fencer Bill Hoskyns from 1956–76. Durward Randolph Knowles (b. 2 Nov 1917) competed in yachting for Britain in 1948 and in the following six Games for the Bahamas.

Orienteering

Origins ■ The first indications of orienteering as a competitive sport have been found in the Swedish army (1888) and the Norwegian army (1895). The first civilian competition seems to have been organised on 31 Oct 1897 (with eight participants) by the sport club Tjalve, outside Oslo, Norway. In spite of a number of other small events up to 1910, the sport died out in Norway but in Sweden survived World War I. On 25 Mar 1919, the first large competition with more than 200 participants was organised in the forest of Nacka, outside Stockholm. From there the sport spread rapidly throughout Sweden and later (about 1925) to Finland, Norway and (especially post-1945) to other countries in Europe and elsewhere. The initiator was Major Ernst Killander, who is known as 'The Father of Orienteering'. World Championships were instituted in 1966. Annual British Championships were instituted in 1967 following the formation of the British Orienteering Federation.

Most titles *World* ■ The men's relay has been won a record six times by: Sweden, between 1966 and 1979; and Norway, between 1970 and 1987. Sweden have won the women's relay seven times, 1966, 1970, 1974, 1976, 1981, 1983 and 1985. Three women's individual titles have been won by Annichen Kringstad-Svensson (Sweden) (b. 15 Jul 1960), 1981, 1983 and 1985. The men's title has been won twice by: Åge Hadler (Norway) (b. 14 Aug 1944), in 1966 and 1972; Egil Johansen (Norway) (b. 18 Aug 1954), 1976 and 1978; and Øyvind Thon (Norway) (b. 25 Mar 1958), in 1979 and 1981.

British ■ Geoffrey Peck (b. 27 Sep 1949) won the men's individual title a record five times, 1971, 1973, 1976–7 and 1979 as well as the over-35s title in 1985–6 and over-40s in 1989. Carol McNeill (b. 20 Feb 1944) won the women's title six times, 1967, 1969, 1972–6. She also won the over-35s title in 1984 and 1985.

Lorna Collett (b. 2 Sep 1922) of South Ribble OC and Terry Dooris (b. 22 Sep 1926) of Southern Navigators have both competed in all 23 British individual championships 1967–89.

Most competitors ■ The most competitors at an event in one day is 22 510 on the first day of the Swedish O-Ringen at Småland on 18 Jul 1983.

Ski Orienteering ■ Seven World Championships in ski orienteering have been held. Sweden have won the men's relay four times (1977, 1980, 1982, 1984) and Finland have won the women's relay four times (1975, 1977, 1980, 1988).

Parachuting

See also page 126

Parachuting became a regulated sport with the institution of World Championships in 1951. A team title was introduced in 1954 and women's events were included in 1956.

Most titles *World* ■ The USSR won the men's team title in 1954, 1958, 1960, 1966, 1972, 1976 and 1980, and the women's team title in 1956, 1958, 1966, 1968, 1972 and 1976. Nikolay Ushamyev (USSR) has won the individual title twice, 1974 and 1980.

British ■ Sgt Ronald Alan 'Scotty' Milne (b. 5 Mar 1952) of the Parachute Regiment won the British title five times in 1976–7, 1979–81. Rob Colpus and Geoff Sanders have each shared ten British titles for Relative Work parachuting, the 4-Way and 8-Way titles won by their team 'Symbiosis' in 1976–7, 1979, 1981–2.

Greatest accuracy ■ Jacqueline Smith (GB) (b. 29 Mar 1951) scored ten consecutive dead centre strikes (10 cm *4 in* disc) in the World Championships at Zagreb, Yugoslavia on 1 Sep 1978. At Yuma, Arizona, USA, in March 1978, Dwight Reynolds scored a record 105 daytime dead centres, and Bill

Wenger and Phil Munden tied with 43 night time DCs, competing as members of the US Army team, the Golden Knights. With electronic measuring the official FAI record is 50 DCs by Aleksandr Aasmiae (USSR) at Ferghana, USSR in October 1979.

The Men's Night Accuracy Landing record on an electronic score pad is 27 consecutive dead centres by Cliff Jones (USA) in 1981.

Parascending ■ Andrew Wakelin (GB) at Artesia Airport, New Mexico, USA on a Sorcerer 33 canopy on a 488 m *1600 ft* line on 1 Aug 1985 set records for distance: 7300 m *23 950 ft*, and height gain: 400 m *1312 ft*. The duration record is 21 min 8 sec by Pat Sugrue on a Paramount 9 in South Wales on 12 Apr 1986.

Nigel Horder scored four successive dead centres at the Dutch Open, Flevhof, Netherlands on 22 May 1983.

Pétanque

The origins of pétanque or boules can be traced back over 2000 years, but it was not until 1945 that the *Fédération Française de Pétanque et Jeu Provençal* was formed, and subsequently the *Fédération Internationale* (FIPJP). The first recognised British club was formed on 30 Mar 1966 as the Chingford Club de Pétanque and the British Pétanque Association was founded in 1974.

World Championships ■ Winner of the most World Championships (instituted 1959) has been France with nine titles to 1988. The first women's World Championships were held in 1988 when the winners were Thailand.

Highest score in 24 hours ■ Chris and Richard Walker scored a record 2109 points in 24 hours (172 games) at the Gin Trap, Ringstead, Norfolk on 24–25 Jun 1988.

Pigeon Racing

Origins ■ Pigeon racing developed from the use of homing pigeons for carrying messages. The sport originated in Belgium from commercial services and the earliest long-distance race was from London to Antwerp in 1819, involving 36 pigeons.

Longest flights ■ The longest confirmed distances, flown in opposite directions, by a single pigeon were north from Rome, Italy, 1474·38 km *916·16 miles*, and south from The Faroes, 1178·82 km *732·5 miles*, by a dark cock, GB83X 03693, to the loft of Marley Westrop of Hitchin, Hertfordshire. The greatest claimed homing flight by a pigeon was for one owned by the 1st Duke of Wellington (1769–1852). Released from a sailing ship off the Ichabo Islands, West Africa on 8 April, it dropped dead a mile from its loft at Nine Elms, Wandsworth, London on 1 Jun 1845, 55 days later, having apparently flown an airline route of 8700 km *5400 miles*, but an actual distance of possibly 11 250 km *7000 miles* to avoid the Sahara Desert. The official British duration record (into Great Britain) is 1887 km *1173 miles* in 15 days by *C.S.O.*, owned by Rosie and Bruce of Wick, in the 1976 Palamos Race. In the 1975 Palamos Race, *The Conqueror*, owned by Alan Raeside, homed to Irvine, Strathclyde, 1625 km *1010 miles*, in 43 hr 56 min. The greatest number of flights over 1000 miles flown by one pigeon is that of *Dunning Independence*, owned by D. Smith, which annually flew from Palamos to Dunning, Perthshire, 1662 km *1039 miles*, between 1978 and 1981.

Highest speeds ■ In level flight in windless conditions it is very doubtful if any pigeon can exceed 96 km/h *60 mph*. The highest race speed recorded is one of 2952 m *3229 yd* per min (177·14 km/h *110·07 mph*) in the East Anglian Federation race from East Croydon, Surrey on 8 May 1965 when the 1428 birds were backed by a powerful south-southwest wind. The winner was owned by A. Vigeon & Son, Wickford, Essex.

The highest race speed recorded over a distance of more than 1000 km *621·37 miles* is 2224·5 m *2432·7 yd* per min (133·46 km/h *82·93 mph*) by a hen in the Central Cumberland Combine race over 1099·316 km *683 miles 147 yd* from Murray Bridge, South Australia to North Ryde, Sydney on 2 Oct 1971.

24-hr records ■ The world's longest reputed distance in 24 hr is 1292 km *803 miles* (velocity 1394 m *1525 yd* per min) by E. S. Petersen's winner of the 1941 San Antonio R.C. event in Texas, USA.

The best 24-hr performance into the United Kingdom is 1165·3 km *724 miles 219 yd* by E. Cardno's *Mormond Lad*, on 2 Jul 1977, from Nantes, France to Fraserburgh, Grampian. Average speed was 1507 m *1648 yd* per min (90.41 km/h *56·18 mph*).

Career records ■ Owned by R. Green, of Walsall Wood, West Midlands, *Champion Breakaway* won 59 first prizes from 1972 to May 1979.

The greatest competitive distance flown is 32 318 km *20 082 miles* by *Nunnies*, a chequer cock owned by Terry Haley of Abbot's Langley, Hertfordshire.

Highest-priced bird ■ Champion racing pigeons commonly change hands for £30 000 or more. Currency fluctuations mean that a record price in sterling may not reflect the true price paid. Recent high-priced pigeons include *Keiser* sold by Arthur Leflere to Masahiko Ohta of Japan in 1985; *Sproetekop*, also sold by Arthur Leflere to Japan in 1986, and *Peter Pau* sold by Silvere Toye of Belgium to Louis Massarella of Loughborough, Leicestershire in 1986.

Polo

Origins ■ Polo can be traced to origins in Manipur state *c.* 3100 BC when it was played as *Sagol Kangjei*. Other claims are of it being of Persian origin, having been played as *Pulu c.* 525 BC. The game was introduced to British officers at Cachar by the Manipur Maharaja, Sir Chandrakirti Singh, and the earliest club was the Cachar Club (founded in 1859) in Assam, India. The oldest club still in existence is the Calcutta Polo Club (1862). The game was introduced into England from India in 1869 by the 10th Hussars at Aldershot, Hampshire and the earliest match was one between the 9th Lancers and the 10th Hussars on Hounslow Heath, Greater London in July 1871. The earliest international match between England and the USA was in 1886. The game's governing body is the Hurlingham Polo Association, which drew up the first English rules in 1875.

Most titles ■ The British Open Championship for the Cowdray Park Gold Cup (instituted 1956) has been won five times by Stowell Park, 1973–4, 1976, 1978 and 1980.

Highest handicap ■ The highest handicap based on eight 7 ½ min 'chukkas' is ten goals introduced in the USA in 1891 and in the UK and in Argentina in 1910. A total of 55 players have received ten-goal handicaps and there are five currently playing in Britain, one Mexican and four Argentinians. The last (of six) ten-goal handicap players from the UK was Gerald Balding in 1939. A match of two 40-goal teams was staged, for the only time, at Palermo, Buenos Aires, Argentina in 1975. The highest handicaps of current UK players is nine by Howard Hipwood (b. 24 Mar 1950). Claire J. Tomlinson of Gloucestershire attained a handicap of five, the highest ever by a woman, in 1986.

Highest score ■ The highest aggregate number of goals scored in an international match is 30, when Argentina beat the USA 21–9 at Meadow Brook, Long Island, New York, USA in September 1936.

Pool

Pool or championship pocket billiards with numbered balls began to become standardised *c.*

1890. The greatest exponents were Ralph Greenleaf (USA) (1899–1950), who won the 'world' professional title 19 times (1919–37), and William Mosconi (USA) (b. 27 Jun 1913), who dominated the game from 1941 to 1957.

The longest consecutive run in an American straight pool match is 625 balls by Michael Eufemia at Logan's Billiard Academy, Brooklyn, New York, USA on 2 Feb 1960. The greatest number of balls pocketed in 24 hr is 16 009 by Paul Sullivan at Selby, North Yorkshire on 8–9 Apr 1989.

The record times for potting all 15 balls in a speed competition are: (men) 37·9 sec by Rob McKenna at Blackpool, Lancashire on 7 Nov 1987 and (women) 53·29 sec by Susan Thompson at Oldham, Greater Manchester on 5 Jun 1988.

A record break of 132 for 14–1 pool was set by Ross McInnes at Pontin's, Heysham, Lancashire on 3 Oct 1984.

Powerboat Racing

A petrol engine was first installed in a boat by Jean Joseph Etienne Lenoir (1822–1900) on the River Seine, Paris, France in 1865. Actual powerboat racing started in about 1900, the first prominent race being from Calais, France to Dover, Kent in 1903. International racing was largely established by the presentation of a Challenge Trophy by Sir Alfred Harmsworth in 1903. Thereafter, racing developed mainly as a 'circuit' or short, sheltered course type competition. Offshore or sea-passage races also developed, initially for displacement (non-planing) cruisers. Offshore events for fast (planing) cruisers began in 1958 with a 273 km *170 mile* passage race from Miami, USA to Nassau, Bahamas. Outboard motor, i.e. the combined motor/transmission detachable propulsion unit type racing began in the USA in about 1920. Both inboard and outboard motor boat engines are mainly petrol fuelled, but since 1950 diesel (compression ignition) engines have appeared and are widely used in offshore sport.

Highest speeds ■ The highest speed recorded

by a propeller-driven boat is 368·52 km/h *229 mph* by *The Texan*, a Kurtis Top Fuel Hydro Drag boat, driven by Eddie Hill (USA) (see also Motor Racing; Drag Racing) on 5 Sep 1982 at Chowchilla, California, USA. He also set a 440 yd *402 m* elapsed time record of 5·16 sec in this boat at Firebird Lake, Arizona, USA on 13 Nov 1983. The official American Drag Boat Association record is 360·29 km/h *223·88 mph* by *Final Effort*, a Blown Fuel Hydro boat driven by Robert T. Burns at Creve Coeur Lake, St Louis, Missouri, USA on 15 Jul 1985 over a 402 m *¼ mile* course.

The fastest speed recognised by the *Union Internationale Motonautique* for an outboard-powered boat is in Class (e): 285·83 km/h *177·61 mph* by P. R. Knight in a Chevrolet-engined Lautobach hull on Lake Ruataniwha, New Zealand in 1986. Robert F. Hering (USA) set the world Formula One record at 266·085 km/h *165·338 mph* at Parker, Arizona, USA on 21 Apr 1986.

The fastest speed recorded for a diesel (compression ignition) boat is 218·26 km/h *135·62 mph* by the hydroplane *Iveco World Leader*, powered by an Aifo-Fiat engine, driven by Carlo Bonomi at Venice, Italy in 1985.

Highest race speeds ■ The highest speed recorded in an offshore race is 166·22 km/h *103·29 mph* by Tony Garcia (USA) in a Class I powerboat at Key West, Florida, USA in November 1983.

Fastest offshore powerboat ● The fastest speed recognised for an offshore boat is 248·537 km/h *154·438 mph* for one way and 238·559 km/h *148·238 mph* for two runs by Tom Gentry (USA), in his 15 m *49 ft* catamaran, powered by four Gentry Turbo Eagle V8 Chevrolets. (Photo: All-Sport/Oli Tennent)

Longest races ■ The longest offshore race has been the Port Richborough London to Monte Carlo Marathon Offshore international event. The race extended over 4742 km *2947 miles* in 14 stages from 10–25 Jun 1972. It was won by *H.T.S.* (GB) driven by Mike Bellamy, Eddie Chater and Jim Brooker in 71 hr 35 min 56 sec for an average of 66·24 km/h *41·15 mph*. The longest circuit race is the 24-hour race held annually since 1962 on the River Seine at Rouen, France. The 1983 winners François Greens, Jan van Brockels and Roger Robin of Belgium drove a Johnson outboard-engined Piranha boat at an average speed of 75·02 km/h *46·63 mph*.

Longest jetboat jumps ■ The longest ramp jump achieved by a jetboat has been 36·57 m *120 ft* by Peter Horak (USA) in a Glastron Carlson CVX 20 Jet

Longest powerboat circuit race ● Instituted in 1962, the 24-hour race on the River Seine at Rouen, France is currently the longest circuit race in the world. (Photo: All-Sport/Vandystadt)

Deluxe with a 460 Ford V8 engine (take-off speed 88 km/h *55 mph*) for a documentary TV film, at Salton Sea, California, USA on 26 Apr 1980. The longest leap on to land is 38·7 m *172 ft* by Norm Bagrie (New Zealand) from the Shotover River on 1 Jul 1982 in the 1½ ton jetboat *Valvolene*.

Rackets

There is record of the sale of a racket court at Southernhay, Exeter, Devon dated 12 Jan 1798. The game, which is of 17th-century origin, was played by debtors in the Fleet Prison, London in the middle of the 18th century, and an inmate, Robert Mackay, claimed the first 'world' title in 1820. The first closed court champion was Francis Erwood at Woolwich, London in 1860.

World Championships ■ Of the 22 world champions since 1820 the longest reign is by Geoffrey Willoughby Thomas Atkins (b. 20 Jan 1927) who held the title, after beating the professional James Dear (1910–81) in 1954, until retiring, after defending it four times, in April 1972.

Most Amateur titles ■ Since the Amateur Singles Championship was instituted in 1888 the most titles won by an individual is nine by Edgar Maximilian Baerlein (1879–1971) between 1903 and 1923. Since the institution of the Amateur Doubles Championship in 1890 the most shares in titles has been eleven by: David Sumner Milford (1905–84), between 1938 and 1959; and John Ross Thompson (b. 10 May 1918), between 1948 and 1966; they won ten titles together. Milford also won seven Amateur Singles titles (1930–51), an Open title (1936) and held the World title from 1937 to 1946. Thompson additionally won an Open Singles title and five Amateur Singles titles.

Racketball

Racquetball using a 12 m × 6 m *40 ft × 20 ft* court was invented in 1950 by Joe Sobek at the Greenwich YMCA, Connecticut, USA, originally as Paddle Rackets. The International Racquetball Association was founded in 1968 by Bob Kendler (USA). John Treharne won three British titles, 1981–3.

Racketball using a 9·75 m × 6·4 m *32 ft × 21 ft* court (as for squash) was introduced to Britain by Ian Wright in 1976. The British Racketball Association was formed and staged inaugural British National Championships in 1984. Three titles have been won at the women's event by Bett Dryhurst, 1985–7.

Rodeo

Origins ■ Rodeo, which developed from 18th-century *fiestas*, came into being in the early days of the North American cattle industry. The sport originated in Mexico and spread from there into the cattle regions of the USA. Steer wrestling came in with Bill Pickett (1870–1932) of Texas in 1900.

The largest rodeo in the world is the National Finals Rodeo (first held in 1959 in Dallas, Texas, USA), organised by the Professional Rodeo Cowboys Association (PRCA). The 1988 Finals at Las Vegas, Nevada, USA had a paid attendance of 165 467 for ten performances. In 1989 a record $2·3 million in prize money was offered for the event, staged in Las Vegas.

Most world titles ■ The record number of all-around titles in the PRCA World Championships is six by Larry Mahan (USA) (b. 21 Nov 1943) in 1966–70 and 1973 and, consecutively, 1974–9 by Tom Ferguson (b. 20 Dec 1950). Roy Cooper (b. 13 Nov 1955) has record career earnings on $1 119 622, 1976–89. Jim Shoulders (b. 1928) of Henryetta, Oklahoma, USA has won a record 16 World Championships at all events between 1949 and 1959. The record figure for prize money in a single season is $166 042 by Lewis Feild (b. 28 Oct 1956) in 1986.

Feild won a record $75 219 for one rodeo ($47 449 for saddle bronc riding and $27 770 for bareback riding) at the 1987 National Finals Rodeo, Las Vegas, Nevada, USA.

Youngest champions ■ The youngest winner of a world title is Metha Brorsen of Oklahoma, USA, who won the International Rodeo Association cowgirls barrel-racing event in 1975 at 11 years old. The youngest champion in Professional Rodeo Cowboys Association/Women's Professional Rodeo Association competition is Jackie Jo Perrin of Antlers, Oklahoma, USA, who won the barrel-racing title in 1977 at age 13.

Time records ■ Records for PRCA timed events, such as calf-roping and steer-wrestling, are not always comparable, because of the widely varying conditions due to the sizes of arenas and amount of start given the stock. The fastest time recorded for roping a calf is 5·7 sec by Lee Phillips at Assiniboia, Saskatchewan, Canada in 1978, and the fastest time for overcoming a steer is 2·4 sec by: James Bynum, at Marietta, Oklahoma, USA in 1955; Carl Deaton at Tulsa, Oklahoma, USA in 1976; and Gene Melton at Pecatonica, Illinois, USA in 1976.

Bull riding ■ Jim Sharp of Kermit, Texas became the first rider to ride all ten bulls at a National Finals Rodeo at Las Vegas in December 1988.

The highest score in bull riding was 98 points out of a possible 100 by Denny Flynn on *Red Lightning* at Palestine, Illinois, USA in 1979.

The top bucking bull *Red Rock* dislodged 312 riders, 1980–8, and was finally ridden to the eight-second bell by Lane Frost (World Champion Bull Rider 1987) on 20 May 1988. *Red Rock* had retired at the end of the 1987 season but still continued to make guest appearances.

Champion bronc ■ Traditionally, a bronc called *Midnight* owned by Jim McNab of Alberta, Canada was never ridden in 12 appearances at the Calgary Stampede.

Roller Skating

The first roller skate was devised by Jean Joseph Merlin (1735–1803) of Huy, Belgium in 1760 and demonstrated by him in London but with disastrous results. James L. Plimpton of New York produced the present four-wheeled type and patented it in January 1863. The first indoor rink was opened in the Haymarket, London in about 1824.

Most titles *Speed* ■ The most world speed titles won is 18 by two women: Alberta Vianello (Italy), eight track and ten road 1953–65; and Annie Lambrechts (Belgium), one track and 17 road 1964–81, at distances from 500 m to 10 000 m. The most British national individual men's titles have been won by Michael Colin McGeogh (b. 30 Mar 1946) with 19 in 1966–85. Chloe Ronaldson (b. 30 Nov 1939) won 40 individual and 14 team women's senior titles from 1958 to 1985.

Figure ■ The records for figure titles are: five by Karl Heinz Losch in 1958–9, 1961–2 and 1966; and four by Astrid Bader in 1965–8, both of West Germany. The most world pair titles is four by Dieter Fingerle (West Germany) in 1959, 1965–7 with two different partners.

Speed skating ■ The fastest speed put up in an official world record is 43·05 km/h *26·75 mph* when Patrizio Sarto (b. 19 Jan 1964) recorded 25·088 sec for 300 m on a road at Bogotá, Colombia in 1984. The world records on a rink for 10 000 m are: (men) 15 min 49·7 sec, Roberto Marotta (Italy) (b. 6 Mar 1948) at Inzell, West Germany 1968; (women) 16 min 30·484 sec, Annie Lambrechts (Belgium) at Louvain, Belgium on 1 Jul 1985. Lambrechts went on to skate 37·097 km *23·051 miles* in 1 hr and 50 km in 1 hr 21 min 25 sec. The men's 1-hour record on a track is 37·230 km *23·133 miles* by Alberto Civolani (Italy) (b. 16 Mar 1933) at Inzell, West Germany on 28 Sep 1968. He went on to skate 80·46 km *50 miles* in 2 hr 20 min 33·1 sec.

Largest rink ■ The greatest indoor rink ever to operate was located in the Grand Hall, Olympia, London. Opened in 1890 and closed in 1912, it had an actual skating area of 6 300 m² *68 000 ft²*. The current largest is the main arena of 3250 m² *34 981 ft²* at Guptill Roll-Arena, Boght Corner, New York, USA. The total rink area is 3844 m² *41 380 ft²*.

Endurance ■ Theodore James Coombs (b. 1954) of Hermosa Beach, California, USA skated 8357 km *5193 miles* from Los Angeles, California to New York and back to Yates Center, Kansas from 30 May to 14 Sep 1979.

Land's End to John o'Groats ■ Steve Fagan, 20, roller skated the distance, 1488 km *925 miles*, in 9 days 10 hr 25 min from 1–10 May 1984, averaging 157 km *98 miles* a day. The fastest time by a woman was 12 days 4 hr 15 min by Cheryl Fisher, 17, from 19 Sep–1 Oct 1987.

ROLLER HOCKEY

Roller hockey (previously known as rink hockey in Europe) was introduced to Britain as rink polo, at the old Lava rink, Denmark Hill, London in the late 1870s. The Amateur Rink Hockey Association was formed in 1908, and in 1913 became the National Rink Hockey (now Roller Hockey) Association. England won the first World Championships, 1936–9, since when Portugal has won most titles with 12 between 1947 and 1982. Portugal also won a record 16 European (instituted 1926) titles between 1947 and 1987.

Rowing

The Sphinx stela of Amenhotep II (1450–1425 BC) records that he *stroked* a boat for some three miles. The earliest established sculling race is the Doggett's Coat and Badge, which was first rowed on 1 Aug 1716 from London Bridge to Chelsea as a race for apprentices, and is still contested annually. Although rowing regattas were held in Venice in 1300 the first English regatta probably took place on the Thames by the Ranelagh Gardens, near Putney in 1775.

Most Olympic medals ■ Six oarsmen have won three gold medals: John B. Kelly (USA) (1889–1960), father of the late HSH Princess Grace of Monaco, Single Sculls (1920) and Double Sculls (1920 and 1924); his cousin Paul Vincent Costello (USA) (b. 27 Dec 1894), Double Sculls (1920, 1924 and 1928); Jack Beresford, Jr (GB) (1899–1977), Single sculls (1924), Coxless fours (1932) and Double Sculls (1936), Vyacheslav Ivanov (USSR) (b. 30 Jul 1938), Single Sculls (1956, 1960 and 1964); Siegfried Brietzke (GDR) (b. 12 Jun 1952), Coxless Pairs (1972) and Coxless Fours (1976, 1980); and Pertti Karppinen (Finland) (b. 17 Feb 1953), Single Sculls 1976, 1980 and 1984.

World Championships ■ World rowing championships distinct from the Olympic Games were first held in 1962, at first four yearly, but from 1974 annually, except in Olympic years.

The most gold medals won at World Championships and Olympic Games is six by the GDR oarsmen: the twins Bernd and Jörg Landvoigt (b. 23 Mar 1951); Joachim Dreifke (b. 26 Dec 1952); Karl-Heinz Bussert (b. 8 Jan 1955); Ulrich Diessner (b. 27 Dec 1954); Siegfried Brietzke (b. 12 Jun 1952); and Wolfgang Mager (b. 24 Aug 1952); and at lightweight events by Ruggero Verroca (Italy) (b. 3 Jan 1961).

The most wins at Single Sculls is five, by Peter-Michael Kolbe (West Germany) (b. 2 Aug 1953), 1975, 1978, 1981, 1983 and 1986,and by Pertti Karppinen, 1979 and 1985 with his three Olympic wins (above), and in the women's events by Christine Hahn (*née* Scheiblich) (GDR) (b. 31 Dec 1954), 1974–5, 1977–8 (and the 1976 Olympic title).

Boat Race ■ The earliest University Boat Race, which Oxford won, was from Hambledon Lock to Henley Bridge on 10 Jun 1829. Outrigged eights were first used in 1846. In the 135 races to 1989,

Cambridge won 69 times, Oxford 65 times and there was a dead heat on 24 Mar 1877.

The race record time for the course of 6·779 km *4 miles 374 yd* (Putney to Mortlake) is 16 min 45 sec by Oxford on 18 Mar 1984. This represents an average speed of 24·28 km/h *15·09 mph*. The smallest winning margin has been by a canvas by Oxford in 1952 and 1980. The greatest margin (apart from sinking) was Cambridge's win by 20 lengths in 1900.

Boris Rankov (Oxford, 1978–83) rowed in a record six winning boats. Susan Brown (b. 29 Jun 1958), the first woman to take part, coxed the winning Oxford boats in 1981 and 1982. Daniel Topolski coached Oxford to ten successive victories, 1976–85.

The tallest man ever to row in a University boat has been Gavin Stewart (Wadham, Oxford) (b. 25 Feb 1963) at 2·04 m *6 ft 8½ in* in 1987–8. The heaviest was Toby Backhouse (Magdalene, Cambridge) (b. 10 Jun 1969) who weighed 106·5 kg *235 lb* in 1989. The lightest oarsman was the 1882 Oxford Stroke, Alfred Herbert Higgins, at 60 kg *9 st 6½ lb*. The lightest coxes, Francis Henry Archer (Cambridge) (1843–89) in 1862 and Hart Parker Vincent Massey (Oxford) (b. Canada, 30 Mar 1918) in 1939, were both 32·6 kg *5 st 2 lb*.

The youngest 'blue' ever was Matthew John Brittin (Cambridge) (b. 1 Sep 1968) at 18 yr 208 days, in 1986.

Head of the River ■ A processional race for eights instituted in 1926, the Head has an entry limit of 420 crews (3780 competitors). The record for the course Mortlake–Putney (the reverse of the Boat Race) is 16 min 37 sec by the ARA National Squad in 1987.

Henley Royal Regatta ■ The annual regatta at Henley-on-Thames, Oxfordshire, was inaugurated on 26 Mar 1839. Since then the course, except in 1923, has been about 2112 m *1 mile 550 yd*, varying slightly according to the length of boat. In 1967 the shorter craft were 'drawn up' so all bows start level.

The most wins in the Diamond Challenge Sculls

Henley Royal Regatta ● The famous regatta celebrated its 150th anniversary in 1989 having been inaugurated on 26 Mar 1839. It was the result of the local interest in rowing which began when the first Oxford and Cambridge Boat race was held in 1829 and which attracted some 20 000 spectators to Henley.

Despite four changes, the course length has remained 1 mile 550 yd throughout its history (except in 1923) and this curious distance relates to the fact that it was the longest stretch of water available in 1839.

The premier event at Henley, the Grand Challenge Cup for eights, dates from the first regatta. (Photo: All-Sport/Oli Tennent)

(instituted 1844) is six consecutively by Stuart A. Mackenzie (Australia and GB) (b. 5 Apr 1937), 1957–62. The record time is 7 min 23 sec by Vaclav Chalupa (Czechoslovakia) on 2 Jul 1989. The record time for the Grand Challenge Cup (instituted 1839) event is 5 min 58 sec by Hansa Dortmund, West Germany on 2 Jul 1989.

Sculling ■ The record number of wins in the Wingfield Sculls (Putney to Mortlake) (instituted 1830) is seven by Jack Beresford, Jr from 1920 to 1926. The fastest time for the course has been 20 min 16 sec by Steven Redgrave (b. 23 Mar 1962) in winning his fifth Wingfield Sculls in 1989.

Highest speed ■ The highest recorded speed on non-tidal water for 2000 m *2187 yd* is by an American eight in 5 min 27·14 sec (22·01 km/h *13·68 mph*) at Lucerne, Switzerland on 17 Jun 1984. A crew from Penn AC, USA, was timed in 5 min 18·8 sec (22·58 km/h *14·03 mph*) in the FISA Championships on the River Meuse, Liège, Belgium on 17 Aug 1930.

24 hours ■ The greatest distance rowed in 24 hours (upstream and downstream) by an eight is 209 km *130 miles* by members of the Renmark Rowing Club, South Australia on 20–21 Apr 1984.

Cross Channel ■ Ivor Lloyd sculled across the

English Channel in a record 3 hr 35 min 1 sec on 4 May 1983.

River Thames ■ Malcom Knight, Simon Leifer and Kevin Thomas rowed the navigable length of the Thames, 299·14 km *185·88 miles*, from Lechlade Bridge, Gloucestershire to Southend Pier, Essex in 39 hr 27 min 12 sec in a skiff from 10–11 May 1988. The fastest time from Folly Bridge, Oxford to Westminster Bridge, London (180 km *112 miles*) is 14 hr 25 min 15 sec by an eight from Kingston Rowing Club on 1 Feb 1986.

Longest race ■ The longest annual rowing race is the annual Tour du Lac Leman, Geneva, Switzerland for coxed fours (the five-man crew taking turns as cox) over 160 km *99 miles*. The record winning time is 12 hr 52 min by LAGA Delft, Netherlands on 3 Oct 1982.

International Dragon Boat Races ■ Instituted in 1975 and held annually in Hong Kong, the fastest time achieved for the 640 metres *700 yd* course is 2 min 27·45 sec by the Chinese Shun De team on 30 Jun 1985. The best time for a British team was 2 min 49·22 sec by the Kingston and Wey Dragon Boat Crew on 26 Jun 1988. Teams have 28 members – 26 rowers, one steersman and one drummer.

Rugby League

There have been four different scoring systems in Rugby League football. For the purpose of these records all points totals remain as they were under the system in operation at the time they were made.

The Northern Rugby Football Union was formed on 29 Aug 1895 at the George Hotel, Huddersfield, West Yorkshire. Twenty-one clubs from Yorkshire and Lancashire were present and all but one agreed to resign from the Rugby Union. Payment for loss of wages was the major cause of the breakaway and full professionalism was allowed in 1898. A reduction in the number of players from 15 to 13 took place in 1906. The title 'Rugby Football League' was adopted in 1922.

Most titles ■ There have been eight World Cup Competitions. Australia have most wins, with five, 1957, 1968, 1970, 1977 and 1988 as well as a win in the International Championship of 1975.

The Northern Rugby League was formed in 1901. The word 'Northern' was dropped in 1980. Wigan have won the League Championship a record ten times (1909, 1922, 1926, 1934, 1946, 1947, 1950, 1952, 1960 and 1987).

In the Rugby League Challenge Cup (inaugurated 1896/7 season) a record ten titles have been won by; Leeds, 1910, 1923, 1932, 1936, 1941–2 (wartime), 1957, 1968, 1977–8; and Wigan, 1924, 1929, 1948, 1951, 1958–9, 1965, 1985, 1988–9. Oldham is the only club to appear in four consecutive Cup Finals (1924–7).

Since 1974 there have been five major competitions for RL clubs: Challenge Cup, League Championship, Premiership, John Player Special Trophy and County Cups. Wigan has a record 45 wins in these competitions, and won four, the League Championship, John Player Special Trophy, Lancashire Cup and Premiership in 1986/7.

Three clubs have won all possible major Rugby League trophies in one season: Hunslet, 1907/8 season, Huddersfield, 1914/15 and Swinton, 1927/8, all won the Challenge Cup, League Championship, County Cup and County League (now defunct).

HIGHEST SCORES

Senior match ■ The highest aggregate score in a game where a senior club has been concerned was 121 points, when Huddersfield beat Swinton Park Rangers by 119 (19 goals, 27 tries) to 2 (one goal) in the first round of the Northern Union Cup on 28 Feb 1914. The highest score in League football is 112 points by Leeds v. Coventry (nil) on 12 Apr 1913. St Helens beat Carlisle 112–0 in the Lancashire Cup on 14 Sep 1986.

Challenge Cup Final ■ The highest score in a Challenge Cup Final is 38 points (8 tries, 7 goals) by Wakefield Trinity v. Hull (5) at Wembley, Middlesex on 14 May 1960. The record aggregate is 52 points when Wigan beat Hull 28–24 at Wembley on 4 May 1985. The greatest winning margin was 34 points when Huddersfield beat St Helens 37–3 at Oldham, Greater Manchester on 1 May 1915.

International match ■ The highest score in an international match is Australia's 70–8 defeat of Papua New Guinea in World Cup match at Wagga Wagga, Australia on 20 Jul 1988. Great Britain's highest score in an international is the 53–19 win over New Zealand at Hameau, Paris, France on 4 Nov 1972.

Touring teams ■ The record score for a British team touring Australasia is 101 points by England v. South Australia (nil) at Adelaide in May 1914. The record for a touring team in Britain is 92 (10 goals, 24 tries) by Australia against Bramley 7 (2 goals and 1 try) at the Barley Mow Ground, Bramley, near Leeds on 9 Nov 1921.

Most points *Season* ■ Leigh scored a record 1436 points (258 tries, 199 goals, 6 drop goals) in the 1985/6 season, playing in 43 Cup and League games.

HIGHEST INDIVIDUAL SCORES

Most points, goals and tries in a game ■ George Henry 'Tich' West (1882–1927) scored 53 points (10 goals and a record 11 tries) for Hull Kingston Rovers (73) in a Challenge Cup tie v. Brookland Rovers (5) on 4 Mar 1905.

The record for a League match is 39 (5 tries, 12 goals) by Jimmy Lomas (1880–1960) in Salford's 78–0 win over Liverpool City on 2 Feb 1907.

The most goals in a Cup match is 22 kicked by James 'Jim' Sullivan (1903–77) for Wigan v. Flimby and Fothergill on 14 Feb 1925. The most goals in a League match is 15 by Michael Stacey (b. 9 Feb 1953) for Leigh v. Doncaster on 28 Mar 1976. The most tries in a League match is ten by Lionel

Cooper (b. Australia, 1922–87) for Huddersfield v. Keighley on 17 Nov 1951.

Most points *Season & career* ■ The record number of points in a season was 496 by Benjamin Lewis Jones (Leeds) (b. 11 Apr 1931), 194 goals, 36 tries, in 1956/7.

Neil Fox (b. 4 May 1939) scored 6220 points (2575 goals including 4 drop goals, 358 tries) in a senior Rugby League career from 10 Apr 1956 to 19 Aug 1979, consisting of 4488 for Wakefield Trinity, 1089 for five other clubs, 228 for Great Britain, 147 for Yorkshire and 268 in other representative games.

Most tries *Season & career* ■ Albert Aaron Rosenfeld (1885–1970) (Huddersfield), an Australian-born wing-threequarter, scored 80 tries in 42 matches in the 1913/14 season.

Brian Bevan (b. Australia, 24 Apr 1924), a wing-threequarter, scored 796 tries in 18 seasons (16 with Warrington, two with Blackpool Borough) from 1945 to 1964. He scored 740 for Warrington, 17 for Blackpool and 39 in representative matches.

Most goals *Season & career* ■ The record number of goals in a season is 221, in 47 matches, by David Watkins (b. 5 Mar 1942) (Salford) in the 1972/3 season.

Jim Sullivan (Wigan) kicked 2867 goals in his club and representative career, 1921–46.

Most consecutive scores ■ David Watkins (Salford) played and scored in every club game during seasons 1972/3 and 1973/4, contributing 41 tries and 403 goals – a total of 929 points, in 92 games.

Individual international records ■ Jim Sullivan (Wigan) played in most internationals (60 for Wales and Great Britain, 1921–39), kicked most goals (160) and scored most points (329).

Michael Sullivan (no kin) (b. 12 Jan 1934) of Huddersfield, Wigan, St Helens and York played in 51 international games for England and Great Britain and scored a record 45 tries, 1954–63.

Michael O'Connor (b. 30 Nov 1960) scored a record 30 points (4 tries, 7 goals) for Australia v. Papua New Guinea at Wagga Wagga, Australia on 20 Jul 1988.

Most Challenge Cup Finals ■ Eric Batten (b. 13 Jun 1914) (Leeds, Bradford Northern and Featherstone Rovers) played in a record eight Challenge Cup Finals including war-time guest appearances between 1941 and 1952 and was on four winning sides.

Eight players have been in four Challenge Cup winning sides – Alan Edwards, Eric Batten, Alex Murphy, Brian Lockwood, Mick Adams, Keith Elwell, Eric Hughes and Andy Gregory. Alan Edwards (b. 15 May 1916) was the only one to do so with four different clubs, Salford 1938, Leeds 1942, Dewsbury 1943, Bradford Northern 1949.

Youngest and oldest players ■ Harold Spencer Edmonson (1903–82) played his first League game for Bramley at 15 yr 81 days. The youngest representative player was Harold Wagstaff (1891–1939) who played for Yorkshire at 17 yr 141 days, and for England at 17 yr 228 days.

The youngest player in a Cup Final was Shaun Edwards (b. 17 Oct 1966) at 17 yr 201 days for Wigan when they lost 6–19 to Widnes at Wembley on 5 May 1984. He became the youngest Great Britain international when he played against France at Headingley, Leeds on 1 Mar 1985 at 18 yr 135 days.

The oldest player for Great Britain was Jeffrey Grayshon (b. 4 Mar 1949) at 36 yr 250 days v. New Zealand at Elland Road, Leeds on 9 Nov 1985.

Most durable player ■ The most appearances for one club is 774 by Jim Sullivan for Wigan, 1921–46. He played a record 928 first-class games in all. The longest continuous playing career is that of Augustus John 'Gus' Risman (b. 21 Mar 1911), who played his first game for Salford on 31 Aug 1929 and his last for Batley on 27 Dec 1954.

Keith Elwell (b. 12 Feb 1950) played in 239 consecutive games for Widnes from 5 May 1977 to 5 Sep 1982. In his career, 1972–85, he received a record 28 winners' or runners-up medals in major competitions.

Most and least successful teams ■ Wigan won 31 consecutive league games from February 1970 to February 1971. Huddersfield were undefeated for 40 league and cup games in 1913/14. Hull is the only club to win all League games in a season, 26 in Division II 1978/9. Doncaster holds the record of losing 40 consecutive League games from 16 Nov 1975 to 21 Apr 1977.

Record transfer fee ■ The highest transfer fee between two rugby league clubs has been £155 000 (plus VAT) paid by Leeds to Hull for centre Gary Edward Schofield (b. 1 Jul 1965) on 23 Oct 1987.

Jonathan Davies joined Widnes from the rugby union club Llanelli on 5 Jan 1989. The signing-on fee was reported at being in the region of £200 000 but has never been confirmed.

Greatest crowds ■ The greatest attendance at any Rugby League match is 102 569 for the Warrington v. Halifax Challenge Cup Final replay at Odsal Stadium, Bradford on 5 May 1954.

The record attendance for any international match is 70 204 for the First Test between Australia and England on the Sydney Cricket Ground on 6 Jun 1932. The highest international attendance in Britain is 50 583 for the First Test between Great Britain and Australia at Old Trafford, Manchester on 25 Oct 1986.

AMATEUR RUGBY LEAGUE

The British Amateur Rugby League Association (BARLA) was formed in 1973 'to foster, develop,

extend and control amateur rugby league football in Great Britain'. Prior to that year the ultimate control of amateurs as well as professionals rested with the Rugby Football League. A National League was formed in 1986/7.

National Cup ■ Pilkington Recreation (St Helens, Merseyside) have won the National Cup four times (1975, 1979, 1980, 1982). John McCabe (b. 26 Jan 1952) has played in a record five National Cup finals, winning on each occasion. He played for Pilkington Recreation in each of their four successes and captained Thatto Heath (St Helens, Merseyside) to victory in 1987.

Highest score *Major competition* ■ Humberside beat Carlisle by 138 points to nil in the second round of the National Inter-league Competition on 20 Oct 1984.

Rugby Union

Records are determined in terms of present-day scoring values, i.e. a try at 4 points; a dropped goal, penalty or goal from a mark at 3 points; and a conversion at 2 points. The *actual* score, in accordance with whichever of the eight earlier systems was in force at the time, is also given, in brackets.

Although there are records of a game with many similarities to rugby dating back to the Roman occupation, the game is traditionally said to have originated from a breach of the rules of the football played in November 1823 at Rugby School by William Webb Ellis (later the Rev.) (c. 1807–72). This handling code of football evolved gradually and was known to have been played at Cambridge University by 1839. The Rugby Football Union was founded on 26 Jan 1871. The International Rugby Football Board (IRFB) was founded in 1886.

WORLD CUP

The inaugural World Cup was contested in Australia and New Zealand by 16 national teams in 1987. The final in Auckland on 20 Jun 1987 was won by New Zealand, who beat France 29–9. The highest team score was New Zealand's 74–13 victory over Fiji at Christchurch on 27 May 1987. They scored ten goals, two tries and two penalty goals. The individual match record was 30 (3 tries, 9 conversions) by Didier Camberabero (France) (b. 9 Jan 1961) v. Zimbabwe at Auckland on 2 Jun 1987. The leading scorer in the tournament was the New Zealand goal-kicker Grant James Fox (b. 6 Jun 1962), with 126 points.

INTERNATIONAL CHAMPIONSHIP

The International Championship was first contested by England, Ireland, Scotland and Wales in 1884. France first played in 1910.

Wales has won a record 21 times outright and tied for first a further 11 times to 1988. Since 1910 Wales

has 15 wins and ten ties and England 15 wins and seven ties. The most Grand Slams, winning all four matches, is eight by England. Wales also have eight but these include two in 1908–9, before the entry of France.

Highest team score ■ The highest score in an International Championship match was set at Swansea on 1 Jan 1910 when Wales beat France 49–14 or 59–16 on present-day scoring values (8 goals, 1 penalty goal, 2 tries, to 1 goal, 2 penalty goals, 1 try).

Season's scoring ■ Jean-Patrick Lescarboura (France) (b. 12 Mar 1961) scored a record 54 points (10 penalty goals, 6 conversions, 4 dropped goals) in 1984.

Individual match records ■ William John 'Billy' Bancroft (1871–1959) kicked a record nine goals (8 conversions and 1 penalty goal) for Wales v. France at Swansea in 1910.

HIGHEST TEAM SCORES

Internationals ■ The highest score in any full international was when New Zealand beat Japan by 106–4 at Tokyo, Japan on 1 Nov 1987, although New Zealand did not award caps. France beat Paraguay 106–12 at Asuncion, Paraguay on 28 Jun 1988.

The highest aggregate score for any international match between the Four Home Unions is 69 when England beat Wales by 69 points (7 goals, 1 drop goal and 6 tries) to nil at Blackheath, London on 19 Feb 1881. (Note: there was no point scoring in 1881.) The highest score under the modern points system between IRFB members is 63, when New Zealand beat Wales 54–9 at Auckland, New Zealand on 11 Jun 1988. The highest score by any overseas side in an international in the British Isles is 53 points (7 goals, 1 drop goal and 2 tries) to nil when South Africa beat Scotland at Murrayfield, Edinburgh on 24 Nov 1951 (44–0).

Tour match ■ The record score for any international tour match is 125–0 (17 goals, 5 tries and 1 penalty goal) (103–0) when New Zealand beat Northern New South Wales at Quirindi, Australia on 30 May 1962. The highest under scoring in use for the game is 117–6 for New Zealand's defeat of South Australia on 1 May 1974.

Match ■ In Denmark, Comet beat Lindo by 194–0 on 17 Nov 1973. The highest British score is 174–0 by 7th Signal Regiment v. 4th Armoured Workshop, REME, on 5 Nov 1980 at Herford, West Germany. Scores of over 200 points have been recorded in school matches, for example Radford School beat Hills Court 214 points (31 goals and 7 tries) to nil (200–0) on 20 Nov 1886. The highest score in the Courage Club Championship is 146–0 by Billingham against Hartlepool Athletic in a Durham/Northumberland Division 3 match at Billingham, Durham on 3 Oct 1987.

Season ■ The highest number of points accumulated in a season by a club is 1917 points (including a record 345 tries) in 47 games by Neath, West Glamorgan in 1988/9.

MOST INTERNATIONAL APPEARANCES

Country	Caps	Player	Years
FRANCE	70†	Serge Blanco (b. 31 Aug 1958)	1980–89
IRELAND	69	Cameron Michael Henderson Gibson (b. 3 Dec 1942)	1964–79
NEW ZEALAND	55	Colin Earl Meads (b. 3 Jun 1936)	1957–71
WALES	55*	John Peter Rhys 'JPR' Williams (b. 2 Mar 1949)	1969–81
SCOTLAND	51	Andrew Robertson Irvine (b. 16 Sep 1951)	1973–82
	51	James Menzies 'Jim' Renwick (b. 12 Feb 1952)	1972–83
AUSTRALIA	49	Simon Paul Poidevin (b. 31 Oct 1958)	1980–88
ENGLAND	43	Anthony Neary (b. 25 Nov 1948)	1971–80
SOUTH AFRICA	38	Frederick Christoffel Hendrick Du Preez (b. 28 Nov 1935)	1960–71
	38	Jan Hendrik Ellis (b. 5 Jan 1943)	1965–76

* *Gareth Owen Edwards (b. 12 Jul 1947) made a record 53 consecutive international appearances, never missing a match throughout his career for Wales, 1967–78. Willie John McBride also had 53 consecutive appearances during his 63 games for Ireland.*

† *France enumerate international caps against all nations, whereas the figures for the seven members for the IRFB include only matches against each other. Blanco has played 51 matches v. IRFB member nations, for which the French record is 52 by Roland Bertranne (b. 6 Dec 1949).*

HIGHEST INDIVIDUAL SCORES

Internationals ■ Phil Bennett (Wales) (b. 24 Oct 1948) scored 34 points (2 tries, 10 conversions, 2 penalty goals) for Wales v. Japan at Tokyo on 24 Sep 1975, when Wales won 82–6. The highest individual points score in any match between members of the International Board is 26 by Allan Roy Hewson (b. 6 Jun 1954) (1 try, 2 conversions, 5 penalty goals and a drop goal) for New Zealand against Australia at Auckland on 11 Sep 1982.

Patrice Lagisquet (b. 4 Sep 1962) scored seven tries for France v. Paraguay on 28 Jun 1988. The most tries in an international match between IRFB members is five by George Campbell Lindsay (1863–1905) for Scotland v. Wales on 26 Feb 1887, and by Douglas 'Daniel' Lambert (1883–1915) for England v. France on 5 Jan 1907. Ian Scott Smith (Scotland) (1903–72) scored a record six consecutive international tries in 1925, comprising the last three v. France and two weeks later, the first three v. Wales. The most tries in an international career is 32 by David Campese (b. 21 Oct 1962) for Australia, 14 Aug 1982–June 1989.

In all internationals Hugo Porta (b. 1951) scored a record 479 points in 48 matches for Argentina, 1973–88, including 376 in 39 against IRB teams. Andrew Robertson Irvine (Heriots) (b. 16 Sep 1951) scored 301 points, a career record in inter-IRFB internationals, 273 for Scotland (including 12 v. Romania) and 28 for the British Lions, from 1973 to 1982.

Season ■ The first-class season scoring record is 581 points by Samuel Arthur Doble (1944–77) of Moseley, in 52 matches in 1971/2. He also scored 47 points for England in South Africa out of season.

Andy Higgin (b. 4 Mar 1963) scored a record 28 drop goals in a season in first-class rugby, for the Vale of Lune in 1986/7.

Career ■ William Henry 'Dusty' Hare (b. 29 Nov 1952) scored 7337 points in first-class games from 1971–88, comprising 1800 for Nottingham, 4427 for Leicester, 240 for England, 88 for the British Lions and 782 in other representative matches.

Most tries ■ Alan John Morley (b. 25 Jun 1950) has scored 473 tries in senior rugby in 1968–86 including 378 for Bristol, a record for one club. John Huins scored 85 tries in 1953–4, 73 for St Luke's College, Exeter and 12 more for Neath and in trial games.

Match ■ Jannie van der Westhuizen scored 80 points (14 tries, 9 conversions, 1 dropped goal, 1 penalty goal) for Carnarvon (88) v. Williston (12) at North West Cape, South Africa on 11 March 1972.

In a junior house match in February 1967 at William Ellis School, Edgware, Greater London, between Cumberland and Nunn, Thanos Morphitis, 12, contributed 90 points (13 tries and 19 conversions) (77) to Cumberland's winning score.

All-rounder ■ Canadian international Barrie Burnham scored all possible ways—try, conversion, penalty goal, drop goal, goal from mark—for Meralomas v. Georgians (20–11) at Vancouver, BC on 26 Feb 1966.

Most international appearances ■ Cameron Michael Henderson Gibson (b. 3 Dec 1942) played in 69 internationals for Ireland, 1964–79, a record for matches between the seven member countries of the 'International Rugby Football Board' and France. Including 12 appearances for the British Lions, he played in a total of 81 international matches. Willie John McBride (b. 6 Jun 1940) made a record 17 appearances for the British Lions, as well as 63 for Ireland.

Youngest international ■ Edinburgh Academy pupils Ninian Jamieson Finlay (1858–1936) and Charles Reid (1864–1909) were both 17 yr 36 days old when they played for Scotland v. England in 1875 and 1881 respectively. However, as Finlay had one less leap year in his lifetime up to his first cap,

the outright record must be credited to him. Daniel Brendan Carroll (b. 17 Feb 1892) was aged only 16 yr 149 days when he played for Australia in the 1908 Olympic Games rugby tournament—not considered to be a 'full' international.

County Championships ■ The County Championships (instituted 1889) have been won most often by Gloucestershire with 15 titles (1910, 1913, 1920–2, 1930–2, 1937, 1972, 1974–6 and 1983–4). The most individual appearances is 104 by Richard Trickey (Sale) (b. 6 Mar 1945) for Lancashire between 1964 and 1978.

Club Championships ■ The most outright wins in the RFU Club Competition (John Player Cup, 1971–87, now Pilkington Cup) is five by Bath, 1984–7, 1989. In the latter season they completed the double having won the English league title, the Courage Clubs Championship, which was founded in the 1987/8 season, when the winners were Leicester. The most wins in the Welsh Rugby Union Challenge Cup (Schweppes Welsh Cup, instituted 1971/2) is six, by Llanelli, 1973–6, 1985 and 1988. The most wins in the Scottish League Division One (instituted 1973/4) is ten by Hawick between 1973 and 1987.

Seven-a-sides *Origins* ■ Seven-a-side rugby dates from 28 Apr 1883 when Melrose RFC Borders, in order to alleviate the poverty of a club in such a small town, staged a seven-a-side tournament. The idea was that of Ned Haig, the town's butcher.

Hong Kong Sevens ■ This, the world's most prestigious international tournament for seven-a-side teams, was first held in 1976. The record of five wins is held by Australia, 1979, 1982–3, 1985 and 1988.

Middlesex Seven-a-sides ■ The Middlesex Seven-a-sides were inaugurated in 1926 and have been won a record 12 times by Harlequins, 1926–9, 1933, 1935, 1967, 1978, 1986–9.

Greatest crowd ■ The record paying attendance is 104 000 for Scotland's 12–10 win over Wales at Murrayfield, Edinburgh on 1 Mar 1975.

Highest posts ■ The world's highest rugby union goal posts are 33·54 m *110 ft ½ in* high at the Roan Antelope Rugby Union Club, Luanshya, Zambia. The posts at Brixham RFC, Devon are 17·37 m *57 ft* high with an additional 0·30 m *1 ft* spike.

Longest kicks ■ The longest recorded successful drop goal is 82 m *90 yd* by Gerald Hamilton 'Gerry' Brand (b. 8 Oct 1906) for South Africa v. England at Twickenham, Greater London, on 2 Jan 1932. This was taken 6 m *7 yd* inside the England

'half', 50 m *55 yd* from the posts, and dropped over the dead ball line.

The place kick record is reputed to be 91 m *100 yd* at Richmond Athletic Ground, London, by Douglas Francis Theodore Morkel (1886–1950) in an unsuccessful penalty for South Africa v. Surrey on 19 Dec 1906. This was not measured until 1932. In the match Bridlington School 1st XV v. an Army XV at Bridlington, Humberside on 29 Jan 1944, Ernie Cooper (b. 21 May 1926), captaining the school, landed a penalty from a measured 74 m *81 yd* from the post with a kick which carried over the dead ball line. The record in an international was set at 64·22 m *70 yd 8½ in* by Paul Huw Thorburn (b. 24 Nov 1962) for Wales v. Scotland on 1 Feb 1986.

Fastest try ■ The fastest try in an international game was when Herbert Leo 'Bart' Price (1899–1943) scored for England v. Wales at Twickenham on 20 Jan 1923 less than 10 sec after kick–off.

Longest try ■ The longest 'try' ever executed by a team of 15, was by the Royal Military Police Training Centre RFC who ran a try of 2737·123 km *1700·816 miles* at Chichester, West Sussex from 1–11 Jan 1989. There were no forward passes or knock-ons, and the ball was touched down between the posts in the prescribed manner (Law 12).

Most successful team ■ The Feilding senior 4ths of New Zealand played 108 successive games without defeat from 1984–9. The Chiltern Under-11 mini rugby side have, since their formation as an Under-8 side, played 180 games without defeat to the end of the 1989 season. They have conceded points in only 13 of these matches and averaged 25·7 points a match.

GUINNESS HAVE PUBLISHED **RUGBY: THE RECORDS** CHRIS RHYS £8.95

Shinty

Origins ■ Shinty (from the Gaelic *sinteag*, a bound) has roots reaching back more than 2000 years to the ancient game of *camanachd*, the sport of the curved stick, the diversion of the heroes of Celtic history and legend. It was effective battle training, exercising speed and co-ordination of eye and arm along with aggression and cool self-control. In spite of the break-up of the clan system in the Highlands of Scotland, the 'ball plays', involving whole parishes, without limit in number or time except the fall of night, continued in areas such as Lochaber, Badenoch and Strathglass. Whisky and the inspiration of the bagpipes were important ingredients of these occasions. The ruling body of this apparently ungovernable game was established in 1893 when the Camanachd Association was set up at Kingussie, Highland.

Most titles ■ Newtonmore, Highland has won the Camanachd Association Challenge Cup (instituted 1896) a record 28 times, 1907–86. Johnnie Campbell, David Ritchie and Hugh Chisholm, all of Newtonmore, have won a record 11 winners' medals. In 1923 the Furnace Club, Argyll won the cup without conceding a goal throughout the competition.

In 1984 Kingussie Camanachd Club won all five senior competitions, including the Camanachd Cup Final. This feat was equalled by Newtonmore in 1985.

Highest scores ■ The highest Scottish Cup Final score was in 1909 when Newtonmore beat Furnace 11–3 at Glasgow, Dr Johnnie Cattanach scoring eight hails or goals. In 1938 John Macmillan Mactaggart scored ten hails for Mid-Argyll in a Camanachd Cup match.

Shooting

The Lucerne Shooting Guild (Switzerland) was formed c. 1466 and the first recorded shooting match was at Zurich in 1472.

Most Olympic medals ■ The record number of medals won is 11 by Carl Townsend Osburn (USA) (1884–1966) in 1912, 1920 and 1924, consisting of five gold, four silver and two bronze. Six other marksmen have won five gold medals. The only marksman to win three individual gold medals has been Gudbrand Gudbrandsönn Skatteboe (Norway) (1875–1965) in 1906. Separate events for women were first held in 1984.

Bisley ■ The National Rifle Association was instituted in 1859. The Queen's (King's) Prize has been shot since 1860 and has only once been won by a woman, Marjorie Elaine Foster (1894–1974) (score 280) on 19 Jul 1930. Arthur George Fulton (1887–1972) won three times (1912, 1926, 1931). Both his father and his son also won the Prize.

The highest score (possible 300) for the final of the Queen's Prize is 295 by Lindsay Peden (Scotland) on 24 Jul 1982. The record for the Silver Medals is 150 (possible 150) by Martin John Brister (City Rifle Club) (b. 1951) and (Lord) John Swansea (b. 1 Jan 1925) on 24 Jul 1971. This was equalled by John Henry Carmichael (WRA Bromsgrave RC) on 28 Jul 1979 and Robert Stafford on 26 Jul 1980, with the size of the bullseyes reduced.

Small-bore ■ The National Small-Bore Rifle Association, of Britain, was formed in 1901. The British team record (1966 target) is 1988 × 2000 by Lancashire in 1968–9 and London in 1980–1. The British individual small-bore rifle record for 60 shots prone is 600 ×600, first achieved by John Palin (b. 16 Jul 1934) in Switzerland in 1972. Richard Hansen shot 5000 bullseyes in 24 hr at Fresno, California, USA on 13 Jun 1929.

Clay pigeon ■ Most world titles have been won by Susan Nattrass (Canada) (b. 5 Nov 1950) with six, 1974–5, 1977–9, 1981. The record number of clay birds shot in an hour is 2312 by Colin Hewish at the Street and District Gun Club, Ivythorn, Somerset on 8 May 1988.

The maximum 200/200 was achieved by Ricardo Ruiz Rumoroso at the Spanish Clay Pigeon Championships at Zaragossa on 12 Jun 1983.

Noel D. Townend achieved the maximum 200 consecutive down-the-line targets at Nottingham on 21 Aug 1983.

Bench rest shooting ■ The smallest group on record at 914 m *1000 yd* is 11·11 cm *4·375 in* by Earl Chronister with a ·30–378 Weatherby Mag at Williamsport, Pennsylvania, USA on 12 Jul 1987.

Highest score in 24 hr ■ The Easingwold Rifle and Pistol Club team of John Smith, Edward Kendall, Phillip Kendall and Paul Duffield scored 120 242 points (averaging 95·66 per card) on 6–7 Aug 1983.

Skiing

The most ancient ski in existence was found well preserved in a peat bog at Hoting, Sweden, dating from c. 2500 BC. The earliest recorded military use of skiing was at the Battle of Isen, near Oslo, Norway in 1200. The Trysil Shooting and Skiing Club, founded in Norway in 1861, claims it is the world's oldest. The oldest ski competitions are the Holmenkøllen Nordic events which were first held in 1866. The first downhill races were staged in Australia in the 1850s. The International Ski Federation (FIS) was founded on 2 Feb 1924, succeeding the International Skiing Commission, founded at Christiania (Oslo), Norway on 18 Feb 1910. The Ski Club of Great Britain was founded on 6 May 1903. The National Ski Federation of Great Britain was formed in 1964 and changed its name to the British Ski Federation in 1981.

Most titles *World/Olympic Championships—*

Alpine ■ The World Alpine Championships were inaugurated at Mürren, Switzerland, in 1931. The greatest number of titles won has been by Christel Cranz (b. 1 Jul 1914) of Germany, with seven individual – four slalom (1934, 1937–9) and three downhill (1935, 1937, 1939), and five combined (1934–5, 1937–9). She also won the gold medal for the Combined in the 1936 Olympics. The most won by a man is seven by Anton 'Toni' Sailer (Austria) (b. 17 Nov 1935), who won all four in 1956 (giant slalom, slalom, downhill and the non-Olympic Alpine combination) and the downhill, giant slalom and combined in 1958.

World/Olympic Championships—Nordic ■ The first World Nordic Championships were those of the 1924 Winter Olympics in Chamonix, France. The greatest number of titles won is nine by Galina Kulakova (USSR) (b. 29 Apr 1942) in 1970–8. The most medals is 21 by Raisa Smetanina (USSR) (b. 29 Feb 1952) including six gold, 1974–88. The most titles won by a man is ten by Gunde Svan (Sweden) (b. 12 Jan 1962), individual; 15 km 1989, 30km 1985, 50 km 1985 and 1989, and Olympics, 15 km 1984, 50 km 1988: and relays; 4 × 10 km, 1987 and 1989, and Olympics, 1984 and 1988. Johan Grøttumsbraaten (1899–1942) of Norway won six individual titles (two 18 km cross-country, four Nordic combined) in 1926–32. The record for a jumper is five by Birger Ruud (b. 23 Aug 1911) of Norway, in 1931–2 and 1935–7. Ruud is the only person to win Olympic events in each of the dissimilar Alpine and Nordic disciplines. In 1936 he won the Ski-jumping and the Alpine downhill (which was not then a separate event, but only a segment of the Combined event).

World Cup ■ The World Cup was introduced for Alpine events in 1967 and for Nordic events in 1981. The most individual event wins is 86 (46 giant slalom, 40 slalom) by Ingemar Stenmark (Sweden) (b. 18 Mar 1956) in 1974–89, including a men's record 13 in one season in 1978/9, of which 10 were part of a record 14 successive giant slalom wins from 18 Mar 1978, his 22nd birthday, to 21 Jan 1980. Franz Klammer (Austria) (b. 3 Dec 1953) won a record 25 downhill races, 1974–84. Annemarie Moser (née Pröll) (Austria) (b. 27 Mar 1953) won a women's record 62 individual event wins, 1970–9. She had a record 11 consecutive downhill wins from Dec 1972 to Jan 1974. Vreni Schneider (Switzerland) (b. 26 Nov 1964) in the 1988/9 season won a record 13 events and a combined including all seven slalom events.

SHOOTING–INDIVIDUAL WORLD RECORDS

In 1986, the International Shooting Union introduced new regulations for determining major championships and world records. Now the leading competitors undertake an additional round with a target sub-divided to tenths of a point for rifle and pistol shooting, and an extra 25 shots for trap and skeet. The table below shows the world records for the 13 Olympic shooting disciplines, giving in brackets the score for the number of shots specified plus the score in the additional round.

MEN

Event	Score	(Breakdown)	Name	Place	Date	Year
FREE RIFLE 50 m 3 × 40 shots	1283·4	(1183 +100·4)	Petr Kurka (Czechoslovakia)	Seoul, South Korea	1 Oct	1987
FREE RIFLE 50 m 60 Shots Prone	704·9	(599 +105·9)	Petr Kurka (Czechoslovakia)	Zürich, Switzerland	2 Jun	1987
	704·9	(598 +106·9)	Goran Maksimovic (Yugoslavia)	Münich, West Germany	21 Oct	1988
AIR RIFLE 10m 60 shots	699·2	(595 +104·2)	Yuriy Fedkin (USSR)	Zürich, Switzerland	7 Jun	1989
FREE PISTOL 50m 60 shots	666	(571 +95)	Igor Bassinskiy (USSR)	Seoul, South Korea	27 Sep	1987
RAPID-FIRE PISTOL 25m 60 shots	698	(598 +100)	Afanasiy Kuzmin (USSR)	Seoul, South Korea	23 Sep	1988
AIR PISTOL 10m 60 shots	690·3	(590 +100·3)	Sergey Pyzhyanov (USSR)	Sarajevo, Yugoslavia	30 Apr	1989
RUNNING GAME TARGET 50m 30 +30 shots	691	(594 +97)	Sergey Luzov (USSR)	Suhl, GDR	7 Sep	1986
	691	(596 +95)	Nikolay Lapin (USSR)	Lahti, Finland	25 Jul	1987

WOMEN

Event	Score	(Breakdown)	Name	Place	Date	Year
STANDARD RIFLE 50m 3 × 20 shots	691·6	(587 +104·6)	Vessela Letcheva (Bulgaria)	Münich, West Germany	22 May	1987
AIR RIFLE 10m 40 shots	504	(399 +105)	Vessela Letcheva (Bulgaria)	Suhl, GDR	30 May	1987
SPORT PISTOL 25m 60 shots	695	(595 +100)	Nino Salukvadze (USSR)	Seoul, South Korea	28 Sep	1987
AIR PISTOL 10m 40 shots	489·5	(389 +100·5)	Jasna Sekaric (Yugoslavia)	Seoul, South Korea	21 Sep	1988

OPEN

Event	Score	(Breakdown)	Name	Place	Date	Year
TRAP 200 targets	224	(199 +25)	Miroslav Bednarik (Czechoslovakia)	Suhl, GDR	14 Sep	1986
SKEET 200 targets	224	(199 +25)	Matthew Dryke (USA)	Suhl, GDR	8 Sep	1986
	224	(199 +25)	Luca Scribani (Italy)	Bologna	11 Jun	1988
	224	(200 +24)	Ribor Ole Rasmussen (Denmark)	Bologna, Italy	11 Jun	1988

Ski-jumping ■ The longest ski-jump ever recorded is one of 194 m *636 ft* by Piotr Fijas (Poland) at Planica, Yugoslavia on 14 Mar 1987. The women's record is 110 m *361 ft* by Tiina Lehtola (Finland) (b. 3 Aug 1962) at Ruka, Finland on 29 Mar 1981. The longest dry ski-jump is 92 m *302 ft* by Hubert Schwarz (West Germany) at Berchtesgarten, West Germany on 30 Jun 1981.

Highest speed ■ The official world record, as recognised by the International Ski Federation for a skier, is 223·741 km/h *139·030 mph* by Michael Prufer (Monaco) and the fastest by a woman is 214·413 km/h *133·234 mph* by Tarja Mulari (Finland), both at Les Arcs, France on 16 Apr 1988. On the same occasion, Graham Wilkie (GB) (b. 21 Sep 1959) set a British men's record of 219·914 km/h *136·651 mph* and Patrick Knaff (France) set a one-legged record of 185·567 km/h *115·309 mph*. On 18 Apr 1987, a British women's record was set by Divina Galica (b. 13 Aug 1944) at 191·99 km/h *119·30 mph*, also at Les Arcs, France. The highest average speed in the Olympic downhill race was 104·53 km/h *64·95 mph* by William D. Johnson (USA) (b. 30 Mar 1960) at Sarajevo, Yugoslavia on 16 Feb 1984. The fastest in a World Cup downhill is 107·82 km/h *67·00 mph* by Harti Weirather (Austria) (b. 25 Jan 1958) at Kitzbühl, Austria on 15 Jan 1982.

Highest speed—cross-country ■ Bill Koch (USA) (b. 13 Apr 1943) on 26 Mar 1981 skied ten times round a 5 km *3·11 mile* loop on Marlborough Pond, near Putney, Vermont, USA. He completed the 50 km in 1 hr 59 min 47 sec, an average speed of 25·045 km/h *15·57 mph*. A race includes uphill and downhill sections; the record time for a 50 km race in World Championships or Olympic Games is 2 hr 4 min 30·9 sec by Gunde Svan (Sweden) in 1988, an average speed of 24·09 km/h *14·97 mph*.

Closest verdict ■ The narrowest winning margin in a championship ski race was one hundredth of a second by Thomas Wassberg (Sweden) over Juha Mieto (Finland) (b. 20 Nov 1949) in the Olympic 15-km cross-country race at Lake Placid, New York, USA on 17 Feb 1980. His winning time was 41 min 57·63 sec.

Highest altitude ■ Jean Afanassieff and Nicolas Jaeger skied from 8200 m *26 900 ft* to 6200 m *20 340 ft* on the 1978 French expedition on Everest.

Most World Cup titles ● Gunde Svan (Sweden) (b. 12 Jan 1962) has won a record five Nordic cross-country World Cup titles and a record-equalling four Olympic golds. (Photo: All-Sport/Pascal Rondeau)

Steepest descent ■ The steepest descents in alpine skiing history have been by Sylvain Saudan. At the start of his descent from Mont Blanc on the north-east side down the Couloir Gervasutti from 4248 m *13 937 ft* on 17 Oct 1967 he skied to gradients of *c.* 60°.

Longest run ■ The longest all-downhill ski run in the world is the Weissfluhjoch-Küblis Parsenn course, near Davos, Switzerland, which measures 12·23 km *7·6 miles*. The run from the Aiguille du Midi top of the Chamonix lift (vertical lift 2759 m *9052 ft*) across the Vallée Blanche is 20·9 km *13 miles*.

Most competitors *Alpine* ■ 1700 downhill skiers competed at Åre, Jämtland, Sweden on 30 Apr 1984.

The most competitors in a skiing competition in Britain are the 450 who took part in the Army Ski Association Championships at Aviemore, Highland from 29 Feb–5 Mar 1988.

Longest races *Nordic* ■ The world's greatest Nordic ski race is the Vasaloppet, which commemorates an event of 1521 when Gustav Vasa (1496–1560), later King Gustavus Eriksson, fled 85·8 km *53·3 miles* from Mora to Sälen, Sweden. He was overtaken by loyal, speedy scouts on skis, who persuaded him to return eastwards to Mora to lead a rebellion and become the king of Sweden. The re-enactment of this return journey is now an annual event at 89 km *55·3 miles*. There were a record 10 934 starters on 6 Mar 1977 and a record 10 633 finishers on 4 Mar 1979. The fastest time is 3 hr 48 min 55 sec by Bengt Hassis (Sweden) on 2 Mar 1986.

The Finlandia Ski Race, 75 km *46·6 miles* from Hämeenlinna to Lahti, on 26 Feb 1984 had a record 13 226 starters and 12 909 finishers.

The longest downhill race is the *Inferno* in Switzerland, 15·8 km *9·8 miles* from the top of the Schilthorn to Lauterbrunnen. The record entry was 1401 in 1981 and the record time 15 min 26·44 sec by Ueli Grossniklaus (Switzerland) in 1987.

Long-distance Nordic ■ In 24 hours Seppo-Juhani Savolainen covered 415·5 km *258·2 miles* at Saariselkä, Finland on 8–9 Apr 1988. The women's record is 330 km *205·05 miles* by Sisko Kainulaisen at Jyväskylä, Finland on 23–24 Mar 1985.

In 48 hours Bjørn Løkken (Norway) (b. 27 Nov 1937) covered 513·568 km *319 miles 205 yd* on 11–13 Mar 1982.

Longest lift ■ The longest gondola ski lift is 6239 m *3·88 miles* long at Grindelwald-Männlichen, Switzerland (in two sections, but one gondola). The longest chair lift in the world was the Alpine Way to Kosciusko Chalet lift above Thredbo, near the Snowy Mountains, New South Wales, Australia. It took from 45 to 75 min to ascend the 5·6 km *3·5 miles*, according to the weather. It has now collapsed. The highest is at Chacaltaya, Bolivia, rising to 5029 m *16 500 ft*.

Ski-bob *Origins* ■ The ski-bob was the invention of J. C. Stevenson of Hartford, Connecticut, USA in 1891, and patented (No. 47334) on 19 Apr 1892 as a 'bicycle with ski-runners'. The *Fédération Internationale de Skibob* was founded on 14 Jan 1961 in Innsbruck, Austria and the first World Championships were held at Bad Hofgastein, Austria in 1967. The Ski-Bob Association of Great Britain was registered on 23 Aug 1967. The highest speed attained is 166 km/h *103·4 mph* by Erich Brenter (Austria) (b. 1940) at Cervinia, Italy in 1964.

World Championships ■ The only ski-bobbers to retain a world championship are: men – Alois Fischbauer (Austria) (b. 6 Oct 1951), 1973 and 1975, Robert Mühlberger (West Germany), 1979 and 1981; women – Gerhilde Schiffkorn (Austria) (b. 22 Mar 1950), 1967 and 1969, Gertrude Geberth (Austria) (b. 18 Oct 1951), 1971 and 1973.

Snowmobile ■ A record speed of 239·1 km/h *148·6 mph* was set by Tom Earhart (USA) in a Budweiser-Polaris snowmobile designed and owned by Bob Gaudreau at Lake Mille Lacs, Minnesota, USA on 25 Feb 1982. (*See also p. 114*).

GRASS SKIING

Grass skis were first manufactured by Josef Kaiser

MOST WORLD CUP TITLES
ALPINE
MEN

OVERALL	4	Gustavo Thoeni (Italy)	1971–3, 1975
DOWNHILL	5	Franz Klammer (Austria)	1975–8, 1983
SLALOM	8	Ingemar Stenmark (Sweden)	1975–81, 1983
GIANT SLALOM	7	Ingemar Stenmark	1975–6, 1978–81, 1984
SUPER GIANT SLALOM	3	Pirmin Zurbriggen (Switzerland)	1987–9

Two men have won four titles in one year: Jean-Claude Killy (France) (b. 30 Aug 1943) won all four possible disciplines (downhill, slalom, giant slalom and overall) in 1967; and Pirmin Zurbriggen (Switzerland) (b. 4 Feb 1963) won four of the five possible disciplines (downhill, giant slalom, Super giant slalom [added 1986] and overall) in 1987.

WOMEN

OVERALL	6	Annemarie Moser (Austria)	1971–5, 1979
DOWNHILL	7	Annemarie Moser	1971–5, 1978–9
SLALOM	4	Erika Hess (Switzerland)	1981–3, 1985
GIANT SLALOM	3	Annemarie Moser	1971–2, 1975
	3	Lise-Marie Morerod (Switzerland)	1976–8
	3	Vreni Schneider (Switzerland)	1986–7, 1989
SUPER GIANT SLALOM	1	Four women	

NORDIC
MEN

JUMPING	4	Matti Nykänen (Finland)	1983, 1985–6, 1988
CROSS-COUNTRY	5	Gunde Svan (Sweden)	1984–6, 1988–9

WOMEN

CROSS-COUNTRY	3	Marjo Matikainen (Finland)	1986–8

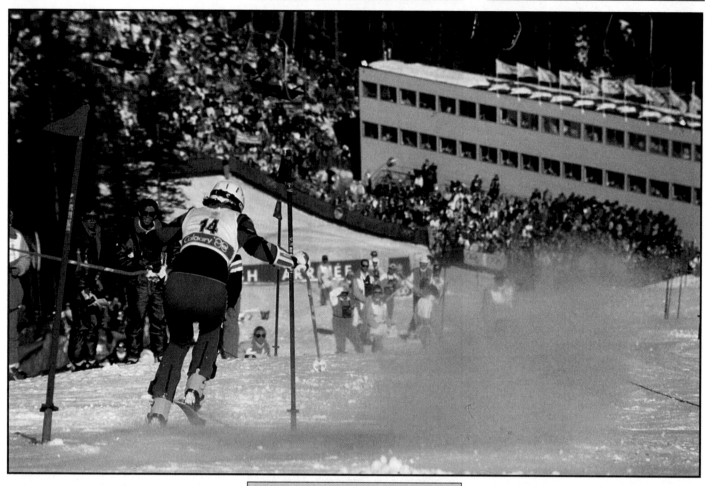

(West Germany) in 1963. World Championships (now awarded for Super G, giant slalom, slalom and combined) were first held in 1979. The most titles won is nine by Ingrid Hirschhofer (Austria) 1979–87. The most by a man is seven by Erwin Gansner (Switzerland) 1981–7.

The speed record is 86·88 km/h *53·99 mph* by Erwin Gansner on 5 Sep 1982; the British record is 79·49 km/h *43·39 mph* by Laurence Beck on 8 Sep 1985, both at Owen, West Germany.

Most wins in a World Cup season ● Vreni Schneider (Switzerland) (b. 24 Nov 1964) completed a clean sweep of all the seven women's slalom events during the 1988/9 World Cup season and in total won a record 14 events. Here she is in action during the 1988 Olympic slalom event when she won the gold medal. (Photo: All-Sport/Steve Powell)

MOST OLYMPIC TITLES

MEN

ALPINE	3	Anton 'Toni' Sailer (Austria) (b. 17 Nov 1935)	Downhill, slalom, giant slalom, 1956
	3	Jean-Claude Killy (France) (b. 30 Aug 1943)	Downhill, slalom, giant slalom, 1968
NORDIC	4[1]	Sixten Jernberg (Sweden) (b. 6 Feb 1929)	50 km, 1956; 30 km, 1960; 50 km and 4 × 10 km, 1964
	4	Gunde Svan (Sweden) (b. 12 Mar 1962)	15 km and 4 × 10 km, 1984; 50 km and 4 × 10 km, 1988
	4	Thomas Wassberg (Sweden) (b. 27 Mar 1956)	15 km, 1980; 50 km, 1984; 4 × 10 km, 1984, 1988
Ski-jumping	4	Matti Nykänen (Finland) (b. 17 Jul 1963)	70 m hill, 1988; 90 m hill, 1984, 1988; Team, 1988

WOMEN

ALPINE	2	Andrea Mead-Lawrence (USA) (b. 19 Apr 1932)	Slalom, giant slalom, 1952
	2	Marielle Goitschel (France) (b. 28 Sep 1945)	Giant slalom, 1964; slalom, 1968
	2	Marie-Thérèse Nadig (Switz) (b. 8 Mar 1954)	Downhill, giant slalom, 1972
	2[2]	Rosi Mittermaier (now Neureuther) (West Germany) (b. 5 Aug 1950)	Downhill, slalom, 1976
	2[3]	Hanni Wenzel (Liechtenstein) (b. 14 Dec 1956)	Giant slalom, slalom 1980
	2	Vreni Schneider (Switzerland) (b. 26 Nov 1964)	Giant slalom, slalom 1988
NORDIC	4[4]	Galina Kulakova (USSR) (b. 29 Apr 1942)	5 km, 10 km and 3 ×5 km relay, 1972; 4 ×5 km relay, 1976
(individual)	3	Marja-Liisa Hämäläinen (Finland) (b. 10 Aug 1955)	5 km, 10 km and 20 km 1984

[1] *Most medals* 9, Sixten Jernberg, four golds, three silver and two bronze
     9, Raisa Smetanina, three gold, five silver and one bronze at women's Nordic skiing 1976–88.
[2] *Also won silver medal in giant slalom in 1976.*
[3] *Wenzel won a silver in the 1980 downhill and a bronze in the 1976 slalom.*
[4] *Kulakova also won two silver and two bronze medals in 1968, 1976 and 1980.*

Skipping

MARATHON

The longest recorded skipping marathon (5 min per complete hour breaks) was one of 31 hr 46 min 48 sec by Frank Oliveri (USA) at Bowling Green State University, Ohio, USA on 26–27 May 1989.

10 MILE RUN-SKIP Ken Solis skipped 10 miles *16·09 km* in 71 min 54 sec at Johnstown, Pennsylvania, USA on 6 Aug 1988.

Other records made without a break:

MOST TURNS IN 10 SEC 128 by Albert Rayner (b. 19 Apr 1923), Stanford Sports, Birmingham, England, 19 Nov 1982.

MOST TURNS IN 1 MIN 418 by Tyrone Krohn at Middletown High School, New York, USA, 10 Jul 1984.

MOST DOUBLES (WITH CROSS) 2411 by Ken Solis (USA) at the North Shore-Elite Fitness and Racquets Club, Glendale, Wisconsin, USA, 29 Mar 1988.

DOUBLE TURNS 10 709 by Frank Oliveri at Rochester, New York, USA, 7 May 1988

TREBLE TURNS 423 by Shozo Hamada, Saitama, Japan, 1 Jun 1987.

QUADRUPLE TURNS 51 by Katsumi Suzuki, Saitama, Japan, 29 May 1975.

QUINTUPLE TURNS 6 by Hideyuki Tateda (b. 1968), Aomori, Japan, 19 Jun 1982.

DURATION 2034 km *1264 miles* by Tom Morris, Brisbane-Cairns, Queensland, 1963.

MOST ON SINGLE ROPE (minimum 12 turns obligatory) 181 by a team at the International Rope Skipping Competition, Greeley, Colorado, USA, 28 Jun 1988.

MOST TURNS ON SINGLE ROPE, TEAM OF 90 160 by students from the Nishigoshi Higashi Elementary School, Kumamoto, Japan, 27 Feb 1987.

ON A TIGHTROPE 58 (consecutive) by Bryan Andro (*né* Dewhurst), TROS TV, the Netherlands, 6 Aug 1981.

MOST TURNS IN 1 HOUR 13 310 Randall Schneider at Clinton, Wisconsin, USA, 1 Apr 1989.

Skittles

24 hours ■ The highest score at West Country skittles by a team of eight is 99 051 by the 'Alkies' Skittles team at Courtlands Holiday Inn, Torquay, Devon on 4–5 Apr 1987; they reset the skittles after every ball. The highest hood skittle score in 24 hr is 118 951 pins by 12 players from the White Hart, Grafton Regis, Northamptonshire on 9–10 April 1986. The highest long alley score is 65 658 by a team of eight called 'The Robins' at The Canterbury Inn, Tewkesbury, Gloucestershire on 10–11 Mar 1989. The highest table skittle score in 24 hr is 90 446 skittles by 12 players at the Finney Gardens Hotel, Hanley, Staffordshire on 27–28 Dec 1980.

Snooker

Origins ■ Research shows that snooker was originated by Colonel Sir Neville Francis Fitzgerald Chamberlain (1856–1944) as a hybrid of 'black pool', 'pyramids' and billiards, in Jubbulpore, India in 1875. It did not reach England until 1885, where the modern scoring system was adopted in 1891. Championships were not instituted until 1916. The World Professional Championship was instituted in 1927.

Most titles *World* ■ The world professional title was won a record 15 times by Joe Davis, on the first 15 occasions it was contested, 1927–40 and 1946. The most wins in the Amateur Championships (instituted 1963) have been two by: Gary Owen (England) in 1963 and 1966; Ray Edmonds (England) 1972 and 1974; and Paul Mifsud (Malta) 1985–6.

Women ■ Maureen Baynton (*née* Barrett) won a record eight Women's Amateur Championships between 1954 and 1968, as well as seven at billiards.

World Championships *Youngest* ■ The youngest man to win a world title is Jimmy White (GB) (b. 2 May 1962), who was 18 yr 191 days when he won the World Amateur Snooker Championship in Launceston, Tasmania, Australia on 9 Nov 1980. Stacey Hillyard (GB) won the Women's World Amateur Championship in October 1984 at the age of 15. The youngest winner of a major title was Stephen Hendry (b. 13 Jan 1969) at 18 yr 285 days, when he won the Rothmans Grand Prix on 25 Oct 1987.

Highest breaks ■ Over 200 players have achieved the 'maximum' break of 147. The first to do so was E. J. 'Murt' O'Donoghue (b. New Zealand 1901) at Griffiths, New South Wales, Australia on 26 Sep 1934. The first officially ratified 147 was by Joe Davis against Willie Smith at Leicester Square Hall, London on 22 Jan 1955. The first achieved in a major tournaments were by John Spencer (b. 18 Sep 1935) at Slough, Berkshire on 13 Jan 1979, but the table had oversized pockets, and by Steve Davis (b. 22 Aug 1957), who had a ratified break of 147 against John Spencer in the Lada Classic at Oldham, Greater Manchester on 11 Jan 1982. The youngest to score a competitive maximum was Gary Hill (b. 29 Sep 1968) at 20 yr 249 days during the World Junior Championship at Reykjavik, Iceland on 5 Jun 1989. Cliff Thorburn (Canada) (b. 16 Jan 1948) has scored two official 147 breaks on 23 Apr 1983 and 8 Mar 1989. Steve Duggan (b. 10 Apr 1958) made a break of 148 in a witnessed practice frame in Doncaster, South Yorkshire on 27 Apr 1988. The break involved a free ball, which therefore created an 'extra' red, when all fifteen reds were still on the table. In these very exceptional circumstances, the maximum break is 155.

The world amateur record break is 147 by Geet Sethi (India) in the Indian Amateur Championships on 21 Feb 1988.

Three consecutive century breaks were first compiled in a major tournament by Steve Davis: 108, 101 and 104 at Stoke-on-Trent, Staffordshire on 10 Sep 1988. Doug Mountjoy (b. 8 Jun 1942) equalled the feat: 131, 106 and 124 at Preston, Lancashire on 27 Nov 1988. Jim Meadowcroft (b. 15 Dec 1946) made four consecutive frame clearances of 105, 115, 117 and 125 at Connaught Leisure Centre, Worthing, West Sussex on 27 Jan 1982.

The first century break by a woman in competitive play was 114 by Stacey Hillyard (b. 5 Sep 1969) in a league match at Bournemouth on 15 Jan 1985.

Softball

Origins ■ Softball, the indoor derivative of baseball, was invented by George Hancock at the Farragut Boat Club of Chicago, Illinois in 1887. Rules were first codified in Minneapolis, Minnesota, USA in 1895 as Kitten Ball. The name Softball was introduced by Walter Hakanson at a meeting of the National Recreation Congress in 1926. The name was adopted throughout the USA in 1930. Rules were formalised in 1933 by the International Joint Rules Committee for Softball and adopted by the Amateur Softball Association of America. The International Softball Federation was formed in 1950 as governing body for both fast pitch and slow pitch. It was reorganised in 1965.

Most titles ■ The USA has won the men's world championship (instituted 1966) four times, 1966, 1968, 1976 (shared), and 1980. The USA won the women's title (instituted 1965) in 1974, 1978 and 1986. The world's first slow-pitch championships for men's teams was held in Oklahoma City, USA in 1987, when the winners were the USA.

Speedway

Motorcycle racing on large dirt track surfaces has been traced back to 1902 in the United States. The first fully documented motorcycle track races were at the Portman Road Ground, Ipswich, Suffolk on 2 Jul 1904. Two heats and a final were contested, F. E. Barker winning in 5 min 54·2 sec for three miles. Modern speedway has developed from the 'short track' races held at the West Maitland (New South Wales, Australia) Agricultural Show on 22 Dec 1923, by Johnnie Hoskins (New Zealand) (1892–1987). He brought the sport to Britain, where it evolved with small diameter track racing at Droylsden, Manchester on 25 Jun 1927 and a cinder track event at High Beech, Essex on 19 Feb 1928.

British championships ■ League racing was introduced to British speedway in 1929 and consisted of a Southern League and Northern Dirt Track League, the National League was formulated in 1932 and continued to 1964. The Wembley Lions who won in 1932, 1946–7, 1949–53, had a record eight victories. In 1965 it was replaced by the British League which Belle Vue have won four times, including three times in succession (1970–2). Wimbledon is the only club to have competed every year since 1929 in Southern, National and British Leagues.

In league racing the highest score recorded was when Berwick beat Exeter 78–18 in the 16-heat formula for the National League on 27 May 1989. A maximum possible score was achieved by Bristol when they defeated Glasgow (White City) 70–14 on 7 Oct 1949 in the National League Division Two. The highest number of League points scored by an individual in a season was 563 by Hans Hollen Nielsen (b. 26 Dec 1959) for Oxford in the British League in 1988. The League career record is 6471 points by Nigel Boocock (b. 17 Sep 1937), 1955–80.

Oxford set a record of 28 successive wins in the British League in 1986.

Belle Vue (Manchester) had a record nine victories (1933–7, 1946–7, 1949 and 1958) in the National Trophy Knock-out Competition (held 1931–64). This was replaced in 1965 by the Knock-Out Cup, which has been won six times by Cradley Heath. The highest recorded score in this competition is 81–25, when Hull beat Sheffield in 1979.

The British League riders Championship was instituted in 1965 and is an annual event contested by the top scorers from each team. Ivan Gerald Mauger (New Zealand) (b. 4 Oct 1939) holds the records for appearances, 15 and points scored, 146, 1965–79. The National League Riders Championship was instituted in 1968. Stephen Lawson (b. 11 Dec 1957) has made a record nine appearances and John Jackson (b. 26 Jun 1952) has scored a record 67 points.

World championships ■ The World Speedway Championship was inaugurated at Wembley, London on 10 Sep 1936. The most wins have been six by Ivan Mauger in 1968–70, 1972, 1977 and 1979. Barry Briggs (New Zealand) (b. 30 Dec 1934) made a record 17 consecutive appearances in the finals (1954–70) and won the world title in 1957–8, 1964 and 1966. He also scored a record 201 points in world championship competition from 87 races.

England has most wins in the World Pairs Championship (instituted 1968) with seven. The World Team Cup (instituted 1960) has been won a record eight times by England / Great Britain and Denmark. Poland uniquely competed in 21 successive World Team Cup finals, 1960–80 and in a 22nd in 1984. Maximum points (then 30) were scored in the World Pairs Championship by: Jerzy Szczakiel (b. 28 Jan 1949) and Andrzej Wyglenda (Poland) at Rybnik, Poland in 1971; and Arthur Dennis Sigalos (b. 16 Aug 1959) and Robert Benjamin 'Bobby' Schwartz (USA) (b. 10 Aug 1956) at Liverpool, New South Wales, Australia on 11 Dec 1982.

Ivan Mauger also won four World Team Cup, two World Pairs (including one unofficial) and two world long track titles. Ove Fundin (Sweden) (b. 23 May 1933) won 12 world titles: five individual, one Pairs, and six World Team Cup medals in 1956–70. Erik Gundersen (Denmark) (b. 8 Oct 1959) became in 1985 the first man to hold simultaneously world titles at individual, pairs, team and long-track events.

Tests —*maximum points* ■ The only rider to have scored maximum points in every match of a Test series was Arthur 'Bluey' Wilkinson (b. 27 Aug 1911) in five matches for Australia v. England in Sydney in 1937–8.

Squash Rackets

Although rackets (US spelling racquets) with a soft ball was played in 1817 at Harrow School, Harrow, London, there was no recognised champion of any country until John A. Miskey of Philadelphia, Pennsylvania, USA won the American Amateur Singles Championship in 1907.

World Championships ■ Jahangir Khan (Pakistan) (b. 10 Dec 1963) won 6 World Open (instituted 1976) titles, 1981–5 and 1988, and the ISRF world individual title (formerly World Amateur, instituted 1967) in 1979, 1983 and 1985. Geoffrey B. Hunt (Australia) (b. 11 Mar 1947) won four World Open titles, 1976–7 and 1979–80 and three World Amateur, 1967, 1969 and 1971.

Pakistan have won five men's team titles, 1977, 1981, 1983, 1985 and 1987. Three women's titles have been won by Australia, 1976, 1981 and 1983, and by Great Britain, 1979, 1985 and 1989.

Most titles *Open Championship* ■ The most wins in the Open Championship held annually in Britain, is eight by Jahingir Khan, in successive years, 1982–9 and by Geoffrey Hunt in 1969, 1974, 1976–81. Hashim Khan (Pakistan) (b. 1915) won seven times, 1950–5 and 1957, and also won the Vintage title six times in 1978–83.

The most British Open women's titles is 16 by Heather Pamela McKay (*née* Blundell) (Australia) (b. 31 Jul 1941) from 1961 to 1977. She also won the World Open title in 1976 and 1979.

Amateur Championship ■ The most wins in the Amateur Championship is six by Abdelfattah Amr Bey (Egypt) (b. 14 Feb 1910), who won in 1931–3 and 1935–7. Norman Francis Borrett (b. 1 Oct 1917) of England won in 1946–50.

Unbeaten sequences ■ Heather McKay was unbeaten from 1962 to 1980. Jahangir Khan was unbeaten from his loss to Geoff Hunt at the British Open on 10 Apr 1981 until Ross Norman (New Zealand) ended his sequence in the World Open final on 11 Nov 1986.

Longest and shortest championship matches
■ The longest recorded competitive match was one of 2 hr 45 min when Jahangir Khan beat Gamal Awad (Egypt) (b. 8 Sep 1955) 9–10, 9–5, 9–7, 9–2, the first game lasting a record 1 hr 11 min, in the final of the Patrick International Festival at Chichester, West Sussex on 30 Mar 1983. Lucy Soutter (GB) beat Hugolein van Hoorn (Netherlands) in just 7 ½ min (9–0, 9–0, 9–0) in the British Under-21 Open Championship at Lamb's Squash Club, London on 17 Jan 1988.

Most international appearances ■ The men's record is 122 by David Gotto (b. 25 Dec 1948) for Ireland. The women's record is 77 by Marjorie Croke (*née* Burke) (b. 31 May 1961) for Ireland, 1981–9.

Highest speed ■ In tests at Wimbledon Squash and Badminton Club in January 1988, Roy Buckland hit a squash ball by an overhead service at a measured speed of 232·7 km/h *144·6 mph* over the distance to the front wall. This is equivalent to an initial speed at the racket of 242·6 km/h *150·8 mph*.

Largest crowd and tournament ■ The finals of the ICI 'Perspex' World Team Championships at Royal Albert Hall, London had a record attendance for squash of 3526 on 18 Apr 1988.

The InterCity National Squash Challenge was contested by 9588 players in 1988, a knock-out tournament record.

Surfing

The traditional Polynesian sport of surfing in a canoe (*ehorooe*) was first recorded by Captain James Cook, RN, FRS (1728–79) on his first voyage at Tahiti in December 1771. Surfing on a board (*Amo Amo iluna ka lau oka nalu*) was first described as 'most perilous and extraordinary ... altogether astonishing and is scarcely to be credited' by Lt (later Capt.) James King, RN, FRS in March 1779 at Kealakekua Bay, Hawaii Island. A surfer was first depicted by this voyage's official artist John Webber. The sport was revived at Waikiki by 1900. Hollow boards were introduced in 1929 and the light plastic foam type in 1956.

Most titles ■ World Amateur Championships were inaugurated in May 1964 at Sydney, Australia. The most titles is three by Michael Novakov (Australia) who won the Kneeboard event in 1982, 1984 and 1986. A World Professional series was started in 1975. The men's title has been won five times by Mark Richards (Australia), 1975 and 1979–82 and the women's title (instituted 1979) four times by Freida Zamba (USA), 1984–6, 1988.

Highest waves ridden ■ Waimea Bay, Hawaii reputedly provides the most consistently high waves, often reaching the ridable limit of 9–10 m *30–35 ft*. The highest wave ever ridden was the *tsunami* of 'perhaps 50 ft *15·24 m*', which struck Minole, Hawaii on 3 Apr 1868, and was ridden to save his life by a Hawaiian named Holua.

Longest ride *Sea wave* ■ About four to six times each year rideable surfing waves break in Matanchen Bay near San Blas, Nayarit, Mexico which makes rides of *c.* 1700 m *5700 ft* possible.

River bore ■ The longest recorded rides on a river bore have been set on the Severn bore, England. The official British Surfing Association record for riding a surfboard in a standing position is 4 km *2·5 mile* by David Lawson from Lower Rea to Lower Parting on 27 Sep 1988. The longest ride on a

surfboard standing or lying down is 4·73 km *2·94 miles* by Colin Kerr Wilson (b. 23 Jun 1954) on 23 May 1982.

The bore on the Ch'ient'ang'kian (see p.59) was ridden for the first time by Stuart Matthews (GB) on 26 Sep 1988. The wave on this occasion was 3·6–4·5 m *12-15 ft* high and was ridden in the standing position for 600 m *656 yd*.

Swimming

In Japan, swimming in schools was ordered by Imperial edict of Emperor Go-Yozei (1586–1611) in 1603 but competition was known from 36 BC. Seawater bathing was fashionable at Scarborough, North Yorkshire as early as 1660. The earliest pool was Pearless Pool, north London, opened in 1743. In Great Britain competitive swimming originated from at least 1791. Swimming races were particularly popular in the 1820s in Liverpool, where the first pool opened at St George's Pier Head, in 1828.

Largest pools ■ The largest swimming pool in the world is the sea-water Orthlieb Pool in Casablanca, Morocco. It is 480 m *1574 ft* long and 75 m *246 ft* wide, and has an area of 3·6 ha *8·9 acres*. The largest land-locked swimming pool with heated water was the Fleishhacker Pool on Sloat Boulevard, near Great Highway, San Francisco, California, USA. It measured 304·8 × 45·7 m *1000 × 150 ft* and up to 4·26 m *14 ft* deep and contained 28 390 hectolitres *7 500 000 US gal* of heated water. It was opened on 2 May 1925 but has now been abandoned. The greatest spectator accommodation is 13 614 at Osaka, Japan. The largest in use in the United Kingdom is the Royal Commonwealth Pool, Edinburgh, completed in 1970 with 2000 permanent seats, but the covered over and unused pool at Earls Court, London (opened 1937) could seat some 12 000 spectators.

Fastest swimmer ■ In a 25 m pool, Dano Halsall (Switzerland) achieved a speed of 8·85 km/h *5·50 mph* at Hendon, Greater London on 24 Feb 1989. The women's fastest is 7·21 km/h *4·48 mph* by Yang Wenyi (China) in her 50 m world record (see World Record table).

Most gold medals ● Kristin Otto (GDR) (b. 7 Feb 1965) won a women's record six swimming gold medals at the 1988 Olympics in Seoul. Uniquely she won individual titles at three different strokes—freestyle, backstroke and butterfly. (Photo: All-Sport)

Most world records ■ Men: 32, Arne Borg (Sweden) (1901–87), 1921–9. Women: 42, Ragnhild Hveger (Denmark) (b. 10 Dec 1920), 1936–42. Under modern conditions (only metric distances in 50 m pools) the most is 26 by Mark Andrew Spitz (USA) (b. 10 Feb 1950), 1967–72, and 23 by Kornelia Ender (GDR) (b. 25 Oct 1958), 1973–6.

Most world titles ■ In the World Championships (inst 1973) the most medals won is ten by Kornelia Ender with eight gold and two silver in 1973 and 1975. The most by a man is eight by Ambrose 'Rowdy' Gaines (USA) (b. 17 Feb 1959), five gold and three silver, in 1978 and 1982. The most gold medals is six by James Montgomery (USA) (b. 24 Jan 1955) in 1973 and 1975. The most medals at a single championship is seven by Matthew Biondi (USA), three gold, one silver, three bronze, in 1986.

OLYMPIC RECORDS

Most medals *Men* ■ The greatest number of Olympic gold medals won is nine by Mark Spitz (USA): 100 m and 200 m freestyle 1972; 100 m and 200 m butterfly 1972; 4 × 100 m freestyle 1968 and 1972; 4 × 200 m freestyle 1968 and 1972; 4 × 100 m medley 1972. All but one of these performances (the 4 × 200 m freestyle of 1968) were also new world records. He also won a silver (100 m butterfly) and a bronze (100 m freestyle) in 1968 for a record 11 medals. His record seven medals at one Games in 1972 was equalled by Matthew Biondi (USA) who took five gold, one silver and one bronze in 1988.

Women ■ The record number of gold medals won by a woman is six by Kristin Otto (GDR) (b. 7 Feb 1965) at Seoul in 1988: 100 m freestyle, backstroke and butterfly, 50 m freestyle, 4 × 100 m freestyle and 4 × 100 m medley. Dawn Fraser (Australia) (b. 4 Sep 1937) is the only swimmer to win the same event, the 100 m freestyle, on three successive occasions (1956, 1960 and 1964).

The most medals won by a woman is eight by: Dawn Fraser, four golds: 100 m freestyle 1956, 1960 and 1964, 4 × 100 m freestyle 1956 and four silvers: 400 m freestyle 1956, 4 × 100 m freestyle 1960 and 1964, 4 × 100 m medley 1960, Kornelia Ender, four golds: 100 m and 200 m freestyle, 100 m butterfly and 4 × 100 m medley in 1976 and four silvers: 200 m individual medley 1972, 4 × 100 m medley 1972, 4 × 100 m freestyle 1972 and 1976 and Shirley Babashoff (USA) (b. 3 Jan 1957), who won two golds (4 × 100 m freestyle 1972 and 1976) and six silvers (100 m freestyle 1972, 200 m freestyle 1972 and 1976, 400 m and 800 m freestyle 1976, 4 × 100 m medley 1976).

Most individual gold medals ■ The record number of individual gold medals won is four by: Charles M. Daniels (USA) (1884–1973) (100 m freestyle 1906 and 1908, 220 yd freestyle 1904, 440 yd freestyle 1904); Roland Matthes (GDR) (b. 17 Nov 1950) with 100 m and 200 m backstroke 1968 and 1972; Mark Spitz and Kristin Otto, and the divers Pat McCormick and Greg Louganis (see below).

Most medals *British* ■ The record number of gold medals won by a British swimmer (excluding water polo, *q.v.*) is four by Henry Taylor (1885–1951) in the mile freestyle (1906), 400 m freestyle (1908), 1500 m freestyle (1908) and 4 × 200 m freestyle (1908).

Henry Taylor won a record eight medals in all with a silver (400 m freestyle 1906) and three bronzes (4 × 200 m freestyle 1906, 1912, 1920). The most medals by a British woman is four by M. Joyce Cooper (now Badcock) (b. 18 Apr 1909) with one silver (4 × 100 m freestyle 1928) and three bronze (100 m freestyle 1928, 100 m backstroke 1928, 4 × 100 m freestyle 1932).

Closest verdict ■ The closest verdict in the Olympic Games was in Los Angeles on 29 Jul 1984, when Nancy Hogshead (b. 17 Apr 1962) and Carrie Steinseifer (b. 12 Feb 1968) (both USA) dead-heated for the women's 100 m freestyle gold medal in 55·92 sec. In the 1972 men's 400 m individual medley Gunnar Larsson (Sweden) (b. 12 May 1951) beat Tim McKee (USA) (b. 14 Mar 1953) by just 2/9 1000 th second, just 3 mm. Now timings are determined only to hundredths.

DIVING

Most Olympic medals ■ The most medals won by a diver are five (three gold, two silver) by Klaus Dibiasi (b. Austria, 6 Oct 1947) (Italy) in the four Games from 1964 to 1976. He is also the only diver to win the same event (highboard) at three successive Games (1968, 1972 and 1976). Two divers have won the highboard and springboard doubles at two Games: Patricia McCormick (*née* Keller) (USA) (b. 12 May 1930), 1952 and 1956 and Greg Louganis (USA) (b. 29 Jan 1960), 1984 and 1988.

British ■ The highest placing by a Briton has been the silver medal by Beatrice Eileen Armstrong

(later Purdy) (1894–1981) in the 1920 highboard event. The best placings by male divers are the bronze medals by Harold Clarke (b. 1888) (plain high diving, 1924) and Brian Phelps (b. 21 Apr 1944) (highboard, 1960).

Most world titles ■ Greg Louganis (USA) won a record five world titles, highboard in 1978, and both highboard and springboard in 1982 and 1986, as well as four Olympic gold medals in 1984 and 1988. Three gold medals at one event have also been won by Phil Boggs (USA) (b. 29 Dec 1949), springboard 1973, 1975 and 1978.

Highest scores ■ Greg Louganis (USA) (b. 29 Jan 1960) achieved record scores at the 1984 Olympic Games in Los Angeles, California, USA with 754·41 points for the 11-dive springboard event and 710·91 for the highboard. At the world championships in Guayaquil, Ecuador in 1984 he was awarded a perfect score of 10·0 by all seven judges for his highboard inward 1 ½ somersault in the pike position.

The first diver to be awarded a score of 10·0 by all seven judges was Michael Finneran (b. 21 Sep 1948) in the 1972 US Olympic Trials, in Chicago, Illinois, for a backward 1 ½ somersault, 2 ½ twist, from the 10 m board.

CHANNEL SWIMMING

The first to swim the English Channel from shore to shore (without a life jacket) was the Merchant Navy captain Matthew Webb (1848–83) who swam from Dover, England to Calais Sands, France, in 21 hr 45 min from 12.56 p.m. to 10.41 a.m., 24–25 Aug 1875. He swam an estimated 61 km *38 miles* to make the 33 km *21 mile* crossing. Paul Boyton (USA) had swum from Cap Gris-Nez to the South Foreland in his patent life-saving suit in 23 hr 30 min on 28–29 May 1875. There is good evidence that Jean-Marie Saletti, a French soldier, escaped from a British prison hulk off Dover by swimming to Boulogne in July or August 1815. The first crossing from France

SWIMMING—WORLD RECORDS (*set in 50 m pools*)

MEN

Event	Time	Name, country and date of birth	Place	Date	
FREESTYLE					
50 metres	22·14	Matthew Nicholas Biondi (USA) (b. 8 Oct·1965)	Seoul, South Korea	24 Sep	1988
100 metres	48·42	Matthew Nicholas Biondi (USA)	Austin, Texas, USA	10 Aug	1988
200 metres	1:47·25	Duncan D'Arcy Armstrong (Australia) (b. 7 Apr 1968)	Seoul, South Korea	19 Sep	1988
400 metres	3:46·95	Uwe Dassler (GDR) (b. 11 Feb 1967)	Seoul, South Korea	23 Sep	1988
800 metres	7:50·64	Vladimir Salnikov (USSR) (b. 21 May 1960)	Moscow, USSR	4 Jul	1986
1500 metres	14:54·76	Vladimir Salnikov (USSR)	Moscow, USSR	22 Feb	1983
4×100 metres relay	3:16·53	United States (Christopher Jacobs, Troy Dalbey, Tom Jager, Matthew Nicholas Biondi)	Seoul, South Korea	23 Sep	1988
4×200 metres relay	7:12·51	United States (Troy Dalbey, Matthew Cetlinski, Douglas Gjertsen, Matthew Nicholas Biondi)	Seoul, South Korea	21 Sep	1988
BREASTSTROKE					
100 metres	1:01·65	Steven K. Lundquist (USA) (b. 20 Feb 1961)	Los Angeles, California, USA	29 Jul	1984
200 metres	2:13·34	Victor Davis (Canada) (b. 19 Feb 1964)	Los Angeles, California, USA	2 Aug	1984
BUTTERFLY					
100 metres	52·84	Pedro Pablo Morales (USA) (b. 5 Dec 1964)	Orlando, Florida, USA	23 Jun	1986
200 metres	1:56·24	Michael Gross (West Germany) (b. 17 Jun 1964)	Hannover, West Germany	28 Jun	1986
BACKSTROKE					
100 metres	54·51	David Berkoff (USA) (b. 30 Nov 1966)	Seoul, South Korea	24 Sep	1988
200 metres	1:58·14	Igor Polyanskiy (USSR) (b. 20 Mar 1967)	Erfurt, GDR	3 Mar	1985
MEDLEY					
200 metres	2:00·17	Tamas Darnyi (Hungary) (b. 3 Jun 1967)	Seoul, South Korea	25 Sep	1988
400 metres	4:14·75	Tamas Darnyi (Hungary)	Seoul, South Korea	21 Sep	1988
4×100 metres relay	3:36·93	United States (David Berkoff, Richard Schroeder, Matthew Nicholas Biondi, Christopher Jacobs)	Seoul, South Korea	25 Sep	1988

WOMEN

Event	Time	Name, country and date of birth	Place	Date	
FREESTYLE					
50 metres	24·98	Yang Wenyi (China) (b. 11 Jan 1972)	Guangzhou, China	10 Apr	1988
100 metres	54·73	Kristin Otto (GDR) (b. 7 Feb 1965)	Madrid, Spain (relay first leg)	19 Aug	1986
200 metres	1:57·55	Heike Friedrich (GDR) (b. 18 Apr 1970)	East Berlin, GDR	18 Jun	1986
400 metres	4:03·85	Janet Evans (USA) (b. 28 Aug 1971)	Seoul, South Korea	22 Sep	1988
800 metres	8:17·12	Janet Evans (USA)	Orlando, Florida, USA	22 Mar	1988
1500 metres	15:52·10	Janet Evans (USA)	Orlando, Florida, USA	26 Mar	1988
4×100 metres relay	3:40·57	GDR (Kristin Otto, Manuela Stellmach, Sabine Schulze, Heike Friedrich)	Madrid, Spain	19 Aug	1986
4×200 metres relay	7:55·47	GDR (Manuela Stellmach, Astrid Strauss, Anke Möhring, Heike Friedrich)	Strasbourg, France	18 Aug	1987
BREASTSTROKE					
100 metres	1:07·91	Silke Hörner (GDR) (b. 12 Sep 1965)	Strasbourg, France	21 Aug	1987
200 metres	2:26·71	Silke Hörner (GDR)	Seoul, South Korea	21 Sep	1988
BUTTERFLY					
100 metres	57·93	Mary Terstegge Meagher (USA) (b. 27 Oct 1964)	Milwaukee, Wisconsin, USA	16 Aug	1981
200 metres	2:05·96	Mary Terstegge Meagher (USA)	Milwaukee, Wisconsin, USA	13 Aug	1981
BACKSTROKE					
100 metres	1:00·59	Ina Kleber (GDR) (b. 29 Sep 1964)	Moscow, USSR	24 Aug	1984
200 metres	2:08·60	Betsy Mitchell (USA) (b. 15 Jan 1966)	Orlando, Florida, USA	27 Jun	1986
MEDLEY					
200 metres	2:11·73	Ute Geweniger (GDR) (b. 24 Feb 1964)	East Berlin, GDR	4 Jul	1981
400 metres	4:36·10	Petra Schneider (GDR) (b. 11 Jan 1963)	Guayaquil, Ecuador	1 Aug	1982
4×100 metres relay	4:03·69	GDR (Ina Kleber, Sylvia Gerasch, Ines Geissler, Birgit Meineke)	Moscow, USSR	24 Aug	1984

BRITISH NATIONAL RECORDS

— MEN —

Event	Time	Name and date of birth	Place	Date	
FREESTYLE					
50 metres	23·13	Mark Andrew Foster (b.12 May 1970)	Crystal Palace, London	1 Aug	1987
100 metres	50·57	Andrew David Jameson (b. 19 Feb 1965)	Orlando, Florida, USA	25 Mar	1988
200 metres	1:51·22	Paul Tony Howe (b. 8 Jan 1968)	Seoul, South Korea	18 Sep	1988
400 metres	3:50·01	Kevin Thomas Boyd (b. 23 Jun 1966)	Seoul, South Korea	23 Sep	1988
800 metres	8:01·87	Kevin Thomas Boyd	Orlando, Florida, USA	26 Mar	1988
1500 metres	15:17·56	Kevin Thomas Boyd	Seoul, South Korea	24 Sep	1988
4 × 100 metres relay	3:21·71	GB (Andrew David Jameson, Mark Andrew Foster, Michael Wenham Fibbens, Roland Lee)	Seoul, South Korea	23 Sep	1988
4 × 200 metres relay	7:24·78	GB (Neil Cochran, Paul Robert Easter, Paul Tony Howe, Andrew Astbury)	Los Angeles, California, USA	30 Jul	1984
BREASTSTROKE					
100 metres	1:01·78	Adrian David Moorhouse (b. 24 May 1964)	Orlando, Florida, USA	26 Mar	1988
200 metres	2:14·12	Nicholas Gillingham (b. 22 Jan 1967)	Seoul, South Korea	23 Sep	1988
BUTTERFLY					
100 metres	53·30	Andrew David Jameson	Seoul, South Korea	21 Sep	1988
200 metres	2:00·21	Philip Hubble (b. 19 Jul 1960)	Split, Yugoslavia	11 Sep	1981
BACKSTROKE					
100 metres	57·72	Gary Abraham (b. 8 Jan 1959)	Moscow, USSR	24 Jul	1980
200 metres	2:04·16	John Philip Davey (b. 29 Dec 1964)	Crystal Palace, London	30 Jul	1987
MEDLEY					
200 metres	2:03·20	Neil Cochran (b. 12 Apr 1965)	Orlando, Florida, USA	25 Mar	1988
400 metres	4:24·20	John Philip Davey (b. 29 Dec 1964)	Crystal Palace, London	31 Jul	1987
4 × 100 metres relay	3:42·01	GB (Neil Cochran, Adrian David Moorhouse, Andrew David Jameson, Roland Lee)	Strasbourg, France	23 Aug	1987

— WOMEN —

Event	Time	Name and date of birth	Place	Date	
FREESTYLE					
50 metres	26·39	Caroline Cooper (b. 26 May 1966)	Austin, Texas, USA	12 Jun	1985
100 metres	56·60	June Alexandra Croft (b. 17 Jun 1963)	Amersfoort, Netherlands	31 Jan	1982
200 metres	1:59·74	June Croft	Brisbane, Australia	4 Oct	1982
400 metres	4:07·68	Sarah Hardcastle (b. 9 April 1969)	Edinburgh, Lothian	27 Jul	1986
800 metres	8:24·77	Sarah Hardcastle	Edinburgh, Lothian	29 Jul	1986
1500 metres	16:43·95	Sarah Hardcastle	Montreal, Canada	18 Apr	1985
4 × 100 metres relay	3:49·65	England (Caroline Cooper, Nicola Fibbens, Zara Letitia Long, Annabelle Cripps)	Edinburgh, Lothian	27 Jul	1986
4 × 200 metres relay	8: 3·70	England (Annabelle Cripps, Sarah Hardcastle, Karen Marie Mellor, Zara Letitia Long)	Edinburgh, Lothian	25 Jul	1986
BREASTSTROKE					
100 metres	1·10·39	Susannah 'Suki' Brownsdon (b. 16 Oct 1965)	Strasbourg, France	21 Aug	1987
200 metres	2:31·57	Jean Cameron Hill (b. 15 Jul 1964)	Strasbourg, France	19 Aug	1987
BUTTERFLY					
100 metres	1:01·48	Nicola Fibbens (b. 29 Apr 1964)	Los Angeles, California, USA	2 Aug	1984
200 metres	2:11·97	Samantha Purvis (b. 24 Jun 1967)	Los Angeles, California, USA	4 Aug	1984
BACKSTROKE					
100 metres	1:03·61	Beverley Rose (b. 21 Jan 1964)	Los Angeles, California, USA	31 Jul	1984
200 metres	2:14·87	Katharine Read (b. 30 Jun 1969)	Coventry, West Midlands	30 May	1986
MEDLEY					
200 metres	2:17·21	Jean Cameron Hill	Edinburgh, Lothian	21 Jul	1986
400 metres	4:46·83	Sharron Davies (b. 1 Nov 1962)	Moscow, USSR	26 Jul	1980
4 × 100 metres relay	4:12·24	GB (Helen Jameson, Margaret Mary Kelly (now Hohmann), Ann Osgerby, June Alexandra Croft)	Moscow, USSR	20 Jul	1980

to England was made by Enrico Tiraboschi, a wealthy Italian living in Argentina, in 16 hr 33 min on 12 Aug 1923, to win the *Daily Sketch* prize of £1000.

The first woman to succeed was Gertrude Caroline Ederle (USA) (b. 23 Oct 1906) who swam from Cap Gris-Nez, France to Deal, England on 6 Aug 1926, in the then overall record time of 14 hr 39 min. The first woman to swim from England to France was Florence Chadwick (USA) (b. 1918) in 16 hr 19 min on 11 Sep 1951. The first Englishwoman to succeed was Mercedes Gleitze (later Carey) (1900–81) who swam from France to England in 15 hr 15 min on 7 Oct 1927. The first twins to complete the crossing were Carole and Sarah Hunt (b. 23 Aug 1962) who swam from England and landed together in France after 9 hr 29 min on 6 Aug 1988.

Fastest ■ The official Channel Swimming Association (founded 1927) record is 7 hr 40 min by Penny Dean (b. 21 Mar 1955) of California, USA, from Shakespeare Beach, Dover to Cap Gris-Nez, France on 29 Jul 1978. The fastest France-England time is 8 hr 5 min by Richard Davey (b. 23 Jun 1965) in 1988.

The fastest crossing by a relay team is 7 hr 17 min, by six Dover lifeguards, from England to France on 9 Aug 1981.

Earliest and latest ■ The earliest date in the year on which the Channel has been swum is 6 Jun by Dorothy Perkins (England) (b. 1942) in 1961, and the latest is 28 Oct by Michael Peter Read (GB) (b. 9 Jun 1941) in 1979.

Youngest and oldest ■ The youngest conqueror is Thomas Gregory (GB) (b. 9 Oct 1976) who swam from Cap Griz-Nez to Shakespeare Point, Dover in 11 hr 54 min on 6 Sep 1988, when he was aged 11 yr 333 days. The youngest girl is Samantha Claire Druce (GB) (b. 21 Apr 1971) who was 12 yr 119 days on 18 Aug 1983 when she swam from Dover to Cap Gris-Nez in 15 hr 27 min.

The oldest has been Bertram Clifford Batt (b. 22 Dec 1919), of Australia at 68 yrs 241 days when he swam from Cap Gris-Nez to Dover in 18 hr 37 min from 19–20 Aug 1987. The oldest woman was Stella Ada Rosina Taylor (b. 20 Dec 1929) aged 45 yr 350 days when she did the swim in 18 hr 15 min on 26 Aug 1975.

Double crossing ■ The first double crossing was by Antonio Abertondo (Argentina) (b. 1919), in 43 hr 10 min on 20–22 Sep 1961. Kevin Murphy (b. 1949) completed the first double crossing by a Briton in 35 hr 10 min on 6 Aug 1970. The first swimmer to achieve a crossing both ways was Edward Harry Temme (1904–78) on 5 Aug 1927 and 19 Aug 1934.

The fastest double crossing was in 16 hr 10 min by

SHORT-COURSE SWIMMING WORLD BESTS (*set in 25 m pools*)

——— MEN ———

Event	Time	Name		Date	
FREESTYLE					
50 metres	21·81	Dano Halsall (Switzerland)	Geneva, Switzerland	16 Jun	1989
100 metres	48·20	Michael Gross (West Germany)	Offenbach, West Germany	2 Jan	1978
200 metres	1:43·95	Giorgio Lamberti (Italy)	Bonn, West Germany	14 Feb	1988
400 metres	3:41·74	Giorgio Lamberti (Italy)	Bonn, West Germany	13 Feb	1988
800 metres	7:38·75	Michael Gross (West Germany)	Bonn, West Germany	8 Feb	1985
1500 metres	14:37·60	Vladimir Salnikov (USSR)	Göteberg, Sweden	19 Dec	1982
4 × 50 metres relay	1:27·95	West Germany	Bonn, West Germany	14 Feb	1988
4 × 100 metres relay	3:16·11	USA			1978
4 × 200 metres relay	7:05·17	West Germany		9 Feb	1986
BACKSTROKE					
50 metres	25·17	Daishi Suzuki (Japan)	Bonn, West Germany	14 Feb	1988
100 metres	54·20	Dirk Richter (GDR)	Den Bosch, Netherlands	15 Dec	1985
200 metres	1:56·60	Tamas Darnyi (Hungary)	Bonn, West Germany	8 Feb	1987
BREASTSTROKE					
100 metres	59·75	Adrian Moorhouse (GBR)	Bonn, West Germany	8 Feb	1987
200 metres	2:08·82	Victor Davis (Canada)	Bonn, West Germany	7 Feb	1987
BUTTERFLY					
50 metres	24·25	Pablo Morales (USA)	Bonn, West Germany	14 Feb	1988
100 metres	52·9*	Michael Gross (West Germany)	Offenbach, West Germany	24 Nov	1984
200 metres	1:54·78	Michael Gross (West Germany)	Bonn, West Germany	9 Feb	1985
MEDLEY					
200 metres	1:58·18	Pablo Morales (USA)	Los Angeles, California, USA	26 Apr	1987
400 metres	4:09·64	Alex Baumann (Canada)	Halifax, Canada	7 Mar	1987
4 × 50 metres relay	1:38·72	USA	Bonn, West Germany	14 Feb	1988

——— WOMEN ———

Event	Time	Name		Date	
FREESTYLE					
50 metres	24·81	Liviu Copariu (Romania)	Sibiu, Romania	9 Apr	1989
100 metres	53·48	Liviu Copariu (Romania)	Sibiu, Romania	8 Apr	1989
200 metres	1:56·35	Birgit Meineke (GDR)	Indianapolis, USA	7 Jan	1983
400 metres	4:02·05	Astrid Strauss (GDR)	Bonn, West Germany	8 Feb	1987
800 metres	8:15·34	Astrid Strauss (GDR)	Bonn, West Germany	6 Feb	1987
1500 metres	15:43·31	Petra Schneider (GDR)	Indianapolis, USA	11 Jan	1982
4 × 50 metres relay	1:42·51	GDR	Bonn, West Germany	7 Feb	1987
4 × 100 metres relay	3:38·77	GDR	Monte Carlo, Monaco	12 Dec	1987
BACKSTROKE					
100 metres	59·89	Betsy Mitchell (USA)	Los Angeles, California, USA	26 Apr	1987
200 metres	2:07·74	Cornelia Sirch (GDR)	Indianapolis, USA	9 Jan	1983
BREASTSTROKE					
100 metres	1:07·05	Silke Hörner (GDR)	Bonn, West Germany	8 Feb	1986
200 metres	2:22·92	Susane Börnike (GDR)	Bonn, West Germany	11 Feb	1989
BUTTERFLY					
50 metres	27·69	Birte Weigang (GDR)	Bonn, West Germany	14 Feb	1988
100 metres	58·91*	Mary T. Meagher (USA)	Gainesville, Florida, USA	3 Jan	1981
200 metres	2:05·65	Mary T. Meagher (USA)	Gainesville, Florida, USA	2 Jan	1981
MEDLEY					
200 metres	2:10·60	Petra Schneider (GDR)	Gainesville, Florida, USA	8 Jan	1982
400 metres	4:31·36	Noemi Lung (Romania)	Paris, France	31 Jan	1987
4 × 100 metres relay	4:02·85	GDR	Indianapolis, USA	8 Jan	1983

* *slower than long-course bests.*

Philip Rush (New Zealand) (b. 6 Nov 1963) on 17 Aug 1987. In setting this record, Philip Rush completed the fastest ever crossing by a man, 7 hr 55 min (England to France). He went on to complete the fastest ever triple crossing in 28 hr 21 min on 17–18 Aug 1987. The women's record is 18 hr 15 min by Irene van der Laan (Netherlands) (b. 27 Dec 1960) on 18 Aug 1983. The first British woman to achieve the double crossing was Alison Streeter (b. 29 Aug 1964) in 21 hr 16 min on 4 Aug 1983. The fastest by a relay team is 15 hr 36 ½ min by the six-man West One International Team (GB) on 24 Sep 1985.

Triple crossing ■ The first triple crossing was by Jon Erikson (USA) (b. 6 Sep 1954) in 38 hr 27 min on 11–12 Aug 1981. Fastest, see Double crossing.

Most conquests ■ The greatest number of Channel conquests is 31 by Michael Read (GB) from 24 Aug 1969 to 19 Aug 1984, including a record six in one year. The most by a woman is 19 (including five

two-way) by Cynthia 'Cindy' M. Nicholas (Canada) (b. 20 Aug 1957) from 29 Jul 1975 to 14 Sep 1982.

LONG–DISTANCE SWIMMING

Longest swims ■ The greatest recorded distance ever swum is 2938 km *1826 miles* down the Mississippi, USA between Ford Dam near Minneapolis and Carrollton Ave, New Orleans, Louisiana, by Fred P. Newton, (b. 1903) of Clinton, Oklahoma from 6 Jul to 29 Dec 1930. He was 742 hr in the water.

The greatest distance covered in a continuous swim is 481·5 km *299 miles* by Ricardo Hoffmann (b. 5 Oct 1941), from Corrientes to Santa Elena, Argentina in the River Parana in 84 hr 37 min on 3–6 Mar 1981.

The longest ocean swim is one of 207·3 km *128·8 miles* by Walter Poenisch Snr (USA) (b. 1914) who started from Havana, Cuba, and arrived at Little Duck Key, Florida, USA (in a shark cage and wearing flippers) 34 hr 15 min later on 11–13 Jul 1978.

In 1966 Mihir Sen of Calcutta, India uniquely swam

the Palk Strait from Sri Lanka to India (in 25 hr 36 min on 5–6 Apr); the Straits of Gibraltar (in 8 hr 1 min on 24 Aug); the length of the Dardanelles (in 13 hr 55 min on 12 Sep); the Bosphorus (in 4 hr on 21 Sep), and the length of the Panama Canal (in 34 hr 15 min on 29–31 Oct).

Irish Channel ■ The swimming of the 37 km *23 mile* wide North Channel from Donaghadee, Northern Ireland to Portpatrick, Scotland was first accomplished by Tom Blower of Nottingham in 15 hr 26 min in 1947. A record time of 9 hr 53 min 42 sec was set by Alison Streeter on 22 Aug 1988. The first Irish-born swimmer to achieve the crossing was Ted Keenan on 11 Aug 1973 in 11–13°C *52–56°F* water in 18 hr 27 min. The first Scottish-born was Margaret Kidd, 22, in 15 hr 25 min 3 sec on 23 Aug 1988.

Bristol Channel ■ The first person to achieve a crossing of the Bristol Channel was Kathleen Thomas (now Mrs Day) (b. Apr 1906) who swam from Penarth, South Glamorgan to Weston-super-

Table Tennis

Mare, Avon in 7 hr 20 min on 5 Sep 1927. The record for the longer swim from Glenthorne Cove, Devon to Porthcawl, Mid-Glamorgan is 10 hr 46 min by Jane Luscombe (b. 13 Jan 1961) of Jersey on 19 Aug 1976.

Lake swims ■ The fastest time for swimming the 36·5 km *22·7 mile* long Loch Ness is 9 hr 57 min by David Trevor Morgan (b. 25 Sep 1963) on 31 Jul 1983. The first successful swim was by Brenda Sherratt (b. 1948) of West Bollington, Cheshire on 26–27 Jul 1966. David Morgan achieved a double crossing of Loch Ness in 23 hr 4 min on 1 Aug 1983. In 1988 he also uniquely swam Loch Ness in 11 hr 9 min on 16 Jul, Loch Lomond 34·6 km *21·5 miles* in 11 hr 48 min on 18 Jul and the English Channel in 11 hr 35 min on 20–21 Jul. The fastest time for swimming Lake Windermere, 16·9 km *10·5 miles* is 3 hr 49 min 56 sec by Karen Toole, 17, of Darlington on 5 Sep 1981. The fastest time for the Lake Windermere International Championship, 26·5 km *16·5 miles*, is 6 hr 10 min 33 sec by Mary Beth Colpo (USA) (b. 1961) on 5 Aug 1978.

24 hours ■ Evan Barry (Australia) swam 96·7 km *60·08 miles*, in a 50 m pool, at the Valley Pool, Brisbane, Australia on 19–20 Dec 1987.

The women's record is 82·1 km *51·01 miles* by Irene van der Laan (Netherlands) at Amersfoort, Netherlands on 20–21 Sep 1985.

Greatest lifetime distance ■ Gustave Brickner (b. 10 Feb 1912) of Charleroi, Pennsylvania, USA in 59 years to November 1986 had recorded 61 977 km *38 512 miles*.

Long–distance relays ■ The New Zealand national relay team of 20 swimmers swam a record 182·807 km *113·59 miles* in Lower Hutt, New Zealand in 24 hours, passing 160 km *100 miles* in 20 hr 47 min 13 sec on 9–10 Dec 1983. The 24 hours club record by a team of five is 154·93 km *96·27 miles* by the City of Newcastle ASC on 16–17 Dec 1986. A women's team from the club swam 143·11 km *88·93 miles* on the same occasion. The most participants in a one-day swim relay is 2135, each swimming a length, organised by Syracuse YMCA in Syracuse, New York, USA on 11 Apr 1986.

The longest duration swim relay was 233 hr 15 min for 903·7 km by a team of 15 from Maccabi Water Polo team at Sydney Football Stadium swimming pool, Sydney, Australia on 1–11 Dec 1988.

Underwater Swimming ■ Paul Cryne (GB) and Samir Sawan al Awami of Qatar swam 78·92 km *49·04 miles* in a 24 hr period from Doha, Qatar to Umm Said and back on 21–22 Feb 1985 using sub-aqua equipment. They were swimming underwater for 95·5 per cent of the time. A relay team of six swam 151·987 km *94·44 miles* in a swimming pool at Olomouc, Czechoslovakia on 17–18 Oct 1987.

Tony Boyle, Eddie McGettigan, Laurence Thermes and Gearoid Murphy swam a relay of 535·71 km *332·88 miles* underwater in 168 hr using sub–aqua equipment at the Mosney Holiday Centre, Co. Meath, Ireland, 22–29 Jun 1985. The first underwater cross-Channel swim was achieved by Fred Baldasare (USA) (b. 1924), who completed a 67·5 km *42 mile* distance from France to England with scuba equipment in 18 hr 1 min on 10–11 Jul 1962.

Sponsored swimming ■ The greatest amount of money collected in a charity swim was £108 040 in 'Splash '89' organised by the Royal Bank of Scotland Swimming Club and was held at the Royal Commonwealth Pool, Edinburgh, Lothian on 28–29 Jan 1989, 3012 swimmers took part. The record for an event staged at several pools was £548 006.14 by 'Penguin Swimathon '88'. It took place at 43 pools throughout London on 26–28 Feb 1988, 5482 swimmers participated.

Table Tennis

Origins ■ The earliest evidence relating to a game resembling table tennis has been found in the

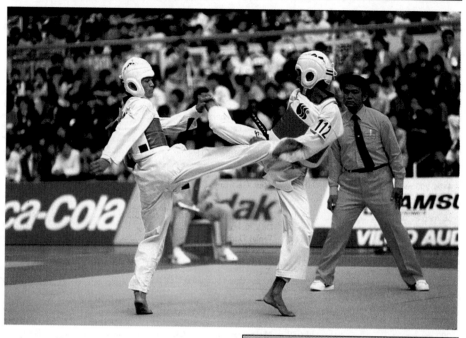

catalogues of London sports goods manufacturers in the 1880s. The old Ping Pong Association was formed in 1902 but the game proved only a temporary craze until resuscitated in 1921. The International Table Tennis Federation was founded in 1926 and the English Table Tennis Association was formed on 24 Apr 1927. Table Tennis is to be included at the Olympic Games for the first time in 1988.

Most English titles ■ The highest total of English men's titles (instituted 1921) is 20 by G. Viktor Barna (1911–72) (b. Hungary, Gyözö Braun). The women's record is 17 by Diane Rowe (b. 14 Apr 1933), now Mrs Eberhard Scholer. Her twin Rosalind (now Mrs Cornett) has won nine (two in singles).

The most titles won in the English Closed Championships is 23 by Desmond Douglas (b. 20 Jul 1955), a record ten men's singles, 1976 and 1979–87, nine men's doubles and four mixed doubles. A record seven women's singles were won by Jill Patricia Hammersley (now Parker, *née* Shirley) (b. 6 Dec 1951) in 1973–6, 1978–9, 1981.

Internationals ■ The youngest ever international was Joy Foster, aged 8 when she represented Jamaica in the West Indies Championships at Port of Spain, Trinidad in Aug 1958. The youngest ever to

Taekwon-Do ● Taekwon-Do was staged as a demonstration sport for men and women at the 1988 Olympic Games with South Koreans winning nine of the sixteen events. (Photo: All-Sport / David Cannon)

TEAM AND INDIVIDUAL TABLE TENNIS CHAMPIONSHIPS

— MOST WINS IN WORLD CHAMPIONSHIPS —

Event	Name and Nationality	Times	Years
MEN			
Singles (St Bride's Vase)	G. Viktor Barna (Hungary) (1911–72)	5	1930, 1932–5
Doubles	G. Viktor Barna (Hungary)	8	1929–35, 1939
Mixed Doubles	Ferenc Sido (Hungary) (b. 1923)	4	1949–50, 1952–3
WOMEN			
Singles (G. Geist Prize)	Angelica Rozeanu (Romania) (b. 15 Oct 1921)	6	1950–5
Doubles	Maria Mednyanszky (Hungary) (1901–79)	7	1928, 1930–5
Mixed Doubles	Maria Mednyanszky (Hungary)	6	1927–8, 1930–1, 1933–4

G. Viktor Barna gained a personal total of 15 world titles, while 18 have been won by Maria Mednyanszky. Note: With the staging of championships biennially the breaking of the above records would now be very difficult.

— MOST TEAM TITLES —

Event	Team	Times	Years
MEN (Swaythling Cup)	Hungary	12	1927–31, 1933–5, 1938, 1949, 1952, 1979
WOMEN (Marcel Corbillon Cup)	China	9	1965, eight successive 1975–89 (bienially)

— MOST WINS IN ENGLISH OPEN CHAMPIONSHIPS —

Event	Name and Nationality	Times	Years
MEN			
Singles	Richard Bergmann (Austria, then GB) (1920–70)	6	1939–40, 1948, 1950, 1952, 1954
Doubles	G. Viktor Barna (Hungary, then GB)	7	1931, 1933–5, 1938–9, 1949
Mixed Doubles	G. Viktor Barna (Hungary, then GB)	8	1933–6, 1938, 1940, 1951, 1953
WOMEN			
Singles	Maria Alexandru (Romania) (b. 1941)	6	1963–4, 1970–2, 1974
Doubles	Diane Rowe (GB) (now Scholer) (b. 14 Apr 1933)	12	1950–6, 1960, 1962–5
Mixed Doubles	Diane Rowe (GB)	4	1952, 1954, 1956, 1960

play for England was Carl Prean (b. 20 Aug 1967), aged 14 yr 191 days, against Portugal at Lisbon on 27 Feb 1982.

Jill Parker played for England on a record 413 occasions, 1967–83.

Counter hitting ■ The record number of hits in 60 sec is 170 by English Internationals Alan Cooke (b. 23 Mar 1966) and Desmond Douglas at Scotswood Sports Centre, Newcastle–upon–Tyne on 28 Feb 1986. The women's record is 168 by the sisters Lisa (b. 9 Mar 1967) and Jackie (b. 9 Sep 1964) Bellinger at Crest Hotel, Luton, Bedfordshire on 14 Jul 1987. With a bat in each hand, Gary D. Fisher of Olympia, Washington, USA completed 5000 consecutive volleys over the net in 44 min 28 sec on 25 Jun 1979.

Highest speed ■ No conclusive measurements have been published but in a lecture M. Sklorz (West Germany) stated that a smashed ball had been measured at speeds up to 170 km/h *105·6 mph.*

Taekwon-Do

The founder and father of this martial art is General Choi Hong Hi 9th Dan, the highest dan awarded. Taekwon-Do was officially recognised as part of Korean tradition and culture on 11 Apr 1955. The International Taekwon-Do Federation was formed in 1966, and has staged world championships from 1974.

The highest dan in Britain is Master Rhee Ki Ha 8th Dan, the Chief Instructor of the United Kingdom Tae- kwon-Do Association.

Tennis (Lawn)

Origins ■ The modern game is generally agreed to have evolved as an outdoor form of the indoor game of tennis (see Tennis [Real]). 'Field tennis' is mentioned in an English magazine – *Sporting Magazine* – of 29 Sep 1793. The earliest club for such a game, variously called Pelota or Lawn Rackets, was the Leamington Club founded in 1872 by Major Harry Gem. The earliest attempt to commercialise the game was by Major Walter Clopton Wingfield (1833–1912) who patented a form called 'sphairistike' on 23 Feb 1874. It soon became called lawn tennis. Amateur players were permitted to play with and against professionals in 'open' tournaments in 1968.

Grand Slam ■ The grand slam is to hold at the same time all four of the world's major championship singles: Wimbledon, the United States, Australian and French championships. The first man to have won all four was Frederick John Perry (GB) (b. 18 May 1909) when he won the French title in 1935. The first man to hold all four championships simultaneously was John Donald Budge (USA) (b. 13 Jun 1915) in 1938, and with Wimbledon and US in 1937, he won six successive grand slam tournaments. The first man to achieve the grand slam twice was Rodney George Laver (Australia) (b. 9 Aug 1938) as an amateur in 1962 and again in 1969 when the titles were open to professionals.

Four women have achieved the grand slam and the first three won six successive grand slam tournaments: Maureen Catherine Connolly (USA) (1934–69), in 1953; Margaret Jean Court (*née* Smith) (Australia) (b. 16 Jul 1942) in 1970; and Martina Navratilova (USA) (b. 18 Oct 1956) in 1983–4. The fourth was Steffi Graf (West Germany) (b. 14 Jun 1969) in 1988, when she also won the women's singles Olympic gold medal. Pamela Howard Shriver (USA) (b. 4 Jul 1962) with Navratilova won eight successive grand slam tournament women's doubles titles and 109 successive matches in all events from April 1983 to July 1985.

The most singles championships won in grand slam tournaments is 24 by Margaret Court (11 Australian,

5 USA, 5 French, 3 Wimbledon), 1960–73. She also won the US Amateur in 1969 and 1970 when this was held as well as the US Open. The men's record is 12 by Roy Emerson (Australia) (b. 3 Nov 1936) (6 Australian, 2 each French, USA, Wimbledon), 1961–7.

The most succesful doubles partnership has been Althea Louise Brough (USA) (b. 11 Mar 1923) and Margaret Evelyn Du Pont (*née* Osborne) (USA) (b. 4 Mar 1918) who won 20 grand slam tournaments, (12 USA, 5 Wimbledon, 3 French), 1942–57.

WIMBLEDON CHAMPIONSHIPS

Most wins *Women* ■ Billie-Jean King (USA) (*née* Moffit) (b. 22 Nov 1943) won a record 20 titles between 1961 and 1979, six singles, ten women's doubles and four mixed doubles. Elizabeth Montague Ryan (USA) (1892–1979) won a record 19 doubles (12 women's, 7 mixed) titles from 1914 to 1934.

Men ■ The greatest number of titles by a man has been 13 by Hugh Laurence Doherty (GB) (1875–1919) with five singles titles (1902–6) and a record eight men's doubles (1897–1901, 1903–5) partnered by his brother Reginald Frank (1872–1910).

Singles ■ Helen Newington Moody (*née* Wills) (USA) (b. 6 Oct 1905) won eight in 1927–30, 1932–3, 1935 and 1938, a record shared with Martina Navratilova, 1978–9, 1982–7. The most men's singles wins since the Challenge Round was abolished in 1922 is five consecutively, by Björn Borg (Sweden) in 1976–80. William Charles Renshaw (GB) (1861–1904) won seven singles in 1881–6 and 1889.

Mixed doubles ■ The male record is four titles shared by: Elias Victor Seixas (USA) (b. 30 Aug 1923) in 1953–6; Kenneth Norman Fletcher (Australia) (b. 15 Jun 1940) in 1963, 1965–6, 1968; and Owen Keir Davidson (Australia) (b. 4 Oct 1943) in 1967, 1971, 1973–4. The female record is seven by Elizabeth Ryan (USA) from 1919 to 1932.

Most appearances ■ Arthur William Charles 'Wentworth' Gore (1868–1928) (GB) made a record 36 appearances at Wimbledon between 1888 and 1927. In 1964, Jean Borotra (b. 13 Aug 1898) of France made his 35th appearance since 1922. In 1977 he appeared in the Veterans' Doubles aged 78.

Youngest champions ■ The youngest champion was Charlotte 'Lottie' Dod (1871–1960), who was 15 yr 285 days when she won in 1887. The youngest male champion was Boris Becker (West Germany) (b. 22 Nov 1967) who won the men's singles title in 1985 at 17 yr 227 days. The youngest ever player at Wimbledon was reputedly Mita Klima (Austria) who was 13 yr in the 1907 singles competition. The youngest player to win a match at Wimbledon was Kathy Rinaldi (USA) (b. 24 Mar 1967), at 14 yr 91 days on 23 Jun 1981.

Oldest champions ■ The oldest champion was Margaret Evelyn du Pont (*née* Osborne) (USA) (b. 4 Mar 1918) at 44 yr 125 days when she won the mixed doubles in 1962 with Neale Fraser (Australia). The oldest singles champion was Arthur Gore (GB) in 1909 at 41 yr 182 days.

Greatest crowd ■ The record crowd for one day was 39 813 on 26 Jun 1986. The record for the whole championship was 400 032 in 1986.

UNITED STATES CHAMPIONSHIPS

Most wins ■ Margaret Evelyn du Pont (*née* Osborne) won a record 25 titles between 1941 and 1960. She won a record 13 women's doubles (12 with Althea Louise Brough), nine mixed doubles and three singles. The men's record is 16 by William Tatem Tilden, including seven men's singles, 1920–5, 1929 – a record for singles shared with: Richard Dudley Sears (1861–1943), 1881–7; William A. Larned (1872–1926), 1901–2, 1907–11, and at women's singles by: Molla Mallory (*née* Bjurstedt) (1892–1959), 1915–16, 1918, 1920–2, 1926; and Helen Moody (*née* Wills), 1923–5, 1927–9, 1931.

Youngest and oldest ■ The youngest champion was Vincent Richards (1903–59), who was 15 yr

Grand Slam tournament titles ● Martina Navratilova and Pam Shriver celebrate winning the 1989 Australian Open women's doubles. It was their seventh Australian Championship and their nineteenth major tournament title overall (4 French, 5 Wimbledon, 3 US). They are one title short of the record which is held by Althea Louise Brough (USA) and Margaret Evelyn Du Pont (*née* Osborne) (USA), 1942–57. (Photo: All-Sport/David Cannon)

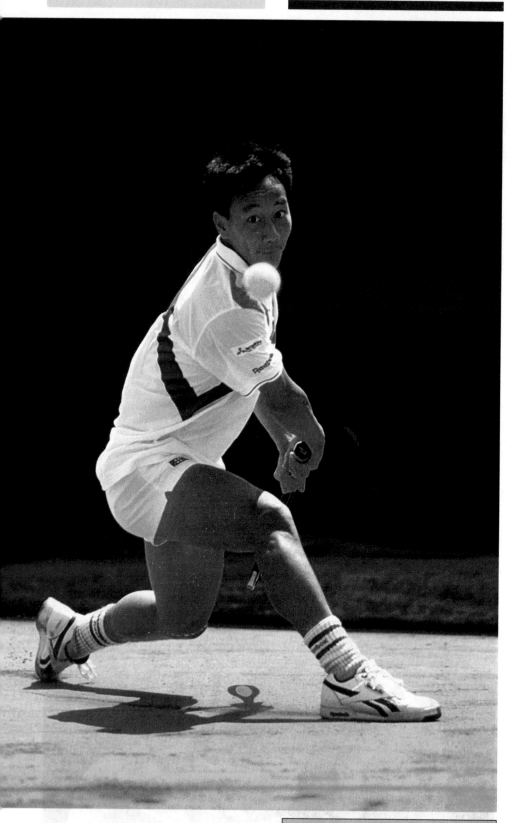

AUSTRALIAN CHAMPIONSHIPS

Most wins ■ Margaret Jean Court (*née* Smith) (b. 16 Jul 1942) won the women's singles 11 times (1960–6, 1969–71 and 1973) as well as eight women's doubles and two mixed doubles, for a record total of 21 titles. A record six men's singles were won by Roy Stanley Emerson (Qld) (b. 3 Nov 1936), 1961 and 1963–7. Thelma Dorothy Long (*née* Coyne) (b. 30 May 1918) won a record 12 women's doubles and four mixed doubles for a record total of 16 doubles titles. Adrian Karl Quist (b. 4 Aug 1913) won ten consecutive men's doubles from 1936 to 1950 (the last eight with John Bromwich) and three men's singles.

Longest span, oldest and youngest ■ Thelma Long won her first (1936) and last (1958) titles 22 years apart. Kenneth Robert Rosewall (b. 2 Nov 1934) won the singles in 1953 and in 1972 was, 19 years later, at 37 yr 62 days, the oldest singles winner. The oldest champion was (Sir) Norman Everard Brookes (1877-1968), who was 46 yr 2 months when he won the 1924 men's doubles. The youngest champions were Rodney W. Heath, aged 17, when he won the men's singles in 1905, and Margaret Smith, who won the women's singles at 17 yr 5 months in 1960.

GRAND PRIX MASTERS

The first Grand Prix Masters Championships were staged in Tokyo, Japan in 1970. They have been held in New York, USA annually from 1977. Qualification to this annual event is by relative success in the preceding year's Grand Prix tournaments. A record five titles have been won by Ivan Lendl, 1982–3, two in 1986 (January and December) and 1987. He appeared in nine successive finals, 1980–8. James Scott Connors (USA) (b. 2 Sep 1952) uniquely qualified for 14 consecutive years, 1972–85. He chose not to play in 1975, 1976 and 1985, and won in 1977. He qualified again in 1987 and 1988, but did not play in 1988.

A record seven doubles titles were won by John Patrick McEnroe (b. 16 Feb 1959) and Peter Fleming (b. 21 Jan 1955) (both USA), 1978–84.

OLYMPIC GAMES

Tennis was re-introduced to the Olympic Games in 1988, having originally been included at the Games from 1896 to 1924. It was also a demonstration sport in 1968 and 1984.

A record four gold medals as well as a silver and a bronze, were won by Max Decugis (France) (1882–1978), 1900–20. A women's record five medals (one gold, two silver, two bronze) were won by Kitty McKane (later Mrs Godfree) (GB) (b. 7 May 1897) in 1920 and 1924.

INTERNATIONAL TEAM COMPETITIONS

Davis Cup (instituted 1900) ■ The most wins in the Davis Cup, the men's international team championship, has been 28 by the USA. The most appearances for Cup winners is eight by Roy Emerson (Australia), 1959–62, 1964–7. The British Isles/Great Britain have won nine times, in 1903–6, 1912, 1933–6.

Nicola Pietrangeli (Italy) (b. 11 Sep 1933) played a record 163 rubbers (66 ties), 1954 to 1972, winning 120. He played 109 singles (winning 78) and 54 doubles (winning 42). The record number of rubbers by a British player is 65 (winning 43) by Michael J. Sangster (b. 9 Sep 1940), 1960–8; the most wins is 45 from 52 rubbers by Fred Perry, including 34 of 38 singles, 1931–6.

Wightman Cup (instituted 1923) ■ The annual women's match has been won 50 times by the

139 days when he won the men's doubles with Bill Tilden in 1918. The youngest singles champion was Tracy Ann Austin (b. 12 Dec 1962) who was 16 yr 271 days when she won the women's singles in 1979. The oldest champion was Margaret du Pont who won the mixed doubles at 42 yr 166 days in 1960. The oldest singles champion was William Larned at 38 yr 242 days in 1911.

FRENCH CHAMPIONSHIPS

Most wins (from international status 1925) ■ Margaret Court won a record 13 titles, five singles, four women's doubles and four mixed doubles, 1962–73. The men's record is nine by Henri Cochet (France) (1901–87), four singles, three men's doubles and two mixed doubles, 1926–30. The

> **Youngest champion** ● Michael Chang (USA) (b. 22 Feb 1972) became the youngest male singles winner of any of the four grand slam tournaments when he won the French Open, beating Stefan Edberg (Sweden) 6-1, 3-6, 4-6, 6-4, 6-2, on 11 Jun 1989. (Photo: All-Sport)

singles record is seven by Chris Evert, 1974–5, 1979–80, 1983, 1985–6. Bjørn Borg won a record six men's singles, 1974–5, 1978–81.

Youngest and oldest ■ The youngest champions were the 1981 mixed doubles winners, Andrea Jaeger (b. 4 Jun 1965) at 15 yr 339 days and Jimmy Arias (b. 16 Aug 1964) at 16 yr 296 days. The youngest singles winner was Michael Chang (USA) (b. 22 Feb 1972) at 17 yr 109 days in 1989. The oldest

United States and 10 times by Great Britain. Virginia Wade (GB) (b. 10 Jul 1945) played in a record 21 ties and 56 rubbers, 1965–85. Christine Marie Evert (USA) (b. 21 Dec 1954) won all 26 of her singles matches, 1971 to 1985.

Federation Cup (instituted 1963) ■ The most wins in the Federation Cup, the women's international team championship, is 12 by the USA. Virginia Wade (GB) played each year from 1967 to 1983, in a record 57 ties, playing 100 rubbers, including 56 singles (winning 36) and 44 doubles (winning 30). Chris Evert won her first 29 singles matches, 1977–86. Her overall record, 1977–87 is 35 wins in 37 singles and 16 wins in 18 doubles matches.

Longest span as national champion ■ Keith Gledhill (b. 17 Feb 1911) won the US National Boys' Doubles Championship with Sidney Wood in August 1926. Sixty-one years later he won the US National 75 and over Men's Doubles Championship with Elbert Lewis at Goleta, California, USA in August 1987.

Dorothy May Bundy-Cheney (USA) (b. September 1916) won 180 US titles at various age groups from 1941 to March 1988.

International contest *Longest span* ■ Jean Borotra (France) (b. 13 Aug 1898) played in every one of the twice yearly contests between the International Club of France and the I.C. of Great Britain from the first in 1929 to his 100th match at Wimbledon on 1–3 Nov 1985. On that occasion he played a mixed doubles against Kitty Godfree (GB) (b. 7 May 1896). Both were former Wimbledon singles champions, and aged 87 and 89 respectively.

Highest earnings ■ Ivan Lendl (Czechoslovakia) (b. 7 Mar 1960) won a men's season's record $2 028 850 in 1982 and has career earnings of $14 003 118 by 26 Jun 1989. The season's record for a woman is $2 173 556 in 1984 (including a $1 million Grand Slam bonus) by Martina Navratilova. Earnings from special restricted events and team tennis are not included. Navratilova's lifetime earnings by 26 Jun 1989 reached $14 331 150.

The one-match record is $583 200 by Ivan Lendl (Czechoslovakia) when he beat Pat Cash (Australia) in the final of the four-man Stakes Match tennis exhibition at West Palm Beach, USA on 30 Nov 1987. The highest total prize money was $4 371 500 for the 1988 US Open Championships.

Greatest crowd ■ A record 30 472 people were at the Astrodome, Houston, Texas, USA on 20 Sep 1973, when Billie-Jean King (*née* Moffitt) (USA) (b. 22 Nov 1943) beat Robert Larimore Riggs (USA) (b. 25 Feb 1918). The record for an orthodox tennis match is 25 578 at Sydney, New South Wales, Australia on 27 Dec 1954 in the Davis Cup Challenge Round (first day) Australia *v.* USA.

Fastest service ■ The fastest service timed with modern equipment is 222 km/h *138 mph* by Steve Denton (USA) (b. 5 Sep 1956) at Beaver Creek, Colorado, USA on 29 Jul 1984. The fastest *ever* measured was one of 263 km/h *163·6 mph* by William Tatem Tilden (USA) (1893–1953) in 1931.

Longest game ■ The longest known singles game was one of 37 deuces (80 points) between Anthony Fawcett (Rhodesia) and Keith Glass (GB) in the first round of the Surrey Championships at Surbiton, Surrey on 26 May 1975. It lasted 31 min. Noëlle van Lottum and Sandra Begijn played a game lasting 52 min in the semi-finals of the Dutch Indoor Championships at Ede, Gelderland on 12 Feb 1984.

The longest tiebreak was 26–24 for the fourth and decisive set of a first round men's doubles at the Wimbledon Championships on 1 Jul 1985. Jan Gunnarsson (Sweden) and Michael Mortensen (Denmark) defeated John Frawley (Australia) and Victor Pecci (Paraguay) 6–3, 6–4, 3–6, 7–6.

The longest rally in tournament play was one of 643 times over the net between Vicky Nelson and Jean Hepner at Richmond, Virginia, USA in October

1984. The 6 hr 22 min match was won by Nelson 6–4, 7–6. It concluded with a 1 hr 47 min tiebreak, 13–11, for which one point took 29 minutes.

Will Duggan and Ron Kapp (both USA) performed a rally of 6202 strokes which took 3 hr 33 min at Santa Barbara Municipal Stadium, California, USA on 12 Mar 1988.

Tennis (Real/Royal)

The game originated as *jeu de paume* in French monasteries *c.* 1050. A tennis court is mentioned in the sale of the Hôtel de Nesle, Paris bought by King Philippe IV of France in 1308. The oldest of the surviving active courts in Great Britain is that at Falkland Palace, Fife built by King James V of Scotland in 1539.

Most titles *World* ■ The first recorded world tennis champion was Clerge (France) *c.* 1740. Jacques Edmond Barre (France) (1802–73) held the title for a record 33 yr from 1829 to 1862. Pierre Etchebaster (1893–1980), a Basque, holds the record for the greatest number of successful defences of the title with eight between 1928 and 1952.

The first two Women's World Championships in 1985 and 1987 were won by Judith Anne Clarke (Australia) (b. 28 Dec 1954) .

British ■ The Amateur Championship of the British Isles (instituted 1888) has been won 16 times by Howard Rea Angus (b. 25 Jun 1944) 1966–80 and 1982. He also won eight Amateur Doubles Championships with David Warburg (1923–1987), 1967–70, 1972–4 and 1976, and was world champion 1976–81.

Tiddlywinks

National Championships ■ Alan Dean (b. 22 Jul 1949) has won the singles title six times, 1971–3, 1976, 1978 and 1986, and the pairs title six times. Jonathan Mapley (b. 1947) has won the pairs title seven times, 1972, 1975, 1977, 1980, 1983–4 and 1987.

Potting records ■ The record for potting 24 winks from 18 in *45 cm* is 21·8 sec by Stephen Williams (Altrincham Grammar School) in May 1966. Allen R. Astles (University of Wales) potted 10 000 winks in 3 hr 51 min 46 sec at Aberystwyth, Dyfed in February 1966.

A record 35 winks were potted in relay in three minutes (24 in two minutes) by Duncan Budd, Tim Hedger, Alex Satchell and Nick Inglis of the Cambridge University Tiddlywinkers Club at Queen's College, Cambridge on 20 Jul 1987.

Track and Field Athletics

The earliest evidence of organised running was at Memphis, Eygpt *c.* 3800 BC. The earliest accurately dated Olympic Games was in July 776 BC, at which celebration Coroibos won the foot race. The oldest surviving measurements are a long jump of 7·05 m *23 ft 1 ½ in* by Chionis of Sparta in *c.* 656 BC and a discus throw of 100 cubits (about 46·30 m *152 ft*) by Protesilaus.

Fastest speed ■ An analysis of split times at each 10 metres in the 1988 Olympic Games 100 m final in Seoul on 24 Sep 1988 won by Ben Johnson (Canada) in 9·79 (average speed 36·77 km/h *22·85 mph* but later disallowed as a world record due to his positve drugs test for steroids) from Carl Lewis (USA) 9·92, showed that both Johnson and Lewis reached a peak speed (40 m–50 m and 80 m–90 m respectively) of 0·83 sec for 10 m, i.e. 43·37 km/h *26·95 mph*.

Highest jump above own head ■ The greatest height cleared above an athlete's own head is 59 cm *23 ¼ in* by Franklin Jacobs (USA) (b. 31 Dec 1957), who cleared 2·32 m *7 ft 7 ¼ in* at New York, USA, on

First 80 m javelin throw by a woman ● Petra Felke (GDR) (b. 30 Jul 1959) set her fourth world record at 80·00 m *262 ft 5 in* at Potsdam, GDR on 9 Sep 1988. She then went on to win the Olympic title in Seoul with an Olympic record throw of 74·68 m *245 ft*. (Photo: All-Sport / Tony Duffy)

27 Jan 1978. He is 1·73 m *5 ft 8 in* tall. The greatest height cleared by a woman above her own head is 30·5 cm *12 in* by Cindy John Holmes (USA) (b. 29 Aug 1960), 1·525 m *5 ft* tall, who jumped 1·83 m *6 ft* at Provo, Utah, USA on 1 Jun 1982.

Most Olympic titles *Men* ■ The most Olympic gold medals won is ten (an absolute Olympic record) by Ray C. Ewry (USA) (1874–1937) in the standing high, long and triple jumps in 1900, 1904, 1906 and 1908.

Women ■ The most gold medals won by a woman is four shared by: Francina 'Fanny' E. Blankers-Koen (Netherlands) (b. 26 Apr 1918) with 100 m, 200 m, 80 m hurdles and 4 × 100 m relay, 1948; Betty Cuthbert (Australia) (b. 20 Apr 1938) with 100 m, 200 m, 4 × 100 m relay, 1956 and 400 m, 1964; and Bärbel Wöckel (*née* Eckert) (GDR) (b. 21 Mar 1955) with 200 m and 4 × 100 m relay in 1976 and 1980.

Most wins at one Games ■ The most gold medals at one celebration is five by Paavo Johannes Nurmi (Finland) (1897–1973) in 1924; 1500 m, 5000 m, 10 000 m cross-country, 3000 m team and cross-country team. The most at individual events is four by Alvin C. Kraenzlein (USA) (1876–1928) in 1900: 60 m, 110 m hurdles, 200 m hurdles and long jump.

Most Olympic medals *Men* ■ The most medals won is 12 (nine gold and three silver) by Paavo Nurmi (Finland) in the Games of 1920, 1924 and 1928.

Women ■ The most medals won by a woman athlete is seven by Shirley de la Hunty (*née* Strickland) (Australia) (b. 18 Jul 1925) with three gold, one silver and three bronze in the 1948, 1952 and 1956 Games. A recently discovered photo-finish indicates that she finished third, not fourth, in the 1948

WORLD RECORDS MEN

World records for the men's events scheduled by the International Amateur Athletic Federation. Fully automatic electric timing is mandatory for events up to 400 metres.

RUNNING	min	sec	Name and country	Place	Date	
100 metres		9·83*	Ben Johnson (Canada) (b. 30 Dec 1961)	Rome, Italy	30 Aug	1987
200 metres		19·72A	Pietro Mennea (Italy) (b. 28 Jun 1952)	Mexico City, Mexico	12 Sep	1979
400 metres		43·29	Harry Lee 'Butch' Reynolds (USA) (b. 8 Aug 1964)	Zürich, Switzerland	17 Aug	1988
800 metres	1:41·73		Sebastian Newbold Coe (GB) (b. 29 Sep 1956)	Florence, Italy	10 Jun	1981
1000 metres	2:12·18		Sebastian Newbold Coe (GB)	Oslo, Norway	11 Jul	1981
1500 metres	3:29·46		Saïd Aouita (Morocco) (b. 2 Nov 1959)	West Berlin, West Germany	23 Aug	1985
1 mile	3:46·32		Steven Cram (GB) (b. 14 Oct 1960)	Oslo, Norway	27 Jul	1985
2000 metres	4:50·81		Saïd Aouita (Morocco)	Paris, France	16 Jul	1987
3000 metres	7:32·1		Henry Rono (Kenya) (b. 12 Feb 1952)	Oslo, Norway	27 Jun	1978
5000 metres	12:58·39		Saïd Aouita (Morocco)	Rome, Italy	22 Jul	1987
10 000 metres	27:13·81		Fernando Mamede (Portugal) (b. 1 Nov 1951)	Stockholm, Sweden	2 Jul	1984
20 000 metres	57:24·2		Josephus Hermens (Netherlands) (b. 8 Jan 1950)	Papendal, Netherlands	1 May	1976
25 000 metres	1 hr 13:55·8		Toshihiko Seko (Japan) (b. 15 Jul 1956)	Christchurch, New Zealand	22 Mar	1981
30 000 metres	1 hr 29:18·8		Toshihiko Seko (Japan)	Christchurch, New Zealand	22 Mar	1981
1 hour	20 944 m 13 miles 24 yd 2 ft		Josephus Hermens (Netherlands)	Papendal, Netherlands	1 May	1976

* Ben Johnson ran 100 m in 9·79 sec at Seoul, South Korea on 24 Sep 1988, but was subsequently disqualified on a positive drugs test for steroids. He later admitted to having taken drugs over many years, and this may invalidate his 9·83 sec. The next best is 9·92 sec by Frederick Carlton 'Carl' Lewis (USA) (b. 1 Jul 1961) at Seoul on 24 Sep 1988.
A This record was set at high altitude—Mexico City 2240 m 7349 ft. Best mark at low altitude: 200 m: 19·75 sec, Carl Lewis, Indianapolis, Indiana, USA, 19 Jun 1983 and Joseph Nathaniel DeLoach (USA) (b. 5 Jun 1967) at Seoul, South Korea on 28 Sep 1988.

HURDLING

110 metres (3' 6" 106 cm)	12·93	Renaldo Nehemiah (USA) (b. 24 Mar 1959)	Zürich, Switzerland	19 Aug	1981
400 metres (3' 0" 91·4 cm)	47·02	Edwin Corley Moses (USA) (b. 31 Aug 1955)	Koblenz, West Germany	31 Aug	1983
3000 metres steeplechase	8:05·35	Peter Koech (Kenya) (b. 18 Feb 1958)	Stockholm, Sweden	4 Jul	1989

RELAYS

4×100 metres	37·83	United States National Team: Sam Graddy, Ronald James Brown, Calvin Smith, Frederick Carlton Lewis	Los Angeles, California, USA	11 Aug	1984
4×200 metres	1:20·26†	University of Southern California, USA: Joel Andrews, James Sanford, William Mullins, Clancy Edwards	Tempe, Arizona, USA	27 May	1978
4×400 metres	2:56·16A	United States: Vincent Edward Matthews, Ronald J. Freeman, George Lawrence James, Lee Edward Evans	Mexico City, Mexico	20 Oct	1968
	2:56·16	United States: Danny Joe Everett, Steven Earl Lewis, Kevin Robinzine, Harry Lee 'Butch' Reynolds	Seoul, South Korea	1 Oct	1988
4×800 metres	7:03·89	Great Britain: Peter Elliott, Garry Peter Cook, Steven Cram, Sebastian Newbold Coe	Crystal Palace, London	30 Aug	1982
4×1500 metres	14:38·8	West Germany: Thomas Wessinghage, Harald Hudak, Michael Lederer, Karl Fleschen	Cologne, West Germany	17 Aug	1977

† Texas Christian University ran 1:20·20 at Philadelphia, Pa, USA on 26 Apr 1986. This time could not be ratified as their team was composed of different nationalities: Roscoe Tatum (USA), Andrew Smith (Jamaica), Leroy Reid (Jamaica), Greg Sholars (USA).

FIELD EVENTS	m	ft	in	Name and country	Place	Date	
High Jump	2·43	7	11½	Javier Sotomayor (Cuba) (b. 13 Oct 1967)	Salamanca, Spain	8 Sep	1988
Pole Vault	6·06	19	10½	Sergey Bubka (USSR) (b. 4 Dec 1963)	Nice, France	10 Jul	1988
Long Jump	8·90A	29	2	Robert Beamon (USA) (b. 29 Aug 1946)	Mexico City, Mexico	18 Oct	1968
Triple Jump	17·97	58	11	William Augustus 'Willie' Banks (USA) (b. 11 Mar 1956)	Indianapolis, USA	16 Jun	1985
Shot 7·26 kg 16 lb	23·06	75	8	Ulf Timmermann (GDR) (b. 1 Nov 1962)	Khania, Greece	22 May	1988
Discus 2 kg 4 lb 6·55 oz	74·08	243	0	Jürgen Schult (GDR) (b. 11 May 1960)	Neubrandenburg, GDR	6 Jun	1986
Hammer 7·26 kg 16 lb	86·74	284	7	Yuriy Georgiyevich Sedykh (USSR) (b. 11 Jun 1955)	Stuttgart, West Germany	30 Aug	1986
Javelin 800 g 28·22 oz	87·66†	287	7	Jan Zelezný (Czechoslovakia) (b. 16 Jun 1966)	Nitra, Czechoslovakia	31 May	1987

†With the new javelin, which has the centre of gravity moved back, introduced in 1986. The best performance with the old javelin was 104·80 m 343 ft 10 in by Uwe Hohn (GDR) (b. 16 Jul 1962) at East Berlin, GDR on 20 Jul 1984.
A Set at high altitude; the low altitude best: 8·79 m 28 ft 10 ¼in, Carl Lewis at Indianapolis, Indiana, USA on 19 Jun 1983.

DECATHLON

8847 points — Francis Morgan 'Daley' Thompson (GB) (b. 30 Jul 1958) — Los Angeles, California, USA — 8–9 Aug 1984
(1st day: 100 m 10·44 sec, Long Jump 8·01 m 26' 3½", Shot Put 15·72 m 51' 7",High Jump 2·03 m 6' 8", 400 m 46·97 sec) (2nd day: 110 m Hurdles 14·33 sec, Discus 46·56 m 152' 9", Pole Vault 5·00 m 16' 4¾", Javelin 65·24 m 214' 0", 1500 m 4:35·00 sec)

200 metres event, thus unofficially increasing her medal haul to eight. Irena Szewinska (née Kirszenstein) (Poland) (b. 24 May 1946) won three gold, two silver and two bronze in 1964, 1968, 1972 and 1976, and is the only woman athlete to win a medal in four successive games.

Most Olympic titles *British* ■ The most gold medals won by a British athlete (excluding tug of war and walking, *q.v.*) is two by: Charles Bennett (1871–1949) (1500 m and 5000 m team, 1900); Alfred Edward Tysoe (1874–1901) (800 m and 5000 m team, 1900); John Rimmer (1879–1962) (4000 m steeplechase and 5000 m team, 1900); Albert George Hill (1889–1969) (800 m and 1500 m, 1920); Douglas Gordon Arthur Lowe (1902–81) (800 m 1924 and 1928); Sebastian Newbold Coe (b. 29 Sep 1956) (1500 m 1980 and 1984) and Francis Morgan 'Daley'

Thompson (b. 30 Jul 1958) (decathlon 1980 and 1984). Daley Thompson was also world champion at the decathlon in 1983.

Most Olympic medals *British* ■ The most medals won by a British athlete is four by Guy M. Butler (1899–1981) gold for the 4×400 m relay and silver for 400 m in 1920 and bronze for each of these events in 1924, and by Sebastian Coe, who also won silver medals at 800 m in 1980 and 1984. Three British women athletes have won three medals: Dorothy Hyman (b. 9 May 1941) with a silver (100 m, 1960) and two bronze (200 m, 1960 and 4×100 m relay, 1964), Mary Denise Rand (now Toomey, née Bignal), (b. 10 Feb 1940) with a gold (long jump), a silver (pentathlon) and a bronze (4×100 m relay), all in 1964 and Kathryn Jane Cook (née Smallwood) (b. 3 May 1960), all bronze – at 4×100 m relay 1980 and 1984, and at 400 m in 1984.

Olympic champions *Oldest and youngest* ■ The oldest athlete to win an Olympic title was Irish-born Patrick J. 'Babe' McDonald (USA) (1878–1954) who was aged 42 yr 26 days when he won the 25·4 kg 56 lb weight throw at Antwerp, Belgium on 21 Aug 1920. The oldest female champion was Lia Manoliu (Romania) (b. 25 Apr 1932) aged 36 yr 176 days when she won the discus at Mexico City on 18 Oct 1968. The youngest gold medallist was Barbara Pearl Jones (USA) (b. 26 Mar 1937) who at 15 yr 123 days was a member of the winning 4×100 m relay team, at Helsinki, Finland on 27 Jul 1952. The youngest male champion was Robert Bruce Mathias (USA) (b. 17 Nov 1930) aged 17 yr 263 days when he won the decathlon at the London Games on 5–6 Aug 1948.

The oldest Olympic medallist was Tebbs Lloyd

WORLD RECORDS *WOMEN*

World records for the women's events scheduled by the International Amateur Athletic Federation. The same stipulation about automatically timed events applies in the six events up to 400 metres as in the men's list.

RUNNING	min sec	Name and country	Place	Date
100 metres	10·49	Delorez Florence Griffith-Joyner (USA) (b. 21 Dec 1959)	Indianapolis, USA	16 Jul 1988
200 metres	21·34	Delorez Florence Griffith-Joyner (USA)	Seoul, South Korea	29 Sep 1988
400 metres	47·60	Marita Koch (GDR) (b. 18 Feb 1957)	Canberra, Australia	6 Oct 1985
800 metres	1:53·28	Jarmila Kratochvilova (Czechoslovakia) (b. 26 Jan 1951)	Münich, West Germany	26 Jul 1983
1000 metres	2:30·6	Tatyana Providokhina (USSR) (b. 26 Mar 1953)	Podolsk, USSR	20 Aug 1978
1500 metres	3:52·47	Tatyana Kazankina (USSR) (b. 17 Dec 1951)	Zürich, Switzerland	13 Aug 1980
1 mile	4:15·61	Paula Ivan (Romania) (b. 20 Jul 1963)	Nice, France	10 Jul 1989
2000 metres	5:28·69	Maricica Puica (Rumania) (b. 29 Jul 1950)	Crystal Palace, London	11 Jul 1986
3000 metres	8:22·62	Tatyana Kazankina (USSR)	Leningrad, USSR	26 Aug 1984
5000 metres	14:37·33	Ingrid Kristiansen (*née* Christensen) (Norway) (b. 21 Mar 1956)	Stockholm, Sweden	5 Aug 1986
10 000 metres	30:13·74	Ingrid Kristiansen (Norway)	Oslo, Norway	5 Jul 1986

HURDLING		Name and country	Place	Date
100 metres (2′ 9″ *84 cm*)	12·21	Yordanka Donkova (Bulgaria) (b. 28 Sep 1961)	Stara Zagora, Bulgaria	20 Aug 1988
400 metres (2′ 6″ *76 cm*)	52·94	Marina Styepanova (*née* Makeyeva) (USSR) (b. 1 May 1950)	Tashkent, USSR	17 Sep 1986

RELAYS		Name and country	Place	Date
4 × 100 metres	41·37	GDR: Silke Gladisch (now Möller), Sabine Rieger (now Günther), Ingrid Auerswald (*née* Brestrich), Marlies Göhr (*née* Oelsner)	Canberra, Australia	6 Oct 1985
4 × 200 metres	1:28·15	GDR: Marlies Göhr (*née* Oelsner), Romy Müller (*née* Schneider), Bärbel Wöckel (*née* Eckert), Marita Koch	Jena, GDR	9 Aug 1980
4 × 400 metres	3:15·17	USSR: Tatyana Ledovskaya, Olga Nazarova, Maria Pinigina (*née* Kulchunova), Olga Bryzgina (*née* Vladykina)	Seoul, South Korea	1 Oct 1988
4 × 800 metres	7:50·17	USSR: Nadezha Olizarenko (*née* Mushta), Lyubov Gurina, Lyudmila Borisova, Irina Podyalovskaya	Moscow, USSR	4 Aug 1984

FIELD EVENTS	m	ft in	Name and country	Place	Date
High Jump	2·09	6 10¼	Stefka Kostadinova (Bulgaria) (b. 25 Mar 1965)	Rome, Italy	30 Aug 1987
Long Jump	7·52	24 8¼	Galina Chistyakova (USSR) (b. 26 Jul 1962)	Leningrad, USSR	11 Jun 1988
Shot 4 kg *8 lb 13 oz*	22·63	74 3	Natalya Lisovskaya (USSR) (b. 16 Jul 1962)	Moscow, USSR	7 Jun 1987
Discus 1 kg *2 lb 3·27 oz*	76·80	252 0	Gabriele Reinsch (GDR) (b. 23 Sep 1963)	Neubrandenburg, GDR	9 Jul 1988
Javelin 600 g *24·74 oz*	80·00	262 5	Petra Felke (GDR) (b. 30 Jul 1959)	Potsdam, GDR	9 Sep 1988

HEPTATHLON		Name and country	Place	Date
7291 points		Jacqueline Joyner-Kersee (USA) (b. 3 Mar 1962)	Seoul, South Korea	23–24 Sep 1988

(100 m hurdles 12·69 sec; High Jump 1·86 m *6 ft 1¼ in*; Shot 15·80 m *51 ft 10 in*; 200 m 22·56 sec; Long Jump 7·27 m *23 ft 10 in*; Javelin; 45·66 m *149 ft 9 in*; 800 m 2 min 08·51 sec)

Johnson (1900–84), aged 48 yr 115 days when he was third in the 1948 50 000 m walk. The oldest woman medallist was Dana Zátopková (b. 19 Sep 1922) aged 37 yr 348 days when she was second in the javelin in 1960.

World Championships ■ Quadrennial World Championships, distinct from the Olympic Games, were inaugurated in 1983, when they were held in Helsinki, Finland. The most medals won is five gold and one silver by Carl Lewis (b. 1 Jul 1961), gold at 100 m, long jump, 4 × 100 m relay in 1983 and the latter two also in 1987, when he took the silver at 100 m. He has also won six Olympic golds, four in 1984 and two in 1988.

World record breakers *Oldest and youngest* ■ For the greatest age at which anyone has broken a world record under IAAF jurisdiction *see p. 220.* The female record is 36 yr 139 days for Marina Styepanova (*née* Makeyeva) (USSR) (b. 1 May 1950) with 52·94 sec for the 400 m hurdles at Tashkent, USSR on 17 Sep 1986. The youngest individual record breaker is Wang Yang (China) (b. 9 Apr 1971) who set a women's 3000 m walk record at age 14 yr 334 days with 21 min 33·8 sec at Jian, China on 9 Mar 1986. The youngest male is 17 yr 198 days Thomas Ray (1862–1904) when he pole-vaulted 3·42 m *11 ft 2¾ in* on 19 Sep 1879 (prior to IAAF ratification).

Most records in a day ■ Jesse Owens (USA) (1913–80) set six world records in 45 min at Ann Arbor, Michigan on 25 May 1935 with a 9·4 sec 100 yd at 3.15 p.m., a 8·13 m *26 ft 8¼ in* long jump at 3.25 p.m., a 20·3 sec 220 yd (and 200 m) at 3.45 p.m. and a 22·6 sec 220 yd low hurdles (and 200 m) at 4.00 p.m.

Most national titles *Great Britain* ■ The most

national senior titles won by an athlete is 27 by Judith Miriam Oakes (b. 14 Feb 1958) at the shot with nine WAAA outdoor, ten WAAA indoor and eight UK titles, 1977–89. The greatest number of senior AAA titles (excluding those in tug of war events) won by one athlete is 14 individual and one relay title by Emmanuel McDonald Bailey (Trinidad) (b. 8 Dec 1920), between 1946 and 1953. The most won outdoors in a single event is 13 by Denis Horgan (Ireland) (1871–1922) in the shot put between 1893

World record ● Olga Bryzgina (USSR) and Florence Griffith-Joyner (USA) set off on the final leg of the 4 × 400 m relay Olympic final at Seoul on 1 Oct 1988. Bryzgina, who had previously won the individual 400 m title, successfully held off the challenge of the American and helped set a new world record time of 3 min 15·17 sec. Griffith-Joyner, in winning a silver, equalled the women's record of four athletics medals at one celebraton, having already won three golds, 100 m, 200 m and 4 × 100 m. (Photo: All-Sport / Bob Martin)

Fastest hurdler ● Colin Jackson (b. 18 Feb 1967) is the current holder of the British record for the indoor 60 m hurdles, 7·41 sec. He also holds the outdoor record for 110 m hurdles. (Photo: All-Sport / Gray Mortimore)

and 1912. 13 senior titles were also won by: Michael Anthony Bull (b. 11 Sep 1946) at pole vault, eight indoor and five out, and by Geoffrey Lewis Capes (b. 23 Aug 1949) at shot, six indoor and seven out.

The greatest number of WAAA outdoor titles won by one athlete is 14 by Suzanne Allday (*née* Farmer) (b. 26 Nov 1934) with seven each at shot and discus between 1952 and 1962. She also won two WAAA indoor shot titles.

Most international appearances ■ The greatest number of international matches contested for any nation is 89 by shot-putter Bjørn Bang Andersen (b. 14 Nov 1937) for Norway, 1960–81.

The greatest number of full Great Britain international appearances (outdoors and indoors) is 73 by Verona Marolin Elder (*née* Bernard) (b. 5 Apr 1953), mostly at 400 m, from 1971 to 1983. The men's record is 67 by shot-putter Geoff Capes, 1969–80. At pole vault and decathlon Mike Bull had 66 full internationals or 69 including the European Indoor Games, before these were official internationals. The most

UNITED KINGDOM (NATIONAL) RECORDS MEN

RUNNING

	min sec	Name	Place	Date	
100 metres	9·97	Linford Christie (b. 10 Apr 1960)	Seoul, South Korea	24 Sep	1988
200 metres	20·09	Linford Christie	Seoul, South Korea	28 Sep	1988
400 metres	44·50	Derek Antony Redmond (b. 3 Sep 1965)	Rome, Italy	1 Sep	1987
800 metres	1:41·73	Sebastian Newbold Coe (b. 29 Sep 1956)	Florence, Italy	10 Jun	1981
1000 metres	2:12·18	Sebastian Newbold Coe	Oslo, Norway	11 Jul	1981
1500 metres	3:29·67	Steven Cram (b. 14 Oct 1960)	Nice, France	16 Jul	1985
1 mile	3:46·32	Steven Cram	Oslo, Norway	27 Jul	1985
2000 metres	4:51·39	Steven Cram	Budapest, Hungary	4 Aug	1985
3000 metres	7:32·79	David Robert Moorcroft (b. 10 Apr 1953)	Crystal Palace, London	17 Jul	1982
5000 metres	13:00·41	David Robert Moorcroft	Oslo, Norway	7 Jul	1982
10 000 metres	27:23·06	Eamonn Thomas Martin (b. 9 Oct 1958)	Oslo, Norway	2 Jul	1988
20 000 metres	58:39·0	Ronald Hill (b. 25 Sep 1938)	Leicester	9 Nov	1968
25 000 metres	1 hr 15:22·6	Ronald Hill	Bolton, Lancashire	21 Jul	1965
30 000 metres	1 hr 31:30·4	James Noel Carroll Alder (b. 10 Jun 1940)	Crystal Palace, London	5 Sep	1970
1 hour	12 miles 1268 yd *20 472m*	Ronald Hill	Leicester	9 Nov	1968

HURDLING

		Name	Place	Date	
110 metres	13·11A	Colin Ray Jackson (b. 18 Feb 1967)	Sestriere, Italy	11 Aug	1988
400 metres	48·12A	David Peter Hemery (b. 18 Jul 1944)	Mexico City, Mexico	15 Oct	1968
3000 metres Steeplechase	8:07·96	Mark Robert Rowland (b. 7 Mar 1963)	Seoul, South Korea	30 Sep	1988

RELAYS

		Name	Place	Date	
4 × 100 metres	38·28	United Kingdom: Elliot John Bunney, John Paul Lyndon Regis, Michael Anthony McFarlane, Linford Christie	Seoul, South Korea	1 Oct	1988
4 × 200 metres	1:21·29	UK : Marcus Adam, Adeoye Mafe, Linford Christie, John Paul Lyndon Regis	Birmingham	23 Jun	1989
4 × 400 metres	2:58·86	United Kingdom: Kriss Akabusi, Derek Anthony Redmond, Todd Bennett, Philip Andrew Brown	Rome, Italy	6 Sep	1987
4 × 800 metres	7:03·89	United Kingdom: Peter Elliott, Gary Peter Cook, Steven Cram, Sebastian Newbold Coe	Crystal Palace, London	30 Aug	1982
4 × 1500 metres	14:56·8	United Kingdom: Alan David Mottershead, Geoffrey Michael Cooper, Stephen John Emson, Roy Wood	Bourges, France	24 Jun	1979

A *Record set at high altitude, best at low altitude: 110 m hurdles, 13·20 Colin Jackson at Nice, France on 10 Jul 1989; 400 m hurdles, 48·52 David Hemery at München, West Germany on 2 Sep 1972.*

FIELD EVENTS

	m	ft	in	Name	Place	Date	
High Jump	2·31	7	7	Dalton Grant (b. 8 Apr 1966)	Seoul, South Korea	25 Sep	1988
	2·31	7	7	Dalton Grant	Portsmouth, Hampshire	11 Jun	1989
(Indoors)	2·35	7	8	Dalton Grant	Budapest, Hungary	4 Mar	1989
Pole Vault	5·65	18	6½	Keith Frank Stock (b. 18 Mar 1957)	Oslo, Norway	7 Jul	1981
Long Jump	8·23	27	0	Lynn Davies (b. 20 May 1942)	Bern, Switzerland	30 Jun	1968
Triple Jump	17·57	57	7¾	Keith Leroy Connor (b. 16 Sep 1957)	Provo, Utah, USA	5 Jun	1982
Shot 7·26 kg *16 lb*	21·68	71	1½	Geoffrey Lewis Capes (b. 23 Aug 1949)	Cwmbran, Gwent	18 May	1980
Discus 2 kg *4 lb 6·55 oz*	64·32†	211	0	William Raymond Tancred (b. 6 Aug 1942)	Woodford, Essex	10 Aug	1974
Hammer 7·26 kg *16 lb*	77·54	254	5	Martin Girvan (b. 17 Apr 1960)	Wolverhampton, West Midlands	12 May	1984
Javelin 800 g *28·22 oz*	85·24‡	279	8	Michael Christopher Hill (b. 22 Oct 1964)	Stockholm, Sweden	30 Jun	1987

† *William Raymond Tancred threw 64·94 m 213 ft 1in at Loughborough, Leicestershire on 21 Jul 1974 and Richard Charles Slaney (b. 16 May 1956) threw 65·16 m 213 ft 9 in at Eugene, Oregon, USA on 1 Jul 1985 but these were not ratified.*
‡ *New javelin; best with old javelin 91·40 m 299 ft 10 in by Arne-Roald Bradstock (b. 24 Apr 1962) at Arlington, Texas, USA on 4 May 1985.*

DECATHLON

8847 points ..... Francis Morgan 'Daley' Thompson (GB) (b. 30 Jul 1958) ..... Los Angeles, California, USA ..... 8–9 Aug 1984
(1st day: 100 m 10·44 sec, Long Jump 8·01 m *26 ft 3½in* (2nd day: 110 m Hurdles 14·33 sec, Discus 46·56 m *152 ft 9 in,*
Shot Put 15·72 m *51 ft 7 in,* High Jump 2·03 m *6 ft 8 in,* Pole Vault 5·00 m *16 ft 4¾in,* Javelin 65·24 m *214 ft 0 in,*
400 m 46·97 sec) 1500 m 4:35·00 sec)

outdoors is 61 by hammer thrower Andrew Howard Payne (b. South Africa, 17 Apr 1931) from 1960 to 1974.

Oldest and youngest internationals ■ The oldest full Great Britain international was Hector Harold Whitlock (1903–85) at 50 km walk at the 1952 Olympic Games, aged 48 yr 218 days. The oldest woman was Christine Rosemary Payne (*née* Charters, now Chimes) (b. 19 May 1933) at discus in the Great Britain *v.* Finland match on 26 Sep 1974, aged 41 yr 130 days. The youngest man was high jumper Ross Hepburn (b. 14 Oct 1961) *v.* the USSR on 26 Aug 1977, aged 15 yr 316 days, and the youngest woman was Janis Walsh (b. 28 Mar 1960) *v.* Belgium (indoor) at 60 m and 4×200 m relay on 15 Feb 1975, aged 14 yr 324 days.

Longest career ■ Duncan McLean (1884–1980) of Scotland set a world age (92) record of 100 m in 21·7 sec in August 1977, over 73 years after his best ever sprint of 100 yd in 9·9 sec in South Africa in February 1904.

Longest winning sequence ■ Iolanda Balas (Romania) (b. 12 Dec 1936) won a record 140 consecutive competitions at high jump from 1956 to 1967. The record at a track event was 122 at 400 metres

British records ● Sally Gunnell of Essex Ladies is the current British record holder at both 100 metres hurdles and 400 metres hurdles. (Photo: All-Sport / Gray Mortimore)

hurdles by Edwin Corley Moses (USA) (b. 31 Jul 1955) between his loss to Harald Schmid (West Germany) (b. 29 Sep 1957) at Berlin, West Germany on 26 Aug 1977 and that to Danny Harris (USA) (b. 7 Sep 1965) at Madrid, Spain on 4 Jun 1987.

London to Brighton race ■ Ian Thompson (b. 16

Oct 1949) (Luton United H) won the 87·4 km *54·3 miles* race (instituted 1951) in 5 hr 15 min 15 sec on 28 Sep 1980, averaging 16·62 km/h *10·33 mph.* The most wins is four by Bernard Gomersall (b. 28 Aug 1932) in 1963–6.

The womens' London to Brighton record is 6 hr

BIRMINGHAM

UNITED KINGDOM (NATIONAL) RECORDS *WOMEN*

RUNNING

	Min sec	Name and country	Place	Date	
100 metres	11·10	Kathryn Jane Smallwood (now Cook) (b. 3 May 1960)	Rome, Italy	5 Sep	1981
200 metres	22·10	Kathryn Jane Cook (*née* Smallwood)	Los Angeles, California, USA	9 Aug	1984
400 metres	49·43	Kathryn Jane Cook (*née* Smallwood)	Los Angeles, California, USA	6 Aug	1984
800 metres	1:57·42	Kirsty Margaret McDermott (now Wade) (b. 6 Aug 1962)	Belfast, N. Ireland	24 Jun	1985
1000 metres	2:33·70	Kirsty Margaret McDermott (now Wade)	Gateshead, Tyne and Wear	9 Aug	1985
1500 metres	3:59·96	Zola Budd (b. 26 May 1966)	Brussels, Belgium	30 Aug	1985
1 mile	4:17·57	Zola Budd	Zürich, Switzerland	21 Aug	1985
2000 metres	5:29·58	Yvonne Carol Grace Murray (b. 4 Oct 1964)	Crystal Palace, London	11 Jul	1986
3000 metres	8:28·83	Zola Budd	Rome, Italy	7 Sep	1985
5000 metres	14:48·07	Zola Budd	Crystal Palace, London	26 Aug	1985
10000 metres	31:06·99	Elizabeth McColgan (*née* Lynch (b.24 May 1964)	Oslo, Norway	2 Jul	1988

RELAYS

		Name and country	Place	Date	
4 × 100 metres	42·43	United Kingdom: Heather Regina Hunte (now Oakes), Kathryn Jane Smallwood (now Cook), Beverley Lanita Goddard (now Callender), Sonia May Lannaman	Moscow, USSR	1 Aug	1980
4 × 200 metres	1:31·57	United Kingdom: Donna-Marie Louise Hartley (*née* Murray), Verona Marolin Elder (*née* Bernard), Sharon Colyear (now Danville), Sonia May Lannaman	Crystal Palace, London	20 Aug	1977
4 × 400 metres	3:25·51	United Kingdom: Michelle Scutt (*née* Probert), Helen Catherine Barnett (now Burkart), Gladys Taylor, Joslyn Yvonne Hoyte-Smith	Los Angeles, California, USA	11 Aug	1984
4 × 800 metres	8:23·8	Great Britain: Joan Florence Allison (*née* Page), Sheila Janet Carey (*née* Taylor), Patricia Barbara Lowe (now Cropper), Rosemary Olivia Stirling (now Wright)	Paris, France	2 Oct	1971

HURDLING

		Name and country	Place	Date	
100 metres	12·82	Sally Jane Janet Gunnell (b. 29 Jul 1966)	Zürich, Switzerland	17 Aug	1988
400 metres	54·03	Sally Jane Janet Gunnell	Seoul, South Korea	28 Sep	1988

FIELD EVENTS

	m	ft	in	Name and country	Place	Date	
High Jump	1·95	6	4¾	Diana Clare Elliot (now Davies) (b. 7 May 1961)	Oslo, Norway	26 Jun	1982
Long Jump	6·90	22	7¾	Beverly Kinch (b. 14 Jan 1964)	Helsinki, Finland	14 Aug	1983
Shot 4 kg *8 lb 13 oz*	19·36	63	6¼	Judith Miriam Oakes (b. 14 Feb 1958)	Gateshead, Tyne and Wear	14 Aug	1988
Discus 1 kg *2 lb 3·27 oz*	67·48	221	5	Margaret Elizabeth Ritchie (b. 6 Jul 1952)	Walnut, California, USA	26 Apr	1981
Javelin 600 g *21.16 oz*	77·44	254	1	Fatima Whitbread (b. 3 Mar 1961)	Stuttgart, West Germany	28 Aug	1986

HEPTATHLON

6623 points	Judy Earline Veronica Simpson (*née* Livermore)	Stuttgart, West Germany	29–30 Aug 1986

(b. 14 Nov 1960) (100 m hurdles 13·05 sec; High Jump 1·92 m *6 ft 3½in* ; Shot 14·75 m *48 ft 4ft* ; 200 m 25·09 sec; Long Jump 6·56 m *21 ft 6¼in* ; Javelin 40·92 m *134 ft 3 in* ; 800 m 2 min 11·70 sec)

37 min 8 sec by Ann Franklin (b. 26 Apr 1951) on 25 Sep 1983.

'End to end' ■ The fastest confirmed run from John o' Groats to Land's End is 10 days 15 hr 27 min by Don Ritchie (GB) from 1–12 Apr 1989. A faster 10 days 3 hr 30 min was claimed by Fred Hicks (GB) for 1410 km *876 miles* on 20–30 May 1977. The fastest by a women is 13 days 17 hr 42 min by walker Ann Sayer (see Walking). A relay team of 10 from Aberdeen A. A. C. covered the distance in 77 hr 26 min 18 sec from 3–6 Apr 1982.

Longest running race ■ The longest races ever staged were the 1928 (5507 km *3422 miles*) and 1929 (5898 km *3665 miles*) trans-continental races from New York City, NY to Los Angeles, California, USA. The Finnish-born Johnny Salo (1893–1931) was the winner in 1929 in 79 days, from 31 Mar to 18 Jun. His elapsed time of 525 hr 57 min 20 sec (averaging 11·21 km/h *6·97 mph*) left him only 2 min 47 sec ahead of Englishman Pietro 'Peter' Gavuzzi (1905–81).

The longest race staged annually is Australia's Westfield Run from Paramatta, New South Wales to Doncaster, Victoria (Sydney to Melbourne). The distance run has varied slightly, but the record is by Yiannis Kouros (Greece) (b. 13 Feb 1956) in 5 days 2 hr 27 min 27 sec in 1989, when the distance was 1060 km *658 miles*.

Greatest mileage ■ Douglas Alistair Gordon Pirie (GB) (b. 10 Feb 1931), who set five world records in the 1950s, estimated that he had run a total distance of 347 600 km *216 000 miles* in 40 years to 1981.

WORLD INDOOR RECORDS

From 1 Jan 1987, the International Amateur Athletics Federation recognised world indoor records. The best performances made before that date have been noted as world bests, and world records must better these to be officially accepted. Track performances around a turn must be made on a track no longer than 200 metres.

Event	min:sec	Name and country	Place	Date
RUNNING				
50 metres	5·55	Ben Johnson (Canada) (b. 30 Dec 1961)	Ottawa, Canada	31 Jan 1987
60 metres	6·41	Ben Johnson (Canada)	Indianapolis, USA	7 Mar 1987
200 metres	20·36	Bruno Marie-Rose (France) (b.20 May 1965)	Liévin, France	22 Feb 1987
400 metres	45·41	Thomas Schönlebe (GDR) (b. 6 Aug 1965)	Vienna, Austria	9 Feb 1986
800 metres	1:44·84	Paul Ereng (Kenya) (b. 1967)	Budapest, Hungary	4 Mar 1989
1000 metres	(2:16·4 officially) 2:16·62	Robert Druppers (Netherlands) (b. 1964)	The Hague, Netherlands	20 Feb 1988
1500 metres	3:35·6	Marcus O'Sullivan (Ireland) (b. 22 Dec 1961)	East Rutherford, New Jersey, USA	10 Feb 1989
	3:35·4 *u	Marcus O'Sullivan (Ireland)	East Rutherford, New Jersey, USA	13 Feb 1988
1 mile	3:49·78	Eamonn Coghlan (Ireland) (b. 21 Nov 1952)	East Rutherford, New Jersey, USA	27 Feb 1983
3000 metres	7:39·2	Emiel Puttemans (Belgium) (b. 8 Oct 1947)	West Berlin, West Germany	18 Feb 1973
5000 metres	13:20·4	Suleiman Nyambui (Tanzania) (b. 13 Feb 1953)	New York, USA	6 Feb 1986
50 metres hurdles	6·25	Mark McKoy (Canada) (b. 10 Dec 1961)	Kobe, Japan	5 Mar 1986
60 metres hurdles	7·36‡	Greg Foster (USA) (b. 4 Aug 1958)	Indianapolis, USA	16 Jan 1987
	7·36	Roger Kingdom (USA) (b. 26 Aug 1962)	Piraeus, Greece	8 Mar 1989
RELAYS				
4 × 200 metres	1:22·32	Italy	Turin, Italy	11 Feb 1984
		(Pierfrancesco Pavoni, Stefano Tilli, Giovanni Bongiorni, Carlo Simionato)		
4 × 400 metres	3:05·21	USA	Glasgow, Strathclyde	10 Mar 1989
		(Clarence Daniel, Charles 'Chip' Jenkins, Kenneth Lowery, Mark Rowe)		
WALKING				
5000 metres	18:15·91	Mikhail Shchennikov (USSR)	Gomel, USSR	4 Feb 1989
	18:11·41u	Roland Weigel (GDR) (b. 8 Aug 1959)	Vienna, Austria	13 Feb 1988

FIELD EVENTS	m	ft in	Name and country	Place	Date
High Jump	2·43	7 11½	Javier Sotomayor (Cuba) (b. 13 Oct 1967)	Budapest, Hungary	4 Mar 1989
Pole Vault	6·03	19 9½	Sergey Bubka (USSR) (b. 4 Dec 1963)	Osaka, Japan	11 Feb 1989
Long Jump	8·79	28 10	Carl Lewis (USA) (b. 1 Jul 1961)	New York, USA	27 Feb 1984
Triple Jump	17·76	58 3¼	Mike Conley (USA) (b. 5 Oct 1962)	New York, USA	27 Feb 1987
Shot	22·66	74 4¼	Randy Barnes (USA) (b. 16 Jun 1966)	Los Angeles, California, USA	20 Jan 1989

OCTATHLON 7084 points Christian Plaziat (France) (b. 28 Oct 1963) Vittel, France 11– 12 Feb 1989
(60 m 6·78 sec; Shot, 14·73 m; High jump, 2·10 m;
400 m, 49·38 sec; Long jump, 7·64 m; 60 m hurdles,
7·91 sec; Pole vault, 4·80 m; 1000 m 2:48·08)

WOMEN

RUNNING	min:sec	Name and country	Place	Date
50 metres	6·06	Angella Issajenko (Canada) (b. 28 Sep 1958)	Ottawa, Canada	31 Jan 1987
60 metres	7·00	Nelli Cooman-Fiere (Netherlands) (b. 6 Jun 1964)	Madrid, Spain	23 Feb 1986
200 metres	22·27	Heike Dreschler (GDR) (b. 16 Dec 1964)	Indianapolis, USA	7 Mar 1987
400 metres	49·59	Jarmila Kratochvilova (Czechoslovakia) (b. 26 Jan 1955)	Milan, Italy	7 Mar 1982
800 metres	1:56·40	Christine Wachtel (GDR) (b. 6 Jan 1965)	Vienna, Austria	13 Feb 1988
1000 metres	2:34·8	Brigitte Kraus (GDR) (b. 12 Aug 1956)	Dortmund, West Germany	19 Feb 1978
1500 metres	4:00·8	Mary Decker-Slaney (USA) (b. 4 Aug 1958)	New York, USA	8 Feb 1980
1 mile	4:18·86	Doina Melinte (Romania) (b. 27 Dec 1956)	East Rutherford, New Jersey, USA	13 Feb 1988
3000 metres	8:33·82	Elly van Hulst (Netherlands) (b. 9 Jun 1957)	Budapest, Hungary	4 Mar 1989
5000 metres	(mixed race) 15:19·84	Lesley Welch (USA) (b. 12 Mar 1963)	Boston, Massachusetts, USA	25 Jan 1986
	15:25·02u	Brenda Webb (USA) (b. 30 May 1954)	Gainesville, Florida, USA	30 Jan 1988
50 metres hurdles	6·58	Cornelia Oschekenat (GDR) (b. 29 Oct 1961)	Berlin, GDR	21 Feb 1988
60 metres hurdles	7·73	Cornelia Oschekenat (GDR)	Vienna, Austria	25 Feb 1989
RELAYS				
4 × 200 metres	1:32·55	S. C. Eintracht Hamm (West Germany)	Dortmund, West Germany	19 Feb 1988
		(Helga Arendt, Silke-Beate Knoll, Mechthild Kluth, Gisela Kinzel)		
4 × 400 metres	3:34·38	West Germany	Dortmund, West Germany	30 Jan 1981
		(Heide-Elke Gaugel, Christina Sussiek, Christiane Brinkmann, Gaby Bussmann)		
WALKING				
3000 metres	12:01·65	Kerry Saxby (Australia) (b. 2 Jun 1961)	Budapest, Hungary	4 Mar 1989

FIELD EVENTS	m	ft in	Name and country	Place	Date
High jump	2·06	6 9¼	Stefka Kostadinova (Bulgaria) (b. 25 Nov 1965)	Piraeus, Greece	20 Feb 1988
Long jump	7·37	24 2¼	Heike Dreschler (GDR) (b. 16 Dec 1964)	Vienna, Austria	13 Feb 1988
Triple jump†	14·45	47 5	Galina Chistyakova (USSR) (b. 26 Jul 1962)	Lipetsk, USSR	29 Jan 1989
Shot	22·50	73 9¼	Helena Fibingerova (Czechoslovakia) (b. 13 Jul 1959)	Jablonec, Czechoslovakia	19 Feb 1988

*u not officially recognised. * hand timed. ‡ adjudged by observers to have been with a rolling start, but officially ratified. † not yet official event.*

ULTRA LONG DISTANCE WORLD RECORDS

TRACK (Men)

Event	hr:min:sec	Name	Place	Date	
50 km	2:48:06	Jeff Norman (GB)	Timperley, Manchester	7 Jun	1980
50 miles	4:51:49	Don Ritchie (GB)	Hendon, London	12 Mar	1983
100 km	6:10:20	Don Ritchie (GB)	Crystal Palace, London	28 Oct	1978
100 miles	11:30:51	Don Ritchie (GB)	Crystal Palace, London	15 Oct	1977
200 km	15:11:10†	Yiannis Kouros (Greece)	Montauban, France	15–16 Mar	1985
200 miles	27:48:35	Yiannis Kouros (Greece)	Montauban, France	15–16 Mar	1985
500 km	60:23:00	Yiannis Kouros (Greece)	Colac, Australia	26–29 Nov	1984
500 miles	105:42:09	Yiannis Kouros (Greece)	Colac, Australia	26–30 Nov	1984
1000 km	136:17:00	Yiannis Kouros (Greece)	Colac, Australia	26 Nov–1 Dec	1984

kilometres					
24 hours	283·600	Yiannis Kouros (Greece)	Montauban, France	15–16 Mar	1985
48 hours	452·270	Yiannis Kouros (Greece)	Montauban, France	15–17 Mar	1985
6 days	1023·200	Yiannis Kouros (Greece)	Colac, Australia	26 Nov–1 Dec	1984

ROAD (Men)

Where superior to track bests and run on properly measured road courses.

	hr:min:sec				
50 km	2:43:38	Thompson Magawana (SAf)	Claremont–Kirstenbosch	12 Apr	1988
50 miles	4:50:21	Bruce Fordyce (SAf)	London–Brighton	25 Sep	1983
1000 miles...	10d 10hr 30min 35sec	Yiannis Kouros (Greece)	New York, USA	21–30 May	1988

kilometres					
24 hours	286·463	Yiannis Kouros (Greece)	New York, USA	28–29 Sep	1985
6 days	1028·370	Yiannis Kouros (Greece)	New York, USA	21–26 May	1988

TRACK (Women)

	hr:min:sec				
15 km	49:44·0	Silvana Cruciata (Italy)	Rome, Italy	4 May	1981
20 km	1:06:55·5	Rosa Mota (Portugal)	Lisbon, Portugal	14 May	1983
25 km	1:29:30	Karolina Szabo (Hungary)	Budapest, Hungary	23 Apr	1988
30 km	1:47:06	Karolina Szabo (Hungary)	Budapest, Hungary	23 Apr	1988
50 km	3:35:42	Ann Franklin (GB)	Barry, South Glamorgan	9 Mar	1986
50 miles	6:17:30†	Monika Kuno (FRG)	Vogt, West Germany	8–9 Jul	1983
100 km	8:01:01	Monika Kuno (FRG)	Vogt, West Germany	8–9 Jul	1983
100 miles	14:29:44	Ann Trason (USA)	Santa Rosa, USA	18–19 Mar	1989
200 km	20:09:28†	Eleanor Adams (GB)	Honefoss, Norway	12–13 Jul	1986
200 miles	39:09:03	Hilary Walker (GB)	Blackpool, Lancashire	5–6 Nov	1988
500 km	86:26:02	Eleanor Adams (GB)	Colac, Australia	24–28 Feb	1986
500 miles	143:11:23	Eleanor Adams (GB)	Colac, Australia	24 Feb–2 Mar	1986

kilometres					
1 hour	18·084	Silvana Cruciata (Italy)	Rome, Italy	4 May	1981
24 hours	229·459‡	Marion Savage (GB)	Birmingham	2–3 Jul	1988
	226·237	Angela Mertens (Belgium)	Izegem, Belgium	2–3 Jul	1988
48 hours	366·512	Hilary Walker (GB)	Blackpool, Lancashire	5–7 Nov	1988
6 days	838·800	Eleanor Adams (GB)	Colac, Australia	16–22 Nov	1987

†Timed on one running watch only.
‡Unratified as it was paced some of the time.

ROAD (Women)

Where superior to track bests and run on properly measured road courses.

	hr:min:sec				
30 km	1:38:27	Ingrid Kristiansen (Norway)	London	10 May	1987
50 km	3:08:39	Frith van der Merwe (SAf)	Claremont-Kirstenbosch	17 Dec	1983
40 miles	4:43:22	Marcy Schwam (USA)	Chicago, USA	3 Oct	1982
50 miles	5:59:26	Marcy Schwam (USA)	Chicago, USA	3 Oct	1982
100 km	7:26:01*	Chantal Langlacé (France)	Migennes, France	17 Jun	1984
	7:30:49	Ann Trason (USA)	Santander, Spain	1 Oct	1988
100 miles	14:49:34	Hilary Walker (GB)	Preston, Lancashire	27–28 Aug	1988
200 km	20:05:50	Hilary Walker (GB)	Preston, Lancashire	27–28 Aug	1988
500 km (actually 518 km)	82:10	Annie van der Meer (Hol)	Paris–Colmar, France	8–11 Jun	1983
24 hours	236·453 km	Hilary Walker (GB)	Preston, Lancashire	27–28 Aug	1988
1000 miles...	14d 20hr 45min 16sec	Sandra Barwick (N. Zealand)	New York, USA	21 May–3 Jun	1988

It should be noted that road times must be assessed with care as course conditions can vary considerably.

* On a road course of uncertain measurement.

Dr Ron Hill (b. 21 Sep 1938), the 1969 European and 1970 Commonwealth marathon champion, has not missed a day's training since 20 Dec 1964. Since then he has run twice a day, except once on Sundays and 23 Dec 1964. His meticulously compiled training log shows a total of 190 794 km *118 557½ miles* from 3 Sep 1956 to 31 May 1989. He has finished 112 marathons, all sub 2:52 and has raced in 50 nations.

The greatest competitive distance run in a year is 8855 km *5502 miles* by Malcolm Campbell (GB) (b. 17 Nov 1934) in 1985.

1000 Hours ■ Ron Grant (Australia) ran 2·5 km within an hour, every hour, for 1000 consecutive hours at Caboolture Sports Centre, Queensland, Australia from 18 Jan–1 Mar 1989.

Mass relay records ■ The record for 100 miles *160·9 km* by 100 runners from one club is 7 hr 53 min 52·1 sec by Baltimore Road Runners Club, Towson, Maryland, USA on 17 May 1981. The women's record is 10 hr 47 min 9·3 sec on 3 Apr 1977 by the San Francisco Dolphins Southend Running Club, USA. The record for 100 × 100 m is 19 min 37·52 sec by a team from Antwerp at Willebroek, Belgium on 8 Oct 1988.

The longest relay ever run was 16 936 km *10 524 miles* by 2660 runners at Trondheim, Norway from 26 Aug–20 Oct 1985. Twenty members of the Melbourne Fire Brigade ran 15 059 km *9357 miles* around Australia on Highway No. 1 in 43 days 23 hr 58 min, 10 Jul–23 Aug 1983. The most participants is 4800, 192 teams of 25, in the Batavierenrace, 167·2 km *103·89 miles* from Nijmegan to Enschede, Netherlands on 23 Apr 1983. The greatest distance covered in 24 hr by a team of ten is 425·595 km *264·459 miles* by Gerrit Maritz High School at Johannesburg, South Africa on 28–29 Aug 1987.

Highland Games ■ The weight and height of cabers (Gaelic *cabar*) vary considerably. Extreme values are 7·62 m *25 ft* and 127 kg *280 lb*. The Braemar caber (5·86 m *19 ft 3 in* and 54·4 kg *120 lb*) in Grampian was untossed from 1891 until 1951 when it was tossed by George Clark (1907–86). The best authentic mark recorded for throwing the 56 lb weight for height, using one hand only is 5·23 m *17 ft 2 in* by Geoffrey Lewis Capes (GB) (b. 23 Aug 1949) at Lagos, Nigeria on 5 Dec 1982. The best throw recorded for the Scots hammer is 46·08 m *151 ft 2 in* by William Anderson (b. 6 Oct 1938) at Lochearnhead on 26 Jul 1969.

Backwards running ■ Anthony 'Scott' Weiland, 27, ran the Detroit marathon backwards in 4 hr 7 min 54 sec on 13 Oct 1982. Donald Davis (USA) (b. 10 Feb 1960) ran 1 mile backwards in 6 min 7·1 sec at the University of Hawaii on 21 Feb 1983. Ferdie Adoboe (USA) ran 100 yd backwards in 12·8 sec (100 m in 14·0 sec) at Amherst, Massachusetts, USA on 28 Jul 1983.

Arvind Pandya of India ran backwards across America, Los Angeles to New York, in 107 days, 18 Aug–3 Dec 1984. He also ran backwards from John O'Groats to Land's End, 1416·2 km *880 miles* in 29 days 5 hr 39 min, 2–31 Oct 1985.

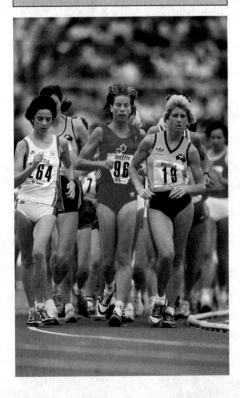

World records ● Kerry Ann Saxby (No. 19) (Australia) (b. 2 Jun 1961) has set a host of women's walking records, starting in 1985, at distances from 3 km to 20 km. (Photo: All-Sport / Gray Mortimore)

THE LONG

SEATTLE 21 Sep 1987

21 October 1987

21 Aug 1987

During the run, Sarah travelled through 35 States and experienced a wide variance of temperature. The coldest temperature being −50°C *−58°F* in Concord, New Hampshire on 15 Jan 1988 **A**, the hottest, 51°C *124°F* near Baker, California on 27 Jul 1988 **B**. The main picture shows her the day before the hottest day experienced, running through the Devil's Playground in the East Mojave Desert, near Kelso, California. Her major injury sustained on the run, surprisingly, was only a callous on the left hand from carrying a water bottle.

The effort expended can best be understood by the clothing Sarah wore out during the run, more than some joggers would use in a lifetime ......
26 pairs of running shoes, 20 T-shirts, 15 pairs of shorts and 6 sweatsuits.

SAN FRANCISCO

LAS VEGAS
21 July 1988
B

21 Sep 1988

LOS ANGELES

FINISH
2 OCTOBER 1988
L.A. COLISEUM
Raiders v Bengals

START
21 JULY 1987
NATIONAL FITNESS CENTRE
Irvine CA

21 August 1988

EL PASO 21 June 1988

OTHER LONG RUNS

Robert J. Sweetgall (USA) (b. 8 Dec 1947) ran 17 072 km *10 608 miles* around the perimeter of the USA starting and finishing in Washington, DC, 9 Oct 1982–15 Jul 1983. Ron Grant (Australia) (b. 15 Feb 1943) ran around Australia, 13 383 km *8316 miles* in 217 days 3 hr 45 min, running every day from 28 Mar to 31 Oct 1983. Max Telford (NZ) (b. Hawick, Scotland, 2 Feb 1935) ran 8224 km *5110 miles* from Anchorage, Alaska to Halifax, Nova Scotia, in 106 days 18 hr 45 min from 25 Jul to 9 Nov 1977.

The fastest time for the cross-America run is 46 days 8 hr 36 min by Frank Giannino Jr (USA) (b. 1952) for the 4989 km *3100 miles* from San Francisco to New York from 1 Sep–17 Oct 1980. The women's trans-America record is 69 days 2 hours 40 min by Mavis Hutchison (South Africa) (b. 25 Nov 1924) from 12 Mar–21 May 1978.

R U N . . . .

The longest run by an individual is one of 11 134 miles *17 918 km* around the USA by Sarah Covington-Fulcher (USA) (b. 14 Feb 1962). She began at the United States Fitness Academy, Laguna Hills, California on 21 Jul 1987 and then ran every day for the next 438 days (an average of 25·42 miles *40·9 km* a day and the map shows her monthly progress) to finish at the Los Angeles Coliseum on 2 Oct 1988.

21 Jan 1988

MINNEAPOLIS

2 Nov 1987

NEW YORK

21 December 1987

CHICAGO

21 February 1988

ATLANTA

21 March 1988

HOUSTON

21 April 1988

21 May 1988

MIAMI

(Inset Photo: Stan Honda Map: Rob and Rhoda Burns)

ROAD WALKING WORLD BEST PERFORMANCES

It should be noted that severity of road race courses and the accuracy of their measurement may vary, sometimes making comparisons of times unreliable.

MEN

20 km: 1 hr 18 min 54 sec, Yevgeniy Misyulya (USSR) (b. 1964) at Sochi, USSR on 19 Feb 1989
30 km: 2 hr 03 min 06 sec, Daniel Bautista (Mexico) (b. 4 Aug 1952) at Cherkassy, USSR on 27 Apr 1980.
50 km: 3 hr 38 min 17 sec, Ronald Weigel (GDR) (b. 8 Aug 1950) at Potsdam, GDR on 25 May 1986.

WOMEN

10 km: 41 min 30 sec, Kerry Ann Saxby (Australia) (b. 2 Jun 1961) at Canberra, Australia on 27 Aug 1988.
20 km: 1 hr 29 min 40 sec, Kerry Saxby at Värnamo, Sweden on 13 May 1988.
50 km: 5 hr 01 min 52 sec, Lillian Millen (GB) (b. 5 Mar 1945) at York on 16 Apr 1983.

BRITISH BEST PERFORMANCES

MEN

20 km: 1 hr 22 min 03 sec, Ian Peter McCombie (b. 11 Jan 1961) at Seoul, South Korea on 23 Sep 1988.
30 km: 2 hr 7 min 56 sec, Ian Peter McCombie at Edinburgh, Lothian on 27 Apr 1986.
50 km: 3 hr 57 min 48 sec, Leslie Morton (b. 1 Jul 1958) at Yelverton, Devon on 30 Apr 1989.

WOMEN

10 km: 45 min 42 sec, Lisa Martine Langford (b. 15 Mar 1967) at New York, USA on 3 May 1987.
20 km: 1 hr 40 min 45 sec, Irene Lillian Bateman (b. 13 Nov 1947) at Basildon, Essex on 9 Apr 1983.

MARATHON

The marathon is run over a distance of 42·195 km *26 miles 385 yd*. This distance was that used for the race at the 1908 Olympic Games, run from Windsor to the White City stadium, and which became standard from 1924. The marathon (of 40 km) was introduced to the 1896 Olympic Games to commemorate the legendary run of Pheidippides (or Philippides) from the battlefield of Marathon to Athens in 490 BC. The 1896 Olympic marathon was preceded by trial races that year. The first Boston marathon, the world's longest-lasting major marathon, was held on 19 Apr 1897 at 39 km *24 miles 1232 yd* and the first national marathon championship was that of Norway in 1897.

The first championship marathon for women was organised by the Road Runners Club of America on 27 Sep 1970.

TRACK WALKING—WORLD RECORDS

The International Amateur Athletic Federation recognises men's records at 20 km, 30 km, 50 km and 2 hours, and women's at 5 km and 10 km. This table also includes world bests for other standard outdoor distances.

Event	Time hr:min:sec	Name, country and date of birth	Place	Date	
MEN					
10 km	38:02·6	Jozef Pribilinec (Czechoslovakia) (b. 6 Jul 1960)	Banska Bystrica, Czechoslovakia	30 Aug	1985
20 km	1:18:40·0	Ernesto Canto (Mexico) (b. 18 Oct 1959)	Fana, Norway	5 May	1984
30 km	2:07:59·8	Jose Marin (Spain) (b. 21 Jan 1950)	Barcelona, Spain	8 Apr	1979
	2:06:07·3 †	Maurizio Damilano (Italy) (b. 6 Apr 1957)	San Donato Milanese, Italy	5 May	1985
50 km	3:41:38·4	Raul Gonzalez (Mexico) (b. 29 Feb 1952)	Fana, Norway	25 May	1979
1 hour	15 547 m	Josef Pribilinec (Czechoslavakia)	Hildesheim, W. Germany	6 Sep	1986
2 hours	28 165 m	Jose Marin (Spain)	Barcelona, Spain	8 Apr	1979
	28 565 m†	Maurizio Damilano (Italy)	San Donato Milanese, Italy	5 May	1985
WOMEN					
3 km	12:13·75	Kerry Ann Saxby (Australia) (b. 2 Jun 1961)	Sydney, Australia	8 Feb	1989
5 km	20:27·59	Ileana Salvador (Italy) (b. 16 Jan 1962)	Trento, Italy	3 Jun	1989
10 km	42:39·2	Ileana Salvador (Italy)	Rome, Italy	17 Jun	1989
	42:14·2 ‡	Kerry Saxby (Australia)	Canberra, Australia	26 Jan	1988

† unratified. ‡ mixed race.

Fastest ■ There are as yet no official records for the marathon, and it should be noted that courses may vary in severity. The following are the best times recorded, all on courses whose distance has been verified.

The world records are: (men) 2 hr 6 min 50 sec by Belayneh Dinsamo (Ethiopia) (b. 1965) at Rotterdam, Netherlands on 17 Apr 1988 and (women) 2 hr 21 min 6 sec by Ingrid Kristiansen (*née* Christensen) (Norway) (b. 21 Mar 1956) at London on 21 Apr 1985. The British records are: (men) 2 hr 7 min 13 sec by Stephen Henry Jones (b. 4 Aug 1955) at Chicago, Illinois, USA on 20 Oct 1985 and (women) 2 hr 25 min 56 sec by Véronique Marot (b. 16 Sep 1955) at London on 23 Apr 1989.

Most competitors ■ The record number of confirmed finishers in a marathon is 22 587 in the London marathon on 23 Apr 1989. A record 93 men ran under 2 hr 20 min at London in 1983, a record 35 under 2 hr 15 min in the World Cup marathon at Hiroshima, Japan on 14 Apr 1985, and a record 6 men ran under 2 hr 10 min at Fukuoka, Japan on 4 Dec 1983 and at London on 23 Apr 1989.

A record 9 women ran under 2 hr 30 min in the first Olympic marathon for women at Los Angeles, USA on 5 Aug 1984.

World record ● Ulf Timmermann (GDR) (b. 1 Nov 1962) set a new shot record of 23·06 m *75 ft 8 in* at Khania, Greece on 22 May 1988. He went on to win the Olympic title at Seoul, setting an Olympic record of 22·47 m *73 ft 8 in*. (Photo: All-Sport/Tony Duffy)

Most run by an individual ■ Sy Mah (USA) (1926–88) ran 524 marathons of 26 miles 385 yd or longer from 1966 to his death in 1988. He paced himself to take 3½hr each run.

Three in three days ■ The fastest combined time for three marathons in three days is 8 hr 22 min 31 sec by Raymond Hubbard (Belfast 2 hr 45 min 55 sec, London 2 hr 48 min 45 sec and Boston 2 hr 47 min 51 sec) on 16–18 Apr 1988.

Highest altitude ■ The highest start to a marathon was one run in the Himalayas on 27 Nov 1987. It began at Gorak Shep, 5212 m *17 100 ft* and ended at Namche Bazar, 3444 m *11 300 ft*. The winner from the field of 45 was Stewart Dutfield (GB), aged 32, in a time of 4 hr 53 min 10 sec.

Oldest finishers ■ The oldest man to complete a marathon was Dimitrion Yordanidis (Greece), aged 98, in Athens, Greece on 10 Oct 1976. He finished in 7 hr 33 min. Thelma Pitt-Turner (New Zealand) set the women's record in August 1985, completing the Hastings, New Zealand marathon in 7 hr 58 min at the age of 82.

WALKING

Most Olympic medals ■ Walking races have been included in the Olympic events since 1906. The only walker to win three gold medals has been Ugo Frigerio (Italy) (1901–68) with the 3000 m in 1920, and 10 000 m in 1920 and 1924. He also holds the record of most medals with four (he won the bronze medal at 50 000 m in 1932), a total shared with Vladimir Golubnichiy (USSR) (b. 2 Jun 1936), who won gold medals for the 20 000 m in 1960 and 1968, the silver in 1972 and the bronze in 1964.

The best British performance has been two gold medals by George Edward Larner (1875–1949) for the 3500 m and the 10 miles in 1908, but Ernest J. Webb (1872–1937) won three medals, being twice 'walker up' to Larner and finishing second in the 10 000 m in 1912.

Most titles ■ Four-time Olympian, Ronald Owen Laird (b. 31 May 1938) of the New York AC, USA, won a total of 65 US national titles from 1958 to 1976, plus four Canadian Championships. The greatest number of UK national titles won by a British walker is 27 by Vincent Paul Nihill (b. 5 Sep 1939) from 1963 to 1975.

Longest race ■ The Paris–Colmar, until 1980 Strasbourg–Paris, event (instituted 1926 in the reverse direction), now about 519 km *322 miles*, is the world's longest annual race walk.

The fastest performance is by Robert Pietquin (Belgium) (b. 1938) who walked 507 km *315 miles* in the 1980 race in 60 hr 1 min 10 sec (after deducting 4 hr compulsory stops). This represents an average speed of 8·45 km/h *5·25 mph*. Roger Quémener (France) has won a record seven times, 1979, 1983, 1985–9. The first woman to complete the race was Annie van der Meer (Netherlands) (b. 24 Feb 1947), who was 10th in 1983 in 82 hr 10 min.

'End to end' ■ The fastest Land's End to John o'Groats walk is 12 days 3 hr 45 min for 1426·4 km *886·3 miles* by WO2 Malcolm Barnish of the 19th Regiment, Royal Artillery from 9–21 Jun 1986. The women's record is 13 days 17 hr 42 min by Ann Sayer (b. 16 Oct 1936), 20 Sep–3 Oct 1980. The Irish 'end to end' record over the 644 km *400·2 miles* from Malin Head, Donegal to Mizen Head, Cork is 5 days 22 hr 30 min, set by John 'Paddy' Dowling (b. 15 Jun 1929) on 18–24 Mar 1982.

London to Brighton ■ The record time for the 85 km *53 mile* walk is 7 hr 35 min 12 sec by Donald James Thompson (b. 20 Jan 1933) on 14 Sep 1957. Richard Esmond Green (b. 22 Apr 1924) completed the course a record 44 times from 1950 to 1980.

24 hours ■ The greatest distance walked in 24 hr is 226·432 km *140 miles 1229 yd* by Paul Forthomme (Belgium) on a road course at Woluwé, Belgium on 13–14 Oct 1984. The best by a woman is 202·3 km

125·7 miles by Annie van der Meer at Rouen, France on 30 Apr–1 May 1984 over a 1·185-km lap road course.

Backwards walking ■ The greatest ever exponent of reverse pedestrianism has been Plennie L. Wingo (b. 24 Jan 1895) then of Abilene, Texas, USA who completed his 12 875 km *8000 mile* transcontinental walk from Santa Monica, California, USA to Istanbul, Turkey from 15 Apr 1931 to 24 Oct 1932. The longest distance recorded for walking backwards in 24 hr is 135·18 km *84·0 miles* by Anthony Thornton (USA) in Minneapolis, Minnesota, USA on 31 Dec 1985–1 Jan 1986.

Trampolining

Trampolines were used in show business at least as early as 'The Walloons' of the period 1910–12. The sport of trampolining (from the Spanish word *trampolin*, a springboard) dates from 1936, when the prototype 'T' model trampoline was developed by George Nissen (USA).

Most titles ■ World Championships were instituted in 1964. A record five titles were won by Judy Wills (USA) (b. 1948) in the women's event, 1964–8. Five men have won two titles.

A record seven United Kingdom titles have been won by Wendy Wright (1969–70, 1972–5, 1977). The most by a man has been five by Stewart Matthews (b. 19 Feb 1962) (1976–80).

Youngest international *Great Britain* ■ Andrea Holmes (b. 2 Jan 1970) competed for Britain at 12 yr 131 days in the World Championships at Montana, USA on 13 May 1982.

Somersaults ■ Christopher Gibson performed 2506 consecutive somersaults at Victory Hall, University of Technology, Loughborough, Leicestershire on 10 Mar 1989.

The most somersaults completed in one minute is 78 by Zoe Finn of Chatham, Kent at BBC Television Centre, London for *Blue Peter* on 25 Jan 1988.

Triathlon

The Triathlon combines long–distance swimming, cycling and running. Distances for each of the phases can vary, but for the best established event, the Hawaii Ironman (instituted 1978), competitors first swim 3·8 km *2·4 miles*, then cycle 180 km *112 miles*, and finally run a full marathon of 42·195 km *26 miles 385 yards*. Record times for the Hawaii Ironman are: (men) 8 hr 28 min 37 sec Dave Scott (USA) (b. 1953) on 19 Oct 1986; (women) 9 hr 1 min 1 sec Paula Newby-Fraser (USA) on 23 Oct 1988. Dave Scott has won a record six races, 1980, 1982–4 and 1986–7.

World Championships ■ After earlier abortive efforts a world governing body L'Union Internationale de Triathlon (UIT) was founded at Avignon, France on 1 Apr 1989, staging the first official World Championships in August 1989.

A 'World Championship' race has been held annually in Nice, France from 1982; the distances 3200 m, 120 km and 32 km respectively, with the swim increased to 4000 m from 1988. Mark Allen (USA) has won six times, 1982–6, 1989.

Largest field ■ The largest field in a triathlon race has been 3888 finishers in the Bud Lite US Triathlon race at Chicago in 1987. This series encompasses races over 1500 m, 40 km and 10 km for the three phases.

Tug of War

Origins ■ Though ancient China and Egypt have been suggested as the originators of the sport, it is known that Neolithic flint miners in Norfolk practised 'rope-pulling'. The first rules were those

framed by the New York AC in 1879. Tug of War was an Olympic sport from 1900 until 1920. In 1958 the Tug-of-War Association was formed to administer Britain's 600 clubs. World Championships have been held annually from 1975, with a women's event introduced in 1986.

Most titles ■ The most successful team at the World Championships have been the Sheen Farmers, competing for England, who won at 640 kg in 1975–6 and at 720 kg in 1977–8 and 1980.

The Wood Treatment team (formerly the Bosley Farmers) of Cheshire won 20 consecutive AAA Catchweight Championships 1959–78, two world titles (1975–6) and ten European titles at 720 kg. Hilary Brown (b. 13 Apr 1934) was in every team. Trevor Brian Thomas (b. 1943) of British Aircraft Corporation Club is the only holder of three winners' medals in the European Open club competitions and added a world gold medal in 1988.

Longest pulls *Duration* ■ The longest recorded pull (prior to the introduction of AAA rules) is one of 2 hr 41 min when 'H' Company beat 'E' Company of the 2nd Battalion of the Sherwood Foresters (Derbyshire Regiment) at Jubbulpore, India on 12 Aug 1889. The longest recorded pull under AAA rules (in which lying on the ground or entrenching the feet is not permitted) is one of 24 min 45 sec for the first pull between the Republic of Ireland and England during the world championships (640 kg class) at Malmo, Sweden on 18 Sep 1988. The record time for 'The Pull' (instituted 1898), across the Black River, between freshman and sophomore teams at Hope College, Holland, Michigan, USA, is 3 hr 51 min on 23 Sep 1977, but the method of bracing the feet precludes this replacing the preceding records.

Distance ■ The longest tug of war is the 2·6 km *1·616 miles* Supertug across the Little Traverse Bay, Lake Michigan, USA. It has been contested annually since 1980 between two teams of 20 from Bay View Inn and Harbor Inn.

Volleyball

The game was invented as *mintonette* in 1895 by William G. Morgan at the YMCA gymnasium at Holyoke, Massachusetts, USA. The International Volleyball Association was formed in Paris in April 1947. The Amateur (now English) Volleyball Association of Britain was formed in May 1955.

Most world titles ■ World Championships were instituted in 1949 for men and 1952 for women. The USSR has won six men's titles (1949, 1952, 1960, 1962, 1978 and 1982) and four women's (1952, 1956, 1960 and 1970). Japan (1962, 1967, 1974 and 1987) have also won four women's titles.

Most Olympic titles ■ The sport was introduced to the Olympic Games for both men and women in 1964. The USSR has won a record three men's (1964, 1968 and 1980) and four women's (1968, 1972, 1980 and 1988) titles. The only player to win four medals is Inna Ryskal (USSR) (b. 15 Jun 1944), who won women's silver medals in 1964 and 1976 and golds in 1968 and 1972. The record for men is held by Yuriy Poyarkov (USSR) (b. 10 Feb 1937) who won gold medals in 1964 and 1968 and a bronze in 1972, and by Katsutoshi Nekoda (Japan) (b. 1 Feb 1944) who won gold in 1972, silver in 1968 and bronze in 1964.

Most internationals *Great Britain* ■ Ucal Ashman (b. 10 Nov 1957) made a record 153 men's international appearances for England, 1976–86. The women's record is 171 by Ann Jarvis (b. 3 Jun 1955) for England, 1974–87.

Water Polo

Water polo was developed in England as 'water soccer' in 1869 and first included in the Olympic Games in Paris in 1900.

Most Olympic titles ■ Hungary has won the Olympic tournament most often with six wins in 1932, 1936, 1952, 1956, 1964 and 1976. Great Britain won in 1900, 1908, 1912 and 1920.

Five players share the record of three gold medals; Britons George Wilkinson (1879–1946) in 1900, 1908, 1912; Paulo 'Paul' Radmilovic (1886–1968), and Charles Sidney Smith (1879–1951) in 1908, 1912, 1920; and Hungarians Deszö Gyarmati (b. 23 Oct 1927) and György Kárpáti (b. 23 Jun 1935) in 1952, 1956, 1964. Paul Radmilovic also won a gold medal for the 4×200 m freestyle swimming in 1908.

World Championships ■ First held at the World Swimming Championships in 1973. The USSR is the only double winner, 1975 and 1982. A women's competition was introduced in 1986, when it was won by Australia.

Most goals ■ The greatest number of goals scored by an individual in an international is 13 by Debbie Handley for Australia (16) v. Canada (10) at the World Championship in Guayaquil, Ecuador in 1982.

Most international appearances ■ The greatest number of international appearances is 412 by Aleksey Barkalov (USSR) (b. 18 Feb 1946), 1965–80. The British record is 126 by Martyn Thomas, of Cheltenham, Gloucestershire, 1964–78.

Water Skiing

The origins of water skiing derive from walking on planks and aquaplaning. A 19th–century treatise on sorcerers refers to Eliseo of Tarentum who, in the 14th century, 'walks and dances' on the water. The first report of aquaplaning was on America's Pacific coast in the early 1900s. At Scarborough, Yorkshire on 15 Jul 1914, a single plank-gliding contest was won by H. Storry.

The present day sport of water skiing was pioneered by Ralph W. Samuelson (1904–77) on Lake Pepin, Minnesota, USA, on two curved pine boards in the summer of 1922, although claims have been made for the birth of the sport on Lake Annecy (Haute Savoie), France at about the same time. The first world organisation, the *Union Internationale de Ski Nautique*, was formed in Geneva on 27 Jul 1946.

Most titles ■ World Overall Championships (instituted 1949) have been won four times by Sammy Duvall (USA) in 1981, 1983, 1985 and 1987 and three times by two women, Willa McGuire (*née* Worthington) of the USA in 1949–50 and 1955 and Elizabeth 'Liz' Allan-Shetter (USA) in 1965, 1969 and 1975. Liz Allan-Shetter has won a record eight individual championship events and is the only person to win all four titles—slalom, jumping, tricks and overall in one year, at Copenhagen, Denmark in 1969. The USA have won the team championship on 16 successive occasions, 1957–87.

The most British Overall titles (instituted 1953) won by a man is seven by Michael Hazelwood (b. 14 Apr 1958) in 1974, 1976–9, 1981, 1983; the most by a woman is nine by Karen Jane Morse (b. 14 Aug 1956) in 1971–6, 1978, 1981, 1984.

Highest speed ■ The fastest water skiing speed recorded is 230·26 km/h *143·08 mph* by Christopher Michael Massey (Australia) on the Hawkesbury River, Windsor, New South Wales, Australia on 6 Mar 1983. His drag boat driver was Stanley Charles Sainty. Donna Patterson Brice (b. 1953) set a feminine record of 178·8 km/h *111·11 mph* at Long Beach, California, USA on 21 Aug 1977. The fastest recorded speed by a British skier over a measured kilometre is 141·594 km/h *87·984 mph* (average) on Lake Windermere, Cumbria on 14 Oct 1987 by Steven Moore (b. 3 Mar 1963). The fastest speed recorded by a British woman is 141·050 km/h *87·647 mph* by Nikki Carpenter on Lake Windermere, Cumbria on 18 Oct 1988.

Longest run ■ The greatest distance travelled is 2126·14 km *1321·16 miles* by Steve Fontaine (USA) on 24–26 Oct 1988 at Jupiter Hills, Florida, USA.

Cross Channel ■ Steve Butterworth (GB) skied across the English Channel in a record time of 57 min 57 sec from New Romney to Boulogne on 19 Sep 1988. He also went on to complete a double crossing in 1 hr 55 min 8 sec.

Most skiers towed by one boat ■ A record 100 water skiers were towed on double skis over a nautical mile by the cruiser *Reef Cat* at Cairns, Queensland, Australia on 18 Oct 1986. This feat, organised

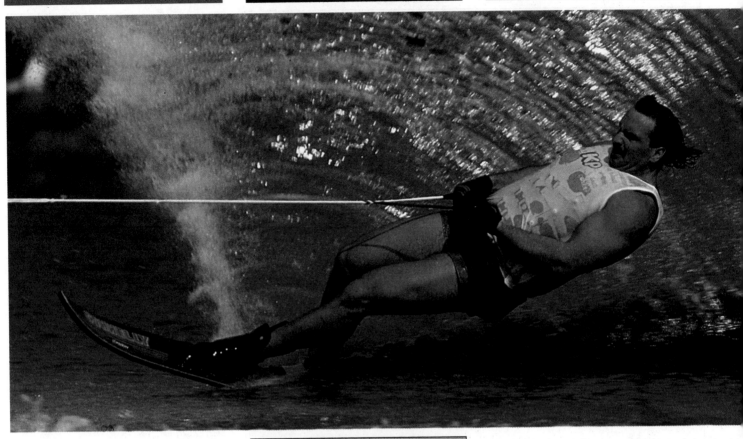

by the Cairns and District Powerboat and Ski Club, was then replicated by 100 skiers on single skis.

Barefoot ■ The first person to water ski barefoot is reported to be Dick Pope Jr at Lake Eloise, Florida, USA on 6 Mar 1947. The barefoot duration record is 2 hr 42 min 39 sec by Billy Nichols (USA) (b. 1964) on Lake Weir, Florida, USA on 19 Nov 1978. The backward barefoot record is 39 min by Paul McManus (Australia). The British duration record is 67 min 5 sec by John Doherty on 1 Oct 1974. The official barefoot speed record is 192·08 km/h *119·36 mph* by Scott Michael Pellaton (b. 8 Oct 1956) over a quarter-mile course at Chowchilla, California, USA on 4 Sep 1983. The fastest by a woman is 118·56 km/h *73·67 mph* by Karen Toms (Australia) on the Hawkesbury River, Windsor, New South Wales on 31 Mar 1984. The British records are: (men) 114·86 km/h *71·37 mph* by Richard Mainwaring (b. 4 Jun 1953) at Holme Pierrepont, Nottinghamshire on 2 Dec 1978; (women) 80·25 km/h *49·86 mph* by Michele Doherty (b. 28 May 1964) (also 71·54 km/h *44·45 mph* backwards), both at Witney, Oxfordshire on 18 Oct 1986. The fastest official speed backwards barefoot is 100 km/h *62 mph* by Robert Wing (Australia) (b. 13 Aug 1957) on 3 Apr 1982.

The barefoot jump record is: men 20·50 m *67 ft 3 in* by Quentin Posthumus (South Africa) at Kimberley, South Africa on 5 Apr 1986 and women 12·40 m *40 ft 8¼ in* by Jacqueline Pfeiffer (Switzerland) at Lago di Orta, Italy on 28 Jun 1986. The British record is: men 19·10 m *62 ft 8 in* by Chris Harris in Germany in 1986 and women 9·9 m *32 ft 5¾ in* by Michele Doherty at Thorpe Park, Surrey in 1986.

Weightlifting

Competitions for lifting weights of stone were held in the ancient Olympic Games. The first championships entitled 'world' were staged at the Café Monico, Piccadilly, London on 28 Mar 1891 and then in Vienna, Austria on 19–20 Jul 1898, subsequently recognised by the IWF. Prior to that time, weightlifting consisted of professional exhibitions in which some of the advertised poundages were open to doubt.

WATER SKIING RECORDS

WORLD

SLALOM
MEN: 5 buoys on a 10·75 m line, Bob La Point (USA) at Shreveport, Florida, USA, 1984; Andy Mapple (GB) (b. 3 Nov 1958), USA, September 1985
WOMEN: 5 buoys on a 11·25 m line, Jennifer Leachman (USA)

TRICKS
MEN: 10 710 points, Cory Pickos (USA)
WOMEN: 8350 points, Ana Maria Carasco (Venezuela), September 1984

JUMPING
MEN: 62·5 m *205 ft*, Sammy Duvall (USA) at Shreveport, Florida, USA in August 1988
WOMEN: 47·5 m *156 ft*, Deena Mapple (*née* Brush) (USA) in 1988

BRITISH

SLALOM
MEN: (see World Listing)
WOMEN: 5 buoys at 12 m, Philippa Roberts, Grand Der, France, August 1986

TRICKS
MEN: 8650 points, John Battleday (b. 1 Feb 1957) at Lyon, France on 5 Aug 1984
WOMEN: 6820 points, Nicola Rasey (b. 6 Jun 1966) at Martigues, France on 27 Oct 1984

JUMPING
MEN: 61·9 m *203 ft* Michael Hazelwood at Birmingham, Alabama, USA on 30 Jun 1986
WOMEN: 44·9 m *147 ft*, Kathy Hulme (b. 11 Feb 1959) at Kirtons Farm, Reading, Berkshire on 1 Aug 1982

The *Fédération Internationalé Haltérophile et Culturiste*, now the International Weightlifting Federation (IWF), was established in 1905, and its first official championships were held in Tallinn, Estonia on 29–30 Apr 1922.

There are two standard lifts: the 'snatch' and the 'clean and jerk' (or 'jerk'). Totals of the two lifts determine competition results. The 'press', which was a standard lift, was abolished in 1972.

Most Olympic medals ■ Norbert Schemansky (USA) (b. 30 May 1924) won a record four Olympic medals: gold, middle-heavyweight 1952; silver, heavyweight 1948; bronze, heavyweight 1960 and 1964.

Most titles *World* ■ The most world title wins, including Olympic Games, is eight by: John Davis (USA) (1921–84) in 1938, 1946–52; Tommy Kono (USA) (b. 27 Jun 1930) in 1952–9; and by Vasiliy Alekseyev (USSR) (b. 7 Jan 1942), 1970–7.

Youngest world record holder ■ Naim Suleimanov (later Neum Shalamanov) (Bulgaria) (b. 23 Nov 1967) (now Naim Suleymanoglu of Turkey) set 56-kg world records for clean and jerk (160 kg) and total (285 kg) at 15 yr 123 days at Allentown, New Jersey, USA on 26 Mar 1983.

Most successful British lifter ■ The only British lifter to win an Olympic title has been Launceston Elliot (1874–1930), the open one-handed lift champion in 1896 at Athens. Louis George Martin (b. Jamaica, 11 Nov 1936) won four world and European mid-heavyweight titles in 1959, 1962–3, 1965. He won an Olympic silver medal in 1964 and a bronze in 1960 and three Commonwealth gold medals in 1962, 1966, 1970. His total of British titles was 12.

Heaviest lift to body weight ■ The first man to clean and jerk more than three times his body weight was Stefan Topurov (Bulgaria), who lifted 180 kg *396¾ lb* at Moscow, USSR on 24 Oct 1983. The first man to snatch two-and-a-half times his own body weight was Naim Suleymanoglu (Turkey), who lifted 150 kg *330½ lb* at Cardiff, South Glamorgan on 27 Apr 1988. The first woman to clean and jerk more than two times her own body weight was Cheng

WORLD WEIGHTLIFTING RECORDS

Bodyweight class	Lift	kg	lb	Name and country	Place	Date	
52 kg 114½lb	Snatch	120	264½	Sevdalin Marinov (Bulgaria)	Seoul, South Korea	18 Sep	1988
FLYWEIGHT	Jerk	153	337¼	He Zhuoqiang (China)	Ostrava, Czechoslovakia	6 Sep	1987
	Total	270	595¼	Sevdalin Marinov (Bulgaria)	Seoul, South Korea	18 Sep	1988
56 kg 123¼lb	Snatch	134·5	296½	Liu Shoubin (China)	Kemerovo, USSR	1 Mar	1989
BANTAMWEIGHT	Jerk	171	377	Neno Terziiski (Bulgaria)	Ostrava, Czechoslovakia	6 Sep	1987
	Total	300	661¼	Naim Suleimanov (Bulgaria)	Varna, Bulgaria	11 May	1984
60 kg 132¼lb	Snatch	152·5	336	Naim Suleymanoğlü (Turkey)*	Seoul, South Korea	20 Sep	1988
FEATHERWEIGHT	Jerk	190	418¾	Naim Suleymanoğlü (Turkey)*	Seoul, South Korea	20 Sep	1988
	Total	342·5	755	Naim Suleymanoğlü (Turkey)*	Seoul, South Korea	20 Sep	1988
67·5 kg 148¾lb †	Snatch	158·5	349¼	Israel Militosyan (USSR)	Athens, Greece	24 May	1988
LIGHTWEIGHT	Jerk	200·5	442	Mikhail Petrov (Bulgaria)	Ostrava, Czechoslovakia	8 Sep	1987
	Total	355	782½	Mikhail Petrov (Bulgaria)	Seoul, South Korea	5 Dec	1987
75 kg 165¼lb	Snatch	170	374¾	Angel Guenchev (Bulgaria)	Miskolc, Hungary	11 Dec	1987
MIDDLEWEIGHT	Jerk	215·5	475	Aleksandr Varbanov (Bulgaria)	Seoul, South Korea	5 Dec	1987
	Total	382·5	843¼	Aleksandr Varbanov (Bulgaria)	Plovdiv, Bulgaria	20 Feb	1988
82·5 kg 181¼lb	Snatch	183	403¼	Asen Zlatev (Bulgaria)	Melbourne, Australia	7 Dec	1986
LIGHT-HEAVYWEIGHT	Jerk	225	496	Asen Zlatev (Bulgaria)	Sofia, Bulgaria	12 Nov	1986
	Total	405	892¾	Yurik Vardanyan (USSR)	Varna, Bulgaria	14 Sep	1984
90 kg 198¼lb	Snatch	195·5	431	Blagoi Blagoyev (Bulgaria)	Varna, Bulgaria	1 May	1983
MIDDLE-HEAVYWEIGHT	Jerk	235	518	Anatoliy Khrapatiy (USSR)	Cardiff, South Glamorgan	29 Apr	1988
	Total	422·5	931¼	Viktor Solodov (USSR)	Varna, Bulgaria	15 Sep	1984
100 kg 220¼lb	Snatch	200·5	442	Nicu Vlad (Romania)	Sofia, Bulgaria	14 Nov	1986
	Jerk	242·5	534½	Aleksandr Popov (USSR)	Tallinn, USSR	5 Mar	1988
	Total	440	970	Yuriy Zakharevich (USSR)	Odessa, USSR	4 Mar	1983
110 kg 242½lb	Snatch	210	462¾	Yuriy Zakharevich (USSR)	Seoul, South Korea	27 Sep	1988
HEAVYWEIGHT	Jerk	250·5	552¼	Yuriy Zakharevich (USSR)	Cardiff, South Glamorgan	30 Apr	1988
	Total	455	1003	Yuriy Zakharevich (USSR)	Seoul, South Korea	27 Sep	1988
Over 110 kg 242½lb	Snatch	216	476	Antonio Krastev (Bulgaria)	Ostrava, Czechoslovakia	13 Sep	1987
SUPER-HEAVYWEIGHT	Jerk	266	586¼	Leonid Taranenko (USSR)	Canberra, Australia	26 Nov	1988
	Total	475	1047	Leonid Taranenko (USSR)	Canberra, Australia	26 Nov	1988

* Formerly Naim Suleimanov or Neum Shalamanov of Bulgaria

† Angel Guenchev (Bulgaria) achieved 160 kg snatch, 202·5 kg jerk for a 362·5 kg total at Seoul, South Korea on 21 Sep 1988 but was subsequently disqualified on a positive drugs test.

Youngest world record holder ● Naim Suleymanoğlü (Turkey) (b. 23 Nov 1967) was a mere 15 yr 123 days when he first set world records in the 56 kg class. In winning the gold in the 60 kg class at the 1988 Olympics he set records in all three categories (snatch, jerk and total) to bring his world record total to 38. (Photo: All-Sport/ Simon Bruty)

Jinling (China), who lifted 90 kg *198 lb* in the 44 kg class of the World Championships at Jakarta, Indonesia in December 1988.

Heaviest weight ■ The greatest weight ever raised by a human being is 6270 lb *2844 kg* (2·80 tons *2·84 tonnes*) in a back lift (weight raised off trestles) by the 26 st *165 kg* Paul Anderson (USA) (b. 17 Oct 1932), the 1956 Olympic heavyweight

champion, at Toccoa, Georgia, USA on 12 Jun 1957. The greatest lift by a woman is 3564 lb *1616 kg* with a hip and harness lift by Josephine Blatt (*née* Schauer) (1869–1923) at the Bijou Theater, Hoboken, New Jersey, USA on 15 Apr 1895.

Women's World Championships ■ These are held annually, first at Daytona Beach, USA in October 1987.

Women's world records have been ratified for the best marks at these championships. The heaviest lift for any of the nine weight categories has been the 132·5 kg *292 lb* jerk by Han Changmei (China) (b. 21 Dec 1965) for over 82·5 kg at Jakarta, Indonesia on 4 Dec 1988.

POWERLIFTING

The sport of powerlifting was first contested at national level in Great Britain in 1958. The first US Championships were held in 1964. The International Powerlifting Federation was founded in 1972, a year after the first, unofficial world championships were held. Official championships have been held annually for men from 1973 and for women from 1980.

The three standard lifts are squat, bench press and dead lift, the totals from the three lifts determining results.

Most world titles ■ The winner of the most world titles is Hideaki Inaba (Japan) with 14, at 52 kg 1974–83, 1985–8. The most by a British lifter is seven by Ron Collins: 75 kg 1972–4, 82 kg 1975–7 and 1979. The most by a women is six by Beverley Francis (Australia) (b. 15 Feb 1955) at 75 kg 1980, 1982; 82·5kg 1981, 1983–5.

Powerlifting feats ■ Paul Anderson, as a professional, reportedly achieved 1200 lb *544 kg* in a squat so aggregating, with a 627 lb *284 kg* bench press and an 820 lb *371 kg* dead lift, a career total of 2647 lb *1200 kg*. Lamar Gant (USA) was the first man to deadlift five times his own body weight, lifting 299·5 kg *661 lb* when 59·5 kg *132 lb* in 1985.

The greatest power lift by a woman is a squat of 285 kg *628 lb* by Lorraine Constanzo (USA) at Dayton, Ohio, USA on 21 Nov 1987. Cammie Lynn Lusko (USA) (b. 5 Apr 1958) became the first woman to lift more than her body weight with one arm, with 59·5 kg *131 lb* at a body weight of 58·3 kg *128·5 lb*, at Milwaukee, Wisconsin, USA on 21 May 1983.

24-hr and 1-hr lifts ■ A deadlifting record of 2 392 150 kg *5 273 699 lb* in 24 hr was set by a team of ten from HM Prison Frankland at Finchale Weightlifting Club, Co. Durham on 8–9 May 1987. The 24 hr deadlift record by an individual is 358 925 kg *791 280 lb* by Manjit Singh at the City and Health Yoga Centre, Leicester on 9–10 Mar 1989.

A bench press record of 3 869 011 kg *8 529 565 lb* was set by a nine-man team from the Hogarth Barbell Club, Chiswick, London on 18–19 Jul 1987. A squat record of 2 168 625 kg *4 780 919 lb* was set by a ten-man team from St Albans Weightlifting Club and Ware Boys Club, Hertfordshire on 20–21 Jul 1986.

A record 76 048 arm-curling repetitions using three 22 kg *48¼lb* weightlifting bars and dumb-bells were achieved by a team of nine from HMS Osprey at Portland, Dorset on 1–2 Dec 1988.

Michael Williams achieved 1438 repetitions of his bodyweight (67 kg *147·7 lb*) in one hour by bench presses at Don Styler's Gymnasium, Gosport, Hampshire on 17 Apr 1989.

Strandpulling ■ The International Steel Strandpullers' Association was founded by Gavin Pearson (Scotland) in 1940. The greatest ratified poundage to date is a super-heavyweight right-arm push of 815 lb *369·5 kg* by Malcolm Bartlett (b. 9 Jun 1955) of Oldham, Lancashire. The record for the back press anyhow is 645 lb *292·5 kg* by Barry Anderson, of Leeds, in 1975. A record 22 British Open titles have been won by Ian Storton (b. 2 Feb 1951) of Morecambe, Lancashire, 1974–88.

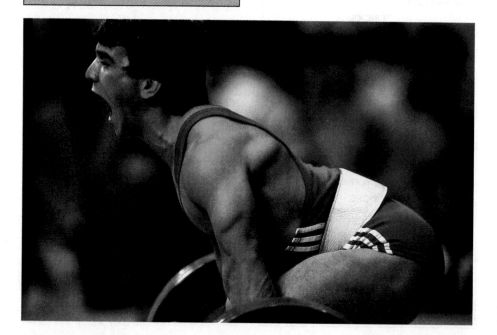

BRITISH WEIGHTLIFTING RECORDS (in kg)

MEN

Class	Snatch		Date		Jerk		Date		Total		Date	
52 kg	92·5	Precious McKenzie	25 Jan	1974	122·5	Precious McKenzie	25 Jan	1974	215	Precious McKenzie	25 Jan	1974
56 kg	105	Dean Willey	15 Jun	1981	132·5	Geoff Laws		1982	235	Geoff Laws		1982
60 kg	122·5	Dean Willey	26 Feb	1983	152·5	Dean Willey	26 Mar	1983	272·5	Dean Willey	26 Feb	1983
67·5 kg	145	Dean Willey	26 Jul	1986	170	Dean Willey	1 Aug	1984	315	Dean Willey		1985
75 kg	155	David Morgan	11 Nov	1986	190	David Morgan	11 Nov	1986	345	David Morgan	11 Nov	1986
82·5 kg	165·5	David Morgan	9 Jul	1988	205	David Morgan	13 Jun	1987	365	David Morgan	13 Jun	1987
90 kg	162	David Mercer			202·5	David Mercer			360	David Mercer		
100 kg	165	Andrew Davies			212·5	Peter Pinsent	17 Sep	1983	362·5	Peter Pinsent	17 Sep	1983
110 kg	195	Andrew Davies	25 Jun	1989	220	Andrew Davies	30 Apr	1988	405	Andrew Davies	30 Apr	1988
Super	190	Andrew Davies	9 Jul	1988	220	Andrew Davies	9 Jul	1988	410	Andrew Davies	9 Jul	1988

WORLD POWERLIFTING RECORDS (All weights in kilograms)

Class	Squat		Bench Press		Deadlift		Total	
MEN								
52 kg	243	Hideaki Inaba (Jap) 1986	146·5	Joe Cunha (USA) 1982	237·5	Hideaki Inaba 1987	587·5	Hideaki Inaba 1987
56 kg	242·5	Hideaki Inaba 1988	160	Hiroyaki Isagawa (Jap) 1988	289·5	Lamar Gant (USA) 1982	625	Lamar Gant 1982
60 kg	295	Joe Bradley (USA) 1980	180	Joe Bradley 1980	310	Lamar Gant 1988	707·5	Joe Bradley 1982
67·5 kg	300	Jessie Jackson (USA) 1987	200	Kristoffer Hulecki (Swe) 1985	313	Daniel Austin (USA) 1987	750	Daniel Austin 1988
75 kg	327·5	Mike Bridges (USA)	217·5	James Rouse (USA) 1980	333	Jarmo Virtanen (Finland) 1988	850	Rick Gaugler (USA) 1982
82·5 kg	379·5	Mike Bridges (USA) 1982	240	Mike Bridges 1981	357·5	Veli Kumpuniemi (Fin) 1980	952·5	Mike Bridges 1982
90 kg	375	Fred Hatfield (USA) 1980	255	Mike MacDonald (USA) 1980	372·5	Walter Thomas (USA) 1982	937·5	Mike Bridges 1980
100 kg	410	Ed Coan (USA) 1988	261·5	Mike MacDonald 1977	377·5	James Cash (USA) 1982	1000	Ed Coan 1988
110 kg	393·5	Dan Wohleber (USA) 1981	270	Jeffrey Magruder (USA) 1982	395	John Kuc (USA) 1980	1000	John Kuc 1980
125 kg	412·5	David Waddington (USA) 1982	278·5	Tom Hardman (USA) 1982	387·5	Lars Noren (Swe) 1987	1005	Ernie Hackett (USA) 1982
125 + kg	445	Dwayne Fely (USA) 1982	300	Bill Kazmaier (USA) 1981	406	Lars Noren 1988	1100	Bill Kazmaier 1981
WOMEN								
44 kg	142·5	Delcy Palk (USA) 1988	75	Teri Hoyt (USA) 1982	165	Nancy Belliveau (USA) 1985	352·5	Marie Vassart (Bel) 1985
48 kg	147·5	Keiko Nishio (Japan) 1987	82·5	Michelle Evris (USA) 1981	182·5	Majik Jones (USA) 1984	390	Majik Jones 1984
52 kg	173	Sisi Dolman (Neth) 1986	95	Mary Ryan (USA) 1984	197·5	Diana Rowell (USA) 1984	427·5	Diana Rowell 1984
56 kg	190	Vicki Steenrod (USA) 1984	115	Mary Jeffrey (née Ryan) 1988	200	Diana Rowell 1984	485	Mary Jeffrey 1988
60 kg	200·5	Ruthi Shafer (USA) 1983	105	Vicki Steenrod 1985	213	Ruthi Shafer 1983	502·5	Vicki Steenrod 1985
67·5 kg	230	Ruthi Shafer 1984	115	Heidi Wittesch (Aus) 1987	244	Ruthi Shafer 1984	565	Ruthi Shafer 1984
75 kg	222·5	Sumita Laha (Ind) 1988	140	Beverley Francis (Aus) 1981	228	Liz Odendaal (Neth) 1989	565	Liz Odendaal 1989
82·5 kg	230	Juanita Trujillo (USA) 1986	150	Beverley Francis 1981	227·5	Vicky Gagne (USA) 1981	577·5	Beverley Francis 1983
90 kg	252·5	Lorraine Constanzo (USA) 1988	130	Lorraine Constanzo 1988	227·5	Lorraine Constanzo 1988	607·5	Lorraine Constanzo 1988
90 +kg	262·5	Lorraine Constanzo 1987	135	Myrtle Augee (GB) 1988	237·5	Lorraine Constanzo 1987	622·5	Lorraine Constanzo 1987

BRITISH POWERLIFTING RECORDS (All weights in kilograms)

Class	Squat		Bench Press		Deadlift		Total	
MEN								
52 kg	217·5	Phil Stringer 1980	130	Phil Stringer 1981	225	John Maxwell 1988	530	Phil Stringer 1982
56 kg	235	Phil Stringer 1982	137·5	Phil Stringer 1983	229	Precious McKenzie 1973	567·5	N. Bhairo 1982
60 kg	247·5	Tony Galvez 1981	142·5	Clint Lewis 1985	275	Eddy Pengelly 1977	645	Eddy Pengelly 1979
67·5 kg	275	Eddy Pengelly 1981	165	Hassan Salih 1979	295	Eddy Pengelly 1982	710	Eddy Pengelly 1982
75 kg	302·5	John Howells 1979	185	Peter Fiore 1981	310	Robert Limerick 1984	760	Steve Alexander 1983
82·5 kg	337·5	Mike Duffy 1984	210	Mike Duffy 1981	355	Ron Collins 1980	855	Ron Collins 1980
90 kg	347·5	David Caldwell 1985	227·5	Jeff Chandler 1985	350·5	Ron Collins 1980	870	David Caldwell 1985
100 kg	380	Tony Stevens 1984	225	Tony Stevens 1985	362·5	Tony Stevens 1984	955	Tony Stevens 1984
110 kg	372·5	Tony Stevens 1984	235	John Neighbour 1987	380	Arthur White 1982	940	John Neighbour 1987
125 kg	385	Sean Spillane 1985	240	Sean Spillane 1985	372·5	David Carter 1989	957·5	Steven Zetolofsky 1984
125 +kg	380	Steven Zetolofsky 1979	258	Terry Purdoe 1971	377·5	Andy Kerr 1982	982·5	Andy Kerr 1983
WOMEN								
44 kg	120	Helen Wolsey 1989	60	Helen Wolsey 1989	137·5	Helen Wolsey 1989	317·5	Helen Wolsey 1989
48 kg	127·5	Karen Cameron 1989	75	Suzanne Smith 1985	140	Karen Cameron 1989	325	Suzanne Smith 1985
52 kg	143	Jenny Hunter 1988	82	Jenny Hunter 1988	173·5	Jenny Hunter 1988	395	Jenny Hunter 1988
56 kg	158	Jenny Hunter 1988	88	Jenny Hunter 1988	182·5	Jenny Hunter 1988	420	Jenny Hunter 1988
60 kg	163	Rita Bass 1988	87·5	Hayley Trafford 1989	182·5	Rita Bass 1989	420	Rita Bass 1986
67·5 kg	175	Debbie Thomas 1988	86	Debbie Thomas 1988	190	Amanda Smith 1987	435	Amanda Smith 1988
75 kg	202·5	Judith Oakes 1989	115	Judith Oakes 1989	215	Judith Oakes 1989	532·5	Judith Oakes 1989
82·5 kg	215	Judith Oakes 1988	117·5	Judith Oakes 1988	210	Judith Oakes 1986	542·5	Judith Oakes 1988
90 kg	195	Beverley Martin 1989	115	Joanne Williams 1989	202·5	Beverley Martin 1989	485	Joanne Williams 1989
90 +kg	215	Myrtle Augee 1989	137·5	Myrtle Augee 1989	225	Myrtle Augee 1989	560	Myrtle Augee 1989

Wrestling

The earliest depictions of wrestling holds and falls on wall plaques and a statue indicate that organised wrestling dates from c. 2750–2600 BC. It was the most popular sport in the ancient Olympic Games and victors were recorded from 708 BC. The Greco-Roman style is of French origin and arose about 1860. The International Amateur Wrestling Federation (FILA) was founded in 1912.

Most titles *Olympic* ■ Three Olympic titles have been won by: Carl Westergren (Sweden) (1895–1958) in 1920, 1924 and 1932; Ivar Johansson (Sweden) (1903–79) in 1932 (two) and 1936; and Aleksandr Medved (USSR) (b. 16 Sep 1937) in 1964, 1968 and 1972. Four Olympic medals were won by: Eino Leino (b. 7 Apr 1891) at freestyle 1920–32; and by Imre Polyák (Hungary) (b. 16 Apr 1932) at Greco-Roman in 1952–64.

World ■ The freestyler Aleksandr Medved (USSR) won a record ten World Championships, 1962–4, 1966–72 at three weight categories. The only wrestler to win the same title in seven successive years has been Valeriy Rezantsev (USSR) (b. 2 Feb

1947) in the Greco-Roman 90 kg class in 1970–6, including the Olympic Games of 1972 and 1976.

Most titles and longest span *British* ■ The most British titles won in one weight class is ten by heavyweight Kenneth Alan Richmond (b. 10 Jul 1926) between 1949 and 1960. The longest span for BAWA titles is 24 years by George Mackenzie (1890–1957) between 1909 and 1933. He represented Great Britain in five successive Olympiads, 1908 to 1928.

Most wins ■ In international competition, Osamu Watanabe (b. 21 Oct 1940), of Japan, the 1964 Olympic freestyle 63 kg champion, was unbeaten and unscored-upon in 189 consecutive matches. Outside of FILA sanctioned competition, Wade Schalles (USA) won 821 bouts from 1964 to 1984, with 530 of these victories by pin.

Longest bout ■ The longest recorded bout was one of 11 hr 40 min when Martin Klein (Estonia representing Russia) (1885–1947) beat Alfred Asikáinen (Finland) (1888–1942) for the Greco-Roman 75 kg 'A' event silver medal in the 1912 Olympic Games in Stockholm, Sweden.

Heaviest heavyweight ■ The heaviest wrestler in Olympic history is Chris Taylor (1950–79), bronze medallist in the super-heavyweight class in 1972, who stood 1·96 m *6 ft 5 in* tall and weighed over 190 kg *420 lb*. FILA introduced an upper weight limit of 130 kg *286 lb* for international competition in 1985.

SUMO WRESTLING

The sport's origins in Japan date from *c.* 23 BC. The heaviest ever *rikishi* is Samoan-American Salevaa Fuali Atisnoe of Hawaii, *alias* Konishiki, who in 1988 had a peak weight of 252 kg *556 lb*. He is also the first foreign *rikishi* to attain the second highest rank of *ozeki* or champion. Weight is amassed by over-alimentation with a high-protein stew called *chankonabe*.

The most successful wrestlers have been *yokozuna* Sadaji Akiyoshi (b. 1912) *alias* Futabayama, winner of 69 consecutive bouts in the 1930s, *yokozuna* Koki Naya (b. 1940) *alias* Taiho ('Great Bird'), who won

Top wrestler ● One of the top sumo wrestler is *Yokozuna* Mitsugu Akimoto *alias* Chiyonofuji. He has dominated the Kyushu Basho, winning for eight successive years, 1981-8. (Photo: Gerry Toff)

the Emperor's Cup 32 times up to his retirement in 1971 and the *ozeki* Tameemon Torokichi *alias* Raiden (1767–1825), who in 21 years (1789–1810) won 254 bouts and lost only ten for the highest ever winning percentage of 96·2. Taiho and Futabayama share the record of eight perfect tournaments without a single loss. The youngest of the 62 men to attain the rank of *yokozuna* (grand champion) was Toshimitsu Ogata (b. 16 May 1953) *alias* Kitanoumi, in Jul 1974 aged 21 years and two months. He set a record in 1978 winning 82 of the 90 bouts that top *rikishi* fight annually and had a record 804 wins in the top *Makunouchi* division.

Yokozuna Mitsugu Akimoto (b. 1 Jun 1955), *alias* Chiyonofuji, set a record for domination of one of the six annual tournaments by winning the Kyushu Basho for eight successive years, 1981–8. Hawaiian-born Jesse Kuhaulua (b. 16 Jun 1944), now a Japanese citizen named Daigoro Watanabe, *alias* Takamiyama, was the first non-Japanese to win an official top-division tournament, in Jul 1972 and in 1981 he set a record of 1231 consecutive top-division bouts. He weighed in at 204 kg *450 lb* before his retirement in 1984.

Yukio Shoji (b. 14 Nov 1948), *alias* Aobajo, did not miss a single bout in his 22-year career, 1964–86, and contested a record 1631 consecutive bouts. Kenji Hatano (b. 4 Jan 1948) *alias* Oshio, contested a record 1891 non-consecutive bouts in his 26-year career, 1962–88, the longest in modern sumo history. He holds the record for the most career wins with 964.

Yachting

Yachting in England dates from the £100 stake race between Charles II and his brother James, Duke of York, on the Thames on 1 Sep 1661 over 23 miles from Greenwich to Gravesend. The oldest club in the world is the Royal Cork Yacht Club which claims descent from the Cork Harbour Water Club, established in Ireland by 1720. The oldest active club in Britain is the Starcross Yacht Club at Powderham Point, Devon. Its first regatta was held in 1772. The oldest exsiting club to have been truly formed as a yacht club is the Royal Yacht Squadron, Cowes, Isle of Wight, instituted as 'The Yacht Club' at a meeting at the Thatched House Tavern, St James's Street, London on 1 Jun 1815.

Olympic titles *World* ■ The first sportsman ever to win individual gold medals in four successive Olympic Games was Paul B. Elvström (Denmark) (b. 24 Feb 1928) in the Firefly class in 1948 and the Finn class in 1952, 1956 and 1960. He also won eight other world titles in a total of six classes. The lowest number of penalty points by the winner of any class in an Olympic regatta is three points (five wins, one disqualified and one second in seven starts) by *Superdocious* of the Flying Dutchman class (Lt. Rodney Stuart Pattisson, RN (b. 5 Aug 1943) and Iain Somerled Macdonald-Smith (b. 3 Jul 1945)) at Acapulco Bay, Mexico in October 1968.

British ■ The only British yachtsman to win in two Olympic regattas is Rodney Pattisson in 1968 (see above) and again with *Superdoso* crewed by Christopher Davies (b. 29 Jun 1946) at Kiel, West Germany in 1972. He gained a silver medal in 1976 with Julian Brooke Houghton (b. 16 Dec 1946).

Admiral's Cup and ocean racing ■ The ocean racing series with the most participating nations (three boats allowed to each nation) is the Admiral's Cup held by the Royal Ocean Racing Club. A record 19 nations competed in 1975, 1977 and 1979. Britain has a record eight wins.

Modern ocean racing (in moderate or small sailing yachts, rather than professionally manned sailing ships) began with a race from Brooklyn, New York, USA to Bermuda, 630 nautical miles *1166 km* organised by Thomas Fleming Day, editor of the magazine *The Rudder* in June 1906. The race is still held today in every even numbered year, though the

course is now Newport, Rhode Island, USA to Bermuda.

The race still regularly run with the earliest foundation for any type of craft and either kind of water (fresh or salt) is the Chicago to Mackinac race on Lakes Michigan and Huron, first sailed in 1898. It was held again in 1904, then annually until the present day, except for 1917–20. The record for the course (333 nautical miles *616 km*) is 1 day 1 hr 50 min (average speed 12·89 knots *23·84 km/h*) by the sloop *Pied Piper*, owned by Dick Jennings (USA) in 1987.

The current record holder of the elapsed time records for both the premier American and British ocean races, the Newport, Rhode Island, to Bermuda race and the Fastnet race: the sloop *Nirvana*, owned by Marvin Green (USA). The record for the Bermuda race, 635 nautical miles *1176 km*, is 2 days 14 hr 29 min and for the Fastnet race, 605 nautical miles *1120 km*, is 2 days 12 hr 41 min, an average speed of 10·16 knots *18·81 km/h* and 9·97 knots *18·45 km* respectively.

Longest race ■ The longest regular sailing race is the quadrennial Whitbread Round the World race (instituted August 1973) organised by the Royal Naval Sailing Association. The distance for 1989–90 is 32 000 nautical miles *59 239 km* from Southampton and return, with stops and re-starts at Punta del Este, Fremantle, Auckland and Punta del Este. The record (sailing) time, obtained by adding the elapsed time of the three legs of the previous shorter course of 26 180 nautical miles *48 465 km*, is 117 days 14 hr 31 min by *UBS Switzerland*, skipper Pierre Fehlmann (Switzerland), finishing on 9 May 1986 (*see also p. 105*).

Greatest distance ■ The greatest distance claimed for a day's run under sail was set by the trimaran *Fleury–Michon VIII* (skipper Philippe Poupon) at 520 nautical miles *963 km* on 16–17 Jun 1987 during a transatlantic crossing (7 days 12 hr 50 min), thus averaging 21·67 knots *40·10 km/h*.

America's Cup ■ The America's Cup was originally won as an outright prize by the schooner *America* on 22 Aug 1851 at Cowes and was later offered by the New York Yacht Club as a challenge trophy. On 8 Aug 1870 J. Ashbury's *Cambria* (GB) failed to capture the trophy from the *Magic*, owned by F. Osgood (USA). The Cup has been challenged 27 times, the United States were undefeated winning 77 races and only losing eight until 1983 when *Australia II*, skippered by John Bertrand and owned by a Perth syndicate headed by Alan Bond beat *Liberty* 4–3, the narrowest series victory, at Newport, Rhode Island, USA.

The most times a single helmsman has steered a cup defender is in three separate series. This was achieved by Charlie Barr (USA) who defended in 1899, 1901 and 1903 and again by Harold S. Vanderbilt (USA) in 1930, 1934 and 1937. Dennis Conner (USA) has been helmsman of American boats four times in succession: in 1980, when he successfully defended; in 1983, when he steered the defender, but lost; in 1987 when the American challenger regained the trophy, and in 1988, when he again successfully defended. On 28 Mar 1989, however, the American Supreme Court judge, Justice Carmen Ciparick ruled that Conner's use of the catamaran *Stars and Stripes* against the New Zealanders monohull had violated the Deed of Gift governing the race. This decision, however, was subject to legal appeal.

The largest yacht to have competed in the America's Cup was the 1903 defender, the gaff rigged cutter *Reliance* with an overall length of 43·89 m *144 ft*, a record sail area of 1501 m² *16 160 ft²* and a rig of 53·3 m *175 ft* high.

Regattas ■ The most consistently sailed regatta is that at Cowes, where the first race for a gold cup took place on 10 Aug 1826. Since then there has been a regatta with one or more races in early August every year except for 1915–18 and 1940–5.

At present, Cowes 'Week' runs for 9 days and there are about 20 races for different classes of yacht each day.

Yacht and dinghy classes ■ The oldest racing class still sailing is the Water Wag class of Dublin, formed in 1887. The design of the boat was changed in 1900 to that which is still used today.

The oldest classes in Britain, both established in 1898 and both still racing in the same design of boat are the Seabird Half Rater, centreboard sailing dinghy of Abersoch and other north-west ports, and the Yorkshire One-design keel boat which race from the Royal Yorkshire Yacht Club at Bridlington, Humberside.

The first international class for racing dinghies was the 14 foot International, whose principal trophy in Britain is the Prince of Wales Cup which has been contested annually since 1927 (except 1940–5).

The most win is 12 by Stewart Morris between 1932 and 1965.

Highest speeds ■ The highest speed reached under sail on water by any craft over a 500-metre timed run is by a boardsailer Eric Beale (GB) at 40·50 knots *75 km/h* in a 35-knot wind at Saintes Maries de-la-Mer, Camargue, France on 14 Nov 1988.

The women's record was set at the same venue Brigitte Gimenez (France) achieved 36·81 knots *68·17 km/h* on 14 Dec 1988.

The sailing speed record prior to speeds achieved by boardsailers was 36·04 knots (41·50 mph *66·78 km/h*) by the 22·40 m *73 ½ ft* proa *Crossbow II* over a 500 m *547 yd* course in Portland Harbour, Dorset, on 17 Nov 1980. The vessel (sail area 130·06 m² *1400 ft²*) was designed by Rod McAlpine-Downie and owned and steered by Timothy Colman. In an unsuccessful attempt on the record in October 1978, *Crossbow II* is reported to have momentarily attained a speed of 45 knots (51 mph *83 km/h*).

Most competitors ■ The most boats ever to start in a single race was 2072 in the Round Zeeland

(Denmark) race on 21 Jun 1984, over a course of 235 nautical miles *435 km*.

The greatest number to start in a race in Britain was 1781 keeled yachts and multihulls on 17 Jun 1989 from Cowes in the Annual Round-the-Island Race. The fastest time achieved in this annual event is 3 hr 55 min 28 sec by the trimaran *Paragon*, owned and sailed by Michael Whipp on 31 May 1986.

The largest trans-oceanic race was the ARC (Atlantic Rally for Cruisers), when 204 boats of the 209 starters from 24 nations completed the race from Las Palmas de Gran Canaria to Barbados.

Highest ■ The greatest altitude at which sailing has taken place is 4910 m *16 109 ft* on Laguna Huallatani, Bolivia, in Mirror Dinghy 55448, variously by Peter Williams, Gordon Siddeley, Keith Robinson and Brian Barrett, on 19 Nov 1977.

BOARDSAILING

The High Court ruled on 7 Apr 1982 that Peter Chilvers (when aged 12) had devised a prototype of a boardsailer in 1958 in England. In 1968 Henry Hoyle Schweitzer and Jim Drake pioneered the sport, often termed windsurfing, in California, USA.

World Championships were first held in 1973 and the sport was added to the Olympic Games in 1984 when the winner was Stephan van den Berg (Netherlands), who also won five world titles 1979–83.

English Channel ■ The record time for boardsailing across the English Channel is 1 hr 4 min 33 sec by Baron Arnaud de Rosnay (France) on 4 Jul 1982 from Cap Gris Nez to Dover at an average speed of 16·9 knots (19·5 mph *31·3 km/h*). After 45 min rest he returned to Wissant, France in 1 hr 4 min 37 sec.

Longest sailboard ■ The longest 'snake' of boardsails was set by 60 windsurfers in tandem at the 'International Windsurfing Week' event in Balk, Netherlands on 2 Jul 1985.

The world's longest sail board, 50·2 m *165 ft*, was constructed at Fredrikstad, Norway, and first sailed on 28 Jun 1986.

THE COMMONWEALTH GAMES

The Commonwealth Games are multi-sport competitions, held every four years, and contested by sportsmen representing the nations of the British Commonwealth. They were first staged as the British Empire Games at Hamilton, Canada, opening on 16 August 1930. The eleven nations participating were Australia, Bermuda, British Guiana, Canada, England, Ireland, Newfoundland, New Zealand, Scotland, South Africa and Wales. Six sports were included, but there were women's events only in swimming.

The idea of staging such an event was first put forward by a Yorkshireman, Rev. J. Astley Cooper in the magazine *Greater Britain* in 1891. The first Inter-Empire Sports meeting was held at Crystal Palace, London in 1911, when events were held at four sports – athletics, boxing, swimming and wrestling. This event was part of the celebrations for the Coronation of King George V.

YEAR	VENUE	SPORTS	COUNTRIES	COMPETITORS MEN	WOMEN
1930	Hamilton, Canada	6	11	c.400	-
1934	London, England	6	16	c.500	-
1938	Sydney, Australia	7	15	378	88
1950	Auckland, New Zealand	9	12	495	95
1954	Vancouver, Canada	9	24	568	94
1958	Cardiff, Wales	9	35	967	163
1962	Perth, Australia	9	35	727	136
1966	Kingston, Jamaica	9	34	854	196
1970	Edinburgh, Scotland	9	42	1095	288
1974	Christchurch, New Zealand	9	39	977	299
1978	Edmonton, Canada	10	46	1149	326
1982	Brisbane, Australia	10	46	1179	400
1986	Edinburgh, Scotland	10	26	1179	483
1990	Auckland, New Zealand	-	-	-	-

ATHLETICS
Lisa Martin
(Australia)

ATHLETICS - Contested at all Games - Games best performances

MEN

Event	Performance	Athlete	Year
100 metres	10·02 sec †	Allan Wells (Scotland)	1982
	10·07 sec	Ben Johnson (Canada)	1986
200 metres	20·12 sec †	Allan Wells (Scotland)	1978
	20·43 sec	Allan Wells & Mike McFarlane (England)	1982
400 metres	45·01 sec	Charles Asati (Kenya)	1970
800 metres	1 min 43·22 sec	Steve Cram (England)	1986
1500 metres	3 min 32·16 sec	Filbert Bayi (Tanzania)	1974
5000 metres	13 min 14·4 sec	Ben Jipcho (Kenya)	1974
10000 metres	27 min 46·40 sec	Richard Tayler (New Zealand)	1974
Marathon	2 hr 9 min 12 sec	Ian Thompson (England)	1974
3000m steeplechase	8 min 20·67 sec	Ben Jipcho (Kenya)	1974
110 metres hurdles	13·31 sec †	Mark McKoy (Canada)	1986
	13·37 sec	Mark McKoy (Canada)	1982
400 metres hurdles	48·83 sec	Alan Pascoe (England)	1974
4x100 metres relay	39·15 sec	Nigeria	1982
	39·15 sec	Canada	1986
4x400 metres relay	3 min 02·8 sec	Trinidad & Tobago (at 4 x 440 yards)	1966
30 kilometres walk	2 hr 7 min 47 sec	Simon Baker (Australia)	1986
High jump	2·31 m	Milt Ottey (Canada)	1982
	2·31 m	Stephen Wray (Bahamas)	1982
Pole vault	5·30 m	Andrew Ashurst (England)	1986
Long jump	8·13 m	Gary Honey (Australia)	1982
Triple jump	17·81 m †	Keith Connor (England)	1982
	16·87 m	Mike Makin (England) (2nd)	1986
Shot	20·74 m	Geoff Capes (England)	1978
Discus	64·04 m	Brad Cooper (Bahamas)	1982
Hammer	75·08 m	Robert Weir (England)	1982
Javelin	80·62 m	David Ottley (England)	1986
	(old) 89·48 m	Michael O'Rourke (New Zealand)	1982
Decathlon	8663 points	Daley Thompson (England)	1986

WOMEN

100 metres	10·92 sec †	Angella Taylor (Canada) (& 11·00 heat)	1982
200 metres	22·19 sec †	Merlene Ottey (Jamaica)	1982
	22·50 sec	Raelene Boyle (Australia)	1974
400 metres	51·02 sec	Marilyn Neufville (Jamaica)	1970
800 metres	2 min 00·94 sec	Kirsty Wade (Wales)	1986
1500 metres	4 min 06·34 sec	Mary Stewart (England)	1978
3000 metres	8 min 45·53 sec	Anne Audain (New Zealand)	1982
10000 metres	31 min 41·42 sec	Elizabeth Lynch/McColgan (Scotland)	1986
Marathon	2 hr 26 min 7 sec	Lisa Martin (Australia)	1986
100 metres hurdles	12·78 sec †	Shirley Strong (England)	1982
	13·07 sec	Lorna Boothe (England) (heat)	1982
400 metres hurdles	54·94 sec	Debbie Flintoff (Australia)	1986
4x100 metres relay	43·15 sec	England	1982
4x400 metres relay	3 min 27·19 sec	England	1978
High jump	1·93 m	Katrina Gibbs (Australia)	1978
Long jump	6·91 m †	Shonel Ferguson (Bahamas)	1982
	6·73 m	Sheila Sherwood (England)	1970
Shot	19·00 m	Gael Martin (Australia)	1986
Discus	62·98 m	Margaret Ritchie (Scotland)	1982
Javelin	69·80 m	Tessa Sanderson (England)	1986
Heptathlon	6282 points †	Judy Simpson (England)	1986

† - wind assisted

BADMINTON
contested since 1966
BOWLS
contested each year except 1966
BOXING
contested each year
CYCLING
contested each year since 1934
FENCING
contested 1950–1970
GYMNASTICS
contested 1978
ROWING
contested 1930, 1938–62
SHOOTING
contested 1966, 1974–86

ATHLETICS
Steve Cram
(England)

ARCHERY
Neroli Fairhall
(New Zealand)

WEIGHTLIFTING - contested since 1950 - Games Records for 2-lift totals:

BODYWEIGHT	kg		
52kg	215	Precious McKenzie (England)	1974
56kg	245	Nick Voukelatos (Australia)	1986
60kg	267·5	Dean Willey (England)	1982
67·5kg	315	Dean Willey (England)	1986
75kg	312·5	Stephen Pinsent (England)	1982
82·5kg	350	David Morgan (Wales)	1986
90kg	350	Keith Boxell (England)	1986
100kg	360	Denis Garon (Canada)	1986
110kg	375	Kevin Roy (Canada)	1986
110kg +	392·5	Dean Lukin (Australia)	1986

WRESTLING - contested each year

ARCHERY - contested only in 1982

MEN	2446	Mark Blenkarne (England)	1982
WOMEN	2373	Neroli Fairhall (New Zealand)	1982

SWIMMING & DIVING - contested each year - Games Records:

MEN	min sec		
100m freestyle	50·95	Gregory Fasala (Australia)	1986
200m freestyle	1:50·57	Robert Gleria (Australia)	1986
400m freestyle	3:52·25	Duncan Armstrong (Australia)	1986
1500m freestyle	15:12·62	Jason Plummer (Australia)	1986
100m breaststroke	1:02·56	Victor Davis (Canada) (heat)	1986
200m breaststroke	2:16·25	Victor Davis (Canada)	1982
100m butterfly	54·07	Andrew Jameson (England)	1986
200m butterfly	1:57·27	Anthony Mosse (New Zealand)	1986
100m backstroke	56·45	Mark Tewksbury (Australia)	1986
200m backstroke	2:02·55	Alexander Goss (Canada)	1986
200m ind. medley	2:01·80	Alex Baumann (Canada)	1986
400m ind. medley	4:18·29	Alex Baumann (Canada)	1986
4x100m freestyle	321·58	Australia	1986
4x200m freestyle	7:23·49	Australia	1986
4x100m medley	3:44·00	Canada	1986

SWIMMING & DIVING - contested each year - Games Records:

WOMEN	min sec		
100m freestyle	56·97	June Croft (England)	1982
200m freestyle	1:59·74	June Croft (England)	1982
400m freestyle	4:07·68	Sarah Hardcastle (England)	1986
800m freestyle	8:24·62	Tracey Wickham (Australia)	1978
100m breaststroke	1:10·84	Allison Higson (Canada)	1986
200m breaststroke	2:31·20	Allison Higson (Canada)	1986
100m butterfly	1:01·22	Lisa Curry (Australia)	1982
200m butterfly	2:11·29	Michelle Ford (Australia)	1978
100m backstroke	1:03·48	Lisa Forrest (Australia)	1982
200m backstroke	2:13·46	Lisa Forrest (Australia)	1982
200m ind. medley	2:16·94	Lisa Curry (Australia)	1982
400m ind. medley	4:45·82	Suzanne Landells (Australia)	1986
4x100m freestyle	3:48·45	Canada	1986
4x200m freestyle	8:12·09	Australia	1986
4x100m medley	4:13·48	England	1986

WATER POLO - contested 1950

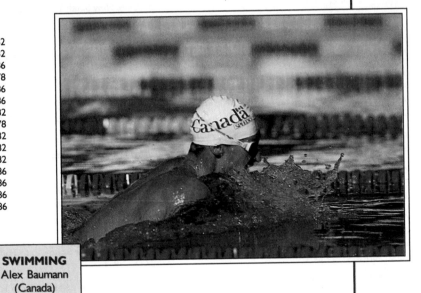

SWIMMING
Alex Baumann
(Canada)

MEDALS - GENERAL

The most gold medals won is nine by fencer Bill Hoskyns of England and swimmer Michael Wenden of Australia. Hoskyns won three individual épée titles and six team golds (at all weapons) between 1958 and 1970. Wenden won the freestyle 100m in 1966, 1970 and 1974, the 200m in 1974 and was in the winning Australian freestyle relay teams at 4 x 100m in 1966 and 1970 and at 4 x 200m in all three years. He also won three silver and one bronze medal, and would have won another gold but for the Australian medley relay team being disqualified after finishing first in 1966.

The most medals won of any colour is 13 by Wenden (above) and by fencer Ivan Lund of Australia, three gold, six silver and four bronze, from 1950 to 1962. The woman's record is eight by Australian swimmer Dawn Fraser, six gold and two silver, 1958 and 1962. The most medals won at one Games is six by swimmer Graham Smith of Canada in 1978.

The youngest gold medallist of whom the date of birth is known for certain is Jenny Turrall (Australia) who won the women's 400m freestyle swimming at 13 years 262 days in 1974. Ved Prakash (India) won the light-flyweight wrestling title in 1970 aged probably 14, although one report gave his age as 12.

COMMONWEALTH GAMES MEDALS BY NATION
1930-86: TOP TWELVE NATIONS

NATION	GOLD	SILVER	BRONZE	TOTAL
England	373	328	326	1027
Australia	345	320	266	931
Canada	252	260	263	775
New Zealand	77	107	134	318
Scotland	51	67	99	217
South Africa*	60	44	47	151
Wales	22	36	48	106
Kenya	29	16	30	75
India	24	28	20	72
Northern Ireland	14	17	29	60
Jamaica	18	14	16	48
Nigeria	14	12	19	45

*No longer member of the Commonwealth

With the increase in length of endurance events to the extent that they often last *days*, the quality of play in the activity in question has frequently declined to such a level that it is questionable that the essence of the game is being played at all. For this reason this is the last edition of *The Guinness Book of Records* which will list sports events when the duration is the only criterion for inclusion.

BACKGAMMON ■ **159 hr 45 min** Matthew Denton and Peter Royle at St Anselm's College, Wirral, Merseyside, 15–22 Aug 1988.

BADMINTON ■ **Singles: 83 hr 25 min** Henry Marais and Jaco Visser at Quartermaster, Pretoria, South Africa, 1–4 Jan 1988.

Doubles: 89 hr Henry Marais, Jaco Visser, Anton Smith and Frikkie Bosman at Sunny City Shopping Centre, Pretoria, 30 May–2 June 1988.

BAR BILLIARDS ■ **110 hr 48 min** David Lillie and Mark Whitehart at The Waggon and Horses, Sudbury, Suffolk, 23–28 Mar 1989.

BASKETBALL ■ **102 hr** Sigma Nu Fraternity at Indiana University, Pennsylvania, USA, 13–17 Apr 1983.

BOARDSAILING ■ **107 hr 7 min** Laurie Dummett (GB) on Suffolk Water Park, Ipswich, Suffolk, 15–19 Sep 1988.

BOWLING (*TEN PIN* **)** ■ **195 hr 1 min** Jim Webb at Gosford City Bowl, New South Wales, Australia, 1984.

BOWLS ■ **Outdoor: 105 hr 33 min** Two teams from Woolston Park Bowling Club, Woolston, New Zealand, 23–27 Mar 1989.

Indoor: 113 hr 16 min Two teams from R.O.T.A. Bowling Club, Ramelton, Letterkenny, Republic of Ireland, 9–14 May 1988.

BRIDGE (*CONTRACT* **)** ■ **186 hr 38 min** Johnathan Noad, Jeremy Cohen, Robert Pinder and Andrew Bale at Ariel Hotel, Hayes, Middlesex, 20–28 Sep 1986.

CHESS ■ **200 hr** Roger Long and Graham Croft at Dingles, Bristol, Avon, 11–19 May 1984.

CRIBBAGE ■ **124 hr 15 min** Four students from St Anselm's College, Wirral, Merseyside, 14–19 Jul 1986.

CRICKET ■ **316 hr** Two teams from Belper, Derbyshire, 14–27 Aug 1983. **Indoor: 129 hr 40 min** Two teams from Isandis CC, Edenvale, South Africa, 14–19 Jul 1987.

CROQUET ■ **120 hr 25 min** Jane Langan, Miles Harbot, Jo Gill and Daryl Shorthose at Birmingham University, 14–19 Jun 1986.

CURLING ■ **4 Players: 67 hr 55 min** Capital Winter Club, Fredericton, New Brunswick, Canada, 9–12 Apr 1982. **2 Players: 48 hr** Rob Warren and Brent Vernon at Newmarket, Ontario, Canada, 31 Mar–2 Apr 1988.

DARTS ■ **182 hr 1 min** Allen Chaperlin and Ian Melton at The Eagle Tavern, Oxford, 11–18 Nov 1988.

DOMINOES ■ **150 hr 5 min** Neil Thomas and Tim Beesley at St Anselm's College, Wirral, Merseyside, 5–11 Aug 1985.

DRAUGHTS ■ **170 hr 2 min** Tom Relph and Edward Roper at St Anselm's College, Wirral, Merseyside, 15–22 Aug 1988.

DUNGEONS & DRAGONS (*TSR* **)** ■ **209 hr** A team from Ogden, Utah, USA in 1983.

FIVES ■ **40 hr** Craig Webster, Robert Lonsdale, Stuart Parker and Mike Wycherley at Shrewsbury School, Shropshire 30 May–1 Jun 1989.

FOOTBALL ■ **75 hr 30 min** Two teams from Roy High School, Roy, Utah, USA, 8–12 Aug 1988. **Outdoor 5-a-side: 74 hr 30 min** Two teams at Liswerry Leisure Centre, Newport, Gwent, 23–26 Jun 1983. **Indoor 5-a-side: 108 hr 10 min** Two teams from The Republic of Ireland Soccer Supporters Club at Greendale Community School, Kilbarrack, Co Dublin, 23–28 Mar 1989.

GAELIC FOOTBALL ■ **60 hr 5 min** Two teams from Kilcornan GAA. Club, Kilcornan, Co. Limerick, Ireland, 23–25 May 1986.

HANDBALL ■ **45 hr 50 min** Castlebridge Handball Club, Castlebridge, Co. Wexford, Ireland 26–28 Sep 1986.

HOCKEY ■ **Outdoor: 50 hr** Two teams from Belper Hockey Club at Belper Sports Centre, Derbyshire, 28–30 Apr 1989. **Indoor: 56 hr** Two teams from Old Kingstonian Hockey Club, Roehampton Recreation Centre, Surrey, 28–30 Apr 1989.

HORSEMANSHIP ■ **149 hr 45 min** Henry Perry at Langdon Hill, Victoria, Australia, 7–13 Nov 1988.

ICE SKATING ■ **109 hr 5 min** Austin McKinley at Christchurch, New Zealand, 21–25 Jun 1977.

JUDO ■ **245 hr 30 min** A team at Smithfield RSL Youth Club, New South Wales, Australia, 3–13 Jan 1984.

NETBALL ■ **45 hr 25 min** Two teams from the Farnham Sports Centre, Farnham, Surrey, 22–24 Jul 1988.

POOL ■ **363 hr 9 min** Sheena Thompson and Geoff Ham at Beacon Vale Institute, Carrbrook, Greater Manchester, 26 Aug–10 Sep 1988.

RACQUETBALL ■ **56 hr 30 min** Brian Leahy and Daryl Houlden in Rochester, Australia, 14–17 Jul 1988.

ROLLER CYCLING ■ **85 hr 24 min** Gilbert Bil at De Weesper, Amsterdam, Netherlands, 10–14 Oct 1986.

ROLLER SKATING ■ **344 hr 18 min** Isamu Furugen at Naha Roller Skate Land, Okinawa, Japan, 11–27 Dec 1983.

RUGBY UNION ■ **24 hr** Tongario High School and Taupo-Nua-A-Tia Grade College School at Turangi Park, New Zealand, 27–28 Mar 1987.

SCRABBLE® ■ **153 hr** Peter Finan and Neil Smith at St Anselm's College, Wirral, Merseyside, 18–25 Aug 1984.

SKIING (*ALPINE* **)** ■ **138 hr** Luc Labrie at Daie Comeau, Quebec, Canada, 20–25 Feb 1984. **With no waiting for lifts – 87 hr 28 min** John Mordini at Kissing Bridge, New York, USA, 11–14 Jan 1988.

SKITTLES ■ **168 hr** Gloucester & District Irish Society at Gloucester, 15–22 Aug 1981.

SNAKES & LADDERS ■ **260 hr** A team from Essex Young Farmers Club, West Mersea, Essex, 29 Jan–9 Feb 1982.

SNOOKER ■ **366 hr 49 min** Peter Hughes and

Andrew Scott at Princess Square, Bracknell, Berkshire, 7–22 Oct 1988.

SOFTBALL ■ **Fast Pitch: 60 hr** Two teams from Campbelltown District Association at Ingleburn, New South Wales, Australia, 6–8 Dec 1986. **Slow Pitch: 111 hr 2 min** Brigade Service Support Group-1 and Marine Aircraft Group-24 at Kareohe Marine Corps Air Station, Hawaii, USA, 3–8 Sep 1986.

SQUASH ■ **133 hr 2 min** John McLachlan and Norman Ingledew at Old Parktonian Minetec Squash Club, Randburg, South Africa, 21–26 Sep 1988.

SUBBUTEO® ■ **100 hr 1 min** Graham Larkin and Kieran Mulrooney at RAF Staff College, Bracknell, Berkshire, 16–20 Mar 1989.

TABLE FOOTBALL ■ **72 hr 20 min** Binesh Lad and Spencer Hughes at Marcher Sound, Wrexham, Clywd, 1–4 Apr 1988.

TABLE TENNIS ■ **Singles: 147 hr 47 min** Shaun Unterslak and Jay Boccia at Dewaal Hotel, Cape Town, South Africa, 12–18 Nov 1983. **Doubles: 101 hr 1 min** Lance, Phil and Mark Warren and Bill Weir at Sacramento, California, USA, 9–13 Apr 1979.

TENNIS (*LAWN* **)** ■ **Singles: 120 hr 9 min** Mark Humes and Bill Victor at The City of Reno Plumas Tennis Centre, Reno, Nevada, USA, 20–25 May 1987. **Doubles: 111 hr** Mike Graff, Paul Vrzal, Mark and Jim Pinchoff at One on One Athletics Club, West Bloomfield, Michigan, USA, 22–26 Nov 1988.

TIDDLYWINKS ■ **300 hr** Southampton University Tiddlywinks Club, Hampshire, 20 Feb–5 Mar 1981.

TRAMPOLINING ■ **266 hr 9 min** Jeff Schwartz at Glenview, Illinois, USA, 14–25 Aug 1981.

TRIVIAL PURSUIT™ ■ **141 hr 56 min** Six students at St Anselm's College, Wirral, Merseyside, 9–15 Aug 1987.

VOLLEYBALL ■ **118 hr 30 min** Students from Krugersdorp High School, Krugersdorp, South Africa, 30 Mar–4 Apr 1988.

WATER POLO ■ **26 hr** Two teams from University of California, San Diego, USA, 8–9 Apr 1989.

NON-STOP

CYCLING ■ Carlos Vieira cycled for 191 hr 'non-stop' at Leira, Portugal from 8–16 Jun 1983. The distance covered was 2407·64 km *1496·04 miles* and he was moving 98·7 per cent of the time.

RUNNING ■ Bertil Järläker (Sweden) (b. 1936) ran 568 km *352·9 miles* in 121 hr 54 min at Norrköping, Sweden, 26–31 May 1980. He was moving for 95·04 per cent of the time.

SWIMMING ■ The longest duration swim ever achieved was one of 168 continuous hours, ending on 24 Feb 1941, by the legless Charles Zibbelman, *alias* Zimmy (b. 1894) in a pool in Honolulu, Hawaii, USA. The longest duration swim by a woman was 129 hr 45 min by Vicki Keith (Canada) at the Artillery Pool, Kingston, Ontario, Canada from 5–10 Jun 1986

WALKING ■ Georges Holtyzer (Belgium) walked 673·48 km *418·49 miles* in 6 days 10 hr 58 min, 452 laps of a 1·49-km circuit, at Ninove, Belgium from 19–25 Jul 1986. He was not permitted any stops for rest and was moving 98·78 per cent of the time.

Stop Press

THE HUMAN BEING

Memory ● (p. 16) George Uhrin of Houston, Texas, USA memorised a random sequence of thirty separate packs of playing cards (1560) which had been shuffled together on a single sighting with only two errors at the Texas Commerce Tower, Houston, Texas on 15–16 Jul 1989.

Fastest talker ● (p. 17) Sean Shannon, a Canadian now living in Oxford, recited Hamlet's soliloquy 'To Be Or Not To Be' in a time of 26·8 seconds at BBC Radio Oxford on 24 Jul 1989.

Backwards talking ● (p. 17) David A Fuhrer at Trax Recording Studio, California, USA recited the entire lyrics of Queen's 1975 album *A Night at the Opera* in a time of 10 min 19 sec on 28 Jul 1989.

THE LIVING WORLD

Oldest cat ● (p. 32) Britain's oldest cat 'Kitty' died in June 1989, just weeks after her 32nd birthday. Her total of known kittens was 218.

Bird-spotter ● (p. 35) By August 1989 Harvey Gilston (b. 12 Oct 1922) of Lausanne, Switzerland had logged 6640 of the 9016 bird species.

THE NATURAL WORLD AND SPACE

Caves ● (p. 57) The longest cave system in Great Britain is the Ease Gill system, West Yorks which by June 1989 had 63·5 km *39½ miles* of explored passage.

Largest asteroids ● (p. 68) The closest approach of an asteroid to the Earth was 690 000 km *430 000 miles* by 1989 FC on 22 Mar 1989. Although probably less than 400 m *1312 ft* in diameter, impact would have resulted in a crater up to 7 km *4 miles* in diameter.

SCIENCE AND TECHNOLOGY

'Pi' ● (p. 73) It was reported in August 1989 that Mr. Y Kanada had calculated 'pi' to 536 870 000 decimal places. It took 67 hr 13 min to run the program and 80 hr 39 min to verify the results.

Clock – most expensive ● (p. 82) A record price of £880 000 was paid for an unknown Thomas Tompion at Christie's, London on 5 Jul 1989.

Largest telephone ● (p. 82) The world's largest operational telephone was exhibited at a festival on 16 Sep 1988 to celebrate the 80th birthday of Centraal Beheer, an insurance company based in Apeldoorn, Netherlands. It was 2·74 m *8 ft 1 in* high and 6·06 m *19 ft 11 in* long, and weighed 3·5 tonnes. The handset, being 7·14 m *23 ft 5 in* long, had to be lifted by crane in order to make a call.

BUILDINGS AND STRUCTURES

Advertising hoarding ● (p. 98) Bassat, Ogilvy Promotional Campaigns erected the world's largest hoarding for Ford España measuring 145 m *475 ft 9 in* in length and 24 m *78 ft 9 in* wide at Plaza de Toros Monumental de Barcelona, Barcelona, Spain.

The world's largest illuminated sign measures 60 m × 20 m *196 ft 7¹/₂in × 65 ft*. It was erected by Abudi Signs of Israel.

TRANSPORT

Marine circumnavigation records – Fastest sail with stops W–E, solo in multihull ● (p. 105) Olivier de Kersauson (France) achieved a record time of 125 days 19 hr 32 min 33 sec (gross) in his 22·9 m *75 ft* trimaran sloop *Un Autre Regard*, leaving Brest, France on 28 Dec 1988 and returning to Brest on 5 May 1989 after 3 stops en route.

Trans-Atlantic records – Fastest power W–E ● (p. 106) Tom Gentry (US) achieved a record time of 2 days 14 hr 7 min 47 sec in his 33·5 m *110 ft* powerboat *Gentry Eagle*, leaving from Ambrose Light Tower at 13.49 BST on 24 Jul 1989 and reaching Bishop Rock Light at 03.56 on 27 Jul 1989.

Most powerful tugs ● (p. 107) In April/May 1989 the tugs 0268 and 0269 *Nikolay Chiker* and *SB-153* were

Javier Sotomayor (Cuba) became the first high jumper to clear the eight foot barrier at San Juan, Puerto Rico on 29 Jul 1989. (Photo: All-Sport)

delivered to V/O Sudoimport, USSR. Their horse power is 26 710 and their bollard pull is over 260 tons.

Fastest road car ● (p. 110) The highest road-tested acceleration for the 0 –60 mph *0 –96·5 km/h* dash is 3·98 sec for a Ferrari F40 owned by Nick Mason and driven by Mark Hales of *Fast Lane* magazine at Millbrook, Beds on 9 Feb 1989.

Circumnavigational drive ● (p. 112) Surgeon Lt.Comdr (Mrs) Rupali Roy and co-driver husband Capt Ranjan Roy, both of the Indian Navy, driving an Indian 796 cc Mini Maruti car, covered four continents (32 countries) and a distance of 42 429 km *26 369 miles* between 14 Apr – 10 Aug 1989.

Round UK 72 Counties drive ● (p. 112) June Laird (driver/leader) together with Jim Laird and Robert Nottger (drivers) completed 4131·2 km *2582 miles* in a record time of 97 hr 35 min. Their journey commenced on 21 Jul 1989 at Lerwick, Shetland and finished on 25 Jul 1989 at Stornoway, Lewis.

Battery powered vehicle ● (p. 112) The Land Speed Record was last broken in an electric car by Camille Jenatzy in *La Jamais Contente* in April 1899 with a speed of 105·87 km/h *65·79 mph* over a flying kilometre in one direction. Ninety years later this was beaten by D J S Lambert in a replica of the original car with a speed of 108·82 km/h *67·62 mph*, on 25 Mar 1989 at RAF Elvington, North Yorks.

Most economical car ● (p. 112) On 9 Aug 1989 motoring writer Stuart Bladon driving a Citroen AX 14DTR achieved a distance of 180·26 km *112·01 miles* using one gallon of fuel driving on the M11 motorway in a test run arranged by Lucas Diesel Systems.

Oldest driver ● (p. 112) Holder of the earliest driving licence Reginald 'Gerry' Bond died on 12 Jun 1989.

Longest motorcycle ● (p. 115) Les Nash of Coventry, West Midlands constructed a 'self made' machine with a Rover 3·5 litre V-8 engine measuring 3·81 m x 1·22 m *12 ft 6 in x 4 ft* and weighing more than 226·8 kg *500 lb*. It may legally be used on public roads.

Smallest motorcycle ● (p. 115) Magnor Mydland of Norway constructed a motorcycle with a wheelbase of 120 mm *4·72 in*, a seat height of 148 mm *5·82 in* and with wheels of 38 mm *1·49 in* (front) and 49 mm *3·39 in* (back) in diameter. He rode a distance of 525 m *1722 ft* attaining a speed of 16 km/h *9·94 mph*.

Fastest wheelie ● (p. 116) Steve Burns of Manchester on his Suzuki GXS 1100 engine, Spondon achieved a speed of 241 km/h *150 mph* at Bruntingthorpe Proving Ground, Leics on 3 Jul 1989.

Smallest plane ● (p. 121) Robert H. Starr of Arizona, USA designed and built *Bumble Bee Two*. It was 2·64 m *8 ft 10 in* long, with a wing span of 1·68 m *5 ft 6 in*, and weighed 179·62 kg *396 lb*. The highest

speed attained was 305·8 km/h *190 mph*. On 8 May 1988 it flew to a height of approximately 1312 m *400 ft*, crashed and was totally destroyed.

Longest flights ● (p. 122) The longest delivery flight by a commercial jet is 18 001 km *9719 nautical miles* from London to Sydney by a Qantas Boeing 747-400 'Longreach', using 179 500 kg *176·6 tons* of specially formulated Shell Jet A-1 high-density fuel, in 20 hr 9 min on 16–17 Aug 1989. It is the first time this route has been completed non-stop by an airliner.

Fastest climb ● (p. 123) Heinz Frick of British Aerospace took a Harrier GR5, powered by a Rolls-Royce 11-61 Pegasus engine, from a standing start to 12 000 m *39 370 ft* in 126·63 sec at the Rolls-Royce flight test centre, Bristol, Avon on 15 Aug 1989.

Paper aircraft ● (p. 127) The largest paper aeroplane was constructed by Werner Heise and Beat Schück at Kongresshaus, Zürich, Switzerland on 18 Dec 1988. With a wing span of 3·04 m *10 ft* it was launched from a 3·04 m *10 ft* high platform and flew for a distance of 21·36 m *70 ft*.

THE BUSINESS WORLD

Largest takeover ● (p. 130) Hanson Trust won control of Consolidated Gold Fields (founded in 1897) on 7 Aug 1989 with a bid of £3500 million. The largest bid ever made for a British company is £13 000 million for BAT Industries on 11 Jul 1989 by Hoylake, lead by Sir James Goldsmith, Jacob Rothschild and Kerry Packer.

Largest financial services institution ● (p. 130) The now merged Price Waterhouse Andersen jointly generated global revenues in 1988 of $4830 million.

Largest cheque ● (p. 135) The greatest amount paid by a single cheque in the history of banking was one for £1 088 524 128.30p. Issued on 30 Aug 1988 and signed by Conrad Milton, Assistant General Manager of the Royal Bank of Scotland, it represented the call monies due from clients of the bank in respect of the BP share issue.

Sheep shearing ● (p. 138) The British record for 9 hr has been set at 1038 (sheep caught *by* shearers) by Nicky Beynon (521) and Wyn Jones (517) at Pant Farm, Merthyr Cynog, Powys on 1 Jul 1989.

Barley ● (p. 138) A yield of 12 200 kg/ha *97·22 cwt/acre* of Winter Barley was achieved on 2 Aug 1989 by farmers Stockton Park Leisure Ltd, Chirnside, Berwickshire from 21·29 ha *52·6 acres*.

Combine harvesting ● (p. 139) Philip Baker of West End Farm, Merton, Bicester, Oxon harvested 165·6 tonnes of wheat in 8 hr using a Massey Ferguson MF 38 combine on 8 Aug 1989.

Straw baling ● (p. 139) Svend Erik Klemmensen of Trustrup, Djursland, Denmark baled 200 tonnes of straw in 9 hr 54 min using a Hesston 4800 baling machine on 30 Aug 1988.

Heaviest chicken ● (p. 140) A White Ross I rooster named 'Bruno' owned by John Steele of Kirkhills Farms, Boyndie, Banff recorded a weight of 10·02 kg *22 lb 1 oz* on 4 Jul 1989.

THE ARTS AND ENTERTAINMENT

Largest poster ● (p. 145) A poster measuring 10 808 m² *116 070 ft²* was constructed by 10 000 schoolchildren from Lancaster, Morecambe, Garstang, Kendal and Windermere on the sands of Morecambe Bay, Lancs on 25 Jun 1989.

Antiques – Carpet ● (p. 145) The highest price ever paid at auction for a carpet is £384 230 for a Louis XV Savonnerie at Christie's, Monaco in June 1989.

Antiques – Furniture ● (p. 146) The highest price paid for an item of English furniture was £1·1 million at Christie's, London on 6 Jul 1989 for a George III ormolu mounted mahogany dressing and writing commode, attributed to John Channon and made *c.* 1760.

Antiques – Typewriter ● (p. 146) The highest price paid for an antique machine is £9900 for an 1890 black enamel Guhl & Harbeck machine auctioned at Christie's, London on 10 Aug 1989.

Longest palindromes ● (p. 148) By 18 Jul 1989 Edward Benbow's palindromic composition contained 88 888 words.

Most letters to an editor ● (p. 151) David Green's total reached 123 by 17 Jul 1989.

Christmas card exchange ● (p. 151) Warren Nord of Mesa, Arizona, USA and Thor ('Tut') Andersen (d. 11 Sep 1988) exchanged the same Christmas card every year from 1930 to 1987.

Highest advance ● (p. 152) The highest advance paid by a British publisher to an author is £2 million by Hodder & Stoughton for two 'horror' novels by James Herbert in August 1989.

Fastest publisher ● (p. 153) A thousand bound copies of Sir Frederick Mason's village history *Ropley – Past and Present* were produced in 12 hr 26 min from raw disk by publishers Scriptmate Editions in conjunction with printers Scan Laser Ltd.

Most durable pianist ● (p. 155) The longest international career in the history of western music was crowned by Mieczyslaw Horszowski (b. Poland, July 1892) with a recital of Bach, Chopin, Mozart and Schumann at the Aldeburgh Festival, Suffolk on 15 Jun 1989. He played before Emperor Franz-Joseph in Vienna in 1899.

Double bass ● (p. 156) Sixteen musicians from Blandford, Dorset played a double bass simultaneously (five fingering and eleven bowing) in a rendition of Strauss' *Perpetuum Mobile* at Blandford Town Hall on 6 Jun 1989.

Highest box office gross ● (p. 164) On 24 Jun 1989 *Batman* (Warner Brothers) grossed $14 600 000 for a single day record. The highest opening gross was also scored by *Batman* on 23 Jun 1989 with a take of $13·1 million.

Highest paid film actor ● (p. 164) Jack Nicholson stood to receive up to $60 million for playing 'The Joker' in Warner Brothers' $50 million *Batman* through a percentage of the film's receipts in lieu of salary.

Longest continuous TV transmission under a single director ● (p. 167) On 10–11 Jun 1989 Mark Dickson directed a 40 hr 1 min 24 sec show hosted by Gerry Kaminski on Maclean Hunter Cable TV, Detroit, Michigan, USA.

Most successful telethon (see also Economics p. 136) ● (p. 168) The highest figure raised within Britain is £22 800 000 by ITV Telethon '88 with Michael Aspel in 27 hours over the May Bank Holiday.

HUMAN ACHIEVEMENTS

Golden weddings ● (p. 172) The Gresl golden weddings record was equalled by the six sons and four daughters of George and Eleonora Hopkins of Patrick County, Virginia, USA all celebrating their golden weddings between November 1961 and October 1988.

Balloon release ● (p. 173) The British record is 128 966 helium balloons released simultaneously on 1 Jul 1989 from Alton Towers, Staffs.

Band, one-man ● (p. 173) Rory Blackwell played 108 different instruments (19 melody and 89 percussion) simultaneously in Dawlish, Devon on 29 May 1989.

Beer keg lifting ● (p. 174) Denis McKeown raised a keg of beer weighing 62·5 kg *137·79 lb* above his head 612 times in the space of 6 hr at Blackrock, Co Louth, Ireland on 30 Jul 1989.

Bricklifting ● (p. 174–5) Russ Holland of Mansfield Woodhouse, Notts lifted 28 bricks on 24 Jul 1989.

Coin balancing ● (p. 175) Hiem Shda of K. Mozkien, Israel stacked a pyramid of 847 coins on the edge of a coin freestanding vertically on the base of a coin which was on a table on 30 Jul 1989.

Cardiopulmonary resuscitation ● (p. 176) Three teams of two, consisting of David Bailey and Les Williams, Angie Drinkard and Rich Martel, and Michelle Tyler and Sherri Johnson, all completed CPR marathons of 120 hr 6 min from 1–6 Sep 1988 in Melbourne, Florida, USA.

Escalator riding ● (p. 177) The record for travelling a pair of 'up' and 'down' escalators is 101 hr, by David Beattie and Adrian Simons at Top Shop, Oxford Street, London from 17–21 Jul 1989. They each travelled 214·34 km *133·19 miles*.

Field to loaf ● (p. 177–8) The fastest time for producing loaves from growing wheat is 30 min 45 sec by Tendring Hundred Farmers' Club and millers Read Woodrow at Wix, Essex on 3 Aug 1989.

Gold panning ● (p. 178) The fastest time for 'panning' eight planted gold nuggets in a 25·4 cm *10 in* diameter pan is 7·55 sec by Don Roberts of Diamond Bar, California, USA in the 27th World Gold Panning Championship on 16 Apr 1989 at Dahlonega, California.

Hamburger ● (p. 178) The largest hamburger on record was one of 2503 kg *5520 lb*, made at the Outagamie County Fairgrounds, Seymour, Wisconsin, USA on 5 Aug 1989.

Milk shake ● (p. 179) The largest milk shake was a chocolate one of 6803·8 litres *1500 gal*, made at 'Taste New Haven', an annual food festival held in New Haven, Connecticut, USA on 20 Aug 1988.

Hay bale rolling ● (p. 180) Michael Priestley and Marcus Stanley of Heckington Young Farmers Club rolled a 1·2 m *3 ft 11 in* wide cylindrical bale over a 50 m *164 ft* course in 18·06 sec at the Lincolnshire Federation of Young Farmers' Clubs annual sports day at Sleaford, Lincs on 25 Jun 1989.

Human centipede ● (p. 182) The largest 'human centipede' to move 30 m *98 ft 5 in* (with ankles firmly tied together) consisted of 552 people. Not one single person fell over in the course of the walk, which took place on 10 Mar 1989 at Belgrave High School, Tamworth, Staffs.

Magician, fastest ● (p. 182) Julian Lincow performed 98 different tricks in 1 min 57·9 sec at Claremont, Cape Town, South Africa on 31 Mar 1989.

Musical chairs ● (p. 183) The largest game on record was one starting with 8238 participants, ending with Xu Chong Wei on the last chair, which was held at the Anglo-Chinese School, Singapore on 5 Aug 1989.

Omelette making ● (p. 183) The greatest number of two-egg omelettes made in 30 min is 379 by Christopher Bracken at Madison, Connecticut, USA on 19 Jun 1989.

Riding in armour ● (p. 183) The longest recorded ride in armour is one of 334·7 km *208 miles* by Dick Brown, who left Edinburgh, Lothian on 10 Jun 1989 and arrived in his home town of Dumfries, Dumfries and Galloway four days later. His total riding time was 35 hr 25 min.

Sand sculpturing ● (p. 184) The long-est sand sculpture ever made — with a mound of sand piled up and the sculpture meticulously carved out — was the 4591 m *15 063 ft* long GTE Directories/Sun Fun 'Never Ending Fantasy' which was constructed at Myrtle Beach, South Carolina, USA on 2 Jun 1989 by 1613 volunteers. The tallest was the 'Invitation to Fairyland' which was 17·12 m *56 ft 2 in* high, and was built by 2000 local volunteers at Kaseda, Japan on 26 Jul 1989 under the supervision of Gerry Kirk of Sand Sculptors International of San Diego and Shogo Tashiro of Sand Sculptors International of Japan.

Singing ● (p. 184) The longest recorded solo-singing marathon is one of 262 hr by Pastor S. Jeyaseelan at the Asian Glass House Building, Ramnad, India from 22 Apr–3 May 1989.

Stamp licking ● (p. 185) John Kenmuir licked and affixed 328 stamps in 4 min at George Square Post Office, Glasgow, Strathclyde on 30 Jun 1989.

Talking ● (p. 185) The longest recorded after-dinner speech was one of 37 hr 55 min by Rev Clive Southerton at Prestatyn, Clwyd from 31 Mar–1 Apr 1989.

Writing minuscule ● (p. 187) Jugal-chandra Kundu of Calcutta, India wrote a poem consisting of 437 characters on a single grain of rice at Kalamazoo, Michigan, USA on 10 Jul 1989.

Yodelling ● (p. 187) The most protracted yodel on record was one of 27 hr by Ashrita Furman of Jamaica, New York, USA from 20–22 May 1989.

Bottle caps ● (p. 187) On 23 Jun 1989 Helge Friholm's collection contained 54 540 bottle caps from 162 countries.

Candle ● (p. 187) A candle constructed by Enham Industries at the Charlton Leisure Centre, Andover, Hants on 2 Jul 1989, measured 30·99 m *101·7 ft* high.

Card ● (p. 187) Seven members of Oceanway PTA, Jacksonville, Florida, USA constructed a greeting card measuring 11·35 m × 16·69 m *37 ft 3 in × 54 ft 9 in*. It was delivered by the US Postal Service to Oceanway Seventh Grade Center on 21 Apr 1989.

Lantern ● (p. 191) A 3·7 m *12 ft 1¼ in* high lantern with a 12 m *39 ft 4 in* circumference was made on 29 Apr 1989 by members of the Lotus Lantern International Buddhist Centre and staff of the Seoul Hilton Hotel, South Korea.

Sofa ● (p. 192) In April 1987 a 4·77 m *15 ft 6 in* long black suede sofa was specially manufactured by Kingcome Sofas, London at their Devon workshops.

THE HUMAN WORLD

Longest term of office ● (p. 201) Andrey Andreyevich Gromyko died on 2 Jul 1989.

Highest bail — British ● (p. 210) David Mitchell was remanded on £750 000 bail on 16 Jun 1989 at Guildhall Magistrates' Court, London, in connection with charges over the collapse of Barlow Clowes.

Greatest damages, personal injury – British ● (p. 210) Martin Harrop, 22, was awarded £1 200 000 in the High Court, London on 9 Aug 1989 against Manuel Fernandez, the driver of a car which had been involved in a crash.

Art robbery ● (p. 213) The two remaining Van Gogh paintings, *Dried Sunflowers* and *Potato Eaters*, were returned to the museum on 13 Jul 1989 by lawyers representing one of the four persons arrested.

Prison sentences – longest sentences ● (p. 214) Chamoy Thipyaso, a Thai woman known as the queen of underground investing, and seven of her associates were each jailed for 141 078 years by the Bangkok Criminal Court, Thailand on 27 Jul 1989 for swindling the public through a multi-million dollar deposit-taking business.

SPORTS, GAMES AND PASTIMES

Archery ● (p. 225) Women's world records, FITA 1369/1440: 70 m 336/360: 60 m 347/360 all by Kim Soo-nyung (South Korea) at the World Championships at Lausanne, Switzerland in July 1989. British record, FITA 1299/1440 by Joanne Franks (later Evans) also at the World Championships.

Board Games ● (p. 229) Scrabble® ; Most titles, Russell Byers (b. 21 Apr 1955) won the British National Championships for a record-equalling second time in 1989. He won previously in 1982.

Bowling ● (p. 230) Highest score, 24 hours; A team of six scored 87 722 at Bitburg Bowling Center, Bitburg, West Germany on 9–10 Jun 1989.

Boxing ● (p. 232) Mike Tyson won his 37 th fight on 21 Jul 1989, stopping Carl 'The Truth' Williams (USA) after just 93 seconds.

Card Games ● (p. 233) Biggest tournament; The Epson World Bridge Championship, held on 9 Jun 1989, was contested by 85 100 players playing the same hands at centres in 90 countries. It was won by Wojciech Blegajlo and Dariusz Zembrzuski of Warsaw, Poland, with 79·17 per cent.

Cricket ● (p. 238) Wicket-keeping; Most catches in a match, Warren Kevin Hegg (b. 23 Feb 1968) of Lancashire equalled the record of eleven (seven in the first innings, four in the second), against Derbyshire at Chesterfield on 9–11 Aug 1989.

Cycling ● (p. 241) World record; Men, indoor 1 km unpaced standing start,

1:02·579 by Aleksandr Kirichenko (USSR) at Moscow, USSR on 2 Aug 1989
Tour de France; The closest race ever was in 1989 when after 3250 km *2019·5 miles* over 23 days (1–23 Jul) Greg LeMond (USA) (b. 26 Jun 1960), who won with a time of 87 hr 38 min 35 sec, beat Laurent Fignon (France) (b. 12 Aug 1960) in Paris by only 8 sec.

Football ● (p. 248) Transfer fees; The highest transfer fee for a British player is the estimated £4·5 million paid by Olympique Marseille of France to Tottenham Hotspur for Chris Waddle (b. 14 Dec 1960) on 6 Jul 1989.

Gliding ● (p. 251) Hang Gliding, World Championships; Great Britain won for a third time at Fiesch, Switzerland in July 1989.

Golf ● (p. 253) Most balls hit in one hour; 1165 (from 1524 attempts) by David Morris at Bannel Golf Range, Buckley, Clwyd on 24 Jun 1989.

(p. 254) Highest earnings, Women; Betsy King (USA), winner of the 1989 US Open, has won $503 794 in the 1989 season to 16 Jul 1989.

Gymnastics ● (p. 256) Most squats in one hour; 2352 by Manjit Singh (GB) at the City Health & Yoga Centre, Leicester on 10 Jun 1989. Most parallel bar dips in one hour; 3118 by Manjit Singh at City Health & Yoga Centre, Leicester on 3 Jul 1989.

Horse Racing ● (p. 259) Major Races; Dick Hern trained a fifth winner in the King George VI and Queen Elizabeth Diamond Stakes, *Nashwan*, on 22 Jul 1989.

Motor Racing ● (p. 268) Most successful drivers; Alain Prost (France) (b. 24 Feb 1955) has scored 567·5 Grand Prix points and 38 Grand Prix victories. Ricardo Patrese (Italy) (b. 17 Apr 1954) has started 186 Grand Prix races, both to 13 Aug 1989. Manufacturers, Ferrari have won 95 races from 450 Grand Prix to 13 Aug 1989.

Skipping ● (p. 282) Most turns in 1 hour; 13 783 by Bob Commers at the Woodbridge Mall, Woodbridge, New Jersey, USA on 13 May 1989: Most on single rope (minimum 12 turns obligatory) 200 by a team at the International Rope Skipping Competition, Greeley, Colorado, USA, 30 Jun 1989.

Swimming ● (p. 285) World records: Men, 200 metres freestyle, 1:46·69 by Giorgio Lamberti (Italy) (b. 28 Jan 1969); 100 metres breastroke, 1:01·49 by Adrian Moorhouse (GB) (b. 24 May 1964), both at Bonn, West Germany on 15 Aug 1989; 200 metres breastroke, 2:12·90 by Mike Barrowman (USA) (b. 4 Dec 1968) at Los Angeles, California, USA on 3 Aug 1989.

Track and Field Athletics ● (p. 292) World records: Men, 110 m hurdles 12·92 by Roger Kingdom (USA) (b. 26 Aug 1962) at Zürich, Switzerland on 16 Aug 1989; High Jump 2·44 m *8 ft* by Javier Sotomayor (Cuba) (b. 13 Oct 1967) at San Juan, Puerto Rico on 29 Jul 1989

(p. 293) Women 1 mile 4:15·61 by Paula Ivan (Romania) (b. 20 Jul 1963) at Nice, France on 10 Jul 1989.

(p. 294) British records: Men, 110 m hurdles, 13·11 by Colin Jackson at Crystal Palace, London on 14 Jul 1989, *equals record and replaces his low altitude best*; High jump 2·33 m *7 ft 7¼ in* by Dalton Grant at Birmingham, West Midlands on 13 Aug 1989; Javelin 85·86 m *281 ft 8 in* by Stephen Backley (b. 12 Feb 1969) at Budapest, Hungary on 8 Aug 1989.

Yachting ● (p. 306) Admiral's Cup; Britain won the ocean racing series for a record ninth time on 10 Aug 1989.

Endurance marathons ● (p. 310) Basketball: 120 hr by two teams at South Towne Mall, Sandy, Utah, USA from 22–27 Aug 1988. Football Outdoor 5-a-side: 75 hr 30 min by two teams at the Coca-Cola Plant, Dublin, Republic of Ireland, 2–5 Jun 1989. Hockey Indoor: 56 hr 10 min by two teams at the YMCA, Bendigo, Australia, 23–25 Jun 1989. Table Football: 90 hr by Terence Madigan and Don Maher at The Coach Inn, Kilcornan, Co. Limerick, Republic of Ireland, 17–21 May 1989.

Index

An asterisk indicates a further reference in the Stop Press

ABBREVIATION, longest 148
A-BOMB see Atomic Bomb
ABSEILING, longest descent 183
ACCELERATOR, most powerful 75
ACCENTS, word with most 148
ACCIDENTS, worst world, UK 196-7, sports 221
ACCORDION, marathon 173
ACCOUNTANCY, largest firm 130
ACE, air 202-3
ACROBATIC RECORDS, 175
ACRONYM, longest 148
ACTOR, most durable, most roles 160, most in family 165
ACTRESS, most durable 160
ADDRESS, longest legal 210, highest-numbered postal 137
ADMIRAL, longest serving 208
ADVANCE, to an author, greatest 152
ADVERTISER, most durable 154, biggest 130
ADVERTISING, highest rate, expenditure 154-5, highest TV rates 168, largest agents 130, sign: greatest ever*, largest, highest world, Great Britain 98
ADVOCATE, most successful 211
AERIALIST, feats 175
AEROBATICS, 221
AEROFLORA, 52
AEROPLANE, see Aircraft
AEROSPACE COMPANY, largest 130
AGE, see Longevity
AGRICULTURE, 138-40
AIR ACE, top-scoring, world, UK, top jet, top woman 202-3
AIRCRAFT, earliest flights 120, Mach scale, supersonic, trans-Atlantic first, first trans-Pacific, circumnavigation: first, fastest, smallest aircraft, largest wing span, heaviest, solar-powered, ultralight 121, heaviest, largest bombers 121-2, airliner: largest, fastest, most capacious, largest propeller, longest*, shortest scheduled flight 122, speed records: 122-3, greatest altitude, flight duration record 123, helicopter: fastest, largest, greatest load, smallest*, highest, circumnavigation, autogyros: earliest, speed, altitude, distance records, flying-boat: fastest, airship: earliest, largest, greatest passenger load, distance, duration 124, model aircraft: speed, duration records, altitude, first cross-Channel flight, smallest, paper aircraft duration record*, take-offs and landings, human-powered 127
AIRCRAFT CARRIER, largest, most landings 104
AIRCRAFT DISASTER, worst world 196
AIRCRAFT MANUFACTURER, largest 130
AIR FORCE, earliest, greatest 208
AIRLINE, largest commercial, most passengers, greatest mileage of routes, oldest 130-1
AIRLINER, largest, fastest, most capacious 122
AIRPORT, largest, busiest, highest, lowest, farthest, nearest to city centre, longest runway 123-4
AIRSHIP, earliest, largest rigid, British, non-rigid hot air, greatest passenger load, distance, duration records 124
AIR SPEED RECORDS, world 122-3
AIR SUPPORTED BUILDING, largest 88
ALBATROSS, largest wing span 33, longest incubation 35
ALBUMS (RECORD), biggest sellers, chart records, fastest selling 163, Grammy awards 163-4
ALCOHOL, most in blood 17, strongest, weakest, most expensive wine, spirits 179-180
ALCOHOLIC, greatest 17
ALE, yard of 187
ALIMONY, highest awards, suit 211
ALL SPORTS records 220-1
ALPHABET, oldest, longest, shortest 147

ALPHORN, longest 156
ALTITUDE RECORDS, bird 34, man, woman, rocket 84, aircraft 123, helicopter 124, balloon 124-5, canoe 233, cycling 242, gliding, hang gliding 251, golf course 252, mountaineering 271, skiing 281, yachting 307
ALUMINIUM, largest producer 131
AMBER, largest piece 65
AMBULANCE, largest 113
AMERICAN FOOTBALL, 221-3
AMPHIBIANS, largest, smallest, longest lived, rarest, highest, lowest, most poisonous, largest, smallest frog, longest frog jump, largest, smallest toad 37-38, earliest, largest extinct 46
AMPHIBIOUS VEHICLE, first circumnavigation 111
AMPHITHEATRE, earliest 159-60, largest 160
AMPLIFIER, biggest 187
AMUSEMENT RESORT, largest 92
ANAESTHESIA, earliest 20
ANAGRAM, longest 148
ANCIENT MONUMENT, newest 100
ANGLING, 223-4
ANIMAL, kingdom 22-46, strongest, most prodigious eater, largest, heaviest mammal, deepest dive 22, largest land, largest marine, tallest, smallest, rarest 23, fastest land 23-4, fastest marine, slowest, sleepiest, longest hibernation, oldest, highest living, largest herds, longest, shortest gestation, largest litter, youngest breeder 24, largest, smallest dinosaurs 44, fastest 45, largest footprints 45-6, most brainless, largest eggs, largest claws, largest skull, largest flying creature, earliest of their types 46, man-eating 196 see also Mammals
ANNUAL GENERAL MEETING, largest 130
ANTARCTIC CONTINENT, most northerly iceberg 56, first ship, first sighting, landing, conquest South Pole, first woman, first crossing, longest sledge journey 170-1
ANTELOPE, fastest 26, largest, smallest, rarest, oldest 29
ANTHEM, National, oldest, longest, shortest, longest rendition 156
ANTIQUE, records* 145-6, 187
ANTLERS, largest span 29, 46
APPEAL, most successful TV 168
APPENDICECTOMY, earliest 20
APPLE, biggest, heaviest 48
APPLE PEELING, record 173
APPLE PICKING, record 173
APPLE PIE, largest 178
AQUARIUM, largest 52
AQUEDUCT, longest ancient, modern, 95-96
ARACHNIDS, see Spiders
ARBITRATION, longest 210
ARCH, longest natural 59
ARCHERY*, 224-5
ARCHIPELAGO, greatest 56
ARCTIC CONTINENT, most southerly iceberg 56, first crossing 171
ARIA, longest 158
ARMED FORCES, largest 208
ARMOUR, thickest battleship 104, longest ride in* 183, most expensive 187
ARMY, largest, oldest, oldest old soldier, youngest soldiers, conscript, tallest soldier, oldest British regiment, most senior, greatest mutiny, longest march, drill 208
ARREST, greatest mass 214
ART, largest 'works of art' 144, painting 144-5, sculpture 145-6
ART AUCTIONEERING, largest, oldest firm, most profitable session 131
ART GALLERY, largest 144
ARTICHOKE, biggest 48
ARTIFICIAL MOUND, largest 100
ARTIFICIAL SEAWAY, longest 96
ARTILLERY, see Gun, Cannon
ART NOUVEAU, highest auction price 145
ARTS FESTIVAL, biggest world 160
ASCENDANTS, most 13
ASPARAGUS, longest 49

ASPIDISTRA, largest 47
ASSETS, business, greatest 130
ASSOCIATION, largest world 131, oldest club 136
ASSOCIATION FOOTBALL, 245-50
ASTEROIDS, largest, only visible, closest, most distant 68
ASTRONAUT, earliest, first woman, first fatality, walk 83-4, longest flight, oldest, youngest, most journeys 84
ASYLUM, see Mental Hospital
ATHLETICS* 291-301
ATLANTIC CROSSING, smallest boat, first rowing, fastest solo boat –USA, fastest solo sail, marine records* 106, first, fastest 109, first amphibious vehicle 111, first air, non-stop, solo, most 121, fastest 123, first balloon 124
ATLAS, most expensive 151
ATOLL, largest, largest land area 57
ATOMIC BOMB, most casualties 196, most deadly, largest arsenal 208
ATOMIC PILE, earliest 77
ATOMIC POWER STATION, largest 77, worst disaster 196
ATOMIC REACTOR, largest 77
ATOM SMASHER, see Accelerator
AUCTION, greatest art 131, greatest company 132, highest price art 144-5, largest one man 173, wine 180
AUDIENCE, greatest, pop festival, concert 157, smallest theatrical 160, television 167
AURORA (Borealis and Australis), noctilucent clouds 66
AUTHOR, see Writer
AUTOGRAPH, earliest royal, most expensive 151, rarest and most valuable, 152
AUTOGYROS, earliest, speed, altitude, distance records 124
AUTOMOBILE, see Car
AVALANCHE, greatest, 59-60, 196
AVENUE (trees), longest 52
AVIATION, oldest, youngest passengers 126, see also Flight
AWARDS, versatility showbusiness 166, youngest recipient 203, largest annual 203-4, see also Medals
AXEMANSHIP, records 186-7

BABIES, most by one mother 11, heaviest, most bouncing, lightest 11-12, test tube 12, multiple births 12-13
BACKGAMMON, 228,310
BACTERIA, largest, smallest, free-living, highest, longest lived, fastest, toughest 52, biggest disaster 196
BADGER, largest 27
BADMINTON, 225, 310
BAG-CARRYING, 173
BAGPIPES, fastest playing 156, longest duration 173
BAIL, highest world, GB* 210
BALANCE, finest 74
BALANCE OF PAYMENTS, highest, lowest 134
BALANCING ON ONE FOOT, 173
BALLET DANCING, records 159
BALLOON, earliest, distance record 124, highest unmanned 124-5, manned 125, largest hot-air 126, inflating meteorological 182
BALLOON FLIGHTS (toy), biggest release* 173
BALLOONING, earliest, distance record 124, highest 124-5, largest, hot-air distance, altitude, endurance records 126
BALLOT PAPER, largest 200
BALLROOM DANCING, marathon record, most successful champions 176
BAMBOO, tallest, fastest growing 49
BANANA SPLIT, longest 178
BAND, largest, largest marching, most successful brass 157, longest playing, greatest one-man* 173-4
BANK, largest, largest building, biggest bail out 131, biggest fraud 213
BANK-NOTE, earliest, oldest surviving, largest, smallest, highest denomination, lowest denomination, highest circulation 135, greatest forgery 213

BANK RATE, lowest, highest 134
BANK ROBBERY, greatest 213
BANKRUPTCY, greatest 130
BANQUET, largest world outdoor, indoor, most expensive 131
BAR, longest 94
BARBECUE, largest 178
BAR BILLIARDS, 228,310
BAREFOOT WATERSKIING, 303
BARGE, largest 107
BARLEY, record yield* 138
BARN, largest, longest tithe GB 98
BAROMETER, largest 73
BAROMETRIC PRESSURE, highest, lowest 64
BARONET, oldest 204
BARRACKS, oldest 90
BARREL-JUMPING, greatest number 174
BARROW, largest, largest long 100
BARROW PUSHING, heaviest load 174
BARROW RACING, fastest 174
BARTER DEAL, greatest 132
BASEBALL, 225-6
BASIN, largest river 59
BASKET, biggest 187
BASKETBALL, 226-7, 310*
BATH TUB RACING, fastest, greatest distance 174
BATON TWIRLING, 174
BATS, smallest mammal 23, 29, largest, rarest, fastest, longest lived, highest detectable pitch, deepest roost 29
BATTERY, largest, longest lasting 77, powered vehicle* 112
BATTLE, earliest, longest, bloodiest, shortest 204-5, Britain, last pitched land, clan, worst, worst in Britain 205
BATTLE HONOURS, most 208
BATTLESHIP, largest world, Britain, largest guns, thickest armour 104
BAY, largest world, GB 54
BEACH, pleasure, largest 92
BEAK, largest, longest 35
BEANS, largest 48
BEARD, longest 15
BEAUTY, feminine 177
BED, most expensive 145, largest, heaviest 187
BED MAKING, fastest 174
BED OF NAILS, duration record on 174
BED PUSHING, record push 174
BED RACE, 174
BEECH, tallest hedge 50
BEEFBURGER, largest 178
BEER, strongest, weakest 179
BEER CANS, largest collection, most expensive 187
BEER KEG, lifting* 174
BEER LABEL COLLECTING, largest collection 187
BEER MAT FLIPPING, 174
BEER MATS, largest collection 187
BEER STEIN CARRYING, fastest 174
BEER TANKARD, largest 187
BEES, biggest mantle of 182
BEETLES, largest, heaviest, smallest 40, highest g force 41
BELL, oldest, heaviest, largest, heaviest carillon 156-7
BEETROOT, heaviest 48
BELL-RINGING, most changes rung 157
BELLY DANCING, 176
BEQUEST, greatest 135
BEST MAN, most often 174
BEST SELLER, world non-fiction, fiction 152, gramophone records 162-3
BETTING, 250-1
BIATHLON, 266
BIBLE, earliest printed 150, most valuable, oldest, longest and shortest books, longest, shortest psalm, verse, total letters, words, longest name 151, print figures 152
BICEPS, largest 16
BICYCLE, earliest 116, longest tandem 116-17, smallest, largest, fastest, endurance record, tallest unicycle, wheelie, penny-farthing record, underwater cycling 117, biggest manufacturers 131, most on one 174, eating 176, fastest 240
BIG WHEEL, largest 92

BILLIARDS, 227-8
BILLIONAIRES, 134
BINGO, 250
BIOGRAPHY, longest 152
BIPLANE, fastest 123
BIRD, largest wing span, smallest, most abundant, longest lived 33, rarest 33-4, largest, heaviest 33-5, fastest, slowest flying, fastest and slowest wing beat, longest lived, longest flights 34, highest flying 34-5, most airborne, fastest swimmer, most acute vision, highest g force, longest, most feathers, largest, smallest egg, longest, shortest incubation, longest bill, earliest and latest cuckoo, largest, smallest nests, heaviest chicken, flying record, most talkative 35, extinct, earliest, largest 46, most expensive stuffed 153, highest priced 273
BIRD SPOTTER, champion* 35
BIRTH DATES, coincident 12
BIRTH RATE, highest, lowest, natural increase 195
BIRTHS, 11-13, most southerly, test tube 12, multiple 12-13
BISHOP, oldest Church of England, Roman Catholic, youngest 217-18
BISHOPRIC, longest tenure 217
BITE, strongest 15, animal 22
BLACK HOLE, 69
BLACK OUT, biggest 78
BLADES, penknife with greatest number 191
BLANKET, most expensive 145, largest 187
BLAST FURNACE, largest 78
BLINDNESS, Colour, highest and lowest rate 16
BLOOD, groups, richest, most alcohol in 17
BLOOD ANTIBODY, highest count 17
BLOOD DONOR, champion plasmapheresis 17
BLOOD GROUP, commonest, rarest 17
BLOOM, see Flower
BOARD GAMES*, 228-9
BOARDSAILING, 310
BOAT, see Ship
BOAT RACE, 275-6
BOAT TROT, largest 174
BOBSLEIGH, 229-30
BOILER, largest 77
BOMB, heaviest conventional, most powerful atom, largest nuclear weapons, biggest 'conventional' explosion 208
BOMBER, heaviest, fastest 121-2
BOMBING, worst in world 196-7
BONE, oldest fragment 6, longest, smallest human 16
BONFIRE, largest 98
BOOK, oldest mechanically printed, largest, smallest printed 150, most valuable 151, best sellers: world, non-fiction, fiction 152, slowest seller, fastest published*, most overdue 153
BOOK SHOP, largest 131
BOOKMAKER, largest 250-1
BOOMERANG, greatest throws 174
BORES, River, greatest world, GB 59
BORING, deepest world 75-6
BOTTLE, largest 179-80, smallest (spirit) 180, message in 182, largest collections 187
BOTTLE CAP, largest collection* 187
BOUNDARY, see Frontiers
BOUQUET, largest 49
BOWLING (Ten-Pin)*, 230, 310
BOWLS, 230, 310
BOX, tallest hedge 50
BOXING*, 231-3
BOX-OFFICE, biggest film* 164
BRAIN, (human) heaviest, lightest 16, (animal) least 46
'BRAIN OF BRITAIN', youngest, oldest 166
BRASS, oldest monumental, 217
BRASS INSTRUMENT, largest 155-6
BREACH OF PROMISE, highest damages 210
BREAKWATER, longest world, UK 98
BREEDER, youngest 26, fastest 28
BREWERY, oldest, largest world, Europe, GB 131

BRICK CARRYING, record for man, woman 173
BRICKLAYING, fastest 174
BRICKLIFTING, greatest number* 174-5
BRICK THROWING, greatest distance 175
BRICKWORKS, largest 131
BRIDE, oldest, most married 172
BRIDEGROOM, oldest, most married 172
BRIDGE, longest 59, oldest, longest suspension, cantilever, steel arch, floating, longest covered, railway longest, longest bridging, widest, highest 95
BRIDGE, Contract, 233, 310
BRIDGE TUNNEL, longest 97
BROAD BEAN, longest 48
BROADCAST, (radio), first advertised, trans-Atlantic, longest 166, (television) first 167
BROADCASTER, fastest 17, most durable (radio), most heard (radio and television) 166
BROADCASTING, see Radio
BROADMOOR, longest detention 214
BROADSHEET, highest price 151
BROCCOLI, heaviest 48
BROTHERS, most knighted 204
BRUSH, finest 144
BRUSSELS SPROUT, heaviest 48
BUBBLE, longest 175
BUBBLE CHAMBER, largest world 74
BUBBLE GUM, blowing 175
BUDGERIGAR, oldest 35
BUDGET, largest world, GB, greatest surplus, deficit 133
BUILDING, (see also Structure), earliest, largest 86, tallest, highest, northernmost, southernmost 87, wooden 87-8, air-supported 88, for living 88-91, entertainment 92-4, tallest (progressive records) 94, largest demolished by explosive 98, largest theatre 160, largest cinema 166, university: oldest, largest 215, religious 216-17
BUILDING CONTRACTOR, largest 131
BUILDING SOCIETY, largest 131
BULB, most powerful, most durable light 74
BULL, highest-priced 139, heaviest 140
BURIAL ALIVE, record 175
BUS, earliest 113-14, longest, longest route 114
BUSINESS, oldest, greatest assets, profits, losses, sales 130
BUTTER FAT, record lifetime, one lactation, day yields 142
BUTTERFLY, largest 41-2, smallest, rarest, most acute sense of smell 42
BUTTERFLY FARM, largest 42
BYPASS, longest world 127

CABARET, highest fee 160
CABBAGE, heaviest 48
CABER TOSS, see Highland Games, 297
CACTUS, largest* 47
CAKE, largest and tallest 178
CALF, highest birthweight 140, most at one birth 142
CAMBRIDGE, Union presidents 204
CAMERA, earliest, largest, smallest, fastest cine, most expensive 164
CAMP, concentration 211, largest penal 214
CAMPANOLOGY, 156
CAMPING OUT, longest 175
CANAL, earliest, longest, busiest big ship, inland waterways, irrigation, largest cut 96, longest tunnel world, Britain 97-8
CANAL JUMPING, longest 175
CANCER, most durable patient 20
CANDLE, biggest* 187
CANNON, largest 209
CANNONBALL, Human, record distance 182
CANOEING 223, Atlantic crossing 106
CANS, biggest pyramid of 187
CANTILEVER BRIDGE, longest 95
CANYON, deepest 59
CAPE HORN, fastest solo rounding 105
CAPITAL CITY, oldest 196, largest, highest, northernmost, southernmost 197

CAPITAL PUNISHMENT, see Execution
CAPSULE, TIME, largest 192
CAR, largest ferry 107, earliest 109-10, earliest and most expensive registrations, fastest*, largest world, largest engine, most powerful, heaviest, longest, lowest, most durable 110, most expensive 110-11, cheapest, longest in production 111, longest tow, longest skid marks 113, solar powered 114, largest manufacturers world, GB, largest single plant, salesmanship record 132, wrecking 175, greatest T-bone dive 185, see also Driver
CARAVAN, longest journey, largest, fastest 114
CARD, memorising 16*, biggest 187-9
CARDINAL, oldest, youngest, longest serving 218
CARD GAMES*, 233-4, 310
CARDIO-PULMONARY RESUSCITATION*, 176
CARD THROWING, longest 175
CAR FERRY, largest 107
CARGO VESSEL, largest 107
CARILLON, largest, heaviest 156-7
CAR MANUFACTURER, largest world, GB, largest single plant 132
CARNIVORE, largest land 26-7, sea, smallest, largest, smallest feline 27, largest fish 38
CAR PARK, largest 112
CAR PARKING METERS, earliest 127
CARPET, most expensive* 145, earliest, largest, most finely woven 189
CARRIAGE DRIVING, 175
CARRIER, typhoid, most notorious 18
CARROT, heaviest 48
CARTOON STRIP, earliest, most widely syndicated 154
CAR WRECKING, record 175
CASH, most found and returned 135
CASINO, biggest world 250
CASTLE, earliest, largest, thickest walls 88
CAT, largest litter 31, population, heaviest world, UK, smallest, oldest*, oldest twins, most prolific, most valuable, best climber, mousing 33, see also Feline
CATALYST CRACKER, largest 78
CATAMARAN, circumnavigation records 105
CATAPULTING, record distance 175
CATERPILLAR, most prodigious eater 22
CATHEDRAL, tallest (progressive records) 90, largest, smallest 216, longest nave, tallest spire 217
CATTLE, longest horns 30, heaviest 140, prolificacy record 142
CATTLE STATION, largest 138
CAULIFLOWER, heaviest 48
CAVE, most extensive system*, deepest by countries 57
CAVING, 57
CELERY, heaviest 48
CELLO, most valuable 156
CEMETERY, largest world, UK 98
CENTENARIAN, oldest 13
CENTIPEDE, longest, shortest, most legs, fastest 42
CENTRIFUGE, fastest 74
CERAMICS, auction record 145
CHAIN STORE, largest department, grocery 131
CHAIR, largest 189
CHAMBER POT, most expensive 145
CHAMPAGNE, cork flight, tallest fountain 175, largest bottles 180
CHAMPIONS (Sports), youngest and oldest world, longest and shortest reign 220
CHANCELLORSHIP, longest, shortest tenure, most appointments 201
CHANDELIER, largest 189
CHANNEL CROSSING, see Cross-Channel
CHAPEL, smallest UK 217
CHARITY COLLECTION, largest 136
CHARITY SWIM, most raised 288
CHARITY WALK, most raised 136
CHARLESTON, duration record 176
CHEESE, heaviest eaters, biggest producer, oldest, varieties, most expensive 142, largest 178

CHEETAH, fastest 26
CHELONIANS, largest, smallest, longest lived, fastest, slowest diving, rarest 36, largest prehistoric 46
CHEMICAL COMPOUNDS, most lethal 72
CHEMIST SHOP, largest chain 131
CHEQUE, largest* 135-6
CHERRY PIE, largest 178
CHEST MEASUREMENT, largest 16
CHESTNUT, greatest girth 50
CHICKEN, largest ranch 138, heaviest*, flying 140, fastest growing, highest egg laying 142
CHILDREN, greatest number of siblings 11
CHILDREN'S HOSPITAL largest UK 196
CHILLI PLANT, tallest 49
CHIMNEYS, tallest 87
CHOCOLATE, largest factory 131, largest model 178
CHOIR, greatest 157
CHORISTER, longest serving 218
CHORUS LINE, longest 160
CHRISTMAS, most recent 'white' 81, most cards, most parsimonious* 151, largest cracker 189
CHRISTMAS PUDDING, largest 178
CHRISTMAS TREE, tallest 51
CHRYSANTHEMUM, largest 49
CHURCH, tallest (progressive records) 90, oldest, largest, smallest 216-17, tallest spire 217
CIGAR, box balancing 175, largest, most expensive 189
CIGARETTE, consumption, highest tar/nicotine content, most popular, longest and shortest, largest collection, most expensive lighter, earliest, rarest packets (cartons) 189
CIGARETTE CARD, most expensive 145, earliest, largest collection 189
CINEMA, earliest, largest output, most, least expensive film, film rights, longest film, longest running, highest box-office gross, largest loss, most violent, highest earning actor, stuntman, longest series 164, character most portrayed, largest studios, most prolific director 165, most Oscars 165-6, oldest, largest, most seats, highest attendance by population, biggest screen 166
CIRCLE, unsupported 186
CIRCULAR STORM, worst in world, UK 196-7
CIRCULATION, highest, newspaper, periodical 154
CIRCUMNAVIGATION, first orbital 83, sea earliest, first solo, motorboat, woman, non-stop, fastest solo*, longest voyage, submarine 105, car 111, amphibious, air fastest, smallest aircraft, without refuelling 121, fastest commercial flight, fastest scheduled flights 122, helicopter 124, walking 170, first polar 171
CIRCUS, largest, acrobatic records 175
CITY, oldest world 196, GB 196-7, largest, smallest, highest world, GB, lowest, northernmost, southernmost, capitals, farthest from sea, most populous 197
CIVIL DAMAGES, greatest 210
CIVIL WAR, bloodiest 205
CLAMS, largest shell, longest lived 43
CLAPPING, longest continuous 175
CLAWS, largest 46
CLIFFS, highest 59
CLOCK, largest world, oldest, most accurate, most expensive* 81-2
CLOTH, finest 190
CLOUDS, 63, noctilucent 66
CLOVER, most-leafed 49
CLOWN, oldest 175
CLUB, oldest UK 136
CLUB SWINGING, duration record 175
COACHING, 109
COAL CUTTING, record 175
COAL MINE, largest open-cast, oldest UK 77
COAL MINER, most durable 173
COAL SHOVELLING, record 176
COAT HANGER, biggest 189
COCKROACH, largest 40
COCKTAIL, biggest 178

COIN, oldest, earliest dated, heaviest, lightest, smallest, rarest, most expensive, greatest collection, hoard, largest mint, largest charity collection, longest, most valuable line of 135-6, balancing*, snatching 175
COLLEGE, oldest, largest, university, most expensive 215
COLLISION, biggest marine 109
COLOUR BLINDNESS, highest, lowest rate 15-16
COLOUR SENSITIVITY, 15-16
COLUMN, tallest monumental, tallest, tallest stone 98-9, 100
COLUMNIST, most syndicated 154
COMA, longest 18
COMET, earliest, speed, closest, largest, shortest, longest period 67
COMIC STRIP, most durable 154
COMMERCE, 130-3
COMMERCIAL, (television), most takes, highest fee 168
COMMERCIAL BUILDING, biggest 86, shallowest 87
COMMUNIST PARTY, largest 200
COMPACT DISCS, 163
COMPANY, oldest, greatest assets, greatest profit, loss, largest employer, greatest sales, largest takeover, greatest bankruptcy, number of companies registered, most directorships 130, largest manufacturing 132, most highly valued UK 136, largest investment house 137
COMPENSATION, (legal) greatest 210
COMPETITIONS, champion winner, largest single prize 175
COMPETITOR, oldest sports 220
COMPOSER, most prolific, most rapid 157
COMPOSITION, longest piano, longest silence 158
COMPUTER, human* 16, longest computation 73, oldest, most powerful, fastest, megabits 81, largest company 131, fraud 213
CONCENTRATION CAMP, worst 211
CONCERT, greatest attendance, most successful tour 157
CONDIMENT, rarest 178
CONDUCTOR, most durable 157
CONGA, longest 176
CONKER, most conquering 50
CONSCIENTIOUS OBJECTOR, most determined 209
CONSCRIPT, youngest 208
CONSONANTS, language with most, least 147
CONSTELLATIONS, largest, smallest 69
CONSTITUTION, oldest 199
CONSTRUCTION PROJECT, largest 87
CONSULTATION FEE, highest 135
CONTAINER SHIP, largest 107
CONTINENT, largest, smallest 56
CONTRACT, biggest TV 168
CONTRACT BRIDGE, 233, 310
CONVEYOR BELT, longest 78
COOLING TOWERS, largest 87
COPPER MINE, largest underground, open-cast 77
CORAL, largest 43
CORK, champagne distance record 175
CORN, record yield 139
CORPORAL PUNISHMENT, last 214
CORPORATION, greatest sales, profit and loss 130
CORRESPONDENCE, shortest 151
COSMONAUT, see Astronaut
COSTS, highest legal 211
COSTUMES, largest number, most expensive 165
COUNTRY, poorest 134, total number of, largest, smallest, most impenetrable boundary, flattest and most elevated, most frontiers, longest, shortest frontiers, population: largest, smallest, densest, sparsest 195
COUNTRY DANCING 176
COUPS, most 200-1
COW, record price 139
COW CHIP, tossing record 175-6
COW SHED, largest 138
CPR*, 176
CRAB, largest 39, smallest 39-40, most abyssal 40,

CRANE, most powerful, most powerful gantry, tallest mobile, greatest weight lifted 78
CRATER, largest volcano 61, meteoric, largest and deepest lunar 66
CRAWL, longest 176
CRAWLER, 113
CREDIT CARD, largest collection 189
CREMATORIUM, oldest UK, first legal cremation, largest world 99
CRESTA RUN, records 229-30
CRIBBAGE, 234, 310
CRICKET, first-class 234, batting 234, 236, bowling 234-6, fielding 238, wicket-keeping 237, County Championship 238, one-day matches 238, women's 239, minor 239, endurance 310
CRIME AND PUNISHMENT, 211-15
CRIMINAL ORGANISATION, largest 212
CRISPS, largest 179
CROCHET, 176
CROCODILE, largest, smallest, oldest, rarest 35-6, largest extinct 46, disaster 196
CROQUET, 239, 310
CROSS-CHANNEL, fastest ferry 109, earliest flight 120, canoeing 233, swimming 285-7
CROSS-COUNTRY RUNNING, 239-40
CROSSWORD, first, longest, largest, fastest, slowest, most durable compilers 154
CROWD, largest 218, sports 221
CRUSTACEANS, largest, smallest, deepest, longest lived 39-40
CRYPT, church, largest 216
CUCKOO, earliest, latest 35
CUCUMBER, heaviest 48, 49, slicing 176
CURLING, 240, 310
CURRENT, greatest, strongest 55-6, most powerful electric 74
CURTAIN, largest, largest functional 189
CURTAIN CALLS, most 159
CUSTARD PIE, throwing record 176, largest 178
CUT, finest 75, largest canal 97
CUTLERY, biggest 75
CYCLE SPEEDWAY, 242
CYCLING*, 116-17, 240-2, 310
CYCLO-CROSS, 242

DAHLIA, tallest 48
DAISY CHAIN, longest 49
DAM, earliest, most massive, largest concrete, highest, longest river, sea, strongest 97
DAMAGES, personal injury* 210, civil damages, breach of promise, defamation 210-11, wrongful imprisonment, alimony, divorce, greatest patent infringement, largest suit, highest costs 211
DAM DISASTER, worst world, UK 196-7
DANCE, largest 176
DANCING, records 176-7
DANCING MANIA, worst outbreak 176
DARTS, 242-3, 309
DEATH, leading cause of 18
DEATH DUTIES, highest 134
DEATH RATE, highest, lowest, infant mortality 195
DEATH ROW, longest stay 214
DEBATE, most protracted 176
DEBT, largest national, most foreign 134
DECAPLETS, 12
DECATHLON, world record 292, UK 294
DECORATIONS, see Medals 202-4
DEEP-SEA DIVING, record depth 171
DEER, largest wild 23, fastest, largest herd 26, largest, largest antler span, smallest 29, rarest 29-30, oldest 30, record heads 245
DEFAMATION, highest damages 210
DEFENCE, world expenditure 205
DEGREES, most honorary 204
DELTA, largest 59
DEMOLITION WORK, by hand 176
DEMONSTRATION, largest 195
DENTISTS, most dedicated 15, most 196

DEPARTMENT STORE, *largest world, UK, most profitable, most* 131
DEPRESSIONS, *deepest world, GB, largest* 57
DESCENDANTS, *most* 13
DESPATCHES, *most mentions* 202
DESTROYER, *fastest* 104
DIAMOND, *largest, rarest coloured, price, highest auction price, smallest, largest cut* 65
DIARY, *longest* 151
DICTIONARY, *largest* 150
DIESEL ENGINE, *most powerful* 78
DINING OUT, 172
DINOSAUR, *largest, smallest, longest trackway, fastest, largest footprints, earliest, most brainless, largest eggs, largest claws, largest skull, largest flying creatures* 44-6
DIRECTOR, *most prolific film, oldest* 165
DIRECTORSHIPS, *most* 130
DISASTERS AND ACCIDENTS, *earthquakes* 60, *worst world, UK* 196-7, *sports* 221
DISCO, *dancing marathon* 176
DISEASE, *commonest, rarest, most infectious, Parkinson's* 18
DISH, *largest* 178
DISTILLERY, *largest* 131
DIVE, *deepest animal* 22-3, *highest* 180
DIVING, *deep-sea, record depth, deepest salvage* 171, *flexible dress* 171-2, *(sport)* 285
DIVORCE, *oldest* 172, *highest rate* 195, *longest case* 210, *highest settlements* 211
DOCK, *largest dry, largest gate* 117
DOCTORATE, *youngest* 215
DOCTORS, *most in family* 173, *highest percentage* 196
DOG, *canine population, heaviest, tallest* 30, *smallest* 30-1, *oldest, strength and endurance, rarest, guide, largest litter, most prolific, most valuable, highest and longest jump, ratting record, tracking feat record, top show dog* 31, *top trainer* 31-2, *drug sniffing* 32
DOG SHOW, *largest* 31
DOLLS, *most expensive* 146
DOME, *largest world, UK* 99
DOMESTICATED ANIMALS, 30-3, *birds* 35
DOMINOES, 176, 310
DON, *most durable* 216
DONKEY, *lowest price* 140
DOOR, *largest, oldest* 99
DOUBLE BASS, *largest, most players** 156
DOW JONES AVERAGE, *peak* 136-7
DOWRY, *biggest* 135
DRAGLINE, *largest* 78
DRAGON, *longest dancing* 176
DRAGONFLY, *largest, smallest* 41
DRAG RACING 270
DRAUGHTS, 228-9, 310
DRAWING, *highest price* 145
DREAM, *longest* 18
DREDGER, *largest* 108
DRESS, *most expensive* 189
DRILLING, *deepest world* 75-6, *deepest ocean* 76, *progressive records* 77
DRINK, *top-selling brand (spirits)* 131, *(soft)* 132, *biggest round* 176, *strongest, weakest beer* 179, *most alcoholic, oldest vintage wine, most expensive wine, greatest wine auction, biggest tasting, most expensive spirits* 180
DRINKER, *hardest* 17
DRIVER, *(car) oldest** 109-10, *youngest, most durable* 112, *worst* 127
DRIVING, *fastest round the world** 111, *most in one year* 111-12, *trans Americas Cape to Cape, round Britain economy, fastest mountain driving, farthest in reverse, battery-powered, longest, fastest on two wheels* 112, *longest tow* 113, *motor racing* 268-70
DRIVING TEST, *most failures* 112
DROUGHT, *longest* 65
DRUG, *most powerful* 16, *most prescribed* 77, *haul* 213
DRUG SNIFFING, *top dog* 32
DRUM, *largest kit, largest drum* 156
DRUMMING, *duration record* 176
DRY DOCK, *largest* 99
DUCK, *most eggs* 142
DUCKS AND DRAKES, 176
DUMPER TRUCK, *largest* 114

DUNGEONS AND DRAGONS, 310
DWARF, *shortest, lightest* 8-9, *oldest, most variable stature* 9
DWARF BEAN, *largest* 48

EAR, *longest rabbit* 33
EARNINGS, see **Income**
EARTH, *largest diameter, greatest circumference, area, axial rotation, weight, density, volume, most abundant element* 54, *deepest penetration* 75-6 *(see also* **Structure and Dimensions** 54-60)
EARTH MOVER, *largest* 78
EARTHQUAKE, *highest seismic (tidal) wave* 55, *greatest* 61, *worst world, UK* 196-7
EARTHWORK, *most massive, most extensive single site GB* 99
EARTHWORM, *longest in world, GB* 43
EASTER EGG, *heaviest and tallest* 178
EATING, *most prodigious animal* 22, *records* 177
EATING OUT, *world champion* 172
ECHO, *longest* 74
ECLIPSES, *earliest, longest, most and least frequent* 67
ECONOMICS, 133-8
EDITORSHIP, *longest* 154
EDUCATION, 215-16
EELS, *most electric* 39, *largest caught* 223
EGG, *largest, smallest bird* 35, *most, least (fish)* 39, *largest dinosaur* 46, *laying records* 142, *biggest drop, hunt, shelling, longest distance thrown* 177
EGG AND SPOON RACE, *marathon* 177
ELECTION, *largest, closest, most decisive, most bent, highest personal majority, UK records, European* 200, *parliament* 201
ELECTORATES, *most mature* 200, *European parliament* 201
ELECTRIC CURRENT, *most powerful* 74, *highest voltage* 75
ELECTRIC GENERATOR, *largest* 77
ELECTRIC LIGHT BULB, *most durable* 80, *smallest* 186
ELECTRIC PLANE 121
ELECTRIC RAILWAY, *first, fastest train* 118, *longest line underground* 120
ELECTRONIC BRAIN, see **Computer**
ELECTRON MICROSCOPE, *most powerful* 74
ELEMENTS, 72
ELEPHANT, *largest* 23, *longest lived, longest gestation period* 26, *longest, heaviest tusks* 30
ELEVATOR, *worst disaster* 196, **Grain,** *largest, largest collection* 87, **Lock,** *largest* 96-7
EMBASSY, *largest* 87
EMBROIDERY, *longest* 192
EMERALD, *largest, highest price* 65
EMIGRATION, *most UK, most* 195
EMPEROR, *longest dynasty* 197
EMPLOYER, *largest* 130
EMPLOYMENT, *highest* 136
EMPLOYMENT AGENCY, *biggest* 131
ENCORE, *longest operatic* 159
ENCYCLOPAEDIA, *earliest, largest, most comprehensive* 150
ENDOWMENT, *biggest educational* 216
ENDURANCE MARATHONS, *(sport)* 310
ENERGY, *world average, highest, lowest consumption* 136
ENGAGEMENT, *longest* 172
ENGINE, *(car) largest* 110
ENGINE, *(jet) see* **Jet Engine**
ENGINE, *(military) largest* 209
ENGINE, *(railway) first* 118, *fastest electric* 118-19, *steam, most powerful* 119
ENGINE, *(ship) earliest steam* 104
ENGINE, *(steam) oldest* 77
ENGINEERING 78-82
ENGLISH CHANNEL, *(first crossing) aircraft* 120, *canoeing* 233, *rowing* 276, *swimming* 285-7
ENTERTAINER *most honoured* 166, *most highly paid TV* 168
EQUESTRIAN SPORTS, 243-4, *horsemanship marathon* 310

EQUITY, *largest, smallest* 137
ERUPTION, *greatest volcanic* 60
ESCALATOR, *first, longest* 78, *longest ride** 177
ESCAPE, *deepest underwater* 171, *longest prison, greatest gaol break* 215
ESCAPOLOGY, *greatest artist* 177
ESKIMO ROLLS, 233
E.S.P., *best performance* 20
ESTUARY, *longest* 59
ETON FIVES, 245
EUROPEAN PARLIAMENT, *election records* 201
EVACUATION, *greatest military* 205
EXAMINATIONS, *youngest 'A' level achiever* 215, *most 'O' and 'A' levels passed* 216
EXCAVATOR, *largest* 78
EXECUTION, *most, largest hanging, last public hanging* 213, *last public guillotining, youngest* 213-14, *oldest, longest stay on Death Row* 214
EXECUTIONER, *longest in office* 214
EXECUTIVE, *highest-paid* 135
EXHIBITION, *largest centre* 87
EXPECTATION OF LIFE, *highest and lowest at birth* 195
EXPLOSION, *greatest volcanic* 60, *largest 'conventional', worst world, UK* 196-7, 208
EXTINCT ANIMALS, *earliest* 44, *largest* 44-5, *smallest dinosaur, longest trackway, fastest* 45, *largest footprints* 45-6, *most brainless, largest dinosaur eggs, largest claws, largest skull, flying creature, marine reptile, crocodile, chelonians, tortoise, longest snake, largest amphibian, insect, largest bird, largest mammal, mammoth, largest primate, longest, heaviest tusks, antlers, greatest span* 46
EXTRA-SENSORY PERCEPTION, see **E.S.P.**
EYE, *smallest visible object* 15, *colour sensitivity, colour blindness* 15-16

FABRIC, *earliest, most expensive, finest cloth* 190
FACTORY, *largest whale ship* 107, *earliest motor-cycle* 115, *largest chocolate* 131
FAIR, *earliest, largest, record attendance, big wheel, fastest, longest switchback, longest slide* 92
FALL, *greatest altitude without parachute* 126
FAMILY, *richest* 135
FAMILY TREE, *largest* 177
FAMINE, *worst world, UK* 196-7
FAN, *largest* 190
FANGS, *largest (snake)* 37
FARM, *earliest site, largest* 138
FASHION SHOW, *most prolific producer* 160, *longest* 177
FAST, *longest* 19
FATTEST, *man* 9-10, *woman* 10
FAUX PAS, *greatest* 177
FEATHERS, *longest, most* 35
FEES, *highest* 135
FEET, *largest* 15
FELINE, *largest, smallest* 27, *see also* **Cat**
FELL RUNNING, 271
FENCE, *longest, highest* 99
FENCING, 244-5
FERN, *largest, smallest* 49
FERRET, *largest litter* 31
FERRY, *largest car* 107, *fastest cross-Channel* 109
FICTION, *best seller* 152
FIDDLER, *most durable* 156
FIELD, *oil* 76, *largest wheat, hop* 138
FIELD GUN, *competition* 177
FIELD SPORTS, 245
FIGURE SKATING, see **Ice Skating**
FILIBUSTER, *longest* 199
FILLING STATION, *largest, largest concentration, highest* 113
FILM, *earliest, most, least expensive, most expensive rights, longest, longest running, highest box-office gross**, *largest loss, most violent, longest series, longest make-up jobs* 164, *largest studios* 165, *most Oscar awards* 165-6, *most seen* 166
FINE, *heaviest* 214
FINGER NAILS, *longest* 15
FINGERS, *most sensitivity of* 15
FIRE, *human endurance* 19, *worst disaster* 196-7

FIREBALL, *brightest* 66
FIRE BREATHER, *most voracious* 19
FIRE EXTINGUISHER, *most voracious* 19
FIRE ENGINE, *most powerful* 114
FIRE PUMP, *greatest gallonage, pulling* 178
FIREWORK, *largest* 190, *worst disaster* 196-7
FIRST NIGHTS, *most* 160
FISH, *largest**, *smallest, fastest, longest lived, oldest goldfish, shortest lived, most abundant* 38, *most, least eggs, most valuable, most venomous, most electric* 39, *largest prehistoric* 46, *deepest* 138-9
FISH AND CHIPS, *largest shop* 132
FISHERIES, *highest recorded catch* 131
FISHING, see **Angling**
FIVES, 245, 310
FJORD, *longest* 54
FLAG, *oldest, largest* 190
FLAGSTAFF, *tallest* 99
FLAME, *hottest* 74
FLAMENCO, *fastest dancer* 176
FLARE, *greatest* 76
FLATS, *tallest block, largest, most expensive, mobile* 90
FLEA, *largest, longest and highest jumps* 41
FLIGHT, *fastest, longest* 34, *highest (bird)* 35, *space* 82-4, *hovercraft* 109, *aircraft, earliest, cross-Channel* 120, *jet-engined* 120-1, *supersonic, trans-Atlantic, first non-stop, solo, most flights, first trans-Pacific, circumnavigational, fastest* 121, *duration record* 123, *greatest distance human-powered* 126, *kite* 182, *gliding* 251
FLOAT, *largest* 190
FLOATING BRIDGE, *longest* 95
FLOOD, *worst world, UK, alluvian* 196-7
FLOTATION, *greatest* 137
FLOWER, *rarest, northernmost, southernmost, highest, slowest flowering plant* 47, *tallest dahlia, gladiolus, hollyhock, lupin, petunia, sunflower* 48, *earliest, largest* 48-9, *most valuable, largest arrangement, largest, tallest, smallest, highest priced orchid, largest rhododendron, largest rose* 49
FLUTE, *marathon* 178
FLYING-BOAT, *first North Atlantic air crossing, largest aircraft wing span* 121, *fastest, highest* 124
FLYING CREATURE, *largest extinct* 46
FLYING DISC, *records* 178
FLYING TRAPEZE, 175
FOG, *longest* 65
FOOD, *survival without* 19, *most expensive* 178, *heaviest, longest, tallest* 178-9
FOOT-AND-MOUTH DISEASE, *worst outbreak* 138
FOOTBAG, *records* 178
FOOTBALL, *American* 221-2, *association** 245-50, *World Cup* 248, *Gaelic* 250, 310, *rugby league* 276-8, *rugby union* 278-9, *seven-a-side* 279, *five-a-side** 310
FOOTBALL POOLS, 250
FOOTBALL STADIUM, *largest* 92
FORD, *longest in England* 109
FOREIGN AID, *total given by US* 133
FOREIGN DEBT, *most* 134
FOREIGN SECRETARYSHIP, *longest tenures* 201-2
FOREST, *largest world, GB* 51-2
FORGERY, *greatest* 213
FORGING, *largest* 78
FORK-LIFT TRUCK, *largest* 78
FORT, *largest* 88
FOSSIL, *oldest human* 6, *biggest animal* 44
FOUNTAIN, *tallest* 99, *tallest champagne* 175
FOXHUNTING, 245
FRAUD, *biggest bank, largest computer, biggest maritime* 213
FREEDOMS, *most conferred* 204
FREEZE, *longest* 61
FREIGHT TRAIN, *longest, heaviest* 119
FREQUENCY, *highest* 74
FRICTION, *lowest* 74
FROG, *rarest, most posionous* 37, *largest, smallest, longest jump* 38

FROGMAN, *farthest underwater* 171, *longest submergence* 185
FRONTIERS, *most impenetrable, longest continuous, shortest, country with most* 194
FROST FAIR, *first recorded* 61
FRUIT, *record dimensions and weight UK* 48, *most and least nutritive, biggest, peach, pineapple* 49, *most expensive* 178
FUEL ECONOMY, *world car record* 112
FUEL RANGE, *longest car* 112
FUMIGATION, *largest* 99
FUNERAL, *largest attendance* 218
FUNGUS, *largest, most poisonous* 52
FURNACE, *solar* 77, *(blast) largest* 78
FURNITURE, *most expensive* 146, *largest item* 190
FUSION POWER 77

GAELIC FOOTBALL, 250, 310
GALAXIES, *most distant, number of, Milky Way, progressive records, farthest visible* 69
GALLANTRY, *civilian* 203, *see also* **Medals**
GALLERY, *largest art* 144
GALLEY, *largest* 104
GAMBLING, 250-1
GAME RESERVE, *largest* 52
GAME SHOOTING, 245
GAOL, see **Prison**
GARAGE, *largest, largest bus* 112-13, *see also* **Filling Station**
GARBAGE DUMP, *biggest* 99
GARDEN, *largest community* 138
GAS, *most powerful nerve, lightest, heaviest, commonest* 72, *lowest melting point* 73
GAS DEPOSIT, *largest* 76
GAS FLARE, *greatest* 76
GAS HOLDER, *largest* 99
GAS PIPELINE, *longest* 81
GASTROPODS, *largest* 43-4, *fastest* 44
GAS TURBINE, *largest* 77
GASWORKS, *largest* 77-8
GAUGE, *widest and narrowest railway track, highest standard, highest GB* 119
GEMS, *largest opal**, *amber, largest, rarest, smallest, largest cut, most expensive diamond, largest jade, topaz, largest gold nugget, largest emerald, ruby, pearl, most expensive sapphire* 65
GENERATING PLANT, see **Power Station**
GENERATOR, *largest* 77
GENOCIDE, *greatest* 196, 211-12
GERBIL, *largest litter* 31, *oldest* 32
GESTATION PERIOD, *mammalian longest and shortest* 26
GEYSER, *tallest* 61
G FORCE, *highest sustained, momentary* 19, *highest bird* 35, *highest insect* 41
GHOSTS, *most durable* 20
GIANT, *tallest* 6-7
GIANTESS, *tallest* 7-8
GIRNING, *records* 178
GLACIER, *longest* 59
GLADIATOR, *greatest combat* 178
GLADIOLUS, *tallest* 48
GLASS, *largest sheet* 102, *auction record* 146, *most priceless example* 190
GLASSHOUSE, *largest UK* 87
GLIDING*, 251
GLOBE, *largest revolving* 99
GNOME, *earliest garden* 190
GOAT, *highest priced* 139, *largest* 140, *record milk yield* 142
GO-KART, *highest mileage* 114
GOLD, *largest nugget* 65, *greatest reserves, accumulation* 134, *coffin* 190, *biggest robbery* 213
GOLDEN DISC, *earliest, most awarded* 162
GOLDEN HANDSHAKE, *biggest* 135
GOLDEN WEDDINGS*, 172
GOLDFISH, *oldest* 38, *most expensive* 39
GOLD MINE, *largest world, GB, richest, chief area* 77
GOLD PANNING*, 178
GOLD PLATE, *highest auction price* 146
GOLD RESERVES, *greatest* 134
GOLF*, *longest drives* 252, *clubs, courses* 252-3, *fastest rounds, championship records* 253, *scores* 253-4, *holes in one* 255

GOLF BALL BALANCING, *178*
GOOSE, *oldest 35, biggest egg* 140-1
GOOSEBERRY, *heaviest 48*
GORGE, *largest 59*
GORILLA, *largest, strength 27*
GOURD, *heaviest 48*
GRADIENT, *steepest, shallowest railway 119*
GRADUATE, *youngest, most in family 215*
GRAIN ELEVATOR, *largest, largest collection 87*
GRAMMY AWARDS, *record number 166*
GRAMOPHONE, *60*
GRAMOPHONE RECORDS, *biggest store 132, earliest 160-1, smallest, oldest 161, largest library, phonographic identification, earliest jazz records 161-2, most successful solo artists, platinum disc award, most successful group, golden disc award, most recordings 162, biggest seller 162-3, best-sellers' charts, top-selling albums, fastest-selling albums, advance sales 163, Grammy awards 163-4, longest-running radio programme 166*
GRANDPARENTS, *most greats 13*
GRAPEFRUIT, *heaviest 48*
GRAPES, *largest bunch 48, catching 178*
GRASS, *commonest, fastest-growing, longest, shortest 49, pollen count 52*
GRAVE DIGGING, *record 178*
GREAT GRANDPARENTS, *multiple 13*
GREENHOUSE, *largest 87*
GREYHOUND RACING, *255*
GRILL, *longest 190-1*
GROCERY STORE, *largest chain 131*
GROSS NATIONAL PRODUCT, *largest 134*
GROUND FIGURES, *145*
GROWTH, *fastest 22, slowest animal 43, fastest grass 49, fastest, slowest tree 50*
GUILLOTINING, *last public 214*
GUINEA PIG, *biggest litter 31, oldest 32*
GUITAR, *largest, most expensive 156, longest solo marathon 178*
GULF, *largest 54*
GUM BOOT, *throwing 178*
GUM WRAPPER, *longest chain 180*
GUN, *most expensive 146, earliest, largest, greatest range 209*
GUN RUN, *competition record 180*
GUSHER, *oil, most prolific 76*
GYMNASTICS*, *256-7*

HABITATION, *highest, northernmost, southernmost 87*
HAEMODIALYSIS, *longest 18*
HAGGIS, *largest 178, throwing 180*
HAIL DISASTER, *196-7*
HAILSTONES, *heaviest 65*
HAIR, *longest, 15*
HAIRDRESSING, *duration record 180*
HAIR SPLITTING, *180*
HAMBURGER, *largest 178*
HAMMOCK, *biggest 191*
HAMSTER, *largest litter 31, oldest 32*
HANDBALL, *257, 310*
HANDBELL RINGING, *longest recital 180*
HANDBUCKING, *see* Sawing
HANDCLAPPING, *175*
HANDSHAKING, *world records 180*
HANGAR, *largest 87*
HANG GLIDING, *251*
HANGING, *see* Execution
HARBOUR, *biggest artificial 99-100*
HARE, *largest 33*
HAREM, *largest 92*
HARNESS RACING, *257*
HAT, *most expensive 146*
HAY BALE, *rolling* 180*
H BOMB, *see* Bomb
HEAD OF STATE, *oldest, youngest 196, female 199*
HEADMASTER, *youngest 216*
HEARING RANGE, *limits 17*
HEART, *artificial human 20*
HEART STOPPAGE, *longest 18*
HEART TRANSPLANT, *first, longest surviving, youngest 20*
HEAT, *human endurance of 18-19*
HEDGE, *tallest 50, hedge laying 180*
HEIGHT, *tallest man 6-7, woman 7-8, couple 8, most variable stature 9*

HELICOPTER, *fastest, largest, greatest load, smallest, highest circumnavigation 124, worst disaster 196-7*
HERB, *most heavily consumed 49*
HERD, *(animals) largest 26*
HIBERNATION, *longest animal 26*
HICCOUGHING, *longest attack 18*
HIGH DIVING, *highest 180*
HIGH KICKING, *180*
HIGHLAND GAMES, *297*
HIGH WIRE, *highest act 180*
HIJACK RANSOM, *greatest 213*
HILL, *steepest 58*
HILL FIGURE, *largest, oldest, ground 145*
HILL-FORT, *largest Celtic 100*
HITCH-HIKING, *records 180*
HOARD, *largest coin 136*
HOARDING, *largest* 98*
HOCKEY, *257-8, 310, ice 262, roller 275*
HOD CARRYING, *record 180*
HOLE, *smallest 74, deepest in world, UK 75-6*
HOLES IN ONE, *see* Golf
HOLLYHOCK, *tallest 48*
HOLY BIBLE, *see* Bible
HOMEWORK, *latest 180*
HOMINID, *earliest 8*
HOMOPHONES, *most 148*
HONORARY DEGREES, *most 204*
HONOURS, DECORATIONS AND AWARDS, *202-4*
HOOP ROLLING, *world record 180*
HOP FIELD, *largest 138*
HOP-SCOTCH, *marathon 180*
HORNS, *longest 30, longest musical 156*
HORSE, *largest, heaviest draught 27-8, tallest, smallest, oldest, strongest draught 30, draught 140, show-jumping 243-4, highest price 258-9, racing* 258-62*
HORSEBACK, *most travelled man 170, longest ride 244*
HORSEMANSHIP, *marathon 310*
HORSEPOWER, *(car) highest 110*
HORSE RACING*, *258-262, Derby 261, Grand National 261*
HOSPITAL, *longest stay 20, largest world, GB, mental, maternity, children's 196*
HOTEL, *largest 88-9, tallest, most remote 89, most expensive 89-90, mobile 90*
HOTELIER, *largest company 131-2*
HOUSE, *earliest 88, largest, most expensive, oldest, smallest, most visited 90*
HOUSE OF CARDS, *largest number of storeys, tallest tower 180*
HOUSE OF COMMONS, *see* Parliament
HOUSE OF LORDS, *see* Parliament
HOUSING, *90, 196-7*
HOUSING ESTATE, *largest UK 90*
HOVERCRAFT, *inventor, earliest patent, first flight, largest, fastest warship, longest flight, altitude 109*
HULA-HOOPING, *182*
HUMAN CANNON BALL, *record distance 182*
HUMAN CENTIPEDE, *longest* 182*
HUMAN FLY, *greatest climb 182*
HUMAN MEMORY, *most retentive* 16*
HUMIDITY, *and discomfort 61, 63*
HUNGER STRIKE, *longest 19*
HURLING, *261-2*
HYDRO-ELECTRIC PLANT, *largest world, GB 77*
HYDRO-ELECTRIC TUNNEL, *longest 97*
HYDROFOIL, *largest 107-8*
HYDROPLANE, *fastest 109*
HYMN, *earliest, longest, shortest, most prolific writer 156*

ICE, *thickest 61*
ICEBERG, *largest, tallest, most southerly Arctic, most northerly Antarctic 56*
ICEBREAKER, *most powerful, largest 108*
ICE-CORE DRILLING, *deepest 76*
ICE CREAM SUNDAE, *biggest 178*
ICE HOCKEY, *262*
ICE RINK, *largest 263*
ICE SHOWS, *most costly 160*
ICE SKATING, *262-4*
ICE SLED, *rocket-powered 110*

ICE SLED, *rocket-powered 110*
ICE YACHTING, *264*
ICON, *most expensive 146*
ILLNESS, *commonest, rarest 18*
IMMIGRATION, *most in US 195*
IMPEACHMENT, *longest 210*
IMPRISONMENT, *compensation for wrongful 211, longest world, GB 214*
INCOME, *richest country, lowest, highest individual, highest in one year, world, lowest 134, actor 164, sport 231*
INCOME TAX, *lowest rate 134, see also* Taxation
INCUBATION, *longest, shortest 35*
INCUMBENCY, *longest 218*
INDEX, *longest 150*
INDUSTRIAL DISPUTE, *earliest, largest, most serious, longest 136*
INDUSTRIAL STRUCTURES, *largest building 86, tallest chimneys, largest cooling tower 87*
INDUSTRY, *oldest 130*
INFANT MORTALITY, *lowest, highest 195*
INFLATION, *worst, least 134*
INFLUENZA, *worst 196-7*
INJECTIONS, *most 20*
INJURY, *personal, highest damages, world, GB 210*
INLAND WATERWAYS, *longest GB, country with greatest, greatest navigable length 96*
INQUIRY, *longest 210*
INSECT, *heaviest, largest cockroach, longest, smallest, rarest, fastest flying 40, fastest moving, highest g force, longest lived, loudest, fastest, slowest wing beat, largest termite mound, largest, smallest dragon fly, largest flea, longest flea jump 41, largest extinct, earliest 46*
INSECTIVORES, *largest 28-9, smallest, longest lived 29*
INSTRUMENTS, *(musical) oldest, largest, loudest 155, highest and lowest notes, easiest and most difficult 156, greatest number played in single tune 173-4*
INSTRUMENTS, *(surgical) largest, smallest 20*
INSURANCE COMPANY, *largest in world, GB, largest life policy, highest payout, marine insurance 132*
INTERNATIONAL, *(sport) youngest and oldest 220*
INTERVIEWER, *of most heads of state 152*
INVASION, *most recent British, greatest airborne, seaborne 205*
INVESTMENT COMPANY, *largest 137*
IRONING, *duration record 182*
IRON LUNG, *longest in 18*
IRON MINE, *largest 77*
IRRIGATION CANAL, *longest 96*
IRRIGATION TUNNEL, *longest 97*
ISLAND, *largest, largest freshwater, remotest, greatest archipelago, northernmost 56, southernmost 56-7, newest island, largest atoll 57*
ISOLATION, *farthest 170*

JACKING SYSTEM, *greatest lift 78*
JADE, *largest piece 65, highest price 146*
JAI-ALAI, *264*
JAIL, *see* Prison
JAZZ RECORD, *earliest 161-2*
JELLY, *largest 178*
JELLYFISH, *largest, most venomous 44*
JET ACE, *most kills 202*
JET AIRCRAFT, *first 120-1, fastest airliner 122, fastest 123, fastest flying-boat 124*
JET ENGINE, *fastest car 110, earliest, first flight 120-1, fastest 123*
JETTY, *longest 99-100*
JEWELS, *biggest auction 132, highest price 146, record theft 213, see also* Gems
JEWS, *world total 216*
JIG-SAW, *earliest, largest 191*
JIVING, *duration record 177*
JOCKEY, *lightest, youngest, oldest, most successful 258-61*
JOKE CRACKING, *longest 182*
JUDGE, *oldest, youngest, most 211*
JUDICIAL CODE, *earliest 209*
JUDO, *264-5*
JUGGLING, *records 175, football 250*

JUMBLE SALE, *largest 182*
JUMP, *highest horse and longest kangaroo 30, dog 31, frog 38, flea 41, high and long jump, see* Track and Field Athletics
JUMPING, *canal, pogo stick 175*
JUNCTION, *(railway), busiest 120*
JUNK, *largest 109*

KALE, *tallest 48*
KANGAROO, *largest, highest and longest jump 30*
KARATE, *265, demolition work 176*
KARTING, *highest mileage 114*
KEBAB, *longest* 178*
KETTLE, *biggest antique 191*
KIDNAPPING, *highest ransom, youngest 213*
KIDNEY, *longest on dialysis 18, earliest transplant 20*
KIDNEY STONE, *largest 18*
KILLINGS, *greatest mass 211-12*
KING, *longest reign, shortest reign, longest lived, youngest, most children, British records 198, heaviest 199*
KISS, *most prolonged screen, marathon 182*
KISS OF LIFE, *see* Cardio Pulmonary Resuscitation*
KITCHEN, *largest 100*
KITE FLYING, *records 182*
KNIGHT, *youngest, oldest, most dubbed, most brothers 204*
KNITTING, *most prolific hand-knitter, fastest sheep-to-shoulder 182*
KNOT TYING, *fastest 182*

LABELS, *oldest matchbox 191*
LABOUR CAMPS, *total number 203*
LABOUR DISPUTES, *see* Strike
LACROSSE, *265-6*
LAGOON, *largest 59*
LAKE, *largest, deepest, highest, lake in a lake, underground 59*
LAMP, *most powerful 74*
LAMPPOST, *tallest 100*
LAND, *remotest spot from 54, Earth's land surface, remotest from the sea, northernmost 56, southernmost 56-57, newest 57, largest owner, longest tenure, highest values, highest price, highest rent 132*
LAND DIVING, *180*
LANDOWNER, *largest 132*
LAND'S END TO JOHN O'GROATS, *hitch-hiking 180, cycling 241-42, running 296, walking 301*
LANDSLIDE, *worst world, UK 196-7*
LAND SPEED RECORDS, *111*
LAND YACHTING, *264*
LANGUAGE, *earliest, oldest, English words 146, commonest 146-47, rarest, most complex, most and least irregular verbs, rarest and commonest sounds, vocabulary, greatest linguist, oldest alphabet, longest, shortest alphabet, most and least consonants and vowels, largest, smallest letter 147, longest words 147-48, longest palindromes, longest scientific name, longest anagram, abbreviation 148*
LANTERN, *largest* 191*
LASER, *highest frequency, first illumination of Moon, brightest light, most accurate 74, highest note 75*
LATHE, *largest 78*
LAUNDRY, *most 182*
LAVA FLOW, *longest 60*
LAW, *209-15*
LAW CASE, *longest 210*
LAW FIRM, *largest 211*
LAWN BOWLS, *230, 310*
LAWN MOWER, *largest, racing, longest drive 114*
LAWN TENNIS, *289-91, 310*
LEAD, *largest mine 77*
LEAF, *largest, clover 49, most on tree 51*
LEAP-FROGGING, *182*
LEASE, *longest 211*
LECTURING, *top rate 173*
LEEK, *heaviest 48*
LEGAL COSTS, *highest English 211*
LEGISLATION, *most, least time-consuming 200, greatest amount 202*
LEGISLATORS, *highest-paid, longest span 199*
LEGISLATURE, *see* Parliament
LEGS, *creatures with most 42*
LEGO, *largest statue 192*
LEMON, *48*
LEPIDOPTERA, *see* Butterfly

LETTERS, *most (alphabet), largest, smallest 147, most frequently used in English 148, total in Bible, longest and most, longest and most to an editor*, shortest, most personal mail, most durable pen pals, highest price, most sent 151*
LETTERS, *most post-nominal 203*
LETTUCE, *heaviest 48*
LEVEES, *largest 97*
LIBRARY, *earliest, largest, most overdue book 153, largest gramophone 161*
LICENCES, *driving* 112*
LIEN, *largest 211*
LIFE, *greatest saving of 212*
LIFEBOAT, *most medals 203*
LIFE EXPECTATION, *highest and lowest at birth 195*
LIFE POLICY, *largest 132*
LIFE SAVING, *most 182, 212*
LIFT, *greatest mechanical 78, fastest passenger world, longest GB 78-9*
LIGHT, *brightest artificial, shortest pulse 74*
LIGHT BULB, *most durable 74*
LIGHTHOUSE, *most powerful, brightest, remotest, tallest 100, earliest vessels 108*
LIGHTNING, *62, most times struck 182, worst disaster 196-7*
LIGHT VESSEL, *earliest 108*
LIMBO DANCING, *lowest bar 182*
LINER, *passenger largest, fastest, longest 104*
LINGUIST, *greatest 147*
LION, *heaviest African 27*
LION TAMING, *most lions mastered 182*
LIQUOR, *most alcoholic, largest 180, smallest bottle, largest collection 187*
LITERARY LUNCHEONS, *150*
LITERATURE, *150-55, oldest 150, longest literary gestation 152*
LITIGATION, *most protracted, in person 210*
LITTER, *largest 26, puppies 31, kittens, rabbits, guinea pigs, hamsters, mice, gerbils and ferret 31*
LITTER COLLECTION, *182*
LIVING STANDARD, *highest income per head 134*
LIZARD, *largest, smallest, oldest, fastest 36*
LOAD, *heaviest draught 30, heaviest and largest (overland) 115, heaviest (railway) 119, greatest helicopter 124, heaviest pushed in a barrow 174, parachute 126*
LOAF, *longest 178, field-to-loaf record 177-8*
LOCAL GOVERNMENT, *service duration records 202*
LOCH, *longest sea 54, largest, longest, deepest, highest 59*
LOCK, *largest, deepest, highest lock elevator, longest flight 96-7*
LOG ROLLING, *longest contest 182*
LOLLIPOP, *largest iced 178*
LONGEVITY, *human 13-14, dwarfs 9, mammal 26, pets 32, bird 34*
LOSS, *greatest company 130, greatest personal 137*
LOUGH, *largest 59*
LUGEING, *230*
LUNAR CONQUEST, *84*
LUPIN, *tallest 48*
LYNCHING, *worst, last in GB 214*

MACHINERY, *oldest, slowest 78*
MACH NUMBER, *scale for aircraft speeds 120*
MAGAZINE, *largest circulation 154, highest advertising rates 154-5*
MAGICIAN, *fastest* 182*
MAGNET, *strongest and heaviest 74*
MAGNETIC FIELD, *strongest, weakest 74*
MAIL, *most personal 151, greatest robbery 213, largest 137*
MAJORITY, *electoral see* Elections, *parliamentary see* Parliament
MAKE-UP JOBS, *longest 164*
MAMMALS, *22-31, largest, heaviest 22, deepest dive 22-3, largest land, marine, tallest, smallest, rarest 23, fastest 23-6, slowest, sleepiest, longest hibernation, oldest, highest living, largest herds, gestation periods, largest litter, youngest breeder 26, earliest, largest prehistoric 46, see also* Animal Carnivore
MAMMOTH, *largest, longest, heaviest tusks 46*

MAN, tallest 6-7, shortest 8-9, most variable stature 9, heaviest, thinnest, lightest, greatest slimming feat, greatest weight gain, greatest differential 9-10, earliest 6, oldest 13-14, largest chest 16, least toes, longest finger nails, longest hair, longest beard, moustache 15, richest natural resources, most alcoholic 17, highest, lowest temperature 18, first space flight 83, most travelled, most isolated 170, most married 172, richest in world, Britain 134, highest salary 134, most statutes 204
MANGOLD, heaviest 48
MANUFACTURING COMPANY, largest 132
MANUSCRIPT, highest price at auction 151, most rejected 152
MAP, oldest, largest 151
MARATHON, 300-1 see also **Endurance Marathons**
MARBLES, 266
MARCH, (military) longest, fastest 208, (musical) 157, 183
MARINE DISASTER, worst world, UK 196-7
MARITIME FRAUD, biggest 213
MARQUEE, largest 100
MARRIAGE, tallest married couple 8, most disparate married couple 10, most, oldest bride and groom, longest, golden weddings, most married, youngest married, largest mass ceremony, most expensive 172, lowest, highest average ages 195
MARROW, heaviest 48
MARSUPIALS, largest, smallest, longest lived, highest, longest jumps, fastest speed 30
MASSACRES, greatest 211-2
MASS ARREST, greatest 214
MASS KILLINGS, greatest 211-2
MASS POISONING, 212
MASS SUICIDE, 212
MASS WEDDING, largest 172
'MASTERMIND', records 168
MASTER OF THE ROLLS, longest 211
MASTS, radio and TV, tallest world, GB 90, ship 109
MATCHBOX LABELS, oldest 191
MATCHSTICK, longest 191
MATERNITY HOSPITAL, largest world, GB 196
MATHEMATICAL CONSTANT, newest 73
MATHEMATICAL PUZZLE, oldest 73
MATHEMATICIAN, most prolific 73
MAYORALTY, longest 202
MAYPOLE, tallest 100
MAZE, largest 100
MEASURE OF LENGTH, earliest 73
MEASURE OF TIME, longest, shortest 73
MEASURE OF WEIGHT, earliest 73
MEAT PIES, largest 178
MEDALS, VC—most bars, youngest, longest lived 202, highest price 203, most decorated 202, most mentions in despatches, highest decorations USSR, Germany, USA 203, most Olympic 272
MEDICAL CENTRE, largest 196
MEDICAL FAMILY, most 173
MEGABITS, 81
MELON, heaviest 48
MEMBER OF PARLIAMENT, longest speech British electoral records 199, youngest, oldest, longest, briefest span of service, women MPs, heaviest, tallest MP 202
MEMORIAL, tallest (progressive records), tallest 90, highest structures in GB 113
MEMORY, (human) most retentive* 16
MENHIR, tallest 100
MENSWEAR STORE, largest 132
MENTAL ARITHMETIC, greatest feat 16
MENTAL HOSPITAL, largest 196, longest sentence in Broadmoor 214
MERCHANT SHIPPING, world total, largest fleet 109
MERRY-GO-ROUND, marathon 182
MESSAGE, in bottle 182
METEOR, greatest shower 66
METEORITE, oldest, largest 66, largest craters 66

METEOROIDS, 65-6
METEOROLOGICAL BALLOON, inflating 182
MICROLIGHTING, 266
MICROPHONE, smallest 75, earliest radio 166
MICROSCOPE, most powerful 74, 75
MIDGET, shortest 8-9, lightest 10
MILESTONE, oldest 128
MILITARY ENGINE, largest 209
MILK BOTTLE BALANCING, greatest distance 182
MILKING, record by hand 142
MILK SHAKE, biggest* 179
MILK YIELD, cows: lifetime, one lactation, day; goats 142
MILLIONAIRES, highest income, most 134
MILLIONAIRESSES, world, UK, youngest 134
MILLIPEDE, longest, shortest, most legs 42
MINARET, tallest 217
MINCE PIE, largest 179
MINE, earliest, deepest, fastest drilling, largest copper, lead, gold, richest gold, largest iron, platinum, uranium, tungsten, spoil heap, largest open-cast, oldest coal 77, greatest depth, shaft-sinking record 172
MINERALS, see **Gems**
MINERAL WATER, largest firm 132
MINIMUM LENDING RATE, lowest, highest 134
MINING, disaster world, UK 196, greatest depth, shaft-sinking record 172, most durable miner 173
MINT, largest 136
MIRAGE, largest 63
MIRROR WRITING, 187
MISER, greatest 135
MISPRINTS, most newspaper 154
MISSILES, 82
MISS UNIVERSE, contest 177
MISS WORLD, contest 177
MOATS, world's largest 88
MOBILE, most massive 145
MODEL AIRCRAFT, records 127
MODEL BOATS, 109
MODEL RAILWAYS, duration record, longest train 120
MODERN PENTATHLON AND BIATHLON, 266
MOLLUSC, largest 43, longest lived, shells: largest, smallest, most valuable 43, snail: largest 43-4, speed 44
MONARCH, longest descent 197-8, longest reign 198, shortest reign, longest lived 198-9, youngest, heaviest, most prolific 199, British records 198
MONETARY VOTE, largest parliamentary 204
MONEY, richest people 134-5, denominations 135, coin records 135-6
MONKEY, largest, smallest, oldest, rarest 28
MONUMENT, largest prehistoric, tallest, youngest ancient 100
MOON, deepest craters, highest mountains, temperature extremes 66, eclipses: earliest, longest, most, least frequent 67, first man on 84
MORSE, highest speed 183
MORTALITY, highest 18, infant, lowest, highest 195
MORTAR, largest 209
MOSAIC, largest 144
MOSQUE, largest 217
MOSS, smallest, longest 48
MOTH, largest 41-2, smallest, rarest, most acute sense of smell 42
MOTHER, most prolific 11, oldest 10-11
MOTIONLESSNESS, longest 19
MOTOR BOAT, circumnavigation records 105, Atlantic crossing 106
MOTOR CAR, see **Car**
MOTOR CARAVAN, longest journey 114
MOTOR RACING*, 268-70
MOTOR RALLY, earliest, longest 268
MOTORCYCLE, earliest, earliest factory, fastest production road machine, fastest racing machine, highest speeds, most expensive, smallest* 115, duration record 115-16, biggest pyramid, backwards riding, wheelie*, two wheel side car riding, most on one machine 116, fastest, most successful 267-8
MOTORCYCLE RACING, 266-68
MOTOR VEHICLE, see **Car**

MOTORWAY, most complex interchange 127, highest 128
MOUND, largest artificial 100
MOUNTAIN, highest submarine 54, highest 57, greatest ranges, longest lines of sight, greatest plateau 58, sheerest wall, lowest hill, highest halite 58, lunar 66, climbing, racing 271
MOUNTAIN DRIVING, fastest 112
MOUNTAIN ENDURANCE RUNNING, 271
MOUNTAINEERING, worst disaster world, UK 196, also 270-1
MOUNTAIN RACING, 271
MOUSE, smallest 28, largest litter 31, oldest 32, Field mouse 139
MOUSING, cat record 33
MOUSTACHE, longest 15
MULE, largest 30
MUMMY, oldest 14
MURAL, earliest, largest, longest, 144
MURDER, trial: longest, shortest, best attended 210, highest, lowest rate, most prolific murderer, world, GB 212
MURDERESS, most prolific 212
MUSCLE, largest, smallest 16, fastest movements 18
MUSEUMS, oldest, largest, most popular 153
MUSHROOM, largest 48, largest farm 138
MUSIC, 155-9
MUSICAL BOX, most expensive 146
MUSICAL CHAIRS, largest game* 183
MUSICAL INSTRUMENTS, oldest, earliest, largest, loudest 155, highest and lowest notes, easiest, most difficult 156
MUSICAL MARCH, longest 183
MUSICAL NOTATION, oldest 155
MUSICAL NOTE, generated by laser beam 75, highest and lowest orchestral 156
MUSICAL SHOW, longest, shortest run 160
MUSICIANS, most durable 155, highest-paid 158
MUTINY, greatest 208

NAILS, (finger) longest 15
NAME, longest star 69, scientific 148, place: earliest, longest, shortest, most spellings 149, personal: earliest 148-9, longest pedigree, longest, most, shortest, commonest, 'Macs', most versions, most changed, most contrived 149, longest biblical 151, of trade union, longest 136, shortest, commonest pub 94, longest company 137, commonest street 128
NARCOTICS, greatest haul 213
NATION, largest 194, richest, poorest 134
NATIONAL ANTHEM, oldest, longest, shortest, longest rendition 156
NATIONAL DEBT, largest 134
NATIONAL INCOMES, highest 134
NATIONAL PRODUCT, largest 134
NATIONAL WEALTH, total 134
NATURAL BRIDGE, longest, highest 59
NATURAL INCREASE, (population) highest, lowest rates 195
NATURISTS, first and largest camps 100
NAVAL BATTLE, greatest 205
NAVE, longest, world, UK 217
NAVY, largest 208, greatest battle 205
NECK, longest 16; (extinct) animal 45
NEEDLE, earliest 191
NEEDLE THREADING, record strands 183
NEGATIVE, photographic largest 164
NEON SIGNS, largest 98
NERVE, fastest impulses 18
NERVE GAS, most powerful 72
NEST, largest, smallest 35
NETBALL, 271, 310
NEWSPAPER, oldest 153, largest 153-4, smallest, most expensive British, most in world, longest editorship, most durable feature, most syndicated columnist, earliest, most durable comic strip, most misprints, most durable advertiser, highest circulation, most read 154, highest advertising rates 154-5
NEW TOWN, largest 90

NIGHT CLUB, oldest, largest 92, lowest 92-4
NOBEL PRIZE, earliest, most, oldest laureates 203, youngest laureates 203-4, highest, lowest cash value 204
NOISE, highest levels 17, loudest 74
NON STOP RECORDS, 310
NOODLE MAKING, most 183
NONUPLETS, 12
NORTH POLE, conquest 170
NOTE, highest and lowest attained by human voice 17, highest generated by laser beam 75, highest and lowest orchestral 156
NOVEL, longest 150, most written, highest sales 152
NOVELIST, most prolific, top-selling, oldest 152
NUCLEAR ARSENAL, largest 208
NUCLEAR DELIVERY VEHICLES, most 209
NUCLEAR EXPLOSION, greatest 208
NUCLEAR POWER STATION, largest 77
NUCLEAR REACTOR, largest 77, accident 196-7
NUCLEAR WEAPONS, largest 208
NUDIST CAMP, first, largest 100
NUGGET, largest gold 65
NUMBER, fastest calculating 16, highest named, lowest and highest prime, lowest and highest perfect, most innumerate people, most decimal places 73
NUMBER PLATE, (car) earliest, most expensive 110
NUMEROLOGY, expression of large numbers 73
NUT, (engineering) largest 78
NYLON, sheerest 191

OARS, earliest 104
OBELISK, oldest, largest 100
OBJECT, smallest visible to human eye 15, farthest visible, remotest (universe) 69, sharpest, smallest man-made 75, largest stolen 213
OBSERVATORY, highest, oldest 70
OCEAN, (see also **Sea**), largest, deepest, remotest spot from land, most southerly, temperature 54, crossings 109, greatest descent 171
OCEANARIUM, earliest, largest 52
OCEAN DRILLING, deepest 76
OCTOPUS, largest 43
OFFICE BUILDING, largest 87, tallest, 86-7
OIL FIELD, largest world, greatest gusher 76
OIL GUSHER, most prolific 76
OIL PIPELINE, longest world, most expensive 76
OIL PLANT, offshore disaster, worst world, UK 196-7
OIL PLATFORM, largest 76
OIL REFINERY, largest 132
OIL SPILL, greatest 76
OIL TANK, largest 78
OLD SOLDIERS, oldest 208
OLYMPIC GAMES, 271-2
OMELETTE, largest 179, greatest number* 183
OMNIVORE, greatest 176
ONION, heaviest 48, peeling record 183
OPAL, largest, most expensive 65
OPERA, longest, shortest, longest aria, youngest, oldest singers 158, longest encore, most curtain calls 159
OPERA HOUSE, largest, most tiers 158
OPERATION, longest, most, oldest subject, heart, kidney, five organ transplants, earliest appendicectomy, anaesthesia, most durable cancer patient, tracheostomy, largest tumour, instruments 20
OPTICAL FIBRE, longest distance transmitted 82
ORANGE, heaviest world 48
ORCHESTRA, highest and lowest notes 156, largest, largest attendance 157
ORCHID, tallest, largest flower, smallest, highest priced, smallest seed 49
ORDER, oldest 202
ORDERS OF MERIT, longest lived holder, oldest recipient, youngest recipient 203
ORDERS AND MEDALS, 202-4

ORGAN, largest, loudest stop 155, marathon 183, highest and lowest notes 156
ORGANIST, most durable 155
ORIENTEERING, 273
OSCARS, most 165-6
OSTRICH, largest egg 35
OWL, rarest 34
OX, heaviest, England 140
OXFORD, Union presidents, 204
OYSTERS, opening 183

PA SYSTEM, largest 155
PACIFIC CROSSING, fastest 109, earliest flight 121, marine records 107
PADDLE BOAT, longest voyage 183
PAELLA, largest 179
PAGODA, tallest, oldest 217
PAINTER, most prolific, most repetitious portraitist, oldest, youngest RA, youngest exhibitor 144
PAINTING, earliest, largest, most valuable, highest price auction, abstract, highest price miniature, modern, living artist, oldest; youngest RA, youngest exhibitor, earliest, largest mural painting 144
PALACE, largest 88
PALINDROME, longest* 148
PANCAKE, tossing 183, largest 179
PANDEMIC, worst world, UK 196-7
PANGRAM, shortest 148
PANIC, worst world, UK 196-7
PAN PIPES, largest 155
PAPER COMPANY, largest 132
PAPER MILL, largest 132
PAPER MONEY, earliest, largest, smallest notes, highest denomination, highest value, lowest denomination, highest circulation 135. See also **Banknote**
PAPERWEIGHT, highest auction price 146
PARACHUTING, longest fall without parachute, parachuting records 126, sport 273
PARASCENDING, 273
PARISH, longest incumbency, largest, smallest 218
PARISH PRIEST, oldest 218
PARISH REGISTER, oldest 218
PARK, largest 52
PARKING METERS, earliest 127
PARKINSON'S DISEASE, most protracted case 18
PARLIAMENT, world: earliest, oldest, smallest quorum, highest-paid legislators, longest UN speech, filibusters, oldest treaty, oldest constitution, women's suffrage, UK, earliest, longest, shortest 199-200, longest sittings 199, longest speech, greatest petition, most, least time-consuming legislation, Private Members' bills, most divisions, largest elections, closest, most decisive, most bent, highest personal majority, communist parties, largest ballot paper, voting age extremes 200, most coups 200-1, prime ministers, world, longest lived 201, English records 199, longest term, European records, party majorities, Lords: oldest, youngest member, prime ministerial records, Chancellorship 201-2, Foreign Secretaryship 201-2, Speakership, MPs youngest, oldest, longest, briefest span, earliest women, heaviest, tallest, MP 202
PARROT, most talkative 35
PARSNIP, heaviest 48
PARTICIPANTS, (sport) most 221
PARTICLE, number, lightest and heaviest sub-nuclear, newest, shortest lived nuclear 72
PARTICLE ACCELERATOR, most powerful 75
PARTY GIVING, most expensive, largest 173
PASS, highest 128
PASSENGER, oldest, youngest air 126
PASSENGER LIFT, fastest world, longest UK 78-9
PASSENGER LINER, largest, longest 104, 107
PASTRY, longest 179
PATENT, earliest radio 166, television 167, earliest H Bomb, earliest English, most applications, shortest, longest 210, greatest infringement damages 211
PEACH, largest 49
PEAPOD, longest 48

PEAR, heaviest 48
PEARL, largest, most expensive 65
PEELING, records, onion, potato 183
PEERAGE, most ancient, oldest creation, longest, shortest, highest numbering, most creations, most prolific 204
PEERESS, most prolific 204
PERFECT NUMBERS, 73
PELOTA VASCA, 264-5
PEN, most expensive 191
PENAL CAMPS, largest 214
PENDULUM, longest 82
PENINSULA, largest 56
PENKNIFE, most blades 191
PENNINE WAY, cycling 242, fell running 271
PENNY-FARTHING, records 117
PENPALS, most durable 151
PENSION, longest 173
PERFECT DEALS, (bridge) 233
PERFORMER, biggest audience 157, highest-paid TV 168
PERFUME, most expensive 72
PERIODICAL, oldest, largest circulation, annual 154, highest advertising rates 154-5
PERMAFROST, deepest 61
PERSONAL INJURY, highest damages world, GB 210
PERSONAL NAMES, 148-9
PETANQUE, 273
PETITION, greatest parliamentary 200
PETROL, consumption 112, first unleaded 113
PETUNIA, tallest 48
PHARMACEUTICALS, biggest sales 132
PHILODENDRON, largest 49
PHONE, see Telephone
PHONOGRAPH, see Gramophone
PHOTOGRAPH, most expensive 164, with stars 191
PHOTOGRAPHIC STORE, largest 132
PHOTOGRAPHY, earliest world, UK, earliest aerial, largest negative 164
PHYSICIANS, most, highest, lowest proportion, 196
PHYSIOLOGY, 15-20
Pi, number of places memorised 16-17 most accurate, inaccurate version 73
PIANIST, highest-paid, greatest span 158
PIANO, earliest, grandest, most expensive, smallest 155, highest notes 156
PIANO COMPOSITION, longest 158
PIANO PLAYING, world, UK 183
PIANO SMASHING, record 183
PIANO TUNING, record 183
PIE, largest apple, cherry, custard, meat 178, mince, pizza 179
PIER, oldest, longest, most, pleasure, world 92, GB, longest 100
PIG, highest price, heaviest 140, prolificacy 142
PIGEON RACING, 273
PIGGERY, largest 138
PILLAR BOX, oldest 137
PILLARBOX STANDING, record number of people 183
PILL TAKER, greatest 20
PILOT, most flying hours, most take offs and landings, oldest and youngest, human-powered flight 126, ace 202-3
PINEAPPLE, largest 49
PINNIPEDS, largest, smallest, most abundant, rarest, fastest, deepest dive, longest lived 28
PIPELINE, longest oil, submarine, natural gas, water, most expensive 79
PIPE SMOKING, duration record 183
PISTOLS, most expensive 191, highest auction price 146
PITCH, (sound) highest detectable 17, bat 29, (sport) highest 220
PIZZA PIE, largest 179
PLACE NAMES, earliest, longest, shortest, most spellings 149
PLAGUE, most infectious disease 18
PLANE PULLING, 183
PLANET, largest, smallest, coldest, outermost, highest orbital speed, hottest, nearest, surface features, brightest and faintest, densest and least dense, conjunctions 67, largest scale model 67-8
PLANETARIUM, first, largest, earliest world, GB 70

PLANT KINGDOM, 47-51, oldest, rarest, northernmost, southernmost, highest, roots 47, worst weeds 46, most spreading 46-7, smallest flowering, fruiting, fastest growth, slowest flowering, oldest pot plant, biggest collection, earliest flower 47, GB 48
PLATEAU, greatest 58
PLATE SPINNING, record 183
PLATFORM, Railway, longest 120
PLATINUM, largest mine 77
PLATINUM DISC, unique award 162
PLAY, longest runs, shortest runs, Shakespeare 160
PLAYING CARDS, rarest and most expensive 146
PLEASURE BEACH, biggest 92
PLEASURE PIER, earliest, longest, most 92
PLOUGHING, championship, greatest acreage ploughed, fastest 139
POEM, longest, most successful 152
POET LAUREATE, youngest, oldest 152
POGO-STICK JUMPING, 179
POISON, most potent 72 (also most poisonous snake 37, most poisonous amphibian 37, most poisonous toadstool 52, most active frog venom 39, most venomous fish 39, most poisonous spider 40), mass poisoning 212-13
POLAR CONQUESTS, first North, South, first at both poles, first circumnavigation 170-1
POLAR LIGHT, see Aurora
POLDER, largest 97
POLE SITTING, records 183
POLICY, Life assurance, largest, highest pay out 132
POLITICAL DIVISION, largest 194
POLITICAL SPEECH, longest on record 199-200
POLLEN COUNT, highest GB 52
POLO, 273
POOL, 273-4, 310
POPCORN, largest container 179
POPE, longest, shortest reign, longest lived, oldest, youngest, last non-Italian, last ex-Cardinalate, English, last married, quickest and slowest election 218
POP FESTIVAL, greatest attendance 157
POP GROUP, most successful 163, non-stop playing 183
POPULATION, world, largest, smallest 194, densest, UK, sparsest 195, cities 197
PORT, largest, busiest 109
PORTRAIT, most expensive miniature 144
POST OFFICE, northernmost UK, and southernmost, oldest, longest counter 137
POSTAGE STAMPS, see Stamps
POSTAL SERVICE, largest and highest average letter mail, highest-numbered address, oldest pillar boxes, northernmost and southernmost, oldest post office, longest counter 137
POSTCARDS, 191
POSTER, largest*, highest priced 145
POTATO, record display 49, dimension, weight 48, record yield 138, peeling record 183
POTATO CRISPS, largest 179
POTATO MASH, largest serving 179
POT LID, highest price 146
POT PLANT, oldest 47, largest 77
POVERTY 134-5
POWDER, finest 72
POWERBOAT RACING, 274-5
POWER FAILURE, greatest 78
POWERLIFTING, 305
POWER PRODUCERS, 77-8
POWERSTATION, largest, largest atomic, solar, tidal 77
PRAM PUSHING, record distance 183
PREGNANCY, longest, shortest 11
PREHISTORIC ANIMALS, see Extinct Animals
PREHISTORIC MONUMENT, largest 100
PREMIER, see Prime Minster
PREMIUM, Insurance, largest 132
PRESS, largest 79
PRESS-UPS, 256

PRESSURE, highest, lowest barometric 64, laboratory 73-4
PRIMATE, largest 27, heaviest, smallest 27-8, rarest, longest lived, strongest 28, earliest 6, 44, largest extinct 46
PRIME MINISTER, oldest, longest term of office* 201, UK, records 201
PRIME NUMBERS, lowest, highest 73
PRINT, record price 145
PRINTER, largest 90, fastest 79
PRINTING, earliest, earliest books, largest, smallest, most valuable books 151, highest print order 151, 152
PRISON, longest sentences, longest time served, longest detention, escapes from Broadmoor, largest GB, highest population, most secure, most expensive 214, longest escape, greatest break 215
PRISONER, oldest, most convictions 214
PRIZE, largest radio 166, TV 168, competition 175, most valuable annual 204, largest ever offered 73
PROCARYOTA, 52
PRODUCER, youngest Broadway 160, most prolific TV 168
PROFESSOR, youngest, most durable 215
PROFIT AND LOSS, greatest 130
PROMISE, Breach of, highest damages 210
PROOF, (mathematical) longest 73
PROP, (movie) most expensive 165
PROPELLER, largest ship 107, largest aircraft 116
PROTISTA, largest, smallest, fastest-moving, fastest reproduction 52
PROTOPHYTE, smallest 52
PROTOZOAN, largest, smallest, fastest-moving, fastest reproduction 52
PSALM, longest, shortest 151
PSYCHIATRIST, most 196, fastest 183
PSYCHIC FORCES, 20
PUBLICATION, largest 150
PUBLIC HOUSE, largest, smallest, longest bars, longest name, shortest name, commonest name, most visits 93, 94
PUBLIC RELATIONS, largest firm 132
PUBLISHERS, fastest*, oldest, most prolific 153
PUBLISHING, largest enterprise 132
PULSARS, first, fastest 69
PULSE RATES, highest, lowest 18
PUMPING, (fire) greatest gallonage 178
PUMPKIN, heaviest 48
PUMP-TURBINE, largest 77
PURGE, greatest 211
PURZLE, mathematical, oldest 73
PYGMIES, smallest 9
PYRAMID, tallest 90, oldest, largest 100, 102, motorcycle 116, human 175

Q.C., see Queen's Counsel
QUADRUPLETS, oldest 14, heaviest, most sets 12
QUARRY, deepest, largest world, England 77
QUASAR, 69
QUEEN, longest lived 198, youngest 199, British records 198
QUEEN'S COUNSEL, youngest, most successful 211
QUIETEST PLACE, 75
QUILT, world's largest 191
QUINDECAPLETS, 13
QUINTUPLETS, heaviest 12, test tube 13
QUIZ, largest TV prize 168, most participants, most protracted 183
QUOIT THROWING, record 183
QUORUM, smallest parliamentary 199

RABBITS, largest litter 33, largest breed 33, heaviest specimen 33, smallest 32, 33, most prolific 33, longest ears 33, oldest 30
RACKETBALL, 275, 310
RACKETS, 275
RADAR INSTALLATION, largest 79

RADIO, origins, earliest patent, earliest broadcast, earliest trans-Atlantic, longest broadcast, topmost prize, most durable programmes, earliest antipodal reception, most assiduous ham, most stations, highest listenership, highest response, smallest set 166, tallest masts 90
RADIO DISH, largest 70
RADIO INSTALLATION, largest 70
RADIO-MICROPHONES, earliest 166
RADIO TELESCOPE, first fully steerable, largest 70
RADISH, heaviest 48
RAFT, longest survival 167, Atlantic crossing 106, Pacific crossing 107
RAIL FERRY, largest 107
RAILWAY, longest, highest bridge 95, tunnel, subway tunnel 97, earliest 118, fastest 118-19, longest non-stop, most powerful engine, greatest load, longest freight train, longest run, longest straight, widest, narrowest gauge, highest, lowest, steepest, shallowest gradients, busiest rail system, country with greatest length 119, railroad handcar pumping 119-20, stations, largest, oldest, busiest, highest, largest waiting rooms, longest platform, underground: most extensive, busiest subway, model railway: duration record, longest run, most miniature 120
RAILWAY DISASTERS, worst world, UK 196-7
RAILWAY ENGINE, see Engine, (Railway)
RAINBOW, longest lasting 63
RAINFALL, most intense 61, greatest 63, least 65
RAINY DAYS, most 64-5
RALLY, (motor) earliest, longest 268-70
RAMP JUMPING, longest 183
RANSOM, highest 213
RAPPELING, longest descent 183
RAT, oldest 32
RATTING, record by dog 31
REACTION, fastest human 18
REAL TENNIS, 291
RECORD, Gramophone, see, Gramophone Record
RECORD BREAKERS, (sport) youngest and oldest 220, most prolific 220
RECORDED SOUND, 160-4, earliest 160-1, oldest, smallest 161, jazz records 161-2, earliest tape 161, most successful artist, group, earliest, most golden discs, most recordings 162, biggest sales 162-3, fastest-selling album, singles, greatest advance sales, compact discs 163, Grammy awards 163-4
RECORDING ARTIST, most successful, earliest, most golden discs, most recordings 162, best-selling 163, charts, fastest sellers, greatest advance sales 163, Grammy awards 163-4
RED CABBAGE heaviest 48
REED, tallest 49
REEF, longest 57
REFINERY, (oil) largest 132
REFLECTING TELESCOPE, largest and most powerful 69-70
REFLEXES, fastest 18
REFRACTING TELESCOPE, largest 70
'REFUSENIK', most patient 195
REGENERATION, powers, animal 22
REGIMENT, British, oldest, most senior 208
REGISTRATION PLATE, earliest, most expensive 110
REIGN, number lived through 14, longest, shortest, highest post-nominal numbers 198, longest lived 'royals' 198-9, British records 198
REJECTIONS (publishers) greatest number 152
RELIGION, oldest, largest, Christian, largest non-Christian, total world Jewry, Roman Catholic records, earliest, oldest buildings, largest temple, largest, smallest cathedral, largest church 216, smallest church, synagogue, mosque 217
RENT, highest, land 132

REPTILE, crocodilians: largest 35, smallest, oldest, rarest 36, lizards: largest 36, smallest, oldest, chelonians: largest, smallest, longest lived, fastest, rarest, slowest, snakes: longest, shortest 36, oldest, fastest, most venomous 37, heaviest 36-7, longest fangs, rarest 37, largest extinct 46, most brainless, largest extinct egg, winged, marine, earliest 46
REPUBLIC, smallest 194
RESERVOIR, largest, deepest 97
RESTAURANT, earliest, largest, highest 94, biggest fish and chip 132
RESTAURATEURS, largest 132
RETAILER, largest 132
RETIREMENT, longest pension 173
RETURN OF CASH, 135
RHODODENDRON, largest 49
RHUBARB, heaviest 48
RIBBON WORMS, longest 44
RICE, biggest farm 138
RICHEST, man 134, family 135
RICK, largest 139
RIDING IN ARMOUR,* 183
RINK, largest 263, roller 275
RIOT, worst disaster 213-14
RIVER, longest 58, shortest 58, largest basin, longest sub-tributary, longest estuary, largest delta, greatest flow, longest submarine, subterranean, greatest bores 59, longest dam 96, longest navigable 58
RIVER BARRIER, tidal 102
RIVER BOAT, largest 108
RIVETING, world record 183-4
ROAD, longest tunnel 97, oldest, first motorway UK, greatest length 128, vehicle density, worst jams 127, widest, longest world 128, longest bypass, most complex interchange 127, longest street, commonest name, narrowest, shortest street, steepest street, highest, lowest 128, longest viaduct, biggest, oldest square, first traffic lights, parking meters 127, worst driver 127-8, oldest milestone, longest ford 128
ROAD DISASTER, worst world, UK 196-7
ROAD LOAD, heaviest 115
ROAD TUNNEL, longest, largest diameter 97
ROAD VEHICLE, 109-17 (see also individual road vehicles), most driving test failures 112, heaviest and largest load 115, longest skid marks 113, greatest density per mile, worst traffic jams 127
ROBBERY, greatest, art, bank, mail-train, jewels 213
ROCK, oldest, largest 56
ROCK, band, longest-playing 183
ROCK, stick of 179
ROCK PINNACLE, highest 56
ROCKET, earliest, longest ranges 82, most powerful world 84, velocity 82
ROCKING CHAIR, duration record 184
RODENTS, largest, smallest, rarest, longest living, fastest breeder 28
RODEO, 275
ROLLER CYCLING, 242, 310
ROLLER HOCKEY, 275
ROLLER SKATING, 275, 310
ROLLING PIN, woman's greatest throw 184
ROMAN OCCUPATION, emperors 198
ROOF, largest 94
ROOST, deepest bat 29
ROOTS, deepest 47
ROPE, longest, strongest, heaviest wire 79-80, largest and longest 191
ROPEWAY, 79-80
ROSE TREE, largest 49
ROUND OF DRINKS, biggest 176
ROUND THE WORLD, see Circumnavigation
ROUNDING THE HORN, fastest, solo 105
ROWING, Atlantic crossing 106, Pacific 107, sport 275-6
ROYAL ACADEMICIAN, oldest, youngest 144
ROYAL SOCIETY, longest term 204
ROYALTY, oldest ruling house 197-8, longest, shortest reign, longest lived, youngest, most children, British monarchy records 198
RUBY, value, largest 65
RUGBY FIVES, 245, 310
RUGBY LEAGUE, 276-8
RUGBY UNION, 278, 310

RULER, most durable 198-9, richest 134
RULING HOUSE, oldest 197-8
RUNNER BEAN, longest 48
RUNNING, see Track and Field Athletics and Cross Country running
RUNWAY, longest world, UK 124

SACRED OBJECT, most valuable 217
SAIL, largest 109
SAILING, ice and sand 264, yachting 306-9
SAILING SHIP, earliest vessel 108-9, largest 108, largest junks, longest day's run, highest recorded speed, largest sails 109, see also Yachting
SAINT, total, most and least rapidly canonized 217
ST SWITHIN'S DAY, falsest 61
SALAMANDER, longest lived, largest 37, human 19
SALAMI, largest 179
SALARY, highest world, GB 134
SALE, longest wait for 131
SALES, corporation, greatest 130
SALESMANSHIP, automobile record 132
SALVAGING, deepest operation 171, record recovery 171-2
SAND CASTLE, biggest 184
SAND DUNES, 59
SAND SCULPTURE, largest* 184
SAND YACHTING, 264
SAPPHIRE, largest, most expensive 65
SATELLITE, ARTIFICIAL, earliest manned, first woman in space, fatalities 83, first walk in space 83-4, largest manned space flight, oldest, youngest astronaut, most journeys 84
SATELLITE, NATURAL, most, least, largest and smallest 68
SAUSAGE, longest 179
SAVING OF LIFE, greatest 212
SAWING, world record 186-7
SCALES, most accurate 74
SCARECROW, biggest 100-1
SCARF, longest 191
SCENIC RAILWAY, see Switchback
SCHOOL, oldest, largest 215, most expensive 215-16, earliest comprehensive, oldest PTA, most attended, most 'O' and 'A' level exams, youngest headmaster, most durable teacher, don 216, Sunday school 218
SCIENTIFIC BUILDING, largest 86
SCIENTIFIC INSTRUMENT, most expensive antique 146
SCIENTIFIC NAME, longest 148
SCOOTER RIDING, greatest distance covered 184
SCORPION, largest, smallest, most venomous 40
SCRABBLE*, 229, 310
SCREEN, biggest cinema 166
SCRIPTWRITER, most prolific TV 168
SCUBA DIVING, 171
SCULPTURE, earliest, most expensive, largest, ground figures, hill figures 145, most expensive ancient 145
SEA, (see also Ocean), largest, remotest spot from land, temperature 54, highest wave 55, inland 59
SEAL, see Pinnipeds
SEA-LION, see Pinnipeds
SEA-LOCH, longest world, GB 54
SEAMOUNT, highest 54
SEARCH, longest 13
SEARCHLIGHT, most powerful 74
SEAWAY, longest artificial 96
SEAWEED, longest, deepest 48
SEED, largest, smallest 49, most viable 50
SEE-SAW, duration record 184
SEGMENTED WORMS, longest, shortest, worm charming 43
SEISMIC SEA WAVE, highest, fastest 55
SENSITIVITY, of touch 15, colour 15-16
SENTENCE, shortest holoalphabetic 148, longest prison, world, UK, longest time served 214
SEPTUPLETS, 12
SERMON, longest 184
SERVICE, longest religious 218
SETTLEMENT, highest legal 210
SEVEN WONDERS OF THE WORLD, 102

SEWAGE WORKS, largest world, GB 87
SEWERAGE TUNNEL, longest 97
SEX RATIO, largest woman surplus, shortage 195
SEXTUPLETS, 12
SHAFT, deepest world, UK 77, sinking record 172
SHAKESPEARE, longest play 160
SHALLOT, biggest 48
SHARES, see Stock Exchange
SHARK, largest 38, 223
SHARPEST OBJECTS, 75
SHAVING, fastest barber 184
SHEAF TOSSING, best performance 184
SHEARING, (sheep) fastest*, biggest total 138
SHEEP, largest station, move, shearing record*, survival 138, highest birthweight 140, prolificacy record 142, highest price auction 139, oldest, heaviest 140
SHEET MUSIC, top selling 156
SHELL, smallest, largest, most expensive 43
SHINTY, 279-80
SHIP, 104-9, earliest, largest, longest, active liner, largest battleships, guns, thickest armour, fastest destroyer, largest aircraft carrier, largest, fastest, deepest submarine 104, largest tanker, cargo vessel, container ship, most powerful tug, largest car ferry 107, largest hydrofoil 107-8, largest river boat, fastest building, most powerful icebreakers, most expensive yacht, largest dredger, heaviest, longest wooden ship, biggest human-powered, light vessel, largest sailing 108, longest day's run, highest speed, largest sails, largest collision, earliest, fastest Atlantic crossing, fastest Pacific crossing, fastest cross-Channel 109, circumnavigation records 105-6, largest object stolen 213
SHIP-BUILDING, annual launching, leading firm, largest shipyard 132
SHIP CANAL, longest, busiest 96
SHIPPING, largest merchant fleet 132-3, 109
SHIPPING LINE, largest 132-3
SHOE, most expensive, largest 191
SHOE-SHINING, 184
SHOOTING, 280
SHOP, largest book 149, largest department store world, GB, most profitable department store, longest wait for a sale 131, largest shopping centre, largest store, supermarket, toy shop 133
SHOPPING CENTRE, largest 133
SHORTHAND, speed records 184
SHOUTING, 181, 17
SHOVEL, largest 80
SHOW, (dog) largest 31, (theatre) longest run, shortest run, one-man 160, (televison) most durable 167
SHOW BUSINESS, versatility awards 166
SHOWERING, most prolonged bath 184
SHOW JUMPING, 243-4
SHRINE, oldest 216
SIAMESE TWINS, original, rarest 12
SIEGE, longest 205
SIGN, (advertising) greatest ever, largest, highest world, neon 98
SIGNALLING, Morse, record receiving 183
SIGNATURE, see Autograph
SILENCE, longest musical 158
SILK, see Queen's Counsel
SILVER, most expensive piece 146, largest pieces 191
SINGER, most successful, worst 94-5, youngest and oldest opera 158, most successful pop 162
SINGING, longest marathon* 184
SINGLE, (record) biggest seller, chart records, top ten sellers 163
SITTING, pole 183
SIT-UPS, 256
SKATEBOARDING, 184
SKATING, Ice, 262-4, 310
SKATING, Roller, 275, 310
SKI-BOB, 281
SKI LIFT, worst disaster 196-7, longest 281
SKID MARKS, longest 113
SKIING, Alpine, Nordic, grass 280-2, 310
SKI JUMPING, 281
SKIPPING*, 282

SKITTLES, 283, 310
SKULL, oldest 6, most expensive 17, largest 45, 46
SKY-JACK RANSOM, greatest 213
SKYSCRAPERS, tallest 87
SLAG HEAP, largest 77
SLEDGE JOURNEY, longest, longest Antarctic 171
SLEEPLESSNESS, longest period 18
SLEEPWALKING, 19
SLIDE, longest 92
SLIMMING, greatest feat 9-10, animal 22
SLINGING, greatest distance 184
SLOGAN, most successful 152
SLOTH, slowest 26
SMELL, most acute sense of 42, smelliest substance 72
SMOG, excess deaths from 196-7
SMOKER, heaviest 19
SMOKE RING BLOWING, most rings 184-5
SMOKESTACK, tallest world, UK 87
SMOKING, heaviest 189
SNAIL, fastest, largest 43-4
SNAKE, longest, heaviest 36, heaviest 36-7, oldest, fastest 37, most venomous* 37, longest, shortest venomous, longest fangs, rarest 37, longest extinct 46
SNAKES AND LADDERS, 310
SNEEZING, longest fit, highest speed 18
SNOOKER, 283, 310
SNORING, loudest 18
SNOW AVALANCHE, greatest 196-7
SNOW CONSTRUCTION, largest 100
SNOWFALL, greatest 64
SNOWMAN, largest 100
SNOWMOBILE, longest journey 114, fastest speed 281
SNOW PLOUGH BLADE, 80
SNOW SHOEING, 185
SNUFF, most expensive 191
SNUFF BOX, record price 146
SOCCER*, see Football
SOFA, largest* 192
SOFTBALL, 283, 310
SOFT DRINK, top-selling 133
SOLAR FURNACE, largest world 77
SOLAR POWER, fastest vehicle 114, first aircraft 121, largest plant 77
SOLAR SYSTEM, 65-7
SOLAR TELESCOPE, largest 70
SOLDIER, oldest old, youngest, youngest conscript, tallest 208
SOLICITOR, most durable 211
SOLITAIRE, 229
SOMERSAULTS, 175, 256-7, 301
SONG, oldest, most frequently sung, top-selling, most successful writers 156
SONGWRITER, most successful 156
SOUND, lowest, highest pitch 17, musical instrument, highest and lowest 156, rarest and commonest (speech) 147
SOUTH POLE, first crossing, sighting 170, landing 170-1, conquest, women, first both poles 171
SPA, largest, highest 90
SPACE FLIGHT 82-4, earliest manned 83-4, worst disaster 196
SPACE TELESCOPE, first, largest 70
SPAN, greatest on piano 158
SPEAKER, most boring of the year 173, (House of Commons) longest in office 202
SPEAR THROWING, greatest distance 185
SPEECH, fastest 17, earliest 146, longest filibuster, longest parliamentary, UN 199, longest non-political* 185
SPEED RECORDS, fastest bird 34, animal 23-4, highest velocity 84, car 110, 270, motorcycle 115, 268, railway 118-19, bomber, airliner 122, aircraft 122-3, fastest man, woman 84, car, fastest water 109, autogyros 124, fastest sport 220, cycling 241, greyhound 255, racehorse 259, pigeon 273, skiing 282, swimming 284, running 291, water skiing 302, sailing 306
SPEED SKATING, 263-4
SPEEDWAY, 283
SPELLINGS, most at one word 148, most of one place name 149
SPICE, most expensive, hottest 179

SPIDERS, largest, smallest, fastest, most common, rarest, oldest, largest, smallest web, most poisonous 40
SPIKE DRIVING, fastest 185
SPINNING, (balance wheel) duration record 185
SPIRE, tallest cathedral, church 217
SPIRIT, highest strength, most expensive 180, top-selling brands 131
SPITTING, greatest distance 185
SPOIL DUMP, largest 77
SPONGE, largest, smallest, deepest 44
SPOONS, record price 146
SPORT, earliest, fastest, slowest, longest 220 (see also individual sports) most participants 221
SPORTS DISASTER, worst in world, UK 221
SPORTSMAN, youngest, oldest record breaker, youngest, oldest champion, internationals 220, most versatile 220-1, longest, reign, heaviest 221
SQUARE, biggest, oldest 127
SQUARE DANCE, longest calling 182
SQUASH RACKETS 283-4, 310
SQUID, largest 43
STADIA, 92, 157
STAG, heaviest 29
STAGE, largest 160
STAINED GLASS, (window) oldest, largest 217
STAIRS, longest 100-1, climbing record 185
STALACTITE, longest 57
STALAGMITE, tallest 57
STAMPS, Postage, 137, 138, licking record* 185
STANDARDS OF LIVING, 134 .
STANDING, endurance record 185
STARS, 68-9
STARFISHES, largest, smallest, most destructive, deepest 39
STATE, see Country
STATELY HOME, most visited 90
STATION, RAILWAY, most visited 119, largest, oldest, busiest 120
STATUE, tallest, longest 102, most 204
STATURE, most variable 9
STATUTE, oldest 209, longest UK 209-10, shortest, most inexplicable 210
STEAM CAR, fastest 110
STEAM ENGINE, 77
STEAMER, oldest 104
STEAM LOCOMOTIVE, fastest, most powerful 119
STEEL ARCH BRIDGE, longest 95
STEEL COMPANY, largest, largest works 133
STELLAR PLANETS, 69
STILTS, highest mastered 185
STOCK EXCHANGE, 136-7
STONE, human largest 18
STORE, see Shop
STORM, circular, worst world, UK 196-7
STOWAWAY, most rugged 185
STRAITS, longest 54-5, broadest, narrowest 55
STRANDPULLING, 304
STRAWBERRY, heaviest 48, most expensive 178
STRAWBERRY BOWL, largest 179
STREET, longest, narrowest, steepest, world, commonest name, shortest 128
STRETCHER BEARING, 185
STRIKE, earliest, largest, most serious, biggest annual total, longest 136
STRING BALL, largest 185
STRINGED INSTRUMENTS, largest 156
STRUCTURE (see also Buildings), earliest known human, largest 86-7, tallest 87, 90, 94, tallest tower 94, tallest (progressive records) 87, 90, oldest religious 216
STUFFED BIRD, most expensive 146
STUNTMAN, highest-paid 164
SUBBUTEO, 310
SUBMARINE, largest, fastest, deepest 104, first circumnavigation 105, most anti-submarine kills, most successful captain 203
SUBMARINE DISASTER, worst world, UK 196-7
SUBMERGENCE, record, human greatest descent, deep-sea diving 171, endurance 185

SUBSTANCES, smelliest, most expensive, most poisonous, most absorbent 72
SUBWAY, longest tunnel 97, busiest 120
SUGAR BEET, heaviest 48, record yield 139
SUGAR MILL, highest output 133
SUGGESTION BOX, most prolific user 185
SUICIDE, highest, lowest rate, mass 212
SUIT, most expensive 192, longest lawsuit 210, longest lawsuit 211
SUMMER, best and worst British 61
SUMO WRESTLING, 306
SUN, distance extremes 66, temperature, dimensions 66-7, sunspot 67, closest approach by rocket 82, eclipses: earliest, longest, most and least frequent 67
SUNDAE, largest 178
SUNDAY SCHOOL, longest attendance 218
SUNDIAL, largest 82
SUNFLOWER, tallest 48, smallest 49
SUNSHINE, maximum, minimum 64
SUNSPOT, largest, most frequent 67
SUPERMARKET, largest UK 133
SUPERNOVA, brightest 69, newest 67, 69
SUPERSONIC FLIGHT, Mach scale, first 121, bomber, airliner 122, speed records 122-3
SURFING, 284
SURGICAL INSTRUMENTS, largest, smallest 20
SURNAME, longest, shortest 148-9, commonest, most versions, most contrived 149
SURTAX, highest 208, highest taxation rates 133-4, highest tax demands 134
SUSPENSION BRIDGE, longest, highest 95
SWALLOWING, compulsive swallowing, sword swallowing 19
SWAMP, largest 59
SWEDE, heaviest 48
SWEETS, top-selling 179
SWIMMING, (bird) fastest 35, fastest 284, most medals 284-8, diving 285, Channel and long-distance swimming 285-8, non-stop 310, world records* 285, British records 286
SWIMMING POOL, largest 284
SWING, tallest 102
SWINGING, 185
SWITCHBACK, fastest, longest, longest ride 92
SWITCHBOARD, largest telephone 82
SWORD, highest price 146
SWORD SWALLOWING, longest 19
SYMPHONY, longest 157
SYNAGOGUE, largest world, GB 217
SYNONYMS, most 148

TABLE, longest 192
TABLE CLOTH, largest 192
TABLE FOOTBALL, largest*
TABLE TENNIS, 288-9, 310
TAEKWON-DO, 289
TAILORING, fastest-made suit 185
TAKE-OVER, largest 130
TALKING, fastest* 17, backwards* 17, longest non-stop* 185, birds 35
TANDEM BICYCLE, longest 116
TANK, (military) earliest 208, heaviest and fastest 208-9
TANK, (oil) largest 78
TANKER, largest 107, largest wreck 109
TAP DANCING, fastest rate 177
TAPE RECORDING, earliest 161
TAPESTRY, earliest, largest, largest 192, most expensive 146
TARTAN, earliest 192
TATTOOS, most 20
TAXATION, least taxed country 133, highest world 133-4, highest demand, highest, lowest rates in GB 134
TAXI, largest fleet 114
T-BONE DIVE, greatest 185
TEACHING, longest career 216
TEETH, oldest 6, earliest, most, earliest false, strongest bite, most valuable 15
TEETH-LIFTING, greatest weight pulled 185-6
TEKTITE, largest 66

TELEPHERIQUE, 79-80
TELEPHONE DIRECTORIES, *tearing in half* 82
TELEPHONES,* 82
TELESCOPE, *earliest* 69, *largest reflecting* 69-70, *refracting, largest radio, largest space* 70
TELETHON, *most successful* 168
TELEVISION, 167-8, *tallest mast (progressive records)* 90, *transmitting tower* GB 87
TEMPERATURE, *highest, lowest* 63, *most equable, greatest ranges, longest freeze, upper atmosphere* 61, *humidity and discomfort* 61-2, *highest shade, lowest screen* 63, *progressive extremes* 61, *lunar* 66, *Sun* 69, *man-made, highest, lowest* 73-4
TEMPERATURE, *human, highest, lowest* 18, *highest endured* 18
TEMPERATURE, *sea* 54
TEMPLE, *largest* 216, *oldest and tallest, Chinese* 217, 99
TENNIS, *(lawn)* 289-91, 310, *(real or royal)* 291
TEN-PIN BOWLING, 230, 310
TERMITE MOUND, *largest* 41
TERRORISM, *greatest loss of life* 197
TEXT, *oldest written, printed, largest book, publication, dictionary, smallest, longest novel* 150, *most valuable book, broadsheet, manuscript, atlas* 151
TEXTBOOKS, *most successful writer* 152
THEATRE, *records* 159-60
THEFT, *greatest, largest object stolen* 213
THEOREM, *most proved* 73
THERMOMETER, *smallest* 73
THIMBLE, *most expensive* 146
THREE PEAKS RECORD, 271
THROWING, *longest* 186, *baseball* 226, *cricket ball* 238
THUNDER-DAYS, *most* 64
TICKET, *smallest* 192, *longest air* 124
TIDAL MILL, 78
TIDAL POWER STATION, *world's first* 77
TIDAL RIVER BARRIER, *largest* 102
'TIDAL' WAVE, *highest, fastest* 55
TIDDLYWINKS, 291, 310
TIDE, *greatest* 55, 56
TIERS, *most in opera house* 158
TIGER, *man-eating* 19
TIGHTROPE WALKING, *greatest walker, endurance record, distance record, highest and steepest* 186, *high-wire act* 186
TIME, *longest, shortest measure* 73
TIME CAPSULE, *largest* 192
TIME MEASURER, *most accurate* 82
TIPSTER, *racing* 251
TITHE BARN, *longest Britain* 98
TITLE, *most titled person* 202
TOAD, *largest, smallest* 38
TOADSTOOL, *most poisonous* 52
TOASTMASTERS, 173
TOBACCO, *largest company* 133, *heaviest smokers* 189, *most expensive snuff* 191
TOBOGGANING, 229-30
TOES, *(human) most, least* 15
TOMATO, *largest, tallest plant* 48
TOMB, *largest* 102
TOP, *longest spin* 186
TOPAZ, *largest* 65
TORNADO, *highest speed, strongest* UK 63, *worst world,* 196, UK 197
TORTOISE, *largest, longest lived* 36, *fastest, slowest, rarest* 36, *largest extinct* 46
TOSSING THE CABER, *see* **Highland Games**
TOTE WIN, *biggest* 250
TOTEM POLE, *tallest* 102
TOUCH, *sensitivity* 15
TOURISTS, *most, highest spending* 195
TOW, *(car) longest* 113
TOWER, *tallest* 94

TOWN, *largest new* 90, *earliest walled, oldest, world,* GB 196, *largest, smallest, highest, lowest, northernmost, southernmost, most remote from sea, most populous, progressive records* 197
TOXIN, *most deadly* 75
TOY, *most expensive antique* 146, *longest* 192
TOY CONSTRUCTION, *tallest* 192
TOY SHOP, *biggest world* 131
TOY SOLDIER, *most expenisve* 146
TRACK AND FIELD ATHLETICS*, 291-301
TRACHEOSTOMY, 20
TRACKING, *greatest feat (dog)* 31
TRACTOR, *largest, most powerful* 114
TRADE UNION, *oldest, largest world,* GB, *smallest* 136
TRAFFIC, *highest density* 127, *worst jams* 127, *lights — first in UK* 127
TRAIN, *see,* **Railway**
TRAINER, *top dog* 31-2, *top horse* 260, 261
TRAIN SPOTTER, *champion* 186
TRAM, *longest journey, oldest* 114, *most extensive system* 115
TRAMPOLINING, *(circus)* 175, *(sport)* 301, 310
TRANS-ATLANTIC CROSSING, *see* **Atlantic Crossing**
TRANSFER FEES, *associaton football* 148, *rugby league* 278
TRANSFORMER, *largest* 80
TRANSISTOR, *fastest* 81
TRANSMISSION LINE, *longest, highest, highest voltage* 80
TRANSMISSIONS, *earliest radio broadcasts, earliest trans-Atlantic wireless* 166, *television, earliest, earliest trans-Atlantic* 167
TRAPEZE, 175
TRAVEL, *(person) most on land, on horseback* 170, *by rail* 119
TREASURE TROVE, 136
TREATY, *oldest* 199
TREES, 50-1
TREE CLIMBING, *fastest* 185, 186
TREE SITTING, *longest* 186
TREE TOPPING, 186
TRIAL, *fastest, longest, shortest, murder, shortest, longest divorce trial, best attended* 210
TRIATHLON, 301
TRIBES, *tallest, shortest* 9
TRIBUNAL, *longest* 210
TRIFLE, *largest* 179
TRIMARAN, *circumnavigation record* 105, *Atlantic crossing* 106
TRIPLETS, *oldest* 14, *heaviest, most* 12, *fastest birth* 13
TRISHAW, *longest parade* 116
TRIVIAL PURSUIT, 310
TROLLEY BUS, 114
TROTTING AND PACING, 257
TRUCK, *most powerful* 114
TSUNAMI, *highest, fastest* 55
TUBA, *largest* 155-6
TUBE, *see* **Underground**
TUBING, *smallest* 75
TUG, *first power-driven vessel* 125, *most powerful* 107
TUG OF WAR, 301, 220
TUMOUR, *largest* 20
TUNGSTEN MINE, *largest* 77
TUNNEL, *longest rail, subway, road, largest, longest hydro-electric, irrigation, longest bridge-tunnel, longest canal* 97, *oldest navigable* 97-8, *worst disaster* 196, *tunnelling record* 98
TURBINE, *first ship* 104, *largest, reversible pump* 77
TURKEY, *most expenisve* 140, *largest farm* 138, *heaviest* 140
TURNIP, *heaviest* 48
TURTLE, *largest, smallest, longest lived, fastest* 36, *largest extinct* 46
TUSKS, *longest, heaviest* 30, *(extinct animals)* 46-7

TWINS, *tallest* 7-8, *shortest* 9, *oldest* 14, *lightest* 12, *heaviest* 10, 12, *Siamese, rarest* 12, *most sets* 12, *most geographically, longest separated* 13, *longest interval between* 13, *boxing champions* 232
TWO-SIDE-WHEEL DRIVING, 112, *motorcycle side car* 116
TYPEWRITER, *earliest* 192, *most expensive*** 146
TYPEWRITING, *fastest, longest* 186
TYPHOID CARRIER, *most notorious* 18
TYRE SUPPORTING, *record* 186
TYRES, *largest* 113

U-BOAT, *see* **Submarine**
ULTRALIGHT, *air records* 121
UNDERGRADUATE, *youngest* 215
UNDERGROUND LAKE, 59
UNDERGROUND RAILWAYS, 120
UNDERTAKER, *biggest world* 133
UNDERWATER, *longest stay* 19, *cycling* 117, *deepest escape* 171, *swimming* 288
UNEMPLOYMENT, *highest, lowest,* UK 136
UNICYCLE, *tallest, distance records, place to place* 117, *sprint* 117
UNION, *see* **Trade Union**
UNITED NATIONS (UN), *longest speech* 199
UNIT OF LENGTH, *earliest* 73
UNIVERSE, *farthest visible object, quasars, pulsars, remotest object, age of* 69
UNIVERSITY, *records* 215, *Union presidents* 204, *boat race* 275-6
UNSUPPORTED CIRCLE, *biggest* 186
URANIUM, *largest mine* 77

VACUUM, *highest* 75
VALVE, *largest* 80
VASE, *most expensive, largest* 192
VAT, *largest* 102
VC, *see* **Victoria Cross**
VEGETABLES, *record dimensions and weights, world,* UK, 48, 49 *potato display* 49
VEHICLE, *battery-powered* 131, *solar powered* 133, *extraterrestrial* 84, *road, see* **Road Vehicle**
VEIN, *largest human* 17
VELOCIPEDE, *see* **Bicycle**
VELOCITY, *highest rocket* 83, *highest* 74
VENOM, *most active snake* 37, *frog* 37, *fish* 39, *spider* 40, *jellyfish* 44
VERBS, *most forms, most and least irregular* 147
VERSE, *longest, shortest Bible* 151
VIADUCT, *longest* GB 127
VICTORIA CROSS, *most bars, youngest person awarded, longest lived, most versatile winner* 202
VIDEO TAPE, *top selling, most rented* 168, *first recording, fastest production* 167
VILLAGE, *most haunted* 20, *shortest name* 149, *oldest, smallest, highest, northernmost, southernmost* 197
VINE, *largest* 48
VINEYARD, *most northerly, southerly* 48, *largest* 168
VINTAGE, *oldest* 180
VINTNERS, *oldest* 133
VIOLENCE, *most film* 164
VIOLIN, *most valuable* 156
VIOLINIST, *most durable* 156
VIRUS, *largest, smallest* 52
VISCOSITY, *lowest* 75
VISION, *smallest, visible object, colour sensitivity (human)* 15-16, *most acute (bird)* 35
VOCABULARY, *richest* 147
VOICE, *highest, lowest* 17, *greatest range* 17

VOLCANO, *records* 60-1, 196
VOLLEYBALL, 301, 310
VOLTAGE, *highest* 75, 146
VOTE, *largest parliamentary* 199, *monetary* 204
VOWELS, *language with most, least* 147
VOYAGE, *longest by sailing boat* 166

WAIST, *smallest* 16
WAIT, *for a sale, longest* 131
WAITING ROOM, *(railway) largest* 120
WALKING, *in space* 83, *longest walks* 186, *tightrope* 183, *on hands* 170, *non-stop* 310, *on water* 186, *track records* 300-1, 296, *backwards walking* 301
WALKING STICK, *most expensive* 146
WALL, *greatest, sheerest mountain* 58, *thickest* 109, *longest* 102, *climb* 271
WALL OF DEATH, *endurance feat* 186
WALLET, *most expensive* 192
WALRUS, *see* **Pinnipeds**
WAR, *records* 204-5
WARDEN, *oldest church* 218
WARSHIPS, *largest, fastest* 104
WASP, *smallest, smallest eggs* 40
WATCH, *oldest, largest, smallest, thinnest, most expensive* 82
WATER, Fresh, *survival without* 19
WATERFALL, *highest, greatest, widest* 58
WATER MILL, *oldest* 78
WATER PIPELINE, *longest* 79
WATER POLO, 301-2, 310
WATER SKIING, 302-3
WATER SPEED RECORDS, 109, 274
WATERSPOUT, *highest* 63
WATER SUPPLY TUNNEL, *longest* 97
WATER TOWER, *tallest* 102
WATERWAY, *(inland) longest, artificial seaway, irrigation canal* 96, *country with greatest navigable length, longest navigable river* 58
WATER WELL, *deepest world, Britain, greatest flow* 76
WATERWHEEL, *largest world,* GB 102
WAVE, *highest* 55, *highest, longest ridden* 284
WEALTH, *national* 134, *individual* 134-5
WEATHER, *records* 61-5
WEB, *largest, smallest* 40
WEDDING CEREMONY, *golden*, largest mass, most expensive* 172
WEED, *worst* 47
WEIGHT, *heaviest men* 9, *women* 10, *twins* 10, 12, *lightest, slimming, weight gaining, greatest differential* 10-11, *greatest lifted* 78, 304
WEIGHTLIFTING, 303-6
WEIGHT-MEASURE, *earliest* 73
WELL, *deepest oil world, British, deepest water world,* GB 76
WHALE, *fastest growth, largest* 23, *heaviest, deepest dive* 22, *fastest* 26, *rarest* 23
WHALE FACTORY SHIP, *largest* 107
WHEAT, *largest field* 138, *record yield* 138, *field-to-loaf record* 177-8
WHEELIE, *truck* 112, *motorcycle** 116, *bicycle* 117
WHIP, *longest cracked* 186
WHISKY, *smallest bottle, largest collection* 192
WHISTLE, *greatest range* 17, *loudest and longest* 186
'WHITE' CHRISTMAS, 61
WHITE HORSE, *oldest in Britain* 145
WHO'S WHO, *longest entry, youngest entrant, American entries* 150
WILL, *shortest, longest* 211, *greatest in UK, Ireland* 134

WINDIEST PLACE, 65
WINDMILL, *largest, earliest, oldest still complete* 78
WINDOW, *largest* 102, *stained glass, oldest, largest* 217, *cleaning record* 186
WIND-SPEED, *highest surface* 64
WINDSURFING, *see* **Boardsailing**
WIND TUNNEL, *largest* 81
WINE, 180
WINE CELLAR, *largest* 102
WING BEAT, *fastest, slowest (bird)* 34, *fastest, slowest (insect)* 41
WING SPAN, *longest (bird)* 33, *(aeroplane)* 121
WING WALKING, 186
WINKLING, *fastest picking* 186
WIRE, *high and low* 186
WIRELESS, *see* **Radio**
WIRE-ROPE, *longest, strongest, heaviest* 80-1
WIRE SLIDE, *longest* 186
WOMAN, *tallest* 7-8, *shortest* 8, *heaviest* 10, *oldest* 14, *reproductivity* 11-13, *smallest waists, longest necks* 16, *lowest temperature, longest coma* 18, *first astronaut* 83, *longest delayed, oldest, parachute drop* 126, *greatest altitude and speed* 84, *richest* 134-5, *most beautiful* 177, *leading air ace* 202, *first prime minister* 201, *first president* 199, *greatest surplus, shortage* 195, *earliest suffrage* 199, *most titles* 202, *MPs* 202
WOMEN'S CRICKET, 239
WOMEN'S HOCKEY, 258
WOMEN'S LACROSSE, 266
WONDERS OF THE WORLD, Seven, 102
WOOD, *heaviest, lightest* 52
WOOD CUTTING, *world record, sawing* 186
WOODEN BUILDINGS, *largest, oldest* 87-8
WOODEN SHIP, *heaviest, longest* 108
WOOL, *highest price* 139, *fastest production* 184
WORD PROCESSOR, *smallest* 81
WORDS, 146, 147-8, *total in Bible* 151
WORKING CAREER, *longest* 171
WORKING WEEK, *longest, shortest* 173
WORLD CUP, 247 *(football)*
WORLD RECORD BREAKERS, *(Sport) youngest and oldest* 220
WORM, *longest, shortest, earthworm, charming* 43, *longest ribbon, immolation* 44
WORSHIP, *oldest places* 216
WREATH, *largest* 49, *costliest* 192
WRECK, *largest* 109, *oldest ship* 104
WRECKER, *most powerful* 115
WRESTLING, 220, 305-6
WRIST WATCH, *earliest, most expensive, largest* 82
WRITERS, 152
WRITING, *handicapped, minuscule** 187

YACHT, *most expensive* 108, *racing disaster* 196, 197
YACHTING, *Atlantic crossing, circumnavigation records* 105, *Pacific crossing* 107, *sport** 306-7, *see also* **Sailing ship**
YACHTING, *ice and sand* 264
YARD-ARM, *last execution* 213
YARD OF ALE, 187
YAWNING, *most persistent* 18
YEW, *tallest hedge* 50, *oldest* GB 51
YODELLING*, 187
YOLKS, *most* 140
YORKSHIRE PUDDING, *largest* 179
YO-YO, *records* 187

ZIP-FASTENER, *longest* 192
ZIGGURAT, *largest* 102
ZOO, *records* 52

*T*HE *GUINNESS WORLD OF RECORDS*